sixth edition

A HISTORY OF CIVILIZATION

Volume II: 1648 to the Present

CRANE BRINTON

JOHN B. CHRISTOPHER
University of Rochester

ROBERT LEE WOLFF

ROBIN W. WINKS
Yale University

Prentice-Hall, Inc., Englewood Cliffs, New Jersey 07632

Library of Congress Cataloging in Publication Data
Main entry under title:

A History of civilization.

    Rev. ed. of: A history of civilization / Crane
Brinton, John B. Christopher, Robert Lee Wolff. c 1976.
    Includes bibliographies and indexes.
    Contents: v. 1. Prehistory to 1715   v. 2. 1648
to the present.
    1. Civilization—History. I. Brinton, Clarence
Crane, 1898–1968. A history of civilization.
CB69.H58 1984   909   83-13830
ISBN 0-13-389866-0 (v. 1)
ISBN 0-13-389874-1 (v. 2)

"Let us learn those things here on earth,
the knowledge of which will continue into the heavens."

Editorial supervision: Serena Hoffman
Cover and interior design: Lee Cohen
Development: Gerald Lombardi
Acquisitions editor: Stephen Dalphin
Art and photo research: Joelle Burrows
Manufacturing buyer: Ron Chapman
Cover photograph: Eiffel Tower—Vic Cox/Peter Arnold

Printed in the United States of America
10 9 8 7 6 5 4 3 2 1

ISBN 0-13-389874-1

Prentice-Hall International, Inc., *London*
Prentice-Hall of Australia Pty. Limited, *Sydney*
Editora Prentice-Hall do Brasil, Ltda., *Rio de Janeiro*
Prentice-Hall Canada Inc., *Toronto*
Prentice-Hall of India Private Limited, *New Delhi*
Prentice-Hall of Japan, Inc., *Tokyo*
Prentice-Hall of Southeast Asia Pte. Ltd., *Singapore*
Whitehall Books Limited, *Wellington, New Zealand*

contents

boxes

maps

preface

Each generation writes its own history and finds that the present is best decoded by a different approach to the past. By the end of World War II North Americans found that they were expected to be the leaders of "the West"—which was generally taken to mean of Western civilization—and they extended their study of history to include non-Western societies in Africa and Asia, both because these societies deserved to be studied for their own sakes, and also as a simple matter of prudence. Diplomatic history moved into the space often reserved for political or administrative history, and intellectual history (most especially the history of art and of thought) also became both important and popular—which are not the same thing. As a result, a textbook used by thousands of readers in hundreds of schools, colleges, and universities, known familiarly as "Brinton, Christopher, and Wolff," went through periodic revision to keep pace with changing expectations.

The present edition represents the first wholesale revision of this text in nearly a decade. That decade has been filled with perhaps the most exceptional array of changes seen in the discipline of history since the nineteenth century—changes both in the way people think about history as well as in our knowledge of its content. Economic and intellectual history have been transformed, and social history has altered our entire way of looking at ourselves and at our past. Historical scholarship must now embrace statistics, psychohistory, geography, and the arguments usually reserved to political science, sociology, and anthropology. Yet the historian and the student must not forget that the purpose of history is to explain how we came to be as we are: why we find ourselves in our present predicaments, how we achieved our present triumphs, how we have developed across centuries through a *process* to a specific point in time—*our* specific point in time—when a savage light known as the present beats down upon us.

This present edition, therefore, is three things at once. It is, first, a body of information, argument, and interpretation that is meant to help the reader understand humanity's long search for security, for meaning, for purpose in life. Second, it is a book by which students may locate themselves in time, decoding in their own way the relevance of the past for the present. And third,

it is a document that demonstrates the state of historical learning at the level of broad generalization and for the broadest general need in the 1980s. Thus, this text is intended to preserve the great strengths in breadth, depth, and grasp of the original editions of Brinton, Christopher, and Wolff, retaining for these distinguished authors (two of them no longer with us, for Robert Lee Wolff died in 1980, twelve years after the death of Crane Brinton) their many loyal readers, while also reflecting new trends in the study of history.

To summarize the significant changes in this new edition, much material has been reordered and combined in different ways and with different emphases, especially in Volume II, with a resulting total of 28 chapters instead of the fifth edition's 33. Volume I ends at 1715 with Chapter 15, "The Problem of Divine-Right Monarchy"; but that chapter also forms the first one of Volume II, which now begins at 1648. Among many other changes, nineteenth-century imperialism has received added emphasis; the chapter on events between the two World Wars has been restructured; and material on events since World War II has been compressed and brought up to date in the context of the perspectives and events of the past ten years.

A new feature, outlines at the beginning of the chapters, includes many dates in order to provide a simplified overview of a particular historical terrain before elaborating on its topographical detail. But the most obvious change to one familiar with earlier editions will be the addition of two new elements: brief boxed-off sections throughout the text that provide selections from sources and documents contemporary with the events in the text, but that also discuss matters of cultural and historiographic interest; and short summaries at the end of each chapter designed to recapitulate its major ideas and events.

A particular effort has been made to tie the illustrations more closely to the text through captions that explain and put in context the works illustrated as well as identifying them. There are several new maps, and all maps have been updated and revised with the intention of including important place names mentioned in the text. The Suggested Readings that appear at the end of each volume have been redone from scratch so as to include the most recent scholarship and to enable readers to move beyond the text as their interests dictate. In an effort to make the index more useful, the major discussion for each entry has been printed in **boldface** type. The index has been expanded to include concepts as well as events and to provide a pronunciation guide for foreign or difficult names of persons and places.

Much appreciated criticism and guidance was provided by the following reviewers, who saw rough drafts of the manuscript: Elizabeth Carney, Clemson University; Douglas McCullough, Dekalb Community College; Charles Connell, West Virginia University; David Lukowitz, Hamline University; R.V. Burks, Wayne State University; and John Donnelly, Marquette University.

The greatest challenge to the historian today is to understand movement through time, even at its most technical or controversial, without losing sight of the essential nature of history itself. History is a narrative. History is concerned foremost with major themes, even as it recognizes the significance of many fascinating digressions. Because history is largely about how and why people behave as they do, it is also about patterns of thought and belief. Ultimately, history is about what people believe to be true. To this extent, virtually all history is intellectual history, for the perceived meaning of a specific treaty, battle, or scientific discovery lies in what those involved in it and those who came after thought was most significant about it. History makes it clear that we may die, as we may live, as a result of what someone believed to be true in the relatively remote past.

A History of Civilization is about how we, as readers studying the past through the traditions and biases of the West, have come to think about civilization. Neither the title nor the content is meant to imply that there are not equally complex, challenging, and productive civilizations elsewhere. But we must recognize, even as material relating to the Far East, South Asia, or Africa is incorporated into the present edition, that we read history to understand *our own* ancient beginnings (Volume I) or *our* modern heritage (Volume II). Though this is our primary reason for studying Western civilization, we must also recognize that it is impossible to do justice to all civilizations in a single text. If these volumes enable us to understand history as a process, and if they illustrate the methodology of history, then they will surely lead us to appreciate other civilizations as well. The text is, therefore, implicitly but not explicitly comparative. Western civilization may not be typical, nor need we conclude that our ways are either "right" or "wrong" simply because they are ours and are known to us. They are the views by which we perceive our world; they are the windows on the world that our own historical experience has opened for us. And since Western societies have had so great an impact on the non-Western world in recent centuries, there is a sense in which world history is also quite legitimately viewed through the windows of Western history.

We cannot each be our own historian. In everyday life we may reconstruct our personal past, acting as detectives for our motivations and attitudes. But formal history is a much more rigorous study. History may give us some very small capacity to predict the future. More certainly, it should help us arrange the causes for given events into meaningful patterns. History also should help us be tolerant of the historical views of others, even as it helps to shape our own convictions. History must help us sort out the important from the less important, the relevant from the irrelevant, so that we do not fall prey to those who propose simple-minded solutions to vastly complex human problems. We must not yield to the temptation to blame one group or individual for our problems, and yet we must not fail to defend our convictions with vigor.

To recognize, indeed to celebrate, the equality of all civilizations is essential to the civilized life itself. To understand that we see all civilizations through the prism of our specific historical past—for which we feel affection, in which we feel comfortable and secure, and by which we interpret all else that we encounter—is simply to recognize that we too are the products of history. That is why we must study history and ask our own questions in our own way. For if we ask no questions of our past, there may be no questions to ask of our future.

Robin W. Winks
For the Sixth Edition

THE VALUE OF HISTORY
AND
OF HISTORICAL
CONTROVERSY

History is a series of arguments to be debated, not a body of data to be recorded or a set of facts to be memorized. Thus controversy in historical interpretation—over what an event actually means, over what really happened at an occurrence called "an event," over how best to generalize about the event—is at the heart of its value. Of course history teaches us about ourselves. Of course it teaches us to understand and to entertain a proper respect for our collective past. Of course it transmits to us specific skills—how to ask questions, how to seek out answers, how to think logically, cogently, lucidly, purposefully. Of course it is, or ought to be, a pleasure. But we also discover something fundamental about a people in what they choose to argue over in their past. When a society suppresses portions of its past record, as the Soviet Union does today, that society (or its leadership) tells us something about itself. When a society seeks to alter how the record is presented, well-proven facts notwithstanding, we learn how history can become a two-edged sword.

Who controls history, it is written, controls the past, and who controls the past controls the present. Those who would close off historical controversy with the argument that we either know all that we need to know about a subject, or that what we know is so irrefutably correct that anyone who attacks the conventional wisdom about the subject must have destructive purposes in mind, is in the end intent upon destroying the very value of history itself—that value being that history teaches us to *argue productively* with each other.

Obviously, then, history is a social necessity. It gives us our identity. It helps us to find our bearings in an ever more complex present, providing us with a navigator's chart by which we may to some degree orient ourselves. When we ask who we are, and how is it that we are so, we learn skepticism and acquire the beginnings of critical judgment. Along with a sense of narrative—just as an autobiography is a narrative—history also provides us with tools for explanation and analysis. It helps us to find the particular example, to see the uniqueness in a past age or past event, while also helping us to see how the particular and the unique contribute to the general. History thus shows us humanity at work and play, in society, changing through time, in ways that we may approve, praise, share, or even comprehend. By letting us experience other lifestyles, history shows us the values of both subjectivity and objectivity—those twin conditions of our individual view of the world in which we live, conditions between which we constantly, and usually almost without knowing it, move. Thus history is both a form of truth and a matter of opinion, and the close study of history should help us to distinguish between the two. It is important to make such distinctions, for as Sir Walter Raleigh wrote, "It is not truth but opinion that can travel the world without a passport."

Far too often what we read and perceive as truth—in our newspapers, on our television sets, from our friends—is opinion, not fact.

History is an activity. That activity asks specific questions as a means of arriving at general questions. A textbook such as this is concerned overwhelmingly with general questions, even though at times it must ask specific questions or present specific facts as a means of stalking the general. The great philosopher Karl Jaspers once remarked, "Who I am and where I belong, I first learned to know from the mirror of history." It is this mirror which any honest textbook must reflect.

To speak of "civilization" (of which this book is a history) is at once to plunge into controversy, so that our very first words illustrate why some people are so fearful of the study of history. To speak, as we do here, of "Western civilization" is even more restrictive, too provincial in the eyes of some historians. Yet if we are to understand history as a process, we must approach it through a sense of place: our continuity, our standards, our process. Still, we must recognize an inherent bias in such a term as "Western civilization," indeed two inherent biases: first, that we know what it means to be "civilized" and have attained that stature; and second, that the West as a whole is a single unitary civilization. This second bias is made clearer when we recognize that most scholars and virtually all college courses refer not to "Eastern civilization" but to "the civilizations of the East"—a terminology that suggests that while the West is a unity, the East is not. These are conventional phrases, buried in our Western perception of reality, just as our common geographical references show a Western bias. The Near East or the Far East are, after all, "near" or "far" only in reference to a geographical location focused on western Europe. The Japanese do not refer to London as being in the far West, or Los Angeles as being in the far East, though both references would be correct, if they saw the world as though they stood at its center. Though this text will accept these conventional phrases, precisely because they are traditionally embedded in our Western languages, one of the uses of history—and of the study of a book such as this one—is to be alert to the biases inherent in language, even when necessity requires that we continue to use its conventional forms of shorthand.

But if we are to speak of Western civilization, we must have, at the outset, some definition of what we mean by "being civilized." Hundreds of books have been written on this subject. The average person often means only that others, the "noncivilized," speak a different language and practice alien customs. The Chinese customarily referred to all foreigners as barbarians, and the ancient Greeks spoke of those who could not communicate in Greek as *bar-bar*—those who do not speak our tongue. Yet today the ability to communicate in more than one language is a hallmark of a "civilized" person.

Thus definitions of civilization, at least as used by those who think little about the meaning of their words, obviously change.

For our purposes, however, we must have a somewhat more exacting definition of the term, since it guides and informs any textbook that attempts to cover the entire sweep of Western history. Anthropologists, sociologists, historians, and others may reasonably differ about the essential ingredients of a civilization. They may also differ as to whether, for example, there is a separate American civilization that stands apart from, say, a British or Italian civilization, or whether these civilizations are simply particular variants on one larger entity, with only that larger entity—the West—entitled to be called "a civilization." Such an argument is of no major importance here, although it is instructive that it should occur. Rather, what is needed is a definition sufficiently clear to be used throughout the narrative and analysis to follow. This working definition, therefore, will hold that "civilization" involves the presence of several (though not necessarily all) of the following conditions within a society or group of interdependent societies:

1. There will be some form of government by which people administer to their political needs and responsibilities.
2. There will be some development of urban society, that is, of city life, so that the culture is not nomadic, dispersed, and thus unable to leave significant and surviving physical remnants of its presence.
3. A form of literacy will have developed, so that group may communicate with group, and more important, generation with generation in writing.
4. Human beings will have become toolmakers, able through the use of metals to transform, however modestly, their physical environment, and thus, their social and economic environment as well.
5. Some degree of specialization of function will have begun, usually at the work place, so that pride, place, and purpose function as cohesive elements in the society.
6. Social classes will have emerged, whether antagonistic to or sustaining of one another.
7. There will be a concept of leisure time—that life is not solely for the work place, or for the assigned class function or specialization—so that, for example, art may develop beyond (though not excluding) mere decoration.
8. There will be a concept of a higher being, though not necessarily through organized religion, by which a people may take themselves outside themselves to explain events and find purpose.
9. There will be a concept of time, by which the society links itself to a past and to the presumption of a future.
10. There will have developed a faculty for criticism. This faculty need not be the rationalism of the West, or intuition, or any specific religious or political mechanism, but it must exist, so that the society may contemplate change from within, rather than awaiting attack and possible destruction from without.

Not all these conditions are essential to civilization, Western or otherwise. Not all may be present in any society that we could, nonetheless, call civilized, nor do they need to arise in the order suggested here. But through its activities and beliefs the society that is becoming a civilization, or attached to a civilization, will have provided a series of declarations of intent about its aspirations. To be sure, historians lean toward what can be studied and measured through the written record, though they would be quite wrong to rely solely upon such a record. A common Western bias is to measure "progress" through technological change and to suggest that societies that show (at least until quite recently in historical time) little dramatic technological change are not civilized. In truth, neither a written record nor dramatic technological changes are essential to being civilized, though both are no doubt present in societies we would call civilized. Perhaps, as we study history, we ought to remember all *three* of the elements inherent in historical action as recorded by the English critic John Ruskin: "Great nations write their autobiographies in three manuscripts, the book of their deeds, the book of their words, and the book of their art."

The issue here is not whether we "learn from the past." Most often we do not, at least at the simpleminded level; we do not, as a nation, decide upon a course of action in diplomacy, for example, simply because a somewhat similar course in the past worked or did not work. We are wise enough to know that circumstances alter cases and that new knowledge brings new duties. Of course individuals "learn from the past"; the victim of a purse snatching takes precautions in the future. To dignify such an experience as "a lesson of history," however, is to turn mere individual growth from child into adult into history when, at most, such growth is a personal study in biography.

We also sometimes learn the "wrong lessons" from history. Virtually anyone who wishes to argue passionately for a specific course of future action can find a lesson from the past that will convince the gullible that history repeats itself and therefore that the past is a map to the future. No serious historian argues this, however: general patterns may, and sometimes do, repeat themselves, but specific chains of events do not. Unlike those subjects that operate at the very highest level of generalization (political science, theology, science), history simply does not believe in ironclad laws. But history is not solely a series of unrelated events—not simply "one damn thing after another." There are general patterns, clusters of causes, intermediate levels of generalization that prove true. History works at a level uncomfortable to many: above the specific, below the absolute.

If complex problems never present themselves twice in the same or even in recognizably similar form, if, to borrow a frequent image from the military world, generals always prepare for the last war instead of the next one, then does the study of history offer society any help in solving its problems? The answer surely is yes—but only in a limited way. History offers a rich collection of clinical reports on human behavior in various situations—individual and collective, political, economic, military, social, cultural—that tell us in detail how the human race has conducted its affairs and that suggest ways of handling similar problems in the present. President Harry S Truman's secretary of state, a former chief of staff, General George Marshall, once remarked that nobody could think about the problems of the 1950s who had not reflected upon the fall of Athens in the fifth century B.C. He was referring to the extraordinary history of the war between Athens and Sparta written just after it was over by Thucydides, an Athenian who fought in the war. There were no nuclear weapons, no telecommunications, no guns or gunpowder in the fifth century B.C.; the logistics of the war were altogether primitive, yet twenty-three hundred years later one of the most distinguished leaders of American military and political affairs found Thucydides indispensable to his thinking.

History, then, can only approximate the range of human behavior, with some indication of its extremes and averages. It can, though not perfectly, show how and within what limits human behavior changes. This last point is especially important for the social scientist, the economist, the sociologist, the executive, the journalist, or the diplomat. History provides materials that even an inspiring leader—a prophet, a reformer, or a columnist—would do well to master before seeking to lead us into new ways. For it can tell us something about what human material can and cannot stand, just as science and technology can tell engineers what stresses metals can stand. History can provide an awareness of the depth of time and space that should check the optimism and the overconfidence of the reformer. For example, millions of hours are wasted teaching children to read English, with its absurd spelling and its overrefined punctuation; yet the slightest background in history would show that societies usually resist changes like the reform of spelling, or accept them only during revolutions (as when the metric system was introduced during the French Revolution), or under dictatorships (as when the Turkish alphabet was changed from Arabic to Roman in the 1920s by the dictator Kemal Atatürk).

We may wish to protect the environment in which we live—to eliminate acid rain, to cleanse our rivers, to protect our wildlife, to preserve our majestic natural scenery. History may show us that most peoples have failed to do so, and may provide us with some guidance on how to avoid the mistakes of the past. But history will also show that there are substantial differences of public and private opinion over how best to protect our environment; or that there are many people who do not believe such protection is necessary; or that there are people who accept the need for protection but are equally convinced that lower levels of protection must be traded off for higher levels of productivity from our natural resources. History can provide the setting by which we may understand differing opinions, but recourse to history will not get the legislation passed, the angry made happy, the future made clean and safe. History will not define river pollution, though it can provide us with statistics from the past for comparative measurement. The definition will arise from the politics of today and our judgments about tomorrow. History is for the long and at times for the intermediate run, but seldom for the short run.

So, if we are willing to accept a "relevance" that is more difficult to see at first than the immediate applicability of science, and more remote than direct action, we will have to admit that history is "relevant." It may not actually build the highway or clear the slum, but it can give enormous help to those who wish to do so. And failure to take it into account may lead to failure in the sphere of action.

But history is also fun, at least for those who enjoy giving their curiosity free rein. Whether it is historical gossip we prefer (How many lovers did Catherine the Great of Russia actually take in a given year, and how much political influence did their activity in the imperial bedroom give them?), or the details of historical investigation (How does it happen that the actual treasures found in a buried Viking ship correspond to those described in an Anglo-Saxon poetic account of a ship-burial?), or more complex questions of cause and effect (How influential have the writings of revolutionary intellectuals been upon the course of actual revolutions?), or the relationships between politics and economics (How far does the rise and decline of Spanish power in modern times depend upon the supply of gold from the New World colonies?), or cultural problems (Why did western Europe choose to revive classical Greek and Roman art and literature instead of turning to some other culture or to some altogether new experiment?), those who enjoy history will read almost greedily to discover what they want to know. Having discovered it, they may want to know how we know what we have learned, and may want to turn to those sources closest in time to the persons and questions concerned—to the original words of the participants. To read about Socrates, Columbus, or Churchill is fun; to read their *own* words, to visit with them as it were, is even more so. To see them in context is important; to see how we have taken their thoughts and woven them to purposes of our own is at least equally important. Readers will find their path across the mine-studded fields of history helped just a little by extracts from these voices—voices of the past but also of the present. They can also be helped by outlines, summaries, bibliographies, pictures, maps—devices through which historians share their sense of fun and immediacy with a reader.

In the end, to know the past *is to know ourselves*—not entirely, not enough, but a little better. History can help us to achieve some grace and elegance of action, some cogency and completion of thought, some harmony and tolerance in human relationships. Most of all, history can give us a sense of excitement, a personal zest for watching and perhaps participating in the events around us which will, one day, be history too.

THE PROBLEM OF DIVINE-RIGHT MONARCHY

The Peace of Westphalia in 1648 ended the Thirty Years' War but also marked the end of an epoch in European history. It ended the Age of the Reformation and Counter-Reformation, when wars were both religious and dynastic in motivation, and the chief threats to a stable international balance came from the Catholic Hapsburgs and from the militant Protestants of Germany, the Netherlands, and Scandinavia. After 1648 religion, though continuing to be a major source of friction in France and the British Isles, ceased to be a significant international issue elsewhere. The main force jeopardizing the European balance thereafter was the entirely secular ambition of Bourbon France on the Continent and abroad. For seventy-two years (1643-1714) France was under a single monarch, Louis XIV, who inherited the throne when only four.

Louis was the embodiment of the early modern form of royal absolutism—monarchy by divine right—and he was the personification of royal pride, elegance, and luxury. To the French, Louis XIV was the *grand monarque*. His long reign brought to an end the *grand siècle*, that great century begun under Cardinal Richelieu in the twenty years before Louis's accession that was marked by the international triumph of French arms and French diplomacy and, still more, of French ways of writing, building, dressing, eating—the whole style of life of the upper classes in France, which called itself *la grande nation*.

While French culture went from triumph to triumph, Louis XIV's bid for political hegemony was ultimately checked. His most resolute opponent was England, still in the throes of the greatest political upheaval in its history, an upheaval that resulted from the collision between the forces of the Stuart monarchy and High Church Anglicanism, on the one hand, and those of Parliament and the Puritans, on the other. The final settlement, after decades of violence and change, was a compromise weighted in favor of the parliamentary side, with one English king executed and another forced into exile. While France appeared stable, England was racked by revolution and insecurity.

The seventeenth century, during which the struggle for stability could be seen in most societies of early modern Europe, was an age of crisis. In England the aristocracy faced unique challenges; a steady decline in population in war-ravaged Germany and in Spain changed society drastically, and the years after 1648 were marked throughout most of Europe by a severe depression, by social upheavals, and by a struggle between the capitalism espoused by the rising middle class and the agrarian traditions of the landed classes, who feared displacement. Revolution seemed almost commonplace—successful, abortive, plotted, rumored—in England, France, Portugal, Spain, and elsewhere. Still, since the province or an even smaller local unit generally remained relatively self-sufficient economically, these broad generalizations about trends are open to many exceptions. And as always, amidst change there was continuity.

It was also a century of intellectual ferment, as writers, philosophers, theologians, painters sought to justify monarchy by divine right or revolution by various groups that saw themselves as "the people," and as the basic intellectual underpinnings of society were changed. The seventeenth century is often called "the century of the genius," for so many innovative ideas sprang forth during it: from explorers and conquerors, from simple sailors and soldiers, from figures like Bacon, Descartes, Pascal, Newton, or Locke, as well as from inventors who drew upon the theories of Galileo and others. According to different historians, "modern history" began with a different event or development, but nearly all agree that the 1600s were the century when Western civilization passed into what is known as the Modern Age.

The intimations of popular revolution in the seventeenth century, the impact of new ideas on a broader public, and the slow but certain change of even traditional peasant culture, which was becoming more articulate, more observable through the printed record, were yet another dividing line between the Middle Ages and the modern period. Before 1700 most people apparently were basically illiterate; a century later, literacy was apparently far more widespread.

I BOURBON FRANCE

Louis XIII and Richelieu, 1610-1643

In 1610 the capable and popular Henry IV was assassinated in the prime of his career by a madman who was believed at the time to be working for the Jesuits—a charge for which there is no proof. The new king, Louis XIII (1610-1643), was nine years old; the queen mother, Marie de' Medici, served as regent but showed little political skill. Her Italian favorites and French nobles, Catholic and Huguenot alike, carried on a hectic competition that threatened to undo all that Henry IV had accomplished. During these troubles the French representative body, the Estates General, met in 1614 for what was destined to be its last session until 1789. Significantly, the meeting was paralyzed by tensions between the noble deputies of the second estate and the bourgeois of the third. Meanwhile, Louis XIII, though barely into his teens, tried to assert his personal authority and reduce the role of his mother. Poorly educated, sickly, masochistic, and subject to depression, Louis needed expert help.

This illustration from Abraham Bosse's "Le Palais Royal" (1640) provides a good picture of French fashions and tastes. Bosse (1602-1676) took a particular interest in etchings that showed how the upper middle class dressed. Furniture also evolved in new styles to accommodate the new clothing.

He was fortunate in securing the assistance of the remarkably talented duc de Richelieu (1585-1642), who was an efficient administrator as bishop of the remote diocese of Autun. Tiring of provincial life, Richelieu moved to Paris and showed unscrupulous skill in political maneuvering during the confused days of the regency. He emerged as the conciliator between the king and his mother and was rewarded, first, by being made a cardinal and then, in 1624, with selection by Louis as his chief minister. While the king maintained a lively interest in affairs of state, Richelieu was the virtual ruler of France for the next eighteen years. He proved to be a good Machiavellian, subordinating religion and every other consideration to *raison d'état* (reason of state)—a phrase that he may have coined himself.

Richelieu had four goals for the France of Louis XIII: to eliminate the Huguenots as an effective political force; to remind the nobles that they were subordinate to the king; to make all of France conscious of a sense of national greatness; and, through these measures, to make the monarchy truly rather than only theoretically absolute. *Raison d'état* made the ruin of the Huguenots the first priority, for the political privileges they had received by the Edict of Nantes made them a major obstacle to the creation of a centralized state. The hundred fortified towns they governed, chiefly in the southwest, were a state within the state, a hundred centers of potential rebellion. Alarmed, the Huguenots rebelled. The fall of La Rochelle, their chief stronghold, in 1628 and Richelieu's unexpectedly humane approach—by which the political and military clauses of the Edict of Nantes were revoked while partial religious toleration continued—helped Richelieu neutralize the Huguenots.

The siege of La Rochelle was prolonged because France had no navy worthy of the name. Over the next

LE GRAND MONARQUE

At age twenty-two Louis XIV already displayed an impressive royal presence, as reported by Madame de Motteville (d. 1689), an experienced observer of the French court:

As the single desire for glory and to fulfill all the duties of a great king occupied his whole heart, by applying himself to toil he began to like it; and the eagerness he had to learn all the things that were necessary to him soon made him full of that knowledge. His great good sense and his good intentions now made visible in him the rudiments of general knowledge which had been hidden from all who did not see him in private. . . . He was agreeable personally, civil and easy of access to every one; but with a lofty and serious air which impressed the public with respect and awe . . . , though he was familiar and gay with ladies.

Memoirs of Madame [Françoise Bertaut] de Motteville on Anne of Austria and Her Court, trans. Katherine Prescott Wormeley (Boston: Hardy Pratt, 1902), III: 243.

As she noted, the young king never laughed in games or at play, and he said of himself that he must be "perfect in all things" and never be found "to fail in anything."

ten years Richelieu created a fleet of warships for the Atlantic and a squadron of galleys manned by European slaves for the Mediterranean. Meanwhile, he guided France expertly through the Thirty Years' War, committing French resources only when concrete gains seemed possible and ensuring favorable publicity by supplying exaggerated accounts of French victories to the *Gazette de France*.

Few official portraits from this period have survived. The only ones about which knowledge is certain are those of Louis XIII and Richelieu. Philippe de Champaigne (1602-1674) often depicted Richelieu, and in this triple portrait he sought to emphasize the rationalism of the age. The painting is now in the National Gallery, London.

Next Richelieu tried to humble the nobles, with only partial success, by ordering the destruction of some of their fortresses and forbidding private duels. More effective was his transfer of supervision of local administration from the nobles and officeholders of doubtful loyalty who had purchased their posts to more reliable royal officials called *intendants*. These officials had existed earlier but had performed only minor functions; now they were given greatly increased powers over justice, the police, and taxation.

Richelieu made possible *la grande nation* of Louis XIV by building an efficient, centralized state. But in a sense he built too well, making the French government so centralized, so professionally bureaucratic, that it became too inflexible for the give and take of politics. Moreover, Richelieu did little to remedy the chronic fiscal weakness of the government, particularly the corruption in tax collection and the recurrent deficits. His concentration on *raison d'état* led him to take a callous view of the subjects on whose loyal performance of their duties the strength of the state depended. He believed that the masses were best kept docile through hard work, that leisure led to mischief, and that the common people ought to take pride in the splendors of the monarchy, in the accomplishments of French literary culture, and in victories over the monarch's enemies. Individual hardship, especially among the lower classes, was to be accepted in the interests of national glory—a common ingredient of nationalism.

Mazarin

The deaths of Richelieu in 1642 and Louis XIII in 1643, the accession of another child king, and the regency of the hated queen mother, Anne of Austria (actually a

Hapsburg from Spain, where the dynasty was called the house of Austria), all seemed to threaten a repetition of the crisis that had followed the death of Henry IV. The new crisis was dealt with by the new chief minister, Jules Mazarin (1602-1661), a Sicilian who had been picked and schooled by Richelieu himself and was exceptionally close to Anne. Mazarin, too, was a cardinal (though not a priest, as Richelieu had been) and a supreme exponent of *raison d'état*. Mazarin was also careless about the finances of France, but, unlike Richelieu, he amassed an immense personal fortune during his career. He antagonized both branches of the French aristocracy: the nobles of the sword, descendants of feudal magnates, and the nobles of the robe (the reference is to the gowns worn by judges and other officials), descendants of commoners who had bought their way into government office. The former resented being excluded from the regency by a foreigner; the latter, who had invested heavily in government securities, particularly disliked Mazarin's casual way of borrowing money to meet war expenses and then neglecting to pay the interest on the loans.

In 1648 discontent boiled over in the *Fronde* (named for the slingshot used by Parisian children to hurl pellets at the rich in their carriages), one of several midcentury uprisings in Europe. Some of the rioting involved the rural peasantry and the common people of Paris, impoverished by the economic depression accompanying the final campaigns of the Thirty Years' War and deeply affected by the peak famine years of 1648-1651. But the Fronde was essentially a revolt of the nobles, led first by the judges of the Parlement of Paris, a stronghold of the nobles of the robe, and then, after the Peace of Westphalia, by aristocratic officers returned from the Thirty Years' War. Various "princes of the blood" (relatives of the royal family) confusingly intervened with private armies. Though Mazarin twice had to flee France and go into exile, and though the royal troops had to lay siege to Paris, and despite concessions Mazarin felt forced to make, the end result of what was in reality two revolts in one—of the Parlement and of the nobles—was to weaken both. The Fronde prepared the way for the personal rule of Louis XIV, with the mass of ordinary citizens in Paris supporting the queen and her son when they returned in triumph in October of 1652. Essentially, the Fronde failed because it had no real roots in the countryside, not even in the rising middle classes of the provincial cities. Rather, it was essentially a struggle for power, pitting Mazarin and his new bureaucracy against the two privileged groups of nobles, each of which distrusted the other. All Mazarin had to do was to apply the old Roman maxim, "Divide and rule."

Louis XIV, 1643-1714

When Mazarin died in 1661, Louis XIV began his personal rule. He had been badly frightened during the Fronde when rioters had broken into his bedroom, and he was determined to suppress any challenge to his authority, by persuasion and guile if possible, and by force if necessary. In 1660 he married a Spanish princess for political reasons; after a succession of mistresses, he married again, in 1685, to a devout former Huguenot, Madame de Maintenon, the governess of his illegitimate children, and she did much to assure dignified piety at court for the rest of his reign.

Louis XIV, the Sun King, succeeded as the *grand monarque* because by education, temperament, and physique he was ideally suited to the role. He had admirable self-discipline, patience, and staying power. He never lost his temper in public and went through long daily council meetings and elaborate ceremonials with unwearied attention and even enjoyment, to which his conspicuous lack of a sense of humor may have contributed. He had an iron physical constitution, which enabled him to withstand a rigorous schedule, made him indifferent to heat and to cold, and allowed him to survive both a lifetime of gross overeating and the crude medical treatment of the day.

He was five feet five inches tall (a fairly impressive height for that day) and added to his stature by shoes with high red heels. To provide a suitable setting for the Sun King, to neutralize the high nobility politically by isolating it in the ceaseless ceremonies and petty in-

Engraving was a particularly important art form in the seventeenth century, for acids and etching tools had been greatly improved. The French were proud of their public buildings, which were often used as subjects for engravings, as with this work by P. Menant, showing the Palace of Versailles. The foreground emphasizes that the palace was in the countryside, well outside Paris.

trigues of court life, and also to prevent a repetition of the rioters' intrusion into his bedroom in Paris, he moved the capital from Paris to Versailles, a dozen miles away. There, between 1668 and 1711, he built a vast palace more than a third of a mile long, set in an immense formal garden with fourteen hundred fountains, supplied by water which had to be pumped up from the River Seine at great expense. Versailles housed, mainly in cramped, uncomfortable quarters, a court of ten thousand, including dependents and servants of all sorts. This was self-conscious government by spectacle, and it would be copied by every monarch who could afford it—and some who could not.

Divine-Right Monarchy

The much admired and imitated French state, of which Versailles was the symbol and Louis XIV the embodiment, is also the best historical example of divine-right monarchy. Perhaps Louis never actually said, "*L'état c'est moi*" (I am the state), but the phrase clearly summarizes his convictions about his role. In theory, Louis was the representative of God on earth—or at least in France. He was not elected by the French, nor did he acquire his throne by force of arms; rather, he was born to a position God had planned for the legitimate male heir of Hugh Capet who had been king of France in the tenth century. As God's agent his word was final, for to challenge it would be to challenge the structure of God's universe; disobedience was a religious as well as a political offense. Thus the origins of divine right were a logical extension of Gallicanism.

In some ways the theory that justified divine-right monarchy looked back to the Middle Ages, to the view that right decisions in government are not arrived at by experiment and discussion, but by "finding" the authoritative answer provided for in God's scheme of things. In other ways the theory was "modern" or forward-looking, in that it derived from expectations about national loyalties and the growth of a sense of nationalism. Henry IV, Richelieu, and Louis XIV sought to fuse the sixteen million inhabitants of France into a single national unit. The problem was to make these millions think of themselves as French and not as Normans, Bretons, Flemings, Alsatians, Burgundians, Gascons, Basques, and Provençaux. The makers of the Bourbon monarchy could not rely on a common language, for only a minority spoke the standardized French that the French Academy tried to foster. Nor could they rely on a common education, a common national press, or a common participation in political life. They could, and did, attempt to set the king up as the symbol of common Frenchness. The king collected taxes, raised armies, and touched the lives of his subjects in a hundred ways. The French had to believe that the king had a right to do all this, and that he was doing it for them rather than to them.

Divine-right monarchy, with its corollary of unquestioning obedience on the part of subjects, was thus one ingredient in the growth of the modern centralized nation-state. It was an institution that appealed to old theological ideas, such as the biblical admonition to obey the powers that be, for "the powers that be are ordained of God." But it was also inspired by the newer ideas of binding people together in a productive, efficient, and secure state. Naturally, in practice the institution did not wholly correspond to theories about it. Louis XIV was not the French state, and his rule was not absolute in any true sense of that word. He simply did not have the physical means to control in detail everything his subjects did; but his policies could touch their daily lives by bringing relative prosperity or hardship, peace or war. And Louis XIV could endeavor, in the majesty of his person, to act out the theories of those like Bishop Jacques Bossuet (1627-1704), who provided the intellectual foundations for a universal history that justified divine-right arguments.

Increasingly, the chief opposition to such ideas came not from the various religions but from the feudal nobles, so that in both France and England the seventeenth century brought a crisis to the aristocracy. The degree to which the nobility was integrated into the new state machinery was of crucial importance in the development of modern Europe. In Hapsburg Spain and in the Hapsburg lands of central Europe the old nobility generally accepted the new strength of the Crown, but maintained many of their privileges and all of their old pride of status. In Prussia they were more successfully integrated into the new order, becoming servants of the crown, yet with a social status that set them well above bourgeois bureaucrats. In England the nobility achieved a unique compromise with the Crown. In France the nobles of the sword were deprived of most major political functions, but they were allowed to retain social and economic privileges and important roles as officers in the king's army.

This process of reducing the old French nobility to relative powerlessness in national political life had begun during the fifteenth century and had been hastened by the religious and civil wars of the next century. An important part of the nobility, perhaps nearly half, had become Protestant, in large part from sheer opposition to the Crown. The victory of Henry IV, purchased by his conversion to Catholicism, was a defeat for the nobility. Under Richelieu and Louis XIV the process was completed by the increasing use of commoners to run the government, from the great ministers of state, through the intendants, down to local administrators and judges. These commoners were usually elevated to the nobility of the robe, which did not at first have the social prestige of the nobility of the sword. But the Fronde had shown that these new nobles could not be counted upon as loyal supporters of the Crown, and among the old nobles they aroused contemptuous envy. Though at times they were able to work together, they posed no long-term threat to the Crown.

Louis XIV was sixty-three and at the height of his power when Hyacinthe Rigaud (1659-1743) painted this strikingly posed portrait. In the background Rigaud has invoked memories of another great empire, Rome, while showing Louis's strength and sense of elegance in the flowing robe, the great ceremonial sword of office, and the coiffed wig. This portrait hangs in the Louvre in Paris.

Nor did the church. Under Louis XIV the French clergy continued to possess important privileges; they were not subject to royal taxation; they contributed a voluntary grant of money that they voted in their own assembly. Carefully the Crown fostered the evolution of a national Gallican chuch, firmly Catholic though controlled by the monarchy. The Gallican union of throne and altar reached a high point in 1682, when an assembly of French clerics drew up the Declaration of Gallican Liberties, asserting in effect that the "rules and customs admitted by France and the Gallican church" were just as important as the traditional authority of the papacy. Louis XIV thereupon took as the goal of his religious policy the application of a French motto—*un roi, une loi, une foi* (One king, one law, one faith).

Where Richelieu had attacked only the political privileges of the Huguenots, Louis attacked their fundamental right of toleration and finally revoked the Edict of Nantes in 1685. Fifty thousand Huguenot families fled abroad, notably to Prussia, Holland, the Dutch colony in southern Africa, England, and British North America. The practical skills and the intellectual abilities of the refugees strenghtened the lands that received them, and the departure of industrious workers and thousands of veteran sailors, soldiers, and officers weakened France. Some Huguenots remained in France, worshiping secretly despite persecution.

Within the Catholic church itself, Louis had to contend with two important elements that refused to accept Gallicanism. Both groups saw themselves as countering the Counter-Reformation while remaining within the Catholic church. The Quietists, a group of religious enthusiasts led by Madame Jeanne Marie Guyon (1648-1717), sought a more mystical and emotional faith and believed in direct inspiration from God and perfect union with him, so that a priesthood was not needed; but their tendency to exhibitionism and self-righteousness combined with their zeal for publicity belied their name and offended the king's sense of propriety. The Jansenists, sometimes called the Puritans of the Catholic church, were a high-minded group whose most distinguished spokesman was the scientist and philosopher Blaise Pascal. Named for Cornelius Jansen (1585-1638), bishop of Ypres, the Jansenists took an almost Calvinistic stand on predestination. They stressed the need to obey God rather than man, no matter how exalted the position of the particular man might be. They therefore questioned the authority of both king and pope, and attacked the pope's agents, the Jesuits. On the surface, Louis repressed both Quietists and Jansenists, but the latter survived two papal bulls of condemnation (1705, 1713) to trouble his successors in the eighteenth century.

The Royal Administration

Of course, in a land as large and complex as France, even the tireless Louis could do no more than exercise general supervision. At Versailles he had three long conferences weekly with his ministers, who headed departments of War, Finance, Foreign Affairs, and the Interior. The king kept this top administrative level on an intimate scale; he usually had only four ministers at one time and gave them virtually permanent tenure. Jean Colbert (1619-1683) served as controller general for eighteen years, and Michel Le Tellier (1603-1685) was secretary of state for the army for thirty-four years, a post later entrusted to his son, who had been ennobled as the marquis de Louvois (1639-1691). All told, only sixteen ministers held office during the fifty-four years of Louis's personal reign. Yet in practice the royal administration was full of difficulties and contradictions. There were many conflicting jurisdictions, survivals of feudalism; the officials of Louis XIV, being nobles of the robe, had a privileged status they could hand down to their heirs. The thirty key provincial administrators, the intendants, were agents of the Crown, but many of them exercised considerable initiative on their own, despite being moved about from one administrative unit to another.

A particularly important potential for trouble existed in the parlements, the supreme courts of appeal in the various provinces. The Parlement of Paris enjoyed special prestige and power from its place in the capital and from the size of its territorial jurisdiction—almost half of France. The judges who staffed these courts headed the nobility of the robe, owned their offices, and could not be removed by the king. Besides the usual work of a court of appeals, the parlements also had to register royal edicts before they went into force. They thus claimed the right to refuse an edict if they thought it not in accord with the higher law of the land. Although this claim negated theoretical royal absolutism, Louis got around it in his own lifetime by using another old institution, the *lit de justice* (literally, "bed of justice"), in which he summoned the Parlement of Paris before him in a formal session and ordered the justices to register a royal edict. In this way, for instance, he enforced measures against Jansenism, which was strong among the judges. But the parlements were also to continue to plague his eighteenth-century successors.

Mercantilism and Colbert Divine-right monarchy was not peculiarly French, of course, nor was the mercantilism practiced by the France of Louis XIV. But like divine-right rule, it flourished most characteristically under the Sun King. Mercantilism was central to the early modern effort to construct strong, efficient political units. The mercantilists aimed to make their nation as self-sustaining as possible, as independent as possible of the need to import goods from other nations, which were its rivals and potential enemies. The mercantilists held that production within a nation should provide all the necessities of life for a hard-working population, and also provide the power needed to fight and win wars. They believed that these goals required planning and control from above. They wished to sweep away such medieval remnants as the manor and the guild, which, they felt, reduced the energies and abilities needed in an expanding economy. But they did not believe, as free-trade economists would later argue, that people should be free to do whatever they thought would enrich themselves. Instead, the mercantilists would channel the national economic effort by protective tariffs, by government subsidies, by grants of monopolies, by industries run directly by the government, and by scientific and applied research.

The mercantilists viewed overseas possessions as a particularly important part of France that should be run from the homeland by a strong government. Many foodstuffs and raw materials were more easily available overseas than in Europe. Colonies therefore should be encouraged to provide necessities, so that the mother country need not import them from competitors. In return, the mother country would supply industrial goods to the colonies and have a monopoly over colonial trade. This mercantilistic approach to colonies was followed not only by France and Spain but by the less absolutist governments of England and Holland.

The great French practitioner of mercantilism was Colbert, who had served his apprenticeship under Mazarin and advanced rapidly to become controller general early in the personal reign of Louis. He never quite attained the supremacy reached by Richelieu and Mazarin; he was the collaborator, never the master, of Louis XIV, since other great ministers, especially, Louvois for military affairs, stood in the way of his supremacy. Yet Colbert was influential in all matters affecting the French economy, most interested in foreign trade and in the colonies, and therefore in the merchant marine and in the navy. His hand was in everything: in invention, in technological education, in designing and building ships, in attracting foreign experts to settle in France.

Among the industries Colbert fostered were the processing of sugar, chocolate, and tobacco from the colonies; the production of military goods by iron foundries and textile mills; and the manufacture of the luxuries for which the French soon became famous. The fifteenth-century Gobelins tapestry enterprise in Paris was taken over by the state and its output expanded to include elegant furniture, for which the king was a major customer. Glassblowers and lacemakers were lured away from Venice, despite strenuous efforts by the Venetian republic to keep their valuable techniques secret. In a blow against French competitors, Colbert imposed heavy tariffs on some Dutch and English products. To promote trade with the colonies and also with the Baltic and the Mediterranean, he financed trading companies, of which only the French India Company eventually succeeded.

At home, Colbert encouraged reforestation, so that iron foundries could have abundant supplies of charcoal (then essential for smelting); he also promoted the planting of mulberry trees to nourish the silkworms vital to textile output. He even attempted—vainly, as it turned out—to control quality by ordering that defective goods be prominently exhibited in public, along with the name of the offending producer, and that the culprit be exhibited for a third offense. He also endeavored, again for the most part in vain, to break down the barriers to internal free trade, such as provincial and municipal tariffs or local restrictions on the shipment of grain to other parts of France. He did, however, successfully sponsor the construction of important roads and canals; the Canal du Midi, linking the Atlantic port of Bordeaux with the Mediterranean port of Narbonne, reduced transport charges between the two seas by three-fourths and was described as the greatest engineering feat since Roman days.

Whether the great prosperity France achieved in the first thirty years of Louis's reign came about because of, or despite, the mercantilist policies of Colbert is difficult to decide. Under the mercantilist regime France did attain undoubted leadership in European industry and commerce. That lead was lost in part because the last two wars of Louis XIV were ruinously expensive, in part because in the eighteenth century France's rival, England, introduced new methods of power machinery and concentrated on large-scale production of inexpensive goods, while France clung to the policies set by Colbert, favoring relatively small-scale production of luxuries and other consumer goods. But the difference between French and English industry was also a difference in the focus of national energies; France, like Spain before it, spent an exceptional proportion of its national product in an unfruitful effort to dominate through the force of arms both Europe and the known overseas world.

French Expansion

France was the real victor in the Thirty Years' War, acquiring lands on its northeastern frontier. In a postscript to the main conflict, it continued fighting with Spain until the Peace of the Pyrenees in 1659, securing additional territories. Prospering economically, France was ready for further expansion when the young and ambitious Louis XIV began his personal rule in 1661. Louis hoped to complete the gains of 1648 and 1659 and secure France's "natural frontiers" along the Rhine and the Alps. As his sense of confidence grew, he waged a mercantilist war against France's major economic competitors, Holland and England. At the height of his prestige, Louis probably wanted to revive the multinational empire that Charlemagne had ruled nine hundred years earlier. He was also keenly aware of cultural imperialism, and he wanted the French language, French taste in the arts, and French customs to spread their influence over Europe.

Louis XIV and his talented experts fashioned splendid instruments to support this aggressive foreign policy. In 1661 half a dozen men made up the whole Ministry of Foreign Affairs; half a century later it had a large staff of clerks, archivists, coders (and decoders) of secret messages, secret agents, and great lords and prelates who lent their dignity to important embassies. The growth of the French army was still more impressive, from a peacetime force of twenty thousand to a wartime one almost twenty times larger. Louis and his lieutenants almost revolutionized the character of France's fighting forces. At the Ministry of War the father and son team of Le Tellier and Louvois grouped regiments in brigades under a general to bring them under closer control. They also introduced two new ranks of officer, major and lieutenant colonel, to give more opportunity to talented commoners; these new commissions were awarded only for merit and were not available for purchase, like the ranks of colonel or captain. Supplies were more abundant, pay was more regular, and an effort was made to weed out the lazy. The inspector general of infantry, Jean Martinet (d. 1672), was so rigorous in drilling and discipline that his name added a word to the modern vocabulary. The armies showed particular strength in artillery, engineering, and siege techniques, all important in the days when armies moved ponderously and did much fighting in the waterlogged Low Countries. The French boasted an engineer of genius, Marshal de Vauban (1633-1707), of whom it was said that a town he besieged was indefensible and a town he defended was impregnable. And though military medical services remained crude and sketchy, a large veteran's hospital, Hôtel des Invalides, was built in Paris.

The First Two Wars of Louis XIV The main thrust of this vast effort was northeast, toward the Low Countries and Germany. Louis XIV sought also to secure Spain as a French satellite with a French ruler. Finally, French commitments overseas in North America and in India drove him to attempt, against English and Dutch rivals, to establish a great French empire outside Europe.

The first war of Louis XIV was a minor one, with Spain, and it ended quickly with the peace of Aix-la-Chappelle in 1668. Furious at the Dutch because of their economic ascendancy, their Calvinism, and their republicanism, Louis resolved to teach them a lesson for entering into an alliance with England and Sweden against him. He bought off Sweden and England, and in 1672 French forces invaded Holland. The terrified Dutch turned to the youthful William III of Orange (1650-1702), great-grandson of the martyred hero of Dutch independence, William the Silent. But the French advance was halted only by the extreme measure of opening the dikes.

Thereupon, Spain, the Holy Roman Empire, and Brandenburg-Prussia joined against France and her allies. French diplomacy separated this ineffective coalition at the six treaties of Nijmegen (Nimwegen) in 1678-1679. Holland was left intact at the cost of promising to remain neutral, and the French gave up Colbert's tariff on Dutch goods; Spain ceded to France the Franche Comté (county of Burgundy), part of the Hapsburgs' Burgundian inheritance, plus some towns in Belgium; Prussia, which had defeated Louis's ally, Sweden, at Fehrbellin (1675), was nonetheless obliged by French pressure to return Swedish lands in Germany. The power and prestige of France were now at their peak, as rulers all over Europe, and in particular the host of minor German princes, tried to copy the standards of Versailles.

The Last Two Wars But in the last three decades of Louis's reign most of his assets were consumed. Not content with the prestige he had won in his first two wars, Louis took on most of the Western world in what looked like an effort to destroy the independence of Holland and most of western Germany and to bring the Iberian peninsula under a French ruler. As a prelude to new military aggression special courts, "chambers of reunion," were set up by the French in the early 1680s to tidy up the loose ends of the peace settlements of the past generation. And there were loose ends aplenty on the northern and eastern frontiers of France, a zone of political fragmentation and confused feudal remnants, many of which were technically within the Holy Roman Empire. After examining the documents in disputed cases, the chambers of reunion "reunited" many strategic bits of land to territories controlled by France. In this way the former free city of Strasbourg, the chief town of Alsace, passed under French control.

Continued French nibbling at western Germany and Louis's assertion of a dynastic claim to most of the lands of the German elector Palatine set off the third of his wars, the War of the League of Augsburg, 1688-1697. This league against Louis was put together by his old foe, William of Orange, who after 1688 shared the throne of England with his wife, Mary, daughter of James II. Thereafter England was thoroughly against Louis. The League also included Spain, the Holy Roman Empire, and Savoy, which was threatened by Louis's tactics of "reunion." The English won a great naval victory at Cape La Hogue in 1692, but William was repeatedly defeated on land in the Low Countries, though never decisively crushed. In Ireland, French (and thus Catholic) attempts to restore the deposed English king, James II, were foiled at the battle of the Boyne in 1690. France and England also exchanged blows in India, the West Indies, and North America, where the colonists called the conflict King William's War. The Treaty of Ryswick ended the war in a peace without victory, an agreement to hold to the status quo.

In 1701 Louis XIV took a step that led to his last and greatest conflict, the War of the Spanish Succession (1701-1714). Charles II, the Hapsburg king of Spain and Louis's brother-in-law, had died in 1700 without a direct heir. For years diplomats had been striving to arrange a succession that would avoid putting on the throne either a French Bourbon or an Austrian Hapsburg. Although they had agreed on a Bavarian prince, he had died in 1699, and plans were made to partition the Spanish inheritance between Hapsburgs and Bourbons. Charles II left his lands intact to Philip of Anjou, grandson of Louis XIV. Louis accepted on behalf of Philip, even though he had signed the treaty of partition. This threat to the balance of power was neatly summarized in the remark a gloating Frenchman is supposed to have made, "There are no longer any Pyrenees." England, Holland, Savoy, the Holy Roman Empire, and many German states formed the Grand Alliance to preserve a separate Spain.

In the bloody war that followed, the French were gradually worn down. In North America they lost Nova Scotia to the English, and in Europe they were beaten by the allies in four major battles, beginning with Blenheim in 1704 and concluding with Malplaquet in 1709. The allied armies were commanded by two great generals, the French-born Prince Eugene of Savoy (1663-1736) and the English John Churchill (1650-1722), first duke of Marlborough. But the French were not annihilated, and Malplaquet cost the allies twenty thousand casualties, at least as many as the French suffered. By scraping the bottom of the barrel for men and money, the French still managed to keep armies in the field.

Moreover, the Grand Alliance was weakening. The English, following their policy of keeping any single continental power from attaining too strong a position, were almost as anxious to prevent the union of Austria and Spain under a Hapsburg as to prevent the union of France and Spain under a Bourbon. At home they faced a possible disputed succession to the throne, and the mercantile classes were sick of a war that was injuring trade and seemed unlikely to bring any compensating gains. In 1710 the pro-peace party won a parliamentary majority and began negotiations that culminated in a series of treaties at Utrecht in 1713.

Utrecht was a typical balance-of-power peace, which contained France without humiliating it. France lost Newfoundland, Nova Scotia, and the Hudson Bay territories to England, while preserving Quebec, Louisiana, and its Caribbean islands. In a sense Louis gained what he had gone to war over, for Philip of Anjou was formally recognized as King Philip V of Spain and secured the Spanish lands overseas. However, the French and Spanish crowns were forbidden ever to be held by the same person, so the allies too had won their point. Furthermore, England took from Spain the Mediterranean island of Minorca and the great Rock of Gibraltar guarding the Atlantic entrance to the Mediterranean. The English also gained the *Asiento*, the right to supply slaves to the Spanish colonies—a right that also gave them opportunities for smuggling. The Austrian Hapsburgs were compensated with Belgium and the former Spanish possessions of Milan and Naples. In Belgium—now the Austrian Netherlands—the Dutch were granted the right to garrison certain fortified towns, "barrier fortresses," for better defense against possible French aggression. For faithfulness to the Grand Alliance, the duke of Savoy was eventually rewarded with Sardinia and the title of king. The elector of Brandenburg was also rewarded with a royal title, king *in* (not *of*) Prussia, which lay outside the Holy Roman Empire.

Yet the rivalry between France and England for empire overseas was undiminished. After Utrecht, in India, as in North America, each nation would continue to try to oust the other from land and trade. In Europe the Dutch did not feel secure against the French, while the Austrian Hapsburg emperor, Charles VI (1711-1740), never gave up hope of becoming "Charles III" of Spain. The distribution of Italian lands satisfied no one, Italian or outsider, and the next two decades were filled with acrimonious negotiations over Italy. In short, the peace was fatally flawed.

French Aggression in Review

Proponents of the view that Europe underwent a severe crisis during the seventeenth century can find much evidence in the horrors resulting from Louis XIV's aggressions. The total cost of his wars in human lives and economic resources was very great, especially in the deliberate French devastation of the German Palatinate during the War of the League of Augsburg. The battle of Malplaquet, which left forty thousand men wounded, dying, or dead in an area of ten square miles, was not surpassed in bloodshed until Napoleon's Russian campaign a century later. There was also much suffering behind the lines notably in the great famine that struck France in 1693-1694. And the year of Malplaquet, 1709, was one of the grimmest in modern French history, as bitter cold, crop failures, famine, skyrocketing prices, and relentless government efforts to stave off bankruptcy by collecting more taxes caused almost universal misery. The Parisians complained bitterly in a mock *Paternoster:* "Our Father which art at Versailles, thy name is hallowed no more, thy kingdom is great no more, thy will is no longer done on earth or on the waters. Give us this day thy bread which on all sides we lack. . . ."*

Louis set himself up as a champion of Catholicism, especially after the revocation of the Edict of Nantes in 1685, and William of Orange was hailed as a Protestant champion. Yet Louis, unlike his predecessor in aggression, Philip II of Spain, had no real hope of stamping out Protestantism among the Dutch. William's Protestant victory at the Boyne brought new hardship to Irish Catholics, and in England and New England the French were hated because they were Catholics. In the end, however, the Grand Alliance against Louis was a complex mixture of Catholic and Protestant in which religion played a comparatively minor role. Louis XIV had achieved no permanent stability for Europe or France, and his authority would die with him; his funeral procession was mocked as it passed through the streets of Paris, though he remained a figure of veneration to the rural masses who made up the majority of France.

II STUART ENGLAND

To the extent that English government utilized the new methods of professional administration developed in the fifteenth and sixteenth centuries, it was potentially as absolute as any divine-right monarchy. But the slow growth of representative government checked this potential, generating a set of rules not to be altered easily by the ordinary processes of government. These rules might be written down, but they might also be unwritten, being a consensus about certain traditions. These rules came to be regarded as limiting the authority not only of the king but even of a government elected by a majority of the people—a guarantee to individuals that they had "civil rights" and might carry out certain acts even though those in authority disapproved. Without such rules and habits of constitutionalism, and without the powerful and widespread human determination to back them up, the machinery of English parliamentary government could have been as ruthlessly absolute as any other government.

*G.R.R. Treasure, *Seventeenth Century France*, 2nd ed. (London: J. Murray, 1981), p. 441.

French kings and ministers could govern without the Estates General. In England, however, King Charles I, who had governed for eleven years without calling Parliament, felt obliged in 1640 to summon it and, though he dismissed it at once when it refused to do his bidding, he had to call another in the same year. This was the Long Parliament, which sat—with changes of personnel and with interruptions—for twenty years, and which made the revolution that ended the threat of absolute divine-right monarchy in England.

Charles was ultimately obliged to call Parliament for two basic reasons that go back to medieval history. First, in the English Parliament the House of Commons represented two different social groups not brought together in one house elsewhere: the aristocratic knights of the shire and the burgesses of the towns and cities. The strength of the Commons lay in the practical working together of both groups, which intermarried quite freely and, despite economic and social tensions, tended to form a single ruling class, with membership open to talent and energy from the lower classes. Second, local government continued to be run by magistrates who were not directly dependent on the Crown. True, England had its bureaucrats, its clerks and officials in the royal pay, but where in France and in other continental countries the new bureaucracy tended to take over almost all governmental business, especially financial and judicial affairs, in England the gentry and the higher nobility continued to do important local work. The Elizabethan Poor Law of 1601 put the care of the needy not under any national ministry but squarely on the smallest local units, the parishes, where decisions lay ultimately with the amateur, unpaid justices of the peace, recruited from the local gentry. In short, the privileged classes were not, as in France, thrust aside by paid agents of the central government; nor did they, as in Prussia, become agents of the Crown. Instead, they preserved secure bases in local government and in the House of Commons. When Charles I tried to govern without the consent of these privileged classes, when he tried to raise money from them and their dependents to run a bureaucratic government, they had a solid institutional and traditional basis from which to resist his unusual demands.

Because Elizabeth I was childless, she was succeeded by the son of her old rival and cousin, Mary, Queen of Scots, in 1603. James Stuart, already king of Scotland as James VI, became James I of England (1603-1625), thus bringing the two countries, still legally separate, under the same personal rule. James was a well-educated pedant, sure of himself, and above all certain that he ruled by divine right. As a Scottish foreigner, he was an object of distrust to his English subjects. He totally lacked the Tudor heartiness and tact, the gift of winning people to him. His son Charles I (1625-1649), under whom the divine-right experiment came to an end, had many more of the social graces of a monarch than his father, but he was still no man to continue the work of the Tudors. Although he was quite as sure as his father had been that God had called him to rule England, he could neither make the compromises the Tudors made nor revive their broad popular appeal. Thus an accident of personality was also important in shaping the outcome of divine-right theories in England.

The business of state was also gradually growing in scope and therefore in cost. The money required by the Stuarts—and indeed by the Bourbons, Hapsburgs, and all monarchs—did not only go for high living by royalty and to support hangers-on; it also went to run a government that was beginning to assume many new functions. Foreign relations, for example, were beginning to take on modern forms, with a central foreign office, ambassadors, clerks, travel allowances, and the like, all requiring more money and personnel. James I and Charles I failed to get the money they needed because those from whom they sought it, the ruling classes, had succeeded in placing the raising and spending of it in their own hands through parliamentary supremacy. The Parliament that won that supremacy was a kind of committee of the ruling classes; it was not a democratic legislature, since only a small fraction of the population could vote for members of the Commons.

In this struggle between Crown and Parliament, religion helped weld both sides into cohesive fighting groups. The struggle for power was in part a struggle to impose a uniform worship on England. The royalist cause was identified with High Church Anglicanism, that is, with bishops and a liturgy and theology that made it a sacramental religion relatively free from left-wing Protestant austerities. The parliamentary cause, at first supported by many moderate Low Church Anglicans, also attracted strong Puritan or Calvinist elements; later it came under the control of Presbyterians and then of extreme Puritans, the Independents or Congregationalists. The term *Puritanism* in seventeenth-century England is confusing because it covered a wide range of religious groups, from moderate evangelical Anglicans all the way to radical splinter sects. But the core of Puritanism went back to Zwingli and Calvin, to the repudiation of Catholic sacramental religion and the rejection of most music and the adornment of churches; it emphasized sermons, simplicity in church and out, and "purifying" the tie between the worshiper and God.

James I, 1603-1625

In the troubled reign of James II there were three major points of contention—money, foreign policy, and religion. In all three issues the Crown and its opposition each tried to direct constitutional development in its own favor. In raising money James sought to make the most of revenues that did not require a parliamentary grant; Parliament sought to make the most of its own control over the purse strings by insisting on the principle that it had to approve any new revenues. When James levied an import duty without a parliamentary grant, an importer of dried currants refused to pay; the case was decided in favor of the Crown by the Court of Exchequer, and the decision attracted much attention because the

judges held the king's powers in general to be absolute. Then a royal appeal for a general "benevolence"—a euphemism for a contribution exacted from an individual—was resisted with the support of the chief justice, Sir Edward Coke (1552-1634). James summarily dismissed Coke from office for asserting the independence of the judiciary and thereby drew attention once again to his broad use of the royal prerogative.

The Tudors had regarded foreign affairs as entirely a matter for the Crown. The delicate problem of a marriage for Elizabeth I, for instance, had concerned her Parliaments and the public; but Parliament made no attempt to dictate a marriage, and Elizabeth was careful not to offend her subjects in her own tentative negotiations. On the other hand, when James I openly sought a princess of hated Spain as a wife for his son Charles, the Commons in 1621 petitioned publicly against the Spanish marriage. When James rebuked them for meddling, the House drew up the Great Protestation, the first of the major documents of the English Revolution, in which they used what they claimed were the historic privileges of Parliament to assert what was in fact a new claim for parliamentary control of foreign affairs. James responded by dissolving Parliament and imprisoning four of its leaders. The Spanish marriage fell through, but the betrothal of Charles in 1624 to the French princess Henrietta Maria, sister of Louis XIII, who was also Catholic, was hardly more popular with the English people.

Though refusing to permit public services by Catholics and Puritans, Elizabeth had allowed much variety of practice within the Anglican church. James summed up his policy in the phrase "no bishop, no king"—by which he meant that the enforcement of the bishops' authority in religion was essential to the maintenance of royal power. James at once took steps against what he held to be Puritan nonconformity. He called a conference of Anglican bishops and leading Puritans at Hampton Court in 1604, at which he presided in person and used the full force of his scholarship against the Puritans. After the conference dissolved with no real meeting of minds, royal policy continued to favor the High Church, anti-Puritan party.

Despite James's failure to achieve anything like religious agreement among his subjects, his reign is a landmark in the history of Christianity among English-speaking peoples, for in 1611, after seven years' labor, a committee of forty-seven ministers authorized by him completed the English translation of the Bible that is still the most widely used. The King James version was a masterpiece of Elizabethan prose, perhaps the most remarkable literary achievement a committee has ever made.

Charles I, 1625-1642

Under Charles I all his father's difficulties came to a head very quickly. England was involved in a minor war against Spain, and though the members of Parliament hated Spain, they were most reluctant to grant Charles funds to support the English forces. Meanwhile, despite his French queen, Charles became involved in a war against France, which he financed in part by a forced loan from his wealthier subjects and by quartering troops in private houses at the householders' expense. His financial position was tenuous; as a French observer remarked, "They wish for war against heaven and earth, but lack the means to make it against anyone." The military preparations were the greatest since 1588, when there had been a visible enemy; in 1626-1628 Charles's subjects were less certain of the need for extraordinary measures. Consequently, in 1628 Parliament passed the Petition of Right—"the Stuart Magna Carta"—which for the first time explicitly stated some of the most basic rules of modern constitutional government: no taxation without the consent of Parliament; no billeting of soldiers in private houses; no martial law in time of peace; no imprisonment except on a specific charge and subject to the protection of regular legal procedures. All these principles were limitations on the Crown.

Charles consented to the Petition of Right to secure new grants of money from Parliament. But he also collected duties not sanctioned by Parliament, which thereupon protested not only against his unauthorized taxes but also against his High Church policy. The king now switched from conciliation to firmness. In 1629 he had Sir John Eliot (1592-1632), mover of the resolutions, arrested, together with eight other members. He then dissolved Parliament, in part for refusing to vote supplies to the king, in part because he felt Parliament was meddling in matters of religion beyond its authority, and in part because Eliot intended to appeal over the king's head to the country. Eliot died a prisoner in the Tower of London, the first martyr in the parliamentary cause, having in effect driven Charles I to take a calculated risk.

For the next eleven years, 1629-1640, Charles governed without a Parliament. He squeezed every penny he could get out of royal revenues that did not require parliamentary authorization, never quite breaking with precedent by imposing a wholly new tax but stretching precedent beyond what his opponents thought reasonable. For example, ship money had been levied by the Crown before, but only on coastal towns for naval expenditures in wartime; Charles now imposed ship money on inland areas and in peacetime. John Hampden (1594-1643), a rich member of Parliament from inland Buckinghamshire, refused to pay it. He lost his case in court (1637) but gained wide public support for challenging the king's fiscal expedients.

In religious matters Charles was guided by a very High Church archbishop of Canterbury, William Laud (1573-1645), who systematically enforced Anglican conformity and deprived even moderate Puritan clergymen of their pulpits. Puritans were sometimes brought before the Star Chamber, an administrative court that denied the accused the safeguards of the common law. In civil matters Charles relied on an opportunist conservative, Thomas Wentworth, first earl of Strafford (1593-

1641), who had deserted the parliamentary side and went on to become Lord Lieutenant of Ireland, a source of continued conflict and expense.

England was seething with repressed political and religious passions underneath the outward calm of these years of personal rule. Yet to judge from the imperfect statistics available, the relative weight of the taxation that offended so many Englishmen was less than on the Continent, and far less than taxation in any modern Western state. The members of Parliament who resisted the Crown by taking arms against it were not downtrodden, poverty-stricken people revolting out of despair, but self-assertive people defending their concept of civil rights and their own forms of worship, as well as seeking power and wealth.

Why, then, was there a revolution? Historians are not agreed, especially about the economic motivations of the English revolutionaries. There is evidence that the more capitalistic gentleman farmers—rural bourgeois—supported the Puritans; but other scholars argue that the elements from the gentry who supported the Puritans were those who saw themselves sinking on the economic scale, because of inflation, because of the enclosure of once common lands for sheep farming, and because of competition by the new secular owners of the old monastic lands. This debate about the nature and role of the gentry illustrates two problems faced by the historian: first, that of definitions, since the debate turns in part on how social classes are defined, or defined themselves in the past; second, that two historians examining the same evidence, or different evidence that overlaps at certain points, may arrive at quite different conclusions about the meaning of that evidence. Was the English Revolution caused by despair—a declining gentry seeking to turn the clock back, so that the revolution was actually conservative in its goals—or was it caused by the perception of the need to modernize, to change the institutions of governments to more rational, efficient purposes—that is, the final stage of the long movement away from feudalism?

The English Revolution did not, in fact, greatly alter the face of England. The laboring poor played almost no role in the Revolution. Nonetheless, a precedent of great significance was established, for a king was brought to trial and executed and his office abolished; an established church was disestablished and its property taken; less emphasis was placed on deference. All this would later be undone, the monarchy and the established church restored. Yet in the process, many would perceive that human beings could alter their world if they chose, and many would see the importance of the political process. And they would see that the Crown was neither rational nor truly responsible in various aspects of finance: in government credit, in the use of improper taxes for purposes considered immoral, and in placing the government's financial interest before its social responsibilities. Thus religion, economics, and politics would prove inseparable, a linked chain of causation.

Charles I could perhaps have weathered his financial

Sir Anthony Van Dyck (1599-1641) painted King Charles I hunting. Probably completed in 1638 and now in the Louvre, this portrait shows the king informally dressed, having dismounted from his horse. The arrogant pose, with hand on hip and cane, was used from medieval times to represent nobility. Contrast the dress and compare the pose with Rigaud's portrait of Louis XIV (p. 11) and with Charles III (p. 76).

difficulties if he had not had to contend with the Scots. Laud's attempt to enforce the English High Church ritual and organization came up against the three-generations-old Scottish Presbyterian "kirk" (church). In 1638 a Solemn League and Covenant bound the members of the kirk to resist Charles by force if need be. Charles marched north against the Scots and worked out a compromise with them in 1639. But even this mild campaign was too much for the treasury, and in 1640 Charles had to call Parliament back into session. This Short Parliament denied him any money until the piled-up grievances against Charles and his father were settled; it was dissolved almost at once. Then the Scots went to war again, and Charles, defeated in a skirmish, bought them off by promising the Scottish army £850 a day until peace was made. Since he could not raise the money, he had to call another Parliament, which became the Long Parliament of the revolution.

Since the Scottish army would not disband until it was paid off, the Long Parliament held it as a club over Charles's head and put through a series of reforms striking at the heart of the royal power. It abolished ship money and other disputed taxes and disbanded the unpopular royal administrative courts, such as the Star Chamber, which had become symbols of Stuart absolutism. Up to now Parliament had been called and dismissed at the pleasure of the Crown; the Triennial Act of 1640 required that Parliament be summoned every three years, even if the Crown did not wish to do so. Parliament also attacked the royal favorites, whom Charles reluctantly abandoned; Archbishop Laud was removed, and Strafford was declared guilty of treason and executed in May 1641.

Meanwhile, Strafford's harsh policy toward the Irish had led to a rebellion that amounted to an abortive war for national independence by Irish Catholics and caused the massacre of thirty thousand Protestants in the northern Irish region of Ulster. Parliament, unwilling to trust Charles with an army to put down this rebellion, drew up in 1641 a Grand Remonstrance summarizing all its complaints. Charles now made a final attempt to repeat the tactics that had worked in 1629. Early in 1642 he ordered the arrest of five of his leading opponents in the House of Commons, including Hampden of the ship-money case. The five took refuge in the privileged political sanctuary of the City of London, where the king could not reach them. Charles left for the north and in the summer of 1642 rallied an army at Nottingham. Parliament simply took over the central government, and the Civil War had begun.

During these years of political jockeying, signs were already evident that strong groups in England and in Parliament wanted something more than a return to the Tudor balance between Crown and Parliament, between religious conservatives and religious radicals. In politics the Nineteen Propositions that Parliament submitted to the king in June 1642 would have established parliamentary supremacy over the army, the royal administration, the church, and even the rearing of the royal children. Charles turned down the propositions, and they became the principal foundation of the war that followed. In religion a Root and Branch Bill, introduced in 1641 but not enacted into law, would have radically reformed the Church of England, destroying "root and branch" the bishops and much of what had already become traditional in Anglican religious practices. In the midst of such extreme contentiousness, a middle path seemed impossible to find.

The Civil War, 1642-1649

England was split along lines that were partly territorial, partly social and economic, and partly religious. Royalist strength lay largely in the north and west, relatively less urban and less prosperous than other parts, and largely controlled by gentry who were loyal to throne and altar. Parliamentary strength lay largely in the south and east, especially in London and in East Anglia, where Puritanism commanded wide support. The Scots were a danger to either side, distrustful of an English Parliament but equally distrustful of a king who had sought to put bishops over their kirk.

In the field, the struggle was at first indecisive. The royalists, or Cavaliers, recruited from a class used to riding, had the initial advantage of superior cavalry. What swung the balance to the side of Parliament was the development of a special force recruited from ardent Puritans in the eastern counties and gradually forged under strict discipline into the Ironsides. Their leader was a Puritan, Oliver Cromwell (1599-1658), who won a crucial battle at Marston Moor in 1644. The parliamentary army, reorganized into the New Model Army and staffed by radicals in religion and politics, stood as Roundheads (from their short-cropped hair) against the Cavaliers. At the battle of Naseby in 1645, the New Model Army was completely victorious, and Charles in desperation took refuge with the Scottish army, who turned him over to the English Parliament in return for their £400,000 back pay.

A situation now arose that was to be repeated, with variations based on time and place, in the French Revolution in 1792 and the Russian Revolution in 1917. The moderates who had begun the revolution and who controlled the Long Parliament were confronted by a much more radical group who controlled the New Model Army. In religion the moderates, seeking to retain some ecclesiastical discipline and formality, were Presbyterians or Low Church Anglicans; in politics they were constitutional monarchists. The radicals, who were opposed to churches disciplined from a central organization, were Independents or Congregationalists, and they already so distrusted Charles that they were thinking about a republican England. The situation was further complicated by the Presbyterian Scots, who regarded the Roundheads as religious anarchists.

The years after 1645 were filled with difficult negotiations, during which Charles stalled for time to gain Scottish help. In 1648 Cromwell beat the invading Scots at Preston, and his army seized the king. Parliament, with the moderates still in control, now refused to do what the army wanted—to dethrone Charles. The Roundhead leaders then ordered Colonel Thomas Pride (d. 1658) to exclude by force from the Commons ninety-six Presbyterian members. This the Colonel did in December 1648, with no pretense of legality. After "Pride's Purge" only some sixty radicals remained of the more than five hundred original members of the Long Parliament; this remnant was known thereafter as the Rump Parliament. The Rump brought Charles to trial before a special high court of radicals, fifty-nine of whom condemned him to death. On January 30, 1649, Charles I was beheaded. To the end he insisted that a king could not be tried by any superior jurisdiction on earth, that his cause was the cause of the people of England, and that if he could be silenced, so might all others. The monarchs of Europe now had their own martyr, and Parliament was, in the eyes of many in England, stained by a clearly illegal act.

Cromwell and the Interregnum, 1649-1660

The next eleven years are known as the Interregnum, the interval between two monarchical reigns. England was now a republic under a government known as the Commonwealth. Since the radicals did not dare to call a free election, which would almost certainly have gone against them, the Rump Parliament continued to sit. Thus, from the start, the Commonwealth was a dictatorship of a radical minority come to power through the tight organization of the New Model Army. From the start too, Cromwell dominated the new government. In religion an earnest and sincere Independent, a patriotic Englishman, strong-minded, stubborn, if now power-mad, still by no means unwilling to compromise, Cromwell was nevertheless a prisoner of his position.

Cromwell faced a divided England, where the majority was royalist at heart and certainly sick of the fighting, the confiscations, the endless confusing changes of the last decade. He faced a hostile Scotland and an even

Oliver Cromwell is invariably depicted as stern and dedicated, staring into the future. This painting by Samuel Cooper (1609-1672), who specialized in miniature portraits of figures from the Commonwealth and Restoration, emphasizes Cromwell's sense of force by focusing solely on the head, devoid of background or distracting detail.

By 1651 the House of Commons was depicted on the Great Seal of England as used by the Commonwealth—testimony to the symbolic significance that Cromwell attached to the House. This scene is a Dutch rendition of Cromwell's dissolution of Parliament in 1653. The owl and small lion made to look like a dog are intended as a satirical commentary on the debate and the dissolution.

more hostile Ireland, where the disorders in England had encouraged the Catholic Irish to rebel once more in 1649. In 1650 Charles II, eldest son of the martyred Charles I, landed in Scotland, accepted the Covenant (thereby guaranteeing the Presbyterian faith as the established Scottish kirk), and led a Scottish army against the English. Once more the English army proved unbeatable, and young Charles took refuge on the Continent after a romantic escape in disguise. Cromwell then faced a war with Holland (1652-1654) brought on by the Navigation Act of 1651, which forbade the importation of goods into England and the colonies except in English ships or in ships of the country producing the imported goods, thus striking at the Dutch carrying trade.

In time Cromwell mastered all his foes. He himself went to Ireland and suppressed the rebellion with extreme bloodshed. In the so-called Cromwellian Settlement of 1652-1654, he dispossessed rebel Irish landholders in favor of Protestants, achieving order in Ireland but not peace. He brought the naval war with the Dutch to a victorious close in 1654. Later Cromwell also waged an aggressive war against Spain (1656-1658), from whom the English acquired the rich Caribbean sugar island of Jamaica. Even in this time of troubles, the British Empire kept growing.

Cromwell, however, could not master the Rump Parliament, which brushed aside his suggestions for an increase in its membership and a reform of its procedures. In April 1653 he forced its dissolution by appear-

ing in Parliament with a body of soldiers. In December he took the decisive step of inaugurating the regime called the Protectorate, with himself as lord protector of England, Scotland, and Ireland, and with a written constitution—the only one Britain has ever had—as the Instrument of Government. It provided for a Parliament with a single house of four hundred and sixty members, who were chosen solely by Puritan sympathizers since no royalist dared vote. Even so, the lord protector had constant troubles with his parliaments, and in 1657 he yielded to pressure and modified the Instrument to provide for a second parliamentary house and to put limits on the lord protector's power. Meanwhile, to maintain order, Cromwell had divided the country into twelve military districts, each commanded by a major general.

Oliver Cromwell died in 1658 and was succeeded as lord protector by his son Richard, who was a nonentity. The army soon seized control, and some of its leaders regarded the restoration of the Stuarts as the best way to end the chronic political turbulence. To ensure the legality of the move, General George Monck (1608-1670), commander of the Protectorate's forces in Scotland, summoned back the Rump and readmitted the surviving members excluded by Pride's Purge. This partially reconstituted Long Parliament enacted the formalities of restoration, and in 1660 Charles Stuart accepted an invitation to return from exile and reign as Charles II.

The Revolution in Review

At the height of their rule in the early 1650s some Puritans had attempted to enforce on the whole population the austere life of the Puritan ideal. This enforcement took the form of "blue laws": prohibitions on horse racing, gambling, cock fighting, bear baiting, dancing on the greens, fancy dress, the theater, and a host of ordinary pleasures of daily living. Yet this attempt to legislate morality, coming too early for modern techniques of propaganda and regimentation, was not entirely effective. Many an Anglican clergyman, though officially "plundered"—that is, deprived of his living—continued worship in private houses, and many a cock fight went on in secluded spots. Nevertheless, the strict code was there, with earnest persons to try to enforce it and with implacable enemies to oppose it. The remark of the great Victorian historian T. B. Macaulay (1800-1859)—that the Puritans prohibited bear baiting not because it gave pain to the bear but because it gave pleasure to the spectators—showed the deep hostility that survived in England toward the reign of the Puritan "saints" two centuries later.

Despite this negative judgment, the events of 1640-1660 are of major importance in the history of the West. For the first time a monarch was challenged in a major revolt by politically active private citizens. Though the Stuarts were ultimately restored, no English king could ever hope to rule again without a Parliament, or revive the Court of Star Chamber, or take ship money, benevolences, and other controversial taxes. Parliament thereafter retained that critical weapon of the legislative body in a limited monarchy, control of the public purse by periodic grants of taxes.

Another basic freedom owes much to this English experience. Freedom of speech was a fundamental tenet of the Puritans, even though at the height of their power they did not observe it themselves. It received its classic expression in 1644 by the poet John Milton (1608-1674), who was the secretary of the Commonwealth, in his *Areopagitica*. While Milton defended free speech principally for an intellectual and moral elite, one of his arguments was characteristically pragmatic and English, namely, that attempts to curb free expression just would not work.

The voluminous pamphlet literature of the early years of the great turmoil was a lively manifestation of free speech in action. The extraordinary rise of radical minorities foreshadowed modern political and social thought. One such group, the Levelers, found many sympathizers in the revolutionary army and advanced a program later carried by emigrants to the American colonies. They called for political democracy, universal suffrage, regularly summoned parliaments, progressive taxation, separation of church and state, and the protection of the individual against arbitrary arrest. There were even hints of economic equality, a goal then closely tied to biblical ideas. The Diggers, for example, were a small sect that preached the sharing of earthly goods in a kind of communism. They advocated plowing up common and waste land throughout England, regardless of ownership, in the interests of social reform. Fifth Monarchy advocates, Millenarians, and a dozen other radical sects preached the Second Coming of Christ and the achievement of a utopia on earth.

Still more important, there emerged from the English Revolution, even more clearly than from the religious wars on the Continent, the concept of religious tolera-

BLACKSTONE ON THE LAW

By the eighteenth century the English recognized that a unique constitution had evolved from the period of their Civil War. Basically unwritten, rooted in the common law, this constitution would contribute to a remarkable period of political stability. In 1765 an English jurist, William Blackstone (1723-1780), would prepare a lengthy set of commentaries on the laws of England in which the process dramatically accelerated by the English Revolution was described by him:

And herein indeed consists the true excellence of the English government, that all the parts of it form a mutual check upon each other. In the legislature, the people are a check upon the nobility, and the nobility a check upon the people; by the mutual privilege of rejecting what the other has resolved: while the king is a check upon both, which preserves the executive power from encroachments. And this very executive power is again checked and kept within due bounds by the two houses, through the privilege they have of inquiring into, impeaching and punishing the conduct (not indeed of the king, which would destroy his constitutional independence; but, which is more beneficial to the public,) of his evil and pernicious counsellors. Thus every branch of our civil polity supports and is supported, regulates and is regulated, by the rest. . . . Like three distinct powers in mechanics, they jointly impel the machine of government in a direction different from what either, acting by itself, would have done . . . a direction which constitutes the true line of the liberty and happiness of the community.

Blackstone, *Commentaries on the Laws of England*, 15th ed. (London: A. Stralan, 1809), I, 153.

MILTON ON FREEDOM OF EXPRESSION

An early, and ringing, defense of freedom of expression was written by John Milton in his *Areopagitica* in 1644. He argued that liberty took three forms: ecclesiastical, domestic, and civil. The first would come through reform of the church. The second and third became merged in Milton's personal concerns, for he wrote a series of tracts defending divorce as a private matter not to be regulated by the state, since he was deeply unhappy in his own marriage. In August 1644 Parliament reapplied, through a new ordinance, the old principle of censorship of the press, and ordered that the author of the tracts on divorce should be found. Milton replied in November with his "Speech for the Liberty of Unlicensed Printing, to the Parliament of England," phrasing his defense of freedom of expression as though he were a Greek orator, addressing the representative Athenian assembly of the Areopagus, hence the title, *Areopagitica:*

There have been not a few since the beginning of this Parliament, both of the Presbytery and others, who by their unlicensed books, to the contempt of an Imprimatur, first broke that triple ice clung about our hearts, and taught the people to see day; I hope that none of those were the persuaders to renew upon this bondage which they themselves have wrought so much good by contemning. But if neither the check that Moses gave to young Joshua, nor the countermand which our Saviour gave to your John, [*Luke*, ix, 49, 50] who was so ready to prohibit those whom he thought unlicensed, be not enough to admonish our elders how unacceptable to God their testy mood of prohibiting is; if neither their own remembrance what evil hath abounded in the church by this let of licensing, and what good they themselves have begun by transgressing it, be not enough, but that they will persuade, and execute the most Dominican part of the Inquisition over us, and are already with one foot in the stirrup so active at suppres-

sing, it would be no unequal distribution, in the first place, to suppress the suppressors themselves; whom the change of their condition hath puffed up, more than their late experience of harder times hath made wise. . . .

This I know, that errors in a good government and in a bad are equally almost incident; for what magistrate may not be misinformed, and much the sooner, if liberty of printing be reduced into the power of a few; but to redress willingly and speedily what hath been erred, and in highest authority to esteem a plain advertisement more than others have done a sumptuous bribe, is a virtue, honored Lords and Commons, answerable to your highest actions, and whereof none can participate but greatest and wisest men.

Milton, *Areopagitica*, ed. John W. Hales (London: Clarendon Press, many editions with differing pagination). The extracts are the third from last and last paragraphs respectively.

tion. The Independents, while they were in opposition, stood firmly for the right of religious groups to worship God as they wished. Though in their brief tenure of power they showed a readiness to persecute, they were never firmly enough in the saddle to make England into a seventeenth-century version of Calvin's Geneva. At least on sect, the Quakers, led by George Fox (1624-1691), held to the idea and practice of religious toleration as a positive good. The Quakers denounced all worldy show, finding even buttons ostentatious. They found the names of the days and months indecently pagan, the polite form "you" in the singular a piece of social hypocrisy, and the taking of legal oaths impious. Hence they met for worship on what they called the First Day, rather than the day of the sun god, they addressed each other as "thee" or "thou," and they took so seriously the Protestant doctrine of the priesthood of the believer that they eliminated any formal ministry. In the Religious Society of Friends, as they were properly known, any worshiper who felt the spirit move might testify—give what other sects would call a sermon. The Friends felt too deeply the impossibility of forcing anyone to see the "inner light"

for them to force people to accept their faith. They would abstain entirely from force, particularly from war, and would go their own way in Christian peace.

The Restoration, 1660-1688

The Restoration of 1660 left Parliament essentially supreme, but attempted to undo some of the work of the Revolution. Anglicanism was restored in England and Ireland, though not as a state church in Scotland. Protestants who would not accept the Church of England were termed dissenters. Although they suffered many legal disabilities, dissenters remained numerous, especially among artisans and middle-class merchants. As time went on they grew powerful, so that the noncomformist conscience became a major factor in English public life. Indeed, the three-century progression of names by which these non-Anglican Protestants were called shows their rise in status: the hostile term "dissenter" became "nonconformist" in the nineteenth century, and "Free Churchman" in the twentieth.

The Restoration was also a revulsion against Puritan

ways. The reign of Charles II (1660-1685) was a period of moral looseness, of lively court life, of Restoration drama with its ribald wit, and of the public pursuit of pleasure, at least among the upper classes. But the new Stuarts were not as adept at public relations as the Tudors had been. Charles II dissipated some of the fund of good will with which he started by following a foreign policy that seemed to patriotic Englishmen too subservient to Louis XIV. Yet Charles's alliance with Louis in 1670 did result in the extinction of any Dutch threat to English sea-power, and it confirmed an important English acquisition, that of New Amsterdam, now New York, first taken in the Anglo-Dutch War of 1664-1667.

What really undid the later Stuarts and revealed their political ineptitude was the Catholic problem. Charles II had come under Catholic influence through his French mother and probably became a Catholic before he died in 1685. Since he left no legitimate children, the crown passed to his brother, James II (1685-1688), who was already an open Catholic. To enlist the support of the dissenters for the toleration of Catholics, James II issued in 1687 a Declaration of Indulgence, granting freedom of worship to all denominations in England and Scotland. While this was, in the abstract, an admirable step toward full religious liberty, to the majority in England Catholicism still seemed a great menace, and it was always possible to stir them to an irrational pitch by an appeal to their fear of "popery." Actually, by the end of the seventeenth century the few remaining Catholics in England were glad to accept the status of the dissenters and were no real danger to an overwhelmingly Protestant country. In Ireland, however, the Catholics remained an unappeasable majority, and Ireland posed a genuine threat.

The political situation was much like that under Charles I: the Crown had one goal, Parliament another. Although James II made no attempt to dissolve Parliament or to arrest its members, he went over Parliament's head by issuing decrees based on what he called the "power of dispensation." Early in his reign he had used a minor rebellion by the duke of Monmouth, a bastard son of Charles II, as the excuse for two ominous policies. First, his judges punished suspected rebel sympathizers with a severity that seemed out of all proportion to the extent of the rebellion. Second, he created a standing army of thirty thousand men, part of whom he stationed near London in what appeared as an attempt to intimidate the capital. To contemporaries it looked as though James were plotting to force both Catholicism and divine-right monarchy on an unwilling England.

The Glorious Revolution and Its Aftermath, 1688-1714

The result was the Glorious Revolution, a coup d'état engineered at first by a group of James's parliamentary opponents who were called Whigs, in contrast to the Tories, who tended to support at least some of the policies of the later Stuarts. The Whigs were the heirs of the moderates of the Long Parliament, and they represented an alliance of the great lords and the prosperous London merchants.

James II married twice. By his first marriage he had two daughters, both Protestant—Mary, who had married William of Orange, the Dutch opponent of Louis XIV, and Anne. Then in 1688 a son was born to James and his Catholic second wife, thus apparently making the passage of the crown to a Catholic heir inevitable. The Whig leaders responded with propaganda, including rumors that the queen had never been pregnant, that a baby had been smuggled into her chamber in a warming pan so that there might be a Catholic heir. Then the Whigs and some Tories negotiated with William of Orange, who could hardly turn down a proposition that would give him the solid assets of English power in his struggle with Louis XIV. He accepted the invitation to take the English crown, which he was to share with his wife, the couple reigning as William III (1689-1702) and Mary II (1689-1694). On November 5, 1688, William landed at Torbay on the Devon coast with some fourteen thousand soldiers. When James heard the news he tried to rally support in the West Country, but everywhere the great lords and even the normally conservative gentry were on the side of a Protestant succession. James fled from London to France in December 1688, giving William an almost bloodless victory.

Early in 1689 Parliament (technically a convention, since there was no monarch to summon it) formally offered the crown to William. Enactment of a Bill of Rights followed. This document, summing up the constitutional practices that Parliament had been seeking since the Petition of Right in 1628, was, in fact, almost a short written constitution. It laid down the essential principles of parliamentary supremacy: control of the purse, prohibition of the royal power of dispensation, and frequent meetings of Parliament.

Three major steps were necessary after 1689 to convert Britain into a parliamentary democracy in which the Crown is the purely symbolic focus of patriotic loyalty. These were, first, the concentration of executive direction in a committee of the majority party in the Parliament, that is, a Cabinet headed by a prime minister, achieved in the eighteenth and early nineteenth centuries; second, the establishment of universal suffrage and payment to members of the Commons, achieved in the nineteenth and twentieth centuries; and third, the abolition of the power of the House of Lords to veto legislation passed by the Commons, achieved in the early twentieth century. Thus democracy was still a long way off in 1689, and William and Mary were real rulers with power over policy.

Childless, they were succeeded by Mary's younger sister Anne (1702-1714), all of whose many children were stillborn or died in childhood. The exiled Catholic Stuarts, however, did better; the little boy born to James II in 1688 and brought up near Paris grew up to be known as the "Old Pretender." Then in 1701 Parliament passed an Act of Settlement that settled the crown—in default of heirs to Anne, then heir presumptive to the sick William III—not on the Catholic pretender, but on the Protestant Sophia of Hanover or her issue. Sophia was a granddaughter of James I and the daughter of Frederick of the Palatinate, the "Winter King" of Bohemia in the Thirty Years' War. On Anne's death in 1714, the crown passed to Sophia's son George, first king of the house of Hanover. This settlement made it clear that Parliament, and not the divinely ordained succession of the eldest male in direct descent, made the kings of England.

To ensure the Hanoverian succession in both Stuart kingdoms, Scotland as well as England, the formal union of the two was completed in 1707 as the United Kingdom of Great Britain. Scotland gave up its own parliament and sent representatives to the parliament of the United Kingdom at Westminster. Although the union met with some opposition from both English and Scots, on the whole it went through with ease, so great was Protestant fear of a possible return of the Catholic Stuarts.

The Glorious Revolution did not, however, settle the other chronic problem—Ireland. The Catholic Irish rose in support of the exiled James II and were put down at the Battle of the Boyne in 1690. William then attempted to apply moderation in his dealings with Ireland, but the Protestants there soon forced him to return to the Cromwellian policy. Although Catholic worship was not actually forbidden, many galling restrictions were imposed on the Catholic Irish, including the prohibition of Catholic schools. Moreover, economic persecution was added to religious, as Irish trade came under stringent mercantilist regulation. This was the Ireland whose deep misery inspired the writer Jonathan Swift (1667-1745) in 1729 to make his satirical "modest proposal," that the impoverished Irish sell their babies as articles of food.

Absolutism was thus almost universal in Europe. On the Continent enlightened despots ruled with an often intelligent but determined hand. In England a tenuous balance had been struck, though for those outside the United Kingdom the rule of the monarch was no less absolute and perhaps less enlightened. While writers of genius might criticize governments, Everyman still had no way of doing so, save through peasant revolts.

III CENTURY OF GENIUS/ CENTURY OF EVERYMAN

In the seventeenth century the cultural, as well as the political, hegemony of Europe passed from Italy and Spain to Holland, France, and England. Especially in literature, the France of the *grand siècle* set the imprint of its classical style on the West through the writings of Corneille, Racine, Molière, Boileau, Bossuet, and a host of others. Yet those writers who exerted the greatest influence on modern culture were not exclusively French and were philosophers and scientists (see Chapter 13). Their arguments were expressed in political and eco-

nomic constructs that justified or attacked the conventional wisdom of the age. In all fields of intellectual endeavor the seventeenth century saw such a remarkable flowering that historians have called it "the century of genius."

Progress and Pessimism

Scientists and rationalists helped greatly to establish in the minds of the educated throughout the West two complementary concepts that were to serve as the foundations of the Enlightenment of the eighteenth century: first, the concept of a "natural" order underlying the disorder and confusion of the universe as it appears to unreflecting people in their daily life; and, second, the concept of a human faculty, best called reason, which is obscured in most of humanity but can be brought into effective play by good—that is, rational—perception. Both of these concepts can be found in some form in the Western tradition at least as far back as the ancient Greeks. What gave them novelty and force at the end of the seventeenth century was their being welded into the doctrine of progress—the belief that all human beings can attain here on earth a state of happiness, of perfection, hitherto in the West generally thought to be possible only in a state of grace, and then only in a heaven after death.

Not all the great minds of the seventeenth century shared this optimistic belief in progress and in the infallibility of reason. The many-sided legacy of this century of genius is evident, for example, in the contrast between two of the most important political writings issuing from the English Revolution: Thomas Hobbes's *Leviathan* and John Locke's *Second Treatise of Government*. Published in 1651 and much influenced by the disorders of the English Civil War, *Leviathan* was steeped in Machiavellian pessimism about the inherent sinfulness of human beings. The state of nature, when people live without government, is a state of war, Hobbes argued, where people prey upon each other and human life is "solitary, poor, nasty, brutish, short." The only recourse is for people to agree among themselves to submit absolutely to the Leviathan—an all-powerful state that will force peace upon humankind.

Hobbes (1588-1679) turned the contract theory of government upside down by having people consent to give up all their liberties; Locke (1632-1704) put the contract right side up again. Locke was a close associate of the Whig leaders who engineered the Glorious Revolution. In his *Second Treatise of Government*, published in 1690 as a defense of their actions, Locke painted a generally hopeful picture of the state of nature, which suffers only from the "inconvenience" of lacking an impartial judicial authority. To secure such an authority, people contract among themselves to accept a government—not an omnipotent Leviathan—that respects a person's life, liberty, and property; should a king seize property by imposing unauthorized taxes, then his subjects are justified in overthrowing their monarch. Locke's relative optimism and his enthusiasm for constitutional government nourished the major current of political thought in the next century, culminating in the American and French revolutions. But events after 1789 brought Hobbesian despair and authoritarianism to the surface once more.

Meantime, exponents of the older Christian tradition continued to flourish on the Continent. One example is Blaise Pascal, a one-man personification of the complexities of the century of genius. He won an important place in the history of mathematics and physics by his work with air pressure and vacuums and, at the practical level, by his invention of the calculating machine and his establishment of the first horse-drawn bus line in Paris. Yet he was also profoundly otherworldly and became a spokesman for the high-minded, puritanical Jansenists, whose doctrines he defended with skill and fervor. He

dismissed as unworthy the concepts of God as mere master geometer or engineer and sought instead for the Lord of Abraham and the Old Testament prophets. He advocated acts of charity, especially by those with wealth and status, for God's incomprehensible love had placed on them the obligation to look after the weak and poor. One night in November 1654, he underwent a great mystical experience in which he felt with absolute certainty the presence of God and of Christ. He spent his final years in religious meditation.

Another example is Baruch Spinoza (1632-1677), the century's most controversial thinker, who was the son of a Jewish merchant in Amsterdam. Spinoza tried to reconcile the God of Science and the God of Scripture. He constructed a system of ethical axioms as rigorously Cartesian and logical as a series of mathematical propositions. He also tried to reunite the Cartesian opposites—

This is the illustration from the title page of Hobbes's *Leviathan*. While it shows the ruler in absolute control over the land, his body symbolically consists of all those individuals whose self-interest is served by their consent to accept the collective rule of the state for the general welfare. All look to him, and each loses individuality; but the mass is, nonetheless, composed of individual figures. This title page is considered to be a masterpiece, summarizing a philosopher's view in a single illustration. The Latin quotation from the book of *Job* translates, "Upon the earth there is not his like."

PASCAL ON ERROR

Pascal left unfinished at his death one of the most remarkable works of Christian apologetics in existence, the *Pensées* ("Thoughts"). In it he wrote:

Man is but a being filled with error. This error is natural, and, without grace, ineffaceable. Nothing shows him the truth; everything deceives him. These two principles of truth, reason and the senses, besides lacking sincerity, reciprocally deceive each other. The senses deceive reason by false appearances: and just as they cheat reason they are cheated by her in turn: she has her revenge. Passions of the soul trouble the senses, and give them false impressions. They emulously lie and deceive each other.

Thoughts, Letters, and Opuscules, trans. O. W. Wight (New York: Hurt and Houghton, 1869), p. 192.

matter with mind, body with soul—by asserting that God was present everywhere and in everything. His pantheism led to his ostracism in Holland by his fellow Jews and also by the Christians, who considered him an atheist; his rejection of rationalism and materialism offended intellectuals. Spinoza found few admirers until the romantic revolt against the abstractions and oversimplifications of the Enlightenment over a century later.

Literature

Just as Henry IV, Richelieu, and Louis XIV brought greater order to French politics after the civil and religious upheavals of the sixteenth century, so the writers of the seventeenth century brought greater discipline to French writing after the Renaissance extravagance of a genius like Rabelais. It was the Age of Classicism, which insisted on the observance of elaborate rules, on the authority of models from classical antiquity, and on the employment of a more polite, stylized vocabulary. In the early 1600s the example of greater refinement in manners and speech was set by the circle who met in the Paris *salon* (reception room) of an aristocratic hostess, the marquise de Rambouillet (1588-1665). Later proper behavior was standardized by the court ceremonial at Versailles, and proper vocabulary by the famous dictionary of the French language that the experts of the academy founded by Richelieu finished compiling in the 1690s, after more than half a century of labor. Nicholas Boileau (1636-1711), the chief literary critic of the day, set the rules for writing poetry with his Cartesian pronouncement, "Think well, if you wish to write well." Exaggerated notions of propriety outlawed from polite usage the French counterparts of such terms as *spit* and *vomit* and obliged writers to seek euphemisms for dozens of commonplace activities. Indeed, many of our concepts of which words are vulgar or obscene derive from this time, though they were later reinforced by Victorian prudery and class concern for "nicety" in the nineteenth century. Already there were indications of the social divisions that would produce the Revolution of

1789 in the enormous gap between the classical French speech of the court and the plainer, coarser language of the average French person.

On the other hand, the linguistic standards of the seventeenth-century court also brought substantial benefits to literature. Without its discipline, French would not have won its unique reputation for clarity and elegance. The leading tragic dramatists of the *grand siècle* made observance of all the classical do's and don'ts not an end in itself but a means to probe deeply into the endless variety of human personalities. Pierre Corneille (1606-1684) and Jean Racine (1639-1699) created moving portraits of people upholding exalted ideals of honor or crushed by overwhelming emotion. The French tragedies of the seventeenth century were worthy successors to the Greek dramas of the fifth century B.C., not merely because of their classical form but also because of their powerful rhetoric, complex structure, psychological insight, and clarity of expression.

As a writer of comedies, Jean Baptiste Molière (1622-1673), the other great French dramatist of the age, was less constrained to employ a dignified vocabulary and to heed the other rules of classicism. The main characters of his satirical comedies were not only sharply etched personalities but social types as well—the overrefined pedantic ladies of the salons, the hypocrite in *Tartuffe* (1664), the ignorant and self-important newly rich in *Le Bourgeois Gentilhomme* (1670). In Molière, as in all good satire, there is more than a touch of moralizing, and didactic overtones are also present in two other characteristic works of the Great Century: the *Fables* of Jean de La Fontaine (1621-1695) reworked in lively fashion tales borrowed from antiquity; the *Maxims* of the duc de la Rochefoucauld (1613-1680) were even more disenchanted in their estimates of human nature. "Judged by most of its reactions, love is closer to hatred than to friendship." "Men would not get on for long in society if they did not fool one another." "In general, we give praise only that we may get it." But la Rochefoucauld could also write, "Perfect courage means doing unwitnessed what we would be capable of with the world looking on," and "The fame of great men should always be judged by the methods they employed to achieve it."*

Seventeenth-century English literature also had its cynics, notably William Wycherley (c 1640-1716), William Congreve (1670-1729), and other playwrights who wrote witty, bawdy, and disillusioned Restoration comedies. Under Charles II and his successors the pendulum of public taste and morality made a particularly violent swing as a reaction to the midcentury Puritans who had closed down the theaters as dens of sinfulness. One of those Puritans, John Milton, the secretary of Oliver Cromwell, produced his major work of literature, *Paradise Lost* (1667), the only English epic in the grand manner that still attracts many readers, after going blind. Though Milton was a classical scholar of great learning, his often complex style and his profound belief in Christian humanism really made him a belated representative of an earlier literary age, the last great writer of the English Renaissance.

What was needed to prepare for the classical age of English letters was the modernization of the English language by pruning the elaborate flourishes, standardizing the chaotic spelling, and eliminating the long flights of rhetoric characteristic of Elizabethan and early seventeenth-century prose. Under the influence of John Dryden (1631-1700), English began to model itself on French, adopting a straightforward word order, comparatively brief sentences, and the polish, neatness, and clarity of the French school. English letters were entering the Augustan Age, which lasted through the first half of the eighteenth century.

The Baroque Era

Baroque, the label usually applied to the arts of the seventeenth century, probably comes from the Portuguese *barroco*, an irregular or misshapen pearl. Some critics have seized upon the suggestion of deformity to criticize the impurity of seventeenth-century art in contrast with the purity of the Renaissance. Especially among Protestants, the reputation of baroque suffered because it was identified with the Counter-Reformation, and many of its leading artists appeared to be propagandists for Rome. Many viewers were also repelled by the flamboyance of baroque works.

Baroque art was closely associated with the Jesuits, with the successors of Philip II in Spain, and above all with Rome during the century following the Council of Trent. Catholic reformers enlisted the arts in propagating the faith and endowing it with greater emotional intensity. But not all the baroque masters were Catholic—Rembrandt, for instance, was a Mennonite, and Sir Christopher Wren an Anglican—nor were all their patrons Catholic prelates or grandees. Portraits of the Protestant Charles I of England brought Van Dyck fame and wealth; and in the Dutch Republic, where the Calvinist churches frowned on all ornamentation, paint-

ers won support from the business community and sometimes became prosperous businessmen themselves.

The unprecedented financial success of some artists is one of the distinguishing characteristics of the baroque period. Rubens, Van Dyck, Wren, and Bernini lived like lords, in contrast to the relatively austere existence of such Renaissance masters as Leonardo and Michelangelo. A second characteristic is the baroque stress on sheer size, as exemplified by the vast canvases of Rubens, the immense palace of Versailles, and Bernini's decorative canopy over the high altar in Saint Peter's in Rome. A third characteristic is theatricality, as painters intensified the illusion of brilliant lighting and placed figures in the immediate foreground of a canvas to draw the spectator into the scene. A final characteristic is the realistic depiction of a wide range of humanity—clowns, beggars, gypsies, card sharps, cripples, and dwarfs, as well as ordinary people, praying, laughing, or eating. In France, for example, Georges de La Tour (1593-1652) took everyday subjects and people—a woman retrieving a flea as she undresses, a hurdy-gurdy player, and, at the height of the seventeenth century devotional cult of Mary Magdalen, a painting of her

Diego Velásquez (1599-1660) painted many portraits of Spain's King Philip IV, but perhaps his most famous royal painting is "The Maids of Honour." Here is Princess Margarita, only four years old, dressed as the times and her station required. With her are two young noblewomen, the court jester, a female dwarf, and others. The child is receiving cold, perfumed water to drink.

The Maxims of La Rochefoucauld, trans. Louis Kronenberger (New York: Random House, 1959), maxims 72, 87, 146, 216, 157.

pensively contemplating a candle—and executed them in a nighttime setting that permitted dramatic contrasts of light and shadow.

Painting The most restrained baroque painter was probably Diego Velásquez (1599-1660), who spent thirty-four years at the court of Philip IV of Spain. Velásquez needed all his skill to soften the receding chins and thick lips of the Hapsburgs and still make his portraits of Philip IV and the royal family instantly recognizable. His greatest feat of technical wizardry is *The Maids of Honor* (see p. 27). A little princess, having her portrait painted, is surrounded by a pet dog, dwarfs, and other attendants; it is the moment when the royal parents are looking in on the scene, but only their reflections are seen in a mirror at the rear of the room. As Velásquez turns to greet them and looks at the viewer, the latter realizes he is standing where the royal couple must have stood. Painted with the adroit use of mirrors, *The Maids of Honor* is a splendid example of baroque attempts to make the spectator an active participant.

Unlike the aristocratic Velásquez, the Flemish Peter Paul Rubens (1577-1640) was the baroque counterpart of the Renaissance universal man. A diplomat, a linguist, and a student of antiquity and archaeology, he amassed a fortune from his painting and collected such impressive honors as being knighted by Charles I of England and elevated to the nobility by the king of Spain. Rubens made his studio, with its two hundred students, a factory of art. He himself is estimated to have contributed to over two thousand pictures, whose subjects ranged from simple portraits to ambitious political themes. He was commissioned by Marie de' Medici, widow of Henry IV of France, to execute a series of canvases glorifying Henry and herself. As monarchs by divine right, Henry and Marie were portrayed more as mythological figures than as mere mortals.

One of Rubens's pupils was a fellow Fleming, Anthony Van Dyck (1599-1641), whose portraits of Charles I captured the casual elegance and confident authority of the Stuart monarch. Although courtly style was not highly valued by the Flemings' northern neighbors in the Netherlands, the officers of Dutch civic guards, the governing boards of guilds, and other important organizations of Dutch merchants liked to be portrayed for posterity. Dutch middle-class families favored small,

Peter Paul Rubens (1577-1640) painted his "Massacre of the Innocents" about 1635. The painting shows King Herod's decree that all children under age two should be killed in order to eliminate the new-born Christ, being carried out with ruthless bloodshed. But Rubens was also recording current events, for in 1635 France prolonged the Thirty Years' War by its entry. Thus, a historical and biblical scene, a contemporary scene, and an allegory were all represented in a single painting, for in the background Rubens showed angels with flowers, to suggest that a heavenly hand still guided earthly events.

Rembrandt used light and facial expression as well as the position of the figures in his paintings to capture a sense of psychological truth. Here, in "The Anatomy Lesson of Dr. Tulp," the first commission he completed after moving from Leiden to Amsterdam, he showed a demonstration given by the leading professor of anatomy of the time. Those around him are members of the surgeons' guild. Each figures is individually realized, as Rembrandt draws attention to the developing science of pathology.

cheerful pictures, preferably showing the leisure activities cherished by these hard-working people. The consequence was a veritable explosion of artistic output that coincided with the heyday of Dutch prosperity during the first two-thirds of the century. With the French invasion of the 1670s, both the economic and artistic hegemony of the Dutch began to fade.

Seventeenth-century Dutch painters were admired both for their subtle depiction of light and color in landscapes and for their realistic representations of the interiors of Dutch houses, with their highly polished or well-scrubbed floors and their strong contrasts of light and shade. The best-known baroque painters in the Netherlands were Frans Hals (c 1580-1666) and Rembrandt Van Rijn (1606-1669). Hals used bold strokes to paint cheerful contingents of civic guards, laughing musicians, and tavern drunks. As he aged, he himself became a chronic drinker; yet in his eighties, a penniless inmate in a poorhouse, he painted the most remarkable group portrait in baroque art—*The Women Regents of the Haarlem Hospital*—dour, formidable, and aging matrons in all their Calvinist severity.

Rembrandt too attained fame early, then slipped into obscurity and poverty; he documented his troubles in a series of moving self-portraits. He also executed famous group portraits—*The Night Watch* and *The Syndics of the Drapers' Guild*. Rembrandt painted an exceptional scientific subject, *The Anatomy Lesson of Dr. Tulp*, in which a physician is explaining the structure of blood vessels

and tendons in the arm of an executed criminal, the only kind of cadaver available to anatomists.

Architecture and the Art of Living Baroque architecture and urban planning were at their most flamboyant in Rome, where Urban VIII (1623-1644) and other popes sponsored churches, palaces, gardens, fountains, avenues, and piazzas in their determination to make their capital once again the most spectacular city in Europe. The Church of Saint Peter's, apart from Michelangelo's dome, is a legacy of the baroque rather than the Renaissance.

In the last third of the century the France of Louis XIV set the trends in architecture, landscape gardening, town planning, and furniture—especially at Versailles and in Paris. Vienna, Munich, Madrid, Warsaw, and

In the famous church of St. Peter's at Rome, the proportions of Michelangelo's Greek-cross design were altered when a greatly lengthened nave was constructed in the early 1600s. With the vast space of the nave leading into the space beneath the dome, it was imperative to find a way of filling the latter. Urban VIII entrusted the commission to a young architect, Gian Lorenzo Bernini (1598-1680), who hit upon the ingenious solution of the *baldachin,* or tabernacle, an enormously magnified and strengthened version of the canopy used to cover the sacrament. This 85-foot structure made elaborate use of the Barberini family symbols and was supposedly modeled on Solomon's temple. To obtain bronze for the columns and canopy, Urban VIII had the bronze roof of the Pantheon—the best preserved of Rome's ancient monuments—melted down.

The great Piazza Obliqua was added to St. Peter's by Bernini in 1657-1666, completing a masterpiece of the baroque. This was the first large open space within a city, in contrast to the enclosed squares typical of the Renaissance, the great colonnades providing a massive space that focuses on St. Peter's itself.

St. Paul's Cathedral in London, built between 1673 and 1710, became an architectural model for much public architecture well into the nineteenth century.

Prague also became major baroque cities, though their styles tended to be imitative of the Italian or French. Great architectural feats sometimes took two generations or more, and the post-1630 period (known as high baroque) was marked by constant building, even in lesser cities like Würzburg or Dresden.

In England baroque building was much diluted by classicism. Under Charles II the chief architect was Sir Christopher Wren (1632-1723), a talented engineer and astronomer who was deluged with commissions after a great fire destroyed much of London in 1666. Saint Paul's Cathedral, in particular, drew upon his capacity to fuse varying styles into a harmonious whole.

The arts of good living made substantial progress in the seventeenth century, despite the ravages of disease and famine that reduced the European population by at least 15 percent between 1648 and 1713. The expansion of Europe overseas made available the new beverages of coffee, tea, and cocoa, the new cotton fabrics, and luxuries like Chinese porcelain and lacquer ware. Exotic tropical woods were used to inlay and veneer furniture. On the whole, furniture was becoming more specialized: dining chairs replaced dining benches; chairs were made both with arms and, to accommodate hoopskirts, without. Table napkins came into use; individual plates and glasses replaced communal bowls and goblets. Families of moderate means could afford these innovations, as well as a teapot, a pitcher, and a few items of plain silver, and thus shared in what amounted to a revolution in domestic arrangements.

Music Baroque composers, especially in Italy, moved further along the paths laid out by their Renaissance predecessors. In Venice Claudio Monteverdi (1567-1643) wrote the first important operas. The opera, a characteristically baroque mix of music and drama, proved so popular that Venice soon had sixteen opera houses, which focused on the fame of their chief singers rather than on the overall quality of the supporting cast and the orchestra. The star system reached its height at Naples, where conservatories (originally institutions for "conserving" talented orphans) specialized in voice training. Many Neapolitan operas were loose collections of songs designed to show off the talents of the individual stars. The effect of unreality was heightened by the custom of having male roles sung by women and some female roles sung by *castrati*, male sopranos who had been castrated as young boys to prevent the onset of puberty and the deepening of their voices.

In England Henry Purcell (c 1659-1695), the organist of Westminster Abbey, produced a masterpiece for the graduation exercises of a girls' school, the beautiful and moving *Dido and Aeneas.* Louis XIV, appreciating the obvious value of opera in enhancing the resplendence of his court, imported from Italy the talented Jean-Baptiste Lully (1632-1687). In his operas Lully united French and Italian musical, dance, and literary traditions, and took over the artificiality, gaiety, and weight of court ballet. No artist of the time was more representative, and none was more distant from the concerns of the people who, though they might admire the majesty of the court from a distance, could know no part in it—the common people, who saw little if any of the art and architecture, read none of the literature, and heard none of the music of baroque high society.

Social Trends

Throughout the seventeenth century the laborer, whether rural or urban, faced repeated crises of subsistence, with a general downturn beginning in 1619 and a widespread decline after 1680. Almost no region escaped plague, famine, war, depression, or even all four. Northern Europe and England suffered from a general economic depression in the 1620s; Mediterranean France and northern Italy were struck by plague in the 1630s; and a recurrent plague killed 100,000 in London in 1665. The "little ice age"—a gradual onset of acute cold too severe for most crops—began in the late sixteenth century and made harvests unpredictable until 1650, and for a decade there was a perceptible advance of glacial ice. Population increase slowed dramatically, and general stagnation was the norm, despite important regional exceptions. Given the emphasis on high fashion at the French court, the gap between the rich and the poor was perceived as growing.

HISTORY AND CHANGE

In his *Pensées* Pascal remarked upon the transitions in history:

Rivers are roads which move, and which carry us wither we desire to go.

When we do not know the truth of a thing, it is of advantage that there should exist a common error which determines the mind of man, as, for example, the moon, to which is attributed the change of seasons, the progress of diseases, etc. For the chief malady of man is restless curiosity about things which he cannot understand; and it is not so bad for him to be in error as to be curious to no purpose.

Thoughts, Letters, and Opuscules, trans. O.W. Wight (New York: Hurt and Houghton, 1869), p. 211.

In France and Russia the sixteenth century was marked by peasant revolts. In France the revolts were directed against the tax collectors, who raised revenues "for the needs of the state"—needs which were felt to be a pretext for enriching a few private persons. The peasants especially resented the tax-farmer, who was a vigorously efficient tax collector because he kept part of what he raised. They also resented the tendency toward centralization which the new taxes, and most especially the *gabelle*, a tax on salt, represented. Peasant revolts in 1636, 1637, 1639, and 1675 underscored the general discontent.

Discontent and fear also help explain the renewal of the search for witches. Witches had once been part of the general belief in magic and religion. In the fifteenth century a substantial handbook on the detection and interrogation of witches had been widely read, and by 1669 it was in its twenty-ninth edition. Witchcraft combined sorcery and heresy; the first was to be feared and the second condemned. Though skeptics and rationalists doubted the existence of witches or the Devil, theologians and the great mass of people did not. Moreover, both law and medicine accepted witchcraft, and even the English jurist Blackstone would seriously discuss witchcraft as an issue in the 1730s.

Between 1580 and 1650 witchcraft trials were commonplace; there probably were nearly 100,000 such trials, amounting to epidemics of mass hysteria. Even in England, where the common law prohibited torture to extract confessions, there were over a thousand trials. Although concern for witches was almost universal, the greatest number of executions took place in Calvinist areas. Historians are not agreed on why an outbreak of witch persecutions would occur in one place rather than another—in Scotland and New England, in Switzerland and France—except to say that where popular magic was commonplace, so was the fear of witches. Trials also usually followed a period of fear about the future and concern over apparent changes in ordered and stable conditions. Nor were the educated spared—indeed, they were often in the lead when a community sought out a witch.

In 1691, in Massachusetts, the strange behavior of two small girls led the community of Salem into a mass witchhunt that did not stop until twenty persons had been executed. Historians believe the hallucinations of the children thought to be under the influence of witches were induced by ergot poisoning from a fungus that grows on barley in a moist season. Elsewhere fertility cults were accused of performing black magic. In southern France witchcraft may simply have been a form of rural social revolt in which the Mass could be mocked and the church hierarchy challenged.

The clergy did not have all the needed answers for the peasant, and were often challenged by astrologers, village wizards, "cunning folk." Popular magic often seemed to provide a more ready remedy for illness, theft, unhappy personal relationships, or a world in which meanings were shifting. In the seventeenth century magic declined in relation to religion; increased popular literacy, improved communications, the slow recognition that diseases such as epilepsy were open to human investigation instead of partaking of the supernatural, the failures of divination, and perhaps reaction against the horrors of the witchcraft craze, all contributed to the turn toward rationalism that occurred first in the cities.

Still, there was continuity amid change. The old traditional rhythms continued in marriage, child-rearing, death, and burial. As feast and famine alternated, people continued to try to explain insecurity, sought for stability, and realized that their lives were racked by events not only beyond their control but beyond their understanding. These fears were also true of the upper classes. Indeed, in some matters the lower classes had more control over their lives. The children of those who owned no property were freer to choose a spouse, since their parents had little economic leverage over them, having nothing to bequeath to them, than were the children of the aristocracy, who had to make carefully calculated marriage alliances to hold on to or increase family property.

By the seventeenth century the position of women with respect to property was improving. On the Continent perhaps 20 percent of families had daughters and no sons; when women inherited land, the social implications were far-reaching, since ownership might pass to a different family at every generation. By the eighteenth century the "female presence" in land holding had become very important in England, finally matching the position women had held in ancient Sparta. Marriages were thereby encouraged between persons of similar status and wealth, hardening class lines. Since a second spouse would diminish the interest of the first, the economy joined the church in working against polygamy. The marriage of a widow had become of great importance to her adult children, since it would influence the estate.

When other siblings were excluded from the land, younger children had to be given an equivalent share in some other way. Thus the custom grew of a younger son's buying a commission in the army, or of entering the church, or of joining the faculty of a university, or of being given a stake in business. However, since the family name remained attached to the land, the aristocracy remained one of land rather than of wealth or of intelligence, so that being a "counter jumper" (a merchant, or "in trade") might lead to far more income but much less prestige. Since common people were unlikely to be able to break into the aristocracy of prestige, successful commoners cast their lot with the merchant class and with capitalism, which was increasingly open to talent rather than to inherited wealth.

Increasingly, the law was used to hold society in balance: to keep people in their place, to assure that the poor did not poach upon the land of the rich, to define acts of social unrest as crimes. The growth in individualism—whether among contributors to the "century of genius" or among those who emerged from "Every-

WHO BUILT THE TOWERS OF THEBES?

In the seventeenth century the underclasses, that unspoken for and, for the historian who relies solely on written records, unspeaking mass of humankind, began to speak and to answer the questions posed in the twentieth century by a radical German dramatist and poet, Bertolt Brecht (1898-1956):

Who built Thebes of the seven gates?
In the books you will find the names of kings.
Did the kings haul up the lumps of rock?
And Babylon, many times demolished
Who raised it up so many times? In what houses
Of gold-glittering Lima did the builders live?
Where, the evening that the Wall of China was
    finished
Did the masons go? Great Rome
Is full of triumphal arches. Who erected them?
    Over whom
Did the Caesars triumph? Had Byzantium, much
    praised in song
Only palaces for its inhabitants? Even in fabled
    Atlantis
The night the ocean engulfed it
The drowning still bawled for their slaves.

The young Alexander conquered India.
Was he alone?

Caesar beat the Gauls.
Did he not have even a cook with him?

Philip of Spain wept when his armada
Went down. Was he the only one to weep?
Frederick the Second won the Seven Years' War.
Who Else won it?

Every page a victory.
Who cooked the feast for the victors?
Every ten years a great man.
Who paid the bill?

So many reports.
So many questions.

B. Brecht, "Questions from a Worker Who Reads," trans. Michael Hamburgh, in John Willett and Ralph Manheim, eds., *Bertolt Brecht Poems* (London: Eyre Methuen, 1976), pp. 252-53.

man"—led to greater variation in human behavior. As a result, there was a perceived need to use laws to define appropriate behavior, with greater interference by the state (as well as the church) in matters relating to sexuality, bastardy, and marriage. Mere nakedness was not yet considered indecent, nor was drunkenness thought to be a public vice. Destruction of the family unit, however, by failing to observe the laws of inheritance was a clear offense against continuity and propriety. It remained one small area of stability that rich and poor could, to some extent, control.

Perhaps we speak today of the seventeenth century as "the century of genius" because so much that is still central to our thought—in politics, economics, literature, art, and science—can be traced most immediately to the great thinkers of that century. But the seventeenth century was also the century of the inarticulate, of the far-less-than-great, of common people who labored for themselves, their families, their church, and, often and increasingly, for their nation. The Fronde was not a popular uprising, but there were many peasant revolts in the seventeenth century and thereafter. The English Civil War was not a "war of people," but the people were intimately touched by its events.

Much of history as written has been criticized for being the history only of great men (and, increasingly, women). Both the criticism and the tactic are sound for the premodern age. The great, the powerful, the visible, the influential shaped the outlines of history through their actions; and yet without the tacit response and support of the mass of humanity, those actions would have taken a different course. By the seventeenth century popular culture—whether in the witchcraft craze or the slow process of a growing literacy—also deeply influenced the course of history. Personality has always played an important role in history, but now not just the personalities of monarchs, generals, philosophers, and great merchants were important, but the collective personality of the common people also helped define national identities. However far back into the past one might press the beginnings of the modern age, or however far into the present one might advance those beginnings, the seventeenth century was most clearly a crucial threshold.

SUMMARY

The seventeenth century was dominated by France. During the reign of Louis XIII, Cardinal Richelieu created an efficient centralized state. He eliminated the Huguenots as a political force, made nobles subordinate to the king, and made the monarchy absolute. Louis XIV built on these achievements during his long reign. Louis XIV moved his capital from the turbulence of Paris to Versailles, where he built a vast palace and established elaborate court rituals that further limited the power of the nobles.

From Versailles, the Sun King demanded unquestioning obedience from his subjects, seeing himself as the representative of God on earth and ruling by divine right. In religion, Louis XIV encouraged the evolution of the Gallican church. In 1685, he revoked the Edict of Nantes, ending toleration of Huguenots. Mercantilism, practiced by Colbert, was central to French economic policy. Colbert's policies promoted foreign trade and the expansion of industry.

Hoping to expand France to its "natural frontiers," Louis XIV pursued an aggressive foreign policy that embroiled the nation in numerous wars. In the War of the Spanish Succession (1701-1714), England, Holland, the Holy Roman Empire, and German states joined forces to prevent a union of Spain and France. The treaty of Utrecht (1713) preserved the balance of power in Europe but left many unresolved issues.

In England, the Stuart monarchs James I and Charles I violated traditions limiting royal authority and protecting individual rights. Their attempts to rule without Parliament brought matters to a revolution between the Crown and Parliament. During the Civil War (1640-1648), England was split between royalists and parliamentarians. Under Puritan leader Oliver Cromwell, the New Model Army decisively defeated the king. Radicals in the Rump Parliament tried and condemned the king to death in 1649.

During the Interregnum, England was a republic dominated by Oliver Cromwell and the Puritans. They faced opposition at home and abroad. In 1660, the monarchy was restored. But the Interregnum marked the first successful challenge to a monarch by a politically active citizenry. Moreover, the events of the Civil War affirmed the existence of an unwritten constitution rooted in English common law. Belief in freedom of speech and religious toleration also emerged in this period.

During the Restoration, Parliament was supreme. The Catholic sympathies of James II so alienated his subjects that he was toppled by the Glorious Revolution of 1688, which put William of Orange on the throne. Parliament then enacted the Bill of Rights of 1689 that embodied the principles of parliamentary supremacy. In the next three hundred years, England would become a parliamentary democracy.

The seventeenth century was an age of intellectual ferment dominated by France, Holland, and England. Two concepts underlay thought: the idea of a natural order and the importance of reason. In England, Thomas Hobbes in the *Leviathan* (1651) and John Locke in his *Second Treatise of Government* (1690) set out ideas on government and human nature that would greatly influence political thought. On the continent, Pascal and Spinoza made equally significant contributions to Western thought.

During the Age of Classicism, French dramatists such as Corneille, Molière, and Racine dominated literature just as the court of Louis XIV influenced all of Europe. In *Paradise Lost,* John Milton combined classical scholarship and profound Christian faith.

Baroque masters produced flamboyant works of art that emphasized size and theatricality. Flemish and Dutch painters including Rubens, Rembrandt, and Van Dyck won widespread acclaim.

In the seventeenth century, laborers faced hardships of plague, famine, and warfare. An epidemic of witchhunts and witch trials reflected a pervasive fear. Yet belief in popular magic declined as literacy spread. The property rights of women were recognized, thereby helping to improve their position. Despite gradual change, traditional patterns of life continued, and law was used to affirm social rights and traditions.

THE OLD REGIMES

Long years of peace appeared to be in prospect for Europe in 1715. In the West the Utrecht settlement of 1713 had ended Louis XIV's prolonged threat to the balance of power, and in the Baltic the long Great Northern War between Russia and Sweden was nearing a settlement. The death of Louis XIV in 1715 gave fresh promise of international stability, for the crown of France passed to his great-grandson, Louis XV, a boy of five. During a long regency France could be expected to be too preoccupied with internal matters to attempt foreign aggression. Finally, the last war of Louis XIV had exhausted both his own state and his victorious opponents.

The term "Old Regime" is used to describe the institutions prevailing in Europe, and especially in France, before 1789. This was the "Old Regime" of the eighteenth century, in contrast to the "New Regime" that was to issue from the French Revolution. On the surface, the Old Regime followed the pattern of the Middle Ages, though the forces that were to transform the economy, society, and politics of modern Europe were already at work. To be sure, the economy was still largely agrarian, for most Europeans lived in farming villages and retained the localized outlook of the peasant. Although in western Europe most peasants had been free of serfdom for several centuries, in eastern Europe—notably in Germany beyond the Elbe and in Hungary, Poland, and Russia—most were still serfs.

The social foundations of the Old Regime rested on the medieval division of society into the first estate of the clergy, the second estate of the nobility, and the third estate of the commoners, which included the urban bourgeoisie and working people as well as the peasantry. Within the third estate, only those at the top exerted much political influence—well-to-do business leaders in England and Holland, French lawyers or merchants wealthy enough to purchase government office, women who had married well or who had the ear of the influential people who attended their salons. Generally, bourgeois influence diminished as one moved eastward; generally, too, the titled nobles and the landed gentry of the second estate still exerted substantial influence and wanted to regain some of their lost power. Every government in Europe tended to represent the interests of the few rather than the many. In this respect, it made little difference whether it was an absolute monarchy like France or Prussia, a developing constitutional monarchy like Britain, or a republic like the Dutch United Provinces.

The apparent stability of 1715 proved to be increasingly deceptive, however, as the eighteenth century advanced. The political and social status quo came under increasing attack from the leaders of the intellectual movement known as the Enlightenment (see Chapter 17). The economic foundations of the Old Regime were eroding under the pressure of revolutionary change, and the balance of power achieved by the Utrecht settlement was undermined. The defeat and death of Louis XIV did not end the worldwide rivalry of England and France, who began another phase of their long conflict in 1740. Meanwhile, further shifts in the international balance resulted from the appearance of two important newcomers: Russia was moving out of semi-isolation to take an active role in war and diplomacy, and the German state of Brandenburg-Prussia was becoming a first-class military power, apparently intent on expansion.

I THE ECONOMIC "REVOLUTIONS"

The changes that undermined the Old Regime affected commerce, agriculture, and industry and were most evident in western Europe, particularly in France, the Low Countries and, above all, Britain. They were in some respects economic revolutions, though many historians dislike the term because it suggests a more sudden upsurge of economic energy and technological inventiveness than actually occurred. In the eighteenth century the pace of economic change was slower than it would be in the nineteenth or twentieth, and it provided less drama than such political upheavals as the American and French revolutions. Yet in the long run the consequences of the economic "revolutions" were fully as revolutionary as were the political and social ones of 1776 and 1789.

Commerce and Finance, 1713-1745

Many of the basic institutions of European business life had developed before 1715—banks and insurance firms in the Renaissance, for example, and chartered trading companies in the sixteenth century. Mercantilism, the loosely defined set of principles determining governmental policies toward commerce, had matured in the Spain of Philip II, in the France of Louis XIV and Colbert, and in Britain between 1651 and the early eighteenth century. The steady growth of seaborne trade, stimulated by an increasing population and a rising demand for food and goods, was a main force in quickening the pace of commerce. Many ports enjoyed a great boom—in England: London, Bristol, and Liverpool; in France: Nantes and Bourdeaux on the Atlantic coast, nourished by the colonial trade, and Marseilles, nourished by trade with the eastern Mediterranean; in Italy: Leghorn, established as a free port by the Grand Duchy of Tuscany; and in Germany: Hamburg, whose prosperity attested to the shift in economic focus of northern Europe from the Baltic to the Atlantic.

The growing maritime trade increased the demand for insurance on ships and cargoes. In London early in the century marine insurance brokers gathered at Edward Lloyd's coffeehouse in Lombard Street to discuss business, news, and politics; they continued to meet there after Lloyd's death in 1713. Thus was born Lloyd's of London, a firm that developed the standard form of policy for marine insurance and published the first detailed and accurate shipping newspaper. Another great London institution to emerge from the informal atmosphere of the coffeehouse was the stock exchange, for buying and selling shares in joint-stock companies.

Marine insurance prospered in part because improved charts and the installation of lighthouses and buoys made navigation safer. Captains could determine their geographical position at sea by using two new instruments, the sextant and the chronometer. The sextant, an elaboration of the telescope, showed the altitude of the sun at noon and thus indicated the ship's latitude. The chronometer, a clock unaffected by the motion of the ship, was kept on Greenwich Mean Time (the time at the meridian running through Greenwich near London). The two new instruments also made it possible to calculate the ship's longitude.

On land, improvements in communication and transport came much more slowly. Except for the relatively good highways of France, European roads were scarcely more than wide paths. The shipment of goods overland remained slow, unsafe, and expensive until after 1750, when the construction of turnpikes and canals gradually improved the situation. The pioneer English canal, built in 1759-1761, cut in half the cost of moving coal from mines to a new factory town, Manchester.

Business people faced the handicaps imposed by restrictive guild regulations, by the many different coins, weights, and measures, and by the numerous local tolls. Sweden, for example, minted only copper money, including a coin weighing 43 pounds. Baden, one of the smaller German states, had 112 separate measures for length, 65 for dry goods, 123 for liquids, and 163 for cereals, not to mention 80 different pound weights. A German merchant who shipped timber down the Elbe

THE COFFEEHOUSE

The thriving maritime trade changed public taste, as it brought a variety of new produce into the British and continental markets. A dramatic example is the rise of the coffeehouse and the drinking of tea at home. In the seventeenth and early eighteenth centuries the coffeehouse was referred to as the "penny university," for the price of entry, which was a penny (and two pennies extra for the coffee itself), admitted one to a room where the daily newspaper could be found and where animated political discussion was taking place. The Turks had called coffeehouses "schools of the wise," and the tendency for them to become centers for subversion led the Russians to attempt to suppress them.

In 1675 England's Charles II tried to close coffeehouses, acting upon the pretext that coffee was injurious to health, as a pamphlet, *The Women's Petition Against Coffee, representing to public consideration the grand inconveniences accruing to their sex from the excessive use of the drying and enfeebling Liquor,* had argued. In truth, as his proclamation showed, Charles was more concerned that "in such Houses . . . divers False, Malitious and Scandalous Reports are devised and spread abroad, to the Defamation of his Majestie's Government, and to the Disturbance of the Peace and Quiet of the Realm." Eleven days later the king withdrew the edict of prohibition on the grounds of "royal compassion." Until the end of the reigns of the early Georges, the coffeehouse, at least in London, remained a male social center: in Queen Anne's time there were five hundred such houses.

In Ned Ward's *Wealthy Shopkeeper,* published in 1706, a typical day of a well-to-do Londoner was laid out:

[R]ise at 5; counting-house till 8; then breakfast on toast and Cheshire cheese; in his shop for two hours then a neighbouring coffee house for news; shop again, till dinner at home (over the shop) at 12 on a "thundering joint"; 1 o'clock on Change; 3, Lloyd's Coffee House for business; shop again for an hour; then another coffee house (not Lloyd's) for recreation, followed by "sack shop" to drink with acquaintances, till home for a "light supper" and so to bed, "before Bow Bell rings nine."

G.M. Trevelyan, *Illustrated English Social History.* Vol. III: *Eighteenth Century* (London: Longmans, Green, 1951), p. 30.

Europe in 1750

━━━━━━ Boundary of the Holy
········· Roman Empire

■ Battle sites

NORWAY

SWE

Oslo

Stockholm

North Sea

DENMARK

Copenhagen

Baltic

SWEDISH POMERANIA

Danzig

SCOTLAND

Edinburgh
Berwick

ULSTER

IRELAND

Drogheda
Boyne R.
Dublin
Limerick

Preston
Liverpool
Manchester

Marston Moor

KINGDOM OF GREAT BRITAIN

Hamburg
Bremen

HANOVER

Elbe R.

BRANDENBURG

Berlin

Oder R.

SHROPSHIRE

ENGLAND

Naseby

Nottingham

EAST ANGLIA

London
Thames R.
Dover

Bristol

UNITED NETHERLANDS

Ryswick
Utrecht
Nimwegen
(Aix-la-Chapelle)

Ypres
Oudenarde

WEST-PHALIA

SAXONY

SILESIA

Prague

BOHEMIA

MORAVIA

THE EMPIRE

C. la Hogue

AUSTRIAN NETHERLANDS

Ramillies
Aachen

Rouen
Malplaquet

HESSE-KASSEL

Würzburg

Rhine R.

Seine R.

Paris

Versailles

Verdun

Metz

Toul

LORRAINE

ALSACE

Strasbourg

Blenheim

BADEN

Augsburg

BAVARIA

Vienna

AUSTRIA

STYRIA

Nantes

Blois
Orléans

Loire R.

Autun

FRANCE

FRANCHE-COMTÉ

SWITZERLAND

Geneva

Rhône R.

TYROL

CARINTHIA

CARNIOLA

Atlantic Ocean

Bordeaux

Garonne R.

SAVOY

PIEDMONT

MILAN

Po R.

Venice

VENETIAN REPUBLIC

Adriatic Sea

Ragu

Genoa

Parma

Avignon
(to the papacy)

Narbonne
Marseilles

Florence

Leghorn

TUSCANY

PAPAL STATES

Rome

Burgos

Ebro R.

PYRENEES

PORTUGAL

S P A I N

Lisbon
Tagus R.
Madrid

Barcelona

Seville
Guadalquivir R.

Granada

Valencia

Gibraltar
(Br.)

BALEARIC IS.

MINORCA
(Br.)

CORSICA
(to Genoa)
(to France, 1768)

SARDINIA
(to Austria, 1714;
to Savoy, 1720)

NAPLES

Naples

Palermo

SICILY
(to Savoy, 1714;
to Austria, 1720)

Mediterranean Sea

ALGERIA

TUNIS

MALTA

0   500
|————————————————|
Miles

FINLAND

L. Onega

L. Ladoga

Gulf of Finland

St. Petersburg

Narva   INGRIA

ESTONIA   Novgorod   Volga R.

N

LIVONIA

Riga

RLAND   W. Dvina R.

Moscow

Oka R.

Vilna   Smolensk

LITHUANIA

POLAND   RUSSIA

Kiev

Dnieper R.   Volga R.

Dniester R.   Don R.

TRANSYLVANIA   Caspian Sea

MOLDAVIA

GARY

CRIMEA

WALLACHIA   Black Sea   PERSIA

Passarowitz

Danube R.

BULGARIA

OTTOMAN   Constantinople

Vardar R.

Salonika   EMPIRE   Tigris R.

Aegean Sea

Athens   Euphrates R.

RHODES

CYPRUS

CRETE

Growth of France, 1559-1769

ENGLAND

Calais

ARTOIS   ALSACE
1659   1648-1681

Paris

LORRAINE
1766

FRANCHE-COMTÉ
1678

1601

FRANCE

Rhône R.

ROUSSILLON   Avignon
1659

SPAIN   CORSICA
1768

THE EMPIRE

— Boundary of the empire, 1559

River from Dresden in Saxony to Hamburg had to sell so many planks to pay tolls to the towns and principalities along the way that of sixty planks floated at Dresden, only six would reach Hamburg. Even in France, a relative model of uniformity and centralization, all sorts of local taxes and other obstacles to internal trade persisted.

The survival of local vested interests showed the limitations of the power of the mercantilist state. Although mercantilism required the regulation of trade on a national basis, no eighteenth-century government had the staff needed to make national regulation effective. Austria, Prussia, and some other German states endeavored to assimilate mercantilism into a more systematized policy called *cameralism* (from *camera*, the council or chamber dealing with expenditures and income). Though the cameralists took a broad view of government's economic responsibilities and activities, their main effort was directed toward planning state budgets, especially the increase of revenues. States outside the cameralist bloc often relied heavily on private companies and individuals to execute economic policies.

Thus the English and Dutch East India companies exercised not only a trading monopoly in their colonial preserves but also virtual sovereign powers, including the right to maintain soldiers and conduct diplomacy. Inventors worked on their own, not in government facilities, although the state occasionally offered prizes on matters of critical importance to the business community. When the English Parliament promised £20,000 for the invention of a reliable seagoing clock, the inventor of the chronometer had to wait twenty-five years to collect his prize money. On the whole, private initiative accomplished more than governments did, though it could also get out of control, as demonstrated by two speculative booms early in the century—the Mississippi Bubble in France and the South Sea Bubble in England.

In 1715 hardly a state in Europe could manage the large debts that had piled up during the recent wars. Yet all of them had to find some way of meeting at least part of the large annual interest on bonds and other obligations or else go bankrupt. The governments of France and England chose to experiment. They transferred the management of state debts to joint-stock companies, which they rewarded for their risk-taking with trading concessions. The commerce of the companies, it was hoped, would prove so lucrative that their profits would cover the interest charges on government bonds.

John Law (1671-1729), a Scottish mathematical wizard and financier, presided over the experiment in France. Law agreed with the mercantilist doctrine that the strength of a state depended upon the quantity of money it possessed; but, he asserted, the limited supply of silver and gold made it difficult to increase the amount of specie (coined money) circulating in any country, and therefore made it difficult to promote business. Paper money, Law concluded, was the solution—paper money backed by a nation's wealth in land and trade. The quantity of paper money in circulation could easily be raised or lowered to meet the needs of business. Trading companies would prosper; the whole country would prosper; in the general prosperity, government debts would be paid off.

The death of Louis XIV gave Law his opportunity. The regent for the young Louis XV, the duke of Orléans, permitted Law to set up a central bank in Paris. Whereas the value of French money had been sinking as the government progressively debased the coinage, Law's bank (following the practice of the Bank of Amsterdam) issued paper notes of stable value. Business activity at once increased. Next, Law set up the Compagnie des Indes, commonly called the Mississippi Company, which received a monopoly of commerce to and from the Louisiana colony, promoted colonization, and absorbed the other French colonial trading companies.

Law's system reached to almost every corner of the French economy, and Law himself became the economic dictator of France. Merging with the royal bank, his company took over the government debt and agreed to accept government bonds in partial payment for shares of Mississippi stock. Many bondholders responded enthusiastically to Law's offer because the bonds had depreciated to 20 percent or less of their face value. Law, however, had to sell additional shares of Mississippi stock to obtain sufficient working capital for his company. To attract cash purchasers, he promoted a boom in Mississippi stock, painting the company's prospects in the brightest colors. Investors, large and small, caught the fever of speculation, and by the close of 1719 Mississippi stock was selling at forty times its par value.

The Mississippi Bubble soon burst, for Law's paper money could not stand the pressure. As the price of Mississippi shares rose higher and higher, cautious investors decided to cash in. They sold their shares, received payment in banknotes, then took the notes to Law's bank and demanded their redemption in specie. The bank exhausted its reserves of gold and silver and suspended specie payments in February 1720. Law was forced to resign in May 1720; he fled France shortly thereafter.

The bursting of the Mississippi Bubble had international repercussions, for within a few weeks of Law's resignation the South Sea Bubble burst in London. Management of the English government's debt had been assigned to the Bank of England. Founded in 1694 as a private institution, the Bank issued notes and performed other services for the government during the last wars against Louis XIV; but in negotiations for the privilege of managing the debt, the Bank was outbid by the new South Sea Company, which paid the government an exorbitant sum. The resources of the company were slim, consisting largely of the right to exploit the trading concessions that Britain obtained under the Asiento agreement at the end of the War of the Spanish Succession. These privileges were limited to furnishing Spain's American colonies with 4,800 slaves annually and sending one ship a year to Panama for general trade.

The South Sea Company, like the Mississippi Company, invited government creditors to transfer their

This engraving by William Hogarth shows London during the South Sea Bubble. Done in 1721, the work depicts the artist's vision of a corrupt society. The sign above the door at the upper left says, "Raffleing for Husbands with Lottery Fortunes—in Here." Frenzied financial speculation goes on through every form of gambling.

bonds into company stock. The directors of the company bought and sold shares in secret to create a more lively market, encouraged purchases of stock with a down payment of only 10 percent in cash, and spread reports of forthcoming sailings by the company's ships on voyages that did not take place, creating a speculative boom. Dozens of other promoters sprang into action, advertising schemes for wheels of perpetual motion, for making saltwater fresh, and "for carrying on an undertaking of great advantage, but nobody to know what it is." The gullibility of the investing public, though remarkable, was not inexhaustible. South Sea shares fell; Parliament ordered an investigation and, to protect the company's creditors, seized the estates of its directors, who had meantime destroyed the company's books and fled the country.

Yet the Bubbles were by no means total misfortunes. They were an extreme instance of the economic growing pains suffered as the states of Europe groped for solutions to new and baffling financial problems. Law's system released French business from the depression induced by the defeats of Louis XIV. It also stimulated settlement in Louisiana. The Mississippi Company, reorganized after 1720, consistently made a large profit. In England the strongest institutions rode out the bursting of the South Sea Bubble; the East India Company continued to pay an annual dividend of 5 to 10 percent, and the Bank of England, no longer having to compete with the South Sea Company for government favor, again became the financial mainstay of the realm.

In the political shakeup following the collapse of the Bubble, the Whig statesman Robert Walpole (1676-1745) came to power with a program of honoring the debt as a *national* debt. This was a novel concept in an age when most states treated their debts as the monarch's personal obligation, to be acknowledged or repudiated as he saw fit. No subsequent stock crisis assumed the proportions of that of 1720, and thereafter British banking grew rapidly and on a stable foundation. This growth was central to the future of Britain's agricultural and industrial development, which would overtake France by the end of the century.

Agricultural Improvements

The agricultural revolution—the second of the forces transforming the modern economy—centered on improvements that enabled fewer farmers to produce more crops. The application of technological discoveries to agriculture was as old as the irrigation ditches of ancient Mesopotamia and the improved plows and horse-collars of the Middle Ages. What was revolutionary in the eighteenth century was the faster tempo of the advance in farming techniques. The Netherlands, both Dutch and Austrian, were the leaders, producing the highest yields per acre while also pioneering in the culture of new crops like the potato, the turnip, and clover. Turnips furnished feed for livestock until the spring pasturing season began, thus eliminating the necessity for massive slaughtering of stock at the onset of winter. Clover, by fixing nitrogen in the soil, increased the fertility of the land and ended the need to have fields lie fallow every third year. Livestock breeding was also improved.

In England the new crops were taken up by Lord "Turnip" Townshend (1674-1738), whose plan for a four-year rotation—planting a field in turnips, barley, clover, and wheat in successive years—became standard on many English estates. Townshend and other "improving landlords" in England were the great publicists of the new agriculture. Jethro Tull (1674-1741) studied French truck-gardens and vineyards, where farmers obtained heavy yields from small plots by planting seeds individually and by carefully hoeing the soil around each plant and vine. Tull adapted French methods to the grain fields of England. In place of the inefficient custom of scattering seed broadcast, he planted it deep in regular rows with a horse-drawn hoe. The improvements of Tull and Townshend won enthusiastic praise from Arthur Young (1741-1820), who published lengthy reports on his frequent trips through the farming districts of Britain and the Continent. Young won an international following that included George III, George Washington, the marquis de Lafayette, and Catherine the Great.

Before 1789, however, only the most enterprising landlords supported the new agriculture, and even in Britain it was practiced mainly by the holders of large estates. Yet uneven though it was, the agricultural revolution of the eighteenth century came close to ending wholesale famines in Europe, even if it did not prevent recurring food shortages. It also marked an important stage in the gradual shift from the largely self-sufficient manor of the Middle Ages to the capitalist farm producing specialized crops. The improving landlords needed large amounts of capital and large plots of land that were not subdivided into long, narrow strips for individual cultivators or otherwise used in common by many farmers. Since these old ways hampered the new agriculture, there was a mounting demand that common fields be fenced off as the private lands of single landlords. Enclosures, which in Tudor England were introduced to extend sheep pastures, were now sought to increase cropland. The new enclosure movement reached its peak in the late eighteenth and the early nineteenth centuries, when Parliament passed hundreds of separate enclosure acts affecting several million acres.

Enclosure created large farms well suited to drill-planting, horse-hoeing, and crop rotation, and enabled Britain to feed a growing population by increasing agricultural output. But it probably created widespread social misery. In Georgian England, as in ancient Greece and Rome, the development of large estates ruined many small farmers, or yeomen, who could not survive without the right to use common lands, and who could not afford to buy tools, install fences, and become improving landlords themselves. Many of them became hired hands on big farms or sought work in the expanding towns. Some, deprived of their land, became poachers, illegally taking game from the great estates. In 1723 Parliament passed the Waltham Black Act, creating fifty new capital offenses and aimed at controlling new crimes that were, in effect, socially defined, such as being armed with weapons and appearing in forests or enclosed lands with faces blackened, which was taken as evidence of the intention to steal or kill animals, to take crops or wood, or to set fire to the property of the owners. The Hanoverian Whigs moved quickly to assure stability for the landed estates in the face of growing social unrest created by the techniques of the improving landlords.

The Beginnings of the Industrial Revolution, to 1789

By increasing productivity and at the same time releasing part of the farm labor force for other work, the revolution in agriculture contributed to that in industry. Industry also required raw materials (supplied in part by colonies overseas), markets (also supplied in part by colonies), and capital (much of it supplied by merchants) to finance the building and equipping of factories. Thus the prosperity of commerce also nourished the growth of industry.

The first major changes were in textile manufacture, where the making of yarn and cloth had long been organized under the *domestic system*, in which spinners and weavers worked at home with wheels and looms. Often they did not buy their own raw materials or market their finished products, but worked as wage-laborers for someone who furnished the raw materials and sold the finished products. In other industries, however, production was sometimes organized in simple factories, which brought together many laborers in a large workshop, though hand processes rather than machines were still used. These factories were particularly common in enterprises requiring close supervision for reasons of state, like cannon foundries, or because they used expensive materials, like gold or silver threads for luxury cloth.

The Industrial Revolution made the domestic system obsolete and transformed the early factory system. Machines superseded the spinning wheel, hand loom, and other hand tools, and water or steam replaced human muscle and animal energy as the chief source of power. Because power-driven machines were often cumbersome and complicated, larger factories were needed to house them. By 1789 these revolutionary changes had affected only a handful of industries, but these were of critical importance: textiles, metallurgy, and munitions.

Coal mining was becoming a big business, largely because of increased demand for coke by iron smelters, which had previously used charcoal to make ore into iron. Although charcoal continued to be used in Sweden and other countries that had an abundant supply of wood, in England, where many of the great forests had been cut down, the price of charcoal was 80 percent of the cost of producing iron. By 1750, despite the abundant local supply of ore, the output of English smelters was declining rapidly, and the country was importing more and more iron. Ordinary coal could not replace charcoal as smelter fuel because the chemicals in coal

James Hargreaves's Spinning Jenny revolutionized the textile industry. Put into use about 1764, it rapidly increased the production of thread. It also assured women a place in the work force, a boon at first to hard-pressed families.

made the iron too brittle. The Darby family of Shropshire discovered how to remove the chemical impurities from coal by an oven process that converted it into coke. In England the Darbys and other private firms were the pioneers in metallurgy. On the Continent governments took the lead; France and Prussia met their requirements for large quantities of munitions by setting up state-financed foundries and arms factories.

The revolution in textiles focused on the cheaper production of cotton cloth. The flying shuttle, a technical device first applied to the hand loom in England (1733), enabled a single weaver to do work that had previously required the services of two. Looms equipped with the flying shuttle used up the supply of hand-spun thread so rapidly that a private organization, the London Society for the Encouragement of Arts, Manufacturers and Commerce, offered a prize for improving the spinning process. James Hargreaves (d. 1778) won the prize in 1764 with his spinning jenny, a series of wheels geared together to make eight threads simultaneously. Soon the jenny was adapted to water power, and its output was increased to more than a hundred threads at once. The eventual emancipation of industry from dependence on unreliable water power was foreshadowed in the 1760s when the Scotsman James Watt (1736-1819) introduced the steam engine.

Although Britain had nearly 150 cotton mills in 1789, woolens and dozens of other basic commodities were still made by hand. Full industrial development would not occur until the canals and railroads permitted cheap transport of heavy freight and until shortages of capital and skilled labor were overcome. A Swedish inventor of the early 1700s designed excellent machines for cutting wheels and files but could not raise the money to put them into operation. And in Britain the difficulty of making precisely machined parts for Watt's engine delayed its production in large quantities. Although the

eighteenth century had taken many of the initial steps in the Industrial Revolution, it remained for the next century to apply them on a truly revolutionary scale.

II THE ESTABLISHED POWERS

Britain, 1714-1760

Leadership in the economic revolutions was making Britain the wealthiest nation in the world. British bankers, strengthened by the Bank of England and by careful management of the national debt, extended credit to business enterprises at the relatively low interest rate of 5 percent. London challenged Amsterdam's position as the international capital of trade and finance; in the eighteenth century British merchants outdistanced their old trading rivals, the Dutch, and gradually took the lead over their new competitors, the French. Judged by the touchstones of mercantilism—commerce, colonies, and sea power—Britain was the strongest state in Europe.

The British colonial empire, however, was not a mercantilist undertaking in the fullest sense. Supervision of the colonies rested with a government department, the Board of Trade, which followed a policy of "salutary neglect," in contrast to the rigid controls exerted by other colonial powers over their possessions. In the long run, as the American Revolution was to show, salutary neglect did not satisfy the colonists, who found British policy neither salutary nor neglectful, but in the short run it promoted the colonists' prosperity and self-reliance.

The Royal Navy enjoyed the assets of a disciplined officer corps and more ships than any other power possessed. Future captains went to sea at the age of sixteen or even younger and passed through long practical training before receiving commissions. Although their ships were inferior in design to those of France and Spain in the midcentury wars, there were more of them. Britain had a 2 to 1 advantage over France in number of warships, a 6 to 1 lead in merchant ships, and a 10 to 1 lead in total number of experienced seamen, merchant and naval. In wartime the fleet could draw on the merchant marine for additional sailors and auxiliary vessels. Even though service in the Royal Navy had its grim aspects—monotonous and unhealthy food, severe punishments—the British navy held a comparative advantage.

The British army, by contrast, was neither large nor impressive. Its officers were reputed to be the worst in Europe, and many of its soldiers were mercenaries from the German state of Hesse-Cassel, or Hessians. Neglect of the army was a deliberate decision. The British Isles were relatively safe from invasion; moreover, the English people feared a standing army as an instrument of potential absolutism, for they remembered the uses that Cromwell and James II had made of this resource. The Glorious Revolution, which in its preliminary stage had done much to confirm distrust of the army,

CABINET GOVERNMENT DEVELOPS IN BRITAIN

Historians continue to debate the actual origins of the British cabinet, though there is no disagreement that by the time of Robert Walpole an early form of cabinet existed. In 1741 a debate took place in both the House of Lords and the House of Commons on the possibility of removing Walpole from office. In the debate it is clear that the general principle of chief ministers, prime minister, and cabinet are understood. Following is an extract from the speech made by Lord Carteret (1690-1763), who violently opposed Walpole and who took office himself the next year:

As members of this house, we are in duty bound to have a watchful eye over the public measures his majesty is advised to pursue, and over the chief ministers he is pleased to employ in the administration of public affairs. And when we are of opinion that the measures he is advised to pursue are wrong, or that the ministers he is pleased to employ are weak or wicked, it is our duty and our business, while we sit here, to warn our sovereign of his danger and to remove weak or wicked counsellors from about his throne. As to the parliamentary methods of removing a minister, I need not acquaint your lordships that they are of several kinds, and that all but one tend to punish as well as remove. When we proceed by impeachment, by bill of attainder [a legislative pronouncement of guilt against a person without a trial], or by bill of pains and penalties, the design is to punish as well as remove; but there is another way of proceeding in parliament which tends only to remove the minister from the king's counsels without inflicting any real punishment upon him, and that is by an humble address to our sovereign that he would be graciously pleased to remove such a one from his counsels.

I believe, my lords, it will not be questioned that either house of parliament may offer such advice to the crown by way of humble address. I believe it will not be said that it is unusual or unprecedented, and therefore I shall not trouble your lordships with calling to your remembrance any of the precedents that may be found in the journals of parliament. I shall only take notice of the difference between the methods of proceeding by impeachment, by bill of attainder, or bill of pains and penalties, and this method of proceeding by way of humble address to the crown. When we proceed by impeachment, by bill of attainder, or by bill of pains and penalties, some particular criminal facts must be alleged, and there must be some sort of proof of those facts. But when we proceed by way of address to the

king, that he would be graciously pleased to remove such a minister from his counsels, a general view of that minister's conduct, a general view of public affairs, may afford just cause for such an address, and common fame is a sufficient proof; for, when no particular fact is insisted on, it is impossible to bring any particular proof. This, my lords, is the difference; and the reason of this difference is very plain. When a man is to be punished, either in his person, his freedom, or estate, some crime or criminal neglect ought to be not only alleged but proved by a legal proof, or by strong presumptions. But as his not being employed in the king's counsels neither affects his person, his freedom, nor his estate, therefore weakness alone, or a general bad character, may be a good cause for removing him. A weak man is certainly in any country very unfit for being in the king's counsels; and in a popular government a man who has incurred the general odium of the people ought not to be continued in the king's counsels, because the unpopularity of the minister may at last affect the throne itself and render the people disaffected to their sovereign.

I must therefore desire your lordships to take particular care to distinguish between the method of proceeding against a minister by impeachment, by bill of attainder, or bill of pains and penalties, and the method of proceeding against a minister by address only; because, if you do not take care to fix this distinction in your minds, you may expect from me what I do not intend to give, and what the nature of the motion I am to make renders it not only unnecessary but unfit for me to give. I am to move only for an humble address to his majesty that he would be graciously pleased to remove a minister—I may say, the minister—from his counsels. . . .

Carl Stephenson and Frederick George Marcham, eds., *Sources of English Constitutional History* (New York: Harper & Brothers, 1937), pp. 629-30.

had also confirmed Britain's unique asset—the supremacy of Parliament. Parliament had approved the accession of William and Mary in place of James II. When Anne, Mary's sister and the last Stuart monarch, died in 1714, Parliament had already arranged for the succession of the House of Hanover. Under the first kings of the new house—George I (1714-1727) and George II (1727-1760)—the cabinet, the institution that would ultimately ensure parliamentary supremacy, was beginning to mature.

Under the first two Hanoverian kings the cabinet was only starting to gain authority. George I and George II by

no means abdicated all the old royal prerogatives. They took a direct interest in the South Sea Bubble and other financial matters, and they often intervened in the conduct of war and diplomacy. George II was the last English monarch to command troops in person on the battlefield—in 1743, during the War of the Austrian Succession. The two Georges chose their cabinet ministers from the Whig party, then in control of the Commons. They did so, however, not because they were required to, but because it suited their convenience and because they distrusted the Tories, some of whom were involved in Jacobite plots to restore to the throne the descendants of James II (Jacobite from *Jacobus*, Latin for James). The Whigs, on the other hand, had engineered the Glorious Revolution and had arranged the Hanoverian succession.

From 1721 to 1742 Robert Walpole, who led the Whigs in the Commons, headed the cabinet; he was in fact prime (or first) minister, although the title was still unofficial. Walpole was a master politician who maintained his majority in the Commons by skillful manipulation. The task was not easy, for party discipline did not yet exist. The terms *Whig* and *Tory* referred to shifting interest groups, not to parties in a formal sense. In 1733, when Walpole forced the resignation of ministers opposed to his plan for radical fiscal reform, he took a major step toward establishing the principle of the need for cabinet unanimity on a crucial issue.

Under the first two Georges the Whigs were a coalition of landed and "funded" gentry; that is, of nobles and squires from the country and of business and professional men from London and provincial towns. The Whigs thus renewed a political alliance that had first appeared in the later Middle Ages when the knights of the shire had joined the burgesses to form the Commons. In the Whig parliaments the country gentlemen predominated by sheer numbers; in 1754, for instance, they outnumbered 5 to 1 the merchants and lawyers sitting in the House of Commons. Family ties, common political aims, and common respect for property bound together the rural and urban Whigs.

What did terms like "gentry," "gentlemen," and "squire" connote about social class in the eighteenth century? Historians generally agree that they referred to a class just below the titled nobility. The ranks of the gentry included the younger sons of nobles, technically not nobles themselves since a seat in the House of Lords passed only to the eldest son. They also included other owners of landed estates, all of whom were addressed verbally as "sir" and in writing as "Esquire" (originally meaning a shield bearer, the lieutenant of the feudal knight). Historically, the gentry lived off the revenues of

William Hogarth was especially known for his satirical view of the political and social customs of the English. He intended to be a silversmith but became an engraver of satirical prints for publishers instead; he then extended his work to moral commentaries on everyday life. His Election series shows both fine draftsmanship and skill as a caricaturist. Here he shows a campaign in progress, in "Canvassing for Votes" (1754).

landed property, but by the eighteenth century many of them also had a stake in commerce. Successful businessmen sometimes bought country estates, set themselves up as gentlemen, and were often accepted as such by the local gentry. This intermingling of country gentlemen with men of business and the intermarriage of the two classes demonstrated that Britain was experiencing greater social mobility than were the states of the Old Regime on the Continent.

In its social and political structure the Britain of Walpole was not democratic. Only gentlemen could hope to rise in the professions, to become army and navy officers, lawyers, clergymen, and physicians. In local affairs the landed gentry alone supplied the justices of the peace, who presided over courts, fixed wage scales, superintended the relief of the poor, maintained bridges and highways, and defended the propertied classes. Until the 1740s only gentlemen had the right to vote for members of Parliament. The small number of voters in many constituencies encouraged corruption, particularly in the "rotten" or "pocket" boroughs, which had such a tiny electorate that control of their vote reposed in the "pocket" of some wealthy lord. Politicians often bribed voters outright or else promised them places on the government payroll. One immensely rich Whig, the duke of Newcastle, controlled the outcome of elections in four counties and in seven pocket boroughs.

Thus in Britain, as on the Continent, the ruling classes governed the generally voteless masses. And the masses were sometimes worse off materially than were their continental counterparts, as in the case of the landless agricultural workers whose numbers mounted with the enclosure movement. London was already big enough to have an early version of all the troubles of a modern metropolis—slums, crimes of violence, traffic jams—accompanied by an almost complete lack of police and fire protection. Life was harsh for the poor and grew more so by the end of the century. Children generally began to work when they were eight years old, and while literacy was growing on the Continent, it did not do so in England. Yet the British ruling classes, selfish and narrow though they often were, had at their best a sense of public spirit and civic-mindedness toward the less fortunate. Furthermore, the memory of Cromwell's rebellion and the recurrent food riots because of the effects of the enclosure movement also provided sharp incentives for the nobility to maintain political control. Within the aristocracy of land and trade there were fewer explicit social barriers than on the Continent, and the English gentry were on the whole more responsive than were their continental counterparts to the need for change and reform.

France, 1715-1774

Where Britain was strong, France was weak. In the France of Louis XV (1715-1774) barriers to social mobility were more difficult to surmount, though commoners who were rich or aggressive enough did overcome them.

France suffered particularly from the rigidity of its colonial system, the inferiority of its navy, and the mediocre abilities of most of its statesmen. The ministry of the navy, which ruled the overseas empire, regarded these possessions as so many warships permanently at anchor. It refused to allow the colonies any significant administrative control of their own affairs, and it applied the same regulations to all, despite their differences. The numerous controls stifled the initiative of the colonists. The mother country, however, prospered, as commercial activity doubled in the ports, and refineries were set up to process the raw sugar imported from the plantations of Guadeloupe and Martinique.

The French navy needed greater resources and better leadership. Its well-designed warships were too few. Since Dutch and British vessels carried much of French commerce, the merchant marine was small. French naval officers, rigorously trained in the classroom, lacked the practical experience gained by captains with a lifetime at sea. Moreover, officers from the aristocracy thwarted the rise of those from the middle class.

French rulers neglected the navy in favor of the army, since France was, above all, a land power, and its vulnerable northeastern frontier invited invasion. Except in size, however, the army of Louis XV scarcely lived up to the traditions of Louis XIV. The troops were poorly trained and the organization was top-heavy; there was one officer to fifteen men, compared with one to thirty-five in the more efficient Prussian army. Many aristocratic officers regarded a commission as simply a convenient way of increasing their personal wealth.

Both the navy and the army were reformed after the defeats suffered by France in the Seven Years' War (1756-1763). The number of warships was increased, the army officer corps was cleared of much deadwood, and more aggressive military tactics were introduced. These improvements accounted in part for the excellent showing made by France in the American Revolutionary War and in the military campaigns resulting from its own revolution. They came too late, however, to save the vanishing prestige of the Old Regime.

The Old Regime was weakest in the monarchy itself. The pleasure-loving duke of Orléans, regent from 1715 to 1723, supported John Law's scheme and gambled with the nation. He tried to get the nobility to play an active role in government, creating councils on which nobles were to work with the professional bureaucrats. This proved a failure, for the nobles, who had been reduced by Louis XIV to ceremonial roles, lacked the knowledge and ability to apply themselves to the daily routine of government. The French second estate had, it seemed, outlived its usefulness. The period of the regency proved that the nobles could no longer govern; the midcentury wars proved that they could no longer lead French armies to victory.

The remaining stronghold of the nobles of the robe were the important courts (known as parlements) in Paris and in some provincial capitals. The parlements took advantage of the regency to extend their claim to register government edicts before they were published and enforced. A papal bull condemned the doctrines of the influential French Catholic minority of Jansenists, who had family ties with the judges of the parlements; when the Parlement of Paris refused to register the bull, Orléans held a special royal session obliging the Parlement to follow the royal command. The judges of the parlements in Paris and elsewhere retaliated by going on strike, refusing to carry on their normal court business. There followed a crippling feud between the king and the judges. In the 1760s the parlements suppressed the Jesuits, the great foe of the Jansenists, and in the last years of his reign Louis XV tried to suppress the parlements in turn, seeking to substitute new courts that would be more under royal control.

In 1726 power passed to one of the few able statesmen of prerevolutionary France, Cardinal Fleury (1653-1743), who remained chief minister until his death. Fleury, who had been tutor to Louis XV, was the last of the great cardinals to exercise supreme ministerial power for the king. He brought together the most able team of ministers in eighteenth-century France and set out to put royal finances in order by avoiding foreign wars. He stablizied the coinage, restricted tax farmers to a comparatively modest profit, made loans more readily available by establishing state pawnshops in the chief cities of France, encouraged new industries with subsidies and other privileges, embarked on a new program for building roads and bridges, and restored relative peace and prosperity to the countryside. Still, when he died at age ninety, his reforms were swept away, for they had not been fundamental, depending largely on his own personal influence. Even before his death, and against his advice, France had entered another ruinous war by intervening in the conflict between Austria and Prussia.

Louis XV began his personal rule in 1743. Intelligent but timid, lazy, and pleasure loving, Louis XV did not have the interest or patience to supervise the details of government. He appointed and dismissed ministers on personal whim or at the bidding of his mistresses and court favorites. In thirty years he had eighteen different foreign secretaries and fourteen chief fiscal officers. Each change in personnel meant a shift in policy, and Louis aggravated the instability by conspiring against his own appointees. France sometimes had two conflicting foreign policies: that of the diplomatic corps, and that of the King's Secret, conducted by royal agents who operated at cross purposes with the regular diplomats.

Nevertheless, France remained a great power. Still the most populous country in Europe, France possessed great reserves of strength; its army, though enfeebled, was the largest in the world, and its navy was the second largest. France led the world in overseas trade until Britain forged ahead in the last quarter of the eighteenth century. French tastes, French thought, and the French language retained the international preeminence they had won in the age of Louis XIV.

Other States of Western Europe

Spain was the only other state in western Europe with a claim to great-power status. Sweden and the Dutch Republic could no longer sustain the major international roles they had undertaken during the seventeenth century. The Great Northern War had withered Sweden's Baltic empire. The Dutch, exhausted by their wars against Louis XIV, could not afford a large navy or an energetic foreign policy. When William III of Orange (and England) died in 1702, many of the Dutch provinces had permitted his quasi-monarchical office of stadholder to stand vacant, and dominance passed to the rich merchants. This was a swing of the political pendulum that had occurred twice before in the history

SAINT-SIMON ON LOUIS XV

The same Saint-Simon who had commented favorably on the splendor of Louis XIV's court came to feel that Louis XV and the nobility were failing the nation, showing themselves unable to govern:

The design was to begin to put the nobility into the ministry, with the dignity and authority appropriate to them, at the expense of the high civil servants and nobles of the robe, and to guide affairs wisely by degree and according to events, so that little by little those commoners would lose all those administrative duties that are not purely judicial . . . in order to submit to the nobility all modes of administration. The difficulty was the ignorance, the frivolity, and the inattentiveness of the nobility who were accustomed to being good for nothing except getting killed, rising in war only by seniority, and romping around for the rest of the time in the most mortal uselessness; as a result they were devoted to idleness and disgusted with all knowledge outside war by their conditioned incapacity for being able to provide themselves with anything useful to do. It was impossible to make the first step in this direction without overturning the monster that had devoured the nobility, the controller general and the secretaries of state.

Duc de Saint-Simon, *Mémoires* (Paris, 1879-1930), xxvii, 8-9, trans. Robin W. Winks; cited in John Lough, *An Introduction to Eighteenth Century France* (New York: David McKay Company, Inc., 1970), pp. 135-36.

AN AGE OF MANNERS

Much of Louis XV's time was spent with his mistresses, official and unofficial, and they exercised great influence over him and over affairs of state. While the first official mistress, Madame de Pompadour (1721-1764), was noted for her cultivation, knowledge, and beauty, as well as for her ambition, she was followed by mistresses who were far less able, and the monarchy further declined in prestige because of the low moral tone attributed to it by the general public. Much time was taken up with questions of manners, court etiquette, and relations between small subclasses within the nobility. The notions of "correct behavior" worked out during the reign of Louis XIV became worthy subjects of satire.

In 1729 a French guide to behavior for the "civilized Christian" covered such subjects as speech, table manners, bodily functions, spitting, nose-blowing and behavior in the bedroom. This guide to good manners was reissued with increasingly complex advice through 1774, though with significantly changing emphases, as certain behavior (blowing one's nose into a kerchief no longer worn about the neck but now carried in the hand, hence *handkerchief*) became acceptable, and other behavior more closely regulated. These guides emphasized class differences, pointing out that behavior that was acceptable in the presence of one's social inferiors was to be avoided in the presence of one's equals or social superiors:

It is a part of decency and modesty to cover all parts of the body except the head and hands. You should take care...not to touch with your bare hand any part of the body that is normally uncovered.... You should get used to suffering small discomforts without twisting, rubbing, or scratching.... It is far more contrary to decency and propriety to touch or see in another person, particularly of the other sex, that which Heaven forbids you to look at yourself. When you need to pass water, you should always withdraw to some unfrequented place. And it is proper (even for children) to perform other natural functions where you cannot be seen. It is very impolite to emit wind from your body when in company, either from above or from below, even if it is done without noise. ... It is never proper to speak of the parts of the body that should be hidden, nor of certain bodily necessities to which Nature has subjected us, nor even to mention them.... You should avoid making a noise when blowing your nose.... Before blowing it, it is impolite to spend a long time taking out your handkerchief. It shows a lack of respect toward the people you are with to unfold it in different places to see where you are to use it.

LaSalle, *Les Règles de la bienséance et de la civilité Chrétienne* (Rouen, 1729), as quoted in Norbert Elias, *The History of Manners.* vol. I: *The Civilizing Process*, trans. Edmund Jephcott (New York: Pantheon, 1982), pp. 132, 156.

By 1774 these expectations were so well known that the guide to civility spoke of them only in passing and emphasized the need to apply the rules in particular to children: "Parents should correct them carefully." Slowly household objects once seen quite openly—the bed, the commode, the spittoon—were removed into increasingly "private" parts of the home. Objects of "shame" changed as manners helped to redefine the role of the individual within the group and the group in society.

of the Dutch Republic. Still, Dutch seaborne trade remained substantial, and the republic settled down to a life of relative prosperity and decreased international significance.

Spain suffered comparatively little damage from the great War of the Spanish Succession of the early 1700s. The loss of Belgium and parts of Italy in the Utrecht settlement of 1713 reduced the unwieldy Spanish domains to more manageable size, and the Bourbon kings proved to be a marked improvement over the Spanish Hapsburgs. Philip V (1700-1746), the first Bourbon monarch, infused fresh life into the country's traditional institutions by importing French advisers schooled in the system of Louis XIV. Philip and his advisers cut down the excessive formalities and long delays of Spanish administration, reasserted the authority of the monarchy over the nobility and clergy, improved the tax system, encouraged industry, built up the navy, and fortified strategic points of the Spanish empire in America.

This new administration, however, did not strike at

the root causes of Spanish decline. The greed of governors and the restrictions of mercantilism still checked the growth of the colonies. The mother country remained impoverished, burdened with noble and clerical castes, and hampered by inadequate resources. Philip V himself was neurotic (refusing, for instance, to cut his toenails, which grew so long that he limped), and he was dominated by his strong-willed second wife, Elizabeth Farnese. Since Philip's son by his first marriage would inherit Spain, Elizabeth was determined to find thrones for her own two sons, and her persistent attempts to secure Italian states for them repeatedly threatened the peace of Europe. Not until the accession of Charles III (r. 1759-1788) did Spain have a monarch devoted to administration and improvements, and by then it was too late for Spain to reassert its dominant role in the balance of power.

During this time Spain was also preoccupied with events in Italy. By 1715 the Italian states had lost much of the political and economic power they had enjoyed during the Renaissance. The opening of new lands overseas and the rise of the Atlantic powers had diminished the importance of the Mediterranean. In the Mediterranean itself, the Ottoman Turks and their satellites in North Africa had long menaced Italian shipping and trade. Moreover, from the time of the French invasion of 1494, Italy had been threatened with conquest by one or another of the new national monarchies.

It was the Spanish Hapsburgs who had made that conquest. For almost two centuries they ruled Milan, Naples, and Sicily directly, and dominated the rest of the peninsula. In the readjustment of the European balance in 1713, Italy exchanged one foreign master for another, as the Austrian Hapsburgs took over the Italian possessions of the Spanish Hapsburgs. By 1720, Austria was firmly established in Lombardy, flanked by the decaying commercial republics of Venice and Genoa. In the mountainous northwest was the small but rising state of Piedmont-Savoy (technically the Kingdom of Sardinia after its acquisition of that island in 1720). Farther down the peninsula were the Grand Duchy of Tuscany (formerly the Republic of Florence), the Papal States, and the kingdom of Naples and Sicily. None of these states was more than a minor power.

Yet Italy could not be written off as a negligible quantity in the eighteenth century. Rome remained the capital of Catholicism, Venice still produced fine painters, and Naples remained the school for European musicians. Lombardy, Tuscany, and Naples all contributed to the economic and intellectual advances of the century. Meantime, Italy was a major stake in balance-of-power politics, a perennial source of dissension and spoils. In 1720, to counter the ambitions of Elizabeth Farnese, the Austrian Hapsburgs took over the island of Sicily, which had gone to Piedmont in the Utrecht settlement; in return, Piedmont secured Sardina, originally assigned to Austria. In the 1730s a series of exchanges gave Naples and Sicily to Elizabeth's older son, while the Austrians

Beautiful, intelligent, and ambitious, Madame de Pompadour was Louis XV's most powerful mistress. This portrait, by François Boucher (1703-1770), a master of the rococo style, provides the historian with valuable details concerning clothing, hair styles, decoration, and furniture.

gained the right to succeed the last Medici grand duke of Tuscany. In 1768 Genoa sold the island of Corsica to France. Italy was, in an old phrase, merely "a geographical expression"—not a single political entity but a series of parts manipulated by ambitious dynasts and empire-builders from outside the penninsula.

In some respects Germany deserved even more to be called a geographical expression, for it was divided into three hundred states. The Peace of Westphalia in 1648 had enhanced the soverign rights of the particular German states and virtually extinguished the authority of their nominal overlord, the Holy Roman Emperor. Unlike Italy, however, Germany did include two considerable powers—one long established (Austria) and one newcomer (Prussia).

The Hapsburg rulers of Austria won a series of military and diplomatic victories in the two decades before 1715. In 1699, by the peace of Karlovitz, they had recovered Hungary from the Ottoman Turks. In 1713, though they failed to keep the old Hapsburg crown of

Growth of Prussia, 1740—1795

- Prussian territory at accession of Frederick the Great, 1740
- Territory acquired 1740–1786
- Territory acquired 1786–1795
- Boundary of the Empire, 1786

COURLAND
Memel
SWEDEN
Baltic Sea
Niemen R.
North Sea
DENMARK
EAST PRUSSIA
Königsberg
E. FRIESLAND
(to Sweden)
MECKLENBURG
POMERANIA
Danzig
WEST PRUSSIA
NEW EAST PRUSSIA
Stettin
NETHERLANDS
Ems R.
MINDEN
Magdeburg
BRANDENBURG
Berlin
Posen
Warsaw
Bug R.
CLEVES
RAVENSBERG
Weser R.
SOUTH PRUSSIA
MARK
Rhine R.
Hubertusburg
SAXONY
P O L A N D
Breslau
T H E   E M P I R E
S I L E S I A
AUSTRIAN NETHERLANDS
BAYREUTH
Elbe R.
Oder R.
Vistula R.
Cracow
BOHEMIA
ANSBACH
MORAVIA
FRANCE
Danube R.
Elbe R.
0   100   200
Miles

Spain from going to the Bourbon Philip V, they were compensated with Spain's Belgian and Italian territories. Yet these last acquisitions were distant from the main bloc of Hapsburg lands in central Europe.

Charles VI (1711-1740), aware that his title of Holy Roman Emperor conferred little real authority, concentrated on the Hapsburg family possessions. He spent much of his reign persuading his own noble subjects to ratify the Pragmatic Sanction; the constitutional agreement that established the principle of linking together the scattered family territories, whereby, in the absence of sons, Charles's daughter Maria Theresa (1717-1780) would succeed him in all his lands. Much, however, remained to be done to consolidate Hapsburg rule over an assemblage of lands that represented many different nations and would never be forged into a single national monarchy. In three key national areas—German Austria, Czech Bohemia, and Magyar Hungary—the nobles still kept most of their medieval prerogatives and, by controlling local estates and diets, controlled grants of taxes and the appointment of officials. The financial and

military weakness of the Hapsburg regime was underlined by the fact that when Charles VI died in 1740, the treasury was nearly empty and the pay of both army and civil service was more than two years overdue. The army was well short of its paper strength of 100,000 men as it faced the great test of strength with Prussia that came in 1740.

III THE NEWCOMERS

Prussia and the Hohenzollerns, 1715-1740

Prussia's territories were scattered across north Germany from the Rhine on the west to Poland on the east. Consisting in good part of sand and swamp, these lands had meager natural resources and supported relatively little trade. With fewer than three million inhabitants in 1715, Prussia ranked twelfth among the European states in population. Its capital city, Berlin, had few of the obvious geographical advantages enjoyed by Constantinople, Paris, London, and other great capitals. The Hohenzollerns had been established since the fifteenth century as electors of Brandenburg, which lay between the Elbe and Oder rivers. A Hohenzollern was the last master of the Teutonic Knights, the crusading order which in the thirteenth century had pushed the Germanic frontier beyond the Vistula to the land called Prussia at the southeast corner of the Baltic Sea. In 1618, when East Prussia fell to the Hohenzollerns, it was separated from Brandenburg by Polish West Prussia and was still nominally a fief held from the Polish king. In western Germany in the meantime (1614), the Hohenzollerns had acquired Cleves, Mark, and some other parcels in the lower Rhine valley and Westphalia. Thus, when Frederick William, the Great Elector (1640-1688), succeeded to the Hohenzollern inheritance as the Thirty Years' War was drawing to a close, his lands consisted of a nucleus in Brandenburg with separate outlying regions to the east and west. With extraordinary persistence, the rulers of Brandenburg-Prussia for the next two hundred years devoted themselves to the task of making a solid block of territory out of these bits and pieces.

The Great Elector was the first in a line of able Hohenzollern rulers. In foreign policy he won recognition from Poland as the full sovereign of Prussia. He also tried, with less success, to dislodge the Swedes from the Pomeranian territories between Brandenburg and the Baltic that they had acquired in 1648. In the various wars against Louis XIV, he shifted repeatedly from the French to the anti-French side and back.

In domestic policy his accomplishements were more substantial. He had found his domains largely ruined by war, the farms wasted, the population cut in half, the army reduced to a disorderly rabble of a few thousand men. The Great Elector repaired the damage thoroughly. To augment the population, he encouraged the immigration of Polish Jews and other refugees from religious persecution, among them twenty thousand French Huguenots to whom he gave partial exemption from taxation. He built a small, efficient standing army that enabled Prussia to command large foreign subsidies for participating in the campaigns for or against Louis XIV. In peacetime he assigned the soldiers to the construction of public works, including a canal between the Elbe and the Oder.

In administration the great Elector affirmed the Hohenzollern pattern of militarized absolutism—a policy in which he was assisted by a Lutheran state church and an educational tradition that taught the virtues of obedience and discipline. On his accession he found that in all three territories—Prussia, Brandenburg, and Cleves-Mark—the authority of the ruler was limited by the estates, medieval assemblies representing the landed nobles and the townspeople. In all three territories he battled the estates for supremacy and won, thereby delaying for two centuries the introduction of representative government into the Hohenzollern realm. He gradually gathered into his own hands the crucial power of levying taxes. Much of the actual work of collecting taxes and performing other administrative functions was done by the war office and the army; policing, too, was done by the military.

Like Louis XIV, the Great Elector reduced the independence of the aristocracy; unlike Louis, however, he relied not on bourgeois officials but on a working alliance with the landed gentry, particularly the Junkers of East Prussia. He confirmed the Junkers' absolute authority over the serfs on their estates and their ascendancy over the towns, and he encouraged them to serve the state, especially as army officers. In contrast with other monarchies, the absolutism of the Hohenzollerns rested on the cooperation of the sovereign and the aristocracy, not on their mutual antagonism.

The Great Elector's son, Frederick I (1688-1713), made a significant gain in prestige in 1701 by assuming the title "King of Prussia" and insisting on international recognition of his new status as the price for his entry into the War of the Spanish Succession. Though technically Frederick was king only in East Prussia, which lay outside the boundaries of the Holy Roman Empire, even a limited royal title conferred added dignity on the Hohenzollerns.

The next king, Frederick William I (1713-1740), returned to the policies of the Great Elector and devoted himself entirely to economy, absolutism, and the army. He reiterated the order *Ein Plus machen* ("Make a surplus"), and he bequeathed a full treasury to his son. His frugality enabled him to undertake occasional projects that he thought worthwhile, such as financing the immigration of twelve thousand South German Protestants to open up new farmlands in eastern Prussia.

To strenghten royal control over the apparatus of state, Frederick William I instituted a small board of experts charged both to administer departments of the central government and to supervise provinces. The arrangement detached provincial administration from local interests and brought it under closer royal control. The king, who insisted on hard work and punctuality, treated the experts of this General Directory as he treated lesser officials, paying them poorly and belaboring them for slovenly performance of their duties.

Frederick William I doubled the size of the standing army and established state factories to provide guns and uniforms. To conserve the strength of the laboring force in his underpopulated state, he furloughed troops to work on the farms nine months a year. The army prompted his sole extravagance—a regiment of grenadiers, all six feet tall or over, who wore special caps more than a foot high to increase the impression of size. In recruiting his beloved "giants," the king threw economy to the winds, employing scores of scouts in other states, paying exorbitant prices, and trading royal musicians and prize stallions for especially tall soldiers.

Frederick William was too cautious to undertake an adventurous foreign policy; his only significant military campaign was against Sweden in the last phase of the Great Northern War, whereby Prussia obtained in 1720 part of Swedish Pomerania and also the important Baltic port of Stettin at the mouth of the Oder River. Thus Frederick William advanced the Great Elector's old aim of liquidating the Swedish possessions in Germany.

Eighteenth-century observers rightly called the Prussia of Frederick William an armed camp and criticized its army for being a "gigantic penal institution" in which minor infractions of regulations brought the death penalty. The king himself, obsessed with military matters, neglected the education of his subjects, showed little concern for the arts, and in particular despised everything French. He carried miserliness to the extreme of refusing pensions to soldiers' widows, and the meager fees he permitted judges and lawyers encouraged corruption and lethargy. Yet in terms of power, his regime worked extremely well. The Junkers, although feudal in outlook, were intensely loyal to the Hohenzollerns and made excellent officers. The army, though smaller than those of France, Russia, or Austria, was the best drilled and disciplined in Europe. When Frederick William I died in 1740, the Prussian David was ready to fight the Austrian Goliath.

Russia and Peter the Great, 1682-1725

Even more spectacular than the rise of Prussia was the emergence of Russia as a major power during the era of Peter the Great (1682-1725). In 1682, at the death of Czar Fëdor Romanov, Russia was still a backward country, with few diplomatic links with the West and very little knowledge of the outside world. Contemporaries, Russians as well as foreigners, noted the brutality, drunkenness, illiteracy, and filth prevalent among all classes of society. Even most of the clergy could not read.

Czar Fëdor died childless in 1682, leaving a retarded brother, Ivan, and a capable sister, Sophia, both children of Czar Alexis (1645-1676) by his first wife. The ten-year-old Peter was the half-brother of Ivan and Sophia, the son of Alexis by his second wife, and as bright and vigorous as Ivan was debilitated. A major court feud developed between the partisans of the family of Alexis's first wife and those of the family of the second. At first the old Russian representative assembly, the Zemski Sobor, elected Peter czar. But Sophia, as leader of the opposing faction, won the support of the *streltsi*, or musketeers, a special branch of the military, many of whom belonged to the conservative schismatic sect of the Old Believers. Undisciplined and angry with their officers, some of whom had been cheating them, the streltsi were a menace to orderly government. Sophia encouraged the streltsi to attack the Kremlin, and the youthful Peter saw the infuriated troops murder some of his mother's family. For good measure, they killed many nobles living in Moscow and pillaged the archives where the records of serfdom were kept. Though their movement had social implications, it was primarily a successful bid for power by Sophia, who now served as regent for both Ivan and Peter, who were hailed as joint czars. In the end, however, the streltsi deserted Sophia, who

was shut up in a convent in 1689; from then until Ivan's death in 1696 Peter and his half-brother technically ruled together.

The young Peter was almost seven feet tall and extremely energetic. Fascinated by war and military games, he had set up a play regiment as a child, staffed it with full-grown men, enlisted as a common soldier in its ranks (promoting himself from time to time), ordered equipment for it from the Moscow arsenals, and drilled it with unflagging vigor. When he discovered a derelict boat in a barn, he unraveled the mysteries of rigging and sail with the help of Dutch sailors living in Moscow. Maneuvers, sailing, and relaxing with his cronies kept him from spending time with his wife, whom Peter had married at sixteen and eventually sent to a convent. He remained to the generally conservative Muscovites a crude figure. He had been taught to read and write by a drunken tutor, and this was reflected in his speech and prose; he smoked (which was thought to be contrary to biblical teachings), drank, caroused, and seemed almost without focus; at various times he took up carpentry, shoemaking, cooking, clock making, ivory carving, etching, and dentistry. Preferring to wear shabby work-clothes, driving his own horses, neglecting formal obligations, and paying little attention to court and church ceremony, Peter was a shock to Muscovites, and not in keeping with their idea of a proper czar. Society was further scandalized when Peter took as his mistress a girl who had already been mistress to many others; after she gave birth to two of his children, he finally married her in 1712. This was the empress Catherine

This contemporary caricature shows Peter the Great clipping the beard of a boyar as part of his campaign to modernize Russia.

PETER THE GREAT

Interpretations of Peter the Great vary enormously. Voltaire considered him to be the model of the "enlightened despot." Nicolai M. Karamzin (1766-1826), who was Russia's first widely read novelist, attacked the Petrine myth and argued that Peter was subverting traditional Russian values:

At this point Peter appeared. In his childhood, the license of the lords, the impudence of the *Streltsy*, and the ambition of Sophia had reminded Russia of the unhappy times of boyar troubles. But deep inside of him the youth already had the makings of a great man, and he seized hold of the helm of state with a mighty hand. He strove toward his destination through storms and billows. He reached it—and everything changed!

His goal was not only to bring new greatness to Russia, but also to accomplish the *complete* assimilation of European customs. . . . Posterity has praised passionately this immortal sovereign for his personal merits as well as for his glorious achievements. He was magnanimous and perspicacious, he had an unshakable will, vigor, and a virtually inexhaustible supply of energy. He reorganized and increased the army, he achieved a brilliant victory over a skillful and courageous enemy, he conquered Livonia, he founded the fleet, built ports, promulgated many wise laws, improved commerce and mining, established factories, schools, the academy, and, finally, he won for Russia a position of eminence in the political system of Europe. And speaking of his magnificent gifts, shall we forget the gift which is perhaps the most important of all in an autocrat: that of knowing how to use people according to their ability? Generals, ministers, or legislators are not accidentally born into such and such a reign—they are chosen. . . . To choose good men one must have insight; only great men have insight into men. Peter's servants rendered him remarkable assistance on the field of battle, in the Senate, and in the Cabinet. But shall we Russians, keeping in mind our history, agree with ignorant foreigners who claim that Peter was the founder of our political greatness? . . . Shall we forget the princes of Moscow, Ivan I, Ivan III, who may be said to have built a powerful state out of nothing, and—what is of equal importance—to have established in it firm monarchical authority? Peter found the means to achieve greatness—the foundation for it had been laid by the Moscow princes. And, while extolling the glory of this monarch, shall we overlook the pernicious side of his brilliant reign?

Let us not go into his personal vices. But his passion for foreign customs surely exceeded the bounds of reason. Peter was unable to realize that the national spirit constitutes the moral strength of states, which is as indispensable to their stability as is physical might. This national spirit, together with the faith, had saved Russia in the days of the Pretenders. It is nothing else than respect for our national dignity. By uprooting ancient customs, by exposing them to ridicule, by causing them to appear stupid, by praising and introducing foreign elements, the sovereign of the Russians humbled Russian hearts. Does humiliation predispose a man and a citizen to great deeds? The love of the fatherland is bolstered by those national peculiarities which the cosmopolite considers harmless, and thoughtful statesmen beneficial. Enlightenment is commendable, but what does it consist of? The knowledge of things which bring prosperity; arts, crafts, and sciences have no other value. The Russian dress, food, and beards did not interfere with the founding of schools. Two states may stand on the same level of civil enlightenment although their customs differ. One state may borrow from another useful knowledge without borrowing its manners. These manners may change naturally, but to prescribe statutes for them is an act of violence, which is illegal also for an autocratic monarch. The people, in their original covenant with the king, had told them: "Guard our safety abroad and at home, punish criminals, sacrifice a part to save the whole." They had not said: "Fight the innocent inclinations and tastes of our domestic life." In this realm, the sovereign may equitably act only by example, not by decree.

Karamzin's Memoir on Ancient and Modern Russia, trans. Richard Pipes (Cambridge, Mass.: Harvard University Press, 1959), pp. 120-22. Copyright 1959 by the President and Fellows of Harvard College. Reprinted by permission.

(c 1684-1727), a hearty and affectionate woman who was able to control her difficult husband as no one else could.

Meantime, anxious to try his hand at war, Peter led a campaign against the Turks around the Black Sea. With the help of Dutch experts, he sailed a fleet of river boats down the Don and defeated the Turks at Azov in 1696. Much curiosity was aroused abroad by this Russian contribution to the war with the Turks in which the Austrians had so long been engaged. The project of forming an anti-Turkish league with the states of western Europe now gave Peter a pretext for the first trip outside Russia taken by a Russian sovereign since the Kievan period. What fascinated him was Western technology, especially in naval matters, and he planned to go to Holland, England, and Venice, where (in his opinion) the best ships came from, to find out how they were built. He hired several hundred technicians to work in Russia, raised money by selling the monopoly of tobacco sales in Russia to an English peer, and on his journey visited every sort of factory, museum, or printing press he could find.

Before Peter reached Venice, his trip was interrupted by news that the streltsi had revolted again (1698); Peter rushed home and personally participated in their punishment. Though many innocent men suffered torture and death, Peter broke the streltsi as a power in Russian life. He was more determined than ever to modernize his country, and on the day of his return summoned the court jester to assist him as they went about clipping off courtiers' beards. This was an act full of symbolism, for the tradition of the Orthodox church held that God was bearded; if man was made in the image of God, man must also have a beard; and if he was deprived of it, he became a candidate for damnation. Peter now decreed that Russian nobles must shave or else pay a substantial tax for the privilege of wearing their beards. Peter also commanded that all *boyars* (members of the gentry class) and the city population in general must abandon long robes with flowing sleeves and tall bonnets, and adopt Western-style costume. The manufacture of traditional clothes was made illegal, and Peter took up his shears again and cut off the sleeves of people wearing them. The enactments on beards and dress were regarded by the victims as an assault on precious customs and a forcible introduction of hated foreign ways.

Peter's policies at home can be understood only in light of his ever-mounting needs to support virtually incessant warfare, together with his intense desire to modernize Russia. His plan for an international crusade

Russian Expansion in Europe, 1689-1796

- Acquired by Peter the Great, 1689-1725
- Acquired 1730-1740
- Acquired by Elizabeth, 1741-1762
- Acquired by Catherine, 1762-1796
- ■ Battle sites

against the Turks collapsed when the Austrians and the Ottoman Empire agreed to the treaty of Karlovitz in 1699. Feeling that Austria had betrayed Russia, Peter made a separate peace with the Turks in 1700. By then he was already planning to attack Sweden, whose large Baltic empire seemed particularly vulnerable since the throne had recently passed to a youth of fifteen, Charles XII (1697-1718). Peter's allies in the enterprise were Denmark and Poland, the latter under its elected king, who was also elector of Saxony. The three partners might have reconsidered had they seen Charles XII strengthening his sword arm by beheading at a single stroke sheep driven down his palace corridors.

Charles won the opening campaigns of the Great Northern War (1700-1721). He knocked Denmark out of the fighting, frustrated Poland's attempt to take the Baltic port of Riga, and completely defeated a larger but ill-prepared Russian force at Narva (1700), capturing the entire supply of cannon of which Peter was so proud. Instead of taking advantage of Peter's helplessness and marching into Russia, however, Charles detoured into Poland, where he spent seven years pursuing the king, who finally had to abandon both the Russian alliance and the Polish crown. Charles thereupon secured the election of his protégé as king of Poland.

In the interim, Peter rebuilt his armies and took from the Swedes the Baltic provinces nearest to Russia—Ingria and Livonia—in the first of which he founded in 1703 the city of St. Petersburg, to which he eventually moved the court from Moscow. In 1708 Charles swept far to the south and east into the Ukraine in an effort to join forces with the Cossacks, whose leader was his ally. Exhausted by the severe winter, the Swedish forces were defeated by the Russians in the decisive battle of Poltava (1709). Peter now reinstated his king of Poland, but he was not able to force the Turks to surrender Charles, who had taken refuge with them after Poltava.

To avenge his defeat Charles engineered a war between Turkey and Russia (1710-1711), during which the Russians made their first appeal to the Balkan Christian subjects of the Turks on the basis of their common faith. Bearing banners modeled on those of Constantine, first emperor of Byzantium, Russian forces crossed into the Ottoman Danubian province of Moldavia. Here the Ottoman armies trapped Peter in 1711 and forced him to surrender; the Turks could have taken him captive but proved unexpectedly lenient, requiring only the surrender of the port of Azov and the creation of an unfortified no man's land between Russian and Ottoman territory.

On the diplomatic front Russia made a series of matrimonial and other alliances with petty German courts, involving itself in central European questions remote from its national interest. The death of Charles XII in 1718 cleared the way for peace negotiations, though it took a Russian landing in Sweden proper to force a decision. At Nystadt (1721) Russia handed back Finland and agreed to pay a substantial sum for the former Swedish possessions along the eastern shore of the Baltic. The opening of this "window on the West" meant that seaborne traffic no longer had to sail around the northern edge of Europe to reach Russia. Next, Peter undertook a brief campaign against Persia (1722-1723). At his death in 1725, Russia had been at war for almost all of his thirty-five-year reign and had risen from a little-known land to become a major military power capable of affecting the destinies of the western European states.

Constant warfare requires constant supplies of men and money. Peter's government developed a form of conscription according to which a given number of households had to supply a given number of recruits. Although more of these men died of disease, hunger, and cold than at the hands of the enemy and although desertion was commonplace, the very length of the Great Northern War meant that survivors served as a tough nucleus for a regular army. Peter also built a Baltic fleet at the first opportunity, but a Russian naval tradition never took hold. From eight hundred ships (mostly very small) in 1725, the fleet declined to fewer than twenty a decade later; there was no merchant marine at all. The apprehensions of the English and the Dutch that Russian emergence on the Baltic would create a new maritime nation proved unfounded. It remained land bound.

To staff the military forces and the administration, Peter rigorously enforced the rule by which all land-owners owed service to the state. For those who failed to register he eventually decreed "civil death," which removed them from the protection of the law and made them subject to attack with impunity. State service became compulsory for life; at the age of fifteen every male child of the service nobility was assigned to his future post in the army, in the civil service, or at court. When a member of this class died, he was required to leave his estate intact to one of his sons, not necessarily the eldest, so that it would not be divided anew in every generation. Thus the class of service nobility—which now included the survivors of the nobility of ancient birth, the old boyars—was brought into complete dependence upon the czar. The system opened the possibility of a splendid career to men with talent, for a person without property or rank who reached a certain level in any branch of the service (for example, major in the army) was automatically ennobled and received lands. The nobility of ancient birth viewed this as a cheapening of their position, but under Peter there was little they could do about it.

To raise cash, Peter debased the currency, taxed virtually everything—sales, rents, real estate, tanneries, baths, and beehives—and appointed special revenue-finders to think of new levies. The government held a monopoly over a variety of products, including salt, oil, coffins, and caviar. However, the basic tax on each household was not producing enough revenue, partly because the number of households had declined as a result of war and misery, and partly because households were combining to evade payment. Peter's government therefore substituted a head tax on every male—the soul tax—making it useless for people to conceal themselves statistically in households. This innovation required a new census, which produced a most important, and unintended, social result. The census takers classified as serfs many who were between freedom and serfdom; these people thus found themselves and their children labeled as unfree, to be transferred from owner to owner. At great cost of human exploitation, Peter's government managed in its later years to balance the budget.

In administration, new ministries (*prikazy*) were first set up to centralize the handling of funds received from various sources. A system of army districts adopted for reasons of military efficiency led to the creation of the first provinces—eight, then nine, then twelve—embracing all Russia. Each province had its own governor, and many of the functions previously carried on inefficiently by the central government were thus decentralized. With the czar often away from the capital and many of the former prikazy abolished, decentralization had gone so far that Russia seemed at times to have little central government.

Ultimately, Peter copied the Swedish system of central ministries to supersede the old prikazy and created nine "colleges"—for foreign affairs, the army, justice, expenditure, and the like—each administered by an eleven-man collegium. This arrangement discouraged corruption by making any member of a collegium subject to checking by his colleagues; but it caused delays in final decisions, which could only be reached after lengthy deliberations. When Peter attempted to model local government on the Swedish example, the experiment failed because of the enormous differences between the two countries in literacy, size, tradition, and attitudes toward civic responsibility.

To educate future officers and also many civil servants, Peter established naval, military, and artillery academies. Because of the inadequacy of Russian primary education, which was still controlled by the church, foreigners had to be summoned to provide Russia with scholars. At a lower level, Peter continued the practice, begun long before him, of importing technicians and artisans to teach their skills to Russians. The czar shaped many of the mercantilist ideas of the age and offered the inducements of protective tariffs and freedom from taxation to encourage manufacturing. Though sometimes employing many laborers, industrial enterprises, chiefly in textiles and iron, remained inefficient. Factory owners could buy and sell serfs (otherwise a privilege restricted to the gentry) if the serfs were bought or sold as a body together with the factory itself. This "possessional" industrial serfdom did not provide much incentive for good work. Russian produce continued to be inferior to comparable foreign goods.

Peter also brought the church under the collegiate system. Knowing how the clergy loathed his new regime, he began by failing to appoint a successor when the patriarch of Moscow died in 1700. In 1721 he placed the church under an agency called at first the spiritual college and then the Holy Directing Synod, headed by a layman. Churchmen of the conservative school were more and more convinced that Peter was the Antichrist himself, as they beheld the increase of foreigners in high places and saw the many innovations imported from the distrusted West.

The records of Peter's secret police are full of the complaints his agents heard as they moved about listening for subversive remarks. Peasant husbands and fathers were snatched away to fight on distant battlefields or to labor in the swamps building a city that only Peter appeared to want. The number of serfs increased with the imposition of the new soul tax and the multiplication of land grants to service men. Service men found themselves condemned to work for the czar during the whole of their lives and were seldom able to visit their estates. Nobles of ancient birth found themselves treated no differently from the upstarts who were flooding into their class from below.

Among the lower orders of society resistance took the form of peasant uprisings, which were punished with extreme brutality. The usual allies of the peasant rebels, the Cossacks, suffered mass executions and sharp curtailment of their traditional independence. The leaders of the noble and clerical opposition focused their hopes on Peter's son by his first wife, the young heir to the throne, Alexis, who they believed would stop the expensive foreign wars, move back to Moscow, and resume traditional ways. An alcoholic, Alexis was not stable enough to lead a conspiracy against his father, but he fanned the hopes of the opposition by indicating that he shared their views. Eventually, he fled abroad and sought asylum from his brother-in-law, the Austrian emperor Charles VI. Promising him fair treatment and forgiveness, Peter lured Alexis back to Russia and then had him tortured to death in his presence.

Among later generations of Russians, both those who welcomed Peter's Westernizing policies and those who condemned them assumed that what he did was drastic and revolutionary. Yet in many respects Peter simply fortified already existing Russian institutions and characteristics. He made a strong autocracy even stronger, a universal service law for service men even more sringent, a serf more of a serf. His trips abroad, his fondness for foreign ways, his regard for advanced technology, his mercantilism, his wars, all had their precedents in Russian history before his reign. Before he attacked it, the church had already been weakened by the schism of the Old Believers, itself the result of Western influences. Perhaps Peter's true radicalism was in the field of everyday manners and behaviors. His attacks on beards, dress, the calendar (he adopted the Western method of dating from the birth of Christ and abandoned the traditional dating from the supposed year of the Creation), his hatred of ceremony and fondness for manual labor—these were indeed new; so too were the exceptional vigor and passion with which he acted. They were decisive in winning Peter his reputation as a revolutionary—Peter the Great.

In foreign affairs Russia found itself persistently blocked, even by its allies; whenever Russia tried to move into central or western Europe, Prussia or Austria would desert any alliance with the Russians. As a result, Russian rulers distrusted European diplomacy and followed an essentially defensive policy. Having learned the skills of war from the Swedes and from foreign generals, as well as from translations of foreign works on military science that Peter had commissioned, the Russians had become a formidable military power capable of doubling their artillery in a single year, with perhaps the best infantry and most able gunnery in Europe by the mid-eighteenth century. A lack of heavy horses held back the cavalry, as did the undisciplined nature of Cossck warfare, which increasingly proved to be a liability on the battlefield. But by the time the Russians occupied East Prussia (from 1758-1761), they too were noted for their discipline, and European monarchs, fearful of Russian influence, increasingly used propaganda against the czars, even when allied to them.

The Polish and Ottoman Victims

By the early eighteenth century, Russia was thus the only great power in eastern Europe. Poland and the Ottoman Empire still bulked large on the map, but both states suffered from incompetent government, a backward economy, and from the presence of large national and religious minorities. The Orthodox Christians in Catholic Poland and Muslim Turkey were beginning to look to Russia for protection. Moreover, the evident decay of both states stimulated the aggressive appetites of their stronger neighbors. Poland would disappear as an independent power before the end of the century, partitioned by Russia, Austria, and Prussia. Turkey would hold on, but was already beginning to acquire its reputation as "the Sick Man of Europe."

The Polish government was a political curiosity. The monarchy was elective; each time the throne fell vacant, the Diet chose a successor, usually the candidate who had offered the largest bribes, and sometimes even a foreigner. Once elected, the king was nearly powerless. The Diet was dominated by the nobility and since the 1650s had practiced the *liberum veto*, whereby any one of its members could block any proposal by shouting "I do not wish it!" The Diet was not a parliament but an assembly of aristocrats, each of whom acted as a power unto himself; unanimity was therefore almost impossible. This loosely knit state had no regular army, no diplomatic corps, no central bureaucracy. Unlike the English gentry or Prussian Junkers, the dominant nobles had no concept of service to the Crown; they also helped destroy a once-flourishing urban middle class by persecuting Jewish shopkeepers and foreign merchants, and they treated their serfs worse than the Russians did.

The Ottoman Empire was still a functioning state, yet it was falling further and further behind the major European powers, particularly in fiscal stability and technology. Not until the nineteenth century did it produce a sultan who would attempt the kind of massive assault on tradition that Peter the Great had mounted. In the eighteenth century, with rare exceptions, the sultans were captives of harem intrigue and could do little to discipline such powerful groups as the Janissaries, who exploited their privileges and neglected their soldierly duties. This backward government did at least govern, however, and it showed considerable staying power in war. The Sick Man was to linger on throughout the century, kept alive in part by Ottoman vitality and in part by the rivalry between two would-be heirs of the Turkish inheritance, Russia and Austria. The so-called Polish and Turkish questions would dominate international politics for the next half-century.

IV WAR AND DIPLOMACY, 1713-1763

In the early eighteenth century the international balance was precarious. Should the strong states decide to prey upon the weak, the balance was certain to be upset. One such upset resulted from the Great Northern War, which enabled Russia to replace Sweden as the dominant power in the Baltic. The expansion of Russia continued to threaten the balance during most of the eighteenth century, and the chief victims were Poland and Turkey. A second major threat to the balance came from the expansion of Prussia at the expense of Austria, Poland, and Sweden. A third arose out of the colonial and commercial rivalry between Britain and the French and Spanish Bourbons.

These were not the only international issues of the day. The old competition between Austria and France, which dated back to the Hapsburg-Valois wars of the 1500s, remained lively. It was complicated by the ambitions of Elizabeth Farnese, second wife of Philip V of Spain, who won the support of France and threatened Austrian power in Italy. The Austrian Hapsburgs were vigorous expansionists, aiming to drive the Turks from the Danube and extend their own domains southeast to the Black Sea.

Although the interplay of all these rivalries led to frequent shifts in power, an international balance was generally maintained. Indeed, eighteenth-century war and diplomacy are often cited as the classic case history of balance-of-power politics in operation. The limited financial resources of the governments of the Old Regime generally permitted only limited warfare. On the battlefield, generals were reluctant to risk losing soldiers who represented a costly investment in training; they favored sieges executed according to conventions well understood by all belligerents. At the peace table diplomats were reluctant to destroy an opponent; they generally sought to award a bit of territory or a minor throne as compensation for a greater loss. Total war and unconditional surrender were not eighteenth-century concepts. A few of the most successful statesmen, notably Frederick the Great of Prussia and William Pitt of Eng-

land, did not always act according to these conventions, however, and the custom of compensating the loser was ignored when Poland was partitioned out of existence late in the century. But earlier in the century, the powers' handling of the Polish and the Turkish questions afforded clear examples of conventional international politics in operation.

The Turkish and Polish Questions, 1716-1739

In 1716 the Ottoman Empire became embroiled in a war with Austria that resulted in the Treaty of Passarowitz (1718), by which Charles VI recovered the portion of Hungary still under Turkish rule, plus some other Ottoman lands in the Danube valley. Another Austro-Turkish war, 1735-1739, modified the Passarowitz settlement and disclosed the growing infirmity of the Hapsburg army. In this second war Austria was allied with Russia, but, in a fashion foreshadowing later struggles of the two powers for control of the Balkans, they fell to quarreling over division of the prospective spoils. In the end there was little to divide, and Charles VI had to hand back to Turkey the Danubian lands annexed in 1718. During the negotiations leading to the Austro-Turkish settlement of 1739, France gave the Ottoman Empire powerful support to redress the balance of power. In the early 1730s Bourbons and Hapsburgs also chose opposing sides in a crisis over the kingship of Poland. The stage was set for the War of the Polish Succession (1733-1735), pitting a Polish contender, Stanislas Leszczyński, protégé of Charles XII, plus France and Spain, against Augustus III, a protégé of Peter the Great, who also had Austrian support.

The diplomats quickly worked out a compromise settlement. Much to the satisfaction of Austria and Russia, Augustus III secured the Polish throne. Yet from the French standpoint, Stanislas Leszczyński was well compensated for his loss. He acquired the duchy of Lorraine on the northeastern border of France, with the provision that when he died Lorraine would go to his daughter, Marie, wife of Louis XV of France, and thence to the French crown. France would thus move one step closer to filling out its "natural" frontiers. The incumbent duke of Lorraine, Francis, future husband of the Hapsburg heiress Maria Theresa, was awarded the Grand Duchy of Tuscany, where the Medici dynasty of grand dukes died out in 1737. Finally, as a byproduct of the settlement, Elizabeth Farnese of Spain capped twenty years of maternal perseverance by procuring the Kingdom of Naples for her elder son.

The War of the Polish Succession may well seem like much ado about a kingship possessing no real power; and the postwar settlement, which affected chiefly Italy and Lorraine, may appear to be a striking case of diplomatic irrelevance. Yet the whole Polish crisis neatly illustrates the workings of dynastic politics and the balance of power. Statesmen regarded thrones as diplomatic prizes, to be assigned without reference to the wishes of the populations involved. No politician of the Old Regime would have contemplated canvassing Neapolitan sentiment or holding a referendum to find out whether Poles preferred Stanislas or Augustus. The complicated arrangements of the 1730s preserved the balance of power by giving something to almost everyone. Although the diplomats had not prevented a little war over Poland, they did keep it from becoming a big one.

Indeed, from 1713 to 1739 diplomacy averted or localized wars. Britain and France took the lead in the campaign to keep any one power from upsetting the balance. To frustrate Elizabeth Farnese's attempts to oust the Hapsburgs from Italy in the late 1710s, the French dispatched an army and the British deployed a fleet. The British also sent a squadron to the Baltic during the last part of the Great Northern War, so that Czar Peter's gains would not be too great. To prevent the dismemberment of Ottoman territories in Europe, Britain intervened in the negotiations between Turkey and Austria at Passarowitz in 1718, and the French revived their Ottoman alliance in the 1730s.

The Austrian Succession, 1739-1748

Britain and France collaborated in the 1720s and 1730s because both Walpole and Fleury sought stability abroad to promote economic recovery at home. The partnership, however, collapsed over the competition between the two Atlantic powers for commerce and empire. Neither Walpole nor Fleury could prevent the worldwide war between Britain and the Bourbon monarchies that broke out in 1739 and that lasted, with intervals of peace, until the final defeat of Napoleon in 1815. This "Second Hundred Years' War" had, in fact, already begun half a century earlier, in the days of Louis XIV. The Utrecht settlement of 1713 had not fully settled the rivalry between Britain and France (and France's Bourbon partner, Spain). Thus the war of 1739 was as much the renewal of an old struggle as the onset of a new one.

The specific issue behind the crisis of 1739 was the comparatively minor question of British disappointment over the results of the Asiento privilege. As the South Sea Company discovered, the Asiento gave Britain only a token share in the trade of the Spanish American colonies. What British captains could not get legitimately they got by smuggling, and Spain retaliated with a coast guard patrol in American waters to ward off smugglers. British merchants complained of the rough treatment handed out by the Spanish guards, and in 1736 they exhibited to Parliament a Captain Robert Jenkins (fl. 1731-1738), who claimed that Spanish brutality had cost him an ear, which he duly produced, preserved in salt and cotton batting. Asked to state his reaction on losing the ear, he replied, "I commended my soul to God and my cause to my country." In October, to the joyful pealing of church bells, Britain began the War of Jenkins' Ear against Spain. The British fleet lost the opening campaign in the Caribbean, and France showed every sign of coming to Spain's assistance. Dynastic ties had

already brought the two Bourbon monarchies into alliance during the Polish war; now French economic interests were at stake, for France supplied the bulk of the wares Spanish galleons carried to America, which cheaper British contraband was driving out of the Spanish colonial market.

In 1740 a chain of events linked the colonial war to the great European conflict over the Austrian succession. On the death of Charles VI in 1740, the Hapsburg dominions passed to his twenty-three-year-old daughter, Maria Theresa (r. 1740-1780). Expecting to outwit Maria Theresa because of her political inexperience, the German princes ignored the Pragmatic Sanction guaranteeing her succession and looked forward to partitioning the Hapsburg inheritance. The elector of Bavaria, a cousin of the Hapsburgs, also hoped to be elected Holy Roman Emperor, defeating Maria Theresa's husband, Francis of Lorraine and Tuscany. The first of the German princes to strike, however, was Frederick the Great (1740-1786), who had just inherited the Prussian throne from Frederick William I. In December 1740 Frederick suddenly invaded the Hapsburg province of Silesia. Though Frederick advanced a flimsy family claim to Silesia, Europe generally regarded his invasion as an act of simple aggression.

In the ensuing War of the Austrian Succession, England and Austria were ranged against France, Spain, Prussia, and Bavaria. Frederick won an emphatic victory in the campaigns on the Continent. The Prussian army astounded Europe by its long night marches, sudden flank attacks, and other surprise tactics quite different from the usual deliberate warfare of sieges. Frederick, however, antagonized his allies by repeatedly deserting them to make secret peace arrangements with Austria. And he did little to support the imperial aspirations of the Bavarian elector, who enjoyed only a brief tenure as Emperor Charles VII.

The Anglo-Austrian alliance worked no better than the Franco-Prussian one. Many of the English felt that George II was betraying their interests by entangling them in the Austrian succession and other German problems, such as the defense of Hanover (from 1714 to 1837 the kings of England were also rulers of Hanover). Nevertheless, British preference for the Hanoverians over the Stuarts was evident when Bonnie Prince Charles, grandson of the deposed James II, secured French backing and landed in Britain in 1745. He won significant recruits only among the chronically discontented highlanders of Scotland, where he was thoroughly defeated at Culloden in 1746. The Stuart cause was now dead.

Outside Europe the fighting of the 1740s was indecisive. The New England colonists took Louisburg, the French naval base on Cape Breton Island commanding the approach to the St. Lawrence River. On the other side of the world, the French took the port of Madras from the English East India Company. In 1748 the Treaty of Aix-la-Chapelle restored both Louisburg and Madras to their former owners, and Britain later agreed to give up the troublesome Asiento privilege.

In central Europe, on the other hand, the war was a

decisive step in the rise of Prussia to the first rank of powers. The new province of Silesia brought not only a large increase in the Prussian population but also an important textile industry and large deposits of coal and iron. Maria Theresa got scant compensation for the loss of Silesia; although her husband, Francis, won recognition as Holy Roman Emperor, she had to surrender Parma and some other territorial crumbs in northern Italy to Philip, the second son of Elizabeth Farnese.

The peace made in 1748 lasted only eight years. Then another and greater conflict, the Seven Years' War of 1756-1763, broke out, caused partly by old issues left unsettled at Aix-la-Chapelle and partly by new grievances arising from the War of the Austrian Succession. The worldwide struggle between Britain and the Bourbons persisted in the undeclared warfare waged during the years of nominal peace after 1748. In Asia the English and French East India companies fought each other by taking sides in the rivalries of native princes in southern India. By 1751 the energetic French administrator Joseph Dupleix (1697-1763) had won the initial round in the battle for supremacy in the subcontinent. Then the English, led by the equally energetic Robert Clive (1725-1774), seized the initiative. In 1754 Dupleix was called home by the directors of the French company, who were unwilling to commit costly resources to his aggressive policy.

In North America English colonists from the Atlantic seaboard had already staked out claims to the rich wilderness between the Appalachians and the Mississippi. But the French, equally intent on mastering the area, moved first and established a string of forts in western Pennsylvania from Presqu'Isle (later Erie) south to Fort Duquesne (later Pittsburgh). In 1754 a force of Virginians under a youthful George Washington (1732-1799) tried unsuccessfully to dislodge the French from Fort Duquesne, initiating a war that would end in a British victory.

The Diplomatic Revolution and the Seven Years' War, 1756-1763

In Europe the dramatic shift of alliances called the Diplomatic Revolution immediately preceded the formal outbreak of the Seven Years' War, which had already begun in the colonies. In the new war the fundamental antagonisms were the same as in the old—Britain versus France, Prussia versus Austria—but the powers reversed their alliances. Britain, which had joined Austria against Prussia in the 1740s, now paired off with Frederick the Great. And in the most dramatic move of the Diplomatic Revolution, France, which had sided with Frederick before, not only turned against him but also joined with its hereditary enemy, Hapsburg Austria.

The Diplomatic Revolution reflected the resentment of the powers at the disloyal behavior of their old partners in the War of the Austrian Succession. The French had bitter memories of Frederick's repeated desertions and secret peace arrangements. Britain deplored Austrian reluctance to defend English continental interests, which included maintaining the territorial integrity of Hanover and excluding the French from the Austrian Netherlands. Austria regarded Hanover and Belgium as peripheral to its main concern, the recovery of Silesia.

In 1755, the British touched off this Diplomatic Revolution. To enlist a second power in the task of defending Hanover, they concluded a treaty with Russia, which had taken a minor part in the War of the Austrian Succession as an ally of England. The Anglo-Russian treaty alarmed Frederick the Great, who feared an eventual conflict between Prussia and Russia for control of the Baltic and Poland. In January 1756 the Prussian king concluded an alliance with Britain that detached it from Russia. The alliance between England and Prussia isolated France and gave the Austrian chancellor the opportunity he had been waiting for. What Austria needed to avenge itself on Frederick and regain Silesia was an ally with a large army; this required an alliance with France, not Britain. Using the Anglo-Prussian alliance as an argument, the Austrians convinced Louis XV and his mistress, Madame de Pompadour, to drop the traditional Bourbon-Hapsburg feud in favor of a working partnership. The last act of the Diplomatic Revolution occurred when Russia joined the Franco-Austrian alliance. The Russian empress Elizabeth (1741-1762) hated Frederick the Great and feared his aggression all the more now that he had deprived her of her English ally.

The new war, like its predecessor, was really two separate wars—one continental, the other naval and colonial. In the European campaigns of the Seven Years' War, Frederick the Great faced a formidable test, confronting the forces of Austria, France, and Russia, whose combined population was more than fifteen times larger than Prussia's. Frederick had almost no allies except Britain, which supplied financial subsidies but little actual military assistance. The frugal traditions of the Hohenzollerns enabled Prussia to survive. Frederick's iron resolution led him to adopt any expedient to gain his end in the face of his strategic disadvantages. To fill up the depleted ranks of his army, he violated international law by impressing soldiers from Prussia's smaller neighbors, Mecklenburg and Saxony. (Prussian "recruiters" had a habit of surrounding churches at the close of Sunday services.) Since British subsidies covered only a fraction of his war expenses, he seized Saxon, Polish, and Russian coins and melted them down for Prussian use.

A final factor in saving Prussia was the shakiness of the apparently formidable coalition arrayed against it. Fortunately for Frederick, his enemies could never exploit their military success to deliver a knockout blow. Russia's generals were unexpectedly timid, and those of France and Austria proved incompetent. Moreover, the French, the strongest of the allies, had to fight a two-front war, in Europe and overseas, without the financial resources to do both.

The grand alliance created by the Austrian chancellor, Prince von Kaunitz (1711-1794), suffered to an unusual extent from the frictions, mistrust, and cross purposes typical of wartime coalitions. In fact, the coalition did not last out the war. When Elizabeth of Russia died in January 1762, she was succeeded by Czar Peter III, a passionate admirer of Frederick the Great, who at once deserted Elizabeth's allies and placed Russia's forces at Frederick's disposal. Although he occupied the Russian throne only until July, Peter's reign marked a decisive turning in the Seven Years' War. In 1763 Prussia won its war, and Austria agreed to the Peace of Hubertusburg, confirming the Hohenzollern retention of Silesia.

Meanwhile, Frederick's British partner was losing abroad. During the first year and half of the fighting the British suffered setbacks on almost every front. At sea they lost the important Mediterranean base of Minorca in the Balearic Islands. In North America the British lost time and again, but the most dramatic of Britain's misfortunes occurred in India. In June 1756, the nawab of Bengal, an ally of the French, crowded 146 British prisoners at Calcutta into a small room with only two windows. The resulting incident, as described by an officer of the English East India Company, came to be known as the Black Hole:

> It was the hottest season of the year, and the night uncommonly sultry. . . . The excessive pressure of their bodies against one another, and the intolerable heat which prevailed as soon as the door was shut, convinced the prisoners that it was impossible to live through the night in this horrible confinement; and violent attempts were immediately made to force the door, but without effect for it opened inward. At two o'clock not more than fifty remained alive. But even this number were too many to partake of the saving air, the contest for which and for life continued until the morn. . . .

> An officer . . . came with an order to open the prison. The dead were so thronged, and the survivors had so little strength remaining, that they were employed near half an hour in removing the bodies which lay against the door before they could clear a passage to go out one at a time; when of one hundred and forty-six who went in no more than twenty-three came out alive. . . .*

It was William Pitt (1708-1778) who turned the tide in favor of Britain. Pitt strengthened the Anglo-Prussian alliance by sending Frederick substantial subsidies and placing English forces in Hanover under an able Prussian commander. Pitt replaced blundering generals and admirals and took energetic measures that transformed the naval and colonial campaigns.

After the Royal Navy defeated both the French Atlantic and Mediterranean squadrons (1759), Britain commanded the seas. Britain could thus continue trading abroad at a prosperous pace, while French overseas trade rapidly sank to one-sixth of the prewar rate. Cut off from supplies and reinforcements from home and faced by generally superior British forces, the French colonies

*Robert Orme, *A History of the Transactions of the British Nation in Indostan* (London: J. Nourse, 1778), pp. 74 ff.

fell in quick succession. In Africa Britain's capture of the chief French slaving stations ruined the slavers of Nantes; in India Clive and others avenged the Black Hole by punishing the nawab of Bengal and capturing the key French posts near Calcutta and Madras; in the West Indies the French lost all their sugar islands except for Santo Domingo. In North America the 65,000 French, poorly supplied and poorly led, were helpless against the million British colonists, fully supported by their mother country. Fort Duquesne was taken at last and was renamed after Pitt, and the British went on to other triumphs in the war that the English colonists called the French and Indian War after their enemies. In Canada the English general James Wolfe (1727-1759) took Louisburg (1758); in the next year he lost his life but won immortal fame in a great victory on the Plains of Abraham above Quebec. When the remaining French stronghold, Montreal, fell in 1760, France's American empire was over.

North America and the Caribbean, 1763
Situation after the Seven Years' War

British Territory:
- Held before 1763
- Acquired from France
- Acquired from Spain
- Proclamation line of 1763

This succession of victories led the British to expect sweeping gains in the postwar settlement; however, their expectations were soon disappointed. Though Pitt had won the war, he did not make the peace; the accession of the obstinate and ambitious George III in 1760 (reigned to 1820) led to Pitt's dismissal the next year. In the Peace of Paris (1763) the French recovered their islands in the West Indies, highly valued as a major source of sugar. While British planters in the Carribean were much relieved, since their markets had been flooded by sugar from captured French islands during the war, it seemed to outraged patriots as though Britain had let a grand prize slip through its fingers.

France, however, lost all its possessions on the mainland of North America. Britain secured both Canada and the disputed territories between the Appalachians and the Mississippi. Moreover, Spain, which had joined France in 1762 when the war was already hopeless, ceded to Britain the peninsula called East Florida and the coast of the Gulf of Mexico as far as the Mississippi called West Florida. In compensation, France gave Spain the city of New Orleans and the vast Louisiana territories west of the Mississippi. In India France recovered its possessions on condition that it would not fortify them or continue the old policy of manipulating the politics and rivalries of native states. For Britain the Seven Years' War marked the beginning of virtually complete ascendency in India; for France it marked the virtual end of its "old Empire."

The International Balance in Review

The peace settlements of Hubertusburg and Paris ended the greatest international crisis that was to occur between the death of Louis XIV and the outbreak of the French Revolution. New crises were to arise soon after 1763: in 1768 a Russo-Turkish war (which Russia won); in 1772 the first partition of Poland; in 1775 the American War of Independence. The new crises in the East did not fundamentally alter the international balance; they accentuated the shifts that had long been underway. And although American independence cost Britain thirteen of its colonies the maritime and imperial supremacy it had gained in 1763 was not otherwise seriously affected.

Thus the international balance established in 1763 remained largely unchanged until 1789. In the incessant struggle for power during the eighteenth century, the victorious states were Britain, Prussia, and Russia. France, Spain, Austria, Turkey survived, though they suffered serious losses. As a Spanish diplomat observed early in the century, the weakest units, Poland and Italy, were being "pared and sliced up like so many Dutch cheeses." The duke de Choiseul (1719-1785), foreign minister for Louis XV during the Seven Years' War, remarked that the "true balance of power resides in commerce."

The world struggle between Britain and the Bourbon empires did much to justify the mercantilist view that conceived of international relations in terms of incessant competition and strife. According to the mercantilist doctrine of the fixed amount of trade, a state could enlarge its share of the existing supply only if it reduced the shares held by rival states, either through war or, in time of peace, through smuggling and retaliatory legislation. All this was borne out by British success (and French failure) in maintaining overseas trade during the Seven Years' War. Yet the concept of economic warfare was only beginning to take shape. During the War of the Austrian Succession English visitors continued to arrive in Paris, and London brokers supplied both insurance and information on naval movements to French shipowners.

Economics did not wholly explain the changes in the international balance during the century. For example, increasingly efficient utilization of Prussian resources played its part in the victories of Frederick the Great. But his success depended still more on his own brilliant and ruthless leadership and the discipline of the society that he headed. Britain seemingly offers the most compelling evidence to support Choiseul's contention about the supreme power of commerce, as Pitt turned its formidable financial and commercial assets to practical advantage. Yet Pitt himself cannot be explained solely in economic terms, for his accession as prime minister in the dark days of 1757 was made possible by a political system, social concepts, and a pragmatic approach to leadership that enabled the right man—irritable, arrogant, yet a genius—to come forward at the right time.

The eighteenth century, despite its wars, was an interlude of comparative calm between the period of religious strife that had preceded it and the storms of liberalism and nationalism that would be loosed by the French Revolution. The prospect in 1715 of long years of peace and quiet had not been wholly deceptive. The Seven Years' War, for example, did not begin to equal in destructive force the Thirty Years' War, in more ways than just the relative shortness of the war: few of the combatants had the feeling of fighting for a great cause, like Catholicism or Protestantism or national independence; the fighting itself was conducted in a more orderly fashion than it had been a hundred years before; soldiers were better disciplined and armies were better supplied; troops lived off the land less often and no longer constituted such a menace to the lives and property of civilians. Even warfare reflected the order and reason characteristic of the Age of Enlightenment.

And yet below the reality of this relative sense of order—of reason and compromise, of enlightened despots and rational, even cynical, diplomacy—the great mass of the population continued to live in debt, disease, deprivation, and destitution. The competitive state system, increasingly efficient at the top, seemed increasingly makeshift at the bottom.

SUMMARY

The Old Regime, the institutions that existed in France and Europe before 1789, exhibited features of both the medieval and early modern worlds. The economy was largely agrarian, but serfdom in western Europe had disappeared. The social foundations of the Old Regime were based on three estates. Increasingly, the economic, social, and political order of the Old Regime came under attack in the eighteenth century.

The economic foundations of the Old Regime were challenged in part by the quickening pace of commerce. European states were hard pressed to service debts accumulated in the wars of the seventeenth century. In France, John Law attempted to restore monetary stability by issuing paper money backed by the nation's wealth. Both in France and England, attempts to manage the national debt caused chaos when these experiments resulted in huge speculative bubbles that burst. The failure of the South Sea Company rocked England, but forced the government to establish a more secure banking system.

Another economic revolution occurred in agriculture. Improvements in farming techniques and the use of new crops such as turnips enabled farmers to produce more food. Increased production ended widespread famines in Europe. In England, enclosures caused widespread social dislocations but created a new labor pool.

A third economic revolution was the beginning of the Industrial Revolution, notably in the textile industry. New machines enabled rapid production and led to the organization of simple factories. New techniques in metallurgy helped make coal mining into a big business.

Britain took the lead in these economic revolutions, becoming the wealthiest nation in the world. Under the first two Hanoverian kings, Parliament was supreme, and the cabinet system took shape under Walpole. Yet Britain was not democratic because only "gentlemen" had the right to vote. For the masses, especially in the growing urban slums of London, life was extremely harsh, but the ruling class was responsive to the need for change.

In the eighteenth century France suffered from mediocre leadership. Cardinal Fleury was the exception. He pursued economic policies designed to stabilize coinage and encourage industry. Despite the failure of Louis XV to institute needed reform, France remained a great power, and French culture dominated Europe.

By the eighteenth century Spain was no longer dominant in the European balance of power. Spanish rulers were preoccupied with Italy, where their claims clashed with those of the Austrian Hapsburgs.

Since the midseventeenth century, the Hohenzollern rulers of Prussia had worked hard to increase their territories and gain international recognition. Their efforts centered on the economy, absolutism, and the army. The miserly Frederick William I built the Prussian army into the finest force in Europe.

Under Peter the Great (1682-1725), Russia emerged as a great power. Fascinated by Western technology, Peter brought foreign experts to teach Russians modern skills. In foreign policy, Peter expanded Russia by engaging in constant warfare. As a result of the Great Northern War against Sweden (1700-1721), Peter gained his "window on the West." His economic and social policies fortified the autocracy.

The expansion of Russia and Prussia, rivalry between Britain and France, and competition between Austria and France frequently threatened the balance of power in the eighteenth century. In the early 1700s Britain and France cooperated diplomatically to maintain the balance. By 1740, however, colonial and commercial rivalry set the two powers at odds. Thus, in the War of the Austrian Succession (1739-1748), Britain and Austria were allied against France, Prussia, and Spain.

A diplomatic revolution occurred on the eve of the Seven Years' War (1756-1763), when Britain and Prussia were paired off against France and Austria, traditional enemies. In the power struggles of the eighteenth century, Britain, Prussia, and Russia were the winners. France, Spain, Austria, and Turkey suffered losses.

chapter seventeen

THE ENLIGHTENMENT

Reason, natural law, progress—these were key words in the eighteenth century. It was the Age of Enlightenment, when it was widely assumed that human reason could cure past ills and help achieve utopian government, perpetual peace, and a perfect society. Reason would enable humanity to discover the natural laws regulating existence, and thereby assure progress.

The intellectuals who professed this optimistic creed were known by the French name of *philosophes*, though some of them were not French and few of them were philosophers in the strict sense. The philosophes were critics, publicists, economists, political scientists, and social reformers. Actually, they were not particularly optimistic about human progress, and they disliked how their ideas were vulgarized to conform to the simple description above. The most famous philosophe, Voltaire, in his most famous tale, *Candide*, ridiculed optimists who thought that all was for the best in the best of all possible worlds. Many intellectuals followed Voltaire in stressing the unreasonable aspects of human behavior and the unnatural character of human institutions.

Nevertheless, though many pessimistic crosscurrents eddied beneath the surface, the main current of the age was optimistic. On the whole the Enlightenment was based on the belief that people could correct the errors of their ways, once these errors had been pointed out to them. An illustrative instance was the American Declaration of Independence, which listed the pursuit of happiness as a fundamental human right, along with the enjoyment of life and liberty. The idea that humanity was entitled to pursue happiness and might even attain it was indeed revolutionary—a profound departure from the traditional Christian belief that happiness could never be expected on earth.

The philosophes derived their basic principles from the writers of the preceding "century of genius." Their faith in natural law came from Isaac Newton, and their confidence in the powers of human reason in part from René Descartes, who had deduced a whole philosophy from the fact that he thought at all. But it was John Locke (1632-1704) to whom the rationalists particularly turned. In a celebrated defense of England's Glorious Revolution, the *Second Treatise of Government* (1690), Locke contended that people are "by nature all free, equal, and independent," and that they submit to government because they find it convenient to do so, not because they acknowledge any divine right on the part of the monarchy.

The new psychology that Locke advanced in the *Essay Concerning Human Understanding* (1690) also strengthened his argument against absolute monarchy. Defenders of political and religious absolutism had contended that the inclination to submit to authority was present in the human mind from birth; Locke's *Essay* denied the existence of such innate ideas. He called the newborn mind a *tabula rasa*, a blank slate upon which experience would write. The two "fountains of knowledge" were environment, rather than heredity, and reason, rather than faith. Locke's empiricism (that is, reliance on experience) places him among the rationalists. He believed that human reason, though unable to account for everything in the universe, could explain all that one needs to know. "The candle that is set up in us," he wrote, "shines bright enough for all our purposes."

Locke also pointed the way to a critical examination of the Old Regime. The philosophes read and admired both his political writings and the *Essay Concerning Human Understanding*. They submitted existing social and economic institutions to the judgment of common sense and discovered many to be unreasonable and unnecessarily complex. Locke's psychology suggested to them that teachers might improve human institutions by improving the thinking of the rising generation. The philosophes sought, in effect, the right kind of chalk to

Voltaire was among the intellectual giants of the age. His contemplative, bemused skepticism is captured here in a remarkable bust by Jean Antoine Houdon (1741-1828). Houdon traveled widely, and in 1785 he went to America to create one of the most famous busts of George Washington.

LOCKE AND THE *TABULA RASA*: A THEORY OF EDUCATION

Let us then suppose the mind to be . . . white paper, void of all characters, without any ideas. How comes it to be furnished? Whence comes it by that vast store, which the busy and boundless fancy of man has painted on it with an almost endless variety? Whence has it all the materials of reason and knowledge? To this I answer, in one word, from experience. . . . Our observation, employed either about external sensible objects, or about the internal operations of our minds, perceived and reflected on by ourselves, is that which supplies our understandings with all the materials of thinking. These two are the fountains of knowledge, from whence all the ideas we have, or can naturally have, do spring.

John Locke, "Essay Concerning Human Understanding," in Edwin A. Burtt, ed., *The English Philosophers from Bacon to Mill* (New York: Modern Library Edition, 1939), p. 248.

use on the blank slates of young minds; their search brought them to accept the view of the universe that has been termed the Newtonian world-machine.

The Enlightenment seized on Newton's discoveries as revelations of ultimate truth. Newton had disclosed the natural force—gravitation—that held the universe together; in so doing, he made the universe make sense. The philosophes believed that comparable laws could be found governing and explaining all human activity. They saw themselves as the Newtons of statecraft, justice, and economics, who would reduce the most intricate institutions to formulas of almost mathematical exactness. The world, they argued, resembled a giant machine whose functioning had hitherto been impeded because the machinery was not properly understood; once the basic laws that governed it were grasped, the world-machine would operate as it should.

The optimistic implications of the belief were expressed most completely in *The Progress of the Human Mind* (1794) by the marquis de Condorcet (1743-1794), written when he was in hiding from political persecution during the French revolutionary Reign of Terror. Condorcet asked:

If men can predict, with almost complete assurance, the phenomena whose laws are known to them . . . why should it be regarded as a vain enterprise to chart, with some degree of probability, the course of the future destiny of mankind by studying the results of human history? Since the only basis of belief in the natural sciences is the idea that the general laws, known or unknown, regulating the phenomena of the universe are regular and constant, why should this principle be any less true for the development of the intellectual and moral faculties of man than for the other operations of nature?*

"Nature has placed no bounds on the perfecting of the human faculties," Condorcet concluded, "and the progress of this perfectibility is limited only by the duration of the globe on which nature has placed us."** He

*Condorcet, *Esquisse d'un tableau historique des progrès de l'esprit humain* (Paris: Agasse [1775]), p. 203. Our translation.
**Ibid, p. 5.

foresaw a society that would enjoy a much higher standard of living, more leisure, and more equality among people in general and between the sexes in particular. War would be given up as irrational, and disease would be so effectively conquered by medicine that the average life span would be greatly lengthened.

A shortcut to utopia was proposed by the advocates of enlightened despotism, who believed that rulers should act as benevolent reformers on the model of the tyrants of ancient Greece or such Renaissance despots as Cosimo and Lorenzo de' Medici. Like a new Solon, the enlightened despot should clear away the accumulation of artificial law that was choking progress and permit natural laws decreed by God to be applied freely. Many monarchs, among them Frederick the Great of Prussia, Catherine II of Russia, and Joseph II of Austria, took up the program of enlightened despotism because it gave them the opportunity to act as the champions of reason and progress while making royal authority more absolute. This interplay between reason and reason of state, however, made their kingdoms uncertain laboratories in which to test the practicality of the reforms proposed by the philosophes. A better test would come with the revolution in the British North American colonies. Yet by the time the Constitution of the United States had embodied the ideas of the Enlightenment, Europe was preoccupied with revolution in France, and the Enlightenment itself was under increasing attack as too rational and too simple.

I THE PHILOSOPHES AND THEIR PROGRAM OF REFORM, 1690-1776

The philosophes hailed improvements in industry and agriculture and the continued advance of science, especially in biology and chemistry. A Swedish botanist and physician, Carolus Linnaeus (Carl von Linné, 1707-1778—he observed the old custom of Latinizing his name), proposed a system for classifying plants and

Antoine Lavoisier, often referred to as the creator of modern chemistry, wrote in a clear and elegant French prose. This sense of elegance is captured here in a portrait of Lavoisier with his wife in his laboratory.

animals by genus and species, establishing the system that biologists still follow today. Modern chemical analysis started with Black and Lavoisier. Joseph Black (1728-1799), a Scottish professor, exploded the old theory that air was composed of a single element by proving the existence of several discrete gases. Black's French contemporary, Antoine Lavoisier (1743-1794), continued the study of gases and demonstrated that water was made up of hydrogen and oxygen (the last a name that he invented from a Greek root meaning "acid" because the element was thought to be present in all acids). Lavoisier asserted that all substances were composed of a relatively few basic chemical elements, of which he identified twenty-three.

In the eighteenth century astronomy and physics consolidated the advances they had made in the seventeenth. The marquis de Laplace (1749-1827), "the Newton of France," rounded out Sir Isaac's investigation of celestial mechanics and explained the movements of the solar system in a series of mathematical formulas and theorems. In the American colonies Benjamin Franklin (1706-1790) showed that electricity and lightning were really the same. He obtained an electrical charge in a key attached to the string of a kite flown during a thunderstorm in Philadelphia. This experiment, which aroused

a lively interest in Europe, was repeated at Versailles for the French royal family.

Almost everyone who was anyone in the eighteenth century attempted experiments. Voltaire made a serious hobby of chemistry; Montesquieu studied physics; and a noble French lady reportedly kept a cadaver in her carriage so that she might dissect and study anatomy during her travels. Almost every state in Europe had its philosophes and its royal or learned society to promote the progress of knowledge. Intellectual life was by no means limited to the capitals and big cities; by the middle of the eighteenth century, for example, many provincial towns in France had academies with reading rooms and lending libraries. Intellectuals paid scant attention to national frontiers and, even in wartime, continued to visit enemy countries and correspond with their citizens.

French Leadership

The cosmopolitan qualities of the century were expressed in the Enlightenment, which had its roots in France and Britain and extended its branches throughout Europe and to the New World. Yet the Age of Reason also marked the high point of French cultural leadership, when, as the American philosophe Thomas Jefferson put it, every man had two homelands, his own and France. The French language was the medium of communication for the Enlightenment, while the salons of Paris helped set the tone of enlightened writing.

By the eighteenth century French was the accepted international language. Louis XIV had made it supreme in diplomacy; the writers of his age, like Boileau, La Rochefoucauld, Racine, and Molière, had made it pre-eminent in literature. There was much justice in the claim that "a dangerous work written in French is a declaration of war on the whole of Europe." Almost everywhere, even in distant Russia, rulers, aristocrats, and intellectuals preferred French to their native tongues. Even as nations warred with each other, the French language bound their respective upper classes to each other, setting the lower classes even further aside as they clung to their native languages.

The great organ of the philosophes was the *Encyclopédie*, begun in 1751. When it was completed a generation later, it totaled twenty-two folio volumes of text and eleven of art, and its contributors included Voltaire, Montesquieu, Rousseau, Condorcet, Quesnay, and Turgot. For years its editor-in-chief, Denis Diderot (1713-1784), worked fourteen hours a day to advance his views of reason and progress. He commissioned fine engravings to show the details of the new industrial machines and learned to operate some of the machines himself. He did not intend to compile an objective compendium of information; rather, he and his encyclopedists sought to assemble knowledge and experience "in order that the labors of past centuries should not prove useless for succeeding centuries; that our descendants, by becom-

The Parisian salons of this period taught writers precision and brought them together for elegant, stylized conversation. The salon was most often the reception room of a large private home, where guests assembled under the guidance of a hostess, a wealthy woman from the nobility or the upper bourgeoisie. In the salon good conversation could flourish, and new ideas were encouraged. Pressure from the salons helped determine who was elected to the French Academy, which passed under the control of the philosophes in the 1760s, and thus the women who presided over the salons often became the arbiters of good taste. The salon shown here is from the time of Louis XVI.

ing better informed, will at the same time become happier and more virtuous."

The purposes of the *Encyclopédie* were didactic, the effect subversive: to expose and thereby ultimately to destroy what its contributors saw as the superstition, the intolerance, and the gross inequalities of the Old Regime and to instruct the public in the virtues of natural law and the wonders of science. It accomplished its purposes, antagonizing many defenders of the Old Regime while gaining enough subscribers to prove a profitable business venture. Louis XV tried to prevent its being printed or circulated, the Church condemned it for its materialism and skepticism, and even the publishers, without consulting Diderot, ordered the printers to cut out passages likely to cause offense—to no avail. The indignation of Diderot, the ridicule leveled by the philosophes at their enemies, the loyalty of the subscribers to the *Encyclopédie*, and the help given the editors by Choiseul, the foreign minister, and Madame de Pompadour, the king's mistress, frustrated the censors. The *Encyclopédie* reached a substantial reading public.

Laissez-Faire Economics

The economic program of the philosophes was introduced in articles written for the *Encyclopédie* by the versatile François Quesnay (1694-1774), biologist, surgeon, and personal physician to the French court. Quesnay headed a group of publicists who adopted the name Physiocrats—believers in the rule of nature. The Physiocrats expected that they would, as Quesnay claimed, discover natural economic laws "susceptible of a demonstration as severe and incontestable as those of geometry and algebra." And to arrive at such laws, the "sovereign and the nation should never lose sight of the fact that land is the only source of wealth, and that agriculture increases wealth."[*]

This new Physiocratic concept of natural wealth clashed with the mercantilist doctrine of equating money (or bullion) and wealth. "The riches which men

[*]F. Quesnay, "Maximes Générales du Gouvernement Economique d'un Royaume Agricole," in Eugène Daire, ed., *Physiocrates* (Paris: Guillamin, 1846), I, 82. Our translation.

need for their livelihood do not consist of money," Quesnay argued; "they are rather the goods necessary both for life and for the annual production of these goods." Mercantilist states, in his judgment, therefore placed excessive emphasis on the accumulation of specie. They tried to regulate commerce when they should have freed it from controls. They made goods more expensive by levying tariffs and other indirect taxes, whereas they should have collected only a single, direct tax on the net income from land. "*Laissez faire, laissez passer,*" the Physiocrats urged—"Live and let live; let nature take its course." They repudiated the controlled economy of mercantilism and enunciated what became known as the "classical" or "liberal" doctrine of a free economy: the state ought not to disturb the free play of natural economic forces; most of all, it ought not to interfere with private property, so necessary to produce agricultural wealth.

The classic formulation of laissez-faire economics was made by the Scotsman Adam Smith (1727-1790) in his *Inquiry into the Nature and Cause of the Wealth of Nations*, published in 1776. Smith too leveled a vigorous attack on mercantilism, maintaining that it was wrong to restrict imports by tariffs intended to protect home industries. Like the Physiocrats, Smith attributed the wealth of nations to the production of goods; but, as befitted a resident of Britain, the leading commercial and industrial state of the day, he took a less agrarian view of the matter. For Adam Smith production depended less on the soil (the Physiocratic view) than on the labor of farmers, artisans, and mill hands. Like the Physiocrats, he minimized the role of the state, claiming that people who were freely competing for their own wealth would be led to enrich their whole society, as if they were guided by "an invisible hand"—that is, by nature. A government should act mainly as a passive policeman.

The mercantilists had raised the state over the individual and had declared a ceaseless trade warfare among nations. Adam Smith and the Physiocrats, reversing the emphasis, proclaimed both economic liberty for the individual and free trade among nations to be natural laws. The laissez-faire program of the Enlightenment marked a revolutionary change in economic thought. It did not, however, revolutionize the economic policies of the great powers, who remained stubbornly mercantilist. Anne Robert Turgot (1727-1781), the chief practical exponent of Physiocratic doctrine, tried in vain to free French agriculture and French business from traditional restrictions during his brief tenure as chief minister of Louis XVI in the 1770s. The Physiocrats neglected what so many philosophes neglected; they overlooked the difficulty of accommodating the simple and reasonable dictates of natural law to the complexity of politics and the apparent irrationality of human nature.

Justice and Education

The disposition to let nature take its course also characterized the outlook of the philosophes on questions of justice. They believed that legislation created by humans prevented the application of the natural laws of justice. They were horrified by the cumbersome judicial procedures of the Old Regime and by its antiquated statutes. New lawgivers were needed to simplify legal codes, and a new science was needed to make the punishment of crime both humane and effective. The new science, which laid the foundations of modern sociology, was promoted by Cesare Beccaria (1738-1794), an Italian philosophe and the author of *Essay on Crimes and Punishments* (1764). Beccaria formulated three natural laws of justice, examples of the Enlightenment belief that common sense would lead humanity to nature's truths.

First, punishments should aim to

prevent the criminal from doing further injury to society, and to prevent others from committing the like offense. Such

---

ADAM SMITH ON FREE TRADE AND THE ROLE OF GOVERNMENT

It is the maxim of every prudent master of a family, never to attempt to make at home what it will cost him more to make than to buy. The taylor does not attempt to make his own shoes, but buys them of the shoemaker. The shoemaker does not attempt to make his own clothes, but employs a taylor. . . . What is prudence in the conduct of every private family, can scarce be folly in that of a great kingdom. If a foreign country can supply us with a commodity cheaper than we ourselves can make it, better buy it of them with some part of the produce of our industry. . . .

According to the system of natural liberty, the sovereign has only three duties to attend to: . . . first, the duty of protecting the society from the violence and invasion of other independent societies; secondly, the duty of protecting, as far as possible, every member of the society from the injustice and oppression of every other member of it, or the duty of establishing an exact administration of justice; and, thirdly, the duty of erecting and maintaining certain public works and certain public institutions, which it can never be for the interest of any individual, or small number of individuals, to erect and maintain. . . .

The Wealth of Nations (New York: Modern Library Edition, 1937), pp. 424, 651.

punishments, therefore, . . . ought to be chosen, as will make the strongest and most lasting impressions on the minds of others, with the least torment to the body of the criminal.

Second, justice should act speedily

because the smaller the interval of time between the punishment and the crime, the stronger and more lasting will be the association of the two ideas of Crime *and* Punishment.

And last:

Crimes are more effectively prevented by the certainty *than by the* severity *of the punishment. . . . The certainty of a small punishment will make a stronger impression than the fear of one more severe. . . .**

Beccaria attacked both torture and capital punishment because they deviated from these natural laws. The use of torture falsely assumed that "pain should be the test of truth, as if truth resided in the muscles and fibres of a wretch in torture." Jail sentences, not execution, should be imposed as punishments. But punishment alone was not enough; the best method of preventing crime was to "let liberty be attended with knowledge," to "perfect the system of education."

In education too the Old Regime failed to pass the philosophes' tests of reason and natural law. They deplored the almost universal church control of teaching and demanded that more stress be placed on science and less on theology; more on modern languages and less on Greek and Latin; more on modern history and less on ancient.

Most universities contributed very little to the Enlightenment; prestigious institutions like Oxford, Cambridge, and the Sorbonne were stagnating under clerical influence. But there were a few exceptions. Two of the liveliest institutions of the period were recently founded German universities—Göttingen in the electorate of Hanover, and Halle in Brandenburg. The medical schools at Vienna, at Leiden in Holland, and at Edinburgh in Scotland also brought distinction to their universities.

In primary education the most sweeping revisions were proposed by the great nonconformist of the Enlightenment, Jean-Jacques Rousseau (1712-1778). Rousseau rebelled against the strict and disciplined society of his birthplace, Calvinist Geneva. He rebelled against the intensive bookish studies he had been forced to pursue as a young boy and against the polite conventions he later encountered in the Paris salons. The result was his book *Emile* (1762), half treatise and half romance, a fervent plea for progressive education. *Emile* had two heroes— Emile, the student, and Rousseau, the teacher. The training that Rousseau prescribed for his pupil departed in every particular from eighteenth-century practice: "Life is the trade I would teach him. When he leaves me,

I grant you, he will be neither a magistrate, a soldier, nor a priest; he will be a man."* Rousseau followed a laissez-faire policy toward his pupil. He did not argue with Emile, or discipline him, or force him to read at an early age. Emile observed the world of nature from firsthand experience, not in books. He learned geography by finding his own way in the woods (with his tutor's help), and agriculture by working in the fields. And when in his teens he was at last taught to read, his first assignment was "the best treatise on an education according to nature," Daniel Defoe's *Robinson Crusoe*, published in 1719.

Rousseau's educational program had many faults. It was impractical, for it assumed that every child could have the undivided attention of a tutor twenty-four hours a day. And it fostered the permanent dependence of pupil upon teacher; when Emile married and became a father, he implored his tutor to remain at his post: "I need you more than ever now that I am taking up the duties of manhood." and yet *Emile* was a most important book, because Rousseau returned to the Renaissance concept of the universal man and to the ancient Greek ideal of the sound mind in the sound body. His theoretical program was adapted to the practical requirements of the classroom by the Swiss educator Johann Pestalozzi (1746-1827), who set an influential example by teaching geography, drawing, and other novelties in his experimental school. Still more influential was the reaction of Pestalozzi against the tradition of drilling lessons into the pupil through endless repetition and punishment.

The Attack on Religion

Attacks on clerical teaching soon formed part of a vigorous and growing body of criticism against the role of the clergy in the Old Regime. In denouncing fanaticism and superstition, the philosophes singled out the Society of Jesus, the symbol and the instrument of militant Catholicism. Pressure for the dissolution of the Jesuits gained the support of Catholic rulers, who had long been annoyed by Jesuit intervention in politics, and in the 1760s the Jesuits were expelled from several leading Catholic countries, including Portugal, France (at the insistence of the parlements rather than of Louis XV), and the homeland of Loyola himself, Spain. Pope Clement XIV (1769-1774) dissolved the Society in 1773; it would not be revived until half a century later, when the political and intellectual climate had become less hostile.

As champions of tolerance, the philosophes showed a particular affinity for the religious attitude called deism (from the Latin *deus*, "god"). Deist doctrines arose in seventeenth-century England, the England of the Civil War and Newtonian science, where the deists hoped to settle religious strife by reason rather than by arms. All persons, they asserted, could agree on a few broad religious principles. Since the Newtonian world-

*C. Beccaria, *Essay on Crimes and Punishments*, reprint ed. (Stanford, Calif.: Stanford University Press, 1953), pp. 47, 75, 93.

*J. Rousseau, *Emile*, (New York: Everyman Edition, 1911), p. 9.

machine implied the existence of a master mechanic, the deists accepted God as the creator of the universe; some of them also believed that he would preside over a Last Judgment. But they limited his role to the distant past and the remote future, and they doubted that he had any concern with day-to-day human activities or would answer prayer and bestow grace. The deists particularly denounced as superstition Christian beliefs and practices arising from mysteries and miracles, such as the Trinity, the Virgin Birth, and the Eucharist.

The chief exponent of deism in France was François-Marie Arouet, who took the pen name of Voltaire (1694-1778). He poured forth letters, plays, epics, histories, and essays. Clear, witty, and often bitingly satirical, his writings were enormously popular, so much so that they were often printed under an assumed name or outside France to evade censorship. It was Voltaire who made Frenchmen aware of English writers like Locke, Newton, and Shakespeare, and it was Voltaire who broadened the writing of history to include economics and culture as well as war and politics. He was also a highly successful and sometimes unscrupulous businessman.

Voltaire coined the anticlerical watchword *Ecrasez l'infâme!* Crush the infamous thing, crush bigotry, superstition, perhaps the church itself. He had experienced political intolerance at first hand. As a young man he had spent a year as a prisoner in Paris and three years of exile in England because he had criticized the French government and had offended a powerful nobleman. The religious and political freedom of Britain made an immense impression on the refugee: "If there were just one religion in England, despotism would threaten; if there were two religions, they would cut each other's throats; but there are thirty religions, and they live together peacefully and happily."*

Back home, Voltaire carried on a lifelong crusade for tolerance. In 1762 a Protestant merchant of Toulouse, Jean Calas, was accused of having murdered his son to prevent his conversion to Catholicism. Calas was executed by being broken on the wheel—the prolonged agony usually prescribed for non-nobles, since only aristocrats were allowed the swift punishment of beheading. Voltaire discovered that the accusation against Calas was based almost wholly on rumor, and he believed that the court condemning him had acted out of anti-Protestant hysteria. Voltaire campaigned for three years until the original verdict was reversed and the name of Calas was cleared.

The existence of evil—of injustices like that suffered by Calas—confronted the Age of Reason with a major problem. Few of the philosophes accepted the traditional Christian teaching that evil arose from original sin, from the fall of Adam and Eve. If God were purely benevolent, they asked, why then had he created a world in which evil so often prevailed? Could a perfect God produce an imperfect creation? Voltaire took his stand in his most famous work, *Candide* (1759), which showed the disasters abounding in the best of all possible worlds.

A real disaster had inspired the writing of *Candide*—a great earthquake, tidal wave, and fire that engulfed the city of Lisbon on November 1, 1755, killing over ten thousand people.

Deism enabled Voltaire to effect a reconciliation between a perfect God and an imperfect world. Voltaire believed that God was indeed the Creator:

> *When I see a watch . . . , I conclude that an intelligent being arranged the springs of this mechanism so that the hand should tell the time. Similarly, when I see the springs of the human body, I conclude that an intelligent being has arranged these organs to be kept and nourished in the womb for nine months; that the eyes have been given for seeing, the hands for grasping, etc.**

But, Voltaire concluded, there was no way to determine whether God would attempt to perfect his creation. Even so, Voltaire had no doubts about the usefulness of religion for the masses. "Man," he stated, "has always needed a brake. . . . If God did not exist, He would have to be invented."

Political Thought

"In politics as in religion, toleration is a necessity," decreed Voltaire. To him, therefore, the relatively tolerant Britain seemed utopia, and he paid the British constitution the most flattering compliment at the command of the age when he claimed that it "might have been invented by Locke, Newton, or Archimedes." The baron de la Brède et de Montesquieu (1689-1755), an aristocratic French lawyer and philosophe, set out to analyze the political virtues of Britain. In his major work, *The Spirit of the Laws* (1748), Montesquieu laid down the premise that no one system of government suited all countries. Laws, he wrote,

> *should be in relation to the climate of each country, to the quality of its soil, to its situation and extent, to the principal occupation of the natives, whether husbandmen, huntsmen, or shepherds: they should have relation to the degree of liberty which the constitution will bear; to the religion of the inhabitants, to their inclinations, riches, numbers, commerce, manners, and customs.***

Montesquieu cautioned against supposing that old customs could simply be decreed out of existence, citing Peter the Great's failure to impose Western ways on Russia.

In spelling out the influence of tradition and environment upon forms of government, Montesquieu concluded that republics were best suited to small and barren countries, limited monarchies to the middle-sized and more prosperous, and despotisms to vast empires. Britain, being middle-sized and prosperous, was quite properly a monarchy limited by aristocracy. A hereditary nobility sat in the House of Lords; a nobility of talent, the elected representatives, sat in the Commons.

Lettres Philosophiques, No. 6. Our translation.

Le Traité de Métaphysique, chap. 2. Our translation.

**The Spirit of the Laws*, trans. Thomas Nugent (New York: Everyman Edition, 1949), book 1, chap. 3.

All this was admirable in Montesquieu's view, for he pronounced the mass of people "extremely unfit" for government. If only the French monarchy had let the aristocracy retain its old political functions, he intimated, France would never have sunk to its low state.

Montesquieu found another key to the political superiority of Britain in the concept of checks and balances. In Parliament the Lords and Commons checked each other; in the government as a whole, the balance was maintained by means of the separation of powers. Here Montesquieu failed to take into account a development that was not yet obvious in the mideighteenth century: the British constitution was moving toward a concentration of powers in the House of Commons rather than their greater separation, since the cabinet was becoming the instrument of legislative supremacy over the executive.

Yet it was Jean-Jacques Rousseau who inspired the radicals of the French revolution. Rousseau's ideas proceeded from a sweeping generalization: whereas nature dignifies people, he contended, civilization corrupts them; people would be corrupted less if civilized institutions followed nature more closely. Rousseau's major political work, *The Social Contract* (1762), attempted to

Rousseau and Voltaire were very different in temperament, though they shared the Enlightenment ideal of reshaping the environment so that human beings might not be corrupted. This contemporary print shows them in sharp argument, each in defense of his own writing.

reconcile the liberty of the individual and the institution of government through a new version of the contract theory of government. Earlier theories of contract, from the Middle Ages to Hobbes and Locke, had hinged on the agreement between the people to be governed, on the one hand, and a single governor or small group of governors, on the other. Earlier theories postulated a political contract; Rousseau's contract was social in that a whole society agreed to be ruled by its general will: "Each of us puts his person and all his power in common under the supreme direction of the general will, and, in our corporate capacity, we receive each member as an indivisible part of the whole." "Each individual," Rousseau continued "may have a particular will contrary or dissimilar to the general will which he has as a citizen." If a person insists on putting self-interest above community interest, that person must be forced to observe the general will: "This means nothing less than that he will be forced to be free."* Thus, the general will was moral as well as political in nature, for it represented what was best for the whole community, what the community ought to do.

Formulating this general will, Rousseau believed, was the business of the whole people. The power of legislation, he argued, could never be properly transferred to an elected body. Executing the general will, however, could legitimately be the business of a smaller group. Like Montesquieu, Rousseau believed that the number of governors should vary inversely with the size and resources of the state—monarchy for the wealthy, aristocracy for the state of middling size and wealth, and democracy for the small and poor. Rousseau doubted, however, that any state was ready for the absolute form of democracy in which the people themselves actually executed the laws. "Were there a people of gods, their government would be democratic. So perfect a government is not for men."**

Almost every radical political doctrine in the past two centuries has owed something to Rousseau. Socialists justified collectivism on the basis of his insistence that "the fruits of the earth belong to us all." Patriots and nationalists hailed him as an early prophet of the creed that nations do—and should—differ. Throughout his writings, he referred to "the dear love of country." Indeed, *The Social Contract* concluded with a plea for the establishment of a "civil religion," which would displace the traditional faith. The moral code of early Christianity might be retained, Rousseau thought, but the state should no longer have to compete with the church for the allegiance of citizens.

When reconstructed at a later time, Rousseau's concept of the general will arouses conflicting interpretations. Because it is ethical in character, it seems to represent more than the sum of individual wills—the whole appears to be more than the sum of its parts. Many, therefore, saw in Rousseau a man who exalted the welfare of the nation over that of the citizens composing

*Rousseau, *The Social Contract and Discourses* (New York: Everyman Edition, 1913), pp. 13, 15.
**Ibid., p. 56.

AN ENLIGHTENED DESPOT DESCRIBES HIMSELF

Frederick the Great laid down the fundamental requirements for an enlightened despot:

Princes, sovereigns, kings are not clothed with supreme authority to plunge with impunity into debauchery and luxury. . . . [The prince] should often remind himself that he is a man just as the least of his subjects. If he is the first judge, the first general, the first financier, the first minister of the nation, . . . it is in order to fulfill the duties which these titles impose upon him. He is only the first servant of the state, obliged to act with fairness, wisdom, and unselfishness, as if at every instant he would have to render an account of his administration to his citizens.

"Essai sur les Formes de Gouvernement et sur les Devoirs des Souverains," *Oeuvres Posthumes* (Berlin: Voss et fils, 1788), VI, 64, 83-84. Our translation.

---

it, a man who worshiped the state. Dictators justified their totalitarianism by asserting that they had a special insight into the general will; a police state might be justified on the grounds that it was doing its subjects a favor by "forcing them to be free." Such authoritarian interpretations indicate some of the possible consequences of Rousseau's ideas, but they overlook both the strongly idealistic and democratic tone of his writings and his personal hostility toward the absolutism of the Old Regime.

A political prescription more practical than *The Social Contract* and clearly more in keeping with existing monarchical institutions was enlightened despotism. The Physiocrats, chief theorists of enlightened despotism, did not share the concern of Montesquieu and Rousseau for the status of the legislative power. In the Physiocratic view, God was the legislator, nature preserved the divine legislation, and the sole duty of government was to administer these natural laws. Democracy and autocracy alike had the fatal weakness of delegating administrative authority to individuals whose short-term selfish aims clashed with the permanent welfare of the nation. By contrast, the Physiocrats explained, the personal interests of a hereditary monarch coincided with the national interests through "co-ownership" of the territories the monarch ruled. This amounted to saying that, since the whole kingdom was in a sense the king's property, whatever he did would be right, so long as it was both reasonable and natural. This came close to being a secular restatement of divine-right theory, and it is not surprising that many eighteenth-century monarchs proclaimed themselves to be enlightened despots.

II ENLIGHTENED DESPOTS

Frederick the Great, 1740-1786

Of all the eighteenth-century rulers, Frederick II the Great, king of Prussia from 1740 to 1786, appeared best attuned to the Enlightenment. As a youth he had rebelled against the drill-sergeant methods of his father, Frederick William I. He delighted in music and played the flute, which he took with him even on military campaigns. An attentive reader of the philosophes, he exchanged letters with them and brought Voltaire to live for a time as his pensioner in his palace at Potsdam, near Berlin. He wrote a pamphlet denouncing the immorality of Machiavelli's *The Prince*.

Frederick shunned luxury, wore stained and shabby clothing, and toiled long hours at his desk. Yet he conducted foreign and military affairs with cunning and guile: "The principle of aggrandizement is the fundamental law of every government,"* he wrote. At home, in his Potsdam palace where he conducted the business of state by correspondence, he drove his subordinates mercilessly. Viewed as a general, diplomat, and the master mechanic of Prussian administration, Frederick the Great was efficient and successful, but, if enlightened, he was also quite clearly a despot.

No Physiocrat could have done more than Frederick to improve Prussian agriculture. From western Europe he imported clover, potatoes, crop rotation, and the iron plow. He drained the swamps of the lower Oder valley, opened up farms in Silesia and elsewhere, and brought in 300,000 immigrants, mainly from other areas of Germany, to settle the new lands. After the ravages of the Seven Years' War, Frederick gave the peasants tools, stock, and seed to repair their ruined farms. He also nursed along the German tradition of scientific forestry, then still in its infancy.

Frederick, however, was hostile to the doctrine of laissez faire and cut imports severely to save money for his army. His mercantilism stimulated the growth of Prussian industry, particularly the textiles and metals needed by the army; but it also placed a staggering burden of taxation on his subjects and produced several economic paradoxes. He tried to make Prussia grow its own tobacco, for which the climate was not suited. Since the growing German consumption of coffee required a

---

*Quoted by G. Ritter, *Frederick the Great: A Historical Profile* (Berkeley: University of California Press, 1968), p. 7.

large outlay of money abroad, he laid a heavy duty on imported coffee beans and established a special corps of French "coffee smellers" to trap smugglers.

The religious and social policies of Frederick the Great combined the Age of Reason at its most reasonable with the Old Regime at its least enlightened. A deist, Frederick prided himself on religious tolerance. When the Jesuits were expelled from Catholic states, he invited them to seek refuge in predominantly Lutheran Prussia. He gave the Catholic minority, particularly important in Silesia, virtually full equality, urging them to build their church steeples as high as they liked, and set the example by constructing a large new Catholic church in the center of Berlin. He boasted that he would build a mosque in his capital if Muslims wanted to settle there. Yet Frederick alleged that Jews were "useless to the state"; he levied special taxes on his Jewish subjects and tried to exclude them from the professions and from the civil service. His concern was, in fact, less for religious tolerance as such than for encouraging new groups of settlers to settle in rural areas.

Frederick also rendered Prussians a great service by his judicial reforms, which freed the courts from political pressures. He ordered a reduction in the use of torture, and he put an end to the unusual custom of turning over appeals from the ordinary courts to university faculties, setting up a regular system of appellate courts instead. He mitigated the practice of bribing judges by insisting that gratuities received from litigants be placed in a common pool, from which each judge should draw only his fair share as a supplement to his meager salary.

Yet the same Frederick took a medieval view of the merits of social caste, in part because of his own convictions about the patriotic duties required of both ruler and subjects. Although he abolished serfdom on the royal domains, he did little to loosen the bonds of serfdom generally, except to forbid the sale of serfs without land in East Prussia in 1773. When he gave the peasants material assistance and urged them to become literate, his aims were utilitarian. Peasants were to learn nothing beyond the rudiments of reading and writing; otherwise, they might become discontented. He regarded the middle class too with disdain. At the close of the Seven Years' War he forced all bourgeois officers in the army to resign their commissions; business and professional men were to be exempt from military service but subject to heavy taxation. He opposed membership in the Academy of Berlin for the leading German writer of his age, G.E. Lessing (1729-1781), because his dramas defended middle-class values of social and political freedom and were written in German, not French. Even the favored Junkers did not escape Frederick's bureaucratic absolutism. Although he appointed only Junkers as army officers, he discouraged their marrying so as to reduce the number of potential widows to whom the state would owe a pension.

Frederick's will directed that he be buried beside his pet dogs. "Such," remarked a French observer, "is the last mark of contempt he thought proper to cast upon mankind." That verdict has been sustained by many historians, who pronounce Frederick's supposed enlightenment a mere propaganda device, an attempt to clothe the nakedness of his absolutism with the intellectual garments of the age. It is fairer to recognize that Frederick espoused two often-conflicting philosophies—the Spartan traditions of the Hohenzollerns and the humane principles of the Enlightenment. The grim overtones of the former kept him from sharing the latter's optimistic estimate of human nature and potentiality. Frederick was an enlightened despot in his general religious toleration and his reform of court procedure and criminal law, but he was contradictory and bent on centralization that enhanced the Prussian kingship.

Maria Theresa, Joseph II, Leopold II, 1740-1792

Frederick's decisive victory in the War of the Austrian Succession laid bare the basic weaknesses of the Hapsburgs' dynastic empire. The empress Maria Theresa (1740-1780) believed in the need for reform and often took as her model the institutions of her hated but successful rival, Frederick II of Prussia. She had the advice of capable ministers. The empress and her experts increased taxes, especially on the nobility, and strengthened the central government at the expense of local aristocratic assemblies, building up departments for central administration. They obliged the non-German provinces to accept the domination of German officials (and of the German language). She also took the first steps toward the eventual abolition of serfdom by placing a ceiling on the amount of taxes and of labor service that the peasants could be compelled to render, and in the 1770s she moved against the general European trend in which the conditions of the peasantry declined. While personally devout, she subjected the Church to heavier taxation, confiscated monastic property, and expelled the Jesuits. But she was fundamentally out of sympathy with the Age of Reason. Lady Prayerful, as Catherine the Great called her, banned the works of Rousseau and Voltaire from her realm and even forbade the circulation of the Catholic *Index*, lest that list of forbidden books arouse the curiosity of her subjects and lead them to pry into the undesirable. It was her eldest son, Joseph II, who instituted the major reforms associated with the enlightened despots.

Joseph (1765-1790), who became emperor in 1765, ruled jointly with his mother until her death in 1780. Earnest, industrious, and puritanical, Joseph promised to make "philosophy the legislator of my empire." Thwarted and restrained by Maria Theresa in her lifetime, seeking solace in work for the grief caused by the death of his young wife, the impatient emperor plunged into activity after his mother died. During his ten years as sole ruler (1780-1790) eleven thousand laws and six thousand decrees issued from Vienna. This

Pompeo Batoni (1708-1787) painted Joseph II with the future emperor Leopold II, then grand duke of Tuscany, in 1769 in Rome. This painting hangs in the Kunsthistorisches Museum in Vienna. The background and many details show Batoni's interest in the neoclassical.

frenzied pace gave the mileading impression that the son's policies ran counter to the mother's; actually, their goals were often identical, but Joseph's methods were less cautious and conciliatory than Maria Theresa's.

For the first time in the history of Catholic Austria, Calvinists, Lutherans, and Orthodox Christians gained full toleration. The emperor took measures to end the ghetto existence of the Jews, exempting them from the special taxes applied to them and lifting the requirement of wearing a yellow patch as a badge of inferiority. On the other hand, Joseph continued his mother's moves to increase state control over the Church in Austrian lands—a control that now went by the name of Josephism because of the emperor's insistence that he and not the pope was the supreme arbiter of ecclesiastical matters in Hapsburg territories. He encouraged what he considered socially useful in Catholicism and dealt ruthlessly with what he judged superfluous or harmful. Thus he established hundreds of new churches while reducing the number of religious holidays. Calling monks "the

most dangerous and useless subjects in every state," he cut in half the number of monks and nuns; of twenty-one hundred monasteries and nunneries, he suppressed seven hundred, chiefly those run by contemplative orders, sparing houses engaged in educational or charitable work. The government sold or leased the lands of the suppressed establishments, applying the revenue to the support of the hospitals that were beginning to earn Vienna a reputation as a great medical center.

Unlike Frederick the Great, Joseph believed in popular education and social equality. His government provided teachers and textbooks for primary schools. More than a quarter of the school-age children in Austria actually attended school—the best record of any country in late eighteenth-century Europe. Everyone in Vienna, high and low, was invited to visit the Prater, the great public park of the capital, the entrance to which bore the inscription, "A place of pleasure for all men, prepared for them by their friend." The new Austrian legal code followed the recommendations of Beccaria in abolishing capital punishment and most tortures and in prescribing equality before the law. Aristocratic offenders, like commoners, were sentenced to stand in the pillory and to sweep the streets of Vienna.

Joseph's policy toward the peasants marked the climax of his equalitarianism. He freed the serfs, abolished most of their obligations to manorial lords, and deprived the lords of their traditional right of administering justice to the peasantry. He also experimented with the collection of a single tax on land, as recommended by the Physiocrats—a revolutionary innovation from the social as well as the economic point of view, because the estates of the aristocracy were to be taxed on the same basis as the farms of the peasantry.

Joseph's economic and political policies, however, often followed the paths of absolutism. In economics he practiced mercantilism, notably in the erection of high protective tariffs and in the government's close supervision of economic life. In politics Joseph extended his mother's efforts to diminish the influence of the nobility by appointing commoners to high governmental posts. Continuing her Germanizing program, he customarily spoke German, patronized German writers, and made the French playhouse in Vienna a German-language theater. He also attempted to terminate the autonomous rights of his non-German possessions, notably Belgium, Bohemia, and Hungary.

Both Joseph's enlightened reforms and his Germanizing measures aroused mounting opposition. Devout peasants, almost oblivious to his attempts to improve their social and economic status, resented his meddling with old religious customs. The nobility clamored against his equalitarian legislation; their opposition to the single-tax experiment was so violent that he had to revoke the decree a month after it was issued. Hungary and Belgium rose in open rebellion against his centralizing efforts and forced him to confirm their autonomous liberties.

In foreign policy too his ambitious projects miscarried. By supporting Russian plans for the dismemberment of Turkey, Austria gained only a narrow strip of Balkan territory. Joseph also attempted to annex lands belonging to the neighboring south German state of Bavaria, where the death of the ruler opened another succession quarrel. But Frederick the Great was determined to check any advance of Hapsburg power in Germany. In the half-hearted "Potato War" of the late 1770s, Austrian and Prussian troops spent most of their time foraging for food, and Joseph secured only a tiny fragment of the Bavarian inheritance.

Joseph II worked himself to death, as one of his friends observed, "by governing too much and reigning too little." Where his mother had often sought to flatter her opponents out of their opposition, Joseph simply laid down the law. He defended his practice of interfering personally in almost every detail of government:

What else can I do in this country devoid of mind, without soul, without zeal, without heart in the work? I am killing myself because I cannot rouse up those whom I want to make work; but I hope I shall not die until I have so wound up the machine that others cannot put it out or order, even if they try to do so.*

Joseph died convinced that he had pursued the proper course, yet believing that he had accomplished nothing. In fact, his course was too insensitive to the feelings of others; but he attempted more in ten years than Frederick attempted in almost half a century, and not all of Joseph's attempts failed. Though some of his major reforms, such as the abolition of serfdom, were repealed soon after his death, others survived.

The reforms that survived profited from the conciliatory policies of Joseph's successor, his younger brother Leopold II (1790-1792), who was an enlightened despot in his own right. As grand duke of Tuscany (1765-1790), he improved the administration of his Italian duchy, which included the busy port of Leghorn and the cities of Florence and Pisa. He also introduced economic reforms along Physiocratic lines and judicial reforms in keeping with the recommendations of Beccaria on the abolition of torture and the death penalty. Unlike his brother, Leopold actively enlisted the participation of his subjects in affairs of state; and, unlike any other enlightened despot, he contemplated establishing a representative assembly in Tuscany, studying the constitution of the state of Virginia in the newly independent United States of America for guidance.

Charles III, Pombal, Gustavus III, 1759-1792

Earlier, another Italian state had profited from the political apprenticeship of another enlightened despot. That state was Naples, where from 1735 to 1759 King Charles carried on a successful struggle against clerical-

ism and feudalism. In 1759 he inherited the Spanish kingship on the death of his half-brother, and Naples passed to his son Ferdinand I, who was married to a daughter of Maria Theresa, moving southern Italy out of the Bourbon Spanish orbit and into that of Hapsburg Austria.

As king of Spain (1759-1788), Charles III energetically advanced the progressive policies begun under his father, Philip V, with the help of advisers from Naples and of lawyers from the lower ranks of the Spanish nobility. Though a pious Catholic, Charles objected strongly to the political activities of the church and forced the Jesuits out of Spain. He reduced the authority of the aristocracy, extended that of the crown, and made Spain more nearly a centralized national state. He curbed the privileges of the great sheep ranchers, whose almost unlimited grazing rights made Spanish agriculture uncompetitive. To give new life to the economy, he undertook irrigation projects, reclaimed waste lands, and established new roads, canals, textile mills, and banks. Spain's foreign commerce increased five-fold during the reign of Charles III. His successor, however, abandoned many of his policies, and Spain soon began to return to its aristocratic and clerical ways, although the influence of the Enlightenment was never entirely extinguished.

In Spain's neighbor, Portugal, the representative of enlightened despotism was not the monarch but the marques de Pombal, the first minister of King Joseph I (1750-1777). Pombal (1699-1782) secured his reputation by the speed and good taste with which he rebuilt Lisbon after the earthquake of 1755. The Portuguese economy depended heavily on income from the colonies, especially Brazil, and on the sale of port wine to and the purchase of manufactured goods from Britain. Pombal tried to enlarge the economic base by fostering local industries and encouraging the growth of grain production. In an attempt to weaken the grip of clericalism, he ousted the Jesuits, advanced religious toleration, and modernized the curriculum of the national University of Coimbra. To weaken the nobles, he attacked their rights of inheritance. But Pombal's methods were high handed, and when he fell from power in 1777 the prisons released thousands of men whom he had confined years earlier for their alleged involvement in aristocratic plots.

Equally high handed in the long run was Sweden's benevolent despot, Gustavus III (1771-1792), a nephew of Frederick the Great. Like his uncle, Gustavus admired French ideas, and when he inherited the Swedish crown he proclaimed his devotion to the Age of Reason. He also resolved not to be cramped by the noble factions that had run the country since the death of the warrior king, Charles XII, early in the century. While he distracted Swedish party leaders at the opera one evening, his soldiers staged a coup that enabled him to revive royal authority and to dissolve the factions. In economics and religion his enlightenment outdistanced that of his uncle in Prussia, for he removed obstacles to both domestic and foreign trade and extended toleration to both Jews

---

*Quoted in C.J. de Ligne, *His Memoirs, Letters, and Miscellaneous Papers* (Boston: Hardy Pratt, 1902), II, 132. Prince Charles Joseph de Ligne (1735-1814) was an Austrian courtier and field marshal noted for his charm; his memoirs are an important source for understanding court life at the time.

Francisco Goya (1746-1828) shows Charles III of Spain (1716-1788) in hunting costume. Goya sought to analyze character as shown by social position, and he became increasingly less subtle in intimating human capacity for evil through his canvasses. Living at the royal court, he became disillusioned by the later corruption of Charles IV, and his work took a savage turn. Compare this hunting portrait with Van Dyck on Charles I of England (p. 18).

and non-Lutheran Christians. Success, however, went to his head. As the king became more and more arbitrary, the nobles determined to recover their old power; in 1792 Gustavus was assassinated at a masquerade in Stockholm.

The Limitations of Enlightened Despotism

The structure of enlightened despotism was impaired by the problem of succession. So long as monarchs came to the throne by the accident of birth, there was nothing to prevent the unenlightened or incapable from succeeding the enlightened and able. This happened in Spain, where the well-meaning but feeble Charles IV (1788-1808) succeeded Charles III; it happened in Sweden,

where the weak Gustavus IV (1792-1809) succeeded Gustavus III; and it happened in Prussia under Frederick the Great's unenlightened nephew, Frederick William II (1786-1797). In Austria, Leopold was followed by his very conservative son, Francis II (1792-1835).

Even the least of the enlightened despots deserves credit for having reformed some of the bad features of the Old Regime; but not even the best of them could strike a happy balance between enlightenment and despotism. Joseph II was too doctrinaire, too inflexible in his determination to apply the full reform program of the Age of Reason. Pombal and Gustavus III were too arbitrary. Frederick the Great, obsessed with strengthening the Crown, entrenched the power of the Junkers, who were hostile to the Enlightenment. And in Russia events during the century after the death of Peter the Great furnished another lesson in the difficulty of applying rational principles to political realities.

III RUSSIA, 1725-1825

Russia had two sovereigns who could be numbered among the enlightened despots: Catherine II the Great (1762-1796) and her grandson Alexander I (1801-1825). For the thirty-seven years between the death of Peter the Great and the accession of Catherine the autocracy was without an effective leader as the throne changed hands seven times. More important than the individuals who governed during these years were the social groups contending for power and the social processes at work in Russia. The guards regiments founded by Peter came to exercise a decisive influence in the series of palace overturns, and the service nobility, no longer restrained by the czar, became dominant.

Nobles and Serfs, 1730-1762

A deeply dissatisfied social group that had the power to make and unmake autocrats, the nobility naturally had a program for the redress of its own grievances. In 1730 the gentry set out to emancipate itself from the servitude placed upon it by Peter. By 1762 the nobles no longer needed to serve at all unless they wished to do so; simultaneously, the authority of noble proprietors over their serfs was increased. The former became the government's agents for collecting the poll tax; the latter could no longer obtain their freedom by enlisting in the army, and could not engage in trade or purchase land without written permission from their masters. Masters could deport their serfs to Siberia and could punish them physically in any way they wished.

To understand the revolutionary nature of the liberation of the nobles from the duty to give military service, one must remember that they had historically obtained their lands and serfs only on condition that they would serve. Now they could keep their lands and serfs with no obligations. Yet the service that had been hated when it was compulsory became fashionable when it was optional. There was really little else for a Russian noble to do except serve the state and to tighten controls over the serfs.

In these middle decades of the eighteenth century, successive waves of foreign influence affected the Russian nobility. It was not only the influx of foreigners that brought in Western habits; there was also the involvement of Russia in European wars and the increased travel abroad by Russians. German influence gave way to French, and with the French language came French literature. French styles of dress were copied by both men and women, and some gentlemen claimed that it would be impossible to fall in love with a woman who did not speak French. Quite literally, nobles and peasants no longer spoke the same language, and this deep rift between the Frenchified gentry and the Russian people was later to prove of critical importance.

Catherine the Great, 1762-1796

Brought up in a petty German court, Catherine II found herself transplanted to St. Petersburg as a young girl, living with a husband she detested, and forced to pick her way through the intrigues that flourished in the Russian capital. Catherine wrote plays, edited a satirical journal, and steeped herself in the literature of the Enlightenment. Both before and after ascending the throne she had many lovers, several of whom played important roles in affairs of state.

Catherine was particularly concerned that Western leaders think well of her and of the condition of Russia under her rule; hence her voluminous correspondence with Westerners. She invited Diderot (who declined) to edit the *Encyclopédie* in Russia; then she bought his library, but he kept his books and received a pension— favorable publicity for the Russian empress. When Diderot visited Russia in 1773, he reported that Catherine had the soul of Brutus and the charms of Cleopatra, while she complained that in the excitement of conversation, her guest had pinched her legs until they were black and blue. Voltaire judiciously stayed out of Russia but accepted Catherine's bounty, in return for which he called her "the north star" and "the benefactress of Europe."

Catherine would perhaps have liked to reform conditions in Russia, but as a woman, a foreigner, and a usurper (she owed her throne to a conspiracy that deposed and murdered her husband, Peter III), she could not act upon her inclinations. Depending as she did upon the good will of the nobility, she could not interfere with serfdom. She had to reward her supporters with vast grants of state land, inhabited by hundreds of thousands of state peasants, who now became privately owned serfs who could be sold. Even in theory, Catherine felt that Russia was so large that its only possible form of government was an autocracy, and as an autocrat she was as arbitrary as any of her predecessors.

Once firmly established on the throne, however, Catherine decided to convoke a commission to codify the laws of Russia, for the first time since 1649. With the help of advisers, Catherine herself spent three years composing the *Instruction* to the delegates, full of abstract argument drawn from Montesquieu's *Spirit of the Laws* and Beccaria's *Crimes and Punishments*. The 564 delegates to the commission were elected by organs of the central government and by every social class in Russia except the serfs. Each delegate—noble, townsman, crown peasant, Cossack—was charged to bring with him a collection of written documents from his neighbors presenting their grievances and demands for change.

Each class of representatives was eager to extend the rights of that class: the free peasants wanted to own serfs; the townspeople wanted to own serfs and be the only class allowed to engage in trade; the nobles wanted to engage in trade and have their exclusive right to own serfs confirmed. After 203 sessions lasting over a year and a half devoted to inconclusive debate, Catherine ended the labors of the commission in 1768. It had not codified the laws, but from Catherine's own point of view it had been a success; she knew that most of her

Portrait of Catherine the Great, Empress of Russia, who was born in a German-speaking state and who cultivated the philosophes.

subjects supported her as absolute autocrat. The commission was the last effort by czardom to consult the Russian people as a whole until the early twentieth century.

Catherine turned the work of the legislative commission to good advantage in her later reforms, which resulted from the great rebellion of the Cossacks under the leadership of Yemelyan Pugachev in 1773-1775. Pugachev (d. 1775) roused the frontiersmen to revolt against Catherine's cancellation of their special privileges. Pretending to be her murdered husband, Czar Peter III, and promising liberty and land to the serfs who joined his forces, Pugachev swept over a wide area of southeastern Russia and marched toward Moscow. Like the disturbances of the seventeenth century, Pugachev's revolt revealed the existence of bitter discontent in Russia—a discontent directed at the supreme autocrat but even more at the landlords and local officials.

Catherine took action. Her reorganization of local government (1775) created fifty provinces where there had been twenty before. She thus replaced a small number of unwieldly units with a larger number of small provinces, each containing roughly three to four hundred thousand inhabitants. While the reform of 1775 gave the nobles the lion's share of provincial offices, it also subjected them to the close direction of the central government. The revolt was brutally crushed.

In a charter of 1785 the nobles again received exemption from military service and taxation and secured absolute mastery over the fate of their serfs and their estates. A charter to the towns in the same year disclosed Catherine's sympathy with the tiny but growing urban middle class and established the principle of municipal self-government, although it remained a dead letter because of the rigorous class distinctions maintained in the urban centers of Russia. For the serfs, however, there was no charter.

Paul, 1796-1801, and Alexander I, 1801-1825

Catherine's son Paul succeeded her in 1796 at age forty-two. All his life his mother had distrusted him, fearing that there might be a conspiracy to oust her and install him, ostensibly a true Romanov. Consequently, when Paul did become czar, he appeared to be motivated chiefly by a wish to undo his mother's work. He exiled some of her favorites and released many of her prisoners. Paul's behavior, however, was erratic. On the one hand, he imposed a strict curfew on St. Petersburg and forbade the importation of sheet music because he feared that all of it might be as revolutionary as the French *Marseillaise*. On the other hand, in a decree in 1797 he observed that most owners of serfs generally required only three days of labor per week, and he prohibited the requirement of labor on Sunday. Later this passing observation was viewed as having stated a

norm for service, though it might be exceeded during harvest season. In any case, he continued to give away state lands and transformed some half a million state peasants into privately owned chattels.

What was probaly fatal to Paul was his policy of toughness toward the nobility. "A noble," he is said to have remarked, "is the man I am talking to at the moment, and he ceases to be a noble when I stop talking to him." This definition could scarcely have appealed to the privileged landowners. Paul restored compulsory service from the nobles and curtailed their powers in the provinces. Nobles were forced to meet the bills for public buildings and to pay new taxes on their lands; they were also subjected to corporal punishment for crimes. Paul wanted to Prussianize the army and especially to develop in its officers a sense of responsibility for their men. The guards regiments detested such programs, and a conspiracy of guardsmen resulted in the murder of Paul and the succession of Alexander in 1801.

Educated by a liberal Swiss tutor, Alexander I had absorbed much of the new eighteenth-century teachings. Yet the application of liberal principles in Russia would directly challenge the most powerful forces in society and would also require the czar to relinquish some of his own power. Alexander hesitated, compromised, and in the end accomplished very little. First he gathered a small group of young men which he called "the unofficial committee." One of the members had been active in the French Revolution, and two others greatly admired the English system of government. The committee took as its self-appointed task the preparation of a constitution for Russia. But when the committee stopped meeting in 1803, it had done nothing about serfdom. The czar himself did sponsor a law creating a new category of free farmers—serfs who had been freed by their masters—and prescribing that if a proprietor freed an entire village of serfs, he must also confer their lands upon them. This mild initiative depended on the voluntary cooperation of the proprietors, and it resulted in freeing fewer than forty thousand of the many millions of serfs.

After the first major war with Napoleon (1805-1807), Alexander had as his chief mentor a remarkable figure, Michael Speransky (1772-1839), son of a Russian priest, intelligent, well educated, and conscientious. Utilizing Montesquieu's principle of the separation of powers, Speransky drafted for Alexander a constitutional project that would have made Russia a limited monarchy. A series of elected assemblies, beginning at the lowest level of administrative subdivision and continuing on up through district and province, would culminate in a great national assembly, the Duma. A similar pyramid of courts and a new set of executive institutions were also planned. The Duma would have to approve any law proposed by the czar and would be a Russian parliament. The franchise Speransky proposed would have enormously favored the nobility and excluded the serfs, whose emancipation was not included in his proposal. One of the most critical moments in Russian history

Alexander I of Russia was interested in the thought of the philosophes and began his reign expecting to carry out liberal reforms. He soon found that traditional autocracy served his interests best, however, and he became increasingly reactionary. Vain, he often had his portrait painted in full regalia. This portrait was by the French artist François Gérard (1770-1837).

came when Alexander balked at implementing the project he had commissioned.

Why did Speransky fail? He had instituted a reform of the civil service, requiring examinations and a system of promotion by merit, which disturbed many of the almost illiterate men in high office. He also had proposed that the nobility pay an income tax. Friends and intimates of the czar spread slander about Speransky, who had engineered the fated alliance with Napoleon; when Napoleon invaded Russia in 1812, Speransky was exiled. At bottom Alexander was unwilling to act on his own alleged beliefs. Speransky's scheme was shelved, except for two elements that in no way diminished the power of the czar. A council of state was created to advise the czar, but since he appointed and dismissed its members and was not obliged to take its advice, the effect was simply to increase imperial efficiency, not to limit imperial authority. Further efficiency was achieved through the reorganization of the ministries, whose duties were set out clearly for the first time, eliminating overlapping.

During the last decade of Alexander's reign, 1815-1825, the most important figure at court was Count Alexsey Arakcheev (1769-1834), an efficient and brutal officer who reformed the army and organized a hated system of "military colonies," drafting the population of whole districts to serve in the regiments quartered there.

When not drilling or fighting, these soldiers were to work their farms, and their entire lives often were subject to the whims of their officers. By the end of Alexander's reign, almost 400,000 soldiers were living in these harsh military camps.

Though Alexander gave Russia no important reforms, he did act as the "liberal czar" in his dominions outside Russia proper. Made king of a partially restored Poland in 1815, he gave the Poles an advanced constitution, with their own army and officials and the free use of their own language. After the annexation of Finland from Sweden in 1809, he allowed the Finns to preserve their own law codes and the system of local government introduced during the long period of Swedish rule.

Foreign Policy, 1725-1796

Between the death of Peter the Great and that of Catherine, Russian foreign policy still pursued the traditional goals of expansion against Sweden, Poland, and Turkey. But as a new member of the European power constellation, Russia found that these goals increasingly involved it with the states of central and western Europe. In the War of the Polish Succession (1733-1735) Russian forces were allied with those of Austria in supporting Augustus III and forcing the abdication of Stanislas Leszczyński. The Russians and Austrians then became allies in a new war against the Turks from 1735 to 1739. Though the Russians invaded the Crimea successfully, their territorial gains were limited to Azov. The Austrians failed to cooperate in an invasion of the Danubian principalities and made it clear that they did not relish a Russian advance toward the Hapsburg frontiers. Prussian influence, which was anti-Austrian, manifested itself with the appearance of the future Peter III as heir and with the selection of the German Catherine, whose father was a Prussian general. Thus, during the War of the Austrian Succession there was much jockeying for Russian assistance. The advance of Frederick the Great along the Baltic shore alarmed the Russians, and a Russian corps was slowly moving westward to join the fighting as the war ended.

The Russians remained loyal to Austria and fought the Prussians in the Seven Years' War. Russian forces invaded East Prussia and in 1760 entered Berlin; the accession of the pro-Russian Peter III early in 1762 led the Russians to change sides and join the Prussians briefly against the Austrians and the French. When Catherine, on her accession, withdrew Russian forces, Russia was excluded from the peace conferences of 1763.

In foreign policy Catherine the Great was vigorous and unscrupulous in pursuing Russia's traditional goals. When the throne of Poland fell vacant, Catherine secured the election of her former lover, a pro-Russian Pole, Stanislas Poniatowski, who became Stanislas II (1764-1795). Frederick the Great then joined with Catherine in a campaign to win rights for the Lutheran and Orthodox minorities in Catholic Poland. One party of Polish nobles, offended at foreign intervention, secured the aid of

France and Austria, who adopted the strategem of pressing Turkey into war with Russia to distract Catherine from Poland.

In the Russo-Turkish War (1768-1774) the Russian Baltic fleet sailed into the Mediterranean and, with the help of British naval advisers, destroyed the Turkish fleet in the Aegean (1770). The Russians then shifted their operations again to the Crimea and to what is now Romania. While Russians and Turks were discussing peace terms, Frederick the Great concluded that Russia's success with the Turks might lead it to seize most of Poland unless he acted quickly; he therefore arranged the first partition of Poland (1772), which lost to Russia, Prussia, and Austria almost one-third of its territory and one-half of its population. Frederick's share was the smallest but included the strategic region that had previously separated Brandenburg from East Prussia.

Maria Theresa abandoned her Turkish and Polish allies to obtain the southern Polish province of Galicia. Russia received a substantial area of what became Belorussia, or White Russia.

Two years later the Russians imposed upon the Turks the humiliating treaty of Kutchuk Kainardji (1774). Catherine annexed much of the formerly Turkish stretch of Black Sea coast; the Crimea was separated from the Ottoman Empire and annexed by Russia in 1783. She also obtained something the Russians had long coveted—freedom of navigation on the Black Sea and the right of passage through the Bosporus and the Dardanelles. A vaguely worded clause gave her various rights to protect the Christian subjects of the sultan, thus providing a justification for later Russian intervention in Turkish affairs.

Now Catherine began to dream of expelling the Turks

**Partitions of Poland,
1772, 1793, 1795**

	1772	1793	1795
To Prussia			
To Russia			
To Austria			

from Europe and reviving the Byzantine Empire under Russian protection. As part of this Greek project, she had her younger grandson christened Constantine and imported Greek-speaking nurses to train him in the language. She also proposed to set up a kingdom of Dacia (the Roman name for Romania), to be ruled by her very able general Gregory Potemkin (1739-1791). By way of preparation, in 1783 Catherine built a naval base at Sebastopol in the newly annexed Crimea. To achieve these grandiose designs, Catherine sought the consent of Austria and took Joseph II on a boat tour of the recently acquired territories of the Russian southwest. However, in a second Russo-Turkish war (1787-1791) Catherine's Austrian allies again provided feeble assistance and soon became embroiled in a conflict of interest with Russia over the European lands of the sultan. In the end Catherine abandoned her Greek project and contented herself with acquiring the remaining Turkish lands along the northern coast of the Black Sea.

Before her death Catherine participated in two more partitions of Poland, made possible largely by the mounting preoccupation of the Western powers with the French Revolution. The second partition came as the result of a Polish constitutional movement, supported by the Prussians in opposition to Russian interests. Catherine intervened on the pretext of defending the established order in Poland and fighting revolution. In 1793 both the Russians and Prussians took large slices of Polish territory; the Austrians did not participate in this partition. An attempted Polish revolution against the reduction of their state to a remnant dominated by foreigners was followed by the third and final eighteenth-century partition in 1795, by which Poland disappeared from the map. This time Austria joined the other two powers and obtained Krakow; Prussia got Warsaw, and Russia got Lithuania and other Baltic and east Polish lands.

The spectacular successes of Catherine meant the transfer to Russia of millions of people—Poles, Lithuanians, Belorussians, Tatars—who hated the Russians, and it left a legacy of instability and insecurity. It also meant that Russia had destroyed the useful buffers of the Polish and Tatar states, and now had common frontiers with its potential enemies, Prussia and Austria.

IV GEORGE III AND AMERICAN INDEPENDENCE

Though Catherine the Great failed to apply the ideas of the Age of Reason, her name often appears on lists of enlightened despots. Another name is at times added to the list—George III, king of Great Britain (1760-1820). "Farmer George" showed very little personal enlightenment beyond taking an interest in the agrarian revolution. In politics, however, he attempted a course that was a diluted form of enlightened despotism, or a reassertion of the monarch's authority. The first of the

Hanoverian monarchs born and raised in England, George III proposed to reassert some of the royal prerogatives that had lapsed under the first two Georges. He tried to wrest control of the House of Commons from the long-dominant Whig oligarchy and retain it through patronage and bribery.

Virtuous as a person and devoted to his family, George as a monarch was stubborn, short-sighted, and in the long run unsuccessful. It was easy for him at first to exploit the factional strife among the Whigs, maneuver William Pitt out of office in 1761, and make his friend and tutor, Lord Bute (1713-1792), the head of the cabinet. Bute and the king, however, found it hard to justify their failure to deprive France of its sugar-rich West Indian islands in the Peace of Paris, which brought the Seven Years' War to a conclusion. The Commons approved the treaty, but George dismissed Bute to appease the critics of British diplomacy.

The harshest criticism came from John Wilkes (1727-1797), a member of Commons, who dubbed the Peace of Paris "the peace of God, for it passeth all understanding." Wilkes's attack on the treaty in his paper, the *North Briton*, infuriated the king; bowing to royal anger, the Commons ordered the offending issue of the paper burned. Later, Wilkes ran for Parliament three separate times, and three times the Commons, under royal pressure, threw out his election. When Wilkes finally took his seat again in 1774, he was a popular hero, and riots occurred in defense of "Wilkes and Liberty."

A wiser king would have reconsidered his course, but George III did not relax his determination to manage both Parliament and cabinet. After seven years of short-lived, unstable ministries (1763-1770), George finally found a man to fill Bute's old role and do the king's bidding—Lord North, who headed the cabinet until 1782. Under North royal intervention in domestic politics at first stiffened, then wavered, and at length collapsed in the face of a revolt.

Background of the American Revolt, 1760-1776

The breach between the colonies and Britain first became serious after the Seven Years' War, when Britain began to retreat from the old policy of salutary neglect and to interfere more directly and frequently in colonial matters. By 1763 the colonies had become accustomed to regulating their own affairs, though the acts of their assemblies remained subject to the veto of royally appointed governors or of the king himself. The vast territories acquired in 1763 in Canada and west of the Allegheny Mountains brought Britain added opportunities for profitable exploitation and added responsibilities for government and defense. When an uprising of Indians under Pontiac (c 1720-1769) threatened frontier posts in the area of the Ohio Valley and the Great Lakes, colonial militias failed to take effective action, and British regulars were brought in. The continuing threat prompted the royal proclamation of October 1763 forbidding "all our loving subjects" to settle west of a line running along the summit of the Alleghenies. To His Majesty's "loving subjects" in the seaboard colonies, however, the proclamation seemed deliberately designed to exclude them from the riches of the West.

The colonies resented still more keenly the attempt by Parliament to raise revenue in North America. The British government had very strong arguments for increasing colonial taxes: the national debt had almost doubled during the Seven Years' War; the colonies' reluctance to recruit soldiers and raise taxes themselves had increased the cost of the war to British taxpayers; now the mother country faced continued expense in protecting the frontier. Surely the Americans would admit the reasonableness of the case for higher taxes, the members of Parliament thought.

That, however, was precisely what the Americans did not admit. The first of the new revenue measures, the Sugar Act of 1764, alarmed the merchants of the eastern seaboard because the customs officers actually undertook to collect duties on molasses, sugar, and other imports. Here was a departure from the comfortable laxity of salutary neglect. And here was a threat to the colonial economy, for the import duties had to be paid out of the colonies' meager supply of coins. The second revenue measure, the Stamp Act of 1765, imposed levies on a wide variety of items, including legal and commercial papers, liquor licenses, playing cards, dice, newspapers, calendars, and academic degrees. These duties further drained the supply of coins, which sank so low that some merchants claimed they faced bankruptcy.

The revenue measures touched off a major controversy. Indignant merchants in the New World boycotted all imports rather than pay the duties, and in October 1765 delegates from nine of the colonies met in New York City as the Stamp Act Congress. The Congress, complaining that the new duties had "a manifest tendency to subvert the rights and liberties of the colonists," proclaimed the principle that there was to be no taxation without representation. Britain surrendered on the practical issue, but did not yield on the principle. The appeals of London merchants, nearly ruined by the American boycott against British goods, brought about the repeal of the Stamp Act in 1765. In 1766, however, Parliament passed a Declaratory Act asserting that the king and Parliament could indeed make such laws affecting the colonies.

For the next decade Britain adhered firmly to the principles of the Declaratory Act, and colonial radicals just as firmly repeated their opposition to taxation without representation. Parliament again tried to raise revenue, this time by the Townshend duties (1767)—named after Charles Townshend (1725-1767), chancellor of the exchequer—on colonial imports of tea, paper, paint, and lead. Again the merchants of Philadelphia, New York, and Boston organized boycotts. In 1770 Lord North's cabinet withdrew the Townshend duties except for a three-penny tariff on a pound of tea, retained as a symbol of parliamentary authority over the colonies. Three years later the English East India Company attempted to sell surplus tea in North America, hoping to overcome American opposition to the hated duty by making the retail price of East India tea, duty included, far cheaper than that of Dutch tea smuggled by the colonists. The result was the Boston Tea Party. On December 16, 1773, to the cheers of spectators lining the waterfront, a group of Bostonians who had a large financial stake in smuggled tea disguised themselves as Indians, boarded three East India ships, and dumped chests of tea worth thousands of pounds into the harbor.

Britain answered defiance with force and the colonists met force with resistance. The Quebec Act (1774), incorporating the lands beyond the Alleghenies into Canada, bolted the door to the westward expansion of colonial frontiers. The Intolerable Acts (1774)—so called because taken together the colonists found them intolerable—closed the port of Boston to trade and suspended elections in Massachusetts. At Lexington and

THE STAMP ACT CONGRESS ASSERTS THE RIGHT OF LOCAL REPRESENTATION

The Stamp Act Congress met in New York City in October 1765 and declared:

That His Majesty's liege subjects in these colonies are entitled to all the inherent rights and liberties of his natural born subjects within the kingdom of Great Britain.

That it is inseparably essential to the freedom of a people, and the undoubted right of Englishmen, that no taxes be imposed on them but with their own consent, given personally or by their own representatives.

That the people of these colonies are not, and from their local circumstances cannot be, represented in the House of Commons in Great Britain.

That the only representatives of these colonies are persons chosen therein by themselves, and that no taxes ever have been, or can be constitutionally imposed on them, but by their respective legislatures.

Documents of American History, 9th ed., Henry S. Commager, ed. (Englewood Cliffs, N.J.: Prentice-Hall, Inc., 1973). p. 58.

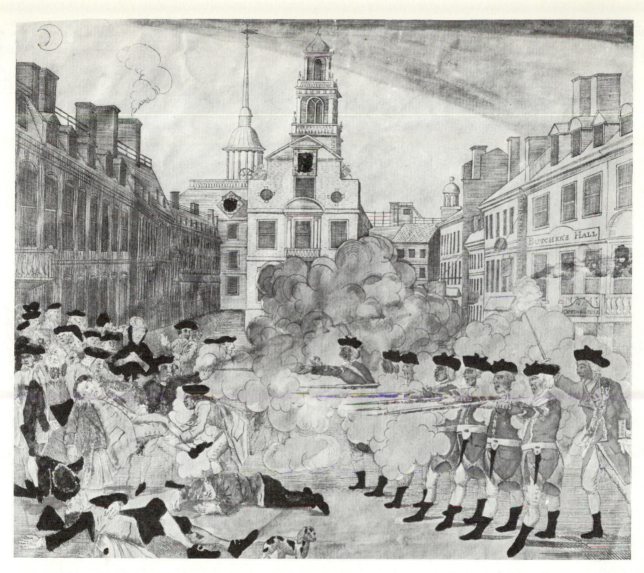

Paul Revere's drawing of "The Bloody Massacre" in Boston, which now hangs in the Metropolitan Museum of Art.

Concord in April 1775 the farmers of Massachusetts fired the opening shots of what became the War of Independence. At Philadelphia on July 4, 1776, delegates to a Continental Congress formally declared thirteen of the American mainland colonies independent of Great Britain.

Implications of the Revolution

For the mother country the American Revolution implied more than the secession of thirteen colonies. It involved Britain in a minor world war that jeopardized Britain's dominance abroad and weakened the power and prestige of King George III at home. The most crucial battle in North America came early in the war—the surrender at Saratoga in 1777 of the British forces under General John Burgoyne (1722-1792), who had been marching south from Montreal to drive a wedge

between New England and the other rebellious colonies. Burgoyne's surrender convinced the French that support of the American colonists would give them an excellent chance to avenge the humiliation of 1763. Entering the war in 1778, France soon gained the alliance of Spain and eventually secured the help or friendly neutrality of most other European states.

French intervention prepared the way for eventual victory. In the peace signed at Paris in 1783, Britain recognized the independence of the former colonies. To Spain she handed back Florida, which she had taken in 1763, and the strategic Mediterranean island of Minorca. But she kept Gibraltar, which the Spanish had also hoped to recover, and she ceded only minor territories to France.

During the early years of the war, the British public was intensely anti-American; but the temper of opinion changed as the strength of American resistance became

LOCKE AND THE AMERICAN REVOLUTION

The colonists claimed that they were only following the example set by the English in 1688 and defended by John Locke. The ideas of Locke and Newton were as well known and as much respected in North America as they were in Europe. They were the basis of the Declaration of Independence:

When in the course of human events, it becomes necessary for one people to dissolve the political bands which have connected them with another, and to assume among the Powers of the earth, the separate and equal station to which the Laws of Nature and of Nature's God entitle them, a decent respect to the opinions of mankind requires that they should declare the causes which impel them to the separation.

The opening paragraph of the Declaration expressed the concept of a world-machine ruled by the Laws of Nature; the next paragraph applied Locke's theory of contract and his justification of revolution to the colonies:

We hold these truths to be self-evident, that all men are created equal, that they are endowed by their Creator with certain unalienable Rights, that among these are Life, Liberty, and the pursuit of Happiness. That to secure these rights, Governments are instituted among Men, deriving their just powers from the consent of the governed. That whenever any Form of Government becomes destructive of these ends, it is the Right of the People to alter or to abolish it, and to institute new Government. . . .

evident. Instances of British mismanagement piled up, while most of Europe rallied to the rebellious colonies. By 1780 George III and his policies were so unpopular that the House of Commons passed a resolution declaring that "the influence of the Crown has increased, is increasing, and ought to be diminished."

And the influence of the Crown *was* diminished. In 1782 Lord North, who had been imploring the king for three years to accept his resignation, finally stepped down. In the next year the post of prime minister fell to William Pitt the Younger (1759-1806), son of the heroic Pitt of the Seven Years' War. Though only in his twenties, Pitt was a seasoned parliamentarian who was to head the cabinet for the next eighteen years. With the advent of Pitt, control of British politics shifted away from the king and back to professional politicians. George III briefly contemplated abdication and gradually resigned himself to the more passive role of constitutional monarch.

Support of the revolution in the colonies was by no means unanimous. Many well-to-do colonists, including southern planters and Pennsylvania Quakers, either backed the mother country or took a neutral position in the struggle; New York supplied more recruits to George III than to George Washington. Some of these Loyalists, or Tories, were to flee to Nova Scotia or Canada when independence became a fact. However, revolutionary sentiment ran particularly high in Virginia and New England and among social groups who had the habit of questioning established authority—many merchants, pioneers living on the frontier, and the numerous religious groups who had come to the New World in protest against the Old.

At the heart of the draft composed by the delegates to the Constitutional Convention at Philadelphia in 1787 was the separation of the executive, legislative, and judicial arms of government—a separation of powers which had been proposed by Locke and Montesquieu as a guarantee against tyranny. Each of the branches of government had the power to check the other two. Since these balancing devices were in part derived from Montesquieu, it may be argued that the future tensions between president and congress originated in the American adaptation of an eighteenth-century French misreading of British constitutional practice. The Founding Fathers of the American republic sought guidance not only from Montesquieu's *The Spirit of the Laws*, of course, but also from the constitutions of the thirteen original states and from English precedents. The first ten amendments to the United States Constitution (1791), guaranteeing freedom of religion, freedom of the press, and other basic liberties, were taken mainly from the English Bill of Rights of 1689.

V CHALLENGES TO THE ENLIGHTENMENT

Philosophes—and Philosophers

Elsewhere the Enlightenment seldom produced such concrete political results as it did in the United States. On the whole, the philosophes expected people to see reason when it was pointed out, to give up the habits of centuries, and to revise their behavior in accordance with natural law. But as Joseph II discovered to his sorrow, people often chose, instead, to cling to irrational customs and traditions. The rationalism of the Enlightenment tended to omit from its calculations the unpredictable complexities of human nature. A minor philosophe, the Abbé de Mably, propagandist for the American colonies in France, got at this central problem when he asked: "Is society, then a branch of physics?" Most of the philosophes and their followers believed that it was, and they applied to unpredictable people the mathematical methods used in the physical sciences. The Physiocrats, for example, tried to reduce the complexities of human economic activities to a few simple agricultural laws. Like the stars in their courses, humanity was assumed to fit neatly into the Newtonian world-machine.

A few outspoken critics, however, already disagreed. The Italian philosopher Giovanni Vico (1668-1744) published in 1725 the *Scienza Nuova* (New Science), which looked at the state not as a piece of machinery subject to natural laws but as an organism with a pattern of growth, maturity, and decay imposed by its own nature. Vico's views attracted little attention until the nineteenth century, when organic interpretations leaning on biological metaphors became popular.

A Scottish philosopher, David Hume (1711-1776), shared the philosophes' critical attitude toward existing institutions. He dramatized his opposition to mercantilism and his advocacy of free international trade by avowing that he prayed for the prosperity of other nations. Yet his profound skepticism and his corrosive common sense caused him to make short work of the philosophes' appeals to nature and reason. To Hume the laws of justice, for instance, were not unalterable but varied with circumstances and, in an emergency, might yield entirely to "stronger motives of necessity and self-preservation. Is it any crime, after a shipwreck, to seize whatever means or instrument of safety one can lay hold of, without regard to former limitations of property?"* Nor, Hume argued, could human conduct be analyzed "in the same manner that we discover by reason the truths of geometry or algebra."

*It appears evident that the ultimate ends of human actions can never, in any case, be accounted for by reason, but recommend themselves entirely to the sentiments and affections of mankind, without any dependance on the intellectual faculties. Ask a man why he uses exercise: he will answer, because he desires to keep his health. If you then enquire, why he desires health, he will readily reply, because sickness is painful. If you push your enquiries farther, and desire a reason why he hates pain, it is impossible he can ever give any.***

Immanuel Kant (1724-1804), who taught philosophy at the University of Königsberg in East Prussia, raised the debate to the level of metaphysics. While advocating many of the doctrines of the Enlightenment, Kant also believed in a higher reality reaching ultimately to God.

He called the eternal verities of the higher world *noumena* (from a Greek word meaning "things thought"), in contrast to the *phenomena* of the material world that are experienced through the senses. Knowledge of the noumenal realm, Kant believed, reached us through reason—reason, however, not as the Enlightenment used the term, not as common sense, but as intuition. The highest expression of the Kantian reason was the "categorical imperative." This was the moral law within the conscience implanted by God. Kant's redefinition of reason and his rehabilitation of conscience exemplified the growing philosophical reaction against the dominant rationalism of the Enlightenment. The popular reaction, on the other hand, was an evangelical revival.

Pietists and Methodists

The evangelical revival began with the German Pietists. The Pietists deplored both the growing concern of Lutherans with the external formalities of religion and the emphasis of deists upon natural law. They asserted that religion came from the heart, not the head, and that God was far more than a watchmaker, more than the remote creator of the world-machine. One of the chief

John Wesley was one of the most noted preachers of the age; he traveled widely and his dramatic sermons commanded large audiences. He is shown here preaching at Nottingham to an audience segregated by sex, as a nonconformist—that is, one not conforming to the tenets of the Church of England.

---

*D. Hume, *An Enquiry Concerning the Principles of Morals* (1751), ed. L. A. Selby-Bigge (Oxford: Clarendon Press, 1935), p. 186.

**Ibid., p. 293.

leaders of Pietism was the German Count Nikolaus Zinzendorf (1700-1760), founder of the Moravian Brethren, who set up a model community based on Christian principles. Moravian emigrants to America established a colony at Bethlehem, Pennsylvania, helping to create the reputation for thrift, hard work, and strict living enjoyed by the Pennsylvania Dutch (Dutch meaning *Deutsch*, German).

In England the example of Zinzendorf and other Pietists inspired John Wesley (1703-1791). Ordained in the Church of England, Wesley at first stressed the ritualistic aspects of religion, but then felt his own faith evaporating after the failure of his ministry to the new colony of Georgia (1736-1737), which was settled by prisoners forcibly transported from Britain. Pietism converted Wesley to the belief that he would find faith through inner conviction. For more than fifty years Wesley labored to share his discovery, preaching throughout the British Isles in churches, in the fields, at the pitheads of coal mines, and in jails. When Wesley died, his movement had already attracted more than a hundred thousand adherents, called Methodists because of their methodical devotion to piety and to plain dress and plain living. Though Wesley always considered himself an Anglican, the Methodists eventually set up a separate organization—a nonconformist Chapel in contrast to the established Church of England. The new sect won its following almost entirely among the lower and middle classes, among people who sought the religious excitement and consolation they did not find in deism or in the Church of England.

Although the beliefs of the Methodists diverged entirely from those of the Enlightenment, they too worked to improve the condition of society. Where the philosophes advocated public reform, the Methodists favored private charity; where the philosophes attacked the causes of evils, the Methodists accepted these evils as part of God's plan and sought to mitigate their symptoms. They began agitation against drunkenness, the trade in slaves, and the barbarous treatment of prisoners, the insane, and the sick. John Wesley established schools for coal miners' children and opened dispensaries for the poor. The Methodists' success derived in part from their social programs and in part from the magnetism of John Wesley and his talented associates. His brother Charles (1707-1788) composed more than 6,500 hymns, and in America Methodist missionaries flourished under the dynamic leadership of Francis Asbury (1745-1816). The number of colleges called Wesleyan and the number of churches and streets called Asbury testify to the significance of Methodism in North American social history.

Literature and the Arts

The literary landmarks of the century included both the classical writings of the French philosophes and the English Augustans, and new experiments in the depiction of realism and "sensibility," that is, the life of the emotions. In England the Augustan age of letters took its name from the claim that it boasted a group of talents comparable to those of Vergil, Horace, and Ovid, who had flourished under the emperor Augustus in Rome.

The greatest of the Augustans was Jonathan Swift (1667-1745), a pessimistic and sometimes despondent genius whose convictions about human depravity and folly went far beyond the moderation of the classical spirit. In his great work, *Gulliver's Travels* (1726), the broad and savage satirization of scientific endeavors and the startling contrast between the noble and reasonable horses, the Houyhnhnms, and the brutish and revolting human Yahoos were intended as attacks on easy assumptions of rational human behavior.

Much closer to the classical temper of the other Augustans and of the Enlightenment were two magnificent works from the latter part of the eighteenth century: Edward Gibbon's *History of the Decline and Fall of the Roman Empire* (1788) and Dr. Johnson's *Dictionary*. Gibbon (1737-1794) made history the excuse for a sustained Voltairean attack on Christian fanaticism. The lexicographer Samuel Johnson (1709-1784) expressed another concern of the age in the preface to his *Dictionary*:

> When I took the first survey of my undertaking, I found our speech copious without order and energetick without rules; wherever I turned my view, there was perplexity to be disentangled and confusion to be regulated; choice was to be made out of a boundless variety, without any established principle of selection; adulterations were to be detected, without a settled test of purity; and modes of expression to be rejected or received, without the suffrages of any writers of classical reputation or acknowledged authority.

Dr. Johnson succeeded admirably in his aim of becoming a Newton of the English language.

Meantime, the rapid development of the novel as a literary form greatly increased the popularity of more down-to-earth and emotional reading. Two of the earliest examples of the new type of fiction were by Daniel Defoe—*Robinson Crusoe* (1719) and *Moll Flanders* (1722)—both purporting to be autobiographies. They were in fact novels, and both were far removed from the refinements and elevated feelings of classicism. Realism was also evident in two celebrated midcentury novels: Tobias Smollet (1721-1771), in *Roderick Ransom* (1748), drew an authentic picture of life in the British navy, with its cruelty and hardship; in the next year Henry Fielding (1707-1754) published the first truly great social novel, *Tom Jones*, with convincing portraits of the toughs of London slums and the hard-riding, hard-drinking country squires.

Fielding also delighted in parodying the sentimental fiction of Samuel Richardson (1689-1761), who created three giant novels cast in the form of letters by the hero or heroine. An example was *Clarissa Harlowe* (1748), which described in 2,400 pages the misfortunes of Clarissa, whose lover was a scoundrel and whose greedy relatives were scheming to secure her property. Clarissa's laments were read aloud at family gatherings, and whenever some new disaster overwhelmed her, the

STORM AND STRESS: A ROMANTIC VIEW OF THE WORLD

A play gave its name to a whole movement by young German writers in the 1770s. The hero of *Sturm und Drang* ("Storm and Stress"), finding himself incapable of settling down, flees Europe to fight in the American Revolution:

Have been everything. Became a day-labourer to be something. Lived on the Alps, pastured goats, lay day and night under the boundless vault of the heavens, cooled by the winds, burning with an inner fire. Nowhere rest, nowhere repose. See, thus I am glutted by impulse and power, and work it out of me. I am going to take part in this campaign as a volunteer; there I can expand my soul, and if they do me the favour to shoot me down—all the better.

F. M. von Klinger, *Sturm und Drang* (1776), quoted in Kuno Francke, *A History of German Literature as Determined by Social Forces*, 4th ed. (New York: Henry Holt, 1931), p. 309.

---

members of the family might withdraw to their various rooms for solitary weeping. With all Richardson's excessive emotionalism and preachiness, his descriptions of passion and conscience carried such conviction to a growing reading public that his novels did much to establish the tradition of moral earnestness in English fiction and public discussion.

In France the novel of sensibility came into its own with the very popular *Manon Lescaut* (1731) of Antoine François Prévost, a tale that still deferred to the moderation of the classical spirit in relating the adventures of a young woman sent to the colony of Louisiana. Much closer to Richardson in style and tone was Rousseau's long novel about the conflict of love and duty, *La Nouvelle Héloïse* (1761), which ranked next to *Emile* as his most popular work before 1789. Because of the strict sexual morality Rousseau preached, the new Héloïse, unlike her medieval namesake in the affair with Abelard, died in time to avoid adultery. Increasingly readers were turning to such fiction, rather than to the Church, for guidance on moral and especially sexual questions.

In Germany the most important literary works were not the Frenchified writings favored by Frederick the Great but the dramas of Lessing and the outpourings of writers associated with the *Sturm und Drang* ("storm and stress") movement. Lessing (1729-1781) combined the sensibility of Richardson and French comedies with an enlightened devotion to common sense and toleration. In *Nathan the Wise* (1779) he dramatized the deistic belief that Judaism, Christianity, and Islam are all manifestations of a universal religion.

Yearning, frustration, and despair characterized the most successful work of the Sturm und Drang period, *The Sorrows of Young Werner* (1774), a short novel that made the youthful Johann Wolfgang von Goethe (1749-1832) famous overnight. Napoleon claimed to have read it seven times, weeping copiously on each occasion when the hero shoots himself because the woman he loves is already married. The book was widely translated, even into Chinese. The themes of self-pity and self-destruction, so at odds with the Enlightenment's cheerful belief in progress, were to be prominent in the romantic movement that swept over Europe at the close of the eighteenth century.

The classicism of the century more strongly affected its art. Gibbon's history, the researches of scholars and archaeologists, and the discovery in 1748 of the ruins of Roman Pompeii, well preserved under lava from Vesuvius, raised interest in antiquity to a high pitch. For the scholars of the Enlightenment, the balance and symmetry of Greek and Roman temples represented, in effect, the natural laws of building. Architects retreated somewhat from the theatricalism of the baroque style and adapted classical models with great artistry and variety.

In painting neoclassicism had an eminent spokesman in Sir Joshua Reynolds (1723-1792), president of the Royal Academy and the artistic arbiter of Georgian England. Beauty, Sir Joshua told the academy, rested "on the uniform, eternal, and immutable laws of nature," which could be "investigated by reason, and known by study." This was the golden age of English portraiture, the age of Reynolds, Thomas Gainsborough (1737-1788), George Romney (1734-1802), and Sir Thomas Lawrence (1769-1830). But it was also the age of William Hogarth (1697-1764), who cast aside the academic restraints of neoclassicism to do in art what Fielding did in the novel. Instead of catering to a few wealthy patrons, Hogarth created a mass market for the engravings that he turned out in thousands of copies, graphic sermons on the vices of London—*Marriage à la Mode*, *The Rake's Progress*, *The Harlot's Progress*, and *Gin Lane*.

The realism of Hogarth was not the only exception to the prevailing neoclassicism. In France the decorative style called *rococo* prevailed during the reign of Louis XV. It was even more fantastic than the baroque, but lighter, airier, more delicate and graceful, addicted to the use of motifs from bizarre rock formations and from shells. In painting the rococo was a return to Peter Paul Rubens's concern for flesh tones, combined with a light, quick touch that suggested improvisation. The style captured the social graces of the period, for it was elegant while superficial, elaborate while stereotyped, and, at its best, cheerfully playful while, at its worst, florid and self-conscious.

Meanwhile, three artistic fashions that were to figure significantly in the forthcoming age of romanticism were already catching on—the taste for the oriental, for the natural, and for the Gothic. Rococo interest in the exotic created a vogue for things Chinese—Chinese wallpaper, the "Chinese" furniture of Thomas Chippendale (c 1718-1779), and the delicate work in porcelain or painted scrolls that is called *chinoiserie*. Eighteenth-century gardens were bestrewn with pagodas and minarets, and gardeners abandoned Louis XIV's geometrical landscaping for the natural English garden. Even the dominance of neoclassical architecture was challenged. At Strawberry Hill near London, Horace Walpole (1717-1797), the son of Robert, endowed his house with an abundance of Gothic "gloomth"—battlements in the medieval style and "lean windows fattened with rich saints in painted glass."

But music was the queen of the arts in the eighteenth century, made so by a flood of great composers and by rapid advances in techniques and instruments. A German choirmaster, Johann Sebastian Bach (1685-1750), perfected the baroque techniques of the seventeenth century. He mastered the difficult art of the fugue, an intricate version of the round in which each voice begins the theme in turn while other voices repeat it and elaborate upon it. Bach composed fugues and a wealth of other material for the organ; for small orchestras he created the Brandenburg Concertos, in which successive instruments are given a chance to show off their potential. His sacred works included many cantatas, the Mass in B minor, and two gigantic choral settings of the Passion of Christ, according to Saint Matthew and to Saint John. His religious music, dramatic and deeply felt, was a world apart from the anticlericalism of the Enlightenment.

Bach's quiet provincial life contrasted sharply with the stormy international career of his countryman George Frederick Handel (1685-1759). After studying in Italy, Handel spent most of his adult years in London trying to run an opera company. He wrote more than forty operas and used themes from the Bible for *The Messiah* and other vigorous oratorios arranged for large choruses and directed at a mass audience. These elaborate works differed greatly from the simple earlier oratorios designed for the tiny Italian chapels called oratories.

Although Bach and Handel composed many instrumental suites and concertos, it was not until the second half of the century that orchestral music really came to the fore. New instruments were invented, notably the piano, which greatly extended the limited range of the older keyboard instrument, the harpsichord. New forms of instrumental music were also developed—the sonata and the symphony—largely the work of an Austrian, Franz Joseph Haydn (1732-1809). Haydn wrote more than fifty piano pieces in the form of the sonata, in which two contrasting themes are started in turn, developed, interwoven, repeated, and finally resolved in a *coda* (Italian for "tail"). Haydn then arranged the sonata for the orchestra, grafting it onto the Italian operatic overture to create the first movement of the symphony.

The operatic landmark of the early century was John Gay's (1685-1732) *Beggar's Opera* (1728), a tuneful work caricaturing the London underworld. Later, the German Christoph Gluck (1714-1787) revolutionized the technique of the tragic opera, making opera a well-constructed musical drama, not just a vehicle for the display of vocal skill. He kept to the old custom of taking heroes and heroines from classical mythology, but he tried to invest these figures with new vitality.

Opera, symphony, concerto, and chamber music all reached a climax in the works of another Austrian, Wolfgang Amadeus Mozart (1756-1791). As a boy Mozart was exploited by his father, who carted him all over Europe to show off his virtuosity on the harpsichord and his amazing talent for composition. Overworked throughout his life, and in his later years burdened with debts, Mozart died a pauper at the age of thirty-five. Yet his youthful precocity ripened steadily into mature genius, and his facility and versatility grew ever more prodigious.

Of all the arts, music came closest to resolving the great conflict in eighteenth-century culture—the tension between reason and emotion, between the abstractions of the Enlightenment and the flesh-and-blood realities of human existence. In other realms, however, as the century drew toward its close, the lines were drawn for the vigorous prosecution of the conflict. In thought, the ideas of Kant and Hume were challenging the optimistic rationalism of the philosophes. Romantic artists and writers were beginning to defy the defenders of classicism. And in politics, as the century ended, the European powers sought to thwart the supreme effort to realize on earth the Enlightenment's dream of reason, natural law, and progress—the French Revolution.

SUMMARY

French cultural leadership in the eighteenth century was preeminent. The key concepts of the eighteenth-century philosophes, or intellectuals, were reason, natural law, and progress. Philosophes, who expressed optimism in human abilities to apply reason, owed a debt to John Locke for their ideas on government and human psychology. Under the direction of Diderot, philosophes produced the thirty-three volume *Encyclopédie*, advancing views on progress and reason, exposing superstition and ignorance, and denouncing inequality in the light of natural law and science.

François Quesnay and Adam Smith summed up the economic principles of those philosophes known as Physiocrats. The Physiocrat's program of laissez faire, or let nature take its course, clashed with traditional mercantilist doctrines.

In justice and education, philosophes sought reforms based on reason and natural law. They championed tolerance and attacked superstition. The well-known philosophe Voltaire professed belief in God but rejected intolerance and furthered deist doctrine.

Like many other philosophes, Montesquieu in *The Spirit of the Laws* (1748) expressed admiration for British ideas on government. In *The Social Contract* (1762), Jean-Jacques Rousseau set out his theory of the general will to reconcile the needs of the individual and the institution of government. Rousseau's ideas have formed the basis of radical political doctrines ever since.

Enlightenment despots of the period displayed a mix of Enlightenment ideas and absolute monarchy. Frederick the Great (1740-1786) read the works of philosophes and promoted Physiocratic ideas in agriculture. But he rejected laissez faire ideas. In religion and social policy, he inaugurated a measure of tolerance and supported judicial reforms but did not move to reduce social inequality.

Joseph II of Austria, Charles III of Spain, as well as rulers in Portugal and Sweden instituted enlightened reforms. However, the successors of these enlightened rulers did not continue their programs.

In Russia, Catherine was an absolute autocrat who liked the idea of reform. She tried to codify laws based on enlightened ideas, reorganized local government, and introduced some municipal reform. But under Catherine, serfdom grew as the nobility gained increased authority over their serfs.

Czar Alexander I had absorbed enlightened ideas but was hesitant and accomplished little despite good intentions. Russia continued its expansionist foreign policy. Catherine annexed the Crimea and participated in the partitions of Poland.

In Britain, George III, stubborn and shortsighted, tried to reassert royal prerogative. After the Seven Years' War, a breach divided Britain and its North American colonies. Colonists' resistance to Britain's attempt to raise revenue in North America resulted in the issuing of the Declaration of Independence on July 4, 1776.

With French help, the colonists won their independence, which was recognized in 1783 at the Peace of Paris. The successful revolt of the American colonists weakened the power and prestige of George III. The Declaration of Independence appealed to the laws of nature described by Locke, while the new Constitution of the United States reflected Montequieu's ideas on the separation of powers.

Philosophes failed to take into account the complexities of human nature. Their appeals to the laws of nature and reason did not reform states. David Hume and Immanuel Kant reflected the philosophic reaction to rationalism. Popular reaction to the Enlightenment was expressed in German Pietism and the Methodist movement in England.

A new type of fiction appeared in the works of Daniel Defoe and the social novels of Henry Fielding. In Germany, Goethe's *Sorrows of Young Werther* embodied the frustration of the *Sturm und Drang* movement. Neoclassicism influenced the arts, but the age of romanticism was foreshadowed in the growing taste for the oriental, natural, and Gothic.

chapter eighteen

THE FRENCH REVOLUTION AND NAPOLEON

In France, as in Britain's North American colonies, a financial crisis preceded a revolution. There was not only a parallel but also a direct connection between the revolution of 1776 and that of 1789. French participation in the War of American Independence enormously increased an already excessive governmental debt, for support to the American colonists had cost two and a half times the normal annual revenue. Furthermore, the example of America fired the imagination of those French who were discontented. To them Benjamin Franklin, the immensely popular American envoy to France, was the very embodiment of the Enlightenment, and the new republic overseas promised to become the utopia of the philosophes. Turgot wrote of Franklin, "He stole thunder from the heavens and the scepter from tyrants." Yet it would be going too far to claim that the American Revolution actually *caused* the French Revolution; rather, it speeded up developments in France that had long been under way. And, just as the reasons for revolution were more deeply rooted and more complicated in France than in America, so the revolution itself was to be more violent and more sweeping.

The immediate cause of the great French Revolution, then, was financial. King Louis XVI vainly tried one expedient after another to avert bankruptcy and at last reluctantly summoned the Estates General, the central representative assembly that had not met for 125 years. Once assembled, the deputies of the nation initiated reforms that were to destroy the Old Regime in France. The more deep-rooted causes of the Revolution, however, also reached into France's society and economy and into her political and intellectual history. Behind the financial crisis of the 1780s lay many decades of fiscal mismanagement; the government had been moving toward insolvency since the last years of Louis XIV. The nobles and clergy, jealously guarding their traditional privileges, refused to pay the necessary share of the taxes. Resentment against inequitable taxation and inefficient government built steadily among the unprivileged—the peasantry, the workers, and above all, the bourgeoisie.

What translated bourgeois resentment into demands for reform and the potential for revolution was the program of change put forward by the philosophes. Apologists of the Old Regime argued that the revolution was essentially a plot hatched by a small minority who had been unsettled by the destructive ideas of the Enlightenment. Their center of operations was a network of six hundred Masonic lodges that had grown up in France since Freemasonry was first brought from England in the early eighteenth century. Modern scholarship has demonstrated the inadequacy of this conspiracy thesis. The Frenchmen who belonged to Masonic lodges did include many influential nobles and bourgeois, and the lodges themselves fostered enlightened ideas, but so did the provincial academies, the local discussion groups called *Sociétés de Pensée*, (Thought Societies), the *Encyclopédie*, and all the other writings of the philosophes. What happened in 1789 and subsequent years was not the result of a plot but was the end of a long drama in which every element of French society—king and noble, priest and Freemason, bourgeois and peasant, artisan and apprentice—played an important role.

I THE CAUSES OF REVOLUTION

France, the home of the Enlightenment, had not been ruled by an enlightened despot; except for suppressing the parlements, Louis XV had refused to take decisive steps to remedy the abuses associated with the Old Regime. What Louis XV would not do, his grandson and successor, Louis XVI (ruled 1774-1792), could not do. When the new king, aged nineteen, learned that his grandfather had died of smallpox, he is said to have exclaimed: "What a burden! At my age! And I have been taught nothing!" The emperor Joseph II, his brother-in-law, later commented that Louis treated petty intrigues with the greatest attention and neglected important affairs of state. Honest, earnest, and pious, but also clumsy, irresolute, and stubborn, Louis XVI was most at home hunting, eating, or tinkering with locks. He also labored under the severe handicap of a politically unfortunate marriage to a Hapsburg. Marie Antoinette (1755-1793), the youngest of the empress Maria Theresa's sixteen children, was badly educated, extravagant, and completely isolated in the artificial social world of Versailles. To French patriots she was a constant reminder of the ill-fated alliance with Austria during the Seven Years' War.

For want of a good administrator, the machinery of centralized royal absolutism was gradually falling apart. That it functioned at all could be credited to a few capable administrators, notably the intendants who ran so much of provincial France. The most efficient of the intendants, like the Physiocrat Turgot at the china and ceramics manufacturing center of Limoges, provided a sense of direction, but most could do little to slow the disintegration of the central government.

The whole legal and judicial system required reform. The law needed to be codified to eliminate obsolete medieval survivals and to end the overlapping of the two legal systems—Roman and feudal—that prevailed in France. The courts needed a thorough overhaul to make them swift, fair, and inexpensive. Many judges and lawyers purchased or inherited their government positions and regarded them as a means to private enrich-

Marie Antoinette's sense of regal isolation from the larger problems of the French nation is unintentionally illustrated by this flattering portrait of her and her children at Versailles. The artist, Elisabeth Vigée-Lebrun (1755-1842), was a leading court painter who emphasized the sense of grace so important to royalty at the time. After the Revolution she emigrated to Italy and then to Russia. The painting hangs today in the Musée de Versailles.

ment and elevation to the nobility of the robe. Louis XV had permitted his ministers to attack the strongholds of these vested interests, the parlements which existed in Paris and in a dozen provincial centers. One of the last acts of his reign had been their replacement by new high courts of royal appointees. One of the first moves taken by Louis XVI was to restore the parlements, a popular measure because many of the French viewed the parlements as a check on absolute monarchy, but they often failed to see that the parlements were also an obstacle to social and economic reform.

The Clergy and the Nobility

The first estate, the clergy, occupied a position of conspicuous importance in France. Though only .5 percent of the population, the clergy controlled about 15 percent of French lands. They performed many essential public functions—running schools, keeping records of vital statistics, and dispensing relief to the poor. The French church, however, was a house divided. The lower clergy came almost entirely from the third estate; humble, poorly paid, and generally hardworking, the priests resented the wealth and arrogance of their ecclesiastical superiors. The bishops and abbots held to the outlook of the noble class into which they had been born; although some of them took their duties seriously, others regarded clerical office simply as a way of securing a large private income. Dozens of prelates turned the administration of their bishoprics or monasteries over to subordinates, kept most of the revenue themselves, and lived in Paris or Versailles.

Taxpayers hated the tithe levied by the church, even though the full 10 percent implied by the word "tithe" was seldom demanded. They also complained about the church's exemption from taxation and about the meager size of the "free gift" voted by the clergy to the government instead of taxes. There were complex urban social services that cried out to be performed, and the church neither did them nor made it possible for them to be done. While the peasants remained moderately faithful Catholics and regarded the village priest, if not the bishop, with esteem and affection, the bourgeoisie increasingly accepted the anticlerical views of the philosophes.

Like the higher clergy, the wealthy nobles of the Old Regime, the second estate, were increasingly unpopular. Although less than 2 percent of the population, they held

Jacques Louis David (1748-1825) sketched the queen on her way to the guillotine. This simple drawing, in sharp contrast to the serenity of Marie Antoinette's official portrait, was made as her tumbril passed the artist's window.

about 20 percent of the land. They had virtual exemption from taxation and monopolized army commissions and appointments to high ecclesiastical office. The French aristocracy, however, was not a single social unit but a series of differing groups. At the top were the hereditary nobles—a few descended from royalty or from feudal lords of the Middle Ages, but more from families ennobled within the past two or three centuries. These "nobles of the sword" tended to view most of their countrymen, including the lesser nobility, as vulgar upstarts. They dreamed of the day when they might rule France again, as the feudal nobles had ruled in the Middle Ages. Many of them, clustered at Versailles, neglected their duties as the first landlords of the realm.

Below the nobility of the sword came the "nobility of the robe," including the justices of the parlements and other courts and a host of other officials. The nobles of the robe, or their ancestors, had originally become nobles by buying their offices. But since these offices were then handed down from father to son, the mercenary origins of their status had become somewhat obscured over time. By the late eighteenth century there was often little practical distinction between the nobility of the robe and of the sword; marriages between members of the two groups were common. On the whole, the nobles of the robe were, in fact, richer than the nobles of the sword, and their firm hold on key governmental positions gave them more power and influence. The ablest and most tenacious defenders of special privilege in the dying years of the Old Regime were the rich judges of parlement, not the elegant and ineffectual courtiers of Versailles.

Many noblemen, however, had little wealth, power, or glamor. They belonged to the lowest level of French aristocracy—the *hobereaux*, or the "little falcons." Hard pinched by rising prices, they felt trapped on their country estates, since they could not afford the expensive pleasures of the court. In an effort to conserve at least part of their traditional status, almost all of the hobereaux insisted on the meticulous collection of the surviving feudal and manorial dues from the peasantry. Their search through old documents to justify levies sometimes long forgotten earned them the abiding hatred of the peasants and prepared the way for the document burning that occurred during the Revolution.

Of course, not every noble was a selfish defender of the status quo. Some hobereaux drifted down the social ladder to become simple farmers. Some nobles of the robe, attracted by the opportunities for profit, took part in successful and innovative business ventures. Even the loftiest noble families produced enlightened spirits, like the marquis de Lafayette, who returned from the American War of Independence to champion reform at home.

The Third Estate

The first two estates included only a small fraction of the French nation; over 97 percent of the population fell within the third estate. Most of these commoners were peasants, whose status was in some respects more favorable in France than anywhere else in Europe. Serfdom, still prevalent in central and eastern Europe, had disappeared almost entirely except in Lorraine and the Franche-Comté, both relatively recent annexations. While enclosures were gradually pushing small farmers off the land in England, small peasant holdings existed by the millions in France; three out of every four adult peasants probably held some land.

Nevertheless, rural misery was widespread. The peasants did not understand the many wars in which France had been engaged, which had led to heavier taxation, but they could see how the nobility and clergy lived lavishly while they themselves existed at the subsistence level. This was especially so when, faced by rapid population growth, the peasantry had little or no surplus agricultural produce to sell. Thus they could not weather the periodic crises that arose from poor harvests or from rural unemployment, as when the textile spinners fell into serious decline in the face of more efficient production elsewhere. Although the degree of agrarian distress varied greatly from province to province, the overall picture was bleak. Part of the trouble lay with such economic fundamentals as backward methods of farming, the shortage of land, and overpopulation. The efficient techniques of the agricultural revolution evident elsewhere made little headway in France before 1789. Vast areas were not cultivated at all or lay fallow every second or third year in accordance with medieval practice. Restrictions on the free movement of grain within France, traditionally imposed to keep local flour for local consumption, promoted hoarding and speculation and increased the danger of local famines if a crop failed. Landless peasants drifted to the cities or turned to brigandage, and the constantly increasing rural population simply could not find steady employment or a decent livelihood.

Financially the peasants saw themselves as in decline. Inflation hurt them; the upward trend of prices in France throughout the eighteenth century brought prosperity to many urban merchants and manufacturers, but most farmers found that the prices of the products they sold rose less swiftly than those of the goods they had to buy. Moreover, the peasants owed a heavy burden of taxes and other obligations—the tithe to the church, feudal and manorial dues to the nobility, and to the state a land tax, an income tax, a poll tax, and other duties, of which the most widely detested was the *gabelle*, the obligatory purchase of salt from government agents, usually at an exorbitant price. Unemployment and poverty had created a revolutionary temper among the peasants. But they did not demand a change in the form of government; they were ignorant of the reform program of the Enlightenment. They most emphatically wanted more land, if need be at the expense of the clergy and the nobility; they wanted an end to obsolete manorial dues; and they wanted relief from a system of taxation that bore hardest upon those who could least afford to pay.

The other members of the third estate—the urban

workers and the bourgeoisie—were also increasingly alienated, though for a time less intensely so. Nearly every major city was faced with discontented wage earners and apprentices who were seriously disadvantaged by the pinch of rising prices. This was especially true of day laborers, who were not allowed to organize unions and who turned to badly led strikes, particularly in the textile industry, where France's first factory system was just beginning. Apprentices and journeymen found their way blocked along the normal if slow path to master carpenter, bookbinder, or ribbon weaver, and these groups as well as stocking-frame weavers, journeymen hatters, dyers, and workers in the building trades resorted to strikes. In the cities, and especially in Paris, a displaced population of floating, seldom-employed workers was growing. The working classes, who had seen themselves as divided into distinct groups, were now beginning to think of their problems in common despite their specialized trades or the gap between semiskilled, manual, and technically trained workers. In time this group, known as the *sans-culottes* ("those without knee breeches"), whether men (such as the furniture makers and masons) or women (such as the *poissardes*, or fishwives), were united by a common fear that they could not buy bread and would starve.

However, it was the bourgeoisie that focused these discontents and ultimately provided the leadership. The bourgeoisie included people of varied resources and interests—rich merchants and bankers in the cities, storekeepers and lawyers in country towns and villages, doctors and other professionals, and thousands upon thousands of crafts workers running their own little businesses. Implacable hostility to the privileged estates and warm receptiveness to the propaganda of the philosophes cemented this sprawling middle class into a political force. The bourgeoisie suffered fewer hardships than the peasants and workers did, but they resented the abuses of the Old Regime perhaps even more keenly. Though they paid a smaller proportion of their incomes in taxes, they violently denounced the inequality of tax assessments. While profiting by the rise in prices and able to buy up some landed estates, the wealthier and more enterprising business people complained of guild regulations and other restrictions on free commercial activity. They found it galling to be snubbed by the nobility, treated as second-class subjects by the monarchy, and excluded from posts of power in government, church, and army. Wealthier, better educated, and more articulate than the peasants and wage earners, the middle class at first took the lead in formulating the grievances of the entire third estate. These grievances were compiled in statements called *cahiers* and were submitted to the Estates General in 1789.

The Financial Emergency, 1794-1788

The chronic financial difficulties of the French monarchy strengthened the hand of the middle-class reformers. The economic crisis was severe and nearly universal; the only sector of the economy not struck by panic was overseas trade, which benefited only a few

This illustration from Diderot's *Encyclopédie* illustrates how bread, the staple food for most of the population, was made in eighteenth-century France. The dough was kneaded in a wooden trough, weighed, formed into loaves, and baked in an oven.

THOMAS JEFFERSON IS AN EYEWITNESS TO THE BEGINNING OF THE FRENCH REVOLUTION

The Réveillon riot in Paris in April 1789 was witnessed by Thomas Jefferson, then the American minister to France:

The Fauxbourg St. Antoine is a quarter of the city inhabited entirely by the class of day-laborers and journeymen in every line. A rumor was spread among them that a great paper manufacturer . . . had proposed . . . that their wages should be lowered to 15 *sous* a day [three quarters of a *livre* or perhaps fifty cents in 1980s currency]. . . . They flew to his house in vast numbers, destroyed everything in it, and in his magazines and workshops, without secreting however a pin's worth to themselves, and were continuing this work of devastation when the regular troops were called in. Admonitions being disregarded, they were of necessity fired on, and a regular action ensued, in which about 100 of them were killed, before the rest would disperse.

Autobiography of Thomas Jefferson, ed. P.L. Ford (New York: G.P. Putnam, 1914), pp. 133-34.

---

port cities and profiteers. The government debt, already large at the accession of Louis XVI, tripled between 1774 and 1789. The budget for 1788 had to commit half the total estimated revenues to interest payments on debts already contracted; it also showed an alarming deficit in the face of continued high expenditures to support the court. Turgot had forecast the crisis twelve years before, if the trend toward deficits was not ended, but despite innovative and sometimes drastic measures that showed some promise of success, Turgot was dismissed through the influence of the vested interests in the Old Regime, seconded by Marie Antoinette. In 1786 the bankers, disturbed by the movement of prices and convinced of governmental mismanagement, refused to make new advances to the French government, which was caught between the third estate's demands for tax relief and the other estates' refusal to yield their fiscal exemptions. The monarchy had temporized and borrowed until it could afford neither fresh delays nor new loans. The finance minister proposed to meet the crisis by reviving Turgot's reforms. Thus, in the hope of persuading the first two estates to consent to heavier taxation, the Assembly of Notables was convened in 1787. But the Notables declined to be persuaded, whereupon the king dissolved them and dismissed his minister.

The new chief minister was an enlightened archbishop who made new attempts at reform. Late in 1787 an Edict of Toleration restored the civil rights of French Protestants, to the annoyance of the clergy. Serious trouble arose in 1788 when the king tried to levy a uniform tax on all landed property without regard to the social status of the holder. The clergy replied by reducing their "free gift" for the year to one-sixth the usual amount, and the Parlement of Paris declared the new tax law illegal and asserted that only the nation as a whole assembled in the Estates General could make so sweeping a change. The king and his minister next resorted to Louis XV's expedient of shifting judicial authority from the parlements to new royal appellate courts. Again,

however, there was a storm of disapproval and an outbreak of rioting, led by both aristocrats and bourgeois in several provincial cities. The king retreated, dismissed his minister, and announced that the Estates General would be summoned for the spring of 1789.

The Estates General, 1789

In summoning the Estates General Louis XVI revived a half-forgotten institution that he thought was unlikely to initiate drastic social and economic reforms. The three estates, despite their immense variation in size, had customarily received equal representation and equal voting power, so that the two privileged orders could be expected to outvote the commoners.

The Estates General of 1789, however, met under unique circumstances. Its election and subsequent meetings took place during an economic crisis marked by a continued influx of unemployed peasants into the cities, especially Paris, and by continued inflation, with prices rising at twice the rate of wages. There was also severe unemployment in some textile centers as a result of the treaty of 1786 with England, which increased British imports of French wines and brandies in return for eliminating French barriers to importing cheaper English textiles and hats.

A final difficulty was the weather. Hail and drought had reduced the wheat harvest in 1788, and the winter of 1788-1789 was so bitter that the Seine froze over at Paris, blocking arrivals of grain and flour by barge, the usual way of shipping bulky goods. Half starved and half frozen, Parisians huddled around bonfires provided by the municipal government. By the spring of 1789 the price of bread had almost doubled—a very serious matter, for bread was the mainstay of the diet, and workers normally spent almost half their wages on bread for their families. Now they faced the prospect of having to lay out almost all their wages for bread alone.

France had survived bad weather and poor harvests many times in the past without experiencing revolution;

this time, however, the economic hardships were the last straw. Starving peasants begged, borrowed, and stole, poaching on the hunting preserves of the great lords and attacking their game wardens. The concern over meat and bread in Paris erupted in a riot in April 1789 at the establishment of Réveillon, a wealthy wallpaper manufacturer. The riot, a major challenge to public order occurring only a week before the meeting of the Estates General, increased the deputies' sense of urgency.

The method of electing the deputies aided the champions of reform. The suffrage was wide, especially in rural areas, where almost all males twenty-five years of age or older met the additional requirement of having their names on the tax rolls. Probably more French men voted in 1789 than in any subsequent election or referendum during the revolutionary era. In each district of France the third estate made its choice directly by choosing electors at a public meeting who later selected a deputy. Since this procedure greatly favored the articulate over the inarticulate, middle-class lawyers and government administrators won control of the commoners' deputation. The reforming deputies of the third estate found some sympathizers in the second estate and many more in the first, where the discontented poorer priests had a large delegation. Moreover, in a departure from precedent, the king agreed with his adviser's plan to "double the third," giving it as many deputies as the other two estates combined to forestall dominance by the aristocracy. Altogether, a majority of the deputies stood prepared to demand drastic changes in the practices of the Old Regime.

In all past meetings of the Estates General, each estate (or order) had deliberated separately, with the consent of two estates and of the Crown required to pass a measure. In 1789 the king and privileged orders favored retaining this "vote by order," but the third estate demanded "vote by head," with the deputies from all the orders deliberating together, each deputy having a single vote, at least on tax questions. "What is the third estate?" asked the abbé Emmanuel Siéyès (1748-1836) in an influential pamphlet of the same name. "Everything," he answered.

> *If votes were taken by order, five million citizens will not be able to decide anything for the general interest, because it will not please a couple of hundred thousand privileged individuals. The will of a single individual will veto and destroy the will of more than a hundred people.**

Siéyès continued, "What has [the third estate] been in the political order? Nothing. What does it demand? To become something."

The question of procedure became crucial after the Estates General convened on May 5, 1789, at Versailles. Siéyès, a priest, and Count Honoré Mirabeau (1749-1791), a renegade nobleman, both deputies of the third estate, led the campaign for counting votes by head. On June 17 the assemblage cut through the procedural impasse by accepting Siéyès's invitation to proclaim itself a National Assembly. The third estate invited the deputies of the other two estates to join its sessions; a majority of the clerical deputies, mainly parish priests, accepted, but the nobility, leaders of the early phases of the reform movement, refused. When the king barred the commoners from their usual meeting place, the deputies of the third estate and their clerical sympathizers assembled at an indoor tennis court nearby. There, on June 20, they swore never to disband until they had given France a constitution. Louis replied to the Tennis Court Oath by commanding each estate to resume its separate deliberations. The third estate and some deputies of the first disobeyed. Louis, vacillating as ever, gave in to the reformers, especially when he realized that the royal troops were unreliable. On June 27 he directed the noble and clerical deputies to join the new National Assembly. The nation, through its representatives, had successfully challenged the king and the vested interests. The Estates General was dead, and in its place sat the National Assembly, pledged to reform French society and give the nation a constitution. The Revolution had begun.

Even now historians disagree on why the Revolution occurred as it did. One school of thought sees a series of class revolts, begun by the aristocracy and continued by a separate bourgeois revolution, culminating in a popular revolution in the cities and finally a revolution of the peasants—that is, a revolution begun by a minority class for limited ends that was transformed, consciously or unconsciously, into a far-reaching revolution of an entire people. Another school sees these classes as all playing a role in the growing momentum of revolutionary fervor, but never agreeing on common goals, so that in the end the French Revolution was a series of contests between class interests. Still other schools argue that the only "true" revolution was that which centered on the demands of a particular group: the bourgeoisie, the sansculottes, the beggars of the countryside, and so forth.

In short, the French Revolution is a fine example of the tendency of some historians to interpret the past in the light of how they view the present and their hopes for the future. Many problems about the Revolution are yet to be resolved. Was the initial goal simply a constitutional monarchy? Were the various stages of the Revolution manipulated by specific leaders, or were they largely spontaneous and broadly based? Was manipulation, where it occurred, necessarily for selfish ends? What were the king's motives at various stages? Was there even a bourgeoisie that could mount a bourgeois revolt? In what fundamental ways did the Revolution differ in Brittany, in Provence, in Strasbourg, in Lyon—that is, in specific regions and specific cities? And in each, who were "the crowd"? What movements in prices disrupted stability and challenged security? What steps might have been taken to forestall a movement, or movements, which in time appeared to become unnegotiable and irrepressible? Few develop-

---

*Emmanuel Siéyès, *Qu'est-ce Que le Tiers Etat?*, ed. Edme Champion (Paris: Sociétié de l'histoire de la révolution française, 1888), p. 82. Our translation.

In this painting David combined tension, emotion, classical composition, and historical accuracy compellingly. Here he shows members of estates that had previously opposed each other symbolically joining hands as equals. The populace throngs the window spaces as the presiding officer, Jean Sylvain Bailly (1736-1793), leads the estates in taking the Tennis Court Oath. Soon after, Bailly became mayor of revolutionary Paris.

ments in modern history present so many challenges to the historian's ability to generalize, and as yet there is no agreement on many fundamental issues relating to the causes and significance of the Revolution.

II THE DISSOLUTION OF THE MONARCHY

Popular Uprisings, July-October 1789

The National Assembly had barely settled down to work when a new wave of rioting swept over France, further undermining the position of the king. Economic difficulties grew more severe in the summer of 1789.

Unemployment increased, and bread seemed likely to remain scarce and expensive, at least until after the harvest. Meanwhile, the commoners feared that the king and the privileged orders might attempt a counter-revolution. Large concentrations of troops appeared in the Paris area early in July—to preserve order and protect the National Assembly, the king asserted. But the Parisians suspected that Louis was planning the forcible dissolution of the Assembly. Suspicion deepened into conviction after Louis dismissed Jacques Necker (1732-1804), a popular Swiss banker who had been serving as the chief royal adviser.

Reaction to Necker's dismissal was immediate. On July 12 and 13 the Parisian electors formed a new municipal government and a new militia, the National Guard, both loyal to the National Assembly. Paris was forging the weapons that made it the leader of the

Revolution. Crowds were roaming the streets, demanding cheaper bread and parading busts of Necker draped in black. On July 14 they broke into government buildings in search of arms. They found one arsenal in the Invalides, the great military hospital, and they hoped to find another in the Bastille, a fortress-prison in the eastern part of the city.

An armed group several hundred strong stormed the Bastille, killing part of the garrison and suffering many casualties themselves. The legend, cherished by defenders of the Old Regime, that participants in the assault were simply "rabble" or a "mob" is untrue. An official list of participants compiled some time after the event showed that most were neighborhood merchants and artisans, especially woodworkers. The fall of the Bastille, though of little practical value, was of enormous symbolic significance. Though there were only seven prisoners to be released, all of whom deserved to be in prison, an aroused people had demonstrated what it could accomplish. The capture and subsequent demolition of the Bastille did much to ensure the destruction of the Old Regime, as rioting spread throughout France in July 1789. Thus the Fourteenth of July became the great French national holiday, the counterpart of the American Fourth of July, marking the moment when perhaps more than a quarter-million Parisians were united and under arms.

Parts of the countryside, meantime, were experiencing the Great Fear, an extraordinary attack of mass delusion. From village to village word spread that "brigands" were coming, aristocratic hirelings who would destroy the now ripe crops and force the National Assembly to preserve the status quo. There were in fact no bands of brigands, only an occasional starving farmhand trying to steal food and, at certain points, foraging national guardsmen. But the peasants in several districts went berserk, grabbing hoes and pitchforks, anything resembling a weapon, and driving many of the nobility to flight and emigration. They attacked châteaux and broke into other buildings that might house a hoard of grain or the hated documents justifying collection of manorial dues. Some nobles voluntarily gave the peasants what they wanted; others saw their barns and archives burnt; a few were lynched. The Great Fear, beginning as a psychological aberration among the politically gullible, ended as an uprising of the peasantry against its traditional oppressors.

The October Days, the last crisis of a tumultuous year, again demonstrated the impotence of Louis XVI and the power of his aroused subjects. The harvest of 1789 had been good, but a drought crippled the operation of watermills for grinding flour from the wheat. Thus, as autumn drew on, Parisians still lined up for bread and still looked suspiciously at the royal troops stationed near their city. Rumors of the queen's behavior at Versailles further incensed them: Marie Antoinette made a dramatic appearance at a banquet of royal officers, clutching the heir to the throne in her arms, striking the pose that her mother, Maria Theresa, had employed to

win the support of the Hungarians in the 1740s. And on hearing that the people had no bread, she was reported to have remarked callously, "Let them eat cake." This story was false, but it was repeated in the lively new Paris papers that delighted in denouncing the queen.

The climax came on October 5, when an array of determined marketwomen and fishwives, neatly dressed milliners, and even middle-class "ladies with hats" marched from Paris to Versailles in the rain to demand bread. They disrupted the National Assembly and penetrated the palace, where they might have lynched Marie Antoinette if she had not taken refuge with the king. The next day the women marched back to Paris, escorting the royal family, who took up residence in the Tuileries Palace. More important, the National Assembly also moved to Paris. Thus Paris, the most revolutionary place in France, had captured both the head of the Old Regime and the herald of the new.

Forging a New Regime

The outlines of the new regime were already starting to take shape before the October Days. The Great Fear prompted the National Assembly to abolish in law what the peasants were destroying in fact. On the evening of August 4, 1789, the deputies voted that taxation would be paid by all inhabitants of the kingdom in proportion to their revenues, and that public expenses would be borne equally by all. The clergy also gave up tithes, and the liberal minority of the second estate surrendered the nobility's game preserves and manorial dues and courts. The Assembly abolished the remnants of serfdom, forbade the sale of justice or of judicial office, and decreed that "all citizens, without distinction of birth, can be admitted to all ecclesiastical, civil, and military posts and dignities." The Old Regime was dead.

Three weeks later, on August 26, the National Assembly formulated the Declaration of the Rights of Man. "Men are born and remain free and equal in rights," it asserted. "These rights are liberty, property, security, and resistance to oppression." It called property "an inviolable and sacred right," and liberty "the exercise of

This contemporary work shows the march of the fishwives to Versailles in October of 1789.

the natural rights of each man" within the limits "determined by law." "Law," the Declaration stated, "is the expression of the general will. All citizens have the right to take part, in person or by their representatives, in its formation." Further, "Any society in which the guarantee of rights is not assured or the separation of powers not determined has no constitution."*

The Declaration of the Rights of Man mirrored the economic and political attitudes of the middle class, though it was also attractive to many aristocrats, including the marquis de Lafayette. It insisted on the sanctity of property, and it proclaimed that "social distinctions may be based only on usefulness," thus implying that some social distinctions were to be expected. It committed the French to the creed of constitutional liberalism affirmed by the English in 1688-1689 and by the Americans in 1776, and it incorporated the key phrases of the philosophes: natural rights, general will, and separation of powers. The National Assembly made a resounding statement of the ideals of the Enlightenment; yet, as the subsequent history of the Revolution demonstrated, it found no formula by which to translate these ideals into practice.

The economic legislation of the National Assembly provided a case in point. Belief in the theory of equal taxation did not solve urgent financial problems, for the new and just land tax imposed by the deputies could not be collected. Tax collectors had vanished in the general liquidation of the Old Regime, and peasants now assumed that they owed the government nothing. Once again, the French state borrowed until its credit was exhausted, and then, in desperation, the National Assembly ordered the confiscation of church lands (November 1789). "The wealth of the clergy is at the disposition of the nation," it declared, explaining that ecclesiastical lands fell outside the bounds of "inviolable" property as defined in the Declaration of the Rights of Man because they belonged to an institution and not to private persons.

The government thus acquired assets worth at least two billion livres. On the basis of this collateral it issued *assignats*, paper notes used to pay the government's debts, which temporarily eased the financial crisis. Unfortunately, the Revolution repeated the mistake of John Law at the time of the Mississippi Bubble; it did not know when to stop. As the state sold parcels of confiscated land—that is, as it reduced the collateral securing its paper money—it was expected to destroy the same amount of assignats. But the temptation not to reduce the number of assignats proved too great to resist, and inflation resulted. The assignats, progressively losing their solid backing, depreciated until in 1795 they were worth less than 5 percent of their face value.

The state sold at auction the property seized from the Church and from aristocratic *émigrés* (those who had left the country). Some peasants profited by the opportu-

*Georges Lefèbvre, *The Coming of the French Revolution*, trans. R.R. Palmer (Princeton: Princeton University Press, 1976), pp. 221-23.

nity to enlarge their holdings, and many bourgeois also bought up land, sometimes as a short-term speculation. The poor and landless, however, gained nothing, since they could not afford to buy, and the National Assembly made no move to help them. Following laissez-faire doctrines, the Assembly abolished the guilds and the tariffs and tolls on trade within France. And deeming the few simple organizations of labor unnatural restrictions on economic freedom, it abolished them too. In June 1791, after an outbreak of strikes, it passed a law banning both strikes and labor unions.

Reforming the Church

Since the suppression of tithes and the seizure of ecclesiastical property deprived the church of its revenue, the National Assembly agreed to finance ecclesiastical salaries. The new arrangement made the French church subject to constant government regulation. Few difficulties arose from the Assembly's prohibition of monastic vows or from the liquidation of some monasteries and convents, since many of these establishments were already far gone in decay, but an uproar arose over legislation altering the status of the secular clergy.

The Civil Constitution of the Clergy (June 1790) redrew the ecclesiastical map of France. It reduced the number of bishoprics by more than a third, making the remaining dioceses correspond to new civil administrative units. It transformed bishops and priests into civil officials, paid by the state and elected by the population of the diocese or parish. Since the right to vote in these elections was extended to some non-Catholics as well as Catholics, the measure was a significant step in granting toleration to Protestants and Jews. A new bishop was required to take an oath of loyalty to the state, and the Civil Constitution stipulated that he might not apply to the pope for confirmation, though he might write to him as the Visible Head of the Universal Church.

These provisions stripped the pope of effective authority over the French clergy and ran counter to the tradition of the Roman church as an independent ecclesiastical monarchy. Naturally the pope denounced the Civil Constitution. When the National Assembly then required that every member of the French clergy take a special oath supporting the Civil Constitution, only a few bishops and fewer than half the priests complied. Thus a breach was opened between the leaders of the Revolution and a large segment of the population. From Louis XVI down to humble peasants, Catholics rallied to the non-juring clergy, as those who refused the special oath were termed. The Civil Constitution of the Clergy, supplying an issue for rebellion, was thus the first great blunder of the Revolution.

The Constitution of 1791

The major undertaking of the National Assembly was the Constitution of 1791. To replace the bewildering complex of provincial units that had existed under the

Old Regime, the assembly devised an orderly system of local government in the spirit of the Enlightenment. It divided the territory of France into eighty-three departments of approximately equal size; each department was small enough for its chief town to be within a day's journey of outlying towns. The departments were subdivided into *arrondissements*, or districts, and the districts into communes—that is, municipalities. In the communes and departments, elected councils and officials enjoyed considerable self-government. Thus the administration of the new France was meant to be far more decentralized than that of the Old Regime.

As for the central government, the principle of the separation of powers was applied. The Constitution established an independent, elected judiciary to replace the parlements and other courts of the Old Regime. It vested legislative authority in a single elected chamber. Although the king still headed the executive branch, his actions now required the approval of his ministers. The ministers, in turn, were responsible only to the king and not to the legislature, as they generally are in a parliamentary or cabinet government. Although the king received the power of veto, it was only a suspensive veto that could block legislation for a maximum of four years. Louis XVI, no longer the absolute king of France, acquired the new constitutional title "King of the French," as if to show that he was no longer the sole proprietor of the real estate called France and now had French citizens to reckon with. The new constitution undertook to give France a uniform code of law (an undertaking completed by Napoleon), declared marriage a civil contract rather than a religious sacrament, and promised free public education.

While the Constitution of 1791 went a long way toward popular government, implementing slogans of popular sovereignty and social equality, it stopped well short of full democracy. It created two classes of citizens—active and passive—and limited the right of voting to those citizens who annually paid in taxes an amount equal to at least three days' wages for unskilled labor in their locality. The passive citizens, numbering about a third of the male population, enjoyed the full protection of the law but did not receive the vote. Moreover, the new legislature was chosen by indirect election. Active citizens voted for electors, who were required to be men of substantial wealth and who ultimately elected the deputies. It was still assumed that property determined political wisdom.

But the majority in the National Assembly suffered a fate often experienced by political moderates in a revolution: they were squeezed out by extremists. Despite moderate intentions, the majority were driven to enact some drastic legislation, notably the Civil Constitution of the Clergy, which weakened their own position. And they failed to develop an effective party organization in the face of the radical minority, called Jacobins. The Jacobins—so named because they belonged to the Society of the Friends of the Constitution, which maintained its Paris headquarters in a former Jacobin (Dominican) monastery—wanted to abolish the monarchy and to set up a republic based on universal suffrage. Their network of political clubs, which extended throughout the provinces, was the only nationwide party organization in France. Almost everywhere, Jacobins captured control of the new department and commune councils. In local elections, as in the elections of the Estates General, an able and determined minority soon prevailed over a politically inexperienced majority.

The defenders of the Old Regime unwittingly helped the Jacobins. After the summer of 1789, alarmed prelates and nobles, including the king's brothers, fled France, leaving behind more rich estates to be confiscated. Many émigrés gathered in the German Rhineland to intrigue for Austrian and Russian support of a counterrevolution. The king's misgivings about the Civil Constitution of the Clergy prompted his disastrous attempt to join the émigrés on the Franco-German frontier. In June 1791, three months before the completion of the new constitution, Louis and Marie Antoinette left the Tuileries disguised as a valet and governess. But a local official along the route recognized Louis; the alarm was sent ahead, and a detachment of troops forced the royal party to make a hot, dusty, dispirited journey back to Paris. After the abortive flight, the revolutionaries viewed Louis XVI as a potential traitor and kept him closely guarded in the Tuileries. Thus the experiment in constitutional monarchy began under most unfavorable conditions.

The Legislative Assembly

On October 1 the first and only Legislative Assembly elected under the new constitution began deliberations. No one faction commanded a majority in the new assembly, though the Center had the most seats.* Since they occupied the lowest seats in the assembly hall, the deputies of the Center received the derogatory nickname of the Plain or Marsh. The capable politicians of the Left soon captured the votes of the Plain, following the leadership of a loose grouping of Jacobins known in time as Girondins (because some of them came from Bordeaux, in the department of the Gironde). Their chief spokesman was Jacques Brissot (1754-1793), an ambitious lawyer, journalist, and champion of reform causes, including emancipation of the slaves. The Girondins were held together by their patriotic alarm over France's situation at home and abroad.

Accordingly, the Girondins specialized in fervent nationalist oratory. They pictured revolutionary France as the intended victim of a reactionary conspiracy, engineered by the émigrés, aided at home by the non-juring clergy and the royal family, and abetted abroad by a league of monarchs under Leopold II, the Austrian emperor and brother of Marie Antoinette. The sudden

---

*In the practice followed by most continental European assemblies, the Right sat to the right of the presiding officer as he faced the assembly, the Left to his left, and the Center in between; thus the common usage of "left" for radical and "right" for conservative parties.

death of Leopold in March 1792 and the accession of his inexperienced and less cautious son, Francis II (1792-1835), increased the Austrian threat. At the same time mounting war fever in France convinced Louis XVI that he should choose Girondin ministers. On April 20 the Legislative Assembly declared war on Austria; the war was to continue, with a few brief intervals of peace, for the next twenty-three years.

Partly because the emigration of many nobles had depleted the corps of French officers, the war went badly for France at the outset. Prussia soon joined Austria, and morale sagged on the home front when Louis dismissed the Girondin ministers because they had proposed to banish non-juring priests, and appointed more conservative replacements. Spirits began to rise in July, especially with a great celebration of the third anniversary of the assault on the Bastille. Paris was thronged with national guardsmen from the provinces on the way to the front, and the contingent from Marseilles introduced to the capital a patriotic hymn which became the national anthem of republican France.

It was not only the stirring of words of the *Marseillaise* that improved morale. On July 25 the Prussian commander issued a manifesto (drafted by an émigré) stating the war aims of the allies:

> To put a stop to the anarchy within France, to check the attacks delivered against throne and altar, to reestablish legal authority, to restore to the king the security and freedom of which he has been deprived, and to place him in a position where he may exercise the legitimate authority which is his due.*

If the Tuileries were attacked, then Paris would witness "a model vengeance, never to be forgotten." This foolish manifesto stiffened the already firm determination of republicans to do away with the monarchy.

Through the early summer of 1792 the Jacobins of Paris had been plotting an insurrection. They won the support of a formidable following—army recruits, national guardsmen, and the rank and file Parisians who were angered by the depreciation of assignats and by the high price and short supply of food and other necessities. One by one the forty-eight wards into which the city was divided came under the control of Jacobins, who advertised their democratic sympathies by inviting unfranchised citizens to take part in political activity. The climax came on the night of August 9-10, when the regular municipal authorities were ousted from the Paris city hall and the Jacobins installed a new and illegal commune.

The municipal revolution had immediate and momentous results. On the morning of August 10 the forces of the new commune, joined by national guardsmen, attacked the Tuileries and massacred the king's Swiss guards, while the royal family took refuge with the Legislative Assembly. The uprising of August 10 sealed the doom of the monarchy and made the Assembly little

Le Moniteur Universel, August 3, 1792. Our translation.

more than the errand boy of the new Paris commune. With most of the deputies of the Right and the Plain absent, the Assembly voted to suspend the king from office, to imprison the royal family, and to order the election of a constitutional convention. Until this new body should meet, the government was to be run by an interim ministry staffed largely by Girondins, but in which the strong man was Georges Danton (1759-1794), a radical and an exceptional orator.

III THE FIRST REPUBLIC

The weeks between August 10 and the meeting of the Convention on September 21 were a time of extreme tension. The value of the assignats depreciated by 40 percent during August alone. Jacobin propagandists, led by Jean Paul Marat (1743-1793), an embittered Swiss physician turned journalist, continually excited the people of Paris. Excitement mounted still higher when the news arrived that Prussian troops had invaded northeastern France. In the emergency, Danton, the minister of justice, won immortality by urging patriots to employ "boldness, more boldness, always boldness."

In Paris, boldness took the form of the September Massacres, mass killings of supposed traitors and enemy agents made possible by the collapse of normal police authority. For five days, beginning on September 2, mobs moved from prison to prison; at each stop they held impromptu courts and summary executions. Neither the new Paris commune nor the national ministry could check the hysterical wave of killings. The number of victims exceeded a thousand and included ordinary criminals and prostitutes as well as aristocrats and non-juring priests, who were often innocent of the treason charged against them. The crowning horror was the mutilation of the princess de Lamballe, the queen's maid of honor, whose severed head was paraded on a pike before the window of the royal prison, so that Marie Antoinette might see "how the people take vengeance on their tyrants." The September Massacres foreshadowed the terror to come.

On September 20 a rather minor French victory, grandly styled "the miracle of Valmy," turned the enemy forces back from the road to Paris; more solid French successes in Belgium, Savoy, and the Rhineland followed in late 1792. Then the tide turned again, washing away the conquests of the autumn. By the summer of 1793 a half-defeated France faced a hostile coalition including almost every major power in Europe. An atmosphere of perpetual emergency surrounded the Convention.

Gironde and Mountain, 1792-1793

In theory the election of deputies to the National Convention in 1792 marked the beginning of political democracy in France. Virtually all male citizens were invited to the polls. Yet only 10 percent of the potential electorate of seven million actually voted; the rest abstained or were turned away from the polls by the watchdogs of the Jacobin clubs, ever on the alert against "counterrevolutionaries." The Convention was numerically dominated by the Center, or the Plain, but again, as in the Legislative Assembly, the Plain was politically irresolute, though now sympathetic to a republic. Many ties existed between the Gironde on the Right and the Mountain (so named because its deputies sat high up in the meeting hall), who made up the Left. Deputies from both factions had Jacobin ties, came mainly from middle-class professions like the law, were steeped in the ideas of the philosophes, and usually regarded the sans-culottes with some distrust.

Gironde and Mountain united to declare France a republic on September 21, 1792. The Girondins wanted a breathing spell in revolutionary legislation; they also defended provincial interests against possible encroachments by Paris. The Gironde, therefore, favored a large

Jacques Louis David's dramatic and symbolic painting, "The Death of Marat" (1793), hangs in The Royal Museum of Fine Arts in Brussels. David drew upon the conventions of classical art while imposing a sense of dramatic realism on his work. The details of the composition provide narrative drive to the scene. Marat, David's friend, is seen as a betrayed hero. He was stabbed to death in his bath by a political enemy, Charlotte Corday (1769-1793), who was admitted to Marat's bath chamber on the basis of the letter he still holds.

measure of federalism—which meant decentralization in the revolutionary vocabulary, and a national government limited by many checks and balances. The details were set forth in a draft constitution completed early in 1793 by the marquis de Condorcet: the executive and the legislature would be independent of each other and separately elected; the results of elections would be adjusted according to proportional representation; laws would be submitted to a popular referendum; and voters could recall unworthy officials. But the leaders of the Mountain denounced federalism and advocated an all-powerful central government.

The chief spokesman for the Mountain was Maximilien Robespierre (1758-1794). This earnest young lawyer did not look like a revolutionary. He powdered his hair neatly and wore the knee-breeches of the Old Regime. Yet Robespierre was a political extremist whose speeches were lay sermons couched in the language of a new faith. Apparently Robespierre was sure that he knew the general will, and that it demanded a Republic of Virtue. If the French would not act in a free and virtuous fashion voluntarily, then, as Rousseau had recommended, they should be "forced to be free."

Robespierre and the Republic of Virtue triumphed. The Mountain won out over the Gironde in the Convention. The first step came when, after one hundred hours of continuous voting, the Convention declared the king, "Citizen Louis Capet," guilty of treason, and by a narrow margin sentenced him to the guillotine without delay. Louis XVI died bravely on January 21, 1793. Although most of the French population probably disapproved of the king's execution, they did not control the Convention. The Girondin deputies split their votes on the issue. Those opposed to the death penalty took a stand in defense of their reading of the humanitarian principles of the Enlightenment, but also exposed themselves to the charge of being counterrevolutionaries.

Now events at home and abroad destroyed the divided Gironde. In February the Convention rejected Condorcet's draft constitution and declared war on Britain, Spain, and the Netherlands. France now faced a formidable coalition of opponents, including Austria and Prussia. In March the French army suffered a series of defeats in the Low Countries, and in April its Girondin commander deserted to the enemy. Marat now loudly denounced many Girondists as traitors; the Girondin deputies countered by calling for the impeachment of Marat, who was brought before a special tribunal and triumphantly acquitted. In July Marat was assassinated in his bath by Charlotte Corday, a young woman wielding a butcher's knife who was convinced that she was a new Joan of Arc called to deliver France from Jacobin radicalism.

By then, however, the Girondins had been completely vanquished. In the face of unemployment, high prices, and shortages of food, soap, and other necessities, they had little to prescribe except more laissez faire. The sections of Paris demanded price controls and food requisitioning; they also pressed for the expulsion of

THE DEATH OF A KING

The carriage proceeded thus in silence to the Place de Louis XV,* and stopped in the middle of a large space that had been left round the scaffold: this space was surrounded with cannon, and beyond, an armed multitude extended as far as the eye could reach. . . . As soon as the King had left the carriage, three guards surrounded him, and would have taken off his clothes, but he repulsed them with haughtiness: he undressed himself, untied his neckcloth, opened his shirt, and arranged it himself. The guards, whom the determined countenance of the King had for a moment disconcerted, seemed to recover their audacity. They surrounded him again, and would have seized his hands. "What are you attempting?" said the King, drawing back his hands. "To bind you," answered the wretches. "To bind *me*," said the King with an indignant air. "No! I shall never consent to that: do what you have been ordered, but you shall never bind me. . . ."

Many voices were at the same time heard encouraging the executioners. They seemed reanimated themselves, in seizing with violence the most virtuous of Kings, they dragged him under the axe of the guillotine, which with one stroke severed his head from his body. All this passed in a moment. The youngest of the guards, who seemed about eighteen, immediately seized the head, and shewed it to the people as he walked round the scaffold; he accompanied this monstrous ceremony with the most atrocious and indecent gestures. At first an awful silence prevailed; at length some cries of "Vive la République!" were heard. By degrees the voices multiplied, and in less than ten minutes this cry, a thousand times repeated, became the universal shout of the multitude, and every hat was in the air. . . .

*Now the Place de la Concorde.

From *English Witnesses of the French Revolution*, ed., J.M. Thompson (Oxford: Basil Blackwell, 1938), pp. 230-31.

Girondins from the Jacobin clubs and the Convention. Finally, on June 2, 1793, a vast crowd of armed sans-culottes from the sections, following the precedent of August 1792, invaded the hall and forced the arrest of twenty-nine Girondin deputies. Backed by these armed Parisians, the Mountain intimidated the Plain, and the Convention consigned the arrested Girondins to the guillotine. The Reign of Terror had begun.

The Reign of Terror, 1793-1794

How was it that the advocates of democracy now imposed a dictatorship on France? Let Robespierre explain:

To establish and consolidate democracy, to achieve the peaceful rule of constitutional laws, we must first finish the war of liberty against tyranny. . . . We must annihilate the enemies of the republic at home and abroad, or else we shall perish.

*If virtue is the mainstay of a democratic government in time of peace, then in time of revolution a democratic government must rely on virtue and terror. . . . Terror is nothing but justice, swift, severe, and inflexible; it is an emanation of virtue. . . . It has been said that terror is the mainstay of a despotic government. . . . The government of the revolution is the despotism of liberty against tyranny.**

The Convention duly voted a democratic constitution, drawn up by the Mountain, granting universal manhood suffrage and giving supreme power, unhampered by Girondin checks and balances, to a single legislative

*Le Moniteur Universel, February 7, 1794. Our translation.

chamber. The Constitution of 1793 was approved by a large majority in a referendum attracting double the participation of the election of 1792, but its operation was deferred, and it never came into force.

The actual government of the Terror centered on a twelve-man Committee of Public Safety, composed of Robespierre and other stalwarts largely from the Mountain. Though nominally responsible to the Convention, the Committee of Public Safety exercised independent authority and acted as a kind of war cabinet. Never under the dominance of a single member, it really functioned as a committee—"The Twelve Who Ruled." A second committee, that of Public Security, supervised police activities and turned suspected enemies of the republic over to the new Revolutionary Tribunal. To speed the work of repressing dissent, the sixteen judges and sixty jurors of the tribunal were eventually divided into several courts.

The Mountain scrapped much of the local self-government inaugurated under the Constitution of 1791. It also whittled away steadily at the prerogatives assumed by the Paris sections, or wards. Local Jacobin clubs purged department and commune administrations of members considered politically unreliable. Special local courts supplemented the grim labors of the Revolutionary Tribunal. To make provincial France toe the line, the Mountain sent out trusted "deputies on mission." From the standpoint of administration, the Terror marked both an anticipation of twentieth-century dictatorship and a return to the age-old French principle of centralization.

The "swift, severe, and inflexible justice" described by Robespierre took the lives of nearly twenty thousand

The guillotine was the symbol of the Reign of Terror. As crowds watched, prisoners were decapitated and their heads held up for display. Popular engravings were sold to townspeople unable to witness the executions so that they could be reminded of them. In this illustration Marie Antoinette is executed, her head ceremonially held out to the assembled revolutionary army.

French men and women. Although the Terror claimed such social outcasts as criminals and prostitutes, its main purpose was military and political—to clear France of suspected traitors, including Marie Antoinette (executed in Paris on October 16, 1793), and to purge the Jacobins of dissidents. It fell with the greatest severity on the clergy, the aristocracy, and the Girondins, by no means always in Paris. Many of its victims came from the Vendée, a strongly Catholic and royalist area in western France that had risen in revolt. Prisoners from the Vendée were among the two thousand victims of drownings at Nantes, where the accused were manacled and set adrift on the River Loire in leaky barges. Equally grisly was the suppression of an uprising of Girondin sympathizers at Lyons, which claimed some two thousand victims.

The wartime hysteria that helped to account for the excesses of the Terror also inspired a very practical patriotism. The army drafted all bachelors and widowers between the ages of eighteen and twenty-five. Hundreds of open-air forges were installed in Paris to manufacture weapons. Since the war prevented importation of the saltpeter needed for gunpowder, the government also sponsored a great campaign to scrape patches of saltpeter from cellars and stables.

By the close of 1793 the forces of the republic had driven foreign troops from French soil. Credit for this new shift in the tide of battle did not rest solely with the Jacobins. The military successes of the republic reflected in part the improvements made in the army during the dying years of the Old Regime; they resulted still more from the weaknesses of the coalition aligned against France. Yet they could scarcely have been achieved without the new democratic spirit that allowed men of the third estate to become officers and that made the French army the most determined and enterprising in Europe.

Total mobilization demanded equality of economic sacrifice. To combat inflation and scarcity, the Terror issued "maximum" legislation, placing ceilings on prices and wages. In theory, wages were held at a maximum 50 percent above the wage rate of 1790, and prices were halted at 33 percent above the price level of 1790. The government rationed meat and bread, forbade the use of the more expensive white flour, and directed all patriots to eat *pain d'égalité* ("equality bread"), a loaf utilizing almost the whole of the wheat. Finally, early in 1794 the Convention passed the Laws of Ventôse, named for the third winter month in the new revolutionary calendar. These laws authorized seizure of the remaining properties of the émigrés and other opponents of the republic

JACOBIN NATIONALISM

On August 23, 1793 the Convention issued a decree that epitomized the democratic nationalism of the Jacobins:

From this moment, until the time when the enemy shall have been driven from the territory of the Republic, all Frenchmen are permanently requisitioned for the service of the armies.

Young men will go into combat; married men will manufacture arms and transport supplies; women will make tents and uniforms and will serve in the hospitals; children will make old linen into bandages; old men will be carried into the public squares to arouse the courage of the soldiers, excite hatred for kings, and inspire the unity of the republic.

Le Moniteur Universel, August 24, 1793. Our translation.

and recommended their distribution to landless French citizens.

The "maximum" regulations did not prove very effective. Attempts by the government to enforce wage ceilings enraged Parisian workers. And though the "maximum" on prices temporarily checked the depreciation of the assignats, many price-controlled articles were available only on the black market, which even the government had to patronize. Moreover, the redistribution of property permitted by the Laws of Ventôse was never implemented. When the laws were proposed, a spokesman for the Committee of Public Safety explained that no general assault on property was intended:

*The revolution leads us to recognize the principle that he who has shown himself the enemy of his country cannot own property. The properties of patriots are sacred, but the goods of conspirators are there for the unfortunate.**

The Terror presented its most revolutionary aspect in its drastic social and cultural reforms. The Convention abolished slavery in the colonies (though it was to be reintroduced by Napoleon a decade later). At home, clothing, the arts, amusements, the calendar, religion, all were changed, for the Republic of Virtue could tolerate nothing that smelled of the Old Regime. Even the traditional forms of address, "Monsieur" and "Madame," gave way to "Citizen" and "Citizeness." The Convention also introduced the metric system as more in keeping with the Age of Reason; a special committee, including Condorcet, Laplace, Lavoisier, and other distinguished intellectuals, devised new weights and measures based on the decimal system rather than on the haphazard accumulations of custom. In August 1793 a decree made the meter the standard unit of length, and supplementary legislation in 1795 established the liter as the measure of volume and the gram as the unit of weight.

Sometimes the forces of tradition resisted the Terror, which tried to destroy the old religion but never suc-

ceeded in legislating a new faith. Many churches were closed and turned into barracks or administrative offices; often their medieval glass and sculpture were destroyed. Some of the Jacobins launched a "de-Christianization" campaign to make Catholics into philosophes and their churches into "Temples of Reason." Robespierre, however, disliked the cult of Reason; the Republic of Virtue, he believed, should acknowledge an ultimate author of morality. The Convention therefore decreed in May 1794 that "the French people recognize the existence of the Supreme Being and the immortality of the soul." At a festival of the Supreme Being on June 8, 1794, Robespierre set fire to figures representing Vice, Folly, and Atheism, and from the embers a statue of Wisdom emerged. But the audience laughed. A deistic supreme being was too remote to satisfy most people's religious needs.

Indeed, the Republic of Virtue itself was too abstract in ideals and too violent in practice to retain popular support. Like the Geneva of Calvin, the France of Robespierre demanded superhuman devotion to duty and inhuman indifference to hardship and bloodshed. During the first half of 1794 Robespierre pressed the Terror so relentlessly that even the members of the Committees of Public Safety and General Security began to fear that they would be the next victims. The Law of the 22 Prairial, Year II (that is, June 10, 1794) enormously expanded the definition of "enemies of the people" who were subject to punishment by the Revolutionary Tribunal so as to include the following: "those who have sought to disparage the National Convention," "who have sought to impede the provisioning of Paris," "to inspire discouragement," "to mislead opinion, to deprave morals," and "those who, charged with public office, take advantage of it in order to serve the enemies of the Revolution, to harass patriots, or to oppress the people."*

Thus Robespierre began to lose his following both in the Convention and in the two powerful committees. More and more of his former supporters favored moder-

*Louis de Saint-Just (1767-1794), in *Le Moniteur Universel*, February 26, 1794. Our translation.

*J.H. Stewart, ed., *A Documentary Survey of the French Revolution* (New York: Macmillan, 1951), pp. 528-29.

ation and argued that the growing French success in the war called for less, not more, terror. The crucial day was the Ninth of Thermidor (the month of Heat, or July 27, 1794), when shouts of "Down with the tyrant!" and the refusal of the presiding officer to give Robespierre the floor blocked his efforts to address the Convention. The convention ordered his arrest, and on the next day he went to the guillotine. The sans-culottes of Paris made no effective attempts to come to his rescue, for only a few days earlier the government had begun a new effort to enforce the "maximum" on wages and to control the economy generally.

Why had Robespierre fallen so quickly? He lost control because of the very situation he had created. An idealist who believed, with Rousseau, that a political society must guarantee the natural rights of humanity, he also believed that a Supreme Being must protect the oppressed and punish their oppressors. He had concluded that it was temporarily necessary to suspend the institutions in which he believed in order to break the chains imposed by tradition, to return in time to a life based on the principles he espoused. He sought, therefore, to destroy each faction systematically as it arose against him. But the charges he brought against others who could be considered as idealistic as he, and the summary justice meted out by his followers, angered and frightened opposition groups in his own party. They united to fight back, both to protect the principles they felt he had abandoned and to protect their own lives, since opposition to Robespierre had been viewed by him as another sign of the factionalism he was committed to root out.

The Thermidorean Reaction and the Directory, 1794-1799

The leaders of the Thermidorean Reaction, or the move toward moderation, many of them former Jacobins, now dismantled the machinery of the Terror. They disbanded the Revolutionary Tribunal, recalled the deputies on mission, and deprived the Committees of Public Safety and General Security of their independent authority. They closed the Paris Jacobin club and invited the surviving Girondin deputies to resume their old seats in the Convention. They took the first step toward restoring Catholicism by permitting priests to celebrate Mass, though under state supervision and without state financial support. The press and the theater recovered their freedom, and pleasure seekers again flocked to Paris, now liberated from the somber Republic of Virtue.

But instability, personal insecurity, and class and caste hatred were by now rife. In Paris long-haired young bourgeois calling themselves the *jeunesse dorée* ("gilded youth") went about dressed like dandies and carrying long sticks, which they used to attack suspected Jacobins. They organized the destruction of busts of Marat and forced the removal of his remains from their burial place. In southern and western France a counter-revolutionary White Terror, equaling the great Terror in fury, claimed many lives, not only of supporters of the

Mountain (or *Montagnards*), but also of purchasers of former church and noble lands. The leaders of Thermidor caused an acute inflation by canceling the economic legislation of the Terror; no longer checked by the maximum, the prices of some foods rose to a hundred times the level of 1790, and the assignats sank so low in value that businesses refused to accept them. Popular suffering became more intense than it had ever been under the Terror. Desperate, half-starving Parisians staged several demonstrations against the Thermidoreans during 1795, clamoring for bread and lower prices.

The Thermidorean Reaction concluded with the passage of the Constitution of 1795, the last major act of the Convention. The Thermidoreans wanted both to retain the republic and to assure the dominance of the propertied classes. The new constitution therefore denied the vote to the poorest quarter of the nation and required that candidates for public office possess considerable property. It established two legislative councils, the Five Hundred and the Elders. The Council of Five Hundred nominated and the Elders chose five persons who headed the executive Directory, which otherwise was almost totally independent of the legislative councils.

The Constitution of 1795 demonstrated that the most radical phase of the Revolution had passed. But three weeks before it was to go into operation, more trouble broke out in Paris, exploited by the *jeunesse dorée* and other conservatives in hopes of ending the First Republic and restoring the monarchy (as had happened in England in 1660). The counterrevolutionary insurgents were put down in the massacre of Vendémiaire (October 5, 1795), dispersed in part by the young Napoleon Bonaparte, who commanded troops loyal to the Thermidorean Convention. The first winter of the Directory (1795-1796) brought France the most intense popular suffering of the revolutionary period as a consequence of inflation, chronic shortage of food, and extreme and icy cold. Thereafter, the situation steadily improved, thanks to good harvests and the Directory's vigorous attack on economic problems.

The new regime levied high protective tariffs, both as a war measure against England and as a concession to French business. Again responding to business pressure, it destroyed the plates used to print the assignats and in 1797 withdrew paper money from circulation. The return to hard money required stringent government economies, which the Directory instituted. Tax collection was made more efficient, and France enjoyed considerable loot from victorious wars. The Directory eased the crushing burden of the national debt by repudiating two-thirds of it and gave the old unit of currency, the livre, a new and lasting name, the franc.

The Directory easily suppressed the amateurish Conspiracy of the equals (1796-1797), sponsored by François Gracchus Babeuf (1760-1797), who has come down in socialist teachings as the first modern communist. The Directory experienced much greater difficulty, however, steering a cautious middle course between the two extremes of restoring the monarchy and reverting to

Jacobin terrorism. The Constitution of 1795 was repeatedly violated, as the directors and the legislative councils clashed, with each seeking to shift the political balance in its own favor. The councils fired directors before their terms were finished, and directors refused to allow duly elected council members to take their seats. Disgruntled politicians and apprehensive moderates, fearing the collapse of the regime, began to maneuver for the help of the increasingly successful army. The result was the coup d'état of Brumaire (that is, October) in 1799 and the dictatorship of Napoleon.

IV   NAPOLEON AND FRANCE

Liberals outside France had hailed the peaceful promise of the French Revolution, and conservatives believed that the very intensity of domestic problems would make France incapable of a vigorous foreign policy. As late as 1792 Catherine the Great predicted that ten thousand soldiers would suffice to douse the "abominable bonfire" in France.

The war that broke out in the spring of 1792 soon destroyed such illusions. Almost all the European powers eventually participated, and the fighting ranged far beyond Europe. By the time the war was a year old, Austria and Prussia, the members of the first coalition against France, had been joined by Holland, Spain, and Great Britain. The British had both ideological and strategic interests at stake. They regarded the attack on the Tuileries, the September massacres, and the execution of Louis XVI as outrages against human decency and the institution of monarchy. And the French invasion of the Austrian Netherlands in the fall of 1792 raised the prospect that this Belgian "cockpit of Europe" would fall under French control. By 1794 the French had definitely gained the advantage, and in 1795 French troops occupied Belgium, Holland, and the Rhineland.

One reason for French success was the Convention's energetic mobilization of national resources, which enabled France to have the unprecedented total of a million men under arms by the spring of 1794. Another reason lay in the weakness of the first coalition, which lacked a first-rate commander. The failure to take Paris in 1792 resulted as much from deficient generalship as from the "miracle" of Valmy. Moreover, the partitions of Poland in 1793 and 1795 greatly assisted the French because they kept Russia out of the war and greatly distracted Austria and Prussia. The pick of the Prussian army was diverted to occupy newly annexed Polish provinces. By 1795 mutual mistrust had reached the point where the Prussians dared not attack the French for fear of being attacked themselves by their nominal Austrian allies.

Prussia was the first member of the coalition to make peace. In the Treaty of Basel (1795), Prussia yielded to France the scattered Hohenzollern holdings west of the Rhine on the understanding that it might seek compensation elsewhere in Germany. Spain, which ceded to France the western part of the island of Santo Domingo (today the Dominican Republic), soon deserted the coali-

---

EDMUND BURKE, A CONSERVATIVE, LOOKS AT A RADICAL REVOLUTION

Edmund Burke (1729-1797), the British political theorist, foresaw the long process that culminated in Napoleon's domination of France and Europe. In 1790 Burke warned the French—and his own countrymen—in his *Reflections on the Revolution in France*:

Everything depends on the army in such a government as yours; for you have industriously destroyed all the opinions, . . . all the instincts which support government. Therefore the moment any difference arises between your National Assembly and any part of the nation, you must have recourse to force. Nothing else is left to you. . . .

It is besides to be considered, whether an assembly like yours . . . is fit for promoting the obedience and discipline of an army. It is known, that armies have hitherto yielded a very precarious and uncertain obedience to any sensate, or popular authority. . . . The officers must totally lose the characteristic disposition of military men, if they see with perfect submission and due admiration, the dominion of pleaders [lawyers].

. . . In the weakness of one kind of authority, and in the fluctuation of all, the officers of an army will remain for some time mutinous and full of faction, until some popular general, who understands the art of conciliating the soldiery, and who possesses the true spirit of command, shall draw the eyes of all men upon himself. Armies will obey him on his personal account. There is no other way of securing military obedience in this state of things. But the moment in which that event shall happen, the person who really commands the army is your master; the master . . . of your king, the master of your assembly, the master of your whole republic.

Reflections on the Revolution in France, (New York: Everyman Edition, 1953), pp. 217, 215-16.

NAPOLEON RALLIES HIS TROOPS

In the Italian campaign Major General Bonaparte, still only in his twenties, cleared the Austrians out of their strongholds in one year and made them sue for peace. He showed a remarkable ability to strike quickly and to surprise his opponents before they could consolidate their defenses. He also showed a gift for propaganda and public relations, as this proclamation from the early phases of the campaign illustrates:

Soldiers! In two weeks you have won six victories; you have made 15,000 prisoners; you have killed or wounded more than 10,000 men.

Deprived of everything, you have accomplished everything. You have won battles without cannon, negotiated rivers without bridges, made forced marches without shoes, encamped without brandy, and often without bread. Only the phalanxes of the Republic, only the soldiers of Liberty, would have been capable of suffering the things that you have suffered.

You all burn to carry the glory of the French people;

to humiliate the proud kings who dared to contemplate shackling us; to go back to your villages, to say proudly: "I was of the conquering army of Italy!"

Friends, I promise you that conquest; but there is a condition you must swear to fulfill: to respect the people whom you are delivering; to repress horrible pillaging.

Peoples of Italy, the French army comes to break your chains; greet it with confidence; your property, religion and customs will be respected.

Abridged from *Le Moniteur Universel*, May 17, 1796. Our translation.

---

tion, as did the Netherlands. In 1795 then, France at last secured its "natural frontiers." Besides Belgium and the Rhineland, France had also annexed Savoy and Nice, thereby extending its southeastern border to the crest of the Alps. These conquests, however, belied the ideals of the Revolution. In declaring war on Austria in 1792, France had sworn to uphold a promise of the Constitution of 1791: never to undertake a war of conquest. This was to be "not a war of nation against nation, but the righteous defense of a free people against the unjust aggression of a king." But the conquering armies of the First Republic brought closer the day when nation would fight nation—when the other European nations would invoke "the righteous defense of a free people against the unjust aggression," not of a king, but of revolutionary France.

Bonaparte's Rise

By the close of 1795 only Britain and Austria remained officially at war with France. To lead the attack against Hapsburg forces in northern Italy, the French Directory picked a youthful general who was something of a philosophe and revolutionary, as well as a ruthless, ambitious adventurer. He was born Napoleone Buonaparte on Corsica in 1769, soon after the French acquisition of that Mediterranean island from Genoa, and he retained throughout his life an intense family loyalty and a view of public affairs that was essentially anti-French.

As a boy of nine Napoleon began to attend military school in France and, though he now spelled his name in the French style, was snubbed as a foreigner by some of his fellow cadets. He immersed himself in reading Rousseau and dreamed of the day when he might liberate

Corsica from French control. Later, however, his zeal for Coriscan independence faded in consequence of the rupture between the Bonapartes and the Corsican nationalists who became allies of Britain.

When the Revolution broke out, the young artillery officer helped to overthrow the Old Regime in Corsica and then returned to France to resume his military career. He defended the Convention, but more out of expediency than from conviction, and commanded the artillery in December 1793, when the forces of the Convention recaptured the Mediterranean port of Toulon, which had fallen to the British earlier in the year. After Thermidor he fell under a cloud as a suspected "terrorist" and came close to going with a team of French experts to advise the Ottoman Empire on modernizing its army. But he settled for a desk job in Paris and was available to rescue the Thermidorean Convention in Vendémiaire. He married Josephine de Beauharnais, a widow who was an intimate of the ruling clique of the Directory. The combination of Josephine's connections and Napoleon's talent gained him the Italian command in 1796.

In the Treaty of Campo Formio (1797) ending the Italian campaign, Austria acknowledged the loss of Belgium and recognized two puppet states that Napoleon set up in northwestern Italy: the Ligurian Republic (Genoa) and the Cisalpine Republic (the former Austrian possession of Lombardy). In return, the Hapsburgs received the Italian territories of the Venetian Republic, plus a secret French assurance that Prussia, despite the specific promise made in 1795, would not be permitted to compensate for its losses in the Rhineland by taking lands elsewhere in Germany.

Only Britain remained at war with France. Napoleon

decided to attack it indirectly through Malta and Egypt, the latter a semi-independent vassal of the Ottoman Empire. Seeking new worlds to conquer and talking grandly of digging a canal at Suez—which would give French merchants the monopoly of a new short trade route to India and exact belated retribution from Britain for Clive's victory in the Seven Years' War—Napoleon invited over a hundred archaeologists, geographers, and other scholars to accompany his army and thereby helped to found the study of Egyptology. (The French thus discovered the Rosetta Stone, the first key to the translation of ancient Egyptian hieroglyphics). Napoleon's experts established in Egypt an outpost of French culture that lasted into the twentieth century.

From the military standpoint, however, the campaign failed. Having eluded the British Mediterranean fleet commanded by Horatio Nelson (1758-1805), Napoleon landed in Egypt in July 1798 and routed the Mamluks, the ruling oligarchy. Then disaster struck. On August 1, 1798, Nelson discovered the French fleet moored at Abukir Bay along the Egyptian coast and destroyed it before its captains could weigh anchor. Nelson's victory deprived the French of both supplies and reinforcements. After a year of futile campaigning in the Near East, Napoleon suddenly left Egypt in August 1799 and returned to France.

Napoleon found the situation in France ripe for a decisive political move, for the Directory was shaken by a strong revival of Jacobinism. Several hundred deputies in the legislative councils belonged to the Society of the Friends of Liberty and Equality, essentially the old Jacobin club. Under their influence, the councils in 1799 decreed a forced loan from the rich and passed a Law of Hostages, designed to make the émigrés stop plotting against the Directory by threatening their relatives in France with reprisals. Moderates feared that a new Reign of Terror would soon be unleashed, and they hoped for a stronger executive to prevent this.

Abroad, the Directory had established four new satellite republics with classical names: the Batavian (Holland), the Helvetian (Switzerland), the Roman, and the Parthenopean (Naples). But this new success of French imperialism upset the European balance and provoked the formation of the second coalition, headed by Britain, Austria, and Russia. The Hapsburgs resented the extension of French influence in their former Italian preserve, and Czar Paul I (ruled 1796-1801) feared that Napoleon would damage Russia's Mediterranean interests. The eccentric czar was head of the Knights of Malta, a Catholic order dating back to the Crusades, which Napoleon had expelled from its headquarters on the island of Malta. In the campaign of 1799 Russian troops fought in Italy and Switzerland, and the Russian general Alexander Suvorov (1729-1800), who defeated the French repeatedly, became the hero of western Europe. By August 1799 the French had been expelled from Italy, and most of their puppet republics had been dismantled.

In these circumstances, Napoleon was given a rousing reception on his return from Egypt. Soon he was plotting to overthrow the Directory, with the complicity of two of the five directors. On November 9 and 10, 1799 (18 and 19 Brumaire by the revolutionary calendar), the plot was executed. The three directors not in the plot resigned, and the two legislative councils named Napoleon military commander of Paris. He then barely persuaded the councils to entrust to the two remaining directors and himself the task of drafting a new constitution, and a detachment of troops loyal to Napoleon expelled the hostile deputies. The coup d'état of Brumaire ended the Directory, for the Bonapartist minority in the councils vested full power in the victorious triumvirate.

Consulate and Empire

The Constitution of the Year VIII, drawn up after Brumaire, was the fourth attempt by revolutionary France to provide a written instrument of government, its predecessors being the constitutions of 1791, 1793, and 1795. Based on Siéyès's autocratic maxim, "Confidence from below, authority from above," the new document erected a very strong executive, the Consulate, named (like other bodies set up by the constitution) after institutions of republican Rome. Although three consuls shared the executive, Napoleon as first consul left the other two only nominal power. Four separate bodies had a hand in legislation: the Council of State proposed laws; the Tribunate debated them but did not vote; the Legislative Corps voted them but did not debate; the Senate had the right to veto legislation. The members of all four bodies were either appointed by the first consul or elected indirectly by a process so complex that Bonaparte had ample opportunity to manipulate candidates. The core of this system was the Council of State, inherited from the Revolution and staffed by Bonaparte's handpicked choices, which served both as a cabinet and as the highest administrative court. The three remaining bodies were intended merely to go through the motions of enacting whatever the first consul decreed. Even so, they were sometimes unruly, and the Tribunate so annoyed Napoleon that he finally abolished it in 1807.

Meantime, step by step, Napoleon increased his own authority. In 1802 he persuaded the legislators, allegedly in the interests of stability, to drop the original ten-year limitation on his term of office and make him first consul for life, with the power to designate his successor and to amend the constitution at will. France was now a monarchy again in all but name. In 1804 Napoleon prompted the Senate to declare that "the government of the republic is entrusted to an emperor." A magnificent coronation took place at Notre Dame in Paris on December 2. The pope consecrated the emperor, but, following Charlemagne's example, Napoleon placed the crown on his own head.

Each time Napoleon revised the constitution in a nonrepublican direction, he made the republican gesture of submitting the change to the electorate. Each time the results of the plebiscite were overwhelmingly favorable: in 1799-1800 the vote was 3,011,107 for Napoleon and the Constitution of the Year VIII, and 1,562 against; in 1803 it was 3,568,885 for Napoleon and the life Consulate, and 8,374 against; in 1804 it was 3,572,329 for Napoleon and the Empire, and 2,579 against. Although the voters were exposed to considerable official pressure and the announced results were perhaps rigged a little, the majority in France undoubtedly supported Napoleon. His military triumphs appealed to their growing nationalism, and his policy of stability at home ensured them against further revolutionary crises and changes. Confidence did indeed seem to increase from below as authority increased from above.

Men of every political background now staffed the highly centralized imperial administration. Napoleon cared little whether his subordinates were returned émigrés or ex-Jacobins, so long as they had ability. Besides, their varied antecedents reinforced the impression that narrow factionalism was dead and that the empire rested on a broad political base. Napoleon paid officials well and offered the additional inducement of high titles. With the establishment of the empire he created dukes by the dozen and counts and barons by the hundred. He rewarded outstanding generals with the rank of marshal and other officers with admission to the Legion of Honor, which also paid its members an annual pension. "Aristocracy always exists," Napoleon remarked. "Destroy it in the nobility, it removes itself to the rich and powerful houses of the middle class." The imperial aristocracy at last gave the leaders of the middle class the social distinction that they felt to be rightfully theirs.

Law and Justice

Napoleon revived some of the glamor of the Old Regime but not its glaring inequalities. His series of law codes, the Code Napoléon (1804-1810), declared all men equal before the law without regard to rank and wealth. It extended to all the right to follow the occupation and embrace the religion of their own choosing. It gave France the single coherent system of law that the philosophes had demanded and that the revolutionary governments had been unable to formulate.

The Code Napoléon did not, however, embody the full judicial reform program of the Enlightenment; at times it confirmed the principles of 1789, and at times it betrayed them. It favored the interests of the state over the rights of the individual, and it permitted some use of torture in trial procedure. Judges were appointed by the emperor; jurors were selected by his prefects. Though Napoleon confirmed the revolutionary legislation permitting divorce by mutual consent, the code canceled other revolutionary laws protecting wives, minors, and illegitimate children, and restored the man of the family to his former legal superiority. It also restored slavery in French colonies.

Ambiguity also clouded Napoleon's attitude toward civil liberties. Although he prided himself on welcoming former political heretics into his administration, his generosity always stemmed from expediency, never from fundamental belief in liberty. If he failed to get his way by conciliation, he used force. In the western departments, where royalist uprisings had become chronic since the revolt in the Vendée, he massacred rebels who declined his offer of amnesty in 1800. In 1804 he kidnapped a Bourbon prince from the neutral German state of Baden because the prince was believed to be the choice of monarchist conspirators for the throne of France. Though Napoleon immediately discovered the prince's innocence, he had him executed nonetheless.

Napoleon cared little for freedom of speech as an abstraction, for he wanted to control and channel knowledge. No segment of public opinion escaped Napoleon's manipulation. He reduced by five-sixths the number of Paris newspapers and argued that the theater should become a vehicle for inspiring patriotism. When he wanted to arouse French feelings, he simply started a press campaign, as in 1807:

> A great hue and cry is to be raised against the persecutions experienced by the Catholics of Ireland at the hands of the Anglican church. . . . Bishops will be approached so that prayers will be offered entreating an end to the persecutions of the Anglican church against the Irish Catholics. But the administration must move very delicately and make use of the newspapers without their realizing what the government is driving at. . . . And the term "Anglican church" must always be used in place of "Protestants," for we have Protestants in France, but no Anglican church.*

Religion and Education

Political considerations generally colored Napoleon's decisions on religion. Since French Catholics loathed the anticlericalism of the Revolution, Napoleon sought to appease them by working out a reconciliation with Rome. The Concordat (a treaty with the Vatican) negotiated with Pope Pius VII (1800-1823) in 1801 accomplished this reconciliation. While it canceled only the most obnoxious features of the Civil Constitution of the Clergy, the French state agreed to end the popular election of bishops and priests. The bishops were to be nominated by the government and then consecrated by the pope; the priests were to be appointed by the bishops. But by declaring that Catholicism was the faith of the "great majority of Frenchmen," rather than the state religion, the Concordat implicitly admitted the toleration of Protestants and Jews, both of whom were expected to accept state supervision of their governing councils. Also, by implication the pope accepted such revolutionary measures as the abolition of the tithe and the confiscation of church lands.

Finally, the Concordat made the activities of the church in France subject to the "police regulations" of the state. These regulations were spelled out in the Organic Articles, which Napoleon appended to the Con-

---

*Lettres Inédites à Napoléon (Paris: Klincksiek, 1973), I, 93-94. Our translation.

cordat without consulting the pope. The French government was to supervise the publication of papal bulls, the establishment of seminaries, the content of catechisms, and a host of other details. The Articles also reaffirmed the principle of the special autonomy enjoyed by the French church within Catholicism. Despite all this, the anticlericals opposed the Concordat, and it took all Napoleon's influence to obtain its ratification by the legislative bodies of the Consulate.

The Concordat, then, made the church a ward of the French state. Though it antagonized anticlericals, it conciliated many Catholics, and it remained in force until 1905. The Concordat, however, did not bring complete peace between France and the Vatican, for Napoleon insisted that the pope render unto Caesar the things that were Caesar's. When Pius VII objected to Napoleon's making a French satellite of the Papal States, the new Caesar lectured him on the proper division of authority between the spiritual and temporal powers. Pius passed the last years of the Napoleonic regime as a prisoner, in northern Italy and then in France.

The Revolution and Napoleon also cost the church its monopoly over education. The Constitution of 1791 had promised France a system of state schools. The Thermidorean Convention, while doing little to apply this principle to primary education, set up institutions for advanced training, incuding a school in Paris for engineers. In each department of France it also established a "central school" to provide secondary education of good quality at relatively low cost to students. Napoleon abolished these central schools in 1802 and replaced them with a smaller number of central lycées open only to the relatively few pupils who could afford the tuition or who received state scholarships. The change had a political motive, as changes in educational structure often do, for Napoleon intended the lycées to groom capable and loyal administrators. The students wore uniforms and marched to military drums, and the curriculum too served the ends of patriotic indoctrination. To provide for the supervision of all schools, lay and clerical, in 1808 Napoleon founded a body with the name University, for universal. He neglected primary schooling almost completely, yet, building on the revolutionary base, he did advance the construction of secular schools. The way was open for bitter educational competition between church and state in nineteenth-century France.

Economics

Political aims also governed the economic program of an emperor determined to promote national unity. French peasants wanted to be left alone to enjoy the new freedom acquired in 1789. Napoleon did little to disrupt them, except to raise army recruits, though in time this proved destructive. The middle class wanted a balanced national budget and the end of revolutionary experiments with paper currency and a controlled economy. Napoleon continued the sound money of the Directory and, unlike the Directory, balanced the budget, thanks in part to the plunder that he gained in war. He greatly improved the efficiency and honesty of tax collectors and established the semiofficial Bank of France (1800) to act as the government's financial agent. He strengthened the curbs placed on strikes and labor unions by the Le Chapelier Law of 1791 and obliged every worker to carry a *livret* (booklet), in effect an identify card recording the worker's jobs and general reputation. Though seaports suffered from the decline of overseas trade, rich war contracts and subsidies kept employment and profits generally high. As the war went on and on, however, Napoleon found it increasingly difficult to keep the peasantry and the bourgeoisie contented, and the seaport populations suffered grievously. Despite the levies on conquered countries, he had to draft more soldiers from the peasantry and increase the already unpopular taxes on salt, liquor, and tobacco.

In summary, the domestic policies of Napoleon I had something in common with the methods of all one-man rulers. Like Caesar in Rome, Napoleon paid lip service to the republic while subverting republican institutions; he used prefects to impose centralized authority as Louis XIV had used intendants; and like twentieth-century dictators, he scorned free speech. Yet Napoleon was an enlightened despot. His law code and some of his educational reforms would have delighted the philosophes. He ended civil strife without sacrificing the redistribution of land and the equality before the law gained in 1789 and the years following. Abandoning some revolutionary policies, modifying others, and completing still others, Napoleon regimented the Revolution without wholly destroying it.

V NAPOLEON AND EUROPE

To many in France, Napoleon was and remains the Man of Destiny, the most brilliant ruler in French history. To many Europeans, on the other hand, Napoleon was a sinister Man on Horseback, enemy of national independence, the foreigner who imposed French control and French reforms. As French conquests accumulated, and as nominally free countries became French puppets, Europe grew to hate the insatiable imperialism of Napoleon. Napoleonic France succeeded in building up a vast and generally stable empire, but only at the cost of arousing the enmity of other European nations, thus contributing to French insecurity.

The War, 1800-1807

Napoleon had barely launched the Consulate when he took to the field again. The second coalition, which had reached the peak of its success in August 1799, was now falling to pieces. Czar Paul of Russia alarmed Britain and Austria by his interest in Italy, and Britain offended him by retaining Malta, the headquarters of his Knights.

This romantic portrait of Napoleon, also by Jacques Louis David, shows him pausing after working early into the morning (note the clock behind him) on his famous Code Napoléon. He appears to be exceeding even his own demand for "two o'clock in the morning courage." He wears the insignia of the Legion of Honor (which he created) and the epaulettes of a general. Upon seeing this flattering portrait, Napoleon said to David, "You have understood me. By night I work for the welfare of my subjects, and by day for their glory." The painting is in The National Gallery in Washington.

Accordingly, the czar formed a Baltic League of Armed Neutrality linking Prussia, Sweden, and Denmark with Russia against Britain. He even contemplated joining with France to drive the British out of India; this scheme collapsed when he was murdered in 1801 and succeeded by his son, Alexander I. The Baltic League disintegrated in the same year after Nelson violated Denmark's neutrality to bombard its fleet in port at Copenhagen. A year earlier, in the spring of 1800, Napoleon had crossed the Alps with much fanfare; his public relations releases sounded as though no one had ever made the passage before. He defeated the Austrians in Italy and negotiated the Treaty of Lunéville (1801), whereby Austria recog-

nized the reconstituted French satellites in Italy and agreed that France should have a hand in redrawing the map of Germany.

After Lunéville, Britain again remained alone at war with France. British taxpayers, however, wanted relief from their heavy burden; British merchants longed to resume trading with the continental markets partially closed to them since 1793. Though Britain had been unable to check Napoleon's expansion in Europe, it had very nearly won the colonial and naval war by 1801. The British had captured former Dutch and Spanish colonies, and Nelson's fleet had expelled the French from Egypt and Malta. The British cabinet was confident that it held a strong bargaining position and could obtain favorable terms from Napoleon. Yet in the Peace of Amiens (1802) the British promised to surrender part of their colonial conquests and got nothing in return. The French failed either to reopen the Continent to British exports or to relinquish Belgium, which remained, in Napoleon's phrase, "a loaded pistol aimed at the heart of Britain."

The one-sided Peace of Amiens provided only a year's truce in the worldwide struggle of France and Britain. Napoleon soon aroused British exporters by a more stringent tariff law and jeopardized British interests in the Caribbean by a grandiose project for a colonial empire based on Haiti and on the vast Louisiana territory ceded back to France in 1800 by Spain. In Haiti, where the expectations of the black majority had been raised by the Convention's abolition of slavery, the blacks revolted against the efforts of the Consulate to reimpose slavery. Stubborn black resistance under François Toussaint L'Ouverture (c 1744-1803) and Jean Jacques Dessalines (c 1758-1806), ex-slaves, and an outbreak of yellow fever took a fearful toll of French troops and forced Napoleon to abandon the American project. In 1803 he sold to the United States for 80,000,000 francs (about $16,000,000) all of Louisiana, which later formed the whole or part of thirteen states.

When the Louisiana Purchase was completed, France and Britain were again at war. Napoleon interned many of the British tourists who had flocked to Paris since the Peace of Amiens, thus striking a new note of "total" war, in contrast with the eighteenth-century custom that permitted enemy citizens to circulate relatively freely even during hostilities. From 1803 through 1805 Napoleon actively prepared to invade England. He assembled more than a hundred thousand troops and a thousand landing barges on the French side of the Straits of Dover. In 1805 he sent Admiral Pierre de Villeneuve (1763-1806) and the French fleet to the West Indies to lure the British fleet away from Europe. Then Villeneuve was to slip back to Europe to escort the French invasion force across the Channel while Nelson was still combing the Caribbean in search of the French fleet.

Villeneuve failed to give Nelson the slip; back in European waters, he put in at a friendly Spanish port instead of heading directly for the Channel, as Napoleon had ordered. Nelson engaged the combined French and Spanish fleets off Cape Trafalgar at the southwest corner

This nearly contemporary engraving shows a supposed Napoleonic scheme for the invasion of England in 1804, by flotilla, aerial balloon, and a cross-channel tunnel. The English are shown putting up kites as an early form of anti-aircraft defense.

of Spain (October 1805). He lost his own life, but not before he had destroyed half of his adversaries' ships without sacrificing one of his own. The Battle of Trafalgar gave the British undisputed control of the seas and blasted French hopes of a cross-Channel invasion.

By the time of Trafalgar, Austria and Russia had joined with Britain in a third coalition. Austria in particular had been alarmed by Napoleon's efforts to promote a major revision of the political map of Germany by abolishing more than a hundred German city-states and small ecclesiastical principalities. The chief beneficiaries of this readjustment were south German states that Napoleon clearly intended to form into a bloc dominated by France, as opposed to Austria and Prussia.

Bonaparte routed the continental members of the coalition in the most dazzling campaign of his career. At Ulm, on the upper Danube (October 1805), he captured 30,000 Austrians who had moved westward without waiting for their Russian allies. He met the main Russian force and the balance of the Austrian army near the village of Austerlitz. The ensuing battle (December 2, 1805) fittingly celebrated the first anniversary of Napoleon's coronation as emperor. Bringing up reinforcements secretly and with great speed, Napoleon completely surprised his opponents; their casualties were three times greater than his own. Within the month he forced the Hapsburg emperor, Francis II, to sign the humiliating Treaty of Pressburg, giving the Austrian Tyrol to Bavaria, and Venetia to the Napoleonic puppet kingdom of Italy.

A still harsher fate awaited the Prussians, brought back into the war for the first time since 1795 by Napoleon's repeated interventions in German affairs. The fact that the Prussian commander was the same inept general who thirteen years before had lost the battle of Valmy indicated how much the army had deteriorated since the days of Frederick the Great. In October 1806 the French smashed the main Prussian contingents in the twin battles of Jena and Auerstädt and occupied Berlin. But Napoleon postponed a final settlement with Prussia until he had beaten his only remaining continental opponent. Russia went down at Friedland in June of 1807.

Even though Napoleon's great string of victories against the third coalition resulted partly from the blunders of his enemies, the French army was now the most seasoned and feared force in Europe. New recruits were furnished by conscription, which raised an average of 85,000 men a year under Napoleon, and they were quickly toughened by being assigned in small batches to veteran units—a process called the *amalgame* and developed during the Revolution to meet the emergencies of the war against the first coaliton. French officers were promoted on the basis of ability, rather than seniority or infuence, and they were, on the whole, more concerned with maintaining the morale of their men than with imposing strict discipline. Bonaparte seldom risked an engagement unless his forces were the numerical equal of the enemy's; then he staked everything on a dramatic surprise, as at Austerlitz. Yet even his seemingly invincible French army had defects. The medical services were poor, so that most deaths on campaigns were from disease or improperly treated wounds. Pay was low and irregular, and supplies were also irregular, since it was

UNITED KINGDOM
OF GREAT BRITAIN
AND IRELAND

SCOTLAND

North Sea

Edinburgh

IRELAND

WALES

ENGLAND
Oxford ● ● Cambridge
London ●

Atlantic Ocean

45

15

40

10

SWEDEN

Ba

KINGDOM OF DENMARK AND NORWAY

Hamburg

Oldenburg

HANOVER

Berlin

Leiden

PRU

NETHERLANDS

K. OF
WESTPHALIA

Antwerp
Waterloo ●
BELGIUM
Amiens

Rhine R.

Göttingen ● Halle

CONFEDERATION

OF

Weimar
Weser R.
Auerstädt

Leipzig

THE

Meuse R.

Jena
Erfurt

Seine R.

Paris

Varennes

Longuyon

RHINE

Prague

BOHEMIA

Versailles

Valmy

LORRAINE

Nantes

Orléans

Luneville

Heidelberg

EM

Austerlitz

VENDEE

Loire R.

ALSACE

Strasbourg

Ulm

Danube R.

Wagram ●

Vienna

FRANCE

Gironde R.

Limoges

Geneva

SWITZERLAND

BAVARIA

TYROL

Bordeaux ●

Lyon

Payrac ●

Avignon

Rhône R.

PIEDMONT

SAVOY

Marengo ●

Genoa

LOMBARDY
Milan

Po R.

Campoformio

VENETIA

Venice ●

IL

Nice

PARMA
MODENA

KINGDOM OF ITALY

Adriatic

Marseilles

CORSICA
(FRANCE)

Pisa

TUSCANY

Florence
Leghorn

BALEARIC IS.

MINORCA

ELBA

PAPAL STATES

Rome ●

SARDINIA

KINGDOM
OF
NAPLES

Naples ●

Coimbra ●

PORTUGAL

Lisbon ●

SPAIN

Madrid ●

Tagus R.

Ebro R.

Guadalquivir R.

Cape Trafalgar

Gibraltar
(BRITAIN)

Palermo ●

SICILY

MALTA
(Br.)

Napoleonic Europe, and After

Empire of France
French satellites
Allied with France
■ Battle sites

FINLAND

L. Ladoga

30

35

40

Gulf of Finland

St. Petersburg

LIVONIA

COURLAND

W. Dvina R.

Vitebsk

Borodino

Moscow

Oka R.

55

Smolensk

Vilna

Niemen R.

Napoleon's route, 1812

dland

Kiev

R U S S I A

Dnieper R.

WHITE RUSSIA

Don R.

Dniester R.

Azov

Pruth R.

UKRAINE

Volga R.

45

Caspian Sea

Sebastopol

40

B l a c k   S e a

Morava R.

Danube R.

Kutchuk - Kainarji

TE-
GRO

P E R S I A

O T T O M A N   E M P I R E

Vardar R.

Bosporus

Istanbul

Tigris R.

35

Dardanelles

Aegean Sea

Euphrates R.

CRETE

CYPRUS

M e d i t e r r a n e a n   S e a

A R A B I A

Abukir Bay

Alexandria

25

E G Y P T

Cairo

35

40

45

Western Europe, 1798

GREAT
BRITAIN

BATAVIAN
REPUBLIC

GERMANY

P R U S S I A

R U S S I A

F R A N C E

A U S T R I A

SWITZ.

CISALPINE REP.

LIGURIAN REP.

OTTOMAN
EMPIRE

SPAIN

CORSICA

PARTHENOPEAN
REPUBLIC

50

Extent of French influence

115

French policy to have men and horses live off the land as much as they could to save the expense and delay of bringing up elaborate supply trains.

Napoleon reached the pinnacle of his career when he met Czar Alexander I on the "neutral ground" of a raft anchored in the Niemen River at Tilsit, on the frontier between East Prussia and Russia. There, in July 1807, the two emperors drew up a treaty dividing Europe between them. Alexander acknowledged France's hegemony over central and western Europe and secured in return the recognition of eastern Europe as the Russian sphere. Napoleon pledged Russia a share in the spoils of the Ottoman Empire if it were dismembered. He demanded no territory from the defeated czar, only a commitment to cease trade with Britain and to join the war against it. The Tilsit settlement, however, made Alexander bitterly unpopular at home, where Russian propaganda had been denouncing Napoleon as satanic.

While the two emperors negotiated on the raft, Frederick William III (1797-1840), the Prussian king, nervously paced the banks of the Nieman. He had good cause to be nervous, for Tilsit cost him almost half his territory. Prussia's Polish provinces formed a new puppet state, the Grand Duchy of Warsaw, which Napoleon assigned to a French ally, the king of Saxony. Prussian territory west of the Elbe River went to Napoleon to dispose of as he wished. Napoleon also stationed occupation troops in Prussia and fixed the maximum size of its army at 42,000 men.

Thus all Europe was divided into three parts: first came the French Empire, including France proper and the territories annexed since 1789; second were the satellites, ruled in many cases by relatives of Napoleon; and third came Austria, Prussia, and Russia, forced by defeat to become allies of France. The only powers remaining outside the Napoleonic system were Britain, Turkey, and Sweden; and in 1810 Count Bernadotte, one of Napoleon's marshals, was invited by the Swedes to become crown prince for their childless king. Ironically, he then proceeded to turn Swedish policy against Napoleon, whom he had always regarded as an upstart.

In central Europe Napoleon decreed a further reduction in the number of German states, and in 1806 he aided the formal dissolution of that museum piece, the Holy Roman Empire. Francis II, the reigning Hapsburg, last of the Holy Roman emperors, now called himself emperor of Austria. To replace the vanished empire, Napoleon created the Confederation of the Rhine, which included almost every German state except Austria and Prussia. At the heart of this confederation Napoleon carved out for his brother Jerome the Kingdom of Westphalia, which incorporated the Prussian holdings west of the Elbe seized at Tilsit.

Napoleon longed to give dignity and permanence to his creations. It was not enough that his brothers and his in-laws should sit on thrones; he himself must found a dynasty, must have the heir so far denied him in fifteen years of childless marriage. He divorced Josephine, therefore, and in 1810 married Marie-Louise, the daughter of the Hapsburg Francis II. In due time Marie-Louise bore a son, called "the king of Rome," but destined never to rule in Rome or anywhere else.

The Continental System

Nowhere was Napoleon's imperialism more evident than in the Continental System. This was an attempt to regulate the economy of the whole Continent through a self-blockade that tied political, military, and economic goals into a single European policy. It had a double aim: to build up the export trade of France and to cripple that of Britain. The collapse of Napoleon's cross-Channel invasion plans led him to expand the earlier tariff measures against Britain into a great campaign to bankrupt "the nation of shopkeepers." The defeat of the third coalition allowed him to experiment with economic warfare on a continental scale and to carry mercantilism to extremes.

The Berlin Decree, issued by Napoleon in November 1806, forbade all trade with the British Isles and all commerce in British merchandise. It ordered the arrest of all Britons on the Continent and the confiscation of their property. Britain replied by requiring that neutral vessels wishing to trade with France put in first at a British port and pay duties. This regulation enabled Britain to share in the profits of neutral shipping to France. Napoleon retaliated with the Milan Decree (December 1807), ordering the seizure of all neutral ships that complied with the new British policy. The neutrals, as neutrals often are, were caught in the middle; the two decrees effectively instituted a continental blockade.

Napoleon's vassals and allies had to support the Continental System or suffer the consequences. Of all the "un-French" activities countenanced in Holland, the worst, in Napoleon's view, was toleration of Dutch smuggling of English contraband. The emperor also expected the satellites to feed French industrial prosperity. When Italians objected to the regulation of their silk exports, Napoleon lectured his viceroy on the facts of economic life:

> All the raw silk from the Kingdom of Italy goes to England. . . . It is therefore quite natural that I should wish to divert it from this route to the advantage of my French manufacturers: otherwise my silk factories, one of the chief supports of French commerce, would suffer substantial losses. . . . My principle is: France first. . . .
>
> It is no use for Italy to make plans that leave French prosperity out of account; she must face the fact that the interests of the two countries hang together.*

The gigantic attempt to make "France first" failed almost totally. Only a few French industries benefited from the Continental System; the cessation of sugar imports from the West Indies, for example, promoted

---

*Quoted in J.M. Thompson, ed., *Napoleon's Letters* (New York: Everyman Edition, 1942) pp. 241-42.

the cultivation of native sugar beets. But the decline of overseas trade depressed Bordeaux and other French Atlantic ports, and the increasing difficulty of obtaining such raw materials as cotton caused widespread unemployment and produced a rash of bankruptcies. Since the new French markets on the Continent did not compensate for the loss of older markets overseas, the value of French exports declined by more than a third between 1805 and 1813.

The Continental System did not ruin Britain, although it did confront the British with a severe economic crisis. Markets abroad for British exports were uncertain; food imports were reduced; while prices rose sharply, wages lagged behind; and because of hoarding, coins were in such short supply that not enough could be minted to keep pace with the demand. Both farm workers, already pinched by the enclosure movement, and factory workers suffered acutely. Yet Britain, fortified by its leadership in the economic revolutions and by the overwhelming superiority of its navy and merchant marine, rode out the storm. More land was brought under the plow. Factory owners improvised substitute payments for their workers when coins were unavailable. Exporters not only developed lucrative new markets in the Americas, the Ottoman Empire, and Asia but also smuggled goods to old customers on the Continent. Napoleon lacked the naval force to seize smugglers at sea, and he lacked a staff of incorruptible customs inspectors to control contraband in the ports. Moreover,

since the French army simply could not do without some items produced only in British factories, Napoleon violated the principle of his own decrees by authorizing secret purchases of British cloth and leather for uniforms.

The Continental System antagonized both the neutral powers and Napoleon's allies. French seizure of United States merchant vessels in European ports under the terms of the Milan Decree put a dangerous strain on Franco-American relations. But British restrictions also weighed heavily on the Americans. British impressment of American seamen on the pretext that they were deserters from the Royal Navy, together with the designs of expansionists in the United States on Canada, produced an indecisive and minor Anglo-American War in 1812-1814.

The Peninsular War, 1808-1813

In Europe the political and military consequences of the Continental System formed a decisive and disastrous chapter in Napoleonic history; a chapter that opened in 1807 when the emperor decided to impose the system on Britain's traditional ally, Portugal. The Portuguese expedition furnished Napoleon with an excuse for the military occupation of neighboring Spain. In 1808 he overthrew the Spanish royal family and made his brother Joseph his puppet king of Spain. But every measure taken by Napoleon—the removal of the inef-

The Spanish artist Francisco de Goya (1746-1828) had the deepest sympathy for the victims of war and none at all for royalty— including Spain's. It was said that he made his initial sketches in the blood of executed Spanish patriots. Here he shows the point-blank executions of Spaniards by the French in Madrid on May 3, 1808. The painting hangs in the Prado in Madrid; Goya painted it in 1814, in continued protest against war.

fectual Spanish Bourbons, the installation of a foreign monarch, the attempted enforcement of the Continental System, and the suppression of the Inquisition and the curtailment of noble and clerical privileges—violated Spanish customs and offended Spanish pride in the Church and the Bourbon dynasty. The irreconcilable Spaniards began fighting Napoleon when the population of Madrid rose in revolt on May 2, 1808.

Although the uprising in Madrid was brutally repressed, the Peninsular War (named after the Iberian peninsula) rapidly grew from a minor irritation into a deadly cancer on the body of the Napoleonic Empire. The Spaniards employed ambushes and poisoned wells and used other guerrilla devices. The expedition that Britain sent to assist the Spaniards belied all expectations about British inferiority in military, as opposed to naval, matters. It was ably commanded by Sir Arthur Wellesley (1769-1852—later the duke of Wellington) and generously supplied from home. Napoleon poured more than 300,000 troops into the campaign, but his opponents gained the upper hand in 1812, when he detached part of his forces for an invasion of Russia. In 1813 King Joseph left Madrid forever, and Wellington, having liberated Spain, crossed into southern France.

German National Awakening

Napoleonic imperialism aroused a nationalistic reaction among the disunited Germans. German intellectuals launched a campaign to check the great influence that the French language and French culture had gained over their divided lands. Jacob Grimm (1785-1863) and his brother Wilhelm (1786-1859) contributed not only their very popular *Fairy Tales* (1812-1815) but also research designed to prove the superiority of the German language. The philosopher J. G. Fichte (1762-1814), once an advocate of the Revolution, delivered at Berlin the highly patriotic *Addresses to the German People* (1807-1808), claiming that German was the *Ursprache*—the fountainhead of language; and the Germans themselves, Fichte continued, were the *Urvolk*—the oldest and most ethical of nations. Thus the German response at first came largely from the intellectuals and the social elite and then gradually from lower down the social scale.

The new German consciousness was evident even when Austria reentered the war against France in 1809 and for the first time attempted a total mobilization comparable to that decreed by the French Convention in 1793. While the new spirit enabled the Austrians to make a better showing, they were narrowly defeated at Wagram (1809) and for the fourth time in a dozen years submitted to a peace dictated by Napoleon. The treaty of Schönbrunn (1809) stripped them of their coastline on the Adriatic and assigned their Polish territory of Galicia to the Grand Duchy of Warsaw. Francis II gave his daughter to Napoleon in marriage, and his defeated land became the unwilling ally of France. Leadership in the German revival passed to Prussia.

The shocks of Jena and Tilsit jarred Prussia out of the administrative lethargy that had overtaken it since the death of Frederick the Great in 1786. The new University of Berlin, founded in 1810 to compensate for the loss of Halle to Saxony by the Tilsit settlement, attracted Fichte and other prophets of German nationalism, and there they began to lay down the theories of a new German national state. Able generals and statesmen, most of them non-Prussian, came to power. General Gerhard von Scharnhorst (1755-1813) headed a group of officers who reorganized the army on more democratic principles and improved its efficiency. The ceiling of 42,000 soldiers imposed by Napoleon was evaded by the simple device of assigning recruits to the reserve after a fairly brief period of intensive training and then inducting another group of recruits. By 1813 Prussia had more than 150,000 trained men available for combat duty.

The social and administrative reorganization of the Prussian state was inspired by the energetic Baron Heinrich vom und zum Stein (1757-1831), an enlightened aristocrat from the Rhineland. Stein conciliated the middle class by granting towns and cities some self-government. He granted some civil rights to Jews. To improve the status of the peasantry, he sponsored an edict of October 1807 abolishing serfdom in Prussia. The edict, however, did not break up the large Junker estates or provide land for the liberated serfs, many of whom thereafter led a difficult existence as day laborers. Nor did it terminate the feudal rights of justice the junkers exercised over their peasants. Stein and others eliminated only the worst abuses of the Old Regime and left authority where it had traditionally rested—with the king, the army, and the Junkers. The Hohenzollern state was not so much reformed as restored to the traditions of absolutism and efficiency established by the Great Elector and Frederick the Great.

The Russian Campaign, 1812-1813

The event that enabled a still immature German nationalism to turn its force against Napoleon was the French debacle in Russia. French actions after 1807 soon convinced Czar Alexander that Napoleon was not keeping the Tilsit bargain and was intruding on Russia's sphere in eastern Europe. When Alexander and Napoleon met again at the German town of Erfurt in 1808, they could reach no agreement, though they concealed their differences by a show of great intimacy. French acquisitions from Austria in 1809 raised the unpleasant prospect of French domination over the Balkans, and the transfer of Galicia from Austria to the Grand Duchy of Warsaw suggested that this Napoleonic vassal might next seek to absorb Russia's acquisitions from the partitions of Poland. Meanwhile, Napoleon's insistent efforts to make Russia enforce the Continental System increasingly angered Alexander. French annexations in northwest Germany completed the discomfiture of the czar, for they wiped out the state of Oldenburg, where his brother-in-law was the reigning duke. All these griev-ances caused a break between the czar and the emperor and led to the invasion of Russia by the French in 1812.

For the invasion Napoleon assembled a Grande Ar-mée of nearly 700,000 men, most of whom, however, were not French but unwilling conscripts in the service of a foreign master. The supply system for so distant a campaign broke down almost immediately, and the Russian scorched-earth policy made it hard for soldiers to live off the land and impossible for horses to get fodder, so that many of them had to be destroyed. As the army marched eastward, one of Napoleon's aides reported:

*There were no inhabitants to be found, no prisoners to be taken, not a single straggler to be picked up. We were in the heart of inhabited Russia and yet we were like a vessel without a compass in the midst of a vast ocean, knowing nothing of what was happening around us.**

Napoleon had hoped to strike a quick knockout blow, but the battle of Borodino—the first engagement in all these wars to exceed in casualties Louis XIV's Malplaquet of a century earlier—was indecisive. Napoleon entered Moscow and remained in the burning city for five weeks (September–October 1812) in the vain hope of bringing Czar Alexander to terms. But Russian stubbornness, typhus, and the shortage of supplies forced Napoleon to begin a nightmare retreat. Ill-fed, inadequately clothed and sheltered, without medical help, the retreating sol-diers suffered horribly from Russian attacks on strag-glers and from the onslaughts of "General Winter." Less than a quarter of the Grand Army survived the retreat from Moscow; the rest had been taken prisoner or had died of wounds, starvation, disease, or had frozen to death.

The Russian leaders feared that Napoleon would liberate the serfs and turn them against their masters. But the peasants, despite the treatment to which they had been subject for so long, formed guerrilla bands, harassed Napoleon's forces, and proved that their patri-otic sentiments outweighed their class grievances. Field Marshal Mikhail Kutuzov (1745-1813), the victorious Russian commander, now wanted to leave the continua-tion of the war to Russia's allies, but Alexander insisted on pursuing the French and sent Russian armies west-ward beyond the Russian frontiers on the track of Napo-leon's forces.

Napoleon's Fall, 1813-1815

The British had been the first to resist Napoleon successfully, at Trafalgar and on the economic battlefields of the Continental System. Then had come Spanish resistance, followed by Russian. Now in 1813 almost every nation in Europe joined the final coalition

*A.A.L. de Caulaincourt, *With Napoleon in Russia* (New York: Norton, 1935), p. 62.

against the feared French. Napoleon raised a new army, but he could not so readily replace the equipment lost in Russia. In October 1813 he lost the "Battle of the Na-tions," fought at Leipzig in Germany, necessitating his retreat into France. The German troops in his army were deserting, the Confederation of the Rhine collapsed, Italian support was increasingly unreliable, and the mystique of Napoleon, who had now suffered two severe defeats, was blighted. By April 1814 the well-organized forces of the coalition occupied Paris. Faced also with mounting unrest and conspiracy at home, the emperor abdicated when his marshals refused to continue the war. After attempting suicide by poison, which turned out to have lost much of its strength since he had procured it for the Russian campaign, Napoleon was sent into exile as ruler of the island of Elba, off the western coast of Italy.

The statesmen of the victorious coalition gathered in the Congress of Vienna to draw up the terms of peace. The Bourbons returned to France in the person of Louis XVIII, a younger brother of Louis XVI. Realizing that he could not revive the Old Regime intact, the new king issued the Charter of 1814 establishing a constitutional monarchy. The returned émigrés, however, showed no such good judgment. They unleashed a new White Ter-ror against the Revolution and all its works. Then, on March 1, 1815, Bonaparte pulled his last surprise: he landed on the Mediterranean coast of France.

For a hundred days, from March 20, 1815, when Napoleon reentered Paris, the French Empire was re-born. Once again the emperor rallied the French people, this time by promising a truly liberal regime with a real parliament and genuine elections. He never had time, however, to show whether his promise was sincere, for on June 18 the British under the Duke of Wellington and the Prussians under General Gebhard von Blücher (1742-1819) delivered the final blow at Waterloo, near Brussels. Again Napoleon went into exile, this time to the remote British island of St. Helena in the South Atlantic. There in 1821 he died, perhaps from arsenic poisoning. Bonapartism, however, did not die with him, any more than the Caesarism of ancient Rome had died on the Ides of March. A Napoleonic legend arose, fostered at first by the emperor himself on St. Helena. It glossed over the faults and failures of the emperor, depicting him as a champion of liberalism and patriotism, and paved the way for the advent of another Napoleon in 1848.

VI THE LEGACY OF THE REVOLUTION

The Napoleonic legend, with its hero worship and belligerent nationalism, was one element in the legacy bequeathed by revolutionary and Napoleonic France. A second and much more powerful element was the great

TOCQUEVILLE ON THE FRENCH REVOLUTION

Alexis de Tocqueville (1805-1859), an observer of the Napoleonic Revolution, wrote:

. . . the French Revolution, though ostensibly political in origin, functioned on the lines, and assumed many of the aspects, of a religious revolution. Not only did it have repercussions far beyond French territory, but like all great religious movements it resorted to propaganda and broadcast a gospel. This was something quite unprecedented: a political revolution that sought proselytes all the world over and applied itself as ardently to converting foreigners as compatriots. . . .

It was because the Revolution always harked back to universal, not particular, values and to what was the most "natural" form of government and the most "natural" social system that it had so wide an appeal and could be imitated in so many places simultaneously.

No previous political upheaval, however violent, had aroused such passionate enthusiasm, for the ideal the French Revolution set before it was not merely a change in the French social system but nothing short of a regeneration of the whole human race. It created an atmosphere of missionary fervor and, indeed, assumed all the aspects of a religious revival. . . . It would be truer to say that it developed into a species of religion. . . .

The Old Régime and the French Revolution, trans. Stuart Gilbert (Garden City, N.Y.: Doubleday Anchor, 1955), pp. 11-13.

---

revolutionary motto—*Liberté, Egalité, Fraternité*—which inspired later generations in France and elsewhere. Behind the motto was the fact that the French, though not yet enjoying the full democracy of the twentieth century, enjoyed greater liberty, equality, and fraternity in 1815 than they had ever known before 1789. True, Napoleon's censors and prefects gave new force to the old traditions of absolutism and centralization, but the middle class had won its freedom from obsolete restraints, and Protestants, Jews, and freethinkers had gained toleration both in France and in the French satellites. Although French institutions in 1815 did not measure up to the ideals of liberty expressed in the Declaration of the Rights of Man, the ideals had been stated, and the effort to embody them in a new form was to be the main theme of French history in the nineteenth century.

The revolutionary and Napoleonic regimes established the principle of equal liability to taxation. They provided more economic opportunity for the third estate by removing obstacles to the activity of business people, big and little, and by breaking up the large estates of the clergy and nobility; these lands passed mainly to the urban bourgeois and the well-to-do peasants. The only gesture toward full equality of property was the Laws of Ventôse of 1794, and they were never implemented. The Revolution was an important step in the ascendancy of middle-class capitalism, both urban and rural. In this sense the work of the Revolution was not truly democratic, since the sans-culottes had apparently gained so little. Yet the Code Napoléon did bury beyond all hope of return the worst legal and social inequalities of the Old Regime. There was much truth in Napoleon's boast:

Whether as First Consul or as Emperor, I have been the people's king: I have governed for the nation and in its interests, without allowing myself to be turned aside by the outcries or the private interests of certain people.[*]

The Revolution and Napoleon promoted fraternity in the legal sense by making all French men equal in the eyes of the law. In a broader sense they advanced fraternity by encouraging nationalism, the feeling of belonging to a great corporate body, France, that was superior to all other nations. French nationalism had existed long before 1789: Joan of Arc, Henry IV, and Louis XIV had all been nationalists in their ways. But it remained for the Convention to formulate a fervent new nationalistic creed in its decree of August 23, 1793, providing for total mobilization. The Napoleonic empire then showed how easily nationalism on an unprecedented scale could lead to imperialism of unprecedented magnitude.

The Revolution's early adherents were unbending—Robespierre and the Jacobins; its later exponents—the men of Thermidor and Brumaire—were more practical and moderate. Even under Napoleon, however, the Revolution remained a kind of religion, demanding political orthodoxy and punishing heretics by political excommunication. After 1815 the "new religion" of the Revolution and the nationalisms it created or unleashed continued to pour forth "its soldiers, its apostles, and its martyrs over the face of the earth."

[*]Quoted in Caulaincourt, *With Napoleon in Russia*, p. 364.

SUMMARY

Years of fiscal mismanagement contributed to the severe financial crisis that precipitated the French Revolution. Louis XVI, irresolute and stubborn, was unable to meet the overwhelming need for reform. The third estate, which comprised 97 percent of the population, held some land, but rural poverty was widespread. Moreover, they bore the heavy burden of taxation. Discontent was rife among urban workers. The bourgeoisie helped focus this discontent against the privileged estates and called for an end to the abuses of the Old Regime, especially the inequalities of tax assessments.

The financial emergency of the heavily indebted monarchy forced the king to summon the Estates General. Bad weather and poor harvests in the winter of 1788-89 led to demands for drastic change. When the Estates General met, the third estate successfully challenged the king over procedure, transforming the Estates General into a National Assembly charged with writing a constitution.

Popular uprisings pushed the Revolution along at an increasing pace. The National Assembly abolished the abuses of the Old Regime and in August 1789 issued the Declaration of the Rights of Man, embodying the ideals of the Enlightenment.

By 1791 the National Assembly had completed its task and established a government based on a separation of powers. The activities of French émigrés and of Louis XVI and the outbreak of war in 1792 opened a gulf between moderates and extremists. In Paris the Jacobins led a municipal revolution that resulted in the abolition of the monarchy.

In 1793 Robespierre, an advocate of democracy, imposed a dictatorship on France. During the Reign of Terror 20,000 were killed. Calling for total mobilization and economic sacrifice, Robespierre and the Committee of Public Safety organized a drive to push foreign invaders from France.

The excesses of the Terror created the conditions for Robespierre's downfall in July 1794. A new Constitution of 1795 established the Directory, which assured the dominance of the propertied classes.

In 1799 Napoleon engineered a coup d'état ending the Directory and establishing the Consulate. Napoleon became first consul for life in 1802 and emperor in 1804. He moved quickly to centralize imperial administration and appointed talented ministers to office.

The Code Napoléon embodied some ideas of the Old Regime as well as revolutionary principles such as the equality of all citizens before the law.

In religion, Napoleon made peace with the church in the Concordat of 1802. Education was subservient to the state, with lycées established to train administrators. Napoleon established the Bank of France and improved tax collection.

In Europe, Napoleon built a vast empire. He forced Prussia, Russia, and Austria to accept peace terms, leaving only Britain in the war against France. The French Empire was divided into three parts: France and the territories it annexed; French satellite states; and Austria, Prussia, and Russia. In Germany, Napoleon formally dissolved the Holy Roman Empire and created the Confederation of the Rhine.

Napoleon's effort to wage economic warfare against Britain backfired, hurting France and antagonizing neutral powers. Nationalist movements in Spain and Prussia threatened the French Empire after 1808.

When Napoleon's Russian campaign of 1812 ended in disaster for his Grand Army, the nations of Europe formed a new coalition that presided over Napoleon's downfall. In 1814 the Bourbons were restored to power. The Napoleonic legend, however, would haunt France, as would the revolutionary goals of liberty, equality, and fraternity.

chapter nineteen

ROMANTICISM, REVOLUTION, AND REACTION

The origins of the modern West lay in the French Revolution, the rising nationalism stimulated by it and by the conquests of Napoleon, and in the developments of the short, intense period between the Congress of Vienna, by which the post-Napoleonic European settlement was worked out, and the wave of revolutions that moved across Europe in 1848. During this time and into the 1880s, the Industrial Revolution was also transforming Western societies, especially in Britain, Germany, and the United States, while new developments in scientific thought, and especially those associated with the work of Charles Darwin, led to yet another series of dramatic changes in how philosophers, politicians, and scientists perceived the world. Ideology, present though hardly a dominant influence in revolutionary thought in either North America or in France, had attained the status of a new religion in many European nations by 1850. Romanticism, idealism, and materialism well describe the various conflicting, overlapping, and prevailing strands of thought by which people tried to account to themselves for their actions, to provide continuity, security, and stability amid rapid change. A triple revolution—industrial and economic, political and social, intellectual and cultural—was slowly supplanting the values, associated with the Old Regimes of Europe, despite their persistence down to 1914.

The labels *reaction* and *counterrevolution* are often applied to the events of 1815-1830. By 1815 Europe was reacting strongly against the French Revolution, which had made Napoleon possible, and against the Enlightenment, which was believed to have made the Revolution possible. The reaction against the Enlightenment took the form of the romantic movement. Romantic writers and artists protested against the rationalism and classicism of the eighteenth century and championed faith, emotion, tradition, and other values associated with the more distant past. The political counterrevolution came of age at the Congress of Vienna in 1814-1815, where the leaders of the last coalition against Napoleon reestablished the European balance of power and repudiated revolutionary principles. Reason and natural law, in the judgment both of political leaders and of many romantics, had led not only to progress, but also to the Reign of Terror and Napoleonic imperialism.

Yet despite the ascendancy of counterrevolutionary forces, the spirit of 1789 did not die in 1815. It inspired new and progressively more intense outbreaks of revolution in the 1820s, in 1830, and in 1848. The revolutions of 1848, though put down, marked a critical turning point in the development of the liberalism and nationalism bequeathed by the great French Revolution.

I THE ROMANTIC PROTEST

Romanticism and the protest movement associated with it were at their peak between 1815 and 1830. The romantic period (usually dated 1780 to 1830) was one in which political and cultural thought showed such a varied concern for tradition that many historians dispute that there was sufficient unity of thought to refer to a "movement" at all. Moreover, "the romantic school of writers" in Germany was quite different from writers in England or France at the same time; the various romantic thinkers tended to be united by what they disliked more than by what they liked.

There was a general revolt against what many viewed as the "narrowness" of the eighteenth century—the emphasis on the purely logical, on the tightly ordered rules of poetry and prose, on what was felt to be an unimaginative approach to history, science, and politics. The romanticists accused their Enlightenment predecessors of being unduly optimistic about the perfectibility of human nature and argued that pleasure can also be taken from the grotesque, the disorganized, and the irrational in life. The English romantic artist William Blake (1757-1827) subtly attacked the worship of Sir Isaac Newton, seeing him less as a scientific genius of the imagination and more as a materialist who thought he could grasp the world in a pair of compasses—that is, by measurement (a form of "reason") without emotional inspiration. God existed and was to be found in Nature, the romantics argued, not in Science. As opposed to the revolutionary desire to throw off the "dead hand of the past," the romantics saw humanity as having emotional ties to the past, and those ties provided a sense of community and gave stability to human institutions. Reason, while important, took its instructions from intuition.

The romantics' emphasis on the individual ultimately enriched the doctrines of liberalism, and their emphasis on the historical evolution of communities strengthened nationalism. Their emphasis on cultural rather than political history led to broader theories and to a greater attempt to grasp the whole of human motivation, rather than to interpret the causes of events predominantly in political or economic terms. Yet the major immediate political influence of romanticism was exerted in support of God and king and in opposition to republicanism and anticlericalism.

Paradoxically, the revolutionary qualities of the romantics were always evident in literature and the arts, where they rebelled against Jacobin and Napoleonic

France's devotion to the cult of classical antiquity. Revolutionary regimes tend to be quite unrevolutionary in the arts, clinging to traditional standards of expression and being cool or hostile toward innovation and experiment; thus revolutionary France was attached not only to Roman names, furniture, and fashions but also to neoclassical painting and architecture. The romantics were most revolutionary in their disdain for the literary and artistic standards of neoclassicism and their attraction to the medieval and the Gothic, to the colorful and the exotic, to the visually undisciplined and the emotional.

If the protest against reason reached full force during the first third of the nineteenth century, it had been building up for a long time in contemporary challenges to the Enlightenment. Before 1750 Wesley in England and the Pietists in Germany were protesting against the deism of the philosophes and preaching a religion of the heart, not the head. Rousseau proclaimed conscience, not reason, as the "true guide of man." The protest against oversimplification of the individual and society, and the insistence on the intricacy and complexity of humanity, formed the common denominators of romanticism.

An Age of Feeling and of Poetry, 1790-1830

Some movements are best revealed in political thought or in the actions that arise from political argument. Romanticism is best revealed through literature, which was one step removed from action and which also provided the romantics with their best platform. Literary romanticism may be traced back to the mideighteenth century—to novels of "sensibility" like Rousseau's *La Nouvelle Héloïse* and to the sentimental "tearful comedies" of the French stage. In the 1770s and 1780s a new intensity appeared in the very popular works of the German Sturm und Drang, for example, Goethe's morbidly sensitive *Sorrows of Young Werther*, and *The Robbers*, a drama of social protest by J.C.F. von Schiller (1759-1805), who went on to write a series of dramas with exceedingly romantic heroes and heroines: William Tell, Joan of Arc, Mary Stuart.

Goethe (1749-1832) was a good eighteenth-century exponent of reason, interested in natural science and comfortably established in the Grand Duchy of Weimar, an enlightened small German state detached from the political passions sweeping Germany in the revolutionary and Napoleonic age. Yet romantic values lie at the heart of his most famous writings—his short lyrics and, above all, *Faust*, which many have called the greatest work in the German language. Begun when Goethe was in his twenties and finished only when he was eighty, this long poetic drama was a philosophical commentary on the main currents of European thought. According to the traditional legend, the aged Faust, weary of book learning and pining for eternal youth, sold his soul to the Devil, receiving back the enjoyment of his youth for an allotted time, and then, terror-stricken,

going to the everlasting fires. Goethe partially transformed this legend: Faust makes his same infernal compact with Mephistopheles, who points out how disillusioning intellectual pursuits are; but Faust is ultimately saved through his realization that he must sacrifice selfish concerns to the welfare of others. A drama of sinning, striving, and redemption, Goethe's *Faust* reaffirmed the Christian values that the Enlightenment had belittled.

The Enlightenment had also belittled any poetry except that following very strict forms, like the heroic couplets of Racine and Pope. The romantics decried this neoclassicism as artificial and praised the vigor, color, and freedom of the Bible, Homer, and Shakespeare. The result was a great renaissance of poetry all over Europe, especially in England, which produced a galaxy of great poets: Lord Bryon (1788-1824), Percy Bysshe Shelley (1792-1822), John Keats (1795-1821), William Wordsworth (1770-1850), Samuel Taylor Coleridge (1772-1834), and others.

Of them all, Wordsworth and Coleridge pressed furthest in their reaction against classicism and rationalism. In 1798 the two men published *Lyrical Ballads*, the first great landmark of English romanticism, to which Coleridge contributed the *Rime of the Ancient Mariner*, a supernatural tale of the curse afflicting a sailor who slays an albatross. Later he created the very "striking images" of *Kubla Khan*, which has a surrealistic quality and probably was induced by taking drugs. In place of a mathematically ordered world-machine, Coleridge's *Kubla Khan* has its Xanadu:

> Where Alph, the sacred river, ran
> Through caverns measureless to man
>   Down to a sunless sea.

Wordsworth, who had lived in France during the early years of the Revolution and had been disillusioned by the failure of rational reform, abandoned the philosophes' confidence in human perfectibility through reason to put his faith in the "immortal spirit" of the individual. In place of the light shed by Newton's laws, he found "a dark inscrutable workmanship." God was to be found in all things.

The Return to the Past

Wordsworth's almost pantheistic universe and the romantics' enthusiasm for the Middle Ages in general and for the earlier history of their own nations in particular linked the universal (nature) to the particular (the nation-state). Nationalism was an emotional, almost mystical force. The heightened sense of nationalism evident almost everywhere in Europe by 1815 was in part a matter of political self-preservation. In the crisis of the Napoleonic wars, for example, both the Spaniards and the Germans became more aware of their national heritages. However, the romantic return to the national past, though intensified by French expansionism, had begun before 1789 as part of the repudiation of the

SHELLEY ON THE DECAY OF KINGS

In 1817 the English poet Shelley captured the romantic sense of despair in his poem "Ozymandias," which stated anew the biblical warning that the overweening aspirations of arrogant humanity would be as dust to dust. As Lord Byron said, the poet was to remind humanity of "the earthquake that was once below."

I met a traveler from an antique land
Who said: "Two vast and trunkless legs of stone
Stand in the desert. Near them, on the sand,
Half sunk, a shattered visage lies, whose frown,
And wrinkled lip, and sneer of cold command,
Tell that its sculptor well those passions read
Which yet survive, stamped on these lifeless things,
The hand that mocked them, and the heart that fed:
And on the pedestal these words appear:

'My name is Ozymandias, King of Kings:
Look on my works, yet Mighty and despair.'
Nothing beside remains. Round the decay
Of that colossal wreck, boundless and bare
The lone and level sands stretch far away."

Paul Robert Lieder, Robert Morss Lovett, and Robert Kilburn Root, eds., *British Poetry and Prose* (Boston: Houghton Mifflin, 1936), II, 171.

Enlightenment. The pioneers of romanticism tended to cherish what the philosophes detested, notably the Middle Ages and the medieval preoccupation with religion.

The German writer Johann Gottfried von Herder (1744-1803) provided intellectual justification for medieval studies with his theory of cultural nationalism. Each separate nation, he argued, like an organism, had its own distinct personality, its *Volksgeist*, or "folk spirit," and its own pattern of growth. The surest measure of a nation's progress was its literature—poetry in youth, prose in maturity. Stimulated by Herder, students of medieval German literature collected popular ballads and folk tales. In 1782 the first complete text of the *Nibelungenlied* (*Song of the Nibelungs*) was published, a heroic saga of the nation's youth that had been forgotten since the later Middle Ages. By putting a new value on the German literature of the past, Herder helped to free the German literature of his own day from its bondage to French culture. He was no narrow nationalist, however, and he asserted that the cultivated person should also study other cultures; so Herder also helped to loose a flood of translations that poured over Germany beginning about 1800: of Shakespeare, of *Don Quixote*, of Spanish and Portuguese poetry, and of works in Sanskrit.

Other nations also demonstrated that the return to the past meant veneration of the Middle Ages rather than of classical antiquity. In Britain Sir Walter Scott (1771-1832) collected medieval folk ballads and wrote more than thirty historical novels, of which *Ivanhoe*, set in the days of Richard the Lionhearted and the Crusades, is the best known. In Russia the poet Alexander Pushkin (1799-1837) deserted the Slavonic language of the Orthodox church to write the first major Russian literary works in the vernacular: *Boris Godunov* (published in

WORDSWORTH COMMANDS THAT NATURE BE OUR TEACHER

Come forth into the light of things,
Let Nature be your teacher.
. . .
One impulse from a vernal wood
May teach you more of man,
Of moral evil and of good,
Than all the sages can.

Sweet is the lore which Nature brings;
Our meddling intellect
Mis-shapes the beauteous forms of things:—
We murder to dissect.

Enough of Science and of Art;
Close up those barren leaves;
Come forth, and bring with you a heart
That watches and receives.

"The Tables Turned," *The Poetical Works of William Wordsworth*, eds. Ernest de Sélincourt and Helen Darbishire (Oxford: Clarendon Press, 1947), IV, 57.

1831) and *Eugene Onegin* (1832). He took subjects from Russia's past and introduced local color from the newly acquired Crimea and Caucasus. He also celebrated his own great grandfather, Hannibal, an African slave who was a general to Peter the Great.

In France, the home of the "classical spirit," the romantic reaction gathered slowly, beginning in the first years of the new century with the vicomte de Chateaubriand (1768-1848) in *The Genius of Christianity* (1802). In 1811 Madame Germaine de Staël (1766-1817), who was the daughter of the banker Necker, published *De l'Allemagne* (*Concerning Germany*), a plea for the French to remember that they were the descendants not only of ancient Romans but also of Teutonic Franks. The most direct blow against classicism came early in 1830, however, at the first night of the play *Hernani* by Victor Hugo (1802-1885), who flouted the classical rules of dramatic verse. When one of the characters uttered a line ending in the middle of a word, traditionalists in the audience set off a riot, and the issues were fought and refought at the theater and in the press for weeks. In the next year Hugo published his great historical novel, *Notre Dame de Paris*, set in the France of Louis XI.

Music

Romantic musicians, like romantic poets, sought out the popular ballads and tales of the national past; they also sought to free their compositions from classical rules. For color and drama composers of opera and song turned to literature: Shakespeare's plays, Scott's novels, Bryon's poetry, and the poems and tales of Goethe and Pushkin. Yet, although literature and music often took similar paths during the romantic era, there were significant differences. Romantic musicians did not revolt against the great eighteenth-century composers as Wordsworth and Coleridge revolted against their predecessors. Rather, romantic music evolved out of the older classical school.

The composer who played the commanding role in this evolution was Ludwig van Beethoven (1770-1827), who lived most of his life in Vienna. Where earlier composers had indicated tempo with a simple "fast" or "slow," Beethoven added such designations as "appassionato" and "Strife between Head and Heart." Part of the color and passion of Beethoven's works derived from his skill in exploiting the resources of the piano, an instrument that was perfected during his lifetime, and his use of more instruments—especially winds, percussion, and double basses—than was traditional. In his Ninth (and final) symphony, Beethoven introduced a chorus in the last movement to sing his setting of Schiller's *Ode to Joy*.

After Beethoven, orchestral works took on increasingly heroic dimensions. The French composer Hector Berlioz (1803-1869) projected an orchestra of 465 pieces, including 120 violins, 37 double basses, and 30 each of pianos and harps. The *Symphonie Fantastique*, which he supposedly based on Goethe's *Werther*, was completed in 1830, the year of Hugo's *Hernani* (and, as we shall see, of

the July Revolution in Paris). Berlioz's *Requiem* called for a full orchestra, a great pipe organ, four brass choirs, and a chorus of two hundred. The romantic propensity for bigness also affected the presentation of Bach's choral works, like *The Passion According to St. Matthew*, originally composed for relatively few performers but revived with a full orchestra and a large chorus in a precedent-setting performance directed by Felix Mendelssohn (1809-1849) in 1829.

Music for the human voice reflected both the increased enthusiasm for instruments, particularly the piano, and the general romantic nostalgia for the past. In composing songs and arias, romantic musicians devoted as much skill to the accompaniment as to the voice part itself. Franz Schubert (1797-1828), Beethoven's Viennese contemporary, made a fine art of blending voice and piano in more than six hundred sensitive *lieder* (songs), seventy of them musical settings of poems by Goethe. Meantime, Carl Maria von Weber (1786-1826) was striving to create a fully German opera, taking an old legend as the libretto for *Der Freischütz* (*The Freeshooter*, 1821). Its plot ran the romantic gamut of an enchanted forest, a magic bullet, and an innocent maiden outwitting the Devil, and its choruses and marches employed folklike melodies. In Russia Mikhail Glinka (1804-1857) cast aside the Italian influences that had dominated the secular music of his country, to base his opera *Russlan and Ludmilla* (1842) on a poem by Pushkin, embellishing it with dances and choruses derived from Russian Asia.

Perhaps most romantic of all was the Polish composer Frédéric Chopin (1810-1849). Writing almost exclusively for the piano, drawing heavily on the melodic forms of Polish popular music, Chopin best combined romantic music with national idioms, especially in his polonaises, which were written to accompany a Polish dance. His work was technically very demanding, while passionate and stirring, and he made the piano the most popular instrument of the century.

The Arts

In the fine arts the forces of romanticism gained no such triumph as they had won in literature and music. The virtual dictator of European painting during the first two decades of the nineteenth century was the French neoclassicist Jacques Louis David (1748-1825). A deputy of the Convention, president of the Paris Jacobin club, and member of the Committee of General Security, David organized many of the great ceremonies of the Revolution, notably Robespierre's Festival of the Supreme Being (June 1794). He became a baron and court painter under Napoleon, then was exiled by the restored Bourbons. No matter how revolutionary the subject, David employed traditional neoclassical techniques, stressing form, line, and perspective.

The works of the Spaniard Francisco Goya (1746-1828) were much closer to the romantic temper, with their warmth, passion, and sense of outrage. No one

This cartoon of Hector Berlioz shows his dramatic use of percussion, string, and wind instruments to drive out classical modes of art in favor of "radical romanticism." Berlioz was also the founder of modern orchestral conducting, bringing his own dramatic personality onto the podium. This wood engraving, by a German cartoonist, was copied from a French newspaper about 1846.

could have any illusions about Spanish royalty after looking at Goya's revealing portraits of Charles III and his successors. After viewing Goya's etchings of the French suppression of the Madrid insurgents of May 1808, one can understand the story that Goya made his preliminary sketches in the blood of the executed Spanish patriots whose agonies he was portraying.

Romantic painting did not acquire formal recognition until an official Paris exhibition in 1824. Although many of the pictures shown there came from the school of David, two leaders of romantic painting were also represented—the Englishman John Constable (1776-1837) and the Frenchman Eugène Delacroix (1798-1863). Constable took painting out of the studio, studied nature afresh, and produced landscapes that stressed light and color more than classical purity of line, thus paving the way for the impressionists of the later nineteenth century. Even more influential was J.M.W. Turner (1775-1851), precursor of the impressionists, who developed British landscape painting to the heights of the sublime and romantic. Delacroix too championed color and light and urged young painters to study the flamboy-

The Houses
of Parliament in London
were extended and rebuilt
in the romantic style
of late Gothic
by Sir Charles
Barry (1795-1860)
and Augustus Pugin
(1815-1852). Begun
in 1840, the building was
not completed until 1888,
although the first
Parliament opened here
in 1852.

Thomas Jefferson greatly admired Roman architecture and especially a Roman temple found in southern France known as the Maison Carrée, or square house, and he adapted this style to secular purposes for the capitol building of Virginia. He then used the Pantheon as the model for his circular library, which approximated a Roman villa, with rows of smaller structures on both sides.

ant canvases of Rubens, whom David had banished from the ranks of acceptable artists. The purpose of art, Delacroix claimed, was "not to imitate nature but to strike the imagination." By the 1830s French painters were divided into opposing schools: the still-influential disciples of David and the romantic followers of Delacroix.

In architecture also two schools flourished during the first half of the nineteenth century: the neoclassical, looking to Greek and Roman antiquity, and the neo-Gothic or Gothic revival, looking to the Middle Ages. Many architects of the early 1800s mastered both styles, not so much copying ancient or medieval structures as adapting them to the needs and tastes of the day. Generally, basic design was classical in its proportions, while decoration was medieval. The Houses of Parliament in London, rebuilt in the 1830s and 1840s after a disastrous fire, were Gothic in their spires and towers, but they also embodied classical principles of balance and symmetry.

At the beginning of the nineteenth century the Roman vogue, firmly set by the French Revolution, reached its peak in Napoleonic Paris with triumphal arches, columns, and churches patterned after Roman forms. In America Thomas Jefferson, who was a gifted designer, provided the University of Virginia with distinguished academic buildings focused on a circular library derived from the Roman Pantheon (the perfect example of "spherical" architecture). Yet by the second quarter of the nineteenth century neo-Roman was yielding to Greek revival, stirred in part by a wave of enthusiasm for the Greek independence movement.

Religion and Philosophy

The romantic religious revival was marked at the institutional level by the pope's reestablishment in 1814 of the Jesuit order, whose suppression in 1773 had been viewed as one of the great victories of the Enlightenment. On the whole, the romantics were horrified by the religious skepticism of the philosophes; Shelley, an atheist, was an isolated exception. Catholicism gained many converts among romantic writers, particularly in Germany, and the Protestants also made gains. Pietism found new strength in Germany and Russia. In England Coleridge vigorously defended the established church, while also introducing the new German idealist philosophy. Chief among these romantic German philosophers was G.W.F. Hegel (1770-1831), a follower of Kant and a professor at the University of Berlin. Like Kant, Hegel attacked the tendency of the Enlightenment to see in human nature and history only what met the eye. Human history, properly understood, was the history of efforts to attain the good, and this in turn was the unfolding of God's plan for the world. For Hegel, history was a *dialectical* process—that is, a series of conflicts; the two contending elements in the conflict were the *thesis*, the established order of life, and the *antithesis*, a challenge to the old order. Out of the struggle of thesis

and antithesis emerged a *synthesis*, no mere compromise between the two but a new and better way—a combination that was another step in humanity's slow progress toward the best of all possible worlds. In turn, the synthesis broke down by becoming conventional and unproductive; it became locked in conflict with a new antithesis, and the dialectic produced another synthesis—and so on and on.

The death of the Roman Republic allowed Hegel to illustrate the dialectic at work. The thesis was represented by the decadent Republic, the antithesis by despotism, and the synthesis by the Caesarism of the early Roman Empire. Hegel explained that "This important change must not be regarded as a thing of chance; it was *necessary*," a part of God's grand design. Julius Caesar himself Hegel called a "hero," one of the few "world-historical individuals" who "had an insight into the requirements of the time" and who knew "what was ripe for development." This concept of the hero as the agent of a cosmic process was another characteristic of the romantic temper.

The dialectical philosophy of history was the most original and influential element in Hegel's thought; it would help to shape the dialectical materialism of Karl Marx. Still, Hegel was once even more famous as a liberal idealist. His emphasis on duty, his choice of Alexander the Great, Caesar, and Napoleon as "world-historical" heroes, his assertion that the state "existed for its own sake"—all suggest a link with authoritarianism. Yet Hegel foresaw the final synthesis of the dialectic not as a brutal police state but as a liberalized version of the Prussian monarchy.

The Romantic Style

Thus Hegel, like the philosophes, believed in progress and in human perfectibility, though he also believed that the process would require far more time and struggle than an optimist like Condorcet had ever imagined. Indeed, the style of romanticism was not totally at variance with that of the Enlightenment; not only a modified doctrine of progress but also eighteenth-century cosmopolitanism lived on into the nineteenth. Homer, Cervantes, Shakespeare, and Scott won appreciative readers in many countries; giants of the age such as Beethoven and Goethe were not merely Austrian or German citizens but citizens of the world.

Yet despite these similarities and continuities, romanticism did have a decided style of its own—imaginative, emotional, and haunted by the supernatural, the terrific (in the sense of inspiring awe and even terror), and by history. The romantics could no longer view history in Edward Gibbon's terms of a classical golden age followed by long centuries of superstition. Rather, history was, as Herder and Hegel argued, an organic process of growth and development, which was indebted to the Middle Ages for magnificent Gothic buildings, religious enthusiasm, folk ballads, and heroic epics.

Just as the romantics rejected the Enlightenment's view of the past, so they found the Newtonian world-machine an entirely inadequate interpretation of the universe. It was too static, too drab and materialistic. In its place they put a neo-Gothic world of religious mystery, the Hegelian mechanics of dialectic and heroes, the poetic and artistic vision of feeling, color, and impulses in nature. The romantics wanted to recreate a sense of wonder, to inspire a belief in the essential unity of God, man, and nature, to show that humanity lived in a world of endless "becoming."

As broadly persuasive intellectual movements do, romanticism pervaded all forms of thought. As in the early Middle Ages, once again Europeans were fascinated with death, and especially with dying heroically, for one's ideals or nation, in defense of home, to achieve a dramatic purpose. Two immensely popular paintings of the time captured the *frisson*, the chill of pleasure down the spine, that merged romanticism and a form of social realism. One, by a German romantic landscape painter, Caspar David Friedrich (1774-1840), depicted the wreck of the *Hope*, a vessel trapped in ice, never to escape from its destiny. Another, earlier work, by the French artist Théodore Géricault (1791-1824), showed the fate of passengers from the frigate *Medusa*, which had foundered on the way to Senegal. The passengers, 149 in all, were put onto an open raft and cut adrift at sea; a handful lived to tell the tale, and Géricault devoted his life to studying corpses in a morgue so that he might capture this horrific moment of both realistic and romantic revelation.

This was the age of great cemeteries, laid out in rows with huge mausoleums, where relatives and friends could gather around the graves—the age of "the beautiful death." Bryon had a romantic death; in the minds of liberals and radicals, conservatives and counter-revolutionaries, one must defend one's principles to the death—as Byron did. The Italian revolutionary leader Mazzini listed six causes worth dying for: liberty, equality, nationality, conscience, individuality, fatherland. In time contradictions between these abstract principles would emerge.

II THE RECONSTITUTION OF A EUROPEAN ORDER

The romantic movement was too intellectually scattered to provide a blueprint for the reconstruction of Europe after the defeat of Napoleon. The general guidelines, though not the specific details, for reconstruction were to be found in the writings of the English orator Edmund Burke (1729-1797), who set the tone for counterrevolutionary conservatism. Burke strongly believed that some form of divine intent ruled society, and that through individual conscience a chain was forged between rights and duties; there were no rights for those who did not do their duty. He was convinced that civilized society required orders and classes, though movement should be possible between these groups. The only true equality, conservatives felt, was moral equality; any other kind was impossible. If this were so, economic leveling was not economic progress. Because people were governed more by emotion than by reason (as the romantics also argued), some control must be put on the free exercise of the will. Burke felt affection for the variety and mystery of tradition; reform, while at times desirable, should be approached with caution to preserve what was valuable from the past.

Burke therefore welcomed American independence, which he viewed more as a reaffirmation of the glorious English tradition of 1688 than as a revolution. The same reasoning drove him to violently condemn the French Revolution, which destroyed everything, good, bad, and indifferent. Rage and frenzy, he observed, "pull down more in half an hour, than prudence, deliberation and foresight can build up in a hundred years."[*] Society itself is thereby threatened. "Society is indeed a contract," Burke wrote, but he did not mean what Rousseau had meant:

> the state ought not to be considered as nothing better than a partnership agreement in a trade of pepper and coffee, calico or tobacco, or some such other low concern, to be taken up for a little temporary interest, and to be dissolved by the fancy of the parties. It is to be looked on with other reverence; because it is not a partnership in things subservient only to the gross animal existence of a temporary and perishable nature. It is a partnership in all science; a partnership in all art; a partnership in every virtue, and in all perfection. As the ends of such a partnership cannot be obtained in many generations, it becomes a partnership not only between those who are living, but between those who are living, those who are dead, and those who are to be born.[**]

Burke's doctrines were especially welcomed by the émigrés. Among them was Joseph de Maistre (c 1753-1821), a diplomat in the service of the king of Sardinia who had been forced into exile when the French overran Savoy and Piedmont. De Maistre combined Burke's conservatism with a belief in the viciousness of the state of nature and a traditional Catholic view of human depravity and the need for discipline. The French Revolution, he believed, had been God's punishment for the philosophes' arrogance in believing that society could be remade without divine assistance. The postrevolutionary world needed firm control by an absolute monarch and inspired guidance from the church. De Maistre carried the revival of Catholicism to an extreme called Ultramontanism (literally, "beyond the mountains"), asserting for the papacy in Rome a universal authority far beyond the Alps that the popes themselves had not claimed since Innocent III and Boniface VIII.

The force of tradition bore heavily upon the politics of

---

[*] *Reflections on the Revolution in France* (New York: Everyman Edition, 1910), p. 164.
[**] Ibid., p. 93.

post-Napoleonic Europe. Yet it was not so much ideological conviction as political realism, however, that accounted for the conservatism of the man who presided over the actual reconstruction of Europe. That man was Prince Klemens von Metternich (1773-1859), Austrian foreign minister from 1809 to 1848 and the chief figure in European diplomacy during most of his long career. Handsome, dashing, aristocratic, Metternich retained some of the eighteenth century's belief in reform through enlightened despotism; but he also believed that reform should proceed with Burkean caution. His family's estates in the German Rhineland had suffered severely during the French Revolution. Moreover, Metternich served a state that was particularly threatened by the liberal and nationalist energies released by the Revolution. Conservatism, he knew, was the cement that held together the very different parts of the multilingual, potentially multinational realm of the Austrian Hapsburgs.

The Congress of Vienna, 1814-1815

In 1814 and 1815 Metternich was host to the Congress of Vienna, which approached its task of rebuilding Europe with conservative deliberateness, seeking to stifle both liberalism and nationalism. For the larger part of a year, the diplomats indulged in balls and banquets, concerts and hunting parties. "The Congress dances," quipped an observer, "but it does not march." Actually, the brilliant social life distracted hangers-on while the important diplomats settled matters in private conferences.

Four men made most of the major decisions at Vienna: Metternich; Czar Alexander I; Viscount Castlereagh (1769-1822), the British foreign secretary; and Charles Maurice de Talleyrand (1754-1838), the foreign minister of Louis XVIII, the restored Bourbon king of defeated France. Castlereagh, who shared the conservative outlook of Metternich, was less concerned with punishing the French for their past sins than with preventing the appearance of a new Robespierre and other Bonapartes. He was at Vienna, he said, "not to collect trophies, but to bring the world back to peaceful habits." The best way to do this, he believed, was to restore the balance of power and keep the major states, including France, from becoming either too strong or too weak. "No arrangement could be wise that carried ruin to one of the countries between which it was concluded."

At Vienna Talleyrand scored the greatest success of his long career. Originally a worldly bishop of the Old Regime, he had in succession rallied to the Revolution in 1789, become one of the very few bishops to support the Civil Constitution of the Clergy, served as Napoleon's foreign minister, and then, while still holding office, intrigued against him after 1807. This adaptable diplomat soon maneuvered himself into the inner circle at Vienna, and the representatives of the victorious powers accepted the emissary of defeated France as their equal.

METTERNICH ON THE NATURE OF POLITICAL ORDER

Metternich was regarded as brilliant, devious, and an exemplar of the conservative position on world affairs. Among his statements about the nature of the political order are these:

Policy is like a play in many acts which unfolds inevitably once the curtain is raised. To declare then that the performance will not take place is an absurdity. The play will go on, either by means of the actors . . . or by means of the spectators who mount the stage. . . . Intelligent people never consider this the essence of the problem, however. For them it lies in the decision whether the curtain is to be raised at all, whether the spectators are to be assembled and in the intrinsic quality of the play. . . .

Arguing that liberty could not be separated from authority, and that true freedom arose from the reality of order, Metternich wrote,

The world is subject to two influences, the social and the political. . . . The political element can be manipulated; not so the social element whose foundations must never be surrendered.

When near death, Metternich said:

In what times have I lived? . . . Let anyone look at the situations which Austria and all of Europe confronted between 1809 and 1848 and let him ask himself whether one man's insight could have transformed these crises into health. I claim to have recognized the situation, but also the impossibility to erect a new structure in our Empire . . . and for this reason all my care was directed to conserving that which existed.

Aus Metternichs Nachgelassenen Papieren, ed. Alfons von Klinkowstroem (Vienna, 1880), VIII, 190, 340; VII, 640. As quoted in Henry A. Kissinger, *A World Restored: Metternich, Castlereagh and the Problems of Peace, 1812-22* (Boston: Houghton Mifflin, 1957), pp. 41, 191, 213.

Talleyrand was particularly adept in exploiting the differences that divided the victors.

To these differences Alexander I contributed greatly. Metternich called the czar a Jacobin, although Alexander's reputation for enlightenment was only partially deserved. By 1814 the czar had acquired a romantic enthusiasm for religion, spending hours praying in the company of a German mystic, Madame de Krüdener. Under her influence he envisioned a Holy Alliance whereby all states would follow Christian teachings. In the first months at Vienna, however, it was Alexander's Polish policy that nearly disrupted the Congress. He proposed a partial restoration of eighteenth-century Poland, with himself as its monarch; Austria and Prussia would lose their Polish lands. Alexander won the support of Prussia by backing its demands for the annexation of Saxony, whose king had remained loyal to Napoleon. Metternich, however, did not want Prussia to make such a substantial gain. Moreover, both Metternich and Castlereagh disliked the prospect of a large, Russian-dominated Poland.

The dispute over Saxony and Poland gave Talleyrand his chance to fish in troubled waters. Thus in January 1815 the representative of defeated France joined Metternich and Castlereagh in threatening both Prussia and Russia with war unless they moderated their demands. The threat produced an immediate settlement. Alexander obtained Poland but agreed to reduce its size and to allow Prussia and Austria to keep part of their gains from the partitions. Prussia took about half of Saxony, while the king of Saxony was allowed to keep the rest.

Once the Saxon-Polish question was out of the way, the Congress was able to turn to other important dynastic and territorial questions. According to what Talleyrand christened "the sacred principle of legitimacy," thrones and frontiers were to be reestablished as they had existed in 1789. In practice, however, legitimacy was ignored almost as often as it was applied, since the diplomats realized that they could not undo all the changes brought about by the Revolution and Napoleon. Although they sanctioned the return of the Bourbons to the thrones of France, Spain, and Naples in the name of legitimacy, they did not attempt to resurrect the Republic of Venice or to revive all the hundreds of German states that had vanished since 1789. In Germany the Congress provided for thirty-nine states grouped in a weak confederation, which came close to recreating the impotent Holy Roman Empire. The Diet, chief organ of the German Confederation, was to be a council of diplomats from sovereign states rather than a representative national assembly. Its most important members were to be Prussia and Austria, for the German-speaking provinces of the Hapsburg realm were considered part of Germany.

The land exchanges were complex and often cynical, with little or no regard for the wishes of the people. Prussia, besides annexing part of Saxony, added the Napoleonic kingdom of Westphalia to its scattered lands in western Germany, creating the imposing Rhine Prov-

ince, Austria lost Belgium, which was incorporated into the Kingdom of the Netherlands to strengthen the northern buffer against France. But Austria recovered the eastern Adriatic shore and the old Hapsburg possession of Lombardy, to which Venetia was now joined. By holding Lombardy-Venetia and exploiting the close family ties between the Hapsburgs and the ruling dynasties in other Italian states, Austria could dominate Italy. The Congress of Vienna restored the Bourbon Kingdom of Naples, the States of the Church, and, on their northern flank, the Grand Duchy of Tuscany. The Kingdom of Piedmont-Sardinia acquired Genoa as a buttress against France. Another buttress was established in the Republic of Switzerland, now independent again and slightly enlarged. The Congress confirmed the earlier transfer of Finland from Sweden to Russia and compensated Sweden by the transfer of Norway from the rule of Denmark to that of Sweden. This last transfer punished the Danes for their pro-French policy and rewarded Bernadotte for his anti-French policy. Finally, Great Britain received the strategic Mediterranean islands of Malta and the Ionians at the mouth of the Adriatic Sea and, outside Europe, the former Dutch colonies of Ceylon and the Cape of Good Hope, plus some minor French outposts.

France at first was given its boundaries of 1792, which included minor territorial acquisitions made during the early days of the Revolution. Then came Napoleon's escape from Elba and the Hundred Days. The final settlement reached after Waterloo assigned France the frontiers of 1790, substantially those of the Old Regime plus Avignon. The French also had to return Napoleon's art plunder to its rightful owners, pay the victorious allies a vast indemnity, and finance allied military occupation of seventeen frontier fortresses on French soil for not more than five years.

To quarantine any possible new French aggression, Castlereagh conceived the policy of strengthening France's neighbors so that they would be able to restrain the troublemaker in the future. Thus, to the north the French faced the Belgians and the Dutch combined in the single Kingdom of the Netherlands; on the northeast they faced the Rhine Province of Prussia; and on the east, the expanded states of Switzerland and Piedmont. The Quadruple Alliance, signed in November 1815, constituted a second great measure of quarantine. The four allies—Britain, Prussia, Austria, and Russia—agreed to use force, if necessary, to preserve the Vienna settlement. At Castlereagh's insistence, the allies further decided on periodic conferences to consider measures for maintaining "the Peace of Europe."

The Holy Alliance, signed in September 1815, was dedicated to the proposition that "the policy of the powers . . . ought to be guided by the sublime truths taught by the external religion of God our Saviour." Although most of the major European rulers signed the Holy Alliance, only Czar Alexander appears to have taken it seriously. Castlereagh called it "a piece of sublime mysticism and nonsense," and Britain declined to participate—the first sign of the rift that was to open between Britain and the continental powers. The pope, refusing an invitation to join, remarked tartly that the Vatican needed no new interpretations of Christian doctrine by the laity.

Neither the Holy Alliance nor the Quadruple Alliance fulfilled the expectations of their architects. At the first meeting of the Quadruple Alliance, in 1818, the allies agreed to withdraw their occupation forces from France, which had paid its indemnity. Czar Alexander pressed the allies to participate in a vague international union with the potentially contradictory goals of promoting constitutional monarchy everywhere, repressing revolution, fostering disarmament, and supporting an international army to sustain governments and defend existing frontiers. Metternich and Castlereagh refused, the latter deploring the czar's effort "to endow the transparent soul of the Holy Alliance with a body." At the next meeting of the allies, two years later, Metternich and Castlereagh would find themselves ranged on opposite sides on the issue of putting down revolutions under international auspices.

For these revolutions of 1820-1821 the Congress of Vienna was itself partly to blame, through its attempt to suppress liberal and nationalist aspirations. Yet as major international settlements go, that of Vienna was a sound one, in many respects more successful than its two predecessors—Westphalia (1648) and Utrecht (1713)—or the Versailles settlement of 1919-1920. There was to be no war involving several powers until the Crimean conflict of the 1850s, and no major war embroiling the whole of Europe until 1914. Seldom have victors treated a defeated aggressor with the wisdom and generosity displayed in 1815. Most of the leading diplomats at Vienna could have said with Castlereagh that they acted "to bring the world back to peaceful habits."

The Persistence of Revolution, 1820-1823

The revolutionary leaders of the post-Napoleonic generation despised the traditions revered by conservatives. Opposing the counterrevolutionary alliance of throne and altar, they remained firm for liberty, equality, and fraternity. The first two words of the great revolutionary motto continued to signify the abolition of noble and clerical privileges in society and, with few exceptions, laissez-faire economics. They also involved broadening civil rights, instituting representative assemblies, and granting constitutions, which would bring limited monarchy or possibly even a republic.

Fraternity, intensified by the romantic cult of the nation, continued to evolve into the formidable doctrine of nationalism. The nationalists of the post-1815 generation dreamed of a world in which each nation would be free of domination by any other, and all nations would live together harmoniously. In practical terms, this signified movements toward national unity and national independence. It meant growing pressure for the unification of Germany and Italy. And it inspired demands for freedom by peoples living under the control of a foreign power—by Belgians against their Dutch rulers, by Poles against Russians, by Greeks and Serbs against Turks, and by Italians, Hungarians, and Czechs against the Hapsburgs.

The first revolutionary outbreaks after 1815 took place in Spain, Portugal, and the Kingdom of the Two Sicilies. In all three states legitimacy meant a return to the Old Regime at its least enlightened. Yet the great majority of the population responded calmly, even enthusiastically, for the aristocracy were delighted to recover their ancient privileges, and many peasants welcomed the return of comfortable traditions. A small minority, drawn from the middle-class artisans and other workers, the intellectuals, and the army, dissented. This discontented minority produced the revolutionary movement of 1820.

The trouble began in Spain. During the war against Napoleon, representatives from the liberal middle class of Cadiz and other commercial towns had framed the Constitution of 1812. Based on the French Constitution of 1791, this document greatly limited the power of the monarchy, gave wide authority to a Cortes elected by a broad suffrage, and deprived the Spanish church of some of its lands and privileges. The Bourbon Ferdinand VII (r. 1814-1833) suspended the constitution, despite his promise not to do so. Ferdinand also restored the social inequalities of the Old Regime and reestablished the Jesuits and the Inquisition. Army officers, alienated by his highhandedness and clericalism, and merchants, facing ruin because of the progressive revolt of Spanish colonies in the distant New World, joined the liberal opposition.

It was Ferdinand's attempt to subdue the rebellious colonies that triggered revolution at home. The independence movement in Spanish America had been the outcome of the refusal of the colonial populations to accept either Napoleon's brother Joseph as their king or the closer ties between colonies and mother country proposed by patriots in Spain and implicit in the Constitution of 1812. Behind the Spanish-American independence movement lay several other factors: the powerful examples of the American and French revolutions; the sympathetic interest of Great Britain, anxious to free lucrative markets from Spanish mercantilist restrictions; and the accumulated resentment of colonial peoples at centuries of indifferent rule by Spanish governors. The colonial rebels had won their initial success at Buenos Aires in 1810, and their movement spread rapidly to Spain's other American possessions.

Ferdinand determined to crush the rebels by force. To transport troops he bought three leaky hulks from Russia. At the end of 1819 this motley new armada, carrying 20,000 men, was about to sail from Cadiz. It never sailed, for on January 1, 1820, a mutiny broke out at Cadiz led by a liberal colonel, Rafael Riego. Uprisings soon followed in Madrid, Barcelona, and other Spanish cities. Ferdinand, virtually a prisoner, surrendered.

Centers of Revolution

1820–1830

1848–1849

The liberal minorities in Portugal and Naples followed the Spanish lead. An army faction seized control of the Portuguese government in 1820, abolished the Inquisition, and set up a constitution on the Spanish model of 1812. Brazil declared its independence, with a prince of the Portuguese royal house as its emperor. In Naples the revolution was the work of the *Carbonari* (charcoal burners). This secret society, with a membership exceeding 50,000, had been opposed to the French and their reforms in the days of Napoleon, but it now sponsored a vaguely liberal program inspired by the French Revolution and the Spanish Constitution of 1812. King Ferdinand I of the Two Sicilies (1759-1825), who was the uncle of the Spanish Ferdinand VII, gave in at the first sign of opposition in 1820 and accepted a constitution of the Spanish type.

However, the strength of the revolutionary movement of 1820 ebbed as quickly as it had risen. The reforms introduced hastily by the inexperienced liberal leaders in Spain and Naples alienated the bulk of the population at home and so alarmed the conservative leaders of the great powers that they sponsored counterrevolutionary intervention. The Spanish revolutionaries were further weakened by a split between *moderados*, who wanted to keep the Constitution of 1812, and *exaltados*, led by Colonel Riego, who wanted to set up a violently anticlerical republic. Only in Portugal did the revolutionary regime survive, and only because it had British protection.

The revolutions of 1820 tested both the stability of the Vienna settlement and the solidarity of the Quadruple Alliance of Britain, Prussia, Austria, and Russia. Though legitimacy was restored in Spain and Italy, the Quadruple Alliance was split in two. While the continental allies increasingly favored armed intervention to suppress revolution, Britain inclined toward nonintervention. The split became evident at the conference of the Quadruple Alliance meeting at Troppau in Silesia late in 1820. Castlereagh, knowing that the Neapolitan revolution

threatened the Hapsburg hegemony in Italy, was willing to see Austria intervene in Naples, but without the backing of the Alliance. The Alliance, Castlereagh declared, was never designed "for the superintendence of the internal affairs of other states," and Britain refused to participate formally in the Troppau meeting. Metternich, supported by Alexander, pressed for a blanket commitment from the Alliance, and the result was the Troppau Protocol, signed by Austria, Prussia, and Russia. It declared war on all revolutionary governments that threatened European stability. Under the terms of the Troppau Protocol, an Austrian army toppled the revolutionary government of Naples in 1821. In 1823 a French army restored the absolute authority of Ferdinand VII, who then executed Riego and hundreds of his followers.

French intervention in Spain provoked the strong opposition of Great Britain and ended the Quadruple Alliance. George Canning (1770-1827), who became British foreign minister when the overworked Castlereagh committed suicide in 1822, suspected that the continental powers might now help Spain recover its former American colonies; so did the United States, which had recognized the independence of the new Latin American republics. But America also feared a possible Russian move southward from its outpost in Alaska along the Pacific coast or an attempt by Britain to extend its possessions in the Caribbean. Therefore, when Canning proposed a joint Anglo-American statement to ward off European interference in Latin America, the government of President James Monroe (1758-1831) refused the invitation. However, in a message to the American Congress in December 1823, the President included a statement that later became known as the Monroe Doctrine. Although this document marked an important assertion of policy by the youthful American republic in opposing European intervention in the Americas, it had little immediate international signficance, except to provoke Metternich to note that the United States wished to set "power against power . . . altar against altar." The Americans, he said, "lend new strength to the apostles of sedition, and reanimate the courage of every conspirator." The European powers were not fully committed to restoring Spain's American empire in any event. So far as they were deterred from that venture, it was by Canning and the possible actions of the British fleet.

Serbian and Greek Independence, 1804-1829

The British fleet was soon to play an important role in the Greeks' bid for national independence. The Greek revolt was part of the general movement of the Balkan nations for emancipation from their Turkish overlords. The Ottoman Turks had fallen well behind Europe generally in commercial and industrial matters by the eighteenth century. During the last quarter of the eighteenth century many peoples of the Balkan peninsula were awakening to a sense of national identity under the impact of French revolutionary and romantic ideas. They examined their national past with new interest and put particular stress on their native languages and on their Christian religion, which separated them from the Islamic Turks.

The first outbreak against the Turkish authorities came in 1804 among the Serbs, now one of the peoples of Yugoslavia. Ably led by Karadjordje Petrović (c 1752-1817), these early Serbian nationalists knew they would need outside help to win their independence. Some turned to Austria, which was nearby and ruled over their fellow Yugoslavs, the Croats and Slovenes; others looked to distant Russia, which attracted them because it was both Slavic in language and Orthodox in religion, for the Serbs were Orthodox, unlike the other Yugoslavs, who were Roman Catholic. Thus was established a pattern of conflicting Austrian and Russian interests that ulti-

mately erupted in World War I. Napoleon's venture in Austria's Adriatic provinces gave the Yugoslavs a taste of the Enlightenment and stimulated their desire for independence. Abandoned by the Russians in 1812, Karadjordje fled to Austria, and leadership of Serb nationalism passed to his rival, Milosh Obrenovich (1780-1860), who won Russian support and succeeded by 1830 in becoming prince of an autonomous Serbia. Although Milosh still paid tribute to the Ottoman emperor and a Turkish garrison remained in the Serb capital of Belgrade, a major step toward independence had been completed.

Meantine, the Greeks had launched a revolution. Leadership came from two groups—the Phanariot Greeks, named for the quarter where they lived in Istanbul, and the Island Greeks, merchants from the ports and islands of the Aegean. The Phanariots had long held positions of power and responsibility in governing the Orthodox subjects of the Ottoman Empire. The Island Greeks dominated the commerce of the Near East. The Island Greeks revived the old Greek mercantile tradition and some of the old Greek zeal for self-government. From their home islands and from their merchant colonies abroad they poured forth a stream of patriotic exhortation. Greek nationalists sponsored a campaign to purge the modern Greek language of its Turkish and Slavic words and to return it to the classical tongue of the Age of Pericles. A revolutionary secret society was formed in the Russian port of Odessa, patterned after the Carbonari of Italy and headed by Alexander Ypsilanti (1792-1828), a Phanariot who was an officer in the Russian army.

In 1821 Ypsilanti led an expedition into the Danubian provinces of the Ottoman empire that failed to stir up a major revolt. The conspirators were more successful in the Morea (the ancient Peloponnesus), where they launched a peasant uprising. The ensuing war for independence was a ferocious conflict. The Morean peasants slaughtered every Turk they could find; the Ottoman

PRESIDENT MONROE DECLARES THE NEW WORLD OFF LIMITS

In the wars of the European powers in matters relating to themselves we have never taken any part, nor does it comport with our policy so to do. It is only when our rights are invaded or seriously menaced that we resent injuries or make preparation for our defence. With the movements in this hemisphere we are of necessity more immediately connected, and by causes which must be obvious to all enlightened and impartial observers. The political system of the allied powers is essentially different in this respect from that of America. . . . We owe it, therefore, to candor and to the amicable relations existing between the United States and those powers to declare that we should consider any attempt on their part to extend their system to any portion of this hemisphere as dangerous to our peace

and safety. With the existing colonies or dependencies of any European power we have not interfered and shall not interfere. But with the governments who have declared their independence and maintained it, and whose independence we have, on great consideration and on just principles, acknowledged, we could not view any interposition for the purpose of oppressing them, or controlling in any other manner their destiny, by any European power in any other light than as the manifestation of an unfriendly disposition toward the United States.

James D. Richardson, ed., *Compilation of the Messages and Papers of the Presidents, 1789-1897* (Washington, D.C.: U.S. Government Printing Office, 1969), II, 207 ff.

government retaliated by killing or selling into slavery 30,000 Greeks from the prosperous Aegean island of Chios. To help with the repression, the Ottoman sultan called in the forces of his vassals, especially the governor of Egypt. By 1827 when it appeared likely that the Egyptian expedition would recapture the last rebel strongholds, Britain, France, and Russia intervened to save the Greek independence movement at its darkest hour.

The three-power action resulted from the combined pressures of public opinion and strategic interests. In Britain, France, Germany, and the United States, the Philhellenic (pro-Greek) movement had won many supporters. Philhellenic committees sent supplies and money and demanded that their governments intervene directly. But intervention hinged on Russia, for Greek patriots had formed their secret society on Russian soil and with Russian backing. For a time Metternich restrained Russia by pointing out the dangers to the European balance in supporting revolution in one country and repressing it in others. Ultimately, however, Russia's desire to dominate the Balkans won out over its concern for preserving the status quo, and it rallied openly to the Greek cause. Britain and France now felt obliged to take action because of Philhellenic pressure and, still more, because they feared to let Russia gain mastery over the Near East. A three-power intervention seemed the only course that would both rescue the Greeks and check the Russians.

Neither aim was fully achieved. In October 1827 Russian, British, and French squadrons sank the Turkish and Egyptian fleet at Navarino on the southwest corner of the Morea, and thus destroyed the chief Ottoman base. The subsequent Treaty of Adrianople (1829), while allowing Russia to annex outright only a little Turkish territory, arranged that the Ottoman Danubian provinces of Moldavia and Wallachia (the heart of present-day Romania) should become a virtual Russian protectorate. After considerable wrangling, the European powers accorded formal recognition to a small independent Greek kingdom, which left most Greeks still within the Ottoman Empire. Neither nationalism nor liberalism had won a complete victory in the Greek war. Greek patriots now schemed to enlarge the boundaries of their new kingdom. And Greek politicians were to threaten its stability and disillusion Philhellenists abroad by continuing the bitter feuds that had divided them, even in the midst of their desperate struggle for independence.

The Decembrist Revolt in Russia, 1825

Russia, which did so much to determine the outcome of revolutions elsewhere, itself felt the revolutionary wave, but with diminished force. The last period of Czar Alexander's reign, marked by the establishment of the hated military colonies, had thoroughly disappointed Russian liberals. Liberal ideas, however, continued to penetrate the country, spread by the secret societies that flourished in Russia after 1815. The introduction of Freemasonry during the eighteenth century and the secret ritual connected with many of the lodges had enabled nobles to meet on equal terms with men from other ranks of society. Moreover, the contrast between the relatively enlightened West and backward Russia made a deep impression on officers who had served in the campaigns against Napoleon. High-ranking officers at St. Petersburg secretly formed the Northern Society, which aimed to make Russia a limited, decentralized monarchy, with the various provinces enjoying rights somewhat like those of American states. The serfs would receive their freedom but no land. These reforms would be achieved by peaceful means. A second secret organization, the Southern Society, with headquarters at Kiev, included many relatively impoverished officers among its members; its leader was a Jacobin in temperament and an admirer of Napoleon. On every main issue the program of the Southern Society went beyond that of the St. Petersburg group; it advocated a highly centralized republic, the granting of land to liberated serfs, and the assassination of the czar to gain its ends.

Both societies tried to profit by the political confusion following the sudden death of Alexander I in December of 1825. Since Alexander left no son, the crown would normally have passed to his younger brother, Constantine, his viceroy in Poland. Constantine, however, had relinquished his rights to a still younger brother, Nicholas, but in a document so secret that Nicholas never saw it. On the death of Alexander, Constantine declared that Nicholas was the legal czar, and Nicholas declared that Constantine was. While the two brothers were clarifying their status, the Northern Society summoned the St. Petersburg garrison to revolt against Nicholas. Throughout the day of December 26, 1825, the rebels stood their ground in Russia's capital city until Nicholas subdued them. Two weeks later the Southern Society launched a movement that was doomed from the start because its leader had already been placed under arrest.

The Decembrist revolt, for all its ineffectiveness, was an important episode. It thoroughly alarmed Czar Nicholas I (1825-1855), who resolved to follow a severely autocratic policy. Nicholas had five Decembrists executed and exiled more than a hundred others to Siberia, where many of them contributed to the advance of local government and education. The Decembrists were the first in a long line of modern Russian political martyrs, and the program of the Southern Society may be seen as a kind of early blueprint for the Revolution of 1917.

III THE REVOLUTIONS OF 1830

Success in France

The next revolutionary wave, that of 1830, swept first over the traditional home of revolution, France. King Louis XVIII (r. 1814-1824) had given the Bourbon resto-

DISORDER IN THE COUNTRYSIDE

One source of discontent was the forest codes, which reserved to the Crown, or for purposes of taxation to the communes, much forest land that had traditionally been accessible to the peasantry for pasturage. In overpopulated sections of France, peasants disguised themselves as women (known as the *demoiselles*) and began to attack forest guards and *charbonniers* (charcoal burners) in the forests.

The following description recounts the problems confronted by the owner of cutting rights in the forest of Ustou, for which the owner had invested a large sum. In the face of attacks, the owner offered the peasants pasturage on his forest lands, "with the exception of the underbrush," which he proposed to keep, but the peasants declared they must have all or nothing, and he was unable to recover his investment:

At the moment of the completion of this work, when the *charbonniers* were to return to my forge toward two in the morning, a band of armed and disguised madmen appeared before my *charbonniers* and made them promise to abandon their work under the threat of death. Nevertheless, I was able to persuade them to stay in the forest, with the promise to obtain the protection of the authorities. Last Sunday, the 12th, toward four in the afternoon, a crowd of masked and armed men, who were without doubt the same who had appeared before, entered the work area, and, firing rifle shots, chased away fourteen *charbonniers*. The people of Ustou, joyous spectators to this horrible scene, offered no help to the unfortunate *charbonniers*. The mayor of Ustou was sick in bed, and could not find anyone to represent and support him, not even the deputy mayor, who said that he could not go to the scene because he had to be away . . . everyone agrees, the justice of the peace, the mayor, and the *charbonniers*, that the inhabitants of the commune themselves are the authors of similar attacks.

John M. Merriman, ed., *1830 in France* (New York: Franklin Watts, 1975), p. 94. (From the Archives Départementales de l'Ariège.)

---

ration an ambiguous start. He would have preferred to be an absolute ruler, but he knew that returning to the Old Regime was impractical, especially since he was declining in health and suffered from the additional political handicap of having been imposed on the French by their enemies.

The ambiguities of Louis XVIII's policies were most evident in the constitutional charter that he issued in 1814, before Napoleon's post-Elba Hundred Days. Some sections sounded like the absolute monarchy of Louis XIV; for example, the preamble asserted the royal prerogative: "The authority in France resides in the person of the king." But the charter also granted a measure of constitutional monarchy. There was a legislature, composed of a Chamber of Peers, appointed by the king, and a Chamber of Deputies, elected on a very restricted suffrage that allowed fewer than one hundred thousand of France's thirty million the right to vote. "In the king alone is vested the executive power," the charter stated, and the Chambers had no formal right to confirm the king's choices as ministers. Yet since Louis tended to select ministers acceptable to majority opinion in the legislature, this was a kind of functional compromise with parliamentary government. Furthermore, the charter confirmed many of the decisive changes instituted in France since 1789: it guaranteed religious toleration, a measure of freedom for the press, equality before the law, and equal eligibility to civil and miliary office; it also accepted the Code Napoléon and, still more important, the revolutionary property settlement.

The charter, however, greatly irritated the ultraroyal-ist faction, drawn from the noble and clerical émigrés who had returned to France after their revolutionary exile. These Ultras were determined to recover both the privileges and the property they had lost during the Revolution. When the election of 1815 gave the Ultras control of the Chamber of Deputies, they proposed to outlaw divorce and to institutionalize the White Terror already launched by setting up special courts to deal with suspected revolutionaries. At the insistence of the allies, Louis XVIII dismissed the Chamber and held a new election, which returned a more moderate majority. He also chose ministers who worked to pay off the indemnity to the victorious allies and to put French finances in good order.

Events, however, soon strengthened the Ultras' hand. Antirevolutionary fears swept France after the Spanish uprising of 1820 and the killing of the king's nephew by a lone assassin who hoped to extinguish the Bourbon line. The Ultras won control of the Council of Deputies, reimposed censorship of the press, and put through a law giving extra weight to the votes of the wealthiest 25 percent of the already very restricted electorate. In 1821 French education was placed under the direction of the Roman Catholic bishops.

The tempo of the reaction quickened when Louis died, and his brother, the Ultra leader, became King Charles X (r. 1824-1830). Though a man of charm, Charles had little political sense. He tried to revive some of the medieval glamor of monarchy by staging an elaborate coronation; he greatly extended the influence of the church by encouraging the activities of the Jesuits, who were still legally banned from France; and he sponsored a law compensating the émigrés for their confiscated property. The measure could be defended as a sensible political move that lifted the last threat of confiscation from those who had acquired property during the Revolution. But it was widely, if inaccurately, believed that a concurrent reduction of the annual interest on government obligations from 5 to 3 percent was intended to defray the cost of the annuities. Many influential Parisian bondholders were infuriated by the move, as well as by the king's clericalism.

After a brief attempt to conciliate the liberals, Charles X appointed as his chief minister the prince de Polignac, an Ultra-royalist who claimed to have had visions in which the Virgin Mary promised him success. Polignac hoped to bolster Charles's waning prestige by scoring a resounding naval victory. He attacked the dey of Algiers, a largely independent vassal of the Ottoman emperor, who was notorious for his collusion with the Barbary pirates; the capture of Algiers (July 5, 1830) laid the foundation of the French empire in North Africa. Meanwhile, the liberal majority in the Chamber of Deputies had attacked Polignac's ministry as unconstitutional because it did not command the confidence of the legislature. To secure a more favorable Chamber, Charles X arranged new elections, which the liberal opposition won. On July 25, 1830, without securing the legislature's approval, Charles and Polignac issued the Four Ordinances, muzzling the press, dissolving the newly elected Chamber, ordering a fresh election, and introducing new voting qualifications that would have disenfranchised the bourgeois who were the mainstay of the opposition. The king and his chief minister believed that public opinion, mollified by the recent victory at Algiers, would accept these measures calmly. They miscalculated utterly.

Aroused by the protests of liberal journalists, encouraged by the hot summer weather, and impatient from a three-year economic recession, the Parisians initiated a riot that became a revolution. During *les trois glorieuses* (the three glorious days of July 27, 28, and 29) they threw up barricades, captured the Paris city hall, and hoisted the tricolor atop Notre Dame cathedral. Charles X abdicated in favor of his grandson and sailed to exile in England.

The revolutionary rank and file in 1830 came mainly from the lower bourgeoisie and the skilled workers, whose numbers were increasing with the growth of industry in Paris (see Chapter 19). Their leadership came from the parliamentary opponents of Charles X and from cautious young liberals like Adolphe Thiers (1797-1877) and François Guizot (1787-1874), both destined to play important political roles. Thiers edited the opposition paper *Le National*; he had also written a history of the great revolution to show that it had not been all bloodshed but had also had a peaceful and constructive side. Guizot too had written history, a survey of civilization focused on the rise of the bourgeoisie, and he had been instrumental in defeating the Ultras in the elections of 1827 and 1830.

The revolutionaries of 1830, like those of 1789, were not agreed on the kind of regime they wanted. A minority would have liked a democratic republic with universal suffrage; they rallied around Lafayette, who was now in his seventies. But many others, who identified a republic with the Terror, wanted a constitutional monarchy with a suffrage restricted to the wealthy; for them 1830 in France should be the counterpart of 1688 in England. The moderate leaders were ready with a candidate for the throne—Louis Philippe, the duke of Orléans.

Louis Philippe's father had participated in the Paris demonstrations of 1789, had assumed the revolutionary name of Philippe Egalité, and had voted for the execution of Louis XVI, only to be guillotined himself during the Terror. Louis Philippe had fought in the revolutionary army at Valmy in 1792, then had emigrated in 1793 before the worst of the Terror. He claimed to have little use for the pomp of royalty, and he dressed and acted like a sober and well-to-do businessman. Having deceived the influential Lafayette into thinking he was a republican, Louis Philippe (r. 1830-1848) accepted the crown at the invitation of the Chamber.

The Chamber also revised the Charter of 1814, which called Louis Philippe, not "king of France" but, following the precedent of 1791, "king of the French." It also substituted the red, white, and blue revolutionary tricolor for the white flag of the Bourbons. The suffrage was still highly restricted; in 1831 166,000 French men had the right to vote. The July Monarchy, as the new regime was termed, left France far short of realizing the democratic potential of liberty, equality, and fraternity; rather like Whig Britain of the eighteenth century, France functioned on a narrow social base which was almost immediately challenged.

Success in Belgium

Within a month of the July uprising in Paris, a revolution began in Belgium. The union of Belgium and the Netherlands, decreed by the peacemakers of 1815, worked well only in economics. The commerce and colonies of Holland supplied raw materials and markets for the textile, glass, and other manufactures of Belgium, at that time the most advanced industrial area of the Continent. In language, politics, and religion, however, King William I of Holland exerted power arbitrarily. He made Dutch the official language throughout his realm, including the French-speaking Walloon provinces. He denied the pleas of Belgians to rectify the "Dutch arithmetic" that gave the Dutch provinces, with two million inhabitants, and the Belgian, with three and a half million, equal seats in the States-General. He refused to grant special status to the Catholic church in Belgium, and particularly offended the faithful by insisting that the education of priests to be subject to state supervision.

All these grievances tended to create a Belgian nationalism and to forge common bonds between the Catholic Dutch-speaking Flemings of the provinces north of Brussels and the Catholic French-speaking Walloons of the highly industrialized southern provinces. In later years, however, the Flemish-Walloon partnership was to be strained by differences in language and also by the divergence between the devout Flemings and the increasingly anticlerical Walloons, much influenced by the French.

The revolution—one of both nationalism and liberalism—broke out in Brussels on August 25, 1830. Headed by students inspired by the example of Paris (and perhaps incited by French agents), the riots were directed against Dutch rule. The insurgents recruited their fighters chiefly from the industrial workers, many of whom complained of low pay and frequent unemployment and had been virtually dislocated in some way by the Industrial Revolution. However, the better-organized middle-class leadership soon controlled the revolutionary movement and predominated in the Belgian national congress that convened in November 1830.

This congress proclaimed Belgium an independent constitutional monarchy. The new constitution granted religious toleration, provided for wide local self-government (always a touchy issue in Flanders), and put rigorous limits on the king's authority. Although it did not establish universal suffrage, the financial qualifications for voting were lower in Belgium than they were in Britain or France. When the congress chose as king a son of Louis Philippe, Lord Palmerston (1784-1865), the British foreign minister, protested vehemently at what appeared to be an effort to place Belgium within the French orbit. The congress then picked Leopold of Saxe-Coburg (1831-1865), a German princeling and widowed son-in-law of King George IV of Britain. Leopold was well fitted to be a constitutional monarch in a brand-new kingdom. He had already shown his political shrewdness by refusing the shaky new throne of Greece; he now repeated it by marrying a daughter of Louis Philippe, thus easing French disappointment.

The Belgian revolution made the first permanent breach in the Vienna settlement. King William stubbornly tried to reconquer Belgium in 1831-1832. A French army and a British fleet successfully defended the secessionists, however, and prolonged negotiations resulted in Dutch recognition of Belgium's new status in 1839. In 1839 also, representatives of Britain, France, Prussia, Austria, and Russia guaranteed both the independence and the neutrality of Belgium in a document that the German Empire was to term "a scrap of paper" when it invaded Belgium in 1914.

Failure in Poland, Italy, and Germany

The course of revolution in Poland contrasted tragically with that in Belgium. In 1815 the Kingdom of Poland had the most liberal constitution on the Continent; twenty years later it had become a dependency of the Russian Empire. The constitution given to the Poles by Czar Alexander I preserved the Code Napoléon and endowed the Diet with limited legislative power. A hundred thousand Poles received the franchise, more voters than in the France of Louis XVIII, which had a population ten times greater. In practice, however, difficulties arose. Many of the men chosen for official posts in Poland were not acceptable to the Poles; indeed, probably no government imposed by Russia would have satisfied them. Censorship, unrest, and police intervention marked the last years of Alexander I.

The advent of the highly conservative Nicholas I in 1825 increased political friction, although the new czar at first abided by the Polish constitution. Meantime, romantic nationalism made many converts at the universities of Warsaw and Vilna (in Lithuania). Polish nationalists demanded the transfer from Russia to Poland of provinces that had belonged to the prepartition Polish state: Lithuania, White Russia, and the Ukraine. Secret societies on the Carbonari model arose in these provinces and in the Kingdom of Poland.

A secret society of army cadets in Warsaw launched a revolution in November 1830. Leadership of the movement was soon assumed by Polish nobles, but they were at best reluctant revolutionaries who had no intention of emancipating the Polish peasants, long the victims of oppressive landlords. This was a revolution for national independence, not for righting the wrongs of the Old Regime. Radicals in Warsaw and other cities disrupted the revolutionary government, which collapsed in September 1831. Polish misery was intensified by an epidemic of cholera, the first outbreak of this Asian disease in Europe. Once the Russians were in control again, Nicholas I scrapped the Polish constitution, imposed martial law, and closed the universities. Some revolutionaries fled the country, and Paris soon became the capital of these Polish exiles.

In Italy and Germany news of the July Revolution in Paris stimulated abortive, and perhaps imitative, revolutionary efforts. In 1831 Carbonari insurgents briefly controlled the little duchies of Parma and Modena and a sizable part of the Papal States. The revolutionaries counted on French assistance, but the July Monarchy had no intention of risking war with Austria. Again, as in 1821, Metternich sent troops to restore legitimacy in Italy.

Metternich did not require soldiers to preserve legitimacy in Germany; whenever a crisis arose, the Diet of the German Confederation obediently followed the Austrian lead. In Prussia King Frederick William III (1797-1840) had never fulfilled his promise to grant a constitution, though he did set up provincial diets. Only Weimar and a few south German states enjoyed liberal constitutions. After 1815 German university students formed the *Burschenschaft* (Students' Union), and in October 1817 students of the University of Jena held a rally where Luther had worked on his German translation of the Bible, to celebrate both the three hundredth anniversary of the Ninety-Five Theses and the fourth anniversary of the battle of Leipzig. During the rally the Burschenschaft burned books by reactionary writers. In March 1819 one of these writers, August von Kotzebue, who was also a Russian agent, was assassinated by a student. Metternich used the incident to suppress student clubs, getting the Diet of the German Confederation to approve the Carlsbad Decrees (September 1819), which stiffened press censorship, dissolved the Burschenschaft, and curtailed academic freedom.

Despite the Carlsbad Decrees, mild political ferment continued in Germany, and the Burschenschaft reorganized underground. In 1830 and the years following, a few rulers in northern Germany, notably in Saxony and Hanover, were forced to grant constitutions. Excited by these minor successes and by the appearance of Polish refugees, thirty thousand revolutionary sympathizers, including many students from Heidelberg and other universities in the region, gathered at Hambach in the Palatinate in May 1832. There they toasted Lafayette and demanded the union of the German states under a democratic republic. Effective action toward unification was another matter. In 1833 some fifty instructors and students tried to seize Frankfurt, the capital of the German Confederation and seat of its Diet. The insurgents, together with hundreds of other students accused of Burschenschaft activities, were given harsh sentences by courts in Prussia and other German states.

The Lessons of 1830

The revolutionary wave of the 1830s revealed two great facts of political life. First, it widened the split between the West and the East already evident after the revolutions of 1820. Britain and France were committed to support cautiously liberal constitutional monarchies both at home and in Belgium. On the other hand, Russia, Austria, and Prussia were more firmly committed than ever to counterrevolution. In 1833 Czar Nicholas I, Met-

The French artist Eugène Delacroix, in "Liberty at the Barricades" (July 28, 1830), allegorically shows Liberty as a woman moving the flag of liberation forward over the bodies of both the troops and the people. The towers of Notre Dame rise through the smoke as a symbol of the traditions of France. Liberty is joined in revolution by representative Parisian types: a member of the proletariat with cutlass, an intellectual with sawed-off musket, and a street boy with pistols.

ternich, and King Frederick William III formally pledged their joint assistance to any sovereign threatened by revolution, though they were unable to help King William of the Netherlands.

Second, revolution succeeded in 1830 only where it enlisted the support of a large part of the population, owing in part to the dislocations caused by the Industrial Revolution. It failed in every country where the revolutionaries represented only a fraction of the people. In Poland the social policies of aristocratic nationalist leaders alienated them from the peasants. Italian revolutionaries still relied on their romantic Carbonari tradition and on unrealistic hopes of foreign aid. In Germany revolution was a matter of student outbursts and other gestures by a small minority. Conspirators and intellectuals needed to make their doctrines penetrate to the grass roots of society; they needed to develop able political leaders and to mature well-laid plans for political reform. These tasks they undertook after 1830; their success was to be tested in the most extensive chain of political uprisings in the history of nineteenth-century Europe—the revolutions of 1848.

IV THE REVOLUTIONS OF 1848

Nationalism was a common denominator of several revolutions in 1848. It prompted the disunited Germans and Italians to attempt political unification, and it inspired the subject peoples of the Hapsburg Empire to seek political and cultural autonomy. The French revolutionary and Napoleonic upheavals, together with the romantic movement, had stimulated a nationalistic outpouring among most peoples in central and eastern Europe. For the national minorities within the Hapsburg Empire, as for the Christian nationalities within the Ottoman Empire, the new nationalism tended to focus on language. The Czech language, for example, was almost extinct in the late eighteenth century; the population of Bohemia increasingly used the German of their Austrian rulers. By 1848, however, a Czech linguistic and literary revival was in full swing. Patriotic histories and collections of Czech folk poetry kindled a lively interest in the national past and fostered dreams of a Pan-Slavic awakening in which the Czechs would lead their fellow Slavs.

Liberalism, the second common denominator of the revolutions, encompassed a wide range of programs. In central and western Europe, where much of the Old Regime survived, liberals demanded constitutions to limit absolute monarchy and to liquidate feudal rights and manorial dues. In France, which already had a constitutional monarchy, many liberals sought to replace the July Monarchy with a democratic republic. But what did they mean by "democratic"? For some, democracy meant that every man (not yet every woman) should have not only the right to vote but also the "right to work"—a phrase that implied the need for governments to take measures against unemployment and

other social ills aggravated by the alternating prosperity and depression associated with industrial growth.

In the Europe of 1848, as in the France of 1789, an economic crisis helped to catalyze discontent into revolution. A blight ruined the Irish potato crop in 1845 and soon spread to the Continent; the grain harvest of 1846 also failed in western Europe. The consequences were a sharp rise in the price of bread and bread riots; mass starvation occurred in Ireland, and widespread misery affected France, Germany, and Austria. The food crisis was compounded by an industrial depression, touched off in 1847 by the collapse of a boom in railroad construction. The number of unemployed mounted just as food prices were rising, thus intensifying popular suffering.

Scholars generally agree that these revolutions did not arise from conspiracies of Masons, Jews, or radicals, though many observers at the time blamed such scapegoats. While the fermentation of ideas had prepared the soil, and while social problems had created worried, angry populations, the long-term cause was a growing conjunction between political and economic crises. Disturbing demographic shifts, unsettling attacks on traditional social practices, and the apparently little understood though destabilizing dynamism wrought by the growing industrialism of western Europe gave ideas of nationalism and liberalism a force they had not had since 1789.

France

The economic crisis hit industrial France with particular severity. Railroad construction almost ceased, throwing more than half a million out of work; coal mines and iron foundries, in turn, laid off workers. Unemployment increased the discontent of French workers already embittered by their low wages and by the still lower esteem in which they were held by the government of Louis Philippe. Under the July Monarchy, French agriculture experienced a golden age at the same time that industrialization was beginning to develop. The government, however, appeared to be indifferent to the social misery that accompanied the new prosperity. In eighteen years it took only two steps to improve the welfare of the industrial working class: an extension of state aid to primary schools in 1833 and a poorly enforced law in 1841 limiting child labor.

The main beneficiaries of the July Monarchy were the social and economic elite who had the right to vote. Demands for liberalization of the suffrage were met with Guizot's unsympathetic advice: *Enrichissez-vous!*—make yourself rich enough to meet the stiff fiscal qualifications for voting. The government banned labor organizations and harshly repressed the workers of Paris and Lyons who demonstrated in the early 1830s to demand a republic and higher wages.

Opposition to the July Monarchy grew during the next decade. Heading what might be termed the official opposition was Adolphe Thiers. Shelved by Louis Philippe in favor of Guizot, the chief minister from 1840 until 1848, Thiers continued to support the principle of constitutional monarchy.

The republicans formed a second opposition group, which increased in numbers with the growing political awareness and literacy of the working classes (in 1847 two out of three men mustered into the army could read). The third, and smallest, group took in the exponents of various doctrines of socialism, who gained recruits from the economic depression of the late 1840s. Potentially more formidable than any of these, but as yet representing only a vague, unorganized sentiment, were the Bonapartists. The return of the emperor's remains from St. Helena to Paris in 1840, arranged by Thiers as an expedient to improve the image of a sagging regime, revived the legend of a glorious and warlike Napoleon, so different from the uninspiring Louis Philippe.

In the summer of 1847 constitutional monarchists of the Thiers faction joined with republicans to stage a series of political banquets throughout France calling for an extension of the suffrage and the resignation of Guizot. This campaign appeared harmless until a huge banquet was announced for February 22, 1848, to be held in Paris. When the Guizot ministry forbade the banquet, the Parisians substituted a large demonstration. On February 23 Louis Philippe dismissed Guizot and prepared to summon Thiers to the ministry. But his concessions came too late. Supported by workers, students, and the more radical republican leaders, the demonstration of February 22 turned into a riot on the 23rd, in which more than fifty of the rioters were killed or wounded. The number of casualties intensified the revolutionary atmosphere, barricades were thrown up, and Thiers was so unnerved that he made no attempt to form a ministry.

On February 24 Louis Philippe abdicated, and the Chamber set up a provisional government headed by an eloquent, cautious advocate of a republic, the romantic poet Alphonse de Lamartine (1790-1869). Popular unrest, mounting along with unemployment, obliged the provisional government to take in a few socialists. Notable among these was Louis Blanc (1811-1882), an advocate of social workshops which the workers themselves would own and run with the financial assistance of the state. As a gesture toward the "right to work," and also as a measure to restore calm in Paris, the provisional government authorized the establishment of national workshops in the capital. These national workshops, however, were not a genuine attempt to implement the blueprint of Louis Blanc but a relief project organized along semimilitary lines and enrolling more than a hundred thousand unemployed persons from Paris and the provinces.

The future shape of France now hinged on the outcome of the elections of April 23, 1848, when all adult males—nine million, as opposed to a quarter of a million voters in the last days of the July Monarchy—would be qualified to vote for the National Assembly, which would draw up a constitution for the Second French Republic. (The First Republic had lasted officially from September 1792 until Napoleon's coronation in 1804.) In this election—the first in European history based on universal manhood suffrage—eight million, 84 percent of the potential electorate, went to the polls. The conservative peasants, who still made up the bulk of the population, approved the fall of the July Monarchy but dreaded anything resembling an attack by the socialists on the private property they had recently acquired. Of the almost nine hundred deputies elected, therefore, most were either monarchists or conservative republicans.

The Paris radicals refused to accept the decision of the country. Demonstrators invaded the National Assembly and proposed the formation of a new provisional government; alarmed moderates arrested the radical leaders and decided that the national workshops threatened law and order because they had attracted so many desperate people to Paris. The Assembly decreed the orderly closing of the workshops; their workers could either enlist in the army or accept work in the provinces. The poorer districts of the capital responded by revolting from June 23 to June 26, 1848, when they were subdued by the troops brought in from the conservative rural areas by General Louis Eugène Cavaignac (1802-1857), the energetic minister of war who hunted the revolutionaries down in street-to-street fighting.

These June Days were a landmark in modern history, the first large-scale outbreak with clear overtones of class warfare. Most of the insurgents seem to have come not from members of the national workshops, who still generally received their dole, but from the unemployed who had tried vainly to enroll in the workshops and were now desperate. Among them were workers of the new industrial age—mechanics, railroad men, dock workers—as well as winesellers, masons, locksmiths, cabinetmakers, and other artisans of the type who had been prominent in the capture of the Bastille in 1789. The prospect of a social revolution, though it may have been remote as a practical matter, terrified the propertied classes, and peasants, shopkeepers, landowners, and nobles were all poured into Paris by the new railroads to quell the uprising. Panic accounted for the severe repression; about ten thousand were killed or wounded, and about the same number were subsequently deported, chiefly to Algeria. All socialist clubs and newspapers were padlocked, and Louis Blanc fled to England. France became a virtual military dictatorship under General Cavaignac.

The fears of the middle-class moderates were evident in the constitution of the Second French Republic, which the National Assembly completed in November 1848. The Assembly declared property inviolable and refused to include the right to work among the fundamental rights of French citizens. In other respects the constitution seemed to be a daring venture in representative democracy and in experimenting with the combination of a strong president and a powerful legislature. The president was to be chosen by popular election every four years, and the single-chamber legislature was to be elected every three years. Perhaps the venture was less daring than it seemed, since elections of 1848 had already shown that conservatives could outvote radicals.

Circumstances did not favor the success of the Second Republic. In the presidential election of December 1848 fewer than half a million votes were polled by the three genuinely republican candidates; five and a half million votes and the presidency of the republic went to Louis Napoleon Bonaparte (1808-1873). This nephew of the great Napoleon was not an impressive figure. He spoke French with a slight German accent, the result of boyhood exile in Germanic Switzerland, and he had associated with disreputable people. Yet he bore the magical name of Bonaparte and could tap the glamor of the Napoleonic legend. In 1848 he staged a clever campaign to identify himself with the cause of order, stability, and democracy. In domestic politics he would subvert the constitution of the Second Republic in a coup d'état late in 1851 and proclaim himself Emperor Napoleon III a year later. The French Revolution of 1848, like that of 1789, had established a republic that ended in a Napoleonic empire.

Italy

In Italy new reform movements supplanted the discredited Carbonari. By the 1840s three movements were competing for the leadership of Italian nationalism. Two were moderate, agreeing that political power in an Italy free of Hapsburg control should be limited to the nobility and the bourgeoisie, but at odds over the form that a united Italian nation should assume. One of these groups, based in the north, favored the domination of Piedmont; its leader was the eventual unifier of Italy, Count Camillo Cavour (1810-1861), who was an admirer of British and French liberalism. Cavour was the editor of an influential Turin newspaper, *Il Risorgimento* ("resurgence" or "regeneration"), which gave its name to the movement for unification. The other moderate group called themselves Neo-Guelfs because, like the Guelf political faction of the Middle Ages, they hoped to engage the pope in the task of freeing Italy from the control of a German emperor. The Neo-Guelf leader, the priest Vincenzo Gioberti (1801-1852), who was briefly premier of Sardinia, declared that the future depended on "the union of Rome and Turin." The pope would head, and the army of Piedmont would defend, a federation of Italian states, each with its own monarch and constitution.

The third group of liberals, Young Italy—so named because only those under the age of forty could join—asserted that Italy should be unified as a democratic republic. Its founder, Giuseppe Mazzini (1805-1872), hoped to create an organization more effective than the Carbonari, but was frustrated by prolonged exile and the ineptitude of his lieutenants. Nevertheless, Mazzini did win an enduring reputation as the great democratic idealist of modern Italian politics. He also inspired the formation of Young Germany, Young Poland, and similar movements, all joined together in a somewhat romantic federation called Young Europe.

The prospects for reform in Italy brightened in 1846, when a new pope was elected, Pio Nono (Pius IX, 1846-1878), whose initial progressive actions, such as the release of political prisoners and steps to modernize the administration of the Papal States, aroused hopes for a liberalized papal government. In the next year the king of Piedmont relaxed his tight censorship to permit *Il Risorgimento* to publicize Cavour's program for economic and political improvements.

Revolution occurred in Italy before it did in Paris. In January 1848 an uprising in Sicily, at first aimed at independence from Naples, forced King Ferdinand II to grant a constitution on the pattern of the French Charter of 1814 (as revised by the July Monarchy); in mid-February the grand duke of Tuscany was forced to follow suit. News of the rising in Paris quickened the pace of the Italian revolutions, as King Charles Albert of Piedmont (1798-1849) and Pius IX agreed to become constitutional rulers like Louis Philippe. Next came Lombardy and Venetia, where although Hapsburg rule had been relatively mild, the ideas of Young Italy had inspired revolutionary movements. Ever since January 1 citizens of Milan, the capital of Lombardy, had been boycotting cigars as a protest against the Austrian tax on tobacco—a maneuver suggested by a professor's lecture on the Boston Tea Party. Severe rioting resulted. News of revolution in Vienna touched off five days of heavy fighting in Milan, which forced the Austrians to withdraw their forces. At the same time, Venice, the capital of Austria's other Italian province, proclaimed itself the independent Republic of St. Mark.

This rapid collapse of Hapsburg rule in Lombardy-Venetia inspired a national crusade against the Austrians. Charles Albert of Piedmont assumed command of the Italian forces, which included contingents from Naples, Tuscany, and even the Papal States, and refused an offer of help from the provisional government of the French republic. As town and country had opposing views and the Austrians exploited these divisions well, the decision to "go it alone" proved unwise. Piedmont moved too far too fast, annexing Lombardy and the two small north Italian duchies of Parma and Modena. The other Italian states, wanting to protect their particularist traditions, began to fear the imperialism of Piedmont more than they desired the unification of Italy. On April 29 Pius IX announced that his "equal affection" for all peoples obliged him to adopt a neutral position in the war with Austria and to recall his soldiers. The pope could not act both as an Italian patriot and as an international spiritual leader. Moreover, Pius was alarmed by the threats of Austrian and German bishops to create an anti-pope and by the increasingly radical political temper of the Roman population. The Neo-Guelf cause had thus received a fatal blow. In the Two Sicilies, the king scrapped the constitution and followed the papal example in withdrawing his troops from the war. The Austrians, taking the offensive, reconquered

Lombardy and crushed the forces of Charles Albert at Custozza in July.

In Rome adherents of Young Italy rose up in November 1848. After Pius IX fled to Neapolitan territory, they transformed the Papal States into a democratic Roman Republic headed by Mazzini himself, who proved too authoritarian when in power. In March 1849 radicals in Piedmont forced the reluctant Charles Albert to renew the war with Austria, but within the month Austria again prevailed, at the battle of Novara. In August 1849 the Austrians put an end to the Republic of St. Mark after a prolonged siege and bombardment of Venice, which suffered acutely from famine and cholera. Meanwhile, Mazzini's Roman Republic had surrendered to French troops sent by President Bonaparte in a bid for Catholic gratitude. Both the Neo-Guelfs and Young Italy were discredited.

Piedmont, however, had emerged as the leader of Italian nationalism and liberalism. It had defied the hated Austrians, and was also the only Italian state to retain the constitution granted in 1848. When Charles Albert abdicated after the defeat of Novara, the crown passed to Victor Emmanuel II (1820-1878), who was to become the first king of modern Italy.

Germany

The German revolutions in 1848 roughly paralleled those in Italy. In Germany too liberalism and nationalism won initial victories and then collapsed before internal dissension and Austrian resistance. The failure in Germany was the more surprising since the revolutionary movement had begun to recruit support among industrial workers, artisans fearing industrial competition, and peasants seeking to abolish the relics of manorialism that had already been swept away in France. Liberal and nationalist agitation, however, was centered in the well-to-do business and professional classes, especially among university professors, who enjoyed more influence and respect in Germany than elsewhere in Europe. Most German liberals were moderates. They wanted constitutional monarchies in the various German states, a stronger German Confederation, and an end to the repressive hegemony of Metternich.

The hero of German liberals was King Frederick William IV of Prussia (1840-1861). Attractive and cultivated, but unstable and infatuated with romantic concepts of divine-right kingship, Frederick William promised to carry out his father's unhonored pledge to give Prussia a constitution and an elected assembly. However, the meeting of representatives from the provincial diets that he finally convoked in 1847 did little.

It was, in fact, the *Zollverein* (customs union) which constituted Prussia's most solid contribution to German unification before 1848. In 1818 Prussia had abolished internal tariffs within its scattered territories and applied a uniform tax on imports. Membership in the Zollverein proved so profitable that by 1844 almost all the German states except Austria had joined. The Zollve-

rein liberated Germany from an oppressive burden of local tolls and taxes and cleared the way for its phenomenal economic development later in the century. The success of the Zollverein suggested that Prussia might naturally take the initiative in political unification.

Stimulated by the example of Paris, the revolutionaries of 1848 scored their first successes in the western German states early in March; from there the demands for constitutions and civil liberties fanned out rapidly. By mid-March most of the rulers of the smaller German states had yielded to the pressure, and in Berlin demonstrators were erecting barricades. Frederick William IV accepted some of the liberals' demands and appealed for calm, but before his appeal could be publicized, rioting broke out with redoubled violence. More than two hundred rioters, chiefly workers, were killed. The mob broke into the royal palace and forced the king to accept the demands of liberals and nationalists. He summoned an assembly to draw up a constitution, declared Prussia "merged in Germany," and proclaimed himself "king of the free, regenerated German nation."

Drastic reform of the German Confederation now began. In May 1848 a constitutional convention met at Frankfurt, the capital of the Confederation. Its 830 members were elected throughout Germany, but often by electoral colleges and with suffrage restrictions that made the results less than a true popular mandate. The Assembly lacked a broad popular base. Moreover, while its members represented the flower of the German intelligentsia, they lacked political experience and talent for practical statesmanship when they had to decide the geographical limits of Germany. The Confederation included Austria proper but excluded most of the non-German Hapsburg territories; nor did it include the eastern provinces of Prussia, notably those acquired in the partitions of Poland. The Austrian issue divided the assembly into two camps: the "Big Germans," who favored the inclusion of Austria and of Bohemia, with its large Czech population, in the projected German state, and the "Little Germans," who opposed the idea. Austrian objections to a "Big Germany" ensured the assembly's adoption of the "Little Germany" proposal, while the nationalism of the Frankfurt Assembly overcame its liberalism on the question of Prussian Poland. By a large majority it voted to include Prussian areas in which the Poles formed most of the population.

In contrast, in March 1849 the Frankfurt Assembly adopted a liberal national constitution based on the American federal system and British parliamentary practice. The individual states were to surrender many of their powers to the German federal government. The federal legislature would consist of a lower house, elected by universal male suffrage, and an upper house, chosen by the state governments and the legislatures. Ministers responsible to the legislature would form the federal executive. Over all would preside a constitutional monarch, the German emperor.

But the Frankfurt constitution died at birth. The assembly elected the king of Prussia to be emperor, but

Frederick William, ignoring his promises of March 1848 and alarmed by Austrian opposition, rejected the offer, and the Assembly soon disbanded. It had never secured recognition from foreign governments, had never raised a penny in taxes, and had never ruled over Germany. The couplet mocking the host of academic deputies, though it exaggerated their numbers, had been justified:

> Hundert fünfzig Professoren!
> Lieber Gott, wir sind verloren!
> [A hundred and fifty professors!
> Good God, we're sunk!]

German liberalism had suffered a major defeat. After the initial shock of the revolutions, the comfortably situated professional and business classes began to fear the radicalism of the workers and artisans. The Old Regime persisted to World War I.

The Hapsburg Domains

The fate of German and Italian nationalism in 1848 hinged partly on the outcome of the revolutions in the Hapsburg Empire. If these revolutions had immoblized the Hapsburg government for a long period, the Italian and German unification might have been realized. But Austria, though buffeted by revolution, rode out the storm. The success of the counterrevolution in the Hapsburg Empire also assured its victory in Italy and Germany.

The nature and the outcome of the Hapsburg revolutions depended in turn on the complex structure of nationalities within the Austrian Empire. There were several nationalities under Hapsburg rule in 1848:

Nationality (by language spoken)	Percentage of Total Population
German	23
Czech and Slovak	19
Magyar (Hungarian)	14
South (Yugo-) Slav	
Slovene	4
Croat	4
Serb	5
Ruthenian (Little Russian)	8
Romanian	8
Italian	8
Pole	7

These national groups were not always separated geographically, each in its own compartment. For instance, in the Hungarian part of the empire—which had large minorities of Slovaks, Romanians, Serbs, Croats, and Germans—the dominant Magyars fell just short of a majority. Throughout the empire, moreover, the German element, chiefly bureaucrats and merchants, pre-dominated in most of the towns and cities, even in the Czech capital of Prague and the Magyar capital of Budapest.

Among the peoples of the Hapsburg realm in 1848, nationalism ran strongest among the Italians of Lombardy-Venetia, the Czechs of Bohemia, and the Magyars and Croats of Hungary. Language was an important issue among Magyars, as it was with Czechs; the replacement of Latin by Hungarian as the official language of the eastern part of the empire in 1844 marked a victory for Magyar nationalism. Since Hungary was overwhelmingly an agricultural land, nationalism, like all other aspects of political life, was dominated by nobles and gentry who monopolized the seats in the county assemblies and the central diet. The spellbinding orator Lajos Kossuth (1802-1894), an ardent nationalist—though he was of Slovak rather than Magyar background—regarded the linguistic reform of 1844 as but the first in a series of revolutionary projects cutting all ties with Vienna. But Magyar nationalists bitterly opposed the national aspirations of their own Slavic subjects. The most discontented were the Croats, whose national awakening had begun when their homeland was absorbed into Napoleon's empire.

The antagonism between Croats and Magyars revealed an all-important fact about the nationalistic movements within the Hapsburg Empire. Some groups—Italians, Magyars, Czechs, Poles—resented the German-dominated government in Vienna. Others, notably the Croats and Romanians, were less anti-German than anti-Magyar. Here was a situation where the central government in Vienna might apply a policy of divide and conquer, pitting anti-Magyar elements against anti-German Maygars, and subduing both. This was substantially what happened in 1848. A similar policy had already been used in 1846 to suppress a revolt in Austrian Poland. When the Polish landlords had revolted, their exploited Ruthenian peasants had risen against them and received the backing of Vienna.

Liberalism also played a significant part in the Hapsburg revolutions, especially in Austria proper. The expanding middle class desired civil liberties, a voice in government, and the lifting of mercantilist restrictions on business. In Vienna, as in Paris and Berlin, some workers went further and also demanded radical social reforms.

From 1815 to 1848 the Hapsburg government virtually ignored the grumblings and protests that arose in almost every quarter of the empire. Metternich probably wanted to make some concessions to liberal and nationalist aspirations, but though he enjoyed a nearly free hand in foreign affairs, Metternich did not have his way in domestic policy. He was blocked by the emperors—the bureaucratic Francis I (1792-1835) and the weak Ferdinand I (1835-1848)—and by the vested interests of the aristocracy. The Hapsburg government was inefficient; Austria, Metternich accurately stated, was "administered, but not ruled."

The news of the February revolution in Paris shook

the empire to its foundations. Four separate revolutions broke out almost simultaneously in March 1848: in Milan and Venice, in Hungary, in Vienna itself, and in Bohemia. In Hungary Kossuth and his Magyar supporters forced Emperor Ferdinand to give Hungary political autonomy, institute parliamentary government, and substitute an elected legislature for the feudal Hungarian diet. New laws abolished serfdom and ended the immunity of nobles and gentry from taxation. But the laws rode roughshod over the rights of non-Magyars by making knowledge of the Hungarian language a requirement for election as a deputy to the legislature.

Aroused by the Hungarian revolt, university students and unemployed workers rose in Vienna on March 12. On the next day Metternich resigned and fled to Britain. Although the imperial government repeatedly promised reforms, the constitution it granted seemed woefully inadequate to the Viennese insurgents. By May the political atmosphere was so charged that Emperor Ferdinand and his family left the capital for the Tyrol. Pending a meeting of a constituent assembly in July, a revolutionary council ran affairs in Vienna. In the meantime, Austrian forces were at war in Piedmont. In September a Constituent Assembly, meeting in Vienna and representing all the Hapsburg provinces except the Italian and the Hungarian, emancipated the peasants from their obligation to work for the landlords. Rather than giving further momentum to revolution, however, this victory accelerated counterrevolution, for, having achieved their goal, the peasants tended to withhold their support from further radical aims.

Meanwhile, in Prague Czech nationalists were demanding rights similar to those granted the Magyars. In June 1848 the Czechs organized a Pan-Slav Congress to promote the solidarity of Slavic peoples against "Big German" encroachments. The Pan-Slav Congress set off demonstrations, during which the wife of the commander of the Austrian garrison in Prague was accidentally killed. Five days later the commander, after bombarding Prague, dispersed the Czech revolutionaries and established a military regime in Bohemia. The counterrevolution had begun. The imperial government authorized the governor of Croatia to invade central Hungary to put down revolt there. While the Magyars held off the imperial forces, the radicals of Vienna revolted again, proclaiming their support of the Magyars and declaring Austria a democratic republic. But the Hapsburg armies crushed the Vienna revolution (October 31, 1848) and executed the radical leaders.

The forces of counterrevolution could not be stopped. In November 1848 the energetic and unscrupulous prince Felix Schwarzenberg (1800-1852) became the Austrian prime minister. Schwarzenberg arranged the abdication of the incapable Ferdinand I and the accession of Ferdinand's eighteen-year-old nephew, Francis Joseph (r. 1848-1916). Schwarzenberg then declared that the promises made by the old emperor could not legally bind his successor and shelved the projects of the Constituent Assembly, though he honored the emancipation of the peasantry. The Magyars fought on. In April 1849 the Parliament of Hungary declared the country an independent republic and named Kossuth its chief executive. Russia now offered Austria military assistance, for Czar Nicholas I feared that the revolutionary contagion might spread to Russian Poland unless it was checked. In August 1849 Russian troops helped to subjugate the Hungarian republic, and the czar boasted in 1850 that God had assigned him "the mission of delivering Europe from constitutional governments."

MAZZINI ON THE TRIUMPH OF REACTION

In early 1848 enthusiastic liberals had hailed the arrival of "the peoples' springtime." It had been a false spring. Mazzini undertook to explain why. In 1850 he wrote from London:

Why, then, has *reaction* triumphed?

Yes: the cause is in ourselves; in our want of organisation; . . . in our ceaseless distrust, in our miserable little vanities, in our absolute want of that spirit of discipline which alone can achieve great results; in the scattering and dispersing of our forces in a multitude of small centres and sects, powerful to dissolve, impotent to found.

The cause is in the gradual substitution of the worship of material interests . . . for the grand problem of education, which alone can legitimatise our efforts. . . . It is in the narrow spirit of *Nationalism* substituted for the spirit of Nationality; in the stupid presumption on the part of each people that they are capable of solving the political, social, and economical problem alone; in their forgetfulness of the great truths that the cause of the peoples is one; that the cause of the Fatherland must lean upon Humanity. . . . The language of narrow nationalism held at Frankfurt destroyed the German Revolution; as the fatal idea of aggrandisement of the House of Savoy [Piedmont] destroyed the Italian Revolution.

Life & Writings of Joseph Mazzini (London: Smith, Elder, 1870), III, 76-77.

By 1850 almost the whole Continent was being delivered from the regimes of 1848. In France the Second Republic faced a very uncertain future under an ambitious president and a conservative assembly, both concerned with preserving order against liberty. In Prussia Frederick William IV, and in Austria and Italy Prince Schwarzenberg guided the triumphant counterrevolution. Kossuth, Mazzini, and other revolutionaries went into exile.

"The narrow spirit of nationalism" was to grow ever more intense after 1848. It was eventually to destroy the Hapsburg Empire. The failure of the liberals to unify Italy and Germany in 1848 transferred the leadership of the nationalist movements from the amateur revolutionaries to the professional politicians of Piedmont and Prussia. Piedmont, alone among the Italian states, retained the moderate constitution it had secured in 1848; in Germany the antiliberal Count Otto von Bismarck was to achieve through "blood and iron" what the Frankfurt Assembly had not accomplished peacefully.

Equally dramatic was the role of the working class, particularly in France, and of the peasantry, which arose in violent revolt in 1851, only to be crushed. Europe was experiencing the challenge of the forces released by the Industrial Revolution, and new demands for drastic social and economic changes were arising alongside the older demands for political liberties, constitutions, and the end of peasant servitude. The year 1848 was not only the year of abortive revolution but also the year in which Karl Marx and Friedrich Engels published their guidelines for future revolutions in *The Communist Manifesto*.

SUMMARY

Romanticism, materialism, and idealism overlapped as strands of thought in a period of rapid change. Romantics rejected the narrow optimism and mechanistic world of Enlightenment rationalists. The style of the romantics was imaginative, emotional, and haunted by the supernatural and by history. They stressed the individual and emotional ties to the past.

In literature and music, romanticism triumphed. In Germany, the *Sturm und Drang* movement and in England the poetry of Byron, Shelley, Keats and others symbolized the romantic protest. Romantic musicians renounced classical rules and sought out popular ballads and tales of the past.

In the fine arts, romantics shared the stage with neoclassicists. In architecture, neoclassical styles gave way to the Gothic revival. In philosophy, Hegel proposed a theory of history as a dialectical process, an organic process of growth and development.

Politically, reactionaries were in power after 1815. The writings of Burke formed the foundation for the reconstruction of Europe. Conservatives believed society required orders and classes. The forces of tradition and political realism were epitomized by Metternich, Austrian foreign minister from 1809 to 1848.

At the Congress of Vienna, European leaders met to rebuild Europe with conservative underpinnings. Metternich, Alexander I, Castlereagh, and Talleyrand sought to restore the balance of power. Dynastic and territorial questions were settled on the principle of legitimacy. The Quadruple Alliance was formed to hold periodic meetings to maintain the peace of Europe.

The spirit of 1789 persisted, however. In 1820-23, revolutions broke out in Spain, Portugal, and Naples. Revolutionaries fought to abolish the privileges of the nobility and clergy, establish representative assemblies, and write constitutions.

Nationalist aspirations led to independence movements in Serbia and Greece. With the aid of Britain, France, and Russia, Greek nationalists eventually prevailed.

Revolutions erupted again in 1830. In France, riots in Paris against the reactionary forces of Charles X led to a revolution in which the French opted for a constitutional monarchy under Louis Philippe. A nationalist revolt in Belgium succeeded in establishing a separate, independent nation whose neutrality was guaranteed in 1839. Revolts in Poland, Italy, and Germany failed, thereby widening the split between the more liberal governments of western Europe and the repressive regimes in eastern Europe.

In 1848 revolutions inspired by nationalist and liberal agitation again rocked Europe. An economic crisis was the catalyst for revolution in France. During the June days, Paris was the scene of the first large-scale outbreak of class warfare. Using the magical name of his famous uncle, Louis Napoleon was elected president of the Second Republic.

In Italy and Germany, nationalist movements seeking unification failed. However, Piedmont emerged as the leader of Italian nationalist liberal forces.

In the Hapsburg domain, revolts at first immobilized the government, but the Hapsburgs soon reasserted their control. Moreover, the government played on the mutual distrust among the many nationalities to divide and conquer the rebel forces. Although the revolutions of 1848 failed, they left a legacy to be fulfilled later in Italy and Germany.

THE INDUSTRIAL SOCIETY

When the Liverpool and Manchester Railway line opened in September of 1830, the railway train—drawn by the *Rocket*, then the fastest and strongest of the locomotives—ran down and killed William Huskisson, a leading British politician and an ardent advocate of improving transport and communication, who had underestimated its speed. This, the first railway accident in history, was symbolic of the new age to come, which benefited many, brought destruction to some, and transformed society far more rapidly than anyone had predicted. In due course the railroad would tie continents together with ribbons of steel, virtually changing how people calculated distance. After the railway age, travelers in England would speak of distances in terms of the time it took to travel them, rather than in terms of miles.* More than any other new instrument of technology, the railroad was indicative of the changes wrought in human lives by the Industrial Revolution.

The Industrial Revolution would, in time, produce a global economy in which developments in a remote corner of a colonial empire would influence price, population, and social customs in European metropolitan centers. The Industrial Revolution proceeded in stages—none so clearly marked as economic historians once assumed, though with relatively clear links of cause and effect between one industrial, financial, or technological development and another—the speed and sometimes sequence of which differed in different nations. Along with an economic revolution in Britain, a political revolution continued in France, which deeply influenced industrial development. This dual revolution led to patterns of cause and effect that are so complex that philosophers, economists, and political scientists continue to argue about their meanings today. These arguments—in defense of capitalism, in support of socialism, in advocacy of communism—produced ideologies so powerful that their exponents often dominated the intellectual history of their time; Marxism, Leninism, and the array of attacks upon the capitalist mode of production grew out of debates in the Industrial Revolution.

Frequently necessity did prove to be the mother of invention. As each new machine, each new adjustment in manufacturing technique produced the need for yet another new machine or another adjustment in the laboring force, inventors, entrepeneurs, and managers showed remarkable innovative capacity. Urbanization accelerated because industry worked best on the basis of concentrated centers of production. Concentrated in these specific centers of production and often working at the same job, laborers developed a sense of class consciousness. Periodic dislocations in the market, overproduction, or perhaps the failure to procure a needed supply of raw materials sometimes led to unemployment and the insecurity of not knowing whether one would, though employed today, be employed tomorrow. The cities thus became centers for both the laboring classes and "the dangerous classes"—those who through discontent, anger, despair, or the inability to find a role to play in an increasingly complex, specialized working class, turned to lives of crime. Simultaneously, a transportation revolution—the railroad on land and the steamship by sea—brought the problems and the successes of one area ever more quickly to another.

The Industrial Revolution was truly a revolution in both senses of the word. It transformed the lives of millions of people, first in western Europe and the United States but eventually in central and eastern Europe and in the overseas empires of the European powers. And it proceeded to "revolve," to unfold at greater speed, to influence those who thought of themselves as distant from the centers of production or unconcerned with the changes brought to society. Just as mechanization of one stage of textile manufacturing virtually demanded mechanization of the next stage, so did changes in the relationships between stages of production lead to changes in the nature of labor, of the family, of nutrition, and of disease. Even though most nineteenth-century Europeans continued to be agricultural laborers despite industrialization, the great economic crises of the century—in the 1840s, in 1857, and most dramatically in 1873—affected all. By the end of the century the tensions between nations, between classes, and between the various reform-minded and conservative groups became acute. By the 1890s the Industrial Revolution had produced an industrial society.

The industrial society developed different tastes in art, literature, and music. Interest in science became increasingly utilitarian; science that could be applied to industry was valued above science that was purely speculative. In the middle of the nineteenth century the revolutionary theory of evolution—applied originally to biology but quickly adapted to economics, society, and even politics—reinforced an emphasis on competition, on survival by contest. The search for knowledge became less intuitive, less romantic, and more capable of being quantified, more open to statistics, research, and the "objective" gathering of data. Competition between nations, between businesses, even between individuals and teams through organized athletics, would mark the industrial society. Realistic and naturalistic fiction would reflect a growing sense of historical determinism.

*While today the clocks of the Trans-Siberian express that makes its way across the Soviet Union are always set on Moscow time, however far from the capital city the train may be, in the United States the railroads have promoted the idea of time *zones*, reflecting more closely the realities of the position of the sun in relation to the speed of travel, so that California is reckoned to be three hours "earlier" than New York.

The Crystal Palace Exposition was one of the first World's Fairs in which industrial societies displayed their triumphs. Officially called the Great Exhibition of the Works of Industry of All Nations and opened in 1851, the fair housed a variety of technological marvels within another such marvel—a "Crystal Palace" of iron and glass. Six million people visited the Great Exhibition. Queen Victoria is shown at left making a royal procession through the Foreign Nave, where the largest collection of foreign goods ever shown in England was on display.

Yet there would also be a continuity of optimism, from the "springtime of the peoples" in 1848 to "the century of hope"—a widely felt sense that the future held virtually unlimited progress for all humanity.

I STAGES OF INDUSTRIAL GROWTH

Economic change generally takes place gradually, and therefore some historians feel it is misleading to speak of an industrial *revolution*, since the process was clearly evolutionary, rather than revolutionary. However, growth did not proceed at an even pace, and developments in one country or one sector of industry often altered circumstances so rapidly as virtually to transform styles of life and modes of work within a generation or less. Generally, the growth of industry was identified with the introduction of machine production, making mass markets possible and the factory system essential.

Historians once believed that production expanded most rapidly at moments of economic "take-off," when various factors that had blocked sustained growth were removed by the forces of capitalism. Among the factors often credited with the economic take-off that ushered in the nineteenth century were the rise of a merchant class during the Renaissance, colonialism and mercantilism, the American and French revolutions, the rise of the competitive state system, the Protestant emphasis on hard work and material progress as signs of salvation, the rise of modern science, and the social theories of the philosophes. Obviously these all played a role, though historians no longer generally agree that a sharp line

separated the Industrial Revolution from the years that preceded it. They do, however, generally agree that between the 1820s and the 1890s industrialization spread from England across Europe and eventually to Russia in four stages; the textile industry was generally the first to be mechanized, followed by metals, chemicals, and ultimately electricity. The first stage was a transition from agricultural to industrial priorities for society. Industrial expansion accelerated as capital was mobilized, raw materials were secured through treaty or annexation, managerial skills were developed, and unified national states turned to the business of competition for markets, influence, and prestige.

The first developments were in textiles, in which Britain led. The second stage was in metallurgy, in which Belgium joined Britain in leadership until Germany overtook both around 1900 (and the United States, in turn, overtook them). In the third stage the chemical industry developed from improvements in mining techniques. By the 1850s new methods for recovering minerals from the earth meant that potassium, phosphate, sulfur, and rock salt were the center of attention; these, in turn, made the development of new fertilizers possible, vastly increasing the productivity of the soil. The fourth stage came after the 1890s, first in Britain and Germany, when electronics marked the move to a new form of industry based on more specialized skills. By 1914 Germany led the world in the production of lights, cables, generators, transformers, ultimately transforming both public and private life by bringing appliances within reach of thousands of purchasers. The age of the consumer had begun.

As each stage led to another, profits built up, so that capital tended to move from the west, where capital was first amassed, to the east. Investment in industry soon

This rural vista of London by George Samuel (1816) shows the intrusion of factory smoke over an industrializing city. The nostalgic view is from Greenwich Park.

led to significant growth in all forms of transportation and in mining. Thus a factory working class was created throughout Europe, drawn largely from rural areas to cities near the resources most needed: Birmingham in England, Mulhouse in France, Kiev in Russia. Industrial growth occurred in the traditional commercial centers as well.

British Leadership, 1760-1850

The process of industrialization began in Britain. After the 1760s England enjoyed a long period of relative economic prosperity. England's growth rate was little more than one percent a year in the volume of goods and services produced, but this modest growth was constant, and its cumulative effect was substantial. Starting in the sixteenth century, a new group of landed proprietors—squires and townspeople—saw land as an investment; thus they were concerned with improved production and profit. The enclosure movement had, in effect, transformed estates into compact farms, set off from others by fences or hedgerows. Their relatively small, private owners were less interested in family inheritance than in sustained growth. Marginal cottagers and garden farmers were eliminated, landowners were freed from manorial restrictions on farming practices, and the division of markets and of labor stimulated individual and geographically localized productivity.

A sharp rise in the price of grain, caused by wars and by industrialization in local centers such as Manchester,

meant that more land was put into crops, leading to a greater demand for labor. Waste lands were put into production for vegetable crops to feed to animals, and eastern England in particular became a center of experimentation with new fertilizers, crops, and methods of crop rotation. Wealthy, aristocratic proprietors adopted the new methods and also financed canals, roads, mines, and eventually railroads to carry their produce to market. By 1800 English agriculture was probably the most efficient in Europe.

This increased productivity led to a rapid growth in population in England and Wales—from seven and a half million in 1751 to twenty-one million in 1851—creating a large pool of workers for the new industries. A long, sustained series of victories over foreign enemies—the Church of Rome and the Spain of Philip II in the sixteenth century, the Dutch in the seventeenth, and the French in the eighteenth— had given England the self-confidence, unity, and pride to take advantage of economic good fortune.

This good fortune was enhanced not only by ample supplies of capital from foreign and colonial trade but also by the possession of large deposits of coal and iron. The geographical compactness of the British Isles made shipments from mine to smelter and from mill to seaport short, fast, and cheap. The marginal farmers, and also the Irish, driven from their overpopulated and famine-ridden island, formed a large reservoir of eager labor, so that managers could accurately predict levels of productivity and meet orders faithfully, earning Britain an early reputation for dependability in trade. The Napoleonic wars further stimulated the demand for metal goods and the invention of new machines. The construction of great new docks along the lower Thames between 1802 and 1807 further assured London of its position as the economic center of Europe.

Thus the twin needs of economic activity were met: labor and capital. The rising population became a market for simple manufactured goods while also supplying labor. Women and children were employed, especially in the textile industries, because they could be paid less and were best suited to jobs requiring dexterity of hand and eye rather than a strong back. The large landowners had capital to spare, and from their ranks, and even more from the ranks of the middle class, came the entrepreneurs who, though not inventors, knew how to adapt the inventions of others to new problems for a profit. The middle class enjoyed a secure social status, as they did not on the Continent, for the law of primogeniture (by which land passed undivided to the eldest son) prevented the division of estates into uneconomic small parcels. Since second sons could not inherit the estate though they were gentlemen in birth and education, they could enter trade, the military, the church, and the colonial service without serious social stigma. To be a "counter-jumper" (a merchant) while not aristocratic, was no disgrace in England, as it continued to be in parts of the Continent. Economically, socially, and politically, Britain was in an excellent position for the first phase of its Industrial Revolution, from the 1760s to the 1850s.

Textiles, Coal and Iron

The textile industry, based in Lancashire and especially in Manchester, was the first to exploit the potentialities of power-driven machinery. Beginning with the spinning jenny in the 1760s, the use of machinery gradually spread to other processes. In 1793 an American, Eli Whitney (1765-1825), devised the cotton gin, an engine that separated the fibers of raw cotton from the seeds and enabled a single slave to do what had previously required the hand labor of fifty slaves. Meanwhile, British inventors perfected a power-driven loom for weaving cotton thread into cloth. By 1830 Britain operated more than fifty thousand power looms, and cotton goods accounted for half of its exports. By 1851 the British census listed more than half a million workers employed in cotton manufacturing alone.

Advances in mechanical engineering made this rapid expansion possible. Earlier, for instance, the difficulty of procuring exactly fitting parts had restricted the output of Watt's steam engine. Then British engineers, by studying the precision techniques of watchmakers, devised a lathe that turned screws of almost perfect regularity. They also developed machines for sawing, boring, and turning the pulley blocks used by British ships in the Napoleonic wars. Meantime, Eli Whitney undertook important experiments at his arms factory in Connecticut, using the concept of standardized and inter-

Here workers are engaged in spinning in a Lancashire mill in 1834.

changeable parts, one of the basic principles of mass production.

New processes in industry were not uniformly adopted, of course. The revolutionary implications of Whitney's experiments with standardization, for example, were long ignored by manufacturers. The survival of handicraft techniques and the workers' fear that they would be displaced by machines also slowed down the process of mechanization. Even in the cotton industry, weaving on the hand loom continued in areas with an especially large reservoir of cheap labor, like Ireland and central Europe, where peasants could produce cloth in the privacy of their cottages and be paid by the piece. In the woolen and clothing industries, mechanization did not come until the 1850s, when Britain produced a machine for combing wool, and an American, Isaac Singer (1811-1875), popularized the sewing machine.

Coal ranked with cotton as an industry that pioneered in the solution of technical problems. Steam engines were used to pump water from the mines; ventilating shafts and power fans supplied them with fresh air; and safety lamps gave miners some protection against dangerous underground gases. The coal output of Britain, the world's leading producer, rose steadily from about sixteen million tons in 1816 to sixty-five million in 1856. The consumption of coal mounted because of its increased use as a household fuel in wood-short Britain, its importance in producing steam power, and its vital contribution to the expanding iron industry, which required large quantities of coal to make the coke used in smelting.

The efficiency of smelting advanced rapidly after the development of the blast furnace (1828), in which fans provided a blast of hot air to intensify the action of the hot coke on the iron. Thanks to the blast furnace, Britain produced iron strong enough for use in bridges and in factory buildings. Yet the best grade of iron lacked the tremendous strength of steel, which is iron purified of all but a minute fraction of carbon by a process of prolonged, intense heating. Steel for industrial purposes could be made in the early 1800s, but only by ruinously expensive methods. Then in 1856 the Englishman Henry Bessemer (1813-1898) invented the converter, which accelerated the removal of impurities by shooting jets of compressed air into the molten metal. A decade later William Siemens (1823-1883), a German living in England, devised the open-hearth process, which utilized scrap as well as new iron, and which handled larger amounts of metal than the converter could. The inventions of Bessemer and Siemens lowered the cost of making steel so substantially that the world output increased tenfold between 1865 and 1880. The nineteenth century ushered in a new iron age.

Transport and Communication

Steam, coal, and iron brought the railway age. Coal powered the railways and the railways carried coal. Though railways based on wooden rails were known from the sixteenth century, iron and steel rails made it possible to carry huge weights and mount giant locomotives to pull long trains; and three hundred tons of iron were required to lay a single mile of railroad track. Canals and hard-surfaced roads had preceded railroads in Europe and North America. A Scot, John McAdam (1756-1836), had devised a means of surfacing ("macadamizing") roads so that they could be traveled in all weather, but extra heavy shipments nonetheless broke the road's surface. The railway was the answer, once cast iron rails were developed by Abraham Darby's foundry in 1767. By the 1820s only mechanization remained to be accomplished. George Stephenson (1781-1848) and others put the steam engine on wheels and created the modern locomotive. Thus it was that Stephenson's *Rocket* traversed twelve miles in fifty-three minutes on the new Liverpool and Manchester Railway in 1830! The railroad-building boom was soon in full swing: Britain had 500 miles of track in 1838, 6,600 miles in 1850, and 15,500 in 1870.

Steam also affected water transport, though at a less revolutionary pace. Robert Fulton's (1765-1815) steamboat, the *Clermont*, made a successful trip on the Hudson River in 1807, and soon paddle-wheel steamers plied the inland waterways of the United States and Europe. Ocean-going steamships, however, were uneconomical to operate because of the inefficiency of their engines. When the Scot Samuel Cunard inaugurated the first regular transatlantic steamer service (between Liverpool and Boston in 1840), the coal required for the voyage took up almost half the space on his vessels. Conse-

quently, only passengers and mail went by steamship, most freight being handled by sailing ships. Finally, in the 1860s, the development of improved marine engines and the substitution of the screw propeller for the paddle wheel forecast the doom of the commercial sailing vessel.

These many improvements in transport by sea and land promoted industrial expansion by creating the need for machines to make the new equipment, by facilitating shipments of raw materials and finished products, and by opening up almost the whole world as a potential market.

Communications also experienced radical improvement. In 1840 Great Britain inaugurated the penny post, which enabled a letter to go from London to Edinburgh, for instance, at the cost of one penny, less than a tenth of the old rate. This provided an inexpensive means by which a family, perhaps separated by the need to look for work, could stay in touch. More dramatic was the utilization of electricity for instantaneous communica-

As this sketch of the problems of travel in 1842 shows, passengers often had to help the coach on the way. Paved roads and adequate bridges were essential to modernize transport.

tion, beginning with the first telegraph message, from Baltimore to Washington in 1844. Then came the first submarine cable (under the English Channel) in 1851, the first transatlantic cable in 1866, and the first telephone in 1876.

This communications revolution was not limited to Britain. Belgium also used the turnpike principle, establishing all-weather roads financed by tolls, so that by 1850 most major centers were reachable even in the worst weather. The industrializing Rhineland provinces of Prussia improved their roads, as did France, which also built an ambitious system of canals. The Ruhr River valley, made navigable by 1780, was tied in by roads and canals to the rest of Germany, France, and the Low Countries. But canals were frequently built too soon, before there was enough traffic to pay for them. It was the railways, which could satisfy many objectives, such as transporting goods, passengers, and armies, and eventually providing access to seaside resorts as a taste for leisure developed, that truly transformed the Continent as they had Britain.

Though the first British railroad opened in 1830, the rest of Europe was not far behind: France in 1832, Germany and Belgium in 1835, Russia in 1837, Austria in 1838, Italy and Holland in 1839, Denmark and Switzerland in 1847, Spain in 1848. By 1870, 897,000 miles of rails had been laid in western Europe, the United States had its own transcontinental line, and railroads were flourishing in Canada and in faraway Australia. The lines differed in one important respect, however. In

THE RAILWAY SYSTEM IN 1852

Source: Malcolm Falkus and John Gillingham, *Historical Atlas of Britain* (London: Grisewood and Dempsey, 1981), p. 199. Copyright © Grisewood and Dempsey Limited, 1981. Reprinted by permission.

Britain traffic for the lines existed before they were built, and railway companies could easily find private capital for finances. In western Europe and in much of the United States, however, lines were built as traffic grew to require them, and private capital needed a government guarantee or subsidy, since the profit margin was precarious. In eastern Europe lines were built well before there was enough traffic to make them profitable, and state financing was necessary. Thus a varying pattern of private capital, state-aided capital, foreign capital, and state-controlled capital developed. In Britain the railways boosted an industrial revolution already in progress; in western Europe the railways often created the revolution; in eastern Europe, to which the iron, rails, locomotives, engineers, and capital all had to be imported, the railway boom led countries into debt and threatened ruin. Thus the railroad was a true symbol of the diversity of responses to industrialization and modern capitalism.

Money, Banking, and Limited Liability

The exploitation of these new developments required a constant flow of fresh capital. From the first, the older commercial community supported the young industrial community. The slave traders of Liverpool financed the cotton mills of Lancashire, thereby increasing the demand for American cotton fiber and for slaves to work the plantations. Tobacco merchants of Glasgow provided the funds that made their city the foremost industrial center of Scotland, and tea merchants in London and Bristol aided the ironmasters of South Wales. Bankers played such an important role that the Barings of London and the international house of Rothschild were among the great powers of Europe. In the early nineteenth century each of five Rothschild brothers, sons of a German Jewish banker, established himself in an important economic center—London, Paris, Frankfurt, Naples, and Vienna. The Rothschilds prospered because, in an age of frequent speculation, they avoided unduly risky undertakings, and because they facilitated investment by residents of one state in the projects of other states. The Paris Rothschild, for instance, negotiated the investment of British capital in the construction of French railroads during the 1840s.

Banks further assisted economic expansion by promoting the use of checks and banknotes in place of coins. During the Napoleonic wars, when the shortage of coins forced some British mill owners to pay their workers in goods, the British government empowered local banks to issue paper notes supplementing the meager supply of coins. But whenever financial crises occurred—and they came frequently before 1850—dozens of local banks failed, and their notes became valueless. Parliament therefore encouraged the absorption of shaky banks by the more solid institutions, and in 1844 it gave the Bank of England a virtual monopoly on issuing banknotes, thus providing a reliable paper currency. It also applied,

first to railroads and then to other companies, the principle of limited liability (indicated by "Ltd." after the name of British firms). Earlier, the shareholders in most British companies were subject to unlimited liability, and they might find their personal fortunes seized to satisfy the creditors of an unsuccessful company. The practice of limiting each shareholder's liability to the face value of that person's shares encouraged investment by diminishing its risks.

By the midnineteenth century, the tangible signs of Britain's economic predominance were evident on every hand—in the teeming docks and thriving financial houses of London, in the mushrooming factory and mining towns of the Midlands, the north of England, and Scotland, and in other quarters of the globe as well. British capital and thousands of skilled British workers participated in the construction of French railroads. American trains ran on rails rolled in British mills and on the capital from British investors. Cotton goods made in Lancashire clothed a sizable part of the world's population, and British entrepreneurs and investors would finance the opening of great cattle ranches in the American West in the next decades.

Yet Britain, even in the heyday of its leadership, did not monopolize inventive skill. The French, for example, devised the chlorine process of bleaching cloth and the Jacquard loom for weaving intricate patterns. German technicians led the world in agricultural chemistry and in the utilization of the valuable byproducts of coal. And from the United States came Eli Whitney and the cotton gin, Samuel F.B. Morse (1791-1872) and the telegraph, Singer and the sewing machine, and the young Cyrus McCormick (1809-1884), whose reaper (1831) was the first of many agricultural machines developed for the vast agricultural expanse of America. In a sense, the whole North Atlantic world, European and North American, constituted an economic, commercial, and financial community.

British Decline

After 1850 Britain began to lose its advantage in this economic community. Politically its leaders had positioned it well to the forefront. The Reform Act of 1832 had put Parliament into the hands of the propertied classes, so that they might pass legislation favorable to industry. In 1846 Parliament had repealed the Corn Laws (in Britain "corn" meant all forms of grain), which had limited the import of grain, and the nation began eighty-five years of nearly tariff-free trade. But the food supply was no longer keeping up, and while the growing empire—the sheep stations of Australia and New Zealand, the vast stretches of prairie in Canada—might meet the need, nearby supplies from Denmark or Holland were obviously cheaper, especially as dietary needs moved from grain and beef to fruit, poultry, and vegetables. With the abolition of the Corn Laws, Britain accepted the principle of heavy specialization, of full commitment to private initiative, private property, and the mechanism of the market place. But this also made Britain increasingly dependent on others for certain necessities, so that it had to be able to assure itself of a supply of those necessities by colonial or foreign policy.

As the middle class became more comfortable and the working class more demanding, the possibilities for peaceful innovation decreased. A period of prolonged inflation, from 1848 to 1873, and another of depression, from 1873 to 1896, intensified the perception of inequalities of wealth. After 1873 British agriculture could no longer compete with the Continent or the United States; agriculture began to stagnate, and the overall rate of British growth decreased.

In the new phase of the Industrial Revolution in Britain, the initial advantage was slowly lost—to Germany, to Belgium, and to the United States. Britain had become a nation of shopkeepers, teacher to the world, but the world had learned too well and had come to the industrial scene later, with newer and better equipment, while Britain continued to work with methods that, while once innovative, were now outmoded. The lead in developing new techniques passed in agricultural machinery to the Americans, in chemical and steel production to the Germans, in electricity to both. England, and particularly London, remained the undoubted financial center of the world, but by 1890 industrial leadership had passed elsewhere, including to Czarist Russia and to Japan.

Industrial and agricultural changes are often mutually dependent. For sustained growth, industry relies on an efficient agriculture for its raw materials and for additions to its labor force, recruited from surplus workers no longer needed on mechanized farms. Agriculture depends on industry for the tools and fertilizers that enable fewer workers to produce more, and to transform farms into agrarian factories. In the nineteenth century factory-made implements like the steel plow and the reaper improved the cultivation of old farmlands and permitted the opening of vast new areas, like the North American prairies, that could scarcely have been touched if the pioneers had had to rely on hand labor alone. The mechanical cream separator raised the dairy industry to a big business, and railroads and steamers sped the transport of produce from farm to market. The processes of canning, refrigeration, and freezing—all industrial in origin and all first applied on a wide scale during the last third of the century—permitted the preservation of many perishable commodities and their shipment halfway around the world.

Farmers found steadily expanding markets both in the industrial demand for raw materials and in the food required by mining and factory towns. International trade in farm products increased rapidly during the second half of the nineteenth century. The annual export of wheat from the United States and Canada rose from 22,000,000 bushels in the 1850s to 150,000,000 in 1880. Imported flour accounted for a quarter of the bread consumed in Britain during the 1850s and for half by the 1870s. Denmark and the Netherlands increasingly fur-

nished the British table with bacon, butter, eggs, and cheese; Australia supplied its mutton, and Argentina its beef.

Germany now partly assumed Britain's old role as the pioneer of scientific agriculture. Shortly after 1800 German experimenters had extracted sugar from beets in commercially important quantities, thus ending Europe's dependence on the cane sugar of the West Indies. In the 1840s the German chemist Justus Liebig (1803-1873) published a series of influential works on the agricultural applications of organic chemistry. Plant growth, Liebig argued, depended on three basic elements: nitrogen, potassium, and phosphorus. But the production of crops and fodder leached these elements from the soil; they had to be returned to it. Liebig's warnings promoted even wider use of fertilizers: guano from the nesting islands of sea birds off the west coast of South America, nitrate from Chile, and potash from European mines.

Generally, farming progressed and prospered in the nineteenth century as never before. Yet the agricultural revolution exacted a price. Faced with the competition of beet sugar, the sugar-cane islands of the West Indies went into a depression from which they did not recover. In the highly industrialized countries the social and political importance of agriculture began to decline. Farming was no longer the principal occupation of the English in the nineteenth century, and land was no longer the yardstick of wealth and power. The urban

Industrial United States, 1

Coal fields

▲ Iron ore deposits

● Principal manufacturing cities

merchants and manufacturers demonstrated their dominance in British politics when they won, through the Anti-Corn Law League, their campaign to abolish the tariffs on grain, which, they said, kept the price of food high. Decisive in the abolition of the Corn Laws in 1846 was an attack of black rot that devastated the Irish potato crop for two years and made it essential to bring in cheap substitute foods. Even so, the great potato famine in Ireland continued to have disastrous results there, leading to massive abandonment of the land.

Meanwhile, across the Channel, France was industrializing far more slowly. Public finance continued to be unstable, capital formation was far more difficult, and France remained wed to tariff protection, which retarded change. Railways were built far more slowly, and the revolution of 1848, caused by an economic crisis, made French financiers even more hesitant. The French economy remained especially sensitive to movements in world prices, creating more dramatic alterations in growth rates than in Britain. Agriculture remained especially important, and both farm and city workers in France were reluctant to innovate. An "aristocracy of labor" set crafts workers apart from manual laborers, and some of the working class—such as the glassworkers of Carmaux, who occupied an elite position though they lived virtually side by side with lower-class miners—successfully resisted mechanization into the 1890s. To the inhibitions of small farms and inadequate capital

was added the effect of equal inheritance laws, which led to the division of land into tiny parcels so that the peasant could not accumulate capital to take risks on new crops. Businesses were owned by single families, who could not be protected by limited liability laws or easily recruit new managers. Since bankruptcy had to be avoided above all else, owners could not afford to take risks with new products or new methods. Economic and social conservatism thus limited efforts to create large-scale production or a high degree of specialization. The social attitudes of the Old Regime persisted down to 1914, the economic attitudes even into the 1930s.

II ECONOMIC AND SOCIAL CHANGE

The Population Explosion and the Standard of Living

When Britain abandoned any pretense of raising all the basic foods its people needed, its population was growing so rapidly that self-sufficiency was no longer possible. Despite substantial emigration, especially to the colonies, the number of inhabitants in England and Wales more than tripled during the nineteenth century, from about 9,000,000 in 1800 to 32,500,000 in 1900. There is no clear agreement why. Some demographers have attributed this population explosion not to a higher birth rate but to the lowered death rate resulting from the improved food and sanitation—especially cheap, washable cotton materials—brought by industrialism. Others claim that neither diet not sanitation improved until the second half of the century, and that the population increase in the first half may be attributed to the rural areas and not to the cities, which had a much higher death rate. It is also pointed out that in Russia, still an agrarian country in a preindustrial stage, the population increased proportionately (36,000,000 in 1800, about 100,000,000 in 1900) almost as fast as it did in Britain.

A similar controversy is focused on the extent to which the Industrial Revolution improved the standard of living not just of the new capitalist and managerial classes but of the workers themselves. The overall standard of living in Britain did not begin to improve steadily until after the Napoleonic wars and the immediate postwar slump. After about 1820 the purchasing power of the workers seems to have grown very gradually, as more and cheaper goods became available. Opportunities for steady, regular employment also grew, as did chances for laborers to climb up the economic ladder a rung or two by mastering a skill and getting a better-paying job. But all these factors varied in their effect from industry to industry and from one locality to another; they also fluctuated with the ups and downs of the economic cycle. Many people, consequently, appear to have found that their standard of living was declining.

There is little debate about one most important social result of industrialism—the truly revolutionary changes it caused in the structure and distribution of the population. Wherever mines and factories were opened, towns and cities appeared. Large areas of once rural England became urban England, and a similar transformation was beginning in the lowlands of Scotland around Glasgow, in the northern French plain around Lille, in the Rhineland, and along the rivers of the northeastern United States. The growth of an urban population increased the numbers and influence of the two social classes that form the backbone of an industrial society: business people and workers. Industrialists, bankers, investors, managers, and promoters of every sort joined the already established capitalists to form the modern middle class, or bourgeoisie. Millhands, railway workers, miners, some artisans, clerks, and a host of other recruits swelled the ranks of wage-earning workers.

The impact of capital and labor upon the life of industrial nations was becoming increasingly evident by the middle of the nineteenth century. Some of the signs pointed to steady material progress—better food and the conquest of space by the railroad, the steamship, and the telegraph. Other signs, however, foretold serious dislocation and violent change. The repeal of the Corn Laws buried an old agrarian way of life in Britain, and the collapse of the French railroad boom in the late 1840s suggested that economic slumps in an industrial society might have alarming consequences, for the hundreds of thousands thrown out of work aggravated the political unrest that culminated in the June Days of 1848 in Paris (see Chapter 19).

The remarkable rise of population tested the earth's resources and environment even before people thought in these terms. Perhaps ten thousand years ago the total population of the globe was under ten million. By 1750, when the modern rise was beginning, the figure was seven hundred and fifty million. By 1930 it was two billion, and only forty-five years later, in 1975, it was double that. Thus, human population expanded to reach its first thousand million over hundreds of thousands of years; the second thousand million was added in a single century; the third in only thirty years, and the fourth in only fifteen. This uncontrollable explosion in population, with its untold impact on the planet's resources, was made evident in the nineteenth century as people flocked to the cities, which grew far more rapidly than sanitation, police, or education could provide for, creating teeming slums that bred disease, crime, and discontent. Population growth in England and Wales was even more striking than these figures indicate, as England, and later Belgium, became the most crowded nations in the West; indeed, England had already reached a population density as early as 1600 that the United States would not reach until 1961.

In the midst of the Industrial Revolution, fewer people worried about overpopulation than rejoiced in the growth of the labor force and the increase in potential consumers. Changing moral concerns influenced traditional methods of limiting fertility and births. While population increased in many societies, the growing acceptance of contraceptive methods in post-Revolutionary France and a rise in abortions, despite church opposition to both practices, contributed to a decline in the French birth rate. The death rate had declined in France from about 1800; after 1870 both the death and birth rates declined in England and Wales. Birth rates were related in part to marriage rates, which were related to economic circumstances; as real wages increased, so did marriage rates. In Ireland postponement of marriage was increasingly common, reducing the total number of children a woman might bear in her lifetime. Yet by modern standards the mortality rate remained very high in the first half of the century, largely owing to infectious disease, and while families grew larger in Victorian times because the comfortable middle class could afford to clothe, house, and educate larger families, mortality also increased with increasing family size. Many wives died in childbirth, and men frequently had a succession of children by two or three wives. Cholera, in particular, had a devastating impact on urban populations at midcentury.

However, despite crowded living conditions in cities, overall mortality rates declined throughout Europe, especially after 1850. This was due in good measure to a decline in certain communicable diseases, as scientific research found both causes and cures, often as a by-product of research conducted for military or commercial purposes. Murder, infanticide, and death in war remained commonplace, but starvation and infectious disease were slowly reduced as causes of death, as greater agricultural productivity, better nutrition, and more rapid movement of foodstuffs from area of production to area of need reduced starvation to a local phenomenon in the West. Certain airborne diseases increased—bronchitis, pneumonia, influenza—as people lived and worked closer together, and by 1901 the death rate was higher than in 1854. Some diseases were reduced marginally, despite crowded conditions, as medicine developed means of combating them; measles, whooping cough, and scarlet fever were reduced to common occurrences in childhood but did not normally lead to death, as they once had done. The death rate from tuberculosis, diphtheria, and smallpox was cut drastically. Thus a death rate in 1700 of thirty persons per thousand was reduced most dramatically by bringing infectious diseases under control. Deaths from industrial accidents, war, localized famine, and physical attack remained relatively high, however. Since these forms of death could be attributed to a seen, known cause, much of the element of mystery once attached to death through the intervention of an "unseen hand"—unidentified infectious air- or water-borne diseases—was removed. Though death remained a frequent occurrence in any family, and though the consolations of religion remained important at the moment of death, men and women of the industrial society nonetheless had reason to think optimistically of the future.

The expectation of the enjoyment of good health, as distinct from the fear of an early death, also increased in the industrial society. Purification of water, efficient disposal of sewage (both requiring public measures, usually by municipalities), and better hygiene—for example, in the introduction of the water closet, or flush toilet; more frequent bathing as water became more readily available; and cleaner bedding—all helped reduce the incidence of typhus. The condition of food improved, though milk—important to childhood diets—remained unpasteurized until after 1900. Because surgery was increasingly performed in well-equipped hospitals with effective anesthesia and antiseptics, especially after the introduction of ether in 1846, certain medical problems no longer led to death—except on the battlefield, where far more soldiers died of disease and infection during surgery than from their wounds. Epilepsy responded to treatment, and new medicines were introduced for many chronic problems.

From the time of Hippocrates to the nineteenth century, few significant new drugs had been developed, and often treatment was totally wrong, according to present-day medical knowledge, for a specific disease; for example, sufferers from malaria were subjected to leeching (the drawing of blood from the body, often by blood-sucking insects), which caused dehydration at a time when their bodies needed all their strength and an increase in liquids. But the kind of research on a mass basis that is possible to conduct only on the battlefield or in a hospital led first to the isolation of infectious patients in separate hospital wards after 1875, and then to specific studies of specific diseases, so that a modern pharmacopeia began to emerge from research hospitals by 1900. While some diseases increased, notably cancer, the chances of surviving to die of old age were materially greater at the end of the century than at the beginning. For this decline in mortality, most historians credit contraception, medical care, better nutrition, and new drugs; after amputation, for example, in which over 50 percent of patients had customarily died from shock and loss of blood, blood coagulants and anesthetics reduced the death rate to 35 percent. However, since access to such improvements in health often depended upon the ability to pay, death rates varied substantially according to class.

Class Grievances and Aspirations

Both business people and workers nourished grievances—and aspirations. In the Britain of the 1820s, the new industrialists had small opportunity to mold national policy. Booming industrial cities like Manchester and Birmingham sent not a single representative to the House of Commons. A high proportion of business leaders belonged not to the Church of England but to non-Anglican Protestant "chapels"; nonconformists, as these dissenters were termed, still suffered discrimination when it came to holding public office or sending their sons (not to speak of their daughters) to Oxford or Cambridge. Even in France, despite the gains made since 1789, the bourgeoisie often enjoyed only second-class status.

In Western Europe the middle classes very soon won the place they felt they deserved; in Britain a gradual process of reform gave them substantially all they wanted. The high spot was the Reform Bill of 1832, which extended the suffrage to the middle class. In 1830 the French bourgeoisie got their citizen-king, and their Belgian counterparts scored a very great advance in political power. In Piedmont the middle class found a sympathetic leader in the aristocratic Cavour and secured at least a narrowly liberal constitution in 1848. In southern and central Europe, by contrast, the waves of revolution that crested in 1848 left the bourgeoisie frustrated and angry.

The grievances of workers were more numerous than those of their masters, and they seemed harder to satisfy. The difficulties may be illustrated by the protracted struggle of laborers to secure the vote and to obtain the right to organize and to carry on union activities. In Britain substantial numbers of workers first won the vote in 1867, a generation after the middle class did. In France universal male suffrage began in 1848. The unified German Empire had a democratic suffrage from its inception in 1871, but without some other institutions of democracy. Elsewhere, universal manhood suf-

ON THE PROFESSIONS

A revealing view of middle-class complaints and hopes was given in a parable published in 1819 by a French social planner, the comte de Saint-Simon (1760-1825). Saint-Simon hypothesized that France suddenly lost fifty each of its best mechanical engineers, finest architects, doctors, bankers, and so on through a long list of three thousand leaders in business, science, and the arts who, Saint-Simon stated, are "the most useful to their country"; "the nation would become a lifeless corpse as soon as it lost them."

Let us pass on to another assumption. Suppose that France preserves all the men of genius that she possesses in the sciences, fine arts and professions, but has the misfortune to lose in the same day Monsieur the King's brother [and many other members of the royal family]. Suppose that France loses at the same time all the great officers of the royal household, all the ministers . . . all the councillors of state, all the chief magistrates, marshals, cardinals, archbishops, bishops, vicars-general, judges, and, in addition, ten thousand of the richest proprietors who live in the style of nobles. . . .

[T]his loss of thirty thousand individuals, considered to be the most important in the State, would only grieve [the French] for purely sentimental reasons and would result in no political evil for the State.

These suppositions underline the most important fact of present politics . . . that our social organization is seriously defective. . . .

The scientists, artists, and artisans, the only men whose work is of positive utility to society, and cost it practically nothing, are kept down by the princes and other rulers who are simply more or less incapable bureaucrats. Those who control honours and other national awards owe, in general, the supremacy they enjoy, to the accident of birth, to flattery, intrigue and other dubious methods. . . .

These suppositions show that society is a world which is upside down.

H. de Saint-Simon, *Selected Writings*, ed. F.M.H. Markham (New York: Harper & Row, 1952), pp. 72-74.

---

frage came slowly—not until 1893 in Belgium, and not until the twentieth century in Italy, Austria, Russia, Sweden, Denmark, the Netherlands, and the United States.

During most of the nineteenth century, labor unions and strikes were regarded by employers as improper restraints on the free operation of natural economic laws; accordingly, a specific ban on such "combinations," as they were termed, was imposed by the British Combination Acts at the close of the eighteenth century.

Parliament moderated the effect of these acts in the 1820s but did not repeal them until 1876. Continental governments imposed similar restrictions, and the July Monarchy in particular repressed strikes with great brutality. France's Le Chapelier Law of 1791 was only relaxed in the 1860s and repealed in 1884. Everywhere labor slowly achieved full legal recognition of the legitimacy of union activities: in 1867 Austria, in 1872 in the Netherlands, and in 1890 in Germany.

Labor's drive for political and legal rights, however, was only a side issue during the early Industrial Revolution. Many workers faced the more pressing problems of finding jobs and making ends meet on wages that ran behind prices. The modern Western world had long experienced the business cycle, with its alternation of full employment and drastic layoffs; the Industrial Revolution intensified the cycle, making boom periods more hectic and widespread depressions, such as the one in the late 1840s, more severe. At first factories made little attempt to provide a fairly steady level of employment. When a batch of orders came in, machines and workers were pushed to capacity until the orders were filled; this was the "brisk time." Then the factory simply shut down to await the next orders.

Excessively long hours, low pay, rigorous discipline, and dehumanizing working conditions were the most common grievances of early industrial workers. Many plants neglected hazardous conditions, and few had safety devices to guard dangerous machinery. Cotton mills maintained the heat and the humidity at an uncomfortable level because threads broke less often in a hot, damp atmosphere. Many workers could not afford decent housing, and if they could afford it, they could not find it. Some few of the new factory towns were well planned, with wide streets and space for yards and parks. Some had an adequate supply of good water and arrangements for disposing of sewage. But many had none of these necessities, and in rapidly growing London the Thames became an open sewer so foul that riverside dwellers were reluctant to open their windows. The life expectancy of a boy born to a working-class family in Manchester was only half that of one born to rural laborers.

The industrial nations also threatened to remain nations of semiliterates; until they made provision for free public schools during the last third of the nineteenth century, education facilities were grossly inadequate. In England, as often as not, only the Sunday school gave the millhand's child a chance to learn the ABCs. A worker with great ambition and fortitude might attend an adult school known as a "mechanics' institute." In the 1840s a third of the men and half of the women married in England could not sign their names on the marriage register and simply made their mark. And no wonder that Benjamin Disraeli, the Tory reformer, in his novel *Sybil* (1845), called Britain "two nations"—the rich and the poor.

Laborers did attempt to join the ranks of the middle class by adhering to the precepts of thrift, hard work, and self-help. Samuel Smiles (1812-1904) pointed the way in a number of books with didactic titles such as *Character*, *Thrift*, and *Duty*, which preached a doctrine of self-salvation. Through joining a temperance society and by regular attendance at a worker's institute, a laborer might rise to become a master cotton spinner, a head mechanic, even a clergyman, shopkeeper, or schoolmaster. For some, the demands of hard work, self-reliance, and adherence to duty paid off in upward social mobility; for others, whether ill, lazy, unintelligent, rebellious, or simply confused, life was a round of exploitation, poverty, and demoralization. For many, the use of alcohol was a way of forgetting the demands of the day, prostitution a means of income, rigid religious observance a path to peace of mind. Flight into anonymity in another city and perhaps descent into a life of casual crime were equally commonplace. For each

Often entire families had to work as a matter of economic necessity. This drawing shows a girl "hurrying coal"—pulling a loaded wagon of coal weighing between two hundred and five hundred pounds through a low shaft in a Yorkshire mine in 1842.

success story there was a horror story; for each "improving landlord" there was a district of hovels and tenements where rats spread disease; for each great lady who provided alms for the poor there was a lunatic committed to an asylum for failing to adjust to the industrial society.

Preceding the revolutions of 1848, Europeans discussed at length the "social question," or, as it was called in Britain, "the condition-of-England question"; these terms were code language for pauperism and the evident decline of the lower classes. Pauperism was most visible in the cities, though conditions of poverty may in fact have been harsher in the countryside. Many social observers, while welcoming the clear benefits arising from industrialization, predicted that social calamity lay ahead. Some thought overpopulation was the main

A DAY AT THE MILLS

Frequently, entire families had to work as a matter of sheer economic necessity. A factory worker testified before a British parliamentary committee in 1831-1832:

At what time in the morning, in the brisk time, did those girls go to the mills? *In the brisk time, for about six weeks, they have gone at 3 o'clock in the morning, and ended at 10, or nearly half-past, at night.*

What intervals were allowed for rest or refreshment during those nineteen hours of labour? *Breakfast a quarter of an hour, and dinner half an hour, and drinking of ale a quarter of an hour.*

Was any of that time taken up in cleaning the machinery? *They generally had to do what they call dry down; sometimes this took the whole of the time at breakfast or drinking, and they were to get their dinner or breakfast as they could; if not, it was brought home.*

Had you not great difficulty in awakening your children to this excessive labour? *Yes, in the early time we had them to take up asleep and shake them when we got them on the floor to dress them, before we could get them off to their work; but not so in the common hours.*

What was the length of time they could be in bed during those long hours? *It was near 11 o'clock before we*

could get them into bed after getting a little victuals, and then at morning my mistress used to stop all night, for fear that we could not get them ready for the time....

So that they had not above four hours' sleep at this time? *No, they had not....*

Were the children excessively fatigued by this labour? *Many times; we have cried often when we have given them the little victualling we had to give them; we had to shake them, and they have fallen to sleep with the victuals in their mouths many a time.*

Did this excessive term of labour occasion much cruelty also? *Yes, being so very much fatigued the strap was very frequently used.*

What was the wages in the short hours? *Three shillings a week each.*

When they wrought those very long hours what did they get? *Three shillings and sevenpence halfpenny.*

A. Bland, P. Brown, and R. Tawney, *English Economic History: Select Documents* (London: Clarendon, 1915), pp. 510-13.

problem and suggested that "redundant populations" be sent overseas to colonies; others thought the problem lay in the decline of agriculture, forcing mechanically unskilled workers to migrate to the cities; yet others thought the oppressive conditions were limited to specific trades and locations. None could agree whether the overall standard of living was increasing for the majority, if at the cost of the minority—nor can historians agree today.

Historians generally do agree on some conclusions, however. There was an aggregate rise in real wages, which went largely, however, to the skilled worker, so that the working class was really two or more classes. Prices for the most basic foodstuffs declined, so that starvation was less likely. Conditions of housing worsened, however, and the urgency of work increased. Workers in traditional handicrafts requiring specialized skills might now have meat on their table three times a week, but workers displaced by a new machine might not have meat at all. Fear of unemployment was commonplace. A millhand could barely earn enough to feed a family of three children if fully employed; economic necessity compelled him to limit the size of his family, even by means morally repugnant to him, and he had to remain docile at work to assure that he would remain

employed. Dependence on public charity, with its eroding effects on self-confidence, was necessary during periods of layoffs in the factory. Women and children were drawn increasingly into the labor force, since they would work at half a man's wage or less, and this led to tension between the sexes, since men saw their jobs being taken by women. In Britain, France, Belgium, and Germany half the mill employees were boys and girls under eighteen.

Work began at dawn and ended at dusk; there was no time for leisure, and often the only solace was in sex, increasing the size of the family and adding to the economic burdens of the parents. Food consumption was dreary and often unhealthy: bread, potatoes, some dubious milk, turnips, cabbage, on occasion bacon. Meat was a luxury; in the sixteenth century the average German was estimated to consume two hundred pounds of meat in a year: in the nineteenth century, forty pounds. The workingman and workingwoman, as well as the workingchild, lived at the margin of existence. Yet they did live, as their predecessors might not have done. The statistics support both those who are pessimistic—poverty was widespread—and those who are optimistic—life at a minimal level was now more likely for all. The very concept of the cycle of life had changed; there

The Industrial Revolution introduced women into the work force outside the home in a massive way. This contemporary print shows women at work on the assembly line of a pen-grinding factory. The introduction of uniform cheap postage created a heavy demand for pens, and the flow of mail soared to unexpected heights.

was a "hierarchy of wretchedness" that was relative rather than absolute, but now was felt all the more acutely.

III THE RESPONSES OF LIBERALISM

The Classical Economists

Faced with the widening cleavage, both real and psychological, between rich and poor, nineteenth-century liberals at first held to the doctrine of laissez faire:

> Suffering and evil are nature's admonitions; they cannot be got rid of; and the impatient attempts of benevolence to banish them from the world by legislation...have always been productive of more evil than good.*

The thinkers who held to these ideas in the early nineteenth century were the classical economists, the architects of "the dismal science"—so called because of its pessimistic determinism. The most famous were two Englishmen: Thomas Malthus (1766-1834) and David Ricardo (1772-1823).

Educated for the ministry, Malthus became perhaps the first professional economist in history; he was hired by the East India Company to teach its employees at a training school in England. In 1798 he published his *Essay on Population*, a dramatic warning that the human species would breed itself into starvation. In the *Essay*, Malthus formulated a series of natural laws:

> The power of population is indefinitely greater than the power in earth to produce subsistence for man.

> Population, when unchecked, increases in a geometrical ratio. Subsistence only increases in an arithmetical ratio. . . . Through the animal and vegetable kingdoms, nature has scattered the seeds of life abroad with the most profuse and liberal hands. She has been comparatively sparing in the room and the nourishment necessary to rear them. . . . Necessity, that imperious, all-pervading law of nature, restrains them within the prescribed bounds. Among plants and animals its effects are waste of seed, sickness, and premature death. Among mankind, misery and vice**

Misery and vice would spread, Malthus believed, because the unchecked increase in human numbers would lower the demand for labor and therefore lower the wages of labor. The reduction of the human birth rate was the only hope that this prophet of gloom held out to suffering humanity. It was to be achieved by "moral restraint," that is, by late marriage and by "chastity till that period arrives."

---

*The Economist [An English weekly news magazine], May 13, 1848.
**T. Malthus, *First Essay on Population*, reprint ed. (Chicago: Henry Regnery, 1965), pp. 13-15.

Ricardo too was a prophet of gloom. He attributed economic activity to three main forces: rent, paid to the owners of great natural resources like farmland and mines; profit, accruing to enterprising individuals who exploited these resources; and wages, paid to the workers who performed the actual labor. Of the three, rent was the most important in the long run. Farms and mines would become depleted and exhausted, but their produce would continue in great demand. Rent, accordingly, would consume an ever larger share of the "economic pie," leaving smaller and smaller portions for profit and wages.

Ricardo tempered his grim forecasts, however. He did not believe that the size of the economic pie was necessarily fixed, and thus did not subscribe entirely to the mercantilist idea that the total wealth of humanity was severely limited, so that more for one person meant less for another. And yet he did predict eventual stagnation. Whereas Adam Smith had cheerfully predicted an increasing division of labor accompanied by steadily rising wages, Ricardo, in contrast, brought labor and wages under the Malthusian formula. Ricardo's disciples hardened this principle into the Iron Law of Wages, which bound workers to an unending cycle of high wages and large families, followed by an increase in the labor supply, a corresponding increase in competition for jobs, and an inevitable slump in wages. The slump would lead workers to have fewer children, followed by a resulting shortage of labor and rising wages; then the whole cycle would begin again. Ricardo himself, however, regarded the cycle not as an Iron Law, but simply as a probability. Unforeseen factors in the future might modify its course and might even permit a gradual improvement of the worker's lot.

What separated the classical economists of the early nineteenth century from their eighteenth-century predecessors was their pessimism. Like the philosophes, they did not doubt that natural laws were superior to human laws and that laissez faire was the best policy, but, unlike them, they no longer viewed nature as the creation of the beneficent God of the deists. To these adherents of the "dismal science," nature was at best a force indifferent to the fate of humanity, and at worst a malevolent one.

Yet the classical economists were proved wrong. The size of the economic pie expanded far beyond the expectations of Ricardo, as did the portions allotted to rent, to profit, and to wages. Malthus did not foresee that scientific advances would make the output of agriculture expand at a nearly geometrical ratio. He did not foresee that the perils of increasing birth rates would sometimes be averted by contraception or by emigration. Many millions of people moved from crowded Europe to lightly populated North America and Australia during the nineteenth century. The exodus from overcrowded Ireland, in particular, continued so briskly after the famine of the 1840s that by 1900 the Irish population was little more than half what it had been fifty years earlier.

DAVID RICARDO APPLIES THE MALTHUSIAN FORMULA TO WAGES

The market price of labour is the price which is really paid for it, from the natural operation of the proportion of the supply to the demand; labour is dear when it is scarce, and cheap when it is plentiful. . . . It is when the market price of labour exceeds its natural price, that the condition of the labourer is flourishing and happy. . . . When, however, by the encouragement which high wages give to the increase of population, the number of labourers is increased, wages again fall to their natural price, and indeed . . . sometimes fall below it.

On the Principles of Political Economy, chap. 5 in *The Works and Correspondence of David Ricardo*, ed. P. Sraffa (Cambridge, Eng.: Cambridge University Press, 1951), I, 94.

Although the classical economists did not take sufficient account of the immense changes being worked by the agricultural and industrial revolutions, their laissez-faire liberalism won particular favor with the new industrial magnates. The captains of industry were perhaps disturbed by Ricardo's prediction that profits would inevitably shrink; but they could take comfort from the theory that suffering and evil were "nature's admonitions." It was consoling to the rich to be told, in effect, that the poor deserved to be poor because they had indulged their appetites to excess, and that whatever was, was right, or at any rate ordained by nature. The poor did not like to hear that they deserved to be poor, and they sometimes felt that whatever was, was wrong and needed to be remedied, if necessary by interference with natural laws. Working-class leaders attacked supporters of the classical economic doctrines for acting without heart and without conscience, and for advancing economic theories that were only rationalizations of their own economic interests.

The Utilitarians

One path of retreat from the stark laissez-faire doctrines of the "dismal science" originated with a man who was himself the friend and patron of the classical economists—Jeremy Bentham (1748-1832), an eccentric philosopher. Bentham projected dozens of schemes to improve the human race, among them a model prison and reformatory. He coined new words by the dozen too, including *minimize*, *codify*, and *international*.

Bentham founded his social teachings on the concept of utility: that the goal of action should be to achieve the greatest good for the greatest number. Bentham declared the idea of "natural rights" to be "nonsense upon stilts." He dismissed the eighteenth-century theory of political contracts as a mere fiction. Ordinarily, he believed, governments could best safeguard the well-being of the community by governing as little as possible. In social and economic matters, they should act as "passive policemen" and give private initiative a generally free

---

JEREMY BENTHAM EXPLAINS THE PRINCIPLE OF UTILITY

Nature has placed mankind under the governance of two sovereign masters, *pain* and *pleasure*. It is for them alone to point out what we ought to do. . . . They govern us in all we do, in all we say, in all we think: every effort we can make to throw off our subjection, will serve to demonstrate and confirm it. . . . The *principle of utility* recognizes this subjection, and assumes it for the foundation of that system, the object of which is to rear the fabric of felicity by the hands of reason and of law. Systems which attempt to question it deal in sounds instead of sense, in caprice instead of reason, in darkness instead of light. . . .

The interest of the community is one of the most general expressions that can occur in the phraseology of morals: no wonder that the meaning of it is often lost. . . . The community is a fictitious *body*, composed of the individual persons who are considered as constituting as it were its *members*. The interest of the community then is—what? The sum of the interests of the several members who compose it.

It is in vain to talk of the interest of the community, without understanding what is the interest of the individual. A thing is said to promote the interest, or to be *for* the interest, of an individual, when it tends to add to the sum total of his pleasures: or, what comes to the same thing, to diminish the sum total of his pains.

J. Bentham, *An Introduction to the Principles of Morals and Legislation*, ed. W. Harrison (Oxford: Basil Blackwell, 1948), pp. 125-27.

---

hand. Yet Bentham realized that the state might become a more active policeman when the pursuit of self-interest by some individuals worked against the best interests of other individuals, since the goal was the greatest good for the greatest number. If the pains endured by the many exceeded the pleasures enjoyed by the few, then the state should step in. In such a situation Bentham believed the state to be "omnicompetent"—fit to undertake anything for the general welfare.

Twentieth-century doctrines of the welfare state owe a considerable debt to the utilitarianism of analysts like Bentham, James Mill (1773-1836), and the young John Stuart Mill (1806-1873), who later broke with the Benthamites. By the time of his death, Bentham was already gaining an international reputation. He had advised reformers in Portugal, Russia, Greece, and Egypt, and his writings were to exert a broad influence, particularly in France, Spain, and the Spanish-American republics. His most important English disciples, the Philosophic Radicals, pressed for reform of court procedures, local government, and poor relief so as to free humanity from the artificial constraints of the environment. The argument over whether nature (one's genetic inheritance) or one's environment (education, family, and state) most determined one's fate was now fully joined.

Humanitarian Liberalism

The great English novelist Charles Dickens (1812-1870), a compassionate observer of industrial England, stated most eloquently the case against the dehumanized sameness implicit in the teachings of the utilitarians and the laissez-faire liberals. In his novel *Hard Times* (1854), he described Coketown, which might have been any one of England's growing industrial cities:

It contained several large streets all very like one another, and many small streets still more like one another, inhabited by people equally like one another, who all went in and out at the same hours, with the same sound upon the same pavements, to do the same work, and to whom every day was the same as yesterday and tomorrow, and every year the counterpart of the last and the next. . . .

You saw nothing in Coketown but what was severely workful. If the members of a religious persuasion built a chapel there—as the members of eighteen religious persuasions had done—they made it a pious warehouse of red brick. . . . All the public inscriptions in the town were painted alike, in severe characters of black and white. The jail might have been the infirmary, the infirmary might have been the jail, the town-hall might have been either, or both, or anything else, for anything that appeared to the contrary in the graces of their construction. Fact, fact, fact, everywhere in the material aspect of the town; fact, fact, fact everywhere in the immaterial. The M'Choakumchild school was all fact, and the relations between master and man were all fact, and everything was fact between the lying-in hospital and the cemetery, and what you couldn't state in figures, or show to be purchaseable in the cheapest market and saleable in the

This 1872 engraving after Gustave Doré (1832-1883), entitled "Over London by Rail," shows how the city was transformed by the Industrial Revolution. Crowded living conditions, air pollution, and tiny back gardens for breathing space were the most the working class could hope for. The illustration incidentally shows why economists sometimes measured the health of the economy in terms of construction—specifically in terms of the number of bricks manufactured.

dearest, was not, and never should be, world without end, Amen.

Dickens saw what was wrong; John Stuart Mill (1806-1873) thought he knew what could be done to put it right. Mill grew up in an atmosphere dense with the teachings of utilitarianism and classical economics. From his father, who worked closely with Bentham and was a good friend of Ricardo, he received an education almost without parallel for intensity and speed. He began the study of Greek at three, was writing history at twelve, and at sixteen organized an active Utilitarian Society. At the age of twenty the overworked youth suffered a breakdown; as Mill relates in his influential *Autobiography*, he had become "a mere reasoning machine." So he turned for renewal to music and to the poetry of Wordsworth and Coleridge; presently he fell in love with Mrs. Harriet Taylor, to whom he assigned the major credit for his later writings. They remained friends for twenty years, until the death of Mr. Taylor at length enabled them to marry. The intellectual partnership was important to them both, and they endowed the liberal creed with the warmth and humanity it had lacked.

Mill's humane liberalism was expressed most clearly in his *On Liberty* (1859), *Utilitarianism* (1863), *The Subjection of Women* (1869), and his posthumous *Autobiography* (1873). But it is evident too in his more

*Charles Dickens, *Hard Times* (New York: Penguin Edition, 1978), pp. 65-66.

JOHN STUART MILL ON LIBERTY

A government cannot have too much of the kind of activity which does not impede, but aids and stimulates, individual exertion and development. The mischief begins when, instead of calling forth the activity and powers of individuals and bodies, it substitutes its own activity for theirs; when, instead of informing, advising, and, upon occasion, denouncing, it makes them work in fetters, or bids them stand aside and does their work instead of them. The worth of a State, in the long run, is the worth of the individuals composing it: . . . a State which dwarfs its men, in order that they may be more docile instruments in its hands even for beneficial purposes—will find that with small men no great thing can really be accomplished.

J.S. Mill, *Utilitarianism, Liberty, and Representative Government* (New York: Everyman Edition, 1939), pp. 169-70.

---

technical works, notably *Principles of Political Economy*. He first published this enormously successful textbook in 1848 and later revised it several times, each revision departing more and more from the "dismal science" of Ricardo and Malthus. The first edition put the question against the Iron Law of Wages:

How is the evil of low wages to be remedied? If the expedients usually recommended for the purpose are not adapted to it, can no others be thought of? . . . Can political economy do nothing, but only object to everything, and demonstrate that nothing can be done?*

Mill outlined the schemes for curbing overpopulation by promoting emigration to the colonies and "elevating the habits of the labouring people through education."

This one example is typical of the way in which Mill's quest for positive remedies led him to modify the laissez-faire attitude so long associated with liberalism. Although he did not accept the solution of abolishing private property, he sympathized with the French national workshops of 1848 and with some of the socialist proposals. He asserted that workers should be allowed to organize trade unions, form cooperatives, and receive a share of profits. However, these changes could best be secured within the framework of private enterprise, and not by public intervention. But he also believed that there were some matters so pressing that the state would have to step in: to protect laboring women and children and to improve intolerable living and working conditions.

Mill made universal suffrage and universal education immediate objectives. All men should have the right to vote; all should be prepared for it by receiving a basic minimum of schooling, if need be at state expense; women should have the same rights. He proposed the introduction of proportional representation in the House of Commons so that political minorities might be assured of a voice and might not be overwhelmed by the tyranny of the majority. Protection of the rights of the individual became the basis of his essay *On Liberty*.

*J.S. Mill, *Principles of Political Economy*, ed. J.M. Robson (Toronto: University of Toronto Press, 1965), Book 2, chap. 13.

Critics have claimed that Mill's eloquent defense of dissenters had undemocratic implications, for he seemed to mistrust the opinions of the majority and to favor those of the intellectual elite. Yet Mill's fear of excessive state power and the hopes he placed in enlightened individuals kept him firmly in the liberal tradition. He did not so much reject laissez-faire liberalism as endow it with new sensitivity and flexibility. He lived at a time when the defects of industrialism were becoming plain; therefore he found the exceptions to the rule of laissez faire more numerous and urgent than had his predecessors. Liberalism, as it is understood today, is the legacy not of the "dismal scientists," but of Mill and other political thinkers and politicians who have shaped modern Western democracies.

What, in fact, was *liberalism*? Those who thought of themselves as liberals were somewhat less unified than those who referred to themselves as conservatives, though they had certain characteristics of thought in common. They began with the assumption that people ought to enjoy as much freedom as possible, in keeping with an orderly society. And they believed that law was the root cause of that orderliness, and that laws ought to grow from the participation of the governed. They saw humanity essentially in social terms and believed that social organization preceded political organization. They sought to educate the individual, so that in the pursuit of personal ambitions and in the service of personal ideals, a person would also contribute to the general welfare. People must accept rules of conduct on rational grounds and by choice in order to serve society.

Although the liberals spoke of "self-realization" (developing the inner being), "self-improvement" (individualism), and "moral autonomy" (the right to private moral commitments), they saw these individualistic needs of humanity as contributing to a collective sense of community. They believed, therefore, in self-criticism, in free speech, in freedom of worship, and in restraining the state. They recognized the delicate balance needed to protect the coherence of a nation while still preserving the rights of the minority. Depending upon the particular liberal democracy, this balance would fall at different points on a scale; no liberal imagined that one person's utopia would necessarily serve for the next. Hence they tended to be nationalistic, to seek to improve their own societies. In time—especially within the liberal democratic states—they tended to engage in "social engineering" to better the standard of living through improved communications, sanitation, and education (that is, through the application of the positive lessons of the industrial society). Thus, though they professed to believe in the autonomy of differing systems of ethics for different societies, they could not resist the temptation to apply their system of government, their system of education, or their system of commerce to their colonial dependencies. Liberalism contained a host of contradictions, which were often attacked by critics from the left.

IV SOCIALIST RESPONSES: TOWARDS MARXISM

In his later years, Mill referred to himself as a socialist; by his standard, however, most voters today are socialists. Universal suffrage for men and for women, universal free education, the curbing of laissez faire in the interests of the general welfare, the use of the taxing power to limit the unbridled accumulation of private property—all these major changes foreseen by Mill are now widely accepted. But they are not socialistic, as commonly defined. The modern socialist does not stop, as Mill did, with changes in the distribution of wealth, but goes on to propose changes in arrangements for the production of goods. The means of production are to be transferred from the control of individuals to the control of the community as a whole.

Socialism—like fascism, imperialism, liberalism, democracy—is one of those words in the modern political vocabulary so laden with moral connotations and personal convictions that their original meaning is often obscured by emotion. Historians attempt to use such words neutrally, for purposes of description and not of passing judgment or allocating guilt or praise. Historically, socialism denotes any philosophy that advocates the vesting of production in the hands of society and not in those of private individuals. In practice it usually means that the state, acting as the theoretical trustee of the community, owns at least the major industries, such as coal, railroads, and steel. Socialism in its most complete form involves public ownership of almost all the instruments of production, including the land itself, virtually eliminating private property. To varying degrees in the late twentieth century, most states control some industries and the means of public transportation; Canada, Australia, and Sweden are examples of what are referred to as "mixed enterprise economies" or "the middle way."

Today the complete form of socialism is often called *communism*; in the midnineteenth century, however, the terms *socialism* and *communism* were used almost

interchangeably, as they are in some societies today. Over a hundred years of history have gone into making the distinction now drawn between the two. Especially since the Bolshevik revolution in Russia in 1917, a *communist* has come to mean someone who believes that the collectivization of property must be accomplished swiftly and violently, by revolution and direct seizure, often at bloody cost to those defeated in class warfare. A *socialist* has come to mean someone who believes that collectivization should be accomplished gradually and peacefully through democratic political procedures and with compensation to private owners. Though the ends may be similar, the means are worlds apart. This highly significant difference started to become apparent long before 1917, with the development of two divergent schools of socialist thought in the midnineteenth century, often called the Utopian and the Marxian.

The Utopians

Utopian socialists derived their inspiration from the Enlightenment. If only people would apply reason to solving the problems of an industrial economy, if only they would wipe out artificial inequalities by letting the great natural law of brotherhood operate freely—then utopia would be within their grasp, and social and economic progress would come about almost automatically. This was the common belief linking together the four chief Utopians of the early nineteenth century: Saint-Simon, Charles Fourier, Robert Owen, and Louis Blanc.

Saint-Simon belonged to a family so old and aristocratic that it claimed direct descent from Charlemagne. Educated by philosophes, Saint-Simon fought with the French army in the American War of Independence. During the French Revolution he made and lost a large fortune, but despite his own reverses, he never lost his enthusiasm for the enormous potential of the industrial age. In accordance with his parable about the three thousand real leaders of France (see p. 160), Saint-Simon would have given supreme political authority to a Parliament of Improvements, composed of ten industrialists and five each of artists, philosophers, chemists, physiologists, physicists, astronomers, and mathematicians, and presided over by one of the mathematicians. He admonished the members of the new elite: "Christianity commands you to use all your powers to increase as rapidly as possible the social welfare of the poor!"* Reform should come peacefully, through "persuasion and demonstration." Combining the Enlightenment's respect for science with romanticism's zeal for the community, Saint-Simon proclaimed the one science transcending all others to be the application of the Golden Rule. Since men of different nations were all brothers, Saint-Simon envisaged a federation of European states.

"Organization," "harmony," and "industry" were

*H. de Saint-Simon, *Selected Writings*, ed. F.M.H. Markham (New York: Harper & Row, 1952), p. 116.

three of Saint-Simon's catchwords; when all three elements were coordinated, humanity would achieve some of the major improvements he proposed, among them great networks of highways and waterways, and would become a single, rational society. After Saint-Simon's death, his followers focused on the strain of social Christianity in his teaching. Prosper Enfantin (1796-1864) combined local railroads into a Paris-Lyons-Mediterranean trunk line, and another Saint-Simonian, Ferdinand de Lesseps (1805-1894), promoted the building of a Suez Canal and made an abortive start at digging across the Isthmus of Panama.

The vagueness of Saint-Simon's concepts permitted almost every kind of social thinker—from laissez-faire liberal to communist—to cite him with approval. Among his disciples were Giuseppe Mazzini and Louis Blanc, the Russian revolutionary pioneer Alexander Herzen, and the French positivist philosopher Auguste Comte. What was socialistic about Saint-Simon was his goal of reorganizing and harmonizing society as a whole, rather than merely improving the well-being of some of its individual members.

Saint-Simon's compatriot and contemporary, Charles Fourier (1772-1837), also extolled harmony and drew up an elaborate blueprint for achieving it. At the French textile center of Lyons Fourier was shocked by the contrast between the wealth of the silk manufacturers and the misery of their workers. At Paris he was shocked when he found that a single apple cost a sum that would have bought a hundred apples in the countryside. Clearly, he concluded, something was amiss in a society

and economy that permitted such divergences. He compared the historical importance of his apple with that of Newton, and believed himself to be the Newton of the social sciences. Just as Newton had found the force holding the heavenly bodies in a state of mutual attraction, so Fourier claimed to have discovered the force holding the individuals of human society in a state of mutual attraction.

This force was *l'attraction passionnelle*; that is, human beings were drawn to one another by their passions. Fourier drew up a list of passions—sex, companionship, food, luxury, variety, and so on, to a total of 810. Since existing society thwarted their satisfaction, Fourier proposed it be remodeled into units that he called *phalanges* (phalanxes), each containing 400 acres of land and accommodating 500 to 2,000 (though ideally 1,620) persons. Volunteers would form a phalanx by setting up a community company and agreeing to split its profits three ways—five-twelfths to those who did the work, four-twelfths to those who undertook the management, and three-twelfths to those who supplied the capital.

Fourier's phalanx, with its relatively generous rewards to managers and capitalists, fell short of complete equality. Yet it did assign to labor the largest share of the profits, and it foreshadowed many other features of socialist planning. Each phalanx would be nearly self-sufficient, producing in its own orchards, fields, and workshops most of the things required by its inhabitants. Adult workers who performed the most dangerous or unpleasant tasks would receive the highest

This print shows one of Fourier's phalansteries—a "working people's Versailles"—in which the inhabitants were to live and labor.

remuneration. The inhabitants of the phalanx were to live in one large building, a *phalanstère*, which would provide the maximum opportunity for the satisfaction of social passions, and would also make the routine of daily living more efficient by substituting one central kitchen for hundreds of separate ones. The sordid features of housekeeping could be left to little boys, who loved dirt anyway and would cheerfully form squads to dispose of garbage and human refuse.

Places of work would be made as pleasant as possible by frequent, colorful redecoration. Members of the phalanx would change their jobs eight times a day because of the human predisposition to the "butterfly passion"—"enthusiasm cannot be sustained for more than an hour and a half or two hours in the performance of one particular operation." They would work from four to five in the morning to eight or nine at night, enjoying five meals. They would need only five hours of sleep, since the variety of work would not tire them. All would become so healthy that physicians would be superfluous, and everyone would live to the age of 140. While colonies sprang up in which Fourierism was tried, especially in the New World, public opinion, including working-class opinion, remained hostile to surrendering the privacy of the family. Both to eliminate the evil of prostitution and to allow human association the fullest possible scope, Fourier advocated complete sexual freedom in the phalanx; he recommended marriage only for the elderly, whose passions had begun to cool.

Underneath these perhaps foolish and failed details lay significant contributions to socialist theory and social psychology. Some of Fourier's recommendations, like higher pay for dangerous jobs and devices for relieving the tedium of work, have become common practice in modern business. In the short run, however, Utopian socialism came to be identified with free love and therefore, in the popular mind, with the grossest immorality.

Another Utopian and advocate of sexual emancipation was a self-made British businessman, Robert Owen (1771-1858). In 1800 Owen took over the large cotton mills at New Lanark in Scotland and found conditions that shocked him, even though the previous owner had been accounted benevolent by the standards of the day. A large part of the working force in the mills consisted of children who had been recruited from orphanages in Edinburgh when they were between six and eight years old. Although the youngsters did get a little schooling after hours, Owen found many of them "dwarfs in body and mind." Adult laborers at New Lanark fared little better.

Remaking New Lanark into a model industrial village, Owen set out to show that he could increase profits and the welfare of his laborers at the same time. For the adults he provided better working conditions, a ten-and-a-half-hour day, higher pay, and improved housing. He closed down the worst drinking places, making less poisonous alcohol available at cheap prices and punishing offenders who made themselves a public nuisance. He raised the minimum age for employment to ten,

hoping ultimately to put it at twelve, and he gave his child laborers time off for schooling. His educational preferences followed Rousseau; advanced bookish subjects were avoided, while crafts, nature study, and other utilitarian subjects received close attention. A properly educated nation, Owen believed, would refute the gloomy predictions of Malthus, who "has not told us how much more food an intelligent and industrious people will create from the same soil, than will be produced by one ignorant and ill-governed."[*] He hoped through such measures to arouse a class consciousness that would provide workers with a sense of pride in their work without contributing to a "revolutionary class."

In the 1820s Owen visited America to finance an abortive effort to set up a colony at New Harmony, Indiana. Undaunted by this failure, he spent the rest of his career publishing and supporting projects for social reform. He advocated the association of all labor in one big union—an experiment that failed, though the call was taken up later in the United States; and he sought to reduce the workers' expenditures by promoting the formation of consumers' cooperatives—an experiment that succeeded. He too offended many of his contemporaries by his advocacy of sexual freedom, by his attacks on established religion, and by his enthusiasm for spiritualism.

Both Owen and Fourier relied on private initiative to build their model communities. In contrast, Louis Blanc (1811-1882) developed Saint-Simon's vaguely formulated principle of "organization" into a doctrine of state intervention to achieve Utopian ends. Author of a pioneering history of the French Revolution from the socialist standpoint and an implacable critic of the July Monarchy, Blanc outlined his scheme for social workshops in a pamphlet, *The Organization of Labor* (1840), which began with the statement, "The other day a child was frozen to death behind a sentry-box in the heart of Paris, and nobody was shocked or surprised at the event."

"What proletarians need," Blanc wrote, "is the instruments of labor; it is the function of government to supply these. If we were to define our conception of the state, our answer would be that the state is the banker of the poor."[**] The government would finance and supervise the purchase of productive equipment and the formation of social workshops; it would withdraw its support and supervision once the workshops were on their feet. As the workshops gradually spread throughout France, socialistic enterprise would replace private enterprise, private profits would vanish, and labor would emerge as the only class left in society, thereby achieving a classless society.

Much of Louis Blanc's socialism was characteristically Utopian, particularly in his reliance on workers to make their own arrangements for communal living. The

[*]R. Owen, *A New View of Society*, written in 1812-1813 (New York: Penguin Edition, 1969), p. 192.
[**]"L'Organisation du Travail," in *The French Revolution of 1848*, ed. J.A.R. Marriott (Oxford: Oxford University Press, 1913), I, 14. Our translation.

real novelty of his plan lay in the role he assigned to the state and in the fact that he began to move socialism from philanthropy to politics. Ironically, politics was to prove his undoing. Alarmed conservatives identified the national workshops of 1848 as an effort to implement his social ideas, and he was forced into exile.

Marx

With Karl Marx (1818-1883) socialism moved to a far more intense form—revolutionary communism. Whereas the early socialists had anticipated a gradual and peaceful evolution toward utopia, Marx forecast a sudden and violent proletarian uprising by which the workers would capture governments and make them the instruments for securing proletarian welfare. From Blanc he derived the summary of socialist goals: "From each according to his abilities, to each according to his needs."

Marx found three laws in the pattern of history. First, *economic determinism:* he believed that economic conditions largely determined the character of all other human institutions—society and government, religion and art. Second, *the class struggle:* he believed that history was a dialectical process, a series of conflicts between antagonistic economic groups, ideas, and practices. In his own day the antagonists were the "haves" and the "have-nots"—the propertied bourgeois against the propertyless proletarians, who, possessing nothing but their working skills, had nothing to fall back on in bad times and were thus at the mercy of their masters. Third, the *inevitability of communism:* he believed that the class struggle was bound to produce one final upheaval that would raise the victorious proletariat over the prostrate bourgeoisie. As he wrote to a friend in 1852, "What I did that was new was to prove (1) that the *existence of classes* is only bound up with *particular historical phases in the development of production*, (2) that the class struggle necessarily leads to the *dictatorship of the proletariat*, (3) that this dictatorship itself only constitutes the transition to *abolition of all* classes and to a *classless society*."* Here were Saint-Simon and Blanc, the English classical economists, and Hegel all wed into a single system.

Although Marx was born and died in the nineteenth century, he belonged in spirit partly to the eighteenth. Both his grandfathers were rabbis, but his father was a deist and a skeptic who trained him in the rationalism of the Enlightenment. Marx early acquired a faith in natural law, fortified by the materialistic teachings of the German philosopher Ludwig Feuerbach (1804-1872), who proclaimed that *Man ist was er esst* ("One is what one eats") and that all religion was a "symbolic dream." From all this followed the boast made by Marx and his disciples that their socialism alone was "scientific," as opposed to the romantic doctrines of the Utopians.

*Tom Bottomore, ed., *Karl Marx* (Englewood Cliffs, N.J.: Spectrum Books, 1973), p. 144.

Though the ideas of Karl Marx are under constant revision by socialists, especially in the Soviet Union, his basic arguments were to triumph over other socialist views. As modified by later theorists, he would become the father of modern communism.

The romantic philosophy of Hegel, however, provided the intellectual scaffolding of Marxism. Although Hegel had died in 1831, his influence permeated the University of Berlin during Marx's student days there (1836-1841). Marx translated the Hegelian dialectic of thesis/antithesis/synthesis into the language of economic determinism and the class struggle. He believed that capitalistic production and the bourgeoisie comprised the thesis; the antithesis was the proletariat; and the synthesis, issuing from the communist revolution, would be true socialism. He stood Hegel on his head—Hegel, Marx said, made ideas independent of the material world, while to Marx the ideal was "nothing less than the material world reflected by the human mind, and translated into forms of thought."

By age thirty Marx had completed the outlines of his theory of scientific, revolutionary socialism. He had also become a permanent exile from his native Germany. On leaving the University of Berlin, he worked for a newspaper at Cologne in the Prussian Rhineland, then moved to Paris in 1843 after his espousal of atheism had aroused the authorities there against him. Exiled again because the government of Louis Philippe feared his anti-bourgeois propaganda, he went to Brussels in 1845.

Wherever he happened to be, he studied the economists of the past incessantly and talked with the socialists of his own generation. From Adam Smith's labor theory of value he concluded that only the worker should receive the profits from the sale of a commodity, since the value of the commodity should be determined by the labor of the person who produced it. The Iron Law of Wages, however, confirmed Marx's belief that capitalism would never permit the worker to receive this just reward. And from observing the depression of the late 1840s, he concluded that economic crises were bound to occur again and again under a system by which capital produced too much and labor consumed too little. Essentially a scholar and a philosopher, Marx had initially expected that people would see the wisdom behind his ideas; that violence should be committed in his name was not his original intention.

Engels and *The Communist Manifesto*

Meanwhile, Marx began his friendship and collaboration with Friedrich Engels (1820-1895). In many ways, the two men made a striking contrast. Marx was poor and quarrelsome, a man of few friends; except for his devotion to his wife and children, he was utterly preoccupied with his economic studies. Engels, on the other hand, was the son of a well-to-do German manufacturer and represented the family textile business in Liverpool and Manchester. He loved sports and high living, but he also hated the evils of industrialism. When he met Marx, he had already written a bitter study, *The Condition of the Working Class in England*, based on his first-hand knowledge of the situation in Manchester.

Both Engels and Marx took an interest in the Communist League, a small, secret international organization of radical workers. In 1847 the London office of the Communist League requested them to draw up a program. Engels wrote the first draft, which Marx revised; the result, a fifty-page pamphlet in German published in January 1848 in London, since there was no political censorship there, was *The Communist Manifesto*. It remains the classic statement of Marxian socialism.

The *Manifesto* opened with the dramatic announcement that "A spectre is haunting Europe—the spectre of Communism." It closed with a stirring and confident appeal:

Let the ruling classes tremble at a Communistic revolution. The proletarians have nothing to lose but their chains. They have a world to win.

Working men of all countries, unite!

In between it traced a communist view of history: "The history of all hitherto existing society is the history of class struggle." Changing economic conditions determined that the struggle should develop successively between "freeman and slave, patrician and plebeian,

lord and serf, guildmaster and journeyman." The guild system gave way first to manufacture by large numbers of small capitalists and then to "the giant, modern industry." Modern industry would inevitably destroy bourgeois society. It creates mounting economic pressures by producing more goods than it can sell; it creates mounting social pressures by narrowing the circle of capitalists to fewer and fewer persons and depriving more and more people of their property and forcing them down to the proletariat. These pressures would increase to the point where a revolutionary explosion would occur, a massive assault on private property. Landed property would be abolished outright; other forms of property would be liquidated more gradually through the imposition of crushing income taxes and the abolition of inherited wealth.

Eventually, social classes and tensions would vanish, and "we shall have an association in which the free development of each is the condition for the free development of all." The *Manifesto* provided only this vague description of the situation that would exist after the revolution. Since Marx defined political authority as "the organized power of one class for oppressing another," he apparently expected that "the state would wither away" once it had created a classless regime. He also apparently assumed that the great dialectical process of history, having achieved its final synthesis, would then cease to operate in its traditional form. But how? Wouldn't the dialectic continue forever, creating new economic and political theses and antitheses? Wouldn't the state always be necessary? To these questions Marx offered no answer except the implication that somehow the liquidation of bourgeois capitalism would radically alter the course of history and transform humanity.

Marx oversimplified the complexities of human nature by trying to force it into the rigid mold of economic determinism and ignoring nonmaterial motives and interests. Neither proletarians nor bourgeois have proved to be the simple economic stereotypes Marx supposed them to be: labor has often behaved in un-Marxian fashion and assumed a markedly bourgeois outlook and mentality; capital has put its own house in better order and eliminated the worst injustices of the factory system. No more than Malthus did Marx foresee the notable rise in the general standard of living that began in the midnineteenth century and continued well into the twentieth.

Since Marx also failed to take into account the growing strength of nationalism, the *Manifesto* confidently expected the class struggle to transcend national boundaries. In social and economic warfare, nation would not be pitted against nation; the proletariat everywhere would join to fight the bourgeoisie. "Workingmen have no country" and "national differences and antagonisms are vanishing gradually from day to day." In Marx's own lifetime, however, national differences and antagonisms were, in fact, increasing rapidly from day to day. Within a few months of the publication of the *Manifesto*, the revolutions of 1848 disclosed the antagonisms between

Italians and Austrians, Austrians and Hungarians, Hungarians and Slavs, Slavs and Germans. Indeed, the *Manifesto* had little influence on the revolutionaries of 1848.

Nonetheless, *The Communist Manifesto* anticipated the strengths as well as the weaknesses of the communist movement. First, it foreshadowed the important role to be played by propaganda. Second, it anticipated the emphasis to be placed on the role of the party in forging the proletarian revolution. The communists, Marx declared, were a spearhead, "the most advanced section of the working-class parties of every country." In matters of theory, they had the advantage over the great mass of the proletariat of "clearly understanding the line of march, the conditions, and the ultimate general results of the proletarian movement." Third, the *Manifesto* assigned the state a great role in the revolution. Among the policies recommended by Marx were "centralization of credit in the hands of the state," and "extension of factories and instruments of production owned by the state." And, finally, the *Manifesto* clearly established the line dividing communism from the other forms of socialism. Marx's dogmatism, his philosophy of history, and his belief in the necessity of a "total" revolution made his brand of socialism a doctrine apart. Marx scorned and pitied the Utopian socialists. They were about as futile, he wrote, as "organizers of charity, members of societies for the prevention of cruelty to animals, temperance fanatics, hole-and-corner reformers of every kind." Bourgeois revisionists lacked the courage, ruthlessness, and vision to carry out the root-and-branch changes that society required, and Marx soon found himself at war with most other socialists.

Marxism after 1848

From 1849 until his death in 1883, Marx lived in London, where, partly because of his own financial mismanagement, his family experienced the misery of a proletarian existence in the slums of Soho. After poverty and near-starvation had caused the death of three of his children, he eventually obtained a modest income from the generosity of Engels and from his own writings. Throughout this time he revised his writings, setting out his main principles in the *Grundrisse*, a thousand-page manuscript not actually published in the West until 1953, and then departing from the outline thus completed in 1858 to write the first volume of *Das Kapital* in 1867. That he changed his views on several matters is clear; that he was consistent in his basic analysis is also clear; but contradictions between versions of his argument have plagued socialist and communist theoreticians ever since, though those committed to a single view have often attempted to obscure Marx's own sense that his work was not fully complete. Two further volumes of *Das Kapital*, pieced together from his notes, were published after his death.

In *Das Kapital* Marx elaborated the doctrines of the *Communist Manifesto*. He spelled out the labor theory of value according to which the workers created the total value of the commodity that they produced, yet received in the form of wages only a small part of the price for the item. The difference between the sale price and the workers' wages constituted *surplus value*, something actually created by labor but appropriated by capital as profit. It was the nature of capitalism, Marx argued, to diminish its own profits by replacing human labor with machines and thus gradually choke off the source of surplus value. Thus would arise a mounting crisis of overproduction and underconsumption. Marx compared capitalism to an integument, a skin or shell, increasingly stretched and strained from within. One day internal pressures would prove irresistible: "This integument is burst asunder. The knell of capitalist private property sounds. The expropriators are expropriated."*

In 1864, three years before the first volume of *Das Kapital* was published, Marx joined in the formation of the First International Workingmen's Association. This was an ambitious attempt to organize workers of every country and variety of radical belief. A loose federation rather than a coherent political party, the First International soon began to disintegrate; it expired in 1876. Increasing persecution by hostile governments helped to bring on its end; but so too did the factional quarrels that repeatedly engaged its members. And Marx himself set the example, both by his intolerance of disagreement and by his incapacity for practical politics.

In 1889 a Second International was organized; it lasted until World War I and the Bolshevik revolution in Russia. The Second International was more coherently organized and more political in character than the First International had been. It represented the Marxian Socialist or Social Democratic parties, which were becoming important forces in the major countries of continental Europe. Among its leaders were men and women more politically adept than Marx. Yet factionalism continued to weaken the International. Some of its leaders tenaciously defended the precepts of the master and forbade any cooperation between socialists and the bourgeois political parties; these were the orthodox Marxists. Other leaders of the Second International were, from the orthodox standpoint, heretics. Still calling themselves Marxists, they revised his doctrines in the direction of moderation and of harmonization with the views of the Utopians. These "revisionists" believed in cooperation between classes rather than in a struggle to the death, and they hoped that human decency and intelligence, working through the machinery of democratic government, could avert the horrors of outright class war.

Both orthodox and heretical Marxists have persisted to the present day, with the orthodox view itself fragmenting, and the heretical views proliferating, as

---

*Frederick Engels, ed., *Capital. I: A Critical Analysis of Capitalist Production* (London: Swan Sonnenschein, 1887), p. 763. The edition read "Thus integument" but modern commentators believe the original intention was "This integument."

theoreticians and political leaders in Asia, Africa, and Latin America attempted, especially after World War II, to adapt Marxian analysis to the perceived realities of their situations. Marx's views would be significantly added to by V.I. Lenin, so that scholars prefer to speak of Marxism-Leninism when referring to the practices of the principal modern advocate of orthodoxy, the Soviet Union (see Chapter 24).

V APOSTLES OF VIOLENCE AND NONVIOLENCE

The various forms of liberalism and socialism did not exhaust the range of responses to the economic and social problems created in industrial societies. Nationalists reinvigorated old mercantilist ideas, not only advocating tariffs to protect agriculture and industry but also demanding empires abroad to provide new markets for surplus products, new fields for the investment of surplus capital, and new settlements for surplus citizens. Others advocated anarchy and violence, while nonviolent preachers of mutualism, good will, and good works sought to return to primitive Christianity.

Tradition assigns the honor of being the first modern socialists to Gracchus Babeuf and his fellow conspirators under the French Directory in 1796-1797. The equalitarianism of Babeuf was too loosely formulated to be called truly socialist, however; the only direct link between him and later socialist doctrines derives from his followers' belief that human nature could change only through immediate violent action in the manner of the Reign of Terror. The leader of these new terrorists was Auguste Blanqui (1805-1881), a professional revolutionary who participated in the Paris revolts of 1830, 1848, and 1870-1871 (after France's defeat in the Franco-Prussian War). Blanqui believed that the imposition of a dictatorial regime by an elite vanguard of conspirators would be the only way to deal with a bourgeois capitalist society. An inveterate plotter of violence, he spent forty years of his life span of seventy-six in prison. When his movement died out in the 1870s, his followers tended to join the Marxian Socialists. His dedication to activism made him a significant figure in left-wing history; it has been said that Lenin's formula for a successful Bolshevik revolution was Marxism plus Blanquism.

Anarchists

Other apostles of violence called themselves anarchists, believing that the best government was no government at all. For them it was not enough that the state should wither at some distant time, however; such an instrument of oppression should be annihilated at once. The weapon of the anarchist terrorists was the assassination of heads of state, and by the turn of the century they had killed the French president Carnot in 1894, King

Humbert of Italy in 1900, and the American president William McKinley in 1901.

The anarchist ideal exerted an important influence on the proletarian movement. Russian scientist and thinker Prince Peter Kropotkin (1842-1921) made the most complete statement of its theory in his book *Mutual Aid: A Factor in Evolution* (1902). Kropotkin foresaw a revolution that would abolish the state as well as private property, and that would lead to a new society of cooperating autonomous groups wherein workers would achieve greater fulfillment and would need to labor only four to five hours a day. Kropotkin's countryman and fellow anarchist Mikhail Bakunin (1814-1876) helped to shape the Russian revolutionary movement and won the attention of workers from many countries by his participation in the First International. Although Bakunin drew only a vague sketch of his utopia, he made it clear that the millennium was to be achieved through an international rebellion set off by small groups of anarchist conspirators.

Bakunin contributed to the formation of the program known as anarcho-syndicalism (from the French word *syndicat*, which means an economic grouping, particularly a trade union). The anarcho-syndicalists scorned political parties, even Marxist ones; they believed in direct action by the workers to culminate in a spontaneous general strike that would free labor from the capitalistic yoke. Meantime, workers could rehearse for the great day by engaging in acts of anticapitalist sabotage. In 1908 these theories received their most forceful expression in *Reflections on Violence* by a French engineer and anarcho-syndicalist, Georges Sorel (1847-1922), who declared that belief in the general strike constituted a kind of myth that would convert all workers into saboteurs, and that democracy inevitably would lead to the triumph of mediocrity. But the writer most frequently cited by the anarcho-syndicalists was the French publicist Pierre Joseph Proudhon (1809-1865). "What is property?" Proudhon asked in a pamphlet in 1840. "Property is theft," he answered. Thus, where Marx foresaw a revolution in ownership of the means of production, Proudhon foresaw a "revolution of credit," a revolution in financing production.

Christian Socialists and Christian Democrats

Still other efforts to mitigate class antagonisms came from the Anglican and Catholic churches. In England the Christian Socialists, a group of midnineteenth century reformers from the Anglican clergy, urged the Church of England to put aside theological disputes and direct its efforts toward ending social abuses. One of these Christian Socialists was Charles Kingsley (1819-1875), author of children's fiction and didactic social novels. The Christian Socialists attacked materialism and championed brotherly love against unbrotherly strife, association and cooperation against exploitation and competition. They relied far more on private philan-

POPE LEO XIII ATTACKS SOCIALISM

In *Rerum Novarum* Pope Leo pronounced it a "great mistake" to believe

that class is naturally hostile to class, and that the wealthy and the workingmen are intended by nature to live in mutual conflict. . . . Each needs the other: Capital cannot do without Labor, nor Labor without Capital. . . .

Religion teaches the laboring man . . . to carry out honestly and fairly all equitable agreements freely entered into; never to injure the property, nor to outrage the person, of an employer; never to resort to violence . . . ; and to have nothing to do with men of evil principles, who work upon the people with artful promises, and excite foolish hopes which usually end in useless regrets, followed by insolvency. Religion teaches the wealthy owner and the employer that their workpeople are not to be accounted their bondsmen; that in every man they must respect his dignity and worth as a man and as a Christian; that labor is not a thing to be ashamed of, if we lend ear to right reason and to Christian philosophy, but is an honorable calling, enabling a man to sustain his life in a way upright and creditable; and that it is shameful and inhuman to treat men like chattels to make money by, or to look upon them merely as so much muscle or physical power.

The Great Encyclical Letters of Pope Leo XIII (New York: Benziger Bros., 1903), pp. 218, 219.

thropy than on state intervention, however, as did their Catholic counterparts on the Continent, who advocated what they called Christian democracy or social Christianity.

By the second half of the nineteenth century an atmosphere of crisis was enveloping the Roman church. A thousand years of papal rule in central Italy ended when the city of Rome passed to the newly unified Kingdom of Italy in 1870; anticlerical legislation threatened traditional Catholic bulwarks in Italy, France, and Germany; and the materialism of the Industrial Revolution and the new ideologies of science, nationalism, and socialism were all competing for the allegiance of Catholics. The church initially responded to these problems by seeking refuge in the past. Pope Pius IX (1846-1878), whose experiences in 1848 and 1849 had ended his earlier flirtation with liberalism, issued the *Syllabus of Errors* in 1864, condemning many social theories and institutions not consecrated by tradition. While Pius also condemned the materialism implicit in laissez faire, socially minded Catholics were disturbed by his apparent hostility to trade unions and democracy and by his statement that it was an error to suppose that the pope "can and ought to reconcile and harmonize himself with progress, liberalism, and modern civilization."

His successor, Leo XIII (1878-1903), recognized that the church could not continue to turn its back on modernity without suffering serious losses, for as a papal nuncio he had witnessed industrial changes firsthand in Belgium, France, and Germany. He knew that Catholicism was flourishing in the supposedly hostile climate of the democratic and largely Protestant United States. Moreover, his studies of St. Thomas Aquinas convinced him that the church had much to gain by following the middle-of-the-road social and economic policies recommended by that medieval Schoolman. Accordingly, Leo XIII issued a series of modernizing documents, notably an encyclical, *Rerum Novarum* (*Concerning New Things*, 1891).

In *Rerum Novarum* Pope Leo wrote of the defects of capitalism as vigorously as any socialist, and then attacked with equal vigor the socialist view of property and the doctrine of class war. Leo believed that the workers must help themselves, and *Rerum Novarum* concluded with a fervent appeal for the formation of Catholic trade unions.

These Catholic unions exist today, but they are only a minority in the realm of organized labor. Neither the Christian democracy of Leo XIII nor the Christian socialism of the Anglican reformers has achieved all that the founders hoped. Yet the Christian democrats eventually came to play a central part in the politics of Germany, Italy, and other European states, particularly after World War II. And in Britain at the beginning of the twentieth century, both Marxism and the Christian socialist tradition helped to attract workers and middle-class intellectuals to the developing Labour party. It was not, in any case, socialism that had proved to be the major threat to traditional religion, nor the most significant product of the industrial society. The new science, which challenged biblical views of creation, and other essentially materialist philosophies, not necessarily socialist and at times clearly antisocialist in nature, had ushered in an age of materialism.

VI A NEW AGE OF SCIENCE

The industrial society liked to display its accomplishments in great international fairs: in London in 1851, in Paris in 1855 and 1867, and throughout Europe and North America. The telegraph, the submarine cable, the telephone, the massive railroad bridges and tunnels, and the high-speed printing press not only improved communications but also demonstrated the practical utility of science. Chemistry and physics were especially important, and the latter had led to a new percepton of the nature of matter. The study of thermodynamics was fostered by the steam engine, which used heat to create power and led physicists to study the conservation of energy. The first law of thermodynamics held that energy was a form of immortality, for it transformed itself from heat into power and back into heat again. But a second law of thermodynamics held that all energy was ultimately dissipated; though the total amount of energy in the universe remained constant, the amount useful to human beings was capable of being steadily degraded. This in turn led to an interest in the conservation of the resources on which energy was based. Some scientists predicted that the sun would gradually lose its heat and the earth would get colder; some held that the universe was running down. Others believed that new sources for energy could be found, and they were not ready to join the physicists who predicted that the ever-growing pace of energy use would lead humanity to disaster.

Competing theories of the universe argued for continuity, whether based on waves or on atoms. Scientists who studied electricity and magnetism developed a new body of study, electromagnetism; they maintained that light was a series of waves. Since light waves must move through some medium, not empty space, it was hypothesized that space was filled with a conductor, a substance called ether. Many scientists abandoned the Newtonian concept of light as made up of minute particles. If humanity lived in a world of eternal waves, it lived within a continuity. While the waves, like the energy of thermodynamics, were material, those who sought to reconcile science to religion could argue that energy was a Cartesian First Cause and that an initiator, a God, was essential to energy and continuity.

To other physicists, and also chemists, biologists, and physicians, humanity continued to live in a world of particles—a world of atoms. Atoms of one chemical element combined with those of another to form molecules of some familiar substance, such as hydrogen, oxygen, and water. But the process of combination raised some important questions. For example, the volume of hydrogen in water was twice that of oxygen, as indicated by the familiar formula H_2O; but experiments showed that the weight of the oxygen was eight times that of the hydrogen. It seemed evident, therefore, that an atom of oxygen must weigh sixteen times more than an atom of hydrogen. To establish a standard table of atomic weights, an international congress of experts met in 1860 in Germany and devised a table based on the calculations of two Italian scientists. To understand the interactions of atomic weights, scientists felt, was to approach an understanding of the nature of energy in the universe.

The biological counterpart of the atomic theory was the cell theory: all plant and animal structures are composed of living units known as cells. The medical counterpart was the theory of germs (in time further refined into bacilli, viruses, and the like)—a great advance over the older belief that disease was in effect a phenomenon of spontaneous corruption, as shown by the term "consumption" for tuberculosis. Biology, like all other sciences, was international: a German microbiologist discovered the organisms causing tuberculosis and cholera; an American doctor found that the virus responsible for yellow fever was transmitted by a mosquito; in Britain a Quaker physician demonstrated that germs were responsible for the infection of wounds and greatly reduced the mortality rate of surgical and battlefield patients by the application of new antiseptic measures; in France the chemist Louis Pasteur (1822-1895) became a popular as well as a scientific hero by developing a vaccine for inoculating victims of rabies, until then invariably fatal, and by devising a process for sterilizing milk. By the twentieth century the average life expectancy in North America and many European countries was to increase by twenty to thirty years, greatly adding to the world's population.

This painting (1885) shows Pasteur in his laboratory examining the spinal marrow of a rabbit that died of hydrophobia. Such scientific exploration brought medicine, surgery, and public health to a point of impressive growth by 1900.

THE ORIGIN OF SPECIES

Darwin's book began with the true scientist's caution:

When on board H.M.S. "Beagle," as naturalist, I was much struck with certain facts in the distribution of the inhabitants of South America, and in the geological relations of the present to the past inhabitants of that continent. These facts seemed to me to throw some light on the origin of species—that mystery of mysteries, as it has been called by one of our greatest philosophers. On my return home, it occurred to me, in 1837, that something might perhaps be made out on this question by patiently accumulating and reflecting on all sorts of facts which could possibly have any bearing on it. After five years' work I allowed myself to speculate on the subject, and drew up some short notes; these I enlarged in 1844 into a sketch of the conclusions, which then seemed to me probable: from that period to the present day I have steadily pursued the same object. I hope that I may be excused for entering on these personal details, as I give them to show that I have not been hasty in coming to a decision.

Charles Darwin, *On the Origin of Species*, facsimile of the 1st ed. (Cambridge, Mass.: Harvard University Press, 1964), p. 1.

Darwinism, 1859-1871

But for the average person and for its practical effect on the industrial society, it was a revolutionary new theory in biology that most transformed thought, and thus action. In 1859 there was published in London a volume on natural history, Charles Darwin's *On the Origin of Species by Means of Natural Selection*, that was to be one of the seminal books in intellectual history. It rested in the study of natural history, the long record of the hundreds of thousands of years of organic life on earth. Already well established by geologists and paleontologists, this record told of the rise, the development, and sometimes the disappearance of thousands of different forms of plant and animal organisms, or species. The record appeared to contradict the biblical book of *Genesis*, which described all forms of life as having begun in the space of a single week by a Creator about six thousand years ago.

Darwin (1809-1882) found one clue to the past in Malthus's *Essay on Population*, which maintained that organisms tended to multiply to a point where there was not sufficient food for them all. In the intense competition for food, some of these organisms did not get enough and died. This was the germ of the conception Darwin phrased as the *struggle for existence*. He next asked himself what determined that certain individuals would survive and that others would die. Obviously, the surviving ones got more food, better shelter, better living conditions of all sorts. If they were all identical organisms, then the only explanation—apart from the intervention of a supernatural being or force—would have to be some accidental variation in the environment. But it was clear from observation that individual organisms of a given species are not identical. Variations appear even at birth. Thus in a single litter of pigs there may be sturdy, aggressive piglets and also a runt, who is likely to get shoved aside in suckling by the sturdier animals and starve. In the struggle for existence, the runt is proved "unfit."

This was the second of Darwin's key phrases—the *survival of the fittest*. The organism best endowed in its variations to get food and shelter lives to procreate young that will tend to inherit these favorable variations. The variations may be slight indeed, but over generation after generation they are cumulative; finally an organism is produced that is so different from the long-distant ancestor that it can be considered to be a new species. This new species has *evolved* by the working of *natural selection*. Plant and animal breeders had long made use of this process and had even directed it by *artificial* selection, by breeding only the most desirable strains. But this deliberate selection had been done with domesticated plants and animals for only a tiny period of geological time, and with only a few species; over the eons, *natural* selection had been the working force. And for the human animal, according to the Darwinian system, natural selection alone had been at work, since humans had yet to breed their own kind as they bred domestic plants and animals.

Darwin held that the variations in individuals of the same species at birth are accidental, and that they are generally transmitted through inheritance. Those biologists who further developed his doctrine did not believe that the evidence showed that variations produced in an individual organism *during* its life could be transmitted to its offspring; thus orthodox Darwinism denied the inheritance of acquired characteristics. Obviously, a person with an amputated leg will not produce one-legged children. The actual mechanism of heredity we know much better than Darwin did, thanks to the Austrian priest Gregor Mendel (1822-1884), whose experiments with crossbreeding garden peas laid the scientific basis of modern genetics and its study of genes and chromosomes.

Darwin's theory was later modified as scientists concluded that the important variations in the evolutionary process were not so much the numerous tiny ones Darwin emphasized but rather bigger and much rarer ones known as *mutations*. Scientists began to study the effect of various forms of radiation on such mutations. A still-disputed geological theory holds that catastrophic movements of great plates forming the earth's crust have so radically altered the environment as to wipe out whole species and speed up the evolution of others. The emphasis on mutations or on extensive crustal movements tends also to be an emphasis on the sudden and violent rather than on the gradual—an attitude more in keeping with the expectations of the twentieth century than with the nineteenth.

The first edition of *The Origin of Species* was sold out on the day of its publication. The book that Darwin himself considered of interest only to students of natural history became a best seller, reviewed all over the world. The major reason for this attention was almost certainly the challenge that orthodox Christians felt they found in the book. Darwinism was a phase of the so-called warfare of science with theology. Yet Darwin's book was no new denial of fundamentalist beliefs, for natural scientists had for over a century been publishing works that flatly denied the possibility that the earth could be only a few thousand years old. The doctrine of God's special creation of each species had also been challenged long before Darwin.

Darwin received such wide attention because he seemed to provide for the secularist a process (evolution) and a causal agent (natural selection), where before there had been only vague "materialistic" notions that emphasized accident rather than order. He also seemed to have struck a final blow against the argument, still very popular in Victorian times, that the organic world was full of evidence of God, the great designer. The human eye, for instance, the theologians said, was inconceivable except as the design of God, and in the Middle Ages it was believed that one could look into the soul through the eye, hence the need to close or shield it after death. Now Darwin said the eye was the result of millions of years of natural selection working on certain nerve ends more sensitive to light than others. Finally, Darwin gained notoriety because of the frequent, though quite wrong, accusation that he made the monkey the brother of man. Later, in *The Descent of Man* (1871), Darwin carefully argued that *Homo sapiens* was descended not from any existing ape or monkey, but from a very remote common primate ancestor.

The Origin of Species stirred up a most heated theological controversy. Fundamentalists, both Protestant and Catholic, damned Darwin, and, as they came to realize how much his work relied on the experiments of earlier scientists, much of science itself. But the Catholic church and many Protestant bodies eventually viewed Darwinism as a scientific biological hypothesis, neither necessarily correct nor necessarily incorrect. Most Christians tacitly accepted sufficient modification of *Genesis* to accommodate the scientist's time scale, and they adjusted the classic theological arguments from first cause, design, and the like to propose a God who worked through organic evolution. Moreover, it was quite clear to reflective individuals that nothing any scientist could produce could give the ultimate answers to the kind of problems set by the existence of God; it was quite clear to them that just as God's eye is on the sparrow, it must once have also been on the dinosaur. The middle class in particular found no contradiction between attendance at church or chapel and belief in a modified form of Darwinian thought as applied to society about them.

Social Darwinism

This theological conflict had pretty well run its course by the beginning of the twentieth century. More important in the long run was the use made of some of Darwin's basic concepts—or at least of his more smoothly coined phrases—in debates on matters moral, economic, and political. The blanket term *Social Darwinism* covers these transfers of ideas from biology to the social sciences and human relations. The central idea that social and political thinkers took over from Darwin was that of competition among individuals and groups. This was of course a concept already implicit in their thinking, and Darwin buttressed it with the prestige of the natural sciences. Most of these late-nineteenth-century thinkers interpreted the human struggle as the classical economists had done, as a battle for the means of livelihood in which the variations that counted were those that brought success in economic, political, and cultural competition—variations that produced inventors, business moguls, statesmen, leaders in the professions and, perhaps, even in the arts. Darwin's work in natural history confirmed the economists' doctrine of laissez-faire and the liberals' doctrine of individual freedom for all people to do what their individual capacities made possible.

Here was scientific validation of the middle-class conviction that the universe was designed to reward hard work, attention to duty, thrift, intelligence, and self-help, and to punish laziness, waste, stupidity, sexual promiscuity, and reliance on charity. Above all, Darwin seemed to vindicate the notions that the poor were poor because they were unfit, badly prepared by nature for living a competitive life, and that efforts by private charity or by state action to take from the well-to-do and give to the poor were useless attempts to reverse the course of evolution. If a person cannot earn enough to eat, it was argued, that person had better die; lowlier organisms too incompetent to feed themselves certainly die off, to the greater good of the species. Herbert Spencer (1820-1903), an ardent British evolutionist, summed up this view:

Of man, as of all inferior creatures, the law by conformity to which the species is preserved, is that among adults the individuals best adapted to the conditions of their existence shall prosper most, and the individuals least adapted to the conditions of their existence shall prosper least. . . . Pervading all Nature we may see at work a stern discipline which is often a little cruel that it may be very kind. . . . The ultimate result of shielding men from folly is to fill the world with fools.*

*H. Spencer, *Principles of Ethics* (New York: D. Appleton & Co., 1893), sec. 257; *Social Statics* (London: Williams and Norgate, 1851), p. 149; *Autobiography* (London: Williams and Norgate, 1904).

Spencer later decided that the emotions promoted by religion—kindness, compassion, love—were also in accord with the intentions of the laws of the universe as summed up in evolution. Mutual extermination might be the law for tigers, but not for human beings, where nature need not invariably be "red in tooth and claw." Indeed, Spencer and many other Social Darwinists held that the altruistic moral sentiments that impel one toward acts of charity were the highest achievement of the evolutionary process, and that a society with many altruists was thereby shown to be the fittest for survival.

The Social Darwinists were, then, faced with this primary difficulty: Darwin seemed to have shown that the struggle for life within a given species and among rival species was the law of the universe; but human history and human feelings showed that humanity could not look on suffering with indifference. One way out of this dilemma was to humanize and ease the struggle, so that the incompetent were shelved but not destroyed. Many who held this view turned to eugenics, or selective breeding. They sought to encourage child bearing by the fit and to discourage it by the unfit. Darwin had begun his *Origin of Species* with a consideration of the extraordinary success farmers had had with artificial selection in the breeding of plants and animals. Why not do the same thing with human beings? Since, according to strict Darwinian theory, acquired characteristics were not transmitted by heredity, no amount of manipulation of the social environment, no amount of wise planning of institutions, would alter human beings. Therefore, the only way to secure permanent improvement of the race was by deliberate mating of the fit with the fit.

The eugenicists, however, immediately ran up against the fact that people, though they domesticate plants and animals, are still in this respect "wild" animals. In choosing a mate the individual human being is no doubt influenced by many motives, and no master human breeder can decide who shall mate with whom. Eugenicists have urged that the feeble-minded, the insane, the pathologically criminal be prevented, if necessary by compulsory sterilization, from having children. Only a tiny handful of human beings, not enough to affect in the slightest the general course of human physical evolution, have undergone such treatment, and then usually in dictatorships where the safeguards of democracy did not apply. A greater effect might possibly result from recent advances in testing human fetuses in the early stages of pregnancy and aborting those destined to have serious birth defects because the parents are carriers of congenital diseases. However, such attempts run directly counter to deeply held religious convictions about the divinity of life from the moment of conception, so that the clash between the ethics of science and the ethics of religion continues in complex ways to the present day.

Racism

By far the commonest way out of the dilemma facing the Social Darwinists lay in the notion that it is not so much among individual human beings that the struggle for existence really goes on as it is among human beings organized in groups—as tribes, races, or national states. What counts is not the struggle, say, among individual Britons to survive, but that between Great Britain and its rivals. The struggle for existence was thus lifted from the biology of the individual to the politics of the group at a time of growing nationalism and of competition among industrial societies. For the nineteenth century, the group meant the nation-state, perhaps kindred nation-states that could be formed into a single bloc, such as the Nordic, Latin, Slavic, or at the very widest, the Caucasian or white peoples in competition with the "colored" peoples—yellow, brown, or black. Accordingly, a group that defeated another group in war had thereby shown itself to be fitter than the beaten group; it had a right—indeed, in evolutionary terms, a duty—to eliminate the beaten group, seize its lands, and people them with its own fitter human beings. The English imperialist Cecil Rhodes (1853-1902) once held that a world wholly and exclusively peopled with Anglo-Saxons would be the best possible world. Thus racism held that inherent differences among the various races determined cultural and individual achievement, so that one race might be considered superior to another in a given context. It was an easy step for many, such as Rhodes, to conclude that social or political policy should be based in some measure on these racial differences.

Racists like Rhodes believed that *Homo sapiens* had already evolved into what were really separate species. A black skin, for instance, was for them a sign of innate inferiority; and blacks would have to go the way of the dinosaurs, into extinction. Intermarriage between the races was forbidden by custom or by law (as in the United States in the nineteenth century) as contrary to God's intention and, since it was believed that "bad blood" would drive out "good blood," because it would degrade the "higher race." As yet few dared to preach genocide, the wholesale murder of those held to be of inferior race; most racists wished to see the "inferiors" duly subjected to their "superiors," or "kept in their own place," or "among their own kind."

Other Social Darwinists applied their theories to a new form of caste organization that came to be known as *elitism*. The fit were not limited to any one race, but they still carried the stamp of their biological inheritance. They were the master group, the elite, the "supermen," and they should everywhere band together against the dull, average people and dutifully exploit them. The German philosopher Friedrich Nietzsche (1844-1900), who gave currency to the term "superman," was a subtle and difficult thinker, neither racist nor Social Darwinist. But like Darwin he was easily misunderstood by the half-educated who admired him in the late nineteenth and early twentieth centuries and who used distortions of his arguments to further racist and elitist causes. Scientific "objectivity" came for a time to mean measurement of cranial capacities in order to judge the intelligence of entire races. This vulgarization of science reached a new low during World War I when a

Society of Medicine in Paris published a report on "polychesia" and "bromidrosis" (excessive defecation and body odor) "in the German race," which contended that German urine contained 20 percent non-uric nitrogen, while all other races contained 15 percent, so that one could detect German spies by urinalysis!

Though Darwinism and its offshoots could be misread as the basis for a new doctrine of progress to support a belief that humanity would evolve to higher and higher stages of being, and though it supported the industrial societies in their expectation of unlimited growth, essentially Darwinism and much of racism were intensely pessimistic. Darwin had emphasized accident, not order, as the nature of causation. Many commentators on race believed, as the title of a popular American book published in 1916, *The Passing of the Great Race*, suggested, that the "lower races" would eventually triumph, for brute strength would overtake sensitivity. In 1853 the French comte Arthur de Gobineau (1816-1882) published the first part of his *Essay on the Inequality of the Human Races*. Though it argued for the superiority of the "Nordic races," it opened with a pessimistic statement: "The fall of civilization is the most striking and, at the same time, the most obscure of all phenomena of history." Civilizations fell, Gobineau argued, because of racial mixing; he and many others considered the ultimate degradation of civilization to be as inevitable as the second law of thermodynamics dictated for the universe. True strength lay in animality; animality would take over the world; the "great race" would not, in the end, survive. The "lower races" were breeding faster and less selectively, democratic egalitarianism was leveling down the best while encouraging the worst; consequently, evolution was sliding downward rather than heading upward to the stars.

A wide variety of forms of historical determinism accompanied the industrial process. To the pessimism of the Social Darwinists, the racists, and the exponents of the "dismal science" were added determinists who thought they detected a better future: Marxists, nationalists, those who thought that human beings could become machines, or that machines could do humanity's ultimate bidding. These various determinists were convinced that they knew where history was leading, and, being convinced, they felt they had a duty to lead it there more rapidly, despite the opposition of those with a different vision, and at the cost of massive violence over the short run in order to benefit civilization in the long run. The extraordinary acceleration of technological improvements, of scientific research, and of more broadly based education that had produced the Industrial Revolution and the industrial societies lent strength to the view that moral and political improvements could also be speeded up by a drastic redirection of public energies. The doctrine of evolution, though it logically should have lessened the force of utopian faiths, paradoxically added to tensions in society by reinforcing the popular conviction that evolution need not be slow, that one could seize the day and increase the speed of change. Thus evolutionary theory intensified the debates over "Whither Humanity?" and "What was to be the direction of change?" and "How might one—if one ought at all—accelerate that change, assuming the movement was in the right direction?" and "Who had the right, or could exert the power, to say what was, in truth, the right direction?"

One group that felt they could answer these questions was the political philosophers. In the age of science and industry many believed that politics was no longer, if it ever had been, an art. They now spoke of "political science" as they spoke of "the science of society" (which became sociology). Just as Darwinism had a massive public impact in a vulgarized form, so did the most sweeping effort to work out a comprehensive philosophical program for the improvement of humanity—positivism, a school of thought that sought to apply evolutionary theory to human governance.

Auguste Comte and Positivism

It was Auguste Comte (1798-1857), who had served his intellectual apprenticeship with Saint-Simon, who coined the term *positivism*. Though Comte later broke with Saint-Simon, his own recommendations for bettering the human conditions retained some of the utopian and messianic qualities of Saint-Simonian teachings. Comte applied the term *positivist* to the third stage of humanity's attitude toward the world. First, in the infant period of history, humanity was in the theological age, standing in awe and fear of nature and seeking to placate the gods that controlled it. Second, in the adolescence of human history, metaphysical concepts replaced divinities as the perceived controlling forces of the world. Finally, science would enable people to understand nature without recourse to theological or metaphysical intermediaries, so that they might take positive action to manipulate the world to their advantage. The epoch of maturity, the positivist age, one of security and therefore stability, was at hand—or so Comte wrote in 1830-1842.

Comte also ranked according to maturity the sciences that enabled humanity to emancipate itself from theological and metaphysical supports. He gave seniority to mathematics and astronomy, put chemistry and physics next, then biology and psychology, and last and youngest, the science of society, or sociology. However, he believed that it was sociology that would give humanity the key to the positive age.

In many ways Comte was simply restating the Enlightenment's optimistic faith in the miracle-working potential of science; he was a belated philosophe, a "Newton of the social sciences." Yet he also realized that the French revolutionary attempt to build a new society from the blueprints of eighteenth-century intellectuals had ended in terror and dictatorship. Accordingly, Comte concluded, utopia must be achieved peacefully through dedicated teaching, so that the masses could free themselves from their old dependence on theology and metaphysics. Comte envisaged these liberators as preachers of a new "religion of humanity," but his critics argued that they were a new set of priests—propagandists of a new positivist dogma that might be more intolerant than old religious dogmas.

The undemocratic implications of doctrines of leadership by a new elite would continue to concern Western thinkers long after the transient popularity of Comte's teachings had passed. Comte's ultimate failure to base everything on science, his recourse to the language of a "religion of humanity" to wean people away from traditional faiths, foreshadowed the uncertainties and perplexities that the response to science engendered in the intellectual life of the Victorian age. The attraction of Comte's positivism lay in assembling diverse beliefs and arranging them with new emphases. The social problem was growing more urgent every day, he felt, and humanity required a sweeping intellectual system if it was to resolve its problems before destroying itself. Thus his three stages of history had the deterministic quality of Marxism, while his classification of the sciences possessed the encyclopaedic desire derived from the Enlightenment to know all things, to be constantly self-improving, and for individual improvement to lead to collective improvement for society. Comte scorned metaphysical philosophy in favor of systematized common sense, as he called his views. In so calling them, he hoped to appeal to women, to the working class, and to those who were generally thought (wrongly) to be unable to deal with abstract reasoning.

Positivism found clear expression in public issues. In Britain Comte's arguments were used to formulate debate on "the condition of England" issue and also on whether the British ought to intervene directly in their nonwhite colonies in order to effect social change. In France those who rejected both the Revolution and the Restoration found in positivism a way to enjoy bourgeois comforts while rejecting bourgeois values. The movement was solidly middle class, generally professional and academic. In an age acutely aware of history precisely because of the rapidity of change, the positivists believed that they could bring to history and society the predictive abilities of science. This was a comforting doctrine that formed an ethical bridge between science and religion.

Idealism and Realism

The polar antithesis between idealism and realism that runs through the Western philosophical tradition persisted during the nineteenth century. Philosophical idealism was born in its modern form in the Germany of Kant and Hegel, and in the Victorian decades it continued to thrive in the land of its birth, as well as in England. Modern philosophical realism, the opposite of idealism, was at least as widespread. The realists had their roots in the same soil as modern science and the scientific rationalism of the eighteenth-century philosophes. Auguste Comte thought of himself as a realist.

The American philosopher William James (1842-1910) summed up this antithesis of idealism and realism by arguing that people are either "tender minded" or "tough minded." The tough minded are convinced that the world of sense experience is the real world; the tender minded are convinced that the world of sense experience is somehow an illusion, or at any rate a flawed copy of the real world, which exists perfectly only in God's mind. This abstract argument, which was a modern formulation of the ancient debate between the Platonists and the Aristotelians, was also a secular equivalent of the great arguments of the Middle Ages between orthodox Christian beliefs and the multiplicity of heresies that had plagued the unity of the West.

Another distinct note in the thought and language of the period was an emphasis on will, on doing—on the life force that energizes the "struggle for existence." The word appeared everywhere, even as a title—in Nietzsche's *Will to Power*, in William James's *Will to Believe*. It appeared but slightly disguised in the French philosopher Henri Bergson (1859-1941), whose ideas of "creative evolution" and "*élan vital*" were highly influential in leading many people to accept a doctrine of dualism, of "knowing" through both intellect and intuition. The pragmatism of William James was a philosophy of the will. To James reality was not absolute, as in the idealist tradition; indeed, reality was not fixed and certain. Reality was what "works" for human beings, truth was what humanity wanted to, had to, believe. James thought he had saved himself from the obvious danger of this line of thought—that is, of making reality and truth purely subjective, purely a matter of the personal judgment or faith—by granting that not everything we want is practical, that not all desires "work." If my will to believe tells me I can jump three hundred feet, experience, the "pragmatic" test, will prove that I cannot. But to many of James's critics, he had by no means saved himself from subjectivism. Pragmatism remained, for these critics, a doctrine dangerously erosive of traditional values, leading either to an exaltation of mere vulgar success, or to "fideism"—a faith in believing for the sake of believing.

The cult of the will intensified the revolt against reason. This antirationalism is one of the "roots" of twentieth-century totalitarianism, though it is by no means a simple synonym for totalitarianism or fascism. The basic position of antirationalism was a rejection of the Enlightenment's belief that the typical human being is naturally reasonable. Antirationalism also had its positive side—the belief that if people can accept their true nature as human beings, they can lead richer lives than any rationalist ever planned for them; what they must accept is the radical limitation of the potential of their thinking mind, or brain, to which so much of their experience never penetrates.

Moderate antirationalism promoted the growth of modern psychology, beginning with William James and Sigmund Freud (see Chapter 28). This psychology sought to aid human reason by pointing out the difficulties under which it must work. Reason, these thinkers maintained, is limited by instincts or "drives," by the biological inheritance of animality so much emphasized by the evolutionists, and by the sociological inheritance of custom and tradition so much emphasized by historians (and by the conservative followers of Edmund Burke).

To use a metaphor from John Locke, moderate antirationalists regarded human reason as a flickering candle, not as the great white universal light it appeared to be to philosophes like Condorcet. Far from wishing to extinguish this candle, they wanted to keep it alive, to nurse it along to greater brightness. In keeping with the views of the evolutionists, they regarded this process as long and slow, likely to be hindered rather than helped by ambitious plans to hasten it. By contrast, extreme antirationalists would put out the candle of human reason, which they regarded as not only feeble but downright bad. For them, reason was, so to speak, a mistake evolution had made—a wrong turn from which the human race must somehow retrace its steps to a sounder life of instinct, emotion, and faith. Thomas Hardy, the English novelist, remarked: "Thought is a disease of the flesh." There was to be a strong dose of antirationalism in many intense nationalist movements, which distrusted reason as likely to lead to compromise. Such nationalists would come to "think with their blood," and their folk inheritance.

Thus, many of the extreme antirationalists turned violently against democracy, which seemed to them to rest on an altogether false evaluation of what human beings were really like. The democrat believes at bottom that every person can be freed from the weight of erroneous traditions, habits, and prejudices; but because antirationalists hold that most people are by nature incapable of fair, dispassionate thinking and discussion, they favor leadership and rule by an elite.

Elitism

The German philosopher Nietzsche, who did most of his work in the 1880s, was representative of the elitist view. The central line of his thinking led to the concept of a new aristocracy—the "superman." Nietzsche's followers, who were numerous throughout the West in the two decades before 1914, insisted that he meant a *spiritual* aristocracy; the superman would be above the petty materialism and national patriotism of the middle classes. Nietzsche's opponents, who were also many, held that he was a preacher of Nordic superiority. Whichever, Nietzsche was clearly an enemy of democracy, which he held to be second only to its child, socialism, as a society in which the weak unjustly and unnaturally ruled the strong: "I am opposed to parliamentary government and the power of the press because they are the means whereby cattle become masters."*

*Nietzsche, *The Will to Power*, trans. A.M. Ludovici (London: Constable, 1910), II, 206.

By 1914 the broad lines of the social attitudes of the present time were laid out. (Indeed, some historians find the twentieth century markedly unproductive of new thought, for even those figures so often identified with the new century, such as Sigmund Freud, were in fact figures of the nineteenth century.) One line of argument favored some kind of revolutionary elitism, the seizure of power by a minority that believes itself to have the formula whereby the gifted few can bring order to a society threatened with chaos because of attempts to make decisions democratically by counting heads, no matter what is inside them. The variety of these revolutionary formulas was great: some made race the mark of the elite, while others made class the mark; some sought to achieve the "dictatorship of the proletariat," another form of class elitism. Indeed, as Lenin developed Marxian socialism, its elitist implications came out clearly. The enlightened minority would seize power and rule dictatorially in the name of, and in the true interest of, the masses. Others dreamed of a new elite, such as Nietzsche's superman, to be created by a kind of new religion. Still others looked to eugenics to make possible the breeding of the new elite.

A second line of argument favored a more flexible form of elitism, one that tried to conserve democratic values. The leaders of such movements wanted no violent overturns, no seizures of power. They believed in gradualness, even in the basic democratic counting of heads. But all of them had doubts about the political capacity of the average man and woman. They were not for extending New England town-meeting democracy to the millions of citizens of the modern state. They hoped they could persuade the millions to listen to the wise planners, who had studied the social sciences and could devise the new institutions that would make human life better—"Machiavellians on the side of the angels."

A third line sought to preserve and protect an existing elite from democratic drives toward equality, especially in the form of state intervention in economic and social life to promote security for all. Followers of this line believed in progress, and most of them prized material plenty, peace, the industrial society. They maintained that the existing middle classes, the leaders of the business world, and Victorian habits and morals were the best insurance that progress would continue. Above all, they feared planners and planning, at least in political positions. They distrusted the state, for they believed that the evolutionary process depended on the struggle for life among competing individuals, fettered as little as possible by government attempts to influence the struggle. They believed that social evolution could not be hastened, and that attempts to hasten it, no matter how well meant, would in fact retard it by limiting actual human variation and initiative. Accordingly, Herbert Spencer thought compulsory sewage disposal in cities would be an interference with the right of the individual to conduct his own private struggle against typhoid fever.

VII LITERATURE AND THE ARTS IN INDUSTRIAL SOCIETIES

The scientific and industrial revolutions and the debate over idealism and realism, occurring almost simultaneously as they did, had a major impact on the whole cultural life of the West. They helped to stimulate an explosion of creativity and artistic experimentation that transformed the novel, drama, and the fine arts. The gap between "genteel" writing and the cruder and more vigorous forms was widening because so much important work was now, more clearly than ever before in Western history, produced and encouraged by men and women in conscious revolt against the tastes of the politically and economically dominant class of their time—that is, the middle class.

Literature

In literature the last two-thirds of the nineteenth century proved to be a great period for fiction, especially for the novel of realism that depicted the problems and triumphs of the industrial society, drawing upon the stylistic canons of the romantics while pursuing starkly realistic theories. The English novelists Charles Dickens (1812-1870) and William Makepeace Thackeray (1811-1863), the French Honoré de Balzac (1799-1850), and the Russian Feodor Dostoevsky (1821-1881) all reveled in exaggeration and poured out undisciplined torrents of words, often writing under the repeated deadlines of serial publication and taking little time to revise or polish.

Yet they were thoroughly immersed in the world of their time and were in many ways realists. Thackeray subtitled his masterpiece, *Vanity Fair*, "A Novel without a Hero," and the title itself, taken from Bunyan's *Pilgrim's Progress*, was an implicit condemnation of the false values of a money-mad, power-hungry society, as exemplified by Thackeray's heroine, Becky Sharp. The novels that constituted what Balzac called "the human comedy"—*Père Goriot*, *Eugénie Grandet*, *Cousin Bette*, and many others—were a savage exposé of the crassness and corruption of bourgeois society under the July Monarchy. The leading French realist of the next generation, Gustave Flaubert (1821-1880), hated the bourgeois world he wrote about in his masterpiece, *Madame Bovary*, quite as much as the escapist writers of an earlier generation had hated theirs.

By the end of the century, these realists were confronted by writers who sought an almost scientific accuracy of observation in their novels, giving attention (and a sense of power) to minutely observed physical details and social nuances. The Russian Ivan Turgenev (1818-1883), the English George Eliot (1819-1880), and above all, the French Emile Zola (1840-1902) showed clearly the influence of the scientific revolution inspired by Darwin. Zola was not content with the realist's aim to reflect life with total accuracy; he sought to arrive at laws of human development, much as the biologist seeks laws of organic development. He called his twenty volumes about a family the "natural history" of a family. Each novel focused on some problem: *La Terre (The Earth)* on the land and peasantry; *L'Assommoir (The Killer)* on alcoholism; *Germinal* (named for the month of sprouting in the revolutionary calendar) on strikes in a coal mine and radical agitators; and *La Débâcle* on the trauma of the war of 1870. Literature was becoming overwhelmingly a prose literature of discontent and protest, exhibiting a pessimistic strain that has continued ever since.

The pessimists reacted against the eighteenth-century doctrine of the natural goodness of humanity. By the close of the Victorian age, nature apparently had made most people greedy, selfish, combative, and addicted to sexual irregularities. Some writers, like the English novelist Thomas Hardy (1840-1928), built this pessimism from a series of incidents in private lives into a grand, cosmic irony. Hardy's characters were often the victims of coincidence, accident, and other unforeseen circumstances; they could hardly be held responsible for their own misfortunes. Anton Chekhov (1860-1904) in Russia used the prose drama and the short story to show how life harasses everyone. Henrik Ibsen (1828-1906) in Norway and George Bernard Shaw (1856-1950) in England helped to develop that characteristically late-nineteenth-century form of the drama, the problem play. The problem was sometimes one of wide moral and political concern, as in Ibsen's *Enemy of the People* or Shaw's *Man and Superman*, but it was very often concerned mainly with the stupid tangles of private lives. Ibsen shocked his contemporaries in *A Doll's House* by having the play begin at the point where the usual nineteenth-century drama ended, and by permitting his heroine to rebel against the doll-house atmosphere her husband had created for her. Ibsen's *Ghosts* scandalized the public by bringing to the stage the problem of venereal disease.

Most of this realistic or naturalistic writing, even when not Marxist inspired, was hostile to the middle class. The bourgeois was no longer just the Philistine, the puritanical conformist, whom the romantic disliked; the bourgeois was also the rapacious titan of industry, the jingoistic nationalist, the authoritarian browbeater of children, the tasteless addict of conspicuous consumption, and the hypocritical practitioner of a double standard of sexual morality. Shaw found a simple phrase to sum up what was wrong—"middle class morality." Ibsen's *Enemy of the People* was ironically named; the real enemy of the people was the people themselves.

The American poet Walt Whitman (1819-1892) exalted democracy and the common man, employing free verse (which has no regular patterns of rhyme and meter). Whitman was no radical innovator, however, and the common man he celebrated had no trouble understanding his poems. He sang, he said, "of the body electric," and one of his most famous poems was to a

THE SONG OF THE SHIRT

The Industrial Revolution caused poetic protests, the most famous of which was prompted by a London news report of the arrest of a seamstress for pawning articles belonging to her employer. Paid by the piece, she could earn at the maximum seven shillings a week, on which she was expected to support herself and two young children. *The Song of the Shirt*, by the minor English poet Thomas Hood (1799-1845), excerpted here, summed up the writer's protest:

Work—work—work
Till the brain begins to swim;
Work—work—work
Till the eyes are heavy and dim!
Seam, and gusset, and band,
Band, and gusset, and seam,
Till over the buttons I fall asleep
And sew them on in a dream!

O! Men, with Sisters dear!
O! Men! with Mothers and Wives!

It is not linen you're wearing out,
But human creatures' lives!
Stitch—stitch—stitch,
In poverty, hunger, and dirt,
Sewing at once, with a double thread
A Shroud as well as a Shirt.

Paul Robert Lieder, Robert Morss Lovett, and Robert Kilburn Root, eds., *British Poetry and Prose* (Boston: Houghton-Mifflin, 1936), II, 171.

locomotive, comparing it to a horse at rest, filled with the energy of the new industrial society.

Painting

In the nineteenth century the painter faced a formidable competitor in depicting the physical realities of nature and life—the photographer. After Louis J.M. Daguerre (1789-1851) made the daguerreotype commercially possible, the science and art of photography developed until, through the work of the American George Eastman (1854-1932), roll film made it feasible for each person to be an artist. Thus painting moved in two directions, either toward the meticulously exact and technically skillful reproduction of scenes in direct competition with the photograph, or toward impressionism as an expression of the artist's inward feelings about the subject.

The rebellion against academic painting, begun by Delacroix, continued in the midnineteenth century with the French artists Honoré Daumier (1808-1879) and Gustave Courbet (1819-1877), who also protested against the values of laissez-faire capitalism and the social mores of the middle class. Daumier exploited to the full the new technological developments that made it possible to mass produce inexpensive copies of his lithographs. With moral indignation and savage bite, Daumier exposed the evils of French society, especially under the July Monarchy. Courbet upset the academic painters by taking commonplace subjects—wrestlers, stonecutters, nudes who bore no resemblance to classical nymphs—and portraying them without attempting to prettify them. The hostility of the academics reached a peak in 1863, when canvases by followers of Courbet were refused a showing in the annual Paris salon. The rejected artists countered by organizing their own *salon des réfusés*, which gained the backing of Emperor Napoleon III.

That science might encourage as well as impede artistic revolution was evident in the case of the impressionists, whose name was invented by hostile critics after viewing a painting entitled *Impression: Sunrise* by Claude Monet (1840-1926), the leader of the school. The impressionists learned from physics that light was a complex phenomenon put together by the human eye from the prismatic reflections of nature. They proposed to break both light and shadow into their component colors and then allow the viewer's eye to reassemble them. They painted landscapes and seascapes for the most part, using thousands of little dabs of color; the result, when seen from up close, is hardly more than a formless mesh of color, but, when viewed from the proper distance, it is magically transformed into a recognizable scene flooded with light.

Two other qualities augmented the revolutionary impact of impressionist painting. One was the abandonment of traditional conventions of symmetry in favor of an arrangement that put the principal figure well to one side, sometimes even partially cut off. This technique, borrowed from the Japanese print, was employed with telling effect by the Frenchman Edgar Degas (1834-1917) and the American James McNeill Whistler (1834-1903). The other departure was a return to subjects evoking everyday life, rather than the artificial world of the studio. Milliners, prostitutes, cardplayers or solitary drinkers in a café, cabaret and circus performers, and ballerinas in rehearsal populate the canvases of Degas, Henri de Toulouse-Lautrec (1864-1901), Auguste Renoir

Among the paintings of the "réfusés" was *Déjeuner sur l'Herbe (Picnic Lunch)* by Edouard Manet (1832-1883), depicting two fully-dressed young men with a nude female companion. The way in which Manet saw reality shocked contemporary opinion. It did not correspond to what the camera saw; notice how his picture of a luncheon on the grass (top) differs from a conventional photograph of a teaparty in a garden at about the same time (bottom).

Manet's version of the execution of Emperor Maximilian demonstrated the distortions characteristic of modern art. Here Manet placed the firing squad almost on top of its victim and falsified factual accuracy by making the executioners French rather than the Mexicans they actually were, so as to suggest the abandonment of Maximilian by France. By so doing he sought to show that the artist could see reality more profoundly than could any mechanical device. Like Goya, Manet used real objects and events for his artistic purposes, but he moved beyond the idea that art must be representational—that is, that is must represent life precisely as it occurs.

(1841-1919), Vincent Van Gogh (1853-1890), and other masters of the last century. Most of these artists are postimpressionists, in that they went beyond impressionism to further experiments. Paul Cézanne (1839-1906) in particular thought impressionism too obsessed with light at the expense of the geometrical and architectural qualities also to be found in nature, and he proposed to restore these qualities with blocks or chunks of color. Much of twentieth-century painting stems from Cézanne. His was perhaps the single greatest influence in modern painting.

The Other Arts

In contrast to painting, sculpture did not flourish exuberantly in the nineteenth century. An age that had mastered the industrial arts so well produced monumental statues, of which the most famous was *Liberty* in New York harbor, the work of the French sculptor Frédéric Bartholdi (1834-1904), a gift from the Third French Republic to the American Republic. But the statues of statesmen and warriors that came to adorn public places everywhere in the West were conventionally realistic, designed for formal display to honor the subject rather than the artist. Toward the end of the century the French sculptor Auguste Rodin (1840-1917) began to simplify, strengthen, and, to a degree, exaggerate the contours of men and women, treating subjects with less academic convention and more power, using the new techniques, even of the foundry, that the industrial society provided. Inexpensive, small-scale copies of

Rodin's *The Thinker.*

The building of a great bridge, such as the bridge from Manhattan across the East River of New York to Brooklyn, transformed a society. Such a bridge was an engineering triumph, a series of experiments, and an aesthetic achievement. It altered patterns of trade, housing, and work, making possible rapid communication from one borough of New York City to another. Such a symbol of the industrial society provided work for thousands of people (twenty of whom were killed before the bridge was finished) and inspiration for artists and poets. The bridge's designer, John Roebling, died as a result of an accident even before construction began; his son was permanently crippled in another accident at the bridge site, but he supervised the construction of the bridge from an apartment in Brooklyn, from which he could watch the work through a telescope. When the Brooklyn Bridge was opened in 1883, New Yorkers hailed it as the world's greatest technological marvel.

the great sculpture of antiquity and of the Renaissance also became common, and many Victorian drawing rooms boasted a plaster Venus or bronze Mercury. Museums could all afford large plaster casts of classical works, so some exposure to the great artistic achievements of the past was now possible for a very wide general public. In particular, the middle class saw the museum and art gallery as educational institutions and flocked to the new treasure houses as leisure time expanded to view reproductions of works conventionally

labeled "classic." Often the great museums were themselves the most representative works of art.

In architecture, as in painting and sculpture, true innovation began toward the end of the century. Structural steel freed construction from the limitations that had so taxed the Gothic builders; structures could now go almost as high as architects pleased. Thus the first "skyscrapers" were put up in Chicago in the 1880s. The general tendency imposed by the materials was toward simplicity of line. This taste for simplicity began to spread, and by the twentieth century the way was open for modern "functional" architecture. Often the architect was also an engineer, and perhaps the finest and most aesthetic structures of the industrial societies were the great railway bridges, the complex Brooklyn Bridge begun in 1869 by John Roebling (1806-1869) and not completed until 1883, and the massive work of Gustave Eiffel (1832-1923) in France.

Perhaps the least immediate response to the interests and new technical capacities of the industrial society was to be found in music. Here too there was emphasis

Parisians felt that their city offered the world's most advanced feat of engineering when the massive, soaring tower constructed by Gustave Eiffel opened in 1889. Emphasizing the upward thrust and verticality so characteristic of the Gothic cathedral, this gigantic structure was seen as a symbol of the triumph of science over religion—a secular cathedral by which the eye and spirit of the beholder could ascend to heaven.

on monumentality and education—in the founding of many of the great modern symphony orchestras and opera companies, in the creation of touring groups that brought the oratorios of Handel and others to country towns, and in the presence of pianos in thousands of private homes. But in musical taste, most people remained firmly rooted in the era of the romantics.

The most ambitious composer of the age did attempt to break with tradition. Richard Wagner (1813-1883) was stage-struck and regarded the theater as a "demon world," excitingly different from humdrum reality. He called opera "music drama" and set out to make it the supreme synthesis of the arts, with drama, music, costumes, and scenery all fused into one. Wagner sought to combine music and action in a realistic entity. His characteristic device was the *leitmotif*, a recurring melodic theme associated with a given character or symbolizing an element in the drama so that the listener might follow the story line and share in and even anticipate the appropriate emotions. Wagner chose subjects from the Arthurian legends or the heroic epics of medieval Germany. These subjects showed his awareness of the human need for archetypes and myths, the demigods and supermen of the past who still haunt the memory. Ironically, though Wagner considered himself a left-wing liberal and was exiled to Switzerland for thirteen years after taking part in an abortive rebellion against the king of Saxony in 1848, his work would be taken up in the twentieth century by the German fascists as representative of the greatness to which they wanted Germany to return. Wagner's operas were, however, fully representative of Victorian tastes and the industrial societies' technological triumphs, for they were loud, lengthy, and required vast stages with elaborate props and machinery.

The Frenchman Claude Debussy (1862-1918) holds the now conventional title of founder of modern music, conferred upon him by many musicologists. Debussy developed new rhythms, harmonies, and dissonances that were a radical change from conventional composition. In reaction against Wagnerian gigantism, he attempted to convey the subtle, sensuous moods of *The Afternoon of a Faun* or the sounds of the sea (*La Mer*). Debussy's style is often called impressionistic, for he sought to convey the sounds and emotions of a transitory moment, much as the impressionist painters sought to capture its light and color.

This sense of life as transitory, like the colors observed and recorded by the artists, pervaded thought in all its forms by the end of the century. The *fin de siècle*, the last years of the nineteenth century, was marked by materialism and pessimism. Somehow the new and better world promised by the revolutions of 1776 and 1789 and by the remarkable industrial explosion prior to 1850 had not arrived. Even religion, that anchor against the fear that all in life was transitory, was under attack and being replaced by secular messiahs. As the American writer Henry David Thoreau (1817-1862) remarked, people everywhere led lives of quiet desperation. Mental illness and crime seemed on the increase, war was ever more destructive, and the earth's resources were being used too rapidly for replenishment. Fear of such catastrophes, while essentially limited to some intellectuals, was already a worm in the bud of late Victorian optimism. In the United States the great satirist of the age, Mark Twain (1835-1910), who won fame for his apparently sunny books about adolescence such as *Tom Sawyer*, dismissed the entire "damned human race."

The nineteenth century had been called the "century of hope," for most people throughout the West continued to believe in progress. They continued to believe that what the individual wrote, said, and did would bring positive results, that despite all the pleas of the pessimists for elites, for limiting the expansion of democracy, for inhibiting self-expression in art, literature, or politics, or even for restricting the growth of the industrial society, the future was even yet "big with blessings." As always, *Homo sapiens* continued to embrace reasoned argument and, often in the same person, passionate outburst. In the search for security and stability, humanity had again reminded itself of nature and its own ambivalence.

SUMMARY

The Industrial Revolution transformed people's lives in western Europe, the United States, and elswhere. Most historians agree that from the 1820s to the 1890s industrialization proceeded in four stages: mechanization of the textile industry, metals, chemicals, and finally electricity. Each stage led to the next.

Britain held the lead in the early Industrial Revolution from the 1760s to the 1850s. It had developed an efficient agriculture system, accumulated capital from foreign and colonial trade, had extensive iron and coal deposits, and was favored by geographic compactness.

A series of inventions in the textile industry made rapid expansion possible. Coal benefited from new inventions, while transportation and communications were revolutionized by new devices. Banks assisted economic expansion by issuing banknotes in place of coins and checks. Companies limited shareholders' liability, reducing the risk of investment.

After 1850 Britain began to lose its advantages. Its rate of growth decreased, and the lead passed to the United States and Germany by the end of the century.

A major feature of the nineteenth century was rapid population expansion. Controversy surrounds the theories that have been advanced to explain this rapid expansion. Another controversy concerns improvement in the standard of living. That towns and cities grew, however, is true. Moreover, mortality rates in Europe declined after 1850.

During the nineteenth century the middle class in western Europe won political power. Workers struggled for the right to vote and the right to organize and strike. Economic cycles during the Industrial Revolution caused hardships for workers. Gradually real wages, especially for skilled workers, rose; however, the threat of unemployment remained. Women and children were drawn into the work force. Basic food prices declined, but work places were dangerous, unhealthy places.

In response to the social and economic problems caused by the Industrial Revolution, classical economists formulated natural laws based on laissez-faire doctrines. Malthus warned of the dangers of overpopulation. Ricardo and his disciples formulated the Iron Law of Wages that condemned workers to cycles of high wages and large families followed by lower wages and decreasing birth rate.

The utilitarian Jeremy Bentham supported laissez faire but saw some instances where the state might step in to ensure the greatest good for the greatest number. The human liberalism of John Stuart Mill led him to modify his laissez-faire belief and demand that the state protect workers and improve working conditions.

Socialists advocated that the means of production be in the hands of society rather than private individuals. Inspired by Enlightenment ideas, Utopian socialists applied reason to the problems of industrial society and thought that utopia was within reach.

Marx transformed socialism into revolutionary communism, forecasting a violent uprising of the proletariat. In January 1848 Marx and Engels published *The Communist Manifesto,* the classical statement of Marxian socialism that presented the communist view of history. Others responded to the new industrial society by advocating mercantilist ideas, anarchy and violence, or a return to primitive Christianity.

A new age of science produced revolutionary theories in physics and biology. In 1859 publication of Darwin's *The Origin of Species* touched off controversy because his theories challenged orthodox Christian teachings based on the Bible. Social Darwinists transferred ideas of biology to society and human relations. Social Darwinism was used to justify the nationalism and racism of the late nineteenth century.

The late nineteenth century was the age of the novel in literature. Writers depicted the problems and triumphs of the industrial society. Photography and lithography made mass-produced works of art widely available. Painters turned to realism, portraying what they saw. Led by Claude Monet, impressionists developed new techniques that allowed viewers to reassemble light and color. The major innovation in architecture was the use of steel in the building of skyscrapers.

THE MODERNIZATION OF NATIONS

Viewed from a distance, human society is less a diversity than a single whole; with so many characteristics in common, the distinctions become clear only by emphasizing different locales. Yet upon close examination, individual actions, even when part of a broad group, are infinitely varied. For example, at one level of generalization, social groups may appear to clash, while at another level of generalization, they may appear to cooperate; the same may be said for nations, for economies, even for broad intellectual arguments. The highest level of generalization (sometimes called *metahistory*, sometimes *macrocosmic history*) proves so broad and so lacking in differentiation between societies and actions as to be virtually useless in helping us to understand why the world is as it is today. The lowest level of generalization (sometimes called *antiquarianism*, sometimes *microcosmic history*) is so specific, so detailed as to bury a reader in a steady stream of factual data from which no trends emerge. This too is virtually useless. Thus history, to be useful, is largely written at the middle distance—by comparing societies, by examining each in turn, by asking the same questions of each.

In recent years historians have often asked whether the best unit for study is a society or a nation, since many questions relating broadly to demography and society cannot be properly addressed within a single nation's borders. But the reality of language—that we study, learn, write, and speak of history in a language associated with one or more particular countries—generally defeats attempts at genuine comparisons, since no one person can know all languages or consult all sources of information. For this reason, historians still find that they must, when first surveying the history of Western civilization, ask traditional questions—though sometimes in untraditional ways. Moreover, they must also usually ask those questions about conventional units of study, such as the Western democracies taken individually, and then compare those democracies to societies felt to be rather less democratic. This may lead the unwary student to assume that one society is being praised, another condemned, when in fact the historian is most often simply using a base familiar to the reader for the comparison.

Because nationalism was triumphant in western Europe between 1848 and 1914, the nation as a unit of study does appear to make particular sense for this period. As humanity sought to define a sense of security, as it identified that security with a particular nation, church, ideology, economic doctrine, or tribe, both *cooperation*—that is, a bringing together of once-diverse groups into ever larger and self-consciously identified groups—and *competition* between these groups became more intense. This trend, so clear by the late nineteenth century, has continued to the present time, ever more intensely, until conventional wisdom today speaks of there being two superpowers—the United States and the Soviet Union—with or against which most other societies (including those that attempt to define themselves as "neutral") find that they must align themselves.

The Enlightenment, the French Revolution, the Industrial Revolution, and the abortive revolutionary movements of the first half of the nineteenth century had secularized the old beliefs in a coming Golden Age. *Meliorism*, the term for the belief that the world could be improved by human effort, gave a special dynamism to nationalism, imperialism, socialism, communism, and democracy. At the same time, movements and dangers (such as famine) that once affected only a relatively specific place became generalized, in the sense that falling cash crop prices in west Africa, depletion of oil production in the Middle East, or major technological innovations in China could have rapid repercussions in Europe and North America. Technology in the nineteenth and twentieth centuries would alter the world radically, so that within a decade a person might experience more change (and perhaps more psychological insecurity as a result) than an earlier civilization had seen in a century. A single dramatic statistic underscores this fact: there are more scientists alive today than have previously lived in all the history of the world!

Perhaps the most symbolically significant of these earlier scientists was Charles Babbage (1792-1871), an English mathematician and inventor who was overshadowed in his lifetime by the great engineers and speculative scientists who invented the steam engine or the railroad or put forward the theory of evolution. But Babbage invented the digital computer, which in the twentieth century made it possible for human beings to travel in outer space, for governments to amass vast statistics for new social purposes, and for armies to destroy each other though separated by thousands of miles. Often the most significant events are not obvious at the time they occur, and the most telling generalizations must often wait a century or more to become evident. In the nineteenth century societies often measured their sense of progress by the growth of literacy; in the latter part of the twentieth century the parallel of the literate reader is the numerate reader who can understand the "language" of computers. The acceleration of technological change since the midnineteenth century—especially in democratic societies, which particularly encouraged speculation, and in industrial societies, which rewarded the practical application of theoretical insights—marks a special continuity in which historians speak of modern history and "the recent past" as encompassing the last century and a half. Thus this part of our story must be told in greater detail than the earlier parts of our account.

I FRANCE: A SECOND EMPIRE, A THIRD REPUBLIC

Sometime between 1850 and the outbreak of World War I in 1914, rural France joined urban France in expressing a common sense of identity. The persistent rhetoric of the years immediately following the French Revolution became reality. By the end of the century popular and elite cultures were united in their sense of *patrie* (fatherland), of nationality, even when they continued to disagree over the nation's goals. This modernization of France—which took place during a century that was rebellious, increasingly secularized, and constantly changing—at times set one French group against another; equally often, as external forces appeared to threaten France, it strengthened the sense of common identity and community.

The basic argument of Karl Marx, that class is best understood in terms of its relation to the mode of production, was increasingly accepted by various economic theorists; however, those who looked first to social or political realities found that class was better understood in the context of its historical time and its social friction with other contemporary classes. According to Marxism, the middle class was not just middle in the economic spectrum, but middle in sequence—arising out of feudalism and followed by industrial working-class triumphs. Others saw the middle class as the principal impetus for historical change, saw it spreading upwards and downwards, to draw in both the nobility, increasingly interested in commerce, and the skilled artisans, increasingly capable of investing in their future. The persistence of social forms carried over from the Old Regime in France underscored the fact that it was France that was experiencing the most profound demographic, economic, and social changes, even though Britain led the way in the narrower economic phenomenon known as the Industrial Revolution. French culture had been a peasant culture overlaid by a Parisian veneer of great urbanity and sophistication; by 1914 the peasant was on the verge of what the historian would call modernity. This modernization changed the forms of collective action—and thus of collective violence—that had marked the French Revolution. Outside observers often commented upon what they saw as an unchanging France, yet by the end of the century French society had been radically changed.

France's democratic revolution, so optimistically begun in 1848, had by 1852 brought still another Bonaparte to the throne: Napoleon III (1808-1873), nephew of the first Napoleon. As president of the Second Republic,

"Prince" Louis Napoleon soon quarreled with the National Assembly elected in 1849, in which monarchist sentiment favoring restoration of either the Bourbons or the house of Orléans greatly outweighed Bonapartism. The Assembly refused to amend the constitution of 1848 to allow him a second four-year term. Fearful of radicals and socialists, the Assembly also compromised the universal male suffrage of 1848, depriving about three million French men of the vote—an act that enabled the prince-president to denounce the move and act as the champion of democracy.

A Second Empire, 1851-1870

The coup d'état of December 2, 1851, was skillfully timed to conclude with the emotionally charged anniversaries of the coronation of Napoleon I (December 2, 1804) and the greatest Napoleonic victory, Austerlitz (December 2, 1805). In control of the army and the police, Louis Napoleon and his fellow supporters arrested seventy-eight noted anti-Bonapartists, including sixteen members of the Assembly. Street fighting in Paris ended with hundreds of casualties, mainly bystanders fired upon by panicky soldiers. It gave Louis Napoleon the chance to act as the champion of order against armed insurrection. Ironically, the now-classic formulation of rebellion in France was reversed: rural revolutionaries from the center and south of France were opposed by frightened urban conservatives. Paris was no longer the center of revolution, though Louis Napoleon would claim that he detected a socialist plot against him.

He strengthened his position by massive arrests, which ultimately sent twenty thousand to prison or into exile. What Marx called "the eighteenth Brumaire of Louis Napoleon Bonaparte" initiated the destruction of the Second Republic.

Napoleon restored universal male suffrage for a plebiscite; by 7,500,000 votes to 640,000 it gave him the right to draw up a new constitution. The plebiscite was accompanied by skillful propaganda. Many opponents of Napoleon simply did not vote, and a substantial majority of French men over twenty-one were apparently willing to accept authoritarian rule rather than face renewed upheaval. For nearly three decades the full force of fashionable French literature had been at work embellishing the Napoleonic legend and identifying the name of Napoleon with an elite French patriotism. Many voted yes, not to Louis Napoleon, nor to any approval of dictatorship in the abstract, but to the music of the *Marseillaise*, the cannon of Austerlitz, the growing cult of Joan of Arc—to all the intangible glories of France. That which a people preserve often reflects that in which they take pride, and more and more the French sought to preserve the visible symbols of an invisible past.

In 1852 another plebiscite authorized Louis Napoleon to assume the title of emperor and to inaugurate the Second Empire, which he did on December 2. The new constitution sponsored by the two plebiscites set up a

FINLAND

NORWAY

SWEDEN

Oslo

Stockholm

St. Petersburg

Moscow

Kazan

Volga R.

Don R.

Dnieper R.

Oka R.

Divina R.

R U S S I A

POLAND

Warsaw

Königsberg

Memel

Vistula R.

Berlin

Oder R.

Copenhagen

DENMARK

SCHLESWIG

HOLSTEIN

Kiel

Hamburg

HANOVER

Baltic Sea

Kiev

Odessa

Dniester R.

Pruth R.

Danube R.

CRIMEA

Sebastopol

Bololovo

Black Sea

GEORGIA

AZERBAIJAN

Baku

ARMENIA

Tigris R.

Euphrates R.

SYRIA

O T T O M A N   E M P I R E

Constantinople

San Stefano

SERBIA

Belgrade

BOSNIA-
HERZEGOVINA

MONTENEGRO

Aegean Sea

Athens

GREECE

CYPRUS

CRETE

Suez

Cairo

EGYPT

Mediterranean Sea

TRIPOLI

Tripoli

TUNIS

ALGERIA

MOROCCO

AUSTRIAN
EMPIRE

HUNGARY

Budapest

Vienna

BOHEMIA

Olmütz

Prague

Zagreb

Adriatic Sea

Venice

KRAIN

TYROL

SWITZ.

LOMBARDY

PIEDMONT

Turin

Genoa

PARMA

MODENA

TUSCANY

PAPAL
STATES

Rome

Str. of Messina

KINGDOM OF
THE TWO
SICILIES

Naples

SICILY

SARDINIA

CORSICA

KINGDOM OF SARDINIA

GREAT
BRITAIN

SCOTLAND

Edinburgh

Glasgow

IRELAND

ENGLAND

WALES

Lancaster

Liverpool

Manchester

Birmingham

Oxford

Cambridge

Bristol

London

Thames R.

*North
Sea*

NETH.

BELG.

Brussels

LUX.

Lille

Metz

Rhine R.

SAXONY

Frankfurt

RUHR

BADEN

WÜRTTEM-
BERG

BAVARIA

Strasbourg

Mulhouse

FRANCE

Paris

Orléans

Chambord

Loire R.

Seine R.

Bordeaux

Marseilles

Rhône R.

BALEARIC IS.

SPAIN

Madrid

Ebro R.

Guadalquivir R.

PORTUGAL

Lisbon

Atlantic Ocean

500

Miles

0

Europe in the
Midnineteenth Century

—— Boundary of the German Confederation

lightly veiled dictatorship very much like that of Napoleon I. The emperor, who was responsible only to "the nation," governed through ministers, judges, and bureaucrats—whom he appointed. The popularly elected assembly, the *Corps Législatif*, was filled with candidates whose success at the polls was assured by the pressure of the emperor's loyal prefects. The assembly had little power to initiate or amend legislation, though Napoleon III insisted that he was no mere tool of the propertied classes but an agent of genuine reform—an emperor for the masses who would use strong government to realize the great public works and international understanding dreamt of by the early utopian social engineer, Saint-Simon.

Napoleon III did carry out an immense program of public works, bringing to Paris and to many provincial cities great public markets, new boulevards and promenades, and other forms of urban renewal. Urban France still bears the stamp of the Second Empire, especially in Paris, where the emperor's prefect, Georges-Eugène Haussmann (1809-1891) cut broad straight avenues with splendid vistas through the medieval maze of streets. The Second Empire also helped with housing and encouraged workers' mutual aid societies. Still, the legal code of labor in the France of 1860 was less generous than that of Britain, and the standard of living of the working class in French cities remained below that in Britain, Germany, and the smaller European democracies. Although French labor benefited from the general prosperity of the 1850s, the gains in wages were partly offset by rising prices, and by 1868 demonstrations and strikes, once again legal, were commonplace.

The bourgeoisie may have gained the most from the Second Empire, assisted by capital supplied through the government-sponsored Crédit Foncier and Crédit Mobilier, set up to promote investment in real estate and movable property, respectively. Napoleon's government also encouraged improvements in banking facilities, helped the rapid extension of French railways by state guaranties, and in general furthered the rise of industry. Paris, already a major metropolitan area, continued to expand rapidly, and centers such as Lyons and Rouen in textiles, Clermont-Ferrand and St. Etienne in metallurgy, and many others came to have full-fledged industrial economies. Yet both under the Second Empire and under its successor, the Third Republic, many French remained loyal to older methods of doing business, to small firms under family control, to luxury trades in which handicraft skills remained important despite the machine. The industrial growth of France was somewhat slower than that of the leading economic powers in most heavy industry; in the 1860s France was losing its continental leadership in iron and steel production to Germany and ultimately was far outdistanced by the burgeoning economy of the new United States.

The French rate of population growth also lagged between 1840 and the 1880s, and an exodus to the cities from impoverished rural departments, especially in the southern half of the country, accelerated under the Second Empire. At the end of the nineteenth century France was not much more than 50 percent more populous than at the beginning, in great part because of a steep decline in birth rate. Britain, despite considerable outward migration to its empire, had about tripled its population, and Germany too was growing rapidly. Even Italy, with slender natural resources and less industry than France, was growing in population faster than France, despite heavy emigration. Though the reasons for such profound French demographic changes are imperfectly understood, one major factor in a country of many small proprietors appears to have been their determination to avoid the division of already modest inheritances among many heirs. This meant that methods of birth control spread quickly through different social milieus—from larger cities to small towns, and then to small landowners in the countryside. Late marriage, the practice of birth control by *coitus interruptus*, continuing high levels of infant mortality, and sharp boundaries between regions were also features of the French demographic pattern until the 1890s. And while

In 1887 a French civil engineer proposed the first Paris underground railway, or Métro, to carry traffic beneath the clogged streets. After a proposed elevated line, as in New York City, was rejected as unaesthetic, the builders of the Métro had to solve the complex problems of underground ventilation and illumination. In 1892 the Paris Municipal Council approved their scheme. Rejecting the London system in which tubes were run far below the surface, the Paris Métro authority built close to ground level. Construction began in October 1898, and two thousand workers labored day and night to have the system ready for the Paris Exposition of 1900.

the general decline in population was partly offset by a rapid increase in immigration to France, this fell off after the 1880s. Thus some historians link the slow rate of France's industrial growth to its generally slow population growth and its regionally diverse and at times inconsistent patterns.

Despite demographic weakness, the France of the Second Empire was still a great power, and its comparative decline was not clear to contemporaries. Although the French gained little from the Crimean War, they had the satisfaction of playing host to the postwar congress at Paris in 1856. And the Paris Exposition of 1855, a counterpart of the London exhibition in 1851, was an international success that showed Napoleon III at the height of his diplomatic powers. In 1859 he joined Piedmont in a war against Austria for the liberation of Italy. French armies won victories at Magenta and Solferino, but the defeated Austrians refused to yield. Fearful that Prussia might come to Austria's assistance, Napoleon III suddenly made a separate peace with Austria, which agreed to relinquish Lombardy, but not Venetia, to Piedmont. To this extent Napoleon III had furthered the cause of Italian unification.

But in 1860 the Italians set about organizing most of the peninsula, including papal Rome, into a single kingdom. Napoleon depended too much on Catholic support at home to permit the extinction of papal territorial power; moreover, the success of Italian nationalism was threatening the long-maintained European balance of power. Napoleon therefore permitted the union of most of Italy under the house of Savoy, but he protected the pope's temporal power with a French garrison in Rome and left Venetia in Austrian hands. In 1860 as a reward for his services, he received from Piedmont the French-speaking part of Alpine Savoy plus the Mediterranean city of Nice and its hinterland. In the end Napoleon III had offended most Italians, Austria and Prussia, liberals everywhere, and most of his Catholic supporters at home.

To make matters worse, in 1861 Napoleon used the Mexican government's default on payments of its foreign debt as the pretext for what proved to be a foolish imperialist venture. A French expedition installed the Austrian archduke Maximilian, brother of the emperor Francis Joseph, as emperor of Mexico, and French arms and men continued to assist him. The Europeanized Mexican upper classes were in part willing to support this venture, for they admired France and they shared Napoleon's desire to forestall domination of Mexico by the United States. But from the start most other Mexicans resented foreign intruders, and Maximilian had to rely heavily on French support to reach Mexico City, where he was formally proclaimed emperor in June 1863. The United States, preoccupied by a crippling civil war, could do nothing at the time against what Americans regarded as an infraction of the Monroe Doctrine. But after peace had been restored in the United States, the American government protested strongly. The able Mexican republican leader Benito Juarez (1806-

1872) had no difficulty in prevailing, especially after American pressure forced Napoleon to abandon Maximilian and his Mexican supporters. Maximilian fell before a firing squad in 1867.

By this time Napoleon realized that he could not function as a dictator-emperor in France, for despite public support, French unity was highly fragile, and his liabilities were too great. He could not be a republican. Nor could he act as a legitimized monarchist, for much of conservative France was loyal to the Bourbons or to the house of Orléans. He was not seen as a truly devout Catholic, despite the orthodoxy of his wife, the empress Eugénie, for his Bonapartist background was heavily tinged with the anticlericalism of the eighteenth century and his meddling in the Italian problem had deeply offended clericals. He could only head an "official" party, relying on the manipulative skills of his bureaucrats to work the cumbersome machinery of a parliamentary system originally designed, like that of Napoleon I, as a disguise for authoritarian rule.

As the pressure of genuine party differences reflecting moral, social, and economic group interests intensified, Napoleon slowly abandoned the repressive measures with which he had begun. An act of 1860 gave the Legislative Assembly power to discuss freely a reply to an address from the throne, and in 1867 to 1870 these powers were extended in the name of a Liberal Empire. Gradually, political life in France began to assume the pattern of a parliamentary or deliberative government, with parties of the right, center, and left. After the general election of 1869, the government faced a strong legal opposition, many of whom declared themselves to be republicans. On July 12 Napoleon granted the Legislative Assembly the right to propose laws and to criticize and vote on the budget. Some ministerial responsibility to the legislature seemed at hand, as Napoleon entrusted the government to the head of the moderates, Emile Ollivier (1825-1913). A plebiscite in May 1870 overwhelmingly ratified these changes.

The Third Republic, 1870-1914

The Second Empire might have thus converted into a constitutional monarchy with full parliamentary government. Yet the changes had been wrung from an ailing and vacillating emperor by frequent popular agitation in the form of strikes, after the Liberal Empire relaxed the ban on unions imposed in 1791. It is also possible that a radical republican groundswell would have submerged the empire in any case. But a Franco-Prussian War, into which Napoleon III was maneuvered by Otto von Bismarck in July 1870, put an abrupt end to the experiments of the Liberal Empire. Sluggish mobilization and French overconfidence, together with Prussian superiority in arms, gave the Prussians a decisive head start. Within only six weeks Napoleon III and a large French army capitulated humiliatingly at Sedan. Two days later rioting Parisians forced the remnant of the Legislative Assembly to decree the end of the empire, and a Third

Republic was proclaimed. Napoleon III went into captivity in Germany and then into exile in England, where he died in 1873. His only child, the prince imperial, was killed fighting with British troops in South Africa in 1879. All hopes of a Bonapartist restoration died with him.

The new republic tried to continue the war with Prussia, but within a month a second large French force surrendered at Metz. In February 1871 an exhausted nation, sick of the war, elected a National Assembly that met at Bordeaux and sued for peace; however, the special circumstances of the election placed an additional handicap on the new republic. For meanwhile Paris, besieged by the German forces, had resisted desperately, the citizens killing even the zoo animals for food, until starvation brought surrender in January. Even under pressure of the siege, Paris radicals had tried to seize power and revive the old Paris commune, or city government, of 1792. These radicals could not accept the capitulation for which the rest of the country seemed to be preparing. In the elections to the National Assembly their stubbornness helped to turn provincial voters toward more conservative candidates who were not only pledged to make peace but to restore the old monarchy.

On March 1, 1871, the new Assembly voted to accept a peace ceding Alsace and part of Lorraine to Germany and paying an indemnity of five billion francs. The Paris National Guard, which had not been disarmed by the Germans, thereupon went over to the radicals because the National Assembly had suspended its pay. The Assembly and the provisional government it had set up under the veteran Orléanist politician Adolphe Thiers sent troops into Paris in a vain attempt to seize National Guard artillery. Thiers and the Assembly established themselves in Versailles, while in Paris the commune took over the functions of government.

Marxist history consecrates the Paris Commune of 1871 as the first major proletarian government to be suppressed by troops on behalf of the bourgeoisie. Most of the communards were in fact Jacobins—radical anti-clericals and highly patriotic republicans who wanted a democratic society of small independent shopkeepers and artisans, not the abolition of private property. Although some communards were affiliated with the First International, most of these were followers of Proudhon rather than of Marx; some other communards were followers of Auguste Blanqui, the aged champion of revolutionary violence who was arrested in the provinces before he could reach Paris. Neither Proudhonians nor Blanquists were socialists in any modern Marxian sense, but the spectacle of a Paris besieged by the Prussians and then besieged again by fellow countrymen has become the traditional starting point for Marxist historiography. In the Bloody Week of May 21-28 troops of the National Assembly advanced through the barricades to clear the city; twenty thousand died in the fighting, far more than in the June Days of 1848.

The Third Republic, born in the trauma of defeat and civil war, at once came into a heritage of strife. From 1871 to 1879, when the threat of a Bonapartist return ended utterly, French politics see-sawed between the left and right. Most members of the new National Assembly were monarchists, anxious to undo the formal declaration of a republic made in Paris after Sedan. About half the monarchist deputies were pledged to the elder legitimate Bourbon line represented by the count of Chambord, who was childless. The other half supported the younger Orléanist line, represented by the count of Paris, grandson of Louis Philippe. Although Chambord agreed to designate the count of Paris as the eventual heir to the throne, he stubbornly refused to accept the revolutionary blue, white, and red tricolor flag that Louis Philippe had himself accepted as the flag of France, demanding instead the white flag and gold lilies of Bourbon, which for millions meant complete repudiation of all that had happened since 1789.

Political stalemate followed the emotional debates over the symbols of legitimacy, monarchy, and France; in the resulting impasse the republican minority was able to gather strength. Thiers, recognized as "president of the Republic," carried through the final settlement with Germany. In 1873, however, he lost what amounted to a vote of confidence in the assembly over his republican (Orléanist) sentiments, and he was succeeded by Marshal MacMahon (1808-1893), a soldier and a monarchist who was chosen to hold the government together until the monarchist majority of the Assembly could work out a compromise between its wings. The compromise was never achieved, as Chambord continued to insist on the white flag. Ultimately, Thiers's strategy worked, and in 1875 enough Orléanists joined with the republicans for the Assembly to pass a series of constitutional measures formally establishing the Third Republic, with MacMahon as president.

These laws, known collectively as the Constitution of 1875, provided for a president elected by an absolute majority of Senate and Chamber of Deputies sitting together as a National Assembly. The Chamber of Deputies was elected by universal male suffrage; the Senate was chosen, one-third at any given time, by elected members of local governmental bodies. All legislation had to pass both houses, though only the lower could initiate finance bills. The critical point was the responsibility of the ministers, which was not spelled out in the laws of 1875. Had the president been able to dismiss them, a new Napoleon III might easily have arisen to destroy the republic. MacMahon attempted to exercise this power on May 16, 1877, when he dismissed an anticlerical premier. But the Chamber was now antimonarchist and voted no confidence in MacMahon's new premier; MacMahon then dissolved the Chamber and called for a new national election. In the election the republicans retained a majority in the Chamber and could have forced the president to name a republican premier. Disgruntled, MacMahon resigned in 1879 and was succeeded by a conservative republican. This crisis of the *Seize Mai* (May 16) set a precedent for the Third Republic, for no president thereafter dared to dissolve the Chamber, and the presidency became a largely ceremonial office. Nine years after its establishment in name, the Third Republic had become a fact.

In form it was a republican constitutional monarchy, with an ornamental president instead of an ornamental king. The real executive, as in England, was the ministry, which was in effect a committee responsible to the legislature, indeed to the Chamber of Deputies, which soon became the focus of political action, leaving the Senate little real power. Reflecting the political realities of an ideologically volatile country, the Chamber was composed of a dozen or more parties, so that any ministry had to be supported by a coalition subject to constant shifting of personalities and principles. The result was a persistent instability of ministries, whose average life expectancy was scarcely a year.

The day-to-day task of governing was carried on by a civil service—by experts in the law courts and in the educational system as well as in the executive branch. This permanent bureaucracy, subject only to broad policy control from above, preserved the basic continuity in French political action, especially in foreign policy. Functionally, the system was highly democratic, for it could work only through constant and subtle compromise. Compromise, the essence of democratic government, was arrived at in France (and in most of the democratic world outside the English-speaking countries) by the several parties in open debate and voting in the legislature *after* an election. In the English-speaking countries, these compromises were made *before* an election, within each of the two major parties, often in the privacy of the party caucus. In a sense, the Third Republic was thus attempting to reconcile the revolutionary ideas of an earlier France with the continuing conservative institutions.

Bitter antagonisms continued to threaten the Third Republic between 1879 and 1914, but they did not destroy it. On the right, many in the church, the army, and among the wealthy still hoped for government by a single strong man, but they remained divided over the extent of their monarchism. The political left was also divided, between pro- and anti-Marxist socialists, anarchists, and syndicalists. After the accession of Pope Leo XIII in 1878 the Catholics were gradually encouraged to accept the freedom of worship that the constitution of the republic offered them. But many Catholics feared the anticlericalism of the republicans, particularly after a law of 1882 made education free and compulsory for French children to the age of thirteen and forbade religious instruction in public schools. Party fragmentation remained intense, and sodalities, religious associations, semisecret lodges, and other forms of voluntary associations became the focus of both political and social life outside of Paris. Slowly but decisively, communal groups began to be replaced by formal organizations that spoke for special-interest groups, especially for segments of the industrial working class.

In the late 1880s those who feared this shifting, growing fragmentation turned to General Georges Boulanger (1837-1891) in the hope that he might become the single strong, Napoleon-like figure who could unite France under authoritarian leadership. Boulanger was an ambitious soldier who had, as minister of war, catered to French desires for revenge on Germany. But though he commanded a popular following, Boulanger had illegitimate origins and radical friends. As it became clear that if given power he might rush the country into war, his following threatened to desert him. In January 1889 he swept a by-election in Paris, but his nerve failed. Instead of seizing power by force of arms, he waited to see if his followers would act. The Chamber of Deputies took courage and threatened to try him for treason; Boulanger fled to Brussels, where he committed suicide in 1891. The republic had surmounted its first great crisis.

But three major scandals next confronted the republic. The president's son-in-law was implicated in the selling of posts in the Legion of Honor. More fuel was added to the fire in the early 1890s with the Panama scandal, brought on by the failure of Ferdinand de Lesseps's attempt to duplicate in Panama his success in building the Suez Canal. Ministers and deputies had accepted bribes for backing the shaky Panama company. Anti-Semitic propagandists were able to make much of the fact that several Jewish financiers were implicated, including one banker, who either committed suicide or was murdered just before his trial. Bad as it was, the Panama scandal was to pale before the Dreyfus affair, in which the force of modern anti-Semitism first attained worldwide attention.

Captain Alfred Dreyfus (1859-1935), a Jew from a wealthy family that had fled to France when Alsace was lost to Germany, was the almost accidental victim of an espionage intrigue and of the anti-Semitism then prevalent in France, especially in military and Catholic circles. Accused of selling military secrets to the Germans, he was railroaded to trial as a scapegoat because he was the first Jew to serve on the French general staff. He was convicted of treason in 1894 and sentenced to life imprisonment on Devil's Island. In 1896 Colonel Georges Picquart (1854-1914), an intelligence officer, became convinced that the document on which Dreyfus had been convicted was a forgery, and that the real traitor was a disreputable adventurer, Major Ferdinand Esterhazy (1849-1923). Picquart was quietly shipped off to Africa by his superiors, who wished to let sleeping dogs lie, but the Dreyfus family, by independent investigation, arrived at the conclusion that Esterhazy was the traitor and sought to reopen the case. Esterhazy was tried and acquitted, but the affair was now too public for such silencing. In 1898 the famous novelist Emile Zola brought matters to a crisis by publishing his open letter, *J'Accuse*. Zola accused the military leaders, one by one, of deliberately sacrificing an innocent man to save the reputation of the army.

France was now divided into Dreyfusards and Anti-Dreyfusards. Almost all the far left, which had hitherto

Captain Alfred Dreyfus, the only Jewish officer on the French General Staff, was accused of selling military information to the Germans. Here he stands in the dock at his first trial.

held aloof from the affair as just one more example of the rottenness of the bourgeois state, now rallied to the Third Republic. Dreyfus was retried in the midst of a frenzied campaign in the press. The military court, faced with new evidence brought out by the suicide of the forger of the most incriminating of the original documents used to convict Dreyfus, nonetheless again found Dreyfus guilty of treason. However, Dreyfus was then pardoned by the president of the republic, and in 1906, after the tensions had abated, he was acquitted by a civilian court and restored to the army with the rank of major.

The Dreyfus affair divided France as the Paris Commune had done in 1871. But the years of debate brought radicals, socialists, liberals, republicans, anticlericals, and intellectuals—all who were suspicious of the army, of the church, and of anti-Semitism—into a loose alliance. Many on both sides of the question worked themselves into a mass hysteria in which the question of Dreyfus's guilt was wholly submerged in the confrontation between the "two Frances"—the France of the republic, heir to the great revolution and the principles of 1789, and the France of the monarchy, of throne and altar, and of the army, which had never reconciled itself to the great revolution. At the same time, the Dreyfus case led Jewish leaders both in and out of France to return with greater intensity to an old debate: Should Jews in Europe assimilate or seek a homeland of their own?

With the victory of the Dreyfusards, the republic moved to the left and punished the church for supporting the army and the Anti-Dreyfusards. In a series of measures between 1901 and 1905 the triumphant republicans destroyed the Concordat of 1801 between Napoleon I and the pope that had established the Roman Catholic church in a privileged position in the French state. Catholic teaching orders were forced to dissolve, and some twelve thousand Catholic schools, which had been formidable rivals of the state school system, were closed. The state would no longer pay the clergy, and private corporations organized by the faithful would take over the expenses of worship and the ownership and maintenance of the churches. But Catholicism was not outlawed, and worship continued in the churches, even though they were not the full legal property of the faithful. Catholic education, while severely handicapped, was not formally persecuted. Indeed, the separation did not radically alter the fundamental social position of the church in France: the upper classes and the peasantry of the north, northeast, and west remained for the most part loyal Catholics; many of the urban middle and working classes and many peasants in parts of the south, southwest, and center remained what they had become over the last few centuries, indifferent Catholics or determined secularists.

The nonconforming Catholics and the anticlericals formed the backbone of the central supporting party of the republic, the Radical Socialists, who were in fact petty bourgeois. The French republic of the early twentieth century was thus a typically bourgeois state. It made certain concessions to demands from the workers for social security and better living conditions, but not nearly as many as the British constitutional monarchy was then making, nor indeed as many as the partly constitutional German monarchy had already made. A measure initiating a progressive income tax failed passage on the eve of World War I, although this was widely considered the most equitable way of raising revenue in a free-enterprise democracy; it had been accepted by Britain in the budget of 1909 and by the United States in the Sixteenth Amendment in 1913. Although trade unions in France were legal, they had hard going against the reluctance of French workers to pay dues and accept union discipline. Moreover, acclaimed republicans like Clemenceau and Briand (see Chapter 23) had no scruples about using force against strikers; when railroad workers went on strike, they were conscripted into the army so that trains could be kept running under military management, even though it was peacetime.

The Third Republic had become more republican without moving noticeably toward the welfare state. This was hardly surprising in a country that remained essentially a land of small farm-owning peasants, conservative in their agricultural methods, and of relatively small family-controlled industries, conservative in their business methods. French firms put aside far more of their profits as reserves than did the British, whose risk capital rapidly increased. French business owners preferred internal financing because they wished to maintain their independence, either because the firm was part of family property or because they preferred substantial emergency reserves to meet sudden drops in the

EATING WELL IN THE NINETEENTH CENTURY

In June 1867, the Dinner of the Three Emperors brought together Alexander II, czar of Russia, the czarevich (the future Alexander III), and the future emperor William I (then king of Prussia) to dine most royally, as the menu indicates. Guests had a choice of soups and could substitute fritters of beef brain steeped in Seville orange juice for one of the main courses. Otherwise all foods and wines were served to everyone.

SOUPS

Impératrice

Fontanges

INTERMEDIATE COURSE

Soufflé à la Reine
Fillet of sole Venetian

Collops of turbot au gratin
Saddle of mutton with purée bretonne

MAIN COURSE

Chicken à la portugaise
Hot quail pâté

Lobster à la parisienne
Champagne sherbets

ROAST COURSE

Duckling à la rouennaise

Canapés of bunting [a small bird]

FINAL COURSE

Aubergines à l'espagnole
Asparagus
Iced bombe
Fruit

Cassolettes princesse
Cheese

WINES

Madeira 1846
Sherry 1821
Château-Yquem 1847
Chambertin 1846

Château-Margaux 1847
Château-Latour 1847
Château-Lafite 1848

Adapted from Prosper Montagne, *Larousse Gastronomique* (New York: Crown Publishers, 1961), p. 619. Copyright © 1961 Crown Publishers, Inc; © Libraire Larousse Paris; English text © The Hamlyn Publishing Group Limited. Reprinted by permission of The Hamlyn Publishing Group Limited and Crown Publishers, Inc.

market or unexpected technological changes, mostly from outside France.

For many in France, life improved during the second half of the nineteenth century, though at the cost of vast dislocation for others. In the growing cities a wandering population, sometimes turning to crime or to organized violence, contended with the migration of the law-abiding poor, who sought greater security in areas of new industrial growth or in the new labor organizations. The transportation system could not always cope with these shifts in population, so that resources were scarce in various regions at different times, enhancing a common sense of social identity through grievance among the activist and the angry, while making social communication among the provincial well-to-do or the apathetic relatively slow. Increasingly, women became part of the working class, sharing its grievances and its growth, though the only jobs open to them were those that demanded the least skills and were therefore the lowest paid. Such jobs often required heavy physical labor, yet paid up to 50 percent less than men received for equivalent work. Moreover, women were generally barred from unions and associations of artisans. By the second half of the century women would be found in metal foundries, in bleaching mills, potteries, and brickyards, and at the mouths of coal pits and stone quarries. However, most women working outside of agriculture were in the textile industry, the garment industry, or domestic service.

The upper and middle classes ate and lived well, though the petty bourgeois found that inflation often forced economies on them, and the wife became increasingly expert at specialized shopping and cooking. "Second-hand" foods became commonplace—foods that had been prepared and served to one family, with the remainder, often decayed, sold to a poorer family. There was an especially brisk trade in Paris in such leftovers, as population growth moved too rapidly for economic adjustments to provide, or transport to supply, sufficient staples. Secret sales from luxury hotels, public sale of day-old or discarded food, and fraud in the food market were sufficiently commonplace to create a need for the Paris police and municipal authorities to attempt to protect the public. Historians have estimated that of the 1,200,000 Parisians in the Second Empire, perhaps 400,000 ate sufficient and healthy food, while the rest ate poorly, or decaying and rotten foods, adding to the growing problems of public health. Throughout the nineteenth century the policing of food and water supplies was a subject of middle-class concern. The woman working in a textile factory—exposed to dangerous machinery, laboring for fifteen to eighteen hours without sanitary facilities (there were no public or work-place toilets), subjected to chemicals and fibers that brought on brown lung and early death—could hope for little more than food that was, at the least, "ripe." And yet French men and women were devoted to the fatherland, *la patrie*. Their growing sense of nationalism led to an increasing assumption that public authorities must deal with such matters as health, transport, and safety.

II ITALY AND UNION, 1849-1870

Italian national unity seemed remote after Piedmont's two decisive defeats by Austria in 1848-1849, yet it was accomplished by 1870. The three leaders of the Risorgimento in its years of triumph were the romantic nationalist adventurer Giuseppe Garibaldi (1807-1882); Victor Emmanuel II of the house of Savoy (1849-1878), king of Piedmont-Sardinia (and later of a united Italy); and, above all, Victor Emmanuel's chief minister, Count Camillo Cavour (1810-1861). Though of aristocratic origin and trained for the army, Cavour enthusiastically supported the economic revolutions and the aspirations of the business classes. He visited France and England as a young man and was deeply influenced by their economic and political accomplishments. He applied the newest agricultural methods to his family estates and promoted the introduction of steamboats, railroads, industries, and banks to prepare Piedmont for leadership in a unified Italy.

Cavour was a superlatively adept practitioner of the brand of diplomacy often called *Realpolitik*, or the politics of realism and power. As chief minister of Piedmont, he cultivated French and English support, bringing Piedmont into the Crimean War on their side against Russia. He received no immediate reward, for England was unwilling to take steps that would offend Austria, possessor of Lombardy and Venetia. But though bitterly disappointed, Cavour finally persuaded Napoleon III that the Austrian hold in northern Italy was a denial of the principle of nationality. Thus in 1859 France and Piedmont had gone to war with Austria. Meantime, sympathetic nationalistic uprisings in Tuscany and the Papal States seemed likely to bring about their merger into an expanding Piedmont. Dismayed by this prospect and by possible Prussian intervention on Austria's behalf, Napoleon III backed out of the war. At a conference with Francis Joseph, the Austrian emperor, at Villafranca in July 1859, Napoleon arranged his compromise whereby Lombardy was to go to Piedmont, Venetia was to remain Austrian, and the old arrangements were to be restored in the other states. Cavour resigned in bitter protest.

He had, however, already won. The wave of popular agitation rose higher in northern and central Italy; in Parma, Modena, Tuscany, and the Romagna (the most northerly province of the Papal States), bloodless revolutions and plebiscites demanded annexation to Piedmont. Early in 1860 Cavour returned to office to manage the annexations and also to pay off Napoleon III by ceding Savoy and Nice to France. He turned next to the rapidly developing situation in the Papal States and the

GUERRA DELL'INDI——PENDENZA ITALIANA

GIUSEPPE GARIBALDI

I MILLE EROI E L'ILLUSTRE LORO DUCE

Giuseppe Garibaldi was frequently shown on horseback in a romantic pose, leading the "war for Italian independence," as the caption to this 1860 picture states.

south. In May an expedition outfitted in Piedmontese ports, but not formally acknowledged by Cavour's government, set out for Naples and Sicily under Garibaldi.

A republican as well as a nationalist agitator, Garibaldi had served his apprenticeship in Mazzini's Young Italy, then won a reputation as a formidable guerrilla fighter in South America. In 1849 he had defended Mazzini's Roman Republic against a French siege. Cavour deeply distrusted Garibaldi, who he feared might make Italy a republic and so alarm the powers that they would intervene to undo Cavour's own achievements. Cavour therefore sought to control Garibaldi's expedition and exploit its success in the interests of his own policy.

Garibaldi and his thousand redshirts had relatively little trouble in overcoming the feeble opposition of the Bourbon king in Sicily. Recruits swarmed to his flag, and popular opinion throughout the West was overwhelmingly on his side. Garibaldi, who had announced his loyalty to Victor Emmanuel, crossed the Straits of Messina to continue his victorious march on the mainland territories of Naples. He had the support of the British prime minister, Lord Palmerston, with the implication that British naval forces might act to block outside intervention against his movement. Cavour, alarmed lest Garibaldi bring on a new crisis by marching north to take Rome from the pope and offend France and other Catholic powers, sent Piedmontese troops to occupy all the remaining papal territories except Rome and its environs. King Victor Emmanuel soon joined forces with Garibaldi near Naples and assured the triumph of Cavour's policy. In the autumn of 1860 Sicily, Naples, and the papal domains of Umbria and the Marches voted for union with Piedmont.

The result was the proclamation in March 1861 of the Kingdom of Italy—essentially a much enlarged Piedmont-Sardinia, but with Florence as its capital and Victor Emmanuel as its monarch. In June Cavour died, a grave loss for the new kingdom. Territorially, however, the work of the Risorgimento was almost complete. Only two more major areas were needed—Austrian Venetia and Papal Rome. Both were soon acquired through the play of international politics. Venetia came as a reward for Italy's siding with Prussia in the brief war of 1866 in which Prussia defeated Austria; Rome came when the Franco-Prussian War forced Napoleon III to withdraw from papal territory. On October 2, 1870, Rome was annexed to the Kingdom of Italy and became its capital. All the peninsula, save for Trieste and Trent in the north, was now under one rule. These two small bits of *Italia Irredenta* (Unredeemed Italy) were of no small importance, for Italian nationalists remained unreconciled to

Austrian possession of them. Irredentism, as the movement to gain Trieste and Trent was called, did much to bring Italy into World War I against Austria and Germany.

Assets and Liabilities of a United Italy

The new kingdom started out with the asset of favorable public opinion throughout the non-Catholic Western world. Italian national unity seemed natural and desirable, and it had been achieved with little bloodshed through a mixture of Garibaldian romance and Cavourian realism. The enthusiasm that had brought the Risorgimento to fruition was now in the service of a united Italy, where promising beginnings in the new industry of the machine age had already begun in the north.

Yet striking liabilities also impeded the new Italy. The Italians, like the French, were divided between Catholics and anticlericals. Ardent Catholics were deeply embittered by the "Roman question," that is, by the annexation of the Papal States without papal consent. Italy lacked coal and iron; in terms of modern economic competition, Italy was a "have-not" country, as the Italians discovered after unification. Much of the mountainous central Italy and all southern Italy were marginally productive, with a poverty-stricken, illiterate peasantry rooted in conservative local ways greatly different from those of urban life, and with a small but tenacious feudal aristocracy. Neapolitans and Sicilians also resented the new political preponderance of north Italians in the unified kingdom. Moreover, at least half of Italy lacked experience in self-government. It was also a land of deep-seated class antagonisms, profound mistrust of governments, and fervent localism.

Consequently, united Italy moved very cautiously toward greater democracy. Its constitution remained that granted to Piedmont in 1848 by Charles Albert; it put effective checks on the power of the king by making the ministers responsible to the Chamber of Deputies, but it also put severe limitations on the suffrage. After 1881 the property qualification was lowered to the payment of a relatively modest direct tax, so that more than two million Italian men had the franchise, but it was not until 1912 that something close to universal male suffrage was introduced.

As time went on, the Roman question became less bitter. The pope, who refused to accept the legality of the new kingdom, stayed in the Vatican Palace as a "prisoner." The Vatican remained the center of the worldwide organization of the Roman Catholic church, and in no important sense was the pope impeded in the exercise of his powers over the faithful throughout the world. Within Italy, the church forbade Catholics to participate in politics and urged a Catholic boycott of the new state. Gradually, Catholics did take an increasing part in politics, but the "Roman question" itself remained unsettled until 1929, when Benito Mussolini and Pope Pius XI

agreed to set up Vatican City as a tiny sovereign state of 108 acres.

The new kingdom did make appreciable economic progress, however. Railroads built and managed by the state pushed rapidly into the backward south, where some of the seaboard area came, by the twentieth century, to appear prosperous and modern. A new merchant marine and an army and navy gave Italy some standing as a power. Even the national finances seemed for a time, under conservative leadership, to be sound. In politics the 1880s saw the growth of parliamentary corruption and the beginning of a long era of unashamed political opportunism. Meantime, the industrial proletariat was small, labor poorly organized, and the socialists both too few and too divided to be an effective instrument of opposition and reform. Moreover, the economic progress of the north, and especially of the Po valley, achieved in part at the expense of a south both exploited and neglected, increased regional differentiation and helped build up explosive social tensions.

Finally, in the 1880s and 1890s, Italy developed imperial aspirations that proved expensive and embarrassing. Since France and Britain had empires, and since a great power had to have "a place in the sun," some way of territorial expansion had to be found if Italy was to be taken seriously as a "great power." Economic explanations of this imperialist drive make little sense for Italy, a nation with no important exportable capital, with no need for colonial markets, and with many domestic difficulties. True, Italy had a rapidly expanding population that found relatively few economic opportunities at home, especially in the south. But since other countries had a head start in empire-building, very little was left for the Italians, and the leftovers were not regarded as suitable for colonial settlement by Europeans. Nonetheless, Italy acquired two of the poorer parts of Africa in the late nineteenth century: Eritrea on the Red Sea, and Somaliland on the "horn" of Africa where the Red Sea meets the Indian Ocean.

Next Italy attempted to conquer the independent highland empire of Ethiopia (then known as Abyssinia). The Abyssinian War drained the resources of the Italian government and was abruptly ended by the disastrous defeat of the Italian expedition by a larger Ethiopian army at Adowa in 1896. This remote battle was a landmark in the history of European colonialism, much publicized by the press of the world. Although imperial powers had previously suffered temporary setbacks at the hands of local forces, Adowa was the first decisive African victory. It was not until 1935, under Mussolini, that the Italians took Ethiopia, which they then held for only six years.

The disaster at Adowa cast a shadow over Italy that has been compared, with some exaggeration, to that cast over France by the Dreyfus case. The shadow was deepened by a bank scandal and by the general depression of the 1890s. Severe bread riots broke out in Milan in May 1898—the *fatti di Maggio* (Deeds of May). In 1900 King

Unification of Italy, 1859-1870

Kingdom of Sardinia before 1859

To Kingdom of Sardinia
1859
1860

To Kingdom of Italy
1866
1870

Italia Irredenta

■ Battle sites

SWITZERLAND

AUSTRIA

FRANCE

SAVOY

LOMBARDY

Trent

VENETIA

Magenta
Novara
Milan
Solferino

Custozza
Verona
Villafranca
Venice

Trieste

Turin

Po R.

PIEDMONT

PARMA

To France, 1860

Genoa

MODENA

Po R.
Bologna

ROMAGNA

"THE RIVIERA"

NICE

Nice

"THE MARCHES"

D A L M A T I A

Leghorn

Florence

TUSCANY

PAPAL

Tiber R.

UMBRIA

A d r i a t i c   S e a

K I N G D O M

Rome

STATES

KINGDOM

Bari

CORSICA
(French)

O F   S A R D I N I A

OF THE

Naples

A P U L I A

Taranto

ALBANIA

SARDINIA

TWO

Tyrrhenian Sea

SICILIES

C A L A B R I A

M e d i t e r r a n e a n   S e a

Palermo

SICILY

Strait of Messina

Tunis

A F R I C A

MALTA

(Br.)

Tripoli

0   100   200
Miles

Humbert I, who had succeeded Victor Emmanuel II in 1878, was assassinated by an anarchist. The accession of a new king, Victor Emmanuel III (r. 1900-1946), who was believed to have liberal leanings, gave heart to many, and the years just before World War I were years of comparative quiet, prosperity, and partial reconciliation with the church. And in 1890-1914 a vast emigration to North and South America—the number of emigrants exceeded half a million in the peak year of 1913—almost canceled out the serious economic difficulties attendant on a high Italian birth rate and the lack of new industrial employment.

Yet frustrated Italian imperialism was still seeking an outlet. Italy's leaders and millions of their followers could not content themselves with the role, say, of a Mediterranean Sweden—by now quite outside the competition for empire and with no pretensions toward the status of a great power. Denied Tunisia by French occupation in 1881 and then forced out of Ethiopia, Italy finally got from the great powers a free hand in poverty-stricken and parched Tripoli, a fragment of the old Ottoman Empire in North Africa, later to be known as Libya. In 1911 Italy went to war with Turkey for Libya, thus initiating a cycle of Balkan wars that touched off World War I, which in turn would bring Italian nationalism new expectations and fresh frustrations.

The industrial growth of Europe, which had begun in Britain, spread to the Continent after 1880, but Italy presented a pattern of substantial industrialization in some areas and continued sluggishness in others. A variety of nourishing factors helped to determine how different regions went about industrialization: resources, location, trade policies, production methods, the availability of labor, and contending or counterattractive work opportunities. Italy remained on the margin of the industrializing process that was so rapidly transforming Germany, partly for economic reasons but partly because of Cavour's political assumptions and a growing preoccupation with winning an overseas empire. The gap widened between the Italian northern industrial triangle of Genoa, Milan, and Turin and the Italian south. By 1900 the south (which comprised 41 percent of Italian land) had only 17 percent of the industrial workers; it had 26 percent of the population and only 12 percent of the taxable property. The south was unable to supply a market for northern Italian goods, so that Cavour had had to emphasize export sales (a policy his successors continued), while the north could not find work for all its surplus labor. The result was a widespread emigration exceeded in Europe only by the Irish.

Italian unity had arisen from the union of Cavourian diplomacy with the continuing appeal of the 1840s revolutionaries. But demographic and economic factors left Italy divided internally along geographic and class lines. The political left advocated further social reforms to achieve social justice and political equality, but accomplished relatively little because of internal dissension. Monarchical Italy reinterpreted such republican

heroes as Mazzini and Garibaldi to emphasize their nationalism rather than their programs of social reform. The remnants of the left wing of the Risorgimento split into largely non-Marxist factions, and no successful secular reform party emerged from the middle class. Italian parliamentary government remained weak, Italian class structure militated against the development of effective multiple parties, and political debate increasingly appeared to be shaped by intellectuals who purported to speak either for a ruling elite or the Italian masses. Many appeared to assume that Italy was a great power, when in fact it was not.

III GERMANY, THE NATION-STATE

The creation of a united imperial Germany was above all the work of Prince Otto von Bismarck (1815-1898). Brilliant, unscrupulous, ruthless, a genius at maneuvering and at concealing his real intentions, Bismarck often seemed bewilderingly inconsistent in his policies. Sometimes he pursued two apparently contradictory policies at the same time, until the moment came when he had to make a final decision on which policy to follow. His loyalty to the Prussian crown, even when he manipulated it to his own purposes, did not falter during his long years in office, although after his dismissal by William II in 1890 he felt that his work was being undone and often tried to embarrass the emperor and his own successors. He could not endure criticism of himself, and he despised his intellectual inferiors, even when they belonged to his own Junker class, the Prussian landed nobility. Influential before 1862, he towered over Prussia from 1862 to 1871, and over the German Empire thereafter

Prince Otto von Bismarck, the pragmatic German chancellor, told the Prussian Diet in 1862, "Not by speechifying and counting majorities are the great questions of the time to be solved . . . but by iron and blood."

until 1890. Yet his efforts could not have succeeded had they not met with general approval from the German people, who had long hungered for unity. In 1862 he declared, "The great questions of the day will not be settled by speeches and majority decisions—that was the great mistake of 1848 and 1849—but by blood and iron." And on this premise he won his way.

Prussia and the German Confederation, 1848-1862

The first major question facing the leaders of central Europe after the revolutions of 1848 was whether Prussia or Austria would dominate the German Confederation. A creation of the Congress of Vienna of 1814, the Confederation had been temporarily split by the developments of 1848 and now needed to be rebuilt. The "Big German" solution called for federation with Austria; the "Little German" solution called for separation from Austria or even from south Germany. The "Little German" program also meant Prussian domination of the non-Austrian states, and therefore became Bismarck's goal. Austro-Prussian rivalry dominated German politics thereafter.

Prussia was aided and Austria was hindered by the rising sense of nationalism. Austria contained many language groups, each of which hoped for a national destiny of its own, while Prussia became increasingly centralized, having only a relatively small Polish minority with which to contend at home. In the 1850s Prussia moved steadily forward in administrative efficiency, well-planned industrialization, financial prudence, and military strength. Furthermore, despite the constitution of 1850, which technically provided for universal male suffrage, the electorate was divided into three classes on the basis of taxes paid, so that the wealthier voters could continue to control the less well-to-do in the lower house, or *Landtag*. Frederick William IV (1840-1861) had formed a union of princes for military purposes on which political unity might be built, and when he was succeeded in 1857 by his brother, Prince William (who became regent and then king in 1861), a conservative line of royal legitimacy was assured.

The Frankfurt Diet had long since lost the support of artisans and industrial workers, as it espoused increasingly conservative policies and used the troops of the German Confederation to suppress radical assemblies in Frankfurt. From 1851 to 1859 the Prussian minister to the Frankfurt Diet had been Bismarck, who emerged as one of its most effective, if most conservative, leaders. At the Diet Bismarck took every occasion to thwart Austrian designs. He favored Prussian neutrality in the Crimean War (1854-1856), in which Britain and France fought (with Turkey) against Russia, while Austria harassed rather than helped the Russians. Realizing that Austrian behavior was alienating Russia, and that Russian friendship would be valuable later when Prussia came to grips with Austria, Bismarck frustrated those Prussians who hoped that Prussia would enter the war against Russia and thus line up with the West. Counting on a military showdown with Austria, Bismarck also wooed the French emperor Napoleon III, despite the horror that many Prussians felt over dealing with a Bonaparte, whom they regarded as the heir of the French Revolution.

Indeed, these diplomatic and military concerns led directly to the beginning of Bismarck's undisputed domination of Prussian policies. King William I was above all a soldier. His minister of war, a friend of Bismarck's, easily persuaded the king that an army reorganization was necessary. He wanted to increase the number of conscripts drafted each year from 40,000 to 63,000, and to lengthen the term of their service from two to three years. A conscript army took time to mobilize, but a professional army (like Britain's) did not, so size was important. Furthermore, alone among the continental nations, Prussia turned over the planning of new railways to the army general staff, which laid out the lines with an eye to mobilization and transportation in time of war, so that military considerations affected the domestic economy. A liberal majority in the Landtag opposed funds for the increase in troops, and a prolonged political crisis over the budget threatened to block other legislation as well. At the height of the crisis, the king, convinced that Bismarck could outwit the parliament, called him back from Paris, where he was serving as ambassador, and appointed him to the key posts of prime minister of Prussia and minister of foreign affairs.

On the grounds that the constitution permitted the government to use taxes collected for other purposes even when the budget had not been approved by parliament, Bismarck carried out the army reforms. Again and again he dissolved parliament, called new elections, faced another hostile house, and then repeated the process. He suppressed opposition newspapers in defiance of a constitutional provision that the press should be free. He indicted an opposition deputy, himself a judge and a loyal Prussian, despite the constitutional provision that deputies could not be indicted for anything they said on the floor of the house. Yet after four years of this illegal behavior (1862-1866), he got away with everything in the end because of the glittering successes he scored by his unorthodox and daring foreign policy. In 1866 an admiring parliament voted retroactive approval of his unauthorized expenditures, rendering them legal.

Since Bismarck probably intended to overthrow the German Confederation as it was then constituted, he opposed Austrian efforts to reform it. Austria wished to create an assembly of delegates chosen by the parliaments of the member states, besides those named by the princes, and a directorate of six monarchs. In 1862 Bismarck prevented William I from attending a congress of princes called by Austria to discuss these proposals, and thus wrecked the congress. In 1863 he kept Austria out of the *Zollverein*, the German customs union. He also consolidated his good relations with Russia during a Polish revolt by an agreement that allowed the Russians to pursue fleeing Poles onto Prussian territory. Thus

War, it was said, was being made impossible by the rapid development of massive new arms. Here Napoleon III inspects a cannon manufactured in Germany by the Krupp company in 1867. Three years later these cannon would be used by Germany against France.

Bismarck wooed the Russians a second time, as he had during the Crimean War.

War and the Strengthening of German Nationhood, 1863-1871

When the king of Denmark died in late 1863, a controversy over Schleswig-Holstein gave Bismarck further opportunities. (The prime minister of England once remarked that only three men had ever understood this complex problem, and that one was dead and one insane, while he himself, the third, had forgotten all about it!) In brief, the duchies of Schleswig and Holstein at the southern base of the Danish peninsula had been ruled by the king of Denmark, but not as part of Denmark. A fifteenth-century guarantee assured the duchies that they could never be separated from one another. Yet Holstein to the south was a member of the German Confederation; Schleswig to the north was not. Holstein was mostly German in population; Schleswig was mixed German and Danish. In 1852 Prussia joined the other powers in the Protocol of London, agreeing on an heir

who would succeed both to the Danish throne and to the duchies, and recommending that Denmark and the duchies be united by a constitution. But when the constitutional union of Denmark and the duchies was attempted, the duchies resisted, and the Danes tried to incorporate Schleswig alone. German patriots there and elsewhere objected. The Prussians and Austrians wanted the duchies to have special representation in the Danish parliament and insisted that Schleswig not be incorporated into Denmark; nonetheless, the king of Denmark had supported annexation.

In 1863 Bismarck moved to win the duchies for Prussia. He wanted both the prestige that Prussia would gain and the valuable commercial port of Kiel in Holstein. First, he maneuvered Prussia and Austria together into a victorious war against Denmark (1864), cleverly forcing Francis Joseph to give in to the popular clamor in Vienna over the duchies, which were viewed as an issue of pro-German self-determination. Then he quarreled with the Austrians over the administration of the duchies. At the Convention of Gastein in 1865 it was decided that Prussia was to administer Schleswig and that Austria was to administer Holstein, thus denying Kiel to Prussia.

Bismarck next tried and failed to tempt France into an alliance. But he did succeed in signing a secret treaty with the Italians, who obliged themselves to go to war on the side of Prussia if Prussia fought Austria within three months, the stake being Venetia. This was contrary to the constitution of the German Confederation, which forbade members to ally themselves with a foreign power against other members. So distressed was William I at this illegality that he lied flatly when the Austrian emperor asked him if such a treaty existed. Finally, Bismarck suddenly proposed that the German Confederation be reformed, and that an all-German parliament be elected by universal suffrage, which everybody knew he actually opposed.

Bismarck probably advanced this proposal to make it appear that his quarrel with Austria involved more than the Schleswig-Holstein question. Yet the proposal may also have reflected his calculation that enfranchisement of all Germans would weaken the Progressive party, heir to the liberalism of 1848, and would produce many

conservative and royalist votes from the peasantry. He had seen how Napoleon III had risen to imperial power in France on the strength of universal suffrage. And he had been influenced by conversations with Ferdinand Lassalle (1825-1864), a German socialist who argued that universal suffrage would weaken the middle classes.

Historians continue to debate Bismarck's actual intentions, many of them contending that it is from his rise to power that the German states departed from the broad western European movement toward parliamentary democracy. Many of the German states had representative institutions from the Middle Ages, and many municipalities were still governed democratically, but in the period of Bismarck's authority and in the context of the rapid movement toward German unity, what democratic historians look back to as "the true path" was abandoned in favor of tidier, more efficient, and more authoritarian rule.

Austria now laid the Schleswig-Holstein question before the Diet of the Confederation. Bismarck ordered Prussian troops into Holstein and declared that Austrian

Unification of Germany, 1866-1871

- Prussia before 1866
- Annexed by Prussia, 1866
- Other states that joined Prussia to form North German Federation
- ········ Boundary of North German Federation, 1866
- States joining confederation to form German Empire
- Territories annexed by Treaty of Frankfurt
- —— Boundary of the German Empire, 1871   • Battle sites

motions in the Diet were unconstitutional, provoking war with Austria. The result was a German civil war, since Bavaria, Württemberg, Saxony, Hanover (the other four German kingdoms), and most of the lesser German states sided with Austria.

The war lasted only seven weeks and was decided in three. The Austrians, fighting on two fronts, had to commit a substantial part of their forces against Italy. Skillfully using their railway network, the telegraph, and their superior armaments, the Prussians quickly overran the northern German states, invaded Bohemia and defeated the Austrians at Sadowa, defeated the Bavarians, and entered Frankfurt, seat of the German Confederation. Hanover, Hesse-Cassel, and Nassau were annexed to Prussia and their dynasties expelled, and Schleswig and the free city of Frankfurt were taken over by terms of the Peace of Prague in August. Except for the cession of Venetia to Italy in the Peace of Vienna in October, Austria suffered no territorial losses but did pay a small indemnity. Most important from Bismarck's point of view, Austria had to withdraw forever from the German Confederation, which now ceased to exist. Most of Germany north of the Main River was to join a new North German Confederation to be organized by Prussia. While it was stipulated that the German states south of the Main were to be free to form an independent union of their own, Bismarck had previously concluded secret treaties of alliance with the most important south German states—Bavaria, Württemberg, and Baden—who promised to put their armies at the disposal of the king of Prussia in case of war. So the proposed South German union could never come into existence.

An assembly elected by universal manhood suffrage now adopted a constitution for the new North German Confederation, of which the Prussian king was president. The draft that Bismarck submitted showed his determination to "kill parliamentarism through parliament." The future parliament (*Reichstag*) was to have no power over the budget, and the ministers were not to be responsible to it. Instead, a Federal Council (*Bundesrat*) of delegates from the member states, who voted according to instructions from their sovereigns, would reach all key policy decisions in secret and would have veto power over any enactment of the Reichstag. A chancellor would preside over the Bundesrat, but would not have to defend its decisions before the Reichstag. Since Prussia now had not only its own votes in the Bundesrat but also those of the newly annexed states, Bismarck's plan in effect made it possible for the king of Prussia to run Germany. The plan also specified that, beginning five years later in 1872, the size of the army would be fixed by law, and that the Reichstag would have a vote on the budget. However, Bismarck, who became chancellor, saw to it that the debate on the military budget did not take place every year, but that sums were appropriated for several years in advance.

As long as Bismarck needed the benevolent neutrality of Napoleon III, he had hinted that he might not object if Napoleon took Belgium. Now the gullible Napoleon found that Bismarck no longer remembered the matter. Hoping to be compensated for his assistance in making peace between Prussia and Austria, Napoleon III tried to acquire Luxembourg by purchase from the king of Holland. Again he was frustrated by Bismarck. Suddenly confronted with the new Germany, much of the French public and press hoped to get "revenge for Sadowa" and became strongly anti-German. The German press responded in kind. Napoleon III tried to obtain an alliance with Austria and Italy to thwart further Prussian expansion, but the Austrians shied away from a commitment, and the Italians were unable to reach an agreement with the French because of the Roman question (see p. 201).

The Spaniards ousted their queen in 1868, and one of the candidates for the throne was a Hohenzollern prince, whom Bismarck secretly backed by discreetly bribing influential Spaniards. Because of family dynastic practice, it was necessary to secure the consent of king William I of Prussia, a consent Bismarck finally extracted without hinting that war with France might result. Napoleon III, also deep in Spanish intrigue, feared that a Hohenzollern on the Spanish throne would expose France to a two-front attack. French diplomatic pressure was exerted directly on King William, and the Hohenzollern candidate withdrew. At this moment, Bismarck seemed to be defeated.

But the French, made overconfident by their success, now demanded that William publicly endorse the withdrawal of the Hohenzollern candidacy and promise never to allow it to be renewed. William, who was at Ems, courteously refused and sent a telegram to Bismarck describing his interchange with the French ambassador. Bismarck then abridged the Ems telegram and released his doctored version to the press and all the European chanceries. He made it seem that the ambassador had provoked William, who in turn had snubbed the ambassador. Public opinion in Germany was now inflamed, and Bismarck set out to bait the French still further by encouraging a violent campaign against them in the German press. The French, led by a war party eager to stop German expansion, reacted as Bismarck had hoped; they declared war on July 19, 1870.

Within six weeks the Germans had advanced into France, bottled up one French army inside the fortress of Metz, defeated another at Sedan, and captured Napoleon III himself. The protracted siege of Paris followed, ending in surrender early in 1871. A new French government had to sign the treaty of Frankfurt. Bismarck forced the French to pay a massive indemnity, to cede Alsace and much of Lorraine (which the German military wanted as a defense against possible future French attack), and to support German occupying forces until the indemnity had been paid.

Imperial Germany, 1871-1914

Even before this peace had been imposed, King William of Prussia was proclaimed emperor of Germany in the great Hall of Mirrors in Louis XIV's palace at Versailles. Bismarck had to make a few unimportant con-

CELEBRATING GERMAN VICTORY OVER FRANCE

Victory over France brought German national pride to a new height and sense of unity. The baroness Spitzemberg, wife of Württemberg's envoy in Berlin, kept a diary throughout the period of their residence. Extracts from it reflect the emotion and nationalism of the time:

[On September 3, 1870:] A capitulation, whereby the whole army in Sedan has been taken prisoner, has just been concluded. . . . What a turn of events! Any German would be proud to have lived through this day! God be praised!

[On December 31, 1870:] What events this one short year has brought! Immortal glory for our nation, a spirit inconceivably magnificent and majestic, the resurrection of the German Empire—and withal such endless grief, misery, tears, and horror!

[On March 3, 1871:] What a peace treaty for us Germans! More magnificent and glorious than ever! United into one *Reich*, the greatest, the most powerful, the most feared in Europe; great by reason of its physical power, greater still by reason of its education and the intelligence which permeates it! Every German heart hoped for it, none suspected that its dreams would be fulfilled, in this way, so soon and so magnificently. We are fortunate in that we not only saw the star of Germany's greatness and magnificence rise, but are still young enough to warm ourselves under its rays, to enjoy, if God will, the fruits, rich and full of blessings, which grow out of this seed, sown in blood and tears. . . .

From Helmut Böhme, ed., *The Foundation of the German Empire: Select Documents*, trans. Agatha Ramm (London: Oxford University Press, 1971), pp. 236, 249.

cessions to the rulers of the south German states to secure their entry into the new empire, but he never had to consult the Reichstag, which hastened to send its own deputation begging the king to accept the crown. The proclamation took place in a ceremony of princes and soldiers. When a constitution for the new empire was adopted, it was simply an extension of the constitution of the North German Confederation of 1867.

As chancellor of the German Empire from 1871 to 1890, Bismarck became the leading statesman in Europe. He felt that Germany had no further need for territory or for war, as his goals had been attained. As diplomat, he worked for the preservation of Germany's gains against threats from abroad, especially by any foreign coalition against Germany. As politician, he worked for the preservation of the Prussian system against all opposing currents. Until 1878 he favored free trade, worked with the Liberals, and opposed the Catholics; in his last twelve years he reversed himself, favoring protective tariffs, cooperation with the Catholics, and opposition to the socialists.

A multitude of economic and legal questions arose as a result of the creation of the new empire. Working with the moderate Liberal party in the Reichstag, Bismarck put through a common coinage and a central bank, coordinated and further unified the railroads and postal systems, and regularized the legal and judicial systems. In 1871 the Reichstag voted to maintain one percent of the population under arms for three years. In 1874 Bismarck, by threatening to resign, forced the Reichstag to fix the size of the army at 401,000 men until 1881; in 1880 he forced an increase to 427,000 until 1888. The privileged position of the army made a military career ever more attractive and served as a constant spur to German militarism.

But the great drama of the 1870s in Germany was furnished by Bismarck's attack on the Roman Catholic church—the *Kulturkampf* ("battle for civilization"). A *Syllabus of Errors* published by the Vatican in 1864 had denounced toleration of other religions, secular education, and state participation in church affairs. Then in 1870 the Vatican Council, the first general council of the church to meet since the Council of Trent in the sixteenth century, adopted the dogma of papal infallibility. This dogma asserted that the judgments of the pope on questions of faith and morals were infallible. To many non-Catholics, this seemed to say that no state could count on the absolute loyalty of its Catholic citizens.

In Germany the Catholics were a large minority of the population. They had formed a political party, the Center, that quickly became the second strongest party in the empire. The Center defended papal infallibility and wished to restore the pope's temporal power, which had been ended by the unification of Italy. The Center not only had many sympathizers in the Catholic provinces of Germany, but also sponsored a labor movement of its own, which seemed to pose a social threat. Catholic peasants, workers, priests, and nobles opposed the largely Protestant urban middle class and the Prussian military predominance in the state. Bismarck identified his clerical opponents with nominally Catholic France and Austria, the two nations he had defeated in forging the new Germany. He also feared the Center because of its special strength in Bavaria, which would, he thought, promote regional and religious divisiveness.

In collaboration with the Liberals, Bismarck put through laws expelling the Jesuits from Germany, forbidding the clergy to criticize the government, and closing the schools of religious orders. In Prussia civil marriage was required, subsidies for the Catholic church were stopped, and priests were forced to study at secular universities. The pope declared these laws null and void and instructed Catholics to disobey them. As Catholic services stopped in towns and villages, many Catholics were deprived of the sacraments.

By declaring that he would not "go to Canossa," Bismarck summoned up for Protestant Germans the picture of the German emperor Henry IV humbling himself before the pope in 1077. But in the 1880s Bismarck had to repeal most of the anti-Catholic measures he had passed in the 1870s, for by then he needed the support of the Center party against his former allies, the Liberals, whose demands for power he found exorbitant, and against the growing attraction of the Social Democrats, who were moderate socialists. Moreover, the Protestant church itself and many of the conservative Prussian nobility had grown alarmed over the excesses of the anti-Catholic campaign.

In 1877 and 1878 Bismarck had begun a gradual shift in policy, dictated at first by the need for more revenue. The empire obtained its money in part from indirect taxes imposed by the Reichstag on tobacco, alcohol, sugar, and the like. The rest came from the individual states, which controlled all direct taxation and made contributions to the imperial budget. As military costs mounted, the government's income became insufficient, and Bismarck did not want to increase the empire's dependence on the states by repeatedly asking them to increase their contributions. He wanted the Reichstag to vote higher indirect taxes, but its Liberal members suspected that if they acceded he might do to them what he had formerly done to the Prussian parliament—govern without them.

Up to this point German tariff policy had basically been one of free trade, with little protection for German goods. But after a financial panic in 1873, the iron and textile industries put pressure on Bismarck to shift to a policy of protection that would help them compete with England. Moreover, an agricultural crisis led conservatives to abandon their previous support of free trade and to demand protection against cheap grain coming in from eastern Europe. In 1879 Bismarck finally put through a general protective tariff on all imports, a move on which his former allies, the Liberals, were ideologically split on business grounds.

To avoid granting the constitutional guarantees demanded by the Liberals, Bismarck gradually abandoned the Kulturkampf. The Catholic Center favored his protectionist policy; moreover, the lessening of the clerical threat in France and the conclusion of a firm German alliance with Austria in 1879 removed the foreign causes for attacking the church. Bismarck thus secured the support of both the Center and the conservatives and was able to avoid making concessions to the Reichstag. He also launched Germany on an era of protection, and the protectionist policy spurred still further the rapid and efficient growth of industry, especially heavy industry. Politically, the conservative Protestant agrarian forces now grew stronger and also gained many urban votes. But Bismarck never entirely trusted the Center, and he successfully remodeled the Liberals into a staunchly conservative industrialist group.

While he was abandoning the Kulturkampf and swinging toward protection in 1878-1879, Bismarck also began to move against the Social Democratic party. Two Marxists, Wilhelm Liebknecht (1826-1900) and August Bebel (1840-1913), had founded this small party in 1869; in 1875 they enlarged it, much to Marx's disgust, by accepting the followers of Lasalle, an apostle of nonviolence. The German Social Democrats were not nearly as revolutionary as their Marxist phraseology suggested. They had many supporters among intellectuals and former liberals and a substantial trade-union following, polling half a million votes in 1877, about 10 percent of the total electorate. They were prepared to concentrate their efforts on improving working conditions rather than on revolution. But Bismarck needed an enemy against whom he could unify his supporters; besides, he had been deeply impressed by the Paris Commune of 1871 and feared that something similar might occur in Germany.

Using as a pretext two attempts by alleged Social Democrats to assassinate William I, Bismarck called a general election in 1878 and rammed through the Reichstag a bill making the Social Democratic party illegal, forbidding its meetings, and suppressing its newspapers. The Liberals supported this law, but they would not allow Bismarck to make it a permanent statute. He had to apply to the Reichstag for its renewal every two or three years; it was renewed each time, until just before Bismarck's downfall in 1890. Social Democrats were still allowed to run for the Reichstag as individuals, and their votes increased during the years when they were suffering legal restrictions.

But Bismarck felt that "a remedy cannot be sought merely in repression of Socialist excesses—there must be simultaneously a positive advancement of the welfare of the working classes." As a result, during the 1880s the government put forward bills in favor of the workers: compulsory insurance against illness in 1882, and against accidents in 1884. The sickness insurance funds were raised by contributions from both workers and employers; the accident insurance funds were contributed totally by the employers. In 1889 old-age and disability insurance followed, with employers and employees contributing equally, and with an additional subsidy from the state. The German system of social security as developed initially under Bismarck did not reduce the Social Democratic vote, but it did provide much that the workers desired.

Bismarck also moved away from the Liberals because he blamed them for the market crash of 1873. The rage for speculation that had swept Germany, especially after currency reform in 1871, had moved through railways and into the construction industry. The entire nation seemed caught up in the search for pleasure. When the market collapsed in 1873, the Liberals were blamed, for it was they who had revealed the extent of unscrupulous practices that reached up even to Bismarck's personal friends, including the "banker of Empire," Gerson von

Bleichröder (1822-1893), a Jew who would become the richest man in Germany. With confidence weakened, a wave of selling on the stock exchange led to a serious collapse, followed by a depression throughout central Europe. Bismarck used the changed economic climate to justify protectionism and to shift the balance of political forces away from liberalism.

Anti-Semitic attitudes, which had been dormant in Germany since the 1820s, were rekindled by those who identified Jews with the Liberal party, with stock-market manipulation in general, and with unearned capital in particular. Thereafter, the myth of a Jewish conspiracy was a recurring theme of German politics, and neither Bismarck nor his successors did much to stop its growth. In 1880 Berlin had 45,000 Jewish residents (at a time when all of France had only 51,000), and Christian intellectuals in that city and elsewhere were beginning to argue that Jews were an "alien" society. The most respected German historian, Heinrich von Treitschke (1834-1896), a father of modern German nationalism, declared in a much-quoted article late in 1879 that "the Jews are our national misfortune." Though Treitschke based his argument on religious and nationalistic grounds, others were prepared to move to "racial" and ethnic arguments, for he had made anti-Semitism respectable; thereafter, it was never far below the surface of modernizing Germany. Both nationalist and racist bigots would rely upon stereotyping to make the abstract concrete, especially for those unable to comprehend abstractions. Thus rumor, unfounded report, and outright lies often played decisive roles in history.

When William I died at the age of ninety in 1888, his son, Frederick III, already mortally ill, ruled for only three months. The next emperor was Frederick's son, William II (1859-1941), a young man of twenty-nine whose accession his grandfather had greatly feared because of his impulsiveness. William I had allowed Bismarck to act for him, but William II was determined to act for himself. This determination underlay the subsequent controversy between him and Bismarck.

Bismarck believed politics to be "the art of the possible." He accepted the implications of Social Darwinism, that no nation could stand still, but he also believed that all nations would decline in time, however high they might have risen. "It is a principle of creation and of the whole of nature that life consists of strife," he wrote. "Among the plants [Bismarck wrote as a forester] . . . through the insects to the birds, from birds of prey up to man himself: strife is everywhere. Without struggle there can be no life and, if we wish to continue living, we must also be reconciled to further struggles."* The conflict of opposites was part of a divine plan. Since further conflict in the future was inevitable, wisdom dictated moderation toward defeated enemies, for they might be needed one day as allies. Since life threw into conflict a shifting kaleidoscope of social classes, political parties, special-interest groups, sectional loyalties, in-

temperate individuals who had attained positions of power, and entire nations and states, one could not expect to predict with accuracy a nation's future needs in terms of alliances. Therefore, a nation's leaders must always have an alternative course of action ready, a course not too brutally contradicted by any former alliance, so that the middle ground might be credibly taken. After Bismarck, Wilhelmine Germany appeared to lose sight of these principles. If Bismarck had changed the world when in office, the fact that he was no longer in office would change it even further.

On his accession, William proclaimed his sympathy for the workers. When the antisocialist law came up for renewal, the emperor supported a modified version that would have taken away the power of the police to expel certain Social Democrats from their homes. Bismarck opposed the measure, while hoping that the Social Democrats would indulge in excesses that would give him the excuse to suppress them by armed force. He lost, and as a result there was no antisocialist law after 1890. Other differences arose between the chancellor and the emperor over an international workers' conference, over relations with Russia, and over procedures in reaching policy decisions. Finally, in March 1890, William commanded Bismarck to resign, using the state of Bismarck's health as a public pretext.

Although four chancellors succeeded Bismarck during the years before the outbreak of another war in 1914, none of them compared with him in ability and influence. The years 1890 to 1914 belonged to William II. Energetic but unsteady, pompous and menacing but without the intention or the courage to back up his threats, William was ill suited to govern any country, much less the militaristic, highly industrialized imperial Germany, with its social tensions and its lack of political balance.

Tendencies already present under Bismarck, which the Iron Chancellor had been able to control, became more apparent in Wilhelmine Germany. The Prussian army, and especially the reserve officers, came increasingly to exercise great influence on William II. They "mistook bravado for an expression of strength, arrogance and conceit for a manifestation of dignity, and swagger for sensibility. . . ."* Other nations had larger armies, and Britain relied on a more professional line soldier, but Germany had a class of officers who saw themselves as a warrior caste with its own code of honor and regarded their profession as a way of life superior to bourgeois, civilian standards. Most capitalist societies assumed that officers were public servants, carrying out the will of politicians, who determined policy. In Prussia, however, capitalist society seemed ever more willing to accept the decisions of the military caste, forgetting that military figures are essentially technicians. Thus political decision-making passed out of the hands of those elected to make those decisions into the hands of those who felt they made decisions by right.

---

*Otto Pflanze, *Bismarck and the Development of Germany: The Period of Unification, 1815-1871* (Princeton: Princeton University Press, 1963), p. 87.

*Eckhart Kehr, *Economic Interest, Militarism, and Foreign Policy: Essays on German History*, trans. Grete Heinz, ed. Gordon A Craig (Berkeley: University of California Press, 1977), p. 108.

THE GROWTH OF BUREAUCRACY

In the arms race that developed during the 1890s, the large government bureaucracy tended to take over, to become a force in itself for policy making. The "official mind" seldom examined questions in terms of independent judgments, but acted out of tradition and departmental interest, so that crucial matters of state were sometimes decided more on interagency rivalry than on coldly weighed and fully rational calculations. This was no less true of the official mind of British imperialism than of the official mind of the German army or navy. It was a clear trend in all modernizing states, as the great German sociologist and student of bureaucracy, Max Weber (1864-1920), would argue in his exceptionally influential studies of how intellectuals, civil servants, and those who held to any form of group consciousness, whether church or military, made their decisions.

The decisive reason for the advance of bureaucratic organization has always been its purely *technical* superiority over any other form of organization. The fully developed bureaucratic apparatus compares with other organizations exactly as does the machine with the non-mechanical modes of production. Precision, speed, unambiguity, knowledge of the files, continuity, discretion, unity, strict subordination, reduction of friction and of material and personal costs—these are raised to the optimum point in the strictly bureaucratic administration, and especially in its monocratic form. As compared with all collegiate, honorific, and avocational forms of administration, trained bureaucracy is superior on all these points. And as far as complicated tasks are concerned, paid bureaucratic work is not only more precise but, in the last analysis, it is often cheaper than even formally unremunerated honorific service. . . .

Today, it is primarily the capitalist market economy which demands that the official business of public administration be discharged precisely, unambiguously, continuously, and with as much speed as possible. Normally, the very large modern capitalist enterprises are themselves unequalled models of strict bureaucratic organization. Business management throughout rests on increasing precision, steadiness, and, above all, speed of operations. This, in turn, is determined by the peculiar nature of the modern means of communication, including, among other things, the news service of the press. The extraordinary increase in the speed by which public announcements, as well as economic and political facts, are transmitted exerts a steady and sharp pressure in the direction of speeding up the tempo of administrative reaction toward various situations. The optimum of such reaction time is normally attained only by a strictly bureaucratic organization. . . .

The more complicated and specialized modern culture becomes, the more its external supporting apparatus demands the personally detached and strictly objective *expert*, in lieu of the lord of older social structures who was moved by personal sympathy and favor, by grace and gratitude. Bureaucracy offers the attitudes demanded by the external apparatus of modern culture in the most favorable combination. In particular, only bureaucracy has established the foundation for the administration of a rational law conceptually systematized on the basis of "statutes," such as the later Roman Empire first created with a high degree of technical perfection. . . .

The bureaucratic structure is everywhere a late product of historical development. The further back we trace our steps, the more typical is the absence of bureaucracy and of officialdom in general. Since bureaucracy has a "rational" character, with rules, means-ends calculus, and matter-of-factness predominating, its rise and expansion has everywhere had "revolutionary" results . . . , as had the advance of *rationalism* in general. The march of bureaucracy accordingly destroyed structures of domination which were not rational in the sense of the term.

Max Weber, *Economy and Society: An Outline of Interpretive Sociology*, Guenther Roth and Claus Wittich, eds. (Berkeley: University of California Press, 1978), II, 973-75, 1002-1003.

Party structure reflected the strains in German society. The Liberals, a party of big business, usually had little strength in the Reichstag, although many industrialists were on intimate terms with the emperor personally. The Liberals were also divided by local and regional rivalries. The great landowners banded together in protest against a reduction in agricultural duties that was included in a series of trade treaties concluded between Germany and other continental European countries between 1892 and 1894. In 1894 they organized an Agrarian League, which spearheaded conservative measures and became powerful in party politics. In 1902 they forced a return to protection.

The electoral strength of the Social Democrats increased during William's reign from 1,500,000 to 4,250,000, and embraced a third of the voting population by 1912. Freed from interference by the removal of the antisocialist law, they organized trade unions, circulated newspapers, and successfully pressured the regime for more social legislation. The party had no immediate plan for a revolution, although its radical wing expected, especially after a Russian revolution in 1905, that a German revolution would come. The "revisionist" wing, which expected no open conflict between capital and labor, hoped that, by allying themselves with the middle class to attain a majority in the

Reichstag, the Social Democrats might eventually overturn the militarist government peacefully.

In Germany, unlike France and Britain, women were generally given little role to play in the reform movement. Denied the right to vote, they were usually barred from membership in political organizations and trade unions, and Bismarck and his successors generally appeared as eager to combat feminist as socialist movements. Whereas in France women had traditionally been leaders in the arts, in Germany they were denied access to professional training, and there were no secondary schools for women comparable to the excellent and rigorous *Gymnasium* educational system established for males. Until the turn of the century, the only women admitted to German universities were foreigners, and until after World War I no women were permitted to work for higher degrees. The goal set for women was to provide their husbands with "a proper domestic atmosphere."

Those few women who were active politically usually joined socialist associations, since the socialists advocated equal pay for equal work. By 1900 there were over 850 associations working for women's rights in Germany, but during the empire few of their stated goals were achieved. Though the Progressive party endorsed the principle of suffrage for women in 1912, it did nothing to achieve that end. Many women worked in the textile industry, and in 1878 women were admitted to the German civil service—a move prompted not so much by feminist efforts as by the need for a new group of skilled workers. The government owned the means of communication and public transportation, and the new technologies had created a need for people who could operate the telegraph, telephone, and typewriter. Women of the upper middle class—daughters of officials and officers—were thus brought into the work force, though they were paid less than men, given no vacations, and generally employed on a wage rather than a salary basis, so that they could not depend upon annual (as opposed to day-by-day) compensation for their labors. In Austria women textile workers would strike in 1893 and successfully found a union, but not in Germany. Even though 60 percent of the population of Germany, male and female, was urbanized by 1910, the radical transformation of social and political thought that urbanization had brought to France and Britain generally did not occur in the German Empire.

Meanwhile, issues of military, colonial, and foreign policy began to complicate the tense internal politics of Germany. The size of the army rose from 479,000 in 1892 to 870,000 in 1913, and for the first time Germany sought a big navy. After Admiral Alfred von Tirpitz (1849-1930) became minister of the navy in 1897, the emperor and Tirpitz planned a high-seas fleet to replace the naval forces that had originally been designed for coastal and commercial defense. The navy boom was also at least partly intended to supply a market for the expanding steel industry. A Navy League, ostensibly a private organization but constantly hand in glove with the regime, spread propaganda on behalf of the new fleet, and the first rather modest naval law of 1898 provided for a navy that was doubled by the second law of 1900. But the army and navy were only the most obvious weapons of world power. The Colonial Society, founded to support the case for overseas expansion, grew rapidly in membership as Germany acquired territories in the Far East and in Africa, despite the drain on the budget (for the German colonies were never profitable). Pan-Germans planned a great Berlin-Baghdad railway to the Near East and cried for more adventure and more conquest.

However, William's naval and colonial policies embittered Germany's relations with Great Britain. In truth, Britain and Germany had been on divergent paths since the 1880s. Apart from foreign policy considerations, a gap in world view was opening between the two societies that had once had much in common. Britain watched with growing apprehension as this cluster of weak states grew into the dominant power on the continent. Britain's professional army, at first scornful of a conscript army in Germany, came increasingly to respect its capacities after the rapid defeat of France in 1871. So long as Bismarck was in control, the British hoped Germany would limit its goals to altering the existing order of power in Europe; after 1890 it seemed clear that Germany also intended to alter the world balance of power, and the British felt their interests directly threatened.

Foreign policy in both nations was shaped by a complex mixture of social, economic, political, and ideological factors ranging from religious and cultural connections through the changing attitudes of parties, the press, pressure groups, and the bureaucracies of both countries. Leaders in business and politics in both countries worked for a harmonious relationship, but in the end they failed. Slowly German policy drove Britain toward its old enemy, France, and quieted those in Britain who sought to pursue a more conciliatory policy toward the nation that was, in their eyes, stabilizing rather than dominating central Europe.

The Bismarckian era, many historians argue, was a Bonapartist-type dictatorial regime. Whether it was a source of stability or a cause of persistent instability continues to be debated. A reactionary class of landed aristocrats adapted themselves to industrial modernization, as did many members of the urban bourgeois population. A leadership elite emerged that sought to dominate the new Germany Bismarck had forged. After Bismarck the politics of coalition were replaced by growing authoritarianism. The egalitarian results of social change experienced in western Europe were restricted in Germany by a political alliance between authoritarian elites. This alliance, though bent and changed, would continue well into the twentieth century.

Britain had other than diplomatic and military reasons to be apprehensive of German power. By the turn of the century Germany had clearly overtaken Britain industrially, even though many in Britain appeared blind to that fact. This surging development of Germany made its militarism possible, while its militar-

OPENING THE GERMAN CIVIL SERVICE TO WOMEN

While women were brought into the German civil service in the 1870s as part of the general reform program, they confronted prejudice in the forms described in this report, made in 1878 to the Organization of German Working Women:

In October 1873, at the suggestion of her Royal Highness, the Crown Princess, the administration of the Telegraph Center decided to employ ladies in its service. The main idea was to open up a respectable branch of business to ladies of the upper middle class, the daughters of officials and officers. At that time, the administration announced that the ladies, after first passing an examination, were to be employed for a four-week probation period; later, however, they could expect permanent employment with pension rights and housing benefits, just the same as male employees. As to the salary scale, the ladies would draw a yearly remuneration of 750 Marks, payable in monthly installments of Mk. 62.50. In addition, they were promised that they would receive, like the male employees, a special bonus of about Mk. 9 per month for the telegrams processed. After the first year of service the first thirty ladies employed would receive a raise in salary from Mk. 750 to Mk. 900, and after the second year from Mk. 900 to Mk. 1050; those in line after the first thirty ladies would move up into the second salary category. Finally, after three years, they could expect permanent employment and receive housing benefits and pension rights. The work schedule and the work itself is the same as for men, except for night service, for which up to April of this year they were paid extra; now they receive a fixed remuneration. As far as performance is concerned, the ladies have given no cause for reproach. On the contrary, the officials of the Telegraph Service have repeatedly acknowledged that their performance is altogether equal to that of the men. This is confirmed by the fact that the demanding service of the Stock Exchange is also in the hands of ladies.

While the experiment to engage ladies as telegraph employees can be regarded as a complete success, the initial benevolence and the favorable disposition toward them in the upper circles of the Telegraph Service has turned into ill-will. There is little doubt that the Telegraph Administration is intent on making the situation as difficult as possible for the ladies in order to force them to voluntarily resign.

FIRST: Despite the fact that many of the ladies already have more than three years service behind them, only fifteen have been granted the maximum salary after the second year; and when two left the service, no one was moved up to the top salary class. Hence, only thir-

teen ladies now draw the maximum salary of Mk. 1050.

SECOND: Prospective female applicants are not called, even when there is a vacancy. Hence, the ladies are slowly eliminated from the Service.

THIRD: The monthly bonus has been discontinued for all employees; hence for the ladies also; the promise made for compensation seven months ago has not been kept as of today.

FOURTH: Up to the present, and after four years, not a single lady in Prussia has been permanently employed; hence, they are not entitled to housing benefits and pensions. On the contrary, by withdrawing the bonus, the ladies have suffered a monthly loss of Mk. 3 and are now forced more than ever before to supplement their income by taking parttime jobs.

FIFTH: More recently, the ladies off-handedly were given notice that they would no longer draw a yearly salary or compensation, but beginning in October, they would be employed on a day-to-day basis with a daily remuneration of Mk. 2.50. This amounts to saying that they are put in the class of unskilled labor, that they will never have the prospect of permanent employment, will receive no housing benefits, and have no pension rights, in short, that all their expectations are voided. At the same time, they can expect to be dismissed from one day to another. It is doubtful that they will receive their daily wages in case of sickness. At any rate, taking them away or granting them is entirely within the power of the authorities.

SIXTH: Every male employee automatically has the right to a two-week summer vacation. Not so the ladies. If a lady takes a leave of absence on the basis of a medical certificate, she is obliged to pay her substitute the daily remuneration, arbitrarily fixed at a high rate. Last year, it amounted to Mk. 0.75 per day, this year Mk. 1.50.

SEVENTH: In such manner, the service is made almost unbearable for the ladies. Unprofessional deportment is rebuked; conversational exchange prohibited. Formerly, every third Sunday was free, now only every seventh, but who knows how long this will last, for everything is determined by arbitrary decrees.

"Briefe," *Neue Bahnen: Organ des Allgemeinen Deutschen Frauenvereins*, XIII, no. 3 (1878), 21-22, as quoted in Eleanor S. Riemer and John C. Fout, eds., *European Women: A Documentary History, 1789-1945* (New York: Schocken Books, 1980), pp. 40-42. Published in Great Britain by the Harvester Press.

ism in turn fed industrialism. Beginning later and with fewer advantages than England, Germany recognized that it was behind the British commercially and made an early commitment to sophisticated technology. As in Britain, railroads provided the first surge of activity, followed by the opening of the Ruhr valley. Germany soon forged ahead in steel, organic chemistry, and electricity.

Economic issues were always close to the surface in all German political debate. When the Ruhr proved to be rich in coal, and transportation costs were moderate, a mixture of private initiative and state assistance industrialized the region almost before political debate could take shape. Agriculture became more efficient, especially on the large estates east of the Elbe, where grain production could be doubled using new chemical fertilizers. Assisted by an active cooperative movement and by state-supported agricultural schools and experimental stations, German grain growers exported food until 1873. Thereafter, as cheap grain from eastern Europe began to enter Germany, economic policy turned toward protectionism, though never to the extent that France did. National efficiency—whether in the growth of larger and larger factories, firms, and cartels, or in more productive agriculture—became a goal on which nearly all parties could agree. By 1914 Germany was largely self-sufficient in many significant areas of industry, though perhaps 20 percent of Germany's food supply was imported, much of it from the Hapsburg Empire.

IV THE HAPSBURG EMPIRE: DIVIDING HUMANITY INTO NATIONS

Historians continue to explore the concept of nationalism, often in order to challenge the easy, unthinking assumption that, because societies did organize themselves into national identities, such a course was inevitable. Although many language groups did achieve separate nationhood, others did not. Some who achieved it lost it again, and some who never achieved it continue to strive for it today. In a sense, nationalism was a doctrine invented in Europe in the nineteenth century to account for social, economic, and political changes that required a single descriptive term. The notion of nationhood easily led to the assumption that humanity was divided—by divine intent, nature, or the material force of history—into nations, and that therefore the course of history was toward the self-determination of those peoples. The American Declaration of Independence had asserted such a principle, and by the midnineteenth century most people in western Europe appear to have assumed that the only legitimate type of government was that which carried a society toward independence. Thus, the ideal of political independence was attached to the earlier Enlightenment notion of the doctrine of progress.

Most commentators on nationalism argue that certain common characteristics can be identified, so that a "nation" can be objectively defined. These characteristics include a shared language, a common object of love (usually called the homeland), a shared life in a common territory under similar influences of nature and common outside political pressures, and the creation of a state of mind that strives toward a sense of homogeneity within the group. This sense of common identity is fostered by holding to common symbols, rituals, and social conventions through a common language (or variant of it), religion, and sense of mutual interdependence. Usually the positive aspects of such a sense of group identity will be strengthened by a negative emphasis on those who lack such characteristics: those who speak incomprehensible tongues and are therefore presumed to be peculiar; those who resist homogeneity (and the mediocrity that often must accompany enforced conformity or concerted action) and are branded as unpatriotic or subversive to the commonly cherished values; or those who pursue some broadly intellectual value system in art, ideology, or religion outside the cooperative framework within a state.

Thus nationalism is built on hate as well as love. It may be fed by what some historians call "vital lies"—beliefs held to be so true and so central to a sense of identity that to question them at all is to be disloyal. Thus certain historical ideas may be untrue—even lies consciously fostered—but because of widespread belief in them, they have the vitality and thus the function of truth. Americans believe they became independent in 1776 because they assert they did; Japanese believed until after 1945 that their Emperor was divine; many Germans believed after World War I that they could have achieved military victory had they not been betrayed by politicians. Most modern societies think of their way of life as superior to others. Most peoples believe themselves chosen—whether by God, by history, or by the environment and resources they have acquired or inherited.

In the twentieth century such assumptions about national identity and the nation as the source of group and individual security and stability are commonplace. But what now seems natural was, in fact, unfamiliar or still emerging as part of the process of modernization in the nineteenth century. This was especially so among the many language groups of the Hapsburg Empire. For the Hapsburg Empire, "modernization" did not mean unification or any substantial industrialization or democratization. It meant fragmentation, a growing gap between its economy and the standard of living in Germany, France, northern Italy, and Britain, and a trend toward representative government only in relation to divisive nationalisms, not toward new national unities.

For over sixty years, from 1848 to 1916, the German-speaking emperor Francis Joseph sat on the Hapsburg throne. Simple in his personal life and immensely conscientious, he worked hard reading and signing state papers for hours every day. But he was without fire or imagination, uninterested in books or even newspapers, devoted to the rigid court etiquette prescribed for Hapsburgs, inflexibly old-fashioned and conservative. He and most of the Hapsburgs were afflicted by frequent family tragedies. He was intensely pious, and his mere longevity inspired loyalty. His decisions usually came too late and conceded too little. His responsibility for the course of events is large.

Hapsburg history between 1850 and 1914 divides naturally into equal portions at the convenient date 1867, when the empire became the dual monarchy of Austria-Hungary. After the suppression of the Revolution of 1848, there was a decade of repression usually called the Bach System, from the name of the minister of the interior, Alexander Bach (1813-1893), ending in 1859 with the war against Piedmont and France. Eight years of political experimentation followed, from 1859 to 1867, punctuated by the war of 1866 with Prussia.

In 1849 all parts of the empire were for the first time unified and directly ruled from Vienna by German-speaking officials. In 1855 the state signed a concordat with the Catholic church giving clerics a greater influence in education and other fields than they had enjoyed since the reforms of Joseph II. The repressive domestic policies of the Bach period required expensive armies and policemen. Instead of investing in railroads and industry, Austria went into debt to pursue centralization, an enlarged bureaucracy, and Germanization. These expenditures left it at a disadvantage compared with Prussia. Then during the Crimean War, instead of repaying Czar Nicholas I for Russia's aid in subduing the Hungarian Revolution, Francis Joseph failed to assist the Russians and kept them in fear of an attack by occupying the Danubian principalities (modern Romania). In 1857 Austria experienced a severe financial crisis, partly as a result of this long mobilization. Defeat in 1859 at the hands of the French and Italians and the loss of Lombardy with its great city of Milan brought about the end of the Bach system.

War continued to threaten, and the nationalities inside the empire, especially the Magyars, could not be kept in a state of perpetual discontent, which would render their troops unreliable. Several solutions were tried in an effort to create a structure that would withstand the domestic and foreign strains but that would not jeopardize the emperor's position. Francis Joseph listened first to the nobles, who favored loose federalism, and then to the bureaucrats, who favored tight centralism. In 1860 he set up a central legislature to deal with economic and military problems. To it the provincial assemblies (*diets*) throughout the empire would send delegates. All other problems were left to the provincial diets, elected by a system that worked to disfranchise the peasants and to benefit the rich and (in Bohemia) the German townspeople rather than the Czech farmers. This solution, known as the October Diploma, did not satisfy the most influential non-German group, the Magyar nobility of Hungary. Even so, Austrian liberals and bureaucrats felt that the October Diploma gave the Magyars too much. It seemed to them that the empire was being dismembered on behalf of the nobility, who dominated the provincial assemblies. Therefore in 1861 the February Patent reinterpreted the Diploma, creating an even more centralized scheme. A bicameral imperial legislature took over most of the powers the October Diploma had reserved for the provincial assemblies or diets.

Naturally, the Magyars objected to this second solution even more than to the first, and they flatly refused to participate. To the applause of the Germans in Vienna, including the liberals, Hungary returned to authoritarian rule. Czechs and Poles also eventually withdrew from the central parliaments and left only a German rump. Disturbed, the emperor suspended the February Patent and began to negotiate with the Magyars, who were represented by the intelligent and moderate Ferenc Deák (1803-1876). The negotiations were interrupted by the war with Prussia in 1866. The Austrian defeat at Sadowa, the expulsion of Austria from Germany, and the loss of Venetia threatened the entire Hapsburg system. Clearly Austria could not risk war with any combination of Prussia, France, or Russia. Francis Joseph resumed negotiations with the Magyars, with the help of the Magyar count Julius Andrássy (1823-1890), who had been exiled for his role in the revolution of 1848. In 1867, the year Francis Joseph lost his brother Maximilian in Mexico, a formula was found that was to govern and preserve the Hapsburg domain down to the World War of 1914-1918.

The Dual Monarchy, 1867

This formula was the *Ausgleich*, or compromise, which created the unique dual monarchy of Austria-Hungary. The Hungarian Constitution of 1848 was restored, and the entire empire was reorganized as a strict partnership. Austria and Hungary were united in the person of the emperor, who was always to be a Catholic and a legitimate Hapsburg, and who was to be crowned king of Hungary in Budapest. For foreign policy, military affairs, and finance, the two states had joint ministers appointed by the emperor. A customs union, subject to renewal every ten years, united them. Every ten years the quota of common expenditure to be borne by each partner was to be renegotiated. A unique body, the "delegations," made up of sixty members from the Austrian parliament and sixty members from the Hungarian parliament, meeting alternately in Vienna and in Budapest, was to decide on the common budget, which had to be ratified by the full parliaments of both countries. The delegations also had supervisory authority over the three joint ministers and might summon them to account for their activities. In practice, however, the delegations seldom met and were almost never consulted on questions of policy. The system favored Hungary, which had 40 percent of the population but never paid more than a third of the expenses. Every ten years, therefore, when the quota of expenses and the customs union needed joint consideration, a new crisis arose.

One overwhelming problem remained common to both halves of the monarchy: that of the national minorities who had not received their autonomy. Some of these minorities (Czechs, Poles, Ruthenes) were largely in Austria; others (Slovaks, Romanians) were largely in Hungary; the rest (Croats, Serbs, Slovenes) were in both states. These nationalities were at different stages of national self-consciousness. Some were subject to pressures and manipulation from fellow nationals living outside the dual monarchy. All had some leaders who urged compromise and conciliation with the dominant Austrians and Magyars, and others who advocated resistance and even revolution. The result was chronic and often unpredictable instability in the dual monarchy.

The Austrian Constitution of 1867 provided that all nationalities should enjoy equal rights and guaranteed that each might use its own language in education, administration, and public life. And in 1868 the Hungarians abandoned the fierce chauvinism of the patriots of 1848 and passed a law that allowed the minorities to conduct local government in their own language, to hold the chief posts in the counties where they predominated, and to have their own schools. But in practice, neither the Austrians nor the Hungarians respected the statutes, and the minority nationalities suffered inconsistently applied discrimination and persecution.

The Nationality Question in Austria

After 1867 many Czechs felt that they too were entitled to an Ausgleich. They argued that the lands of the Crown of Saint Wenceslaus, a martyred prince of Bohemia (d. 929), possessed rights comparable to those that the Magyars had succesfully claimed for the lands of the Crown of Saint Stephen (c. 975-1038), who had been crowned as first king of Hungary in 1001. But the Czechs never had the power or the opportunity that the Magyars had to bring pressure on the Austrians, although Czech deputies boycotted the Austrian parliament in the hope that Francis Joseph would consent to become king of Bohemia in Prague, as he had become king of Hungary in Budapest.

In 1871 the emperor did indeed offer to be crowned as king of Bohemia. The Bohemian Diet, from which all Germans had withdrawn, drew up proposals that would have produced a triple instead of a dual monarchy. The rage of Austrian and Bohemian Germans, the opposition of Magyar politicians, and a Slavic uprising in southern Austria forced Francis Joseph to change his mind. Deeply disappointed, the Czech nationalist leaders turned to passive resistance.

By 1879, when the Czech deputies finally returned to the Vienna parliament, they were divided into moderate "old Czechs" and radical "young Czechs." In the 1880s and 1890s each time the Czechs won cultural or political gains, the German extremists bitterly opposed them, strengthening the Czech extremists and weakening the moderates. A law requiring all judges in Czech lands to conduct trials in the language of the petitioner led to the development of an experienced body of Czech civil servants, since many Czechs knew German already, while Germans usually had to learn Czech. In 1890 the government and the old Czechs tentatively agreed on an administrative division of Bohemia between Germans and Czechs, but the young Czechs rioted in the Bohemian Diet, and Prague was put under martial law, which lasted until 1897. When a new law was passed requiring that all civil servants in the Czech lands be bilingual after 1901, the Germans in the Vienna parliament forced out the ministry, while Czech extremists began to talk

ominously about a future Russian-led Slavic showdown with the Germans. All moderation vanished in the waves of noise and hatred. No Austrian parliament could stay in session, and the government had to be conducted by decree.

Under the stress of prolonged agitation and influenced by the apparent triumph of constitutionalism in Russia, Francis Joseph finally decided to reform the franchise. In 1907 all male citizens of the Austrian lands were enfranchised and could vote for deputies of their own nationality. Of the 516 deputies in the new parliament, 233 would be German and 107 Czech, a figure nearly proportional to the census figures, since Czechs comprised 23 percent of the Austrian population. Yet in 1913 the Bohemian Diet was dissolved, and in 1914 Czech deputies in the Austrian parliament refused to allow national business to proceed. Thus World War I began with both parliament and the Bohemian Diet dissolved and with the emperor and ministers ruling by themselves. Perhaps chief among the many causes for this general parliamentary breakdown was the failure to give the Czech provinces the full internal self-government they had vainly sought since 1867.

Czech nationalism was fostered by an active Czech-language press, by patriotic societies, by Czech schools, and by the *sokols* (hawks), a physical-training society with strong nationalist leanings. At the ancient Prague University, Czech scholars supported the idea of a separate national identity. Perhaps the most influential was Thomas Masaryk (1850-1937), professor of philosophy and student of Slavic culture, who deeply influenced generations of students and upheld democratic ideals in politics. Masaryk was interested in the theory of nationalism, and he encouraged people to study history, certain that such study promoted patriotism, while he inspired poets and novelists to write of a glorified national past for a popular audience, and helped to define both a Czechoslovak and a Yugoslavian nation. From 1907 he formally led the Czech independence party, convinced that "the ideals of humanity" were best realized through union with a self-defined national identity. In 1918 Masaryk would become president of the new nation whose primary philosopher he had been.

Of all the minority nationalities in the dual monarchy, the Czechs were in the best position to exercise independence. Substantial in population, with a high percentage of artisans skilled in the porcelain, glassware, lace, Pilsen beer, and sugar-beet industries, and with a thriving tourist trade that gave them access to the broader world, the Czechs also were the center of growing heavy industry, especially at the Skoda armament works, which by 1900 were second only to those of Krupp in Essen, Germany. A portion of this industrialized area was shared, however, with the former Poland.

Of all the minorities in Austria, the Poles (18 percent of the population) were the least overtly discontented. Most of them lived in Galicia, where they formed the landlord class and generally oppressed their peasants, especially the Ruthenians (Ukrainians). Like the Czechs, the Galician Poles asked for provincial self-government on the Magyar model and, like the Czechs, they were denied. But they had their own schools, and Polish was the language of administration and the courts. The Poles enjoyed favorable financial arrangements, and after 1871 there was a special ministry for Galicia in Vienna. Since the Poles hated Russia, pan-Slavism never tempted them, as it did the Czechs; they were not yet interested in forming a future independent Poland.

The contrast between this relatively nondiscriminatory treatment of Poles in Austria and the brutality suffered by Poles living in Prussian and Russian Poland led Poles everywhere to look to Austrian Galicia as the center of national life and culture. Polish refugees took refuge in the cities of Kracow and Lemberg (later, Lvov). Here were splendid Polish universities, noble families living grandly (as they always had in Poland), and opportunities to serve the Hapsburg crown in the provincial administration. The universities trained generations of Poles who would be available later for service in independent Poland. Polish literature and the study of Polish history flourished. Slowly, industrialization began, and a promising petroleum industry was launched. Only the Ruthenians and the Jews suffered systematic discrimination and hardship. The Poles eliminated Ruthenians from the Galician Diet and until 1907 also kept them out of the imperial parliament. The Ruthenians themselves were divided into an older pro-Russian generation and a younger generation of Ukrainian nationalists, who hated Poles and Russians alike, and who hoped for their own autonomous status within the monarchy.

The other minorities in Austria were far less numerous: in 1910 less than 3 percent of the population was Italian; about 4½ percent was Slovene; and less than 3 percent was Serb and Croat. The Italians of the south Tyrol and Istria, where their center was the seaport of Trieste, were far more important than their numbers suggest, however, because of the existence of the Kingdom of Italy directly across the border. Almost all of them wanted to belong to Italy, and Italy regarded their lands as Italia Irredenta (see p. 200). Of all the Austrian minorities, the Italians proved to be the most anxious to get out of the Hapsburg monarchy altogether. Both Serbs and Croats in Austria were divided; some preferred autonomy within the empire, and others hoped one day to join a south Slav state.

Minorities in Hungary

In Hungary minority problems were more acute. Magyar behavior toward other national groups grew increasingly oppressive. The Slovaks, the Romanians, and the Serbs and Croats living in Hungary were the worst victims of a deliberate policy of Magyarization, but even the Croatians of Croatia, whose province had its own constitutional special status, suffered. The Magyar aim was to destroy the national identity of the minorities and to transform them into Magyars; the weapon used was language.

Deprived of economic opportunity and sometimes of religious freedom, the peasants of southeastern Europe, like the French Canadians or the Boers of South Africa, found in the languages they spoke living proof of national identity. The Magyars too, who made up only 55 percent of the population of their own country (exclusive of Croatia), had an intense devotion to their own language—an Asian tongue quite unrelated to the German, Slavic, or Romanian languages of the minorities. They tried to force it upon the subject peoples, particularly in education. All state-supported schools, from kindergartens to universities, wherever located, had to give instruction in Magyar, and the state postal, telegraph, and railroad services used only Magyar.

The Slovaks, numbering about 11 percent of the population of Hungary, were perhaps the most Magyarized. Poor peasants for the most part, the more ambitious of them often became Magyars simply by adopting the Magyar language as their own. As time passed, a few Slovaks came to feel a sense of unity with the closely related Czechs across the border in Austria. A Slovak literature had also been developing for a century. The pro-Czechs among the Slovaks were usually liberals and Protestants, while Catholic and conservative Slovaks advocated Slovak autonomy. After Czechoslovakia was formed in 1918, the Catholic movement in Slovakia continued to be anti-Czech and became pro-German in the 1930s.

The Romanians, who lived in Transylvania, amounted in 1910 to about 17 percent of the population of Hungary and were a majority in Transylvania itself. For centuries they had been downtrodden by the Magyars and had fought constantly to achieve recognition of their Greek Orthodox religion. Largely in hope of receiving better treatment, many of them had accepted papal supremacy, but otherwise preserved their own liturgy. Despite laws designed to eliminate the use of the Romanian language, the Romanians fiercely resisted assimilation. Many looked to Vienna, which before the Ausgleich had often been a source of assistance against the Magyars, but it was now committed to give the Magyars a free hand. Some Romanians hoped that Transylvania might again be made autonomous, as it had been in the past. Many pressed for the enforcement of the liberal Hungarian nationalities law of 1868. But when in 1892 they petitioned Vienna on these points, their petition was returned unopened and unread, and when they circulated the petition widely abroad, their leaders were tried and jailed.

Under Magyar rule, some Serbs and Croats lived in Hungary proper and others in Croatia; in 1910 those in Hungary totaled about 600,000, of whom two-thirds were Serbs. Living in a compact mass in the southern and western frontier regions, they were the inhabitants of the old Hapsburg "military frontier" against the

Turks. They had been transferred to Magyar rule in 1869, and they disliked Hungarian administration, hoping to be united with the independent kingdom of Serbia to the south. A greater menace to Hungarian unity was provided by the existence of Croatia itself.

The Croats, though connected since the eleventh century with the Crown of Hungary, had become strongly nationalistic under the impact of the Napoleonic occupation and had fought on the side of the monarchy against the Magyar revolutionaries of 1848. Nonetheless, Francis Joseph, as part of the Ausgleich settlement, handed them back to the Magyars. Croatian nationalists were deeply disappointed. Led by a Roman Catholic bishop, Josef Strossmayer (1815-1905), a man of great intelligence and liberal views, they had hoped for an autonomous Croatia and Dalmatia (the coastal strip along the Adriatic inhabited largely by Croats but governed by Vienna), which would serve as a nucleus to attract all southern Slavs.

Instead, the Magyar moderates, led by Deák, worked out in 1868 an Ausgleich of their own between Hungary and Croatia. All military and economic affairs were to be handled in Budapest by a special cabinet minister for Croatian affairs. Representatives from the Croatian parliaments at the Croatian capital of Zagreb would sit in Budapest whenever Croatian affairs were under discussion. Croatian delegates would be part of the Hungarian "delegation" to the dual monarchy. The Croatian language would be spoken by Croat representatives at the sessions of any body they attended, and the language of command in the Croatian territorial army would be Croatian. The Croats would control their own educational system, their church, their courts, and police; however, taxes would be voted and collected by Budapest.

The Croat Party of the Right wanted a completely autonomous Croatia and scorned as inferior the Serbs and other non-Catholic south Slavs, whom Strossmayer had hoped to attract. Further problems were created in Catholic Croatia by the existence of a Serb Orthodox minority (more than a quarter of the population), which spoke the same language as the Croats. But the Serbs worshiped in different churches and were therefore subject to religious discrimination. The Hungarian-appointed governor fostered this Serb-Croat antagonism by using the Serbs for local offices. He received the support only of those Croats who had become Magyar-speaking, usually great landowners or government officials, creating deep class divisions in Croat society. Yet by 1903 Serbs and Croats were beginning to cooperate against Hungarian rule and to spread pro-Slav propaganda in Dalmatia.

But in 1907 the hopes of moderate leaders on all sides were dashed by an unpopular Railway Servants Act, which forced all railroad workers to speak Magyar. Croats began to boycott Hungarian-made goods; the Croatian Diet refused to collaborate with the new governor, who in 1909 arrested fifty-odd Croats and Serbs and charged them with plotting to unite Croatia and Bosnia

with Serbia. The evidence was inadequate, and the defendants, though condemned, obtained a reversal of the sentences on appeal to a higher court. But these Zagreb trials gave the Slavic press a splendid opportunity to denounce the policy of the dual monarchy.

Also in 1909 a celebrated Austrian historian charged in the Vienna press that politicians in Croatia were plotting with Serbians in Serbia, but he was eventually forced to admit that his documentary sources, which in all probability had been fed to him by the Vienna foreign office, were forgeries. The Zagreb trials and the repeated press attacks from Vienna, Budapest, and Zagreb drove away any remnant of loyal south Slavs. Nationalism soon found expression in terrorism, and in 1912, 1913, and again in 1914, Bosnian students tried to assassinate the Hungarian governor of Croatia.

The region of Bosnia-Herzegovina had a special status in the dual monarchy. By the 1870s these two provinces had been part of the Ottoman Empire for about four centuries. Although solidly south Slavic, the population in 1879 included about half a million Muslims, half a million members of the Orthodox church, and perhaps 150,000 Catholics. Under Turkish rule those who accepted Islam had enjoyed economic advantages. Most of the Orthodox Christians were peasants, working on the estates of Muslim landlords and looking across the frontiers to Serbia in hope of liberation. In 1875 a Herzegovinian uprising against the Turks precipitated a general Balkan Slavic attack on the Turks. Russia too went to war against the Ottoman Empire. At the Congress of Berlin in 1878, the Hapsburgs obtained the right to occupy the provinces, but not to annex them. Until 1908 the dual monarchy occupied both. The sovereignty of the Ottoman sultan was recognized throughout this period, but in fact the provinces were ruled from Vienna, though not as part of either Austria or Hungary. Instead, they were put under the joint Austro-Hungarian minister of finance.

These provinces perpetually threatened to create an explosion. Many observers in Vienna pressed for some sort of all-south-Slav solution that would join Dalmatia, Croatia, and Bosnia-Herzegovina into one south-Slav kingdom under Francis Joseph, with the same status as Hungary—a triple rather than a dual monarchy. However, the advocates of this solution, known as "Trialists," met with violent Magyar opposition.

Then in 1908 a revolution in Turkey led by young army officers gave the Austrian foreign minister a chance to act; fortified by a prior secret agreement with Russia, he annexed the two provinces in October and announced that they would be given a diet of their own. This move precipitated a major European crisis, which threatened world war but which eventually subsided, leaving the Serbs bitterly resentful, the young Turk leaders partially discredited (since Bulgaria took advantage of Ottoman preoccupation to declare its independence), and the Balkan peoples in turmoil.

The discontent of the population of Bosnia—added to the discontent of the Czechs and Italians in Austria and the Slovaks, Romanians, Croats, and other south Slavs in Hungary—goes far to account for the wartime weaknesses and postwar disintegration of the dual monarchy. Yet the minority question, critical though it was, does not provide the entire answer. The Austrian-German and Hungarian majorities were also subject to divisive forces that crippled them individually and together.

Society and Politics in Austria and Hungary, 1867-1914

Since Austria was 90 percent Catholic, it did not experience the strenuous Kulturkampf of Germany. However, liberals did fight clerical conservatives over religious issues and forced through bills legalizing civil marriages, quasisecularized schools, and taxes on church property. Many liberals were discredited by the financial crash of 1873, during which it was revealed that some of them had accepted bribes, and, as in Germany, political anti-Semitism grew. The working class turned toward socialism after the crash, while the Austrian nobles, who often owned great estates which they ran almost like independent rulers, took little interest in the nation's problems. The large size of noble estates was a fundamental reason for the small size of the average peasant holding, and made it necessary even for landowning peasants to seek supplementary employment on a noble's property. The peasants' standard of living and level of literacy were extremely low, so that communication and organization for political unity—essential steps to any "revolution of rising expectations"—were limited. Furthermore, the Austrian clergy remained loyal to the dynasty and worked on behalf of the nobles against possible peasant uprisings.

The middle class was small. Among the bourgeoisie were many Jews, who generally could not be nobles, bureaucrats, or army officers. Forced to enter trade, the professions, and the arts, where they prospered, the Jewish minority gave Viennese life much of its widely hailed, yet often suspect, charm and gaiety, its cultivation, its music, its cafés, its newspapers, its Sacher torte and whipped cream, its high reputation in medicine and science, its image of "the good life" that was so attractive to western European visitors yet so offensive to peasant and noble in the provinces.

Anti-Semitism, fanned by the migration of poorer Jews from regions of eastern Europe where oppression had kept them squalid and illiterate, was general in Austria. Political anti-Semitism grew among the lower middle classes, often unsuccessful competitors in the world of small shopkeeping. Partly out of religious prejudice, partly out of distaste for the liberal politics preferred by the middle-class Jews, the clericals attacked them. One response among the Jews to the swelling chorus of anti-Semitism was Zionism—sponsorship of a future Jewish state—which originated in the dual monarchy. Another response was assimilation, for conversion and intermarriage were especially common in cosmopolitan Vienna.

In the late nineteenth century the stresses and strains inherent in this social structure, aggravated by the problems of the national minorities, produced two important new political movements among the Germans of Austria: Pan-Germanism and the Christian Social party. In the early 1880s, moderate Austrian Germans had wanted to hand over the Slavic lands of Austria to the Hungarians to rule, and then, stripped to the German core, to unite economically with Germany. The Pan-Germans were more radical. They opposed the Hapsburg dynasty and the Catholic church, demanded that Austria become Protestant, and agitated for political union with Germany. The Christian Socialists, however, became the most important Austrian political party. Strongly Catholic and loyal to the Hapsburgs, they appealed to both the peasant and the small business owner by favoring social legislation and by opposing big business. They, like the Pan-Germans, were violently anti-Semitic. At first skeptical of the value of the Christian Social Party, the clergy later made the movement its own.

The most famous Christian Socialist leader was the perennial mayor of Vienna after 1895, Karl Lueger (1844-1910), idol of the lower middle classes of the capital. For years he sponsored public ownership of city utilities, parks, playgrounds, free milk for schoolchildren, and other welfare services, while catering to his followers' hatred of Jews, Marxists, and Magyars. A later German leader, Adolf Hitler, who saw Lueger's funeral procession in 1910, hailed him in his book *Mein Kampf*

Vienna was one of the first major planned modern cities. After the destruction of the old city fortifications, a circle of tree-lined boulevards was constructed to provide the city with breathing space and aesthetically pleasing views. The Ringstrasse, sixty yards wide and two and a half miles long, provided a handsome setting for Hapsburg imperial architecture from 1865. Shown here are the Parliament and Town Hall on the Ringstrasse.

as the greatest statesman of his time. It is impossible to understand the doctrines of German Nazism in the twentieth century without understanding the social and racial structure of the Hapsburg monarchy in which Hitler, born in Austria in 1889, grew to maturity.

To the Pan-Germans and the Christian Socialists, the Austrian Social Democrats, founded in 1888, responded with a Marxist program calling for government ownership of the means of production and for political action organized by class rather than by nationality. But the Austrian Social Democrats were not revolutionaries, and they set as their goals such political and social gains as universal suffrage, fully secular education, and the eight-hour working day. They were usually led by intellectuals, many of them Jewish, but they were followed by an ever-increasing number of workers. On the nationality question, Social Democratic leaders strongly urged democratic federalism. Each nationality should have control of its own affairs in its own territory; in mixed territories, minorities should be protected; and a central parliament should decide matters of common interest. Cultural autonomy of the nationalities of a multinational state was by no means an impractical or solely Marxist idea. Some measure of its practicality was later attested by the Soviet Russians, faced as they were with a similar problem and much influenced by the thinking of Austrian Social Democrats on the question.

Through it all Emperor Francis Joseph continued to treat his dynasty as an impersonal institution which, he believed, was far more benevolent than party government could be. He thought of himself as the last "monarch of the old school," and he faced bitter personal loss time and again. His son Rudolf committed suicide in a scandal in 1889; his wife Elisabeth was killed by an anarchist at Geneva in 1898; and his nephew's assassination at Sarajevo in 1914 would trigger a world war. Still, he reigned with determination far longer than any other European monarch, loyal to the Hapsburg ideal to the end.

Despite imperial tragedy and divisive politics, Vienna was one of the great cities of Europe in the years between 1870 and 1914. Its cosmopolitan air, its rapid growth, its mixture of frivolity and high seriousness were remarkable. Many concepts of modern urban planning began in Vienna, with its great Ringstrasse—a complex of public buildings, private dwellings, and public parks that provided a model for urban reconstruction. Here Sigmund Freud would write *The Interpretation of Dreams* in 1902, a secular personal statement as representative of the new century as St. Augustine's *Confessions* had been for the fourth century. Here controversy over art, literature, dance, music and sexual morality would explode into revolt against the old norms.

As young intellectuals abandoned protest through politics, rejecting political liberalism as irrelevant, they found cultural forms of protest that made Vienna both politically conservative and culturally alive. While in Britain and France the bourgeoisie had come to power by the end of the century or earlier, the bourgeoisie in Austria remained a rival to the old aristocracy, imitating the lifestyle of the nobility rather than substituting a new one. Culture became a substitute for power, and many former liberals took refuge in a cult of inner sensibility and self-fulfillment, to the exclusion of social concerns. In Britain the middle class spoke of duty, in France it spoke of political authority, but in Vienna it spoke of cultural modernity.

In Hungary the situation was rather different. The great landed nobility, owning half of Hungary in estates of hundreds of thousands of acres apiece and loyal to the dynasty, were a small class numerically. Hungary had a much larger class of country gentlemen, the squirearchy or gentry, whose holdings were far smaller and whose social position was lower, but whose political influence as a group was greater. After the emancipation of the serfs in 1848 and during later periods of uncertain agricultural and climatic conditions, many members of the gentry became civil servants or entered the professions. For centuries the towns had been centers for Germans and Jews, but during the nineteenth century the towns became steadily more Magyar, as members of the gentry and peasantry moved into them. At the bottom of the social pyramid was a class (never more than 20 percent of the population) of industrial workers in the cities, mostly in the textile and flour-milling industries. Wages were low, and living and working conditions were abominable, much like those in Russia.

The Jewish population grew rapidly, mostly by immigration from the north and east. In Hungary many Jews were converted and assimilated and became strongly Magyar in sentiment; but, as in Austria, they were disliked, especially among the poorer city population and in the countryside, where they were associated with money lending and tavern keeping, two professions that kept the peasant in their debt. Nonetheless, though anti-Semitism existed in Hungary, it never became as important a political movement as in Austria.

The Catholic church was immensely powerful and rich in Hungary, as in Austria, but in Hungary Catholicism was the faith of only about 60 percent of the population. Some Hungarian magnate families and many of the gentry had never returned to Catholicism after the Reformation, having remained Calvinists. Several hundred thousand Germans, chiefly in Transylvania, were Lutheran, and there also were Magyar Unitarians. Clericalism could never become the dominant force in Hungary that it was in Austria.

Thus, because of its differing social and religious structure, Hungary did not produce strong parties like the Austrian Social Democrats and Christian Socialists. Austria had a relatively liberal franchise before 1907 and universal manhood suffrage thereafter. Hungary, in contrast, never effectively changed its law of 1874, by which only about 6 percent of the population could vote. Moreover, Magyars were united in their determination to subjugate the national minorities in Hungary; therefore, other internal political or social issues did little to determine Hungarian political alignments. The only real source of Magyar political differences was the question of Hungary's position in the dual monarchy. Some,

**Nationalities in
Central and Eastern Europe**
About 1914

——————— Political boundaries, 1914
- - - - - - - Boundary between Austria
and Hungary

followers of Lajos Kossuth (1802-1894), favored complete independence; others, called the Tigers, wished to improve the position of Hungary within the monarchy by securing Hungarian control over its own army, diplomatic service, and finances, and by limiting the tie with Austria to the person of the monarch. While the Tigers were generally victorious, the Kossuthists were able to disrupt the government in 1902, and in 1905 the Kossuthists won a majority. When Francis Joseph refused to

meet the demands of the new majority and appointed a loyal general as premier, the Kossuthists urged patriots not to pay taxes or perform military service, and until 1910 they kept parliament in convulsion. Kossuthists had to be removed by force from parliament, and gag rule had to be imposed. It was in this utterly unstable atmosphere that Hungary received the news on June 8, 1914 that Francis Ferdinand, heir to the throne of the dual monarchy, had been assassinated.

V   RUSSIA, 1825-1914

In Russia, the third and largest of the great eastern European empires, the process of modernization took far longer than in western Europe. There was no parliament in Russia until 1905, and even then the czar was able to weaken and eventually to dominate the new representative body. Serfdom had not been abolished until 1861, and agrarian problems were in some ways intensified by the liberation of the peasants. Each time reform came—in the 1860s and in 1905 and 1906—it came as a result of military defeat abroad, which rendered reform essential, yet suspect. The reforms of Alexander II (1855-1881) arose from Russia's defeat in the Crimean War (1854-1856), and the Revolution of 1905 was made possible by Russia's failure in the Russo-Japanese War (1904-1905). During most of the nineteenth and early twentieth centuries, even after the reforms, the Russian czars claimed for themselves the autocratic rights that Peter the Great and his Muscovite predecessors had exercised. Thus the Russian people experienced long periods of repression and reaction: the entire reign of Nicholas (1825-1855), and a protracted period from 1866 through 1904, including the last fifteen years of Alexander II's reign (1866-1881), the whole of Alexander III's (1881-1894), and the first ten years of Nicholas II's (1894-1916), the last of the czars.

The failure to adjust to the currents of the times and the attempt to preserve autocratic rule produced unparalleled discontent in Russia. Disillusioned and angry intellectuals in the 1830s and 1840s gave way to proponents of social change in the 1850s and early 1860s, and these in turn yielded to determined revolutionaries and terrorists in the late 1860s and the years that followed. Although Marxist literature was known early in Russia and Marxist political groupings existed after 1896, the Marxists were neither numerous nor effective Russian revolutionaries in the nineteenth century. Non-Marxist revolutionary parties performed the killings and other acts of violence that convulsed the regime and won the support of large groups of Russians. It was only V.I. Lenin's transformation and adaptation of Marxist doctrine specifically to Russia that enabled his Bolsheviks to emerge as an important threat. And it was only Lenin's supreme tactical skill and boldness that enabled him to bring the Bolsheviks, still a minority, to power during the Revolution of 1917, a movement that was again made possible by Russian losses in yet another war.

Amid official attempts to preserve sixteenth-century patterns, Russia was experiencing the impact of nineteenth- and twentieth-century industrialization and modernization. New resources were developed, thousands of miles of railroads were built, and many factories were engaged in both heavy and light industry. A new laboring class thronged the cities, as elsewhere in Europe, though it lived and worked under conditions worse than those in any other country. Most Russian revolutionaries looked to the peasants, in traditional Russian fashion, to provide them with their political and social base, and they therefore considered the peasant's problems paramount. The Marxists, on the other hand, recruited their following among this new urban proletariat and focused their attention on its problems; but they relied for their tightly organized leadership almost exclusively on a small body of intellectuals and theorists. And despite censorship and repression, Russia experienced during the nineteenth century a substantial literary flowering, as poets, novelists, and playwrights produced works that rank with the greatest of all time.

Nicholas I, 1825-1855

Coming to the throne amid the disorders of the Decembrist Revolution, Nicholas I presided over the investigation of the revolutionaries and prescribed their punishment. He used their confessions to learn about Russian opinion. Reactionary and autocratic, literal-minded and devoted to military engineering, he lived in fear of future revolution. Nicholas I worked hard at the business of the state and firmly believed that the imperial word was sacred. Although he despised all constitutions, he honored the liberal constitution that his elder brother Alexander had granted to the Poles until the Poles themselves revolted in 1831. He believed that his autocratic power had been ordained by God; the autocrat could not, even if he wished, limit his own authority. He was prepared to make improvements, but not to touch the fundamental institution of the autocracy. Though he was uneasy over the dangers inherent in serfdom, he was afraid to reform it in any significant way, because he feared that concessions would stimulate revolution among his peasants. Nicholas leaned heavily on the nobility as a class, referring to its members as "benevolent police chiefs."

So personal was Nicholas's rule, that his own secretariat became the most important organ of Russian government. He enlarged it by creating several sections, often under close personal friends, including a notorious "third section" for political police activity, which spread rapidly and kept Russian political life under surveillance. This enormous expansion of the czar's secretariat did not result in the abolition of any of the older organs of government; consequently, bureaucratic confusion became great, paperwork was multiplied, and much injustice was done through sheer incompetence. And for the first time since 1649, Russian laws were collected under the direction of Speransky, who was returned from exile in Siberia, but the collection was neither a full codification nor a modernization.

Nicholas favored the improvement of technical schools, but he was deeply worried about the possibility that subversive foreign ideas might penetrate into the universities. After the revolutions of 1848 in Europe, his reactionary minister of education abolished the study of philosophy at the University of St. Petersburg because, as he said, the usefulness of the subject had not been proved, and it might even do harm since it led to speculation about the nature of things. Formulated under the three heads of Autocracy, Orthodoxy, and Nationality—unlimited power of the monarch, sanctity of the Russian church, and conformity with the "Russian national character,"—Nicholas's policies resulted in a police state, complete with censorship and terror, yet not nearly as efficient in the delivery of public services as a twentieth-century despotism.

Nicholas put his faith in dynastic friendships, counting on the alliance with Prussia and Austria without realizing that conflicting national interests were more important than friendships between monarchs. Thus he failed to see that Prussia would oppose his efforts to prevent the unification of Germany, and that Austria's interests conflicted with his own in southeastern Europe. It was partly Nicholas's failure to see the weakness of his own system of alliances that led him into the disastrous Crimean War.

Like other Russian rulers before him, Nicholas confidently expected the collapse of the Ottoman Empire. Russia wished to protect the Orthodox subjects of the sultan and also had important economic interests at stake. The great wheat-producing areas in the south were being developed intensively, and Odessa on the Black Sea had become the major commercial port for the grain trade. Nicholas hoped to establish a Russian sphere of influence in the Balkans and even to take possession of Istanbul itself; thus he intervened in the Greek War of the late 1820s, and when the governor of Egypt, Mehmet Ali, revolted against the Ottoman sultan in 1832 and threatened Istanbul, he landed a Russian army and got credit for saving the sultan's capital.

In 1833 the Turks paid the bill for these services. Instead of wishing to annex large sections of the Ottoman Empire, the czar, under the influence of a well-argued memorandum from his foreign minister, Count Karl Nesselrode (1780-1862), now preferred to maintain a weak and friendly Ottoman Empire that would serve as a buffer between Russia and the Hapsburg Empire, which became apprehensive whenever the Russians seemed about to expand into the Balkans. In the Treaty of Unkiar Skelessi with Russia, Nicholas took the Ottoman Empire under his protection, and the Turks agreed to close the Bosporus and Dardanelles to the warships of any nation.

Alarmed at the control the treaty gave to Russia in an area of the world vital to British imperial and commerical interests, British diplomacy was geared to undoing it. The next time Mehmet Ali revolted (in 1839), the British were able to put him down with their fleet before he came near a Russian land force. In 1841 all the other important powers joined Russia in guaranteeing the integrity of Turkey, thus ending the exclusive position obtained by Russia at Unkiar Skelessi.

In the meantime, in 1839 a Turkish reforming minister, Mustafa Rashid (1802-1858), had realized that the great powers would guarantee the Ottoman Empire only if it set about modernizing itself. He reformed the legal code and established, in the *Tanzimat* (or Beneficial Reforms), changes meant to win back popular opinion and satisfy the European powers. These reforms included new tribunals, new commercial and penal codes based on French models, and a new organization of provinces.

For twelve years (1841-1853) Nicholas tried to reach an agreement with Britain on what should be done with Ottoman territory if Turkey collapsed. The British did not believe that such collapse was imminent, and they hoped to prevent Russia from doing anything to hasten it. By 1853 the czar mistakenly believed that Britain was not opposed to Russian domination of Turkey, and Britain mistakenly believed that the czar would not act in Turkey without consulting her.

Russian relations with the Ottoman Turks were further complicated by religion. The Turks were Muslim. The czar saw himself as the protector of the Orthodox Christians, and the Russian Empire in the Caucasus region was filled with diverse nationalities, several of them followers of Islam. While the Georgians and Armenians had been Christians for centuries, the Muslim subjects of the empire had been under pressure throughout the eighteenth century to accept conversion. The Tatars, centered in Kazan, had risen in the Pugachev rebellion in 1773-1775; Nicholas again focused attention on the Tatars when he broke up the University of Kazan, where Western and Eastern culture had met effectively in a center of high repute, and began urging conversions to Orthodoxy. The Tatars of the Crimea and the Turks of Azerbaijan, who viewed themselves as culturally different from the people of Kazan, were strongly influenced by developments in Turkey. Thus the czar had religious as well as political reasons to assert his authority over the sultan's Christian population.

A dispute arose over whether the Roman Catholics, backed by Napoleon III, or the Orthodox clergy, backed by the czar, should have the right to perform certain functions in the Christian Holy Places in Palestine, which was still part of the Ottoman dominions. This dispute was the immediate cause of the Crimean War, since the sultan ruled in favor of the Roman Catholics. But the underlying cause was the czar's wish to reestablish Russian dominance as in the Treaty of Unkiar Skelessi. Nicholas coupled his demand for Russia's exclusive position with the demand that the Turks settle the dispute over the Holy Places amicably and he occupied the Danubian principalities to enforce his demands. After many months of elaborate diplomatic negotiations in which all the powers strove to work out a suitable formula to avoid war, the drift toward war proved too strong to be checked. Turkey declared war on Russia and lost its fleet. Britain, France, and eventually the Italian kingdom of Sardinia then fought the Russians, ostensibly to protect the Turks though in fact to preserve the balance of power.

Famous in myth and legend as the occasion of the charge of the Light Brigade and of pioneer efforts by Florence Nightingale (1820-1910) to save the lives of sick

In 1855 the Allied fleet gathered in Balaclava harbor in the Crimea. From the ordnance wharf there the seige of Sevastopol was supplied. Control of the Black Sea ports proved crucial to the Allied victory.

and wounded soldiers, the Crimean War consisted mostly of a joint French and British siege of the great Russian naval base at Sevastopol in the Crimea. Military operations on both sides were conducted inefficiently, but eventually the Russians were compelled to surrender. In the Peace of Paris of 1856, Russia was forbidden to fortify the Black Sea coast or to maintain a fleet there. Because this made it impossible for the Russians to defend their own shores or to conduct their shipping in security, it became the paramount object of Russian foreign policy to alter the Black Sea clauses of the treaty. Not only had Russia lost the war, but Prussia had not helped her, and Austria had been positively hostile. Nicholas did not live to see the total failure of his policy. He died during the war and was succeeded by his son, Alexander II (1855-1881).

Alexander II and Reform, 1855-1881

By this time a very substantial segment of Russian public opinion favored reforms, in reaction to the long period of repression at home and abroad. Moreover, the economic developments of the early nineteenth century had rendered the system of serfdom less and less profitable. In the south, where land was fertile and crops were produced for sale as well as for use, the serf usually tilled his master's land three days a week, but sometimes more. In the north, where the land was less fertile and could not produce a surplus, the serfs often had a special arrangement with their masters called *quit-rent*. This meant that the serf paid the master annually in cash instead of in work, and usually had to labor at home as a craftsman or go to a nearby town and work as a factory hand or small shopkeeper to raise the money. Perhaps a quarter of the serfs in all Russia paid quit-rent by 1855. Neither in the south nor in the north was serfdom efficient in agriculture. As industries grew, it became clear to factory owners, who experimented with both serf and free labor, that serf labor was not as productive. Yet free labor was scarce, and the growing population needed to be fed. Many estates were mortaged to state credit institutions because of inefficient management and the extravagance of the landlords.

Serfdom had become uneconomic. But this fact was not widely recognized among Russian landowners, who knew only that something had gone wrong somewhere. Most often when a fundamental social system has become antiquated through economic and demographic

Emancipation of the serfs in Russia preceded the freeing of the slaves in the United States by two years. Here Alexander II's manifesto proclaiming emancipation for the serfs is read to the public in the Caucasian province of Georgia. Alexander I had actually freed some serfs earlier, but in parts of the Caucasus many were not freed until after 1861.

change, those with a stake in the old system refuse to examine carefully whether the old premises are still valid; they prefer to believe that an application of old views, from which there may have been some deviation, or the ferreting out of those who have failed to be loyal to those old views will set society back upon the right track. Equally often, others are convinced of the direction change must take and impatient to begin reformulating society. In Russia the nobility wished to keep things as they were and did not as a class feel that emancipation was the answer. Yet the serfs showed increasing unrest. Abolitionist sentiment spread widely among intellectuals. Conscious of the unrest, Alexander II, though personally almost as conservative as his father, determined to embark on reforms, preferring, as he put it, that the abolition of serfdom come from above rather than from below.

Though a cumbersome arrangement in which local commissions made studies and reported their findings to members of the government, an emancipation law was eventually proclaimed early in 1861. A general statute declared that the serfs were now free, laid down the principles of the new administrative organization of the peasantry, and set out the rules for the purchase of land. Local statutes governed the particular procedure to be followed in the different provinces. All peasants, crown and private, were freed, and each peasant household received its homestead and a certain amount of land, usually the amount the peasant family had cultivated for its own use in the past. The land usually became the property of the village commune, or *obshchina*, which had the power to redistribute it periodically among the households. The government bought the land from the proprietors, but the peasants had to redeem it by payments extending over a period of forty-nine years. The proprietor retained only the portion of his estate that had been farmed for his own purposes.

This statute, liberating more than forty million human beings, has been called the greatest single legislative act in history. There can be no doubt that it made an immense moral contribution to peasant self-respect. Still, there were grave difficulties inherent in so sweeping a change in the nature of society. The peasant had to accept the allotment, and since his household became collectively responsible for the taxes and redemption payments, his mobility was not greatly increased. The commune took the place of the proprietor, and differing local conditions caused great difficulty in administering the law. Moreover, most peasants felt that they got too little land and had to pay too much for it. They did not, for example, get significant forest and pasture lands. An agrarian crisis developed, in part as a result of the law's inadequacies.

The end of the landlords' rights of control and police authority on their estates made it necessary to reform local administration. By statute in 1864, provincial and district assemblies, or *zemstvos*, were created. Chosen by an elaborate electoral system that divided the voters into categories by class, the assemblies gave substantial representation to the peasants. The zemstvos dealt with local finances, education, medical care, scientific agriculture, maintenance of the roads, and other economic and social questions. Starting from scratch in many cases, the zemstvos made great advances in primary education and in improving public health. They brought together peasant and proprietor to work out local problems. They served as schools in citizenship for all classes, and led tens of thousands of Russians to hope that this progressive step would be crowned by the creation of a central parliament, or *duma*. But the duma was not granted, partly because after an attempted assassination of the czar in 1866, the regime swung away from reform and toward reaction.

But before this happened, other advances had been made. The populations of the cities were given municipal assemblies, with duties much like those of the zemstvos in the countryside. The antique Russian judicial system and legal procedure, which were riddled with inequities, were significantly modernized. For the first time juries were introduced, cases were argued publicly and orally, all classes were made equal before the law, and the courts were completely reorganized. Censorship was relaxed, the universities were freed from the restraints that Nicholas had imposed upon them, and the often brutal system of military service was reformed and rendered less severe. And in 1856-1859 provision was made for the use of the Finnish language in public business in the Grand Duchy of Finland (of which the czar was the grand duke).

In foreign policy, Alexander II's record was uneven. The Russians successfully repressed the Polish uprising of 1863. They seized the opportunity provided by the Franco-Prussian War of 1870 and simply tore up the Black Sea provisions of the Treaty of Paris, declaring unilaterally that they would no longer be bound by

The complex and hierarchical social structure of imperial Russia was shown in this satirical cartoon of 1900.

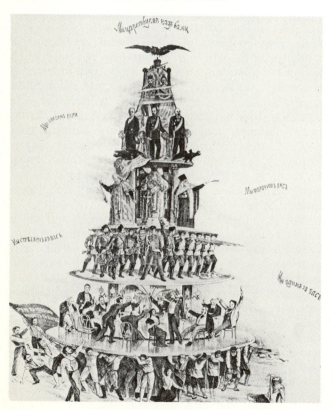

them—an illegal act to which the powers later reluctantly gave their assent. In 1877 the Russians went to war against Turkey once again, now on behalf of the rebellious Balkan Christians of Bosnia, Herzegovina, and Bulgaria. By the Peace of San Stefano, dictated early in 1878 to the defeated Turks, Russia obtained, contrary to her previous agreements, a large, independent Bulgarian state, which Russian policy makers hoped to turn into a useful Balkan satellite. But the powers at the Congress of Berlin later in the same year reversed the judgment of San Stefano. They permitted only about half of the planned Bulgaria to come into existence as an autonomous state, while another portion obtained autonomy separately as East Rumelia and the rest went back to Turkey. Russian public opinion resented the powers' depriving Russia of the gains scored in the Russo-Turkish War. Bitterness ran particularly high among the Pan-Slavs; who hoped to unite all Slavs in some kind of federation.

Meanwhile, encroachments begun under Nicholas I against Chinese territory in the Amur River valley remained undeflected by the Crimean War, and Russian gains were confirmed by the Treaty of Peking in 1860. Russian settlements in the "maritime province" on the Pacific Ocean continued to flourish, and Vladivostok ("Ruler of the East") was founded in 1858 and grew rapidly. In central Asia a series of campaigns conquered the Turkish khanates by 1896 and added much productive land to the Crown. Here, however, the advance toward the northwest frontier of India appeared to threaten British interests and aroused public opinion in Britain against Russia, and after a brutal conquest of the Turkomans in 1881, the Russian Empire was, for the time, complete.

Despite all his accomplishments in a relatively few years, Alexander II became the target for impatient revolutionaries in 1866, and terrorist activity continued throughout the 1870s until assassins finally succeeded in 1881. It is impossible to understand these developments without taking a brief look at Russian intellectual life under Nicholas and Alexander. In the end, the Russian intelligentsia was found wanting in both domestic reform and in foreign policy.

The Idea of an Intelligentsia

Early in Nicholas's reign, Russian professors and students, influenced by German philosophers, were devoting themselves to discussions on art, philosophy, and religion. Russian universities were generally excellent and at the cutting edge of contact with western Europe and the great variety of modernizing ideas associated with the nineteenth century. Many intellectuals outside the universities followed suit. These were the first groups to be known as *intelligentsia*, originally a class limited to Russia, though the concept of the intelligentsia—and even more, of the intellectual, the person who makes a living through mental labor—soon spread to the rest of the European continent. By the 1830s the intelligentsia

A street demonstration in Moscow in 1905.

was beginning to discuss Russia's place in the world, and especially its historical relationship to the West and the proper course for it to follow in the future. Out of its debates arose two important opposing schools of thought: the Westerners and the Slavophiles.

The Westerners stated their case in a document called the *Philosophical Letter*, published in 1836 though written earlier. Its author, Peter Chaadaev (c 1794-1856), lamented the damaging effect of Byzantine Christianity and the Tatar invasions upon Russian development and declared that Russia had made no contribution of importance to the world. He hailed Peter the Great's efforts at Westernizing Russia as a step in the right direction, and he praised the Roman Catholic church as the source of much that was fruitful in the West. Nicholas I had Chaadaev certified as insane and commanded that he be put under house arrest, while the journal in which the letter appeared was banned and its editor sent into exile. Yet despite scorn and censorship, the Westerners would not be silenced. They continued to declare that Russia was a society fundamentally like the West, though far behind it, and that Russia should now catch up.

In contrast, the Slavophiles vigorously argued that Russia had its own national spirit, like the *Volksgeist* that Herder had discovered in the Germans. Russia was, they maintained, essentially different from the West. The Orthodox religion of the Slavs was not legalistic, ra-

tionalistic, and particularistic, like that of the Roman Catholic states of the West, but emotional and organically unified. The Slavophiles attacked Peter the Great for embarking Russia on a false course. The West ought not be imitated, but opposed. The Russian upper classes should turn away from their Europeanized manners and look instead for inspiration to the Russian peasant, who lived in the truly Russian institution of the village commune. Western Europe was urban and bourgeois; Russia was rural and agrarian. Western Europe was materialistic; Russia was deeply spiritual. Like the Westerners, the Slavophiles attached fundamental importance to the national religion and made it the center of their arguments; but they praised where the Westerners damned.

This view, perhaps most ably argued by Ivan Kireevski (1806-1856), also led to a demand for a thorough change in the country, however, and Nicholas viewed it as no less a challenge to his authority. The Slavophiles opposed the tyranny and the bureaucracy of Nicholas I as bitterly as did the Westerners, but they wanted a patriarchal, benevolent monarchy of the kind they argued had existed before Peter the Great, instead of a constitutional regime on the Western pattern. Instead of a central parliament, they looked back to the feudal Muscovite assembly, to the *zemski sobor,* and to other institutions of czardom before Peter. Extremists among them went about the streets dressed in the old boyars' robes that Peter had made illegal. Many intellectuals shifted back and forth between the two camps, and few ever adopted in full the ideas of either side.

Alexander Herzen (1812-1870), for example, began his intellectual career as a Westerner and a devotee of French culture. The illegitimate son of a nobleman, brought up in his father's house, he was charming, engaging, and highly intelligent. Like many Russians, however, he was fascinated with the thought that the structure of Western society might be rotten and doomed. The failure of the Paris revolution of 1848, to which he was an eyewitness, convinced him that this was true, and he became a revolutionary socialist. At the same time, he became convinced that the Westerners must be wrong in assuming that Russia could in a short time pass through the stages of development that the West had taken centuries to experience. So Herzen became a Slavophile. As a revolutionary, he preached the destruction of existing institutions; as a Slavophile, he looked to Russia with its unique institution of the peasant commune, the *mir*, to provide an inspiration for all Europe. Herzen became an influential publicist and issued a Russian-language paper in London, *Kolokol*, which was widely read by Russian intellectuals.

Michael Bakunin (1814-1876) reached roughly the same conclusions as Herzen at roughly the same time. But he was a practical tactician of violence who advocated "anarchism, collectivism, and atheism." He looked forward to a great revolution spreading perhaps from Prague to Moscow and thence to the rest of Europe, followed by a tight dictatorship; beyond this he was entirely vague about the future. Atheism was a fundamental part of his program—not a casual part, as it was to the Marxists. In his long career, Bakunin was to exert from exile abroad a considerable influence on Russian radicals. In 1872 he was expelled from the Marxist-dominated First International. Of the impractical Bakunin, it was said that he would be irreplaceable on the first day of revolution and would be shot on the second.

In the 1860s, and especially after the emancipation of the serfs, the Russian intelligentsia, like intellectuals elsewhere in Europe, reacted against the romanticism of their predecessors. Suspicious of idealism, religion, and metaphysics, they turned to a narrowly utilitarian view of art and society. As one of these young men said, a pair of shoes to him was worth more than all the madonnas of a great Renaissance painter. All art must have a social purpose, and those bonds holding the individual tightly to the traditions of society must be smashed: parental authority, the marriage tie, the tyranny of custom. For these people, the name *nihilist* (a person who believes in nothing) quickly became fashionable. A portrait of a nihilist was drawn by the great novelist Ivan Turgenev (1818-1883) in the figure of Eugen Bazarov in his novel *Fathers and Sons* (1862). Rude and scornful, obstinate and arrogant, Bazarov was accepted as an actual model by intellectual leaders of youth in revolt against established ways of behavior, who generally failed to see that

Turgenev had written with pity of the perennial conflict between generations. Yet nihilism as such was not a political movement.

In the 1860s many of these young Russian intellectuals went to Switzerland, where the Swiss bourgeoisie were scandalized at the men with their hair worn long and the women with their hair cut short, at their loud voices and insolent behavior. Also present in Switzerland were two important Russian revolutionary thinkers, Peter Lavrov and Peter Tkachev. Lavrov (1823-1900) taught his followers that as intellectuals they owed a great debt to the Russian peasant, whose labor had enabled their ancestors to enjoy leisure and had made their own education possible. More gradual in his approach and more realistic in his estimate of the Russian peasant than Bakunin, Lavrov advised the nihilist students to complete their education and then return to Russia and go among the peasants, educating them and spreading among them propaganda for an eventual, not an immediate, revolution of the masses. On the other hand, Tkachev (1844-1886) taught that no revolution could ever be expected from the peasant masses or from student pranksters, but that it would have to come from a tightly controlled, small revolutionary elite, a little knot of conspirators who would seize power. Though not influential at the time, Tkachev would be important in Lenin's later thinking.

Under the influence of these teachers, especially Bakunin and Lavrov, Russian nihilists turned to a new kind of movement, called *populism*. Young men and women of education decided to return to Russia and live among the peasants. When a government decree in 1872 actually summoned them back, they found that a parallel movement had already begun at home. About three thousand young people now took posts as teachers, innkeepers, or store managers in the villages. Some tried to spread revolutionary ideas, others simply to render social service. Their romantic views of the peasantry were soon dispelled, however. Suspicious of their motives, the peasants often betrayed them. The populists became conspicuous and were easily traced by the police, who arrested them. Two mass trials were held in the 1870s, at which the general public for the first time learned about the populist movement. After the trials the populists who remained at large decided that they needed a determined revolutionary organization. With the formation of the Land and Freedom Society in 1876, the childhood of the Russian revolutionary movement was over.

The revolutionaries had been further stimulated by Alexander II's grant of reforms. So great had the discontent become that it is doubtful whether any Russian government could have proceeded fast enough to suit the radicals, who were not satisfied with piecemeal and gradual reform. Stemming from a misreading of John Stuart Mill and from Western Utopian Socialists like Fourier and Robert Owen, Russian socialism was not yet greatly influenced by the gradualism of Marx. It was not urban but rural, not evolutionary but revolutionary, not a mass political party but a conspiracy. Its members lived underground and developed a conspiratorial psychology. They proposed to overthrow a bourgeois society in Russia before such a society ever got started. The movement became more and more radical, and in 1879 those who believed in the use of conspiracy and terror separated from the others and founded a group called the People's Will; the antiterrorists called themselves the Black Partition. The first deeply influenced Lenin's party; the second was an ideological ancestor of Bolshevism.

The members of the People's Will now systematically went on a hunt for Czar Alexander II himself. They shot at him and he crawled on the ground to safety. They mined the track on which his train was traveling, and blew up his baggage train instead. They put dynamite under the dining room of the palace and exploded it, but the czar was late for dinner that night, and eleven servants were killed instead. They rented a shop on one of the streets along which he drove and tunneled under

it. Finally, in March of 1881, they killed him with a handmade grenade, which also blew up the assassin. The supreme irony was that Alexander II had that day signed a document designed to summon a consultative assembly, which was expected to lead to further constitutional reform. His successor, the reactionary Alexander III (1881-1894), refused to confirm the document, and Russia was left to stagnate in renewed repression. The terrorists were rounded up and punished; their organization was smashed.

Of course, not all Russian intellectual life was so directly concerned with the problem of revolution and social reform. Indeed, even some of the clearly revolutionary movements had not started out with the goal of overthrowing the government, and many intellectuals preferred to work within the creative arts. Here too artists tended to be taken up with the kinds of issues that divided the Westerners and the Slavophiles. For example, in music Rimsky-Korsakov had drawn the sounds of folk

---

THE RELATIONSHIP BETWEEN "THE PEOPLE" AND "THE INTELLIGENTSIA"

Intellectuals do not necessarily set themselves apart from the mainstream of the people, though under repression in Russia, literature, philosophy, and the writing of fiction were often the least censored means of political expression. The Western versus Slavophile debate and the romanticism associated with such figures as Bakunin and the nihilists did give Russian thought a marked sensitivity, a feeling of guilt for the misery of the peasant, and a somber and pessimistic tone. Alexander Blok (1880-1921), a leading Russian poet, wrote the following commentary on "The People and the Intelligentsia" in 1909:

The love for the common people that awoke in the Russian intelligentsia during Catherine's reign has never diminished. They keep collecting materials for the study of "folklore"; cram their bookcases with anthologies of Russian songs, epics, legends, incantations, dirges; investigate Russian mythology, wedding and funeral rites; grieve for the people; go to the people; are filled with high hopes; fall into despair; even give up their lives, face execution or starve to death for the people's cause. Possibly they have even come to *understand the people's soul.* But how do they understand it? Isn't understanding *everything* and loving *everything*—even the inimical, even that which requires abjuring what one values most—isn't that the same as understanding *nothing,* loving *nothing?* . . .

Once in a while, on the narrow line where the people and the intelligentsia communicate, great men and important events arise. These men and events always demonstrate . . . that the antagonism is deep and of long standing, that the problem of reconciliation is not an abstract but a practical problem, and that it must be solved in some special way, which we have not found as yet. The men who emerge from the masses and reveal the depths of the people's soul are immediately antipathetic to us, antipathetic because somehow incomprehensible in their innermost being. . . .

What we must do is love Russia, "travel around in Russia." . . . How does one begin to love one's brothers? To love people? The soul wants to love only the beautiful, and poor humanity is so imperfect, there is so little in it that is beautiful! How does one go about it? Begin by thanking God that you are a Russian. For Russians, the way is opening now, and the way is Russia herself. . . .

. . . the sleep [of Russia] is coming to an end, and the quiet is broken by a far-off, gathering rumble, unlike the mixed din of the cities. . . . The rumble, growing so fast that with every passing year we can hear it more distinctly, is nothing else than the "magic ringing" of the troika's bell. What if the troika, around which "the rent air thunders and becomes wind," is *racing straight at us?* When we rush to the people, we are rushing to certain death under the mad troika's hoofs.

From Marc Raeff, ed., *Russian Intellectual History: An Anthology,* trans. Louise and Aylmer Maude, pp. 359-361, 363. Reprinted by permission of Humanities Press, Atlantic Highlands, N.J. 07716, and the Harvester Press, Ltd. The literary references in quotation marks arise from Blok's use of his essay to provide a critique of the work of two major Russian writers, Nikolai Gogol and Maxim Gorky (1868-1936), a social realist who had written *The Lower Depths* in 1902.

Shown here is an artist's reconstruction of the assassination of Czar Alexander II on March 13, 1881. A Nihilist had thrown a bomb at Alexander's carriage, but the emperor was not harmed. He left the carriage to talk to the wounded cossacks, and at that moment a second assassin threw a second bomb under Alexander's feet. Mutilated, Alexander said, "Home to the Palace, to die there," and did so ninety minutes later.

music into his compositions, and in his operatic work Moussorgky had given Russians pride in their national past. Above all, Russian prose writers of the late nineteenth century towered above the cultural landscape. All of Europe read Pushkin, Turgenev, Chekhov, Gogol, or the poet Mikhail Lermontov (1814-1841), who enjoyed a posthumous vogue in France and elsewhere. To non-Russian readers, two writers seemed to best express the romantic sense of despair to be found in the Russian revolutionaries. One, Feodor Dostoevsky, had died in 1881, but his brilliant, disturbed work seemed best to represent the trend of Russian thought: compassion for all humanity, an almost frenzied desire to remake society, coupled with a morbid sense that society was incapable of being remade—a mixture of socialist commitment and religious conviction that was both understandable and exotic to the West. In *Crime and Punishment*, *The Possessed*, and *The Brothers Karamazov*, the last completed in 1880, he had shown himself to be a giant of modern literature who, aware of how the old classes of prereform Russia were breaking up, sought to portray the existential condition of humanity.

The most influential voice of the time in circles outside Russia was that of Count Leo Tolstoy (1828-1910), who had participated in the Crimean War and, in *War and Peace* (1865-1869), had pungently revealed the failings of the Russian nobility during the Napoleonic Wars. In 1876, while writing *Anna Karenina*, a masterpiece of moral tragedy, he underwent what he called a conversion to a belief in Christian love and nonresistance to evil. He shared the romantics' view that the Russian future lay with the peasants, for urban society became inevitably corrupt and violent. He thus became a spokes-

man for pastoral simplicity and Christian anarchism, and he was widely read in Russia and abroad for his advocacy of passive resistance in the face of evil and violence.

The Years of Reaction, 1881-1904

The reign of Alexander III and the first decade of the reign of his son, Nicholas II, formed a quarter-century of consistent policies (1881-1904) of the kind Tolstoy attacked so eloquently (see box). Both czars hated the earlier liberal reforms and were determined that there would be no more. Yet a peasant bank set up under Alexander III made the redemption payments easier for the peasants to pay, and a few pieces of labor legislation, enacted under the influence of Bismarck's example, made working conditions somewhat more tolerable; for example, hours were shortened for women workers. Against these measures were the establishment of a special bank that extended credit to the impoverished nobility, the reinstitution of rigorous censorship, and the institution in the countryside of so-called rural leaders or land captains in place of the elected justices of the peace of Alexander II. Election procedure for the zemstvos and for the city assemblies was made far less democratic. There began a vigorous persecution of the minority nationalities and of Jews, a policy called Russification. The Finns, Poles, Ukrainians, Armenians, and Jews all suffered discrimination, varying from loss of their own institutions, which the Finns had enjoyed, to government-sponsored massacres of Jews. In 1891 20,000 Jews were evicted from Moscow, and most were restricted to the Pale of Settlement, an area roughly identical to Byelorussia and the Ukraine. Official pogroms (organized massacres) were directed against them, especially in Kiev. A quota was applied to Jews, limiting their entry to high schools and universities. One result was massive emigration; over a million Jews, in a population of five million, left, many for America. Another result was that the intellectuals among them joined the various revolutionary movements.

Yet these years were also notable for steady growth. The Donets coal basin was exploited for the first time; the Baku oilfields came into production; steel and cotton output soared. In 1892 Count Sergei Witte (1849-1915) came to the Ministry of Finance, a self-made railroad man who for the next twelve years was responsible for the ever-mounting economic progress. Indeed, in a sense Witte began the true revolution, for as minister of finance until 1903 he undertook to bring Russia out of its backwardness. Witte began the Trans-Siberian Railroad, put Russia on the gold standard, attracted much foreign capital (especially French) for investment, and balanced the budget, in part through a government monopoly of the sale of vodka. The state-owned railroad network doubled in length between 1894 (the year of Nicholas II's accession) and 1904, and the need for rails stimulated the steel industry. Correspondingly, the number of urban workers multiplied, and many strikes were called in protest against wretched working conditions. In 1897 the working day was fixed by the state at eleven hours for adults, and other provisions were adopted to improve and regularize conditions. These laws, however, proved difficult to enforce.

Under the circumstances, many of the young generation of revolutionaries now turned to Marxist "scientific" socialism, embracing the class struggle and predicting the inevitable downfall of capitalism. A small clandestine group of intelligentsia, formed in 1894-1895 at St. Petersburg, proposed to overthrow the regime, working with all opponents of the class system. The members of the group included Lenin, a vigorous young intellectual of upper-middle-class origins, whose brother had been executed for an attempt on the life of Alexander III. In 1898 this group and others formed the Social Democratic party, which in 1900 began to publish its own newspaper. Within party ranks, dissension soon arose over the question of organization. Should the party operate under a strongly centralized directorate, or should each local group of Social Democrats be free to agitate for its own ends? In the tradition of Bakunin and Tkachev, Lenin insisted on a small, tightly knit group of directors at the center. At the party congress of Brussels and London in 1903, the majority voted with him. Lenin's faction thereafter was called by the name *Bolshevik*, meaning majority, as against the *Menshevik*, or minority group, which favored a loose, democratic organization for the party. The Mensheviks held to the ideas of George Plekhanov (1857-1918), who is often called the Father of Russian Marxism, and who had lived abroad since 1882. He felt that Russia would be ripe for socialism only after capitalism and industrialism had progressed sufficiently to fulfill the needs of a Marxist class structure. Both groups remained Social Democrats, or SDs, as they were often called.

Meanwhile, in 1901 the non-Marxist revolutionaries, who were the direct heirs of the People's Will tradition, also organized a political party. They were the Socialist Revolutionaries, or SRs, with their own clandestine newspaper. Whereas the SDs as Marxists were initially interested almost exclusively in the urban workers, the SRs as populists were chiefly interested in the peasantry. Their aim was to redistribute the land, and they continued in their terrorist ways. They assassinated several cabinet ministers between 1902 and 1907, using as their slogan the cry "We don't want reforms. We want reform!"

The moderates and liberals were a third political grouping, not SD or SR in orientation, but mostly veterans of the zemstvos—intellectuals indignant over government repression who favored nothing more radical than compulsory free private education and agrarian reform. The regime stubbornly made no distinction between them and the terrorists and Marxists. Thus the moderates also were forced to organize and to begin their own clandestine paper, favoring a constitution and a national parliament for Russia. In 1905 they took the name of Constitutional Democratic party and were

thereafter usually referred to as *Kadets*, from the Russian initials KD. Faced by this political activity among its radical and moderate opponents, the government only tightened the reins, and by 1904 V.K. von Plehve (1846-1904), the minister of the interior, had adopted the view that a short, victorious war would unite the country.

Trans-Siberian railway construction made it desirable for the Russians to obtain a right-of-way across Chinese territory in Manchuria. The Russians took the initiative in preventing Japan from establishing itself on the Chinese mainland after Japan defeated China in 1895; in exchange, Russia then required the Chinese to allow the building of the new railroad. In 1897 Russia seized Port Arthur, the very port it had earlier kept out of Japanese hands. Further friction with the Japanese took place in Korea, in which both Japan and Russia were interested. Then, after the Boxer Rebellion of 1900 in China, the Russians kept their troops in Manchuria when the other nations withdrew theirs. Although the Russians promised to withdraw their forces by stages, they failed to do so, partly because Russian foreign policy fell into the hands of adventurers, some of whom had a lumber concession in Korea and wanted war with Japan. After it became apparent that the war party had won control in Russia, the Japanese, without warning, attacked units of the Russian fleet anchored at Port Arthur in February 1904. The Russo-Japanese War had begun.

Far from their bases and taken by surprise, the Russians nonetheless stabilized a front on land. But their fleet, which had steamed all the way around Europe and across the Indian Ocean into the Pacific, was decisively defeated by the Japanese in the battle of Tsushima Strait (May 27, 1904). To the Russian people, the war was a mysterious, distant political adventure of which they wanted no part and by which they were now humiliated. Many intellectuals opposed it, and the SRs and SDs openly hoped for a Russian defeat, which they expected would shake the government's position. Alarmed at the growing unrest at home, the Russian government was persuaded by the president of the United States, Theodore Roosevelt, to accept his mediation, which the Japanese also actively wished.

Witte, the go-getting businessman who had opposed the war from the first, was sent to Portsmouth, New Hampshire, as Russian representative. Here he not only secured excellent terms for Russia but also won a favorable verdict from American public opinion, which had previously been strongly pro-Japanese and had thought of Russians as either brutal aristocrats or bomb-throwing revolutionaries. Earlier, Bakunin, who had visited the United States, had argued that the two countries were essentially similar. Though Witte disagreed, he benefited from the perception that both were expansive nations of vast frontiers attempting to stabilize great hinterlands: the United States in Latin America and Russia in eastern Asia. By the Treaty of Portsmouth (1905), Russia recognized the Japanese protectorate over Korea, ceded Port Arthur and the southern half of Sakhalin Island, together with fishing rights in the North

TOLSTOY URGES THE RUSSIAN PEOPLE NOT TO FOLLOW THE PATH OF THE WEST

Writing of the revolution in 1906, Tolstoy said:

The Russian nation now stands, like the hero of the fairy tale, at the parting of two roads, both leading to destruction.

It is impossible for the Russian nation to continue to submit to its government. It is impossible, because having freed themselves from the prestige which has hitherto enveloped the Russian government, and having once understood that most of the miseries suffered by the people are caused by the government, the Russian people cannot cease to be aware of the cause of the calamities they suffer, or cease to free themselves from it.

Besides, the Russian people cannot continue to submit to the government, because now a government—such a government as gives security and tranquility to a nation—no longer exists in reality. . . .

What, then, is the Russian nation to do?

The natural and simple answer, the direct outcome of the facts of the case, is to follow neither this path nor that.

To submit neither to the government which has brought it to its present wretched state; nor, imitating the West, to set up a representative, force-using government such as those which have led those nations to a still worse condition. . . .

For the Russian people to follow the path the Western nations have trodden would be as though a traveler followed a path on which those who went before him had lost their way, and from which the most farseeing of them were already returning. . . .

Whether the Russian nation will accomplish the great task now before it (the task of liberating men from human power substituted for the will of God) or whether, following the path of the Western nations, it will lose its opportunity and leave to some other happier Eastern race the leadership in the great work that lies before humanity, there is no doubt that at the present day all nations are becoming more and more conscious of the possibility of changing this violent, insane, and wicked life for one that shall be free, rational, and good. And what already exists in men's consciousness will inevitably accomplish itself in real life. For the will of God must be, and cannot fail to be, realized. . . .

We of the Eastern nations should be thankful to fate for placing us in a position in which we can benefit by the example of the Western nations: benefit by it not in the sense of imitating it, but in the sense of avoiding their mistakes. . . . Just in this halt in the march along a false path . . . lies the chief and mighty meaning of the revolution now taking place in Russia.

From Marc Raeff, ed., *Russian Intellectual History: An Anthology*, trans. Louise and Aylmer Maude, pp. 335-336, 343, 357. Reprinted by permission of Humanities Press, Atlantic Highlands, N.J. 07716, and the Harvester Press, Ltd.

Pacific, and promised to evacuate Manchuria. Russian prestige as a Far Eastern power was not deeply wounded or permanently impaired by the defeat or by the treaty. Yet the effect of the defeat in Asia was to transfer Russian attention back to Europe, where a world crisis had already begun.

The Revolution of 1905

The most important immediate result of the Russo-Japanese War was its impact on Russian domestic developments. While it was still going on, Plehve was assassinated by an SR bomb in July 1904. His successor was a moderate. The zemstvo liberals, the future Kadets, were encouraged and held banquets throughout Russia to adopt a series of resolutions for presentation to a kind of national congress of zemstvo representatives. Although the congress was not allowed to meet publicly, its program—a constitution, basic civil liberties, class and minority equality, and extension of zemstvo responsibilities—became widely known and approved. The czar issued a statement so vague that all hope for change was dimmed, and took measures to limit free discussion.

Ironically, it was a police agent of the government who struck the fatal spark. He had been planted in the St. Petersburg iron works to combat SD efforts to organize the workers, and to substitute his own union. He organized a parade of workers to demonstrate peacefully and to petition the czar directly for an eight-hour day, a national assembly, civil liberties, the right to strike, and other moderate demands. When the workers tried to deliver the petition, Nicholas left town. Troops fired on the peaceful demonstrators, some of whom were carrying portraits of the czar to demonstrate their loyalty. About a thousand workers were killed on "Bloody Sunday" (January 22, 1905).* The massacre made revolutionaries of the urban workers, and the increasingly desperate moderate opposition joined with the radical opposition.

Amid mounting excitement, the government at first seemed to favor the calling of a zemski sobor—

*All dates in this chapter use the Western, rather than the Russian, calendar.

consultative, not legislative, in the old Russian pattern, rather than the Western parliamentary one, but still a national assembly of sorts. But then even this project was whittled away, as the timid Nicholas II listened to his reactionary advisers. While the czar hesitated, demonstrations occurred throughout the summer of 1905. In October the printers struck. No newspapers appeared, and the printers, with SD aid, formed the first *soviet*, or workers' council. When the railroad workers joined the strike, communications were cut off between Moscow and St. Petersburg. Soviets multiplied and relations between the czar and his subjects collapsed.

The Bolsheviks saw the soviet as an instrument for the pursuit of their program of armed revolt, for the establishment of a provisional government, for the proclamation of a democratic republic, and for the summoning of a constituent assembly. This program differed relatively little from the program of the moderate liberals, who originally had hoped to keep the monarchy and obtain their ends by pressure rather than by violence, until the level of repression forced them to realize that persuasion was a worthless option and that extreme measures were required. At the time, the Bolsheviks, like other Marxists, accepted the view that it was necessary for Russia to pass through a stage of bourgeois democracy before the time for the proletarian revolution could come. They were therefore eager to help along the bourgeois revolution.

Nicholas was faced, as Witte told him, with the alternatves of either imposing a military dictatorship or summoning a truly legislative assembly with veto power over the laws. The czar finally chose the latter course, and in October 1905 he issued a manifesto that promised full civil liberties at once, and a legislative assembly or duma to be elected by universal suffrage. In effect, this October Manifesto ended the autocracy, since the duma was to be superior to the czar in legislation.

Yet the October Manifesto did not meet with universal approval or end the revolution at once. On the right, a government-sponsored party called the Union of the Russian People demonstrated against the manifesto, proclaimed their undying loyalty to the autocrat, and organized their own storm troops, or Black Hundreds, which killed more than 3,000 Jews in the first week after the issuance of the manifesto. The armies that had returned from the Far East remained loyal to the government. Thus the soviets of 1905, unlike those of 1917, included only workers and no soldiers. On the left, the Bolsheviks and SRs made several attempts to launch their violent revolution but failed, and the government was able to arrest their leaders and to put them down after several days of street fighting in Moscow in December 1905. In the center, one group of propertied liberals, pleased with the manifesto, urged that it be used as a rallying point for a moderate program; they were the Octobrists, so called after the month in which the manifesto had been issued. The other moderate group, the Kadets, wished to continue to agitate by legal means for further immediate reforms. But the fires of revolution burned out by early 1906 as Witte used the army to put down any new disturbances.

The Dumas, 1906-1914

Suffrage for the Duma was universal but indirect. Voters chose an electoral college, as in the United States, which then selected the 412 deputies. Although SRs and SDs boycotted the elections out of discontent over the indirect election system, many of them were elected. The Kadets were the strongest party. Contrary to the expectations of the government, the peasant vote was not conservative, but highly liberal. But even before the first Duma had met, Witte was able to reduce its powers. He secured a large French loan, which made the government financially independent of the Duma, and issued a set of "fundamental laws," which the Duma was not to alter. The Crown was to continue to control war and foreign policy; the minister of finance was to control loans and currency. The czar's council of state was transformed by adding members from the clergy, nobility, the zemstvos, the universities, and chambers of commerce. It became a kind of upper house that had equal legislative rights with the Duma and could therefore submit a rival budget, which the government could then adopt in preference to that of the Duma. Finally, the czar could dissolve the Duma at will, provided he set a date for new elections; when it was not in session he could legislate by himself, although his enactments had later to be approved by the Duma.

The first Duma, the "Duma of Popular Indignation," met between May and July 1906. It addressed a list of grievances to the czar, asking for a radical land reform that would give the peasants all state and church land and part of the land still in private hands. The government flatly refused, and after some parliamentary skirmishing the Duma was dissolved. The Kadet membership, maintaining that the dissolution was unconstitutional, crossed the frontier into Finland, and there issued a manifesto urging the Russian people not to pay taxes or report for military service unless the Duma was recalled. Its authors were tried in absentia and declared ineligible for office. Future Dumas were thus deprived of the services of these capable Kadet moderates.

With the dissolution of the first Duma, the highly intelligent and conservative Prince Peter Stolypin (1862-1911) came to power as minister of the interior and stayed in office until 1911, when he was assassinated. Together with Witte, he was the leading statesman of the last period of czarist Russia. Stolypin put through a series of agricultural laws that enabled the peasants to free themselves from the commune. A peasant wishing to detach his property could demand that he be given a single unitary tract. Stolypin called this program the "wager on the strong and sober"; he was encouraging the initiative and enterprise of individual Russian peasants who had the will to operate on their own as successful small farmers. His program accomplished much of what he hoped for; about a quarter of the peasant households of European Russia (almost nine million) emancipated themselves from the communes between 1906 and 1917, when war and revolution kept the process from going further. Lenin and others who hoped for the revolution were deeply suspicious of Stolypin's agrarian reforms; they feared that the peasant grievances would be satisfied, and that no revolution in Russia could succeed without the peasants.

Simultaneously with his agrarian program, Stolypin carried on unremitting war against terrorists and other revolutionaries. He did not hesitate to act unconstitutionally when it suited him. He did everything he could to interfere with elections to the second Duma, but the SRs and SDs were well represented, so that the Duma (March-June 1907) would not work with the government. It was dissolved because it refused to suspend parliamentary immunity of the SD deputies, whom Stolypin wanted to arrest.

After the dissolution of the second Duma, the government illegally altered the election laws, cutting the number of delegates from the peasants and national minorities, and increasing the number from the gentry. By this means the government won a majority, and the third Duma (1907-1912) and the fourth (1912-1917) lived out their constitutional terms of five years apiece. Though unrepresentative and limited in their powers, they were still national assemblies. In their sessions the left-wing members could be heard and could question ministers like any other members. The Dumas improved the conditions of peasant and worker and helped strengthen national defense as World War I drew closer. Their commissions, working with individual ministers, proved extremely useful in increasing the efficiency of government departments. The period of the third Duma, however, was also notable for the continuation of Russification, and the Finns in particular lost their remaining rights (1910).

Under the fourth Duma, the government, with Stolypin dead, tended even more toward reaction. The leftists organized for another revolution, working in unions, cooperatives, evening classes for workers, and a network of other labor organizations. A vast web of police spies challenged them at every turn. Meanwhile, the imperial family drifted into a dangerous situation as the religious and autocratic empress fell under the spell of a half-mad and power-hungry monk from Siberia. This man, Gregory Rasputin (1872-1916), was said to have the mysterious ability, possibly hypnotic, to stop the bleeding of the young heir to the throne, who suffered from hemophilia. Since the empress had enormous influence on her beloved husband, Nicholas II, Rasputin was widely rumored to be the ruler of Russia, much to the horror of loyal supporters of the imperial house, and greatly to the benefit of those who knew how to manipulate rumor. When World War I began, Russia was in the throes of a major crisis precipitated by the government's reactionary policies, the scandal of Rasputin's influence, and the indignation of the loyal Duma.

Thus, by 1914 in Russia, the Hapsburg Empire, and Germany, modern political parties had coalesced around principles. What each party stood for, in France and Italy as well, was determined largely by the peculiar circumstances of the country that gave it birth. Yet certain parallels reached across national boundaries. Although no group in either Germany or Austria was comparable with the Russian populists (Social Revolutionaries), German Liberals, Austrian Liberals, and Russian Kadets or Octobrists had similar views. So had the Pan-Germans and the Pan-Slavs. The Social Democrats were Marxist in all three countries, but becoming less revolutionary in Germany and Austria-Hungary, and more so in Russia.

During this period all five countries experienced economic boom and occasional depression; the Industrial Revolution hit central and eastern Europe late, but with terrific impact. By the start of the twentieth century, Germany had made such advances that its steel production surpassed that of England and was second in the world only to that of the United States. Though far behind Germany both in resources and in technology, Austria-Hungary too was rapidly becoming industrialized. In Russia transport and industry boomed. Yet in these three countries, the landed nobility continued to exercise political influence quite out of proportion to their numbers. Everywhere the existence of a new and underpriviliged class of urban workers stimulated intellectual leaders to form Marxist political groups, to preach the class struggle, and, except in Russia, to strive for immediate improvements in conditions rather than for the violent overthrow of the regime.

Russia emancipated its serfs in 1861, while the most rapidly modernizing nation of the nineteenth century, the United States, freed its slaves two years later in 1863. The United States had stood aloof from the developments on the European continent, avoiding treaty systems, opening and exploiting its own vast frontier regions. But by the end of the century, it too, like the nations of eastern Europe, was moving onto the world scene. Its modernization was extraordinarily rapid, and while its political system bore marked comparisons to that of Britain, and its industrialization to that of Germany, it demonstrated that its path to modernization was in many significant ways unique by the time it became a participant in the great war of 1914-1918.

VI THE UNITED STATES: MODERNIZATION AT TOP SPEED

The United States came to be a great power in isolation. Two sets of statistics dramatically point up the speed of American growth. In 1790 the United States comprised 892,000 square miles, and in 1910, 3,754,000 square miles. Even more important, the population of the United States was 3,929,000 in 1790, and 91,972,000 in 1910—a total greater than that of either of the most powerful European states, Germany and Great Britain, and second only to that of Russia. And, still more important, the combined industrial and agricultural capacities of America by 1910 were greater than those of any other single country.

The Federal Union, 1787-1881

The land that became so powerful in little more than a century was, in the late 1700s, almost empty of cultivation beyond the Alleghenies, save for a relatively few settled areas occupied by Native Americans. Most

observers expected the central parts of the North American continent to fill up eventually with settlers, but few realized how quickly this would occur. Moreover, most commentators felt that the developed and fully occupied continent could not possibly come under one political rule. They expected it to be divided—as the South American continent came to be—into several independent nations on essentially the European model. Some unsympathetic observers did not believe that the thirteen Atlantic seaboard colonies that had gathered together to fight the British could possibly maintain their postwar union. Yet hold together they did. Though the union was

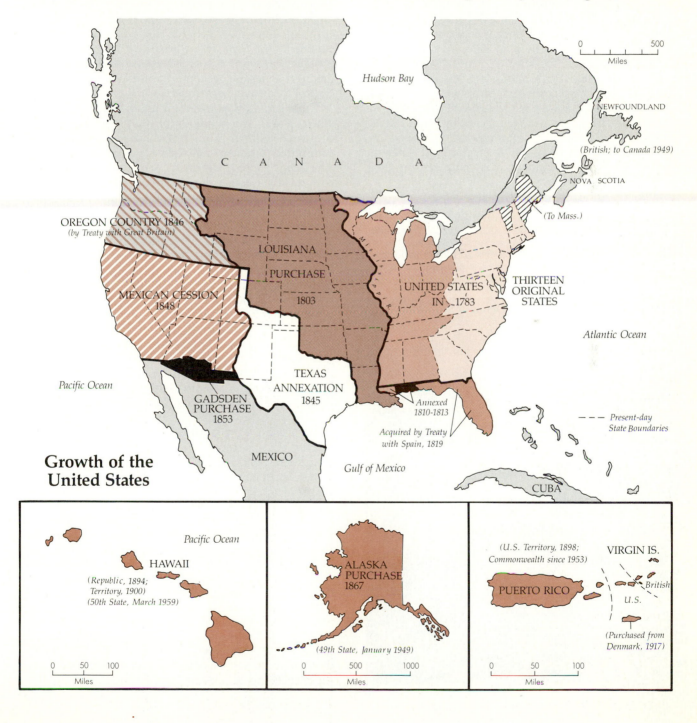

Growth of the United States

OREGON COUNTRY 1846
(by Treaty with Great Britain)

MEXICAN CESSION 1848

LOUISIANA PURCHASE 1803

UNITED STATES IN 1783

THIRTEEN ORIGINAL STATES

GADSDEN PURCHASE 1853

TEXAS ANNEXATION 1845

Annexed 1810-1813

Acquired by Treaty with Spain, 1819

MEXICO

Hudson Bay

CANADA

NEWFOUNDLAND
(British; to Canada 1949)

NOVA SCOTIA

(To Mass.)

Atlantic Ocean

– – – Present-day State Boundaries

Pacific Ocean

Gulf of Mexico

CUBA

HAWAII
(Republic, 1894; Territory, 1900)
(50th State, March 1959)

Pacific Ocean

ALASKA PURCHASE 1867
(49th State, January 1949)

(U.S. Territory, 1898; Commonwealth since 1953)

VIRGIN IS.

PUERTO RICO

British

U.S.

(Purchased from Denmark, 1917)

| 0 | 50 | 100 |
| Miles | | |

| 0 | 500 | 1000 |
| Miles | | |

| 0 | 50 | 100 |
| Miles | | |

often to be sorely tested—once in the bloodiest war Americans ever fought—the process of unification produced a single nation, so that the United States joined Germany and Italy on the path toward nationalism.

Why the United States held together cannot be explained by any one factor. Geography was certainly kinder than in Latin America, for the Appalachians were no real barrier at all; the Rockies were not the barrier the Andes were; and the Mississippi valley, unlike that of the Amazon, helped rather than hindered settlement and communications. The railroad and the telegraph were developed in time to enable goods and ideas to move fast and far enough to hold Americans together. The communications and transportation network already developed by 1860 enabled the North to count on the West in the decisive struggle of the war between the northern and southern states. The sheer size of the new republic after the acquisition of the Mississippi-Missouri valley by purchase from Napoleon in 1803 seemed historically compatible with a loosely held empire of many tongues and peoples, like those of ancient Persia or Rome, but not with a unified nation-state. But modern technology reduced sheer size to manageable proportions. After the first transcontinental railway was completed in 1869,

Perhaps the most famous photograph of Abraham Lincoln was this thoughtful pose by Matthew Brady (c 1823-1896), the most skilled of Civil War photographers. The American Civil War was the first major war to be brought into the homes of civilian populations through extensive photography and the use of battlefield maps in newspapers.

Californians could get to the federal capital at Washington more quickly than New Yorkers had in 1801.

Moreover, the resistance to Britain had helped forge a sense of national patriotism. The colonists, despite contrasts between Puritan New England and Cavalier tidewater South, despite Dutch and German elements in the middle colonies, all recognized one language and one law. Almost all the colonies had frontiers—in the new American sense of the word, not guarded lines with customhouses, as in Europe, but freely accessible areas on their western edges where an expanding population was carving new lands from the wilderness. This frontier population was a powerful force for unity, for it had little attachment to the older, and at times still divisive, colonial centers. The frontier settlers had great confidence in their own "manifest destiny" to keep pushing westward with the blessing and patronage of the new federal government, but with only remote control from that government.

Americans had gained their independence from Britain by a war and a revolution that were rather mild compared with the French Revolution. After the more committed Loyalists had left for Canada or Britain, Americans shared a growing sense of national unity, without any seriously alienated European minorities. At the Philadelphia convention of 1787 and in the campaign for adoption during the next two years, they put together a federal constitution that set up a central government with the ability to tax individuals (not just to ask for contributions from constituent states), to control armed forces, and to conduct all foreign relations. The new constitution, in short, set up a sovereign federal nation, not a mere league of sovereign states. On the whole, this result was achieved under conservative leaders, anxious to preserve their economic and social privileges and afraid that democracy in separate, quasi-independent states might go too far. Furthermore, the threat of continued British control of its remaining North American provinces, especially Canada, helped to limit domestic divisions. The United States developed in its critical earliest years an awareness of the need for union against a possble foreign danger.

Thus the new republic entered the world war of the Napoleonic period in 1812. Neither the French nor the British had been observing the freedom of commerce that the United States claimed as the right of a neutral, but the British—who were by 1812 masters of the sea— seemed to the Americans to be infringing upon neutral rights more seriously than the French were. Moreover, American expansionists saw a possible prize in winning Canada from England, but no comparable prize to be won from France. An American attempt to invade Canada failed, not only from ineptness but from the determined resistance of the Canadians. In isolated combat on the seas, the United States won victories that made up for its failures on land and helped bolster national pride. On the whole, the war was a stalemate, a footnote to the Napoleonic Wars, and the United States experienced no important gains or losses.

A generation later, however, the United States acquired an enormous block of territory, from Texas to California, at the expense of Mexico. This came in part as a result of annexing the Republic of Texas (1845), which had been settled by pioneers from the southern states and had broken away from Mexico in 1836. President James K. Polk (1795-1849) also resolved to acquire Mexican territories west of Texas by purchase and, when negotiations collapsed, launched the Mexican War of 1846-1848, which ended with Mexico's cession of New Mexico and California to the United States in the Treaty of Guadalupe Hidalgo.

Civil War and Reconstruction, 1861-1877

The greatest test of the Federal Union was the war that broke out in 1861 after long years of sectional strife within the union between North and South. The Civil War was really an abortive nationalist revolution, the attempt of the Confederate (Southern) states to set up a separate sovereignty, as the southern Democrats lost political control at the national level. The South was predominantly agricultural, with a society based largely on plantation slavery and on cotton and tobacco, much of which was exported abroad. The North was increasingly industrial, with a society based largely on free labor and independent farm owners, whose business owners preferred protective tariffs, which hurt the South in its competition for markets.

To the conflict of economic interest was added a conflict of ideals, of ways of life. The fires of conflict were fanned by the question of slavery, which seemed immoral to many in the North, and which seemed the order of nature to many in the South. They were fanned still further by writers and preachers on both sides, the northerners thinking of themselves as heirs of the Puritans, the southerners as heirs of the Cavaliers. With the election of Abraham Lincoln (1809-1865) in 1860, the South anticipated an attack on the institution of slavery, which was increasingly defended on ideological grounds that made compromise—always possible when issues are essentially economic—difficult. Upon the secession of South Carolina and its sister states in March of 1861, antagonism reached the point of open war.

In retrospect, the victory of the North has an air of inevitability, especially since by 1861 the middle and upper Mississippi valley was bound firmly to the North by economic and cultural ties. The North was greatly superior in population—especially since the South did not dare use slaves as soldiers—and in industrial resources. Yet aided by an able corps of officers, by the advantages in morale that determined underdogs have, and by disastrous northern overconfidence, the South won initial victories that gave its cause great momentum. But the North thwarted the efforts of Confederate diplomats to secure British intervention and was able to improvise a naval force that gradually established a blockade, shutting off the South from importation of necessary war materials. In the long run, northern determination, manpower, and materials wore the southern armies down by the spring of 1865, and the last Confederate forces capitulated in May. In the previous month, President Lincoln was assassinated.

The road to reunion after 1865 was not easy, and in the first years of the Reconstruction period after the war

General Ulysses S. Grant (1822-1885) ultimately led the North to victory. Willing to accept appalling losses, Grant waged the "first modern war," defeating the Southern commander, Robert E. Lee (1807-1870). Both were graduates of West Point. Grant, born in Ohio, was moved from the Western front into direct confrontation with Lee after his victory at Vicksburg. Lee, born in Virginia, had fought for the United States in the war with Mexico. He was not sympathetic to the Southern secession movement. Offered a field command in the United States Army, Lee resigned his commission when he learned of Virginia's secession and was made commander of Virginia's forces three days later.

During the Civil War free Black troops were brought into action by the North, but the South, fearing a slave insurrection, could make little use of this substantial portion of its population.

it appeared to be almost impossible. With Lincoln's death, a moderate who might have tempered the vengefulness of the northern radicals was lost. The South was occupied by northern soldiers, the former slaves were enfranchised, and a period of political instability, which included impeachment of Lincoln's successor, followed. Yet the Civil War did not end as such wars have often ended, in wholesale reprisals, executions, and exile. There were very few political refugees of the kind that often emerge from defeated causes; the soldiers of the South returned to devastated homes and lost fortunes, but under amnesty. Gradually the crusading fervor of the North subsided over matters of racial freedom, as a generally conservative view prevailed in both major postwar political parties. Conservative, business-conscious northerners were anxious to get back to normal conditions and quite prepared to compromise with like-minded southerners at the expense of racial equality and other democratic ideals. By 1877 the southerners had regained control over their states through a political bargain. Slavery, abolished by Lincoln's proclamation of 1863, was never restored, but blacks were in effect disenfranchised, and "white supremacy" was restored. The racial question assumed complex class and caste forms familiar to the twentieth century, and an era of growing racism followed.

The end of Reconstruction left the Democratic party in control of what came to be called the "solid South."

This was a natural development, for the Republican party had guided the North during the war and had tried to carry through Reconstruction. This situation worked to strengthen the American two-party system, since with so secure a voting block for the Democrats, the Republicans were forced either to make compromises among themselves to preserve their own party unity or lose power; and the northern Democrats were forced to make compromises with their southern wing. Third-party movements, whether radical or reactionary, did not develop as in Europe. Politically minded groups that could offer attractive programs soon found their ideas absorbed by the two main parties. This assured continued political stability, since both parties held to generally centrist or moderate positions, in European terms.

Free Enterprise and Government Regulation, 1865-1917

In 1865 the American economy was still in some respects "colonial"; that is, it produced mainly foods and other raw materials, to be exchanged abroad for manufactured goods. In financial terms, it was dependent on foreign money markets, chiefly London. But in the northern and midwestern states the Industrial Revolution had already accelerated. By 1914 the United States was transformed into a great industrial nation, with its agriculture mechanized to a high degree, and with its financial resources so great that after World War I New York was partly to replace London as a world financial center. This transformation could not have taken place at the rate it did without the existence of an abundant work force, especially after massive waves of new emigration, largely from eastern and southern Europe in the 1890s. Also, the traditions of individual initiative and freedom of enterprise—a product of the "frontier," especially of the frontier as a state of mind—were a basis for a national sense of aggressive and buoyant optimism as the indigenous population was systematically pushed aside in the name of progress. Europe played a significant role in American economic growth by furnishing investment capital and, above all, by sending forth a steady flow of emigrants.

This great expansion in national wealth was achieved in a climate of opinion that overwhelmingly supported the view that the federal government should not interfere directly with business enterprise beyond maintaining public order, enforcing contracts, exercising control over the coinage of money, and, for much of this time, maintaining a protective tariff. Nor were state and local governments supposed to go beyond such limits, though at times some did, since the decentralized nature of the American federation left room for a good bit of experimenting at the state level. This laissez-faire view, generally that of the classical economists, maintained itself more firmly in the twentieth century in the United States than in the other parts of the Western world. It was reinforced by the Fourteenth Amendment to the Constitution, passed in 1866 and designed to protect the freed slaves in the South from state action to deprive them of civil rights. The Amendment contained a "due process" clause: "nor shall any state deprive any person of life, liberty, or property without due process of law." In the era of free enterprise that followed the Civil War, the Supreme Court of the United States interpreted the clause to mean that state governments should not deprive business owners—including corporations as "persons"—of property by regulating wages, prices, conditions of labor, and the like.

Many of the same forces that had produced the Factory Acts in Britain gradually brought to the United States minimum-wage acts, limitation of child labor and women's labor, sanitary regulation, control of hours of labor, and workmen's compensation. Characteristically, and despite the Fourteenth Amendment, these measures were first achieved at the state rather than at the national level, and they varied greatly in the different states. Wisconsin early established a reputation for advanced social legislation, and many of the older northeastern states played an important part in the movement. By the early twentieth century public opinion was ready for increased participation by the national government in the regulation of economic life.

Theodore Roosevelt (1858-1919), Republican president from 1901 to 1909, promised to give labor a "square deal" and to proceed vigorously with *trustbusting*— attacks on great trusts or combinations that had come to

monopolize important sectors of the American economy. Although Roosevelt did not fulfill all his promises, his administration did attack the trusts in railroads and tobacco and did press regulation of great corporations by the federal government. Federal prosecution of John D. Rockefeller's (1839-1937) Standard Oil Company resulted in 1911 in a Supreme court decision dissolving the great holding company. Yet the work of the radicals of 1900 and of the "muckrakers"—who wrote exposés of questionable business practices for popular magazines—was clearly not in vain. American big business in the later twentieth century was bigger than it had been in the day of Theodore Roosevelt, but it was also more aware of its responsibilities to public opinion—or at least, afraid of what might happen if it followed the advice of one of the great nineteenth-century "robber barons," Cornelius Vanderbilt (1843-1899), "The public be damned!"

During 1913-1917, in the first administration of Woodrow Wilson (1856-1929), a Democrat, the process of regulation gained momentum. The Federal Reserve Act of 1913, for example, gave federal officials more control over banking, credit, and currency. Meantime, the Sixteenth Amendment, legalizing a progressive income tax, and the Seventeenth, providing for direct election of senators rather than their appointment by state governments, made the federal republic more democratic in practice. Approval of such measures was not, of course, unanimous, since Americans differed loudly and widely about almost everything, from the use of the environment to organized sports. To outsiders, and to many native critics, American life in the decades between the Civil War and 1917 often seemed one great brawl, a Darwinian struggle for wealth and power. Yet this apparently chaotic society achieved extraordinary material growth and political stability that required the tacit assent of millions of men and women holding to a generally common goal of modernization.

Despite general American distrust of "government"—at times real and at times mythical—government in the United States came to play a larger and larger part in the lives of all. Although this was also true of local and state government, it was especially so for the federal government. The gradually increasing importance of the federal government and the gradually decreasing initiative of state governments were as clear in the period 1789-1917 as was the material growth and increased nationalism of the United States.

The United States Becomes a World Power, 1898-1914

Quite as clear, though still the subject of complex debate among Americans, was the emergence of the United States as a great international power. The United States was never literally "isolated." From the very beginning it had a department of state and a traditional apparatus of ministers, consuls, and, later, ambassadors. The United States was involved in the world war of

240

The new "navalism," which already had assertive advocates in Britain and Germany, derived many of its doctrines from the writings of an American officer, Captain Alfred T. Mahan (1840-1914). Mahan's book *The Influence of Sea Power upon History* (1890), and his later works assigned navies a place of preeminent importance in determining power status and found an influential audience at home and abroad, especially in Germany, Britain, and Japan.

Whether they will or no, Americans must now begin to look outward. The growing production of the country demands it. An increasing volume of public sentiment demands it. The position of the United States, between the two Old Worlds and the two great oceans, makes the same claim, which will soon be strengthened by the creation of the new link joining the Atlantic and Pacific. The tendency will be maintained and increased by the growth of the European colonies in the Pacific, by the advancing civilization of Japan, and by the rapid peopling of our Pacific States with men who have all the aggressive spirit of the advanced line of national progress. Nowhere does a vigorous foreign policy find more favor than among the people west of the Rocky Mountains.

It has been said that, in our present state of unpreparedness, a trans-isthmian canal will be a military disaster to the United States, and especially to the Pacific coast. When the canal is finished the Atlantic seaboard will be neither more nor less exposed than it now is; it will merely share with the country at large the increased danger of foreign complications with inadequate means to meet them. The danger of the Pacific coast will be greater by so much as the way between it and Europe is shortened through a passage which the stronger maritime power can control. The danger lies not merely in the greater facility for dispatching a hostile squadron from Europe, but also in the fact that a more powerful fleet than formerly can be maintained on that coast by a European power, because it can be so much more promptly called home in case of need. The greatest weakness of the Pacific ports, however, if wisely met by our government, will go far to insure our naval superiority there. The two chief centres, San Francisco and Puget Sound, owing to the width and the great depth of the entrances, cannot be effectively protected by torpedoes; and consequently, as fleets can always pass batteries through an unobstructed channel, they cannot obtain perfect security by means of fortifications only. Valuable as such works will be to them, they must be further garrisoned by coast-defense ships, whose part in repelling an enemy will be coördinated with that of the batteries. The sphere of action of such ships should not be permitted to extend far beyond the port to which they are allotted, and on whose defense they form an essential part; but within that sweep they will always be a powerful reinforcement to the seagoing navy when the strategic conditions of a war cause hostilities to center around their port. By sacrificing power to go long distances, the coast-defense ship gains proportionate weight of armor and guns; that is, of defensive and offensive strength. It therefore adds an element of unique value to the fleet with which it for a time acts. No foreign states, except Great Britain, have ports so near our Pacific coast as to bring it within the radius of action of their coast-defense ships; . . . It is upon our Atlantic seaboard that the mistress of Halifax, of Bermuda, and of Jamaica will now defend Vancouver and the Canadian Pacific. In the present state of our seaboard defense she can do so absolutely. What is all Canada compared with our exposed great cities? Even were the coast fortified, she could still do so, if our navy be no stronger than is as yet designed. What harm can we do Canada proportionate to the injury we should suffer by the interruption of our coasting trade, and by a blockade of Boston, New York, the Delaware, and the Chesapeake? Such a blockade Great Britain certainly could make technically efficient, under the somewhat loose definitions of international law. Neutrals would accept it as such.

The military needs of the Pacific States, as well as their supreme importance to the whole country, are yet a matter of the future, but of a future so near that provision should immediately begin.

A.T. Mahan, *The Atlantic Monthly*, LXVI (December, 1890), 22-24.

the Napoleonic era, and by the Monroe Doctrine of the 1820s took the firm position that European powers were not to extend further their existing territories in the Western hemisphere. This was an active expression of American claims to a far wider sphere of influence than the continental United States. Although Americans took no direct part in the nineteenth-century balance-of-power politics in Europe, they showed an increasing concern with a balance of power in the Far East, where they had long traded and wanted an "open door" to commerce. As a result of a brief war in 1898 with Spain that broke out in Cuba, always a strategic and economic concern of the United States because of its proximity to Florida, Americans annexed the Philippine Islands and Puerto Rico from Spain. The newly "independent" Cuba became a veiled American protectorate, and in 1900 Hawaii became a territory of the United States (see Chapter 22). All this seemed to Europeans and Latin Americans, and to North Americans, to constitute an American empire.

Theodore Roosevelt, who owed his rapid political rise partly to his military exploits in the Spanish-American War, was a vigorous expansionist. He pressed the building of the Panama Canal, which opened in 1914, stretched the Monroe Doctrine to justify American military intervention in Latin American republics, upheld the Far Eastern interests of the United States, and advocated a larger navy. Roosevelt wanted to see his country play an active part in world affairs, as exemplified by his arbitrating the peace settlement between Russia and Japan in 1905.

After over a century of expanding wealth and trade, the United States had come to take full part in international commercial relations. Except when the federal government was blockading the Confederacy, it had stood firmly for rights to trade, even though there was a war on somewhere—that is for the rights of neutrals. This fact alone might have brought the United States into the world war of 1914-1918, as it had brought it previously into the world war of 1792-1815. But in 1917 America was, as it had not been in 1812, an active participant in the world state system, even though it had followed the admonition of George Washington's farewell address and had avoided any formal, permanent entangling alliances. The great themes of modern European history—industrialization, modernization, national unity and nationalism, imperialism, intellectual ferment—were all so evident that Americans could not question that they were part of the broad stream of history.

SUMMARY

During the nineteenth century a sense of *patrie,* or commonality, brought the French together. A coup d'état engineered by Louis Napoleon in 1851 ended the Second Republic and gave birth to the Second Empire. Napoleon III promised to reform but did little to improve the standard of living of the working class. Population and industrial growth was smaller in France than in many other western European nations. The Franco-Prussian War ended the Second Empire.

The Third Republic was born amid defeat and civil strife. Antagonism between republicans and monarchists, and scandals such as the Dreyfus affair, mirrored serious rifts in French society.

Garibaldi, Victor Emmanuel, and Cavour led Italy to union. By 1870, only Trent and Trieste remained as part of *Italia Irredenta.* Public opinion in Italy favored the new kingdom, but deep divisions between Catholics and anticlericals and between north and south would pose difficulties for the new government. In the late 1800s Italy industrialized, but industrialization was unevenly distributed. At the same time, efforts at imperialist expansion went badly.

Bismarck, architect of the German state, was a ruthless genius completely loyal to the Prussian crown. He used unorthodox policies to secure his own ends. Between 1864 and 1870 Prussia acquired Schleswig-Holstein, defeated Austria in a brief war, and won a stunning victory over France in the Franco-Prussian War. As a result of this war, France was forced to cede Alsace-Lorraine and pay a massive indemnity.

As chancellor of the German Empire from 1871-1890, Bismarck created a uniform monetary, legal, and judicial system and helped strengthen German militarism. In the late 1880s he introduced accident, health, and later old-age insurance for workers. When William II succeeded to the throne in 1890, he forced Bismarck to resign. By the early 1900s Germany was a strong modern industrial nation with an efficient agricultural system.

The Hapsburg Empire, ruled from 1848 to 1916 by Francis Joseph, consisted of many national minorities. The dual monarchy of Austria-Hungary was created in 1867 to appease nationalist aims of Magyars. However, the formula left the many other national minorities in the empire dissatisfied.

Between 1825 and 1914 modernization proceeded slowly in Russia. Under Nicholas I (1825-1855), Russia became involved in the Crimean War, a balance-of-power conflict over the weakening Ottoman Empire.

Czar Alexander II embarked on reforms, abolishing serfdom in 1861 and reforming the legal and judicial system. His assassination in 1881 led his successors to return to a policy of repression. Intellectual ferment grew into protest movements. Political activity heightened in the early 1900s when Lenin founded the Bolshevik party.

Defeat in the Russo-Japanese War in 1905 sparked an uprising that forced Nicholas II to summon a Duma, or legislative assembly. But the dumas that met between 1906 and 1914 had little power, although czarist ministers such as Stolypin did manage to introduce some reform.

In the nineteenth century the United States expanded, building communication and transportation networks across the continent. By 1914 the United States was an industrial nation with a large labor pool provided by immigrants from Europe. As a result of its war with Spain, the United States became a major world power with territories in the Caribbean and the Pacific.

MODERN EMPIRES AND IMPERIALISM

In the nineteenth century one Western democracy led all others—Britain. It became the first modern nation; by the 1880s, however, its preeminence was slipping away as other nations, especially Germany and the United States, challenged British leadership. In time Britain would become the first of the great industrial nations to pass into a postindustrial phase of economic decline. At its height Britain possessed the greatest empire the world had ever seen. Historians still debate whether this empire was a symbol of Britain's power or a cause of Britain's decline, though all recognize that nineteenth-century imperialism was expressed most typically (and was most extensively disruptive of traditional Asian and African cultures) in the British rather than in the French and other colonial empires. Nineteenth-century Britain grew into a Greater Britain, and its domestic history was inextricably bound up in imperial history, as foreign affairs were yoked to economic and industrial developments. In the age of nationalism and imperialism, it was Britain that most often laid the political foundations for the European balance of power and maintained the concert of Europe—sometimes by war, sometimes by treaty, often by holding aloof from any commitment to either side in a threatened conflict. No one doubted this supremacy from 1815 to 1850; clearly, Britain had challengers in the last half of the century, and equally clearly, by 1914 Britain was no longer preeminent.

Both economic and political factors account for Britain's leadership in the nineteenth century. Britain had become the first industrial nation, the first to experience the Industrial Revolution, with its attendant changes in demography, society, and politics. Thus for a time Britain was in a position to control the spread of the Industrial Revolution. In turn, this meant that Britain was the financial capital of the world, a nation of shopkeepers who created the world's clearinghouse. Less shaken by the depression of 1873 than were France or Germany, Britain grew in financial strength. In 1900 this first modernized state enjoyed a favorable balance of trade of £100 million. Such financial strength meant that Britain was in a better position to use free trade, fair trade (which generally meant free trade within the empire and a degree of protection against competitors outside the empire), and protective tariffs, the last after 1880, as economic conditions appeared to demand them.

But British dominance was based on more than economic factors, which were the product of other conditions, just as they also fed and made possible those conditions. The British parliamentary system became for a time the model for representative government, so that for much of the world—and overwhelmingly for the British Empire—political maturity was taken to mean achieving independence or stability through par-liamentary government on British lines. The growth of constitutional government in western Europe, in Canada, Australia, and New Zealand, and in some measure in Argentina and Brazil, owed a heavy debt to British political thought and practice.

Britain also enjoyed enormous prestige, not alone for its economic leadership and democratic attainments (both flawed, though not so perceived by a nation that became rather more smug than innovative, until shocked into new formulations in the 1930s and after), but also for its influence in statecraft. British diplomacy was the protector of European stability, the Pax Britannica the symbol of a nation that produced numerous statesmen of world stature. Britain succeeded in forcing the other great powers into a position by which they could gain access to the world only by sea—a sea dominated by the British navy. Only Russia and the United States remained outside Britain's circle of maritime dominance, and since both were preoccupied throughout much of the century, that hardly mattered. British statecraft was thus translated into real power and genuine influence that endured into the 1890s.

This influence was reinforced by a very real humanitarian impulse. At its best this impulse led to the abolition of the slave trade (1807), to the abolition of slavery throughout the British Empire (1833), to an extensive network of missionary activity abroad, and to the founding of the world's first systematic private

British industrial output as a percentage of the world total, 1780-1958. E.J. Hobsbawm, *Industry and Empire,* (Pelican Economic History of Britain: 3, 1969), p. 342. Copyright © E.J. Hobsbawm, 1968, 1969. Reprinted by permission of Penguin Books, Ltd.

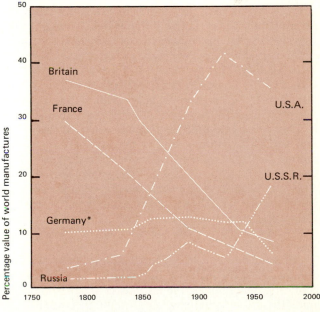

*1958: German Federal Republic only

THE MOTIVES OF ONE IMPERIALIST

The amalgam of humanitarianism, purpose, drive, sacrifice, arrogance, self-righteousness, superiority, Darwinism, progressivism, and muscular Christianity is well captured in this extract from a Visiting Commissioner's report after having traveled up-river in the British colony of The Gambia, on the coast of West Africa, in 1897:

There are higher purposes in life than merely living. Perhaps I shall die here, but I shall die a better man for having been here. These people are degraded, ignorant, swept by disease; how low, how low they stand. Yet, they *stand*. I can help move them that inch higher, give them that direction they need, tell them of that truth that, once grasped, lived, proved, may one day make them right-thinking Englishmen, men with souls as white as any other, men I will have been proud to have known. Lift them, lift them! If I pass through the Gate before them, one day they too will pass through it, and I, there before them, will welcome them as mine.

Visiting Commissioner's Report, "The Gambia" (The Gambian Archives, Banjul), quoted in part in Robin W. Winks, ed., *The Age of Imperialism* (Englewood Cliffs, N.J.: Prentice-Hall, Inc., 1969), p. 76.

philanthropic societies. At its worst this impulse led to direct intervention in the affairs of African and Asian states, allegedly for the good of their people to bring them the fruits of modernization—improved transportation, communication, sanitation, and education—which, however, were often quite destructive, and which could easily serve the cynical manipulation of power. The idea that Britain knew best what "native" people needed, that Britain should engage in social engineering to "improve the lot of the savages," or that Africans or Asians were civilized only if they dressed and spoke as the English did—such ideas fed on and would feed racism.

In part, British preeminence rested on the simple British conviction of their own superiority. It also rested on the presence of vast numbers of Britons around the world. The nineteenth century saw a mass movement of people from Europe, largely to the New World, which was greater than the world had ever known. While much of this movement, especially after 1880, was from southern and eastern Europe, more of it was from the British isles. In 1750 Europe held one-fifth of the world's population; in 1900 it held one-quarter, although its population grew from 140 million to 401 million. Britain's share of Europe's population virtually doubled in this time, and yet Britain saw a greater exodus than any other nation. Nearly 23 million emigrants left Europe between 1850 and 1900; 10 million of these were from Britain. Thus the English language, English, Scots, Welsh, and Irish culture, and British ideas broadly were spread throughout the world in the nineteenth century, and entire new nations were founded on the basis of this great migration.

All these factors were reflected in, contributed to, and supported by the British Empire. Emigrants went to it, founding new nations; the navy used its ports to dominate the seas; humanitarians sought to demonstrate within it the values of British, Christian society. Trade,

finance, and technology migrated to an empire that was both formal and informal (in areas never annexed, though in fact dominated by the British economy, such as Argentine, Uruguay, parts of China, or the cattle kingdom of the United States). Each cause of preeminence fed another; as Britain transformed itself, it transformed other societies, until World War I—a war which it won, and because of winning it, lost the world.

I BRITAIN, THE FIRST MODERN NATION, 1815-1914

In the years immediately after Waterloo, Britain went through an intense postwar economic crisis. Unsold goods accumulated, and the working classes experienced widespread unemployment and misery. Popular suffering increased as a result of the Corn Law of 1815, which was the latest in a series of protective tariffs on grain and forbade the importation of cheap foreign grain until the price of the home-grown commodity rose to a specified level. This assured the profits of the English grain farmer and probably raised the cost of bread for the average English family. Although trade unions were outlawed (see Chapter 21), workers nonetheless asserted themselves in strikes and in popular agitation that helped prepare for the parliamentary Reform Bill of 1832. By the 1820s economic conditions were improving, and Britain embarked on the process of reform that was to make it a modern democratic state.

Slow Democratization, to 1885

The process of democratization is most clearly marked in the milestones of parliamentary reform that transformed the government of Britain from an oligarchy into a political democracy. Britain emerged from the

Napoleonic wars with an executive composed of a prime minister and his cabinet of ministers who were wholly under the control of Parliament. The Crown had become largely decorative. On that decorative post, held for much of the century (1837-1901) by Queen Victoria, were centered the patriotic emotions of loyal British subjects. Victoria never thought of herself as a mere figurehead; she was the most popular British monarch since the days of the Tudors, and her name would be used to describe an entire era, the Victorian age, and the taste and sensibilities that were associated with the dominant values of that age. Queen Victoria was also a dynastic focus, as her many children and grandchildren married into the royal families of the Continent.

Still, real power lay with Parliament, which in the early nineteenth century was very far from being a broadly representative body. The House of Lords, which had equal power with the lower house except over money bills, was composed of the small privileged class of peers born to their seats, with the addition of a relatively few new peers created by the Crown from time to time. The House of Commons, its members unpaid (thus effectively barring those whose first need was to earn a living), was recruited from the gentry, the professional classes, and very successful businessmen, with a sprinkling of sons of peers. It was chosen by less than one-sixth of the adult male population, voting without a secret ballot. The working classes in both town and country and the run of moderately prosperous middle-class people were generally excluded from the franchise, although some few boroughs had a much broader electorate. None included women. Moreover, the largely rural south, once the most populous area of the kingdom, now had more representatives than it warranted, including a large contingent from "rotten boroughs"—towns of very small population or, as with the notorious Old Sarum, once a lively medieval town, with no population at all. Members of Parliament were not required to come from the area of their constituents. The teeming new industrial centers of the north, such as Manchester, Liverpool, and Sheffield, were underrepresented.

Proposals to modernize the structure of representation had come close to being adopted in the late eighteenth century, but the wars with revolutionary and Napoleonic France postponed reform. In wartime and in the immediate postwar years, even moderate reformers were denounced as Jacobins. Several disorders had frightened the upper classes: Luddite (anti-industrial) burnings and an agricultural uprising, followed by a riotous assembly near London in 1816; an abortive uprising in Derbyshire, and a planned, though suppressed, mass march from Manchester to London in 1811; and then, in August 1819, an attack by constables, a troop of hussars, and a detachment of yeomanry in an attempt to arrest a speaker as he addressed a peaceful assemblage of nearly 60,000 people who carried banners advocating parliamentary reform, at St. Peter's Field near Manchester. Eleven persons died and over 400 were wounded in what was called, with a bitter echo of

This regal portrait of Queen Victoria presiding over the House of Lords was copied from the work of Benjamin Constant (1845-1902). It shows her in old age, caught in the radiance of majesty—the epitome of the mystique that still attached to the monarchy.

Waterloo, the Peterloo massacre. Entrenched positions hardened and class antagonisms became more evident. Postwar repression reached its height with Parliament's approval of six "gag acts," which after December 1819 curtailed freedom of speech, prohibited training in the use of firearms, and imposed a stamp tax on political literature.

The Whig party increasingly moved toward conciliation to avert the dangers of revolution. In this campaign the middle class appealed to the lower classes by using the language of popular rights and even of universal male suffrage. Many popular leaders talked as if the Reform Bill would bring immediate political democracy to England. Yet much of the preparation for reform was actually the work not of liberal agitators, but of conservatives. Guided by George Canning and Sir Robert Peel (1788-1850), the Tory governments of the 1820s lifted the restrictions on civil rights imposed during the long war with France and the postwar crisis. They permitted laborers to organize into unions, though not to strike;

they reformed the antiquated criminal code, so that, for example, the theft of a sheep no longer carried with it a death penalty; and they began the reduction in protective tariffs (though not as yet affecting the Corn Laws) that was to lead to free trade. The seventeenth-century Test Act, which, though not observed, legally excluded Protestant dissenters from public life, was repealed. Civil restrictions for Roman Catholics now came under renewed fire, and Wellington and Peel pressed legislation through Parliament in 1829 providing for Catholic emancipation. However, it was a Tory government that fulfilled this Whig pledge, splitting the Tories, since many among the gentry felt that the party had betrayed the Church of England. Now Catholics could enjoy all but the highest offices of state—which were still reserved to the established church. What was to be a peaceful revolution had begun.

The Reform Bill itself was enacted under the leadership of a Whig, the second Earl Grey (1764-1845), backed by a full apparatus of agitation and pressure groups. Tory opponents of parliamentary reform were won over—even the Duke of Wellington was converted at the last moment—until only the Tory House of Lords blocked the measure. At this climax, Lord Grey, as prime minister, persuaded King William IV (1830-1837) to threaten to create enough new Whig peers to put the reform through the Lords. This threat, combined with fears of a run on the Bank of England and of an outbreak of popular violence in Bristol, resulted in passage of the bill on June 4, 1832.

The First Reform Bill is probably the most celebrated single act of legislation passed by Parliament, because it accomplished a potentially revolutionary change without revolutionary violence. It was "revolution by due course of law," and it marked a distinct weakening of the established church and the Crown—two bastions of privilege in continental societies. It demonstrated that the working classes could be won to the cause of parliamentary reform, and that the masses need not be driven into the arms of the Jacobins.

Debate had brought all fears out in the open. Those who opposed the bill feared making concessions to those who could be bought by "bribery and beer"; those who favored the bill readily admitted that they saw it as essential to forestall the kind of revolution overtaking the continent of Europe. Though the country at large clearly welcomed the bill, it was carried on the basis of the Irish members, for by a narrow margin the English representatives had voted it down. Yet by no means did the Reform Bill bring political democracy to Britain. It did diminish the great irregularities of electoral districts, wiping out more than fifty rotten boroughs and giving seats in the Commons to more than forty unrepresented industrial towns. The number of voters was increased by about 50 percent, so that virtually all the middle class got the vote, but the property qualifications for voting excluded the great mass of workers. However, uniform qualifications took the franchise away from some who had enjoyed it in a few exceptionally liberal boroughs; as the bill extended

the suffrage in the counties, which tended to vote Conservative, its impact was not, in fact, as radical as its opponents had feared.

In the partly reformed Parliament, agitation went on for a wider suffrage. The middle class had won its gains, not in the name of its own admission to an oligarchy, but in the name of the right of all competent men to have the vote. With the gradual spread of literacy to the lower classes, and with the rapid expansion of the press, the number of competent men deserving the vote was steadily growing. The more militant workers, however, not content to accept reform piecemeal, wanted immediate direct representation in Parliament to press for legislation that would mitigate the hardships brought on by the Industrial Revolution. These demands were formally drawn up in a People's Charter calling for universal manhood suffrage, the secret ballot, abolition of all property requirements for members of Parliament, payment of members, equal electoral districts, and annually elected Parliaments. The Chartists, who greatly alarmed the conservative classes, were the closest English equivalent of the radical parties that on the Continent carried on the Jacobin tradition of the French Revolution, mingled with elements of early socialism. Chartist strength lay in the urban industrial proletariat, particularly the unions, and was supported by many intellectuals of

Benjamin Disraeli, Lord Beaconsfield, was British prime minister in 1868 and again in 1874-1880. As a novelist Disraeli popularized the idea of Britain consisting of two nations—the rich and the poor. Through his policies he hoped to bring them closer together.

PASSAGE OF THE GREAT REFORM BILL

At three minutes of three in the morning of June 4, 1832, the most crucial vote began in Parliament. An eyewitness described it:

We set up a shout that you might have heard to Charing Cross, waving our hats, stamping against the floor, and clapping our hands. The tellers scarcely got through the crowd: for the House was thronged up to the table, and all the floor was fluctuating with heads like the pit of a theatre. But you might have heard a pin drop as [a member of Parliament] read the numbers. Then again the shouts broke out, and many of us shed tears. I could scarcely refrain. And the jaw of Peel fell; and the face of [the member most vocally in opposition to the middle class] was as the face of a damned soul. . . . We shook hands, and clapped each other on the back, and went out laughing, crying, and huzzaing into the lobby. And no sooner were the outer doors opened than another shout answered that within the House. All the passages, and the stairs into the waiting rooms, were thronged by people who had waited till four in the morning to know the issue. We passed through a narrow lane between two thick masses of them; and all the way down they were shouting and waving their hats, till we got into the open air. I called a cabriolet, and the first thing the driver asked was, "Is the bill carried?" "Yes, by one." "Thank God for it, Sir."

Quoted from George O. Trevelyan, ed., *Life and Letters of Lord Macaulay*, in John Cannon, *Parliamentary Reform* (Cambridge: Cambridge University Press, 1973), pp. 217-18.

varied social and economic backgrounds. The movement presented to Parliament in 1839 a monster petition with several hundred thousand signatures, urging adoption of the People's Charter. Parliament never considered the petition, even after two additional Chartist initiatives in 1842 and 1848. Chartism, like the Anti-Corn Law League, was an extraparliamentary movement that failed in its immediate goal, while making it evident that the Reform Act and Whig reforms in general were unfinished business. The Chartists' major demands were to become law in the next two generations.

By the 1860s the groundswell for more parliamentary reform was so powerful that Benjamin Disraeli (1804-1881), the leader of the Conservatives (as the former Tories were now officially designated), recognized that if his party did not put through the reform, the Liberals (former Whigs) almost certainly would, and that his party had best get the credit. Disraeli (not yet prime minister, even though he was his party's tactician) hoped that the newly enfranchised urban working class, hostile to their middle-class employers, would vote for the Conservatives with the expectation that they would be responsible caretakers of the lower classes. But in 1868, in the first general election after the new reform, Disraeli (now prime minister) and the Conservatives were turned out. In the meantime, a potential embarrassment was removed. Though a Christian convert, Disraeli was of Jewish background, and Jews could not take seats in Parliament, since members were required to swear "on the true faith of a Christian." When the Baron de Rothschild had been elected to Parliament in 1847, the Lords had refused to let him take his seat, though the Commons had, since 1833, sought to remove the restrictive oath. In 1866 a new oath was at last drawn up removing the sectarian reference.

Still, the Reform Bill of 1867 did not introduce full manhood suffrage. Like the first, it was a piecemeal change that brought the electoral districts into greater uniformity and equality, but it still left them divided into boroughs and shires, as in the Middle Ages. It about doubled the number of voters in Britain by giving the vote to householders—that is, settled men owning or paying rent on their dwellings—in the boroughs. But this Second Reform Bill did not give the vote in rural areas to men without the "stake in society" of property— that is, men who did not own a piece of real estate or a bank account, men who were therefore regarded by many upper-class Victorians as irresponsible, willing to vote away other people's property.

The next reforms were put through by the Liberal party under the leadership of William Ewart Gladstone (1809-1898). Bills of 1884 and 1885 again doubled the size of the electorate, particularly by extending the franchise in rural areas. But migrant laborers, domestic servants, and bachelors living in parental households still did not have the vote—and some were beginning to ask whether the vote was worth having. Moreover, the medieval constituencies of borough and shire were finally modernized, and many smaller boroughs were lumped together with surrounding county areas to form single constituencies. The political map of Britain was beginning to be redrawn so that all districts would have roughly the same population. Some striking inequalities continued, however. Workers could scarcely hope to become members of Parliament, for MPs still served without pay; voters with business property in one district and a home in another could vote twice; and graduates of Oxford and Cambridge could vote a second time for special university members. Nor could women vote or, indeed, own property with any security, for the Married Women's Property Act of 1870, despite its title, only assured women of the right to keep money they person-

William Gladstone was Britain's pragmatic prime minister on four occasions—in 1868-1874, in 1880-1885, in 1886, and in 1892-1894. He and Disraeli were locked in a contest for political leadership until 1881. Queen Victoria, who greatly enjoyed Disraeli's company, complained that Gladstone was entirely too earnest and addressed her as though she were a public meeting.

ally earned, so that they were generally unable to acquire the theoretical "stake in society" on which the franchise had been based. Only in two acts, in 1882 and 1893, did women gain the right to separate ownership of property, the first applying to married women, and the second to single women.

By 1885 Britain was, relative to other Western societies, a political democracy in which the majority of males were almost, if not quite, politically sovereign through their representatives in the House of Commons. The House of Lords retained the right to veto most legislative acts until 1911, when a Parliament Act ended the real power of the Lords, leaving them with no more than a delaying or suspensive veto. Other extensions of the logic inherent in the reforms were: the Local Government Act of 1894, in which urban and rural boards and local government parishes were granted wide sanitary and other public service powers, and women, whether married or single, were allowed both to vote and to stand as candidates; the institution of salaries for MPs in 1911;

and a majority act in 1918 that enfranchised all men over twenty-one, gave the vote to women over thirty, and limited plural voting to two votes—a property vote and a university vote. In 1928 women won the vote at twenty-one; after World War II university votes were abolished and the Lords' powers further reduced. Then in 1969 Britain, in common with other Western democracies, lowered the voting age to eighteen. By this time, however, most Western societies were defining democracy less in political and more in economic terms, and people were asking whether extension of the franchise to larger groups necessarily changed the structure of society.

Triumph of the Two-Party System

The dynamics of the process of democratizing British politics is in part explicable in terms of class antagonisms, as the bourgeoisie and then the proletariat gained the vote. But the central human institution working this change, the political party, was more than an instrument for advancing narrow class interests. When the Conservative Disraeli took the "leap in the dark" in 1867, as the risk inherent in the reform bill of that year was called, he hoped that the newly enfranchised workers would, from a sense of deference, vote for their "betters" in his own party. Though he was proved wrong in 1868, in the long run he was partly right, for after his death the Conservatives returned triumphantly to power for a whole decade (1895-1905), largely under Lord Salisbury (1830-1903), despite the still wider franchise of 1885.

Both the Conservative and Liberal parties were very different from their ancestors, the oligarchical eighteenth-century factions of Tories and Whigs. The Conservatives, first under Peel and then primarily under Disraeli, kept their old electoral following among country gentlemen, army and navy officers, and Anglican clergymen, but they added many new supporters among agricultural laborers, tradespeople, and even some of the urban working and white-collar classes. The Liberals, who in the early and middle parts of the century were still led by men like Grey and the Viscount Palmerston (1784-1865) from the great aristocratic Whig families, found many new supporters among businessmen, the Nonconformists, white-collar radicals, and the more politically conscious workers. Both parties frankly appealed to the "people." The Conservatives, with their Primrose League in memory of Disraeli's favorite flower, their appeal to love of queen and country, their record of social legislation against the worst evils of the new factory system, did at least as good a job of building a party machine and getting out the vote as did the Liberals.

The two-party system was almost wholly confined to the English-speaking lands: Britain, the United States, and the British dominions. On the Continent, a multiparty or coalition system usually prevailed—not only in France, Italy, and Germany, but also in the smaller democracies of Scandinavia, Switzerland, Holland, and Belgium, as well as in Spain, which had established a bicameral legislature in 1876. Under the unstable conditions created by the Industrial Revolution, the rapid demographic changes in Western societies, and the always risky foreign policies pursued by those who sought to maintain a delicate balance of power in the nineteenth century, a two-party democracy had clear advantages in promoting continuity, clarity of debate and choice, and a sense of security. In the twentieth century neither two-party systems nor parliamentary governments proved ultimately to be the norm for newly independent and modernizing states, and even in the older democracies more and more voters saw themselves as "independents," casting their votes on issues rather than party loyalty. But in the nineteenth century and in the early and middle stages of modernization, the relative clarity of position, the stability of policy, and the possibilities for direct compromise that arose from two-party government made for relatively greater domestic peace. But it was also in some measure less democratic than a multiparty system, since it generally offered the voter relatively limited choices.

In terms of political psychology, a two-party system means that the millions of individual voters who make up each party must be in greater agreement than disagreement over what the party stands for; or at least when they vote they must feel that their candidate stands for what they want more than for what they are opposed to. Each voter makes some kind of compromise, takes something less in practice than is ideal, or else abstains. The reasons why the British made such compromises must be sought in history. One reason lies in the relative security of the British Isles from external foes during the long years in which political habits of moderation and compromise could mature without the constant pressure of foreign wars. All the continental states were repeatedly exposed to the dangers of war and the threat of invasion. This might have happened in Britain too, had it undergone many repetitions of the kind of alarm raised over the possibilities of subversion by Jacobins and invasion by Napoleon. But it did not, and Britain was not seriously challenged internally or externally until the twentieth century, when problems associated with Ireland and with the need to accommodate a growing racial minority arriving from the West Indian, African, and south Asian parts of the empire placed the British sense of compromise under heavy strain.

Another reason for Britain's relative stability is that continental states in the nineteenth century were still going through popular revolutionary modifications of royal absolutism. They were still torn by major class antagonisms between the privileged nobles (usually backed by orthodox religion) and the middle class. In England the struggle against absolutism had occurred a century and a half earlier. It had left England with a moderate ruling class that was itself the product of a compromise between the old landed gentry and the new commercial classes, a ruling class that would develop within itself reasonable habits of restraint and compromise from which it only occasionally departed,

and to which it held with a strong sense of self-discipline and self-interest. If the upper class were to retreat, as were upper classes everywhere, they at least hoped to influence the pace and direction of that retreat. The deep abyss the French Revolution had dug on the Continent between royalists and republicans and between clericals and anticlericals did not exist in Britain, even though class bias was very real there. Then too, a good bit of the revolutionary fervor felt by the secularized lower-middle class and working class on the continent was poured, in England, Scotland and Wales, into a resurgence of religious interest, especially among nineteenth-century Methodists, reform-minded Quakers, and Welsh Baptists.

Even more important than the individual readiness of Liberals and Conservatives to support their party's policies was the fact that both parties had a wide area of mutual agreement above and beyond party. There was not much ideological difference between the Conservatives and the Liberals. Her Majesty's Government and Her Majesty's Opposition, almost equally loyal to established ways, helped to develop in the British people practices of pragmatic compromise, of respect for law, and of remarkable political stability. This willingness to abide by the law was enhanced by a substantial increase in public services and by the development of the first effective police force on a national scale, through Peel's creation of a metropolitan police for London which, after the migration of criminals into less protected towns, was followed in 1856 by an act that compelled all counties to organize police forces under the control of the Home Office.

The Program of the Utilitarians

The Reform Bill of 1832 was soon followed by other measures that helped make over not merely British political life but British economic and social life as well. Part of the inspiration for these reforms came from a small but influential middle-class group of Utilitarians, the Philosophic Radicals. These disciples of Bentham and of the Enlightenment believed that, if properly educated, people are impelled by rational self-interest and thus automatically do what is best for themselves and their fellows. Under the influence of the Philosophic Radicals, English local government and the English legal system were made simpler and more efficient. Legal procedures, which had been so complicated that the Chancery Court was many years behind in its cases, were speeded up. The Municipal Corporations Act of 1835 vested basic authority in elective councilors who supervised professional civil servants, including the recently established professional police.

Middle-class radicals, arguing that the government governs best which governs least, sought to expedite government rather than to add to its tasks. They believed in education, but not in compulsory public education; in their opinion, private initiative would do well what government would do poorly and tyrannically. Large-scale government reform of British state-supported education had to wait until 1870, and then occurred only at the elementary level. Meanwhile, the private initiative preached by the Utilitarians led to mechanics' institutes and other adult and vocational education institutions. The upper-middle class also sponsored various private schools (which, being paid for by fees from the public, are called "public schools" in Britain). Many of these had grown from medieval religious foundations, and both discipline and education had fallen to low levels in most of them. Their reform began under Thomas Arnold (1795-1842), headmaster of Rugby from 1828 to 1842, who declared that henceforth the fee-supported schools were to teach religious and moral principles and gentlemanly conduct, and were to enhance intellectual ability. New schools founded under his influence restored the "public" schools' prestige, while the new railroads made it easier for parents to send their sons (and later their daughters) away to school: to Marlborough, founded in 1843 chiefly for the sons of the Anglican clergy; to Wellington, founded in 1853, largely for the sons of officers; or to a revitalized Eton, Harrow, or Winchester. These schools fostered snobbery and class consciousness, but they also provided, especially after 1864, the first systematic instruction in the new sciences, introduced entrance by competitive exams, and became the chief nurseries of statesmen and officers. They introduced interschool athletic competition and improved the environment in which education takes place. Not until 1902, when a state-aided system of secondary education was systematically introduced to Britain, did they begin to lose their educational and class leadership.

In the meantime, in London, Manchester, and other cities, new universities that resembled American urban universities in many ways were opened. These new "redbrick" institutions (so called in contrast to the medieval stones of Oxford and Cambridge) broke the centuries-old monopoly of "Oxbridge," though they did not have the same prestige. In time these municipal institutions rose to equality in the sciences and, following a new wave of university reform after World War II, there were ultimately forty-six British universities, all deemed roughly equal in the quality of the education they offered undergraduates. By that time the Utilitarians' reservations about public education had been abandoned, and for those who could qualify for admission, both university and secondary education were virtually free—that is, publicly financed.

The most typical Utilitarian reform, the one that stirred up public opinion most thoroughly, was the New Poor Law of 1834. This bill codified, centralized, and made more coherent a complicated system of public relief that had originated in the Elizabethan Poor Law of 1601 and in earlier Tudor legislation. But it did more; it shifted the base of this relief. The old methods of "outdoor relief" had permitted supplementary payments from the parishes to able-bodied poor working on low wages, supplements for children, and "doles" direct to families living in their own homes. The new system would have none of this encouragement of what the Utilitarians feared was "natural human laziness." The New Poor Law united parishes for greater efficiency, permitted greater supervision by the central government in London, and supplied—in formidable poorhouses in which the sexes were firmly separated—the "indoor relief" by which able-bodied paupers were made as uncomfortable as the limits of decency would allow. Hardship, it was held, would encourage the poor to try to become self-supporting outside.

The New Poor Law set off a controversy over the entire complex and modern issue of welfare payments. Poorhouses offended humanitarians in the upper classes, but to middle-class business interests, they had the alleged merit of making poor relief more efficient. This triumph of Bentham's ideals was a direct cause of the growth of Chartism. The ideology behind the law—that the Poor Law commissioners would teach discipline and restraint to the poor, including restraint in the size of families—was challenged by many, while the inefficiency of the operation of the law was challenged by even more. Clearly it did not work. In 1838 in England and Wales there were something over 80,000 workhouse inmates; by 1843 the figure was nearly 200,000. Poverty grew and deepened.

The most successful of the Utilitarian reforms in its long-term consequences was the repeal of the Corn Laws in 1846, after a long campaign headed by the Anti-Corn Law League. This pressure group wanted Britain to exploit its head start in the Industrial Revolution by adopting free trade, so that it might use exports of manufactured goods to pay for imports of raw materials and food. The victory of the free traders was achieved in 1846 when they persuaded the Conservative leader Peel to abandon traditional Tory protectionism in the face of the tragic potato famine in Ireland and the urgent need for massive importation of cheap grain. Britain thus became the only major free-trade nation in a world that never quite lost its mercantilist preconceptions. The repeal of the Corn Laws had, however, temporarily split the Conservative party into two groups: one, the Peelites, accepted the repeal; the other, soon led by the brilliant young Disraeli, continued to support high tariffs on wheat. Within a decade, however, the Conservatives were reunited in a single party under Disraeli's leadership.

Still another series of reforms helped create the prosperous England of Gladstone and Disraeli. These were the Factory Acts, begun very modestly in 1802 and 1819 with bills sponsored by Peel's father. The Act of 1819 applied only to the cotton industry, forbade night work for children, and limited day work to twelve hours; it did not provide for effective inspection and was violated with impunity by many employers. The Act of 1833—forbidding child labor entirely below the age of nine, and restricting it to nine hours for those below thirteen, and twelve hours for those below eighteen—marked an important stage mainly because it provided salaried inspectors to enforce the law.

These and subsequent acts required the support of both political parties, as well as demands from below and paternalistic or self-interested concern from above. Given the prevailing laissez-faire economic philosophy and the Utilitarians' conviction that the state ought not to interfere with the natural order (by which the poor either bettered themselves through thrift, hard work, and a sense of duty, or else remained forever poor), and given the fact that labor was generally all that the working person had to sell, intervention by Parliament was slow and piecemeal. The single greatest intervention against the concept of personal property—the emancipation of slaves throughout the British Empire in 1833—had the united support of the humanitarians as well as the hard-headed calculations of many business and plantation owners that slavery was no longer economically sound.

To intervene with the free market in labor required a union of quasisocialist and conservative paternalistic views. Such a political alliance ultimately led to a series of acts which, by establishing the principle that Parliament had a responsibility to prevent the most grave of abuses, established a basis on which later reformers could build. The major architects of this legislation were Richard Oastler (1789-1861), a Tory; Sir John Cam Hobhouse (1786-1869), a radical; Michael Sadler (1780-1835), the parliamentary leader behind the bill of 1833 who, on all other matters, was a conservative; and Lord Shaftesbury (1801-1885), a liberal. Oastler led the Anti-Poor Law movement and together with Shaftesbury achieved the passage of the Ten Hours Act in 1847; Shaftesbury himself sponsored legislation that took women and children out of coal mines and that provided for institutionalized care for the insane.

By the end of the nineteenth century, a complex code of labor legislation regulated the hours of labor for everyone, protected women and children, and made employers responsible for worker's compensation in industrial accidents. New unions in the 1880s and 1890s organized the dock workers, gas workers, and other unskilled groups, and in 1892 Kier Hardie (1856-1915), a miner who had turned to journalism, became the first independent worker to win election to Parliament. As the first leader of the new Labour party in Parliament (1906-1907), he broadened the base of the movement. Then in 1911 came the National Insurance Act, which inaugurated compulsory health and unemployment insurance through combined payments from the state, employers, and employees.

Two other areas of entrenched privilege were attacked successfully in the 1870s. One, the requirement that fellows and staff at Oxford and Cambridge take religious tests to confirm their Anglicanism, was abolished by Gladstone with relative ease, since acts in 1854 and 1856 had already enabled non-Anglicans to earn degrees from those universities. Second, although Brit-

Here J.G. Tissot (1836-1902) captured "a heavy swell"—an English gentleman—in 1870. This casual air of superiority was greatly admired and much imitated outside Britain as well.

ain had become a modern state in most matters, the military remained unaltered, though since the 1850s it was increasingly under attack. It would be the sorry showing of the British army in the Crimean War that would at last make it possible for reformers to change the pre-Napoleonic system.

In foreign relations, almost everyone agreed on Britain's fundamental position: maintain the European state system in balance, preferably by diplomatic rather than military action; police the seas with the British navy; open world markets to British goods; maintain and, after 1870 in Africa, extend the vast network of the British Empire. The Liberals were more likely to side with the democratic and nationalist movements in Europe than the Conservatives were. They sympathized with the struggling Italians, Greeks, and Poles, and disliked the great powers, especially Russia. In midcentury the Liberal Palmerston pursued an active policy of near intervention on behalf of oppressed nationalities, and British "benevolent neutrality" was a factor in Italian unification. The Crimean War of 1854-1856, the only European war in which Britain was directly involved between 1815 and 1914, was fought to maintain the balance of power; Britain had joined France to oppose what they judged to be a Russian threat to their Near Eastern interests. They supported the Ottoman Empire, whose treatment of its Christian minorities aroused Liberal indignation under other circumstances. Although the war was mismanaged on both sides, it at least checked Russian advances for a time and made the ultimate disposition of the Balkan regions of the decaying Turkish empire a matter for joint action by all the great powers.

Doctrines of economy and efficiency—so natural to the Utilitarians, to both political parties, and to the concept of the modern state—had clearly not been at work in the bungled Crimean War. Military reform was delayed, for Palmerston opposed it, having been deeply involved in army organization. But in Gladstone's first ministry (1868-1874), his able secretary for war, Edward Cardwell (1813-1886), initiated a series of reforms that increased the efficiency and size of the British army while reducing its cost. In 1868 Cardwell abolished flogging during peacetime. The next year he began withdrawing troops from self-governing colonies, while encouraging the colonies to raise their own militias. In 1870 he abolished bounty money for recruits. He then placed the commander-in-chief under the secretary for war, assuring civilian governance over military matters, and attacked the system by which commissions and promotions were obtained by purchase. Almost all senior officers opposed this last change; in the House of Lords hostility to the bill was so intense that Gladstone asked the queen to abolish purchase by issuing a royal warrant. For the first time the Lords were revealed in complete opposition to the Commons on a class issue; they resorted to full-scale parliamentary obstruction. But demands for democratization of the military were joined by growing fears of Prussian professionalism,

which demonstrated its superiority in military science in the wars of 1866 and 1870. While some in Britain preferred officers who saw war as an art, more wanted a professional service than feared it. Some openly argued that an inefficient army was a protection against an authoritarian state. Gladstone and Cardwell carried the day, however, and the latter quickly began to modernize the army on the basis of the Regulation Bill of 1871. In 1882 the reorganized army would prove itself in the Egyptian campaign, and Lord Salisbury's diplomatic initiatives at the end of the century would be based in part on the knowledge that Britain now had an effective and growing military force.

Issues and Parties in the Early Twentieth Century

The long lead Britain had had in the Industrial Revolution was being lost as other nations acquired the technical skills of large-scale production. Germany, the Low Countries, Switzerland, the United States, and Japan were competing effectively with Britain on the world market. By the 1880s the prosperity, sense of confidence, and general air of political and social innovation associated with early- and mid-Victorian leaders were on the wane. Contemporaries referred to the years 1873 to 1896 as the Great Depression, and while historians now doubt that there actually was a sustained depression, participants at the time thought there was, and they acted on what they believed. There was an undeniable depression in arable farming, a drop in prices for commerce, and a slowing in the rate of industrial growth that was depressing, if not a Depression. A general decline in public and private morals and a move from duty toward frivolity seemed to mark the Edwardian period, named after the pleasure-loving though philanthropic King Edward VII (reigned 1901-1910). Irish troubles, the war in South Africa (in which world opinion generally supported the Boers, not the British), the rising international tensions that were leading to World War I, and the difficulties of raising the additional government revenue to finance both the naval armament race with Germany and the measures inaugurating the welfare state—all confronted the British people at the same time.

Under such conditions, many Britishers came to doubt the wisdom of the free-trade policies that had prevailed in 1846. For the Germans and others were not only underselling the British abroad; they were invading the British home market! Why not protect that market by a tariff system? Few Britishers believed that the home islands, already too densely populated by the 1880s to feed themselves and constitute a self-sufficient economy, could surround themselves with a simple tariff wall. But the empire was worldwide, with abundant agricultural resources. Within it the classical mercantilist interchange of manufactures for raw materials could still (in theory) provide a balanced economic system. Britain could still be, if not the workshop of the world, at least the workshop of that quarter of the world that composed the British Commonwealth and Empire.

A reform leader from Birmingham, Joseph Chamberlain (1836-1914), had resigned from Gladstone's liberals in 1886 over the issue of Irish home rule and had turned his attention to colonial matters, becoming colonial secretary under Lord Salisbury in 1895. Chamberlain had become a leading protectionist, giving special importance to the establishment of a system of imperial preference through which the whole complex of lands under the Crown would work together in a tariff union. Many Conservatives, never wholly reconciled to free trade, welcomed the issue, and Chamberlain's new Unionist party had made protection a major plank in its program. Reversing the aims but imitating the methods of Cobden and the Anti-Corn Law League of the 1840s, Chamberlain organized a Tariff Reform League. In 1903 he made sweeping proposals that would have restored moderate duties on foodstuffs and raw materials (largely to give a basis for negotiating with the dominions, which already had tariff systems of their own) and on foreign manufactured goods. But the new Conservative prime minister, Arthur Balfour (1848-1930), did not dare go so far, and Chamberlain resigned with his bill unpassed. Thus Chamberlain, who had already split the Liberal party on home rule, now split the Conservatives on tariff reform. Although the new Liberal government after 1905 continued free trade in a modified form, the rift Chamberlain had made in the old Liberal party was never really repaired.

The Liberals were, however, increasingly committed to another policy as contrary to the classical philosophy of laissez faire as was protectionism. This was the welfare state—social security through compulsory insurance managed by the state and in part financed by the state, minimum-wage laws, compulsory free public education, and a variety of public works and services. The most dramatic point in working out this program was the "People's Budget" of 1909. It was introduced by a relatively new figure on the political stage, a Welshman who was deeply hostile to all forms of English privilege, David Lloyd George (1863-1945), the Liberal chancellor of the exchequer. This budget, which proposed making the rich finance the new welfare measures through progressive taxation on incomes and inheritances, was no ordinary tax measure. It was a means of altering the social and economic structure of Britain. Its opponents called it "not a budget, but a revolution," especially in its attempt to tax the unearned increment on land values. The bill passed the Commons but was thrown out by the Lords, even though it was a money bill. This rejection led to a general election, which the Liberals won. They then put through the Parliament Act of 1911, which took away from the Lords all power to alter a money bill, and left them with no more than a delaying power of not more than two years over all other legislation. The Liberal program of social legislation was achieved under conditions strongly reminiscent of 1832, for the new king, George V (r. 1910-1936), had promised Prime

Under the youthful David Lloyd George, the Liberal Party emerged as a major force in British politics.

Minister Herbert Asquith (1852-1928) that, if necessary, he would create enough new peers—which might have meant several hundred—to put the Parliament Act through the House of Lords. As in 1832, the threat was enough, and the peers yielded.

The dissenting Liberals who had followed Joseph Chamberlain out of the party in the 1880s did not think these measures were appropriate, and Chamberlain's two sons, Austen and Neville, who played an important part in twentieth-century politics, thought of themselves as conservatives. What happened in the generation after 1880 was a major change in the political orientation of British parties. The Liberals, who had believed that the government governs best which governs least (and least expensively), had come to believe that the state must interfere in economic life to help the underdog, and had adopted Lloyd George's plan for redistributing the national wealth by social insurance financed by taxation. And the Conservatives, who in the midnineteenth century had stood for factory acts and mild forms of the welfare state, were now in large part committed to a laissez-faire program against government "intervention"—a program much like that of the Liberals of 1850.

One factor in this reversal had been the growth of the political wing of the labor movement, which in 1906 won fifty-three seats in the Commons. The political ideas that went into the making of the British Labour party antedated its formal organization, for they derived from the legacy of 1776 and 1789, as modified by Marxist thought, by Christian socialism, and by the rapidly growing trade unions. Labourites wanted the welfare state, and many of them also wanted a socialist state in which at least the major industries would be nationalized. Labour had the backing of many upper- and middle-class people who sympathized with the quest for social justice. From their ranks came intellectuals like G.B. Shaw, H.G. Wells, G.D.H. Cole (1889-1959), and Sidney and Beatrice Webb (1858-1947 and 1858-1943, respectively), who participated in the influential Fabian Society, formed in the 1880s. The Fabians preached the "inevitability of gradualness," the attainment of social democracy through the peaceful parliamentary strategy of advancing one step at a time, as was done by the Roman republican general Fabius to wear down the Carthaginians in the third century B.C.

By the early 1900s Fabianism seemed to be working, for the Liberals, who depended on Labour votes to maintain a majority, put through much important legislation in the interest of the worker: acceptance of peaceful picketing, sanctity of trade union funds, and employer's liability to compensate for accidents (all in 1906); modest state-financed old age pensions (1909); health and unemployment insurance (1911); and minimum wage regulations (1912). In passing this legislation the British were learning from one of their former colonies, New Zealand, which had won responsible government in 1857 and had enacted a series of welfare laws in 1894, some of them well ahead of their British equivalents. Part of the motivation for Liberal social legislation was a desire to forestall Labour initiatives. But over the long run, these tactics worked no better in the twentieth century than they had in the nineteenth, and the workers on the whole stuck by the Labour party. The Liberal party was beginning a long decline that would be hastened by the effects of World War I and would drive its right wing to Toryism and its left wing to

BEATRICE WEBB ON "WHY I BECAME A SOCIALIST"

One of the leading intellectuals in the socialist movement in Britain was Beatrice Potter, who became the wife of the Fabian socialist and administrator Sidney Webb. She described the years of her marriage in *My Partnership*, while the preceding years, in which she addressed the question, "Why I Became a Socialist," she described in *My Apprenticeship*:

Can I describe in a few sentences the successive steps in my progress towards Socialism?

My studies in [London's] East End life had revealed the physical misery and moral debasement following in the track of the rack-renting landlord and capitalist profit-maker in the swarming populations of the great centres of nineteenth-century commerce and industry. It is true that some of these evils—for instance, the low wages, long hours and insanitary conditions of the sweated industries, and the chronic under-employment at the docks, could, I thought, be mitigated, perhaps altogether prevented by appropriate legislative enactment and Trade Union pressure. By these methods it might be possible to secure to the manual workers, so long as they were actually at work, what might be regarded from the physiological standpoint as a sufficient livelihood. Thus, the first stage in the journey—in itself a considerable departure from early Victorian individualism—was an all-pervading control, in the interest of the community, of the economic activities of the landlord and the capitalist.

But however ubiquitous and skilful this State regulation and Trade Union intervention might become, I could see no way out of the recurrent periods of inflation and depression—meaning, for the vast majority of the nation, alternate spells of overwork and unemployment—intensified, if not actually brought about by the speculative finance, manufacture and trading that was inspired by the mad rush to secure the maximum profit for the minority who owned the instruments of production. Moreover, "Man does not live by bread alone"; and without some "socialism"—for instance, public education and public health, public parks and public provision for the aged and infirm, open to all and paid for out of rates and taxes, with the addition of some form of "work or maintenance" for the involuntarily unemployed—even capitalist governments were reluctantly recognising, though hardly fast enough to prevent race-deterioration, that the régime of private property could not withstand revolution. This "national minimum" of civilised existence, to be legally ensured for every citizen, was the second stage in my progress towards socialism.

Beatrice Webb, *My Apprenticeship* (Hammondsworth: Penguin Books, 1938), II, 439-40. Copyright by the London School of Economics and Political Science.

Labour, which by 1914 was the party of the center. Many Liberals were converted from laissez faire to social security, however, for they believed that the logic of their democratic assumptions must lead them to raise the standard of living in Britain by state action.

The imperialist wing of the Liberal party, led originally by Chamberlain, remained unreconciled to this trend, and in 1901 a union between the Fabians and disaffected Liberals began to hint that a new national party was needed to make national efficiency its goal. As the Liberal party fragmented, declined, and sought to hold on to its followers against the rise of Labour, it became more of a coalition than a functioning whole within a two-party system. On one subject it remained reasonably united, however—the significance of the British Empire. As one influential former Liberal Unionist member of Parliament, Halford John Mackinder (1861-1947), the father of geopolitics, noted after his election in 1910, free trade would protect imperialism. He maintained that in preparation for the coming conflict with Germany and eventually with Russia, Britain must transform itself; it must become a nation of "organizers," of workers whose patriotism led them to realize that they existed primarily to serve the national ends of the state. As an aspect of its modernization, Britain was like the nations of the Continent, moving toward increased centralization, and preparing itself for war. In this future conflict the empire, the Liberals hoped, would be a major advantage; but one aspect of the empire—Ireland—would be a major disadvantage. By 1914 Britain was faced with several crises which, though separate, seemed to fall simultaneously and most heavily on the Liberal party and its principles.

An Imperial Issue Close to Home: The Irish Problem

As in eastern Europe, a nationality problem peculiar to Britain grew more acute near the end of the nineteenth century. This was "the Irish problem," as the English called it, which had existed since the Norman-English conquest of Ireland in the twelfth century. The English, and the Scots who came to settle in the northern Irish province of Ulster in the sixteenth and seventeenth centuries, had remained as privileged Protestant landowners over a subject population of Catholic Irish peasants. Although there were also native Irish among the ruling classes, many of them had been Anglicized and had turned Protestant.

For three centuries religious, political, and economic problems in Ireland had remained unsolved. Early in the nineteenth century the English attempted to solve the political problem by a formal union of the two kingdoms, with Irish members admitted to the British Parliament. On January 1, 1801, the United Kingdom of Great Britain and Ireland came into being. Beginning with the Catholic Emancipation Act of 1829, which allowed Irish voters to elect Catholics to office, most of the English reforms were extended to Ireland. The Irish, led by Daniel O'Connell (1775-1847), the Great Emancipator, organized politically to press for repeal of the union and in favor of home rule. They sought not only self-government but also land reform, to break the economic dominance of the Protestant minority, and disestablishment of the Anglican church in Ireland— that is, abolition of a state church supported by taxes levied both on its members and on the Irish majority, who were nonmembers.

Irish hatred for the English was fanned by the disastrous potato famine of the 1840s, when blight ruined a crop essential to the food supply. The British government, with its prevailing laissez-faire reaction to an emergency, did not provide prompt or efficient relief, and twenty-one thousand Irish deaths were attributed directly to starvation. At least a million more, weakened by malnutrition, succumbed to disease. Many of these deaths occurred on ships, as hundreds of thousands of Irish emigrated. Those who survived carried their hatred of the British with them; they formed pressure groups such as the Fenian Brotherhood, organized in New York in 1858, to raise funds to aid Irish resistance against the obdurate and often inept British.

Over the next decades British governments made piecemeal reforms. In 1869 they disestablished the Anglican church in Ireland, and in the next year the Irish Land Act began a series of agrarian measures that were designed to protect tenants from "rack renting" (rent gouging) by landlords, many of them absentee British landlords. The reforms were neither far-reaching nor rapid, intensifying Irish awareness of cultural differences and nationalty. Then in 1875 a brilliant Irish leader, Charles Parnell (1846-1891), himself of Protestant descent but a firm Irish patriot, was elected to the British Parliament. Under his leadership the Irish nationalists in the British Parliament were welded into a firm, well-disciplined party which, though it held fewer than a hundred seats in the House of Commons of the United Kingdom, could often swing the balance between Liberals and Conservatives.

The critical step came in 1885 when Gladstone was converted to the cause of Irish home rule, and in the next year introduced a bill providing for a separate Dublin-based Irish parliament (with some restrictions on its sovereignty) under the Crown. Gladstone's decision split his own Liberal party, and a group led by Chamberlain seceded under the name of Liberal Unionists; in effect, they joined the Conservative party. Gladstone lost the election brought on by the split, and home rule was dropped for the moment.

Agitation continued in Ireland, however, becoming more and more bitter when Parnell, involved in a divorce scandal, was dropped by Gladstone and by some of his own Irish followers. In 1892, however, Gladstone won a close election on the Irish issue, obtaining enough English seats to get a second home rule bill through the Commons with the aid of eighty-one Irish nationalists. However, the bill was defeated in the House of Lords and was dropped once more. The Conservatives, when they came in for a ten-year reign in 1895, sought to "kill home rule by kindness," enacting several land reform bills that helped make Ireland a land of small peasant proprietors.

But Ireland was now beyond the reach of modest reforms, and Irish problems were no longer—if ever they had been—largely economic and administrative. Irish nationalism was now in full flower, nourished by a remarkable literary revival in English and in Gaelic by writers like the poet W.B. Yeats (1865-1939), the dramatist John Millington Synge (1871-1909), and Lady Augusta Gregory (1859-1932), cofounder of the Abbey Theatre, which staged plays with deeply Irish themes. Irish men and women everywhere—including Irish-Americans—would be satisfied with nothing less than an independent Irish state.

The Liberals, back in power after 1905, found that they needed the votes of the Irish nationalists to carry through their proposal for ending the veto power of the Lords. The Liberals struck a bargain: home rule in return for the Parliament Act of 1911. A home rule bill was placed on the books in 1912 but never went into force, for as home rule seemed about to become a fact, the predominantly Protestant north of Ireland, the province of Ulster, bitterly opposed to separation from Great Britain, threatened to resist by force of arms. The home rule bill as passed carried the rider that it was not to go into effect until the Ulster question was settled. The outbreak of the European war in 1914 put such a settlement out of the question, and the stage was set for the Irish Revolution of the 1920s.

II THE GREAT MODERN EMPIRES AND THE QUESTION OF IMPERIALISM

If the transition from medieval to modern history was, in part, a result of the period of European expansion overseas, then the transition from modern to what some scholars refer to as postmodern history is marked by the rise and collapse of the great modern empires. Colonialism and imperialism made the history of Western civilization and world history into one subject, for the complex cultures of Asia, of Africa, and of the Pacific Islands, while moving along their own historically unique path, were also brought into the Western story through the mechanisms of imperialism. The age of maritime exploration and early colonialism had knit the globe together into one intellectual construct; the age of imperialism would give political and economic reality to this set of mental maps. It would also assure that, although *imperialism* is, to the historian, essentially a descriptive term that applies to the impact of higher technologies on lower technologies and to the exploitation of the lands and the labor of non-Western peoples, the word would join others that nonhistorians invariably use for emotional purposes. Terms like *liberalism*, *con-*

servatism, *socialism*, *nationalism*, or *religiosity*—all words likely to evoke emotions in those unwilling to consider them as essentially neutral descriptive terms used to embrace complex ideas—would at least continue to be debated as though there were two sides to the questions posed by them. *Imperialism*, on the other hand, though originally a word used in praise, especially in Britain, would come to be used almost exclusively in negative ways as a consequence of the actions of the imperialists and the interpretations of the nationalistic historians of the newly independent former colonies. Imperialism, both as word and as deed, became part of the power struggle among the Western powers and, in the twentieth century, among non-Western nations as well.

Motives for Empire

Between 1800 and roughly 1870 European nations acquired new territories mainly from other European powers. Britain rested its continuing ascendancy upon sea power, and those colonies it kept after victories over continental nations were retained largely for strategic reasons, such as the need to protect the sea route to India and the Far East. Thus Mauritius was taken from the French because it had the best harbor in the south Indian Ocean, Ceylon from the Dutch for its port of Trincomalee, and Malacca (by treaty in 1824, also from the Dutch) because it controlled the straits to China. Concern for trade routes led the British to found Singapore in 1819 and to retain Gibraltar, Malta, and the Ionian Islands in the Mediterranean. Most of these colonies were without intrinsic importance, being pawns in a game of power; they helped assure the safety of existing colonies of settlement, protected potential trade routes that might displace old ones, and stabilized interior regions through which a rival power might attempt to move.

The principles of free-trade imperialism were compromised toward the end of the century, as the relative position of the industrial nations changed. On the whole, Britain held to a free-trade position from the abolition of the Corn Laws in 1846 until 1932. France moved toward protectionism after Jules Ferry (1832-1893) became leader of the government in 1880; by 1892 he had built high tariff walls that protected home industries from direct colonial competition, while giving colonial produce a degree of protection as well. Germany and Belgium, despite moderate tariffs directed against Britain, generally held to free trade, and the Dutch belatedly went over to it in the 1870s. Britain stood midway, manipulating imperial preferences to its benefit while espousing the general principles of free-trade competition. Thus a modified form of mercantilistic thought came to be applied to the colonies. They would provide cheap raw materials for the industrial machine in Europe, since labor in the colonies cost a fraction of that at home; they would purchase finished products and provide strategic protection for the trade routes by which the bulk of these products moved to other nations; they would become centers for investment, absorbing surplus capital as well as produce; and by helping to eliminate the surpluses that led to domestic cycles of unemployment, they would help to forestall the social revolution many feared.

The modern capitalist state would need new kinds of trading partners capable of sustaining a trend toward consolidation, large-scale marketing, and giant trading firms—a trend that made possible economies of scale that, in turn, either increased profits or lowered prices and broadened markets. Underconsumption at home was the primary cause of low wages, according to the first analyst of imperialism as a phenomenon, John A. Hobson (1858-1904), in his 1902 book *Imperialism: A Study*. Underconsumption prevented the profitable employment of capital at home and forced governments to seek out colonies as an outlet for their surpluses. Hobson saw this as a correctable problem, but another analyst, Lenin, saw it as the inevitable, irreversible, and destructive *Highest Stage of Capitalism*, the subtitle he gave to his own work on *Imperialism* in 1916. This being so, he argued, colonies were adjuncts to capitalist balance-of-power politics, since colonies were needed as outlets for surplus capital.

The European state system had been remolded at the Congress of Vienna around the concept of a balance of power—a projection of an essentially seventeenth-century doctrine into the nineteenth. Louis XIV had wished to create a "universal monarchy"—a condition by which one state could command all others—and European statesmen had feared just this eventuality, if not by the French then by some other nation. To prevent the rise of such a superpower, they sought to assure a distribution of power among many states, so that no one state would be dominant; at best, a nation's leaders wished to have sufficiently greater weight than any other nation so that they would be vital to any coalition and would hold the balance of power. The purpose was to preserve independence of action and to protect national sovereignty. While this balance of power rested largely within Europe until the midnineteenth century, the growing importance of overseas trade—and the emotion and prestige attached to having an imperial "place in the sun"—appeared to shift the balance toward colonial possessions after 1870. The balance of power no longer rested solely upon the question of which nation had the most and largest ships, for prestige could not be measured solely in such terms.

To these economic and political motives for imperial expansion after the midcentury were added more emotional or psychological motivations, of which the desire for national and personal glory was the most evident. Imperialism was closely allied to nationalism. For a nation to be without a colony at the end of the century, even if that colony was an economic liability, was to confess to weakness. As late as 1936, when Italy at last overran Ethiopia, the primary goal was said to be to achieve "manhood among nations." Colonies helped to assert the pride of the nation and to give it security in a Darwinian world "red of tooth and claw." The quest for security on the ground that one's country is dearer than all others and must at all costs be made safe in a competitive world was basic to modern thought.

A related motive for the acquisition of territory was strategic. Islands, river mouths, or peninsulas that dominated trade routes and on which forts might be built were coveted because they could make economic and political goals more accessible. Often colonies were little more than adjuncts to some larger area of an empire; for example, after the completion of the Suez Canal in 1869 Britain took Perim, Aden, and Socotra solely to protect the new route to India and the East, and France annexed large portions of West and Equatorial Africa as strategic hinterlands for the protection of travel routes to the coast, or of the coastal holdings themselves. Strategic considerations also altered with the new technologies—the telegraph, the steamship, and the airplane. An area once important could be traded for another area of greater importance, making indigenous populations pawns in larger, European-based strategic games. Even so, an area was of strategic importance only in relation to the prevailing economic and political theories of the powers, and thus the strategic motive may largely be subsumed under the others. This was especially true in the acquisition of territories in East Africa after 1880 by Britain, France, Germany, and Italy. Britain wished to maintain control in Egypt, although without formal annexation; conquest of the Nile to its headwaters seemed a strategic necessity. To stabilize the Nile holdings, the highlands and parts of Kenya and Tanganyika seemed vital and were therefore taken by Britain and Germany respectively. To maintain control over the Panama Canal route, the United States had to dominate—through dollar diplomacy rather than direct annexation—the Caribbean and Central American republics, and in particular, Cuba.

As strategic needs changed, the tenacity with which a nation held to an area might also have been expected to change, if imperialism were a wholly rational system of world organization. To some extent such changes did occur; Britain slowly lost interest in the West Indies after the abolition of slavery in 1833 and the decline of the sugar market, and the United States' interventionist policies in the Caribbean gradually receded as air began to replace water transport. Yet for the most part empires continued to grow in defiance of economic wisdom and strategic planning. Nonrational impulses to empire were clearly at work.

Foremost among these was the humanitarian desire to reform, to uplift, to help the "little brown brother"—the native who was felt to need more efficient, liberal, or rational forms of government, economic organization, or worship. Christian missionaries desired to save souls, to bring to Christ those whom they regarded as heathen and lost. Evangelical Protestants in particular sent missionaries into China, Africa, and India to educate non-Christians so that they might read the Bible for themselves. Some Christians saw the machine as an instrument of God, and many embraced the new imperialist trinity—railroads, sanitation, and good government—as the pathway to temporal elevation of humanity and ultimately to spiritual triumphs. From the time of John and Charles Wesley, who preached to the colonists in Georgia in the 1730s, independent Methodist churches had grown among the middle and lower class in Britain. The Wesleyan Methodists were revivalist and conservative; they were also competitive, especially where Anglican or Roman Catholic missions were present, as in Indo-China, for example, where they were conscious instruments of French expansion. Most of those missionaries who actively promoted imperialism, however, especially in Africa and the Pacific Islands, did so for their church, not their nation; French missionaries opposed British because the former were Roman Catholic and the latter Protestant.

Humanitarianism also had its ethical, secular goals, as in the campaign to end slavery—a campaign closely allied to the broad doctrine of progress. Indigenous groups often practiced slavery or, as in Malaya, a form of debt bondage. A Western nation would be a powerful secular ally in the battle against cannibalism, *suttee* (the custom of burning widows on the funeral pyre of their husband) child marriage, bride price, and nakedness. Frequently, the central authority of the imperial power was used to improve the physical life of the native population, for the European authorities could intervene in local affairs to protect a local minority against exploitation by a local majority. Although those living in colonies—whether members of dominant tribal or religious groups, or white settlers attempting to press back indigenous populations in Australia, New Zealand, or southern Africa—usually thought of the imperial power as an interfering body, it often interfered to protect the weaker groups. Britain slowed the pace of self-government in Australia in the 1850s in order to speak out for the rights of the aboriginal population, accepted a form of constitutional government for Canada in 1867 only after French-speaking rights were entrenched in the enabling acts, and refused independence to Rhodesia in the 1960s because the blacks there were not accorded a progressively equal political standing with whites in the colony's draft constitution. In the late nineteenth century the United States' federal government sought to slow the growth of statehood in certain western American territories because it feared that, once sovereign, they would create unrepresentative institutions.

In the final analysis, imperialism also rested upon humanity's acquisitive nature, the desire to influence, control, dominate, own, or crush another people. Racism fed upon such desires and also fed them, and racism usually was one facet of imperialism, in the sense that the imperialists held themselves to be superior to nonwhites. Some theorists of empire argued that racial differences were largely environmental; that is, that while the other races might appear inferior to the white, they were so only by virtue of historical circumstance, and that sufficient exposure to more advanced customs and technologies would, in time, make the "lesser breeds" functionally equal within the law. This position helped justify taking and retaining land occupied by another race. Other theorists argued that some races were inherently inferior and would always need the protection of the stronger. The latter tended to think of the indigenous populations as useful labor forces, while the former thought of them as societies in need of

---

RUDYARD KIPLING'S VIEW OF IMPERIALISM

Many were pleased to be called imperialists, determined to "take up the White Man's burden" . . . "To seek another's profit, / And work another's gain." In the words of the poet laureate of empire, Rudyard Kipling (1865-1936), the United States too must:

Take up the White Man's burden—
  Send forth the best ye breed—
Go bind your sons to exile
  To serve your captives' need;
To wait in heavy harness
  On fluttered folk and wild—
Your new-caught, sullen peoples,
  Half devil and half child.

          . . .

Take up the White Man's burden—
  The savage wars of peace—
Fill full the mouth of Famine
  And bid the sickness cease;
And when your goal is nearest
  The end for others sought,

Watch Sloth and heathen Folly
  Bring all your hope to nought.

          . . .

Take up the White Man's burden—
  And reap his old reward:
The blame of those ye better,
  The hate of those ye guard—
The cry of hosts ye humour
  (Ah, slowly!) toward the light:—
"Why brought ye us from bondage,
  "Our loved Egyptian might?"

From *Rudyard Kipling's Verse: Definitive Edition*. Reprinted by permission of the National Trust, Doubleday & Company, Inc., and Macmillan, London, Ltd.

transformation. This nurture-nature debate showed a curious blend of the missionary, humanitarian, wealth-seeking, and prestige-conscious impulses of the West.

These motives were sustained by an infrastructure within most imperial nations that strengthened the ties between mother country and colony. The settlement colonies would absorb surplus population and often draw the military-minded to them. The exploits of the French or British armies created tales of wartime glory that fostered yet more exploits. Civil servants and youthful adventurers, usually sons who could not expect to inherit their father's property, added to the spiral of imperial expansion.

But annexation was not, in any event, necessary to imperial expansion. Not only was annexation expensive, it was also dangerous, perhaps bringing a reaction from another power; it produced shock waves within the interior of an area that might force further annexations to calm and control turbulent frontiers; it led local administrators to intervene in intertribal, interethnic, or interpolitical affairs that might draw a nation far more deeply into moral and political involvement than its population at home would accept. There were, therefore, other "empires" parallel to the formal ones. These were the so-called informal empires.

Informal empires were areas that were technically independent but whose economies, communication systems, and often politics and social life were inextricably bound up with an imperial power. Such power relations were new only in degree, for there had always been client states. The United States exercised such informal control over portions of Latin America and the Pacific. Russia came to hold influence over vast, continuous territories, some of which were eventually absorbed into the Soviet Union. Germany and France sought to dominate much of the eastern end of the Mediterranean prior to World Wars I and II. In the nineteenth century Britain thought of Argentina as virtually another dominion, so closely connected were Argentine rails, beef prices, and minerals to the British Empire's needs, and Argentina remained neutral in World War II partly because this was what Britain preferred. Strikingly, the economies of formal and informal portions of an empire might well differ very little; in the late nineteenth century the economies of New Zealand and of Uruguay—the latter an independent nation, the former a British colony—bore remarkably similar economic relationships to Britain.

Did formal colonies pay? In psychological terms, undoubtedly; in financial terms, generally no. In the nineteenth century, however, many expected them to pay. Cecil Rhodes thought imperialism to be "a bread and butter question," and the neomercantilists of Britain and the Continent agreed. Statistics are difficult to compare, given competing systems of trade, inaccurate data, and the fact that different nations kept their statistics in different ways; nonetheless, for the neomercantilist period, certain conclusions can be drawn. Some historians have asserted, for example, that the profits from

the slave trade paid for nearly 20 percent of Britain's industrial revolution. Others have argued that the mid-century industrial progress of Britain was financed largely from the cheap labor of India. Such judgments are at best guesses, although revenues from the colonies undoubtedly were drained to serve imperial interests. The Dutch drew eighteen million guilders a year from the Dutch East Indies (Indonesia) from 1831 until 1877, at a time when the entire Dutch budget was only sixty million guilders. In 1890 42 percent of Indian revenues went to finance the Indian Army, under British officers, which primarily served imperial purposes, when Britain's entire defense budget was 38 percent of its revenue.

Against such financial gains from empire must be set the heavy costs of the colonies, which ordinarily faced deficit budgets that had to be met by the imperial power, which involved many small wars of great expense, and which were also costly to administer in terms of health. French expenses in Morocco more than wiped out any profits from trade. Italy's colonies cost her 1,300 million lire, more than was produced by all Italian colonial trade between 1913 and 1932. Germany's external trade with her colonies was 972 million marks between 1894 and 1913, while the expenses of the colonies were 1,002 million marks, and at the outbreak of World War I, Germany's empire was taking only 0.5 percent of German overseas trade. Even the Congo was always a small part of Belgium's total overseas trade, never comprising more than 7 percent. For Britain the colonies were more important, but there too the balance was generally unfavorable; in 1850 the empire took 28 percent of Britain's overseas trade and 40 percent in 1934. Of the 1934 figure, however, well over half was with the dominions, that is, Canada, Australia, New Zealand, Newfoundland, South Africa; 7 percent was with India, and only 9 percent was with the remainder of the empire. In short, for Britain the chief economic advantage lay in the former settlement colonies and in India, while the new African possessions were of little importance in economic terms.

Hobson and Lenin argued that the real economic gain from colonies lay in investments. But aside from Britain's self-governing dominions, most capital exports flowed into Europe, Latin America, or the United States, which at the outbreak of World War I were taking 53 percent of all British capital investment, while the dependent colonies took 6 percent, and India, combined with Ceylon, took 22 percent. The figures for France were similar. Nor did the colonial investments pay significantly higher rates of return, for most European investment was in government bonds or debentures with fixed interest, which averaged only 0.5 percent higher returns than noncolonial stocks did.

Yet the nations of Europe, joined after 1808 by the United States, continued to acquire colonial possessions, until by 1930 84 percent of the land surface of the globe was under the control of the Western nations. Clearly there were powerful motivations toward empire, and clearly (in retrospect) they were not truly economic motivations. Yet we must remember that at the time many imperialists felt that the colonies could be made to pay eventually, and that the search for a balance of power lent special credence to those who wished to deny to another nation a new acquisition, initiating preventive annexations and playing the politics of denial.

To these four causes of imperial expansion—the desire for economic gain, whether immediate or deferred; the need to dominate strategic passages; the emotional search for national prestige; the fervor to convert others to a more "civilized" religion or form of government—would be added a fifth, now referred to as the *collaborator model.* During the 1870s official British policy was outspokenly against the acquisition of further territory overseas; yet, that same decade saw the British Empire expand greatly. This "new imperialism," as the post-1870 movement was called, arose in part because of growing British and French relations with indigenous leaders who, for reasons arising from their own political needs, cooperated with the imperialists and, at times deliberately, at times inadvertently, drew reluctant and penny-pinching administrators into costly new acts of expansion and annexation. "Native uprisings" and local conflicts with rival European powers or indigenous leaders were reported in the European press in increasingly emotional terms, and toward the end of the century the British, French and Germans were clamoring for imperial adventure.

The New Imperialism, 1870-1931

The "new imperialism" that spread after 1870 was more emotional and nationalistic than the earlier imperialisms, but it was also more intimately connected to a nation's industry and its cultural consciousness. The Industrial Revolution had now led to a demand for goods aimed at specific markets and appealing to national fashions. Higher-quality goods made for a critical market required European control over the processes of manufacture, over methods of planting and cultivation, over port facilities, storage depots, communications systems, and even local finance. Home industries often related to colonial markets and sources of materials in startling ways. The need for rubber, for instance, led the British to experiment with trees brought from Brazil to Kew Gardens, near London, and then to the introduction of rubber trees into Malaysia; the desire to control prime rubber-growing areas would lead in turn to further British expansion in Southeast Asia. The need for skilled rubber tappers led the British to introduce Indian and Ceylonese laborers into Malaya in the 1920s, creating an ethnic division that plagues Malaysia to this day. European states that professed to be reluctant to add new colonies with their attendant administrative and defense costs nonetheless allowed and then encouraged their citizens to invest capital in underdeveloped regions: in mines, plantations, warehouses, wharves, railroads, steamships, and banks.

European commerce required trained Europeans, who moved to the colonies in greater numbers each year as transient supervisors. Because they were transient and their new environments strange, the Europeans created their own housing compounds, offices, hotels, recreational facilities, schools, and resorts. Few among the local population could afford to use such facilities, even if granted access to them, so that whites came to be physically separated from native populations. Relations once relatively friendly became distant. The local inhabitants became employees of European companies that were in distant European capitals. The whites who supervised them were promoted within their companies largely on the basis of keeping costs low and production high, so that the welfare of local populations was not primary in their priorities. The labor situation was, by its nature, exploitative. Racial differences accelerated the obvious class problems. Where white colonial administrators attempted to meet their responsibilities to native populations, they often clashed with European business people.

Many areas in the tropics were thought to be unsuitable for whites to live in; therefore, they preferred to work through friendly, stable, and powerful local rulers: the Egyptian khedives, the Indian maharajahs, or the shahs of Persia. Such rulers often remained in power only through the money lent to them by Europeans, thus becoming collaborators, puppets on a string, their nations client states of the major powers. With massive investments at stake, European business people often sought to pressure their governments into direct intervention in the affairs of the client states if the pliant rulers appeared to be in danger of being overthrown. Often such intervention was entirely legal, under protective treaties signed by the local rulers who sought outside support for their regimes; where intervention was not legal, sheer force of arms made it possible nonetheless. Equally often, the European powers did not need to land troops, occupy territory, or rattle sabers, for the threat of the use of such force—"gunboat diplomacy"—was sufficient to secure concessions.

Gradually European governments were drawn deeper and deeper into the affairs of Africa and Asia. Most governments preferred not to intervene, but theory and practice did not run parallel. In the 1870s no British colonial secretary favored the annexation of new territories, and yet the Fiji Islands were ceded by King Thakambau to Britain in 1874; Britain left its island base in Southeast Asia, which rested upon the Straits Settlements of Singapore, Malacca, Penang, and Labuan, to intervene directly in the Malayan mainland states of Perak and Selangor in 1875; and the British displaced the Dutch on the Gold Coast (now Ghana), in Africa, in 1872.

Common to these areas of expansion was the recurrence of native turbulence within the hinterlands adjoining areas of importance to European trade. On the Malayan mainland, successive governors sought to avoid expansionism, and yet they expanded, for the Chinese-controlled tin trade was racked by rivalries, and the

TECHNOLOGY AND EMPIRE

The Industrial Revolution in Europe had given the West an immense advantage throughout the world in weaponry, shipping, invention, and health. This advantage would last until air transport and the potential for atomic warfare again changed, by a quantum leap, the technological distance between societies, forcing a new formulation of the definitions of world power. Until that time, national pride was relatively simple in its expressions. Prince Bernhard von Bülow (1894-1929), chancellor of Germany from 1900 to 1909, whose aggressive policies over Morocco helped isolate his country and pave the way for World War I, remarked, "Where I have planted my foot, there shall no one else be permitted to place his." And a British writer, Hilaire Belloc (1870-1953), wrote satirically of how technology—in the form of the machine gun—gave the British victory over the Boers in the South African war:

I never shall forget the way
That Blood upon this awful day
Preserved us all from death.
He stood upon a little mound,
Cast his lethargic eyes around,
And said beneath his breath:

"Whatever happens we have got
The Maxim gun,
and they have not."

Hilaire Belloc, *The Age of Imperialism* (Englewood Cliffs, N.J.: Prentice-Hall, Inc., 1969), p. 59. Reprinted by permission of Gerald Duckworth & Co., Ltd., and Random House, Inc.

Malayan sultanates, upon whom stability within the peninsula lay, were subject to frequent struggles over succession to the thrones. Burma was annexed in 1885 for similar reasons. In South Africa the British expanded north and east time and again, despite an expressed desire not to, because of repeated incursions into white settlement areas by Bantu tribes, equally repeated clandestine raids upon native areas by the Boers, and disruptions by successive Zulu chiefs. The British took such action because the mercantile community wanted peace, stability, and dependable communications with the interior, so that raw materials might flow freely into the ports that Europeans controlled.

The new imperialism was thus far more widespread and far more pervasive than the old, and it often grew out of the barrel of a gun, as the old had grown upon the pages of a ledger. Simple Marxist views that the race for colonies, and World War I, was caused by an imperialist conflict over markets must be rejected; however, the urge to expand that characterized European states before World War I was a psychological symptom of a problem that had economic roots—the intensely competitive nature of nineteenth-century capitalism.

The period from 1815 to 1870 saw a partial decline in imperialist fortunes, as most of Spain's American colonies gained their independence, as Brazil broke away from Portugal (1822), and as Britain took the first major steps leading to the independence of Canada, but other nations surged forward. The French established themselves in Algeria in 1830; the Americans, through a colonization society, established ties with Liberia in

West Africa in 1821; and the British annexed Lagos, the nucleus for Nigeria, in 1861. Russia did not expand overseas and parted with its vast but thinly inhabited possession in North America when the czarist government sold Alaska to the United States in 1867. But Russia began the effective settlement of the great areas east of the Urals and began to push into the borderlands of the Middle and Far East, toward Persia, India, and China.

Throughout the century, the Americas and the old British settlement colonies were generally outside the scramble for empire. The Monroe Doctrine, which European nations increasingly heeded as the strength of the United States grew, helped to keep both American continents free from further annexation by outside powers. So too did the British navy. Competition between Britain and Germany for markets and for fields of investment in South America intensified in the 1890s and was one of many factors that brought these powers to war. Since no state was strong enough to take the older colonies from Britain, throughout the nineteenth century British problems both in colonies of settlement and colonies of exploitation were essentially internal problems of the British system itself, and Britain was slow to recognize that these problems were developing.

One major field of rivalry and penetration was the Near or Middle East, essentially the widespread territories under varying degrees of Turkish control, plus Persia. The whole "Eastern Question," as it was called, revolved around the problem of what was to be done with the Balkan and eastern Mediterranean territories, which were peopled principally by Muslims. They were backward regions by nineteenth-century Western standards, their farmlands exhausted by centuries of simple agriculture and their ancient irrigation systems often in disrepair. They were poor also in natural resources, for their great wealth in petroleum would not be important until the twentieth century. England, France, Austria, and Russia were in active competition over the Near East early in the nineteenth century, and they were later joined by Italy and Germany. The principal issues were diplomatic, dynastic, and strategic, however, rather than imperialistic.

Africa was the scene of the most spectacular imperial rivalry. In 1815, except for the nominally Turkish lands of North Africa, the Dutch settlement at the Cape of Good Hope (formally acquired by the British in 1815), and a string of Portuguese, Spanish, French, and British "factories," or fortified trading posts along the coasts, Africa was untenanted by Europeans and its interior almost unexplored. Islam had penetrated well below the Sahara, expecially in the western Sudan, in Futa Jalon (northern Guinea), and in the empire of the Sokoto (roughly northern Nigeria), from which a flourishing trade had developed. Between 1840 and 1860 trade also developed substantially from the east African centers of Mombasa and Zanzibar, with Indians acting as money-lenders and Arabs leading the caravans that penetrated well into the interior. Traders brought out information about the interior, and the first missionaries, who established themselves in Mombasa after 1844, added to Western knowledge of African customs, geography, and resources. Soon exploration was well under way. In the latter half of the century the great powers—Britain, France, and Germany, as well as Portugal, Italy, and Belgium—blocked out territorial units under their respective flags over most of the continent. The only exceptions were the small Republic of Liberia and the mountainous inland state of Abyssinia (now Ethiopia). Contact with Abyssinia had once been relatively active, and the ruling dynasty claimed descent from King Solomon and the Queen of Sheba, but after the Jesuits were expelled in 1632, contact with outsiders was systematically discouraged. The British invaded the land in 1868 to free some English captives, but then withdrew, and not until 1896 would a European nation seriously seek to breach the Abyssinian kingdom. Then the Abyssinians, under their emperor Menelek II (1844-1913), defeated an Italian army at Adowa and maintained their independence until the Italians tried again under Mussolini in 1935.

The Far East was also a major scene of imperialist rivalries. European powers strengthened their hold on older colonies and acquired new ones in Southeast Asia: the mainland areas of Burma, Indochina, and Malaya, and the island groups of Melanesia and Polynesia. But the ancient, thickly populated, highly complex Chinese Empire was never subjected to actual partition and direct annexation. However, China was not sufficiently united politically or advanced industrially to resist European penetration, and by the end of the century it was subjected to a de facto partitioning among Britain, France, Germany, and Russia. Each power operated from certain treaty ports as centers and exercised some control (basically economic) over considerable areas—*spheres of influence*, as they were called. Often they conducted business through local go-betweens, or *compradors*, who by the end of the century were becoming instrumental in beginning the modernization of China. Rivalry among the European powers and the United States, which favored an Open Door policy of permitting as much free trade in China as was possible and of preserving Chinese sovereignty, served to counterbalance Chinese weakness and left China an independent nation.

Japan had isolated itself from the rest of the world from the midseventeenth to the midnineteenth centuries. This compact island empire was closed to foreigners during the period when European powers strengthened their small holds in China. Then in 1854 an American naval officer, Matthew C. Perry (1794-1858), persuaded Japan to open two ports to outside trade. By adopting some Western ways, particularly economic ways, and by capitalizing on its own military tradition, Japan was able not merely to preserve real independence during the late nineteenth century but to begin its own imperial expansion on the mainland of Asia after winning a brief war with China in 1894-1895. It also began to compete industrially with the West, becoming the first modern nation-state in the Far East.

III THE BRITISH EMPIRE

The United States was the product of an earlier age of imperialism that had brought many Europeans to the first colonies of settlement. American independence had been the eventual result, and while initially the British had felt that they might woo the new republic back into the empire, by 1815 they realized this would not happen. They also recognized that colonies occupied largely by settlers from the British Isles would most likely move toward independence, and therefore they sought to control the pace and nature of this movement in order to assure continued loyalty to the concept of a Greater Britain, rather than try to prevent it altogether.

The colonies of settlement were originally rather thinly inhabited lands. The Europeans were not settling virgin land, however, at least not on the eastern seaboard of North America, and they had to displace a resident population. Though the settlers saw themselves as "civilized" and the indigenous population as "savages," these were relative terms. Scholars disagree over the size of the Indian population; earlier estimates that suggested one million (a figure that encouraged the myth that the New World was basically uninhabited) have now been rather convincingly scaled upward to 10 to 12 million north of the Rio Grand and 80 to 100 million south of that line. There is general agreement that the effects of "the Columbian exchange"—Europe's diseases, firearms, and disruptive practices in exchange for the New World's diseases, foods, and land—reduced the aboriginal population of the New World by 90 percent within a century of European contact. This, then, was the greatest single catastrophe that empire visited upon any land.

In Tasmania, a large island to the south of the Australian mainland, the aborigines were totally wiped out, the last hunted down by dogs in a virtual war of genocide. In Australia, the "blackfellows," as the settlers called them, came close to meeting the same fate. On the north island of New Zealand, the Maoris, who were Polynesians, fought guerilla wars in the 1840s and 1860s in a vain attempt to exclude white settlers from their lands; their numbers shrank from 250,000 to 40,000

during the nineteenth century, perhaps the least catastrophic decline.

Canada, the First Dominion, 1783-1931

The rebellious thirteen colonies of North America had wanted to add a fourteenth or fifteenth, and had tried to win the British colonies of Canada and Nova Scotia, but a complex of causes contributed to leaving both in British hands at the peace in 1783. Most of the precedents by which the British Empire evolved into a commonwealth of self-governing nations were first developed in Canada. Between 1783 and 1931 Canada became the first dominion, fully independent from at least that time and probably earlier, and essentially self-governing from 1867.

North America and the Caribbean, about 1910

Dates indicate year of admittance into Dominion of Canada

The defeat of the British in the American Revolution propelled thousands of loyal Tories northward to start life anew in Canada as United Empire Loyalists. These Loyalists wished protection from the French; they wished to secure their rights as Englishmen, although not to the extent of rebellion against the Crown they had just defended; and they wished to set themselves clearly apart, morally and politically, from the new republic to the south. The result was a history of constitutional changes that provided the pattern for other colonies. Some of these changes arose from Loyalist demands, some from the need to achieve a balance between French-language and English-language interests, and some from the need for protection against an expanding United States. First was the Constitutional Act of 1791, establishing elective assemblies in both Upper and Lower Canada, the new provinces that split the original single structure of Quebec, the first almost exclusively British and the second largely French. A constitutional struggle between the elective assemblies and the governors followed, as in pre-Revolutionary Virginia and Massachusetts, with the central issues being the collecting of revenue, the granting of land for settlement, and the powers of the judiciary. Deadlock resulted by 1837.

Rebellion followed. In Upper Canada William Lyon Mackenzie (1795-1861), "the Firebrand," who had read Tom Paine and lived in the United States, led a popular uprising. In Lower Canada Louis-Joseph Papineau (1786-1871) rallied the disgruntled in Montreal. When the mass of the population remained aloof, the two rebel leaders were easily defeated and fled to the United States. Relations with the republic—which had remained strained since the War of 1812, during which American militia had burned York (present-day To-

ronto), the captial of Upper Canada—deteriorated further. Recognizing the dangers of continued discontent within its North American provinces and of persistent strife with the United States, Britain sought to pacify both situations.

The solution was proposed in the single most fundamental document in the constitutional history of the British Empire: the Durham Report. Lord Durham (1792-1840), a Whig, was sent to Canada by the British to be governor-general with sweeping investigative powers. Concluding that two cultures were "warring within the bosom of a single state," Durham's massive 1839 *Report on the Affairs of British North America* proposed a union of the two Canadas, the British and the French, and the grant of full responsible government to the united colony. Britain would retain control over foreign relations, the regulation of trade, the disposal of public lands, and the nature of the constitution, surrendering all other aspects of administration to local authorities.

The sense of the Durham report was embodied in the Union Act of 1840 and in the governorship of Lord Elgin (1847-54), who in 1849 refused to veto a bill—the Rebellion Losses Bill, intended to compensate those who had suffered losses in the uprisings of 1837, including many of the rebels—that came to him from the assembly. By failing to exercise a power that in theory was his, Elgin showed that responsible government now existed.

The American Civil War sped the next phase of constitutional growth for the British North American provinces. As the conflict continued, many European and Canadian observers predicted that the North would lose the war and then, with its vast standing army—at the time the largest in the world—might invade Canada to compensate for the loss of the Southern states. To this

A MASTERPIECE OF DIPLOMATIC PROSE: A STAGE IN INDEPENDENCE BY EVOLUTION

An important precedent in achieving independence by evolution rather than revolution was marked in Canada, which in 1858-1859 decided to apply tariff barriers against British and American goods in order to promote local industry. The British Privy Council had disallowed earlier efforts by the colonies of New Brunswick and New South Wales (in Australia) to erect tariff structures, and to forestall such a reaction the Canadian finance minister, Alexander T. Galt (1817-1893), sent a carefully constructed message to London which, in its crescendo of warnings, was a superb example of stating the offensive without giving offense. Galt received no reply to his message, and a Canadian tariff was put in force in 1859.

[T]he Government of Canada . . . cannot . . . in any manner waive or diminish the right of the people of Canada to decide for themselves both as to the mode and extent to which taxation shall be imposed . . . even if it should unfortunately happen to meet the disapproval of the Imperial Ministry. Her Majesty cannot be advised to

disallow such acts, unless her advisers are prepared to assume the administration of the affairs of the Colony irrespective of the views of its inhabitants.

Canada, *Sessional Papers*, XVIII (1860), part 4, 4.

fear were added two clear problems: no Canadian administration had been able to govern for long because the parties were so evenly matched that each election produced a near deadlock; and Britain, preoccupied with problems in Europe and hoping to avoid embroilment in colonial wars, threatened to withdraw the imperial troops and counseled some form of regional union for the North American colonies, so that they might be less exposed to American threats.

The result was a series of conferences that by the end of 1865 led to an agreement upon how the weak, separate, and threatened colonies might unite. In 1867 the united Canadas, (now to be called Ontario and Quebec), Nova Scotia, and New Bruswick formed the Confederation of Canada, to be known as a *dominion* (taking the title from the Bible), launching a new nation. Canada was not yet fully independent, but a giant stride toward this goal had been made, a stride that led imperial authorities to associate dominion status with some form of federation between disparate colonies. (When Britain would try to decolonize other portions of its empire after World War II, it would try to do so through a succession of federations, all of which either failed or suffered civil war: the West Indies, Central Africa, Malaysia, South Arabia, and—the one survivor—Nigeria.)

The Canadian confederation held together, however, adding new provinces under the British North America Act of 1867. When British Columbia, which had recently united with the formerly separate colony of Vancouver Island, joined the confederation in 1871, dominion from sea to sea was truly achieved. Thereafter, the interior was progressively settled and new provinces were carved out of the rich agricultural lands. Newfoundland, a separate dominion, had held aloof from unification, but the Great Depression of 1929 forced it into bankruptcy in 1932, and, after reverting to quasicolonial status, it voted to join with Canada in 1949. Meanwhile, Canada had established other precedents by which complete independence from Britain was achieved: the negotiation of a treaty with the United States by which boundary disputes were settled, to which Canada was a signatory (1871); the creation by Canada of its own department for foreign affairs (1909); its assertion of an independent right to sign peace treaties at the end of World War I; its separate membership in the League of Nations (1919); and the removal of any remaining colonial subordination by the Statute of Westminster in 1931. The Canadian government would later renounce the right of its citizens to have royal titles conferred upon them by the English monarch (the only dominion to do so), and would even abandon the title of *dominion* itself in a series of stages after 1950. Thus Canada contrasted with the United States, the other predominantly English-speaking North American frontier society, by achieving its independence through evolution rather than revolution.

Dominion status was applied to other colonies of white settlement. The six provinces of Australia had common British origins and relatively short lives as separate colonies, the oldest, New South Wales, dating from 1788. Nevertheless, they developed local differences and separateness, symbolized by the three different gauges used on the railroads. They gained the essentials of self-government in the Australian Colonies Government Act of 1850, but federal union and dominion status were not achieved until New South Wales, Queensland, Victoria, South Australia, Western Australia, and Tasmania were linked as the Commonwealth of Australia in 1901. The influence of the American example was clear in the constitution of Australia, which provided for a senate with equal membership for each of the six states, a house of representatives apportioned on the basis of population, and a supreme court with certain powers of judicial review. But in Australia, as in the other British dominions, the parliamentary system of an executive (prime minister and cabinet) that could be dismissed by vote of the legislative body was retained. Long before it became a dominion, Australia pioneered in the secret printed ballot; New Zealand (in 1893) and South Australia (in 1894) extended the suffrage to women well in advance of Britain and Canada (1918) or the United States (1920). South Australia also pioneered in legislating compulsory arbitration of industrial disputes, while New Zealand was a social laboratory for the welfare state.

South Africa, 1815-1910

The legacy of empire was particularly complex and ultimately tragic in South Africa, where there were two, not one, white settlement groups. Britain acquired the Cape Colony from the Netherlands in 1815. Because the Cape was strategically important before the opening of the Suez Canal and the climate seemed suited to European settlement, Britishers arrived and soon began to compete for land with the older European colonists, the *Boers* (a Dutch word for farmer). The adoption of English as the sole official language, the abolition of slavery throughout the empire (which took effect in South Africa in 1834), and the attempts by London to protect the aboriginal population went against the grain of the partriarchal Boers, who were fundamentalist Christians who believed that the Bible told them that slavery was ordained of God. Between 1835 and 1837 some ten thousand Boers moved north into sparsely settled country in the Great Trek, a heroic folk migration that would bulk large in South African nationalist feeling. Needing more land to support their custom that each farmhouse should be an hour's walk from any other house (making the average farm six thousand acres in size), and refusing to acknowledge any African rights to the land they were occupying, the Boers pressed against the Bantu and other groups, who had themselves migrated to these lands from the north. After some confused three-cornered fighting among Boers, British, and Zulus, the Boers established two virtually independent states—the Transvaal and the Orange Free State. Located on territory suitable for grazing but not for intensive agriculture, these land-locked, thinly populated states initially posed no threat to the British.

The British settled another province to the east along the Indian Ocean, known as Natal. Cape Colony and Natal, which both had black populations heavily outnumbering the British and remaining Boer residents combined, acquired the self-governing rights that British colonies of settlement elsewhere were acquiring. British South African leaders for the most part wanted to bring the Boer republics under the British flag; but as the London home government swung between Tory and Liberal domination, it also swung between a policy of imperialist expansion and a "Little Englander" policy of leaving the Trekkers alone.

Even as an undergraduate, Cecil Rhodes had in mind a grand plan for the British Empire in Africa. While at Oxford he wrote his "Confession of Faith," which asked, "Why should we not form a secret society with but one object the furtherance of the British Empire and the bringing of the whole uncivilised world under British rule for the recovery of the United States for the making the Anglo-Saxon race but one Empire? What a dream, but yet it is probable, it is possible."

The British Empire at the southern end of the African continent grew reluctantly, caught up in contending policies between ambitious colonial politicians and imperial administrators on the one hand, and indigenous leaders who often saw the British as potential intermediaries on the other. In 1852, by the Sand River Convention, the British (under a Liberal cabinet) acknowledged the independence of Transvaal; soon after they also acknowledged that of the Orange Free State. But in 1877, under Disraeli and the Conservatives, they reversed themselves and annexed Transvaal as a step toward the federation of all South Africa under the British crown. The Boers revolted in 1880, and the Liberal Gladstone, then in power, lived up to his principles by making a treaty with the Boers at Pretoria in 1881 that reestablished the Transvaal as independent, though under the "suzerainty" of Great Britain.

The British were already filtering up through the arid country to the west of the Boer republics when the discovery of gold and the development of a diamond industry in these republics undid Gladstone's work. The Transvaal was no longer a poor and isolated grazing country; it offered a great source of wealth that tempted quite different kinds of settlers. The region about Johannesburg, the Rand, filled up with adventurers and entrepreneurs of a dozen nations, all looking to Britain to protect them from the conservative Boers, to whom they were undesirable *Uitlanders* ("outlander," or foreigners) with differing economic interests.

The simmering conflict came to a head with the Jameson Raid of December 29, 1895.* The British in South Africa were now under the leadership of Cecil Rhodes, prime minister of Cape Colony and a determined imperialist who had made a quick fortune consolidating the chaotic diamond industry. The raid itself, under a follower of Rhodes, Dr. Leander Jameson (1853-1917), was an invasion of Transvaal from British territory and was planned to coincide with an uprising of Uitlanders in Johannesburg. But the uprising did not take place, and the president of Transvaal, Paul Kruger (1825-1904), had no trouble defeating Jameson's handful of invaders. The German kaiser, William II, congratulated the Boer president by telegram, inflaming British public opinion. Boer resistance to the Uitlanders hardened with alien expulsion and immigration restriction acts, and controls were placed over the right of assembly and the freedom of the press. The two Boer republics renewed a defensive alliance, initiated talks with the governor at the Cape, Sir Alfred Milner (1854-1925), and presented an ultimatum to the British government. The ultimatum was rejected, and the Boer War began on October 11, 1899.

The war went badly at first for the British. They did not have enough troops immediately available to put

---

*The seasons are, of course, reversed in the southern hemisphere from those of the northern hemisphere; hence, the December raid took place in midsummer. Overwhelmingly, history has been written from a northern perspective, so that at times historians and readers have forgotten the realities of climate when interpreting events in, say, Argentina, Australia, or South Africa.

Africa and the Middle East, 1910

Belgian
British
French
German
Italian
Portuguese
Spanish

British occupation
Independent

down determined commando fighters, who were on their own ground and were accustomed to the rigors of outdoor life. Western opinion, including that in the United States, generally sided with the underdog Boers, and even in Britain many Liberals and Labourites strongly opposed the war. But in the long run the overwhelming strength of British numbers and technology prevailed. By the middle of 1900 the British had won in the field, but it took another eighteen months to subdue the desperate guerrilla bands into which Boer opposition dissolved, and the British resorted to concentration camps to hold their prisoners, in which disease became a serious problem. In 1902, by the Treaty of Vereeniging, the Boers accepted British rule, with the promise of ultimate self-government. The British ap-

plied Canadian precedents to the Transvaal in 1906 and to the Orange River colony in 1907, and in 1910 they created the Union of South Africa, linking Cape Colony, Transvaal, Orange Free State, and Natal. The seat of the legislature was in the first, at Cape Town; that of the executive in the second, at Pretoria; and that of the judiciary in the third, at Bloemfontein. In the new state the central government was stronger than the member provinces. English and Afrikaans, as the South African Dutch dialect had evolved into, were equal official languages.

Thus, on the eve of World War I South Africa was among the self-governing British dominions. British and Boer seemed to be composing their long quarrel and to be ready to collaborate in developing an increasingly

Egypt and Africa
South of the Sahara, 1859-1914

At the opposite end of Africa, Britain excluded the French from control of Egypt, a semi-independent province of the crumbling Ottoman Empire. French influence had continued there since Napoleon's venture, and in the late nineteenth century French prospects in Egypt seemed particularly bright. Between 1859 and 1869 the private French company headed by Ferdinand de Lesseps built the Suez Canal, which united the Mediterranean with the Red Sea and shortened the sea trip from Europe to India and the Far East by thousands of miles. The British had opposed the building of this canal under French patronage; but now that it was finished, the canal came to be considered an essential part of the lifeline of the British Empire.

The British secured a partial hold over this lifeline in 1875, when Disraeli arranged the purchase of 176,000 shares of stock in the canal company from the financially pressed *khedive* (prince) Ismail (1863-1879). The shares gave Britain a 44 percent interest in the company. Despite the sale of the stock, Ismail's fiscal difficulties increased, for he had spent heavily in his efforts to hurry Egypt into a position of international eminence. The Egyption national debt, which was perhaps £3,300,000 at his accession, rose to £91,000,000 by 1876. That year, with Ismail's bankruptcy threatening, the European powers (from whose private banks Ismail had borrowed large sums at high interest) obliged Egypt to accept the financial guidance of a debt commission that they set up.

Two years later Ismail had to sacrifice still more sovereignty when he was obliged to appoint an Englishman as his minister of finance and a Frenchman as his minister of public works to ensure that his foreign creditors had first claim to his government's revenues. In 1879 Ismail himself was sacrificed when his creditors prevailed on the Ottoman emperor to depose him. Egyptian nationalists, led by army officers whose pay was drastically cut by the new khedive as an economy move, revolted against foreign control and against the government that had made this control possible. Using the slogan "Egypt for the Egyptians!" the officers established a military regime that the powers feared would repudiate Egyptian debts or seize the Suez Canal. France and Britain sent a joint note of concern that was deemed threatening, angering both the khedive and the Ottoman sultan; expecting action against them, in 1882 the British and French sent a naval squadron to Alexandria, ostensibly to protect their nationals. A riot there killed fifty Europeans. The Egyptian military commander began to strengthen the fortifications at Alexandria, but the British naval squadron destroyed the forts and landed British troops, declaring they were present in the name of the khedive to put an end to the disorders. The khedive gave the British authority to occupy Port Said and points along the Suez Canal to ensure freedom of transit. But

The ill-equipped Boers inflicted surprising defeats on the British Army early in the South African War. Here a group of Boers are shown in 1899.

important outpost of the West. But there were ominous signs even then. The Boers resisted being Anglicized, and they were still fundamentally opposed to their partners in empire. The foundations of an intensely divisive policy of racial segregation had been laid, especially in native policy in Natal after 1845, and racial separation was extended by the restriction of immigration from India after 1897. Though South Africa was a frontier, the presence of open land had none of the democratizing effects experienced by settlers in the United States, Canada, and Australia. Because the indigenous African population was a suppressed majority, South Africa would become increasingly troubled over matters of race. As racial barriers were applied to freedom of movement, the very notion of a "frontier" of opportunity failed to arise, and South Africa created for itself a major problem relating to migrant labor. The two European elements together were in a minority of one to four compared with the non-Europeans: the Africans, the East Indians (who had immigrated in great numbers, especially to Natal), and the "colored" peoples of mixed blood.

In 1869 the Suez Canal, a hundred miles in length, was opened to the steamships of the world. The *Illustrated London News* represented the grand convoy to its readers as shown here. Forty-six ships moved through the canal at ten-minute intervals all day long on November 17, with the empress Eugénie's imperial yacht in the lead.

the French held back because of a cabinet crisis at home and also because they were involved in Tunisia, occupied the year before. Thus Britain acted alone and acquired the upper hand in Egypt, taking the canal and occupying Cairo. Dual French-British control was over.

By the eve of World War I Britain exercised virtual sovereignty over Egypt. Legally, Egypt was still part of the Ottoman Empire, and the khedive's government remained; but a British Resident was always at hand to exercise control, and each ministry was guided by a British adviser. For a quarter of a century this British protectorate was in the hands of an imperial proconsul, Sir Evelyn Baring, Lord Cromer (1841-1917), Resident in Cairo from 1883 to 1907. Under Cromer and his successors the enormous government debt was systematically paid off and a beginning made at Westernizing the economic base for Egypt, symbolized by the completion of the first dam on the Nile at Aswan, increasing the amount of water for irrigation and the potential agricultural output. But nationalist critics complained that this was too small a beginning, that too little was being spent on education and public health, and that British policy was designed to keep Egypt in a perpetual colonial economic status, exporting long-staple cotton and procuring manufactured goods from Britain, rather than establishing home industries.

Egyptian nationalists were also offended by British hesitation in permitting experiments in representative government and by British policy toward the Sudan. This vast region to the south of Egypt, today the largest African nation, four and a half times the size of France, had been partially conquered by Muhammad Ali and Ismail, then lost in the 1880s as a result of a revolt by an Islamic leader, Muhammad Ahmad (c 1844-1885), who called himself the *mahdi* (messiah). Fears that France or some other power might gain control over the Nile headwaters prompted Britain to reconquer the Sudan. The reconquest at first went very badly for the British. An

Egyptian army under British leadership was annihilated, and the anti-imperialist Gladstone, again prime minister in Britain, hoped to get out of Egypt, not be drawn further in. The British press trumpeted for revenge, and General Charles George ("Chinese") Gordon (1833-1885) was dispatched to Khartoum, the Sudanese capital. Gordon was a romantic folk hero in Britain, having won his nickname by reorganizing a brigade of Chinese forces under European officers to help put down the Taiping Rebellion in China in 1862-1864. But Gordon proceeded badly, lost the confidence of Gladstone, and was surrounded in Khartoum. A relief expedition to rescue Gordon left too late, and after passing most of 1884 under seige, Gordon fell to the Mahdists on January 26, 1885, sixty hours before relieving steamers arrived. Finding Khartoum occupied by the Mahdists, the expedition retired. When news of Gordon's death reached England, public reaction was intense, rocking the government to its foundations.

National pride required the avenging of Gordon and the reconquest of the Sudan. This was achieved by Lord Kitchener (1850-1916) in an overwhelming victory against the Mahdists at Omdurman in 1898. Between the defeat of Gordon and the battle of Omdurman the British had exploited their technological superiority. They had extended the rail line from Cairo into the heart of the Mahdists' land, using a gauge to match that at the Cape of Good Hope; and they had equipped their troops with new rifles, the Maxim machine gun, and field artillery. The Mahdists were armed with spears and muzzle-loading muskets. At Omdurman the Mahdists were destroyed and the superiority of European arms definitively established. The Mahdists lost 10,800 killed and 16,000 wounded; the Anglo-Egyptian army lost 48 killed and 382 wounded.

A week later news reached Kitchener that French troops were at Fashoda, within the Sudan and on the upper Nile, having crossed from the Atlantic coast. The

The British on the attack at the Battle of Khartoum.

result was a crisis in Anglo-French relations, which led to an assertion of British supremacy over the entire Sudan. Fearing that the French intended to dam the Nile and block new irrigation for Egypt, Kitchener pressed on toward Fashoda. The French, weakened and preoccupied by the Dreyfus affair and unable to depend on their Russian ally, withdrew and renounced all claim to the Nile valley. The British made the Sudan an Anglo-Egyptian condominium (joint rule), of which they were the senior partner. This assured clear British dominance in Egypt, since they now controlled the source of its water supply, and it assuaged public opinion in Britain, which had clamored for war; but it aroused Egyptian nationalists, who feared Egypt had lost a province rightfully belonging to it alone. Thus began a period of progressively better relations with France, which would be cemented by the Anglo-French Entente of 1904. The British had gained one more possession and a vital link in their dream of an all-British route by rail and water from Cairo to the Cape.

Between the Cape and Cairo the British steadily added to their African possessions throughout the century. At its end they had the lion's share of the continent. They had only 4 million square miles out of over 11 million, but they controlled 61 million people out of some 100

million. The most significant areas were in West Africa. Sierra Leone had been founded after a British judge, Lord Mansfield (1772), had decided that slaves could not be held in England. Seeking some place for free blacks, the British established the "province of freedom" in 1787, adding to its population by bringing in freed slaves from the North American colonies after the American Revolution. This, the only black settler colony, would not be encouraged to evolve as the white settler colonies had done, however, and it would not become independent until after World War II. More important in terms of resources and strategic location was the Gold Coast, acquired in three of Britain's seventy colonial wars of the nineteenth century by the defeat of the Ashanti in 1874 and, more completely, in 1896 and 1900. The whole of Ashantiland was formally annexed in 1901.

The most important, however, was the colony and protectorate of Nigeria, to which one of Britain's ablest administrators, Sir Frederick (later Lord) Lugard (1858-1945), applied a method of colonial governance known as "indirect rule," which he had initiated earlier when governor in Uganda, and which became characteristic of British colonial rule in tropical Africa, as well as on the Malay peninsula and in Samoa. Centering on the great River Niger, Nigeria was formally put together from earlier West African colonies in 1914. Northern Nigeria was ruled by Muslim emirs of the Fulani people; southern Nigeria was inhabited by divided groups that had long been harassed by slave raids. The region over which the British asserted control comprised Hausa, Yoruba, and Ibe peoples—the first Muslim, the others increasingly converted by Christian missionaries, and all three in conflict with each other.

In the Americas, Britain maintained its colonial dependencies in the Caribbean in Bermuda and the Bahamas, and on the mainland in British Honduras (now Belize) and British Guiana (now Guyana). Tiny dependencies were held as well in the Atlantic between the Americas and Africa at St. Helena, Tristan da Cunha, and the Falkland Islands; to the last, the independent nation of Argentina periodically asserted a claim. Limited self-government of the seventeenth-century kind, which some of the Caribbean island colonies had lost in the midnineteenth century, was gradually granted them in the twentieth. These were all tropical or semitropical lands, with a relatively small planter class, large black or "brown" lower classes, and often a substantial commercial class from South Asia. The West Indies suffered gradual impoverishment as a result of the competition offered to the local cane sugar crop by the growth in other countries of the beet-sugar industry, together with an increase in population beyond the limited food resources of the region. By 1914 the once proud "cockpit of the British Empire" had become an impoverished "problem area."

As racism grew in most of the West toward the end of the century, the African and West Indian colonies tended to be lumped together in the official mind of British imperialists. Racial disharmony became more common, but it did not reach its peak in the British Empire until the 1920s and early 1930s, when white settlers moved in substantial numbers into Kenya and the Rhodesian highlands. Nor would racist arguments be applied so stringently to the Asian areas of the empire, even though a sense of European superiority became ever more apparent.

India, the "Crown Jewel of Empire," 1815-1915

In India Britain's victory over France in 1763, confirmed by its victory over Napoleon in 1815, left it in sole dominance over the subcontinent of Asia. India was the richest of Britain's overseas possessions, the center and symbol of empire, as the imaginative Disraeli realized when in 1876 he had Queen Victoria proclaimed empress of India. It was over India that the British most often debated the merits of direct intervention versus indirect control, massive social reform imposed from without versus creation of a collaborating elite that would carry out the reforms from within, and whether nature (that is, race) or nurture (that is, environment) most determined a people's future. India figured prominently in British political debate, and especially in Liberal party debate, in a way the rest of the empire did not.

In 1763 India was already a great and well-peopled land, but not, in the Western sense, a single nation. It was a vast collection of identities and religions, ranging from the most cultivated Brahmins to tribes still in the Stone Age technologically. As the nineteenth century began, the two main methods of British control had already become clear. The richest and most densely populated regions, centering on the cities of Calcutta, Madras, and Bombay and on the Punjab, were maintained under direct British rule. The British government

Queen Victoria was made empress of India by Disraeli. Though she did not travel to Asia, she was invested with that title in a magnificent ceremony known as a *durbar*, held in Delhi, India.

did not originally annex these lands; they were first administered by the English East India Company, a chartered enterprise surviving from the great days of mercantilism in the seventeenth and eighteenth centuries. The company in its heyday had taken on enormous territories and made treaties like a sovereign power. In the nineteenth century the company was regarded by most economists and political thinkers as outdated, and the India Office of the central government in London gradually took over the real control and administration of British India. The trading monopoly of the company had long since been undermined. In 1857 the company's native army of Sepoys rebelled. As is true in all major conflicts, the rebellion was brought on by a number of causes. It was fed by rumors that bullets issued to soldiers were coated with grease made from beef fat, repugnant to Hindus, or from pork fat, repugnant to Muslims. But the basic cause was that all the soldiers had come to fear that British ways were being imposed on them, to the destruction of their own ways. The Sepoy Rebellion was put down, but not before several massacres of Europeans had occurred, and not without a serious military effort by the British, which ended in brutally harsh punishment and executions of some of the mutineers. The mutiny ended the English East India Company. In 1858 the British crown took over the company's lands and obligations, announcing that no further annexations were sought in India.

The rest of India—roughly a third of its area and a fourth or a fifth of its population—came to be known as the "feudal" or "native" states. These were left nominally under the rule of their own princes, who might be fabulously rich sultans, as in Hyderabad, or merely local chieftains. The "native" states were governed through a system of British Resident Advisers, somewhat like the system later adapted to Nigeria. The India Office never hesitated to interfere with succession of ruling families, or to disallow acts of princes, or even to assume direct rule when it was thought necessary. While it may not have been Britain's intention, the effect was to allow Britain to "divide and rule" the diverse continent with an authority, and thus a unity, it most likely would not have achieved for itself. One result was to place heavier emphasis on secure routes of passage to India (as with the Suez Canal); another was to make trade with China more secure; yet another was to create an Anglo-Indian class within the subcontinent whose fortune rested on the empire.

Material growth under British rule in India is readily measurable. In 1864 the population of India was about 136 million; in 1904 it was close to 300 million. Although the latter figure includes additional territories in Burma and elsewhere, it is clear that nineteenth-century India experienced a significant increase in total population. In 1901 one male in ten could read and write—a high rate of literacy for the time in Asia; only one in a hundred and fifty women could read and write. On the eve of World War I India had thousands of miles of railroads, telegraph lines, universities (where classes were conducted in English), hospitals, factories, and busy seaports. But in proportion to the total population, India did not have these advantages to anything like the extent that even the poorest of European countries had them. Statistics show a native ruling class sometimes fantastically rich, and an immense peasant class for the most part living as their ancestors had lived, at subsistence level. A middle class was just beginning to form, and like all the middle classes formed in non-European lands under European penetration, it had proportionately far more aspirants to white-collar posts in law, medicine, and other liberal professions than to posts in international trade, engineering, and industry—fields badly needed by modernizing societies.

The total wealth of India increased under British rule and was spread more widely among the Indian populations in 1914 than it had been in 1763. Proportionately less and less wealth went directly from an "exploited" India to an "exploiting" Britain. The familiar English "nabob" of the seventeenth and eighteenth centuries, who made a fortune in India and retired to comfort and perhaps to a peerage in England, almost ceased to exist. Anglo-Indian economic relations typically took the form of trade between a developed industrial and financial society (Britain) and a society geared to the production of raw materials (India). Indians took an increasing part in this trade, and toward the end of the century local industries, notably textile manufacturing, financed for the most part with British capital, began to arise in India. Indians also did much for themselves, for they had always followed commercial pursuits, and the conflict between cultures had injected a sense of competition and frequently a desire for excellence that had its parallels in the West.

Historians debate whether British rule in India brought social revolution or social stagnation. In some areas society seemed little touched by the transfer of power into British hands, yet in others the rate of colonial impact was startling. Historians do agree, however, that the union between British and Indian ideas and energies was unique; the Utilitarians, who early defined policy for India, were compatible with any Indian nationalists who wished to reform their society; the humanitarians and evangelicals from Britain were matched by Indian leaders who added their own Indian ethical standards to the desire for change; those British who saw themselves as trustees or guardians were met by Indians who considered themselves a chosen people and who espoused a caste system; and the Burkeans, who stressed duty and the close study of human institutions before attempting to alter them, found many Indian thinkers already intent upon *dharma* (duty) and self-knowledge. While India had many leaders who drew upon both the British and the Indian ethical arguments, perhaps none blended the several points of view so well as did Mohandas K. Gandhi (1869-1948), who had been admitted to the British bar and had learned of racism firsthand while working for the rights of Indians in South Africa. In 1915 Gandhi returned to India to begin working for the independence of his people.

Throughout the nineteenth century many British—

One of the richest men in India was the gaekwar of Baroda, whose opulent life-style quickly caught the imagination of the British. At that time court photographers were replacing court painters, and Raja Lala Deen Dayal, court photographer to the Nizam of Hyderabad, recorded this photograph of Fateh Singh Rao, the eldest son of the gaekwar, in 1891.

few in proportion to the total population, but numbering in the thousands—"lived off India." Some of them were in private business, but most were military and civilian workers, the generally efficient Indian civil service who "ran" India. Yet Indians were gradually working their way into positions of greater responsibility, into both private and public posts at the policy-making level. Both groups opposed the evolution toward independence for India, because their jobs and sometimes their fortunes depended upon continued colonial status. While the British recognized, at least in theory, the complexity of Indian cultures, and while they acknowledged that one day India, and perhaps the great island off its southern tip, Ceylon, would be independent, they did not expect that day to come soon. One official report released between the world wars predicted that India would require two centuries to pass through the stages of preparation exemplified by Canada.

IV OTHER EMPIRES

The French

The British victory in the "Second Hundred Year's War," capped by the defeat of Napoleon in 1815, had stripped France of all but insignificant remnants of its former empire. Yet during the nineteenth century France acquired a new colonial empire second in area only to that of the British. France, despite frequent revolutionary changes in government, maintained an imperi-

alist policy that added close to three and a half million square miles to the lands under the French flag and some fifty million people. This empire was concentrated in North, West, and Equatorial Africa, and in Indochina.

Little of this second French colonial empire was thought suitable for settlement by Europeans, especially since a third of it was taken up by the Sahara Desert. A major exception was French North Africa: Tunisia, Algeria, and Morocco. These lands were once flourishing parts of the Roman Empire; after France took them over, they reached a greater degree of material prosperity than they had known for nearly eighteen centuries. These lands, with a typically Mediterranean climate, were inhabited chiefly by Berber and Arab peoples of Muslim faith. Though the total indigenous population increased greatly under French rule, over a million European colonists moved in. Mostly French, but including sizable groups of Italians and Spaniards, these *colons* took land from the native groups. Though they added to the total arable acreage by initiating irrigation projects and other improvements, they were hated by the native peoples.

The French got a toehold in North Africa in 1830 through an expedition against Algerian pirates, stayed on, and spent forty years in "pacifying" the hinterland of Algiers in the face of stubborn local resistance. The French then added protectorates over Tunisia to the east (1881) and over Morocco to the west (1912). In 1904 Britain gave the French a free hand in Morocco as compensation for their exclusion from Egypt. In Algeria and Tunisia the French called their policy one of assimilation—in contrast with the British policy of indirect rule. They hoped to assimilate Africans into French civilization, making them ultimately into representatives of the eighteenth-century Enlightenment and the principles of 1789. They hoped to create an empire of "one hundred million Frenchmen," more than half of them overseas, and to draw on abundant local manpower to fill up the ranks of the republic's armies.

In the main, assimilation proved difficult and was only partly achieved. Militarily, the policy worked out pretty much as the French had hoped; black troops from Senegal and *goums* (Moroccan cavalry serving under French or Algerian Muslim officers) gained a reputation as tough fighters. The French, always desirous of spreading their culture, did bequeath their language and laws to part of the indigenous elite. Under the Third Republic they made Algeria politically a part of France itself, organizing it into three departments, each with representatives to the Chamber of Deputies; the franchise was open to the relatively small group of Europeanized Algerians as well as to colons.

In Morocco the French took a somewhat different tack. They sought, in part successfully, to open the area to French business and to the international tourist trade. Casablanca became a great modern city. But even by World War I, it was apparent that economies based in large measure on tourism were chronically dependent and unstable, so that a diversified economic base was badly needed. In 1912 the French colonial administrator Marshall Lyautey (1854-1934) began to apply a "splash of oil" policy; that is, he pacified certain key centers by establishing firm working relations with the local population, and then hoped to let pacification spread over the surface of Morocco like a splash of oil on water. The sultan and his feudal subordinates were maintained in Morocco by the French, left relatively free to carry on traditional functions, but stripped of real power. Tunisia, like Morocco, was formally a regency and was wanted by Italy. Because Tunisia was small and easily pacified, assimilation was pursued more intensively there than in other French possessions, while in Algeria it worked least well. When the three French North African states became independent after World War II, a bloody war broke out between indigenous Algerians and colons.

In 1815 the British had left France its small posts in West Africa at the mouth of the Senegal River, together with a slight foothold on the great island of Madagascar off the East African coast. By 1914 the French had been very successful in the partition of Africa, perhaps because the British preferred French to German aggrandizement, especially after 1870. In 1914 France had nearly as many inhabitants in Africa as in the home territories (about thirty-nine million). Yet outside of North Africa and in certain coastal towns where their administration and business enterprises were concentrated, the French had not achieved much progress toward assimilating or Westernizing their vast districts. Most of their attempts to hasten the economic development of their African lands by organized joint-stock companies, as the British had developed theirs, failed

miserably. Still, in justifying their policy of assimilation, the French claimed an absence of racial prejudice, in contrast with the British, and a willingness to accept blacks as equals.

In Asia, the French took over lands that came to be called French Indochina, which included two rich, rice-growing deltas around Hanoi in the north and Saigon in the south, inhabited by peoples culturally and ethnically related to the Chinese. They also included Cambodia, culturally related to Siam, and the remote mountain peoples of Laos. In the process they made many enemies: the French fought the Vietnamese in 1883, forcing the status of a protectorate on the court at Hué in 1883; fought a war with China in 1884, since Peking claimed Vietnam as its own protectorate; used a puppet at Hué to install French resident advisers throughout Annam; assumed power in Cambodia in the face of a popular revolt; and claimed Laos by promoting a coup that threw off Siamese overlordship in 1893. France also took part in the struggle for control of China proper. The French sphere of influence was in southern China, in particular the province of Yunnan adjoining Indochina; in 1898 the French won a lease on a port on the South China Sea.

The French sought to assimilate the local elite class, and they turned Saigon into a French-style city of broad boulevards. They brought substantial material progress in medicine and hygiene, communications, roads, education, industry, and agriculture. They also applied to proud societies European notions of hierarchy. Nationalist movements, nourished by educated local leaders who held jobs of less dignity and authority than they believed should be theirs, rose in strength as the years went on.

Other Continental Powers

Germany and Italy came late to the imperial scramble, as they came late to national unity. Nevertheless, Germany was clearly a great power, and Italy aspired to be one; hence, both sought to acquire at least token colonies.

Condemned to the role of weakest of the great powers, Italy got very little out of the partition of Africa. Tunis, which Italy coveted, went instead to France. Italy's major effort centered on the lands at the southern end of the Red Sea, but after the defeat by the Abyssinians in 1896, Italy had to be content with a few thousand square miles, most of it desert, in Eritrea and Somaliland. Italian efforts to add to this insignificant empire by taking Tripoli from its nominal Turkish ruler succeeded in 1912. They also secured Rhodes and other islands off the southwestern corner of Anatolia, known collectively as the Dodecanese ("the twelve"). These acquisitions were the fruit of the Italo-Turkish War of 1911-1912. In any case, Italy was not greatly interested in an empire in Africa; of greater concern were territorial aims in the Adriatic and in Albania.

Until the 1880s Bismarck had resisted calls for imperialism, for he felt that domestic unity and military strength on the European continent were paramount. In

1882 a German Colonial League was founded by north German merchants who feared that without overseas expansion Germany would not keep pace with Britain. Two years later Germany signed treaties creating a German protectorate in Southwest Africa, largely as a strategic challenge to Britain, and acquired Togoland and the Cameroons (Kamerun). In 1885 Germany declared an official protectorate over East Africa, urged on by a man as visionary as Rhodes, Karl Peters (1856-1918), who had founded a Society for German Colonization. But only Tanganyika and Zanzibar had any potential economic significance, and the latter was traded to Britain in 1890 for the tiny British-held island of Heligoland, in the North Sea.

In the Pacific, the Germans picked up some small islands, and a large territory on the island of New Guinea. Germany also took part in the attempted partition of China, taking a ninety-nine-year lease on Kiachow Bay, on the north China coast. Germany also had designs on the Portuguese empire, as the French had on the Spanish. The latter two nations came to terms over Morocco in 1910, that portion closest to the Spanish coast being assigned to Spain. But Britain, which also hoped to inherit the huge remnants of the Portuguese empire, successfully blocked the Germans, so that the Portuguese possessions would remain Portuguese and would, in fact, become the last in Africa to be decolonized. The Portuguese had sought to extend their trading activities into the interior of both Angola and Mozambique, and they continued to control the strategic islands of São Tomé and Fernando Po in the Bight of Biafra. The Belgians helped to establish an International African Association 1876, with the purported goal of suppressing the slave trade and gathering scientific information; the association sent Henry Morton Stanley (1841-1904) to open up the region of the Congo, at which he worked persistently until 1884.

The Germans and British feared this expansion, and they also feared that Belgian or French exploration would threaten the Portuguese territories, which controlled the approaches to the Congo River. Thus in 1884 an Anglo-Portuguese treaty guaranteed freedom of navigation on the Congo to all nations; however, British public opinion and the press opposed this support of Portugal. The treaty was shelved, and Bismarck summoned an international convention in Berlin to settle the Congo and Portuguese issues. The Congo basin was declared a free trade area by the conference in 1885, the independent state of the Congo—with King Leopold of Belgium as its sovereign—was recognized, and the Portuguese were left in possession of their territories, though frequently challenged by the British along the borders of Mozambique and the Germans from south of Angola.

Thus Belgium, through the enterprise of its shrewd and ruthless king, Leopold II (1865-1909), managed to acquire a large part of equitorial Africa. This project began as the Congo Free State, with an announced ideal of cooperative European civilizing missions in Africa; it ended up in 1908 simply as the Belgian Congo. Nineteenth-century scandals about forced labor and ruthless exploitation in the Congo called Leopold's experiment to the attention of the world and provided anti-imperialists with fresh arguments. The Belgians developed the Congo into one of the most profitable of colonies, thanks to its copper, rubber, and other riches, and Belgium made no move to prepare the Congolese for eventual self-government.

The Belgian Congo thus became one of the three foci of anti-imperial debate before World War I. The others were the rise of pro-Boer sentiment and opposition to the Boer War in Britain, and a sustained effort in the United States to prevent America from acquiring an empire as the fruit of the Spanish-American War.

The United States

Americans did not regard their westward movement as an exercise in imperialism, but it showed many of the same characteristics. While the industrial powers of Europe were expanding overseas, the United States acquired by purchase and conquest the remainder of its Manifest Destiny—a dominion from sea to sea that was "to bring the blessings of liberty" to the entire continent. The United States believed it had a moral obligation to expand in order to extend the area of freedom against monarchical or dictatorial governments.

The first American empire was solely within the continent. By the end of the century the Indian had been swept aside—into reservations, off ancestral lands—and was a ward of the state. Once the Indian was "pacified"—the last major battle was fought at Wounded Knee in Dakota Territory, in December of 1890—and the frontier was thought to be closed, the main thrust of the westward movement was over, and Americans would have to look elsewhere for new worlds to conquer. By the 1870s a national consensus was emerging that the new frontiers should be sought overseas, especially in trade, and particularly in the Caribbean and the Pacific. The Pacific Ocean had represented the territorial goals of most American presidents through James K. Polk, with control of the harbors of San Diego, San Francisco, and the Juan de Fuca Strait (near present-day Seattle) a primary aim. Such essentially maritime needs strengthened the desire of British and American statesmen to find a peaceful solution to a controversy over the Oregon Territory (1846); and the acquisition of California in 1848 was seen as essential to American advancement into the Pacific.

In 1854 Admiral Perry persuaded the Japanese to open two ports to American vessels by the Treaty of Kanagawa. But if the China trade and the expected Japan trade were to flourish, American vessels needed repair and refueling facilities elsewhere in the Pacific. The Hawaiian Islands now took on added significance, for, besides refuge, they also afforded supplies of sandalwood for the China trade. After the discovery of gold in California in 1848, the islands provided the mainland

In 1854 a Japanese artist portrayed Commodore Matthew Perry as shown here. The caption refers to Perry as "a high official of the North American Republic."

with badly needed sugar and foodstuffs. In 1875 the sugar growers in Hawaii, largely Americans, obtained a reciprocal trading agreement with the United States that stipulated that no part of Hawaii might be given by the Hawaiian Kingdom to any other country. Sugar exports to America increased, until the islands were utterly dependent upon the continental market, and in 1884, when the agreement was renewed, the United States was granted exclusive use of Pearl Harbor as a naval base. In the meantime, the indigenous population declined rapidly, and the planters in need of labor, imported thousands of Chinese, Japanese, and Portuguese.

Hawaii was annexed on July 7, 1898, the first land outside the North American continent to fly the American flag on a permanent basis. Although Hawaii had been within the American economic orbit for three quarters of a century, annexation had waited upon three developments: the overthrow of the Hawaiian monarchy and creation of a republic in which American sugar producers counted heavily; the imposition of a new tariff that put sugar on the free list and thus made Cuban sugar, so much closer to the large eastern cities, competitive; and the victory of American naval forces over Spanish defenders at Manila Bay nine weeks earlier,

accentuating the American need for a midway base between Asia and the West Coast.

The events at Manila Bay would have been of little importance had it not been for a slow, corrosive series of quarrels with Spain in the Caribbean. That Americans chose to quarrel with European nations over their colonial possessions in the New World seemed natural to many, for as early as 1823 the Monroe Doctrine had made it clear that the United States saw itself as exerting a strong moral influence in Latin America. The Monroe Doctrine was given a corollary in 1895, when President Grover Cleveland (1837-1908) intervened in a boundary controversy between Venezuela and Britain, asserting that the United States had an obligation to the free nations of the entire Western Hemisphere to protect them from abuse by European powers. In the same year Cuba revolted against Spain. As the revolt spread, American sugar and tobacco growers and iron mine owners on the island complained of the destruction of their property. Outnumbered by the Spanish troops in Cuba, the revolutionaries turned to guerrilla warfare, hoping to draw the United States into intervening. A new governor, appointed in 1896, sought to limit the effects of guerrilla tactics by forcing large elements of the rural population into concentration camps. There thousands died. While American business opposed direct intervention in so unstable a situation, the "yellow" press, in the midst of intense campaigns to increase circulation, printed atrocity stories that stirred up prorevolutionary sympathy. Then, on February 15, 1898, the U.S. battleship *Maine*, at anchor in Havana harbor as an indication of America's intent to protect its nationals' property, was destroyed by an explosion that killed 260 officers and men.

President William McKinley (1843-1901) sent an ultimatum to Spain demanding an armistice in the revolution and an end to the concentration camps. Spain revoked the camp policy at once, and instructions were sent to the governor ordering an armistice. But the American people were looking for the action and for the adventure they thought war would be. The nation was tense, worried over the lingering depression that had begun in 1893, disturbed over a populist revolt and free-silver agitation, and caught up in an overheated political campaign in 1896 in which both parties had engaged in much rhetoric about what the future of America should be. Without waiting to learn the details of the Spanish armistice order, McKinley presented the Cuban crisis to Congress with the charge that Spain's response had been "disappointing." After lengthy debate, Congress voted recognition of Cuban independence on April 19, authorized the use of American troops to make recognition effective, and pledged "to leave the government and control of the Island to its people." A scenario of escalation was then played out. McKinley signed the resolution, and the United States served an ultimatum upon Spain to grant Cuban independence. Spain broke diplomatic relations; the American navy blockaded Cuban

Asia and the Pacific about 1910–1926

British territory
British protected states
Dutch territory
French territory
German territory
Japan and Japanese territories
United States and possessions

Pacific Ocean

SAMAR
LEYTE
MINDANAO
PHILIPPINE ISLANDS (U.S.)
LUZON
MINDORO
PANAY
NEGROS
PALAWAN
Manila
South China Sea
BORNEO
Miles
200
0

CANADA
UNITED STATES
San Francisco
MEXICO
120

ALASKA (U.S.)
ALEUTIAN IS. (U.S.)
60 (Russia)
60 (U.S.)

R U S S I A
S I B E R I A
Lena R.
L. Baikal
Chita
Krasnoyarsk
Yenisei R.
Irtysh R.
Omsk
Ob R.
Aral Sea
TRANS-SIBERIAN RAILROAD
Amur R.
KAMCHATKA
KURILE IS.
SAKHALIN IS.
Vladivostok

Pacific Ocean
30
INTERNATIONAL DATE LINE

HAWAIIAN ISLANDS (U.S.)
Honolulu
JOHNSTON IS. (U.S.)
KINGMAN REEF (U.S.)
PALMYRA IS.
MIDWAY IS. (U.S.)
WAKE IS. (U.S.)
MARSHALL IS. (Ger.)
HOWLAND (U.S.)
BAKER IS. (U.S.)
PHOENIX IS. (Br.)
GILBERT IS. (Br.)
ELLICE IS. (Br.)
AMERICAN SAMOA (U.S.)
W. SAMOA (Ger.)
FIJI IS. (Br.)
180
NEW ZEALAND
Auckland
Wellington
30

JAPAN
Tokyo
Kyoto
KOREA
Seoul
Port Arthur
MANCHURIA
Peking
Tientsin
Yellow R.
Yangtze R.
Mekong R.
CHINA
Nanking
Shanghai
Wenchow
Foochow
Kiaochow Bay (Ger.)
Canton
Hong Kong (Br.)
Macao (Port.)
OKINAWA
FORMOSA
PHILIPPINE ISLANDS (U.S.)
GUAM (U.S.)
MARIANAS IS. (Ger.)
CAROLINE IS. (Ger.)
BISMARCK ARCH. (Ger.)
SOLOMON IS. (Br.)
NEW GUINEA
MELANESIA
NEW HEBRIDES (Br. and Fr.)
NEW CALEDONIA (Fr.)
150

MONGOLIA
TANNU TUVA
SINKIANG
TIBET
BHUTAN
NEPAL
BURMA
SIAM
LAOS (Fr.)
ANNAM (Fr.)
INDO-CHINA
FED. MALAY STATES (Br.)
Singapore (Br.)
BORNEO
SUMATRA
DUTCH EAST INDIES
CELEBES
JAVA
Batavia
TIMOR (Port.)
AUSTRALIA
WESTERN AUSTRALIA
SOUTH AUSTRALIA
QUEENSLAND
NEW SOUTH WALES
VICTORIA
Brisbane
Sydney
Canberra
Melbourne
Adelaide
Perth
TASMANIA
120

AFGHANISTAN
PERSIA
INDIA
Karachi
Bombay
Goa (Port.)
Damam
Diu (Port.)
Mahé (Fr.)
CEYLON
Madras
Pondicherry (Fr.)
Karikal (Fr.)
Yanaon (Fr.)
Calcutta
Chandernagore (Fr.)
90
Indian Ocean
60

277

ports; Spain declared war against the United States for an act of aggression; and the United States countered with a declaration of war against Spain on April 25, making the declaration retroactive to April 21.

The Spanish-American War lasted 115 days, and the American forces swept all before them. The American army lost 5,462 men, the great majority to disease in their camps rather than to enemy bullets. The Spanish empire was broken, its army crushed, and virtually all of its battle fleet sunk or driven onto the beaches. Five days after war was declared, Admiral George Dewey (1837-1917), forewarned two months earlier by Theodore Roosevelt, then assistant secretary of the navy, to sail for Hong Kong, reached Manila Bay. There he methodically destroyed a larger Spanish fleet, and thirteen days later American troops, reinforced Filipino guerrillas under General Emilio Aguinaldo (1869-1964), occupied Manila, On July 4 remote Wake Island, west of Honolulu, was taken; on July 7 Hawaii was annexed; on July 25 Puerto Rico fell; and the next day Spain asked for peace terms. The Treaty of Paris, by which the Philippines were ceded to the United States, was signed on December 10. Spain surrendered all claim to Cuba, assumed the Cuban debt, ceded Puerto Rico and the Pacific island of Guam to the United States as indemnity, and received $20 million in payment for the Philippines. In one quick step the United States had become a maritime empire with interests in both the Caribbean and the Far East.

American troops remained in control of Cuba until 1902. Before they could be withdrawn, Senator Orville H. Platt (1874-1905) proposed an amendment to the Army Appropriation Bill of 1901 (an amendment later made part of a treaty with Cuba and imbedded in the Cuban constitution at American insistence) providing that Cuba could not enter into any treaty or assume any public debt without American permission, and that the United States might intervene in Cuba at any time "for the preservation of Cuban independence." In effect, Cuba became an American protectorate and the second largest recipient of American investments in the Western Hemisphere. Investment required stability, and from 1917 until the Platt Amendment was abrogated in 1934, the American government made it clear that it would recognize no hostile regime in Cuba.

It was the Pacific that continued to be the testing ground for the growth of an American empire, however. To maintain control over Caribbean areas seemed natural, for Americans had long considered themselves to be the guardian of the New World. To attempt the same in the remote Pacific invited new dangers. The Filipinos showed that they felt betrayed by the continued presence of the American army, and when Aguinaldo learned that the Treaty of Paris had given the Philippines to the United States, he organized an armed revolt that continued as guerrilla warfare until mid-1902. A special commission established by President McKinley recommended ultimate independence for the islands, with American rule to continue indefinitely until the Filipinos

proved themselves "ready for self-government." One condition of such proof was to terminate the rebellion and accept American rule. In 1916 partial home rule was granted to the Philippines; in 1935 the islands became a commonwealth; and in 1946 they were granted full independence (see map on p. 277). They proved to be a financial loss to the American people, and their strategic value was dubious, for while they provided the American navy with a valuable base for Far Eastern operations, they also posed a constant challenge, especially in the 1930s, to the expanding Japanese empire.

On the whole, American imperialism in Asia was nonterritorial, since the British naval presence in the area made outright colonial expansion by the United States difficult and in most cases unnecessary. American policy was best symbolized by the Open Door concept. The Opium War of 1841 between Britain and China, the Sino-Japanese War (1894-1895), and the disintegration of the Manchu Empire in the 1890s had left the Chinese open to demands by European nations for political and economic concessions and the carving up of the China trade into spheres of influence. The British had taken Hong Kong, and the French, Germans, and Russians were on the move. The British suggested that the United States join in guaranteeing equality of commercial access to China for all Western nations. In a circular letter of September 6, 1899, Secretary of State John Hay (1838-1905) asked for assurances from Germany, Russia, and Britain (and later from France, Italy, and Japan as well) that none would interfere with any treaty ports in China, and that none would discriminate in favor of their own subjects when collecting railroad charges and harbor dues. Although he received evasive replies, Hay announced in March 1900 that the principle of the Open Door was "final and definitive." Thus, the United States had gained assurance of at least an equal chance to exploit the China market.

The Panama Canal Zone added a third and final chapter to the American attempt to compromise between economic advantage and political interest. Concluding that intervention in the Caribbean and Central America would continue to be necessary to the United States—now involved in a two-ocean foreign policy and needing to move naval forces quickly from the Atlantic to the Pacific—Theodore Roosevelt moved forward on two fronts. Roosevelt, who had succeeded McKinley as president in 1901 after the latter's assassination saw the election of 1900 as a mandate on imperialism. Desiring canal rights in Central America, he connived a Panamanian revolt against Colombia, immediately recognized the independence of Panama, and in November 1903, the Hay-Bunau-Varilla Treaty, gained perpetual rights of use and control of a canal zone across the isthmus of Panama for the United States, in exchange for $10,000,000 and an annual fee.

A year later "T.R." added a further corollary to the Monroe Doctrine, fearing armed European intervention in Venezuela after that nation had defaulted on debts to Britain and Germany. Roosevelt stated that if Latin

American nations could not administer their own financial affairs, and if they gave European nations cause for intervention, then the United States might be forced to "exercise . . . an international police power" in the Western Hemisphere. This was especially applicable to nations that could threaten access to the canal route, and when the Panama Canal was opened on August 15, 1914, the United States had further reason to protect its Caribbean approches. Under Roosevelt's corollary, Santo Domingo became an American protectorate in 1907, as did Haiti in 1915. American marines were stationed in Nicaragua from 1912 until 1925; in 1916 the United States acquired the right to construct a canal across Nicaragua; and the Virgin Islands were purchased from Denmark in 1917. Even revolution in Mexico—which began in 1913 and led to American intervention at Vera Cruz in 1914 and along the northern border two years later—did not disturb the flow of commerce, investment, and shipping in the Caribbean, which had become "an American lake." Not until an entirely new dimension was added to the tensions among world powers by the cold war between the Soviet Union and the United States was American dominance over the Caribbean breached.

The Japanese Empire

One more empire was being formed during the decades before World War I, the only modern empire to be created by a non-European people—the Japanese. Even during their long, self-imposed isolation the Japanese had maintained an interest in Western developments through the trading station that the Dutch were allowed at Nagasaki, and they had been discovering Europe for themselves for over a hundred years. When Japan opened its ports in 1853, its basic political and economic structure had long been in need of overhauling. The ruling feudal oligarchy was ineffective and unpopular. Discontent was growing, especially among two important social classes. One was the urban middle class of merchants and artisans. Although the Industrial Revolution had not yet reached Japan, the country already had populous cities, notably Tokyo (then called Yedo or Edo). The urban middle class wanted political rights to match their increasing economic power. The other discontented class may be compared roughly with the poorer gentry and lesser nobility of Europe under the Old Regime. These were the *samurai*, or feudal retainers, a military caste threatened with impoverishment and political eclipse. The samurai dreaded the growth of cities and the subsequent threat to the traditional preponderance of agriculture and landlords; many of them also resented their exclusion from positions of power by the prevailing oligarchical regime. These social pressures, more than outside Western influences, forced the modernization of Japan.

Economically, the transformation proceeded rapidly. By 1914 much of Japan resembled a Western country, for it too had railroads, fleets of merchant vessels, a large textile industry, large cities, and big business firms. The industrialization of Japan was the more remarkable in view of its meager supplies of many essential raw materials. But it had many important assets. Japan's geographical position with respect to Asia was very like that of the British Isles with respect to Europe. Japan too found markets for exports on the continent nearby and used the income to pay for imports. The ambitious Japanese middle class, supplemented by recruits from the samurai, furnished aggressive and efficient business leadership. A great reservoir of cheap labor existed in the peasantry, who needed to find jobs away from the overcrowded farms and who were ready to work long and hard in factories for what seemed very low wages by Western standards.

Politically, Japan appeared to undergo a major revolution in the late nineteenth century and to remodel its government along Western lines. Actually, however, the change was by no means as great as it seemed. A revolution did indeed occur, beginning in 1868 when the old feudal oligarchy crumbled. Authority and prestige were restored to the position of *mikado* (emperor), who had been only a figurehead for many years. In 1889 the emperor bestowed a constitution on his subjects, with a bicameral diet composed of a noble House of Peers and an elected House of Representatives. The architects of these changes, however, were not democrats; they were aristocrats and ambitious young samurai, supported by allies from the business world, who were determined to make Japan over from above. The result was to substitute a new oligarchy for the old. A small group of aristocrats dominated the emperor and the state. The Constitution of 1889 provided only the outward appearance of full parliamentary government; the ministry was responsible not to the Diet but to the emperor, and hence to the dominant ruling class. The Diet itself was scarcely representative; the right to vote for members of its lower house was limited to a narrow male electorate, including the middle class but excluding the peasants and industrial workers.

Japan began its overseas expansion by annexing the island of Formosa from China after a short war in 1894-1895. China was also forced to recognize the independence of Korea, which Japan coveted. But Russia, too, had designs on Korea; the result of this rivalry was the Russo-Japanese War of 1904-1905. Japan secured unchallenged control in Korea (which was annexed in 1910), special concessions in the Chinese province of Manchuria, and the cession by Russia of the southern half of the island of Sakhalin, to the north of the main Japanese islands. Thus Japan had the beginnings of an empire, which it would seek to expand further by playing a role on the winning side in World War I. The Japanese saw no reason to accept European notions of racial superiority. By victory in war, first with Russia, then as an Allied nation fighting with Britain and France in World War I, and then most dramatically after the war, they set out to disprove all claims of Western superiority.

Empire Challenged

By 1914 it was quite clear that many non-European peoples were beginning to reject claims of white supremacy, including the colonies of exploitation. The educated classes in the Middle East and Asia were developing a sense of nationalism. They took from the West that particular form of group consciousness that is attached to a territorial political unit and that is shared, in principle at least, by all who live within the unit. This concept of nationalism, new outside of Europe and the Americas, had continued to spread. In the early twentieth century it was most evident in Japan and, to some extent, China, Egypt, and India.

Egyptian, Indian, and Chinese patriots were primarily concerned with getting rid of their European imperial masters; their attitudes were those of oppressed nationalistic groups everywhere. They were organized on a new principle copied in some measure from the West—the secular religion of nationalism. In theory, nationality transcends the dividing lines of profession, social class, and even caste. The *fellah*, the Egyptian peasant whose ancestry reached back more than fifty centuries, could claim to be as good an Egyptian as the aristocratic *pasha*—indeed a better one, since he was uncorrupted by European culture. People began to talk and write of "Arab" nationalism, of a spirit of *négritude* that might unite black Africa, of Irish nationalism, of a separate *canadienne* identity, of a separate Afrikaans language and faith. Imperialism, which had once looked as though it might unite peoples, had by 1914 become another cause of nationalism, even as it had once been, in part, a result.

Imperialist rivalries, especially after 1870, exacerbated the normal rivalries among the European great powers and were thus a major factor in the complex of causes that brought on the war in 1914. This is particularly true of the Anglo-German rivalry, which, unlike that of France and England or of Austria and Russia, had no long historical background. This Anglo-German rivalry was manifested everywhere by 1900—by commercial travelers of both nations trying to sell machinery in South America; by missionaries in Africa; by army and naval officers, editors, labor organizers, all seeking to make either German or British influence prevail. The rivalry extended even to the academic world; there were those who regarded the Rhodes Scholarships for study at Oxford, founded in 1904, as a British attempt to counterbalance the great prestige that German universities had acquired in America. Increasingly, the public, assailed by rumor and political persuasion, found it difficult to separate the silly from the sinister, a task especially essential in a democratic society.

Was imperialism harmful? All forms of imperialism—while often bringing stability, sanitation, education, and improved communications to an area—forced people to change at a pace set by someone else. All imperialisms, including those directed toward the ultimate independence of a colony, implied that only the superior power could name the stages through which the inferior must pass and the degree and speed of that passing. The most pervasive legacy of imperialism was the pernicious assumption that "superior" nations had the unquestioned right to judge the progress of "inferior" nations. Although the short-run physical benefits of imperialsm may have been great for both imperial power and colony alike, the psychological effects ultimately may have been harmful to both.

Imperialism was surely harmful in creating two special classes within colonial and postcolonial societies. The first were the products of racial intermixture—called half-breeds in the United States, *métis* in Canada, *lançados* in Portuguese colonies, *mestizos* in Spanish, and Eurasian, throughout Asia. Such people often found that they were accepted by neither society from which they sprang. Some European societies and some churches showed less racial prejudice than others. Roman Catholics generally tried to ameliorate the condition of slaves and of free nonwhites, although here too there were great differences between orders, the Jesuits practicing greater racial liberality than the Franciscans, for example. The French often intermarried or intermated. And so long as the colonial people assimilated French cultural norms and language, the French practiced relatively less systematic or state-supported discrimination than did other nations. The English and later the Americans, on the other hand, had far deeper fears about "race mixing."

A second half-way group created by imperialism were those now referred to as collaborators—members of the indigenous culture who felt that the future lay with Europe and the colonial power. While some cooperated with the imperial powers for purely personal gain, others collaborated because they shared the European conviction that the values Europe brought to their society outweighed the disadvantages. Some saw the Europeans as peace makers, since they often had the power to enforce peace where local chiefs could not; others chose to work with the conquerors because they were impressed by European forms of representative government. Ironically, nationalist leaders in these colonies would often use the words and techniques of the imperial powers against them—Ceylon arguing against a continued British presence after 1947 in the words of Bentham, Burke, Locke, and Mill, and India's Gandhi and Nehru using British parliamentary practices to achieve national independence. Uruguay would have its senators who were pleased to speak of themselves as British liberals, Africans would take western names, Maoris would accept knighthoods, and an entire class of Anglo-Indians would arise.

Although Western influence was extensive at the surface, in many areas it did not touch the village level, and African and Asian societies remained essentially unchanged at the bottom. But the intellectual and political elites at the top were transmuted in fundamental ways, and even those who did not accept Western culture had to battle against it on Western terms. Military, technological, political, and intellectual patterns throughout the world were Westernized. Non-Western peoples faced crises of identity in Asia and Africa. That essentially European concept, the nation-state, and the rampant nationalism of the twentieth century became a basic heritage of the imperialism of the nineteenth. In this sense the Western impact on traditional societies, if not by 1914 then by 1929, was so great as to constitute an imperial revolution no less pervasive than the scientific, industrial or commercial revolutions. Imperialism became a state of mind and Europe a place name on a worldwide mental map—a map that was to be much altered as a consequence of the Great War of 1914-1918.

SUMMARY

In the nineteenth century Britain emerged as a parliamentary democracy. The Reform Bills of 1832 and 1867 accomplished revolutionary changes without violence. The cabinet controlled Parliament; representation was increased through the extension of suffrage and the reform of rotten boroughs. In the stable political atmosphere of England, the two-party system grew. Disraeli and Gladstone, leaders of Conservatives and Liberals respectively, dominated politics in this age of reform.

By the late 1800s economic difficulties and challenges abroad led to calls for protectionism. Liberals gave up their classical laissez-faire doctrines in exchange for government interference. Conservatives became committed to laissez-faire. While the Liberal party fragmented and declined, the Labour party gained strength.

In Ireland, resistance to English dominance increased as a result of the potato famine. Piecemeal reforms did not satisfy Irish nationalists. The struggle for home rule eventually produced a bill in 1912, but it never went into effect because of the outbreak of World War I.

Between 1800 and 1930, 84 percent of the world's land came under the control of Western nations. Economic, political and psychological motives, including a desire for national glory, contributed to imperialism in the late nineteenth century. Strategic concerns also came into play as imperial powers sought to protect trade routes. A humanitarian impulse was evident in the desire to reform and Christianize other peoples.

Imperial powers acquired both formal and informal empires, exercising control over areas that were technically independent. The new imperialism after 1870 involved emotional and nationalist needs, but it was also tied to industrialization and cultural goals.

In the nineteenth century, the relationship that evolved between Canada and the British Parliament set the pattern for self-government in other white-settled colonies. These changes paved the way for independence without revolution. By 1914, Australia, New Zealand, and South Africa had also achieved self-government.

In Egypt, Britain gained the upper hand with control of the French-built Suez Canal, considered Britain's lifeline to India. Britain expanded into the Sudan and acquired colonies in East and West Africa as well as in the Caribbean and Central and South America.

After 1815 Britain dominated India, which became the symbol of empire when Disraeli had Queen Victoria proclaimed empress of India. The Sepoy Rebellion (1858) allowed the British government to take control of the lands formerly administered by the English East India Company. Other areas were ruled by local princes under the control of British administrators.

In the nineteenth century France acquired a colonial empire in North Africa and Indochina. After achieving national unity, Germany and Italy entered into the scramble for colonies. Italy acquired Tripoli and lands along the Adriatic. Germany acquired colonies in East Africa, southwest Africa, and among the Pacific islands.

Westward movement in the United States had similar characteristics to imperialist expansion elsewhere. The United States pushed through to new frontiers in the Pacific, acquiring Hawaii and the Philippines. In 1900 Americans supported the policy of an Open Door in China to guarantee equal commercial access to the disintegrating Manchu Empire.

After 1853 Japan experienced rapid modernization and industrialization, accompanied by imperial ambitions. In 1895 it annexed Formosa after a war with China, and in 1905 gained control of Korea after its defeat of Russia. Non-Europeans rejected white supremacy, and many patriots worked against imperialist ambitions.

GREAT WAR, GREAT REVOLUTION

On June 28, 1914, the Hapsburg arch-duke Francis Ferdinand, heir to the throne of Austria-Hungary, and his wife, Sophie Chotek, were assassinated in the streets of Sarajevo, capital of the province of Bosnia, which had been occupied by Austria-Hungary since 1878. The assassin, Gavrilo Princip (1895-1918), was a Serbian nationalist, and Bosnia had long been coveted by the Serbs. The Austro-Hungarian government, alarmed by the ambitions of Serbian nationalists, took the occasion of the assassination to issue a severe ultimatum to Serbia. The Serbian government's refusal to accept the ultimatum in its entirety led to an Austrian declaration of war on Serbia on July 28. Within the week, the great states of Europe were engaged in a general war—the Central Powers (Austria-Hungary and Germany, joined by Turkey and, later, Bulgaria) against the Allies (Serbia, Russia, France and Britain, eventually supported by eighteen other nations).

Princip's bullet would eventually cost 36 million casualties in killed, missing, and wounded. This was the first general war, the first war to involve most members of the world state system, since the wars of the French Revolution and Napoleon a century earlier. After the war, and particularly after the failure of the peace settlement and the widespread disillusionment with leaders who apparently had so naively fought a "war to end all wars," much public debate took place about where the greatest responsibility for the war lay. This debate, though appearing to look backward and thus be a matter for historians, in fact looked forward, to help political leaders justify new policies (including fascism) in their nations. This debate over the *causes* of the war became confused with the moral issue of *responsibility* for the war, and once again the public was led to confuse cause with responsibility, and responsibility with guilt. Thus, historians, public leaders, those who spoke for the church, for the press, for pacifism, for rearmament became deeply engaged with sorting out war aims, with tracing how those aims changed during the course of the war (as war aims invariably do), and with using history as a weapon rather than as a tool for analysis, to justify yet another world conflagration. Many saw the two world wars of 1914-1918 and 1939-1945 as a continuity.

On the morning of June 28, 1914, Archduke Francis Ferdinand and his wife set out on a round of ceremonial visits. There had been no signs of danger during the Bosnian tour, but in Sarajevo the archduke was greeted by a bomb attack, in which he was not injured. After completing his ceremonial functions, Ferdinand decided to visit the hospital where an officer wounded in the attack was being treated. The prearranged route for the motorcade was abandoned, and the archduke's car sped along and made a wrong turn. As the chauffeur applied the brakes preparatory to backing up the car, Gavrilo Princip, who apparently by chance was standing on the corner, stepped forward and fired point blank at the archduke and his wife.

Since the great Russian Revolution took place in the context of World War I, and since its results led in time to the great cold war of the midtwentieth century, the period from 1914 to the present comprises, in effect, a remarkable whole which, though brief, has the coherence of the long religious wars of the sixteenth century and after.

I CAUSES OF THE WAR

Shifting National Self-Images

In the long view, one factor that made war more likely was the unification of Germany and Italy. The creation of these two new major states in the 1860s and 1870s altered the always delicate balance of power in the European state system; the efforts of statesmen during the next forty years to adjust the system and to take account of the two new powers ultimately proved unsuccessful. The older established powers were unwilling to give up their own claims. After 1850, with the principle of national sovereignty well established, smaller western European states were no longer open to annexation by the great powers, even through the peaceful means of a change of religious allegiance or a dynastic marriage; there was little territory available in Europe for making adjustments. In the late nineteenth century only the Balkan lands of the weakening Turkish Empire remained as possible territorial pickings for ambitious powers. Even there, the growth of national feeling in Romania, Serbia, Bulgaria, and Greece made formal annexation difficult. Instead, amid intense rivalry, much of Africa, Asia, and the Pacific islands underwent a partitioning that always seemed capable of revision by territorial exchange, annexation, or conquest.

Meantime, influenced by their rivalries in Europe and abroad, the great powers were choosing sides in a series of alliances and agreements. By the early years of the twentieth century two increasingly armed camps existed: the Triple Alliance (Germany, Austria-Hungary, and Italy), and the Triple Entente (France, Britain, and Russia). As many people at the time saw clearly, the system had become so tightly organized that there was almost no free play left; after 1900 almost any crisis might lead to war.

Nationalism and the accompanying shifts in the balance of power both influenced and were profoundly influenced by public opinion. A slowly but persistently widening public base was making itself heard through representative assemblies at the national and local levels; through a rising demand for romantic novels of empire and wartime heroism, the mass sales of which indicated a trend of public taste; and through the public press, which both reflected opinion (since newspaper owners depended on sales and advertising for their revenue) and shaped opinion (since the newly enfranchised and newly literate often tended to trust what they saw in print more than what they heard). Throughout western Europe and in the United States a jingoistic press, often intent on increasing circulation, competed for "news," and not all papers were careful to separate

---

THE BRITISH PRESS GIVES OFFENSE TO THE GERMANS

The rapid growth in printing technology and in newspaper readership meant that public opinion was increasingly expressed by, and influenced by, the press. In October 1908 the German kaiser had granted an interview to a correspondent for the London *Daily Telegraph* by which he hoped to allay British fears about the naval race between the two powers. While the kaiser assured the British of his friendly feelings toward them, the printed version of his remarks so offended the German naval and military leaders that the kaiser found that he had to give way to their demands for more armament. The Russian ambassador reported on this furor:

Encouraged by the undoubted preparedness of the Army and the other strata of society for the war and offended [by the debates caused by the newspaper reports] in their traditional feelings of loyalty towards their Supreme Leader, the war party regards war as the only means to restore the prestige of monarchical power which has been shaken in the eyes of the masses. The mood of military circles is nourished by the conviction that the present superiority of the Army promises Germany the greatest chance of success. Such convictions could entice the present Kaiser to give his foreign policy a militant character. At the same time a victorious war could, at least for an initial period, repel the radical currents among the people pressing for a change of the Prussian as well as the Reich Constitution in a more liberal direction. These are, in general outline, the symptoms of the German domestic situation, which could help to explain the causes of the military preparations.

Quoted in V.R. Berghahn, *Germany and the Approach of War in 1914* (New York: St. Martin's Press, 1973), p. 81.

the verifiable from the rumor, the emotional atrocity story (even when true) from the background account that would explain the context for the emotion.

Technology made printing far cheaper than it had ever been. In 1711 the highly influential English paper *The Spectator* sold two thousand copies a day, and there was only a handful of effective competitors; in 1916 a Paris-based newspaper sold over two million copies a day, and there were hundreds of other newspapers. This revolution in communicating the printed word had taken place in the nineteenth century. That authoritative "Thunderer," *The Times* of London, began to use steam presses in 1814, producing copies four times as fast as before. In Britain and France and later in central Europe, the railway made a national press possible, for the papers of Paris could be read anywhere in France the next day. After the 1840s the invention of the telegraph encouraged the creation of news services and the use of foreign correspondents, so that the same story might appear throughout the nation though in different papers. Taxes on newspapers were removed, as in Britain in 1855. When Richard Hoe (1812-1886), a New Yorker, invented a rotary press in 1847 that could produce twenty thousand sheets an hour, the modern newspaper was born. Linotype and monotype machines were also used to set books, and by 1914 there had been a massive leap in the sale of all reading matter. This in turn gave rise to greater censorship in some societies, and everywhere to an awareness that the printed word could be manipulated to political purposes. By the end of the century, when a newspaper cost a penny, few people were out of reach of that word.

The word was supplemented by photographs, which increasingly replaced drawings. The battle map was introduced to the public in the American Civil War. After 1839 *daguerrotypes* began to replace painting as a means of conveying reality. In the 1880s, with the invention of relatively inexpensive dry plates, mass-produced cameras became available. A simple box camera, the Kodak, was invented in 1888, and with the concurrent commercialization of the halftone screen, newspaper pictures became commonplace. The graphic nature of war was brought into the living rooms of the middle class daily with home delivery of the illustrated newspaper.

Newspapers became more important in political life, especially as elementary education became more commonplace and standardized. In Britain Alfred Harmsworth (1865-1922), in France Charles Dupuy (1844-1919), and in the United States two competitors, Joseph Pulitzer (1847-1911) and William Randolph Hearst (1863-1951), brought all the elements together to create mass journalism. These "press lords" helped to develop mass opinion. The two Americans worked to promote war with Spain in 1898, and all these papers supported the establishment and jingoist views.

The introduction of universal peacetime conscription by the continental powers, made possible by the increased productivity and efficiency of the factory system, further stimulated the introduction of compulsory universal elementary education, and later of universal manhood suffrage. These led to a further growth in the number of readers, to greater political content in the press, and to the quest for technological innovation in rapid typesetting. One could, by 1900, genuinely speak of "public opinion" as a force in world affairs.

Thus the outbreak of war in 1914 saw in each belligerent nation broad public support of the government. Many men marched off to war convinced that war was good. Bands played, crowds shouted, and war seemed romantic as well as necessary. Even the socialists supported the war. Yet, public opinion might as easily have been led against war, had an increasingly complex alliance system not cut off national options and individual leaders not chosen the course they did. For example, in the hectic five weeks after the assassination at Sarajevo, the German kaiser, William II, belatedly tried to avoid a general war. But in the decisive years between 1888 and 1914 he had been an aggressive leader of patriotic expansion, a "White Knight" leading his people to glory, encouraging German youth to believe that while their enemies were numerically superior, Germany's spiritual qualities would more than compensate for brute strength. He was, at the least, a willing and effective figurehead for expansionists and violent nationalists.

German ambitions and German fears had produced an intense hatred of Britain, a hatred that focused on the English upper classes, thought to be perfectly tailored, smug in their effortless superiority, the favorite children of fortune. At first few English returned this hate; the English were still on top despite their dependence on imported foodstuffs. But as the expensive race between Britain and Germany in naval armaments continued, as incident after incident occurred, and as German wares progressively undersold British wares in Europe, in North and South America, and in Asia, the British began to worry about their prosperity and leadership. In India, the greatest British possession, it was already clear that concessions toward self-government would have to be made to the nationalists. Closer to home, the Irish crisis was in an acute phase, with Protestant Ulster in arms against the proposed home rule and British officers stationed there guilty of planning a mutiny in 1914. The British were worried about their obsolescent industrial plants and their apparent inability to produce goods as efficiently as the Germans; they were critical of their commercial failures abroad and their stodgy self-satisfaction. There was, in effect, a crisis of imperialism in British domestic politics. The British were frightened.

In democratic France as in democratic England, prewar opinions on international politics ran the gamut. A large socialist left was committed to pacifism and to an international general strike of workers at the threat of actual war. However, there remained an embittered patriotism of the defeated; the French wanted *revanche*, revenge for the defeat of 1870. They wanted Alsace-Lorraine back. The revanchists organized patriotic

ART IN THE SERVICE OF HATE

Wartime feelings were expressed in the poem "A Chant of Hate Against England" by a lesser German writer, Ernest Lissauer (1882-1937):

French and Russia they matter not,
A blow for a blow and a shot for a shot,
We love them not,
We hate them not,
We hold the Weichsel and Vosges gate,
We have but one and only hate
We love as one, we hate as one,
We have one foe and one alone: —

     . . .

You will we hate with a lasting hate,
We will never forego our hate.
Hate by water and hate by land,

Hate of the head and hate of the hand,
Hate of the hammer and hate of the Crown.
Hate of seventy *millions*, choking down.
We love as one, we hate as one,
We have one foe and one alone:

     England!

Ernst Lissauer, "A Chant of Hate Against England," trans. Barbara Henderson, in Burton E. Stephenson, compiler, *The Home Book of Verse*, 3rd ed. (New York: Holt, 1918), II, 2549-50. Note that this poem was included in a book of English and American verse designed for reading aloud at home. The Vosges and Weichsel were approaches to Germany through France.

societies, edited patriotic journals; since 1871 the statue representing Strasbourg among the cities of France in the Place de la Concorde in Paris had been draped in black. The French, like the British, had supported movements for international peace—the Red Cross, conferences at the Hague in 1899 and 1907, and various abortive initiatives by the international labor movement. But French diplomats continued to preserve and strengthen the system of alliances against Germany, and in July 1914 it was clear that France was ready for war. In short, the armed peace was in danger of degenerating into international anarchy. Nationalism, imperialism, and militarism were emotions not amenable to careful, logical negotiation. Secret diplomacy, entangling alliances, and international crises made compromise ever more difficult.

Triple Alliance and Triple Entente, 1879-1918

After 1891 Bismarck feared a French attempt at revenge and sought to isolate France diplomatically by building a series of alliances from which it was excluded. Germany, he insisted, was by the 1880s a "saturated" power and wanted nothing more in Europe. He sought to keep on good terms with both Austria and Russia, and, what was more difficult, to keep both these powers on good terms with each other. Since both wanted to dominate the Balkans, Bismarck's task was formidable.

Bismarck laid the cornerstone of his diplomatic system by a defensive alliance with Austria-Hungary in 1879, an alliance that held until 1918, and by the League of the Three Emperors (1872-1878, 1881-1889), which bound Germany, Russia, and Austria together. The three powers agreed to act in common when dealing with Turkey, and to maintain friendly neutrality should any

one of them be at war with a power other than Turkey. Next, working skillfully on Italian anger over French expansion in Tunis and on Italian fear that France might join an international effort to restore Rome to papal sovereignty, Bismarck secured an alliance among Germany, Austria-Hungary, and Italy directed chiefly against France—the Triple Alliance of 1882, often renewed, which still existed on paper in 1914.

On this series of tightropes Bismarck maintained a precarious balance through the 1880s. Uppermost in his mind was the danger that the Russians, fearful of Austrian designs upon the Balkans, would desert him and ally themselves with France, always anxious to escape from the isolation that Bismarck had designed for it. In 1887 Russia did refuse to renew the League of the Three Emperors, but Bismarck was able to repair the breach by a secret Russo-German agreement known as the Reinsurance Treaty. The two promised each other neutrality in case either was involved in a war against a third power; but this neutrality was not to hold if Germany made an "aggressive" war against France, or if Russia made an "aggressive" war against Austria. Since Russian nationalist agitation continued against both Austria and Germany, Bismarck in 1888 made public the terms of the Austro-German alliance and allowed the main terms of the Triple Alliance to be known informally as a warning to Russia.

Then in 1890 William II dismissed Bismarck. The emperor's advisers persuaded him not to renew the Reinsurance Treaty with Russia, as it was incompatible with the Dual Alliance, and shortly afterward what Bismarck had worked so hard to prevent came about. After lengthy secret negotiations, Russia and France in 1894 made public an alliance that ended French isolation. It was a defensive agreement by which each was to come to the other's aid in the event that Germany or

Austria made "aggressive" war against either ally. It was supplemented by military agreements between the two general staffs. Against the Triple Alliance there now stood the Dual Alliance of republican France and absolutist Russia, freeing France to follow a more aggressive policy overseas.

Great Britain still remained technically uninvolved by a formal treaty with a European ally, and indeed never undertook any full legal commitment, even with France. The next development in tightening the network was to align Great Britain against the Triple Alliance by informal agreement. After the clashes with France over Fashoda in 1898 and the diplomatic isolation caused by general opposition to the Boer War of 1899-1902, Britain sought first to come to an understanding with Germany; when rebuffed, the British then concluded a formal alliance with Japan (1902) and informal "understandings" (*ententes*) with France (1904) and Russia (1907). What chiefly drove Britain to these actions was the financially burdensome naval race with Germany and the rapid alienation of British public opinion. Fear of Russia rather than fear of Germany inspired Britain's alliance with Japan; in the Entente Cordiale France gave England a free hand in Egypt and England gave France a free hand in Morocco. More important, the base was laid for further collaboration, particularly in advance planning for military and naval cooperation in case of war, especially by relocation of the French fleet.

The final stage in aligning the two camps came in 1907 when Russia, chastened by defeat by Japan and encouraged by the French, came to an understanding with Great Britain. Both countries made concessions in regions where they had been imperialist rivals—Persia, Afghanistan, Tibet—and the British at last made some concessions to Russia's desire to open up the Bosporus and Dardanelles to its warships. The agreement was not based on any genuine sympathy between the two peoples, for the British had been Russophobes for well over a century. The agreement was informal and left Britain less than fully committed to any binding continental alliance system; nevertheless, it rounded out the Triple Entente against the Triple Alliance.

As the Entente took shape, a succession of military and diplomatic crises inflamed public opinion and further circumscribed the room to maneuver. First came a deliberately theatrical gesture by the kaiser, when in 1905 he made a ceremonial visit to Tangier in Morocco as a signal that the Germans would not recognize the Anglo-French assignment of Morocco to France. The British then indicated clearly to the French that they would not support them. Moreover, the British and the French now began informal military and naval conferences, which the French, at least, believed committed Britain to armed support if the Germans attacked. However, France's foreign minister, Théophile Delcassé (in office 1898-1905), had pressed too hard, and when it became evident in the Moroccan crisis that France was not ready to extend the diplomatic arm to its logical length—war—he was forced out of the cabinet. Army

William II is shown here with his military entourage.

morale was at its lowest point, still divided by the Dreyfus affair, and though Delcassé's policy was followed by his successor, the Germans could claim that they had humiliated the French.

French public opinion was infuriated by these events, and at an international conference at Algeciras in Spain (1906) Germany was outvoted, although it had called for the conference; France pursued plans for a protectorate in Morocco, dividing the country with Spain.

The Algeciras conference also marked the beginnings of participation by the United States in the European system, though very tentatively. In 1904 a person thought to be a naturalized American citizen had been seized by a Moroccan chief, and Theodore Roosevelt, in the midst of the Republican party national convention, had sent a truculent cable. Two years earlier, at the urging of Jewish citizens in the United States, the State Department had protested against Romanian persecution of Jews. Given this protest over a domestic Romanian matter, the State Department could not readily refrain from action where an American citizen was thought to be concerned. (In 1911 the United States would end a commercial treaty with Russia over Russian refusal to honor passports carried by American Jews.) Roosevelt sent two representatives to Algeciras, who helped conciliate differences between the two camps. When the Algeciras convention was presented to the Senate, however, it was with the reservation that being a party to the convention meant no departure from the traditional American policy of remaining aloof from European wars.

A decisive turn on the road toward Sarajevo came in 1908 in the Balkans. Austria formally proclaimed the annexation of the Turkish provinces of Bosnia-Herzegovina, already occupied for thirty years. Austria's actions infuriated the Serbs, who hoped to annex Bosnia. It also infuriated the Russians, who did not know that their foreign minister had informally agreed with his

Austrian counterpart to permit the annexation in exchange for Austria's services in opening the Straits to the Russian fleet. But Russia gained nothing, for Britain would not permit the Straits to be opened. The wound to Russian pride was profound.

What directly prompted the Austrian annexation of Bosnia-Herzegovina was the successful rising against the Ottoman sultan in the summer of 1908 by the Young Turks, who wanted the modern industrial achievements of the West, representative government, and international respect. A Pan-Turanian movement was instigated largely by Turks from central Asia (and named for their nomadic Turanian ancestors) whose independent principalities had been conquered by Russia during the reign of Alexander II and who were now undergoing forced Russification; they sought to group the Turkish peoples of central Asia with the Ottoman Turks and Magyars of Hungary. Austria was determined that Serbia and Croatia would remain under its rule and felt it necessary to send such a message in the face of fragmentation elsewhere.

A second Moroccan crisis in 1911 heightened tensions in western Europe and brought the possibility of a general war home to France. The kaiser sent a German gunboat, the *Panther*, to the Moroccan port of Agadir as a protest against French occupation of the old city of Fez. In ensuing negotiations, well publicized in the press, the Germans agreed to give the French a free hand in Morocco, but only at a price the French considered blackmail; part of the French Congo was ceded to Germany. French opposition to this bargain was so intense that the government fell, and thereafter no French ministry dared make concessions to the Germans.

Events followed with bewildering and interlocking impact. In 1911 Italy seized upon the Agadir crisis to demand Tripoli from Turkey, and though Italy and Germany were nominally linked through the Triple Alliance, Germany was preoccupied and, while pro-Turkish, was unable to influence either nation. In the year-long Turco-Italian war that followed, Italian nationalists, led by the writer Gabriele d'Annunzio (1863-1938), at last saw the chance for substantial imperial gains. Italy annexed Tripoli, bombarded the Syrian coast, and occupied Rhodes and the other Dodecanese Islands. Austria held Italy back, refusing to permit attacks in the Balkans or on the Aegean coast, and Russia lost heavily in commerce when the Turks closed the Straits. By the Treaty of Lausanne in October 1912, Italy confirmed its new possessions.

In the meantime, the war over Tripoli (Libya) had proved a prelude to the Balkan Wars of 1912-1913, as the Balkan states struck at a preoccupied Turkey. In the first of these wars, Montenegro declared war on Turkey, as did Bulgaria, Serbia, and Greece ten days later. The war went against the Turks, but Russia warned the advancing Bulgarians not to occupy Constantinople or the Russian fleet would be used against them. The Serbs reached the Adriatic by overrunning Albania; intent on

preventing Serbian access to the sea, the Austrians declared for an independent Albania. Russia supported Serbia, and in November 1912 Austria and Russia began to mobilize, always a slow process. The Russians, belatedly realizing that they were not prepared for war, abandoned the Serbs, who, with Bulgaria, came to terms with Turkey. By a treaty of May 30, Turkey ceded substantial territory in Europe, abandoned its claims to Crete (which was annexed to Greece), and left the status of Albania and the Aegean Islands to the powers. Albanian independence led to an intense dispute over Macedonia.

One month later the second Balkan War erupted when the Bulgarian military commander attacked Serbia and Greece without informing his government. Both nations counterattacked, Romania and Turkey entered the war on their side, and in six weeks, by the Treaty of Bucharest, Bulgaria was stripped of much that it had gained. In a separate treaty with Turkey, Bulgaria was forced to give back Adrianople. During the negotiations Serbia invaded Albania and only withdrew in the face of an Austrian ultimatum, adding to the legacy of contending hatreds.

During this time, the Anglo-German naval race had continued unabated. In February 1912 Lord Haldane (1856-1928), British secretary for war, disturbed over Russian ambitions in Persia and by the Agadir crisis, and knowing that there was a group in Germany eager to come to an agreement with Britain, went to Berlin to suggest that Britain would support German expansion in Africa in exchange for a freeze on the size of the German fleet. Germany refused and the next month published a naval bill that provided for a third squadron of battleships.

Britain now faced a major dilemma. In 1897 its fleet had been the greatest in the world; with the introduction of its massive and expensive *Dreadnought* in 1905, a new standard in armor and armament had been attained. But the Germans, threatened by this new superweapon, even though beginning far behind in the race had matched it, and escalation on both sides had continued. In 1911 Winston Churchill (1874-1965), who was committed to a fully modernized navy, became Britain's first lord of the admiralty. In 1912 a new naval law made it clear that Germany intended to match the British. Both nations were increasingly worried over growth in the Austro-Hungarian and Italian navies. The British concluded that they could halt rising naval expenditures only through a naval agreement with France by which France would control the Mediterranean and Britain would focus on the North Sea, the Straits, and the Near East.

The Final Crisis, July-August 1914

The diplomats and statesmen were drawn into war because they believed that a defeat or loss of face for their nation was worse than war. Austria-Hungary believed (correctly, though without positive proof) that the

Serbian government had had some suspicion of Princip's assassination plot and should have given Austria warning. For this reason, and also because Austria wished to check the Serbian agitation that had long been unsettling the Yugoslav peoples living in the dual monarchy, Austria-Hungary decided to make stiff demands on Serbia after the assassination of Francis Ferdinand on June 28, 1914, with the involvement of agents of the Serbian terrorist organization, the Black Hand. Before doing so, however, Austria consulted Germany, which promised to support whatever policy Austria might adopt toward Serbia—the equivalent of a diplomatic "blank check." Britain, in the meantime, was seriously distracted by violence and gun-running in Ulster, for on June 23 the new effort to achieve home rule for Ireland had gone before the House of Lords.

Encouraged, the Austrian government on July 23 sent Serbia an ultimatum to be answered within forty-eight hours. The ultimatum was exceedingly demanding and may have been designed to be unacceptable. It required that publications hostile to Austria be suppressed, anti-Austrian patriotic organizations be dissolved, teachings that smacked of propaganda be barred from the schools, officials known for conducting anti-Austrian campaigns be dismissed, Serbian officials believed to be involved in the assassination plot be arrested, and a formal apology be made. These demands the Serbs might have accepted, but two others they could not: that Austrian officials work with the Serbians in investigating the plot, and that judicial action be taken against any found guilty by this joint investigation. Serbia probably had some assurance of Russia's help if its partial rejection of the ultimatum led to war. While accepting most points, the Serbian reply was, upon close examination, evasive on the most important, and the Serbs had begun mobilization before delivering it. Serbia apparently hoped this stratagem would allow time for further negotiations, but the Austrian minister immediately left Belgrade, and Austria began to call up its troops. Austria declared war on July 28, after turning down as inconsistent with national honor a European conference proposed by the British foreign minister, Sir Edward Grey (1862-1933). Germany supported Austria in this decision.

But the German diplomats still equivocated, putting pressure on Vienna to act against Serbia while trying to find out whether Britain would remain neutral in a general war—a constant German goal. If war were to come, the Germans wished to place the guilt on Russia. Since Russia was beginning the full mobilization of its armies, the kaiser, on July 29, told Czar Nicholas II in a personal telegram about German attempts to get the Austrians to compromise. Apparently this telegram caused full Russian mobilization to be modified into partial mobilization against Austria and caused the Austro-Russian talks to be resumed on July 30. If German Chancellor Theobald von Bethmann-Hollweg (1856-1921) could make it appear that a full-scale European war was the fault of the Russians, then he still had some hope of Britain's neutrality.

But mobilization was not easy in Russia, a country of vast distances, poor communications, and bureaucratic red tape. The Russian military feared that their enemies would get the lead on them, so the Russian government, probably against the inclinations of the czar himself, decided to renew general mobilization. Germany at once insisted that all Russian mobilization cease, and, when it continued, ordered its own at 4:00 P.M. on August 1. Germany declared war on Russia three hours later.

THE "BLANK CHECK"

There is some debate among historians as to just how sweeping the "blank check" given to Austria by Germany actually was. A report by the Austrian ambassador on his meeting with the Kaiser at Potsdam on July 5, 1914, indicates what the Austrian believed to be the case:

After lunch, when I again called attention to the seriousness of the situation, the Kaiser authorized me to inform our gracious Majesty that we might in this case, as in all others, rely on Germany's full support. He must . . . first hear what the Imperial Chancellor has to say, but he did not doubt in the least that Herr von Bethmann Hollweg would agree with him. Especially as far as our action against Serbia was concerned. . . . Russia's attitude will no doubt be hostile, but to this he had been for years prepared, and should a war between Austria-Hungary and Russia be unavoidable, we might be convinced that Germany, our old faithful ally, would stand at our side. Russia at the time was in no way prepared for war, and would think twice before it appealed to arms. But it will certainly set other powers on to the Triple Alliance and add fuel to the fire in the Balkans. He understands perfectly well that His Apostolic Majesty in his well-known love of peace would be reluctant to march into Serbia; but if we had really recognized the necessity of warlike action against Serbia, he would regret if we did not make use of the present moment, which is all in our favor.

Max Montgelas and Walter Schücking, eds., *Outbreak of the World War: German Documents Collected by Karl Kautsky* (New York: Carnegie Endowment for International Peace, 1924), p. 76.

France, meantime, had determined to stand by its Russian ally, now evidently about to be attacked, and mobilized at 3:55 P.M. on August 1. Having failed to get Britain to guarantee French neutrality, and apparently convinced that France would come to Russia's support, Germany invaded Luxembourg on August 2 and demanded from Belgium permission to cross its territory, in exchange for Belgian neutrality. Belgium refused, and on August 3 Germany declared war on France and invaded Belgium to seize the ports on the English Channel and bear down upon Paris from the west, while a weaker left wing was to draw the French out to the south along the French-German border, thus striking a decisive blow at France before the slow-moving Russians could get their armies into the field.

Britain had been wavering. Although her entente with France did not legally bind the two nations together, it had led to close coordination of defense plans by the French and British military and naval staffs, and so perhaps Britain would have come into the war anyway. What made entry certain was German violation of the neutrality of Belgium, which both Britain and Prussia had joined with other powers to guarantee in 1839, thirty years before German unification. Sir Edward Grey, though opposed by some members of the British cabinet

A British World War I recruiting poster made use of the popularity of Lord Kitchener to launch a campaign for one hundred thousand volunteers. In response to the call, "The First New Army" came into existence.

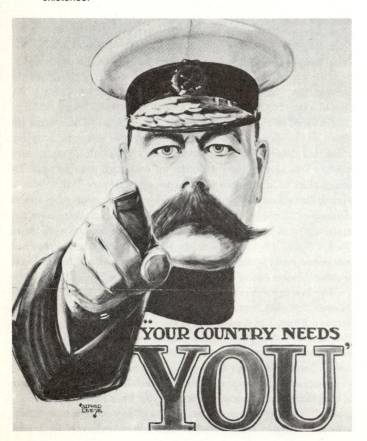

who did not believe the defense of Belgian neutrality worth a war, seized firmly upon the German invasion of Belgium as grounds for action. On August 4 Britain declared war on Germany. Bethmann-Hollweg, informed of this action, let slip the phrase that Britain had gone to war just for a "scrap of paper"—the treaty of 1839 that established Belgian neutrality. This unhappy phrase, seized upon by the press of the world, not only solidified British opinion in favor of the war but was also responsible more than any other single factor for the later charge of war guilt that was laid against Germany.

The Entry of Other Powers

By August 6, when Austria declared war on Russia, all the members of the Triple Alliance and the Triple Entente had entered the war, with the exception of Italy, which declared neutrality. The Central Powers of Germany and Austria-Hungary stood against the Allies— Russia, France, Britain, and Serbia. Japan, desirous of gaining recognition as a major power, hoping to dislodge Germany from the Far East, and aware that distance from the primary field of combat would mean token participation in exchange for rapid industrial and territorial expansion, came in on the side of the Allies late in August. Turkey joined the Austro-German side in November. After receiving competing territorial offers from both Allies and Central Powers, Italy joined the Allies in May 1915. Bulgaria came in on the side of the Central Powers in 1915, and Portugal and Romania on the side of the Allies in 1916. In time much of the world joined in; there were fifty-six declarations of war before the end of 1918.

Late to arrive on the scene but in the end decisive was the United States. Americans had hoped to avoid entanglement in the European conflict, and for a time public opinion was deeply divided. While many Americans sided with Britain and France because they felt these two powers were fighting to assure that democratic government would survive in Europe, many others continued to think of Britain as the traditional enemy. Many American voters remained deeply conscious of their ethnic roots in Europe; the Irish were likely to be anti-British, while eastern Europeans hoped for the defeat of the Central Powers, since this could lead to the breakup of Austria-Hungary and to freedom for the suppressed Balkan nationalities. Even though the United States had entered into many trade agreements with other nations, had fought Spain over issues of empire, and had developed its own informal sphere of influence in the Far East, as well as dominating Central America and the Caribbean, Americans still thought of themselves as upholding a tradition of isolation from Europe's wars. To a considerable extent this was true, for no overseas invader had set foot on American soil since 1815 (or would until 1942, when Japanese troops landed in the Aleutian Islands, off Alaska, in World War II). American troops had served abroad fairly often, but only under rare circumstances, as in the Boxer Rebellion in China, in concert with any other nation. The American government committed itself quickly to a policy of neutrality.

As the war raged in Europe, however, public sympathies increasingly turned against the Central Powers, and against Germany in particular. In a language shared with the English, Americans read of the war through British dispatches, heard atrocity stories that were directed against the Germans, and viewed the Hapsburgs as attempting to suppress legitimate aspirations for the self-determination of peoples—a revolutionary tradition still important to Americans. Furthermore, the European war helped the United States economically, for Britain and France, initially controlling the seas and needing supplies, bought enormous quantities of goods from the United States, which the Central Powers were in no position to do. Within a year after the beginning of the war, the economies of the United States and Allied powers were closely intertwined. A debtor nation at the beginning of the war, the United States had become a creditor nation. American loans to Europe were enormous and entangling.

Still, the American business community had no reason to see the United States actively enter the war, for neutrality, which tended to favor the Allies by the facts of geography, trade, and public opinion, paid handsomely. President Woodrow Wilson (1856-1924) campaigned in the national election in 1916 on a pledge to keep the United States out of the conflict if possible. But he suspected that if the stalemate that had developed on the western front and German desperation over the flow of American foodstuffs to Britain were to continue, avoiding war would be very difficult. This proved to be so. American definitions of neutral shipping seemed to the Germans to openly favor the British. Germany felt obliged to use its most powerful maritime weapon, the submarine, and in 1915 it proclaimed the waters around the British Isles to be a war zone in which enemy merchant ships would be sunk on sight. Neutral vessels entering the zone did so at their own risk. Americans insisted on exercising their rights on the high seas, including traveling on passenger vessels of combatants. On May 7, 1915, the British transatlantic steamer *Lusitania* was sunk by a German submarine; 1,198 people died, including 124 Americans.

The United States protested in the strongest terms. Throughout 1915 German submarines complied, limiting their attacks to freighters. Nonetheless, further incidents followed, and in 1916 Germany formally agreed to abandon unlimited submarine warfare. Late that year Germany initiated peace efforts, but the Allies rebuffed these attempts. Early in 1917 German military leaders gained the upper hand over civilians with respect to wartime decisions. Though Bethmann-Hollweg resisted the resumption of unrestricted submarine warfare, he finally agreed, convinced that the British could be destroyed before American power could be made effective, even if the United States were to be drawn into the war. On February 1 submarine attacks on all neutral and belligerent shipping (with an allowance for a single American vessel to pass to England weekly) became official policy. Three days later an American naval vessel was sunk after warning, and Wilson asked Congress to sever diplomatic relations with Germany. Six more ships were sunk in the next month. In the meantime, on March 12 a new democratic government was set up in Russia, effectively knocking Russia out of the war and potentially releasing German troops from the eastern front to the western. Wilson attacked the German submarine policy as "warfare against humanity," and on April 6 the United States declared war on Germany. Even so, Americans were careful to maintain their separate status from the Allies, not joining them formally and insisting throughout the war on being called merely an Associated Power.

German resumption of submarine warfare was the immediate cause of American entry into the war, but there were, of course, other less obvious causes. Though neutrality had paid well, interest groups in the United States had assumed that war would bring even higher profits. So much had been lent to the Allied nations that American creditors could not afford to see them defeated. Public opinion was outraged by the German submarine policy, and the press was loudly condemnatory. Many Americans feared that their nation's security would be hurt if Germany were victorious; at the least, the world order would be reorganized, and the United States itself might be threatened. Americans could sell to Britain more easily than to Germany, and American supplies would prove critical to the Allied war effort. Perhaps above all, more Americans simply felt emotionally closer to Britain than to the Germans, and they were unprepared to see Europe unified under German domination. By 1917 the French armies were torn by mutinies, Russia was in political turmoil, and Britain had only six weeks' supply of grain left and had privately concluded that at best it could contiinue to fight only another seven months. Wilson no doubt did not believe that he was embarking on a war to "make the world safe for democracy," but he did believe that democracy would not be safe if the Central Powers were victorious. Europe was committing suicide, and he knew this must not be permitted.

II   THE COURSE OF THE WAR

Resources of the Belligerents

On paper even before the American entry, the Allies had an overwhelming superiority in total population and resources. The Central Powers had in their own continental lands not over 150 million people; Britain, France, Russia, and Italy in their own continental lands had at least 125 million more people than their enemies. Moreover, in their overseas possessions, which included the 315 million people of India, the Allies had many millions more. As for material resources, the Central

Powers had, especially in Germany, admirably organized industries and enough coal and iron to fight a long war, but here too the statistics were overwhelmingly in favor of the Allies. Moreover, though German submarines and surface raiders seriously interfered with Allied lines of communication, on the whole the Allies were still able to get indispensable food and other supplies from their overseas sources. And when in 1917 a beaten Russia, in the throes of a revolution, ceased to be of aid, the Allies gained not only the great resources of the United States but direct military participation by American troops.

In the long run, the side with the most men and materials wore down its enemies and won the war, but it was by no means the uneven struggle that the statistics of total population and material resources would indicate. The Central Powers had initially important advantages, won many battles, and seemed at critical moments close to final victory. Germany and Austria adjoined one another and had interior lines of communication, which enabled them to transfer troops rapidly from one threatened front to another. The Germans and Austrians spoke the same language and had for years been firmly allied. Most important of all, Germany was ready for war, with an efficiently organized military machine and a good stock of munitions. When food supplies ran low, German scientists proved highly skillful at creating *ersatz*, artificial substitutes, having a more advanced chemical industry than any of the Allies. The German people were united in support of the war, and they enjoyed the great psychological advantage of being on the offensive, or carrying the war to the enemy. Indeed, no important part of the war was ever fought on German soil; it ended with the German army still intact and the German Fatherland still uninvaded.

By contrast, geography and language separated the western Allies from Russia. German control of the Baltic and Turkish control of the Straits proved a serious obstacle to communication between Russia and its allies, who had to take roundabout and difficult routes through Archangel in Arctic waters and through Vladivostok on the Pacific at the end of the long, slow, single-track Trans-Siberian railway. For the Allies, transfer of troops between eastern and western fronts was militarily almost impossible, even had it been politically possible. It was not, however, possible, and here was one of the greatest weaknesses of the Allies.

Russia, Britain, and France had only recently come together, and then not as close allies. Each had many sources of conflict with the others. They had no experience of mutual cooperation, no common language (as the Germans and Austrians did). France and England were democracies, and though the peoples of both supported the war, Britain, in particular, was unused to centralized military and political control. Unified military planning and administration were never achieved between Russia and the western Allies. Even among Britain, France, and the United States on the western front, unification was not achieved until the French general Ferdinand Foch (1851-1929) was appointed commander in chief in 1918, and then only imperfectly.

Finally, of the three great Allied powers in 1914, only France was ready, and France, with only 39 million people against Germany's 65 million, was the weakest of the Allies in manpower. Britain was well prepared on the sea, but the navy could not be of direct use against the German army. The situation in Ireland still remained tense, and in the midst of the war a short-lived and brutally repressed uprising, the Easter Rebellion of 1916, would add to the unpredictability of Britain's western shore. Russia had universal military service and a huge army, but it had vast distances to overcome, an inadequate railway system, a less developed heavy industry, an army whose morale had been shaken by its recent defeat at the hands of Japan, a people whose morale had been shaken by a recent abortive revolution, and a military and political organization that was riddled with inefficiency and corruption.

Military Campaigns, 1914-1918

The Western Front The German attack through Belgium was the first stage in the plan prepared by Alfred Graf von Schlieffen (1833-1913), chief of the general staff from 1891 to 1906. The strong right wing was to take Paris and fall on the rear of the French, who would be pinned down by the left wing in a so-called Swinging Door. With France quickly eliminated in a short war of movement, the Germans would then unite their forces and attack the Russians, who would still be in the throes of mobilization. Britain, an island nation, would be held off and attacked if necessary, though it might withdraw from the war if its Allies were quickly destroyed.

The German plan almost succeeded. It failed for two reasons, to which many separate tactical factors contributed. First, the German chief of staff, Helmuth von Moltke (1848-1916), who succeeded Schlieffen, had modified the Schlieffen plan by weakening the critical right wing to send divisions to the east. When the German right wing neared Paris, it had too few divisions to take the capital and then turn on the French army as planned, partially because troops were needed in East Prussia against the Russians. Second, the French, though at first preparing an offensive eastward as Germany had hoped, shifted their armies northward and westward in time to meet the invading Germans. With the help of a small British force, the French exploited a gap that opened between the German armies, who lost their first great test, known as the Battle of the Marne (September 5-12, 1914). A short war of movement became a long war of siege.

The German advance, which had been almost continuous since August 2, had been stopped. The opposing forces then engaged in what came to be called the "race for the Channel," with the Germans trying to outflank the Allies and reach the Channel ports first, thus shutting the short sea passage to future British reinforcements. But they failed here too, and throughout the war the ports of Calais and Boulogne and the southwestern corner of Belgium were to remain in Allied hands.

By the autumn of 1914 this western front was stabilized. Between the Channel and the Swiss border of Alsace near Basel, hundreds of thousands of soldiers faced each other in a continuous line. Both sides dug in and made rough fortifications, the central feature of which was a series of parallel trenches deep enough to conceal a man standing upright. As time went on these trenches were greatly improved; they were supplied with parapets, machine-gun nests, and an elaborate network of approach trenches and strong points, until the entire front became one immense fortification. Thousands of local actions in the four years of trench warfare shifted the lines here and there, and a series of partial breakthroughs occurred on both sides, but on the whole the lines held, and the actual fighting in the west was confined to an extraordinarily narrow, though very long, field in which changing weaponry gave the defense increasing advantages over the offense. The Central Powers became a fortress under siege—a fortress that could not be stormed and out of which it was impossible to sally.

The ultimate outcome was decided on the western front, but there were many other fronts that helped determine the final results. Over the long pull, the Germans had fewer men and resources, so the dispersal of energy that these lesser fronts called for, plus the continuous need to bolster their Austrian, Turkish, and Bulgarian allies, were major factors in their defeat. For the belligerents the war was a whole; its far-flung theaters were mutually dependent, with each one influencing the others, even as each front developed its own dynamics.

The Eastern Front   The eastern front, where the Russians faced both the Germans and the Austrians, was crucial to Allied tenacity in the west. Millions of men were involved on both sides, and had the Russians not held out until the end of 1917, the Allies in the west could hardly have withstood the reinforcements that the Germans and Austrians would have been able to send to France and Italy. Though the war in the east was more fluid than the war in the west, even in the east there were long periods of stalemate, especially during the winters, when the opposing armies faced each other in improvised fortifications. The brunt of the attack had to be carried by Germany, for the Dual Monarchy had to deploy many units which were basically Slavic and pro-Russian. Hence Croatian units, for example, could be used only against the Italians.

The Russians began well, throwing huge armies against Austrian Galicia. They took the Galician capital of Lemberg (later the Polish Lwów, now the Soviet Lvov), and by the end of September 1914 they had reached the northern ends of the passes leading into

Hungary through the Carpathian Mountains. That Russia's mobilization was slow hardly mattered against the Germans, who had to defend East Prussia, which jutted into Russian territory. On August 19-20, 1914, the Russians won the battle of Gumbinnen. The alarmed Germans reorganized their eastern command. The brilliant general Erich Ludendorff (1865-1937), under the nominal command of Paul von Hindenburg (1847-1934) and aided by the exceptional staff officer Max von Hoffman (1869-1927), moved successfully against the two Russian armies, which because of French pleading were attempting a premature pincers movement. Late in August at Tannenberg, the Germans decisively defeated a Russian army, taking 100,000 prisoners. The Russian commander committed suicide. Early in September the Germans again won decisively at the Masurian Lakes, taking another 125,000 prisoners.

The Germans' hard-pressed Austrian allies to the south were by now clamoring for help, and the western front was still demanding men. Hindenburg and his aides had to do their best with what they had. In a series of hard-fought battles in Poland, they relieved the pressure on the Austrians. The end of 1914 found the Austrians hanging on in Galicia and the Germans in a good position to push eastward from East Prussian and Polish bases. In two great joint offensives in May and July 1915 the Central Powers won substantial successes, inflicting on the underequipped Russians severe losses from which they never really recovered. At the end of 1915 the battle line ran roughly from near Riga, deep in the Baltic provinces of Russia, to the eastern edge of Galicia.

In 1916 the Russians, with a new commander, General Aleksei Brusilov (1853-1926), undertook a major new offensive against the Austrians in the south. The Russians' need to bolster their failing morale would probably have made some action necessary, but they were also being pressed by the western Allies to do something to help the Italians, who were threatened by the Austrians in the Alps. The Brusilov offensive was begun too soon, without adequate preparation. It scored a striking success at first, in places driving the Austrians back some eighty miles, and taking 200,000 prisoners. Once more the Germans came to the rescue; with fresh troops transferred from the west, they halted Brusilov, costing him a million men and exhausting his supplies.

It was from the backwash of this defeat that the Russian Revolution, which began early in March 1917, was born. During the moderate early phase of that uprising, before the Bolshevik revolution of November 1917, Brusilov undertook one last desperate offensive. But he was soon checked, and the Russian army began to disintegrate; the way was open for the Bolsheviks to carry out their promise to make peace. By the end of 1917 Russia was out of the war. It was forced by the Central Powers to sign the punitive peace of Brest-Litovsk (March 1918), by which Russia lost its Polish territories, its Baltic provinces, the entire Ukraine, Finland, and some lands in the Caucasus. The last went to Turkey; most of the others came under what proved to be the temporary domination of Austria and Germany. This was a catastrophic end to a war in which two million Russian soldiers had been killed, four million wounded, and three million taken prisoner.

The Italian Front In the meantime, in April 1915 Italy had concluded with Britain, France, and Russia the secret Treaty of London, which promised the Italians their long-sought Trent and Trieste plus other lands at Austro-Hungarian and Turkish expense. In May the Italians formally declared war on Austria-Hungary (they did not declare war on Germany until August 1916), and a new front was added along the Austro-Italian frontier at the head of the Adriatic. Since much of this front was mountainous, action was largely confined to some sixty miles along the Isonzo River, where for two years there was a series of bloody but indecisive engagements that pinned down several hundred thousand Austrian troops. Then in the late autumn of 1917, with Russia already beaten, came a blow that very nearly knocked Italy out. Once again the Germans supplied the propulsive force as Ludendorff, now in supreme command, sent six German divisions to the Isonzo. The Germans and Austrians broke through at Caporetto and sent the Italians into retreat across the Venetian plains. French and British reinforcements were hastily rushed across the Alps, but what did most to stop the Austro-Germans was the grave difficulty of supplying their armies in such a rapid advance. The Italians were finally able to hold along the line of the Piave river, almost at the Po.

The Dardanelles and the Balkans Ultimately more significant was the Dardanelles campaign of 1915, which proved to be a bad blow to Allied morale. With the entry of Turkey into the war on the side of the Central Powers in November 1914, and with the French able to hold the western front against the Germans, a group of British leaders decided that British strength should be put into amphibious operations in the Aegean area, where a strong drive could knock Turkey out of the war by the capture of Constantinople. The great exponent of this Eastern Plan was Winston Churchill, first lord of the admiralty. The point of attack chosen was the Dardanelles, the more southwesterly of the two straits that separate the Black Sea from the Aegean. The action is known as the Gallipoli campaign for the long, narrow peninsula on the European side of the Dardanelles that was a key to the action. Allied victory here would have opened communication with Russia through the Black Sea.

The British and French fleets tried to force the Straits in March 1915, but they abandoned the attempt when several ships struck mines. Later landings of British, Australian, New Zealand, and French troops at various points on both the Asian and European shores of the Dardanelles were poorly coordinated and badly backed up. They met fierce and effective resistance from the Turks, whose ranking officer at Gallipoli, one of the young Turks of 1908, Mustafa Kemal (1880-1938), greatly distinguished himself, and in they end they had to withdraw without taking the Straits. The cost of this campaign was enormous: 500,000 casualties, to little effect. The Anzac (Australian and New Zealand) troops felt they had been led into senseless slaughter by British officers who had been seeking an alternative to further attacks on the western front, and at Gallipoli a sense of a separate Australian nationalism was clearly expressed for the first time. Russia remained sealed in by the Straits all during the war.

Serbia's part in the crisis that had produced the war meant that from the start there would be a Balkan front. In the end there were several such fronts, and all Balkan states became involved. The Austrians failed here also, and although they managed to take the Serbian capital, Belgrade (December 1914), they were driven out again. Bulgaria, wooed by both sides, finally came in with the Central Powers in the autumn of 1915. The Germans sent troops and a general, August von Mackensen (1849-1938), under whom the Serbs were finally beaten. The remnant of their armies took refuge on the island of Corfu in still neutral Greece.

To counter this blow in the Balkans, the British and French had already landed a few divisions in the Greek city of Salonika and had established a front in Macedonia. The Greeks themselves were divided into two groups. One was headed by King Constantine (1868-1923), who sympathized with the Central Powers but who for the moment was seeking only to maintain Greek neutrality. The other was a pro-Ally group headed by the able prime minister Eleutherios Venizelos (1864-1936), who had secretly agreed to the Allied landing at Salonika. The Allies rode roughshod over Greek neutrality, and Venizelos did not get firmly into the saddle until June 1917, when Allied pressure compelled King Constantine to abdicate in favor of his second son, Alexander (1893-1920). Greece then declared war on the Central Powers.

Meanwhile Romania, which the Russians had been trying to lure into the war, yielded to promises of great territorial gains at the expense of Austria-Hungary; anticipating Brusilov's continued success, Romania came in on the Allied side in August 1916. The Central Powers swept through Romania and by January 1917 held most of the country, effectively eliminating Romania from the war. When the Russians made the separate Peace of Brest-Litovsk with the Germans in March 1918, the Romanians were obliged to yield some territory to Bulgaria and to grant a lease of oil lands to Germany.

Despite the formal declaration of Greece on the Allied side in June 1917, the Macedonian front remained in a stalemate until the summer of 1918, when, with American troops pouring rapidly into France, the Allied military leaders decided they could afford to build up their forces in Salonika. The investment paid well, for under the leadership of the French general Franchet d'Esperey

(1856-1942), the Allied armies on this front were the first to break the enemy completely. The French, British, Serbs, and Greeks began a great advance in September all along a line from the Adriatic to the Bulgarian frontier. They forced the Bulgarians to conclude an armistice on September 30, and by early November they had crossed the Danube in several places. The armistice in the west on November 11 found the tricolor of France, with the flags of many allies, well on its way to Vienna. This victory, reminiscent of Napoleon, helped inspire in the French the thought that they were once more the dominant nation on the continent of Europe.

The Near East and the Colonies But dominance *in* Europe and dominance *over* Europe would not, in the future, be the same thing, for this truly worldwide war, fought in the Near East, Africa, and the Far East, as well as in every ocean, made it clear that noncontinental events were no longer mere sideshows. The war in the Near East, in particular, would unleash nationalisms that continue to the present day. The Turks, trained and officered by German experts, had often resisted effectively. In April 1916, in a blow to British prestige as bad as the Dardanelles defeat, they forced the surrender of the British forces at Kut in Mesopotamia, and marched up the Tigris-Euphrates Valley. The following year the

British marched north again and took Baghdad, effectively ending Turkish authority in Mesopotamia.

Turkish defeats had always occasioned revolts by the subject peoples of the Ottoman Empire. In 1894 the Armenians had revolted and been brutally suppressed, leading Britain and France to pressure Turkey into promising reforms. The reforms were not put into operation, however, and in part in hopes of Western intervention the Armenian revolt continued. In 1895-1897 eight thousand Armenians were killed. The remaining Armenians in Turkey had bided their time; now they felt that the World War provided them with their opportunity. When the Russians launched an offensive near Lake Van, the Armenians nearby rose, took over the Turkish fortress, and turned it over to the Russians. Declaring that Armenians everywhere were helping the Russians, the Turkish government ordered the removal of all non-Muslims from military areas or lines of communication. In the forced removal thousands of Armenians died of exposure in the desert; Armenian men were massacred, the women raped, and survivors forcibly converted to Islam. Once a thriving culture in Syria and throughout eastern Turkey, the Armenians were reduced to a remnant at the end of the war, an estimated one million having died. Many Armenians who had emigrated to Egypt and the United States or who survived in Russia would thereafter harbor the deepest hatred for the Turks.

Elsewhere the British exploited Arab dislike for the Turks, with the particular assistance of the romantic colonel T.E. Lawrence (1888-1935), who knew the Arabs intimately and helped coordinate an Arab revolt with a British expedition from Egypt under General Sir Edmund Allenby (1861-1936). By the end of 1917 the British held Jerusalem. In September 1918 a great British offensive in Syria was so successful that on October 30 the Turks, isolated by Bulgaria's surrender, concluded an armistice and left the war.

From these campaigns there later emerged not only the independent Arab states but also the Jewish national state of Israel. In November 1917, in the Balfour Declaration, the British promised "the establishment in Palestine of a national home for the Jewish people." This promise bore fruit in the mandate of 1922 from the League of Nations, by which such a home was set up under British protection.

In their overseas colonies the Germans, though cut off from the homeland by the British navy, fought with great skill. In East Africa they managed to hold out in a series of campaigns, so that they still had forces in the field on Armistice Day, November 11, 1918, and their commander did not surrender until November 23. But elsewhere the Germans fought from inadequate bases and with inadequate forces, so that by the end of 1914 the British, Australians, New Zealanders, South Africans, French, and Japanese had pretty well taken over the German overseas possessions. The Allies had won the "colonial war," indeed, the war for empire.

T.E. Lawrence worked among the Arabs, often in their own dress. Soon romantic legend gave him the title of Lawrence of Arabia.

Allied Victory

The War at Sea In the long run British seapower, reinforced by the French and later by the Italian and American navies, together with American supplies, proved decisive. The Allied command of the sea made it possible to draw on the resources of the rest of the world, and in particular to transfer with few losses large numbers of British and later American troops to the crucial western front. Seapower also enabled the Allies to shut Germany and its allies off from overseas resources. The Allied blockade slowly constricted Germany, limiting not merely military supplies for the armies but also food supplies for the civilian population. At the end of the war many Germans were suffering from malnutrition while the death rate among children and old people was soaring, important factors in German willingness to surrender without fighting to the bitter end. Furthermore, it had been American insistence on observing the doctrine of the freedom of the seas, and self-interested British support for this doctrine as a matter of propaganda, that had brought the United States into the war. In this sense Germany lost the war at sea doubly, because the initial technological advantage provided by the submarine created diplomatic problems with which none of the powers had been able to contend. The submarine had made the traditional rules of war on blockade, stop-and-search before attack, and provision for the safety of passengers and crews obsolete. The United States had insisted on their observance, and yet they could not be observed if the submarine was to exploit its main strategy: to remain beneath the surface.

Yet the war at sea was not easy for the Allies and their Associate Power, the United States. The submarine proved as dangerous as British alarmists had feared. When the Germans launched their unrestricted submarine warfare, they made serious inroads against the merchant ships that were essential to Britain. By the end of 1917 some eight million tons of shipping had been sunk by the Germans, most of it by submarines. The submarine menace was only slowly overcome by extensive use of convoys, depth bombs, antisubmarine patrols, and the development of small, fast subchasers and destroyers.

The navy of surface vessels that the Germans had built up since the 1890s and that had proved to be so important in the growth of Anglo-German hostility never played a decisive part in the war itself. German surface raiders caused severe damage in the first year, but in January 1915 British battle cruisers defeated the Germans in the battle of the Dogger Bank, and for the remainder of the year the Germans limited themselves to minelaying and to concentrating on their *Unterseeboot* warfare. In 1916 a new commander sought to use the German High Seas Fleet more effectively; destroyer groups conducted raids, battle cruisers bombarded the English coast, and in May the Germans tried to trap part of the British Grand Fleet in harbor. Forewarned, British Admiral Sir John Jellicoe (1859-1935) put to sea, and in the running battle of Jutland, fought in the North Sea May 31-June 1, 1916, the British forced the Germans to run for port, although British losses were much heavier. The German surface navy never again seriously threatened Britain's command of the sea in European waters. At the war's end the German high command attempted to get the fleet out in a heroic last stand. The German sailors' refusal to take the ships out—their mutiny, in fact—gave a critical push to the German revolution that led to the Armistice of 1918.

The Western Front This war also saw the beginnings of air warfare. German dirigibles (known as Zeppelins) raided London many times in 1916 and 1917, and both sides made airplane bombing raids on nearby towns. But the total damage was relatively light and did not affect the final result. The airplane was more important for scouting, especially for artillery; despite its short range it could also locate submarines. The fighter plane was greatly improved during the war, and a base was laid for the development of the modern air force. The airplane made greater technical strides in the four years of war than it had made since Orville Wright (1871-1948) and his brother Wilbur (1867-1912) first flew at Kitty Hawk in North Carolina in 1903.

Although the invention of the airplane did not alter traditional warfare, a new type of warfare was developed, especially on the western front—trench warfare. The machine gun, the repeating rifle, and fast-firing artillery, with the guidance of spotter planes, could pour in upon an attacking force such deadly fire that it was almost impossible for either side to break through the opposing trench systems on a wide front. Because of the new technology and trench warfare, both sides suffered losses of a magnitude never known before.

Two new weapons almost broke the deadlock. One was poison gas, first used by the Germans in shells in October 1914, with disappointing results. Then in April 1915 the Germans used chlorine gas discharged from cylinders. The overwhelmed French broke in a wave five miles wide, leaving the line completely undefended. But the Germans were not prepared to follow through, and the gap was closed once the gas had dispersed. Meanwhile military technicians developed a simple countermeasure, the gas mask, which became part of the equipment of every soldier on both sides. The age-old balance of attack and defense was once again reestablished. However, a new element of fear had been added to modern warfare, for although in fact only three men died in this first gas attack, the public was told that five thousand men had been killed.

The second new weapon came much nearer to producing decisive success. This was the tank, an armored land battleship. A British invention that had been nursed along in its infancy by Churchill, the tank acquired its name when early models were shipped under tarpaulins, which the curious were told covered water tanks. But the new weapon was used too soon, in inadequate numbers, and before sufficient mechanical tests had been made, in the British Somme offensive of 1916. With substantial modifications, tanks were used again at the Battle of Cambrai late in 1917, when three hundred tanks broke through the German lines. Failure to follow up quickly gave the Germans, who were also developing tanks, a chance to drive the British back, but the battle had clearly shown what tanks could achieve when well used.

The tank was a powerful symbol of the devastating new technology brought on by the exigencies of war. Both sides knew that the entry of the United States, with its fresh forces and vast industrial capacity, would be telling, were the war to last another year. But the Central Powers anticipated victory before American forces could be in the field. The French were crumbling, the burden of fighting having fallen increasingly on the British during 1917, and the Allies attempted "the one big push" on the western front while they still could, in the spring of 1917. The British were successful at Arras, the Canadians at Vimy Ridge, but the French were denied the easy victory promised them by their generals in the ravines of the Aisne, and their exhausted troops mutinied. To contain the Germans, the British general, Sir Douglas Haig (1861-1928), threw his troops into nine successive attacks in waterlogged terrain at Ypres from July 31 to November 15, and except for the Canadian capture of Passchendaele, the British line gained only 9,000 yards at the cost of 30,000 casualties. The Caporetto campaign and the failure to capitalize on Cambrai occurred in the same series of battles, and the Allies were deeply de-

pressed. The establishment of a Supreme War Council in late November to unify Allied strategy did little to bring order to a chaotic and increasingly divisive situation, especially with Russia out of the war.

Thus early in 1918 Germany decided to throw everything it had against the Allies on the western front before the American troops, now trickling in, turned into a wave. American troops had gone into action in October 1917; Germany, on the other hand, now had troops released from the eastern front. General Ludendorff knew that he must drive the British into the sea early in 1918, and he turned to massive application of the barrage, in which a long discharge of artillery would flatten out a section of enemy defenses and the no-man's land in front of the troops, forcing the enemy to retire to rear trenches. The initial barrage would include gas shells to knock out enemy observation posts and guns. A rolling barrage would ensue, advancing one kilometer an hour, with infantry following behind. Used on the Somme in combination with dense fog, this tactic had helped the Germans to pierce the British line along a 41-mile front, capture 80,000 prisoners, inflict 200,000 casualties, and approach Amiens, a major communications link. In the midst of this crisis General Foch, instructed to coordinate the Allied armies, became commander in chief. The American general, John J. Pershing (1860-1948), placed his troops at Foch's disposal, but he insisted that the United States army be kept separate, as befitted an Associate.

Slowly the tide turned. The Germans sustained heavy

American troops were pressed into action along the Hindenberg Line.

WAR IN THE TRENCHES

The war in the trenches was unremitting tedium punctuated by moments of intense action. Long after the war a distinguished British historian, Charles Carrington (1897-1981), who was a young man on the Somme, wrote of his experience:

After a battle you buried your comrades and saw to it that their graves were marked with a wooden cross and a name. If you had time, and if it was not too dangerous, you did as much for other British dead. The enemy came last in priority, and more than once I have cleared a trench of its defunct tenants by throwing them over the parapet where someone might or might not find and bury them when the battle was over. There were so many live inhabitants in the landscape as I saw it at Contalmaison in November 1916 that corpses had been cleared off everyone's premises, unless you went up to the new front where it was too dangerous for burial-parties to work. But in rolling forward the armies left desert areas behind, where no one had either need or inclination to go, in winter dreary beyond description, inhabited only by giant rats, fattened on corpse-flesh, in summer strangely beautiful with carpets of wild flowers and loud with skylarks. Clumps of scarlet poppies sprang up wherever the chalky subsoil had been disturbed by digging or by shell-fire. Long afterwards you could find corpses in nooks and corners of this wilderness as I found one at La Boisselle in 1921. When I was a boy I was very superstitious, suffered from "creepy" feelings when I was alone, and was afraid of the dark. This nonsense was completely obliterated by the genuine horrors of the battlefield and I remember surprise at my own unconcern. I never heard a ghost-story at the front. . . .

The killed and wounded were all lost by harassing fire, mostly on their way up or down the line. Once in position at Le Sars you could not show a finger by daylight, and by night every path by which you might be supposed to move was raked by machine-guns which had been trained on it by day. The entrance to the village, that is the gap in the ruins where the Bapaume Road passed through, the only way, by which you must pass, was under continuous shell-fire. If you could reach your funk-hole, and crouch in it, there was a fair chance of your coming out of it alive next day to run the gauntlet of the Bapaume Road again. In your funk-hole, with no room to move, no hot food, and no chance of getting any, there was nothing worse to suffer than a steady drizzle of wintry rain and a temperature just above freezing-point. A little colder and the mud would have been more manageable. Life was entirely numbed; you could do nothing. There could be no fighting since the combatants could not get at one another, no improvement of the trenches since any new work would instantly be demolished by a storm of shell-fire. I don't remember that we had any "wire" in front of us. We huddled and hid in piles of old brickwork and rafters, or behind hedgerows which once had bonded cottage gardens, scrabbling our way deeper down into mudholes, and painfully trying to keep our rifles clean, dragging out time until the relief came sneaking through the mud, exhausted before their tour of duty began. . . .

Charles Carrington, *Soldier from the Wars Returning* (New York: David McKay, 1965), pp. 127-28, 130-31.

losses as they advanced, and they lacked reserves. The French and British held the Germans after an advance on the Lys River. Ludendorff secretly shifted his troops and pressed on the Marne to within forty miles of Paris, where American and French troops held the south bank of the Marne at Château-Thierry on June 1-4. Ludendorff attacked along the Marne again in July, but by then he had lost 800,000 men, and British, French, and American troops drove the Germans back. On August 8 a surprise attack by the British, using 450 tanks, broke through the German lines near Amiens, and on this, "the black day" (as Ludendorff called it) for the German army, German units refused orders. Then, from September 26 to November 11, a Franco-British attack on the west and a Franco-American attack on the south nearly closed the Germans in a pincers in the Argonne forest and along the Meuse. Ludendorff's troops were in slow and generally orderly retreat, but suffering from low morale and without supplies, and he was determined that Germany itself should not be invaded. On September 29 he asked for an armistice; the German chancellor resigned the following day, and his successor appealed directly to President Wilson to call a peace conference on the basis of Wilson's Fourteen Points (see p. 302). The Allies were reluctant to accept these conditions, and Wilson hinted that the Americans would conclude a separate peace. On October 27 the Austro-Hungarian Empire, which was breaking up, also asked for an armistice. On November 3 mutiny in the German fleet at Kiel and in much of northwest Germany, and on November 7 revolution in Bavaria, made it impossible to continue. Ludendorff had been dismissed, and William II abdicated on November 9 and fled to Holland. Negotiations that had begun on November 8 were concluded at 5:00 A.M. on November 11, when the armistice was signed. All was, at last, quiet on the western front.

World War I turned out to be primarily a battle of goods. The great strategic question was whether the allies could outproduce the Central Powers. The strategy of supply became decisive. This in turn changed the rules of warfare. To maintain a successful blockade against the Central Powers the British had again and again to extend the list of contraband, until even safety pins were listed on it, for virtually everything produced was of importance to this kind of war effort. The distinction between combatant and noncombatant also began to disappear. The submarine could not surface, fire a shot across the bow of a freighter, board and examine the manifest, and, if the cargo were contraband, permit crew and passengers to take to the boats before sinking her. The distinction between belligerent and neutral became nearly useless also. Because of what it supplied to the Allies, the United States was in fact a belligerent almost from the beginning. British seapower was decisive precisely because it made possible an uninterrupted flow of American goods. Germany could not win the battle of goods without resorting to unrestricted submarine warfare, and here she was checkmated by the new antisubmarine warfare techniques.

The new warfare required such intimate coordination of the production and military effort on each side and the losses in manpower and wealth were so huge that the national motivations with which the fighting began became more and more irrelevant. In 1917 the war almost ground to a halt of itself. Whole French divisions refused to return to the line and had to be decimated. Rioters in Berlin had to be shot by the police. Russia left the war, bursting into revolution. There was universal war-weariness. It was at this juncture that America entered the war under the leadership of a president who proclaimed a new set of supranational objectives: a war to end all war, which would mean a peace without victory, so there would be little motive for vengeance; and a world made safe for democracy, for if the people had to choose there would be no war.

III THE HOME FRONTS

In World War I soldiers and sailors were, for the most part, not professionals. They were civilians, drafted from civilian families, and unused to military ways. Behind the front—on the production lines, subject to rationing and regimentation in daily living, subject also to the constant prodding of war propaganda—families too were part of this great "total war." They too bore up under it, though in France in 1917, after the bloody failure of the "one big push," civilian and military discontent, fanned by politicians, almost broke French morale. And in Germany the armistice was the result, in part, of a psychological collapse under intolerable spiritual and material pressures.

The Germans, much influenced by nineteenth-century ideas about the rights of the individual and laissez-faire economics, were slow to organize for total war. They failed notably to ensure the proper and equitable distribution of food supplies, so that as 1918 wore on, whole sectors of the urban population began to suffer from malnutrition. Nor were their finances and war production managed as efficiently as industrial production before the war had led everyone to expect. Rationing, strict control of production, price controls, systematic use of the resources of conquered countries—

these and many other measures were employed by the Germans, but not with the decisiveness and long preparation that were to characterize them in the later conflict of 1939-1945.

Sooner or later, all countries engaged in the war felt obliged to introduce drastic wartime economic planning, which anticipated in some sense a planned economy. In Britain the Defense of the Realm Act—known with wry affection as DORA—clamped down severely on the right to say and do what one liked. In the United States business executives who were working for the government for the first time flocked to Washington and helped build up an enormous new central government, which regulated the economy as it had never been regulated before. And of course all the belligerents engaged in a war of propaganda or, as it came to be called later, psychological warfare.

The Allies won the battle of the production lines, in which the United States played a major part. Allied production was slow in getting started and suffered from mistakes, bottlenecks, and hasty experiments. In the beginning the Allies were often at cross-purposes in production as well as in military strategy. Nevertheless, the Allies eventually fully exploited their potential superiority over the Central Powers in material resources, and by the end of 1917 their military machine was adequately, and in some ways wastefully, supplied.

The Allies also won the most critical phase of the war of propaganda. They sought to convince the neutral world, especially the United States, Latin America and the Swiss, Dutch, Scandinavians, and Spaniards, that the Allies were fighting for the right and the Central Powers for the wrong. This was not a total victory, for important groups in all these countries remained pro-German to the end, and Spain was probably anti-French and anti-English throughout the war. Still, most of the neutral West was early convinced that the cause of the Allies was just, or would at least prove victorious—a conviction strengthened by the public perception of the traditional liberalism of France and Britain, in contrast with the traditional autocracy of the German and Austrian empires, though the presence of the autocratic Russian Empire on the Allied side somewhat handicapped Allied propagandists.

Allied propaganda was one-sided and unfair—as propaganda usually is meant to be—notably in accusing the Germans of frightful atrocities in Belgium. The Germans imposed rigorous military controls on conquered populations, but their record was hardly worse than what was usual in warfare. Allied propaganda also simplified and falsified the complex causes of the war, making it appear that the Germans and Austrians were wholly responsible for its outbreak. This propaganda backfired shortly after the war had ended; revulsion against its unfairness had much to do with the widespread acceptance of the revisionist thesis that Germany had been guiltless of starting the war.

Except in Russia, the four years of war saw no major changes in political structure. The Central Powers retained until their collapse their incompletely responsible

Women working in an American factory during World War I.

parliamentary governments, and the parliaments on the whole were reasonably submissive. Despite the strengthening of the executive in wartime, France, Britain, and the United States carried on their democratic institutions. In Britain the skillful but indecisive Liberal leader Herbert Asquith (1852-1928) proved unable to master events, even though he widened his government into a coalition in May 1915. In December of that year he was succeeded by David Lloyd George, the architect of Britain's social insurance system, who had also proved himself an admirable organizer of war production. Under Lloyd George the coalition really worked, and his position as war leader was to remain unchallenged. Clemenceau—the Tiger, as he was known to his friends and enemies alike—came to power at the end of 1917, at a time when defeatism threatened both the military and the civilian strength of France. He took firm command of the war effort and disposed summarily of the disaffected politicians with decisiveness and disregard for the peacetime "rights of man."

The war brought substantial changes to social life on the home front, however. The fact that it claimed 36 million casualties devastatingly influenced demographic trends. An entire generation of young men, potential leaders in industry and politics, was destroyed in Britain and France. In both countries and in the United States women were employed where men had once worked, to release men to the battlefronts—in factories, on streetcars, at the lower levels of politics, and just behind the lines as nurses in military hospitals. At the end of the war, when demobilized men expected to return to their

jobs, women who had acquired skills were thrown out of work, and many turned to socialism.

Moral codes concerning sexual propriety also changed, for the men felt they might never return from the front, and the old barriers requiring a slow courtship were often cast aside. While the double standard in sexual conduct was intensified—soldiers were expected to violate the conventions of marriage without blame, while women were expected to remain faithful to their departed men—there were many who began to question these conventions. Sexual promiscuity and "social diseases" became more prevalent, as all societies began to challenge the authority of the family, the church, or the school over moral conduct. The Great War would, in modern memory, be the turning point for many social trends, especially in Britain and the United States.

The war produced a remarkable body of antiwar literature of the highest order, in fiction and poetry, and many intellectuals who had initially supported the war seemed permanently disillusioned, as was the British "Tommy" in the trenches. The political leaders had seemed to many only barely equal to the task of guiding the democratic nations through the war. In Britain there was a similar revulsion against the military leaders, and General Haig, in particular, was felt to have demonstrated the inadequacy of traditional methods of command. The public, though filled with euphoria over victory, was also mindful, in the words of the great war poet Wilfred Owen (1893-1918), that "carnage incomparable, and human squander," had devastated all of Europe.

IV THE PEACE SETTLEMENTS

As in Westphalia in 1648, at Utrecht in 1713, and at Vienna in 1815, the warring powers gathered in a great meeting to make the peace settlement. They met at Versailles to settle with the Germans and at other châteaux around Paris to settle with the rest. Peace congresses never meet in a world that is really at peace, for there is always an aftermath of local war, crises, and disturbances; in 1918-1919 these were so numerous and acute that they conditioned the work of the peace congresses. In addition, throughout 1918-1919 an influenza epidemic more devastating than any disease since the Black Death swept across the world, taking 20 million lives and disrupting families and work everywhere.

The most worrisome crises were in Russia—in 1919 deep in the throes of civil war and foreign invasion. No sooner had the Germans been forced to withdraw from the regions they had gained at Brest-Litovsk than the Allies sent detachments to various points along the perimeter of Russia—on the Black Sea, on the White Sea in the far north, and on the Pacific. The Allies still hoped to restore in Russia, if not the monarchy, at least a moderate republic. Their dread of final Bolshevik success (*Bolshevism*, not *Communism*, was the term almost universally used during this period) and of the possible spread of Bolshevism westward added to the tensions at Versailles and strengthened the conservative positions that Clemenceau and Lloyd George were taking there.

Bolshevism was clearly spreading westward. While the German revolution of November 1918 had been carried out under socialist auspices, through the winter of 1918-1919 there were communist riots and uprisings, and in Bavaria in April a soviet republic was proclaimed. The new republican government of Germany put these communist movements down, but only by an appeal to the remnants of the old army and to officers thoroughly hostile to any type of republic. After the breakup of the Austro-Hungarian monarchy in the autumn of 1918, the successor states—Czechoslovakia, Austria, Hungary, Yugoslavia, Romania—were disturbed by deep social and economic upheaval. In Hungary Bela Kun (c 1886-c 1940), who had worked with Lenin in Moscow, won power through a socialist-communist coalition and then set up a Bolshevik dictatorship. In August 1919 a Romanian army forced Kun to flee. Finally, groups of German ex-soldiers—Freikorps ("free corps") made up of embittered officers and recruits who could not adjust to civilian life, and joined by university students—were clamoring for the return of the monarchy and were attacking communists. Two major communist theoreticians, Karl Liebknecht (1871-1919), founder of the Spartacus party, which mounted the 1919 revolt, and Rosa Luxemburg (1870-1919), who had helped found the Communist party in Germany, were killed by soldiers while being taken to prison.

In the Near East the Allies had even greater instability to contend with. Greece was now up in arms against the Turks. Its nationalists had revived the hope of a restored Byzantine Empire, with the Greeks in command of the Straits. Greek armies, with Allied encouragement, landed at Smyrna in Asia Minor in the spring of 1919. The French and British, to whom control over different parts of the former Turkish Empire had been assigned, began at once having trouble with Arab leaders, while Jews were pressing for a national home in Palestine in accordance with the Balfour Declaration, to which the Arabs were bitterly opposed.

In India the aftermath of war was particularly disastrous as the epidemic of influenza swept the subcontinent. Indians had fought well as professional soldiers on the Allied side during the war; educated Indians thought their country was ripe for much more self-rule. Widespread disorders culminated in the Amritsar massacre in April 1919, in which a British general ordered his soldiers to fire on an unarmed crowd, killing or wounding some sixteen hundred people. Amritsar shocked world opinion, adding to the reputation the Allies were already acquiring among liberals everywhere, and knitting India more closely together in opposition to the British.

The situation in China was even less stable. There a revolution in 1911-1912 had ended the rule of the Manchu dynasty and inaugurated a precarious republic. The internal distractions of the Chinese and the weakening of Russia led the Japanese to renew their ambitious plans in north China. The presence of American troops in occupation of Archangel and Murmansk, in north Russia, and within the port at Vladivostok would color future relations with the Soviet Union. But while the British, French, and American interventions in Russia were mainly anti-Bolshevik, the American troops in Siberia were present largely from fear of Japanese aggression.

The world was in turmoil when the Allies assembled to make peace. The problems that faced the peacemakers were worldwide, complex, and often insoluble, in the sense that no decision on a given problem could possibly satisfy all the groups concerned. Yet the world expected more from them than from any previous settlement. Public opinion in the eighteenth and nineteenth centuries had built up a faith in the possibility of a peaceful, just, and happy world. In the minds of many, this war had been a war to "make the world safe for democracy," a "war to end war." It had produced an American president, Woodrow Wilson, who could eloquently articulate the hopes of all humanity.

In 1918 these hopes were embodied in one text— Woodrow Wilson's Fourteen Points—which were widely accepted by people in Allied countries and even in Germany and Austria as a platform for the peace to come, but which were also widely misunderstood and subject to divergent interpretations. Wilson's primary concerns were to secure the freedom of the seas and to create a League of Nations to organize peace thereafter. He and his advisers had formulated the language of the Fourteen Points to make them useful in case of complete victory, a stalemate, or even defeat, for they had been put forward as negotiating points. At the peace conference, however, they became rigid demands. These points were:

1. Open covenants of peace must be openly arrived at.

2. Absolute freedom of the seas must be guaranteed.

3. Economic barriers must be removed to establish equality of trade conditions among nations.

4. Guarantees must be given to reduce national armaments.

5. Colonial claims must be adjusted impartially, with the interests of the colonial populations given equal weight.

6. Russian territory must be evacuated.

7. Belgium must be restored.

8. All French territory should be freed, and Alsace-Lorraine restored to France.

9. The frontiers of Italy should be adjusted in accordance with "nationality."

10. The peoples of Austria-Hungary should be assured of autonomous development.

11. Romania, Serbia, and Montenegro should be evacuated and Serbia given access to the sea.

12. Turkey should be assured its sovereignty, but the nationalities under Turkish rule should be given an opportunity for autonomous development, and the Dardanelles should be opened to free passage.

13. An independent Polish state should be created with secure access to the sea.

14. A general association of nations must be formed to afford mutual guarantees "to great and small states alike."

Other hopes and promises that contradicted the Fourteen Points were not embodied in a single document. There were three categories: the previous diplomatic commitments made by the Allies; the widespread popular hopes fanned by Allied propaganda and promised at the end of the war by some Allied leaders; and the long-established habits and traditions that had become part of the dominant policies and trends of each nation. These countervailing expectations were bolstered by the fact that Wilson's points were at times vague and permissive rather than mandatory.

In the first category, the most difficult of the diplomatic commitments was the contradictory set of promises made to Italy and Serbia by the original Entente, including Russia, about the disposal of Hapsburg lands. There were other commitments, especially in the Balkans, that were very difficult to bring into the open. In the second category were the promises, widely believed by the British and French peoples, that Germany would be made to suffer to the full for its war guilt. Germany would be made to pay the whole cost of the war in reparations, its war criminals would be punished, and it

would be forever rendered incapable of aggression. In the third category were the deeply rooted drives of the various nations—French drives for revenge against Germany, for hegemony in Europe, and for security; Italian Irredentist drives; British longing for Victorian serenity and economic leadership, safe from German commercial competition; and the nationalist aspirations of the new states of central Europe. Important too was the American tradition of isolationism, the desire to be free from European alliances and entanglements as soon as possible.

Peacemaking and Territorial Settlements, 1918-1923

The peace conference first met formally on January 18, 1919. Nearly thirty nations involved in the war against the Central Powers sent delegates. Russia was not represented. None of the victorious great powers wanted to invite the Bolsheviks (by then in power in Moscow) to the peace table, and no Russian government-in-exile seemed suitable for an invitation. The defeated nations took no part in the deliberations; they were simply notified of the final terms and told to sign. The Germans, in particular, were given little chance to comment on or criticize the terms offered them. German publicists soon coined a term for the treaty—*Diktat*, the imposed, the dictated (as distinct from negotiated) peace. German anger over this failure of the Allies to accept their new republic was to play a large part in the ultimate rise of Adolf Hitler.

Although a few Western liberals were from the first disillusioned by the exclusion of communist Russia and the Central Powers from the peace table, the conference got off to a good start. Wilson's reception in Europe had been extremely enthusiastic, and the Fourteen Points already seemed to guarantee peace; it was believed that the proposed association of nations, working together in the freedom of parliamentary discussion, would eliminate the costly burdens of armament. Wilson's hopeful phrases resounded in press and pulpit, and none more loudly than his "open covenants openly arrived at."

More liberals were soon disillusioned, for the conference took on a familiar pattern. The small nations were excluded from the real negotiations; the business of the conference was carried on in private among the political chiefs of the victorious great powers—the Big Four of Wilson, Lloyd George, Clemenceau, and Italian premier Vittorio Orlando (1860-1952) (actually a Big Three, for Italy was by far the weakest of the quartet, and Orlando a less imposing personality than his colleagues). Decisions were made in the traditional way of diplomacy, with only indirect consultation of public opinion and with all the pressures, intrigue, compromises, and bargaining common to earlier peace conferences.

The professional diplomats of the smaller states had probably never expected that they would be treated on equal terms, but the completeness of their exclusion from the work of the conference annoyed them and angered their peoples. This was particularly true of

The Big Four met in Paris in December 1918. Seated from left to right were: Orlando, Lloyd George, Clemenceau, and Wilson.

Greece. More important, all the major powers had large staffs of experts—economists, political scientists, historians, specialists in many fields—who were confident that they would do the real work and make the real decisions. They drew up report after report, but they did not make policy. The disillusionment of these young experts was intense, and did much to discredit the work of the conference, especially among liberal intellectuals everywhere. The most celebrated of these experts was an economist, John Maynard Keynes (1883-1946), who represented the British Treasury at Versailles until he quit in disgust and wrote a highly critical and influential analysis, *The Economic Consequences of the Peace.*

Wilson and his experts were gradually persuaded to accept harsher peace terms. The reparations bill against Germany was lengthened; Poland, Italy, and Japan made claims to lands that could not be justified on the basis of self-determination by the peoples concerned; the victors more openly showed that they proposed to behave as do all victors in war, without compassion. Wilson compromised on a dozen points, but then chose to stand fast against the weakest of the Allies; he would not let the Italians have Fiume, which had once been the sole seaport of Hungary, though Italy might have neighboring Trieste (which was Italian-speaking) and the coveted Trentino, where there were many German or Slavic-speaking peoples. Yet Fiume was Italian-speaking and historically was linked with the great past of Venice; still it had never been part of modern Italy, and it had not been promised to Italy in the secret treaties of 1915. The Italian delegation left the conference in anger, but Wilson was immovable. Thus the fate of Fiume was not settled at the conference; in 1924, by treaty with Yugoslavia, the city went to Italy.

However, Wilson did get his new international organization; the covenant of the League of Nations was an integral part of the Treaty of Versailles. The League was no supranational body, but a kind of permanent consultative system initially composed of the victors and a few neutrals. The way was left open for the Germans and the Russians to join the League, as they later did. But to many liberals Wilson's League looked rather like Metternich's and Castlereagh's congress system of 1815, and not worth the sacrifices Wilson had made to obtain it. The League had an assembly in which each member state had one vote, and a council in which five great powers (Britain, France, Italy, the United States, and Japan) had permanent seats, and to which four other member states were chosen by the assembly for specific terms. A permanent secretariat, to be located at Geneva, was charged with administering the affairs of the League. The League never fulfilled the hopes it had aroused. It did not achieve disarmament, nor did its peacemaking machinery prevent aggression. The great powers simply went their usual ways, using the League only as their policy makers saw fit.

More relevant to the work in Paris was the problem of territorial changes. The peacemakers were confronted not merely with the claims of the victorious Allies but also with those of the new nations that had sprung up from the disintegrating Austrian, Russian, and Turkish empires. They had to try to satisfy diverse land hungers without too obviously violating the Wilsonian principle of "self-determination of peoples." This principle was hard to apply in much of central Europe, where peoples of different language and national consciousness were mixed together in a mosaic of minorities. The result was to multiply the number of sovereign nations. Nationalism, which some people had thought was on the wane, was fanned to intense new life in a dozen states.

France regained Alsace-Lorraine. Clemenceau also hoped to annex the small but coal-rich Saar Basin of Germany as compensation for French coal mines destroyed by the Germans during the war, and to detach from Germany the territory on the left (or west) bank of the Rhine, thereby strengthening French security and

setting up a Rhineland republic that might become a French satellite. Both French hopes, opposed by Wilson and Lloyd George, went unrealized. The Saar was to be separated from Germany for fifteen years as an international ward supervised by the League of Nations. During that period its coal output would go to France, and at its close a plebiscite would determine its political future. The Rhineland remained part of the German Republic, though it was to be demilitarized and occupied for a time by Allied soldiers.

The smaller states received a miscellany of emotionally important rewards. Belgium was given some small towns on the German border. After a plebiscite provided for in the Treaty of Versailles, Denmark recovered the northern part of Schleswig, which the Danish crown had lost to Prussia in 1864. Because Italy redeemed the

World War I and the Territorial Restructuring of Europe, 1914–1926

The Balkans and the Middle East, 1921

Irredenta of Trent and Trieste, thousands of German and Slavic-speaking peoples were now included within the new Italian boundaries. Poland, erased from the map as an independent state in 1795, was restored and given lands that it had possessed before the partitions of the eighteenth century, but that contained large German and other minorities.

The old Hapsburg Empire was completely dismembered. By the end of the war divisive influences within the Austro-Hungarian empire had rent it asunder. Charles I (1887-1922) had come to the Hapsburg throne in 1916 and had sought separate peace negotiations. But the empire broke up under him as ice breaks in a spring river: on October 15, 1918, Poland declared its independence; on October 19 Serbs, Croats, and Slovenes at Zagreb declared the sovereignty of a South Slav government; on November 1 Charles granted Hungary independence. When Austria-Hungary signed a separate armistice on November 3, it had virtually ceased to exist. The heart of its German-speaking area was constituted as the Republic of Austria, which was forbidden to join itself to Germany, and the heart of its Magyar-speaking area became a diminished Kingdom of Hungary. The

Czech-inhabited lands of Bohemia and Moravia were joined with Slovakia, to which were added the Ruthenian lands of the Carpatho-Ukraine frontier further east to form the "succession state" of Czechoslovakia, which included a large and discontented Sudeten German minority.

Another succession state was Yugoslavia, officially the Kingdom of Serbs, Croats, and Slovenes, a union between prewar Serbia and the south Slav territories of the Hapsburgs. Romania, which received the former Hungarian province of Transylvania, was also rewarded with Bessarabia, a Russian province that the Bolsheviks could not defend. Romania thus emerged with doubled territory and some restive non-Romanian minorities. Greece received Thrace at the expense of Turkey and Bulgaria. Wilson's refusal to accept the partition of Albania among Yugoslavia, Italy, and Greece saved that country from destruction.

Out of the former czarist domains held at the end of the war by the Germans besides Poland, the Baltic republics of Estonia, Latvia, and Lithuania were created. In time plebiscites determined other territorial adjustments, notably whether parts of East Prussia and Silesia should go to Poland or remain German. The new Polish state was granted access to the Baltic Sea through the so-called Polish Corridor, a narrow strip of land that had once been Polish and that terminated in the almost wholly German port of Danzig. The Poles wanted Danzig, but the Allies compromised by making it a Free City and by giving the Poles free trade with it. The Polish Corridor now separated East Prussia from the rest of Germany, and Germans had to cross it in sealed trains.

Outside Europe the Near East presented the most acute problems. By the Treaty of Sèvres of October 1920, the Turks were left with only Constantinople and a small area around it in Europe, and with Anatolia in Asia. Mesopotamia (contemporary Iraq) and Palestine were given as mandates to Britain, while Syria and Lebanon were granted as mandates to France. The Greeks were to hold Smyrna and nearby regions in Asia Minor for five years after which the mixed Greek and Turkish population would be entitled to a plebiscite. But the Treaty of Sèvres never went into effect, though it was signed by the sultan. A group of army officers headed by Mustafa Kemal led a popular revolt in Anatolia against the government at Constantinople and galvanized the Turkish people into a renewed nationalism. In the Greco-Turkish War of 1921-1922, the Turks drove the Greek army into the sea and set up a republic with its capital at Ankara in the heart of Anatolia. The Allies were obliged to conclude the Treaty of Lausanne with this new government in 1923; the new treaty transferred the area of Izmir (Turkish for Smyrna) and eastern Thrace from Greek to Turkish control and was much more advantageous to the Turks than the Treaty of Sèvres had been.

The Lausanne settlement included a radical innovation: a formal transfer of populations affecting two million people. Greeks in Turkey, except for Istanbul, were moved to Greece, and Turks in Greece, except for western Thrace, were moved to Turkey. Each government was to take care of the transferred populations, and though much hardship resulted, on the whole the plan worked. No such exchange occurred on Cyprus, the British-controlled island in the eastern Mediterranean, where Greeks outnumbered Turks four to one, and where the two peoples were so thoroughly intermingled in the towns and villages that an exchange would have been extremely difficult. Nor were measures taken to satisfy the national aspirations of two other minorities—the Muslim Kurds of eastern Anatolia and the Christian Armenians, many now dispersed from northeastern Anatolia to northern Syria.

In the rest of the world the straightforward policy of annexing overseas territories of defeated powers, as practiced in 1713, 1763, and 1815, seemed no longer possible in 1919. Opinion both in Europe and in America had already been deeply offended, and Wilson himself would not permit outright annexations. The consequence was the mandate system, in which control over a given territory was assigned to a power by the League of Nations, which undertook to see that the terms of the mandate were fulfilled. This system was designed by its proponents to prepare colonial peoples for eventual independence. Under it the former German overseas territories and the non-Turkish parts of the Ottoman Empire were distributed. Of Germany's African possessions, East Africa (renamed Tanganyika) went to Britain; Southwest Africa went to the Union of South Africa; and both the Cameroons and Togoland were divided between Britain and France. In the Pacific the German portion of New Guinea went to Australia, western Samoa to New Zealand, and the Caroline, Marshall, and Mariana island groups to Japan. In the Near East France secured Syria and Lebanon, while Britain took Palestine, Transjordan, and Iraq (the new Arabic designation for Mesopotamia).

To leaders like Clemenceau, the mandate system may have seemed like disguised annexation. The Japanese, for example, quite openly annexed and fortified their new Pacific islands in defiance of the terms of their mandate. But its advocates maintained that it was what it professed to be, a nursery for eventual nationhood. Apart from Japan, the mandatory powers at least made a show of treating mandated territories in a way that would prepare them for eventual freedom, and by the 1980s, sixty years later, all except Southwest Africa and the Japanese mandates had achieved it.

After land transfers, the most important business of the peace conferences was reparations, which were imposed on Austria, Hungary, Bulgaria, and Turkey, as well as on Germany. It was, however, the German reparations that so long disturbed the peace and the economy of the world. The Germans had to promise to pay for all the damage done to civilian property during the war, and to pay at the rate of five billion dollars a year until 1921, when the final bill would be presented to them. They would then be given thirty years in which to pay the full amount. The amount was left indefinite at Versailles, for the Allies could not agree on a figure, but the totals suggested were astronomical. It was clear from the first that the payments would ultimately have to be in goods—German goods in competition with the goods of the Allies. A Germany prosperous enough to pay reparations could not be the weak and divided nation that men like Clemenceau really wanted. Thus, from the very start the "realists" at Versailles—Lloyd George and Clemenceau—cherished hopes that were quite inconsistent with those of Wilson.

The Versailles settlement also required Germany to hand over many merchant ships to the Allies and to make large deliveries of coal to France, Italy, and Belgium for ten years. Furthermore the German army was to be limited to one hundred thousand troops, and the western frontier zone, extending to a line fifty kilometers east of the Rhine, was to be completely "demilitarized"—that is, to contain neither fortifications nor soldiers. In addition, the Allies could maintain armies of occupation on the left bank of the Rhine for fifteen years or longer. The treaty forbade Germany to have either submarines or military planes and severely limited the number and size of surface vessels in its navy. Finally, Article 231 of the Treaty of Versailles obliged Germany to admit that the Central Powers bore sole responsibility for starting the war in 1914. To the Germans, Versailles was a cruel and humiliating peace, the Diktat, a great national grievance on which Hitler was later to play so skillfully. To liberals of that time and later it seemed an unsound, vengeful peace, disastrous in its unrealistic reparations policy. Yet it was at least a settlement, and one that in the later 1920s seemed a basis for slow improvement in international relations.

The League of Nations was potentially a means by which a new generation of international administrators might mitigate the old rivalries. The reparations could be and were scaled down to be more reasonable. The new succession states were based on a modern, popular, national consciousness that had been developing for at least a century. Though some might protest at the "Balkanization of Europe," it would have been impossible to deny national independence to the Czechs, the Poles, the Baltic peoples, and the south Slavs. Germany, though not treated generously, was not wiped off the map, as Poland had been in the eighteenth century. Versailles was simply a compromise peace.

It contained, however, too many compromises for the American people, who were not used to striking international bargains. The American refusal to ratify the Treaty of Versailles was the result of many forces. Domestic politics were an important part, for the Republicans had won control of Congress in the elections of November 1918. The president was still Wilson, a Democrat, and he made no concessions to the Republicans, either by taking Republicans to Paris with him or by accepting modifications in the treaty that would have satisfied some of his Republican opponents. The Senate feared that the League would drag the United States into future wars, and many were convinced that the League Covenant giving Canada, for example, a separate vote, was merely a device to award Britain two votes. Wilson declared that Article X of the Covenant had turned the Monroe Doctrine into a world doctrine, for it guaranteed "the territorial integrity and political independence" of all League members. But opponents argued that were the United States to sign the Covenant, the League could interfere with American tariffs and with immigration laws that excluded Asians; a group of "irreconcilables" insisted that the League idea be separated entirely from the peace treaty. The Senate thereupon refused to ratify the treaty and ended the technical state of war with Germany by congressional resolution on July 2, 1921. Separate treaties were then signed with Germany, Austria, and Hungary, by which the United States gained all the rights stipulated for it by the Treaty of Versailles.

It is unlikely that even a more pliable and diplomatic American president than Wilson could have won Senate ratification of another important treaty involved in the proposed settlement—a defensive alliance among France, Britain, and the United States. Wilson had been pushed into it as part of the price of getting France to give up proposals for a separate Rhineland republic and for French annexation of the Saar. Without United States participation, Britain refused a mere dual alliance with France against a German attack. France, still seeking to bolster its security, thereupon patched up a series of alliances with the new nations to the east and south of Germany—Poland, and the Little Entente of Yugoslavia, Czechoslovakia, and Romania—a wholly unsatisfactory substitute for Britain and the United States as allies.

The peace left France with uneasy dominance of Europe, dependent on the continued disarmament and economic weakening of Germany, on the continued isolation of Russia, and on the uncertain support of unstable new allies. Moveover, France had been disastrously weakened by the human and material losses of the war, and its posture of leadership was unreal, though it alarmed the British, with their long memories of French rivalry in the past. Germany was in fact still the strongest nation on the Continent. The Great War had checked, but not halted, its potential ability to dominate the Continent.

One most important matter was not directly touched upon by the Versailles settlement: Russia, or the Union of Soviet Socialist Republics (USSR), the formal name of the new communist state. Yet in many senses, the most important result of World War I was the emergence of this Russia, with capabilities greatly increased by the stimulus of successful revolution.

V THE RUSSIAN REVOLUTION OF 1917

The Immediate Background to Revolution, 1914-1917

Though Russia was shaken by domestic crisis in 1914, the country greeted the outbreak of World War I with demonstrations of national patriotism. The Duma supported the war, while the left-wing parties abstained from voting for war loans but offered to assist the national defense. Yet it was the war and the regime's failure to deal with the crises it provoked that precipitated revolution.

Russia was geographically isolated from the munitions and supplies that would otherwise have come from the Allies. Only Vladivostok, on the Siberian Pacific coast, and Archangel and Murmansk, on the White Sea, were available as seaports, and for the first three years of the war Archangel was not connected with the interior by rail. Despite Russia's great resources in agriculture and potential for industry, transportation was inadequate from the beginning, and when the trains were used to move troops, food shortages developed in the cities. Moreover, the imperial government was not only inefficient in mobilizing the resources of Russia for war, but was reluctant to give the existing public bodies—Duma, zemstvos, city governments—the opportunity to exercise authority, sure that such powers, once delegated, would never be recovered.

By 1917 more than 15,000,000 Russians had been drafted into the armies. Losses in battle were staggering from the first; the Russians suffered more than 3,800,000 casualties during the first year of war. On the home front so much criticism was aroused by the inadequate handling of the supply of munitions that the minister of war was tried for high treason. By mid-1915 the center and left groups in the Duma, known as the Progressive Bloc, were urging moderate reforms, such as the end of discrimination against minority nationalities and an increase in the powers of the zemstvos. The empress Alexandra opposed all such measures and kept urging her husband, Czar Nicholas II, to act more autocratically. In the autumn of 1915, in answer to a demand by the Progressive Bloc for a cabinet that would be responsible to it and not to the czar, Nicholas dismissed the Duma and took personal command of the armies in the field, leaving his wife in authority in St. Petersburg. She in turn left matters in the hands of her favorite, Rasputin.

With the empress and Rasputin in control, a gang of shady adventurers, blackmailers, and profiteers bought and sold offices, speculated in military supplies, put in their own puppets as ministers, and created a series of scandals. Confusion, strikes, and defeatism mounted at home during 1916, while the armies at the front, lacking transport, equipment, supplies, and medical care, slowly bled to death. The conservatives began to denounce Rasputin publicly, and in December 1916 he was murdered under gruesome circumstances by a group of monarchists and patricians, acting in what they considered to be the best interests of the absent czar. Despite repeated warnings from moderates in the Duma that the government itself was precipitating a revolution by its failure to create a responsible ministry, the czar remained apathetic. When news of Rasputin's death reached Berlin, the Germans saw a chance to knock Russia out of the war by promoting independence movements in the Ukraine, Poland, and Finland, and by aiding Russian revolutionaries whom, the Germans hoped, they could then control. Independently of one another, relatives of the imperial family and members of the Duma began to plot for Nicholas's abdication. In the early months of 1917 all conditions favored revolution, but the revolutionaries were not prepared.

The March Revolution By February only ten-days' supply of flour was left in the capital, and the regional commander set up a rationing system. Long lines, closed shops, and the prospect of starvation led to disorder. In the Duma "unfit ministers" were attacked, and speakers invoked the French Revolution, though to empty seats, since the president of the council and the ministers refused to attend. The left-wing deputies turned to the secret organizations, which had already been working up public opinion against the government's dismissal of thousands of factory workers after a strike. The strikers demonstrated in the streets, and thousands of other

workers, led by the wives of the workers, massed in a march that was broken up by mounted police. By the third day the Bolsheviks had taken charge of the continuing strikes and parades. The czar's secret police, the *Okhrana*, conducted mass arrests. But the soldiers were now refusing orders to stop the workers as they sought to march across the River Neva from the workers' quarter to the palaces, and on March 10 (February 27 in the old Russian calendar) many soldiers handed their weapons over to the crowd. The insurgents captured the arsenal with 40,000 rifles, and Petrograd (as St. Petersburg was now called) was in their hands. Meanwhile, the czar suspended the Duma, which ignored his orders and went into session, though without any clear leadership or program.

Indeed, the Revolution of February and March 1917, a product of despair and high emotion, remained virtually leaderless and without a program, since those who had been planning revolution were not yet fully prepared. The main Bolshevik leaders were still abroad or in exile, and the radical agrarian group—the Social Revolutionaries (SR)—and the more philosophical Marxists—the Social Democrats (SD)—were also caught by surprise. Nonetheless, by March the Romanov dynasty, which had ruled since 1613, was without hope.

A determining factor in the overthrow of the czar was the disintegrating loyalty of the garrison of Petrograd. When the czar ordered other troops to fire on the rioters, only a few obeyed, and in revulsion against the order, the troops joined the dissidents and began to hunt the police. On March 12 the Progressive Bloc in the Duma formed a provisional government to keep order until there could be a constituent assembly. By March 14, when the czar finally decided to appoint a responsible ministry, it was too late. On March 15 he abdicated in favor of his younger brother, Michael, and on March 16 Michael refused the throne.

Before that, on March 12, leftists, including many released from prison by the mobs, formed a soviet of workers and soldiers, modeled on the 1905 soviet. Its "Army Order No. 1," setting up a committee of soldiers within every unit of the army to control weapons, dealt a blow to military discipline and organization. The soviet created a food-supply commission and published newspapers; its fifteen-man executive committee of SRs and Mensheviks became the policy makers of the revolution. The Soviet located its headquarters in the same building as the Duma and was soon in conflict with it. The Duma wanted to get its provisional government functioning quickly, to restore public order, to get what the liberals called "the Dark People" out of the streets, and to carry on the war with efficiency for the honor of Russia. Some Duma members were monarchists; some wanted to continue the war and receive Constantinople as a reward; most felt the question of citizens' rights was secondary to these more pressing matters. The Soviet, on the other hand, knew that the great mass of Russian people did not care about Constantinople and wanted an immediate peace, as well as land and food.

The Marxists among the Soviet leaders—mainly Men-

The first session of the Duma of the provisional government met in March of 1917. Behind the speaker's platform was an empty frame that had formerly displayed a portrait of the czar.

sheviks—believed in the necessity of a preliminary bourgeois revolution, and they did not yet regard the Soviet itself as an organ of power. Therefore, though they would not participate in the provisional government, they offered it their limited support. Despite their widely differing political and economic aims, both the Duma and the Soviet agreed to grant political liberties immediately and to summon an assembly to establish the future form of government and give Russia a constitution. The provisional government was composed mainly of Kadets (Constitutional Democrats) and other moderates and was headed by the liberal prince Georgi Lvov (1861-1925), chairman of the union of zemstvos and of the Red Cross. It also included one member of the Soviet, the moderate SR Alexander Kerensky (1881-1970), minister of justice, who was a member of the Duma.

The Provisional Government The provisional government—which held office between mid-March and early November 1917—was a total failure. Russian moderates had no experience of authority. They were separated by a great cultural gulf from the lower classes. Their opportunity to rule came amid a fearful war, which they felt they had to pursue while reconstructing and democratizing the enormous and unwieldy Russian Empire. Moreover, the Soviet held many of the instruments of power, yet refused to accept responsibility. Workers and soldiers in the capital supported the Soviet. In the provinces the new governors appointed by the provisional government had no weapon except persuasion to employ against the local peasant-elected soviets, which multiplied rapidly. The provisional government had no means to suppress its opponents.

The two great issues facing the provisional government were agrarian discontent and the continuation of the war. The peasants wanted land, and they wanted it immediately. The provisional government, however, believed in acting with deliberation and according to law. It refused to sanction peasant seizures of land, despite increasing disorder in the countryside. Instead, it appointed a commission to collect material on which to base future agrarian legislation—an act totally inadequate to the emergency. As to the war, the provisional government still unrealistically hoped that Russia might win and thus gain the territories the Allies had promised. But the Soviet subverted discipline in the armies at the front by issuing a "declaration of the rights of soldiers," which virtually ended the authority of officers over enlisted men. But the Soviet did not call for a separate peace. Even the Bolshevik members of the Soviet, who now began to return from exile, demanded only that Russia participate in general peace negotiations, which should begin at once.

Lenin

The most important of the returning Bolshevik exiles was Lenin. His real name was Vladimir Ilyich Ulianov, but in his writings he used the pen name Lenin, to which he sometimes prefixed the initial N, a Russian abbreviation for "nobody," to tell his readers that he was using a pseudonym. Son of a provincial official, Lenin became a revolutionary in the 1880s, and in the early years of the SDs he led the party's Bolshevik wing. He had returned to Russia from abroad for the Revolution of 1905, but he left Russia once more in 1908. From abroad he joined with a small group of socialists in opposing the war and urging that it be transformed into a class war. He had been writing extensively on class war and on the right of nations to self-determination. In 1916 in his subsequently influential *Imperialism, The Highest Stage of Capitalism*, he considered the war to be the product of imperialism, itself produced by capitalism; thus, war, empires, and capitalism must all be destroyed if society was to be reformed. Poor and with few followers, Lenin was in Bern, Switzerland, when the revolution broke out in Russia.

Though he had for a time despaired of living to see a true socialist revolution, Lenin was anxious to get back to Russia. The German general staff thought his return would help disrupt the Russian war effort, so the German military transported Lenin and other Bolshevik leaders across Germany from Switzerland to the Baltic in a sealed railroad car. Lenin arrived at the Finland station in Petrograd on April 16, 1917, a little more than a month after the March revolution.

Most Russian Social Democrats had long regarded a bourgeois parliamentary republic as a necessary preliminary stage to an eventual socialist revolution. Therefore, they were prepared to help transform Russia into a capitalist society, though not without grave doubts that the bourgeois capitalists might be as bad as the czar and the landlords, or that the masses might prefer the new system. They favored the creation of a democratic republic and believed that complete political freedom was absolutely essential for their own rise to power. Despite the Marxist emphasis upon the industrial laboring class as the only proper vehicle for revolution, Lenin early realized that in Russia, where the "proletariat" embraced only about 1 percent of the population, the SDs must seek other allies. During the Revolution of 1905 he had begun to preach the need for limited tactical alliances between the Bolsheviks and the SRs, who commanded the support of the peasantry; when that alliance had served its purpose, the SDs were to turn on their allies and destroy them. Then would come the socialist triumph. Lenin's view, however, was not adopted, even by most Bolsheviks. Together with the Mensheviks, they

SIMPLE ERRORS: THE WEST AND RUSSIAN HISTORY

The way in which certain simple matters of fact are sometimes dealt with in the West when the subject is Russia illustrates the problem of understanding the historical development of a relatively isolated nation. For example, for years some writers insisted that Lenin's first name was Nikolai or Nicholas because of his use of the initial N, not understanding Russian and communist customs concerning abbreviations and pseudonyms. This "discovery" was repeated in the American press as recently as 1983.

Many texts give different dates from those given here for certain events; virtually all disagree over the precise sequence of events and over the nature of leadership in the Duma and the first Soviet. Events that took place in March according to the Western calendar employed throughout this book are frequently referred to as taking place in February because of the different Russian calendar. The number of deaths in any specific demonstration, mutiny, or battle reveal dramatic discrepancies in different books. These inconsistencies in both Soviet and modern Western literature on the Russian Revolution are symptomatic of the degree to which Russia was cut off from the West at the time. Matters of straightforward chronology, of fact, even of names or birth and death dates were subjects of rumor or propaganda both inside and outside Russia. Later, when Soviet leadership ordered the rewriting of much of Russian history so that Russian citizens would not have access to other, and thus confusing, points of view, many aspects of Russian history fell under even greater suspicion.

Russian history clearly represents the problems of accurately recording and intelligently interpreting the past when a society has either been long ignored or cut off from alternative interpretations of its past. It also illustrates how a political leadership may attempt to make history as a discipline serve its own ends by rewriting the past to fit present-day expectations.

continued to urge that a bourgeois revolution and a parliamentary democracy were necessary first steps.

Because Lenin did not trust the masses to make a revolution (by themselves, he felt, they were capable only of trade-union consciousness), he favored a dictatorship of the Bolshevik party over the working class. Because he did not trust the rank and file of Bolshevik party workers, he favored a dictatorship of a small elite over the Bolshevik party. And in the end, because he did not trust anyone's views but his own, he favored, though never explicitly, his personal dictatorship over this elite. Another future Russian leader, the brilliant Lev Davidovich Bronstein, known as Leon Trotsky (1879-1940), early warned that Lenin's views implied one-man dictatorship.

Trotsky, for his part, argued that the Russian bourgeoisie was so weak that the working class could telescope the bourgeois and socialist revolutions into one continuous movement. After the proletariat had helped the bourgeoisie achieve its revolution, the workers could move immediately to power, and could nationalize industry and collectivize agriculture. Although foreign intervention and civil war were to be expected, the Russian proletariat would soon be joined by the proletariats of other countries, who would make their own revolutions. Except for this last point, Trotsky's analysis accurately forecast the course of events, and between 1905 and 1917 Lenin himself accepted Trotsky's view from time to time, as he did the views of other rivals when it was strategic to do so.

Lenin's greatest talent was not as an original thinker but as a skillful tactician. He often seemed able to judge just what was politically feasible in a given situation, and he was not afraid to gamble. Thus, even before he returned to Russia in 1917, he had assessed some of the difficulties facing the provisional government and decided that the masses could take over at once. Immediately upon his arrival, therefore, he hailed the worldwide revolution, proclaiming that the end of imperialism, "the last stage of capitalism," was at hand. Ignoring the positions taken previously by both the Bolsheviks and Mensheviks, he demanded that all power immediately be given to the soviets. These doctrines were known as the April Theses.

Almost no one save Lenin felt that the loosely organized soviets could govern the country or that the war would bring down the capitalist world in chaos. Still, Lenin called not only for the abandonment of the provisional government and the establishment of a republic of soviets, but for the confiscation of estates, the nationalization of land, and the abolition of the army, of government officials, and of the police. He was offering land at once to the impatient peasants, peace at once to the war-weary populace. This program fitted the mood of the people far better than the cautious efforts of the provisional government to bring about reform by legal means. Dogmatic, furiously impatient of compromise, and entirely convinced that he alone had the courage to speak the truth, Lenin galvanized the Bolsheviks into a

This "mug shot" of Leon Trotsky, taken after an arrest, was found by the victorious revolutionaries in the files of the czarist police.

The young Lenin is shown here in a disguise he used on an illegal identification card to escape to Finland.

TO THE FINLAND STATION

On the day Lenin arrived at the Finland Station in Petrograd, he declared that the World War must be transformed into a series of civil wars, the bourgeois revolution into a social revolution, so that a crisis of European capitalism might be precipitated. In a memorable confrontation, he instantly revealed that he would not accept the more moderate expectations of the Petrograd Soviet. The following account is drawn from the notebooks of a journalist who was on the spot:

The train was very late. . . . But at long last it arrived. A thunderous *Marseillaise* boomed forth on the platform, and shouts of welcome rang out. . . . Behind [the master of ceremonies] . . . Lenin came, or rather ran, into the room. He wore a round cap, his face looked frozen, and there was a magnificent bouquet in his hands. Running to the middle of the room, he stopped in front of [N.S.] Chkheidze [(1864-1926), the chairman of the Soviet] as though colliding with a completely unexpected obstacle. And Chkheidze, still glum, pronounced the following "speech of welcome" with not only the spirit and wording but also the tone of a sermon:

"Comrade Lenin . . . we welcome you to Russia. But—we think that the principal task of the revolutionary democracy is now the defence of the revolution from any encroachments either from within or from without. We consider that what this goal requires is not disunion, but the closing of the democratic ranks. We hope you will pursue these goals together with us." . . .

Lenin . . . stood there as though nothing taking place had the slightest connection with him . . . and then, turning away from the Ex[ecutive] Com[mittee] delegation altogether, he made this "reply":

"Dear Comrades, soldiers, sailors, and workers! I am happy to greet in your persons the victorious Russian revolution, and greet you as the vanguard of the worldwide proletarian army. . . . The piratical imperialist war is the beginning of civil war throughout Europe. . . . The hour is not far distant when at the call of our comrade, Karl Liebknecht [who was still alive at the time], the peoples will turn their arms against their own capitalist exploiters. . . . The worldwide Socialist revolution has already dawned. . . . Any day now the whole of European capitalism may crash. The Russian revolution accomplished by you has prepared the way and opened a new epoch. Long live the worldwide Socialist revolution! . . .

To another *Marseillaise*, and to the shouts of the throng of thousands, among the red-and-gold banners illuminated by the searchlight, Lenin went out by the main entrance and was about to get into a closed car, but the crowd absolutely refused to allow this, Lenin clambered on to the bonnet of the car and had to make a speech.

N.N. Sukhanov, *The Russian Revolution, 1917*, trans. Joel Carmichael (London: Oxford University Press, 1955), pp. 272-74, as quoted in M.C. Morgan, *Lenin* (London: Edward Arnold, 1971), pp. 104-106. Sukhanov (1833?-1931?), while in favor of revolution, was anti-Bolshevik. Although Lenin criticized Sukhanov as a Social Democrat who did not understand the workers, he accepted his account of the revolution as factually accurate.

All European socialists who had supported the war had, he said, betrayed the proletariat. The very idea of Social Democracy, as ideology or as party name, "had been desecrated by treason. It was impossible to have anything in common with it, impossible to purge it; it had to be cast aside as the symbol of the betrayal of the working class."

truly revolutionary group waiting only for the right moment to seize power. He also had millions of German marks at his disposal to pay for the party newspaper, *Pravda (Truth)*, for antiwar propaganda, and for armed Red Guard contingents.

The November Revolution

The provisional government how faced a crisis because the Kadet ministers wished to maintain the Russian war aim of annexing the Straits, while the Soviet wanted a peace "without annexations or indemnities." Kerensky, now war minister, emerged as the dominant leader. He failed to realize that it was no longer possible to restore the morale of the armies, which were dissolv-

ing under the impact of Bolshevik propaganda, poor leadership, and exhaustion. A new offensive ordered on July 1 collapsed as soldiers refused to obey orders, deserted their units, and hurried home to their villages, eager to seize the land. Ukrainian separatism also plagued the government. The soviets became gradually more and more Bolshevik in their views, as Lenin and Trotsky worked at recruitment and organization. Although the June congress of soviets in Petrograd was less than 10 percent Bolshevik, the Bolshevik slogans of peace, bread, and freedom won overwhelming support.

An armed outbreak by troops who had accepted the Bolshevik slogans found the Petrograd Soviet professing unwillingness to assume power. While crowds roared outside, the Soviet voted to discuss the matter two weeks later and meanwhile to keep the provisional government in power. The government declared that Lenin was a divisive agent of Germany and, as his supporters wavered, raided the offices of *Pravda*. Lenin went into hiding in Finland to avoid arrest.

Kerensky became premier. General Lavr Georgyevich Kornilov (1870-1918), chosen by Kerensky as the new commander-in-chief of the armies, quickly became the hope of all conservative groups. In August Kornilov plotted a coup, intending to disperse the Soviet. His attitude toward the provisional government was less clear, but had he succeeded he would probably have demanded a purge of its more radical elements. Tension between Kornilov and his superior, Kerensky, mounted. The Soviet backed Kerensky, fearing Kornilov's attack. When Kornilov refused to accept his dismissal as war minister and seemed about to march against Petrograd, the Bolsheviks threw themselves into preparations for defense. Kornilov's troop movements were sabotaged, however, and by September 14 he had been arrested. This threat from the right helped the Bolsheviks greatly, and sentiment in the Petrograd and Moscow soviets became predominantly Bolshevik for the first time, weakening Kerensky.

The Kornilov affair turned the army mutiny into a widespread revolt. Soldiers murdered their officers. In the meantime, the old tradition of the Pugachev revolt

(see p. 223) had been renewed in the countryside; farms were burned, manor houses destroyed, two hundred estates were devastated in the Ukraine, and large land-owners were killed. After the great estates were gone, the peasantry attacked the smaller properties, though they allowed owners in some districts to keep a portion of their former lands through redistribution.

Amid these disorders Lenin returned to Petrograd. Trotsky was warning that Kerensky was planning to surrender Petrograd to the Germans, which enabled Trotsky to gain control over a Military Revolutionary Committee to help defend the city and to transform the committee into a general staff for the revolution. Beginning on November 4, huge demonstrations and mass meetings were addressed by Trotsky, and on November 7 (October 25 on the old Russian calendar) the insurrection broke out as Trotsky intended. The February Revolution, as it is known in Russian historiography, had failed, to be replaced by the October Revolution.

In Petrograd the revolution had been well prepared and proceeded with little bloodshed. Military groups loyal to the Bolsheviks took control of key points in the city. The Bolsheviks entered the Winter Palace, where the provisional government was meeting, and arrested the ministers. Kerensky escaped in a car belonging to the American Embassy. The Military Revolutionary Committee took over. A long-awaited Congress of Soviets,

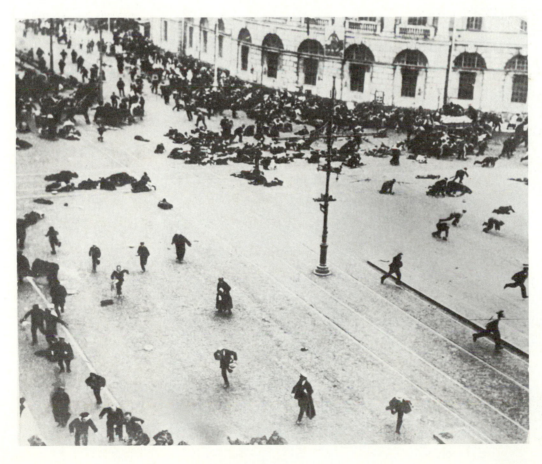

Demonstrators in the streets of Petrograd in July 1917 were fired upon by police and soldiers of the Kerensky government.

representing less than half of the soviets in Russia, opened on November 8. Both Lenin and Trotsky appeared. When the Mensheviks and right-wing SRs walked out, Trotsky called them garbage that would be swept into the trash cans of history. Cooperating with the left-wing SRs and adopting their land program, Lenin abolished the property rights of the church, of landlords, and of the crown. He transferred the land thus affected to local land committees and soviets of peasant deputies, transforming at a stroke the isolated Russian villages by "legalizing" a process already begun. Though Lenin did not approve of the system of individual small holdings that this decree put into effect, he recognized the psychological advantage of appearing to accept what was happening in the countryside in any case. He also urged an immediate peace without annexations or indemnities and appealed to the workers of Germany, France, and England to support him in this demand. Finally, a new cabinet, called a Council of People's Commissars, was chosen, with Lenin as president and Trotsky as foreign *commissar*—terms like "prime minister" or "cabinet" being rejected as too bourgeois in origin.

The Bolsheviks installed as commissar of nationalities a younger man, a Georgian named Joseph Dzhugashvili (1879-1953), who had been a successful organizer of bank robberies in the days when the party treasury was filled in this way, but whose role had otherwise been somewhat obscure. He had taken the name Stalin, suggesting a steel-like hardness. Under Lenin's coaching, Stalin had become the party authority on questions relating to the many minority nationalities and had published a pamphlet on the subject in 1913.

Outside Petrograd the revolution moved more slowly. In Moscow there was a week of street fighting between Bolshevik Reds and anti-Bolshevik Whites, as those opposed to the revolution were called. Elsewhere, in factory towns the Bolsheviks usually won speedily; in nonindustrial centers it took longer. A main reason for the rapid and smooth success of the Bolsheviks was that the provincial garrisons opposed the war and willingly allied themselves with the workers. Local military revolutionary committees were created in most places and held elections for new local soviets. Most of Siberia and central Asia came over, but Tiflis, the capital of Georgia, went Menshevik and passed resolutions calling for a constituent assembly and the continuation of the war. Gradually the town of Rostov-on-Don, near the Sea of Azov, became the main center of White resistance, as Kornilov and other generals together with a number of the leading politicians of the Duma gathered there.

This initial triumph of the revolution did not mean that the population of Russia had been converted to Bolshevism. By sensing the mood of the people, Lenin had given the Bolsheviks a set of slogans around which the people could rally, although some of the slogans did

Lenin was a charismatic speaker, as is apparent even in this photograph of him addressing a crowd in 1919.

not correspond with mainstream Bolshevik views. The Russian people were, in fact, probably generally anti-Bolshevik. But the Bolsheviks had triumphed, and the liberal democratic hopes for freedom of the press and other individual freedoms were doomed to disappointment. Late in November an agreement was reached with the left-wing SRs, three of whom entered the government, and peace negotiations were begun with the Germans. The revolution proper was over and Lenin was in power.

The Russian state, however, was disintegrating and decomposing socially on all sides. The Bolsheviks now spoke of elections for a constituent assembly. Lenin had no use for this sort of democratically chosen parliament, which he considered "inferior" to the Soviet. Yet perhaps because he had so long taunted the provisional government with delaying elections, he felt compelled to hold them. On November 25 the Russian people had the first free election in their history. Lenin accepted as accurate figures showing that the Bolsheviks polled about a quarter of the vote; the other socialist parties, chiefly the SRs, polled 62 percent. As was to be expected, the Bolshevik vote was heaviest in the cities, especially Moscow and Petrograd, while the SR vote was largely rural.

Disregarding the majority cast for his opponents, Lenin maintained that "the most advanced" elements had voted for him. The constituent assembly met only once, in January 1918. Lenin dissolved it the next day by decree and sent guards with rifles to prevent its meeting again. The anti-Bolshevik majority was deeply indignant at this unconstitutional act of force against the popular will, but there was no public outburst and the delegates disbanded. In part this was because the Bolsheviks had already taken action on what interested the people most—peace, bread, and land—and in part because the Russian masses lacked a democratic parliamentary tradition.

War Communism, 1917-1920

The first period of Soviet history, which runs from the end of 1917 to the end of 1920, is usually called the period of war communism or military communism. The term implies that the main features of the period were determined by military events; civil war raged, and foreign powers intervened on Russian soil. But the term is also somewhat misleading. This was a period of militant as well as military communism, symbolized early in 1918 by the change of the party's name from Bolshevik to the Russian Communist party (with the reference to Bolsheviks retained in parentheses, to be dropped only in 1952). The capital was shifted from Petrograd, with its exposed location on the western fringe of Russia, to the greater security of Moscow, in the heart of European Russia. And a newspaper, *The Communist* (which was leftist communist and opposed to Lenin), began publication. The Bolsheviks firmly believed that world revolution was about to begin, probably first in Germany, then spreading to Britain and

ultimately to the United States. This view led the Bolsheviks to hasten the construction of a socialist state in Russia and to take a casual atttitude toward their international affairs, since they expected that relations with capitalist states would be temporary. Many of the decisions that were taken under military pressure were, therefore, also regarded as leading to the new society.

By 1920 the state had taken over all enterprises employing more than ten workers (more than five, if motor power was used). Labor was compulsory and strikes were outlawed. The state organized a system of barter, which replaced the free market. Internal trade was illegal; only the government food commissary could buy and sell. Money disappeared as the state took over distribution as well as production. It expropriated the banks, repudiated the czarist foreign debt, and in effect wiped out savings. Church and state were separated by decree, and judges were removed from office and replaced by appointees of the local soviets. Nine opposition political parties were liquidated (Kadets) or persecuted (SRs and Mensheviks).

The government subjected the peasantry to ever more severe requisitioning. It mobilized the poorer peasants against those who were better off (called *kulaks*, from the word meaning "fist" and used to apply to usurers, as if to say "hardfisted"). By calling for a union of the hungry against the better-fed, the regime deliberately sowed class hatred in the villages and stimulated civil war in the countryside. A decree forming a secret police, the *Cheka* (from the initials of the words meaning "extraordinary commission"), was issued in December 1917, and terror became a weapon in the civil war.

Before the communist government could function at all, peace was necessary, as the army had virtually ceased to exist. Negotiations between the Russians and the Germans and Austro-Hungarians at Brest-Litovsk dragged on into 1918, the Russians hoping that revolution would break out in Germany, and the Germans demanding enormous territorial cessions, stepping up their demands as the Russians delayed. Finally, on March 3, 1918, the Russians signed the Peace of Brest-Litovsk, which deprived them of the entire Ukraine, the Baltic provinces, Finland, and some Caucasian lands, undoing three centuries of Russian territorial expansion. The treaty cost Russia a third of its population, 80 percent of its iron, and 90 percent of its coal. Many communists resigned rather than accept the peace, and the left SRs quit the government. The Germans overran the Ukraine and the Crimea and installed a highly authoritarian regime, against which the communists continued to agitate. The Whites, with German help, put down the Reds in Finland.

Civil War, 1918-1921

During the months following Brest-Litovsk, disorder in the countryside as a result of requisitioning and class warfare was swelled by the outbreak of open civil strife. During the war a legion of Czechs resident in the country and of deserters from the Hapsburg armies had been formed inside Russia. When Russia withdrew from the war, the Czech nationalist leader, Thomas G. Masaryk (1850-1937), wanted to have the Czech corps sent to the French front. Czech, Soviet, and Allied representatives therefore decided to transport the Czech corps to Vladivostok, from which they could sail to France. As the Czechs gathered, the communists became suspicious of their intentions and ordered them to disarm. The Czechs then took control of the Siberian railroad. When the Soviet government tried to take reprisals against the Czechs, who numbered fewer than 35,000 men, the Czechs seized several towns in western Siberia. The local soviets were unprepared, and the SRs were sympathetic to the Czechs. Local anti-Bolshevik armies quickly came into being. In July, in fear that Whites would rescue the former czar and his family, in exile in Ekaterinburg in the Ural Mountains, the leader of the local soviet, encouraged by Lenin, executed Nicholas II, his wife, his son, his four daughters, his doctor, his servants, and his dog.

Shortly before the executions the Allies had decided to intervene in Russia on behalf of the opponents of Bolshevism. The withdrawal of Russia from the war had been a heavy blow to the Allies, and they now hoped to protect the vast amounts of war supplies still at Vladivostok and Archangel, which had never reached the imperial Russian armies. They also wished to create a new second front against the Germans in the East. The idea of a capitalist "crusade" against Bolshevism—later popularized by Soviet and pro-Soviet historians as the sole motive for the intervention—was in fact much less significant, though not without force in some quarters. The Allies had been at war a long time, and their populations were war weary; they were apprehensive over communist efforts to stimulate revolution in all the capitalist nations of the world.

The Czechs overthrew the local soviet in Vladivostok in June 1918, and by early August, British, French, Japanese and American forces had landed. The Americans occupied Vladivostok to safeguard railroad communications in the rear of the Czechs. Of the Allies, only the Japanese had long-range territorial ambitions in the area. In effect, the Bolshevik regime had now been displaced in Siberia. The SRs disbanded the soviets and reestablished the zemstvos, calling for "all power to the constituent assembly." Soon there were three anti-Red governments in three different Siberian centers. In August 1918 a small British and American force landed at Archangel. Then on August 30 an SR assassin killed the chief of the Petrograd Cheka, and Lenin, who was in Moscow, was shot twice. The Bolshevik leadership feared a general counterrevolution in which any doctor might be involved, so the seriously wounded Lenin was taken directly to his apartment rather than to a hospital. The woman who had attempted to kill him was shot without a trial, and since responsibility for her act was never proven, rumors multiplied. Blaming the bourgeoisie, the Moscow Cheka shot six hundred people,

while others felt they detected the British secret service behind the plot. Cheka retaliation elsewhere was massive.

The regime now sped up its military preparations. As minister of war, Trotsky imposed conscription, and by a mixture of appeals to patriotism and threats of reprisals against their families secured the services of about fifty thousand czarist officers. The Red Army, which was Trotsky's creation, grew to over three million strong by 1920. Its recapture of Kazan and Samara on the Volga in the autumn of 1918 temporarily turned the tide in the crisis that seemed about to engulf the Soviet state.

The German collapse on the western front in November 1918 permitted the Bolsheviks to repudiate the Treaty of Brest-Litovsk and move back into parts of the Ukraine, where they faced the opposition of local forces. Elsewhere, the opposition consisted of three main armies. An army of Whites moved from Rostov-on-Don south across the Caucasus and received French and British aid. Other forces in western Siberia overthrew the SR regime in Omsk, where their commander, Admiral Alexander Kolchak (1874-1920), became a virtual dictator. Yet another army, including many former members of the German forces, operated in the Baltic region and threatened Petrograd from the west. Allied unwillingness to negotiate with the Bolsheviks was heightened by the successful Red coup of Bela Kun in Hungary, which seemed to foreshadow the further spread of revolution.

In the spring of 1919 the Reds defeated Kolchak, and by winter took Omsk. In 1920 the admiral was arrested and executed. Though the Reds also reconquered the Ukraine, mutinies in their own forces prevented them from consolidating their victories and from moving, as they had hoped to do, across the Russian frontiers and linking up with Bela Kun in Hungary. In the summer of 1919 the White army took Kiev and struck north, advancing to within two hundred and fifty miles of Moscow itself. A second army advanced to the suburbs of Petrograd, but by the end of 1919 the Reds were able to defeat the White threat, though one White general, Baron Peter Wrangel (1878-1928), retained an army in the Crimea in 1920. Trotsky now called for the militarization of labor to reconstruct the ravaged country.

After the defeat of the Whites, the Reds had to face a new war with the Poles in 1920, led by General Jósef Pilsudski (1867-1935). Pilsudski wanted to reestablish the Polish frontier as it existed in 1772, the year of the first partition. His immediate objective in 1920 was to drive the Bosheviks out of the Ukraine and associate the Ukraine with Poland in a common but federally organized state. Beyond that he intended to bring White Russia, Lithuania, and Latvia into the federation also. The effect on Soviet power in the loss of mineral resources and coastlines would have been substantial, which is why the Western powers in general, fearing the ideological threat from the East, now swung around in support of Pilsudski's enterprise.

Although after an initial retreat the Red Army nearly

0   500
Miles

SIBERIA
TRANS-SIBERIAN RAILROAD
Moscow
Omsk
Vladivostok
ALASKA

Russian territorial losses,
Brest-Litovsk, 1918

Boundaries as of 1914

Curzon Line

Boundary between Poland and the
U.S.S.R., 1920-1939

Archangel

NORWAY

SWEDEN

Gulf of Bothnia

FINLAND

Helsinki

L. Onega

L. Ladoga

Kronstadt

Petrograd
(Leningrad)

Baltic Sea

ESTONIA

LATVIA

LITHUANIA

Danzig

GERMANY

Vilna

Niemen R.

WHITE
RUSSIA

Volga R.

Kazan

Moscow

Samara

Ekaterinburg

Warsaw

POLAND

Bug R.

Brest-
Litovsk

Curzon
Line

Vistula R.

Vienna

AUSTRIA-

Budapest

HUNGARY

Kiev

UKRAINE

Dniester R.

Dnieper R.

R   U   S   S   I   A

Don R.

Tsaritsyn
(Stalingrad
Volgograd)

Volga R.

Pruth R.

Rostov-on-Don

BOSNIA

SERBIA

MONTE-
NEGRO

ROMANIA

Danube R.

CRIMEA

Sea of Azov

Occupied by Germany, 1918

Caspian Sea

ALBANIA

BULGARIA

Black   Sea

GEORGIA

C A U C A S U S

Tiflis

Baku

GREECE

Istanbul

Kars

T U R K E Y

PERSIA

Russia in Revolution, 1917-1921

took Warsaw, it failed to do so, in part because the French assisted the Poles. (This Red Army had probably been intended by Lenin to go on into Germany and set off a revolution there once Polish resistance had been crushed.) Eager to finish off the remnant of the Whites and persuaded that there was no hope for a communist regime in Poland, the Reds now concluded peace in October 1920. The Poles obtained much of White Russia and the western Ukraine. This area was not inhabited by Poles but had been controlled by Poland down to the eighteenth-century partitions. It lay far to the east of the "Curzon line," an ethnic frontier that had been proposed by the British foreign minister, Lord Curzon (1859-1925), during the Versailles negotiations and that Pilsudski had rejected. The final line, established at Riga in 1921, bisected Byelorussia and the Ukraine roughly where the Uniate and Orthodox churches met. The size of the ethnic minorities transferred to Poland under this treaty, combined with their mistreatment by the government in Warsaw, was a principal factor making Poland ungovernable in the interwar years, except by military dictatorship.

The Reds now turned on Baron Wrangel, who had marched northward from the Crimea and had established a moderate regime in the territory he occupied. He was forced to evacuate, assisted by a French fleet, in November 1920. The White movement was virtually over. Many circumstances accounted for the Whites' failure and the Reds' victory. The Whites could not unite on any political program beyond the overthrow of the Reds, for they were deeply divided ideologically. They

Lenin and Stalin together in 1922.

adopted a policy of "nonanticipation," which meant that some future constituent assembly would settle the governmental structure of Russia. Their numbers included everyone from czarists to SRs, and they disagreed so violently on the proper course for Russia to follow that they could agree only to postpone discussion of these critical problems. Their own regimes were often repressive, so that they did not build local followings, and their troops were at times undisciplined. They argued for too long over who was to be their supreme commander. Moreover, although their movement was located on the geographical periphery of Russia—in Siberia, the Crimea, the Ukraine, the Caucasus, and the Baltic—the Whites never reached an understanding with the non-Russian minorities who lived in these regions. Thus they ignored the highly developed separatist sentiments of the Ukrainians and others, to which the Bolsheviks, by contrast, were temporarily willing to cater.

Most important, the Whites could not command the support of the peasantry. Instead of guaranteeing the results of the land division already carried out with Bolshevik approval, the Whites often restored the landlords in areas they temporarily controlled. The peasantry grew sick of both sides. Food production was curtailed. Atrocities were frequent, and peasant anarchist bands committed many of their own. Moreover, the Whites simply did not command as much military strength as did the Reds, who outnumbered them and who had inherited much of the equipment manufactured for the czarist armies. Holding the central position, the Reds had a unified and skillful command, which could use the railroad network to shift troops rapidly. The Whites, moving in from the periphery, were divided into at least four main groups and were denied effective use of the railroads. Finally, the intervention of the Allies on the side of the Whites was ineffectual and amateurish. It probably harmed the White cause, since the Reds could speak as the national defenders and could portray the Whites as the hirelings of foreigners. Without the "capitalist" and White threats in the periphery, the center might not have rallied behind Lenin. Certainly the victorious Reds were to use the charge of Western intervention against communist Russia as further proof of the hostile intentions of all capitalist nations. The presence of British, French, American, and other troops would be frequently invoked in the years ahead to stir the Russian people to a sense of national unity.

The struggle for power in Russia in no sense ended with the civil war. Famine was raging, sanitation had broken down, and class hatreds were exploited on an unparalleled scale. Industry was producing at only an eighth of its prewar output, agricultural output had fallen by 30 percent, and distribution was breaking down. The new regime was losing support in Russia itself. But by early 1921 all major nations in the West were undergoing intense political change, as the postwar effort to absorb returning troops, to restore prewar conditions in the victorious nations, and to live with defeat in others created widespread instability.

The civil war had been fought over ideology, and had succeeded because of Russia's vast size, population, and resources, however badly employed. In the nineteenth century the Russian population had grown nearly 200 percent, changing the Russian countryside from being underpopulated to being overpopulated. While emigration to Siberia had carried off five million people between 1870 and 1914 and another three million had gone to the New World, much of the surplus peasantry had been taken into the towns. Thus Russia had acquired that demographic group essential to the modern state and to its revolution: an urban proletariat. This group existed only in certain centers in Siberia or on the periphery, but it was powerful within the area where Lenin had built his authority. While the World War had cost Russia two million dead, and fourteen million more had died from disease and malnutrition during the revolution and the civil war, which produced a severe birth deficit in the 1920s, Russia continued to grow.

Having put down a serious rebellion of the naval forces at Kronstadt in March 1921, Lenin left a nation on its way toward unity, with a population that despite revolution, war, and famine had regained its prewar levels, and with the expectation of an international communist revolution. Ill from the end of 1921, the man who had reinterpreted Marx tried to prepare his successor—most likely Stalin. Lenin died in January 1924. By then much of the West was aware that the peacemaking at Versailles had not brought security to Europe, and that the Russian Revolution and its aftermath had assured continued instability for much of the world.

SUMMARY

The creation of a unified Italy and Germany altered the balance of power in Europe in the 1860s and 1870s. Nationalism, imperialism, great-power alliances, and public opinion—influenced by newspapers and photos—helped fuel tensions. By the early 1900s the Triple Alliance and the Triple Entente had taken shape. A naval arms race between Germany and Britain as well as diplomatic and military crises in Morocco, the Balkans, and elsewhere contributed to an uneasy peace.

The assassination of Hapsburg archduke Francis Ferdinand, heir to the throne of Austria-Hungary, set off a crisis that led to war. Austria took a strong stand against Serbia, holding it responsible for the assassination. When Serbia rejected demands, Austria declared war. Germany, Russia, France, and Britain aided their respective allies. Italy declared its neutrality but later joined the Allies. Other European nations were drawn into the conflict. By 1917 repeated violations of neutral shipping brought the United States into the war.

The Schlieffen plan for German armies to eliminate France before turning to the Russian front did not succeed. German armies were pinned down on the western front where a stalemate existed throughout much of the war. Millions more were tied down on the eastern front until 1917, when Russia withdrew from the war. The war was fought on other fronts in the Near East, East Africa, and the Far East, as well as on the oceans of the world. The last German offensive in the spring of 1918 could not be sustained, and by that summer the Allies were advancing on the western front. On November 11, 1918, a defeated Germany signed an armistice.

On the home fronts, wartime economic planning anticipated the regulated economies of the postwar era. Both sides waged virulent propaganda warfare. War contributed to changes in social life and in moral codes.

President Wilson's Fourteen Points embodied the hopes for peace. However, conflicting aims among the Allies over reparations, punishment of Germany, and territorial settlements soon disillusioned liberal hopes for peace. Russia and the Central Powers were not represented at Versailles as the Big Four—Wilson, Lloyd George, Clemenceau, and Orlando—bargained, compromised, and established new nations. An international organization, the League of Nations, was set up with a consultative assembly, but it did not fulfill the hopes of its early supporters.

In the end, the United States refused to ratify the treaty. France, weakened by the war, had its way with reparations, while Germany, still potentially the strongest nation in Europe, reluctantly accepted the cruel humiliation of the treaty.

Strikes and shortages of bread as well as huge losses in the war prepared the way for revolution in Russia in 1917. From the outset, the provisional government and soviets were in conflict. When the moderate provisional government failed to meet crises at home and abroad, Lenin, who had returned to Russia from exile, called for a program that appealed to the Russian people.

In November 1917 the Bolsheviks seized power in Petrograd. The Bolshevik Revolution brought great changes to Russia, although the new regime displayed much continuity with old Russia—an autocratic dictator, an elite of bureaucrats and managers, secret police, and Russian nationalism.

chapter twenty-four

BETWEEN THE WARS

A Twenty-Year Crisis

The years between World War I and World War II were marked more by movements to the extreme right than by movements to the extreme left, despite the Western democracies' fear of Bolshevism. Beginning in the early 1920s, fascist regimes took over in Italy, Germany, Spain, Finland, and most of eastern and southeastern Europe, and were firmly in the saddle by the late 1930s. Since these individual fascist states were the products of different societies, they came into power under different circumstances, commanded vastly different resources, and differed in other important respects. But they also had several characteristics in common. The fascist regimes in Italy and Germany in particular were products of the disillusionment with the failure of democratic or even socialist policies to achieve stability and security for increasingly middle-class societies. Economic depressions played a significant role in the rise of dictators almost everywhere. These dictators demonstrated a flair for the dramatic—war cries, special salutes, elaborate ceremonies, uniforms that set the faithful apart from the mass, glorification of a national past. They invariably sought to place the burden of blame for the nation's economic or social problems on some scapegoat group: on other nations (most often Britain or the United States), other ideologies (most often communism), or other special groups (most often the Jews). These various fascisms had in common an aggressive nationalism, a sense of grievance, a totalitarian governmental system, and usually racism.

Europe's age of fascism, from roughly 1919 to 1945, did not envelop France (though it nearly did so at various stages), the Scandinavian kingdoms, Britain, or the United States, though they may have had vigorous fascist parties. Fascism everywhere was essentially a reaction against the devastating impact of the Great War on basically liberal nineteenth-century societies that found that victory had not also brought harmony, as well as on fragmented and conservative societies that had been branded the aggressors in the war. Thus a sense of anger was basic to fascist states. Within each nation puzzled and frightened peoples reached out to each other. They responded with a new nationalism in the face of an international challenge—communism—and an international disaster—universal war followed by universal depression after 1929.

In the phrase of many observers, the twentieth century became an "Age of Anxiety," especially as the European nations began to recognize that they were moving toward economic chaos and political collapse. Having expected benefits from the postwar settlements that had worked to break up the remnants of the aristocracies in the Central Powers, the lower middle classes now wanted power, prestige—benefits that had been denied them by prewar societies. The European nations had been bled far more deeply by World War I than they realized. Nations that were now powers of the second rank sought to continue to behave as though they were powers of the first rank, especially in aggressive foreign policies. Under such conditions renewed clashes, while not inevitable, were highly likely. Given the emotional base for most fascist movements, compromise was equally unlikely, for while nations may compromise on the price of wheat, they generally cannot compromise on what they believe has been ordained by God, or the state, or the will of the people, or "historical destiny."

I THE FIRST TRIUMPH OF FASCISM: ITALY

Although Italy was one of the victorious Allies, it finished the First World War with a sense of defeat. Six hundred and fifty thousand Italians had been killed and a million wounded. Italian industry slumped immediately after the war, and within a few months 10 percent of the industrial workers were unemployed. Prices rose rapidly, and wages failed to keep up. The promised pensions for wounded veterans and families of the killed were long delayed. Strikes and disorders became frequent. Many of the young men were released from the armies with no trade but war and no job to go to; they drifted restlessly, prey for leaders with glittering promises.

Perhaps most important, the Italian government itself, hoping to influence the peace negotiations, began to spread propaganda among the Italian people to the effect that their wartime allies were robbing them of Dalmatia, which had been promised to Italy by the secret Treaty of London (1915) in exchange for Italy's entrance into the war. The United States had never agreed to this arrangement and now would not accept it. Although the Allied leaders at the Paris Peace Conference remained unaffected by the storms of protest arising from Italy, the Italian people came to believe that they had shed their blood in vain.

Some Italians, supporting Gabriele d'Annunzio (1863-1938) seized the city of Fiume, which had not been awarded to Italy by the Treaty of London. D'Annunzio ran his own government in Fiume until the end of 1920, patterning his regime on that of an imaginary medieval commune. In November 1920, when the Italian government signed the Treaty of Rapallo with Yugoslavia by which Fiume was to become a free city, Italian forces drove d'Annunzio out. But d'Annunzio's techniques of force, haranguing of mobs from a balcony,

A COMPARISON OF FASCISM AND COMMUNISM

Though fascism is, at base, an approach to the use of the power of the state that stands at the opposite pole to communism as a way to organize society, both forms of dictatorship have many apparent characteristics in common. In 1964 Klaus Epstein (1927-1967), professor of history at Brown University, attacked this appearance of similarity as follows:

It is a notorious fact that fascist regimes take on many of the features of the Communist enemy they combat (for example, the use of terror, concentration camps, single-party dictatorship, and destruction of man's "private sphere"). Yet it is important to keep communism and fascism sharply distinct for analytical purposes. They differ in their avowed aim, ideological content, circumstances of achieving power, and the groups to which they appeal. Fascists seek the greatness of the nation (which need not exclude a racialist internationalism); Communists, the world triumph of the working class (which need not exclude a strong Russian nationalism). Fascists stand in avowed revolt against the ideas of 1789; Communists pose as the heirs and executors of those ideas. Fascism has a miscellaneous and heterogeneous ideological content; communism prides itself upon the all-embracing logic of its [world view]. Fascism glories in an irrational world of struggle; communism aims ultimately at a rational world of peace and harmony (which does not preclude some pride in the violent methods required prior to the final achievement of utopia). Fascism has triumphed in some highly developed communities through abuse of the electoral process (*e.g.*, Germany); communism typically achieves power through military occupation or successful use of violence in backward communities demoralized by prolonged military strains (Russia, Yugoslavia, China). Fascism has special appeal to the lower middle class and sections of the frightened upper class; communism generally finds its greatest resonance in sections of the working class, peasantry, and intelligentsia. Fascism consists, finally, of a series of national movements lacking centralized overall direction, while communism is a centralized world movement in which each member party obeys the orders emanating from a single center.

Klaus Epstein, "A New Study of Fascism," *World Politics*, XVI (1964), as quoted in Henry A. Turner, Jr., ed., *Reappraisals of Fascism* (New York: Franklin Watts, 1975), p. 10.

straight-arm salute, black shirts, rhythmic cries, plans for conquest, and the "corporative" scheme of the Statutes of Fiume (d'Annunzio's constitution for Fiume based, he thought, on the guilds of the Middle Ages) inspired Benito Mussolini, founder of Italian fascism.

Between 1918 and 1922 Mussolini created and brought to power a new political force in Italy. In October 1922 he was summoned to office by King Victor Emmanuel III (reigned 1900-1946) and gradually created a totalitarian state of which he was the undisputed ruler. Suppressing all opposition at home and threatening the peace abroad, fascist Italy served in some degree as a model for the Nazis in Germany, for the Falangists in Spain, and for totalitarian regimes in virtually all the European successor states of the Hapsburg and Ottoman empires. Eventually Mussolini was forced into an alliance with Hitler; in 1940 this alliance took Italy into World War II.

Mussolini was born in 1883; his father was a socialist who had begun his career as an anarchist under the influence of Bakunin. Trained as an elementary-school teacher, Mussolini was a passionate socialist himself when young, and he was imprisoned for opposing the war against Turkey over Tripoli (1911). In 1912 he became editor of the most important Italian socialist newspaper, *Avanti* (*Forward*).

When World War I began Mussolini opposed Italy's entry. He loathed militarism, was himself a draft-dodger, and urged soldiers to desert the army. He hated monarchy and savagely attacked in his writings the crowned heads of Europe, especially the Italian House of Savoy. A vehement atheist, he also opposed nationalism and referred to the Italian flag as "a rag to be planted on a dunghill." But then, during 1914, Mussolini changed his mind, favoring "relative neutrality"—meaning that socialists should leave themselves free to support Italian entry if such a course seemed likely to prove favorable to them. When the Italian Socialist party refused to follow this idea, he resigned as editor of *Avanti* and founded his own newspaper, *Il Popolo d'Italia* (*The People of Italy*), in Milan and began to advocate an immediate Italian declaration of war on the side of the Allies. For this the Socialist party expelled him.

Ultimately Mussolini was to repudiate almost all his earlier positions. As a fascist, he attacked all left-wing movements; he made his peace with the monarchy and the Church; he became a militant nationalist, a mystic patriot, and a militarist. In fact, Mussolini did not care much for programs; what he wanted was to rule. His switch from isolationism to interventionism in the war of 1914 was only the first of many turnabouts.

After his expulsion from the Socialist party, he agitated for war, speaking to groups of similarly minded young men called *fasci* (the image is of a bundle of rods, a symbol of office in the Roman Republic of antiquity). Soon after Italy entered the war in 1915, Mussolini was drafted and sent to the front. He was wounded in 1917 by an Italian mortar shell that exploded during practice; when out of the hospital, he again edited his newspaper. In 1919 Mussolini founded the first *fasci di combattimento* ("groups for combat"). In Italy the danger of revolution from the left proved to be small, but the fear proved to be great. The peasants seized some land, but they were unprepared to go further, except in the extreme south. The industrial workers, though deeply discontented, knew that Italy had to import most of its raw materials, so any general strike they might launch could be starved out. The Socialist party was in the hands of moderates, and it was forced to compete for the votes of the lower classes with a new Popular party, founded in 1919 by Catholics. Thus the leaders of the Socialist party and of the General Confederation of Labor voted down the proposals of anarchists and communists to turn the workers' sporadic occupation of factories into a revolution.

During 1920 and 1921 the industrialists and landowners, squeezed by taxation and inflation, became bitter. Shopkeepers and tradespeople wanted the street disorders to end, food prices to be regulated, and the cooperative food stores of the Socialist and Catholic parties to be closed as competitors. Professionals and others with fixed incomes suffered, as prices and wages went up and salaries lagged behind. The police grew tired of suppressing local disorders; exservicemen, insulted by anarchists and communists for their war records, grew more patriotic.

All these groups identified those they did not like as Bolsheviks and accepted as an article of faith the myth of an impending Bolshevik revolution. After a series of fascist-socialist street fights and riots, these anti-Bolsheviks began to look to Mussolini's fascist bands to defend their interests. D'Annunzio's defeat left Mussolini as his natural heir. The leftist opposition to Mussolini was further weakened when the communists split off from the Socialist party in 1921. The fascists grew enormously, from 30,000 in May 1920, to 100,000 in

Mussolini was a dramatic public speaker who used theatrical gestures to reinforce his points. As this photograph shows, he made full use of the relatively new medium of radio to reach a mass audience.

February 1921, to more than 300,000 in October 1922. Liberal parliamentary leaders of Italy felt that the fascist bands were teaching the left a useful lesson, so they encouraged army officers to issue rifles, trucks, and gasoline to the fascists and assigned officers to command their operations. The police were encouraged to look the other way during disorders started by fascists, and local judges were urged to help by releasing arrested fascists. Mussolini's newspaper was circulated free to the soldiers in the army as a patriotic sheet.

THE VITAL LIE

Speaking at Naples in October 1922, Mussolini recognized that at the heart of fascism, as at the heart of nationalism, lay a vital lie—a belief held so strongly that it had the force of truth. He referred to this belief as a myth which, if universally accepted, would become reality:

We have created our myth. The myth is a faith, it is passion. It is not necessary that it shall be a reality. It is a reality by the fact that it is a good, a hope, a faith, that it is courage. Our myth is the Nation, our myth is the greatness of the Nation! And to this myth, to this grandeur, that we wish to translate into a complete reality, we subordinate all the rest.

From Herbert Finer, *Mussolini's Italy* (New York: Universal, 1935), p. 218.

A campaign of terror now began against the socialists and Christian Democrats, as the fascist squadrons cruised around Italy in trucks, burning down labor-union offices, newspaper offices, and local Socialist party headquarters, and attacking labor leaders and local antifascist politicians. The fascists forced elected officials to resign. An estimated two thousand people—antifascist and fascist, police and bystanders—died by violence between October 1920 and October 1922. Mussolini had demonstrated that control over sources of information, rapid mobility, and the use of terror and intimidation could effectively silence opposition in a divided and frightened society.

In the elections of May 1921 Mussolini and thirty-four other fascists were elected to the Chamber of Deputies (the lower house of the Italian parliament), along with ten Nationalists, their political allies. The momentum of the fascist movement was now too great to be slowed down. Mussolini abandoned his antimonarchical views, and fascism became a political party in November as a necessary step in the drive for power. Too late, the government became alarmed and tried to take measures against the fascists, but the squadrons were too strong, the police too accustomed to collaborating with them, and the liberal politicians themselves as yet unaware that a tightly directed armed mob could take over the state. The king's cousin had become a fascist sympathizer, as had many generals, the entire Nationalist party, and leading industrialists.

In the fall of 1922 it was clear that the army would not resist a fascist coup in Rome. When a decree of martial law was presented to the king, he refused to sign it, probably influenced by his knowledge that the army would not fight the fascists and that his cousin would gladly take his crown. The cabinet resigned, and on October 29 the king telegraphed Mussolini in Milan to come to Rome and form a cabinet. Mussolini arrived by sleeping-car the next morning, just ahead of thousands of followers who "marched on Rome" by commandeering railroad trains.

Fascist Dictatorship and Corporative State

Mussolini gradually turned his premiership into a dictatorship. A month after coming to office he obtained dictatorial powers that were supposed to last only until the end of 1923. Although the constitution theoretically remained in force, Mussolini took over the administration. He created a fascist militia almost two hundred thousand strong, which owed complete allegiance to him. He enlarged the regular army and required its members to take an oath of personal loyalty to him. Before his dictatorial powers expired, he secured from parliament by pressure a new electoral law that provided that the political party that received the largest number of votes in a general election, if that amounted to at least one-quarter of the vote, should automatically receive two-thirds of the seats in parliament; the rest of the seats would be divided proportionately. This law made the fascists' domination of future parliaments certain. In the election of April 1924 the fascists polled 65 percent of the votes cast; the first all-fascist cabinet was then appointed. Meanwhile, local administration was made secure by the appointment of fascist prefects and subprefects in the provinces; these officials pursued the enemies of fascism with the same weapons of murder and intimidation that had been used before Mussolini's March on Rome.

Early in 1924 the leader of the opposition to Mussolini, the socialist Giacomo Matteotti (1885-1924), published a book, *The Fascists Exposed*, in which he reviewed the outrages the fascists had committed on their way to power. It seemed probable that further revelations were in store, exposing some of Mussolini's cabinet members as corrupt. On June 10 Matteotti was murdered. The crime was traced to Mussolini's immediate circle. This scandal rocked Italy, and for a moment it seemed that Mussolini would fall. But he dismissed from office those who were involved and pledged himself to restore law and order. In protest against the murder and the failure to vigorously prosecute those who had participated, opposition deputies walked out of the Chamber. They were then refused readmission, thereby playing into Mussolini's hand. In effect, the murder of Matteotti marked the beginning of Mussolini's true dictatorship.

Next, a series of the "most fascist laws" tightened control over the press, abolished secret societies like the Freemasons (whom Mussolini had loathed since his socialist youth), and replaced all elected local officials by men appointed from Rome. Opponents of the regime were arrested and exiled to islands off the Italian coast. Early in 1926 Mussolini was empowered to govern by decree. Three attempts on his life led to a new law providing the death penalty for action against the king, the queen, or Mussolini. All opposition political parties were abolished in that same year, and the Fascist party was left as the only legal political party in Italy.

The Italian state and the Fascist party were increasingly coordinated. Mussolini was both the *duce* (leader) of the fascists and the *capo di governo*, the chief of state. At one time he held eight cabinet posts simultaneously. The members of the Fascist Grand Council, about twenty of the highest party functionaries, all appointed by Mussolini, held all the significant posts in the administration that were not held by Mussolini himself. In 1928 the Grand Council was given important constitutional duties: preparing the lists of candidates for election to the Chamber, advising Mussolini, and proposing changes in the constitution or in the succession to the throne. The Grand Council thus became a kind of third house, above the other two houses of parliament, the Senate and the Chamber.

Mussolini believed that the interests of labor and capital should be made to harmonize with the overriding interests of the state, and representation should be based on economic interests organized in "syndicates."

TEN COMMANDMENTS FOR FASCISTS

By 1934 the fascists had pressed their campaign to the point where they could announce a set of ten "secular commandments" that emphasized their militarism, the idea of the garrison state, and the cult of the personality of *il Duce* (the Leader):

1. Know that the Fascist, and in particular the soldier, must not believe in perpetual peace.
2. Days of imprisonment are always deserved.
3. The nation serves even as sentinel over a can of petrol.
4. A companion must be a brother, first, because he lives with you, and secondly because he thinks like you.
5. The rifle and cartridge belt, and the rest, are confided to you not to rust in leisure, but to be preserved in war.
6. Do not ever say, "The Government will pay . . ." because it is *you* who pay; and the Government is that which you willed to have, and for which you put on a uniform.
7. Discipline is the soul of armies; without it there are no soldiers, only confusion and defeat.
8. Mussolini is always right.
9. For a volunteer there are no extenuating circumstances when he is disobedient.
10. One thing must be dear to you above all: the life of the Duce.

Michael Oakeshott, ed., *The Social and Political Doctrines of Contemporary Europe* (Cambridge, Eng.: Cambridge University Press, 1939), p. 180.

Such an idea was not new. The French syndicalist Georges Sorel had already argued in this vein. But Sorel believed in class warfare and in government by syndicates of workers only. Mussolini believed in capitalism, class collaboration, and producers' syndicates as well as workers' syndicates.

In 1925 fascist labor unions were recognized by employers as having the sole right to negotiate labor contracts. In April 1926 the state officially recognized producers' and workers' syndicates in each of six areas—industry, agriculture, commerce, sea and air transport, land and inland waterway transport, and banking—plus a syndicate of intellectuals, making thirteen syndicates in all. Each syndicate could bargain and reach contracts and could assess dues upon everyone engaged in its economic field, irrespective of membership in the syndicate. Strikes and lockouts were forbidden. The syndicates were put under the control of a special Ministry of Corporations; Mussolini was its minister. When labor conditions did not improve, a "charter of labor" promising insurance and other benefits was issued in 1927.

In 1928 the system of parliamentary representation was changed in accordance with fascist syndicalism. A new electoral law provided for a new Chamber of Deputies with 400 instead of 560 members. The national councils of the thirteen syndicates could nominate a total of 800 candidates. Each syndicate had a quota, half to be selected by the employers and half by the employees. Cultural and charitable foundations could nominate 200 more candidates. When the total list of 1,000 was completed, the Fascist Grand Council could either select 400 of them, or strike out names and add names of its own, or even substitute an entirely new list. The voters would then vote in answer to the question: "Do you approve of the list of deputies selected by the Fascist Grand Council?" They could vote yes or no on the *entire* list, but they could not choose from among the candidates. If a majority voted yes, the list was elected; if not, the procedure was repeated. Despite the highly touted role of the syndicate, all the power obviously lay with the Fascist Grand Council. Universal suffrage was abolished, even for this very limited form of election. Payment of a minimum tax or dues to a syndicate was required of each voter; women could not vote. In 1929 the elections under this system produced a yes vote of 8,519,559 and a no vote of 137,761. Between 1930 and 1938 several additional constitutional steps were taken that moved the syndicates to the center of the stage.

In 1938 the impotent Chamber of Deputies replaced itself with the Chamber of Fasces and Corporations. Nothing remained of the old parliamentary constitution that had been set up by Cavour except the Senate, nominally appointed by the king but actually subservient to Mussolini, who on one occasion had the king appoint forty fascist senators at once. This new structure, this *corporative state* (so named because each of the seven syndicate areas had been declared a corporation), was influenced by d'Annunzio's medieval ideas and by Mussolini's own wish to produce innovative political and economic forms. But despite much oratory by fascist sympathizers about the corporative state and its virtues, it appears that the new bodies never had much to do with running the economic or political life of Italy, which remained firmly under the direction of the fascist inner bureaucracy.

During the 1930s the fascist version of the planned economy made its appearance in Italy through this bureaucracy. The government issued or withheld permits for factory construction. A concerted effort was launched to make Italy more nearly self-sufficient in agriculture. In 1932 official figures reported that domestic wheat production could supply 92 percent of the nation's normal needs, and the drive was enlarged to include other cereal products. The government subsidized steamship and air lines, encouraged the tourist trade, and protected Italian industries with high tariffs on foreign products. Marshes were drained and land was reclaimed; the incidence of malaria was reduced. Enormous sums were spent on public works, and great strides were made in hydroelectric power. Public transportation became efficient. Yet Italy's weakness in essential raw materials proved insurmountable.

The state also reached into the life of the individual at almost every point. Though Italy was overpopulated and had for decades relieved the situation by mass emigration, Mussolini made emigration a crime. Beginning in 1926 he pursued a vigorous pro-birth policy, encouraging people to marry and have the largest possible families by reducing their taxes, extending special loans, taxing bachelors, and extending legal equality to illegitimate children. He hoped in this way to swell the ranks of his armies and to strengthen his claim that Italy must expand abroad. Children, the future party members, were enrolled in a series of youth movements beginning at the age of six. Textbooks in the schools, books in the libraries, professors in the universities, plays on the stage, and movies on the screen became vehicles of fascist propaganda. The secret police, OVRA (from the initials of the Italian words for "Vigilance Organization against Anti-Fascist Crimes") endeavored to discover and suppress all opposition movements.

In 1929 Mussolini settled the Roman question—that of the annexation of the Papal States without the Pope's consent—by entering into the Lateran Pact with the papacy. This treaty recognized the independence of Vatican City, over which the pope had temporal power. Mussolini also recognized Catholicism as the state religion and promised to end antipapal propaganda. He gave up the power to tax contributions to the church or the salaries of the clergy, and paid $105,000,000 to compensate the papacy for Italian confiscation of papal territories. An additional concordat legalized religious marriages and extended religious instruction in the schools. On its part, the church agreed not to engage in politics in its publications.

Yet although many church officials viewed the fascist movement sympathetically, difficulties arose after these agreements had been concluded. In an encyclical, Pope Pius XI (1922-1939) indicated his disapproval of Mussolini's economic policies and of the corporations as "serving special political aims rather than contributing to the initiation of a better social order." Mussolini now charged that the church's Catholic Action Clubs were engaged in politics and dissolved them. The pope denied the charges and denounced the Fascist party's practice of monopolizing the time and education of the young. In 1931, however, a further agreement was reached, and the clubs were reopened. Mussolini had thus eliminated a festering sore. In the eyes of many Catholics he had achieved respectability; in the eyes of anti-Catholics he had restricted the pope to a tiny area and had effectively resolved a long-standing dispute. Increasingly, in domestic and in foreign affairs, many Italians regarded Mussolini as a statesman of international repute.

Mussolini's wish to re-create the glories of ancient Rome plus domestic population pressures impelled him to undertake a policy of adventure in the Mediterranean, which he called *Mare Nostrum* ("our sea") as a sign that he was the heir to the Caesars. In time he would send settlers into Libya, which he called Italy's Fourth Shore. This policy of expansion began in 1923, when five Italians working for the League of Nations were assassinated as they marked out the new frontier between Albania and Greece. Mussolini thereupon bombarded and occupied the Greek island of Corfu, just off Albania, and refused to recognize the League's right to intervene until British pressure led to a settlement of the matter.

Most important, Mussolini alienated Italy from its earlier allies, France and Britain. His policy of adventure led him to military aggression in Ethiopia, in Spain, and in Albania (which he dominated during the 1920s and occupied in April 1939). It drove him into an alliance with another fascist, Adolf Hitler, and led him to voice loud claims against the French for Corsica, Tunisia, Nice, and Savoy. Mussolini's grandiose fascist ideology spurred Italy to win a larger degree of self-sufficiency, to rebuild its seaports, and to create a merchant fleet and navy.

The Italian alliance with Germany was also responsible for a striking new departure in fascist domestic policy: the official adoption of anti-Semitism in 1938. With only 70,000 Jews, most of whom had long been resident, Italy had no "Jewish problem" of the kind Hitler was alleging existed in Germany. Italian Jews were entirely Italian in their language and sentiments and were distinguished from other Italians only by their religion. Many of them were prominent fascists; many others were antifascist. There was no widespread sympathy in Italy for the government's adoption of Hitler's racial policies, yet Hitler's dominating influence led Mussolini to expel Jews from the Fascist party and to forbid them to teach or to attend school, to intermarry with non-Jews, or to obtain new licenses to conduct business.

Opportunistic, ruthless, quick-witted, Mussolini loved power, but he also genuinely cared about Italy. Although the lives of many improved under his regime, the lives of others were brutalized. His private views appear inconsistent, his public policies acts of theater by which he presented a new personality almost weekly. Many commentators then and since would find him simple, a man floundering beyond his depth; other commentators would find him shrewd, careful, and well aware of how his unpredictable yet emotionally exciting personality could make him attractive to many and keep him firmly in power. The policies that carried him into war in alliance with Germany in 1940 would end in his death, hanging upside down on a communist gallows, his personality still an enigma in 1945.

II THE WEIMAR REPUBLIC: GERMANY, 1918-1933

Whereas Mussolini took over in Italy less than four years after World War I ended, the Germans worked with their democracy for fifteen years before succumbing to Adolf Hitler. Two days before the armistice of November 11, 1918, the German Social Democrats proclaimed a republic. On July 31, 1919, this republic adopted a constitution drawn up by a national assembly at Weimar; it is therefore known as the Weimar Republic. The republic passed through three phases: a period of political threats from both left and right and of mounting economic chaos, from 1918 to the end of 1923; a period of political stability, fulfillment of the Versailles Treaty requirements, and relative economic prosperity, from 1924 to late 1929; and a period of economic depression and mounting right-wing power, from late 1929 to January 1933, when Hitler became chancellor.

Years of Instability, 1918-1923

Germans were shocked by their defeat in 1918. The military authorities who ran the German Empire during the last years of the war had not revealed to the public the extent of German reverses on the battlefield, and no fighting had taken place on German soil. Now the defeated and demoralized armies came home. Some historians argue that the Allies committed a grave blunder by not marching to Berlin to bring home to the German people the realization that they had actually been defeated. Schooled in reverence for the military, the Germans could not grasp the fact that their armies had lost the war. Moreover, the Allies, under the leadership of Wilson, simply refused to deal with the Supreme Command of the German armies. Field Marshal von Hindenburg, as supreme commander, was never required to hand over his sword to Marshal Foch or to sign the armistice. Rather, it was the civilian politicians who had to bear the disgrace. Thus, the Allies unintentionally did the German military caste a great service.

The generals, led by Hindenburg himself, declared that the German armies had never really been defeated. This was what the public wanted to believe, and the facts—that Ludendorff and Hindenburg had insisted on surrender because the armies could no longer fight—were never effectively publicized. So a legend that Germany had been "stabbed in the back" by civilians—by liberals, socialists, communists, and Jews—took deep root. This legend was widely disseminated by politicians, especially those who had a stake in the old Prussian system—monarchists, large-scale agrarians,

industrialists, militarists. Throughout the period of the Weimar Republic these groups remained hostile toward the government.

In retrospect, the Allies also blundered by including the "war-guilt" clause in the Treaty of Versailles. The German signatories were obliged to acknowledge what none of them believed (and what subsequent historians would disprove): that Germany alone had been responsible for the outbreak of the war. The clause made it harder for the German public to acknowledge defeat, to sweep away the militarists, and to create a republic. Instead, it led many Germans to devote their energies to denying war guilt, to attack the enemies who had saddled them with the charge, and to await a chance to show by force that the generals had been right—that Germany had been betrayed from within.

Threats to stability from the left strengthened the antirepublican forces of the right. Responsibility for launching the republic and for preventing disorder fell upon the "majority socialists," made up of Social Democrats and right-wing Independent Socialists, and led by a Social Democrat, Friedrich Ebert (1871-1925). A moderate group, the Social Democrats made no attack on agrarian property, and they allowed the Junkers to keep their estates and the social and political position that went with them. The Social Democrats concluded collective bargaining agreements with the industrialists that guaranteed an eight-hour day, rather than trying to nationalize German industry.

But the left wing of the Independent Socialists and the communist Spartacists (named for Spartacus, the leader of a slave revolt in ancient Rome) agitated for proletarian revolution on the Russian pattern. Unable to operate effectively through soviets, the left tried to stage a revolution in the winter of 1918-1919, and Ebert called in the army to stop it. The generals used not only regular units, but also the newly formed volunteer units, or "Free Corps," made up mostly of professional soldiers who were embittered by Germany's recent military defeat and who were opposed to the new democracy. To protest the use of troops, the right wing of the Independent Socialists withdrew from the government, and as civil strife continued, the Communists attempted a new coup, which the troops again put down.

Meanwhile, in Catholic Bavaria disorders led to the brief emergence of a Soviet republic, which was liquidated in May, leaving Bavaria subject to a permanent red scare. Thereafter, the Bavarian local authorities encouraged the intrigues of monarchists, militarists, and nationalists. Thus, the forces of the German right, ostensibly crushed by the war, were given a powerful new lease on life.

The old parties of imperial Germany reappeared, often with new labels. The right wing of the old Liberals now emerged as the People's party, including the more moderate industrialists, with a platform of private property and opposition to socialism. Its leader was Gustav Stresemann (1878-1929). Former progressives and left-wing Liberals now formed the new Democratic party, a middle-class, republican, democratic group, including many of Germany's most distinguished intellectuals. The Catholic Center party reemerged with its name and program unchanged. It accepted the republic, rejected socialism, and, under pressure from its trade-union members, favored social legislation, but under pressure from its right wing of aristocrats and industrialists it opposed far-reaching reform. On the right, the former Conservatives reemerged as the National People's party, or Nationalists, dominated by the Junkers as before. The Nationalists had the support of some great industrialists, most of the bureaucrats, and a substantial section of the lower middle class who did not accept the republic.

When the Germans voted for a national constituent assembly in January 1919, the parties supporting the republic won more than 75 percent of the seats, with the Social Democrats alone obtaining nearly 40 percent. The assembly met in Weimar, elected Ebert president of Germany, and formed a government that reluctantly signed the Treaty of Versailles. The assembly also adopted the new constitution. The new Germany was still a federal state, but the central government had great authority to legislate for the entire country. The president might use armed force to coerce any of the states that failed to obey the constitution or national laws. The cabinet was responsible to the lower house, or Reichstag, which was to be chosen by universal suffrage of all citizens (including women) over twenty.

The president, who was to be elected every seven years, was given considerable authority. He was empowered to make treaties, appoint and remove the cabinet, command the armed forces, appoint or remove all officers, dissolve the Reichstag, and call new elections. Furthermore, he could take any measure he deemed necessary to restore order, and might temporarily suspend the civil liberties that the constitution granted. Yet the Reichstag could order such measures repealed. The chancellor was a prime minister, with responsibility for planning policy. The constitution provided for popular initiative, since one-tenth of the electorate could propose a law or an amendment to the constitution. The constitution also provided that the government might socialize suitable enterprises, but it guaranteed both private property and the right of inheritance. The powers of the president made dictatorship a real possibility, while proportional representation required that votes be cast for entire party lists of candidates, and thus prevented independent politicians from obtaining office and encouraged small splinter parties to multiply.

In March 1920 a right-wing *putsch*, or coup, drove the government from Berlin for several days. The commander of the Berlin military district, supported by Ludendorff and Free Corps leaders, had hoped to bring to power an East Prussian reactionary. Ebert defeated the putsch by calling a general strike that paralyzed Germany. An immediate outgrowth of the strike was a communist revolt in the Ruhr. To suppress the commu-

nists, German troops entered the area, which had been demilitarized by the Versailles Treaty; this action led to French military intervention and a brief occupation of the Ruhr and Frankfurt. The elections of June 1920, began the polarization of the electorate, with voters supporting extremists of the right and left.

The Democrats and Social Democrats lost more strength in April 1921 when the Allies presented their bill for reparations, which totaled 132 billion gold marks. The politicians of the right favored outright rejection, while the Weimar parties realistically decided that the threat of invasion made this course impossible. Again the moderates had to take responsibility for a decision that was certain to prove unpopular. The minister for reconstruction, Walter Rathenau (1867-1922), a Democrat and successful industrialist, hoped that a policy of "fulfillment" might convince the Allies that Germany was acting in good faith and might in the long run lead to concessions. An intensely patriotic German, Rathenau was also a Jew, and he attracted the particular venom of anti-Semitic nationalist orators.

Secret terrorist groups on the right now began a campaign of assassination. In August 1921 they murdered the Catholic Center politician who had signed the armistice, a leading moderate. The assassins escaped through Bavaria, and when one of them was caught, the courts acquitted him. When the League of Nations awarded to Poland a substantial area of the rich province of Upper Silesia containing many Germans, the right grew still angrier. Rathenau was killed in June 1922 by men who believed that by murdering a Jew they could avenge the "betrayal" of the German army. In the wake of this assassination, Stresemann's People's party moved away from the Nationalists, who were viewed as tainted with murder, and worked with the Center and Democrats. Declaring the political situation too tense for an election, Hindenburg postponed a scheduled presidential election to 1925.

The political maneuvers to meet the increasing threat from the right were largely nullified, however, by the economic problem posed by steadily growing inflation, which in 1922 and 1923 reached unheard-of extremes. Inflation is a complicated economic phenomenon still not well understood, but the single chief cause for the runaway inflation in Germany was probably the failure of the German government to levy taxes with which to pay the expenses of the war. The imperial regime had expected to win and to make the losers pay Germany's expenses by imposing huge indemnities. So it had paid for only abut 4 percent of the war costs through taxation. As defeat neared, the government borrowed more and more money from the banks. When the loans came due, the government repaid them with paper money that was not backed by gold. Each time this happened, more paper money was put into circulation, and prices rose; each rise in prices led to a demand for a rise in wages, which were paid with more paper money. The inflationary spiral was under way. Instead of cutting purchasing power by imposing heavy taxes, the government permitted buyers to compete with each other for goods that were in short supply, thus causing prices to shoot up even further, and speeding up the whole process of inflation.

Many other forces contributed to inflation. Germany lacked gold to back its currency, having paid in gold for goods bought abroad during the war; meanwhile, the rich sent great sums out of Germany lest the government use them to pay reparations. Raw materials were in short supply; industry was disorganized; credit was curtailed. The armies of occupation had to be maintained at German expense, and reparations payments had to be made. Nationalist Germans maintained that these expenses, especially reparations, were the cause of inflation, but the total sums involved in reparations were never enough to affect German currency until long after the inflation was under way. Indeed, the inflation rate was partly due to the industrialists' wish to avoid paying reparations and to clear their own indebtedness by letting the currency become worthless. When the war ended, the mark, normally valued at 4.2 to a dollar, had fallen to 8.4; in January 1921 it was 45; by that December, 160; by September 1922 it was 1,303, and at the end of the year it was 7,000!

During these months the German government begged for a moratorium on reparations payments and for a foreign loan. But the French were unwilling. They had already spent billions to rebuild those parts of France that the Germans had devastated during the war, and they wanted the Germans to pay the bill. As a guarantee, the French demanded the vitally important German industrial region of the Ruhr. Despite British opposition, the French occupied the Ruhr in January 1923, after the Germans had defaulted on their reparations payments. The French declared their intention to run the mines and factories for their own benefit, and thus make up for the German failure to pay reparations.

The Germans could not resist with force, but they declared the occupation of the Ruhr illegal and ordered its inhabitants to embark on passive resistance—to refuse to work the mines and factories or to deliver goods to the French. This order the people of the Ruhr obeyed. Local tension in the occupied area became serious when the French took measures against German police and workers, and German Free Corps members undertook guerrilla operations against the French. But the most dramatic result of the French occupation of the Ruhr was its effect upon the already desperate German economy. Not only was the rest of Germany cut off from badly needed goods from the occupied area, but the Ruhr inhabitants were idle at the order of the German government and had to be supported at government expense. The printing presses ran off ever-increasing amounts of ever-more-worthless marks. The exchange rate went from thousands of marks to the dollar to millions, to billions, and by December 1923, well up into the trillions!

Such astronomical figures become meaningful only when we realize their personal and social consequences. A student who set off one afternoon for the university with a check for a year's tuition, room, board, and entertainment found, when he arrived the next morning,

Berliners sold discarded tin cans to sidewalk scrap merchants during the inflation of 1923 as a means of earning a few coins.

that the money would only pay for the journey. Lifetime savings were rendered valueless; people were seen trundling wheelbarrows full of marks through the street to buy a loaf of bread. Those who lived on fixed incomes were utterly ruined, and the investments of the middle classes were wiped out. Real estate took on fantastic value, speculation flourished, and some speculators made fortunes.

For the German worker, inflation did not mean the liquidation of savings, because the worker usually had none. But it did mean a great drop in the purchasing power of wages, so that the worker's family suffered from hunger and cold. Since the financial position of the labor unions was destroyed, they could no longer help the workers, who deserted the unions. The great industrialists, however, gained from the inflation, in part because it crippled the labor unions, but still more because it wiped out their own indebtedness and enabled them to absorb small competitors and build giant business combines.

Politically, therefore, inflation greatly strengthened the extremists of both right and left. The middle classes, although pushed down to the economic level of the proletariat, would not support the working-class parties of Social Democrats or Communists. Disillusioned, they would not support the moderate parties that supported the republic—the People's party, the Center, and the Democrats. So the Nationalists, and Hitler's Nazis above all, reaped a rich harvest of the frightened and the discontented. The hardships of the working class led many workers to turn from the Social Democrats to the Communists. But Soviet Russian constraints on the leaders of the German Communist party prevented any concerted revolutionary drive until the fall of 1923, by which time poor organization and strong governmental repression had doomed their efforts.

With the country seething in crisis, Stresemann became chancellor in the fall of 1923 and proclaimed that, because of the economic dislocation, Germany could not keep up passive resistance in the Ruhr. He ordered work to be resumed and reparations to be paid once again. Political troubles multiplied when the right refused to accept the new policy. At the height of the agitation in Bavaria, Adolf Hitler broke into a right-wing political meeting in a Munich beerhall in early November 1923 and announced that the "national revolution" had begun. At gun point he tried to get other local leaders to support him in a march on Berlin, to be compared to Mussolini's march on Rome one year earlier. Troops broke up the demonstration, which Ludendorff had joined, with only a few casualties.

The trials of Ludendorff and Hitler showed the Weimar judicial system's partiality for the right: Ludendorff was respectfully acquitted; Hitler was allowed to use the trial as a propaganda platform for his ideas and was sentenced to the minimum term for high treason—five years. He spent only eight months in jail, during which time he wrote large portions of *Mein Kampf (My Battle)*, soon to be the bible of the Nazis.

In 1921-1922 a new element had emerged among the welter of right-wing organizations in Bavaria. This was the National Socialist Party of the German Workers (called "Nazi" as an abbreviation of the word *National*) led by Hitler, the son of an Austrian customs official, whose real name had been Schicklgruber. Born in 1889, Hitler had early quarreled with his father and seems always to have felt bitter and frustrated. In 1907 he had been rejected by the Vienna Academy of Fine Arts, where he wished to study painting, and he became an odd-job man, hovering on the edge of starvation. His hatred of the Jews began during these years. Lower-middle-class Vienna at the time was deeply devoted to its anti-Semitic Mayor Lueger, whom Hitler admired. Because Karl Marx himself had been of Jewish origin and because many Viennese Jews were socialists, Hitler associated socialism with the Jews and saw both as responsible for his personal troubles.

Hitler drew support for his anti-Semitism from several nineteenth-century theorists. The French count Joseph Arthur de Gobineau (1816-1882) had laid a pseudoscientific foundation for theories of "Nordic" and "Aryan" supremacy. One of Gobineau's most influential readers was the German composer Richard Wagner, whose son-in-law, the Englishman Houston Stewart Chamberlain (1855-1927), wrote *Foundations of the Nineteenth Century*, which glorified the Germans and assailed the Jews; one section argued that Christ had not been of Jewish origin. Chamberlain opposed democratic government and capitalism. Thus he provided Hitler with a potent mixture of racism, nationalism, and radicalism.

Hitler had hated Vienna's cosmopolitan and Jewish character and had moved to Munich in 1913. In 1914 he had enlisted in the German army, fought through the war as a corporal, and returned to Munich, where Ludendorff was the center of reaction. While employed as a political education officer for the troops, Hitler discovered a small political group that called itself the German Workers' party, which espoused nationalism, militarism, and radicalism. Hitler joined the party in 1919 and soon proved himself to be far abler than any of his colleagues. He urged intensive propaganda to unite all Germans in a greater Germany, to eliminate Jews from political life, to guarantee full employment, to confiscate war profits, to nationalize trusts, to encourage small business, and to grant land to the peasants.

Hitler was a charismatic orator with almost hypnotic gifts of capturing a crowd. By 1921 he had made himself the absolute leader, the *Führer* (compare with *Duce*) of the Nazi party, and he had strengthened himself by founding the SA—originally meaning Sports Division, but eventually *Sturmabteilung*, or storm troops—brown-shirted units copied from the black shirts of Italy and recruited largely from the Free Corps. These storm troopers wore arm bands with a swastika emblem, patrolled mass party meetings, and performed other services for the leader. Their commander was also political adviser to the commander of the infantry stationed in

Bavaria; so the Nazis, like the Italian Fascists, could use their sympathizers in the army to obtain illegal access to government arms.

Hitler's closest collaborators included Hermann Göring (1893-1946), a wartime aviator who had shot down twenty Allied planes, who took on the job of giving the SA a military polish; Rudolf Hess (1894-), principal propagandist for Hitler; and Alfred Rosenberg (1893-1946), a Baltic German distinguished for his fanatical hatred of Jews and Bolsheviks, the first editor of the party newspaper. They and others—many associated with the Thule Society, founded in Munich in 1918 and dedicated to "racial purity"—worked out the basic theories of Nazism, including several elements imitative of Marxism, of which the most important was the conviction that bourgeois politicians could not be expected to rescue the German people from their degradation because they could not unite mind and violence in one organization. This Hitler was determined to do, as he felt the Marxists had done, by uniting ideology and terror in one movement. In 1923 his months in jail gave him his opportunity to draw his disordered and contradictory doctrines together.

Economic Recovery, 1923-1929

Communist disorders and the Nazi beerhall putsch marked the last phase of the inflation period. Shortly before Hitler's move, Stresemann had given extraordinary financial powers to two tough-minded centrists, Hans Luther (1879-1962), minister of finance, and Hjalmar Schacht (1877-1970), banker and fiscal expert. All printing of the old currency was stopped. A new bank was opened to issue new marks, which were assigned the value of the prewar mark. The new currency was backed not by gold but by an imaginary "mortgage" on all Germany's agricultural and industrial wealth, a psychological gesture that won public confidence. One trillion of the inflated marks equaled one of the new. Simultaneously, rigorous economies were put into effect in every branch of the government, and taxes were increased. The public protested loudly, but the measures remained in force until they had the intended effect. The cure for inflation produced serious hardships too. Prices fell, and overexpanded businesses collapsed. Unemployment rose sharply, wages stayed low, and workers labored long hours.

During 1924 the Allies at last helped end the crisis in Germany by formulating the Dawes Plan, named for Charles G. Dawes (1865-1951), an American financier and vice-president under Calvin Coolidge (1872-1933). The plan recommended the evacuation of the Ruhr by the French, the establishment of a special bank to receive reparations payments, a gradual increase in annual payments for the first five years, and an international loan to finance the German deliveries in the first year. The Nationalists attacked these proposals as a scheme to enslave Germany to foreign masters, and in the Reichstag elections of May 1924 they scored impressive gains,

as did the Nazis and the Communists, while moderate parties suffered. But a coalition managed to win acceptance of the Dawes Plan in August by promising the Nationalists seats in the cabinet. When new elections were held in December, the Nazis and Communists sustained losses and the Social Democrats and moderates gained. Early in 1925 a Center-People's Party-Nationalist coalition took office; one wing of the Nationalists, however, led by an enormously rich industrial press and film magnate, Alfred Hugenberg (1865-1951), who had made a fortune during the inflation, opposed all cooperation with the republic. Though Germany had moved appreciably to the right, foreign policy remained in the conciliatory hands of Stresemann, who was foreign minister through all governments between November 1923 and his death in October 1929.

During these less-troubled years, economic recovery proceeded steadily, until in 1929 German industrial output exceeded that of 1913. First-rate German equipment, coupled with superb technical skill and systematic adoption of American methods of mass production, created a highly efficient industrial machine. This "rationalization" of industry increased production, but led to overborrowing and some unemployment. *Vertical trusts*—which brought together in one great corporation all the parts of an industrial process from coal- and iron-mining to the output of the finished product—and *cartels*—associations of independent enterprises that controlled sales and prices for their own benefit—became characteristic of the German system. Emphasis was always on heavy industry, which meant that a big armaments program might assure continued prosperity. Throughout, reparations were paid faithfully, with no damage to the German economy. Indeed, more money flowed into Germany from foreign, especially American, investment than flowed out from reparations. Dependence on foreign capital, however, which would cease to flow in bad times, made German prosperity highly vulnerable.

In 1925, after President Ebert died, a presidential election was held in which three candidates competed. The Catholic Center, the Democrats, and the Social Democrats all supported the Center candidate. The Nationalists, People's party, and other right-wing groups supported Field Marshal von Hindenburg, then seventy-seven years old. The Communists ran their own candidate and thus contributed to the election of Hindenburg, who won by a small plurality. The choice of a man so intimately connected with imperial, militarist Germany created dismay abroad; but until 1930 Hindenburg acted fully in accord with the constitution, to the distress of most of the nationalist groups. Though domestic issues of this period aroused great heat, they were settled by democratic process. In the elections of 1928 the Social Democrats were returned to power; prosperity had encouraged moderation and growing support for the republic.

In foreign affairs, this period saw a gradual increase in German participation in the system of collective security. In 1925 Germany signed the Locarno treaties, which took the French armies out of the Rhineland in return for a neutral zone and a frontier guaranteed by Britain and Italy, and set up machinery to arbitrate disputes between Germany and its neighbors. These treaties did not, however, guarantee Germany's frontiers with Poland and Czechoslovakia. In 1926 Germany was admitted to the League of Nations, with a permanent seat on the League's Council. In 1929 Germany accepted the Kellogg-Briand Pact, which outlawed aggressive war.

In 1929 a new reparations plan named after another American, Owen D. Young (1874-1962), chairman of the committee that drew it up, substantially reduced the total originally demanded by the Allies. The Young Plan also established lower rates of payments than those under the Dawes Plan and allowed the Germans a greater role in their collection. Before June 1930 the Rhineland was evacuated by the Allies, four years ahead of the date set by the Treaty of Versailles.

Germany and World Depression, 1929-1933

But the economic depression had begun to knock the foundations out from under prosperity and moderation. An economic depression is a sharp and deep decline in trade and general prosperity. In the worldwide depression of 1873 to 1896, prices had fallen, agricultural distress had intensified—made worse in Europe by bad harvests followed by wet summers, and by competition from Argentine and Australian meat and Canadian and American grain—and banks had collapsed, especially in Austria and France. Indeed, this earlier depression had contributed greatly to Britain's relative decline against Germany and the United States. No one wanted such a period of worldwide strain and destabilization again, but it nonetheless occurred, and while scholars do not agree on the long-range causes of the depression (just as economists do not agree on the causes of inflation or recession today), it was apparent to all that the new "world slump" of 1929-1934, while short, was extremely intense and was particularly destructive of middle-class confidence in the United States, Germany, and Austria.

The depression had, in fact, already begun before the Wall Street crash of the stockmarket in October 1929, for agriculture had declined as overproduction and poor distribution brought prices down, and as speculation on the stockmarket had led to general financial reckless-ness. American banks now withdrew their funds from Europe. The Austrian Kredit-Anstalt, the largest commercial bank in Austria, with many interests throughout central and eastern Europe, was made bankrupt in 1931 when the French, themselves in dire economic need, withdrew short-term credit. In Germany a shortage of capital and foreign credits quickly curtailed industrial production, leading to a decline in exports and a reduced need for transportation (especially shipping), which triggered further widespread unemployment.

The need for economic planning seemed evident, and since totalitarian movements of both left or right generally already had a commitment to long-range economic planning, those most hurt by what quickly became known as the Great Depression turned increasingly away from a free-market economy. For capitalists, the Bolshevik solution was not acceptable; for nationalists, convinced that the depression had been caused by unsound economic practices in another country, one solution was tariffs. Since fascist movements advocated economic nationalism and centralized state planning for the economy, they quickly gained new adherents, especially in the most hard-hit areas of Europe: Austria, Germany, Romania, and Italy. In Germany unemployment insurance cushioned the first shock for the workers; the lower middle classes, painfully recovering from the period of inflation, had no such barrier between them and destitution. Their desperation helped Hitler, whose fortunes during the years of fulfillment had fallen low. Meanwhile, however, Hitler was preparing the instruments of force, especially by creating the *Schutz-staffel* (defense force, or SS), an elite, black-shirted guard of honor under the direction of Heinrich Himmler (1900-1945). The SS membership requirements emphasized "racial purity," and its members would become the nucleus for the *Gestapo*, or secret police.

The coalition government fell in 1930 over a disagreement on unemployment insurance benefits. Hindenburg appointed as chancellor Heinrich Brüning (1885-1970), a member of the Catholic Center party and a fiscal conservative, and instructed him to shape an emergency cabinet not restricted by party allegiance, one that could forestall the military intervention that appeared imminent. President Hindenburg, now eighty-two, had fallen under the influence of General Kurt von Schleicher (1882-1934), an ambitious and clever political soldier who had schemed his way into the president's favor. Hindenburg wanted to rule by decree, as the constitution authorized him to do in an emergency. By failing to pass Brüning's economic program, the Reichstag gave Hindenburg the opportunity he wanted. Brüning agreed, partly because he felt that a genuine emergency existed, but partly because he was determined to keep his bitter political rivals, the Social Democrats, from replacing him in office.

A presidential decree proclaimed the new budget. When the Reichstag protested, Hindenburg dissolved it and called new elections for September 1930. Nazis and Communists fought in the streets and both gained greatly at the expense of the moderates. The Nazis' Reichstag representation rose from 12 to 107 and the Communists' from 54 to 77. Brüning had to carry on against the wishes of the electorate; supported only by Hindenburg, he too now turned authoritarian.

Political matters were now fueled almost exclusively by the deepening economic crisis. To avoid a new government in which Nazis would participate, the Social Democrats decided to support Brüning. When the Reichstag met, Nazis and Communists created disorder

GERTRUDE STEIN MOCKS MONEY

Gertrude Stein (1874-1946), an American-born author, maintained a salon in Paris after 1903 and influenced many writers and artists. Her comment on the problem of world finances was typically oblique and yet to the point:

As a cousin of mine once said about money, money is always there but the pockets change; it is not in the same pockets after a change, and that is all there is to say about money.

Quoted in Charles P. Curtis, Jr., and Ferris Greenslet, eds., *The Practical Cogitator* (Boston: Houghton Mifflin, 1945), p. 313.

on the floor, but voted together against government measures. These measures passed only because the Social Democrats voted for them. In 1931 Brüning tried to arrange an Austro-German customs union to coordinate the tariff policies of the two countries and help them fight the depression, without affecting their political sovereignty. Whether such an arrangement between two countries that were both suffering from unemployment would actually have succeeded cannot be surmised; the impulse for Germany and Austria to unite politically might not have proved overpowering. In any case, the project raised in the minds of the Allies, especially the French, the specter of a "greater Germany," and the scheme was vetoed by the World Court. The collapse of the Kredit-Anstalt in May further deepened the depression, despite a British loan to Austria and despite the one-year moratorium on reparations payments procured for Germany by the American president, Herbert Hoover (1874-1964).

Nazis, Nationalists, the veterans' organization of the Steel Helmets (*Stahlhelm*), the Junkers' Agrarian League, industrialists, and representatives of the former princely houses now formed a coalition against Brüning. This coalition had great financial resources, mass support, and private armies in the SA, the Stahlhelm, and other semimilitary organizations. Because the left was split, nothing stood between this new right-wing coalition and political victory except Hindenburg, who controlled the army. Early in 1932 Hitler was invited to address a meeting of coal and steel magnates, whose financial support he won. Though some of Hitler's followers were now impatient for a new putsch, he curbed them, believing that the Nazis could come to power legally.

In the presidential elections of March 1932, Hitler ran as the candidate of the Nazis, and Hindenburg as the candidate of the Center, Social Democrats, and other moderate parties. The Nationalists nominated a Stahlhelm man, and the Communists ran their own candidate. Hitler polled 11,338,571 votes, and Hindenburg polled 18,661,736, four-tenths of a percent short of the required majority. In the runoff election, the Nationalists backed Hitler, whose total rose to 13,400,000, as against Hindenburg's 19,360,000. The eighty-four-year-old marshal reelected as the candidate of the moderates was, however, no longer a moderate himself, but the tool of the Junkers and the military.

There was an alternative direction in which Hitler could move; denied the presidency, he could become chancellor. Responding to pressure from the state governments, Brüning and Hindenburg tried to ban the SA and SS, while Schleicher orchestrated protests against such a ban. Feeling he had been ill advised, Hindenburg told his chancellor he would not sign any further emergency decrees, and Brüning resigned. Schleicher, eager to stop Hitler, recommended that he himself be included in a coalition government that could take credit for his policies as well as its own, and he persuaded Hindenburg to appoint Franz von Papen (1879-1969), a rich Catholic nobleman and a member of the extreme right wing of the Center, who installed a cabinet composed of other noblemen.

The Center, however, disavowed Papen, who had the support of no political party or group, but whom the Nazis temporarily tolerated because he agreed to lift the ban on the SA and SS. But in foreign policy, Papen succeeded where Brüning had failed, for the Allies scrapped the Young Plan and required Germany to pay only three billion gold marks into a fund earmarked for general European reconstruction. Instead of being bound for many decades to pay reparations, Germany was now freed from all such obligations.

On July 31, 1932, new elections for the Reichstag took place, called by Papen on the assumption that the Nazis had passed their peak, that their vote would decrease, and that they would then cooperate in the government. However, on July 20 Papen had dismissed the government of Prussia, where there had been over five hundred confrontations between storm-troopers and those they saw as their enemies, on the grounds that it could not maintain public order. This played into the hands of the Nazis, who won 230 seats to become the biggest single party in the Reichstag; the Communists gained also, chiefly at the expense of the Social Democrats. The Democrats and the People's party almost disappeared.

Papen had failed. He now wanted to take some Nazis into the government, but the Nazis demanded the chancellorship, which Hindenburg was determined not to hand over to Hitler. Papen decided to dissolve the Reichstag and call new elections. By repeating this process, he hoped to wear down Hitler's strength each time, until he brought Hitler to support him and accept a subordinate place. Papen also put pressure on the industrialists who had been supporting Hitler, and Nazi funds began to dry up, leaving Hitler seriously embarrassed. The election of November 6, 1932, bore out Papen's expectations. The Nazis fell off from 230 seats to 196; and although the Communists gained substantially, Papen too won some support.

Thus emboldened, Papen designed a constitutional change that would have moved the Weimar Republic even closer to the policies of the corporative state: power was to be returned to the hands of the propertied elite. Schleicher persuaded Hindenburg that the plan was naive and tried desperately to form a new majority based on labor organizations—Catholic, Nazi, and independent—with army backing. Failing, he stepped down, leaving the way clear for Hitler as the only person with a program and public support. In turn, Papen, eager for revenge over being displaced by Schleicher, met with Hitler, who led Papen to hope that he would come back into office with Hitler's backing. Hindenburg, too, was enlisted. But when Schleicher resigned on January 28, 1933, after only eight weeks in office, Hitler demanded the chancellorship for himself. Papen consented, provided Hitler undertook to govern in strict accord with parliamentary procedure. Papen was to be vice-chancellor, and still thought he could dominate the government, since only three of its eleven ministers would be Nazis. He therefore persuaded Hindenburg to accept Hitler as chancellor. But Papen underestimated Hitler. Though Hitler swore to Hindenburg that he would maintain the constitution, he did not keep his oath. The Weimar Republic was doomed from the moment Hitler became chancellor on January 30, 1933. Basing his power in local centers, he had taken over the nation; heedless of the law, he had nonetheless achieved a revolution through legal means. He would now set out to change the law to fit his long-range goals.

III GERMANY UNDER HITLER, 1933-1939

Hitler's first weeks in power were devoted to transforming his chancellorship into a dictatorship. He dissolved the Reichstag and called for new elections. During the campaign, opponents of the Nazis were intimidated by violence and threats and were denied radio time and free use of the press. On the night of February 27, a fire mysteriously broke out in the Reichstag building. When he heard the news, Hitler exclaimed, "Now I have them," for he knew that the fire could be blamed on the Communists. By the next morning, 4,000 Communist party members were arrested, and by noon Hitler had persuaded Hindenburg, who was convinced a Bolshevik revolution was at hand, to suspend the basic rights of the citizenry during the emergency. Arrest, indefinite detention, and terror were now embraced by the state. Germany was, in effect, a dictatorship.

Nonetheless, in the election of March 5 the Nazis won only 44 percent of the votes, which gave them 288 seats in the Reichstag. Using the SA as a constant threat, Hitler bullied the Reichstag. Except for 94 Social Democrats (the Communists were denied their seats), all members voted for an Enabling Act on March 23, suspending the Weimar constitution. The act was renewed in 1937 by a subservient Reichstag, and again in 1943.

Now Hitler could act as he chose, unimpeded by the laws. He instituted a ministry of propaganda under Josef Goebbels (1897-1945). He stripped the state governments of their powers and made Germany a strongly centralized state (April 1933) by appointing governors from Berlin who could override the state legislatures.

Like Mussolini, Hitler too was a dramatic speaker who accompanied his explosive delivery with melodramatic body language. He is shown here wearing the swastika armband that became the symbol of his government.

When Hindenburg died in August 1934, Hitler became president as well as chancellor, but he preferred to use the title *Der Führer*. This new move was approved by a plebiscite in which Hitler obtained 88 percent of the votes.

Political parties that opposed Hitler were forced to dissolve. The government banned Communists and Socialists (May 1933); the Nationalists dissolved themselves (June 1933); the government put an end to the Catholic parties (July 1933) and all monarchist groups (February 1934). The Stahlhelm was incorporated into the Nazi party. In July 1933 the Nazis were declared to be the only legal political party in Germany.

The appeal of the Nazis to the German people lay partly in their denunciation of the "disorderly" parliamentary system; a strong man who got things done struck a responsive chord in the public. In the last elections, in November 1933, there were no opposition candidates, 92 percent of the electorate voted Nazi, and there were only two non-Nazi deputies in a chamber of 661. As in fascist Italy and communist Russia, youth groups fed the party, which soon had a powerful regional organization all over Germany and among Germans abroad.

Within the Nazi party itself, however, a difficult situation was created by those who had believed Hitler's more radical pronouncements on social and economic questions. Many of these Nazis were concentrated in the SA, whose members, most of them from the lower classes, were also distressed by how Hitler had treated their organization. The SA had made possible his rise to power, but it was now an embarrassment to Hitler, no longer quite respectable, and certainly not in favor, as were the SS and especially the army, which had remained neutral in January of 1933, thus assuring the triumph of Hitler's forces.

On June 30, 1934, Hitler ordered and personally participated in a "blood purge," or, as he himself called it, "the night of the long knives." Ernst Röhm (1887-1934), founder and leader of the SA, was shot, and so were, by Hitler's own admission, seventy-three others, including the head of Catholic Action, and Schleicher and his wife. (Other estimates of the casualties run as high as one thousand). The killings were ruthless and selective, except in Silesia, where SS units rampaged out of control. Hitler justified the murders, and house arrest for Papen, by declaring that the SA was planning a putsch, and that the opposition and all who offended public morality (for Röhm was a homosexual), must be crushed. After June 1934 there was no effective opposition to Hitler left.

Racism and Political Theory in Practice

Soon after the passage of the enabling law, Hitler struck the first of his many blows against the Jews, whom he had long denounced. In a country of approximately sixty million people, practicing Jews were less than 1 percent of the population. The Jews had become leading members of the professions and the arts and had made outstanding contributions to German culture. Since most Jews were patriotic Germans, many of them would probably have become Nazis if they had been permitted to. Instead, anti-Semitic doctrines required their ruthless elimination.

As with many societies in the past, racism now became part of state policy. The businesses and professions of the Jews were boycotted; Jews were forbidden to hold office (April 1933), although a temporary exception was made for veterans of World War I. In the "Nuremberg laws" of September 15, 1935, a Jew was defined as any person with one Jewish grandparent; all such persons were deprived of the rights of German citizenship. Intermarriage between Jews and non-Jews was forbidden as "racial pollution." Jews might not fly the national flag, write or publish, exhibit paintings or give concerts, act on stage or screen, teach in any educational institution, work in a bank or a hospital, enter any of the government's labor or professional bodies, or sell books or antiques. They were not eligible for unemployment insurance or charity, and the names of Jews who had died for Germany in World War I were erased from war memorials. Many towns and villages, especially in North Germany, under the spur of government-sponsored propaganda refused to permit Jews to live inside their precincts.

In November 1938 a Jewish boy of seventeen, driven to desperation by the persecution of his parents, shot and killed a secretary of the German embassy in Paris. Two days later organized German mobs looted and pillaged Jewish shops all over Germany, burned and dynamited synagogues, and invaded Jewish homes to batter the occupants and steal their possessions. The state then compelled the Jews to restore the damaged properties and pay a fine. Jews were forced to take special names, to wear yellow Stars of David, and to belong to a Reich "Union of Jews." Although some Jews managed to leave Germany, it was usually at the cost of abandoning all their possessions; these proved to be the lucky ones. All measures designed to drive the Jews into ghettos and starvation were but the prelude to their physical extermination in gas ovens by the Nazis during World War II. What distressed many horrified Western observers as much as the actions themselves was the failure of any substantial number of educated non-Jewish Germans or of the churches to register any form of public protest.

Enthusiasm for "racial purity" led to the study of eugenics, to the promotion of widespread athleticism and the cult of physical health, and to the elevation of Hitler in the minds of some into a virtual secular Messiah who had discovered how to save his chosen people. Blond, blue-eyed, ideal "Nordic types" were urged to mate with each other early and to have many children. German motherhood was made the object of paeans of praise; by the time a woman was twenty-four years old she was statistically expected to be a mother. To keep the race pure, sterilization was introduced, supposedly to prevent inherited disease. The carrying out of such a law depended upon the cooperation of the medical and legal

Arms raised, faces white with fear, a group of Jews is led off by Nazi storm troopers during the destruction of Warsaw. This photograph, taken from an SS commander's report to his superior officer, was introduced at the Nuremberg trials as evidence of Nazi brutality. The Germans idealized the blond, blue-eyed "German student" as a physical and intellectual type. Below a handsome Nordic youth holds the flag while the poster urges Germans to join Hitler's National Student Organization for the glory of the Führer and the *volk*—the pure strain of German people.

professions, which soon fell into the hands of charlatans. Medical experimentation of horrifying cruelty and of no verifiable scientific value was practiced during the war on human beings of "inferior" races—Jews, Poles and other Slavs, and gypsies. These practices were the direct outcome of Nazi pseudoscientific "eugenic" legislation.

In foreign affairs, German racism justified the conquest of all territory inhabited by Germans—Austria, the western borderlands (Sudetenland) of Czechoslovakia, Danzig, the Polish corridor, and other less important places. In addition, the doctrine of *Lebensraum* ("living space" for the expanding "Nordic race") justified the incorporation of non-German areas—the rest of Czechoslovakia, Poland, all of southeastern Europe, and much of Russia. Hitler declared that what the Germans needed they were entitled to take, since they were a superior people.

Some German intellectuals had looked back with longing upon the Holy Roman Empire of the Middle Ages, the first Reich. Now that the war had ended the second Reich of William II, they hoped to create a third one, incorporating the old territories, no matter who now lived in them. This is the meaning of Hitler's use of the term "Third Reich" to describe the Nazi state, which he proclaimed would last a thousand years. A "scientific" basis for the Lebensraum theory was supplied by the teachers of "geopolitics," chief among whom was Karl Haushofer (1869-1946), professor of geography, chief theoretician of geopolitics, and teacher of Hitler's close friend and adviser, Rudolf Hess, who in 1933 became Deputy Führer. Haushofer declared that Britain and France were decadent, that small powers must

DER DEUTSCHE STUDENT

FÜR F... ...K

IN DER MANNSCHAFT DES NSD-STUDENTENBUNDES

HITLER JUSTIFIES THE USE OF TERROR

In *Mein Kampf*, Hitler had set forth, from the quiet of his prison cell, the doctrines that would justify National Socialism and the use of terror against his enemies:

. . . we National Socialists must hold unflinchingly to our aim in foreign policy, namely, *to secure for the German people the land and soil to which they are entitled on this earth*. And this action is the only one which, before God and our German posterity, would make any sacrifice of blood seem justified: before God, since we have been put on this earth with the mission of eternal struggle for our daily bread, beings who receive nothing as a gift, and who owe their position as lords of the earth only to the genius and the courage with which they can conquer and defend it. . . . The soil on which some day German generations of peasants can beget powerful sons will sanction the investment of the sons of today, and will some day acquit the responsible statesmen of blood-guilt and sacrifice of the people. . . .

And I must sharply attack those folkish pen-pushers who claim to regard such an acquisition of soil as a "breach of sacred human rights" and attack it as such in their scribblings. . . . By such an attitude they help to weaken and destroy from within our people's will for the only correct way of defending their vital needs. For no people on this earth possesses so much as a square yard of territory on the strength of a higher will or superior right. . . . *State boundaries are made by man and changed by man. . . .*

But we National Socialists must go further. *The right*

to possess soil can become a duty if without extension of its soil a great nation seems doomed to destruction. And most especially when not some little nigger nation or other is involved, but the Germanic mother of life, which has given the present-day world its cultural picture. *Germany will either be a world power or there will be no Germany. . . .*

Here Fate itself seems desirous of giving us a sign. By handing Russia to Bolshevism, it robbed the Russian nation of that intelligentsia which previously brought about and guaranteed its existence as a state. For the organization of a Russian state formation was not the result of the political abilities of the Slavs in Russia, but only a wonderful example of the state-forming efficacy of the German element in an inferior race. . . . For centuries Russia drew nourishment from this Germanic nucleus of its upper leading strata. Today it can be regarded as almost totally exterminated and extinguished. It has been replaced by the Jew. Impossible as it is for the Russian by himself to shake off the yoke of the Jew by his own resources, it is equally impossible for the Jew to maintain the mighty empire forever. . . .

From *Mein Kampf*, trans. Ralph Manheim, pp. 652-55. Copyright 1943 and © renewed by Houghton Mifflin Company. Reprinted by permission of Houghton Mifflin Company. Italics in original.

This unhistorical analysis is representative of Hitler's thought throughout his life. Contained in it are all the elements of his theory—racism, his ignorance of how the United States might limit his expansion, his fear of Bolsheviks and hatred of Jews, and his strategic sense that Germany might, nonetheless, under the right circumstances, conclude an alliance with other elements of the Russian state. Given to fits of depression, at times highly unstable, Hitler could, as here, be coldly reflective. Nothing is so dangerous as a leader who acts upon misconstrued history, and Hitler had laid out his basic misconceptions and his major strategies for all to see, well in advance of taking power.

---

disappear (except for Switzerland, which was leaning toward Germany, and Vatican City), that Germany, preserving its master race purity, must possess the will to power and expand ruthlessly, occupying the "heartland" of Eurasia, and dominate the world.

Another school of thought in Germany argued that Germany's future lay in an alliance with Russia, in which Russia's inexhaustible work force would be joined with Germany's industrial output and military techniques. This notion had been strong in German army circles in czarist days and persisted after the Bolshevik Revolution. Outside the army, other German nationalists retained the Bismarckian attitudes of hostility toward the West and Poland, and of friendship toward Russia, whatever

its regime. Moreover, many German Marxists were highly nationalistic; Hitler's National Socialism succeeded in part because he knew how to use old Marxist clichés to present an essentially nationalist program.

Accordingly, Hitler revamped the German judicial system, abandoning traditional legal principles and substituting "folk" justice, which, Hitler said, totally subordinated the individual to the people (*Volk*). In practice, this mystic doctrine meant that whatever Hitler wanted was German law. People's Courts, to which Hitler appointed the judges, were established (May 1934) to try all cases of treason, a crime that was now logically extended to include many lesser offenses against "the people," such as circulating banned newspapers that were harmful to the people's morality or political judgment. Concentration camps were established for enemies of the state, who could be executed without appeal. The Gestapo (*Geheime Staatspolizei*, Secret State Police), formally established in April 1933 in Prussia, was extended to all of Germany in 1934, with a free hand in opening private correspondence, tapping wires, and spying on citizens.

All economic life was brought under the regime. In agriculture, the Nazis aimed at self-sufficiency and at control of the peasantry. The Junkers were protected, and no effort was made to divide their vast estates. In 1933 a special law protected smaller farms against forced sale and attachment for debt, an act that won the small farmer to Hitler. But the government determined the production required of farms, and fixed farm prices, wages, and fees for distributing farm products. Unused land was put under cultivation, and citizens had to grow vegetables in greenhouses in preparation for war. By 1937 Germany was 83 percent self-sufficient in agriculture, a rise of 8 percent since the Nazis had come to power. Fats and coffee were perhaps the two most important remaining deficiencies.

In industry, taking a leaf out of Russia's book, Hitler proclaimed a Four-Year Plan in 1933 and a second one in 1936. The first was aimed chiefly at economic recovery and at ending unemployment. Labor camps for men and women helped decrease unemployment, as did rearmament and public works. By 1936 unemployment had dropped from about seven million to less than one and a half million. The second plan was designed to prepare for war, and especially to make Germany blockade-proof. Output of raw materials was increased, and the materials were distributed first to armament and other war industries; labor was allocated in a similar way; prices and foreign exchange were controlled. Hermann Göring was put in charge of the plan. He assumed direction of the new Göring Iron Works, designed to make up for the loss of the rich iron resources of Alsace-Lorraine, which yielded three quarters of Germany's pre-1918 supply. To this end, low-content ores were worked, and the government absorbed the higher costs; output went up more than 50 percent in two years. Germany's skilled scientists made up for other deficiencies by devising successful, if expensive, synthetic products. Especially important were the distillation of motor fuel from coal and the production of synthetic rubber. The state also built strategic highways (*Auto-bahnen*), the first modern expressways, for the rapid movement of goods and troops, much as Germany had used its railways in World War I.

The Nazis abolished all labor unions in 1933 and

During Hitler's tour of Rome in 1938, he and Mussolini paid a ceremonial visit to the Galleria Borghese, accompanied by German Foreign Minister von Ribbentrop (far left) and Italian Foreign Minister Ciano (far right). Although the visit went well publicly, Hitler disliked Italian art, which he thought decadent, and he discovered that he also disliked Mussolini, whom he had at first admired.

Powerful leaders have often exploited the human craving for the dramatic, and Hitler, above all others, was a master. "Vaults of light"—great beams that dazzled the eye and gave nighttime crowds a sense of unity and awe—were used skillfully by him to climax many Nazi mass meetings.

employers' associations in 1934. To replace them, a Labor Front was established to include all wage earners, salaried persons, professionals, and employers. Strikes and lockouts were forbidden. Workers were assured of jobs as long as they accepted the system. The Labor Front was also a spy organization, constantly on the alert for anti-Nazis in the factories; it could reduce their pay, fire them, or put them in jail. An adjunct to the Labor Front was the Strength through Joy organization, which provided paid vacation trips for German workers to resorts or tourist centers, and which sponsored concerts and other entertainments.

As the second Four-Year Plan went into effect, the workers became less mobile. They had work books detailing their past training and positions, and they could not get a new job unless the state decided it was more suitable. All graduates of secondary schools had to register with employment authorities, and men and women of working age could be conscripted for labor. Just before the outbreak of war, all agricultural and mining workers and certain industrial workers were frozen in their jobs. Meanwhile, the big cartel became the all-pervasive feature of German industrial organization—a system of profitable monopoly under state control. Interlocking directorates made the system even tighter than it looked; six industrialists, for example,

held among them one hundred and twenty-seven directorates in the largest corporations, were presidents of thirty-two, and all held government posts besides. The minister of economics sat at the top of the economic pyramid, authorizing plant expansion, controlling imports and exports, fixing prices and establishing costs, and allocating raw materials.

These processes of *Gleichschaltung* (coordination) were applied throughout German life, including education and the arts. Göring is said to have remarked, "When I hear anyone talk of culture, I reach for my revolver," a revealing restatement of his belief in the purely practical, for as he also said, "Guns will make us powerful; butter will only make us fat." Hitler's own artistic views were extremely simple: he denounced most modern art as non-Aryan; expressionism, he said, was simply cultural Bolshevism. The school curriculum, especially history, had to be taught in accord with the Nazi doctrine of "blood and soil." Nazi racial doctrine, the great past achievements of Germany, the military spirit, and physical fitness were the cornerstones of the new education, which was to shape a single view of the nation's purpose, with no higher claims to be made on the individual than those made by the state.

The Christian churches, both Protestant and Catholic, were a problem for the Nazis. Extremists among

Hitler's followers favored a return to a mystical paganism and the old German gods celebrated by Wagner's operas. Hitler himself, born a Catholic, had once declared that Germany was his only god. Yet power politics required him to come to terms with the churches, which still commanded the allegiance of most Germans. In the hope of avoiding state domination, the Lutheran ministry in 1933 organized a national synod, which the Nazis almost immediately took over by appointing their own bishop. The efforts of extremist Nazis to purge the Bible and to abandon the crucifix led to discontent. The dissidents, led by pastor Martin Niemöller (1892-   ), objected to Nazi theology and efforts at control. Although Niemöller also pledged his loyalty to Hitler and made no objections to Nazi racism, in 1936 he went to a concentration camp solely to resist dictation over the Lutheran church. The "confessional" movement for which he spoke probably did not extend beyond about 15 percent of the Protestant clergy.

In July 1933 Hitler and the Vatican reached a concordat guaranteeing freedom of worship and permitting religious instruction in the schools. Catholics were to be allowed to form youth groups and to appoint professors of theology. But the Nazis did not live up to these terms. They interfered with the circulation of Catholic magazines, persecuted the youth groups, and insulted Catholic priests in their press as members of a "black international." On the other hand, the Catholic church found much to oppose in the teachings to which Catholic children were exposed in the Hitler youth groups. Rosenberg's books were placed on the Index (a list of books Catholics were forbidden to read without permission), and in 1937 a papal encyclical attacked National Socialism. Still, Catholics supported Hitler's territorial ambitions, and the church took an ambiguous position on his treatment of the Jews, still the subject of much historical controversy. In general, Hitler carefully avoided a direct clash with the churches, and they remained silent. He apparently planned to deal with them when his war was over.

IV AUTHORITARIANISM IN IBERIA AND EASTERN EUROPE

In the troubled years between the wars, nondemocratic authoritarian governments emerged not only in Italy and Germany but also in Spain, in Portugal, in the successor states to the Hapsburg Empire (except Czechoslovakia), and in the other states of eastern and southeastern Europe.

Spain

In 1918 Spain was still a nation in which local loyalties contested with national sentiment. Catalonians and Basques continued to work toward separate states, and

though the Catholic religion had united Spaniards against Muslims in the Middle Ages and against Protestants in the sixteenth and seventeenth centuries, the church was no longer so strong a force for unity, since it was identified with the large landowners and with the voices of social conservatism. While Spain at times approached self-sufficiency in agriculture and industrial raw materials, its soil was poor and its farming antiquated, and the rural areas were suffering from overpopulation relative to resources. As in the south of Italy poverty was commonplace, and the masses were increasingly discontented with their national leadership.

Spain had also suffered from a lowered sense of prestige. It had lost its empire to the United States in the short war of 1898, and in World War I it had remained neutral (as Portugal had not). In 1900 Spain was entering the demographic situation associated with modern states, which much of Europe had entered in 1870: a declining death rate, a slowly falling birth rate, and a lessening of emigration within Europe, though with increased movement overseas. The government had done little to improve agriculture, and farmers in Catalonia could not gain access to sufficient land to support themselves. There were many small landholdings and many large estates, but no middle ground for prosperous farmers. Spanish sheep, once prized, declined in competition against Australian and Argentine breeders, while Spanish grain from Castile cost more in Barcelona because of inadequate transport than did foreign grain from distant North America. While Spain had enjoyed rapid growth in viniculture, especially when French wine exports were virtually wiped out by an attack of phylloxera in the late nineteenth century, the Spanish wine trade was also in serious trouble by 1900. By World War I Spain had no export market to itself in Europe except for cork, which was benefiting the area already best developed, intensifying the sense of disparity among the various regions.

Spanish industry was dominated by textiles, indicative of its early stage in the Industrial Revolution. But Spanish production was largely confined to the home market, where the consumption of cotton was no higher than in eastern Europe. Though it was the most important part of Spain's industries, the cotton industry was unable to stimulate further stages of industrialization, as had occurred in France, Switzerland, and Belgium. Moreover, what small prosperity the textile industry brought to Spain was largely confined to Catalonia. Spain had little coal for heavier industry, and the iron industry in Bilbao used British coal until 1914. Spain also had to rely on British investments for its railroads, and both rails and rolling stock had been imported until the war curtailed them. In short, Spain had not achieved a breakthrough into modern industrialism, the level of agriculture remained low, the gap between the rich and the poor was very great, and there seemed little prospect of change in 1918.

When the Spaniards turned to revolutionary doctrine,

it was chiefly to Bakunin's anarchist beliefs and later to Sorel's syndicalism. Anarchism (and anarchosyndicalism) really took hold only in Spain. The industrial workers of Catalonia and the peasants of Andalusia who no longer attended Mass were anarchist; they wanted to destroy the state utterly rather than conquer and use it. Yet anarchism, which at its peak numbered a million to a million and a half adherents, could only harass governments, not overthrow them, and its positive achievements were limited to securing an occasional increase in wages through strikes. The movement was deeply puritanical and anti-Catholic; its adherents burned churches and killed priests. But terror was not a policy. A wave of assassinations put into office General Miguel Primo de Rivera (1870-1930), who proclaimed martial law, dissolved the Cortes (the Spanish parliament), imposed censorship, drove liberal critics into exile, and ruled from 1923 until 1930, when the world depression revealed that the roads, irrigation projects, and electrification he had brought to Spain had been at the high cost of foreign loans.

In the 1930s Spain also had a growing Marxist Socialist party with its own federation of trade unions parallel to that of the anarchists. The socialists drew their first strength from the urban workers of Castile and from the mining and steel-producing centers of the north. When Spain became a republic in 1931, the socialists added many rural supporters, and the party numbered a million and a quarter in 1934. The socialists were moderates who had refused to adhere to the Comintern in 1920, but who had joined the revived Second International a few years later. Dissidents founded a small Communist party, and Catalonians had their own socialist organization. The church supported labor unions of its own in the north, where it had not become identified with the landlords. The socialist doctrine that each should be rewarded according to need sustained the traditional Spanish contempt for success and property. In fact, Spain had not accepted the capitalist system or the Industrial Revolution any more than it had accepted the Protestant Reformation.

On the extreme right was Carlism. Founded in the nineteenth century as a movement supporting Don Carlos (1788-1855), a pretender to the throne, Carlism called for the restoration of the Inquisition, regarded the railroad and the telegraph as sources of evil, and rejected the Copernican theory of the universe. Carlism had its lower-class followers, too, especially among the rebellious farmers of Navarre in the north.

King Alfonso XIII (reigned 1886-1931), a constitutional monarch strongly ambitious for absolute power, ruled over Spain until 1931. Based on electoral corruption and intimidation, the "liberals" and "conservatives" in his governments took orderly turns at office, and the real power rested with the local political bosses. These alternating governments occupied the political center, which in fact was quite small. Once the prosperity brought by Spain's wartime neutrality was over, the clashes between the anarchists, the left, and the far right

led many people to consider General Primo's rule necessary.

After Primo's resignation and death, King Alfonso restored the constitution. Municipal elections in April 1931 were viewed as a plebiscite on the monarchy. They resulted in a victory for the republicans, representing the lower middle classes of the towns, small traders, intellectuals, teachers, and journalists. The king left the country without abdicating. Elections to a constituent assembly in June 1931 brought in a republican-socialist majority, and in November the assembly forbade the king's return and confiscated his property. Spain was now a republic. The monarchy, having stood only for clergy, army, and aristocracy, had failed.

The assembly adopted a new constitution in December. This provided for a responsible ministry, a single-chamber parliament, and a president to be chosen by an electoral college consisting of parliament and an equal number of electors chosen by popular vote. It was clear that the army would rise against the republic whenever the opportunity presented itself, and that the army would have the support of the church and the large landowners. Moreover, although the republic temporarily had socialist support, it did not have the support of the anarchists. Danger threatened from both the right and the left.

The first crisis arose over a new constitutional law defining the position of the church. The assembly rejected a moderate proposal which would have preserved the church as a special corporation with its own schools and which might have proved acceptable to most Catholics, even though the cardinal-primate of Spain had already denounced the republic. Instead, the assembly's law was more extreme; it closed church schools and ended state grants to the church after two years. This hurt education badly and lost the republicans many supporters, especially among the lower clergy. And although the republic granted Catalonia autonomy, it failed to act decisively on agrarian reform.

The anarchists expressed their dissatisfaction by major uprisings (1933), which the government put down by force. The jails were full and unemployment was as high as ever. Repression of the anarchists lost the republic much support on the left, but failed to gain it support from the right, which came back strongly in the elections of November 1933 as the largest party in parliament. Now the government helplessly swung to the right, and much of its previous legislation, especially laws affecting the church and the working classes, remained unenforced.

Grown more revolutionary, the socialists now competed with the anarchists for the loyalty of Spanish workers. Strikes and disorders multiplied. In October 1934 the socialists called a general strike to protest the inclusion of fascists in the government. Catalonia, declaring itself an independent republic, was deprived of its autonomy. The coal miners of the Asturias region in the north staged a revolt, backed by both anarchists and socialists, which was put down with the loss of more than three thousand lives. The government's use of Muslim troops from North Africa against Spaniards was deeply resented, and intense hatred was directed at the new minister of war, Francisco Franco (1892-1975).

Thus the right lost its public support; and now the left, under the impact of the Asturias uprising and influenced by the Comintern, united in a Popular Front for the elections of February 1936. For the first time anarcho-syndicalists went to the polls and voted for republicans, socialists, and communists. The left won a considerable victory, in part because it promised an amnesty for those involved in past outbreaks. Catalan autonomy, land reform, and anticlerical measures were the first order of business. Instead of entering the cabinet, Francisco Largo Caballero (1819-1946), leader of the left-wing socialists, now played at insurrection, acting as if he intended to seize power. *Pravda* hailed him as a new Lenin. Yet he had no forces of his own. The route to power for left-wing revolutionaries could open up only if the right attempted a military coup, if the government then armed the workers to fight it, and if the workers then won. The Spanish Communist party in 1936 emerged for the first time as a considerable element. The Communists' participation in the Asturias uprising and the Popular Front gained them political strength despite their numerical weakness (three thousand members). They were more moderate in their immediate aims than were the socialists, because they felt the need for a long period of Popular Front cooperation to increase their own power.

Simultaneously in 1936 the *Falange* (phalanx)

During the Spanish Civil War civilians armed themselves and threw up barricades in the streets. They were soon joined on both sides by volunteers from outside Spain.

emerged on the right—a party founded in 1932 by the son of Primo de Rivera, José Antonia (1903-1936), a fascist on the Italian pattern, who did not oppose agrarian reform or other socialist programs. The Falange used as its symbol a bunch of arrows and a yoke, and as its slogan, "*Arriba España*" ("Upward, Spain"). Its program called for national expansion in Africa, the annexation of Portugal, and the building of an empire in South America. It established youth groups and a private army, as Hitler had done. Although the Falange polled relatively few votes in the election of 1936, it worked with army, monarchist, clerical, and Carlist groups for a counterrevolution. Everyone knew a military coup against the government was in the offing. In July it came, under the leadership of General Franco.

The Spanish Civil War (1936-1939) was the first act in the conflict that was to ripen into World War II. Decisively aided by Germany and Italy, Franco's forces pushed on to eventual victory, capturing the republican strongholds of Madrid and Barcelona in 1939. During the war the functions of the weak republican government were usurped by a series of workers' committees, and then a Popular Front regime under Largo Caballero came to office in September 1936. In government territory terror reigned, at first the work of anarchists, and after their suppression, of the communists, who—with Russia behind them—ruthlessly worked against their rival leftist parties in the regime. The right-wing rebels made Franco chief of staff in November 1936, and in their territory terror also took a heavy toll, as republicans were killed. After Franco's triumph the prisons were filled and the executioner was busy. The Spanish Civil War took half a million lives, proportionately as large a loss to Spain's potential leadership as that sustained by Britain in both world wars together.

For all its fascist trappings, the Franco regime still depended after the war upon the same classes that had supported the Spanish monarchy—the landowners, the army, and the Church. The new regime was opposed by the poor in city and country, but the fear of a new civil war, which lay heavily on all classes, prevented open opposition. Franco would rule until his death in 1975.

Portugal

In the meantime, any Falangist designs on Portugal were blocked by the rise to power there of another dictator, Antonio de Oliveira Salazar (1889-1970). Portugal had participated in World War I, and the republican regime, which had driven King Manoel II (reigned 1908-1910) from the country in 1910, governed, though erratically, until forced from office by a military coup in 1926. Two years later Salazar, a little-known professor of economics at the University of Coimbra, became minister of finance on the condition that he be granted sweeping powers over the economy. Salazar's concern for sound finance during the world economic crisis won him many supporters, and in 1932 he became prime minister and progressively used his office to turn his

Pablo Picasso's *Guernica* was an impassioned protest against the Spanish Civil War. Painted in 1937, it was kept from his native country by the artist and exhibited only in the United States until after the death of Franco, when it was finally returned to Spain as a gesture of healing between the opposing sides.

party into the only legal option open to the Portuguese people. Salazar sought to remain neutral in the growing European conflict, and his authoritarian rule, never decked out in the symbols and slogans of full-scale fascism, did not generate effective opposition from the political left. Salazar would step down, Portugal's empire overseas virtually intact, his dictatorship increasingly inert, in 1968.

V SUCCESSOR STATES TO THE HAPSBURG EMPIRE

The triumphs of the authoritarian right in one form or another in eastern Europe are explained partly by the lack of a parliamentary tradition; partly by the failure to solve grievous economic problems, especially after the worldwide depression of 1929; and partly by a popular fear of Bolshevism, sometimes deserved, but skillfully played upon by self-interested leaders. Perhaps as important as all the other factors put together was the initial impression created by the successes of Mussolini and Hitler. The way to succeed, at least after 1935, seemed to be to put on a uniform, proclaim a doctrine of extreme nationalism, and launch a war of nerves against opponents and neighbors by threatening to use violence.

Austria

The Austria that was left at the end of World War I had an almost purely German population of about eight million, about two million of whom lived in Vienna.

Long the market for an enormous hinterland and the supplier of industrial finished goods to the agricultural provinces, Vienna was now cut off from its former territories by political boundaries and tariff walls. Between 1922 and 1925 Austrian finances were under direct League of Nations supervision; a League loan and reconstruction policies brought some recovery. But one possible road to economic salvation—union of Austria with Germany—though voted by the assembly of the new Austrian republic in March 1919, was forbidden on political grounds by the Allies in the Treaty of St. Germain (September 1919).

These two problems, economic survival and union with Germany, were complicated by the continuation in even more violent form of the basic political struggle of imperial Austria between Social Democrats and Christian Socialists. The Social Democrats were a moderate Marxist party with strong urban support, especially in Vienna itself. The Christian Socialists were a conservative clerical party with a mass following in the countryside and among the urban lower middle classes and counted many priests among their leaders.

In the midtwenties the two hostile parties, usually almost evenly balanced in the parliament, organized private armies: the Christian Socialists, the *Heimwehr* (home guard), and the Social Democrats, the *Schutzbund* (defense league). The Social Democrats governed Vienna, introducing measures for relief and for workers' housing, paid for by taxes on the rich. After 1930, when a treaty was signed with Italy, Mussolini supported the Christian Socialists, who grew more fascistic in their outlook. The failure of Brüning's plan for a customs union with Germany and the related collapse of the

Vienna Kredit-Anstalt bank increased tensions in 1931, and in September 1931 the Heimwehr tried its first coup, which failed. Efforts in 1932 to organize a Danubian economic cooperation scheme—an alternative to Austrian union with Germany, and favored by France—were rendered futile by Italian and German opposition. After Hitler came to power in early 1933, many Christian Socialists openly became Nazis.

The Christian Socialist chancellor, Engelbert Dollfus (1892-1934), however, strove to curb the Nazis. To this end he suspended parliamentary government in March 1933, in effect ending parliamentary democracy. He forbade the wearing of uniforms by political groups and tried to expel Nazi agitators. In retaliation, Hitler made it prohibitively expensive for German tourists to visit Austria and thus destroyed one of the most lucrative sources of Austrian income. In the face of Nazi-inspired disorder, Dollfus banned the Nazi party (June 1933). But he also attacked the Social Democrats, banning all parties except his own Fatherland Front, a union of all rightwing groups except the Nazis. A raid on Social Democratic headquarters precipitated a workers' riot. The government then bombarded the workers' new apartment houses in which the Social Democratic leaders had taken refuge (February 1934), breaking the Social Democratic party but alienating the workers of Vienna and uniting them in opposition to the regime. Dollfus had to depend on Italy to support him against the threat from Hitler. After he established himself as a fascist dictator (April 30, 1934), the Nazis assassinated him, and only Italian troop concentrations on the frontier prevented Hitler from taking Austria.

Dolfus's successor, Kurt von Schuschnigg (1897-1981), was committed to the same policies. But Mussolini now needed Hitler's support for Italian aggression in the Mediterranean. Schuschnigg planned a Hapsburg restoration, tried to concentrate armed power in his own hands rather than those of the Heimwehr, and strove to come to an understanding with France and its allies to replace the tie with Italy. But he failed. To stave off violence he had to make concessions to Artur Seyss-Inquart (1892-1946), leader of the Austrian Nazis, and then humble himself by visiting Hitler at his Bavarian mountain retreat at Berchtesgaden. Hitler threatened full-scale invasion, and Schuschnigg agreed to bring the Nazi party into the Fatherland Front and to pursue the foreign policy goals dictated by Hitler. He also agreed to make Seyss-Inquart minister of the interior, the ideal position from which to direct a coup.

When Schuschnigg returned to Vienna, he realized that he had surrendered Austria, and he called for a sudden plebiscite, desperately hoping to win working-class support. This forced Hitler's hand. On March 2 he invaded Austria, even against the advice of Seyss-Inquart, and proclaimed his native land a province of Germany. In April a plebiscite on Austrian union with Germany—called *Anschluss*—resulted in a 99.75 percent yes vote.

Hungary

On October 31, 1918, eleven days before the armistice, Count Michael Károlyi (1895-1955) became prime minister of Hungary, after that country had severed its ties with Austria. One of the richest of the great landed nobles, Károlyi was also a democrat. He proved his sincerity as a social reformer by handing over the fifty thousand acres of his own estate to be divided among the peasants, and by preparing a land-reform law. He made every effort to reach a compromise with the national minorities, but they were past the point where they would trust any Magyar. The French commander of the Allied armies demanded that the Hungarians withdraw from Slovakia. In March 1919 Károlyi resigned in protest over the loss of Transylvania.

Thwarted nationalism now combined with a growing radicalism, stimulated by the news of Bolshevik activities in Russia brought by returning Hungarian prisoners of war. A left-wing government took over, dominated by Béla Kun, Lenin's agent, a Hungarian-born Jew. He put through revolutionary nationalization decrees and installed a soviet political system by terrorist methods, especially in the countryside, where the peasants resented the delay in giving them land. The Allies could not tolerate a Bolshevik in Hungary. The Romanians invaded and drove Kun out; during 1919 and part of 1920 they occupied the country and stripped it of everything they could move. Meanwhile, under French protection, a counterrevolutionary government returned to Budapest, where Admiral Nicholas Horthy (1868-1957), a member of the gentry, became regent and chief of state in March 1920. Hungary was now a kingdom without a king, Horthy an admiral without a fleet. Twice the Hapsburg king Charles tried to regain the throne, but was frustrated largely because Hungary's neighbors objected. The new counterrevolution gave free rein to a White Terror directed largely against Jews, but also against Magyar workers and peasants.

The Treaty of Trianon (June 1920) confirmed Hungary's losses: a small strip of land to Austria, Transylvania to Romania, Slovakia to Czechoslovakia, and Croatia and other Serb and Croat territories to Yugoslavia. Thereafter, the most important political issue for the ruling groups in Hungary was *revisionism*, the effort to revise the treaty and get these lands back. The national motto was now "*Nem, nem, soha*" ("No, no, never").

Most Hungarians, however, who had never cared much about the nationalist questions that had agitated the upper classes, also cared relatively little about revisionism. Hungary had no land reform; the great estates remained intact; nobles and gentry remained dominant. Behind a screen of parliamentary government, an authoritarian dictatorship governed the country for the old ruling groups. It was helped by a swollen bureaucracy, and it became more and more fascist in character as the years went by. In 1927 a treaty with Italy began a close association between Hungary and Mussolini.

ROMANTIC NATIONAL SOCIALISM

One of the most influential fascists in eastern Europe was Ferencz Szalasi (1897-1946), a leading National Socialist in Hungary and an officer on the army general staff. In 1936 he summarized the Hungarian fascist position in a manner that well illustrates the sometimes illogical nature of the fascist movement. Communism claimed to be rigorously logical; fascism, on the other hand, admitted to being vigorously and romantically directed to the emotions:

Hungarism is an ideological system. It is the Hungarian practice of the national socialistic view of the world and time spirit. Not Hitlerism, not fascism, not antisemitism, but Hungarism.

Thus Hungarism means socialism, the tuning together of the moral, spiritual, and material interests of the I and the Us. It has set as its aim not the happiness of the particular privileged individuals or classes, but of the totality of individuals and classes. But Hungarism at the same time also means national socialism, because it fights for the happiness of the most natural community of the people, for the welfare of the nation, and through this of every working individual. . . .

Beside all this, Hungarism is the protector of all the members of its national family who are strewn all over the world and have been forced out by the need to earn a livelihood. Its right and duty is their repatriation into the Great Fatherland. . . .

During history three totalities have developed, first successively and later parallel to each other and strengthening each other. Their common feature is that they demand unconditional obedience, each representing a most ancient dictatorship within a closed society. The oldest is the military totality. Later came the totality of the Church. And after that the economic totality of the leaders of economic life—mainly Jews. Thus morality, spirit, and material things have separately found their most typical representatives, they have progressed separately, but in their great decisions we always find them together.

In national socialism, however, the fourth totality was born: the totality of the nation. This is the most perfect totality, because it can unite the others. . . .

National socialism is the expert of peace, of everybody's peace. Its executor: the Nation. . . .

The socialism of liberalism is capital socialism, the socialism of Marxism is state socialism, while the socialism of the social-national is national socialism. In liberalism the state serves the individual, the individual serves capital; in Marxism the individual serves the state and the state serves capital; while in the social-national capital serves the state, the state serves the nation, and the moral, spiritual, and material interests and values of the national community serve without exceptions for the good and benefit of its every member. . . .

Ferencz Szalasi, *Ut es Cél*, trans. Anne M. Sail (Budapest, 1936), quoted in Eugen Weber, ed., *Varieties of Fascism* (New York: D. Van Nostrand, 1964), pp. 157-61.

While the Italians supplied arms to the Hungarians, Hitler favored Hungarian revisionism along with his own. After Austria had fallen to Hitler, he had Hungary in his pocket, and when he broke up Czechoslovakia in March 1939, the Hungarians seized the extreme eastern portion, Ruthenia, and a small part of Slovakia. To pursue revisionism, the Hungarians had to follow Hitler, since he alone offered the opportunity to redraw the map as they felt it should be drawn; so before war broke out, they had withdrawn from the League of Nations and had enacted anti-Semitic laws in the Nazi pattern. But because Hitler needed Romania too, he would not give the Magyars all of Transylvania. The price they paid for advocating revisionism between the wars was the Soviet-dominated regime installed in Hungary after World War II.

Yugoslavia

In the new Kingdom of the Serbs, Croats, and Slovenes, proclaimed in December 1918, there came together for the first time in one state the former south-Slav subjects of Austria and Hungary with those of the former Kingdom of Serbia. This was in most respects a satisfactory state from the territorial point of view; revisionism therefore was not a major issue. But the new state had to create a governmental system that would satisfy the aspirations of each of its nationality groups. Over this problem democracy broke down and a dictatorship was established. The dictatorship was not of the fascist type, although as German power grew important, Yugoslavian politicians became convinced that the future lay in Hitler's hands and responded accordingly. Most Yugoslavs were peasants deeply devoted to their local freedoms, and they opposed fascism, and, when they got the chance, ousted the politicians who sought to align them with it.

Serbian political ambitions had helped to start the war. The Serbs were more numerous than Croats and Slovenes together, and many Serbs felt that the new kingdom, which their Serbian king ruled from his Serbian capital of Belgrade, should be the "greater Serbia" of which they had so long dreamed. Orthodox in religion, using the Cyrillic alphabet, and having experienced and overthrown Ottoman domination, Serbs tended to look down on the Croats. Roman Catholic in religion, using the Latin alphabet, and having opposed Germans and Magyars for centuries, Croats tended to feel that the Serbs were crude Easterners who ought to give them a full measure of autonomy within the new state. The battle lines were drawn: Serb-sponsored centralism against Croat-sponsored federalism. The Slovenes were less numerous and more conciliatory, but the Serbs forced the acceptance of their answer to the constitutional question. This brought about dictatorship, alienating many Croats.

The Croats, under their peasant leader Stephen Radić (1871-1928), boycotted the constituent assembly of 1920, and the Serbs put through a constitution providing for a strongly centralized state. Both sides refused to compromise, and when Radić was murdered on the floor of parliament in June 1928, a crisis arose that ended only when King Alexander II (ruled 1921-1934) proclaimed a dictatorship in January 1929. Alexander tried to settle the problem by erasing old provincial loyalties. There would be no more Serbia or Croatia, but new administrative units named after the chief rivers that ran through them. The whole country was renamed Yugoslavia, as a sign that there were to be no more Serbs and Croats. But it was still a Serbian government, and the Croats would not forget it. Elections were rigged by the government, and all political parties were dissolved. Croat leaders spent much time in jail, and while this dictatorship of King Alexander passed no racial laws and had no colored shirts, it was unmistakably authoritarian.

One result was to strengthen Croat extremists who had wanted an independent Croatia in the days of the Hapsburgs, and who now combined this demand with terrorism, supported by the enemies of Yugoslavia—Italy and Hungary. The Croat extremists were called *Ustashi* (rebels), and they were assisted by Mussolini. The Ustashi were deeply involved in the assassination of Alexander during a state visit to France in October 1934. Under the regency of Alexander's cousin, the dictatorship continued. As German economic power in the Balkans grew, leading politicians turned more toward Germany, but popular opposition prevented an alliance. In the summer of 1939, on the very eve of war in Europe, an agreement was reached with the Croats that established an autonomous Croatia. But by then it was too late, for war soon engulfed the Balkans.

VI OTHER AUTHORITARIAN REGIMES

In Poland Marshal Josef Pilsudski (1869-1935) led a military coup against the democratic government in 1926 and headed a military dictatorship that became ever more authoritarian, especially after the depression. This coup was made possible largely because of the government's failure to grant concessions to Lithuanians and other national minorities and to deal with the economic problems left by the war and occupation. Tension was heightened when Germany denounced a trade treaty and precipitated a crisis in the Polish coal industry. The violent hatreds that divided the political parties made Pilsudski's rule even easier. Once he had won power, he turned to the great landowners and big industrialists, building his government on their support and on that of his military clique.

In Romania entrenched corruption in political life coexisted with the parliamentary system. There was also widespread anti-Semitism, which was adopted as the chief program of the Iron Guard, a Romanian Nazi party. Greenshirted and wearing small bags of Romanian soil around their necks, the Guard began to assassinate moderate politicians early in the 1930s. Economic dislocation and peasant misery, brought about by the worldwide agricultural depression, strengthened the Guard and other fascist groups. To head off a Guardist coup, King Carol II of Romania, who had returned from exile in 1930, installed his own fascist dictatorship in 1938. Although the Guardist leaders were "shot while trying to escape," Romania could not avoid German pressure. After Hitler had acceded to the Russian seizure of Romanian Bessarabia and northern Bukovina and had given Hungary northern Transylvania (August 1940), Carol had to abdicate, and Hitler's man took over with Iron Guard support.

In Bulgaria, always a strongly pro-Russian country, the threat of communism was a serious problem. Moreover, Bulgaria, like Hungary, was revisionist because of its failure to gain the Macedonian territory given by the peace treaties to Yugoslavia and Greece. The issue was made more intense by the presence of thousands of Macedonian refugees, who tended to join revolutionary terrorist societies. Bulgaria, which had no serious minorities problem, no rich landowners, no aristocracy, and no great industries, nonetheless produced political hostilities even more violent than those in countries where economic inequality prevailed; unparalleled ferocity marked its political life. In 1920-1923 a peasant politician, Alexander Stambolisky (1879-1923), gave the country a period of reasonably popular government. But even he curbed the press as he fought both Macedonian terrorists and communists. His imposition of high income taxes alienated the bourgeoisie, and his conciliatory policies toward Yugoslavia infuriated the army. In 1923 right-wingers murdered him and installed a strongly authoritarian regime. From then on communist plots, bombings, and Macedonian terrorist strife racked the country. After 1930 the Italian marriage of King Boris (r. 1918-1943) led to ties with Mussolini. In 1934 a military coup brought a group of army officers to power who installed a dictatorship of their own. But in 1936 King Boris, like Alexander of Yugoslavia and Carol of Romania, imposed a royal dictatorship, which lasted until his death during World War II.

In Greece between the wars, the main issues were whether the country should be a monarchy or a republic, and how to overcome the economic difficulties caused by the transfer of 1,250,000 Greeks from Turkey. On the constitutional question, the Greeks wavered, voting for a monarchy in 1920, for a republic in 1924, and for a monarchy again in 1935, always by enormous majorities. Economic dislocation strengthened communism among the refugees and in labor groups. Political instability was chronic, and the interwar period was punctuated by a series of coups, some by republican generals, some by monarchists, all more or less authoritarian. The last of these was the most fascist, General John Metaxas (1871-1941), who became dictator in August 1936. Metaxas abolished political parties, instituted censorship and political persecution of his opponents, launched a program of public works, and imitated the Nazis in other ways. But when the Italian invasion came from Albania in October 1940, Metaxas ordered resistance, which was the beginning of Greece's heroic showing in World War II.

None of these regimes in eastern Europe was fascist in the truest sense of the term. In Italy and Germany the regimes rested on considerable popular support, at least initially, even though that support was kept alive by propaganda. In eastern Europe, on the other hand, the dictatorships rested on the police, the bureaucracy, and the army, and not on the support of the masses. Most dictators (Franco was an exception) developed the cult of self. In some of these regimes racism was a genuine issue, in others a red herring. In most, but not all, Jews were systematically persecuted. While the various fascist states had much in common, they also differed, so that fascism never became the universalized international movement that communism explicitly aspired to become. Some authoritarian regimes learned techniques of control from the fascist states without copying all their policies, and the fascist and authoritarian creeds differed in their degree of mysticism and emphasis on duty,

bloodshed, and power. All arose from frightened, angry people, and the source of their anger often could be traced to World War I, to the point that World War II seemed but an extension of World War I, and the twenty years of crisis from 1919 to 1929 simply, as one writer called it, "the bit in between."

VII THE SOVIET UNION

Not all authoritarian regimes were fascist, of course, and perhaps only a few ever sought to be completely so. During the twenty-year crisis between the wars, an already authoritarian government in Russia became a virtual dictatorship, though one of the left rather than the right. The apparent success of this dictatorship, especially under Joseph Stalin (1879-1953), intensified the trend toward authoritarianism on the Continent, both because tight controls over all aspects of human life appeared, for the moment, to be working, and because the right-wing dictatorships were girding themselves for what they viewed as an inevitable conflict with international communism. Stalin's policies cannot be understood outside the context of the events in Europe; equally, the reactions of Hitler and Mussolini, as well as Britain, France, and the United States, cannot be understood outside the context of their fear of Russian expansionism, now no longer territorial but presumably ideological.

From 1914 Russia had been in turmoil, first of war and then of revolution. By 1921, with the end of civil war, sanitation had broken down, famine was widespread, and class hatreds had reached unparalleled heights. Industry and agriculture were crippled, distribution was near a breakdown, and the communist regime was perilously near the loss of public support. When a large-scale anarchist revolt broke out early in 1921 and could not be suppressed until mid-1922, Lenin remarked that

THE IDEA OF CHARISMATIC LEADERSHIP

Hitler, Mussolini, and Stalin all emphasized the cult of personality, focusing national loyalties on themselves. With dramatic, widespread communications available through newsreel photography (and later through television), national leaders could thrust themselves into the limelight. In commentary accompanying a photograph of Mussolini playing the violin, one Italian nationalist writer, Francesco Sapori (1890-1964), wrote in *Amor di Patria*:

Imperial power lies in the flash of the eyes. Every word uttered by the soldier, the politician, or the father who loves his people is monumental; every gesture is conclusive. As a statesman his speeches suddenly become warm-hearted, he smiles in jest, and snaps out an order. He fences. He delicately touches his violin. He is at

the wheel of his favourite car; he likes driving fast. He pilots his own aircraft from one end of Italy to the other.

Quoted in Gillo Dorfles, *Kitsch: The World of Bad Taste* (New York: Universe Books, 1969), p. 123.

he was, at last, deeply frightened for the future of his nation. The mutiny of sailors at the Kronstadt naval base near Petrograd in March 1921 triggered a change in policy. The mutineers called for "soviets without communists," to be chosen by universal suffrage and secret ballot, for free speech and assembly, for the liberation of political prisoners, and for the abolition of grain requisitioning. Trotsky now realized that the proletariat itself was opposing the dictatorship of the proletariat and needed educating. Furthermore, revolution was not going to sweep Europe, for governments everywhere were already suppressing their local Bolsheviks. Russia would be, for a time, an island of revolutionary socialism in a sea of capitalism. Trotsky therefore used the Red Army to crush the rebellion as a showpiece of brutality, while Lenin embarked upon economic reform.

The Kronstadt mutiny led directly to the adoption of the New Economic Policy (always referred to by its initials as the NEP). But the underlying reason for the shift was the need for reconstruction, which seemed attainable only if militant communism were at least temporarily abandoned. Lenin himself referred to "premature" attempts at socialization. It was also necessary to appease the peasants and to avert any further major uprisings. Finally, since the expected world revolution had not taken place, the resources of capitalist states were badly needed to assist Russian reconstruction. The adoption of NEP coincided with the conclusion of an Anglo-Russian trade treaty. Abroad, NEP was optimistically hailed as the beginning of a Russian "Thermidor"—a return to normality like that following the end of the Terror in the French Revolution—though the moderation of policy was primarily strategic and temporary, and it rested on a return to the system of private trade that had developed in czarist Russia.

Under NEP the government stopped requisitioning the peasants' entire crop, taking instead only what was needed to meet the minimum requirements of the army, urban workers, and other non-farm groups. The peasants still had to pay a very heavy tax in kind, but they were allowed to sell the remainder of their crop—to the state if they wished, but to a private purchaser if they preferred. Peasant agriculture became in essence capitalist once more, and the profit motive reappeared. Lenin imitated Stolypin by guaranteeing the peasant permanency of tenure. Thus War Communism was abandoned. The whole system tended to help the rich peasant grow richer and to transform the poor peasant into a hired, landless laborer.

Elsewhere in the economy, under NEP the state retained what Lenin called "the commanding heights"—heavy industry, banking, transportation, and foreign trade. In domestic trade and in light industry, however, private enterprise was once more permitted. This was the so-called "private capital sector" of the economy, in which workers could be paid according to their output and factory managers could swap some of their products for raw materials.

Lenin himself described NEP as a partial return to capitalism and urged the communists to become good at business. Yet NEP was never intended as more than a temporary expedient. Lenin believed that it would take a couple of decades before the Russian peasant could be convinced that cooperative agriculture would be the most efficient. He also argued that a temporary relaxation of government intervention would increase industrial production and give the Russians a useful lesson in managerial skills.

Economic recovery was indeed achieved. By 1928 industrial and agricultural production was back at prewar levels. But NEP was bitterly disliked by leading communists, who were shocked at the reversal of all the doctrines they believed in. By 1924 private business accounted for 40 percent of Russian domestic trade, but thereafter the figure fell off. Those who took advantage of the opportunities presented by the NEP were known as NEPmen. They were often persecuted in a petty way by hostile officials, who tried to limit their profits, tax them heavily, and drag them into court on charges of speculation. The kulak had essentially the same experience. Thus the government often seemed to be encouraging private enterprise for economic reasons and simultaneously discouraging it for political reasons.

Within the Communist party, one group favored the increase of the private sector and the extension of NEP as a new road toward the socialist goal; these were the so-called "right deviationists." Their opponents favored the ending of such concessions, the liquidation of NEPmen and kulaks, and a return to Marxist principles at home and the fostering of world revolution abroad—in short, the pressing of the "socialist offensive"; these were the "left deviationists," who included Trotsky. In the center stood those who attacked both deviations: the right as an abandonment of communism, the left as likely to disrupt the worker-peasant alliance.

The Struggle for Power: Stalin against Trotsky, 1921-1927

But NEP was not the only question to agitate communist leaders in the early twenties. Lenin died in January 1924. During the last two years of his life, he played an ever-lessening role. Involved in the controversy over NEP was also the question of succession to Lenin. Thus an answer to the questions of how to organize industry, what role to give organized labor, and what relations to maintain with the capitalist world depended not only upon an estimate of the actual situation but also upon a guess as to what answer was likely to be politically advantageous. From this maneuvering the secretary of the Communist party, Joseph Stalin, was to emerge victorious by 1928.

The years between 1922 and 1928, especially after Lenin's death, saw a desperate struggle for power between Stalin and Trotsky. Lenin foresaw this struggle with great anxiety. He considered Trotsky abler, but feared that he was overconfident; he knew that Stalin had concentrated enormous power in his hands through his role as party secretary, and he feared that he did not know how to use it. When he learned that Stalin had disobeyed his orders in smashing the Menshevik Republic of Georgia instead of reaching an accommodation with its leaders, he wrote angrily that Stalin should be removed from his post as general secretary. At the moment of his death, Lenin had published a scathing attack on Stalin and had broken off relations with him.

During these years Trotsky argued for a more highly trained managerial force in industry and for economic planning as an instrument that the state could use to control and direct social change. He favored the mechanization of agriculture and the weakening of peasant individualism by encouraging rural cooperatives. As Trotsky progressively lost power, he championed the right of individual communists to criticize the regime. He also concluded that only through the outbreak of revolutions in other countries could the Russian socialist revolution be carried to its proper conclusion. Only if the industrial output and technical skills of the advanced Western countries could be put at the disposal of communism could Russia hope to achieve its own socialist revolution; socialism could not succeed within just one country. Either world revolution must break out or Russian socialism was doomed to failure.

The opponents of Trotsky's "left deviation" found their chief spokesman in Nikolai Bukharin (1888-1938), the extremely influential editor of *Pravda*. A strong defender of NEP, Bukharin softened the rigorous Marxist doctrine of the class struggle by arguing that, since the proletarian state controlled the commanding heights of big capital, socialism was sure of success. This view was not unlike the gradualist position taken by western European Social Democrats. Bukharin did not believe in rapid industrialization; he favored cooperatives, but opposed collectives in which (in theory) groups of peasants owned everything collectively (as, it was argued, most preindustrial and precolonial African societies did). In foreign affairs, he was eager to cooperate abroad with noncommunist groups who might be useful to Russia. Thus he sponsored Soviet collaboration with China and with the German Social Democrats.

In his rise to power Stalin used Bukharin's arguments to discredit Trotsky; then, partly because Bukharin's policies were failing, he adopted many of Trotsky's policies and eliminated Bukharin. Original Stalinist ideas, however, developed during this process. Stalin was not basically a theoretician; he was a party worker. He adopted theoretical positions partly because he thought they would work and partly because he was charting his own course to supreme power. He came to favor rapid industrialization and to understand that this meant an unprecedentedly heavy capital investment. At the end of 1927 he shifted from his previous position on the peasantry and openly sponsored collectivization, since agricultural production was not keeping pace with industry. He declared that agriculture, like industry, must be transformed into a series of large-scale unified enterprises.

Against Trotsky's argument that socialism in one country was impossible, Stalin maintained that an independent socialist state could exist. This view did not imply abandoning the goal of world revolution, for Stalin maintained that the one socialist state (Russia) would inspire and assist communist movements everywhere. But, in his view, during the interim before the communists won elsewhere, Russia could still exist as the only socialist state. In international relations, this doctrine allowed the Soviet Union to pursue a policy of "peaceful coexistence" with capitalist states when that seemed most useful, or a policy of militant support of communist revolution everywhere when that seemed desirable. Stalin's "socialism in one country" also heartened Russian communists, who were disappointed by the failure of revolutions elsewhere. It also meant that Russia, not the West, was to be the center of the new society. Stalin's doctrine reflected his own Russian nationalism, rather than the more cosmopolitan and more Western views of Trotsky. It was Stalin, not Trotsky, who would triumph.

At the end of the civil war, Stalin was commissar of nationalities. In this post he dealt with the affairs of 65,000,000 of the 140,000,000 inhabitants of the new Russian Soviet Republic. He managed the destiny of the Asians, whom he, as one of them, understood. Their local Bolshevik leaders became his supporters; where they did not, as in his native Georgia, he ruthlessly crushed them. Though a Georgian, he identified himself with Russian nationalism in the interests of a centralized Bolshevik state.

Stalin took charge of creating the new Asian "republics," which enjoyed a degree of local self-government, programs of economic and educational improvement, and a chance to use their local languages and develop their own cultural affairs, so long as these were communist managed. In 1922 Stalin proposed the new Union of Socialist Soviet Republics as a substitute for the existing federation of republics. In the USSR, Moscow would control war, foreign policy, trade, and transport, and would coordinate finance, economy, food, and labor. In theory, the republic would manage home affairs, justice, education, and agriculture. A Council of Nationalities, with an equal number of delegates from each ethnic group, would join the Supreme Soviet as a second chamber, thus forming the Central Executive Committee, which would appoint the Council of People's Commissars—the government. Stalin regarded this administrative transformation as an achievement equal to Trotsky's creation of the Red Army.

Stalin was also commissar of the Workers' and Peasants' Inspectorate. Here his duties were to eliminate inefficiency and corruption from every branch of the civil service and to train a new corps of civil servants. His teams moved freely through all the offices of the government, observing and recommending changes. In creating this post Lenin had hoped to clean house, but the same ignorance and the lack of tradition that rendered the czarist and Bolshevik civil service incompetent and

In the early years of the revolution, Russian adults were taught to read, write, and do arithmetic.

corrupt persisted in Stalin's Inspectorate. Although the Inspectorate did not do what it was established to do, it did give Stalin control over thousands of bureaucrats and thus over the machinery of government. Lenin attacked Stalin's work in the Inspectorate just before he died, but by then it was too late.

Stalin was also a member of the *Politburo*—the tight little group of party bosses elected by the Central Committee, which included only five men throughout the civil war. Here his job was day-to-day management of the party. He was the only permanent liaison officer between the Politburo and the *Orgburo*, which assigned party personnel to their various duties in factory, office, or army units. Besides these posts, Stalin became general secretary of the party's Central Committee in 1922. Here he prepared the agenda for Politburo meetings, supplied the documentation for points under debate, and passed the decisions down to the lower levels. He controlled party patronage—all party appointments, promotions, and demotions. He saw to it that local trade unions, cooperatives, and army units were under communists responsible to him. He had files on the loyalty and achievements of all managers of industry and other party members. In 1921 a Central Control Commission, which could expel party members for unsatisfactory conduct, was created; Stalin, as liaison between this

commission and the Central Committee, now virtually controlled the purges, which were designed to keep the party pure.

In a centralized one-party state, a man of Stalin's ambitions who held so many key positions had an enormous advantage in the struggle for power. Yet the state was so new, the positions so much less conspicuous than the Ministry of War, held by Trotsky, and Stalin's manner so often conciliatory that the likelihood of Stalin's success did not become evident until it was too late to stop him. Inside the Politburo he formed a three-man team with two other prominent Bolshevik leaders: the demagogue Gregory Zinoviev (1883-1936) and the expert on doctrine Leo Kamenev (1883-1936). Zinoviev was chairman of the Petrograd Soviet and boss of the Communist International; Kamenev was Lenin's deputy and president of the Moscow Soviet. All three were old Bolsheviks, in contrast to Trotsky, who had been a Menshevik and an independent member of the intelligentsia.

The combination of Stalin, Zinoviev, and Kamenev proved unbeatable. The three used the secret police to suppress all plots against them. They resisted Trotsky's demands for reform, which would have democratized the party to some degree and would have strengthened his position while weakening Stalin's. They initiated the cult of Lenin immediately before his death and kept it burning fiercely thereafter, so that any suggestion for change coming from Trotsky seemed an act of impiety. They dispersed Trotsky's followers by sending them to posts abroad. They prevented the publication of Lenin's "testament," so that the rank and file of the party would not know Lenin's doubts about Stalin. They publicized all Trotsky's earlier statements in opposition to Lenin and revised history to diminish Trotsky.

Early in 1925 Stalin and his allies forced Trotsky to resign as minister of war. Soon thereafter the three-man team dissolved; Stalin allied himself with Bukharin and other right-wing members of the Politburo, to which he began to appoint his own followers. Using all his accumulated power, he beat his former allies on all questions of policy, and in 1926 they moved into a new but powerless alliance with Trotsky. Stalin now deposed Zinoviev from the Politburo, charging him with plotting in the army. Next, Trotsky was expelled from the Politburo, and Zinoviev was ousted as president of the Comintern. In December 1927 a Communist party congress expelled Trotsky from the party and exiled him to Alma Ata in Central Asia, from where he fled abroad. Stalin had won.

Mobilizing the Nation, 1928–1940

The Communist party congress also ended NEP and proclaimed that the new "socialist offensive" would begin in 1928. The thirteen years between 1928 and 1941 were to see massive changes in Russian life—

collectivized agriculture, rapid industrialization, forced labor, great purges, the extermination of all political opposition, the building of an authoritarian state apparatus, and a return of bourgeois standards in almost every aspect of social and intellectual life.

In 1928 the failure of the peasants to deliver as much grain to the cities as was required underlined the dangers inherent in the land divisions of 1917 and in the concessions of NEP. Farm productivity on the small individual holdings was not high enough to feed the city population. Food was expensive, yet the kulaks wanted more land. Grain was hoarded. The government economic plan issued during 1928 set a figure of 20 percent of Russian farms as the maximum to be collectivized by 1933. Yet during 1929 Stalin embarked on immediate full-scale collectivization, declared war on the kulaks, and virtually ended individual farming in Russia.

The government did not have the money or the credit to import food and had no governmental machinery to force farmers to part with food that they were hoarding. Therefore, the government enlisted on its side the small peasants; in exchange for their assistance in locating and turning over the kulaks' crops, the peasants were promised a place on a collective farm to be made up of the kulaks' land and equipped with the kulaks' implements. The kulaks, Stalin declared in late 1929, were to be liquidated as a class. There were about two million households of them, perhaps as many as ten million people in all. Their lands were now to be totally expropriated, and at the same time, they were to be barred from joining the new collectives. Since no provision was

Russian peasants carried banners in support of Stalin's program that demanded liquidation of the kulaks as a class. A group of peasants is shown here initiating the new planting season at their collective farm in 1931.

made for them, this move turned collectivization into an economic and social nightmare.

Peasants were machine-gunned into submission; kulaks were deported to forced labor camps or to desolate regions in Siberia. In desperate revolt the peasants burned crops, broke plows, killed and ate their cattle rather than turn them over to the state, and fled to the cities. More than half the horses in all Russia, 45 percent of the cattle, and two-thirds of the sheep and goats were slaughtered. Land lay uncultivated, and over the next few years millions died of famine. As early as March 1930 Stalin showed that he was aware of the incredible mistakes he had made, and he blamed local officials who, he said, had been too eager to rush through the program. Still, 50 percent of Russian farms had been hastily thrown together into collectives during that year. Only 10 percent more were added during the next three years, so that by 1933 a total of 60 percent had been collectivized. The number rose again, and by 1939 more than 96 percent of Russian farms had been collectivized.

The drive in industry was closely related to the drive in agriculture. Here too Stalin originally had scorned the grandiose plans of the "superindustrializers," and as late as 1927 had proposed an annual increase in industrial production of only 15 percent. But just as he stepped up the frantic pace of collectivizing agriculture, so at first gradually, then suddenly, he shifted to forced draft in industry also. In 1928 the era of five-year plans began, each setting ambitious goals for production over the next five years. In 1929 and 1930 Stalin appropriated ever higher sums for capital investment, and in June 1930 he declared that industrial production must rise by 50 percent in that year. Under the first five-year plan, adopted in 1928, annual pig-iron production was scheduled to rise from 3,500,000 tons to 10,000,000 tons by 1932, but in that year Stalin demanded 17,000,000 tons instead. It was not produced, but Stalin's demand for it was symptomatic of the pace at which he was striving to transform Russia from an agricultural to an industrial country.

Part of the reason for this rapid pace lay in the collectivization drive itself. Large-scale farming, to which Stalin was committing Russia, must be mechanized farming. Yet there were only seven thousand tractors in all Russia at the end of 1928. Stalin secured thirty thousand more during 1929, but industry had to produce millions of machines plus the gasoline to run them. Since the countryside had to be electrified, power stations were needed by the thousands. Millions of peasants had to be taught how to handle machinery. But there was no one to teach them and no factories to produce the machinery.

Another reason for the drive to industrialize lay in the tenets of Marxism itself. Russia had defied all Marx's predictions by staging a proletarian revolution in a country that lacked a proletariat. Yet despite the communists' initial political successes, Stalin felt that capitalism had a firmer basis than communism in Russia, so long as it remained a country of small peasants.

And so the communists were determined to create, as a support for themselves, that massive Russian urban proletariat which did not yet exist. Stalin was determined to make Russia as nearly self-sufficient as possible, in line with his theory of socialism in one country. Underlying all this was a motive at least as intense as any dictated by Marxist doctrine—Russian nationalism.

The goals of the first five-year plan were not attained, although fulfillment was announced anyway in 1932. Immediately, the second plan, prepared by the state planning commission, went into effect and ran until 1937; the third was interrupted by Hitler's invasion. Each plan emphasized the elements of heavy industry—steel, electric power, cement, coal, oil. Between 1928 and 1940 steel production was multiplied by four and one-half, electric power by eight, cement by more than two, coal by four, and oil by almost three. Similar developments took place in chemicals and in machine production. Railroad construction was greatly increased, and the volume of freight carried quadrupled with the production of Russia's own rolling stock. By 1940 Russian output was approaching that of Germany. What the rest of Europe had done in about seventy-five years, Russia had done in about twelve. Enthusiasm was artificially whipped up by widely publicizing the high output of individual workers, called Stakhanovites after a coal miner who had set production records. "Stakhanovites" and "heroes of labor" were richly rewarded, and others were urged to imitate them.

All this was achieved at the cost of dreadful hardship, yet eyewitnesses report that many workers were as enthusiastic as if they had been soldiers in battle. Valuable machinery was often damaged or destroyed by inexperienced workers. The problems of repair, of replacement, of achieving balance between the output and consumption of raw materials, of housing workers in the new centers, of moving entire industries thousands of miles into the Urals and Siberia were unending and cost untold numbers of lives. An American eyewitness estimated that Russia's "battle of ferrous metallurgy alone involved more casualties than the battle of the Marne."

Administratively, the Russian economy was run by the state. The *Gosplan*, or state planning commission, drew up the five-year plans and supervised their fulfillment at the management level. The *Gosbank*, or state bank, regulated the investment of capital. An economic council administered the work of various agencies; its major divisions were metallurgy and chemistry, defense, machinery, fuel and power, agriculture and procurements, and consumer goods. Production trusts controlled the mines, blast furnaces, and rolling mills; these were the so-called *combinats*, or great production complexes. In each plant the manager was responsible for producing the quota set within the maximum cost allowed.

The social effects of this economic program were dramatic. Urban population rose from about 18 percent in 1926 to about 33 percent in 1940. The largest cities,

STALIN ON RUSSIA'S NEED TO CATCH UP

The strength of Stalin's motives is revealed in a speech that he made in 1931:

To slacken the pace means to lag behind, and those who lag behind are beaten. We do not want to be beaten. No we don't want to. . . . Old Russia . . . was ceaselessly beaten for her backwardness. She was beaten by the Mongol Khans, she was beaten by Turkish Beys, she was beaten by Swedish feudal lords, she was beaten by Polish-Lithuanian gentry, she was beaten by Anglo-French capitalists, she was beaten by Japanese barons; she was beaten by all—for her backwardness. For military backwardness, for cultural backwardness, for political backwardness, for industrial backwardness, for agricultural backwardness. She was beaten because to beat her was profitable and went unpunished. . . . We are fifty or a hundred years behind the advanced countries. We must make good this lag in ten years. Either we do it or they crush us.

Quoted in Isaac Deutscher, *Stalin* (New York: Mentor, 1950), p. 328.

Moscow and Leningrad (the new name for Petersburg-Petrograd after the death of Lenin), almost doubled in size, and among smaller cities, for example, Alma Ata grew from 45,000 to 230,000 between 1928 and 1939. The entire demographic picture was radically altered.

The relative freedom to choose one's job that had marked the NEP disappeared. Individual industrial enterprises signed labor contracts with the collectives by which a given number of farm workers were obliged to go to the factories, often against their will. Peasants who resisted collectivization were drafted into labor camps. In the factories the trade unions became an organ of the state. The chief role of the unions was to achieve maximum production and efficiency, to discourage absenteeism and poor work. Trade unions could not strike or quarrel with management, though they could administer the social insurance laws and negotiate to improve workers' living conditions.

Thus, Stalin set himself against the old Bolshevik principles of equality. The Marxist slogan, "From each according to his capacity, to each according to his needs" was shelved in favor of a new one, "From each according to his capacity, to each according to his work." Where Lenin had allowed none of the members of the government to earn more than a skilled laborer, Stalin set up a new system of incentives. A small minority of bureaucrats, skilled laborers, factory managers, and successful collective bosses earned vastly more than the unskilled laborers and peasants. Together with the writers, artists, musicians, entertainers, and athletes who lent their talents to the service of the regime, these people—generally men—became a new elite. They had a vested interest in furthering a regime to which they owed everything. The old privileged class of noble landlords, already weakened at the time of the revolution, had ceased to exist. The industrial, commercial, and financial bourgeoisie, which was just coming into its own at the time of the revolution, was destroyed after 1928, despite the temporary reprieve it had experienced under NEP. Most of the old intelligentsia, who had favored a revolution, could not in the end accept Stalin's dictatorship, and many of them emigrated. Those who remained were forced into line with the new Soviet intelligentsia, which Stalin felt to be a very important class. All were compelled to accept Stalinist dogma and to drop their interest in the outside world. They were expected to concentrate on technical advances and on new administrative devices for speeding the transformation of the country; that is, they were to be "social engineers," high-level bureaucrats, propagandists for the new society who did not question its basic tenets or its direction.

After 1928, therefore, the logic of Stalin's policies forced a systematic mobilization of thought that in time virtually became thought control. Marx had assumed that a radical change in human nature was possible by conditioning of the social environment. Lenin recognized, however, that the new socialist society presumed the existence of a "new man" and "new woman," who would have to be created as part of the revolution. Industrialization and the collectivizing of agriculture could work only if unproductive speculation gave way to applied thinking directed to the needs of the state; this was particularly so in economics, philosophy, and psychology, but history and literature must also be transformed. To transform them, they must be controlled.

Russia was noted for its economists, whose support was essential to give credibility to the NEP. Some economists felt that the potential scope of state planning was severely limited; others thought total planning possible; some were optimistic about how fast industrialization could proceed; others were pessimistic. Those whose arguments were contrary to the political needs of Stalin were accused of trying to undermine the first five-year plan, and one, Vladimir Groman (1873-1957), who had played a major role in Gosplan, was jailed in 1931. Though Stalin had attacked only the economists for their failure to keep pace with practical successes, the philosophers quickly understood his message and also turned to the practical application of philosophy to social problems, eager to eliminate any Menshevik errors of thought and to provide a philosophical defense for the policies of the Communist party.

Before the revolution Russian psychology had been widely influenced by the subjectivist school. But Freudian teachings could not be allowed to prevail, for if socialism demanded that humanity be transformed by changes in the environment, then the unconscious and the subconscious must be ruled out. Soviet psychology therefore turned first to biology. Researchers such as Ivan Pavlov (1849-1936) emphasized how human behavior could be explained in terms of biological reflexes. Psychology also influenced education, and in time educators would argue that four factors determined behavior: heredity, environment, training, and self-training. Schools ceased trying to provide an environment in which the personality might develop and became institutions geared to turning out productive and loyal citizens.

But it was in literature and history and in their explicit censorship that the need to mobilize thought was most apparent. Lenin had felt that literature should, so long as the class struggle lasted, serve the purposes of propaganda. Because literature should not be a means of making money, the idea of the free artist was false. The state must "substitute for a literature which is hypocritically free, but in fact bound to the bourgeoisie, a literature that is really free and *openly* bound to the proletariat." Literature was important because it influenced people, not because it was a path to truth. Declaring that neutral art was impossible, the Central Committee of the party gave its full support to peasant writers. A series of industrial novels, as well as Five-Year Plan novels written to official dictation, sought to energize the people to higher productivity and pride. Maxim Gorky (1868-1936) became editor of a magazine on socialism, and he and others launched a series of histories of factories to focus attention on the nation's industrial triumphs.

History was to take communist partisanship as its guiding principle. At first non-Marxist historians were allowed to continue their work, but with the organization of the Institute of Red Professors (1921) and the Society of Marxist Historians (1925), Soviet historiography became increasingly intolerant of those who did not see history as a science or who continued to write of Peter as "the Great" or of Catherine II as other than a "dissolute and criminal woman." Nonetheless, as Stalin realized that world revolution was increasingly unlikely, and as the need for patriotism to meet Hitler's challenge became more evident, historians were able to return to writing of past figures who would give the Russian people a sense of pride. History, one of Russia's early Marxist historians had written, was "politics projected into the past."

Finally, to make thought control effective and thus change the environment, restrictions and ultimately censorship were necessary. In 1922 a review agency, the Chief Administration for the Preservation of State Secrets in the Press (or *Glavlit*, its Russian abbreviation),

was established to censor the press, manuscripts, photographs, radio broadcasts, lectures, and exhibitions. A subsection, begun in 1923, dealt with theater, music, and other arts. Glavlit placed an official in each publishing house, broadcasting studio, customs house, and so forth, to monitor how the law was being obeyed. Strictly speaking these officials did not censor; they made a preliminary judgment that was acted upon at a higher level. But their presence and the prospect of scrutiny by more powerful officials effectively limited freedom of expression. Some publications, such as the official newspaper of the Soviet, *Isvestiya*, were exempt from Glavlit, and the autonomous republics could establish their own Glavlits.

In an increasingly literate society of the kind Stalin intended, control over the press would prove to be even more important. The government encouraged the establishment of newspapers as a means of informing and educating the people to revolutionary socialism; by 1927 there were 1,105 newspapers and 1,645 periodicals in the Soviet Union; and by 1965 the number had grown to 6,595 and 3,833, respectively, in sixty-five languages. To control this vast outpouring, a decree of 1935 established the Telegraphic Agency of the Soviet Union (or *Tass*) as the central organ for information in the USSR. Until 1961 Tass held a monopoly over the distribution of all foreign information within the USSR and over all information that moved from one Soviet republic to another.

The Authoritarian State, 1931-1943

Stalin's program was not achieved without opposition. The crisis of 1931 and 1932, when industrial goals were not being met and starvation swept the countryside, created discontent inside the regime as well as outside. A few officials circulated memoranda advocating Stalin's removal as general secretary, an act that the party had the right to perform. Stalin jailed them for conspiracy, and one leading Bolshevik committed suicide. Stalin's second wife reproached him at this time for the ravages that the terror was working, and she too committed suicide in 1932. Then, in December 1934, Sergei Kirov (1888-1934), who was rumored to be heir to Stalin's position, was assassinated in Leningrad, probably on Stalin's orders. Using Kirov's death as an excuse, Stalin purged the party of his opponents, having hundreds of Russians shot for alleged complicity in the killings and bringing his old colleagues Zinoviev and Kamenev to public trial in 1936. They and fourteen others either admitted involvement in Kirov's death or signed confessions fabricated for them; they were executed. In a second trial (1937), seventeen other leading Bolsheviks declared that they had knowledge of a conspiracy between Trotsky and the German and Japanese intelligence services by which Russian territory was to be transferred to Germany and Japan. All were executed. Then in June 1937 came the secret liquidation of the top commanders in the Red Army, who were accused of conspiring with "an unfriendly foreign power" (Germany) with a view to sabotage. All were executed after

MAKING LITERATURE "SOCIALLY USEFUL"

In 1928 the Central Committee of the Communist party sent a directive to all publishing houses requiring that writings generally be of a "socially useful character":

The publication of fiction is to be increased, especially of works on present-day themes and directed against bourgeois influences, philistinism, decadence, etc.

Mass-circulation books must be intelligible and accessible.

Such books must be an instrument for the mobilisation of the workers for the tasks of industrialisation and collectivisation.

Publishers should depend for the most part on Communist authors.

In 1931 the Chief Administration for the Preservation of State Secrets in the Press, known as *Glavlit*, was instructed to:

prohibit the issue, publication and distribution of works which
(a) contain agitation and propaganda against the Soviet regime and the dictatorship of the proletariat;

(b) disclose State secrets;
(c) arouse nationalistic and religious fanaticism;
(d) have a pornographic character.

Two years earlier *Glavlit* was authorized to inspect:

All production of the Press, photographic blocks, sets of type, matrices, sound recordings, gramophone records, cylinders, disks and sheets of music for automatic playing on musical instruments, metal counters and badges, coats-of-arms, banners with inscriptions, sculptured figures, bas-reliefs, photographs, films, photographic plates, negatives, light-sensitive paper, manuscripts, documents, plans, drawings, artistic pictures, and sheet music, both for import and export. . . .

Quoted in Robert Conquest, ed., *The Politics of Ideas in the U.S.S.R.* (New York: Praeger, 1967), pp. 34, 43–45.

an announcement that they had confessed. The last of the public trials took place in March 1938, as twenty-one leading Bolsheviks, including Bukharin, confessed to similar charges and were executed.

But these public trials and the secret trial of the generals provide only a faint idea of the extent of the purge that was now transformed into the period known as the Terror. Every member of Lenin's Politburo except Stalin and Trotsky was either killed or committed suicide to avoid execution. Two vice-commissars of foreign affairs and most of the ambassadors in the Soviet diplomatic corps, fifty of the seventy-one members of the Central Committee of the Communist party, almost all the military judges who had sat in judgment and had condemned the generals, two successive heads of the secret police, themselves the leaders in the previous purges, the prime ministers and chief officials of all the non-Russian Soviet Republics—all were killed or vanished.

Not since the days of the witchcraft trials or of the Inquisition—and then not on so grand a scale—had the test of political and ideological loyalty been applied to so many people, and not since the days of the French Revolution had so many died for failing the test. Arrests multiplied tenfold in 1936 and 1937. Anything was used as an excuse for an arrest: dancing too long with a Japanese diplomat, buying groceries from a former kulak, not reporting an Armenian nationalist neighbor.

People simply went out to work one day and did not return—killed or sent to one of many huge anonymous prisons, or banished to Siberia. Most academicians and writers took for granted periods of exile and prison as natural parts of the rhythm of life. A historian could fall from favor for describing Joan of Arc as nervous and tense just when the party line, taking its cue from communist leaders in France, wished her described as calm in the face of death. When a linguistic theory that held that all language derived from four sounds was accepted as official, professors who opposed this view had their books withdrawn. By 1938 at least one million Russians were in prisons, probably eight and a half million people had been arrested and most sent to prison camps and colonies, and perhaps seven hundred thousand Russians had been executed.

Stalin apparently wanted to destroy utterly all possibility of future conspiracies. So he trumped up charges against anyone who could conceivably become a member of a regime that might replace his own. Yet despite the enormous upheaval of the purges, the state did not break down. New bureaucrats were found to replace the old. New Stalin-trained officials filled all top-level positions, and terror had been enthroned as a principle of government, keeping all officials in constant fear for their lives and their jobs. In the end the purgers too were purged, used as scapegoats by Stalin for the Terror they had carried out at his command. Even Trotsky was pursued and killed. Having attacked Stalin from exile in his journal, *The Bulletin of the Opposition*, and having been blamed by Stalin for instigating hundreds of plots against him, Trotsky could not be left free, especially since he was now trying to create a Fourth International. In August 1940 an assassin tracked Trotsky down to his refuge in Mexico and killed him with an ax.

In the midst of the Terror in 1936 Stalin proclaimed a new constitution, the "most democratic in the world." By its provisions no one was disenfranchised, as priests and members of the former nobility and bourgeoisie had previously been. Civil liberties were extended on paper, though they could be modified in the "interest of the toilers." Because the USSR was a one-party state, elections were an expression of unanimity. The right to nominate candidates for the Supreme Soviet belonged to Communist party organizations, trade unions, cooperatives, youth groups, and cultural societies; but all were completely dominated by the party. The party picked the candidates, and no more than one for each post was presented to the voters. The party controlled the soviets, and the party hierarchy and government hierarchy overlapped and interlocked.

Every citizen could apply for membership in the party to a local branch, which voted on the application after a year of trial. Communist children's organizations fed the youth groups, which in turn fed the party. The party was organized both territorially and functionally in pyramid form, with organizations at the bottom level in factory, farm, and government office. These were grouped together by rural or urban local units, and these in turn by regional and territorial conferences and congresses. The party organizations elected the All-Union party congress, which selected the Central Committee of the party, which was in theory the highest policy-making organ, though actually no party congress was held between 1939 and 1954. The Central Committee selected the Politburo. At each level of the party pyramid there were organizations for agitation and propaganda (or "agitprop"), for organization and instruction, for military and political training. The party exercised full control over the government, which simply formally enacted whatever the party had decided upon. The five-year plans, for example, were party programs that went into effect even before they were formally adopted by the government.

The highest organ of the government was the Supreme Soviet, made up of two houses—a Soviet of the Union, based on population, and a Soviet of Nationalities, elected according to national administrative divisions. In theory the Supreme Soviet was elected for a term of four years. The Supreme Soviet itself did little; it appointed a presidium, which issued the decrees and carried on the work of the Supreme Soviet between sessions. It also appointed the Council of Ministers (long called the Council of People's Commissars). This cabinet, rather than the Supreme Soviet or its presidium, enacted most of the legislation and was thus both the legislative and the executive organ of the Russian state. Stalin was chairman of the Council of People's Commis-

sars and of the Politburo, and general secretary of the Communist party. He was also commissar of defense, chief of the State Defense Council, which ran the country during wartime, and supreme military commander.

With the new constitution in place and Stalin's enemies dead or intimidated, the late 1930s brought a softening of revolutionary fervor. Simultaneously with the purges and the new constitution, the bread ration was raised; individual farmers could own their homesteads; new medals and titles were awarded to leading workers in plants and to scientists, engineers, and military officers. In the Red Army, the traditional czarist distinctions between officers and men were restored, and marshals were named for the first time. The standard of living went up as the production of consumer goods was encouraged; and workers were invited to spend their earnings on small luxuries previously unavailable.

Simultaneously, the state rediscovered Russia's past. The standard communist teaching had been that proletarians have no fatherland; now officially controlled organs of opinion extolled love of country and hailed the heroes of the czarist era. The tarnished reputations of the great literary figures of the nineteenth century underwent a similar rehabilitation. Russian nationalism reached its climax during World War II, when the Marxist *Internationale* was dropped as the national anthem.

The early Bolsheviks had destroyed the old school system, abolished homework and examinations, and allowed children to administer the schools collectively with their teachers. Attendance fell off, the schools became revolutionary clubs of youngsters, and the training of teachers was neglected. The universities deteriorated, since anyone could enroll in them at age sixteen. Degrees were abolished, and technical training was stressed, to the exclusion of other subjects. Under NEP this chaotic situation was modified, and the basic problem of increasing literacy was tackled seriously. But the ordinary school curricula were replaced by heavy emphasis on labor problems and Marxist theory. The Communist party itself took over the universities, purged the faculties, and compelled the students to spend one week in three at work in factories.

Now this system again changed drastically. Training of teachers improved, their salaries were raised, and they were admitted to the civil service. The prerevolutionary system of admissions and degrees in the universities was restored, as was the prerevolutionary school curriculum. Emphasis on political education was reduced, and coeducation was abandoned. Tuition fees were restored for secondary schools, the Russian counterpart of the American high school or the French lycée. These fees made higher education difficult to obtain, except for children of the new elite or unusually talented students who won state scholarships. Literacy rose to about 90 percent, increasing the need for firm doctrinal control; nevertheless, such control could never be absolute, since all outside sources of information could not be controlled absolutely and at all times.

Very reluctantly Stalin came last of all to modify the traditional communist position on religion. Militant atheism had been the policy of the early Bolsheviks. Behind their attitude lay more than the standard Marxist feeling that religion was the opium of the masses; in Russia the Orthodox church had always been a pillar of czarism. Many years of attacks on religion, however, had failed to eradicate Orthodoxy from among the people. When in 1937 Hitler built a Russian church in Berlin and took every occasion to speak kindly of the Orthodox church, Stalin had to respond. Declaring that Christianity had contributed to past Russian glory, the government abated its antireligious propaganda and permitted church attendance again. While the early revolutionaries had attacked the family as the backbone of the discredited social order, Stalin rehabilitated the sanctity of marriage and emphasized the family and its growth. In 1943 Stalin received high churchmen; the government lowered taxes on church property, lifted the curfew for Easter, and appointed a new patriarch on whose subservience the regime could count.

Historians still debate the reasons for this relaxation in revolutionary intent, especially in the midst of the Terror. Stalin may have hoped to retain popular loyalty while purging the party, using these concessions as a counterbalance to the tense uncertainties of Soviet life. He may have been preparing for the expected attack from Germany; improved education in scientific and technical skills, the support of the church hierarchy against Hitler, and a growing birth rate all served the state. He was, without doubt, inconsistent, opportunistic, perhaps even irrational. Given the cult of leadership over which he presided, there was no one to demand reasoned explanations from him; such was his authoritarian state.

Karl Marx, who had scorned and disliked Russia, would have been confounded had he lived to see that agricultural land, almost without a proletariat, produce the only major European communist revolution. Perhaps Marx was wrong, or perhaps what happened in Russia was not a Marxist revolution at all. It seems clear that Marx did not correctly estimate the revolutionary force latent in the Russian peasantry. Since Marx died in 1883, he could not foresee the ultimate inadequacy of the czarist regime, the start of effective Russian industrialization, the extent of the tensions created by World War I, or the feebleness of the provisional government of 1917. But it also seems clear that, to bring the Bolsheviks to power, it took Lenin's recognition of the importance of the peasantry, his grasp of the immediate situation, his willingness to risk everything, and his good fortune at being in the right place at the right time with the right weapons.

On the other hand, the revolution was not wholly Marxist. Once the Bolsheviks were in power, it was natural that the real situations they faced would modify their Marxist-Leninist theories. When civil war and foreign intervention brought chaos, the deviation of NEP provided a necessary respite. Stalin combined Marxism, Russian nationalism, and ruthless politics in ways no one could have foreseen. Although it fell short of its goal, Stalin's program created an industrial state able to resist the blows that Hitler was to deal it. Servants of the state though they were, collectivized by force, industrialized by force, purged, terrorized, and struggling by the millions to exist in forced labor camps or to leave the country, the Russians in World War II nonetheless succeeded, with much help from the United States and other nations, in defeating Hitler and his allies.

How much of the loyalty of Russians to Stalin arose from the failure of the German invaders to treat them well, and how much of their support Hitler might have won with a different policy cannot be known. The Russians were facing a coalition of fascist states—Germany, Italy, Hungary, Romania, and others—pledged to the utter destruction of communism. These nations clashed in a war that brought to an end twenty years of uneasy peace, insecurity, and instability, to replace those years with another uneasy peace and new forms of insecurity and instability.

SUMMARY

The period from 1919 to 1945 was marked by the success of movements to the right. Although these movements were products of different societies, they had features in common: disillusionment with democracy for its failure to provide stability, aggressive nationalism, a sense of grievance, totalitarian government, and racism.

Fascism triumphed first in Italy after World War I. Mussolini, a socialist until the war, repudiated his old beliefs and shifted to militant nationalism. In a campaign of terror, Mussolini drove to power in the early 1920s. He established a fascist dictatorship, assuring his dominance by controlling the press and abolishing opposition parties.

Mussolini set up a corporative state in which the needs of labor and capital were subordinate to the interests of the state. Worker and producer syndicates had little real power or influence, which was held by the fascist bureaucracy. Mussolini pursued an aggressive foreign policy in the Mediterranean, Spain, Ethiopia, and Albania.

After World War I, Germany experienced fifteen years of democratic government under the Weimar Republic. However, Weimar Germany went through three distinct phases: in the first, which lasted from 1918-1923, political threats arose from the left and right, and the nation was in economic chaos; in the second, which lasted from 1924-

1929. Germany enjoyed political stability and relative economic prosperity; in the third, which lasted from 1929-1933, the right rose to power under Hitler, and economic depression cut the foundations from prosperity.

Hitler quickly established a dictatorship. He used the threat of a Bolshevik revolution to suspend constitutional government and build a strongly centralized state. He dissolved opposition political parties and crushed opponents within his own party. Once in power, Hitler embarked on a policy of eliminating Jews, and racism became a state policy. In foreign affairs, Nazi racist policies were extended to claiming lands inhabited by Germans.

In Spain, turmoil caused by divisions between left and right increased after the death of King Alfonso in 1931. During the Spanish Civil War (1936-1939), General Franco, aided by Italian and German forces, won a victory over the leftists. Franco established an authoritarian regime supported by landowners, the army, and the Church.

In Portugal, another dictator, Antonio Salazar, rose to power. In eastern Europe, the successor states to the Hapsburg Empire lacked parliamentary traditions. In the interwar period, authoritarian regimes were established in these nations.

After Lenin's death in 1924, a desperate power struggle unfolded in the Soviet Union between Stalin and Trotsky. Stalin used his strong base of support in the party to force Trotsky out of power. Under Stalin, an authoritarian regime of the left was intensified.

By 1928 Communists had rejected Lenin's New Economic Policy, which had aimed at reconstruction after the civil war. Between 1928 and 1941, Stalin imposed massive changes on Russian life: collectivization, industrialization, elimination of opponents, and a return to bourgeois standards in social and intellectual life.

By the late 1930s Stalin had mobilized writers and historians to use Russia's past to increase Russian nationalism. For by then, the Soviet Union faced a coalition of authoritarian fascist regimes pledged to exterminate communism.

chapter twenty-five

THE DEMOCRACIES AND THE NON-WESTERN WORLD

The central fact—and irony—of politics between the two world wars is that the war "to make the world safe for democracy" seemed to make it a very difficult and very dangerous place for democracy. Idealists like President Wilson had expected that the collapse of the Romanov, Hapsburg, and Hohenzollern empires would automatically ensure an increase in the number of democratic states. But, instead, much of Europe came under regimes that were hostile to liberal democracy. Even Italy, which had appeared to be evolving toward a democratic constitutional monarchy, turned fascist. In the 1920s and 1930s the core of democracy remained the great North Atlantic powers—Britain, France, and the United States—the smaller states of Scandinavia, the Low Countries, Switzerland, and the inheritors of the British tradition—Canada, Australia, and New Zealand. Certainly the totalitarian aggressors bore great responsiblity for the unleashing of a second world war. Yet a major factor in the deterioration of the twenty years' truce was the failure of the democracies to present a unified front against those who threatened world peace.

In the 1920s Britain, France, and the United States were preoccupied with domestic problems. In the early 1930s their preoccupation increased as a result of the urgent crisis of the depression. But this was the very time when international problems demanded equally urgent attention. International trade was steadily shrinking in response to the depression and mounting tariff barriers; the prospects for peace were steadily fading in response to resurgent and authoritarian nationalisms. Faced with two sets of problems, the democracies turned first to the domestic ones, only to discover that the international ones would not wait.

Nor was this all. During the twenty years' truce, the democracies faced a third set of problems, less urgent than the other two but of very great potential importance. This third set involved imperial issues—the relations between the democracies and the non-Western peoples, many of whom were still under colonial rule. Particularly in Asia and the Middle East, non-Western peoples were beginning to assert their nationalism and to demand the loosening of imperial ties. This formidable political movement did not reach full intensity until after World War II, when a long procession of former colonies, protectorates, and mandates began to join the ranks of independent states. But the non-Western nationalist movements grew steadily in the 1920s and 1930s.

I GREAT BRITAIN

The Postwar Economic Crisis, to 1921

Besides tragic human losses from the war, Great Britain's economic losses were grave—the incalculable difference between the actual cost of a destructive war and what would otherwise have been a peaceful, productive effort. The national debt after the war was ten times that of 1914. Many British investments abroad, returns on which had been a major factor in Victorian prosperity, had been liquidated to purchase food and war materials. Forty percent of the great British merchant fleet, the income from which had helped to balance Britain's international accounts and pay for her imports, had been destroyed by enemy action. The whole fabric of international trade on which Britain depended was torn in a thousand places in 1918 and could not be rapidly restored in the unsettled postwar world. And finally, to supplement British and French war production, the industrial plants of the United States, Canada, and India had been called on, and that stimulus made them more effective competitors of the British in peacetime. In addition, German industry, nourished in part by loans from America, once more took up the rivalry that had so alarmed the British before the war.

In short, the country that in Victorian days had been the "workshop of the world" had now lost its head start and could no longer provide full employment to its millions of workers. Those workers were in no mood to accept a lower standard of living, for they had made great gains in social security before the war. They had fought the war and won it in the expectation of still better things to come. They had been promised that the defeated enemy would pay the costs of the war and thereby give Britain a new start.

This hope was very early disappointed; no substantial reparations came through. The return to peace caused a sudden boom in production to meet the postwar demand for goods that had been denied to civilians in war time, which was accompanied by a sharp rise in prices and quickly followed by the collapse of the boom, leaving Britain in a severe postwar depression. By the summer of 1921 there were over two million people out of work, more than one-fifth of the labor force. Faced with the rising cost of living, the British government increased the very meager unemployment payments. These payments, soon scornfully called the dole, were strictly speaking not old-fashioned poor relief but payments on unemployment insurance policies that had been part of Lloyd George's prewar social legislation. However, large-scale unemployment continued (it did not drop below one million until World War II, and after that war it escalated again), and some young workers never found jobs. Unemployment insurance could not be maintained on a sound actuarial basis indefinitely, and the payments again became in fact a form of poor relief.

The British economic decline was not yet catastrophic, although some gravely depressed areas, like the coal-mining regions of South Wales, began to show signs of permanent decay. What happened generally, however, was a relative decline, the slowing down of an economy geared to dynamic growth, with a working population conditioned psychologically to a gradually rising standard of living and a middle class similarly conditioned to traditional comforts. Moreover, the tabloid newspaper, the movie, and the radio made the British well aware that Americans and others enjoyed automobiles, radios, refrigerators, and telephones, while they did not.

Britain was suffering from those ills characteristic of postindustrial development, and it was the first nation to do so. There was still a lot of coal in Britain, for example, but much of it was costly to mine, since the most easily and cheaply worked seams were being exhausted. The industry was badly organized, with many small and inefficient mines running at a loss and with machinery and methods that were antiquated in comparison with the newer American and continental mines. Productivity per work-hour over the whole industry was low. Worst of all, the 1920s saw the rapid rise all over the industrialized world of major competitors to coal—oil, and electricity based on water power—with a consequent decline of British coal exports. Since the British Isles had no petroleum (the discovery of oil fields under the North Sea lay in the future) and no very great potential in hydroelectric power, coal, the historic basis of British industrial power, simply had to be mined. But the workers were unionized and in no mood to accept cuts in wages, while owners did not want to run their businesses at a loss. A strike in March 1921, after the government had rejected Labour party proposals for making permanent the wartime nationalization of the coal industry, focused national attention on this problem. The strike was settled in July by the government's consenting to pay subsidies to cover increased wages.

The Conservative and Labour Programs

Against the background of economic depression, British domestic politics during the twenty years' truce continued to display a fairly clear class basis. The Conservatives, still often called Tories, tended to get the support of aristocrats and of middle-class people, who generally wanted to attack new problems with traditional methods and with a minimum of government intervention. The Labour party tended to get the support of trade unionists and of intellectuals from all classes, who demanded that the government intervene more vigorously in the economy. In the struggle between Labour and Conservative, the old Liberal party was an early casualty. The Conservatives, who had won the lion's share of seats in the "khaki election" of 1918—held immediately after the armistice and dominated by returned soldiers—decided in 1922 to withdraw their support from the coalition government headed by the immensely popular Liberal, David Lloyd George. In the ensuing elections the Conservatives won and the Liberals lost heavily, split as they were between the followers of Lloyd George and those of Herbert H. Asquith. For the first time Labour became His Majesty's Opposition.

Both Conservatives and Labour recognized the underlying difficulties of Britain's position. Both were fully aware that twentieth-century Britain had to sell enough goods and services abroad, enough manufactured goods and shipping, insurance, banking, and tourist services, so that income from them would buy food for its people and raw materials for its factories. But the parties could not agree on how to achieve this necessary task. Broadly speaking, the Conservatives wanted to retain private industry, with government and other technical experts helping to make it more efficient. But they were thwarted by high tariffs in the United States and elsewhere, by the drive for economic self-sufficiency all over the world, by the difficulties of trade with communist Russia, and by rising anti-imperial sentiment in India.

The state of world trade drove the Conservatives to advocate protective tariffs against competing foreign goods and to weld the empire and commonwealth, with their vast variety of resources, into a largely self-sufficient trade entity by "imperial preference" agreements. Such agreements would give raw materials from the colonies and dominions preferred treatment in the British market in return for preferred treatment of British manufactures in the colonial and dominion markets. In theory the scheme could have worked, for the commonwealth and empire of the 1920s had the requisite natural and labor resources and offered a potential market capable of supporting Britain in the style to which it was accustomed. In practice the great problem was the unwillingness of the individual parts of the empire and commonwealth to accept the subordinate role of producers of raw materials in exchange for British manufactured goods and services, a role the American colonies had challenged in the eighteenth century. The self-governing dominions, loyal though they had been during the war, were unwilling to assume a role essentially like that of colonies in the old mercantilistic days. They were looking toward independent nationhood, and they wanted their own industries.

The Labour solution was *nationalization*—that is, government purchase and operation of key industries with fair compensation to their private owners. The key industries were transportation, utilities, coal, steel, and perhaps even textiles, cutlery, pottery, and machine tools—all the industries that seemed to thrive best on large-scale organization. Many Labourites wanted nationalization simply because, as socialists, they believed that profits, rent, and interest were forms of capitalist exploitation of the workers and should cease. But many of their leaders realized that even nationalized industries would still face the fundamental problem of selling enough goods abroad to keep the economy going. They argued, therefore, that nationalization would also enable British industries to produce more cheaply and efficiently by doing away with wasteful competition and with the inefficiency so conspicuous in the coal industry, for instance. It would, they believed, force into productive work unnecessary managerial and sales staffs, as well as stockholders and other investors who lived without labor.

Politics between the Wars, 1918-1936

Neither the Conservatives nor the Labourites were able to carry out their full platforms. The Conservatives were frustrated by the refusal of the commonwealth

---

BALDWIN AND CHURCHILL

In manner of speech and in approach to politics, Stanley Baldwin and Winston Churchill stood in dramatic contrast. Although Baldwin accomplished much, to his critics he seemed to have done little. He was generally praised by the more liberal portions of the Conservative party and by the political Left. Baldwin summed up his own views in a speech in February 1923:

Four words of one syllable each are words which contain salvation for this country and for the whole world. They are "Faith," "Hope," "Love," and "Work." No Government in this country today which has not faith in the people, hope in the future, love for its fellow men, and which will not work and work and work, will ever bring this country through into better days and better times. . . .

A historian used the words of the great romantic novelist of empire, John Buchan (1875-1940), to describe Baldwin:

There is a moderation which is in itself a fire, where enthusiasm burns as fiercely for the whole truth as it commonly does for half-truths, where moderation becomes not a policy but an act of religion. . . . The moderate man can never become a barren dogmatist.

And a subsequent leader of the Conservative party, Harold Macmillan, wrote of Baldwin:

The young and progressive wing of his party had a special regard for him. His speeches, particularly on industrial problems, struck just the note which we thought appropriate and illuminating. The fact that the Right Wing and especially the so-called "industrials" had little love for him, confirmed our feelings.

In contrast, the young, flamboyant Winston Churchill was generally disliked, and his approach to politics, which would prove so effective in a time of crisis, was rejected by his party. It was Churchill, however, who most consistently and eloquently warned against unthinking pacifism. Churchill feared that Britain would fail to prepare for the next war on the illogical premise that because an arms race in 1906-1914 had led to a great war, refusal to rearm was the best means of preventing another war. He was seen by many commentators as a warmonger. In 1932, before Hitler came to power in Germany, Churchill wrote:

There is such a horror of war in the great nations who passed through Armageddon that any declaration or public speech against armaments, although it consisted only of platitudes and unrealities, has always been applauded; and any speech or assertion that set forth the blunt truth has been incontinently relegated to the category of "warmonger." . . . The cause of disarmament will not be obtained by Mush, Slush, and Gush. It will be advanced steadily by the harassing expense of fleets and armies and by the growth of confidence in a long peace.

These four extracts are taken from the work of the historian referred to in the second quotation, Robert Rhodes James, *The British Revolution, 1880-1939* (New York: Alfred A. Knopf, 1977), pp. 461-62, 528.

countries to go any further than to accept certain limited imperial preferences. Labour came to power for two brief spans—for ten months in 1924 with Ramsay Mac-Donald (1866-1937), an intellectual and pacifist, as prime minister, and again from 1928 to 1931. In both instances, although Labour won more seats in the Commons than any other party, it did not have an absolute majority. These Labour governments, obliged to rely on the Liberals for parliamentary support, were still too shaky to introduce measures as controversial as the nationalization of any industry.

For a few weeks in 1926 some two and a half million trade-union members attempted a general strike to support coal miners, who were striking to protest a cut in their wages. The general strike failed, but its brief course revealed fundamental British attitudes. Thousands of people from the middle and upper classes volunteered to keep essential services operating when a state of emergency was declared. Both sides remained calm and moderate, the union leaders and the prime minister, Stanley Baldwin (1867-1947), wanting a negotiated settlement, with neither side seeking all-out victory in a class war. When the general strike was called off, the miners eventually had to return to the pits on the owners' terms. In 1927 a Trade Disputes and Trade Union Act set the clock back twenty years, making all sympathetic strikes or strikes against the government illegal, and requiring union members who wanted to contribute to the Labour party to "contract in" instead of "contract out"*—an attack on Labour party finances that was deeply resented.

Meanwhile, two more steps were taken toward the political democratization of Britain that had begun in 1832. In 1918, in preparation for the election, the government had put through a reform bill that eliminated all the old exceptions to universal male suffrage and gave the vote to all males over twenty-one. Culminating a long and spectacular campaign by suffragettes who had gone to jail for women's rights, the bill also gave the vote to women. But it set the voting age for women at thirty years, thus ensuring that there would always be more male than female voters. The distinction was too unsound to last, especially after experience demonstrated that women divided politically about the way men did. In 1928 a new bill gave women the vote at twenty-one.

Although the dole, depressed industries, and other signs of economic ill health persisted, Britain recovered somewhat in the late 1920s. But then came the Great Depression. Britain, already weakened, was one of the first nations to suffer; in eighteen months the number of unemployed jumped from slightly over one million to two and a half million. Faced by a serious government

deficit and unwilling to meet it by cutting the dole and other social services, the second Labour government of Ramsay MacDonald resigned in August 1931.

It gave way to a coalition of Conservatives, Liberals, and right-wing Labourites—headed by the same MacDonald. Many Labourites were dismayed by what seemed to them MacDonald's surrender to the forces of capitalism, and the deep split within the party crippled its effectiveness throughout the 1930s. The "national government," as the coalition cabinet was called, reduced the dole and social services. Late in 1931 it took the decisive step—a hard one in view of Britain's traditional financial leadership and devotion to the gold standard—of going off the gold standard and letting the pound fall in value. In 1932 it made the first firm move away from free trade by enacting protective tariffs, and it also ceased to pay its war debts to the United States, except for a few token payments. These measures did little to help the unemployed or get at the roots of British economic troubles. Nevertheless, partly because of Labour's disarray, two general elections, in October 1931 and in June 1935, returned a majority supporting the national government.

The coalition government was dominated by Conservatives, and after the 1935 election the Conservative leader, Stanley Baldwin, became prime minister. Gradually the British economy pulled out of the worst of the depression, and Baldwin was able to balance the budget. By 1936, however, Mussolini's and Hitler's aggressions were beginning to demand British attention. The economic question and the social question, by no means solved, now seemed less urgent than the threat of another war.

For a few months in 1936 the great issue confronting Baldwin's cabinet was neither social nor diplomatic but constitutional, as the cabinet forced the abdication of King Edward VIII (1894-1972) in the same year as his accession to the throne. Edward had enjoyed a long and successful career as Prince of Wales, displaying a charming and effective manner in public all over the world. He had fallen in love with an American divorcee, however, and wanted to marry her. The royal family, the cabinet, and most of the British people opposed him, and he abdicated (with the title of Duke of Windsor), allowing his brother to become King George VI (r. 1936-1952).

Some of the opposition to Edward's marriage stemmed from dislike of Americans, but much more of it came from a strong feeling against having a divorcee near the throne, since the public regarded the monarchy as a symbol of moral rectitude, and divorce was not yet widely accepted. The dispute attracted worldwide attention at the time and proved seriously distracting to the Baldwin administration throughout "the summer of the King's Matter," when events on the Continent demanded attention. But at the moment of abdication in December, Baldwin proved so strong a leader that he regained total control over a House of Commons that had been in rebellion against him.

---

*This is the concept of the negative checkoff used in all labor unions, health plans or book-of-the-month clubs. You must take a specific action in order *not* to be involved (contracting out), rather than taking an action in order to be involved (contracting in). Since most movements and many advertising campaigns know that people are apathetic, membership is far larger if the movement can legally be based on the contract-out principle.

THE BRITISH UNION OF FASCISTS

In 1932 Sir Oswald Mosley (1896-   ) founded the British Union of Fascists, known also as the Blackshirts. Mosley had been a Labour member of Parliament who felt that the Labour party had not attacked unemployment vigorously enough, and he turned toward the corporations of Italy. He alienated conservative followers by becoming stridently anti-Jewish, though not before his movement had gained twenty thousand adherents and was linked with the effort to convince the British public that war on the Continent was none of their business. Following is a handbill for one of his London meetings:

BRITONS AWAKE!
—— DANZIG IS NOT WORTH ONE DROP OF BRITISH BLOOD.

WHY FIGHT A WAR IN EASTERN EUROPE?

TO STOP ONE LOT OF GERMANS UNITING WITH AN-OTHER. WHY GO TO WAR IN A POLITICIAN'S QUARREL AND TO SAVE THE FINANCIERS' INTEREST?

THE POLITICIANS AND FINANCIERS WANT WAR ——
THE PEOPLE WANT PEACE.

STOP THE MAD DRIFT TO WAR!

NEGLECT OF DEFENCE AND EMPIRE —— MUDDLING INTERFERENCE IN EASTERN EUROPEAN QUARRELS HAVE REDUCED BRITAIN TO A POSITION OF HUMILIATION, AND BROUGHT US TO THE BRINK OF WAR.

STOP the policy of humiliation decadence & defeat. THE WARMONGERS NOW!

SAVE PEACE JOIN WITH BRITISH UNION IN THIS TREMENDOUS DEMONSTRATION FOR BRITAIN, PEACE & PEOPLE IN THE LARGEST HALL IN THE WORLD.

FEW TICKETS LEFT — GET YOURS NOW
ADMISSION FREE
RESERVED SEATS
1/- 2/6 3/- 5/- 7/6 10/6
from
BRITISH UNION
16 Gt. SMITH St.
S.W.1.
OR ANY LOCAL DISTRICT OFFICE

MOSLEY SPEAKS
FOR BRITAIN, PEACE & PEOPLE
EARLS COURT
EXHIBITION HALL
SUNDAY, JULY 16th 7.30 P.M.
—— DOORS OPEN 6:30 PM ——

The Irish Question, 1916-1949

The years between the wars were of great importance for Ireland. In 1916 the British put down the Easter rebellion with grim determination, creating new Irish political martyrs. The British government did not dare extend conscription to Ireland until April 1918, and that attempt led Irish nationalists to boycott the British Parliament. The crisis of 1914, postponed by the war, was again at hand.

But by 1919 home rule as decreed in 1914 was not enough for Irish nationalists. The home-rulers of prewar days had yielded to the *Sinn Fein* (meaning in Gaelic "ourselves alone"), who wanted complete independence. The years 1919-1921 were filled with violence, ambushes, arson, and guerrilla warfare, as the Irish, who now had their own illegal parliament, the *Dail Eireann*, moved into full revolution. The British, tired from four years of world war, were not prepared to use force effectively; the Irish, on the other hand, were admirably organized and ready to fight.

Yet the immediate result of the violent phase of the

revolution was a compromise, for the Sinn Fein split in two. The moderate wing was willing to accept a compromise in which Protestant Ulster would remain under direct British rule and the Catholic counties would be given dominion status. The radical wing, led by Eamon De Valera (1882–1975), insisted that the whole island achieve complete independence as a unified republic. De Valera had raised substantial funds for the republican cause from sympathizers in the United States, but the defeat of the Democratic party there in 1920 and Britain's ability to forestall discussion of Ireland at Versailles and in the League of Nations had weakened his position.

The moderates therefore negotiated with the British, and in 1921 obtained for the twenty-six counties of southern Ireland dominion status under the name of the Irish Free State. The Free State had its own parliament, the Dáil, and was completely self-governing, with its own army and its own diplomatic services. It did, however, accept the British crown as symbolic head. The six predominantly Protestant counties of Ulster maintained their old relationship with Britain, including the right to send members to the Parliament at Westminster, but they also acquired their own parliament at Belfast and considerable local autonomy. Henceforth, Britain was officially known as the United Kingdom of Great Britain and Northern Ireland.

This settlement was unacceptable to De Valera, and the Irish revolution now became a civil war between partisans of the Free State and those of a republic, with a return to burning, ambush, and murder. But when the moderate leader Michael Collins (1890–1922) was assassinated by a republican, public opinion began to turn away from the extremists. De Valera, after refusing to sit in the Dáil because he would have had to take an oath of loyalty to the king, attacked the civil war and ultimately decided to bring his party, the *Fianna Fáil*, into the national parliament in 1927.

De Valera's party won a plurality in the Dáil in 1932 and a majority in 1933; thereupon it abolished the oath of loyalty to the Crown and cut the threads that still tied the Free State to the United Kingdom. In 1938 De Valera became prime minister, and in 1939 the Free State showed that it was free from British domination by maintaining neutrality throughout World War II. In 1949 the final step was taken when Britain recognized the fully independent Republic of Eire (Gaelic for Ireland). There remained, however, the festering problem of Northern Ireland. To Irish republicans, this was irredentist land; to Irish Catholics, the minority there needed the protection of the Catholic majority in the republic; to the dominant Protestants in Ulster (as Northern Ireland was also called), union with Britain remained the only protection against an anticipated religious war and against the loss of entrenched privileges.

The Commonwealth, 1931–1939

No such secession took place elsewhere among the British possessions between the two world wars. On the contrary, constitutional recognition of the essential independence of the dominions seemed to make them more loyal, though at the cost of any central British authority over their economic and foreign policies, at least in law. The climax of the long process begun with the Durham Report nearly a century before was the Statute of Westminster of 1931 (see Chapter 22). The new status acquired by the dominions in 1931 was

---

IRELAND'S DECLARATION OF INDEPENDENCE

On January 7, 1919, twenty-six elected Sinn Fein representatives convened the Assembly of Ireland (the *Dail Eireann*) in the Dublin Mansion House, where a committee drew up a provisional constitution. On January 21 members who were not in prison (as thirty-four were) met to hear the Provisional Constitution of the Dail read out:

Whereas the Irish people is by right a free people: And whereas for seven hundred years the Irish people has never ceased to repudiate and has repeatedly protested in arms against foreign usurpation: And whereas English rule in this country is, and always has been, based upon force and fraud and maintained by military occupation against the declared will of the people: And whereas the Irish Republic was proclaimed in Dublin on Easter Monday, 1916, by the Irish Republican Army, acting on behalf of the Irish people . . . Now, therefore, we, the elected Representatives of the ancient Irish people in National Parliament assembled, do, in the name of the Irish nation, ratify the establishment of the Irish Republic and pledge ourselves and our people to make this declaration effective by every means at our command. . . .

Quoted in George Dangerfield, *The Damnable Question: One Hundred and Twenty Years of Anglo-Irish Conflict* (Boston: Little, Brown, 1976), p. 302.

symbolized by a change in terminology. They were no longer to be considered parts of the British Empire, but free members of the British Commonwealth of Nations (a title reduced to Commonwealth after World War II, in deference to the many new non-Western members, some of which did not recognize the Crown). In this new relationship, Britain would have to negotiate with Canada or Australia about tariffs, trade conditions, or immigration as with foreign countries. It was on the basis of the Statute of Westminster that the Irish Free State became the Republic of Eire.

Although Britain was unable to build a self-sufficient economic unity out of its dominions, still in 1939, as in 1914, the dominions all ultimately came into the war on Britain's side. They made this decision independently, however, for they had the legal right to follow the example of Ireland and remain neutral. Transfer of power to the major dominions was complete.

II FRANCE

The Impact of the War, 1918-1928

In France both World War I and the postwar difficulties caused even more serious dislocation than they did in Britain. France had lost proportionately more in human lives and in material damage than did any other major belligerent. Two million Frenchmen in the prime of life were either killed or so seriously mutilated as to be incapable of normal living. In a land of only thirty-nine million with an already low birth rate, this human loss affected all phases of activity. Three hundred thousand houses and twenty thousand factories or shops were destroyed. In a land of conservative economic organization where most work was done without large-scale machinery, this material setback would long be felt. Psychologically, victory did not compensate for the traumatic losses of the four years of struggle.

France wanted revenge on Germany in every possible way. The French tried to extract reparations to the last possible sum, undeterred by the arguments of economists that Germany could not pay. But France insisted even more on keeping Germany isolated in international relations and without the physical means to wage war. Most of the French would probably have been willing to forego reparations in order to deprive Germany of the economic plant necessary for modern war, preferring this to collecting reparations from a rich and productive Germany. Postwar French leaders attempted to follow both policies simultaneously and failed. The culmination came in January 1923 under the premiership of the conservative Raymond Poincaré (1860-1934), when French and Belgian troops occupied the Ruhr to make Germany pay full reparations, an occupation that brought France only the censure of international opinion. The elections of 1924 resulted in a victory for the *Cartel des Gauches*, a coalition of mildly left-wing par-

ties headed by the Radical Socialists. The French withdrew their last troops from the Ruhr in 1925.

Meanwhile, France was experiencing an inflation that resulted in part from the cost of rebuilding the devastated areas—a cost that drained government finances and that was only partly covered by German payments. It resulted also from the high cost of maintaining armed forces (for the French dared not disarm), from the general disorder of international trade, and from the staggering debts piled up during the war by the French government, which, like the imperial German government, had preferred loans to taxes. By the mid-1920s the franc had slipped from its prewar value of twenty cents against the dollar to a dangerous low of about two cents. In the crisis Poincaré was recalled to power to "save the franc." In 1926 he initiated new taxes and stern economy measures which, together with the gradual restoration of normal international trade after the French withdrawal from the Ruhr, stemmed the decline of the franc. In 1928 it was officially revalued at 3.92 cents.

The French inflation, though mild compared with the German, nevertheless caused economic and social dislocation. Those French who had lent their government francs worth twenty cents were now repaid only one-fifth of their loans. This very considerable loss fell with particular severity on the lower middle class, the *petite bourgeoisie*. The greatest sufferers were those living on their savings or on relatively fixed incomes—on pensions, on the return from bonds, or even on the contents of the wool sock in which the French peasant traditionally hoarded cash. Inflation thus weakened a social class that had long been a mainstay of republicanism in France and added to the social tensions that formed the central theme of French domestic history between the two world wars.

Social and Political Tensions, 1928-1936

During World War I the French had temporarily put aside the great political and social conflict they had inherited from 1789. After the war the "sacred union" of political parties that had carried France through the struggle soon dissolved, and the traditional conflict was resumed. This is sometimes termed the conflict between the "two Frances"—the republican France of the left and the royalistic or authoritarian France of the right. The conflict was not a simple struggle between rich and poor. On the right the wealthier classes, many of them openly hostile to the existence of the parliamentary state, were reinforced by conservative peasants and by small business people and investors. Many of these petit bourgeois were not hostile to the Third Republic as such, but were determined to resist any attempt to extend the social services of the welfare state. As a result of this right-wing resistance, France lagged behind Britain, Germany, Sweden, and other European states in providing measures of social security.

On the left were the champions of the welfare state,

the socialists and the communists, backed by the more radical workers, by many white-collar people, especially in the bureaucracy, and by some intellectuals. The post-war left was hampered by the split between the communists, who followed the Moscow line, and the socialists, who did not, and by a comparable schism within the major trade-union organization, the CGT (*Confédération Générale du Travail*—General Confederation of Labor). Still nominally part of the left, but actually in the political middle and not anxious to extend the welfare state, was the misleadingly named Radical Socialist party, long the main party of the Third Republic. The Radicals were strong among the peasants of southern France and among white-collar and professional workers.

Religious difficulties further embittered French politics. The widely held but unproved assumption that women would vote as the priests told them delayed women's suffrage until after World War II. The traditional anticlericals in France were the leftists, including the Radicals. After World War I they rashly attempted to introduce anticlerical measures into strongly Catholic Alsace, where the separation of church and state that was carried through in France after the Dreyfus crisis had not been applied because Alsace was at the time part of the German Empire. In the long run, the government was obliged to make compromises on the Alsatian question and on other clerical issues. After bitter public debate, it finally decided in the mid-1920s to resume diplomatic relations with the Vatican—relations that had been broken off since 1905.

In the late 1920s, the years of increased prosperity that coincided with the revaluation of the franc, the Third Republic seemed to be getting the better of its internal difficulties. The world economic crisis that began in 1929 was late in striking France, and for a while it looked as though the French economy, less dependent on large-scale industry than that of the United States, Britain, or Germany, might weather the crisis much more easily. But France too depended on international trade, particularly on the export of luxuries. By 1932 the depression had struck, and the government was in serious economic and political difficulties.

The political crisis came to a head in February 1934 as a result of the Stavisky case, a financial scandal reminiscent of the Panama scandal of the 1890s. Serge Stavisky was a swindler with influential connections, particularly in Radical Socialist circles. He was finally exposed in December 1933 and escaped to an Alpine hideout, where he committed suicide—or, as many believed, was killed by the police lest he implicate important politicians. France was rocked by the event and also by the mysterious death of a judge who had been investigating the case. On the extreme right royalists had long been organized in a pressure group known as the *Action Française* and were gaining recruits among upper-class youth. The *Camelots du Roi* (The King's Henchmen), strong-arm squads of the Action Française, went about beating up communists, who in turn re-

sponded with violence. Less fascist in character yet also supporting the right was a veterans' organization, the *Croix de Feu* (Cross of Fire—the reference is to war). During the agitation following the Stavisky case, the Camelots du Roi, the Croix de Feu, and other right-wing groups took part in demonstrations against the government in Paris in February 1934. The left countered with a brief general strike. Fourteen demonstrators were killed, and many feared that France again faced revolution.

The Popular Front, 1936-1937

Once more, however, as in the time of Dreyfus, the republican forces rallied to meet the threat, and once more, after the crisis had been surmounted, France moved to the left. Edouard Daladier (1884-1970), Radical premier, resigned, and a coalition of all parties except the royalists, socialists, and communists formed a national government, including all living former premiers. But the franc was again falling in value. In 1935 a ministry in which the dominant figure was Pierre Laval (1883-1945), a former socialist turned conservative, attempted to cut back government expenditures by measures similar to those that had worked a decade earlier under Poincaré; this time, however, they did not work. The forces of the left responded by forming a Popular Front, which for the first time linked together the Radical Socialist, Socialist, and Communist parties. It also had the backing of CGT, which had temporarily healed the schism between communist and noncommunist unions. In the elections of 1936 the Popular Front won, with the socialists at the top. The premiership was accordingly offered to a socialist, the Jewish intellectual Léon Blum (1872-1950).

The Popular Front came to power with a mandate from voters who wanted the government to distribute wealth more equitably. Many in 1936 also voted left to protest the compromises that French politicians had been making with Hitler and Mussolini. Finally, these were the years when Russia, just admitted to the League of Nations, seemed to want to collaborate with the West against the threat of Nazi Germany. Moscow therefore urged the French communists to cooperate with their old enemies, the socialists. In June 1936 the Blum government introduced an ambitious program of reform. Labor gained a forty-hour work week, higher wages, vacations with pay, and provision for compulsory arbitration of labor disputes. The Bank of France, the railroads, and the munitions industry were all partially nationalized. Quasifascistic groups like the Camelots du Roi and Croix de Feu were ordered to disband.

Impressive as this program was on paper, events conspired to block its successful implementation. The communists did not really cooperate, for they refused to participate in the Blum cabinet and sniped at it in parliament and in the press. Business took fright at the growth of the CGT and at the effectiveness of sit-down strikes of French industrial workers in June 1936—the first widespread use of this formidable economic weapon through which struck plants were occupied by the striking workers, preventing the owners from using their weapon, the lock-out.

The nation was soon bitterly divided between partisans and enemies of the Popular Front. Business and farming classes were traditionally reluctant to pay income taxes, which would have to be raised to meet the costs of social services; the economy was not geared to labor-saving devices; there were competing demands on the nation's money. As the antidemocratic regimes in Germany, Italy, and Spain won new victories, France was driven to expensive rearmament. Capital, however, was rapidly leaving the country to be invested or deposited abroad, and the monied class would not subscribe to the huge defense loans that were essential if the French armed forces were to prepare for the war that seemed to be approaching. Faced by mounting opposition, Blum was obliged to step down as premier in favor of a Radical in 1937. The Popular Front now disintegrated, and the CGT lost millions of its new members and suffered a new schism between communists and anticommunists.

The morale of the French sagged badly after the collapse of the Popular Front. Under the mounting international tensions of 1938 and 1939, the Radical Socialist premier, Daladier, kept France on the side of Britain in unsteady opposition to the Rome-Berlin Axis. Various measures of retrenchment—including virtual abandonment of the forty-hour week—kept the French economy from collapse. But the workers resented the failure of the Popular Front, and as late as November 1938 almost achieved a general strike, which the government combated by putting the railway workers under military orders. The "have" classes, on the other hand, were outraged by Blum's measures. Many of them were convinced that their salvation lay in a French totalitarian state—"Better Hitler than Blum," as their slogan stated, with an anti-Semitic echo from the days of the Dreyfus affair. The France that was confronted with war in 1939 was not only inadequately armed; it was also psychologically and spiritually divided, uncertain of what it was to fight for or against, and its production level was still that of 1929.

Many in France had relied on their great empire to restore the flagging morale and material capabilities of the nation. Colonial troops, particularly from Senegal and North Africa, had helped to replenish the diminished ranks of the army during World War I and might do so again. Enthusiasts spoke of France as a nation of one hundred million, which included the populations of the colonial territories. But the colonial populations were beginning to desire home rule or independence, especially in Algeria, Senegal, and French Indochina. Although some leaders of the French left urged concessions to such desires, little was conceded, except in a compromise fashion to the new mandates of Syria and Lebanon, to which the Cartel des Gauches government in the mid-1920s had given constitutions. In 1936 the Popular Front government negotiated treaties with both,

granting them independence with many reservations, so as to safeguard the primacy of French interests. But this compromise was too much for the Chamber of Deputies, which refused to approve the treaties. Perhaps no policy pursued in the interwar years could have averted the disintegration of the French Empire that occurred during and after World War II, but the unimaginative policy that prevailed did nothing to reconcile the nationalists among the French colonial peoples.

III THE UNITED STATES

Neither the human nor the material losses of the United States in World War I were at all comparable with those of Britain and France. American casualties were 115,000 dead and 206,000 wounded; the comparable French figures were 1,385,000 dead and 3,044,000 wounded in a population one-third as large. Moreover, in purely material terms, the United States probably gained from the war. Heavy industries were greatly stimulated by Allied war orders, in turn made possible by American loans to the Allies. The war made New York a financial center equal to London; the dollar had begun to dethrone the pound sterling. The United States came out of the war victorious and prosperous.

Yet in some ways the American postwar revulsion against the war was as marked as that in Britain, France, and defeated Germany. It helped to unseat the Democrats, who had controlled the federal government since 1913. The Republicans won the presidential elections of 1920 (in which women had the vote for the first time), 1924, and 1928, and three successive Republicans occupied the White House: Warren Harding (1921-1923), Calvin Coolidge (1923-1929), and Herbert Hoover (1929-1933).

Although the election was not close, the campaign of 1928 was notable for the bitterness aroused in many quarters by the unsuccessful candidacy of Democrat Alfred E. Smith (1873-1944). Smith, who had been a progressive governor of New York, was a Roman Catholic and a "wet"—committed to repeal of the Eighteenth Amendment (1919), which had outlawed the sale of alcoholic beverages—while "dry" sentiment was still strong in the mostly Protestant South and Midwest. These two considerations in the election of 1928 well illustrated the fact that the United States was both like and unlike the European nations; as in France, England, and Germany the religion of a political candidate was important. On the other hand, no western European nation had attempted so massive an experiment in social control as that contained in the effort to prohibit the sale (as distinct from efforts to limit the intake) of alcohol.

Isolationism and Internationalism, 1920-1933

American revulsion against war also took the form of isolationism, the wish to withdraw from international politics outside the Western Hemisphere. The country

In 1920 women won the right to vote in the United States. Here suffragettes ride down Pennsylvania Avenue from the Capitol toward the White House.

was swept by a wave of desire to get back to "normalcy," as President Harding phrased it. Many Americans felt that they had done all they needed to do in defeating the Germans, and that further participation in the complexities of European politics would simply involve American innocence and virtue even more disastrously in European sophistication and vice. Just as the French, for example, vacillated between right and left-leaning governments, Americans vacillated between a desire for a strong executive such as Wilson (and Theodore Roosevelt before him) and a relatively weak executive such as Wilson's three successors. Americans were dismayed by the rapidity of political successions in Europe, where ministries might rise and fall in a matter of months, and they tended to forget that they were protected from this instability (while also limited in their options in the interim) by their constitution, which prescribed four-year terms for presidents. American reaction against strong presidents took the form of repudiating all of Wilson's work at Paris as un-American. Furthermore, as the months of negotiation went on in Europe with no final decisions, many Americans began to feel that withdrawal was the only effective action they could take.

The Treaty of Versailles, containing at Wilson's insistence the establishment of the League of Nations, was finally rejected in the Senate on March 19, 1920, and the United States remained technically at war with Germany

until July 1921. Historians still disagree whether this failure to join the League doomed Europe to continued instability and thus to future war, just as they disagree whether the American people as a whole truly embraced isolationism, or whether an effective minority with strong Senatorial leadership achieved the rejection of the Versailles settlement by adroit political maneuvers.

American isolationism was also expressed in these years in other concrete measures. Tariffs in 1922 and 1930 set successively higher duties on foreign goods and emphasized America's belief that its high wage scales needed to be protected from cheap foreign labor. The spirit of isolationism, as well as growing racist movements, also lay behind the immigration restrictions of the 1920s, which reversed the former policy of almost unlimited immigration. The reversal was hastened by widespread prejudice against the recent and largely Catholic and Jewish immigrations from southern and eastern Europe. The act of 1924 set an annual quota limit for each country of 2 percent of the number of nationals from that country resident in the United States in 1890. Since the heavy immigration from eastern and southern Europe had come after 1890, the choice of that date reduced the flow from these areas to a trickle. Northern countries like Britain, Germany, and the Scandinavian states, on the other hand, did not use up their quotas.

Isolationism did not apply to all matters, however. The United States continued all through the 1920s to insist that the debts owed to it by the Allied powers be repaid. It is true that these sums were refunded in a series of agreements, and that in the closely related problem of German reparations Americans generally favored reducing German obligations. But Congress paid little heed to the argument, so convincing to most economists, that the European nations could not repay except with dollars gained by selling their goods in the American market, and that American tariffs continued to make such repayment impossible. Congress tended to reduce the complexities of international debts to President Coolidge's simple dictum: "They hired the money, didn't they?"

Yet the United States did not withdraw entirely from international politics. Rather, as an independent without formal alliances, it continued to pursue policies that seemed to most Americans traditional, but that in their totality gradually aligned them against the major new challengers. In 1928 the Republican secretary of state, Frank B. Kellogg (1856-1937), proposed that the major powers renounce war as an instrument of national policy. Incorporated with similar proposals by the French foreign minister, Aristide Briand (1862-1932), it was formally adopted that year as the Pact of Paris, commonly known as the Kellogg-Briand Pact, and was eventually signed by twenty-three nations. Although the pact, like the reinsurance treaties preceding World War I, proved ineffective, the fact that it arose in part from American initiative, and that the United States was a signatory to it, was clear indication that even if Americans did not wish to enter into any formal alliances, they were still concerned with the problems of worldwide stability and peace.

During the 1920s the United States was hard at work laying the foundations for the position of world leadership it reached after World War II. American businesses were everywhere; American loans were making possible the revival of German industry; American motors, refrigerators, typewriters, telephones, and other products were being sold the world over. In the Far East the United States led in negotiating the Nine-Power Treaty of 1922 that committed it and the other great powers, including Japan, to respect the sovereignty and integrity of China. When the Democratic President Franklin D. Roosevelt resisted the Japanese attempt to absorb China and other Far Eastern territory, he was following a line laid down under his Republican predecessors.

Boom and Bust, 1923-1933

In domestic affairs, the Coolidge era (1923-1929) was a time of frantic prosperity for the many who played the stock market. These were the years of prohibition, of the speakeasy and the bootlegger, when the American media—newspapers, magazines, radio, and motion pictures—gave the impression that the entire nation was absorbed by short skirts, loosened sexual mores,

new dances, and bathtub gin. Such activities occupied only a tiny minority of the people, of course, just as the "whipped cream" culture of turn-of-the-century Vienna had been unrepresentative of most Austrians. But by the 1920s there was a significant difference. Agricultural workers who had never recovered their sense of prosperity and people who still held to Victorian standards of conduct would be led to believe that boundless riches, social vacuity, and sin were typical of the upper classes. The way was being paved for the American concern with public personalities, especially in athletics, entertainment, and scandal, that would fascinate the entire nation. And the way was also being prepared for the introduction of ideas of class warfare from Europe.

But the Coolidge era was also a time of marked industrial progress, of solid advancement of the national plant and productive capabilities, vindicating Coolidge's contention that "the business of America is business." It was an era of the steady expansion of standards of living heretofore limited to the relatively few, standards of living that seemed to some intellectuals vulgar, but that were nevertheless a new thing in the world. Unknown in Europe and envied there, the new lifestyle was much desired by nearly everyone, whether vulgar or not. The United States became, in this era, the first true consumer society.

The era ended with the onset of the Great Depression. In 1928 Wall Street had enjoyed an unprecedented boom. Speculators by the millions were playing the market, buying stocks in hopes of quick resale at huge profits. They paid only a fraction of the cost in cash, borrowing the balance from their brokers, and often borrowing the cash investment as well. Not only stocks but houses, furnishings, automobiles, and many other purchases were financed on borrowed money. Credit swelled until it was no longer on a sound basis in a largely unregulated economy. Eventually, shrewd investors began to sell their holdings in the belief that the bubble would soon burst. The result was a self-fulfilling prophecy: a disastrous drop in stock values, beginning in October 1929 and continuing almost without letup to 1933. Both the speculators and the lenders were ruined.

The immediate cause of the Great Depression, then, was the stockmarket crash. About the more deep-seated causes there is even now no complete agreement, since other recessions and depressions have occurred more recently, and to agree on an explanation for the depression of 1929 has clear implications for future public policy. Yet this much seems certain: Coolidge prosperity was very unevenly distributed among the various sectors of the American economy and American society. Agriculture, notably, suffered a kind of permanent stagnation throughout the 1920s. In 1918 farmers had commanded very high prices for their produce and enjoyed an apparently insatiable market at home and abroad. They expanded their production and borrowed to finance the expansion, often at a reckless rate. Then, as "normalcy" returned in the early 1920s, the foreign market dried up, the home market shrank, farm prices

Even in America, a country that regarded itself as rich, many people were reduced during the Great Depression to the neighborhood soup kitchen, where they might receive a simple free meal.

fell rapidly, and the foreclosure of farm mortgages began. Wage-earning workers, though not as hard hit as the farmers, gained comparatively little increase in their purchasing power during the 1920s. Workers often did raise their standard of living by purchasing a house or a car, but they did it on credit, by assuming the burden of a heavy mortgage or by financing the purchase on long-term installments.

The Great Depression was very severe in many countries throughout the world, but nowhere was it worse over a sustained period than in the United States. Its effects may be measured by the figure of sixteen million Americans unemployed at the low point in the early 1930s—something like one-third of the national labor force. In terms of gross national product (GNP), one widely accepted statistic for calculating the health of an economy, the figure in 1929 had been cut nearly in half in only four years, by 1933.

Yet this grave crisis in the American economy produced almost no organized movements of revolt, no threat of revolution. Some intellectuals of the 1930s did indeed turn to "social consciousness," and Marxism made converts among writers and artists. But the bulk of the population did not abandon their fundamental belief that the solution lay in the legal means provided by existing American institutions. Even before the election of Franklin D. Roosevelt (1882-1945) in 1932, local authorities and private charities did much to soften the worst sufferings of the unemployed. They were helped

by President Hoover's Reconstruction Finance Corporation (RFC), which advanced government credits to release the frozen assets of financial institutions severely affected by the wave of bankruptcies and bank failures. Hoover was generally committed to the philosophy of laissez faire, however, aside from the RFC, and his administration did little to cushion the effects of the depression. People who wanted a more vigorous attack on economic problems voted for the Democrats in 1932; significantly, very few voted for the socialist or communist candidates. In the crisis of the Great Depression, the two-party system continued to meet the basic political needs of most Americans.

The New Deal, 1933-1941

Victory seemed to give the Democrats a clear mandate to marshal the resources of the federal government against the depression. Franklin Roosevelt took office on March 4, 1933, during a financial crisis that had closed banks all over the country. He at once summoned Congress to an emergency session and declared a bank holiday. Gradually the sound banks reopened, and the first New Deal began. Subsequently, under improving economic conditions, many from the American business community turned with bitterness against Roosevelt and all his works. But in the early months of 1933 the mere fact that a national administration was trying to do something about the situation was a powerful boost to

F.D.R.'S FIRST INAUGURAL ADDRESS

The 1930s were a time of charismatic orators: F.D.R., Churchill, Hitler, Mussolini. Roosevelt used his Inaugural Address on March 4, 1933, less to outline a program than to inspire the public to stand behind him in a series of sweeping reforms:

This is a day of national consecration, and I am certain that my fellow Americans expect that on my induction into the Presidency, I will address them with a candor and a decision which the present situation of our nation impels.

This is preeminently the time to speak the truth, the whole truth, frankly and boldly. Nor need we shrink from honestly facing conditions in our country today. This great nation will endure as it has endured, will revive and will prosper.

So first of all let me assert my firm belief that the only thing we have to fear is fear itself—nameless, unreasoning, unjustified terror which paralyzes needed efforts to convert retreat into advance.

In every dark hour of our national life a leadership of frankness and vigor has met with that understanding and support of the people themselves which is essential to victory. I am convinced that you will again give that support to leadership in these critical days. . . .

I favor as a practical policy the putting of first things first. I shall spare no effort to restore world trade by international economic readjustment, but the emergency at home cannot wait on that accomplishment.

The basic thought that guides these specific means of national recovery is not narrowly nationalistic.

It is the insistence, as a first consideration, upon the interdependence of the various elements in, and parts of, the United States—a recognition of the old and permanently important manifestation of the American spirit of the pioneer. . . .

I am prepared under my constitutional duty to recommend the measures that a stricken nation in the midst of a stricken world may require.

These measures, or such other measures as the Congress may build out of its experience and wisdom, I shall seek, within my constitutional authority, to bring to speedy adoption.

But in the event that the Congress shall fail to take one of these two courses, and in the event that the national emergency is still critical, I shall not evade the clear course of duty that will then confront me.

I shall ask the Congress for the one remaining instrument to meet the crisis—broad executive power to wage a war against the emergency as great as the power that would be given me if we were in fact invaded by a foreign foe.

From Henry Steele Commager, ed., *Documents of American History* (New York: Crofts, 1934), pp. 417, 419. Though many editions of Commager's collection of documents have appeared since, it is interesting to note that only a year after Roosevelt had delivered his address, a professional historian already considered it to be one of the basic documents of American history.

national morale. The nation emerged from the bank holiday with a new confidence, repeating the phrase from Roosevelt's inaugural address that there was "nothing to fear but fear itself."

The New Deal was in part a series of measures aimed at immediate difficulties and in part a series of measures aimed at permanent changes in the structure of American society. The distinction between its short-term and long-term aims is in a sense arbitrary, for the men and women who carried both through were not always clear in their own minds exactly what their long-range goals were. Some worked from theory, but most worked from the pragmatic need to solve an immediate problem. The New Deal was the application to the United States, under the special pressures of the Great Depression, of measures that were being tried in European countries, measures often leading to the welfare state.

By releasing the dollar from its tie with gold, the short-term measures of the New Deal aimed to lower the price of American goods in a world that was abandoning the gold standard. They aimed to thaw out credit by extending the activities of the RFC and by creating such new governmental lending agencies as the Home Own-

ers' Loan Corporation. They aimed to relieve unemployment by public works on a large scale, to safeguard bank deposits by the Federal Deposit Insurance Corporation, and to regulate speculation and other stock-market activities by the Securities and Exchange Commission. The National Recovery Act (NRA) of 1933 set up production codes in industry to regulate competition and to ensure labor's right to organize and carry on collective bargaining. The historical significance of many of these innovations rested in the fact that they were undertaken not by private business or by state or local authorities but by the federal government. There was one exception to the rule of widening federal activity. The Twenty-first Amendment to the Constitution (ratified in December 1933) repealed the Eighteenth and abandoned the unsuccessful federal effort to enforce prohibition, leaving the matter of legislating on the public morality of consuming alcohol to the individual states.

The long-term measures of the New Deal were, of course, more important. The Social Security Act of 1935 introduced to the United States on a national scale the unemployment insurance, old-age pensions, and other benefits of the kind that Lloyd George had brought to

Britain. By extending and revising tax structures, including the income tax authorized by the Sixteenth Amendment to the Constitution in 1913, Congress in effect redistributed wealth to some degree, as the Liberal and Labour parties in Britain had advocated. Congress also passed a series of acts on labor relations that strengthened and extended the role of organized labor. A series of acts on agriculture regulated crops and prices and provided subsidies on a large scale. And finally—the showpiece of the New Deal—a great regional planning board, the Tennessee Valley Authority, used government power to make over the economic life of a relatively backward area by checking the erosion of farmlands, instituting flood control, and providing cheap electric power generated at government-built dams.

The presidential election of 1936 gave Roosevelt an emphatic popular endorsement. Maine and Vermont were the only states he failed to carry. Yet the New Deal never regained the momentum it had in his first term. In retrospect, although the New Deal is still a subject of some controversy, it seems evident that the measures taken by the Roosevelt administration, combined with the resilience of American institutions and culture, pulled the United States at least part way out of the depression. Full recovery, however, did not come until the boom set off by the outbreak of World War II. It seems evident too that the New Deal measures also restored a high degree of confidence to Americans. The intellectuals, whose role in modern America has gener-

ally been in opposition to business, in the 1920s had found the United States a crass and vulgar society. But in the 1930s, though some intellectuals turned to Marxism, most supported the New Deal. Intellectuals generally did not, in any event, regard themselves as a class apart, as many did in Europe, and as the Russian intelligentsia had done, and though they generally saw their role as the critics of society—whichever party might be in office—they did not suffer from the sense of disillusionment and alienation common to the intellectual community in much of Europe.

The onset of war in Europe found Americans anxious to remain neutral if Europe should persist in going to war. Roosevelt and his Republican opponents had been for some time exchanging insults. Yet in the pinch of the international crisis of 1939 it became clear that, although the nation was not completely united, it was not deeply divided. As so often in American history, the violence of verbal politics—in which language is often used with more vehemence than in Europe—masked a basic unity. When war came to the United States in 1941, Americans were largely ready for it psychologically and—what is really remarkable in a Western democracy—prepared for it militarily.

When the war came, moreover, the United States had already made many efforts to enlist the support of the Latin American states, so that the New World might once again redress the grievances of the Old. In 1930, before the so-called Roosevelt Revolution in American

F.D.R. inspired confidence in people, and wherever he went crowds reached out to shake his hand. Here, as he waited for his wife, Eleanor, who had been addressing a meeting in December 1933, the president was surrounded by admirers.

diplomacy, President Hoover's State Department issued a memorandum specifically stating that the Monroe Doctrine did not concern itself with inter-American relations, but was directed against *outside* intervention in the affairs of the Western hemisphere. The United States was no longer to land Marines in a Central American republic; rather, American policy was to try to strengthen hemispheric solidarity. On these foundations, President Roosevelt built his celebrated Good Neighbor policy toward the other American nations, withdrawing the United States from Cuba and beginning the liquidation of formal American empire. To that end, in 1934 Congress passed an act promising the Philippine Islands formal independence after twelve years and bestowing a diluted kind of dominion status on the islands during the interim.

IV THE EAST MEETS THE WEST: WESTERN HISTORY AND WORLD HISTORY

The interwar years were marked by a fundamental change in the relations between those nations associated with "Western civilization" and the nations and peoples of Asia and the Middle East, and to a lesser extent, of Africa. Though China had been the object of European wars, though Japan had been "opened" to the West, and though virtually the whole of the world had been brought into the European and American orbits during the age of imperialism, people in the West had not recognized that the societies of Asia and Africa had histories of their own. Even though these histories had impinged upon each other through trade, cultural borrowing, the migration of peoples, and the setting up of empires, the histories of Japan or China, for instance, had not become significant as yet to an understanding of Western history. Now they would become so, and Western history and world history would be virtually indistinguishable.

Japan

Alone among non-Western peoples, the Japanese maintained full political independence during the golden age of imperialism. More than that, as the twentieth century opened, Japan was experiencing the Industrial Revolution and advancing to the status of a great power, a full (if unwelcome) participant in the struggle for imperial position. Since the Japanese made these impressive accomplishments without radically altering their traditional oligarchical and absolutist political structure, they remained fully "of the East," even as they became an integral part of Western history—as one of the Allied nations in World War I, as the first industrialized nation in Asia, and in time as the first so-called "Westernized" nation east of Turkey and north of Australia.

In the decade after World War I, it looked as though Japan might gradually liberalize its political institutions. The cabinets of the 1920s included many businessmen who favored vigorous expansion abroad but who also granted some measure of cautious liberalism at home. The suffrage was gradually extended, for example, and in 1925 all men received the right to vote; women were granted this right in 1949. For the first time, Western-style political parties began to develop, especially in the cities, and seemed likely to give new vitality to the Diet, the relatively weak Japanese parliament. Trade unions also began to win a following.

However, interwar Japan did not evolve into a parliamentary democracy. By the early 1930s political power was falling into the hands of army and navy officers, many of whom were descended from the feudal *samurai* class. This officer clique hated the prospect of liberal civilian government and envied and mistrusted the business class. It found a potent political weapon in the institution of the emperor, who was supposed to possess the kind of political infallibility that Westerners had associated with a divine-right monarch. Putting their own words into the emperor's mouth, the admirals and generals used his pronouncements to further their own ends. And to make doubly sure, they assassinated or terrorized the chief liberal leaders.

The consequence was a military dictatorship in Japan during the 1930s. Although popular elections continued to be held, their results were disregarded; businessmen supported the new regime out of fear or in anticipation of the profits to be secured from its adventures abroad. A cult of emperor worship grew, focusing popular loyalties on the divine mission of the emperor and ensuring popular submission to the will of those who ruled in his name. A corps of ruthless agents, named "thought police," hounded people suspected of harboring "dangerous thoughts." In short, Japan now had a government that exploited many uniquely Japanese traditions, but in its operations also bore a striking resemblance to the totalitarian governments of Europe.

Nowhere was the parallel with European totalitarianism more marked than in the foreign policy of Japan between the two world wars. Like Hitler's Germany or Mussolini's Italy, Japan claimed to be a "have-not" nation. The Japanese too pointed to their steadily growing population, and did all they could to encourage its further growth. The Japanese, having experienced one hundred and twenty-five years of zero-growth before 1853—during which time they had improved their standard of living, consolidated their natural resources, and begun to urbanize and accumulate capital—were well into a sustained period of economic and population growth. Between 1850 and 1950 (despite the intervening wars) the population soared from thirty-two million to eighty-four million. The Japanese too harped on the overcrowding of the homeland, its inadequate resources, and its restricted markets.

Behind these arguments lay real economic problems of sustaining the Japanese economy in the face of the depression and the worldwide disruption of international trade, problems of providing food and work for the sixty million Japanese in 1930. In seeking to solve these problems by imperial expansion, the militarists of the 1930s were following a pattern that had already been set by the West. And they were also following the path marked out by the Japanese officers and politicans who had secured Formosa in 1895 and annexed Korea in 1910. During World War I Japan had tried in vain to subjugate China; by World War II it had apparently almost succeeded in doing so.

China

China, meantime, was engaged in a great struggle to free itself from the hold of the Western colonial powers. The struggle was much more than a simple conflict between nationalists and imperialists. It was complicated by two additional elements in particular—the increasing threat to Chinese independence from an expansionist Japan and increasing communist intervention in Chinese politics. China faced the prospect of simply exchanging one set of imperial overlords for another.

By 1900 the Chinese Empire was well into political decay. Nominally independent under the rule of its Manchu dynasty, it had lost much of its effective sovereignty through concessions of naval bases and economic and political privileges to the European powers and Japan. Following China's defeat by Japan in 1895, European imperialists had engaged in a hectic scramble for further concessions (see Chapter 22). A formidable reaction to this outburst of imperialist activity had erupted within China. The hard-pressed Manchu government had encouraged the formation of antiforeign nationalist secret societies, of which the most important was The Fists of Righteous Harmony. Missionaries called this group the Boxers, and when they revolted, the name was taken up by the Western press. The result of the Boxer Rebellion of 1900, in which more than two hundred foreigners were slain, was the use of troops by the foreign powers, including the United States, to protect their nationals and property against the Boxers. In 1901 they obliged the Manchu government to pay a large indemnity and to grant them rights that further impaired Chinese sovereignty.

The next Chinese rebellion, the revolution of 1911, was directed against the Manchu regime that had proved so incapable of resisting foreign imperialism. The movement was also directed against the West— against Westerners themselves or against local governors who seemed to be agents of the West. But it was a movement inspired at least in part by Western ideas and examples and often led by thoroughly "Westernized" Chinese.

From the start, two chief revolutionary groups displayed conflicting ideas about the nature of the new society that would replace the Manchus. One group formed the Nationalist party, the Kuomintang, led by Sun Yat-sen (1866-1925) and many young intellectuals who had studied and traveled in the West. Its leaders wanted a democratic parliamentary republic modeled on the Western political system, though preserving as far as possible the basic Chinese family and village structure, on to which Western industrial society was to be grafted. The other group, whose leader was Yüan Shih-k'ai (1859-1916), wanted a strong central government basically authoritarian in structure, with authority not in the hands of an emperor and the traditional and highly conservative mandarin bureaucracy, but in the hands of strongmen capable of modernizing China from above.

A struggle for power broke out between the assembly elected after 1911 and Yüan Shih-k'ai. The party of Sun Yat-sen was defeated, and by 1914, after a purge of the Kuomintang members of the assembly, Yü Shih-k'ai issued a constitutional declaration that put him in the presidential office for ten years. Sun Yat-sen and his followers had failed to turn China into a parliamentary democracy. Sun was, however, a gifted leader, and though defeated, he continued to be viewed as the hero of the revolution until well after his death in 1925. Yüan, however, died in 1916, leaving the new republic facing the prospect of the dissolution of all but the shadow of central control and the assumption of real power by regional strongmen. A new era of provincial warlords had begun.

In the same years, China also faced the aggressive attempts of Japan to take over the Far Eastern imperial interests of European powers now at war among themselves. Early in 1915 the Japanese secretly presented to the Chinese government the Twenty-One Demands, which amounted to a demand for something close to a protectorate over China. The Chinese republic, now at the lowest point of its strength, countered by declaring war against the Central Powers, thus securing at least the nominal protection of Britain and France. Unable to defy Western objections, the Japanese contented themselves with taking over the German concessions. At the end of the war the victorious Allies, with the United States in the lead, checked the ambitions of their recent military partner. In 1922 Japan was forced to sign a Nine-Power treaty guaranteeing the independence of China. This rebuff to Japan was one of the first in a long chain of events that intensified the hostility of Japan toward the United States and ended, two decades later, in war.

After World War I, then, the main elements in the Chinese political situation were the Kuomintang, the communists, and the Japanese invaders. After the death of Sun Yat-sen, the Kuomintang came under the leadership of his brother-in-law, Chiang Kai-shek (1887-1975), an army officer trained in Japan. The Nationalists of the Kuomintang were engaged in a constant and unsuccessful struggle to set up an effective central government against the provincial warlords. The Chinese Communist movement began in the early 1920s. At first it was inspired by direct contacts with the Comintern in Mos-

The Western world first became fully aware of Generalissimo Chiang Kai-shek as a significant force in China by this press photo, sent out in December of 1935, when he was chosen as chairman of the Executive Yuan, becoming virtual dictator of China.

cow, guided by Soviet agents, and encouraged by leaders of the Kuomintang itself, since Sun Yat-sen hoped that the example and advice of the successful Russian party might help to strengthen his own faltering organization. For a time the Chinese Communists were little more than the left wing of the Kuomintang, but a breach soon occurred between them and the more conservative elements led by Chiang Kai-shek.

The Communists did badly in this early struggle for power. In 1926 Chiang's forces began a campaign of persecution and assassination against them; in 1927 they were expelled from the Kuomintang. An important reason for this setback was the failure of the Chinese Communists to get effective support from Moscow, for these were the years of the Trotsky-Stalin feud. The conflict between the two Russian titans was intensified by their differences over the "correct" Chinese policy for the Soviet Union to follow. Stalin, who was rapidly gaining the ascendancy, believed that China was not ripe for a proletarian revolution; therefore, he did nothing to help his Chinese comrades.

Nationalists and Communists fought in word and deed for the allegiance or the passive acceptance of nearly five hundred million Chinese, for the most part illiterate peasants. To transform China into a nation in the Western sense required more than building railroads and factories or promoting the study of modern science instead of the Chinese classics. It required getting the Chinese peasants to regard themselves as Chinese citizens. This indispensable process was beginning in the 1920s and 1930s.

The Japanese attack came in September 1931 in Manchuria, an outlying northern province of China that was a particularly tempting target for Japanese aggression. Manchuria had coal and iron; it adjoined Korea, already a Japanese possession; and it had never been fully integrated into China. Moreover, the Japanese regarded themselves as the natural successors of the Russians, whom they had driven from Manchuria in the Russo-Japanese war of 1904-1905. By 1932 the Japanese were strong enough to proclaim Manchuria the "independent" state of Manchukuo, under a puppet ruler, Henry Pu-yi (1905-1967), who as a child had been the last emperor of old China. The Chinese responded by boycotting Japanese goods; the Japanese countered by carrying the war to the Chinese port of Shanghai. Given the weakness of the Kuomintang government, effective Chinese resistance would have required full support from strong outside forces. Neither the Western powers nor the League of Nations gave China more than verbal support; the Chinese had to give up their boycott, and the Japanese remained in Manchuria. Tensions between China and Japan persisted, and the Japanese soon decided to absorb most of the rest of China. The invasion came in July 1937 without a formal declaration of war.

Militarily, the Japanese did very well. By October, when the key southern Chinese city of Canton fell, they had taken the strategic points along the coastal area and the thickly populated river valleys. Chiang Kai-shek took refuge in the interior province of Szechuan, where he set up his capital at Chungking on the upper Yangtze River. There, with Western aid, the Nationalist government held out until the end of World War II and the collapse of Japanese imperialism.

Yet even at the height of their success, the Japanese had achieved no more than the stretching across China of a string of garrisons and the control of great cities like Shanghai and Peking. They held the railroads, subject to guerrilla attack, but away from the relatively sparse lines of modern communication they were helpless. Many Chinese villages in the area that were nominally Japanese never changed their ways during the occupation; nowhere did the Japanese win over the Chinese people.

The Nationalists of the Kuomintang led the resistance to the Japanese from the beginning, but they too ultimately failed to win the full loyalty of the Chinese people. This was partly a military matter, for Chiang's armies were no match for the Japanese, who controlled the few industrial cities in China. During the long exile in Szechuan, moreover, the morale of the Nationalists decayed. The ordeal, far from purifying and strengthening them, emphasized their alienation from the Chinese masses, their own corruption and intrigue, and their inability to live up to the early promise of Sun Yat-sen and the Kuomintang. It was the Communists, not the Nationalists, who succeeded in the end.

THE JAPANESE HONOR THEIR PUPPET, PU-YI

The Japanese invited Pu-yi, now known as the Emperor Kang-teh, to visit Japan. He went alone, for the empress was in the throes of heroin addiction. The Japanese sent one of their largest battleships to take the puppet emperor to Japan, and a fleet of seventy Japanese warships greeted him with ceremonial cannon. To show that he was indeed an emperor, Pu-yi replied with a short poem in the classical manner:

The journey is not only
to admire mountains and waters
but to make our alliance shine
like sun and moon.

After World War II, this emperor would be imprisoned in Siberia and would die in China during the Cultural Revolution of 1967.

Quoted in Arnold C. Brackman, *The Prisoner of Peking* (New York: Van Nostrand Reinhold, 1980), p. 208.

During the 1930s and the early 1940s the relative strength of Communists and Nationalists underwent a decisive shift. Both parties were in a sense totalitarian. Both were organized on the one-party pattern, which left no place for an opposition. The Communists, pursued across much of China during the 1930s, ended up with a base in Yenan in the north; their strategic position somewhat resembled that of Chiang in Szechuan. But there was an important difference. In the long years of Japanese occupation, Chiang remained in Chungking with his army and his bureaucracy. The Communists, on the other hand, managed to extend their network of organized armies and local councils in and around the Japanese in the north, and down to the sea and up through Manchuria. By 1945 the Communists were ready for their successful conflict with the Kuomintang.

After heavy shelling, Japanese units advanced through the war zone around Shanghai in 1937. This dramatic news photo was rushed to the United States by the new trans-Pacific Clipper airmail service.

India

In India World War I had marked a crucial turning point. India made important contributions to the British armies, particularly to their victory over the Turks. Indians, growing in numbers and educated in the Western tradition, responded to Allied propaganda in favor of the war to save the world for democracy. Monetary inflation and other war dislocations fostered growing agitation for self-government. Already during the war the British viceroy and his experts, both British and Indian, were planning reforms. These plans were conditioned by tensions between Hindus and Muslims. About a quarter of the total population of British India was Muslim. In the Indus Basin and part of the Punjab in the northwest and in part of Bengal in the east, the Muslims were a majority; elsewhere they lived scattered among the Hindus and other non-Muslims. Though some of the Muslims belonged to the aristocracy, most were peasants, and on the whole the Muslim community was outstripped financially, industrially, and educationally by the Hindu community.

While they might mix socially and in the civil service or the British bureaucracy, Hindu and Muslim felt strong antipathy toward each other, in part on deeply held religious grounds. Muslims opposed idolatry in all forms and felt that Hindu worship of many gods was unacceptable, and that the depiction of those gods in a variety of human, and often explicitly sexual, forms was sacrilegious. To the Hindu, much in the world was divine, so that the Hindu might worship the cow or other animals, which the Muslim might slaughter. The Hindu regarded Muslim practices as unclean, while the Muslim saw Hindu practices as unholy. It was not surprising, therefore, that after serious attempts to bring Hindu and Muslim into a unified resistance movement against the British, two separate bodies arose in the twentieth century—the Indian National Congress and All-India Muslim League. Immediately after World War I the two bodies often did present a common front against the British, but as time went on their irreconcilability tended to become more evident.

Despite these difficulties, the Indian drive for self-government and independence went on steadily after World War I. For the Hindus, the Congress party was held together effectively and given extraordinary influence over the masses by one of the great leaders of the twentieth century, Mohandas K. Gandhi (1869-1948). Gandhi was not a Brahmin (a member of the highest Hindu caste) but a member of the *bania*, or shopkeeping caste. Educated as a lawyer at Oxford and therefore familiar with the West, trained in the harshness of practical politics as a young lawyer serving the Indian minority in South Africa, Gandhi was admirably equipped to deal with both British and Hindus. Among his own people he appealed by his simple and austere personal life, his fasts, and his use of native costume. He devised the technique of insurrection called *Satyagraha*, or nonviolent noncooperation, which appealed to the fundamental Hindu belief that force is illusory and therefore ineffective. A characteristic measure sponsored by Gandhi was the organized Indian boycott of British goods, backed by his recourse to the spinning wheel to publicize the resources of native cottage industries and by a march to the sea to make salt from it illegally in defiance of British regulations. The Mahatma, as Gandhi was known, also defied Hindu prejudice, directing some of his hunger strikes not against the British but against the status of the untouchables as pariahs outside the caste system.

Other Congress leaders, especially at the local level, were willing to imitate Western methods of agitation, propaganda, and some violent "nonviolence." Concession after concession was wrung from the British, and as the Indians gained political experience in provincial self-government and in civil service, dominion status was thought to be just around the corner. This was the situation at the outbreak of World War II. By the time the war was over, however, the mutual antagonism of Hindus and Muslims seemed to require not a single unified India, but two separate states.

By 1919 Gandhi was urging a policy of noncooperation on all Indian nationalists. In 1921, the year this picture was taken, he made one last attempt to impress upon Britain the need to listen to India's aspirations. "No matter what you do," he said, "no matter how you repress us, we shall one day wring reluctant repentance from you; and see that you do not make the three hundred millions of Indians your eternal enemies."

DEMOCRACY AT THE VILLAGE LEVEL

Gandhi was in pursuit of *Swaraj* (independence), and he wrote of it often. In 1921 he sought to explain "the secret of Swaraj":

The householder has to revise his or her ideas of fashion and, at least for the time being, suspend the use of fine garments which are not always worn to cover the body. He should train himself to see art and beauty in the spotlessly white *Khaddar* and to appreciate its soft unevenness. The householder must learn to use cloth as a miser uses his hoard.

And even when the householders have revised their tastes about dress, somebody will have to spin yarn for the weavers. This can only be done by everyone spinning during spare hours either for love or for money.

Under the pre-British economy of India, spinning was an honourable and leisurely occupation for the women of India. It was an art confined to the women of India, because the latter had more leisure. And being graceful, musical, and as it did not involve any great exertion, it had become the monopoly of women. But it is certainly as graceful for either-sex as is music, for instance. In hand-spinning is hidden the protection of women's virtue, the insurance against famine, and the cheapening of prices. In it is hidden the secret of *Swaraj*. . . . The revival of hand-spinning is the least penance we must do for the sin of our forefathers in having succumbed to the Satanic influences of the foreign manufacturer.

Do I want to put back the hand of the clock of progress? Do I want to replace the mills by hand-spinning and hand-weaving? Do I want to replace the railway by the country cart? Do I want to destroy machinery altogether? These questions have been asked by some journalists and public men. My answer is: I would not weep over the disappearance of machinery or consider it a calamity. But I have no design upon machinery as such. What I want to do at the present moment is to supplement the production of yarn and cloth through our mills, save the millions we send out of India, and distribute them in our cottages. . . .

Just as we cannot live without breathing and without eating, so is it impossible for us to attain economic independence and banish pauperism from this ancient land without reviving home-spinning. I hold the spinning wheel to be as much a necessity in every household as the hearth. No other scheme that can be devised will ever solve the problem of the deepening poverty of the people.

From Anan T. Hingorani, ed., *The Village Reconstruction, by M.K. Gandhi* (Bombay: Bharatiya Vidya Bhavan, 1966), pp. 5-7.

The Middle East

The European powers had a long history of attempts to secure an imperial stake in the Near East—or Middle East, to use the term that gained currency in World War II. Before 1914 the Middle East—Persia and the Asian and African lands that were still nominally part of the decaying Ottoman Empire—was still poverty stricken. But by 1914 the first discoveries of petroleum had been made; today the Middle East contains the richest nations in the world. The whole area was not to share in this new wealth. The major fields were found in southwestern Persia, in the river valleys of Iraq, and along the Persian Gulf. These new-found riches of the Middle East heightened the interest of the European powers, and in the 1930s as American experts began to worry about the depletion of oil reserves in the Western hemisphere, American business entered the area to compete with well-established French and British interests. American oil companies soon joined with British, Dutch, and French companies in developing and marketing Middle Eastern petroleum.

Although the Westerners tried to maintain sufficient control of the Middle East to ensure the orderly exploitation of oil, they also tried to avoid the cruder sort of political imperialism. After World War I the Arab territories of the old Ottoman Empire were administered as Western mandates, not annexed as Western colonies. The French had received the mandates for Syria and for Syria's half-Christian neighbor, Lebanon. The British, who already held a protectorate over Egypt, were given the mandates for Palestine and Iraq. The only major Arab state enjoying anything like full independence was Saudi Arabia. It was an essentially medieval state, the personal creation of a tribal chieftain, Ibn Saud (1880-1953). The postwar mandates, which brought so much of the Arab world under imperial control, frustrated the aspirations of Arab nationalists. In these nationalist movements the usual ingredients—Western education, hatred of Westerners, desire to emulate Western technology—were mixed with a common adherence to Islam and a feeling of a common Arab identity.

Arab nationalism was already focused on the special problem of Palestine, for by the Balfour Declaration of 1917 the British had promosed to open this largely Arab-populated territory as a "national home for the Jewish people." The immigration of Jews into Palestine, especially after the Nazis took power in Germany, raised their proportion of the population from about 10 percent to about 30 percent and caused repeated clashes between Arabs and Jews. Caught between Jewish nationalism (or Zionism) and Arab nationalism, the British tried in vain to placate both sides. On the eve of World War II, mindful of Nazi attempts to woo the Arabs, the British restricted Jewish immigration into Palestine and Jewish purchases of Arab lands in the mandate. The seeds were thus sown for the acute Palestine problem of the postwar period.

The French made few concessions to Arab nationalism, infuriating the Syrians by bombarding their capital of Damascus while quelling an insurrection in 1925 and 1926. A decade later the expectations aroused by the Popular Front's willingness to grant at least some independence to Syria and Lebanon were nullified when the French parliament rejected the draft treaties, intensifying the Arab sense of betrayal. Soon nationalist leaders in Algeria and later in Tunisia were discussing with the Arabs of Syria and Lebanon how to make common cause against the French.

The British attempted a more conciliatory policy by granting some of their dependencies nominal independence and substituting the looser ties of alliance for the older imperial ties. In Egypt nationalist agitation after World War I led Britain to proclaim that country an independent monarchy under King Fuad I (1868-1936). The British, however, still retained the right to station troops there. They also insisted that Westerners resident there be under the jurisdiction not of regular Egyptian courts but of mixed courts, on which Western judges (including one American as well as Europeans) outnumbered Eygptians. In 1936 an Anglo-Egyptian agreement provided for the eventual end of the mixed courts and the eventual withdrawal of British troops from the country, except along the Suez Canal. The controversial question of the future of the Anglo-Egyptian Sudan, which some Egyptians hoped to annex, was left unsettled. Meanwhile, Egypt continued to be closely allied with Britain; in exchange for this alliance, the British did little to moderate Fuad's increasingly autocratic ways which, in turn, gave rise to an opposition party, the Wafd.

Turkey too was undergoing a political renaissance. World War I reduced its territory to a cohesive national unit, the largely Turkish-populated Anatolia. To defend this core against further losses to the Greeks and to the victorious Allies, the Turks launched an ardent nationalist revival, dramatically extending the reforms begun by the Young Turks before 1914. The leader of this new political revolution was the gifted army officer Mustafa Kemal, who drove the Greeks from Anatolia and negotiated more favorable terms with the Allies at Lausanne in 1923. Under his guidance, the Republic of Turkey was proclaimed in 1922, with a constitution modeled on Western parliamentary lines, though with a one-party system. To emphasize the new nationalistic focus of the republic, Kemal moved its capital from cosmopolitan Istanbul to Ankara, in the interior of Anatolia.

Kemal also imposed rapid, wholesale, and sometimes ruthless measures of Westernization. Women received the vote, began to serve as deputies in the parliament, and were, at least in theory, emancipated from Muslim restraints, though even Kemal did not dare to sponsor legislation banning the wearing of the veil in public. He did, however, require men to wear Western garb. The office of caliph, with its memories of medieval Muslim grandeur, was abolished, along with that of Ottoman emperor. The sacred law of Islam was replaced by a European law code; polygamy was banned and civil marriage required; the Western calendar was introduced, with Sunday, not the Muslim Friday, as the weekly day of rest; and the building of new mosques and repair of old ones were discouraged. Justinian's Church of Santa Sophia, which had become a mosque with the Ottoman conquest in 1453, was secularized as a museum. The Turkish language was reformed by the introduction of a Western alphabet—a measure of major importance, for only a fraction of the Turkish people had ever been able to master the old Ottoman Turkish, with its heavy content of Persian and Arabic words and its difficult Arabic script. All Turks were now required to take surnames in the Western manner, and Kemal himself took that of Atatürk, "Father of the Turks." At his death in 1938 Atatürk had revolutionized his country, even though Westernization was only beginning to trickle down to the grass roots of Turkish society where Islamic traditions remained strong. Moreover, he had established its independence of the West, as the neutrality of Turkey during World War II was soon to demonstrate.

The example of Turkey was followed, though less sweepingly and less effectively, by the other traditionally independent major state of the Middle East—Persia, or, as it was officially styled after 1935, Iran (Land of the Aryans). The Iranian revolution began in 1905-1906 in response to the imperialist encroachments by Britain and Russia that were reducing the shahs of the Qajar dynasty in Persia to nonentities. The political structure inherited from the Middle Ages was changed into a limited monarchy with an elected parliament. This Iranian revolution proved to be abortive, however. The country, with its powerful, wealthy landlords, its peasants, and its tribes, did not adapt itself readily to modern Western political institutions. The shah was unwilling to give up his traditional powers, and the British and Russians were unwilling to give up their spheres of influence. During World War I, therefore, they both stationed troops in an ostensibly neutral Persia.

The Russian Revolution eased the czarist threat to Persian sovereignty, and at the end of the war Persian nationalists forced their government to reject a British attempt to negotiate a treaty that would have made the country a virtual British protectorate. The leader of the nationalists was Reza Khan (1878-1944), an able army

NAMING AND NATIONALISM

One aspect of both modernization and nationalism is to change names that have long been used in a way now regarded as derogatory, false, or not properly indicative of the values of the new society. Instances abound throughout this chapter. The great capital city of China, long known as Peking (and so referred to here), is now Beijing because of the modernization of methods for transliterating Chinese characters and their sounds into English. Yet we continue to use the old term. Persia is now officially Iran, though it is nonetheless still correct to refer to the citizens of Iran as Persians, for one is used as a noun and the other as an adjective. The name of the last ruling dynasty in Iran, Pahlavi, was an ancient one, taken by Reza Shah in 1925 to confer magnificence upon his otherwise humble origins. The name of the Boxer Rebellion is a purely Western creation, mildly ludicrous and deeply resented in modern Chinese historiography, since it in no way captures the sense of the *I Ho Chüan*, the Fists of Righteous Harmony.

Thus not only in changing place names, but in their pronunciation, in the creation of titles, in the translation of phrases, history shows its biases and is quickly dated. Even in so apparently simple a matter as the pronunciation of the former British East African colony of Kenya lurks the sound of historical transition, since before independence the colony was pronounced "keen-ya," while the independent nation is properly pronounced "ken-ya." Historians must observe these distinctions if they are to be true to the time they describe.

officer of little education who deeply distrusted the Russians. He used his military successes to become, first, minister of war and then, in 1923, prime minister. Thereafter he tried to manipulate the *Majles*, or parliament, to his purposes, and he won the support of the army and the cabinet. After conferring with the clergy in the holy city of Qum, the forces of Islam also fell into line behind him. In 1925 the Majles deposed the Qajar dynasty and proclaimed Reza to be Reza Shah Pahlavi. Reza Shah lacked familiarity with the West, and his erratic attempts to modernize his isolated country often failed. He ruled in increasingly arbitrary fashion, also demonstrating mounting sympathy for the Nazis,

largely because of his fears of some new British or Russian encroachment on Iranian independence. In 1941, after Hitler's invasion of Russia, the British and Russians sent troops into Iran and forced Reza Shah's abdication in order to secure the important trans-Iranian supply route to the Soviet Union.

The fate of Reza Shah was a reminder that some of the seemingly sovereign states of the non-Western world were not yet strong enough to maintain their independence against great powers. By World War II imperial ties had been loosened but by no means severed or dissolved; the full revolution against imperialism was yet to come.

SUMMARY

Great Britain was the first nation to suffer from the ills of post-industrial development. In the postwar period Conservatives wanted to preserve private industry and advocated protective tariffs against foreign competition. Labour called for nationalization of key industries.

Political democratization continued in Britain with all men over age twenty-one receiving the vote. Women over age twenty-one finally gained equal voting rights in 1928. A slight economic recovery in the later 1920s was followed by the Great Depression.

By 1919 Irish nationalists were demanding complete independence from Britain rather than home rule. In 1921 the twenty-six southern countries became the Irish Free State, while the six Ulster counties remained tied to Britain.

Although Britain recognized the full independence of the Republic of Ireland in 1949, the problem of Northern Ireland remained.

France felt the impact of the war most heavily, both in terms of casualties and material damage. In the 1920s, as the rebuilding effort got underway, France suffered severe inflation as well as other economic and social dislocations. Political divisions inherited from the French Revolution resurfaced in postwar France.

Rocked by economic and political difficulties, French governments compromised with Hitler and Mussolini despite protests from the left. In 1939 France was poorly equipped militarily and psychologically to deal with the threat of war.

People in the French colonies of Algeria, Senegal, and Indochina demanded home rule or independence. The French mandates of Syria and Lebanon were given constitutions but not independence.

In the postwar period, the isolationist mood of the United States was reflected in its tariffs and in the policy of imposing quotas to limit immigration. Nevertheless, the United States was still involved in European and world affairs in the 1920s.

At home, the uneven prosperity of the Coolidge years and the unprecedented speculation on Wall Street ended with the stock market crash of 1929. The Great Depression was worse and lasted longer in the United States than elsewhere. Franklin D. Roosevelt introduced the New Deal to ameliorate conditions. Yet recovery did not occur until the outbreak of World War II.

A liberalizing trend that occurred in Japan after World War I ended in the 1930s when the military acquired political power and imposed a military dictatorship. As in Italy and Germany, the Japanese regime embarked on an expansionist policy, claiming the need for living space, resources, and new markets.

In 1911 a revolution toppled the Manchu regime in China. China struggled to free itself from Western imperialist powers but was distracted by an internal conflict between Nationalist and Communist forces and by the threat of Japanese expansion. In 1931 Japan attacked Manchuria and in 1937 invaded China proper.

Indians agitated for self-government in the 1920s and 1930s, but irreconcilable differences between Hindus and Muslims prevented a united front. Gandhi, leader of the Congress party, advocated nonviolent noncooperation, which appealed to many Hindus.

In the Middle East, European powers were anxious to protect access to petroleum deposits. The mandate system that continued European control in the region frustrated the hopes of Arab nationalists. Although Egypt became independent, Britain had the right to keep troops there. In Turkey, Mustafa Kemal imposed wholesale Westernization. In Iran, Reza Khan's attempt to modernize rapidly met with only limited success.

chapter twenty-six

THE SECOND WORLD WAR AND ITS AFTERMATH

General wars have usually been born of a previous war or of a previous settlement that failed to solve certain important problems. In seeking the origins of World War I, historians go back to 1870, to Bismarck and the "rape of Alsace-Lorraine." World War II was, in many ways, a result of the flawed peace settlement at Versailles, though other causes, such as the Great Depression, also played a role. The cold war following the Second World War was in some ways a continuation in another form of the war of 1939-1945, though it was also in part a reversion to the Western fear of Bolshevism so prevalent in the 1920s. So troubled were international relations for the twenty years after 1919, and so closely in time did the Second World War follow on the First, that the interval between the two is sometimes called the "twenty years' truce." It is likely that historians in the distant future will consider the two wars really one war, as they now consider the wars of the French Revolution and Napoleon essentially one war; but for the present, most historians continue to use the accepted terms: World War I (1914-1918) and World War II (1939-1945). Such usage at least has the advantage of emphasizing the close relationship between the two wars.

I INTERNATIONAL POLITICS BETWEEN THE WARS

During the first part of the twenty years' truce, international leadership of the democratic world rested with Britain and France. Though supported in principle and at times in practice by the United States, they were increasingly unable to stem the rise of powers hostile to their preferred form of government—Italy, Germany, Russia, Japan. In the end, Germany once more waged aggressive warfare against the major Allies of 1918, though this time Germany was allied with two of its former enemies, Italy and Japan, each disappointed with its share of the spoils of 1918.

Why was the peace settlement of 1918 followed in only twenty years by a second great war? Why was it so unlike the last great settlement, that of 1815 following the Napoleonic wars, which inaugurated a long period of general peace, interrupted only by localized and overseas wars? Nazi Germany maintained that the second war was the direct result of what its leaders called the "dictated peace" of Versailles. Supported by many sympathizers, the Nazis claimed that Germany was humiliated by the war-guilt clause, stripped of territories and colonies, saddled with an unpayable reparations bill, denied the normal rights of a sovereign state in armaments—in short, so badly treated that national

dignity made revolt against the *Diktat* and its makers a necessity. The settlement of Versailles did saddle the new German Republic with a heavy burden—a burden that was dictated in part by revenge and fear. With hindsight, a wiser Allied policy would perhaps have been to start the new government off without too great a burden, as the Allies in 1815 had done with the France of Louis XVIII, or as the Allies in 1945 would do with Germany and Japan. But hindsight is not history.

The West

But the Diktat thesis does not contain the whole truth. What breaks down the argument that the iniquities of Versailles alone explain the Second World War is the so-called "era of fulfillment." The landmark of this era was a series of treaties negotiated in 1925 at Locarno in Switzerland. Germany there agreed with France and Belgium on a mutual guarantee of their common frontiers; Britain and Italy agreed to act as guarantors—that is, to provide military aid against the aggressor if frontiers were violated. Germany affirmed its acceptance of the western frontier drawn at Versailles by the Rhineland Treaty. France affirmed the new moderate direction that its German policy had taken since the failure of the occupation of the Ruhr.

In public, the Locarno settlement endured for several years. It was nourished by the general prosperity of the French and the Germans and by the policies of their respective foreign ministers, Briand and Stresemann. In 1926 Germany was admitted to the League of Nations, an event that seemed to signify not only its restoration to international respectability but also its acceptance of the peaceful purposes of League membership. These hopeful impressions appeared to receive confirmation when Germany signed the Kellogg-Briand Peace Pact of 1928. In 1929 the French consented to withdraw the last of their occupation troops from Rhineland by 1930, thus ending the Allied occupation of Germany at a date considerably in advance of the one stipulated in the Versailles Treaty.

Meantime, other international developments were bolstering the "Locarno spirit." The League of Nations began its operations in 1920. Its Council, dominated by the great powers, and its Assembly, representing all members, met regularly at the League's capital in Geneva, Switzerland. The League soon had two achievements to its credit: resolving a dispute between Sweden and Finland over the Aland Islands in 1921, and pacifying a frontier incident involving Greece and Bulgaria in 1925.

Though not a member of the League, the United States took a leading part in furthering one of the League's chief objectives—disarmament. Meeting in

Washington during the winter of 1921-1922, a naval conference of the major sea powers achieved an agreement establishing a ten-year "holiday" in the construction of capital ships (defined as battleships and heavy cruisers). The agreement also set the allowed tonnages of capital ships at a ratio of 5 for the United States, 5 for Britain, 3 for Japan, and 1.67 each for France and Italy. Nations with excess tonnage were to scrap their ships. However, the Washington settlement, while significantly helping to forestall a renewed naval race, would be a source of future conflict, since Japan felt that it was being denied the equality of status it had earned as an Ally in World War I, and since the British, who had hoped to initiate a conference themselves, were reluctant to see any other nation given naval equality.

A conference at London in 1930 had less success in limiting noncapital ships (including submarines, which had proved their destructive capacities in World War I). The partial failure of the London naval conference was a portent. Two years later, after long preparation, the League itself convoked a meeting to address the problem of limiting military armaments. Not only League members but also the United States and the Soviet Union sent representatives to Geneva. The World Disarmament Conference of 1932, however, accomplished nothing; it was wrecked by Franco-German antagonism, by the German demand for equality in armaments with France, and by the French refusal to grant the demand.

By 1932 the Locarno spirit was dead, and the era of fulfillment had ended. One obvious explanation for this failure of the hopes aroused in the 1920s was the worldwide depression that began in 1929. In Germany the depression was decisive in putting Hitler in power. In the democracies too it had serious consequences for the peace of the world, since the depression sapped their morale and made them less confident. Britain, in particular, was struck hard by the depression's impact on armament programs and the capacity to prepare its navy for rapid, full-scale action. In any case, even when the era of fulfillment was most successful, there had been clear warnings that appearances and reality did not fully coincide. The Germans had remained unwilling to accept a Locarno-style settlement of their eastern frontiers; the French had begun to seek out renewed alliances and to build a massive defensive line; and the Germans had begun a secret collaboration with the Russians to bypass the Versailles restriction on armaments.

Another unsettling factor was Soviet Russia. The West regarded Russia as a revolutionary power that could not be fully integrated into the international state system. The Soviet Union was the center of a revolutionary faith hated by Western politicians who feared (often with justification) communist agitation among their own peoples. Westerners simply could not trust a government that was based on the Marxist belief that all Western capitalist democracies were destined to collapse and become communist after a violent class war.

Yet another factor that led to the Second World War was the continuing failure of the three major Western democracies—Britain, France, and the United States—to present a united front. Although each was a capitalist and a democratic state, the nature of their governments differed more than the growing similarity of governments in the fascist nations. The democracies each had a native fascist movement of its own. The United States had widely diverse ethnic communities that traced their origins to Europe and took different positions on the problems emerging there. Britain and France were often at cross-purposes within the League of Nations, and the United States, not being a member, could exercise only modest influence in bringing them together. There was a sense of common apprehension in the three democracies, but not a sense of common policy.

France, exhausted and suffering a decline in population, was trying to play the part of a first-rate power with only second-rate resources, and it lived in growing fear of a revived Germany. The French sought not only to apply in full the economic and political measures of the Versailles Treaty that aimed at keeping Germany weak, but also to make up for Russia's defection as its eastern ally against Germany. Beginning in 1921 France did this by making alliances with the smaller states to the east of Germany—Poland, Czechoslovakia, Romania, and Yugoslavia. All of them wanted French protection against the possible restoration of the Hapsburg Empire, whose former lands made up so much of their own territory. All except Poland were informally linked together as the Little Entente. To British politicians who remembered the long story of Anglo-French conflicts from the Hundred Years' War to Napoleon, the France of the 1920s seemed once more to be aiming at European supremacy, once more to be threatening the traditional British policy of preventing supremacy by any single nation on the Continent.

Some advocates of the old British hope to live in "splendid isolation" had survived the war and made the British—and especially their nearly independent dominions—unwilling to commit themselves to intervene with force in continental Europe. Although Britain did accept Locarno and its commitment to punish any violator, in the previous year the dominions had played a large part in British rejection of the more sweeping Geneva protocol, which had been urged upon Britain by France and which would have committed its signatories to compulsory arbitration of international disputes. Pursuing increasingly independent trade policies, the dominions were not prepared to enter into a tight trading agreement with Britain, and this made balancing the British budget more difficult, adding to the appearance of a militarily weakened Britain. Pacifist sentiment in Britain and the dominions further strengthened the German perception that Britain would not resist limited aggression on the Continent.

The difficulties of the Anglo-French partnership partly explain the weakness of the League of Nations. In addition, the League had no means to enforce its decisions, and it was top-heavy, since the fully representative Assembly counted for less than the smaller Council, which Britain and France dominated. When these two powers disagreed, the League scarcely operated at all. One example of how the grand purposes of the League suffered from Anglo-French friction was the rejection of the Geneva protocol; another was the Corfu incident of 1923, when Mussolini defied the League for a time and set a precedent for the later use of gangster tactics by the dictators. During the Corfu crisis the League was crippled by Anglo-French discord over the Ruhr policy of France. After 1935 Germany was engaged in what some historians have called a "unilateral armaments race," while two of the greatest nations in the world, the United States and the Soviet Union, were generally absent from the overall balance of power.

Soviet Foreign Policy

As the civil war in Russia ended, Lenin realized that world revolution was not going to follow immediately, and that it would be necessary to deal with the capitalist world. In time a coherent Soviet foreign policy would emerge that would have great impact upon the decisions of Western diplomats, especially in Britain. Between 1918 and 1939 this policy was in the hands of two competent men—Georgi Chicherin (1872-1936), a learned aristocrat turned Bolshevik, and Maxim Litvinov (1876-1952), his shrewd and able chief assistant.

But the ultimate goal of world revolution was not abandoned. Lenin in 1919 founded the Third International, known thereafter as the Comintern. It summoned communists all over the world to unite against the "bourgeois cannibals" of capitalism. Gregory Zinoviev was put in charge, and his chief assistants were mainly Russians. Labor, socialist, and anarchist parties in Bulgaria, Norway, Italy, and Spain began to adhere to the new organization, although some idealists withdrew in disgust when it became clear that the Bolsheviks were establishing a dictatorship in Russia through their secret police and army. Yet the Comintern continued to operate side by side with the Soviet Foreign Office, and during the next few years often in apparent contradiction to it. This duality gave Russian foreign policy a unique and at times unpredictable aspect. The Comintern aroused suspicion abroad and made capitalist states reluctant to accord the new Russia even formal diplomatic recognition.

Treaties were concluded between Russia and Poland, the Baltic states, Scandinavia, Germany, and Italy, exchanging trade for a promise not to interfere in the domestic affairs of these states. While binding on the Soviet Foreign Office, these agreements did not, in reality, affect the Comintern. In 1922 the Russians were invited to an international economic conference at Genoa. The British and French assumed that NEP meant a return to capitalism, and they worked out a scheme for investment in Russia as part of a program for the economic reconstruction of Europe. Not only did the Russians reject this plan, but they signed the Treaty of Rapallo (April 1922) with defeated Germany, which provided for the renunciation of all claims for reparations and implied a German willingness to recognize Bolshevik nationalizations of industry. The other powers, especially France, were unwilling to grant such recognition because of the large investments they had in Russia before the revolution. Rapallo relieved Russian isolation and brought German technical knowledge to the service of the Bolsheviks, who permitted the Germans to build and operate armament and aircraft factories on Russian soil in defiance of the Treaty of Versailles.

In 1923 at Lausanne Russia lost a dispute with Britain over international regulation of the Straits, and further friction with Britain arose over Afghanistan. But Britain recognized the Soviet regime in 1924. Many members of the Labour party, while aware of the bloodshed in Russia, had great admiration for the rapidity with which Lenin was modernizing Russian society. Later in 1924 the so-called "Zinoviev letter" was published in England, which purported to instruct the British Communist party in the techniques of revolution. It was probably a forgery, but the Zinoviev letter influenced the British voters to turn Macdonald's Labour party out of office and elect Baldwin's Conservative government. In 1927 a raid on the offices of a Russian firm doing business in London produced further evidence of communist agitation in England, and the British government broke relations with Russia altogether. The Anglo-Russian council of trade unions set up by the communists collapsed when the Russians criticized British modernization in the general strike of 1926. The United States, meantime, had no diplomatic relations with the Soviet regime and did not recognize it until Roosevelt became president in 1933.

During 1918-1927 the Comintern compiled a record of failure. First, the Russians failed to restrain the Italian left in 1921 and thus contributed to the success of Mussolini in the next year. Next, their failure in Bulgaria to collaborate with a liberal agrarian regime allowed a right-wing group to triumph in 1923. Most important, they failed in Germany, where a revolution actually threatened in 1923 as a result of French occupation of the Ruhr. After Lenin's death, the feud between Stalin and Trotsky was reflected in the communist parties of other countries and cost the Comintern heavily.

The Russians also failed in Poland, where they helped Pilsudski gain dictatorial power in 1926, after which he turned against them. They failed in the Muslim and colonial world. But their greatest failure came in China, where in 1923 the Chinese nationalist revolutionary leader, Sun Yat-sen, agreed to take communist advice and received one of the Comintern's best men, Michael Borodin (1884-1953). Borodin helped Sun reorganize the Kuomintang and admit communists to it. In March 1926, Sun having died, Chiang Kai-shek led a coup against the government and began to arrest communists. Stalin now fell back on a theory that the Bolsheviks had not espoused since Lenin's return to Russia in April 1917—that a bourgeois revolution must precede a socialist revolution, and that all the communists could do in China was to help Chiang achieve this first revolution. The eventual result was the massacre of Chinese communists by Chiang and a loss of prestige for Russia.

Stalin had apparently never really believed in the effectiveness of the Comintern as an instrument of world revolution. When he came to power he could not abandon it, however, because of the criticism he would have aroused, and because he sought to dilute and eventually to eradicate the Trotskyite sentiments of some communists in other countries. He therefore applied to the Comintern the same techniques he had used against the party at home, and used the Russian delegation to establish full control over it. (As the representative of the only successful revolutionary country, the Russian delegation enjoyed great prestige.) The Comintern was thus influenced to denounce the enemies of Stalin: Trotsky and the left in 1924, Bukharin and the right in 1928. Thereafter, there was no divergence between the Comintern and the Foreign Office.

Stalin then directed the Comintern into a new period of militant revolutionary activity. The Social Democrats of Western countries were now denounced as "social fascists" and the most dangerous enemies of communism. Yet Stalin's personal belief in the possibility of worldwide revolution seems always to have been slight. This lack of interest in the behavior of communists abroad and his failure to understand the play of forces inside other countries led directly to the triumph of Hitler in Germany in 1933. The communists in Germany, who had been instructed by the Comintern that the Social Democrats and not the Nazis were their worst enemies, fought the Nazis in the streets but allied themselves with them in the Reichstag. They believed that a Nazi triumph would very soon be followed by a communist revolution. Thus even after Hitler came to power, the Russians renewed their nonaggression pact with Germany.

The shock of realization that Hitler had meant precisely what he said about liquidating communists and the fear that Russia itself might be in danger soon led Stalin to support collective security. After Hitler had refused to guarantee the Baltic states jointly with Stalin, Russia entered the League of Nations in September 1934. The Soviet delegate, Litvinov, became an eloquent defender of universal disarmament and of punishment for aggressors. Soon afterward, the Russians began to negotiate for an "eastern Locarno" security pact to balance the agreement reached by the western European nations. Although no such structure could be created because of Polish and German hostility to the USSR, Russia did sign pacts with France and Czechoslovakia in 1935 providing for consultation under the terms of the League and for mutual aid in the event of aggression. However, Soviet aid to Czechoslovakia, if the Czechs became victims of aggression, was to be delivered only if the French, who were bound to the Czechs by an alliance, honored their obligations first.

With the shift in Soviet foreign policy, the Comintern also shifted its line. In 1935 the communists' recent enemies, the Social Democrats and bourgeois liberals of the West, were embraced as allies against the fascist menace. Communists were to join popular fronts against fascism and might welcome anyone, no matter how conservative, who would stand with them on this principle. Revolutionary propaganda and anticapitalist agitation were to be softened. The communists in all the countries of the world now led the fight for the defense budgets that they had previously sabotaged. A Bulgarian communist hero was made head of the Comintern. Inside the Soviet Union, the adoption of this popular-front strategy was related to the purges, since the "right deviationists" were anxious to reach an accommodation with fascist states, while the "left deviationists" insisted on the steady pursuit of world revolution.

Russia and the western European bloc each assumed that the chief purpose of the other was to turn the full force of Hitler's forthcoming attack away from itself and in the opposite direction. That Hitler intended to attack, few doubted. On September 12, 1936, he specifically declared that

> *If I had the Ural mountains with their incalculable store of treasures in raw materials, Siberia with its vast forests, and the Ukraine with its tremendous wheatfields, Germany under National Socialist leadership would swim in plenty.**

There was, then, much reason for the West to hope that the attack would be directed against the Soviets; this Stalin was determined to avert.

Soviet intervention in the Spanish Civil War demonstrated Stalin's real position. General Francisco Franco had obtained aid from Mussolini and Hitler. The Russians, though reluctant to intervene in Spain because of their anxiety to prove their respectability to the Western powers, realized that a failure to help the Spanish republic would cost them support all over the world. But their aid was too little and too late, and it consisted largely of police agents who devoted themselves to fighting Spanish anarchists and Trotskyites. The Russians hoped that the Western powers would also intervene, feeling that if they did so they would be irrevocably committed to fight against Hitler on other battlefields. But Western neutrality in Spain helped convince Stalin that a Western alliance could not be counted on.

Still more important was the Western appeasement of Hitler, which reached its climax in the Munich agreement among Britain, France, Germany, and Italy in September 1938. From the Russian point of view, Munich's grant of Czech lands to Hitler and the French failure to support Czechoslovakia and thus make operative the Russo-Czech alliance could have only one purpose—to drive Hitler east. Stalin was apparently ready to support the Czechs if the French did; when they did not, he apparently decided that he had better sound

*Hitler, *My New Order*, ed. Raoul de Roussy de Sales (New York: Reynal & Hitchcock, 1941), p. 400.

out Hitler for an understanding. Thus a truly effective alliance between Stalin and the West proved impossible between 1935 and 1939.

When the British and French realized that appeasement had failed to stop Hitler, they reluctantly sought a firmer alliance with the Russians. From March to August 1939, Stalin kept open both his negotiations with the West and his slowly ripening negotiations with the Germans, which at first seemed to be concerned only with a trade agreement. The British and French mission, when it finally arrived in Moscow, was not composed of sufficiently high-ranking men to inspire Russian confidence. Moreover, the Western powers would not agree to turn over to Stalin the territories that he wanted as a bulwark against Germany—Finland and the Baltic republics.

The growing eagerness of the Germans to secure a nonaggression pact gave Stalin his opportunity to divert war from Russia. In May 1939 Litvinov was dismissed as foreign minister because he was Jewish and therefore could not negotiate with the Germans; he was replaced by Vyacheslav Molotov (1890-   ). In the pact that Molotov eventually reached with Hitler on August 23, 1939, each power undertook to remain neutral toward the other in the event of war. A secret additional protocol provided for a division between Germany and Russia of Poland, which Hitler was about to attack; this put Russia's frontier farther west in the event of a subsequent German attack. The pact included the statement that it would take effect the day it was signed, a provision only totalitarian leaders with no need to refer their negotiations back to an elected body could have made. The Russians lived up to the economic clauses of the agreement to the letter, although the Germans did not.

The publication of the Hitler-Stalin pact necessitated an abrupt shift in the world communist line, which had remained staunchly popular front. Now it was once more necessary for communists to denounce liberals and Social Democrats as enemies, and to call the war that Hitler launched against Poland within a few days an "imperialist war," in which there was no difference between the two sides and in which communists should not get involved. Thus Russian foreign policy, especially under Stalin, was one major avenue in the road to the war that erupted in September 1939.

II THE ROAD TO WAR, 1931-1939

A First Step:
Manchuria, 1931

The first decisive step along the road to World War II was the Japanese seizure of Manchuria in 1931. Henry L. Stimson (1867-1950), President Hoover's secretary of state, responded to the seizure by announcing that the United States would recognize no gains made by armed force. Stimson hoped that Britain and the other democracies might follow this American lead, but his hopes were largely disappointed. The League of Nations did send a commission headed by the earl of Lytton (1876-1947); the Lytton Report of 1932 condemned the Japanese act as aggression. Neither the United States nor the League, however, fortified its verbal protests by effective action; force was not met by force. Japan, refusing to accept the report, withdrew from the League of Nations in March 1933, making the first formal breach in the League's structure.

A Second Step:
German Rearmament, 1935-1936

The next breach in the League's structure was made by Germany. In October 1933 Hitler withdrew from the League, thereby serving notice on the world of his aggressive intentions. On March 16, 1935, he denounced the clauses of the Treaty of Versailles that limited German armaments and began openly rebuilding the German armed forces.

The response to this illegal act set the pattern for the next few years. On April 17, 1935, the League of Nations formally condemned Germany's repudiation of treaty obligations—and Germany continued to rearm. In May 1935 France and the Soviet Union concluded their treaty of alliance against German aggression—and Germany continued to rearm. In June 1935 the British signed a naval agreement with Germany limiting the German navy to one-third the size of the British, and German submarines to 60 percent of those of Britain.

Hitler's next act drew no more than the customary protests from the signatories of Locarno. This was the "reoccupation" of the Rhineland in March 1936—that is, the sending of German troops into the western German zone demilitarized by the Treaty of Versailles. Britain and France once more did nothing, although many military critics thought that united military action at that point would have worked, since German rearmament was far from complete. In retrospect, this moment in 1936 may have been the last opportunity to avert war in Europe.

A Third Step:
Ethiopia, 1935

Meanwhile, the Italians struck in Ethiopia, where an independent state had precariously maintained itself largely because its imperial neighbors—Britain, France, and Italy—would neither agree to divide it nor let any one of the three swallow it whole. The Italians, who wanted it most, had lost the disastrous battle of Adowa to the Ethiopians in 1896, and this humiliation rankled the fascists, who felt they had to show the world that there was more than rhetoric in their talk about a revived Roman Empire.

In 1934 a frontier incident occurred at a desert post in

Italian Somaliland—or in Ethiopia, for both sides claimed the site. France and Britain were ready to appease Italy, partly because they hoped to align Mussolini with them against Hitler. Over the protests of the Ethiopian emperor, Haile Selassie (1891-1976), they offered Mussolini generous economic concessions in Ethiopia. But since Ethiopia was a member of the League, the French and the British had to insist that its formal independence be observed. This Mussolini would not accept, and in October 1935 his troops invaded Ethiopia. Italian airplanes, artillery, and tanks made it impossible for the Ethiopians to repeat their victory of 1896. Mussolini's poison gas finished the conquest early in 1936, and the king of Italy acquired the coveted title of emperor of Ethiopia.

The League of Nations had already formally condemned the Japanese aggression in Manchuria and the German denunciation of the disarmament clauses of the Treaty of Versailles. In 1935 it promptly declared that, by invading Ethiopia, a League member, Italy had violated its obligations under the Covenant of the League. Now the League made the momentous decision to move from words to deeds. This decision was supported by most of its members and was urged on by the British, the French, and most movingly in a speech delivered to the League in Geneva by Haile Selassie, speaking in Amharic, the language of Ethiopia, while Italian fascists hissed and booed. On October 11, 1935, fifty-one member nations of the League voted to invoke Article 16 of the League Covenant, which provided for economic sanctions against a member resorting to war in disregard of its commitments.

But the sanctions against Italy failed. There were loopholes; oil, for instance, was not included in the list of articles barred from commerce with Italy, which had only meager stockpiles of this vital war material. Mussolini had declared that if the League adopted more drastic sanctions that included oil, a wider war would result. France was too divided to fight, and a sampling of British public opinion in a so-called Peace Ballot revealed that, though the public would support economic sanctions, it also favored disarmament and was not prepared for unilateral action against Italy. The British would agree to collective military efforts, but French premier Laval was willing to grant much of Ethiopia to Italy, and he persuaded the new British foreign secretary, Sir Samuel Hoare (1880-1959), to join him in such a proposal. There was much recrimination among members of the League over what articles should be placed on the prohibited list and over the British and French failure to check Italian movements of troops and munitions through the Suez Canal, which Britain then controlled. Germany was no longer in the League and was wholly unaffected by its decisions. No major power applied sanctions rigorously, so that the effectiveness of economic sanctions was not really tested. The League was hardly a factor in the increasing tensions, and no one was surprised when Italy, like Japan and Germany, withdrew from the League in December 1937.

A Fourth Step:
The Spanish Civil War, 1936-1939

The Spanish Civil War, which broke out in July 1936, was the emotional catalyst that aroused millions of men and women all over the Western world. The war pitted fascists, monarchists, and conservatives of the right against socialists, communists, anarchists, and a few liberals of the left. As in most great civil wars, there was really no center. It was a quasi-religious war, waged with the great violence that marks wars of principle. Almost from the very start it engaged, the emotions of the West through individual foreign enlistments and the active though covert intervention of other nations.

The Spanish Civil War proved to be a rehearsal for the larger war that was approaching, as the fascist nations tested their weapons. One of the first deliberate aerial bombardments of a civilian population took place in April 1937, when low-flying planes, apparently German, devastated the Basque town of Guernica. Intervention by Italy and Germany was decisive and effective; it was less determined and effective by communist Russia; and it was feeblest of all by Britain and France. Early in 1939, with the fall of Barcelona, the Civil War was over, and once more a fascist-leaning group had won.

Meantime, Mussolini signed a pact with Hitler in October 1936 formally establishing the Rome-Berlin Axis, an alliance of fascist Italy and Nazi Germany. Late in 1938 Mussolini orchestrated a public outcry in Italy for the French to hand over certain territories. He demanded not only Nice and Savoy, which had been ceded to Napoleon III in 1860, but also Corsica, which had been French since 1768, and Tunisia, which had never been under Italian rule. These demands came to nothing. Finally, on April 7, 1939, Mussolini attacked Albania, across the Adriatic Sea from Italy and long coveted by the Italians, and quickly subjugated it.

A Fifth Step:
The Marco Polo Bridge, 1937

The war between China and Japan had fallen into a lull when, on the night of July 7, 1937, a skirmish between troops of the two nations at the Marco Polo Bridge near Peking led to full-scale war once again. Neither Chiang Kai-shek nor the Japanese generals wanted war at this point, but junior officers in the field were in command of the situation. Later it would be claimed for propaganda purposes by both parties that the other had instigated the renewed conflict, though only the Japanese had reason to do so. A united anti-Japanese front had taken shape in China. An incident between Japanese and Russian forces on the Amur River the month before had made it clear that the Soviet Far Eastern army need not be feared, and a wave of nationalism in both China and Japan escalated mutual hatreds beyond the capacity of politicians to control them.

As first Peking and then Shanghai fell to the Japanese,

the Chinese government appealed to the League of Nations. Sanctions would work only if the United States joined in them, but the American secretary of state suggested "parallel" rather than "joint" action with Britain, and President Roosevelt, though clearly opposed to Japanese advances in the Far East, called for a "quarantine" of aggressor states. But following a Japanese attack on the American gunboat *Panay* on the Yangtse River, the Americans appeared ready to discuss joint Anglo-American economic action. However, by then Britain wanted a political and military agreement that went further than the United States was prepared to go. This decision appears to have moved Chamberlain to feel that, since the United States was "appeasing" Japan, he might do the same to Germany and Italy in Europe.

A Sixth Step: Anschluss, 1938

The immediate origins of World War II lay, however, in the mounting series of German aggressions. Hitler had begun openly rebuilding the German armed forces in 1935. Three years later he felt strong enough to make his first open effort at expansion. Ever since 1918 there had been a strong movement among Austrians for union (Anschluss) with Germany. This movement had been opposed by Italy and France, though the Rome-Berlin Axis lessened Mussolini's opposition to Anschluss. Early in 1938 Hitler began a violent propaganda campaign by press, radio, and platform against the alleged misdeeds of the Austrian government. In February 1938 he summoned Austrian chancellor Schuschnigg to Berchtesgaden, and in March he moved his troops into Austria, making Anschluss a fact.

A Seventh Step: Czechoslovakia Dismembered, 1938-1939

The Czechoslovak republic was the only state in central or eastern Europe where parliamentary democracy had succeeded after World War I. It faced a difficult problem of national minorities, but had inherited some of the most highly developed industrial regions of the old Hapsburg Empire; consequently, its economy was far better balanced between industry and agriculture than were those of the other states of eastern Europe. This healthy economy was mirrored in the social structure, where a working balance was maintained among peasants, middle classes, and industrial workers. The period immediately after the war and the Great Depression of the 1930s affected Czechoslovakia relatively lightly. Yet these advantages could hardly have preserved democracy in the republic had it not been for the enlightened policies of Thomas Masaryk (1850-1937), chief founder and president of his country until his resignation at the age of eighty-five in 1935.

But the Czech government could not keep the country from ultimately being destroyed by outside pressures working on its sensitive minorities. The Sudeten German minority of three and a quarter million were the heirs of all the Germans who had opposed Czech aspirations within the Hapsburg Empire. They looked down on the Slavic Czechs and resisted the new republic, even when the Prague government tried to satisfy their just grievances. From 1933 on, Nazi agitation became increasingly serious in Czechoslovakia. Early in 1938, having secured Austria, Hitler decided to pursue the Czech conquest next. His Sudeten puppet made demands on the Prague government for what amounted to complete Sudeten autonomy. The Czechs were relying on their French allies and on the British, but by the spring of 1938 Britain and France had decided not to defend the territorial integrity of Czechoslovakia. France felt itself in no position to do so and did not wish to take action if this would draw Russia into action of its own. Opinion in Britain held that Czech independence was not vital to British interests, and the British chiefs of staff argued that attempting to make war on Germany before the air force was ready would be like "a man attacking a tiger before he had loaded his gun."

By the autumn of 1938 Hitler was ready. On September 12 he made a violent speech at Nuremberg, insisting on self-determination for the Sudeten Germans. This was the signal for widespread disorders in Czechoslovakia, followed by the proclamation of martial law by the government of Eduard Beneš (1887-1948). The Conservative British prime minister, Neville Chamberlain (1869-1940), made two preliminary visits to Hitler in Germany in an effort to moderate German demands. Finally, with the help of Mussolini, he persuaded Hitler to call a full conference of the four great Western powers. Hitler, Mussolini, Chamberlain, and Daladier of France met in Munich on September 29, 1938. Russia was not invited; this affront was the last nail in the coffin of the popular-front policy.

Munich was a sweeping victory for Hitler. Czechoslovakia was partially dismembered; its Sudeten borderlands were turned over to Germany; the Czechs were obliged to hand over Teschen and other areas to the Poles; their entire economy and transportation system were weakened; the defense of their frontiers was made impossible by the loss of the border mountains and their fortifications. Slovakia was given autonomy within a federal state, emphasized by the official change in spelling from Czechoslovakia to Czecho-Slovakia.

The Czech leaders had found it impossible to resist the Germans without French and British aid, and their people acquiesced bitterly in the settlement of Munich. The Germans had played skillfully on the differences between the more industrialized Czechs and the still largely agricultural Slovaks. But even had the country been strongly united, Munich would have ruined its morale. Hitler acted quickly. In the very next spring, before the final lines of demarcation set at Munich had actually been drawn, he summoned the Czech president to Germany and announced that the fate of the Czech

Europe on the Eve
of World War II,
August 1939

Neutral nations following
outbreak of war

0   300
Miles

The Axis Powers
Areas annexed by Germany 1935-1939
Areas made "protectorates" of Germany, 1939
Annexed by Italy, 1939

people "must be placed trustingly in the hands of the Führer." In March 1939 Hitler sent his army into Prague and took over the remaining Czech lands, meeting no real resistance. Hungary, anxious to reclaim some of its lost territory, occupied the easternmost province of Czechoslovakia, Ruthenia, with German consent.

The best defense that can be made for Munich and appeasement is that the West was either genuinely trying to avoid war or that it was buying time to prepare for a war that it knew to be inevitable but for which it was not yet ready. In September 1938 the democracies were in a stronger military position relative to that of Germany than they would be in September 1939. It also seems likely that Chamberlain and Daladier, as well as millions all over the world, hoped that the acquisition of the Sudeten Germans would satisfy Hitler, that after Munich he would behave as Bismarck had behaved after Sedan,

and that he would try to preserve the balance of power. Some Westerners even hoped that Hitler might join with them against communist Russia, or get himself so entangled in eastern Europe that he would bring on a Russo-German war. Hitler's words and deeds, however, had given no real basis for such hopes. As early as November 1937 he had announced to his close advisers his unalterable intention of destroying Czechoslovakia and moving on into Poland and the Ukraine.

The actual destruction of Czechoslovakia in March 1939 seems not to have surprised anyone. But the mixture of resignation, condemnation, and resolution with which this action was greeted in the West marks a turning point. The days of appeasement were over, as Britain and France made clear their intentions to guarantee the borders of Poland, and Britain started a peacetime draft. Munich proved to be a catalyst both for professional Western diplomats and for Western opinion generally. Hitler's next aggression would not lead to a Munich. Historians cannot be sure whether Hitler and his aides realized this, or thought they could take still another step without bringing on a general war. Hitler, Göring, and other Nazi leaders made no secret of their feeling that the British and French were decadent, inefficient, and too cowardly to resist an inspired and rejuvenated Germany. Yet there is evidence that Hitler expected at least a local war with Poland, and that he was quite prepared to confront the French and the British if need be. Hitler had strengthened his system on May 22 by concluding an offensive-defensive "Pact of Steel" with Mussolini, who only six weeks before had conquered Albania. Both nations obviously intended further aggression.

The Final Step: Poland, 1939

Poland was clearly going to be Hitler's next victim. The Germans regarded the Polish corridor dividing East Prussia from the rest of Germany as an affront; so too was the separation from Germany of the Free City of Danzig, German in language and tradition, on the edge of the Polish corridor. Hitler's Germans thought of the Poles as inferiors who would benefit from German supervision. Hitler began his Baltic adventure on March 2, 1939, when he took the port town of Memel from Poland's northern neighbor, Lithuania. At the end of the month, the British and French responded by assuring Poland of aid in the event of a German attack.

The critical issue in the tense half-year that led up to the outbreak of war on September 1, 1939, was whether Poland would undergo the same fate as Czechoslovakia and receive no support from the Western democracies. The British government made it clear that it would back away no longer; indeed, in the final week of crisis Chamberlain sent a letter to Hitler in which he made his position clear. Of course, since Britain had not stood firm on earlier occasions, Hitler may have believed that despite its pronouncements, Britain still might, in the end, back down.

The critical issue now was the attitude of Russia. Hitler had an understandable fear of a war on two fronts against major powers to the east and to the west, like the war on which Germany had embarked in 1914. But the Russians deeply distrusted the British Tories under Chamberlain, believing that Tory Britain was fundamentally more hostile to communist Russia than Nazi Germany was. This Russian mistrust of the West was not dispelled by a diplomatic mission that Britain and France sent to Russia in the summer of 1939. The Western powers proposed a mutual assistance pact, but the negotiations were inept and halfhearted. Moreover, Chamberlain's government made a tactless choice of negotiators, one of whom had been involved in the British intervention against the Reds at Archangel in the early days of the Bolshevik state. In any case, the British negotiators lacked high rank. Hitler, who was also negotiating with Russia, put Foreign Minister Ribbentrop himself on the job. The Anglo-French overture to Moscow came to nothing; the Russian leaders had apparently concluded that if they did not come to terms

---

AN END TO APPEASEMENT

Wars often occur because one side or the other is unclear about the intentions of a potential enemy. The language of diplomacy is carefully calculated to permit maximum ambiguity when that is desirable, and extreme clarity when that is necessary. Hitler may have doubted the sincerity of the warnings he was receiving, but by August 22 the British prime minster, Chamberlain, was leaving no room for such doubts. He sent the following message to Hitler:

Your Excellency will have already heard of certain measures taken by His Majesty's Government and announced in the press and on the wireless this evening. These steps have, in the opinion of His Majesty's Government, been rendered necessary by military movements which have been reported from Germany and by the fact that apparently the announcement of a German-Soviet Agreement is taken in some quarters in Berlin to indicate that intervention by Great Britain on behalf of Poland is no longer a contingency that need be reckoned with. No greater mistake could be made. Whatever may prove to be the nature of the German-Soviet Agreement, it cannot alter Great Britain's obligation to Poland, which His Majesty's Government have stated in public repeatedly and plainly and which they are determined to fulfill.

It is alleged that if His Majesty's Government had made their position more clear in 1914, the great catastrophe would have been avoided. Whether or not there is any force in that allegation, His Majesty's Government are resolved that on this occasion there shall be no such tragic misunderstanding.

If the case should arise, they are resolved and prepared to employ without delay all the forces at their command, and it is impossible to foresee the end of hostilities once engaged. . . .

Documents on British Foreign Policy, 1919-1939, 3rd series, E.L. Woodward and R. Butler, eds. (London: Her Majesty's Stationery Office, 1954), VII, 170-172.

with Hitler, he would attack them. Perhaps they also calculated that the French armies would resist the Germans successfully for some time, and the Western powers would thus wear themselves out and enable the Soviets to profit by the consequences, or at least gain valuable time to arm themselves further.

Finally, the Russians were distrustful of the Polish government. The Western policy of encouraging the smaller powers of eastern Europe to act as counterweights to both Germany and Russia had borne fruit. The Polish government would not accept Russia as protector; it would not consent to the passage through Polish territory of Russian troops in case of war with Germany. The Russians, they knew, were tempted by the opportunity to recover lands in eastern Poland that they had lost in World War I and its aftermath.

So, to the horror of the West, on August 23, 1939, Stalin signed a nonaggression pact with Hitler, a pact concluded personally by Ribbentrop and Molotov. This Nazi-Soviet pact freed Hitler's hands. It also stunned Communist party members in most Western countries and led to wholesale desertions from the party, as many intellectuals—who had either remained blind to Stalin's purges or had convinced themselves that such purges, however vicious, were necessary to achieve "socialism in one country"—decided that their new secular god had failed them. Those not committed to ideology were less surprised, for while they recognized that Marxism might be a valuable analytical method, an analytical method does not invariably prescribe an acceptable course of political action. The cynical alliance between the totalitarianism of the right and the totalitarianism of the left shattered the illusions of many followers of communism.

On September 1, 1939, the German army marched into Poland. On September 3 Britain and France honored their obligations and declared war on Germany. The twenty years' truce was at an end. The democracies had not been able to halt a dedicated, ruthless, organized state. Since the Great Depression the Western democracies had been committed to helping their citizens attain minimum standards of material comfort; normally they would produce butter before guns. Their totalitarian opponents, on the other hand, were able to convince or intimidate their people to agree that butter was to be attained in the future—and by making use of the guns if need be. They had persuaded their citizens to go without for the sake of military preparations; democratic states would find it difficult to get such sacrifices from their people until the war had actually begun.

III WORLD WAR II, 1939-1942

The First World War had been one long siege in its main theater, the western front. Since military experts tend to prepare for the last war in planning for the next, both France and Germany in the 1930s built confronting

"Rendezvous" was David Low's cartoon commentary on the Hitler-Stalin pact. Low (1891-1963) was one of the first political (that is, editorial) cartoonists, and his enormous influence in the pages of the mass-circulation London *Evening Standard* was indicative of an important shift in journalism toward the use of comics and political cartoons for serious purposes.

lines of fortifications on their common frontier. The Maginot Line on the French side and the Siegfried Line on the German were far more formidable than were the trenches of 1914 to 1918. With the outbreak of hostilities, most people expected that the war would be decided primarily in the area between France and Germany, and that it would be a closely confined war, perhaps of siege, perhaps quite brief with at most only diversionary activity in other parts of the world.

But the war once more showed the perils of prediction. As Germany was joined by its Axis partners, Italy and Japan, and as the United States entered on the Allied side, the Second World War became much more fully a world war than the First had been. Its outcome was decided on the eastern front in Russia, in the Pacific, and in the Mediterranean quite as much as in France. The entry of new nations, the relative freedom of movement over vast areas, and the special problems presented by a wide-ranging war brought about major technological changes in the nature of warfare.

In 1939 Germany was ready for war to an extent that it had not been in 1914. The reverse was true of the principal Allies, for neither France nor Britain was fully prepared. Moreover, Germany did not need to fight on two major fronts, since the pact with Stalin had neutralized Russia. However, France, which had held only one front in the First World War, now had to maintain troops along the Spanish and Italian borders to guard against an attack by those nations. Still, German success was predicated on a quick victory; otherwise, the United States might once again be drawn into the war, the British would gain time to supply their troops and

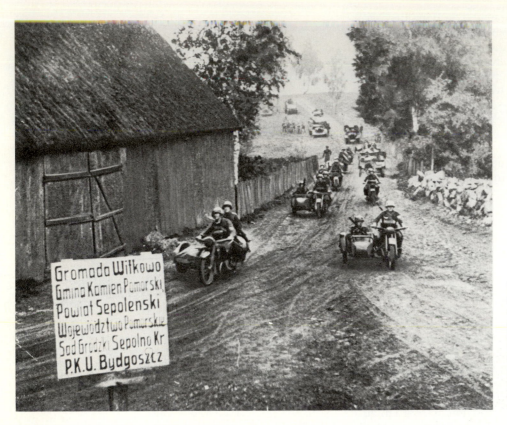

The German motorized cavalry leads the German army into Poland. The sign indicates the invaders are near Bydgoszcz, which was then about a hundred miles inside Poland. This photograph was taken by official photographers with the German army.

resources from their dominions, and the obviously superior British navy would begin to close off German food supplies. In a long war Germany and Italy were vulnerable, for Italy depended upon overseas resources (such as British coal) for industrial power, and Germany could be starved into submission. Aware of this, German scientists had done much imaginative work with *ersatz* (imitation) products, both of foodstuffs and of gasoline and rubber substitutes.

On land, the German forces were undoubtedly superior. They were better equipped than either the French or British. Though the French had refused to cooperate in various disarmament initiatives, they had not prepared themselves for the failure of disarmament. Still, the French army's reputation was excellent, and the German leaders saw the defeat of France as their essential first task. Because the French were known to be especially weak in tanks and antiaircraft defense, the Germans turned to the ideal combination—massive use of tanks in close cooperation with aircraft, especially the Stuka bomber, which could dive bomb enemy positions. This strategy was aimed largely at France, for Britain lay beyond the range of German bombers, at least until airfields in France or the Low Countries could be secured.

Before the outbreak of the war there had been much debate about the likely significance of air power. One school held that aircraft would make trench warfare impossible and that long-range bombers would destroy the economic and military capacities of an enemy and demoralize the civilian population. In most countries the army and navy resisted such arguments; they felt aircraft to be important, but mainly as protective cover for advancing land units and for ships. Yet others felt that airplanes would prove ineffective, that massive bombing would not be sufficiently accurate to disrupt mature industrial states, and that the diversion of industrial capacity to build airplanes would undermine other, more important, needs. Germany had committed itself to its air force, the *Luftwaffe*, even though its army was also well prepared; Britain was still struggling to make itself ready for aerial warfare; France remained largely committed to ground troops. The British accepted the psychological significance of being able to bomb enemy targets, and they developed light bombers, called Mosquitoes, which could fly as far as Berlin.

German plans all focused on moving rapidly by means of the *blitzkrieg*, or lightning war. This became even more true when Mussolini declared himself to be a "nonbelligerent." No one doubted that he stood behind Germany, but he would not actively commit his troops to the war. For Britain and France, ultimate victory rested on delay, forestalling a quick German victory until their lack of preparation could be offset by control of the seas, superior industrial production, and the support of world opinion which, they felt, would be in their favor. Russia remained unpredictable and might be turned around. If Hitler did have to fight a real war on two fronts, the Wehrmacht might be bled deeply and long enough to weaken its western thrust. While this did not seem probable in 1939, this is what did, in fact, happen; as the Russian, or eastern, front wore down Germany's forces, a successful invasion of occupied France became possible by 1944.

On all fronts aerial bombardment—toward the end of the war carried on by German pilotless aircraft and rocket missiles—brought the horrors of warfare to urban civilians. Military experts had been inclined to believe that civilians could not possibly stand aerial bombardment, and that any country whose cities were subject to sustained bombardment would be obliged to sue for peace. Yet European and Asian civilian populations endured months of attack; German civilian deaths from air bombardment alone have been estimated at about 500,000. Organized systems of shelter and partial dispersal of populations enabled the people of heavily bombed cities like London, Berlin, and Tokyo to endure what were in effect front-line conditions. Some cities—Rotterdam in Holland, Coventry in England, Dresden in Germany—were utterly devastated by aerial attack, but so long as conventional weapons were used, the major capitals remained intact.

At the very end of the war, a technical innovation was introduced that radically altered the character of war. This was the atom bomb, developed in secrecy by American, Canadian, and British experts, with scientific support from German and Italian refugees from fascism. It was first used by the United States on the Japanese city of Hiroshima on August 6, 1945; one single bomb destroyed something over half that city. Somewhat less damage was done by a second and different bomb dropped on Nagasaki three days later. Over a hundred thousand people were killed in the two cities by the two bombs, an incidence of death that aroused widespread

WAR AND CIVILIAN POPULATIONS

War had devastated civilian populations before, but aerial bombardment brought World War II to the urban populations of Europe and East Asia to an extent hitherto unknown. Shortly before the outbreak of war, the City of Westminster (part of London) issued the following notice so that children under the age of two might be issued gas masks in the event of attack:

City of Westminster
A.R.P.
GAS HELMETS FOR INFANTS UNDER 2 YEARS

Parents and Guardians residing in Westminster are asked to bring their infants up to two years of age to one of the below - mentioned Centres during the week commencing on Thursday, the 24th August, 1939 — including Saturday and Sunday — between the hours of 10 a.m. and 6 p.m., to be fitted with helmets for protection against the effects of gas :

1. Ebury Bridge Maternity and Child Welfare Centre, S.W.1
2. Bessborough Street Maternity and Child Welfare Centre, S.W.1
3. Marshall Street Maternity and Child Welfare Centre, W.1
4. City of Westminster Health Centre, 121, Marsham Street, S.W.1
5. South Audley Street, Public Library, W.1

Women Wardens, who are able to assist at the Centres, are specially requested to notify their district offices at once of the hours during which they will attend.

Westminster City Hall, W.C.2 22nd August, 1939.

PARKER MORRIS, Town Clerk.

fear that the atom bomb and its still more powerful successor, the hydrogen bomb, had ended any distinctions between military and civilian targets.

Early Successes of the Axis

The first campaign of World War II reached its expected conclusion. No one had seriously expected isolated Poland to stand up for long against the German and Soviet armed forces, or expected Britain and France to act rapidly enough to help their Polish ally decisively. Yet the speed of the German conquest surprised almost everyone. The Luftwaffe soon gained absolute command of the air and used it to disrupt Polish communications and to spread terror with its dive bombers. Special fully motorized German task forces swept through the less mobile Poles.

Anxious to get his share of Poland, Hitler's collaborator, Stalin, hastened to invade Poland from the east; he also occupied and then annexed the Baltic republics of Estonia, Latvia, and Lithuania, which had been created out of Russian provinces at the close of World War I. Fear of Germany and an imperialistic desire to expand also drove the Russians into a war with neighboring Finland in November 1939. The Russians, who had perhaps miscalculated the strength of the Finns, did rather badly at first. For a time the British and French considered massive aid to the Finns. By March 1940, however, Soviet forces had worn down the Finns; they secured bases and annexed Finnish lands that were close to Leningrad. This "winter war" with Finland helped push Hitler toward the fateful decsion in 1941 to make war on Russia, for German military experts concluded from Russian difficulties that an easy victory would be possible.

Meanwhile, in the west what the British called the "phony war" was pursuing an uneventful course. As in 1914 the French and British had mobilized, and as in 1914 the British sent a few divisions to the Continent, but the Germans refused to repeat the pattern of 1914. Busy in Poland, they did nothing in the west. The Germans had no intention of sitting out a defensive war, but their general staff was not yet prepared to undertake a decisive campaign in the west with winter ahead. They waited until spring. In April 1940 the Germans secured their northern flank, as they had not in 1914. Without declaring war, they invaded neutral Denmark and Norway by sea and air. Denmark, totally unprepared, was occupied almost without resistance. Norway, also unprepared but favored by rugged terrain, put up determined opposition. Neither the British nor the French could help with more than token forces, and by the end of April Norwegian resistance had been broken. The Germans now had excellent bases for air and submarine action against the British.

The great blow was struck without warning on May 10, 1940. The German armies, brilliantly supported in the air, invaded the Low Countries and thus bypassed the Maginot Line. Holland, spared in 1914, was invaded this time, so that the Germans might be doubly sure of their northern flank. A carefully planned attack was successful and rapidly opened the way into the Low Countries.

Both the Belgians and the Dutch had been anxious in the 1930s to avoid compromising themselves by planning for joint resistance with Britain and France against a possible German attack. They were now to suffer the full consequences of their policy of attempting to appease Hitler, for the crucial failure to hold the Germans in actual battle came in the Low Countries. Clearly the lack of coordination among French, Belgian, Dutch, and British forces was a major factor in the German success. Thus, the Germans did not have to take the French Maginot Line by frontal assault, but outflanked it at the crucial point where it tapered off along the Franco-Belgian border in the Ardennes hills.

Through the Ardennes the Germans poured their best motorized troops into France. In a blitzkrieg that once more capitalized on the lessons of 1914, the Germans resisted the temptation to drive at once for Paris, but instead pushed straight through northern France to the English Channel, where the port of Boulogne fell on May 26, a little over two weeks after the start of the campaign. By this stroke the Germans separated the British, Belgian, and a large part of the French troops from the main French armies to the south.

Meanwhile, in Britain Chamberlain had resigned on May 8 as a result of the defeat in Norway. He was succeeded as prime minister by Winston Churchill (1874-1965), whose advent was comparable to the replacement of Asquith by Lloyd George in World War I. Chamberlain was neither a man of action nor an appealing or heroic figure; Churchill was to prove himself all this and more.

In despair, the British and French attempted to pinch off the German motorized thrust by a concerted attack from north and south. But the Belgians, badly disorganized, decided to surrender, and neither the French nor the British could rally themselves to carry out the movement. In the last days of May and the first days of June, the British did indeed withdraw some 215,000 British and 120,000 French soldiers by sea to England from the beaches around Dunkirk at the northern tip of France. With protection from the Royal Air Force, an extraordinary flotilla of all sorts of vessels, including private yachts and motorboats, got the men out, though most of their equipment had to be abandoned. Dunkirk was a courageous action and did much to help British morale, even though the hurried retreat from the beaches marked the final stage in a major military defeat.

But from documents captured after the final defeat of Germany, it appears (though the point is still controversial) that the "miracle of Dunkirk" was possible in part because Hitler himself decided not to press home the destruction of the British forces trapped on the coast, since he believed that Britain was no longer a real threat. At the last moment, Hitler gave in to the lure of Paris and decided to push the attack on the French capital at once. Here he was entirely and rapidly successful. The French could not rally, and the Germans marched southward almost unopposed. A clear signal that the rally of 1914 at the Marne would not be repeated was given on June 13, when the French declared Paris an open city and evacuated it without fighting.

The battle of France was thus decided by mid-June 1940. But the French might still have tried to defend the south or, failing that, used their navy and merchant marine to get as many troops as possible across the Mediterranean into French North Africa, where they might have continued the fight against the Germans with British aid. Some French leaders, of whom General Charles de Gaulle (1890-1970) was the most vocal, wished to do this. To persuade them to do so, Churchill made France the extraordinary offer of a complete governmental union of the two countries to continue the struggle. But his offer was not accepted.

On June 16 French premier Paul Reynaud (1878-1966) was supplanted by Marshal Henri Pétain (1856-1951). Pétain and his colleagues were determined on peace at any price, and on June 22, 1940, an armistice was signed at Compiègne at the exact spot where the armistice of November 11, 1918, had been signed. By this armistice the French withdrew from the war, handed over three-fifths of France, including the whole Atlantic and Channel coasts, to German occupation, and retained only the central and Mediterranean regions under strict German supervision. "Unoccupied France" was ruled from the little resort city of Vichy, where Pétain—the hero of the World War I battle of Verdun against the Germans, now very old and thoroughly defeatist—set up an authoritarian, antidemocratic state of which he was chief. His government was known simply as Vichy France.

Some of Pétain's supporters were pro-German. But most of them, even men like the collaborator Pierre Laval (1883-1945), a dominant figure at Vichy, were sure that Hitler had won the war and were coming to terms with what they regarded as the inevitable German total victory. They did not believe that Britain could successfully resist the German war machine that had defeated France, for that nation had never in modern history been so crushed. Their army was demobilized, and their navy either immobilized in France or scattered among North African ports. In retaliation for the humiliation of Germany over reparations, France was to pay for all the costs of the German occupation. The situation of Vichy France was extremely delicate and ambiguous, and the problem of who collaborated and who resisted the Germans would plague the French nation for years after the war was over.

The new Vichy government attempted to remake France along conservative, monarchist lines. Laval declared that "Parliamentary democracy has lost the war. It must disappear and give place to a hierarchical authoritarian regime, national and social." For the slogan "Liberty, Equality, Fraternity," the Vichy regime sub-stituted a new trinity, "Labor, Family, Fatherland." From the start the Vichy regime was compromised by its association with the Germans; born of defeat, it did little before it collapsed in the Allied victory.

Even in the dark days of June 1940, a few French patriots led by Charles de Gaulle, who was flown out to London four days before the armistice, refused to give up the fight. With British aid, de Gaulle, a formidable intellectual and a scientific student of war, set up a French National Committee with headquarters in London. A nucleus of French soldiers taken off the beach at Dunkirk, plus a stream of refugees who left France in the next few years, made up the Free French, or Fighting French. Back in France, a secret Resistance movement gradually formed to prepare for eventual liberation. While North Africa, strongest of the French colonial areas, was controlled by Vichy, some of the colonies rallied to the Free French from the start. Notably in Equatorial Africa, under the leadership of the Cayenne-born black governor, Félix Eboué (1884-1944), a valuable base for Allied operations was secured. Although weak, the Fighting French were at least a rallying point. They set up an effective radio center in England from which they conducted a propaganda campaign against Vichy and the Germans, beamed across the Channel to the homeland.

On June 10, 1940, Mussolini brought the Italians into the war against France and Britain, too late to affect the outcome of the battle of France. This "stab in the back," as Franklin Roosevelt called it, further outraged American opinion, already alarmed by the Nazi successes. Italy, now irrevocably committed to the struggle, was anxious to secure some kind of success that would offset the great gains of its German ally. The war, up to this time confined to northern and western Europe, would soon spread to the Mediterranean.

The Battle of Britain

The Germans had not really worked out a plan for dealing with Britain. Hitler seems to have believed that with France out of the war, Britain would make a separate, compromise peace in which Germany would dominate the continent of Europe and Britain would retain its overseas empire. Hitler assumed that this division of the spoils would be eminently satisfactory because it did not threaten the British Empire. Mixed with his hatred for England was a deep-rooted admiration and an emotional and misleading idea that Germany and England were natural allies. There were no natural allies available to him in Britain, however. Britain had interned all German subjects in the country (including Jewish refugees) and had locked up nearly eight hundred members of the British Union of Fascists, including their leader, Sir Oswald Mosley (1896-1981). For over four centuries Britain had gone to war rather than accept one-power domination over western and central Europe or a hostile occupation of the Low Countries.

During wartime air raids thousands of Londoners slept in the stations of the London Underground system, which, unlike the French Métro, had been placed far below the surface and could, therefore, act as impromptu air-raid shelters. By early 1941 the London Transport Board fitted station platforms with bunks, so that people could sleep while the trains continued to function.

Hitler was counting heavily on the possibility that German submarines could eventually cut off British supplies of food and raw materials from overseas and thus starve it into submission. But this would take a long time, and Hitler was impatient. The obvious thing to do was to attempt a landing in England; however, the Germans had made no real preparation for amphibious warfare and had no specially designed landing craft. Moreover, the German air force and the German navy were at odds over the projected invasion. A hastily assembled flotilla of miscellaneous vessels was badly damaged by British aircraft, and early in August 1940 Hitler and Göring, his air marshal, made the fateful decision to try to do the job solely with air power. But the British could not be certain that Hitler did not intend to invade. Their navy could not resist an invasion for long without air support, and if the Germans came ashore in large numbers the British land forces were not strong enough to repel them. Britain could forestall invasion, the chiefs of staff felt, only through demonstrating superiority in the air, which must be done in any case, lest German bombing destroy the factories that were building British aircraft.

The Battle of Britain that followed had two main phases. First, in August and September, the Luftwaffe attempted in daylight bombing attacks to wipe out merchant ship convoys, British airports, and fighter planes. The Royal Air Force, using the new radar technique to spot the attackers early, proved just barely strong enough to check the Germans, who began full-scale attacks with bomber fleets on August 13. In critical actions in September the level of German losses, always

Perhaps the most famous and effective wartime photograph of the Battle of Britain was this International News Photo, taken late in 1940, of the massive dome of St. Paul's Cathedral rising above the burning city of London during a German incendiary bomb attack. Fire fighters stationed around the dome were able to save the cathedral, and when the photo ran in the influential American magazine *Life* on January 27, 1941, it won thousands of reluctant Americans over to the British cause.

higher than those of the British, became too great to sustain, and on September 17 Hitler postponed any invasion. Germany still had enormous air-strike capacity, but it had failed to win air superiority. This was the "nation's finest hour," as described by Churchill, an exceptionally effective wartime leader and a master at stirring national pride. Though air attacks would continue against Britain until 1942, the aerial Battle of Britain was over. Night bombings continued throughout 1940, but even in Coventry, where the cathedral was destroyed, the city's industrial capacity continued. Nor did civilian morale break. Rather, the night bombings strengthened the British will to resist. In one of his imperishable phrases, Churchill said of the small group of British fighter pilots who had saved Britain, "Never in the field of human conflict was so much owed by so many to so few."

Hitler had also made a mistake in not building aircraft carriers so that his airplanes could be launched nearer to British shores. Equally crucial during the Battle of Britain was the Battle of the Atlantic, since it was essential that convoys from North America bringing needed supplies get through to Britain. The British navy proved equal to the task, shepherding convoys across the ocean, sweeping harbors of mines floated in by the Germans, and seeking out the highly effective German submarines, which could move more rapidly than the convoys. Shipping losses for the British rose alarmingly through 1940 and into 1941, with the German blockade extending as far north as Greenland. Unable to destroy the German submarines by aerial bombing, the British began to hunt them down at sea using radar. The German surface navy initially operated along the French coast and in the Indian Ocean, but it was beaten back from the Atlantic when the heavy battleship *Bismarck*, pursued by the British aircraft carriers *Victorious* and *Ark Royal*, was sunk in May 1941 by a combined air and cruiser attack. Thereafter the British controlled the surface of the sea, while the Germans still prowled beneath the waters. Although Allied and neutral shipping losses ran to twenty-three million tons during the war, radar, sonar, escort carriers, and destroyer groups effectively neutralized the German submarine advantage.

The Mediterranean and Russian Campaigns

Hitler now faced the possibility of a long stalemate. Like Napoleon invading Egypt in 1798, Hitler turned at first to the obvious strategy of getting at Britain through its Mediterranean lifeline to India and the East. His ally Mussolini, already itching to expand in the Mediterranean, invaded Greece from Albania in October 1940 without informing Hitler. The Greeks, however, pushed the Italians back halfway across Albania. But as the Germans came to the rescue of their Austrian ally in the First World War, so they now rescued Mussolini.

Just how far Hitler himself wanted to invest in the Mediterranean is not clear. Certainly he toyed with the

Winston Churchill proved to be a superb wartime leader for the British. His ability to rally them at their darkest hour—the Battle of Britain—showed him at his finest moment. Here Churchill, leaving number 10 Downing Street, gives the press his familiar "V for Victory" sign.

idea of a campaign against the British fortress of Gibraltar through Spain, to be coordinated with Axis attacks in the eastern Mediterranean to clear that sea of the British. But Franco wanted too high a price from the French for his consent to a German march through Spain, and Hitler was unwilling to risk driving Vichy France, which still controlled French North Africa, too far. The Germans had to be content with backing up Mussolini in Greece and attacking Egypt from the Italian colony of Libya. Their efforts to organize local action against the British and French in the Middle East were suppressed without grave difficulty by British and Free French troops in Syria, and Turkey remained neutral.

Nevertheless, the German commitment to help the Italians in Greece took valuable German divisions away from another task in the spring of 1941. Though Hitler forced on a frightened Yugoslav government a treaty allowing German forces free passage across Yugoslavia to Greece, a Serbian uprising overthrew the Yugoslav

European and Mediterranean Theaters, in World War II, 1939-1945

GREAT BRITAIN

IRELAND
Dublin

North Sea

Atlantic Ocean

English Channel

NORWAY

SWEDEN
Stockholm

DENMARK

FINLAND
Helsinki

Oslo

L. Ladoga

Leningrad 1943

KARELIA

ESTONIA

LATVIA

LITHUANIA

Baltic Sea

Königsberg

Danzig

EAST PRUSSIA

POLAND

Warsaw

GERMANY

Berlin
Potsdam

NETH.
Rotterdam

BELG.
Brussels

RUHR
Cologne
Bonn

Hamburg

Elbe R.

Dresden

Prague

CZECHOSLOVAKIA

Munich
Dachau

AUSTRIA

Vienna

Budapest

HUNGARY

Trieste

YUGOSLAVIA

Belgrade

Frankfurt

Stuttgart

SWITZ.

Rhine R.

Dunkirk

NORMANDY

FRANCE

Paris

Seine R.

Loire R.

Vichy France

Lyon

Marseilles

Nice

Bordeaux

Po R.

ITALY

Florence

Rome

Anzio

Monte Cassino

Naples

Salerno

Adriatic Sea

ALBANIA

GREECE

Athens

Aegean Sea

CRETE

Corsica

SARDINIA

BALEARIC IS.

SPAIN

Madrid

Ebro R.

PORTUGAL

Lisbon

Gibraltar

Tangier

MOROCCO (Fr.)

Casablanca

ALGERIA (Fr.)

Oran

Algiers

Bougie

Bône

TUNISIA

Bizerte

SICILY

Palermo

MALTA

Mediterranean Sea

Coventry

London

Volga R.

RUSSIA

Moscow

Don R.

Dnieper R.

Dniester R.

BESSARABIA

ROMANIA

Bucharest

Danube R.

BULGARIA

Sofia

Black Sea

Sevastopol

Yalta

Istanbul

Ankara

TURKEY

CYPRUS

SYRIA

PALESTINE

TRANS-JORDAN

SUEZ CANAL

Nile R.

Cairo

EGYPT

El Alamein 1942

Tobruk 1942

LIBYA

CAUCASUS MTS.

Grozny

Baku

500

Miles

0

★ Sinking of the Bismarck

Stalin-Hitler Pact of August 1939
Axis countries
Greatest military expansion by Axis
Allies
Heaviest Allied bombing
Furthest German advance on the Eastern front

400

regime, and thereafter the Germans had to combat guerrilla resistance and to dismember Yugoslavia. The British did their best to back up their Greek allies, but once more they were not strong enough. German air power crippled British naval power in the Mediterranean, and by June the Axis had conquered the Greek mainland. A spectacular attack on Crete followed, with extensive German use of paratroopers. The British defeat appeared total, but in fact the Germans had invested far too much armament in the Balkan campaign.

The other task for which the German forces were needed in the spring of 1941 was the conquest of Russia. Hitler had firmly resolved not to repeat what he thought was the fateful mistake of Germany in 1914; he would not engage in a war on two fronts. Yet by his invasion of Russia on June 22, 1941—an invasion delayed for perhaps a decisive two months by the Balkan adventure—he committed himself to just such a war. Russia was indeed a tempting goal. The Nazi plan had always looked to the fertile areas of Poland and south Russia as the natural goal of German expansion, the *Lebensraum* (room to breathe) of German destiny. After the successful blitzkriegs in Poland, western Europe, and now Greece, Hitler and his military experts believed that they could beat the Russians in a single campaign before winter set in, a view British and American military advisers privately shared. It was quite clear that neither Britain nor the United States, even if the latter were to enter the war, could land armies in Europe in 1941. Therefore, an attack on Russia, Hitler seems to have told himself, would not really create two fronts. Indeed, once Russia was conquered, the Germans would have little trouble disposing of Britain, and, if necessary, of the distant United States.

Furthermore, Hitler had returned to his old suspicion of Bolshevism. In March he had told the leaders of his forces that communists could never be Germany's friends and that they must be exterminated. He knew that Stalin had agreed to the pact with Germany for opportunistic reasons, and that Russia might well change sides in any event. The pact had destroyed Poland, the natural wall between the two enemies. And Russia had already been expanding in ways that reinforced Hitler's distrust. In June 1940, Stalin had demanded of Romania the province of Bessarabia, whose loss after World War I the Soviets had never recognized, and also northern Bukovina, which had formerly been Austrian, not Russian, territory, but which had a large Ukrainian population and was strategically valuable. The Germans had expected the Russian seizure of Bessarabia, but not of northern Bukovina; they permitted the seizure, however, telling the Romanians that they could expect no help from Hitler. But that was as far as Hitler's cooperation with Stalin in eastern Europe went. The reannexation of Bessarabia had given the Russians the mouth of the Danube, controlling an important artery. The Russians seemed to be moving into southeast Europe, a region in which the Germans were not prepared to let them operate alone.

Only a few weeks after the Russian seizure of Romanian territory, Hitler asserted his own southeastern interests by forcing the Romanians to cede territory to Hungary and then guaranteeing the new Romanian frontiers, a guarantee that could apply only against the Russians. Soon afterward German troops appeared in Finland, "to reinforce the German armies in Norway," Hitler explained. And in the autumn of 1940 German troops entered Romania proper "to guard the Romanian oilfields against British sabotage." These maneuvers on his new frontiers deeply disquieted Stalin. Then in October 1940 Italy attacked Greece, and the war spread to the Balkans; German troops moved into Bulgaria, which Russia regarded as essential to its own defense. With Germany established in Yugoslavia and victorious in Greece by May of 1941, Stalin knew that an invasion of Russia was logically next. To prepare for the worst, in April he concluded a nonaggression pact with Japan, which would make it possible to withdraw Russian troops from the Far East to face Hitler.

Russia was not conquered, but Hitler's plan almost worked. There was a successful blitzkrieg; within two months the Germans were at the gates of Leningrad, and by the end of October they had conquered the Ukraine. Russian losses rose into the millions of killed or captured. In sheer distance, the German armies had pushed more than twice as far as they had in France. Yet as the Russian winter closed in, the Germans had taken neither Moscow nor Leningrad. Much Russian heavy industry had been transferred to the remote Urals, and existing plants there and in Siberia had been strengthened. The vast resources of Russia were still adequate for Russian needs. The government had not collapsed, and national spirit was high. Moreover, the Germans had shown once more, as they had in the Battle of Britain, that their planning was far from perfect. Their troops were not sufficiently equipped to withstand the rigors of a Russian winter. Confident that the summer and autumn would be sufficient to finish the campaign, the German planners had left the winter to take care of itself. In winter fighting between December 1941 and May 1942, the Russians regained much useful ground.

The United States Enters the War

Meanwhile, the Germans had fallen into a second fatal miscalculation. Hitler had sought to keep out of war with the United States. Although the United States had a strong isolationist element and some Nazi sympathizers, American opinion had, from the very beginning of the attack on Poland in 1939, been far more nearly unanimous against the Germans and Italians than it had been against the Central Powers in 1914. With the fall of France in 1940, anti-Axis sentiment grew stronger, reinforced by a growing belief that if Hitler won in Europe, the United States would be his next victim.

Between June 1940 and December 1941, the Roosevelt administration, with the consent of Congress and with

THE FOUR FREEDOMS

In January 1941 President Roosevelt, a leader of exceptional eloquence, had described the "four freedoms" for which the United States stood. As a result of this effective speech, the Four Freedoms were generally accepted as potential war aims.

The happiness of future generations of Americans may well depend upon how effective and how immediate we can make our aid felt. No one can tell the exact character of the emergency situations that we may be called upon to meet. The Nation's hands must not be tied when the Nation's life is in danger. . . .

A free nation has the right to expect full cooperation from all groups. A free nation has the right to look to the leaders of business, of labor, and of agriculture to take the lead in stimulating effort, not among other groups, but within their own groups . . . .

In the future days, which we seek to make secure, we look forward to a world founded upon four essential human freedoms.

The first is freedom of speech and expression—everywhere in the world.

The second is freedom of every person to worship God in his own way—everywhere in the world.

The third is freedom from want—which, translated into world terms, means economic understandings which will secure to every nation a healthy peacetime life for its inhabitants—everywhere in the world.

The fourth is freedom from fear—which, translated into world terms means a world-wide reduction of armaments to such a point and in such a thorough fashion that no nation will be in a position to commit an act of physical aggression against any neighbor—anywhere in the world.

Peace and War: United States Foreign Policy, 1931-1941 (Washington: Government Printing Office, 1943), pp. 610-11.

---

the general backing of American public opinion, took a series of steps "short of war" to aid Britain and later Russia. By conventional standards of international relations, these steps were not in accord with America's status as a neutral; they would have given Hitler ample legal justification for declaring war against the United States. The American government transferred fifty "overage" destroyers to the British in exchange for Atlantic naval bases in British colonies, supplied the British with arms, and used the American navy to help get these supplies across the Atlantic. Above all, in March 1941 by the Lend-Lease Act, the United States agreed to supply materials needed for defense, including food, to "any country whose defense the President deems vital to the defense of the United States." Supplies at once began flowing into Britain and later to other anti-Axis powers without the complications produced by the war-debt methods employed during World War I. This help also went promptly to communist Russia. Churchill and Roosevelt recognized that, despite mutual hostility between the Soviets and the West, it was now in the Allied interest to assist them vigorously.

In 1936 Germany and Japan had concluded an Anti-Comintern Pact, agreeing to assist each other in case of aggression by the Soviet Union. In March 1939, as he prepared for European war, Hitler had pressed the Japanese emperor, Hirohito (1901-), to join a tripartite alliance with Germany and Italy, but the Japanese estimated that they would not be ready for a Pacific war before 1942. Pushed by his army and held back by his navy, Hirohito agreed to a military alliance with Hitler, provided that clauses relating to the democracies be kept secret, and that Japan need not enter a general war until

it felt strong enough to do so. Hitler rejected the latter provision. In September 1940 the two nations agreed that if the United States attacked Germany, Japan would come into the war. But the three-nation Axis would not be truly formed until Japan moved its timetable forward and struck at the United States in December 1941.

Meanwhile, the Japanese took advantage of the fall of France and the Netherlands and of the weakness of Britain to speed up the expansion in Asia that they had begun in Manchuria in 1931. They penetrated into French Indochina (Vietnam) by agreement with Vichy France, even as they continued to press their campaign, the so-called China Incident, on the mainland of China. The American government, which had never been willing to accept Japanese conquests in China, continued to oppose what it considered Japanese aggression, which took the form of trying to create a Greater East Asia Co-Prosperity Sphere under Japanese Management. The Japanese, feeling desperately squeezed and convinced that the United States would never grant them the status of a great power in the Far East, needed rubber and oil to continue their war on the Chinese mainland. Their government fell increasingly into the hands of military leaders who felt that war with the United States was inevitable and who preferred to strike before the American democracy could fully prepare itself. Had the United States been willing to back away from its persistent opposition to Japanese expansion, the war in the Pacific could perhaps have been avoided, but the Americans remained adamant.

In the summer and autumn of 1941 the American government took steps to freeze Japanese credits in the United States, to halt Japanese access to raw materials,

JAPAN TAKES A STAND

On July 2, 1941, the following policy was prepared by the Japanese:

The Imperial Government is determined to follow a policy which will result in the establishment of the Greater East Asia Co-Prosperity Sphere and world peace, no matter what international developments take place.

The Imperial Government will continue its effort to effect a settlement of the China Incident and seek to establish a solid basis for the security and preservation of the nation. This will involve an advance into the Southern Regions and, depending on future developments, a settlement of the Soviet Question as well.

The Imperial Government will carry out the above program no matter what obstacles may be encountered.

U.S. Congress, *Joint Committee on the Investigation of the Pearl Harbor Attack, Hearings* . . . (Washington: Government Printing Office, 1946), pp. 4018-19.

and to get the Japanese to withdraw from China and Indochina. Negotiations toward these ends were going on between the Japanese and Americans when on December 7, 1941 (American date; in Japan it was December 6), the Japanese struck without warning from carrier-based airplanes at the American naval base at Pearl Harbor in Hawaii. Grave damage was inflicted on ships and installations, but American power in the Pacific was by no means destroyed. Moreover, the "day of infamy" produced almost unanimous support in the United States for the immediate declaration of war against Japan. Germany and Italy honored their obligations to their Axis partner by declaring war against the United States on December 11. As 1942 began, the war was literally a world war.

Although the United States was far better prepared now than in 1917, it was still at a disadvantage. Against Germany, it could do no more than increase its aid to Britain and Russia by lend-lease and take part in the struggle against German submarines. Against Japan,

The American Pacific Fleet rode at anchor at Pearl Harbor on December 7, 1941—eight battleships in a row, nine cruisers, twenty-nine destroyers, and five submarines. Three aircraft carriers were on detached duty. The Japanese attack came in two waves, forty-one minutes apart, and it took the Americans completely by surprise. Only four American airplanes got off the ground. The Americans lost five of their battleships and twenty-four hundred men; the Japanese lost twenty-nine of their three hundred and sixty airplanes.

the United States was almost as powerless. Its Pacific outposts of Guam, Wake Island, and the Philippines fell in rapid succession to Japanese arms, despite a courageous defense at Corregidor, near Manila. Nor could the British and the exiled Dutch governments protect their colonies in Southeast Asia, which the Japanese had also attacked. By the spring of 1942, with the fall of Singapore, the Japanese had forced the largest surrender of a British army in history. They had acquired Indonesia from the Dutch, possessed the oil of Borneo, the rubber of Malaya, and had virtual control of Siam (Thailand) and Burma. They seemed poised for an attack on Australia.

The Japanese did not intend to repeat Germany's mistake concerning air and sea power. The Japanese attack on Pearl Harbor had been made possible only by close coordination of air and sea forces. They had, as Hitler had not, the carrier capacity to carry attack bombers close to Australian shores, and they had dramatically demonstrated during their rapid conquest of Malaya that they dominated the seas at least to the mid-Pacific. Singapore had fallen because of inadequate land defenses, but also because British air protection was meager. Public opinion was particularly shaken when the only British capital ships east of Suez, the battleship *Prince of Wales* and the cruiser *Repulse*, were destroyed in the Gulf of Siam by Japanese air attack in a matter of minutes on December 10. The Americans, who understood that they were to carry the primary responsibility for the Pacific War, realized that they must turn the Japanese navy back if their own aerial strike forces were to be able to enter Far Eastern waters.

IV VICTORY FOR THE UNITED NATIONS

There were several turning points in the struggle thereafter. The earliest was a series of naval actions in which Japanese expansion was stopped. In these actions, carrier-based American airplanes played a decisive role. On May 7, 1942, in the battle of the Coral Sea in the southwest Pacific, Allied sea and air power halted a possible Japanese invasion of Australia and its protecting islands. In June American sea and air power dispersed a Japanese fleet that was seeking to conquer Midway Island. Although the Japanese landed on American territory at Attu and Kiska in the Aleutian Islands of Alaska, they never seriously threatened Hawaii or the mainland.

In Europe the Americans and the British were not yet able to respond to Russian pressure for a second front on the Continent. But in November 1942 they did land in French North Africa and were rapidly established in force in Morocco and Algeria. The Libyan segment of the long North African coast had been held by the Germans and their Italian allies since the beginning of the war in the Mediterranean, and there had been seesaw campaigns in these desert areas. At the time of the North

African landings, the British, under General Sir Bernard Montgomery (1887-1976), were holding a defensive line inside the Egyptian frontier near El Alamein. But on October 23, 1942, the British started on a westward offensive, which was planned to coordinate with an eastward offensive by the American General Dwight D. Eisenhower (1890-1969), commander of the Allied forces in French North Africa, in the classic maneuver of catching the enemy in a vise. The vise closed slowly, but in May 1943 Free French, British, and American troops took the last Axis strongholds of Tunis and Bizerte and accepted the surrender of some three hundred thousand Axis troops.

The North African campaign had clearly been a turning point. The Allies had successfully made large-scale amphibious landings, and they had annihilated one of the most renowned of Axis forces, commanded by one of the few German generals of this war to strike the imagination of the world—Erwin Rommel (1891-1944), the Desert Fox. North Africa was by no means the main battleground, but it was nevertheless a major campaign in which the Allies gained confidence and prestige.

The great turning point on land was the successful Soviet defense of Stalingrad (formerly Tsaritsyn and now known as Volgograd). The defense turned into an attack in the same month (November 1942) that saw the Allied landing in North Africa. After their stalemate in Russia in the winter of 1941-1942, the Germans turned their summer offensive of 1942 away from Leningrad and Moscow and toward the oil-rich regions of southeastern Russia. The Germans were already beginning to suffer oil shortages, partly because of Allied bombing, but even more because, though they held the oil fields of Romania, they did not have enough oil for the ravenous demands of mechanical warfare. This push toward the Russian oil fields carried the Germans deep inside the Soviet Union, over a thousand miles from their original starting point. But again it failed, falling just short of the rich oil fields of Grozny and Baku. Russian distance, weather, manpower, and ability to take punishment were too much for the overextended Germans. Their armies were thrown back at Stalingrad, and early in 1943 the Russians started the long march westward that was to take them to Berlin two years later.

A much less spectacular turning point was the Allied victory in the battle of supply, yet this victory was of the greatest importance, since naval and military success ultimately depended on supplies. Even for the Soviets, an important source of supplies was the United States. But the United States was separated from its allies—and its enemies—by vast distances of water, and the precious supplies, had to move across the seas. If the Germans could stop this movement or reduce it greatly, they might still win, despite the overwhelming resources of the Allies. They made important improvements in their submarines, but there were simply not enough of them, and the countermeasures of the Allies—radar, coordination of naval vessels and aircraft, the convoy system—slowly reduced the number of sinkings.

At Stalingrad the Russian forces stopped the German advance, which had moved deep into Soviet territory, and in a long battle, waged from house to house, reversed the tide. Had Stalingrad fallen, Germany would have controlled the Caucasus oil fields. In the summer offensive in Russia, the Germans had suffered 1,200,000 casualties. Those losses and a severe gasoline shortage, as well as the determined Russian resistance, stopped the German advance. Though Hitler ordered the German army to fight to the last man, the German commander surrendered on January 31, 1943.

The Axis on the Defensive

In the last two years of the war the Axis powers were on the defensive. Both in Europe and in Asia the Allies attacked with land forces along definite lines of march—campaigns of the traditional kind. But the way for these armies was made easier by two new factors in warfare: air power and modern propaganda, or psychological warfare. Air bombardment, at least until the atom bomb at Hiroshima, was never the perfect weapon that the prophets of air power had predicted. But as the superior Allied air power grew and was used systematically to destroy enemy capabilities in critical materials like ball bearings, machine tools, locomotives, and oil; and as American airplanes dropped incendiary bombs on the relatively flimsy Japanese cities, air power did much to destroy the Axis will to resist.

The attack by land on Germany and Italy was pressed in three directions—by the Russians from the east, and by the British, French, Americans, and the other Allies from the south and west. In the south the Allies crossed from North Africa to Sicily in a successful amphibious operation (July 1943) within two months of their final victory in Tunisia. From Sicily they moved in another six weeks to the mainland of Italy at Salerno and Anzio. These landings were costly, and troops were pinned down for weeks. German forces kept the Italian campaign going for longer than the Allies anticipated, but the Allied victories of the summer of 1943 were sufficient to put Italy out of the war. Top officers of the Italian army and others close to the king, helped by dissident fascist leaders, engineered a coup in July that brought about the fall and imprisonment of Mussolini and re-

sulted in some negotiations between the Allies and the new government headed by Marshal Pietro Badoglio (1871-1956).

But the Germans were unwilling to abandon their Italian defensive line. A detachment of German troops rescued Mussolini in September 1943 and set him up as the head of a "fascist republic"—a post in which he continued until he was executed by partisans in April 1945. Meantime, Italy had a civil as well as a foreign war on its hands. Many Italians had never favored the war and were now heartily sick of it, but still the war in Italy went on. In June 1944 the Allies succeeded, after particularly severe fighting around Monte Cassino, in breaking through to Rome, which was declared an open city, and by August they were in Florence. They could not effectively move further north, however, until the final collapse of the Germans in their heartland early in 1945.

At a conference of Churchill, Roosevelt, and Stalin in Teheran in December 1943, the decision was made to open the long-delayed second front. The landings in France began on "D-Day," June 6, 1944. The Allies' choice of the Normandy coast surprised the German high command, who believed the landings would come farther north and east along the English Channel. In their four years of occupation the Germans had fortified the French coastline, but the Allies had also used those four years to study, invent, and plan. Allied landing craft, amphibious trucks, naval and air support (by now the Luftwaffe had almost been driven from the skies), artificial harbors, and a well-organized supply system gained a beachhead for the allied land forces. From this beachhead, a little over a month after D-Day they were able to break out at Avranches and sweep the Germans

American troops wade ashore on the Normandy coast on D-Day, June 6, 1944.

back across the Seine in a great flanking movement led by the American general George S. Patton (1885-1945) and his Third Army.

A long-planned auxiliary landing on the French Mediterranean coast, to be followed by a march north up the Rhône-Saône valleys, was launched on August 15, 1944, and met very little opposition. Everywhere the French Resistance movement welcomed the liberating forces, some of whom were heirs of the Free French of 1940. Paris, a symbol as well as a place, was liberated toward the end of August after its inhabitants had staged an uprising in the style of 1848 against the German garrison.

The Germans were beaten back, but not disorganized. In July 1944 conservative elements, both military and civilian, attempted to assassinate Hitler to pave the way for negotiations. But Hitler survived the bomb intended for him, executed the plotters, and retained a firm grip on the German state by killing five thousand people suspected of complicity. The Allies were encouraged by their rapid successes in July and August to try to destroy the German armies before winter, or cut them off from their homeland; however, Patton's mechanized troops ran out of fuel. The new German pilotless planes and rocket-propelled missiles limited Allied use of Antwerp as a port of supply, and by late

autumn the Germans had retired in good order to their own Siegfried line.

Though falling back, the Germans hoped, as in World War I, to prevent an assault on Germany itself. They still had an army of ten million in the field, in large measure because eight million foreign and usually forced laborers maintained war production within Germany. Hitler was pressing the development of the jet plane, which he hoped could still save Germany. To buy another winter, in late September 1944 he called up the last reserves, ordering all able-bodied males between sixteen and sixty into the service. Not wishing to give Hitler the winter, Eisenhower ordered an airborne assault to leap over German defensive lines on the lower Rhine, but plans for a linked ground-air attack went badly, and the airborne army had to be rescued. The allied offensive, having overreached its supplies, was now bogged down, and Hitler ordered a final counteroffensive sweep through the Ardennes Forest on Antwerp, the Allies' supply port. A German armored attack on December 16, with the advantage of fog, snow, systematic infiltration, and complete surprise, threatened to throw the Allies back in the Battle of the Bulge and completely surrounded an American airborne division at Bastogne. As the weather cleared, Allied air strikes and German fuel shortages stopped the German counteradvance.

Germany now had no more men or supplies to throw into the battle. German oil production had been given a death blow, and tanks had to be hauled to the front by oxen. The catastrophic technique of fire bombing which had proved psychologically devastating in an attack on Hamburg in 1943 in which 50,000 civilians had been killed, was being used. The British put Dresden to the torch in a massive incendiary raid on February 13-14, 1945, with the loss of 135,000 lives, many of them refugees pouring in from the east, running from the Russian advance.

The Russians had been pushing on relentlessly ever since Stalingrad. In the campaign of 1943, while the Western Allies were busy in Italy, the Russians won back most of their own territories that had been lost in 1941 and 1942. They kept up the pressure during the winter and started an early spring campaign in the south. By the autumn of 1944 the Russians had been able to sweep across Romania and Bulgaria, only half-hearted allies of Hitler, to a juncture with the Yugoslav communist guerrillas under their leader Marshal Josip Broz, called Tito (1892-1980), and were ready for the attack on Hungary. In the center and north, they had recovered all their own territory and were ready to attack Germany across Poland from the east. Poland, caught between the advancing Russians and the retreating Germans, was devastated. In August the provisional government of Poland in London ordered a mass uprising in Warsaw. The battle within Warsaw continued until October, when the Germans at last succeeded in crushing it, at the cost of over 200,000 Polish casualties. The Russians, on the outskirts of the city, did not intervene, and later they would be accused of wishing to see the Polish Resistance destroyed so that they might create their own collaborators. This was the last German victory.

The rapid conclusion of the Battle of Germany followed. The Russians had not stopped for winter but had pressed on through Poland to menace Berlin early in March. The Western Allies broke through the Siegfried Line in February, crossed the Rhine, and entered the heart of Germany. Early in February 1945, Stalin, Churchill, and Roosevelt held another summit conference, this time at Yalta in the Crimea, and confirmed final plans for the conquest of Germany. It was plain that the Germans, whose key industries had been so riddled from the air that they could no longer support their armies adequately, and whose manpower had been reduced to the very bottom, could not hold out for long. The Allied planners were anxious to halt the race to be the first to arrive in Berlin and wanted to settle peacefully which areas of Germany each of them would occupy and govern after the German defeat. The decision was reached to give the Russians the honor of taking Berlin, a decision that, in effect, confirmed their hold on Poland as well. At the time this view seemed to recognize the fact that during the two years of successful offensive against the Germans, the Russians had pinned down many more German divisions than had the Western Allies. Stalin further demanded that Germany pay $20 billion in reparations, with half the sum to go to war-torn Russia. The Russians fought their way into a Berlin already pulverized by the air power of the Western Allies. Hitler and his mistress shot themselves in his bunker suite, and their bodies were covered with gasoline and burned. On April 30, by Hitler's testament, power in Germany was turned over to Grand Admiral Karl Doenitz (1891-1980).

The Allied advance into Germany now revealed for the first time the full horror of Nazi treatment of slave laborers from conquered lands, of political opponents, and of Jews, Poles, and other German-styled "inferior" peoples. One after another the concentration camps were liberated—Auschwitz, Belsen, Buchenwald, Dachau, Nordhausen, Mauthausen, and others. The world was appalled at the gas ovens that had claimed so many victims, at the piles of emaciated corpses not yet cremated, and at the pitiful state of the prisoners who had survived. This was one of the horrors of war whose reality exceeded the grimmest expectations of Allied opinion.

This discovery of the extent of what is known as the *Holocaust*—a war of genocide fought in particular against the Jews and referred to by the Germans as "the Final Solution"—remains controversial, though no responsible historian doubts the grim facts. In one German camp alone, Buchenwald, 239,000 prisoners were killed. The figures were even more devastating for the camps in Poland. At Auschwitz no one yet knows, or can know, how many died, used as victims in medical experiments, herded into gas ovens, shot down, or starved. The Germans burned their records. The extent of the horror is best indicated by the debate over whether the lowest possible figure might be one million, while other estimates range up to four million.

After the war many people would ask why Germans who knew of this systematic killing had not protested it; why the Russians, as they moved into Poland, had not stopped it; why the Western Allies, who though surprised by the extent but well aware of the camps, had not made them early targets of liberation; why the pope had not spoken out, especially with respect to nominally Catholic countries such as Poland and Austria; or why the Jews themselves had not organized more systematic resistance within the camps. There is little agreement on these questions, though little disagreement about the magnitude of the deaths and the importance of the questions those deaths give rise to. The war Hitler had unleashed in Europe killed seventeen million soldiers and eighteen million civilians at the lowest estimate. No European war in history had been so destructive, so corrosive to the doctrine of progress, to the concept of human beings as rational, to the hopes of humanity.

On May 8, 1945, Churchill and Harry S Truman (1884-1972)—who had become the American president on Roosevelt's death that April—announced the end of German resistance, the day of victory in Europe, V-E Day. It was symbolic of difficulties to come that Stalin was offended because the Western Allies had accepted a

THE FINAL SOLUTION

During the International Military Tribunal, held after the war at Nuremberg to try German war criminals, a German engineer who was an eye witness to a massacre of Jews in the Ukraine, where Ukrainian guards were used, described what proved to be a relatively routine event:

On 5th October 1942, when I visited the building office at Dubno my foreman told me that in the vicinity of the site, Jews from Dubno had been shot in three large pits, each about 30 metres long and 3 metres deep. About 1,500 persons had been killed daily. All the 5,000 Jews who had still been living in Dubno before the pogrom were to be liquidated. As the shooting had taken place in his presence, he was still much upset.

Thereupon I drove to the site accompanied by my foreman and saw near it great mounds of earth, about 30 metres long and 2 metres high. Several trucks stood in front of the mounds. Armed Ukrainian militia drove the people off the trucks under the supervision of an S.S. man. The militiamen acted as guards on the trucks and drove them to and from the pit. All these people had the regulation yellow patches on the front and back of their clothes, and thus could be recognized as Jews.

My foreman and I went directly to the pits. Nobody bothered us. Now I heard rifle shots in quick succession from behind one of the earth mounds. The people who had got off the trucks—men, women and children of all ages—had to undress upon orders of an S.S. man, who carried a riding or dog whip. They had to put down their clothes in fixed places, sorted according to shoes, to clothing, and underclothing. I saw a heap of shoes of about 800 or 1,000 pairs, great piles of underlinen and clothing.

Without screaming or weeping these people undressed, stood around in family groups, kissed each other, said farewells, and waited for a sign from another S.S. man, who stood near the pit, also with a whip in his hand. During the 15 minutes that I stood near I heard no complaint or plea for mercy. . . .

At that moment the S.S. man at the pit shouted something to his comrade. The latter counted off about 20 persons and instructed them to go behind the earth mound. . . . I walked around the mound and found myself confronted by a tremendous grave. People were closely wedged together and lying on top of each other so that only their heads were visible. Nearly all had blood running over their shoulders from their heads. Some of the people shot were still moving. Some were lifting their arms and turning their heads to show that they were still alive. The pit was already two-thirds full. I estimated that it already contained about 1,000 people. I looked for the man who did the shooting. He was an S.S. man, who sat at the edge of the narrow end of the pit, his feet dangling into the pit. He had a tommy-gun on his knees and was smoking a cigarette. . . .

Military Tribunal, *The Trial of German Major War Criminals* (London: Her Majesty's Stationery Office, 1952), XIX, 457.

At Belsen the liberating troops uncovered a mass grave, a scene they would encounter again at each of the German concentration camps.

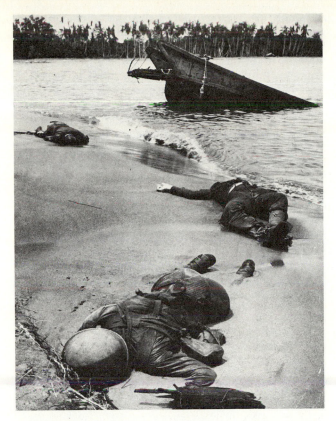

The long, slow, island-hopping campaign in the Pacific was costly in lives on both sides. This photograph of the bodies of American soldiers on Buna Beach, New Guinea, was one of the first the American government permitted the press to use that showed American personnel killed in combat in World War II. It ran in *Life* magazine on September 20, 1943.

formal surrender at Reims in France. He chose to announce separately, on Russia's part, the final victory over Germany, and not until the next day. The hopes of humanity still seemed far away.

The War in the Pacific

V-J Day, the day of victory over Japan, was now the all-out goal of Allied effort. The Soviet Union had refrained from adding Japan to its formal enemies as long as Germany was still a threat. Britain and the United States, on the other hand, were anxious for the Soviets to enter the war against the Japanese. This desire was responsible for many of the concessions made to Stalin in the last months of the German war.

The two years of Allied successes against Germany had also been years of Allied successes against Japan. The attack on Japan had been pressed in three main directions. First, in a process that the American press soon called "island-hopping," the American navy drove straight toward Japan from the central Pacific. One after another, the small island bases that stood in the way were reduced by American naval forces, which used both air support and the amphibious methods that were being worked out simultaneously in Europe and North Africa. Each island required an intense beach assault and pitched battle: Tarawa, Eniwetok, Kwajalein, Iwo Jima, Okinawa, Saipan, and Guam.

Second, the Americans and Australians, with help from other commonwealth elements, worked their way up the southwest Pacific through the much larger islands of the Solomons, New Guinea, and the Philippines. The base for this campaign—which was under the

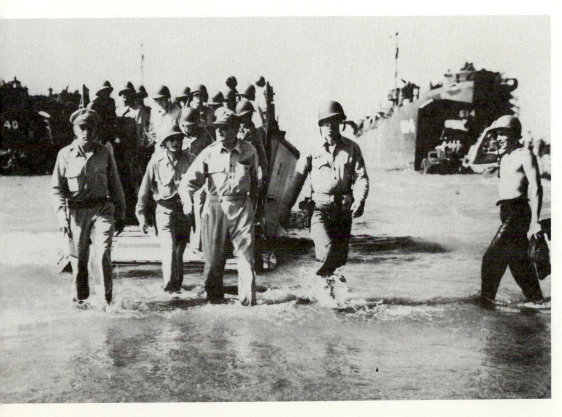

General Douglas MacArthur wades ashore with his troops at Leyte, in the Philippines, in October of 1944, fulfilling his promise that he would return.

command of the American general Douglas MacArthur (1880-1964)—was Australia and such outlying islands as New Caledonia and the New Hebrides. The start of the campaign went back to the first major offensive step in the Far East, the difficult seizure of Guadalcanal in the Solomons by the United States Marines on August 7, 1942. These campaigns involved jungle fighting of the hardest sort, slow and painful work. But by October 1944 the sea forces had won the battle of the Philippine Sea and had made possible the successful landing of MacArthur's troops on Leyte and the reconquest of the Philippine Islands from the Japanese.

The third attack came from the south in the China-Burma-India theater. The main effort of the Allies was to get material support to Chiang Kai-shek and the Chinese Nationalists at Chungking and, if possible, to weaken the Japanese position in Burma, Thailand, and Indochina. After Pearl Harbor, when the Japanese seized and shut the "Burma Road," the only way for the Allies to communicate with Chiang's Nationalists was by air.

Although the Western Allies did not invest an overwhelming proportion of their resources in this China-Burma-India theater, they did help keep the Chinese formally in the fight. And as the final campaign of 1945 drew on, the British, with Chinese and American aid, were holding down three Japanese field armies in this theater.

The end in Japan came with a suddenness that was hardly expected. From Pacific island bases, American airplanes had inflicted crippling damage on Japanese industry in the spring and summer of 1945. The Japanese fleet had been almost destroyed, submarine warfare had almost strangled the Japanese economy, and the morale of Japanese troops was declining. Nonetheless, American leaders were convinced that only the use of their recently invented atom bomb could avert the very heavy casualties expected from the proposed amphibious invasion of the Japanese home islands. Some commentators believe that racism also played a role in the decision to use the bomb on the Japanese rather than on any Euro-

American Marines raised the flag on Mount Suribachi, on Iwo Jima, in February 1945; in May of that year the Soviet banner of victory waved over a destroyed Berlin.

Asian and Pacific Theaters, 1941-1945

Area under Japanese domination, Aug. 1942

U.S.—Australian joint drive

pean people, though the bomb was not, in fact, ready for use in time to affect the European war. No doubt an additional motive for its use was the desire to demonstrate to the Soviet Union, which many feared would turn upon the Allies at the end of the war, just how powerful America's new weapon was. The result was the dropping of the first atom bomb on Hiroshima on August 6, 1945.

On August 8 the Russians, who had agreed to come into the war against Japan once Germany was beaten, invaded Manchuria in full force. Faced with what they felt was certain defeat after the dropping of the second atom bomb on Nagasaki, the Japanese government, unlike the German, decided not to make a last-ditch stand in their own country. On September 2, after brief negotiations, the Japanese formally surrendered in Tokyo Bay. Japan gave up its conquests abroad and submitted to American military occupation. Contrary to the desires of some Allies, the emperor of Japan was not dethroned. Purged of most of its militarists, the Japanese government continued to rule under nominal Allied (actually American) supervision.

The atomic bomb transformed war and diplomacy. First exploded at the White Sands Missile Range in New Mexico in July, 1945, the bomb was used against civilian populations in Hiroshima and Nagasaki during the following month.

The Allied Coalition

The Grand Alliance, as Churchill liked to call it, known in its last years as the United Nations, had mustered overpowering strength against Germany, Japan, Italy, and such collaborators as the Axis powers could secure in the Balkans, Southeast Asia, and western Europe. Britain and the Commonwealth, the Soviet Union, and the United States were the heart of the Allied coalition. Nationalist China, for all its inefficiencies, had tied down hundreds of thousands of Japanese soldiers, and the resources of the French Empire and the French Resistance movements at home and abroad had been valuable. The Allies had been able to count on the resources of many Latin American nations, and Brazil had been an active member of the alliance. In this truly global war, Brazilian troops had fought in Italy, the most cosmopolitan of theaters, along with American (including Japanese-American, or Nisei), French imperial, British imperial, pro-Allied Italian, Polish, and other troops. At the very end of the European war, Argentina too declared war on Germany and Japan, even though its leader, General Juan Peron (1894-1974), the most powerful of a group of fascist colonels who had overthrown the government in 1943, had hoped for a German victory. Hurried declarations of war near the end were

commonplace, so that states might be assured of a seat in the United Nations.

The instruments of Allied union were the summit conferences of the Big Three—Roosevelt, Churchill, and Stalin—with the political and military advisers and experts, plus the more frequent Anglo-American conferences. Even before the United States entered the war, Roosevelt and Churchill met off Newfoundland and issued the Atlantic Charter on August 14, 1941, in which they declared support for the freedom of the seas, equality of access to economic opportunity, abandonment of aggression, and the restoration of rights to conquered peoples. Formal conferences—between Roosevelt and Churchill at Casablanca (January 1943) and Quebec (August 1943), and among the Big Three at Teheran and Yalta—concluded agreements that had been steadily carried on at lower political and military levels. From July 17 to August 17, 1945, a final conference at Potsdam (near conquered Berlin) brought together the United States, Britain, and the Soviet Union. With two new figures attending, President Truman and Prime Minister Clement Attlee (1883-1967), they met to confirm the Yalta decisions.

But there were grave military and political matters to be ironed out. It was not easy to maintain even Anglo-American collaboration, which was perhaps the closest military collaboration ever achieved between two major sovereign powers. For the actual direction of operations in the field, the British and Americans had decided to set up, not just the sort of supreme command the Allies painfully achieved late in World War I, but a complete intermeshing of staffs. All down the line, an American in command always had a Briton as his second, and a Briton in command always had an American as his second. Even the intelligence-gathering apparatus of the two nations was meshed, a virtual abandonment of the sovereign principle of maintaining secrecy in espionage and counterintelligence. At the highest level, the Combined Chiefs of Staff, in close touch with top American and British government officials, did the overall planning. The Russians could not be brought into such close military cooperation, and Soviet troops in the field always fought on their own.

During the war the Allies had agreed that the Axis powers were to be forced into "unconditional surrender." History was responsible for this policy. Hitler had simply taken advantage of widespread German opinion that in World War I Germany had not been defeated in the field but had been betrayed by the false promises of Wilson's Fourteen Points. This time the Allied leaders were determined to give the Germans no excuse for a future psychological ploy of this sort. The Germans must be beaten unmistakably, and Allied troops must enter Berlin as conquerors. There must be no political negotiation at all, simply unconditional military surrender. In Britain and the United States there was some opposition to this policy during the war, partly on humanitarian grounds, but also because people feared that the prospect of unconditional surrender would stiffen the German will to resist and would unite the nation behind Hitler. In retrospect, it seems unlikely that Hitler would ever have negotiated with the Allies; and after the failure of the attempt to kill him in 1944, there was little chance that the Germans themselves would overthrow the Nazi government.

Another political problem created a much clearer rift between the British and the Americans. The underlying issue was just how far anti-German elements in France, Italy, and other occupied lands had to go to prove that they were democratic enough to secure the backing of the Western powers. Here the difference in the underlying tone of American and British policies was evident in the views of Roosevelt and Churchill. Roosevelt was convinced that if the Allies did not interfere to support conservatives and reactionaries in the occupied lands, but instead allowed these peoples to choose their form of government freely, they would choose democracy. Churchill was less idealistic. He was eager to use any elements that were hostile to the Germans, even if their hostility was quite recent, and he had little faith in the desire of peoples like the Italians for Anglo-Saxon democracy. Therefore he was willing to back Badoglio and the monarchists in Italy; Roosevelt insisted that the Italians wanted a republic. Furthermore, Roosevelt began to press Churchill for a commitment to decolonization, especially of India, at the end of the war, while Churchill responded that he would not preside over the dissolution of the British Empire.

In French politics the issue was further complicated by Roosevelt's suspicions of de Gaulle, the chosen leader of the French liberation movement. To Roosevelt, de Gaulle seemed a potential man on horseback, another Napoleon III. To Churchill, de Gaulle was a difficult but indispensable ally. As it turned out, the Gaullists, in collaboration with the organized French Resistance in the homeland, did take over the civilian administration of French territory as it was liberated, and France by free popular vote restored a democratic form of government. In 1946 the Italians also narrowly voted for a republic. What had threatened at one time to be a serious difficulty between American policy and British policy was resolved by the liberated people themselves. However, the anger aroused in de Gaulle himself and in many other French leaders by Roosevelt's policy embittered Franco-American relations for three decades.

But the political issue that bulked largest after World War II was the problem of potential Soviet domination in eastern and southeastern Europe. At Yalta the Western powers had allowed Stalin to push his armies westward, and had relied on his promises to permit free elections in Poland, Hungary, Czechoslovakia, and the Balkans. Most of the smaller eastern European countries had no tradition of Western-style democracy; most of them had moved toward fascist totalitarianism before World War II, and a transition to communist totalitarianism would not be difficult. Churchill, who never trusted Stalin, did not dare risk losing Soviet manpower and material

Churchill, an ailing Roosevelt, and Stalin met in a summit conference at Yalta. Churchill feared there might be war with the Soviet Union, but Stalin was looking ahead to the peace settlement and how to create a protective ring of satellite states in eastern Europe. Roosevelt had just been inaugurated for his fourth term and was counting on four years of allied unity. Churchill wrote at that time that at Yalta Roosevelt had "an air of purification" about him, with "a far-away look in his eyes." Two months later Roosevelt died at Warm Springs, Georgia.

resources during the war. Appeasement of Stalin seemed absolutely essential, not only to Roosevelt, who hoped the Soviets would cooperate with the democracies in the postwar world, but also to Churchill, who seems to have had little hope of such cooperation during the war. At the end of the war, the western European states, though victorious, were so near impoverishment that they could play no major role in the balance-of-power politics that would follow, so that the Russians and Americans soon became the only superpowers. Contrary to its hopes and public expectations, the United States was drawn deeply into European and Asian matters.

But when the war ended, there was no peace. The defeat of Germany and Japan was almost immediately followed by the rise of a new aggressor, the Soviet Union, which had already given clear warning of its intentions. As with so many other wars in the past, once the need for victory against a common enemy no longer held a coalition together, it began almost immediately to fall apart. The long shooting war was followed quickly by sharp antagonisms between the Soviet Union and its former allies, a degree of hostility so intense it was soon called the *cold war*.

V THE COLD WAR BEGINS

The quarter century following World War II, between 1945 and 1970, embraces the period conventionally identified as the cold war, even though in some respects a thaw had set in before 1970, and in others the hostilities of the cold war extend to the present. A source of international insecurity, the cold war nonetheless has marked a period longer than that between World Wars I and II without a renewed world war. However, the number of local and often intensely destructive and largely undeclared wars has increased: wars of liberation in the European colonies, wars of nationalism in the Middle East, repeated wars between Israel and its Arab neighbors, a long war by the United Nations in Korea, a prolonged war in Southeast Asia deeply involving the United States, insurgent wars in Cuba and Central America. Taken together, this warfare has taken more lives than did World War I, so that the interval since 1945 has been referred to by some analysts as a period of perpetual war to assure perpetual peace.

The Postwar Settlement

The devastation wrought by the war, including the war in the Pacific, greatly exceeded that in World War I: at least forty million dead, more than half of them civilians, and more than $2,000 billion in damage. Despite a sharply rising birth rate and vast programs of economic reconstruction, such losses could never be fully repaired. Moreover, new and terrifying problems faced the world. Atomic weapons, hydrogen bombs, and guided missiles made real the fear that a new general war might exterminate all life on this planet. The United

States and the Soviet Union were at first the only powers able to initiate or pursue nuclear warfare. Given the ideology of the communist state and the character of Stalin, the Russians naturally regarded the Americans as their rivals for control of the world, and the Americans were quickly forced to accept the same estimate of the situation. The postwar history of international politics thus became largely a history of Soviet-American rivalry: a cold war between superpowers.

Enemy attack and occupation had caused incalculable devastation inside Russia and left millions of survivors destitute; but Russia's capitalist ally, the United States, had remained unattacked in its heartland and had invented and used atomic weapons. It seemed to Stalin that all the technological advances of the Soviet period, undertaken to bring the Soviet Union up to the industrialized West, had now been wiped out by the United States, and it took him four years (1945-1949) to catch up by making his own atomic bomb. Scientific information given the Russians by agents and spies made some contribution to this achievement, but only the high level of Soviet science and technology and the Soviet capacity to concentrate government investments made it possible at all. Though the Soviet Union and its former Western allies agreed on peace treaties with Italy, Hungary, Romania, and Bulgaria, no such treaty could be concluded with Germany or Japan. The Soviet Union also concluded a peace treaty with Finland in which it took a portion of Karelia. From Romania Russia again took Bessarabia and northern Bukovina, and it annexed part of former East Prussia and the easternmost part of Czechoslovakia.

The chief surviving Nazi leaders were tried at Nuremberg in 1946 and several were executed for war crimes. Defeated Germany was divided into four sections—American, British, French and Russian. The Soviet sector extended from eastern Germany to west of Berlin, which, as the former capital, was also divided into four occupation zones, one for each of the Allies. This arrangement was designed for temporary military occupation, but it continued because no treaty could be reached. It proved extremely dangerous, for it left Berlin as an island surrounded by Soviet-dominated territory, yet an island including zones to which the Western allies were entitled to have military access. The failure to reach any settlement over Germany left the most serious problem in Europe unresolved.

In 1949 the three Western powers promoted the union of their respective sectors as the Federal Republic of Germany—West Germany—with its capital at Bonn. The Russians responded by creating the communist German Democratic Republic—East Germany—with its capital at Pankow outside Berlin. Many West Germans were eager for reunion with their fellow Germans in the Soviet zone. Yet a reunification of Germany under Western capitalist auspices was what the Russians feared most, believing that it would mean a revival of aggression. An all-communist Germany was equally intolerable to the Western powers. Indeed, few French or

THE IRON CURTAIN

Winston Churchill, British wartime prime minister who was voted out of office on the eve of victory, had been consistently suspicious of Soviet intentions. Fearful that Americans would slip back into a stance of isolation, he coined the phrase "iron curtain" in a speech in Fulton, Missouri, on March 5, 1946:

A shadow has fallen upon the scenes so lately lighted by the Allied victory. Nobody knows what Soviet Russia and its Communist international organization intends to do in the immediate future, or what the limits, if any, to their expensive and proselytizing tendencies. . . .

From Stettin in the Baltic to Trieste in the Adriatic, an iron curtain has descended across the Continent. Behind that line lie all the capitals of the ancient state of central and eastern Europe. Warsaw, Berlin, Prague, Vienna, Budapest, Belgrade, Bucharest and Sofia, all these famous cities and the populations around them lie in the Soviet sphere and all are subject in one form or another, not only to Soviet influence but to a very high and increasing measure of control from Moscow. Athens alone, with its immortal glories, is free to decide its future at an election under British, American and French observation. . . . Police governments are prevailing in nearly every case, and so far, except in Czechoslovakia, there is no true democracy. . . .

Vital Speeches of the Day, XII (March 15, 1946), 331-32.

English leaders looked with enthusiasm upon the idea of any reunified Germany.

In Asia the most grievous problem remained that of China. The Chinese communists, who had challenged Chiang Kai-shek's ruling Kuomintang party for power, kept their forces active during the Japanese occupation. The United States unsuccessfully tried in 1946-1947 to bring about an agreement between Chinese nationalists and communists that would end the civil war. By 1949 the communists had defeated Chiang Kai-shek, who took refuge on the island of Formosa (Taiwan), where the communists could not follow because they had no fleet. In the last years of the struggle, Chiang had lost his hold over the Chinese people; the morale of his own forces was low, and an ever-mounting inflation ravaged the economy, already ruined by the long Japanese occupation. By 1950 mainland China had gone communist and formed part of the Soviet bloc, while Chiang's government in Taiwan remained part of the American bloc. American foreign policy had suffered a major defeat. Unaccustomed to defeat, Americans blamed the failure on a conspiracy by subversives within the United States, but the magnitude of the change, the huge numbers of Chinese involved, rendered this explanation unsatisfactory.

Elsewhere, the Soviet Union pursued its goal of world communism through the agencies of individual Communist parties. Communist parties existed in virtually every country, sometimes strong—as in France or Italy—sometimes weak—as in Britain or the United States—often varying in the degree of subservience to the Communist party of the Soviet Union (CPSU) and the Soviet government. The Soviet Union thus had a certain advantage in the cold war, in the competition between the two superpowers for the allegiance and support of the rest of the world. The United States, by contrast, had no ideologically disciplined supporters in most of the world. The two superpowers each became the leader of a great coalition whose members were attached by bonds of self-interest.

The members of the loose American coalition in 1945 included the Western Hemisphere nations, Great Britain, the British Commonwealth, western Europe, Japan, the Philippines. The Soviet coalition included the countries of eastern Europe and, by 1949, China. The border between the two coalitions in Europe—named the Iron Curtain by Winston Churchill in 1946—ran along a north-south line across central Europe. Turkey belonged to the Western coalition, and portions of the Middle East and of Southeast Asia were linked to it by a network of pacts. The dividing line between North and South Korea—with the Soviet Union occupying the north and the United States the south, and with a heritage of troop movement at the end of the war—represented a kind of Asian extension of the long frontier between the two coalitions. Over this long frontier came aggressive Soviet probing operations that led to crises and in several cases to wars.

Repeatedly, the West tried unsuccessfully to ease relations between the two coalitions. In 1946 Stalin refused to join in a United Nations atomic energy commission. In 1947 the United States proposed an international plan of massive American economic aid to accelerate European recovery from the ruin of the war— the Marshall Plan, named for General George C. Marshall, American secretary of state (1880-1959). The Soviet Union refused to accept the aid for itself and would not let its satellites participate in the Marshall Plan. The member nations subsequently formed the nucleus of the North Atlantic Treaty Organization (NATO) in 1949. The Soviet coalition founded the Cominform (Communist Information Bureau) in 1947 as a successor to the former Comintern, and created the Warsaw Pact (1955), binding eastern Europe together, as a reply to NATO. The United States and Britain sought in the 1950s and 1960s to prevent the spread of atomic weapons. Their plan called for a joint Multilateral (Nuclear) Force. Because the Germans would participate, the French rejected MLF and in 1966 withdrew their military forces from NATO and forced NATO headquarters to be moved out of France.

In the Middle East, the Baghdad Pact and its successor, the Central Treaty Organization (CENTO), proved to be no more than a series of unstable agreements among the United States, Britain, Turkey, Iran, and Pakistan. With the withdrawal of Iraq from the Baghdad Pact in 1959, no direct alliances linked the Arab world with the West. The neutral nations remained outside the coalitions. Some, like Switzerland or Sweden, were simply maintaining their traditional policies of not aligning themselves with any grouping of powers. But most were newly independent nations. Of these India was the most influential, taking much-needed economic assistance from both coalitions. As economic aid became an instrument in the cold war, neutral nations tried, often with success, to play one side off against the other. A deeply frightenend United States at first declared that neutrality in a moral crusade was impossible, but by the 1960s the United States came to regard neutrality as often positively helpful to its interests.

Through the years of cold war, the United Nations—formed during World War II from among the opponents of the Axis and chartered in 1945 at San Francisco—served as an international organization where members of both coalitions and neutrals alike could confer. As the direct successor to the League of Nations, though with its headquarters in New York, it inherited the League's duty of keeping the peace; but, like the League, it lacked independent sovereignty or authority over its members. To deal with threats to the peace, its charter created a Security Council with eleven member states, five of which—the United States, the Soviet Union, Great Britain, France, and China—held permanent memberships. The other six were elected to rotating two-year terms by the General Assembly, to which all member states belonged. The secretary general, elected by the Security Council, could exert great personal influence in international affairs. The first three secretaries general were a Norwegian, Trygvie Lie (1896-1968), a Swede, Dag Hammarskjold (1903-1961), and a Burmese, U Thant (1909-1974). The first angered the Russians by involving the United Nations in the Korean conflict and was forced to retire in 1953; the second, realizing how precarious the office was, managed to tread a path sufficiently neutral to survive the attacks of both sides until his death in an airplane crash in Africa in 1961; and the third, being Asian, clearly shifted the office into the neutralist bloc.

But each of the five permanent members of the Security Council could veto any substantive question. Both the Soviet Union and the United States insisted that decisions had to be unanimous before action could go forward. As a result, the Security Council often found itself unable to act because of a veto. Of the eighty vetoes cast in the first decade, the Soviets exercised seventy-seven.

In the mid-fifties new nations joined the UN: some pro-Western, like Austria and Italy (both former Axis states and so originally excluded); some pro-Soviet, like Romania and Bulgaria, former Axis satellites in eastern Europe; and some neutral and mostly former colonies, like Ceylon (Sri Lanka) or Libya. Japan joined in 1956. As the former colonies obtained their independence during the late fifties and early sixties, each joined the United Nations, where the Afro-Asian bloc came to command a majority in the General Assembly. The United States for twenty years successfully opposed the seating of the Chinese communists, which until 1971 left the permanent Chinese seat on the Security Council in the possession of Chiang Kai-shek's representative.

The League of Nations had never been able to put its own forces into the field, but the UN did so repeatedly: in Korea in 1950-1952 (where, because of the absence at the time of the vote of the Soviet representative from the Security Council, the Russians failed to veto the Council's decision to intervene, and the American army fought under the sponsorship of the UN); on the Arab-Israeli frontiers (1956-1967, and again in 1974 and 1982); in the former Belgian Congo; in Cyprus and elsewhere.

Through its functional councils and special agencies—the Economic and Social Council, the Educational, Scientific and Cultural Organization (UNESCO), the World Health Organization, the Food and Agricultural Organization, and the World Bank—the UN advanced loans to governments to initiate new development plans, controlled epidemics, and provided experts on modern farming techniques. The UN proved widely effective in spreading technical information, in helping new nations be heard in a way small countries could not ordinarily have been, and in providing the major states with a forum in which they could cool their anger through public debate and public exposure. But the UN was frequently unable to forestall war, and while it remained a valuable instrument of diplomacy, the high hopes originally entertained for it were not realized. It tended to respond to the actions of others, rather than to initiate actions, and the nations it responded to most often were the superpowers or their client states.

As the nation least injured by World War II because virtually no fighting took place on its home soil, the United States was in the best position to respond immediately. Under President Truman (who had been Roosevelt's vice-president and who, though initially intimidated by the presidency, grew rapidly in strength and vision once in office) a new balance of power began to emerge. As part of that balance, the United States first turned to a policy of containment designed to prevent the Soviet Union from extending its control beyond the limits it had consolidated in 1947. But by about 1952 the belief that inherent weaknesses in the Soviet system would cause it to disintegrate began to be seriously challenged, and many analysts realized that the confrontations between the two great powers would continue. Containment was attacked in the United States by the left, which felt Truman was too hard on the Soviets; by the right, which wanted to roll the Russians back to their original borders; and by the political middle, which argued that containment was only a defensive stance, and that the United States must devise fresh initiatives, to attract the newly independent nations of the so-called Third World.

For a brief time the United States supported the idea of liberation, or "rollback," but was disillusioned after the Hungarian uprising of 1956 in which Americans found they could do very little against Russian domination. At the same time there was a sharp break with Britain over the nation's Suez policy, and the United States turned increasingly toward efforts to encourage diversity within communist states, especially in eastern Europe. Since the first Russian atom bomb test was detected in the West in September 1949, the United States had debated how best to deal with a growing tendency toward stalemate. If the Soviet bloc could be made to loosen its control of its satellites, some liberalization might take place within the Soviet bloc itself without direct Western intervention. Thus attitudes toward the nations of eastern Europe remained in flux, with the great powers trying to manipulate the balance, much as in the years immediately preceding the outbreak of World War I.

The Soviet Union and the West, 1945-1970

Russia moved rapidly to consolidate its territorial position. Using the Red Army, the Russians created "people's republics" in Poland, Romania, Hungary, and Bulgaria, which became Soviet satellites. Yugoslavia organized its own communist government, with Albania as its own satellite. Soviet troops occupied about a third of Germany, roughly between the Elbe and the Oder rivers, where they organized the communist-ruled satellite of East Germany. The part of Germany that lay east of the line formed by the Oder and Neisse rivers, except for the sections of East Prussia directly annexed to the USSR, was handed over by the Russians to their Polish satellite; here a wholesale transfer of population replaced the Germans with Poles. Finland became a hostage to the Russian security system but retained its prewar political institutions and a measure of neutrality. The four Allied powers detached Austria from Germany—thus undoing Hitler's Anschluss of 1938—and divided it, like Germany, into four occupation zones. The presence of Soviet troops in Hungary and Romania was specifically guaranteed to protect the communication lines between Russia and its occupying forces in Austria. In 1948 the communists took over Czechoslovakia by a coup d'état and ousted the government of Edward Beneš, enemy of Hitler in 1938, now betrayed for a second time. Within each satellite the communists aped Soviet policies, moving quickly to collectivize agriculture, impose forced industrialization, control cultural life, and govern by terror.

In other cases, the Soviet Union was rebuffed. In 1946 the Soviets at first refused to withdraw their forces from northwest Iran and yielded only to pressure from the United Nations. A more alarming probe came in Greece, where a communist-dominated guerrilla movement during World War II had attempted to seize control and been thwarted by British troops. In 1946 the Greek communists tried again, backed this time by Albania, Yugoslavia, and Bulgaria. Simultaneously, Stalin pressured the Turks for concessions in the Straits area. In response, President Truman proclaimed that countries facing the threat of communist aggression could count on help from the United States. Under this "Truman Doctrine," he sent American military aid to Greece and Turkey. The threat to the Turks receded, and by 1949, after severe fighting, the Greeks put down the communist uprising with the help of American advisers.

The Russians began one of the most bitter phases of the cold war in 1948 in Germany. By shutting off all major highways from the West to Berlin, they attempted to force the Western Allies to turn Berlin over to them. The Allies stood firm, however, and in the next six months airlifted more than 2.3 million tons of supplies to West Berlin. Though the Russians then gave up and reopened the land routes, the Soviets remained determined to oust the Western powers from Berlin.

The Yugoslav Rebellion Also in 1948, the Russians faced a rebellion from a country that had previously seemed the most pro-Soviet of all the new communist states of eastern Europe—Yugoslavia. Yugoslavia had overthrown a pro-German government in 1941 and throughout World War II remained a scene of intense guerrilla action against the Germans and Italians. There were two main groups of guerrillas: the Chetniks, representing the Serb royalist domination over the south Slav kingdom; and the Partisans, led by Croatian-born, communist Tito. As the war contined, the communist-dominated Partisans gained ground against the Chetniks. Churchill, focusing on the need to beat Hitler, sent Tito supplies, and the United States followed suit. The Russians helped put their fellow communist, Tito, in control in 1944.

Once in power, Tito installed his own communist government, abolished the Yugoslav monarchy, and for three years adopted all the standard Soviet policies. Yet in June 1948 the Russians expelled Tito's regime from the Cominform. The Soviet satellites broke their economic agreements with Yugoslavia, unloosed barrages of anti-Tito propaganda, and stirred up border incidents. Soviet arrogance and insistence on penetrating the Yugoslav army and security organizations had aroused Yugoslav national feeling, never very far below the surface. Stalin believed that he could bully the Yugoslavs into submission. "I will shake my little finger," he said, "and there will be no more Tito."

But Tito remained in power, accepting the aid that was quickly offered him by the United States. Washington recognized that a communist regime hostile to Stalin was a new phenomenon that would deeply embarrass the Russians. Gradually, Yugoslav communism evolved its own ideology, rejecting Stalin's politics and declaring that Tito and his followers were the only true Leninists. Tito decentralized the economy, beginning in the factories, where workers' committees began to participate actively in planning. From the economy, decentralization spread to the local government, then to the central government, and finally to the Yugoslav Communist party, now renamed the League of Yugoslav Communists. Tito also gradually abandoned collectivized agriculture, which, as always, was most unpopular with peasants. Yugoslavia remained communist, however, and suspicious of the Western capitalists who were helping it. Lest this new "national" communism spread to the other regimes, the Soviets directed a series of ferocious purges in eastern Europe, executing leading communists for alleged "Titoism" and thus terrorizing anyone who might hope to establish autonomy within the communist bloc.

The Korean War   After the failures in Greece and Berlin, the Soviet Union embarked on new Asian adventures, as czarist governments had when balked in Europe. Communists had tried and failed to win power in Indonesia, Burma, Malaya, and the Philippines. The Korean War, which broke out in June 1950, was in some measure a Soviet-sponsored operation, although the Russians contributed only support and sympathy and allowed their Chinese ally to take the military lead.

Korea had been a target of Russian interest in the late nineteenth and early twentieth centuries, but the Japanese defeat of the Russians in 1905 had led instead to Japanese annexation of the country in 1910. In 1945 Russian troops occupied the northern part of Korea and American troops the southern part. The country was divided in the middle by a line along the 38th parallel of latitude. A communist-inspired People's Democratic Republic of Korea was set up in the north and an American-inspired Republic of Korea in the south. When all American forces except for a few specialists were withdrawn from South Korea, the North Koreans marched south to unite the nation under communist control.

The communists may have thought the operation would go unchallenged, since incautious official American pronouncements had implied that Korea was outside the American "defense perimeter." But when the invasion began, the United States moved troops into Korea. Under General Douglas MacArthur, they halted the North Korean drive and pushed the enemy back almost to the frontier of China. At this point Chinese

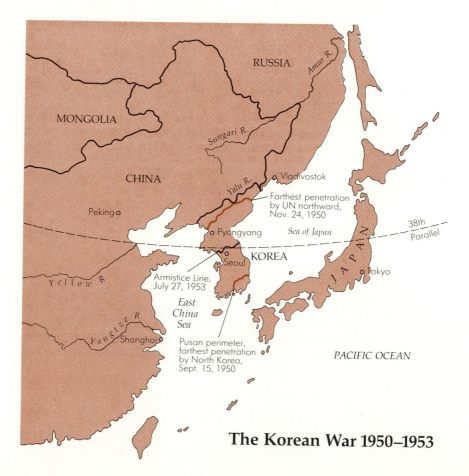

The Korean War 1950–1953

troops joined the North Koreans in pushing the Americans southward again. By 1951 the line of battle had been stabilized roughly along the old boundary between North and South Korea. After prolonged negotiations, an armistice was finally concluded in July 1953.

The Korean settlement did not end the tension between Communist China and the United States, and serious friction developed over Taiwan (Formosa) and smaller offshore islands in the hands of Chiang Kai-shek. Nor did the Korean settlement bring a closer understanding between the Soviet Union and the United States. It was at best a compromise. After all the fighting, the United States had managed to hold on to the devastated southern portion of the country, and the communists had been driven back to the north, which they governed undisturbed. Neither side could call it a victory.

By the time the Korean war ended, Stalin had been dead for more than three months. Stalin's heirs realized that any attack that threatened the vital interests of the United States might well touch off the ultimate disaster. A policy of probing to see just which interests the United States considered vital had already led to the Korean War. Continued tension between the two superpowers required the Soviets to continue to devote their resources to guns rather than butter. To relax the tension would theoretically have meant more butter, but would raise the danger that the Soviet Union would lose its position as leader of the world communist movement. China, in its determination to seize Taiwan and expand in Asia, might take over the leadership of world revolutionary forces and might represent the Russian leaders as old and tired, no longer true Leninists. In the end it proved to be impossible for the Russian leadership to hold all these threats in balance, and the choices they felt forced to make led to a major split in the communist world.

Eastern Europe In eastern Europe, the new first secretary to the Soviet party, Nikita Khrushchev (1894-1971), sought to heal the breach with Tito. In May 1955 he went in person to Belgrade and publicly apologized for the quarrel, taking the blame upon the Soviets and agreeing that "differences in the concrete forms of developing socialism are exclusively matters for the people of the country concerned." Relations between Tito and Moscow improved, although the Yugoslavs never abandoned their ties to the West. Khrushchev even went so far as to declare that many prominent victims of the Titoist purges had been executed wrongly, and he abolished the Cominform, the body that ostensibly had started the quarrel with Tito. But in making these admissions and healing the quarrel Stalin had started, Khrushchev opened the door to new troubles.

In 1956 Khrushchev denounced Stalin and admitted to many past injustices in the Soviet Union. This proved far too stong a brew for the European satellites. Anti-communist riots by workers in Poznan, Poland, in June 1956 were followed by severe upheavals elsewhere in Poland. The uprising was conducted by one wing of the Communist party, that led by Wladislaw Gomulka

(1905-1982), who had been purged for alleged Titoism in 1951. Not even the presence in Warsaw of Khrushchev himself prevented Gomulka's rise to power, although at one moment the Russians seem to have contemplated imposing their will by force. Yet because the new government in Poland was still communist, they allowed it to remain in power until 1970.

In Hungary, however, the upheaval went farther. Starting, like the Polish uprising, as an anti-Stalinist movement within the Communist party, the Hungarian disturbance at first brought Imre Nagy (1895-1958), a communist like Gomulka, into office as premier. But popular hatred for communism and for the Russians got out of hand, and young men and women took up arms in Budapest in the hope of ousting the communists and taking Hungary out of the Soviet sphere. When Hungary denounced the Warsaw Pact, Khrushchev ordered full-fledged military action. In November 1956 Soviet tanks and troops, violating an armistice, swept back into Budapest and put down the revolution in blood and fire. A puppet government was installed and more than 150,000 Hungarian refugees fled to the West. Despite the Soviet charges that the uprising had been trumped up by Western "imperialists" and "fascists," the West in fact had not dared to help the Hungarians for fear of starting a world war.

The Hungarian uprising demonstrated that Khrushchev was unwilling to permit much deviation from the Soviet line, and that he would use military power when that line was crossed. Perhaps most important, it demonstrated to other satellite states that they could not count on aid from the West in the face of Soviet resistance. The effect was to stabilize the Iron Curtain, putting an end to major probes across it by either side.

Chinese influence was apparent in the harshness of the onslaught against Tito's revisionism and in Khrushchev's giving up his efforts to win the Yugoslavs by softness. Eager to play a leading role in world communism, the Chinese had displayed a strong preference for Stalinist orthodoxy and repression. By the spring of 1958 the Chinese and Khrushchev declared that Stalin's original denunciation of the Yugoslavs in 1948 had been correct after all. In June 1958 the Soviet government underlined this decision by announcing the executions of Imre Nagy and other leaders of the Hungarian uprising, in violation of promises of safe conduct.

All the eastern European satellites had been bound together in the Council for Mutual Economic Aid (Comecon) established in 1949, which took measures to standardize machinery and coordinate economic policies and issued blasts against western European efforts at economic cooperation through the Common Market. Yugoslavia never joined Comecon, and after 1958 it was not invited to send observers. In 1958-1959 Comecon called for a specialization plan in which the more developed countries would concentrate on heavy industry, and Romania in particular on the production of raw materials (chiefly food and oil). The Romanian government, communist though it was, protested, pointing to its already considerable achievement in heavy industry; in 1969 Romania openly refused to accept the "principles of the international socialist division of labor" issued at the Twenty-second Congress of the CPSU.

Thus the Romanians, like the Yugoslavs, assumed a more independent position within the communist bloc. They increased their trade with the noncommunist world and remained neutral in the growing Soviet-Chinese quarrel. In 1963 the Russians sanctioned Romania's continued efforts to build a steel industry. Soviet propaganda, however, called for integrating the lower Danube region—which would have meant taking territory from Romania—and denied that the Romanians had contributed to the Allied cause in World War II. The Romanians claimed full credit for their "liberation from fascism" and dared to demand the return of Bessarabia and northern Bukovina. Yugoslav-Romanian cooperation became an important part of Romanian policy. Largely owing to the ruthless balancing skill of the Romanian Communist leaders, first Gheorghe Gheorghiu-Dej (party secretary 1952-1965) and then Nicolae Ceausescu (1918-   ), supported by the traditionally anti-Russian sentiments of Romanians generally, the Romanians demonstrated a measure of independence in foreign and economic affairs.

Berlin But modest liberalization under Khrushchev in Hungary and Czechoslovakia also required a clear show of force against noncommunist states, or in the most important satellite, East Germany. There the Soviet Union had created its most industrially productive European satellite, fully integrated into Comecon. Strategically East Germany was of great importance to the USSR; control over East Germany enabled the Russians to keep Poland surrounded and to keep communist troops within easy reach of West Germany. Every year thousands of East Germans had been escaping into West Berlin, and the East German population had declined by two million between 1949 and 1961. Because West Berlin provided an example of prosperity and free democratic government that was more effective than any propaganda, Krushchev was determined to get the Western powers out of Berlin. He threatened to sign a peace treaty with the puppet government of East Germany, which was not yet recognized by the West, to turn over to it all communications to Berlin, and to support it in any effort it might make to force the Western powers out. Western refusal to abandon agreements concluded during World War II led to a prolonged diplomatic crisis in 1959.

The Western powers could not permit the Soviets to recreate the conditions that led to the airlift of 1948 or accept the suggestion that, once Western troops were removed, Berlin would become a "free city." Defenseless and surrounded by communist territory, Berlin and its two million citizens might soon be swallowed up. Moreover, the Soviet proposal for a confederation of East and West Germany aroused the gravest doubts. How could a state that was a full member of the Western coalition of NATO join with one that belonged to the Soviet coali-

tion's Warsaw Pact? How could a state that stood for capitalist development federate with one completely communized? How could a parliamentary state governed by a multiparty system federate with a communist totalitarian state? From all those complex proposals and counterproposals, Khrushchev hoped at least to gain some measure of Western diplomatic recognition of East Germany, arrange some permanent settlement to his advantage over Berlin, and enhance his prestige in the eyes of rising opposition at home.

While the Berlin threat persisted, the new American president, Dwight D. Eisenhower, and Khrushchev agreed to exchange visits, and Khrushchev made a dramatic tour of the United States. But when the leaders of the two great powers met at the summit in Paris in May 1960, tensions were once again inflamed by a striking incident. A Soviet missile had brought down an American U-2, a lightweight, extremely fast plane that had been taking high-altitude photographs of Soviet territory from bases in Turkey and Pakistan. The Russians had captured the pilot unharmed. After an initial denial, Eisenhower had to admit the truth of the charge; the

In June, 1961, Khrushchev and Kennedy met in Vienna, alternately at the American and (as shown in the picture) Russian embassies.

AMERICAN AND RUSSIAN LEADERS MEET TO DISCUSS THE COLD WAR

When Khruschev and Kennedy met in Vienna, they discussed at length why the two nations had such different views of the future. A special assistant to President Kennedy, Arthur M. Schlesinger, Jr., (1917-   ), on leave from his professorship of history at Harvard University, wrote of the meeting:

Kennedy observed courteously that Americans were impressed by the economic achievement of the Soviet Union; it was a source of satisfaction to the whole world. But, as he saw the problem, it was not that the democracies were trying to eliminate communism in areas under communist control, but that the communists were trying to eliminate free systems in areas associated with the west. Khruschev brusquely rejected this. It was impossible, he said, for the Soviet Union to implant its policy in other states. All the Soviet Union claimed was that communism would triumph; this was not propaganda but a scientific analysis of social development. Communism was superseding capitalism today as capitalism had superseded feudalism in the past. Changes in social systems were bound to come, but they would be brought about only by the will of the people themselves. The Communists believed in their systems, as the President believed in his. In any event, this was a matter for debate, not for war. . . .

The great need, Kennedy commented, was for each side to understand the other's views. The American position was that people should have freedom of choice. When communist minorities seized control against the popular will, the Chairman regarded this as historical inevitability; we did not, and this brought our two nations into conflict. . . .

This led Khruschev into a sententious discourse on intellectual freedom. Did the United States, he asked, plan to build a dam against the development of the human mind and conscience? The Inquisition had burned people but could not burn their ideas, and eventually the ideas prevailed. History must be the judge in a competition of ideas. If capitalism could insure a better life, it would win. If not, communism would win; but this would be a victory of ideas, not of arms. . . .

Kennedy quoted Mao Tse-tung's remark that power came out of the end of the rifle. Khruschev blandly denied that Mao ever said this. Mao was a Marxist, and Marxists were against war. Kennedy repeated that Khruschev must understand the American views: if our two nations failed to preserve the peace, the whole world would be the loser. . . . The greatest danger was the miscalculation by one power of the interests and policy of another.

Arthur M. Schlesinger, Jr., *A Thousand Days: John F. Kennedy in the White House* (Greenwich, Conn.: Fawcett, 1967), pp. 334-36.

---

incident ended both the summit meeting and the plans for his own visit to the Soviet Union.

When Eisenhower's successor, John F. Kennedy (1917-1963), met Khrushchev in Vienna (June 1961), Khrushchev insisted that his country would sign the treaty with East Germany before the end of the year. Tension mounted, and the number of refugees fleeing from East Berlin rose to a thousand a day. On August 13 East German forces cut all communications between East and West Berlin and began to build the infamous Berlin Wall to prevent further departures. Taken by surprise, the United States realized that it could not resort to arms to prevent the closing of the East Germans' own border. The Wall became the symbol of a government that had to imprison its own people to keep them from leaving. Escapes, recaptures, and shootings continued along the Wall for the next two decades, but the immediate crisis proved to be over. Khrushchev had backed away from unilateral cancellation of the Berlin treaties.

Nuclear Tests: Cuba But Khrushchev now probed in another way, announcing in August 1961 that the Soviets would resume atomic testing in the atmosphere, a practice stopped by both powers in 1958. In the two months that followed the Russians exploded thirty bombs, whose total force exceeded all previous American, British, and French explosions. President Kennedy decided that, unless Khrushchev would agree to a treaty banning all tests, the United States would have to conduct its own new tests. Khrushchev refused, and American testing began again in April 1962.

In the summer of 1962 Khrushchev moved to place Soviet missiles with nuclear warheads in Cuba. This former American dependency and economic satellite, which was of great strategic importance and which lay only ninety miles off the Florida coast, was now in the hands of a domestic communist party led by Fidel Castro (1926-   ). Castro had overthrown Cuba's dictator, General Fulgencio Batista (1901-1973), in 1959. Castro's revolution, which had taken nearly six years, had at first seemed romantic and had been supported by many Americans. Once in power, Castro, who may not initially have been a communist, quickly entered into an alliance with the Soviets. Hoping to bring Castro down, anticommunist Cuban exiles in the United States—with the blessing of President Kennedy but without the needed American air support—had attempted a disastrous landing at the Bay of Pigs in 1961.

Castro quickly learned what it meant to be a Soviet satellite during the Cuban missile crisis. He may not have asked for the missiles, but he had accepted them, even though Soviet officers were to retain control over their use. Although their installation would effectively have doubled the Soviet capacity to strike directly at the United States, the chief threat was political. When known, the mere presence of these weapons ninety miles from Florida would shake the confidence of other nations in America's capacity to protect even its own shores, and would enable Khrushchev to blackmail America over Berlin. American military intelligence discovered the sites and photographed them from the air. Khrushchev announced that the Soviet purpose was simply to help the Cubans resist a new invasion from the United States.

But Kennedy could not allow the missiles to remain in Cuba. At first the only course of action seemed an air strike, which might well have touched off a new world war. Instead, Kennedy found a measure that would prevent the further delivery of missiles—a sea blockade ("quarantine") of the island—and he combined it with the demand that the missiles already in Cuba be removed. He thus gave Khrushchev a way to avoid world war and a chance to save face. After several days of great tension, Khrushchev backed down and agreed to halt work on the missile sites in Cuba and to remove the offensive weapons there, while reaffirming the Soviet wish to continue discussions about disarmament.

Kennedy now exploited the American victory to push for a further relaxation in tensions. In July 1963 the United States, the Soviet Union, and Great Britain signed a treaty banning nuclear weapons tests in the atmosphere, in outer space, or under water. The treaty subsequently received the support of more than seventy nations, though France and China—prospective nuclear powers—would not sign it. The installation of a "hot line" communications system between the White House and the Kremlin that enabled the leaders of the two superpowers to talk to each other directly and the sale of surplus American wheat to the Russians marked the final steps Kennedy was able to take to decrease tensions before he was assassinated on November 22, 1963.

Czechoslovakia The administration of Kennedy's successor, President Lyndon B. Johnson (1908-1973), saw no Soviet-American crisis as acute as that over the missiles, but relations between the two superpowers remained tense and suspicious. The war in Vietnam would make relaxation of tension impossible, and the two powers also would take opposite sides in the Middle East. The settlement in 1968 on the terms of a nuclear nonproliferation treaty to prevent the spread of atomic arms beyond the nations that already possessed them seemed to represent a step forward, but Soviet intervention in Czechoslovakia in the summer of 1968 delayed its ratification.

Long the most Stalinist of the eastern European governments, the Czech regime was unpopular at home. Soviet exploitation and the rigidity of communist dogma had crippled the once flourishing Czech economy. Then in 1968 Alexander Dubček (1921-   ), a Slovak communist trained in Russia, took over the Czech Communist party as first secretary and ousted his predecessor. The Dubček government freed the press from censorship, and pent-up protests filled its columns. It appeared that the regime might even allow opposition political parties to exist. Some army officers apparently favored revision of the Warsaw Pact, which enabled the Soviets to hold military exercises in the territory of any member state. Yugoslavia and Romania encouraged the Czechs in this liberal course, and a revival of the old Little Entente between these three countries seemed to be in the making.

However, the Czechs could not put through such a radical liberalization without alarming the Russians and the East German government. In the spring and summer of 1968 the Soviets moved from first denouncing the Dubček regime to intimidating and bullying it, and finally to armed intervention. Soviet and satellite tank divisions, more than 500,000 strong, swept into the country and met no active resistance. Unlike the Soviet attack on Hungary in 1956, that on Czechoslovakia in the summer of 1968 was not directed against a population already in armed rebellion. There was little bloodshed, but there was great shock. Those who had been arguing that the Soviets had outgrown the Stalinist repression of earlier years found themselves proved wrong, and the French and Italian Communist parties joined the Yugoslav and Romanian parties in condemning the invasion.

The return of Stalinism to Czechoslovakia was inexorable. Dubček was ousted from government and party; the Czech government was once more a mere Soviet puppet. A grim purge of Czech intellectuals followed. The Russians had been so alarmed by the Czech cultural, economic, and political ferment and its military and diplomatic implications that they were willing, at least temporarily, to sacrifice much of the international good will that they had been able to accumulate. In 1969 and 1970 discussions between the United States and the Soviet Union over limitations of armaments (SALT, Strategic Arms Limitation Talks) resumed. By then both powers had a compelling interest in reducing their huge expenditures on weapons and obtaining more resources to deal with their internal economies.

VI CONFLICT IN ASIA, 1953-1970

Between Stalin's death in 1953 and Khrushchev's denunciation of Stalin in 1956, Chinese-Soviet relations were basically amicable, and Chinese influence rose in the communist world. The Russians returned Port Arthur and Dairen to China in 1955. But when Krushchev attacked Stalin without consulting Mao Tse-tung (1893-1976), the Chinese Communist leader, the Chinese denounced him for joining with Tito and the revisionists.

Mao had walked a long road to become head of the most populous nation on earth: he had organized the Red Army in 1928, had endured the six-thousand-mile Long March to a stronghold in northwest China in 1934-1936, had helped to repel the Japanese, had defeated Chiang Kai-shek, and had established the People's Republic of China in 1949. An undeviating Stalinist, Mao was convinced that the Soviet Union had deserted the true doctrine, and he was deeply offended at being ignored on so significant a matter as revealing to the world the extent of Stalin's purges and the nature of the Terror. To doctrinal matters Mao added practical grievances; he wanted far more economic aid than the Soviets had been able or willing to provide, especially aid in developing nuclear weapons. In 1957 Mao experimented briefly with a liberated public opinion ("Let one hundred flowers bloom"), but soon resumed a thoroughly leftist militant course. At home he embarked on forced industrialization—the "great leap forward"—with backyard blast furnaces and mass collectivization of the "people's communes," ending in disastrous results to both industry and agriculture. Having been down this road themselves, the Russians disapproved, and the latent disagreements between the two communist giants began to emerge.

The Soviet-Chinese Split

In 1959 Khrushchev told Peking that the Soviet Union would not furnish China with atomic weapons and tried unsuccessfully to unseat Mao. Chinese bombardment of Quemoy and Matsu (1958), offshore islands claimed by Taiwan, plus a savage conquest of Tibet and an invasion of Indian territory in Ladakh were undertaken without consultation between the Chinese and the Soviets. The Russians publicly declared themselves to be neutral between the Chinese and the Indians, and in 1960 Khrushchev withdrew all Soviet technicians from China.

The Chinese tried to influence other communist parties against the Russians and picked up a European satellite—Albania, the smallest and poorest of the Balkan countries. The Albanian Communist party had thrown off Yugoslav domination after Tito's rebellion from Stalin in 1948. More than anything else, the Albanian communists feared renewed control by the Yugoslavs. When Khrushchev made his repeated efforts to conciliate Tito, the Albanians found an ally in the Chinese. Albania was an economic liability, but the Chinese won prestige by wooing a European communist state away from the Russian bloc.

In the midst of the 1962 crisis over Soviet missiles in Cuba, the Chinese chose to attack India again, apparently intending to seize the border regions in Ladakh, including important road communications. The Chinese withdrew when they had what they wanted; but the Soviets, though ostensibly neutral, were clearly pro-Indian. India was of great importance in the eyes of both superpowers, and each preferred to see it nonaligned; thus both feared any possible Chinese conquest there.

When the nuclear test-ban threaty was signed, the Chinese denounced the Russians as traitors to the international communist movement. Khrushchev tried to arrange for a public excommunication of the Chinese by other communist parties, but he was unable to win sufficient support. Mao called for Khrushchev's removal

MAO ON REPRESSION

Mao's militance is indicated by his remarks in 1949, remarks which would be used to justify the liquidation of 800,000 people for "security reasons" between 1949 and 1954, as he admitted in 1957:

Our present task is to strengthen the people's state apparatus—meaning principally the people's army, the people's police, and the people's court—thereby safeguarding national defence and protecting the people's interests. Given these conditions, China, under the leadership of the working class and the Communist Party, can develop steadily from an agricultural into an industrial country and from a New Democratic into a Socialist and, eventually, Communist society, eliminating classes and realizing universal harmony.

Such state apparatus as the army, the police, and the courts are instruments with which one class oppresses another. As far as the hostile classes are concerned, these are instruments of oppression. They are violent and certainly not "benevolent" things.

"You are not benevolent." Exactly. We definitely have no benevolent policies toward the reactionaries or the counterrevolutionary activities of the reactionary classes. Our benevolent policy does not apply to such deeds or such persons, who are outside the ranks of the people; it applies only to the people.

Quoted in Robin W. Winks, *The Cold War from Yalta to Cuba* (New York: Macmillan, 1964), p. 52.

and accused the Russians of illegally occupying eastern European and Japanese territory. By the time of Khrushchev's ouster in a bloodless coup in October 1964, the Chinese had the support of the North Korean and North Vietnamese communist parties and enjoyed a special position of strength in Indonesia and Algeria. In Africa, they had established a predominant influence in two former French colonies, and they took the lead in sponsoring a major rebellion in the former Belgian Congo. In South America, the Chinese supported Castroites within the pro-Soviet Latin American parties in the hope of promoting more active revolutionary movements.

Power, Mao pointed out, came from the barrel of a gun, and he feared that the rising standard of living in the Soviet Union and elsewhere, together with doctrinal revisionism, had led the former world center of international communism to go soft. Maoism had become the cutting edge of international revolutionary communism—in Asia, in Africa, and in the United States. But 1965 brought major Chinese setbacks. A congress scheduled for Algiers, in which they had expected to condemn the Russians, was canceled, in part because the Algerians overthrew their pro-Chinese premier. The Congo revolt was put down. An attempted communist coup in Indonesia failed after the assassination of numerous leading army officers. The Indonesian army took power and revenged itself with the help of the Muslim population upon the Chinese minority and upon the local communists, of whom perhaps five hundred thousand were killed. A Chinese threat to renew the attack on India during the Indian-Pakistani conflict in 1965 evaporated when the United States and the Soviet Union tacitly cooperated in the United Nations to force a temporary ceasefire. Early in 1966 the Soviet premier acted as mediator between India and Pakistan, achieving an agreement to seek a peaceful solution, thus depriving the Chinese of a pretext for intervention while reasserting Soviet influence in Asia.

In part as the result of these successive setbacks abroad, and in part because of persistent failures to meet production goals at home, in 1966 the Chinese regime began to show signs of unbearable tensions. Denunciations and removals of important figures at the top of the government and party were accompanied by a new wave of adulation for Chairman Mao. Young people in their teens—the Red Guard—erupted into the streets, beating and killing older people whose loyalty they professed to suspect, destroying works of art and other memorials of China's precommunist past, and rioting against foreigners and foreign influences. In October 1966 the Chinese successfully fired a guided missile with a nuclear warhead—the third Chinese nuclear explosion in two years—affirming that the political turmoil had not interfered with the development of military hardware. Yet the turmoil continued, and all of China apparently became embroiled. The Chinese educational system was completely halted, and something like civil war raged in some provinces.

This artificially induced cultural revolution died down gradually in 1969, when the Ninth Chinese Communist Party Congress took place. In 1969 and 1970 the mystery that veiled China from the West seemed to thicken. Since Western and even Soviet journalists, scholars, film-makers, missionaries, or business people—the usual sources of information about a closed society—were not allowed in, foreign observers had to rely on guesswork. There is still no clear agreement on what happened during the cultural revolution or its immediate aftermath. Something like a fourth of the top party and government officials had been purged, leaving economic stagnation and ideological disillusionment behind. Chairman Mao himself—nearing the age of eighty—disappeared from the news for months at a time, and when he showed himself it was not as the implacable foe of all revisionism but as a relaxed and genial leader. Though Soviet-Chinese tension twice broke into open fighting on the frontiers, and though the hostile propaganda of both sides reached a shrill pitch, the two countries continued to negotiate.

Behind the series of incidents that revealed the mounting Chinese-Soviet quarrel to the world, there lay theoretical disagreements about the best way to bring communist control to the peoples of Asia, Africa, and Latin America. The Chinese favored direct sponsorship of local communist revolutionary movements; the Russians generally favored peaceful economic competition with the capitalist world for the loyalty and admiration of the emerging peoples. The Russians maintained that the communists could win the competition without world war by helping along local "wars of national liberation"—revolutions at least partly under communist control. The Chinese refused to grant that nuclear weapons had changed the nature of war or imperialism, and they regarded world war as inevitable. "The bourgeoisie," they maintained, "will never step down from the stage of history of its own accord." It must be pulled down.

The Chinese insisted that communists alone must take charge of all revolutionary movements from the beginning and claimed that aid to noncommunist countries was a delusion. They particularly objected to Soviet aid to India, their enemy. They opposed disarmament. They wanted Khrushchev to freeze Soviet living standards at a low level and invest the savings to help the Chinese catch up, but Khrushchev preferred to let his people enjoy some of the fruits of their labors. Remembering their success as a guerrilla operation that first came to control the countryside and then conquered the cities, the Chinese theoreticians extended this lesson to the whole globe, regarding Asia, Africa, and Latin America—the less developed areas—as the countryside and Europe and North America as the cities.

Race was also a factor. The Russians disliked and feared the Chinese, the "yellow peril" on their borders. The huge Chinese masses—soon to number one billion people—who were crowded into territory adjacent to the vast, sparsely populated regions of Siberia and Mon-

AMERICA'S STAKE IN VIETNAM

Because it is such a recent event, debate still continues over nearly all aspects of the long war in Vietnam. There is no clear agreement on what the stakes were for the United States in Vietnam; nor is there agreement on why the Eisenhower and Kennedy administrations felt they had to pick up where the French had left off. In a speech in June 1956, then-Senator John F. Kennedy outlined what would later be known as "the domino theory": that if the democracies allow one free nation to fall, all others in the vicinity will follow:

[Vietnam] represents the cornerstone of the Free World in Southeast Asia, the keystone to the arch, the finger in the dike. Burma, Thailand, India, Japan, the Philippines, and obviously Laos and Cambodia are among those whose security would be threatened if the red tide of Communism overflowed into Vietnam. . . .

Vietnam represents a proving ground for democracy in Asia. However we may choose to ignore or deprecate it, the rising prestige and influence of Communist China in Asia are unchallengeable facts. Vietnam represents the alternative to Communist dictatorship. If this democratic experience fails, if some one million refugees have fled the totalitarianism of the North only to find neither freedom nor security in the South, then weakness, not strength, will characterize the meaning of democracy in the minds of still more Asians. The United States is

directly responsible for this experiment—it is playing an important role in the laboratory where it is being conducted. We cannot afford to permit that experiment to fail. . . .

Vietnam represents a test of American responsibility and determination in Asia. If we are not the parents of little Vietnam, then surely we are the godparents. We presided at its birth, we gave assistance to its life, we have helped to shape its future. . . .

America's stake in Vietnam, in her strength and in her security, is a very selfish one—for it can be measured, in the last analysis, in terms of American lives and American dollars. . . .

American Friends of Vietnam, *America's Stake in Vietnam* (New York: Friends of Vietnam, 1956), pp. 10-11.

golia frightened the Asian Soviets. Because the threat came from another race, the fear increased. Despite protestations to the contrary, the Russians were race-conscious, as the experiences of African students in Moscow testified, and they reserved for the Chinese the deepest dislike of all. In turn, the Chinese openly used race as a weapon in their efforts to win support among Asians, Africans, and Latin Americans, lumping the Soviet Union with the United States as symbols of the white intention to continue dominating the nonwhite world. Firmly convinced of their own superiority to the rest of humankind, the Chinese were racists too. In Russia, in China, in a rapidly industrializing Japan, in the United States, in south Africa, in a Britain absorbing thousands of immigrants from Asia and the West Indies, in Israel, in the Arab states—throughout the world people bolstered their confidence by seeing themselves as superior, as chosen, as needing protection from the modern equivalent of barbarian invaders. Racism, strong in the nineteenth century, at its height in the 1920s and 1930s, experienced a strong resurgence in the insecurity unleashed by the cold war.

Vietnam

A special problem for the Chinese, Russians, and Americans arose in Southeast Asia from the revolt of the Viet Minh (Revolutionary League for the Independence

of Vietnam) against France that broke out in French Indochina after World War II. During the Korean War the United States, fearing that the Chinese communists would strike across the border into northern Indochina, had given substantial assistance to the French. In 1954, when the French had been resoundingly defeated after the fall of their stronghold of Dien Bien Phu, a conference of powers at Geneva recognized the independence of the Indochinese provinces of Cambodia and Laos.

Vietnam, the third and largest portion of the former French colony, was divided roughly along the 17th parallel. The northern portion, with its capital at Hanoi, was governed by the communist Viet Minh party, whose leader was a veteran communist, Ho Chi Minh (1890-1969). The southern portion, with its capital at Saigon, was led by a Catholic nationalist leader, Ngo Dinh Diem (1901-1963). The Geneva agreements promised free elections in two years. Though the United States did not sign the agreements, it endorsed their intent, hoping that the area, in which it had already invested more than $4 billion would not fall to the communists. Ho was receiving aid from Mao, with whom he shared a commitment to doctrine, a proven life of heroism (between 1940 and 1945 he had organized a guerrilla force to expel the Japanese), and the prestige of victory.

Between 1954 and 1959 Diem created the bureaucratic machinery for a new regime, provided for almost a million refugees from the communist North, and resettled in the countryside millions of peasants who had fled to the cities. After the departure of the French in 1956, the Americans assumed the responsibility for financial aid and technical advice. But Diem failed politically. He canceled the scheduled elections and together with his immediate family governed despotically. In 1958 and 1959 communist-led guerrilla activity broke out again. Now known as the Viet Cong (or VC), the guerrillas set up a National Liberation Front. In September 1960 Ho endorsed the Viet Cong movement, which he was already supplying with arms and training; by 1961 the guerrillas were moving almost at will in South Vietnam, overrunning much of the countryside, murdering, looting, and burning.

Neighboring Laos, strategically important, was less a nation than a collection of unwarlike Buddhist groups, where only a small clique of families traditionally managed political affairs. In 1953 a communist-oriented political faction, calling itself the Pathet Lao and supported by Ho Chi Minh, seized the northeastern portion of the country. The United States tried with massive financial and military aid to build a national Laotian army and establish a firm regime, but instead succeeded largely in creating corruption and factionalism. The head of the government, Souvanna Phouma (1901-   ), who was the brother-in-law of the head of the Pathet Lao, agreed in 1957 to set up a coalition government and neutralize the country, absorbing the Pathet Lao into the army. The United States objected, ousting Phouma and introducing a right-wing government. By 1960 Phouma was working with the Russians, and a portion of the army was working with the Pathet Lao. Soviet airlifts of supplies to their side enhanced the possibility that the country would fall to the communists, and that Thailand, Burma, and South Vietnam would also be endangered.

As president, Kennedy sought to neutralize Laos and to convince the Soviets that if his efforts failed, American military intervention would follow. Although the Soviets agreed to neutralization, fighting in Laos between Soviet-backed and American-backed forces continued until mid-May 1961, when Khrushchev apparently realized that the United States was preparing to send in marines from Okinawa. Before an agreement was reached at Geneva in July 1962, Kennedy did send marines to Thailand to stop the Pathet Lao from continuing to violate the truce there. When the decision to neutralize Laos was reached, the Pathet Lao, now a strong force armed with Russian weapons and still supported by Ho Chi Minh, withdrew from the coalition and kept control over its own portion of the country, which bordered on South Vietnam and included the Ho Chi Minh Trail, a supply route from Hanoi to the Viet Cong guerrillas.

Incomplete and unsatisfactory as the Laos arrangement was, it far surpassed any solution that could be reached for South Vietnam. American efforts to get Diem moving politically failed. All that emerged was the strategic-hamlet plan—a program to relocate peasants to fortified villages in the hope that this would provide protection against the guerrillas and thus make the communist campaigns first expensive and then impossible. Meanwhile, protests against Diem's rule increased, often led by Buddhist monks. In August 1963 Diem staged a mass arrest of Buddhists, and in November he and his brother were ousted and murdered in a coup led by dissident generals and permitted by the United States.

Thereafter, the South Vietnamese government changed hands many times, each time by military coup. The longest-lived regime, that of General Nguyen Cao Ky (1930-   ), successfully conducted elections in September 1966, with Ky emerging as vice-president under President Nguyen Van Thieu (1923-   ). But the hamlet program was a failure, and North Vietnamese troops appeared in South Vietnam in support of the guerrillas. More than half a million peasant families were once more made refugees by floods and by terrorism.

Between 1965 and 1967 the United States increased its troops from fewer than a single division to more than 500,000 troops and began bombing North Vietnamese installations. Massive American intervention prevented the Viet Cong from conquering the entire country and assured the United States of bases along the coast. Having increased the American commitment to such a level that none could doubt his intentions, President Johnson, in the hope of bringing Ho Chi Minh to the conference table, then assured the enemy that the United States had no long-range intention of remaining in the country and sought no military bases there. In 1966 Johnson suspended the bombings for a time, but the North Vietnamese insisted that there could be no negotiations until all American troops left the country. And the government in the South, nominally an ally of the United States, became increasingly dictatorial and corrupt.

The Vietnam War was the first in history to be viewed on television in livingrooms half a world away. The horror of the jungle fighting, the misery of the countless fleeing Vietnamese survivors, the ravages of napalm, the corruption of the Saigon government were all brought home vividly to the American public. Two chilling photographs, each a winner of a Pulitzer Prize, did much to make Americans decide that their stake in Vietnam was questionable. The war's mounting costs wrecked President Johnson's widely hailed Great Society program, and more and more voices called for American withdrawal. Mass protests, student strikes, demonstrations at military installations, and a substantial number of refusals to register for the draft underscored the growing divisiveness of the war, as opposing public opinion urged that the war be intensified and won. Intensification of the war threatened a land war in Asia of unprecedented difficulty and unpredictable length; on the other hand, withdrawal meant abandoning the goals for which the United States had fought in Asia in World War II. The communists of the 1970s, like the Japanese militarists of the 1940s, would dominate the Asian continent in open opposition to the United States.

In 1968, as the time for American elections approached, Senator Eugene McCarthy (1916-   ), Democrat of Minnesota, challenged the Johnson administration by announcing his candidacy for the presidency on an antiwar platform. His impressive successes in early primary elections at the state level stimulated another opponent of the war, Senator Robert F. Kennedy (1925-1968), Democrat of New York, one of the assassinated John Kennedy's younger brothers, to enter the race on his own. The strength of the antiwar candidates brought about the withdrawal of President Johnson— who had been expected to run again. Ho Chi Minh, who had always expected that internal American politics would force the United States out of Vietnam, then consented to open peace talks, which began in Paris but dragged on inconclusively. Robert Kennedy was assassinated in Los Angeles, and the Democratic party, now led by Johnson's vice-presidential running mate, Hubert Humphrey (1911-1978) was turned out of office by the Republicans under Richard M. Nixon (1913-), who had served as Eisenhower's vice-president.

The Nixon administration inherited an increasingly unpopular war and the halting negotiations designed to end it. Nixon pledged the eventual withdrawal of all American forces and began substantially to reduce them. He hoped to "Vietnamize" the fighting by rapidly training and supplying South Vietnamese forces, who would replace the Americans in combat but continue to have American assistance, including massive air support, until a settlement could be reached with the North that did not involve the communization of the South. But even the death of Ho Chi Minh in 1969 did not weaken the North Vietnamese government. It seemed prepared to carry on with the war, obviously believing that the Americans had lost faith in the cause, and that the communists would gain more by continuing the war than by ending it through negotiations.

The military picture was further clouded for the United States by the increasing Viet Cong domination of Laos, where the hard-won and tenuous settlement of the early 1960s was in jeopardy, and by the movement of Viet Cong forces into those portions of Cambodia nearest to South Vietnam. The head of Cambodia was a French-educated prince of an old ruling house, Norodom Sihanouk (1922-), who made some effort to maintain Cambodian neutrality despite his belief that in the end China would dominate his part of the world and so must be appeased. These beliefs made him unpopular both in Washington and at home. In 1970 a coup d'état overthrew Sihanouk, who, from Peking, announced the formation of a government in exile.

Not long afterward American and South Vietnamese troops made an "incursion" into Cambodia. The invading forces failed to wipe out the Vietnamese forces believed to be the chief target of the expedition. Public response in the United States to this extension of hostilities was far more negative than President Nixon and his adviser, Henry Kissinger (1923-), had expected. Many of America's allies condemned the action, and anti-American demonstrations were widespread throughout western Europe and Canada. Despite the capture of many North Vietnamese supplies in Cambodia, the American forces failed to find a central enemy

headquarters. Nixon withdrew the forces within the time promised, but there remained much doubt whether the Cambodian operation had been justifiable. During the Cambodian operations the United States had resumed intensive bombing of North Vietnam, the most effective weapon left to the United States as its land forces in Vietnam were reduced.

Probably no war since the religious wars of the Middle Ages has been so complex, has posed so many moral problems, or has proved so unpopular to its participants. The United States could not, for political and military reasons, commit more troops to the war; without more troops, the Americans and South Vietnamese were slowly being pressed back by the invaders from the North. Confused and tired, the American people allowed an alliance of the right and the left to draw them out of Vietnam. Withdrawal was advocated by those who condemned the regime in the South as corrupt and undemocratic, as well as by those who actively favored a communist victory on behalf of the peasants; withdrawal was also advocated by the "realists" who, whatever the moral issues involved, felt the stakes had become too high and that the United States was wasting its resources over an area of less significance to it than Europe, the Middle East, or Latin America; withdrawal was demanded by isolationists who felt the United States had no business trying to resolve what they saw as essentially a civil war in a remote land; withdrawal was called for by racists who thought American lives ought not to be spent on Asians; withdrawal was prayed for by pacifists, who felt that all war was evil. Few voices continued to advocate an all-out American commitment to Vietnam. American troops were pulled back, and a cease-fire was finally arranged in January 1973.

Persistent violations of the cease-fire on both sides accompanied the evacuation of South Vietnamese troops toward Saigon, an evacuation that advancing North Vietnamese turned first into a retreat and then a rout. The city of Saigon fell to the Viet Cong and North Vietnamese on April 30, 1975, as Americans were completing their own evacuation at the last moment by helicopter from their embassy roof. In this long war, sometimes dated from 1964 (when an incident in the Gulf of Tonkin had led President Johnson to escalate America's commitment) to 1975, more American lives were lost than in World War I; South Vietnam's military had lost two hundred and twenty thousand lives; the North had sustained an estimated six hundred and sixty-six thousand deaths, despite victory; civilian deaths had run as high as in World War II. In all, well over a million people had died.

In a sense, with the end of the war in Vietnam the cold war too came to an end. The cold war had grown out of the failure to resolve the tensions of World War II, and for a time the diplomatic and military events associated with it were simply an extension of that war. Then with the war in Vietnam and with the shifting politics of the Middle East, the cold war took on causes and momentums of its own. By the 1970s many new immediate and proximate causes of events had arisen, so that to the extent that the cold war continued, it took on different expectations. While international affairs continued to be important, domestic issues moved to the forefront of concern in the Western democracies: issues of the effec-tiveness of government, the rights of the individual, rapidly inflating economies, and, later, soaring unemployment. Everywhere, it seemed, there was a pause in world affairs in the early 1970s sufficient to set the years that preceded them apart from those that followed.

SUMMARY

Some historians today consider the time between the two world wars as simply a twenty-year truce. Yet the 1920s had offered hope for peace, as evidenced by the Locarno spirit. This hope was dashed by the Great Depression that helped put Hitler in power.

Between 1918 and 1938 Soviet leaders shifted their view on the likelihood of a world communist revolution. Hitler's successful rise to power in Germany posed a threat to the Soviet Union. Stalin tried to counter this threat by negotiation. Both the West and the Soviet Union sought to turn Hitler's aggression against the other.

The period from 1931 to 1939 was marked by various international crises, each of which moved the world closer to war. The major crises included: Japan's seizure of Manchuria (1931); German rearmament (1935-1936); Italian invasion of Ethiopia (1935); German and Italian intervention in the Spanish Civil War (1936-1939); Japanese invasion of China (1937); the Anschluss with Germany (1938); the dismemberment of Czechoslovakia (1938-1939); and the German invasion of Poland (1939)—the final crisis that forced Britain and France to abandon the policy of appeasement.

In September 1939 Germany was ready for war. Hitler had reached an accord with Stalin that gave Germany security from war on two fronts. In the opening stages of the war, the German blitzkreig resulted in a string of victories that gave the Axis powers control of much of western Europe. The use of aerial bombardment brought civilians into the front line of war.

Germany was drawn into the Balkans and the eastern Mediterranean in an effort to weaken Britain by cutting its route to India. In 1941 Hitler also attacked Russia. The Japanese attack on Pearl Harbor brought the United States into the war. By the spring of 1942 Japanese expansion in Asia and the Pacific had reached its height.

The turning point in the war came in 1942. In the Pacific, the battle of the Coral Sea prevented the Japanese invasion of Australia. The successful North African campaign (1942-1943), the Soviet defense of Stalingrad, and the Allied success in maintaining its supply lines forced the Axis powers on the defensive in 1943. The end of the war in Europe revealed the full horrors of extermination camps and opened the controversy over how the Holocaust had been allowed to happen.

In the Pacific, American and Allied forces moved against Japan on several fronts. Finally, the Americans decided to use the newly developed atom bomb to prevent the heavy casualties that would be involved in an attack on the Japanese home islands.

When the war ended there was still no peace. Between 1945 and 1970 a cold war raged between the Soviet Union and its former ally, the United States. Local wars of liberation were fought in European colonies; wars broke out in the Middle East, Southeast Asia, Cuba, and Central America. In China, the civil war ended in a communist victory.

Efforts to ease cold-war tensions failed. The United Nations, successor to the League of Nations, tried to deal with threats to peace but had no authority over its members. The UN did, however, provide effective technical aid to new nations and offered a forum for debate on international issues.

During the cold war, the United States pursued a policy of containment. But when it perceived diversity in the communist world, it encouraged liberalizing trends in Eastern Europe. After Stalin's death and Khrushchev's denunciation of Stalin, a split developed between the Soviet Union and China's communist leader, Mao Tse-tung. The Soviet Union and China vied for influence over communist parties in Africa, Asia, and Latin America.

In Vietnam, Ho Chi Minh, leader of the communist north, received aid from China. The South Vietnamese government was helped by the United States. The United States was increasingly drawn into the conflict between North and South Vietnam. In the 1960s the war spread to Laos and Cambodia. After antiwar protests intensified in the United States, a ceasefire was negotiated in early 1973. By 1975 Vietcong and North Vietnamese forces had defeated South Vietnam. With the end of the war in Vietnam came a marked, if temporary, decline in cold-war tensions.

OUR TIMES

Arriving at the Present

hough dominated by the cold war, the history of the past four decades also speaks of many triumphs. Despite wars, political intimidation, and terror, both population and longevity have increased. Diseases that devastated populations in the Middle Ages have been virtually eradicated, and modern vaccines and medicines promise longer life and better health to millions. In all the Western democracies, concern for the rights of the individual has been heightened, in part because those rights are more visibly threatened. Many societies have questioned their former values and conventional wisdoms, while reaffirming national pride and cohesion, just as others have begun to fragment into smaller units.

Inventions in one part of the globe are quickly known in another part, and technology continues to grow faster than humanity can comprehend: the microchip transforms storage of and access to knowledge; the jet plane shrinks time and distance; and new frontiers are discovered when for the first time humans walk in outer space and reach the moon. Also for the first time societies and governments systematically concern themselves with the conservation of resources, with the provision of a wide array of services for mind and body, and with the grim possibility of mutual and near-total destruction.

Without necessarily infringing upon political sovereignty, the world has become one. All of humanity must be concerned, as were the ancient Greeks Plato and Aristotle, with defining moral, ethical, and legal bases for life, though from different perspectives and out of different historical experiences. The long search for stability and security—never over, never to be over—continues. New players on the stage join the nations of Western civilization in this search.

I WESTERN EUROPE

After 1945 the nations of western Europe successfully preserved the forms of the sovereign state and the politics of nationalism, while also making real attempts to organize a "free Europe" on a level beyond the national state. In 1952, as a first step, France, West Germany, and Italy joined with Belgium, the Netherlands, and Luxembourg in setting up a European Coal and Steel Community. It created for their coal and iron industries a free market area of all six nations, in which a joint administrative body could make certain final and binding decisions without the participation of any government officials. Each nation had given up some part of its sovereignty, and the plan was a success.

By the Treaty of Rome in 1957, these same six countries established the European Economic Community (EEC), better known as the Common Market, with headquarters in Brussels. This was the beginning of closer economic union under a central administration of delegates from each partner nation. The treaty also provided for increasing powers over trade, production, immigration, currency, and the transport of goods for the Common Market, according to a carefully worked out schedule. Each nation moved toward *mixed economy*—free enterprise under government regulation. In combination they represented a trading area and population equal to that of the greatest trading and consuming nation in the world, the United States. By the late 1970s the success of the Common Market—in which Britain, Denmark, Greece, Eire, Spain, and Portugal joined—had made western Europe fully competitive with the United States, giving the European bloc equal weight in many world economic and foreign policy decisions.

The path to this success was not easy. In 1959 Britain had joined with Switzerland, Portugal, Austria, and the Scandinavian countries to establish the European Free Trade Area. In 1961 Britain also sought to join the Common Market, but twice France vetoed Britain's entry and insisted on specific provisions favoring French farmers. The difficulty about British participation in any European supranational arrangement was real, for many British regarded themselves primarily as part of the Commonwealth, and not as Europeans. Furthermore, President de Gaulle of France felt that Britain and the United States were so intertwined that British entry would mean undue American influence. Not until the departure of de Gaulle from French political life in 1969 did the possibility of British entry into the Common Market revive.

Nonetheless, economic integration moved forward and proved successful in many ways. In 1973 Britain joined the Common Market, successfully defending special protection for its most dependent Commonwealth partner, New Zealand. Tariffs between member nations were eliminated, and labor migration among members grew. Visas were abolished, so that citizens of member countries could pass from one to another with ease. Common policies on railway and highway construction, on sign posting, on the adoption of the metric system, and on the relative value of national currencies were adopted. By the 1980s serious discussion of a common currency, the Eurodollar, made it clear that, despite disagreements and disappointments, the basic idea of the Common Market was sound.

Great Britain

In Britain a general election in July 1945—after the war had ended in Europe—ousted Churchill and the Conservative party and for the first time gave the Labour party an absolute majority in the House of Commons. The Liberal party was practically extinguished. The new prime minister was Clement Attlee (1883-1967), a middle-class lawyer of quiet intellect who was committed to major social reform at home and the decolonization of much of the British Empire abroad.

The new government—with a mandate for social change—proceeded to take over, with compensation to the owners, the coal industry, railroads, and parts of commercial road transportation, and began to nationalize the steel industry. Britain already had a well-developed system of social insurance; this was now capped by a system of socialized medical care for all who wished it. The educational system was partly reformed to make it more democratic and to lengthen the period of compulsory education.

Once nationalized, coal and railroads did not become great state trusts, but rather public corporations with a structure similar to that of private industries in the West, run by impartial boards dominated neither by bureaucrats nor politicians. Broad sectors of the economy remained in private hands. When the Conservatives, with Churchill still at their head, were returned to power in 1951 and remained there for twelve years, they halted the nationalization of steel, but otherwise kept intact the socialism of their opponents, including the national health plan. Thus a social revolution was achieved without bitter divisiveness between the parties. However, the parties were much slower to agree on colonial matters. But by 1961 both parties were committed to the end of the empire.

In the postwar years the British were not able to keep up with the extraordinary pace of technological innovation. The British automobile industry, for example, which immediately after the war gained a large share of the world market, yielded the lead in the 1950s to the Germans, with their inexpensive, standardized light car, the Volkswagen. Furthermore, Britain was one of the last countries in Europe to develop a system of super highways, completing its first modern highway only in 1969. The British were falling behind because they had been the first to industrialize, and now their plants were the first to become outdated and inefficient. Observers often found Britain's managers lacking in enterprise and uninterested in research, while workers were relatively undisciplined and unproductive, compared to workers on the continent, regarding management as the enemy. While British management and labor remained bound to traditional ways, the West Germans, buoyed by vast sums of money provided for their economic recovery by their former enemies, and especially by the United States, embarked on new paths, with new equipment replacing that destroyed by the war.

Even in apparent prosperity, Britain remained in economic trouble. The pound, a currency used as standard along with the dollar in the Free World (as the West was increasingly called during the deepening of the cold war), was always in danger. Continued pressure on the pound in the 1960s repeatedly required help from Brit-

ain's allies to maintain its value. This weakness of the pound signaled an unfavorable balance of trade in which the British were buying more from the rest of the world than they could sell. In the fifties and sixties, in what came to be called the "brain drain," some of Britain's most distinguished scientists and engineers left home to find higher pay and more modern laboratories in the United States, Canada, or Australia.

Under Harold Wilson (1916-   ), a shrewd politician often criticized for opportunism, the Labour party came to power in 1964 and governed until 1970. Increasingly, Parliament had ceased to be the supreme governing body in Britain; rather, it was the source of the majority that would determine which party would govern. The machinery of state was more and more in the hands of party leaders, heads of departments, trade-union leaders, outside experts and consultants, and powerful interest groups. In 1966 Wilson froze wages and prices in an effort to restore the balance between what the British spent and what they produced. In his own party, such measures were deeply unpopular and were regarded as exploiting the poor to support the rich. Wilson had to devalue the pound after heavy foreign pressure against it. Despite the unpopularity of his policies, by 1969 the deficits had disappeared and general prosperity continued, along with high taxes and rapid inflation. Prices were rising so fast that the gains from rising wages were largely illusory. The national health plan and education for working-class mothers had freed women for the work force. But a spiral continued with only momentary breaks, regardless of the party in office, and except for a period of prosperity and relative confidence in the late 1960s and early 1970s, Britain's decline in relation to its competitors continued. By the 1980s, when Margaret Thatcher (1925-   ) was prime minister, British inflation had been lessened but still remained dangerously high, unemployment stood at depression levels, and the British standard of living had been surpassed by most nations in western Europe. The British sense of cohesion seemed threatened, by racial violence, a fragmenting though vigorous religious life, the decline of the established church, a separatist movement in Scotland, and persistent violence in Northern Ireland. Britain had become a second-class power.

Even so, conditions of life improved for most people. The Labour government had imposed heavy income taxes on the well-to-do and burdensome death duties on the rich, using the income thus obtained to redistribute goods and services to the poor. An increasing number of new universities (called "red-brick universities," to distinguish them from the older, originally medieval seats of learning with their ancient stone buildings) offered young people of all classes educational opportunities that had previously been available only to the upper and upper-middle classes. Oxford and Cambridge now accepted many working-class students on state scholarships. And secondary education was substantially democratized but at the expense of intense political debate.

A LEADER FALLS BEHIND

By the late 1970s British decline was evident to all. A nation that had been a great power in 1939, despite a relative decline since the nineteenth century, was unable to command substantial attention in foreign affairs. British troops had been withdrawn from east of Suez after the loss of the canal; British production lagged far behind that of both Japan and Britain's European partners; there were grave doubts about whether Britain could fully perform its NATO commitments.

The following comparative figures show this decline in relation to a fellow ally in World War II, France, and a vanquished enemy, Germany.

Growth of Gross National Product, using 1954 as a base point of 100:

	1954	1960	1977
Britain	100	117	175
France	100	133	297
Germany	100	164	310

Share of manufactured goods exported by member countries of Organization for Economic Cooperation and Development (OECD):

	1954	1960	1977
Britain	18.9	15.0	8.5
France	7.2	8.7	8.9
Germany	12.2	17.4	18.8

Number of registered private vehicles in millions:

	1954	1977
Britain	3.2	14.9
France	2.7	16.5
Germany	1.4	20.2

Percentage of labor force in trade unions:

	1977
Britain	50%
France	22%
Germany	44%

Number of days lost in industrial disputes (in thousands):

	1957	1977
Britain	6,012	10,142
France	3,506	2,434
Germany	69	86

The Economist, June 2, 1979, pp. 29-33.

In the postwar years race became a serious issue in Britain for the first time. Indians, Pakistanis, West Indians, and Africans—Commonwealth subjects with British passports—left poor conditions at home and migrated freely to Britain in large numbers to take jobs in factories, public transportation, and hospitals. Dislike for nonwhites rose markedly and affected both political parties. Despite its liberal and antiracist protestations, the Wilson government was forced to curtail immigration sharply. Some Conservative politicians predicted bloody race riots (which, in fact, occurred in 1981, made worse by unemployment) unless black immigration was halted, and some extremists proposed that nonwhites already in Britain be deported. Many working-class people supported these views, which cut across party lines.

Closely related to the race issue at home was the

question of official British relations with southern Africa, to which the Labour government refused to sell arms because of the apartheid policies of the South African regime from the late 1940s. Relations deteriorated quickly after South African police fired upon a mass demonstration at Sharpeville in 1960, killing many black Africans. In 1961, under pressure from the prime ministers of Canada and India and with Britain's approval, the rigidly racist government of South Africa withdrew from the Commonwealth. To this strain was added a major challenge to British authority when the white-dominated government in Southern Rhodesia, unwilling to accept a constitution that provided for full black participation in legislation, unilaterally declared Rhodesia independent of Great Britain, citing the American colonies in 1776 as a precedent. This move led to the imposition of sanctions by the United Nations and years of delicate negotiations punctuated by civil war, until a cease-fire, a constitution, and elections were ultimately accepted by all parties, and the Thatcher government declared Rhodesia independent, as Zimbabwe, in 1980.

Perhaps most persistently debilitating to British security, however, was the Irish problem, long quiescent, which arose again in the late 1960s. In Ulster (the northern counties that were still part of the United Kingdom), an industrial area suffering from deep economic troubles, the Catholics generally formed a depressed class and were the first to lose their jobs in bad times. They were inflamed by the insistence of Protestant extremists (the Orangemen) on celebrating the anniversaries of victories of William III in the 1690s that had ensured English domination over the region. Marching provocatively through Catholic districts, the Orangemen in the summer of 1969 precipitated disorders that began in Londonderry and spread to Belfast and other areas. The regular police were accused by the Catholics of being mere tools of the Protestant oppressor and had to be disarmed. The British army then intervened to keep order.

The government of the Republic of Ireland took a strong interest in the Northern Irish troubles, suggesting that the United Nations be given responsibility for the problem, a suggestion unacceptable to both the Northern Irish and British governments, who regarded the problem as an internal matter. Extremists of the south, the Irish Republican Army (IRA), who had always claimed the northern counties as part of a united Ireland, now revived their terroristic activities. But the IRA itself was split between a relatively moderate wing and the Provisionals (Provos), anarchists dedicated to indiscriminate bombing. Despite infrequent lulls, the level of fighting steadily escalated in Northern Ireland. In 1972 the British suspended the Northern Irish parliament and governed the province directly. In 1981 a group of prisoners, insisting that they not be treated as common criminals but as political prisoners, resorted to hunger strikes; although ten prisoners died, the British government continued to refuse political status to people they viewed as terrorists. By 1983 nearly fifteen hundred people had been killed in Northern Ireland, and no solution appeared in sight.

Yet Britain was by no means wholly gloomy or depressed. Many British products continued to set the world's standards, especially for the upper classes. British liberalization of social attitudes toward dress, sex, and religion was widely felt abroad. Beginning with the enormous popularity and stylistic innovations of the Beatles in the early sixties, England for a time set the style for young people in other countries. Long hair for men, the unisex phenomenon in dress, the popularity of theatrical and eccentric clothes, the whole mod fashion syndrome that spread across the Atlantic and across the Channel started in England. Carnaby Street, Mick Jagger, and the Rolling Stones all had their imitators elsewhere, but the originals were English. Thus Britain continued to play a major role in fashion, music, social attitudes, and in tourism, through a tourist boom that brought millions of visitors to Britain, making it the front-ranking tourist nation in the world. By the 1970s Britain and the United States were growing closer together as a mid-Atlantic pattern of speech, thought, and address emerged.

Most evident was the gradual erosion of rigid class distinctions in England, traditional bastion of political freedom and social inequality. The Beatles were all working-class in origin, and all spoke with a lower-class Liverpool accent; lower class too were most leading English pacesetters of the new styles in song, dress, and behavior. These styles spread not only abroad, but among the middle and upper classes of the young in Britain as well, who were increasingly impatient to have done with the class sentiment that had so long pervaded English thought.

This impatience reflected the growing fragmentation of British social and economic life. The Labour party suffered from chronic disunity, its left wing often in near rebellion. In 1980 some of its members founded an alternative party, the Social Democratic party, hoping to take up the middle ground politically through an alliance with the remnant of the Liberals. Britain was, by the 1980s, a society transformed, mired in depression, bogged down in Northern Ireland, shorn of its empire, and yet still respected for its civility, its commitment to orderly procedures and the parliamentary way, and for its remarkable stability.

France

France too experienced recovery, but this recovery was all the more dramatic for taking place in a nation that, though victorious in war, had also been defeated. In a sense France had the best of both worlds: the psychological uplift of victory that the British experienced, plus the need to lift itself, with some foreign aid, to at least prewar levels of productivity, as the defeated Germans would have to do. By the 1980s France was, for the first time in two hundred years, ahead of its former British rival in standard of living, and it had arrived at a delicate balance between its political right and political left. Contributing to this balance were the loss of its overseas empire, with the United States seeking to replace it in Southeast Asia; the legitimacy given to right-of-center politics by the towering figure of Charles de Gaulle; the independence of its left-of-center political groups, including the communists, who thought more in national than in international terms; and its major role in the emergence of a new European balance of economic power based on the Common Market. All this was possible because of France's need to contend with the deep wound of early defeat in World War II.

Defeat by the Germans, brutal German occupation and economic exploitation, the spectacle of French collaboration with the enemy—all this was followed by a liberation that, despite the part played in it by the Fighting French and the French Resistance movement, was clearly the work of American, British, and Russian arms. Nor had France since the early nineteenth century kept pace with the leading industrial nations in production, finance, or population growth. Only a rising birth rate gave cause for optimism. Hundreds of thousands of French men and women deliberately decided to have children—a clear sign of the recovery that lay ahead. The arrival of nearly a million refugees from the colonial war in Algeria in 1962-1963 and the influx of almost four million foreign workers made France, already a cosmopolitan nation, even more so, and assured the nation a labor supply on which to base its rapid industrial expansion.

The French government-in-exile, led by General de Gaulle, had easily reestablished in liberated France the old republican forms of government, called the Fourth Republic. But after de Gaulle temporarily retired from politics in 1946, the Fourth Republic began to look like the Third. Cabinets lasted on an average only a few months; to the old splinter parties was added a Communist party of renewed strength, openly dedicated to revolutionary change. After nine years of war, Indochina was lost in 1954; in the same year an active rebellion against the French began in Algeria; Morocco and Tunisia were both lost in 1956, and the crisis deepened.

In 1958 de Gaulle took power again, after financial instability, inflation resulting from the war costs in Indochina and Algeria, and rising popular dissatisfaction combined to bring about the fall of the Fourth Republic. When a rightist, military coup d'état took place in Algeria on May 13, 1958, de Gaulle announced that he was willing to come out of retirement. The leaders of the coup wrongly assumed that he would carry out their plan for keeping Algeria French.

A plebiscite in France confirmed a new constitution. The constitution of the new Fifth Republic provided for a president to be elected for a seven-year term by direct popular vote. An absolute majority was required, and, if not achieved in a first election, was to be obtained in a runoff between the two candidates with the most votes. Elected outright in 1958, de Gaulle was reelected to a second term in 1965 in such a runoff. Under the new constitution the French president appointed the pre-

mier, who could dissolve the legislature and order new elections at any time after the first year. Thus the new constitution gave the executive more power, the legislature much less.

De Gaulle's enemies soon called him a dictator, the personification of French haughtiness and superiority. He was obstinate, opinionated, and authoritarian; yet he was also consistent, clear, capable, and utterly committed to creating a stable and progressive French state. He intended that France be taken seriously in world affairs, even to restore it to *la gloire* associated with Louis XIII and XIV. To this end he fought to keep Britain out of the Common Market, worked to prevent what he anticipated would be American dominance in Europe, and sought to establish a creditable French military presence in both conventional weapons and, at least symbolically, in nuclear capacity. He did not want to see France bled by further colonial wars, and though he believed strongly in the unity of all French-speaking peoples (seeking even to establish a separate cultural mission to the French-speaking people of Quebec), he nonetheless worked out a settlement making Algeria independent in 1962, despite repeated terrorist threats against this alleged appeasement.

Starting with Marshall Plan aid in 1947, great economic and social changes began in France. Unlike the United States, Britain, and Germany, France had preserved the small-scale, individualistic methods of production and distribution characteristic of the period before the Industrial Revolution. Now a full-scale reorientation of the economy was undertaken in accordance with the practices of modern industry. Helped by foreign investment, especially American, France began to experience a real boom. Prosperity meant that for the first time the French, by the hundreds of thousands, bought cars, television sets, and record players; that they traveled in ever growing numbers; that they experienced fearful traffic jams and incredible highway accidents; and that those who found the new ways unsettling blamed all the changes—like *le hamburger, le drugstore,* and blue jeans—on the Americans. Those who feared that France would adopt the new British-American culture emphasized the continuity, unity, complexity, and alleged purity of the French language, and looked for their own cultural influences to offset Americanization and "Coca-Colanization."

De Gaulle never forgot the treatment accorded him by Churchill and Roosevelt during World War II, and when he came to power he retained a strong personal dislike of *les Anglo-Saxons.* The thought of such supranational bodies as the Common Market and NATO that could rob France of sovereignty even to a small degree was uncomfortable, and talk of a United States of Europe was totally unacceptable. He spoke instead of *Europe des patries,* a "Europe of fatherlands," that would include even Russia; within the *Europe des patries* France would take the lead. But to do this France must have its own atomic weapons. Therefore de Gaulle refused to join the United States, Great Britain, and the Soviet Union in a treaty barring atomic tests, and France continued to test nuclear weapons in the atmosphere, exploding its first hydrogen bomb in 1968. Vigorously opposed to communism at home, de Gaulle nonetheless came to terms with Russia; the Russians, he argued, no longer represented the threat to the general peace that they had represented in the fifties. In balancing the scales against the industrial and military power of the United States and Britain, France needed friends. To South America, to Canada, to Poland, and to Romania, de Gaulle carried his message that France would be the leader of Europe.

In the spring of 1968, however, while de Gaulle was in Romania, Paris erupted. The French universities—so overcrowded that there were not enough classrooms and no way for students to listen to their lecturers—had been ignored by the regime in a period when the young throughout western Europe were bursting with resentment against "the machine civilization" of the cold-war society. Students in Paris occupied university buildings, fought the police, and eventually drew a reluctant Communist party into the battle in order that it not lose the support of the French workers, who had already begun to strike in sympathy with the students. Similar student anger was evident in Britain, the Netherlands, West Germany, the United States, Japan, and Mexico, where highly vocal minorities attacked universities with ferocity, declaring them to be bulwarks of traditional society—undemocratic and oppressive.

De Gaulle returned to Paris, assured himself of army support, proposed a referendum, which he was obliged to abandon in favor of new elections, and then won a great victory at the polls, obtaining a larger majority in the legislature than before. Thereupon he embarked on a new phase of his regime. His economic and social program called for participation by the workers not only in the profits of industry but in its management. His new minister of education, acknowledging the legitimacy of many of the grievances of the students, pushed through the legislature a reform bill decentralizing the educational system. Having established his strength with the strong support of the right, as in 1958, de Gaulle appeared to be preparing to appease the left, also as in 1958.

De Gaulle now staked his political future on the issue of regional reform in a public referendum—and lost. As he had done before, he withdrew into private life. In the 1969 elections the Gaullists were returned to office with a substantial majority, and Georges Pompidou (1911-1974) became president of France. As in the other Western nations, inflation continued, but on the whole prosperity continued as well. Pompidou maintained de Gaulle's policies but pursued them less flamboyantly. De Gaulle's death in 1970 marked the passing of the last of the great leaders of World War II.

France now entered more readily into competition rather than confrontation with its former allies. To make the French more competitive, the franc was devalued. The veto against Britain's entry into the Common Market was abandoned, and, without rejoining NATO,

France began more formal cooperation with it. An economic recession began in 1973, however, and public confidence, still shaken by the student rebellions of 1968-1969, wavered. France returned to governments that could administer programs only with the help of complex coalitions, as the aristocratic Valéry Giscard d'Estaing (1926-   ) became president. Fearful of the left, and ultimately beset by political scandal, Giscard did not press the social reform his platform had promised. From 1972 to 1977 the Socialist and Communist parties formed a Common Front to oppose the right and center parties, but the communists withdrew in 1977.

In 1981 an able Socialist party regular who had worked to broaden the socialist base by weakening the communists, their traditional enemies, won the presidential election. This man, François Mitterrand (1916-   ), brought four communists into his cabinet, frightening those who felt NATO secrets could no longer be safe if shared with the French, and announced plans to nationalize certain sectors of industry. At the same time, Mitterrand took a strongly anti-Soviet stance over Russia's invasion of Afghanistan in December 1979. He declared himself committed to a mixed-enterprise economy and to cooperation with the Americans in their efforts to renew disarmament talks while seeking to base a nuclear missile force within Europe. To this Germany also agreed.

West Germany

The West German postwar recovery was the most remarkable of all—"the German miracle." The wartime destruction of much of Germany's industrial plant had paradoxically proved beneficial; the new plant was built with the latest technological equipment. The Allied High Commission, mindful of the results of harsh treatment of Germany after World War I and not wishing to see a power vacuum between the Soviet Union's satellites and the West, was never very severe. It gradually abolished controls over German industry, save for atomic energy and certain military restrictions. It provided economic aid and scaled down prewar German debts. By the early 1950s West Germany had a favorable balance of trade and a rate of industrial growth as high as 10 percent a year.

The West German Gross National Product rose from $23 billion in 1950 to $103 billion in 1964, with no serious monetary inflation. This prosperity was spread through all classes of society. The working class in West Germany had begun to enjoy affluence; new buildings rose everywhere, while superhighways grew overcrowded and had to be widened and extended. The economic miracle attracted population into West Germany from southern Europe and drew other Germans out of East Germany into the Federal Republic. East Germany thus had a net loss in population as West Germany boomed. By the late 1960s the German birth rate had fallen, however, and in the 1980s, except for a continuing influx of "guest-workers" from Yugoslavia

French president Charles de Gaulle met with West German chancellor Konrad Adenauer (left) at the Elysée Palace in July 1962 to discuss the political union of Europe and the formation of the Common Market.

and Turkey, the population had stabilized at sixty-two million. This made for a highly industrialized, close-knit, urban nation, as population density rose to be second only to Belgium and the Netherlands. West Germany was, in effect, three times as crowded within its constricted postwar borders as was France.

The independent West German state had a constitution that provided for a legislature whose lower house represented the people directly and whose upper house represented the states (*Länder*). The president, elected by a special assembly for a five-year term, was largely a ceremonial figure. Real executive leadership was vested in the chancellor, a prime minister dependent on a parliamentary majority. The old splinter-party system did not return to plague the new republic. Under the firm leadership of Konrad Adenauer (1876-1967), the Christian Democrats, distant heirs of the old Centrist party, held power until 1961. A Rhineland Catholic, former mayor of Cologne, conservative, pro-French, and democratic, Adenauer was forced to retire only because of age, and continued to wield enough influence to weaken his successor, Ludwig Erhard (1897-1977), a Protestant and professional economist, who remained in

office for five more years. The twenty-year reign of the Christian Democrats was supported by the voters, not the result of one-party totalitarian politics.

Indeed, Germany had been rather successfully "de-Nazified"—a requirement stipulated by the Allied High Commission. As a result of the Nuremburg trials in 1946, seventy-four major Nazi leaders were convicted of war crimes, and ten were hanged. In general, lower-level Nazis were required only to demonstrate that they fully accepted the new democratic government; to have dismissed all civil servants who had held posts under the Nazi regime would have utterly crippled any administrative recovery. Some Nazis who had escaped to other parts of the world, notably South America, continued to be hunted out, and if captured, were tried for war crimes. Some ex-Nazis, though accepting the new constitution, joined with Germans too young to have been active members of the party to agitate for reunion with East Germany, even at the cost of confrontation. And from time to time signs of anti-Semitism, of other old Nazi hopes, or of efforts to conceal former Nazi sympathies hurt various local political leaders. Thus the range of acceptable leaders at the national level, as was true of French leaders who had to be cleared of any taint of collaboration with Vichy, was somewhat limited.

The major political question remained, that of an eventual reunion with communist-dominated East Germany. Neither Germany recognized the other diplomatically. After years during which the East Germans, attracted by better living conditions in West Germany, crossed the border by the tens of thousands, the East German government in August 1961 began building a wall between the two parts of the city. Though on special holidays families in West Berlin were allowed to cross into East Berlin briefly to visit relatives and friends, the wall stood as the visible symbol of a divided Germany. Berlin, in particular, became a battleground of the cold war, a symbol of the failure of the superpowers to conclude a peace.

As a consequence of the cold war, the Americans, British, and French permitted the West Germans to rearm early in the 1950s and to join NATO. Military conscription was introduced in 1955, and by 1970 West Germany had developed a sizable modern military. The government and people supported the armed forces as a necessity, but militarism did not revive among the people at large. Access to the atom bomb was not included in this rearmament. Even so, and despite low-key political leadership, the spectacle of a rearmed Germany caused much concern—in the Soviet bloc, in Britain, and among Jewish voters in all nations, who could not be expected to forget that the Final Solution had very nearly been a reality. Vienna, the Austrian city that once had been a center of Jewish cultural life with a Jewish population in the hundreds of thousands, had perhaps only two thousand Jews in 1980. Those who survived the Holocaust had moved elsewhere—to Israel, to the United States, to Britain—and were deeply suspicious of both the restored republic of Austria and the new and frantically booming Federal Republic of Germany.

Chancellor Erhard's government fell in 1966, when a small disciplined party, the Free Democrats, in coalition with which the Christian Democrats were ruling, refused to support his proposals for higher taxes. The Christian Democrats now proposed a "grand coalition" with their chief opponents, the Social Democrats. The very popular mayor of West Berlin, Willy Brandt (1913-), became vice chancellor and foreign minister. This grand coalition commanded popular support, and it lasted until the elections of 1969.

In these elections Brandt, the Social Democrat, became chancellor and formed a coalition in his turn with the Free Democrats. Brandt moved slowly and cautiously to open discussions with the East Germans. The chief stumbling block was Soviet fear of West Germany. It gradually became apparent that a treaty between West Germany and the Soviet Union in which both renounced the use of force would be one of the necessary preliminaries. In the summer of 1970 Brandt reached agreement with the Russians on the text of such a treaty. It recognized all existing European frontiers, which Germans and Russians agreed never to try to alter by force, leaving open future negotiations. The second step was an agreement with Poland, which Brandt concluded during 1970. Brandt's *Ostpolitik*, or Eastern policy, culminated in a treaty with Czechoslovakia and in the entry of both Germanies into the United Nations in 1973. A form of detente with the Soviet bloc was nearly achieved, when in 1974 Brandt resigned upon the discovery that one of his closest assistants had been an East German spy, a discovery that renewed German fears of the designs of the Soviet bloc.

The 1970s also dimmed the West German economic miracle. While the German inflation rate, roughly 6 percent in 1975, was mild compared to the rest of Europe, and the growth rate continued at over 5 percent, unemployment began to climb, reaching a million. German social services were now among the best in the world, and German per capita income had surpassed the nations that had defeated Germany in Europe in World War II, but a deep-seated memory of the inflation that had destroyed the democratic hopes of Weimar made the Germans cautious and insecure. Waves of terrorism, at first an outgrowth of student protest movements in the late 1960s, while numerically small compared to events elsewhere in the world, further disconcerted the German leadership. Only Brandt, now discredited, and after 1974 Helmut Schmidt (1918-), had seemed to provide the vigorous leadership the Germans had enjoyed under Adenauer. Together with other nations in the west, Germany appeared to lack able new leaders with dramatic solutions to the nation's problems. Although the electorate recognized that the range of dramatic new solutions was severely limited by the constraints of superpower confrontation and an eroding economy, they nonetheles hoped for a renewal of vigor at the top. Politics in the Federal Republic became fragmented when the grand coalition broke up, with powerful leaders emerging on the basis of strong local support. German postwar recovery, based in good measure on consensus politics, appeared threatened, as unions became more militant and unemployment reached record highs. Liberal democracy, it was widely said, was in dire trouble throughout the West. Thus, in 1983 the Christian Democrats won a landslide victory and, paradoxically, were soon confronted with a groundswell of public opinion when they appeared to be overzealous in pursuit of "law and order."

Italy

Unlike Germany, Italy was in turmoil for much of its postwar years. In 1946 a plebiscite showed 54 percent of the voters in favor of a republic, which was therefore established. Some monarchists and fascists remained, but neither group influenced parliamentary politics to any great extent. A strong Christian Democratic party (a Catholic party with a relatively liberal program) held power under a succession of leaders, with support from other groups. The government broke up large landed estates in the south to redistribute the land. A very strong Communist party, the largest in the West, with whom the larger faction of the Socialists was allied, offered a persistent challenge. In the early sixties a series of complicated negotiations began a process the Italians called the *apertura a sinistra*, the opening to the left. In this process the Christian Democrats won over some Socialist support. A further weakening of the extreme left occurred in 1966, when the Socialists—long split between anticommunists and procommunists—reunited as one party.

Italy's economic growth between 1953 and 1966 was so remarkable that the Italians too spoke of an economic miracle. As in France, this growth was achieved with some government ownership and with much government regulation and planning. Membership in the Common Market gave Italian enterprise opportunities that it had never had before. The grave problems of southern Italy, Sardinia, and Sicily were attacked by programs of investments, by providing jobs in the north or in Germany or Switzerland for the surplus workers of the south, and by old-age pensions. In the Italian balance of payments, an income of about $1 billion annually from tourists proved enormously important, as prosperous West Germans, Scandinavians, Americans, and Israelis poured into Italy. Italian fashions, like those of Britain and France, became popular throughout the world, further bolstering both the economy and the national sense of well-being. The Italian motion picture industry began to rival that of France and ultimately overtook the immediate postwar leader, Britain. All these developments depended on projecting a sense of political stability and maturity, which the extreme left and the political terrorists of both right and left hoped to disrupt. Tourism and the centrist political parties became particular targets of attack.

Thus by the late 1960s Italian political stability began to crumble, in part due to severe internal political strains within the Christian Democratic party, and in part due to the uncertainty of the party's relationship with its supposed partners, the Socialists. In part it was also due to the inflation that was plaguing the other Western countries, but that Italy, with its larger poor population and its lack of any tradition of the welfare state, was perhaps less able to bear than were the advanced industrial nations. Strikes occurred sporadically and unpredictably but often, and 1969 was marked by mass strikes. The government seemed frozen in bureaucratic traditionalism.

The Italian bureaucracy was marked by no-show jobs, scandal, corruption, and pettiness. Economic mismanagement became evident in the 1970s, as it had for the United States by 1929. The Italian inflation rate soared above even Britain's; nearly two million Italians were unemployed, and the economic growth rate was inconsistent and unpredictable, though generally declining. By 1974 Italy had a huge trade deficit and had to turn to the International Monetary Fund and to West Germany for credit. The government was unable to restrain demands for wage increases, which ran at 30 percent annually, spurring further inflation in prices and overburdening the middle class. The Mafia, long powerful but also long dormant, began to show itself overtly in Sicily and southern Italy. Terrorists, hoping for the disruption of the state, openly attacked judges, teachers, journalists, and police officers in the streets. In 1978 one group, the Red Brigade, kidnapped former premier Aldo Moro (1916-1978) and murdered him after the Italian government refused to negotiate his release. The universities were in chaos; Rome University, built for 15,000 students, had to accept 165,000 under a new policy of open admissions. There was no place for the students; there were no teachers for them; there was no program; and students throughout the nation went on frequent and prolonged strikes, so that the ablest sought their education in other countries. Of all the nations of western Europe, Italy's experiment with liberal democracy seemed most clearly on trial.

During this time the large Italian Communist party increased in size and organizing skills. In 1976 the Communists polled 35 percent of the popular vote for the Chamber of Deputies. Led by Enrico Berlinguer (1922-   ), the Communists declared their desire to enter into a coalition government with their former enemies and promised to abide by the constitution and to keep Italy in NATO. The United States doubted the sincerity of these promises and supported those Italian leaders best able to block Berlinguer's move toward power. But by entering into what it called a "historic compromise," the Communist party won a new middle-class following. It condemned terrorism, declining to support the various pro-Palestinian, Japanese, and Libyan hit-men who passed through or periodically used Italian airports and cities for their attacks. In 1978 the Communist party was granted equality with other parties in shaping government policies when it promised to support a national unity government. Ministries continued to change hands with bewildering rapidity in Italy, the entire cabinet resigning in 1981 when it was revealed that many officials were members of an illegal and secret Masonic lodge. Scandals in banking and politics, the kidnapping of public officials, instability in leadership, and recurrent social unrest continued to plague Italy deep into the 1980s.

The Vatican

In the eye of the hurricane, one force for continuity seemed clear. The Pope, based in Vatican City, in the heart of Rome, began to assert bold new initiatives in the political sphere, while holding to traditional positions on doctrinal church affairs. The feeling that Pope Pius XII (1939-1958) had not done enough to forestall World War II or to assist beleaguered Jews within the Nazi-controlled nations persisted, and after the war he and his successors sought to take clear positions on world affairs much as their medieval predecessors had done. While some commentators—intent upon the hard-won separation of church and state in their nations and remembering the long period of papal intervention in political developments, especially in Italy—were fearful of these new initiatives, even more commentators appeared to welcome a vigorous papacy that would take moral positions on secular issues.

These positions were defined in the context of substantial changes within the church itself. The most extensive changes were initiated by Pope John XXIII (1958-1963), who in 1959 called the Twenty-first Ecumenical Council of the church, in a tradition begun by Constantine the Great in the fourth century. Known as Vatican II, this council continued to meet under his successor, Pope Paul VI (1963-1978). The council made many changes in the liturgy, encouraged celebration of Mass in the vernacular language, and opened up relations with many other denominations.

While the church continued to be identified in many parts of the world with the forces of conservatism—especially in its opposition to women clergy, in its emphasis on the child-bearing responsibilities of women, and in its support of Catholic dictators in South America—elsewhere the church was increasingly associated with the forces of reform. Radical priests in Central America, innovative church leaders in North America, and activist bishops in the non-Western world were urging the church to face the statistical fact that most Catholics apparently practiced some form of birth control, that the church should be a force for land reforms that would benefit the peasants, and that the nature of the church service needed to be changed even further if the younger generation were to be retained. Pope Paul showed his commitment to racial harmony, in particular, by appointing cardinals from nations throughout the former colonial world. He would not, however, bend on the church's prohibition against contraception or on its requirement of celibacy for priests.

These trends, marked by a concern for public affairs, continued under a dynamic new pope, John Paul II, elected in 1978 as the youngest pope since 1846 and the first non-Italian pope since the sixteenth century. A Pole, Karol Wojtyla (1920-   ), former archbishop of

Kracow, worked to expand the role of the church in the non-Western world. He made extensive overseas visits, including to the United States, where church doctrine was frequently questioned by younger priests, and took strong positions against military aggression and political terrorism. Of particular concern to this pope was the suppression of the Polish Solidarity Movement in 1981-1982. Presumably as an indication of the extent to which John Paul was seen to be a political as well as a religious leader, he was seriously injured in an assassination attempt in Rome in 1981, though he recovered and was able to pay an official visit to Poland in 1983.

Other Western European Countries

The Low Countries shared the general European prosperity and the common problems. In Belgium, which enjoyed great material well-being, the chronic difficulties between the minority of French-speaking Walloons and the majority of Dutch-speaking Flemings continued to worsen and to threaten stability. The Netherlands—the most crowded nation in Europe—at first enjoyed prosperity and stability, though there too student unrest, terrorist outbreaks, and serious environmental pollution created persistent problems. Mass emigration from Indonesia and Surinam, which became independent in 1975, revealed racial prejudices for the first time within the Netherlands. A political scandal over the business activities of Queen Juliana (1962-1980), which contributed to her abdication in 1980 in favor of her daughter Beatrix (1938-   ), challenged even the monarchy.

Spain under Franco had taken major steps toward modernization and a few mild measures to relax political tyranny. Low wages, especially to the depressed coal miners of the north, and bitter government opposition to the Basques prevented full economic or political stability. Five languages were accorded formal recognition: Spanish, Catalan, Basque, Galician (a Portuguese dialect), and Valencian (a Spanish dialect). Franco arranged that after his death the monarchy would be restored under Prince Juan Carlos (1938-   ), grandson of Alfonso XIII, and in 1975 Juan Carlos became king. The actual government remained in the hands of political parties, however, since Juan Carlos was a constitutional monarch, as in the United Kingdom. Still, it was Juan Carlos who presided over the dissolution of many of Franco's institutions.

The first free elections since the Spanish Civil War took place in 1976, returning moderates and democratic socialists. Spain threatened to return to right-wing rule when a military coup erupted in the parliament in February 1981, but the bulk of the army remained loyal to the king. As Spain turned from agriculture to industry, becoming a major industrial nation, and as tourism grew ever larger in its balance of payments, the need for stability became paramount. To this end Spain attempted in 1982 to come to a peaceful settlement with Britain over a long-standing dispute concerning ownership of Gibraltar, and the Spanish government granted substantial home rule to Catalonia and the Basque lands in 1980. Spain too gave up most of the remnants of its empire. The Canary Islands became two of Spain's fifty provinces, and Spain's tiny enclaves on the north Moroccan coast were incorporated into metropolitan Spain. Having long before lost the great bulk of its overseas empire, Spain suffered less than any former colonial power from the wounds of modern decolonization.

Elsewhere in the Mediterranean democracy was also restored. In 1968 the Portuguese dictator Salazar, too ill to continue, passed the government to a successor. In 1974 a military coup by radical Portuguese army officers, embittered by the colonial wars in Angola and Mozambique by which the Portuguese had tenaciously attempted to hold on to their overseas empire, brought down the dictatorship. For a time the army junta worked in alliance with Portuguese communists, who were supported by the trade unions, the peasants of southern Portugal, and much of the press. However, in the elections of 1975 the Socialists under Mario Soares (1924-   ) won the largest following, and at the end of the year he became prime minister. Soares was faced with formidable problems: a continuing colonial war that was feeding the highest rate (34 percent) of inflation in Europe, unproductive agricultural practices, and the absence of a solid industrial base. As the war in Africa went badly, unemployment in Portugal was forced upward by an influx of refugees from the colonies. Portugal became dependent on foreign loans, and Soares had to incorporate the center and some right-of-center elements into a coalition government to remain in office. In the 1980s, with the colonial war over and the former colonies now independent states, the inflation rate began to moderate, but political stability continued to elude the Portuguese people, and when Soares returned to power in 1983, he could govern only with the help of a coalition.

Greece too had been ruled by a military junta. The 1950s and early 1960s had been prosperous years. By 1965 industrialization had become more important than agriculture, tourism was producing a large income, and the Greek merchant fleet prospered. Aid under the Truman Doctrine had stabilized both Greece and Turkey, and the Americans continued to support Greece, regardless of the government in power, as an important bulwark against the Iron-Curtain countries. With the end of the Greek civil war in 1955, a succession of ministries had struggled for authority until April 1967, when several army officers (later called "the colonels") staged a coup and established a right-wing military dictatorship. King Constantine went into exile, the colonels suspended civil liberties, and the government became increasingly brutal, though efficient, until it was sharply challenged by popular demonstrations.

World opinion was turning against the colonels when they decided in 1974 on a gamble intended to win nationalist support. They tried to overthrow Archbishop Makarios III (1913-1977), the president of Cyprus, who had led his people in a bitter war against the British and who, the colonels felt, was not sufficiently aggressive against the Turkish minority on that island. This led to a full-scale Turkish invasion of Cyrpus and its occupation by Turkish forces, subjecting the large Greek majority (75 percent of the population) to military rule. The Greek regime was humiliated. It had lost its war, lost the Greek Cypriots, driven a wedge deep into NATO (since both Greece and Turkey were members), and angered the United States. Elections late in 1974 brought back civilian government under Konstantin Karamanlis (1907-   ). The monarchy was abolished, the galloping inflation rate was brought under reasonable control, and the Western nations attempted to mediate the hostility between Greece and Turkey. However, they were unsuccessful, and the Greek coalition governments of the late 1970s and early 1980s, still under Karamanlis and increasingly socialist, continued to be marked by the political instability now characteristic of much of the West.

The general exception to this instability was Scandinavia. The three constitutional monarchies of Denmark, Norway, and Sweden proved to be progressive, democratic, and highly prosperous; together with Switzerland they proved that political stability was possible. The Scandinavians went further and more rapidly in providing full equality to women than had any other countries in the world; in 1981 Norway elected a woman prime minister (as had Sri Lanka, India, Israel, the United Kingdom, and Iceland earlier). Standards of living soared, to become among the highest in the world. To varying degrees the Scandinavian countries embarked on substantial social-welfare programs. Denmark and Sweden in particular committed themselves to the international marketplace, requiring all school children to learn English, the new international language of trade. Denmark set the pace in design, especially of furniture, kitchenwares, and fabrics. By the 1980s the Danish per capita income was well above that of the United States, once the richest nation in the world.

Sweden, which had enjoyed industrial growth as a neutral during World War II, experienced similar prosperity. Its steel, automobile, shipbuilding, and machine industries were modernized and progressive, as were its labor policies. Heralded as representing "the middle way," Sweden became a democratic and socialist state with a per capita income third only to Denmark and Belgium.

For forty years the Social Democratic party ruled in Sweden until 1976, but by then inflation had begun to soar, and grave doubts about social policy at home and foreign policy abroad introduced a period of modest political instability. By the 1980s the troubles the Swedes had seemed to have avoided were upon them: Soviet submarines were found spying in Swedish waters; the domestic crime rate was rising dramatically; voters supported limited expansion of nuclear energy, after first opposing it; and in 1980 a massive series of strikes almost brought the country to an industrial standstill. While still maintaining one of the world's highest per capita gross national products, Sweden found it was not immune to the problems that plagued other democracies.

II   NORTH AMERICA

The United States

Nor could the largest and most populous of the Western democracies avoid instability even though it was to provide the leadership for the Western alliance and was clearly a superpower in trade and military terms. Though racked by social tensions at times, the United States was, in general contrast to Europe, markedly prosperous and politically stable for much of this period. Nonetheless, significant new elements were introduced to the American scene.

Rather than reverting to isolation, as in 1919, the United States took the lead in 1945 in organizing both the United Nations and a network of alliances. It put through vigorous programs of economic aid to other countries, first through the Marshall Plan, then by direct assistance to the newly independent former colonies, and also by massive assistance through internationally organized financial institutions, such as the International Monetary Fund and the World Bank. Both political parties generally endorsed these programs; not until the American government began to suffer deep economic strains in its domestic programs under the impact of the escalating cost of the war in Vietnam did the sums appropriated for foreign aid begin to be cut.

Agreement between the Republican and Democratic parties on foreign policy was generally shared on domestic issues as well, and both parties were, in European terms, centrist. Broadly, the Democrats, except for their southern wing, were somewhat more committed to interventionist positions in the economy, to social-welfare programs, and to expanding civil liberties. The Republicans were relatively more committed to laissez-faire positions on the economy and government, to somewhat more cautious programs for social welfare, and to the need to more closely match a sense of duty with a sense of rights in civil liberties. However, just as the Conservative party in Britain made no attempt to undo the general program of the Labour party when it was returned to office there, the majority of the Republican party either did not wish to, or did not consider it politically possible to, undo the major programs associated with Roosevelt's New Deal. When the first Republican in twenty years, Dwight D. Eisenhower, attained the White House largely on the strength of his popularity as supreme Allied commander in World War II, he proved to be a shrewd preserver of that which had gone before.

During his eight years as president (1953-1961), Eisenhower not only did not repeal the New Deal enactments of the Roosevelt period but left them intact and even expanded the system of Social Security. Nor, despite an effort to tag the Democrats as a "war party," did the Republicans shift the bases of foreign policy. Eisenhower's secretary of state, John Foster Dulles (1888-1959), spoke of "rolling the Russians back" and "liberating" their satellites in eastern Europe, but when he was challenged by Soviet military intervention in Hungary in 1956, he was unable to do anything, and the Democrats had no counter policy to offer.

The early 1950s brought an episode in which a single senator, Joseph McCarthy (1908-1957) of Wisconsin, attacked American civil servants whom he called communists. The fact that some few American communists had obtained government posts and had passed valuable information to the Russians lent credibility to McCarthy's accusations. A frightened people, not used to defeat, was persuaded that communists in high places had "lost" China or "sold" eastern Europe to the international communist movement. McCarthy's attacks fed upon these unproved fears, as he challenged the civil rights of those he attacked and demoralized the diplomatic service, the movie industry, and university faculties. But he never located a single communist in high places, and he attacked many persons on the flimsiest evidence. McCarthy's tactics were not akin to Stalin's reign of terror; rather, they were similar in emotion and dimension to the Salem witch trials of the seventeenth century, being based on fear and rumor, thus posing a challenge to the constitution's insistence on strict canons of evidence. In 1954 McCarthy was condemned by his fellow senators for abuse of his powers. The spectacle of McCarthy bullying witnesses on television—then a new device—had helped arouse the public against him.

The United States was generally prosperous and productive during the quarter-century following World War II, though with occasional recessions and readjustments. So remarkable was the steady growth of the Gross National Product that it appeared that the Americans had learned how to avoid depression altogether. The general affluence, which made the United States a nearly classless society, did not, however, by any means filter down satisfactorily to its poorest members. President Lyndon Johnson's series of programs to assist the poor had to be abandoned because of the heavy expense of the war in Vietnam. The strains imposed by the war, accompanied by increasing domestic unrest, inflation, and rising unemployment, continued to mount, though unevenly, in the 1970s.

That so many of the poor in the United States were black worsened what was already the gravest American social problem. Though individual blacks had won recognition in the arts, in sports, in entertainment, and often in business and the professions, blacks in general were handicapped by the failure of American society to provide them with equal opportunities for education and for jobs. This was true not only in the South, but also in the cities of the North, where during the war hundreds of thousands of blacks had flocked to work.

CHAOS OR COMMUNITY?

Black American leadership was divided between those who advocated the Gandhian path of nonviolence and those who argued that only violence would change society, as in revolutionary Russia or Hitler Germany. Those who espoused violence were fragmented into various bodies—some anarchist, some Marxist, some Maoist, some simply convinced that a display of anger and acts of self-defense were essential to dignity.

In 1967 Martin Luther King spoke eloquently against the rise of the various groups that tended to be lumped together under the heading of Black Power:

Probably the most destructive feature of Black Power is its unconscious and often conscious call for retaliatory violence. . . .

The problem with hatred and violence is that they intensify the fears of the white majority, and leave them less ashamed of their prejudices toward Negroes. In the guilt and confusion confronting our society, violence only adds to chaos. It deepens the brutality of the oppressor and increases the bitterness of the oppressed. Violence is the antithesis of creativity and wholeness. It destroys community and makes brotherhood impossible. . . .

Returning violence for violence multiplies violence, adding deeper darkness to a night already devoid of stars. Darkness cannot drive out darkness: only light can do that. Hate cannot drive out hate: only love can do that. . . .

Like life, racial understanding is not something that we find but something that we must create. What we find when we enter these mortal plains is existence; but existence is the raw material out of which all life must be created. A productive and happy life is not something that you find; it is something that you make.

Martin Luther King, *Where Do We Go from Here: Chaos or Community?* (New York: Harper & Row, 1967), pp. 54, 61-63, 28.

In 1954 in *Brown vs. Board of Education*, the Supreme Court unanimously declared that the existence of separate compulsory public schools for blacks was unconstitutional. This major decision immediately affected the South, where "separate but equal" education had been the rule, and where the separate black schools had usually been markedly inferior. The Court declared that separate education could not be equal education. The years that followed saw varying degrees of compliance with the new requirement. Most parts of the South were determined to disobey the Court by one means or another, or if they obeyed, to admit only token numbers of black students to white schools. The many efforts to speed compliance met with some success, and by 1970 in some southern cities, such as Atlanta, desegregation was well advanced.

But the existence of black ghettos in the northern cities and the prevalence of neighborhood schools everywhere meant that public education in New York or Boston was often as segregated as in Mississippi. Northern whites often opposed busing children to schools out of their home neighborhoods as a method of balancing the numbers of black and white children just as vigorously as southern whites had opposed desegregation in principle. Southern white support for a Republican, Richard M. Nixon (1913-   ), in the election of 1968 left him with a political debt to southern politicians, and many observers felt that the diminished efforts of the federal government to enforce desegregation during his administration reflected an effort to repay this debt. The problem of equal education for all, including the rapidly increasing number of predominantly Spanish-speaking students, remained a serious one in the 1980s.

The drive to improve conditions for blacks extended far beyond education, however. In the late fifties and early sixties activist whites and blacks worked to increase the registration of black voters in the South and to liberalize real-estate practices in the North. Both drives made considerable headway, though some whites responded with intimidation and terror, others by quietly turning away. Some blacks, feeling that justice would never be gained by gradual means, turned away from organizations such as the National Association for the Advancement of Colored People (NAACP), which had traditionally preferred to work by persuasion, toward more militant groups. The Reverend Martin Luther King (1926-1968)—a nonviolent black minister from the South who in 1955 had sponsored a successful black boycott of segregated buses in Montgomery, Alabama, forcing the bus lines to end segregation, and in 1957 had founded the Southern Christian Leadership Conference to press for nonviolent change throughout the South—lost some of his large following to other groups advocating one form or another of Black Power.

During the summers of 1965 through 1967 severe rioting broke out in Los Angeles, Newark, Detroit, and other northern cities. Blacks burned their own neighborhoods, looted shops, and fought with the police. The passage of a federal Civil Rights Act in 1965 and the

Despite major changes in racial attitudes, racism remained a force in American life. Here the Ku Klux Klan holds a cross-burning ceremony at Stone Mountain, Georgia, in 1973.

outlawing of discrimination in real estate transactions did not calm the stormy situation. Black violence aroused bitter protest, even among white moderates who favored the black advance but were growing more and more anxious about public order. This anxiety was another factor in Nixon's victory in the election of 1968.

The new wave of violence in American life derived not only from the race question. Democrat John F. Kennedy, the first Roman Catholic to be elected president, succeeding Eisenhower and defeating Nixon (1960), was a young man of intelligence, personal elegance, and charm. To the young he seemed to offer a new start and charismatic leadership, and abroad he was widely respected as a potential leader for the West. His New Frontier envisioned federally sponsored medical care for the aged, tax reform, civil rights, and antipoverty measures. But Kennedy had deeply angered the far right, was distrusted by Cuban exiles, who felt he had not supported their efforts to unseat Castro, and was hated for his efforts to fight organized crime and to press forward with civil rights. He was assassinated in 1963 by Lee Harvey Oswald, an apparently psychopathic killer with a rifle. Televised details of the crime came

LET THE WORD GO FORTH

In his Inaugural Address, newly elected President John F. Kennedy demonstrated charismatic powers of oratory. He did more, however, for he also issued a challenge to his fellow Americans that was more dramatic, more sweeping, a tinge more arrogant, and perhaps more idealistic than they had heard, or would hear, for some time. European observers of the role of the United States in the history of Western civilization were inclined to the judgment that Kennedy's thousand days in office, while marked by several failures in the execution of policy, were also noted for the kind of vigorous leadership they had come to expect from America.

Let the word go forth from this time and place, to friend and foe alike, that the torch has been passed to a new generation of Americans, born in this century, tempered by war, disciplined by a hard and bitter peace, proud of our ancient heritage, and unwilling to witness or permit the slow undoing of those human rights to which this nation has always been committed. . . .

Let every nation know, whether it wishes us well or ill, that we shall pay any price, bear any burden, meet any hardship, support any friend, oppose any foe to assure the survival and the success of liberty. . . .

Finally, to those nations who would make themselves our adversary, we offer not a pledge but a request: that both sides begin anew the quest for peace, before the dark powers of destruction unleashed by science engulf all humanity in planned or accidental self-destruction.

We dare not tempt them with weakness. For only when our arms are sufficient beyond doubt can we be certain beyond doubt that they will never be employed.

But neither can two great and powerful groups of nations take comfort from our present course—both sides overburdened by the cost of modern weapons, both rightly alarmed by the steady spread of the deadly atom, yet both racing to alter that uncertain balance of terror that stays the hand of mankind's final war.

So let us begin anew, remembering on both sides that civility is not a sign of weakness, and sincerity is always subject to proof. Let us never negotiate out of fear, but let us never fear to negotiate. . . .

Let both sides seek to invoke the wonders of science instead of its terrors. Together let us explore the stars, conquer the deserts, eradicate disease, tap the ocean depths and encourage the arts and commerce. . . .

All this will not be finished in the first one hundred days. Nor will it be finished in the first one thousand days, nor in the life of this Administration, nor even perhaps in our lifetime on this planet. But let us begin. . . .

In the long history of the world, only a few generations have been granted the role of defending freedom in its hour of maximum danger. I do not shrink from this responsibility; I welcome it. I do not believe that any of us would exchange places with any other people or any other generation. The energy, the faith, the devotion which we bring to this endeavor will light our country and all who serve it, and the glow from that fire can truly light the world.

And so, my fellow Americans, ask not what your country can do for you; ask what you can do for your country.

My fellow citizens of the world, ask not what America will do for you, but what together we can do for the freedom of man.

As quoted in Theodore C. Sorensen, *Kennedy* (New York: Bantam Books, 1966), pp. 275-78. This edition also provides examples of the drafts through which the speech passed.

into every American home, as did the subsequent murder of the assassin.

The failure of the nation to protect its president, of the Dallas police to protect the accused assassin, and of subsequent and repeated investigators to come to a definitive conclusion about the assassination despite a lengthy report by a commission chaired by the chief justice of the United States, added to the national sense of suspicion and fear. The murder of Martin Luther King—also by rifle—in 1968, and the murder by pistol of President Kennedy's brother, Senator Robert F. Kennedy (1925-1968) of New York, while he was campaigning to secure the Democratic nomination for the presidency in 1968, all combined to produce a major public revulsion. Yet crime continued to present a severe and growing problem, and easy access to guns continued

to set the United States apart from all other nations. Some saw the failure to enact strong anti-gun laws as a sign that the United States did not realize it was no longer a frontier society; others felt that the constitution guaranteed the right to bear arms, and they argued that infringements on this right were an attack on a basic civil liberty. These three assassinations, as well as subsequent attempts on other presidents and public figures, would stir a debate that clearly posed the democratic dilemma of how best to define the public good. Where does the line between protecting the individual and protecting the community lie? Americans found themselves, usually without realizing it, repeating arguments that dated back to Plato and ancient Greece.

After the assassination, Lyndon Johnson, John Kennedy's vice-president, assumed office and, in an intensive legislative drive, successfully put through much of the social program that Kennedy had not been able to achieve. His goal, he said, was to create the Great Society. But the gains were outweighed in the public mind by the cost in life and money of the war in Vietnam and by the rising discontent with a society that could not fairly distribute its own affluence. City life, in particular, seemed to degenerate rapidly as prosperity increased. Racial tension and crime, pollution of the air and water, intolerable motor traffic, and strikes by teachers, sanitation employees, air-traffic controllers, and others made urban life a nightmare. Public transit had apparently suffered a substantial breakdown, while municipal government was too often both corrupt and bankrupt. Yet taxes continued to rise faster than income.

Further, children of the well-to-do were "opting out" of society in large numbers. Some took drugs—the increasingly fashionable marijuana, heroin, cocaine, or LSD. Many dropped out of school and left home: the "hippies" of the late 1960s. Behind their veneer of long hair and strange clothing they revealed much about which a thoughtful segment of society worried: that the structure of society was alienating many young people; that the unknown effect of a variety of drugs was making human behavior vastly more unpredictable; that the cost of those drugs was leading to ever higher crime rates; that a gap was opening between generations; that the family as a unit for promoting stability was being threatened; that the same young who professed to be individualists who would not join in what they condemned as the "groupthink" of industrial society were nonetheless removing themselves to communes where another form of groupthink dominated.

Other young people rebelled actively against the institutions of their immediate world—the university and the draft board. Student violence in 1968 and 1969 sometimes took the form of sit-ins or building seizures, accompanied by the disruption of classes, the theft of documents from files, and the attempted intimidation of classmates, professors, or administrators. When university authorities summoned police or the National Guard to quell the violence, the effect often was to turn moderate students into radicals. The universities were thus faced with a painful dilemma: either to submit to intimidation and violence, usually from the left, or to fight, thus vastly increasing the numbers of the disenchanted. When the National Guard fired into a student demonstration at Kent State University in Ohio in 1970,

Martin Luther King led civil rights marchers on the last stage of their march from Selma to Montgomery, Alabama, in 1965. Marching with him were his wife, Coretta, and other civil rights leaders, including his principal aide and successor, Ralph Abernathy.

In May 1970 Ohio National Guardsmen used tear gas and rifle fire to break up a demonstration at Kent State University in Ohio.

killing four white students, and a few days later police in Jackson, Mississippi, killed two more who were black, there was a cry of outrage and guilt on university campuses and in homes throughout the nation.

The racial protests, the campus violence, and the long battle in the media and in Congress between "hawks" (who favored pursuing the war in Vietnam with vigor) and "doves" (who considered the war immoral, impractical, or lost) had injected a high level of apprehension and confusion into the lives of most Americans. By 1967 the total number of casualties in Vietnam had exceeded one hundred thousand. That fall seventy thousand demonstrators picketed the Department of Defense. Though de-escalation of the war began before he took office in 1969, Nixon inherited the domestic chaos of the preceding years.

Nixon moved quickly to effect basic changes in foreign policy, while narrowing the range of newly acquired civil liberties at home. Bismarck, it was said, knew how to be silent in seven languages, but modern American presidents know that the powerful medium of television renders silence impossible. Under the guidance of his national security adviser and eventual secretary of state, Henry Kissinger—an admirer of Metternich and an advocate of pragmatic rather than doctrinaire approaches to foreign relations—Nixon took several bold initiatives. He sped up the de-escalation of American involvement in Vietnam, accepting Kissinger's argument that the conflict there was essentially a civil war from which the United States must slowly extricate itself. Once unencumbered in Southeast Asia, the United States could maintain an equilibrium of power between itself, the Soviet Union, an increasingly assertive China, the growing industrial might of Japan, and the new unity of Europe. To this end, Nixon initiated Strategic Arms Limitation Talks (SALT) with Russia; declared that there must in future be "Asian solutions to Asian problems"; began to withdraw from the Alliance for Progress, through which the United States had channeled substantial aid for economic reform into Latin America, a region Nixon did not regard as especially important; and most dramatically, sent Kissinger on a secret mission to the People's Republic of China in July 1971, and then visited the country himself early in 1972, to "normalize relations" between the two nations. A politician who had based his early reputation on intense anticommunism, Nixon was now ready to recognize the need to do business with those regimes. Nixon thus brought about a diplomatic revolution in which, by the mid-1970s, Communist China appeared to be cautiously aligned with the United States against the Soviet Union. This, in turn, created renewed strains with both Russia and Japan.

Nixon had reasoned that an easing of world tensions and an end to the bloodshed in Vietnam would also ease tensions at home. He was correct. Student protests slackened, an uneasy racial peace was achieved, and the early 1970s were marked by relative tranquility. Perhaps as a result, Nixon was returned to office in a landslide election in 1972, capturing every state save one. But a new instability soon plagued the nation, for early in his second administration it became known that a group of President Nixon's supporters had not only burglarized the headquarters of the Democratic party in the Watergate complex in Washington, but that Nixon's closest

Brought vividly into every American home by news photographs and television, the war in Vietnam proved to be deeply divisive. Thousands of young Americans refused to serve in the military and fled to Canada, as Congress debated the legitimacy, morality, and strategy of the war. Two photographs above all deeply influenced American opinion against continuing the war. One, taken in 1968, showed the South Vietnamese national police chief executing a Viet Cong officer in Saigon; the other showed South Vietnamese children running from a napalm attack by their own government's aircraft.

aides appeared to have had knowledge of the burglary. Soon hearings in the Senate and intense investigative reporting by journalists revealed that the president had tape-recorded conversations in his Oval Office and that the Federal Bureau of Investigation and the Central Intelligence Agency (the latter barred from domestic surveillance activities by law) had been pressed into service to obtain information that would help the Nixon reelection and to cover up the initial revelations about Watergate.

In the midst of this crisis of confidence, Nixon's vice-president, Spiro Agnew (1918-   ), resigned from office in the face of charges of income-tax evasion and bribery. Preoccupied with defending himself against mounting charges that soon enveloped his closest aides, then the attorney general, and finally the presidency itself, Nixon paid little attention to foreign policy, allowing an ominous meeting of ministers from the oil producing and exporting nations (OPEC) to go virtually unnoticed. Facing almost certain impeachment for misconduct in office, President Nixon finally resigned on August 9, 1974. Gerald R. Ford (1913-   ), a respected Republican Congressman from Michigan who had served in the House of Representatives for a quarter of a century and had been appointed vice-president in 1973, succeeded him in the presidency.

The Watergate affair had proved deeply divisive, and President Ford set out to bind up the nation's wounds. He pardoned Nixon to avoid the extended rancor of a trial, although Nixon's assistants were convicted and sentenced to jail. There had been no political scandal of this complexity or dimension in American history, and Europeans looked on in wonder. Ford turned to the problem of inflation, which mounted in 1974 in the face of higher oil prices, and public attention turned to energy policy. Revelations about the involvement of the FBI and CIA in violations of civil rights, the fall of South Vietnam, and the rapidly mounting demand of women for full equality in the nation's economy all undermined faith in Ford's administration. By 1975 44 percent of married women worked, as opposed to only 15 percent in 1940. When in 1973 the Supreme Court upheld a California law that granted women abortions on request, the feminist movement became the new target for hate, replacing the racial-equality movement of the 1960s.

Despite peace in Vietnam and a rise in the stock market, Ford was unable to win a widespread following. Though low by European standards, the American inflation rate still stood at 7.6 percent and unemployment at eight million. An oil embargo against the West by Arab states had revealed that the United States was vulnerable in its consumption of energy. And the right wing of the Republican party was up in arms against what it regarded as a weak American policy in the Middle East, the Panama Canal, in Latin America, and even in Israel, which was thought to be operating too independently, having precipitated the energy crisis by its war against the Arab states in 1973-1974.

Thus a political unknown who had captured the Democratic nomination, James Earl Carter (1924-   ), known even formally as Jimmy Carter, attained the presidency by a narrow margin. The chief issue was the economy. The Voting Rights Act of 1965, which had enfranchised southern black voters, helped Carter, a Georgian; so too did his antiestablishment views, his religious convictions, and the fact that his wife, Rosalynn, was clearly a near-equal partner. Voters were prepared to try a new approach; above all, they wanted to return to a sense of security about the economy.

In this and much else, the Carter presidency disappointed many, returning the nation instead to its sense of deepening confusion. Carter achieved some gains, most notably in environmental legislation, urban redevelopment, and deregulation of some sectors of the economy. Although he brought the Israeli and Egyptian leaders together to sign an accord that appeared to end the long-standing hostility between their nations, Carter's presidency was crippled by an event in far-away Iran. There

The bitter war in Vietnam cost more American lives than any conflict since the Civil War. In one of the war's brighter moments, a family is shown here joyously rushing to greet a former prisoner of war who, having been shot down over North Vietnam in 1967, was freed to return to the United States in 1973.

the United States had long supported the powerful shah, Mohammed Reza Pahlavi (1919-1980), son of Reza Shah, who had abdicated in 1941. Reza Shah had been placed in office through British and American intervention, so that nationalists there would not bar the West from the rich oil fields of Iran. He had remained in power by winning the support of a small but steadily growing middle class, by cautious modernization, by committing himself to the American position against the Russians, and by becoming an autocrat with an emperor's powers. Iran under the Pahlavis was a test case for modernization; to go too fast would alienate the traditional Islamic clergy and the peasantry; to go too slowly would lose the middle class and the Westernized Iranians. Although the shah had instituted a White Revolution—agricultural reforms that gave Iran a steadily rising standard of living—he was seen as corrupt, despotic, enriching himself and his family at the expense of the peasantry. In 1967 he had himself crowned *Shahanshah* (King of Kings) and in 1971 he held an impressive festival at ancient Persepolis to celebrate twenty-five hundred years of Persian monarchy.

The United States failed to see revolution in Iran coming, and when it came, appeared to deal with it falteringly. Fearful of revolution from political radicals, Americans had not become sufficiently aware of the growing discontent of traditional society in Iran. Violence was followed by martial law in 1978. From France the exiled Shi'ite religious leader, the ayatollah Ruhollah Khomeini (1902-   ), orchestrated a rebellion that drove the shah into exile in January 1979. The ayatollah (a title meaning "reflection of God") returned to Iran the next month, and soon his power was virtually absolute.

In 1979 the shah of Iran was forced into exile by a fundamentalist revolution. Huge crowds of demonstrators filled the streets in support of the ayatollah Ruhollah Khomeini. They are shown here in front of the massive monument the shah had built in Teheran to honor the Pahlavi dynasty.

In the meantime, the shah had been admitted to the United States for treatment of cancer. On November 4, 1979, militant students stormed the American embassy in Teheran and seized ninety hostages, including sixty-five Americans, whom they refused to release unless the shah were returned to Iran to stand trial for crimes against the people. The Iranians remained in control of the embassy for four hundred and forty-four days, despite international condemnation, an abortive rescue mission by American forces, and intense diplomatic pressure from the United States. For fifteen months Americans were faced nightly on their television sets with the dramatic (and inflated) spectacle of "America held hostage."

While Carter was faulted for not having taken precautions to protect the American embassy, there was little that he could do thereafter. And it was this very sense of national helplessness that turned the electorate against him. To underscore how they could influence American elections, the Iranians released the hostages on January 20, 1981, just minutes after a new president of the United States, Republican Ronald Reagan (1911-   ), was sworn into office. The turmoil continued in Iran as the revolution passed through phases of vengeance and countervengeance, much like the French Revolution. Waves of executions eliminated Marxists, those who had collaborated with Americans, those who had worked for the shah, and those who opposed the new Islamic Republic's constitution, which had been shaped by the

clergy. Members of the ecumenical, international Bahai faith, which had a following in the United States, were also systematically killed, while the United States stood helplessly by.

Ronald Reagan had been elected on a wave of public frustration. He was a right-wing conservative who offered voters a clear alternative to previous administrations. Once in office, however, he proved to be less conservative than the right wing had hoped, and he soon tempered some of his stands. Reagan appealed to Americans who felt that government had become too big, too interfering, and too central to their lives. He agreed with Thomas Jefferson that the best government was the government that governed least, and he promised deregulation, decentralization, and a restoration of public and private morality. Working against these goals were the risks inherent in an arms race with the Soviet Union, a resurgence of the environmentalist movement, and apparently intractable inflation and unemployment.

In the 1980s the United States was undergong unprecedented change, far more sweeping than that experienced by most European nations. A nation once thought to be committed to isolation was now involved with events virtually everywhere. A nation that once had the highest standard of living in the world, that had taken for granted its unlimited resources and steady progress, had sadly discovered the poor in its midst and was acutely aware of its dependence on other nations for resources such as oil. The United States had fallen to eleventh place in per capita income among Western nations (omitting the oil-rich Arab states), and stood tenth in its health rate. The United States was still the dominant nation in the world, but on the indicators most meaningful in case of war, it was directly challenged by the Soviet Union, and on the indicators most significant in time of peace, it had been marginally—and to Americans, quite unexpectedly—overtaken by several nations.*

Once shaped by a vast open frontier that had made Americans optimistic, expectant of material progress, rudely democratic, and highly mobile, the United States now faced a closed frontier. Once shaped by an economy of abundance, so that each succeeding generation, as well as arriving immigrants, could anticipate a better future, the United States now faced shortages in areas crucial to the economy, rising demands from the less privileged part of the population, and an agonizing awareness of the magnitude of the problems. Once shaped by an illusion of "free security"—security from foreign invasion, virtually free of cost, since neither land neighbor, Canada or Mexico, posed a military threat, and other nations were thousands of miles across the seas—the United States now feared for its security in the

*Economists use many different indicators for measuring standard of living, and per capita income or health rate are only two of them. In many other indicators, the United States was first or second in both. For these statistics, see the figures under each nation in any current edition of *The World Almanac and Book of Facts* (New York: Newspaper Enterprise Association). The above figures are from the 1982 edition and were current to November of that year.

atomic era and could maintain such security as it had only at great cost. Many Americans turned toward their past, nostalgically hoping that these old, formative influences might still work for American society. But by the 1980s many other people were on the path to the future, determined to find an American solution to American problems, to maintain civil liberties and democratic government, to achieve security and stability, and yet to do so without, as Britain had done in the 1950s, as Germany had done in the 1930s, or as the Roman Empire had done in the third century, looking essentially backwards.

Canada and Mexico

One of the nations that briefly surpassed the United States in per capita income was its immediate neighbor, Canada, which enjoyed economic growth in part on the basis of massive postwar immigration. Exploiting its vast hydroelectric resources and oil and mineral wealth, Canada had become a major industrial nation. Between 1954 and 1959 the United States and Canada built an extensive new seaway to join the Great Lakes with the St. Lawrence River, so that Canadian and midwestern

goods could flow to world markets more readily. Yet Canada increasingly asserted an independent foreign policy—independent of both Britain and the United States. Its foreign minister played a major role in mediating the Suez crisis; Canada recognized and traded with communist Cuba and China; and by the 1970s Canadian nationalist leaders were seeking to achieve greater economic independence from the United States.

But in Canada too political instability threatened. French-speaking Canadians continued to lag behind English-speaking Canadians in their standard of living. Because the hundreds of thousands of immigrants were assimilating predominantly into English rather than into French Canada, French Canada felt that its language and culture were under attack. When an Official Languages Act, which made French equal to English in all federal matters, did not satisfy French expectations and was often ignored in the English-speaking provinces of western Canada, terrorist groups kidnapped a British diplomat and killed a Quebec government official. The French-Canadian prime minister, Pierre-Elliott Trudeau (1919-   ), applied emergency powers with such vigor that he further alienated the population of the province of Quebec, where a separatist movement grew in

THE CULTURAL MOSAIC

Most modern nations based largely on settlement from Europe have, like the United States, sought to create a cultural "melting pot" in which newly arrived immigrants have, by the second generation, lost their original cultural identity. In the last two decades this goal has no longer been sought, nor has it been considered achievable, in the United States. Canada, moreover, continues to champion the goal of the "cultural mosaic," in which each ethnic identity remains clearly distinguishable. In 1978 the Canadian prime minister, Pierre Elliott Trudeau, again defended the principle of the mosaic:

The renewal of the Federation must lead to respect for cultural diversity and for the right of every citizen, regardless of ethnic origin, to equal opportunity. Every cultural community should be able to rely on the goodwill of governments in preserving its own cultural heritage and in discovering and appreciating those of other communities.

For more than a century, people of other ethnic origins have come to Canada and settled beside those of British and French ancestry. A large number of them have joined the English-speaking majority and others the French-speaking majority, without in the process losing their individuality.

With the sheer weight of their numbers, it is natural that the French and British cultures occupy a major place in Canada. But there is no question of having only one or two official cultures; Canadian society must promote cultural diversity, clearly and explicitly.

This diversity will only be protected if we ensure that

Canadians of all ethnic origins have equal opportunities and full protection against discrimination.

Our French and British traditions have not been weakened by the multicultural character of our society. On the contrary, by good fortune this increasing diversity has helped to reduce the old rivalry between them. They have also been invaluably enriched and revitalized in all fields—from the arts and sciences to economics and politics. Our two principal cultures will in no way be diminished by the determination of new communities to preserve their own cultural heritage.

We must therefore do more to develop and enhance all the elements of the Canadian mosaic. We must also significantly increase exchanges between our cultures, so that every Canadian has the chance to discover, appreciate, and respect the heritage of his fellow-citizens.

Trudeau, *A Time for Action: Toward the Renewal of the Canadian Federation* (Ottawa: Government of Canada, 1978), pp. 9-10.

strength over the next decade. The *Parti Québécois*, committed to greater autonomy for Quebec, won wavering support within the province and was soundly reelected in 1981. Meanwhile, despite changes in the federal government, Trudeau continued to dominate the national political scene, and in 1980 he embarked on the delicate task of constitutional reform, in which the first essential change was the formal transfer of the right to amend its own constitution from Britain to Canada, completed in 1982. Opposed by eight of the ten Canadian provinces, Trudeau found himself presiding over a nation deeply divided on fundamental issues relating to civil rights, the use of natural resources, the distribution of wealth, and the legitimacy of biculturalism.

Mexico, in the meantime, was also posing a challenge to the United States. Larger and more populous than any country in Europe and point of origin for thousands of immigrants to the United States, Mexico had remained in relative poverty while experiencing political stability. The Institutional Revolutionary party had dominated since 1929; despite its title, it had consistently used strong measures to put down radical opposition. But by the 1970s Mexico's foreign policy was trending to the left. A reversal of reforms in land redistribution after 1976 left a substantial part of the population angry, while the great significance of oil as a bargaining chip in international affairs was giving Mexico far more author-ity in the world's marketplaces. A period of unprecedented prosperity, during which Mexico City grew to be the largest city in the world, was abruptly ended by a severe currency devaluation in 1982. The economic collapse was the worst in fifty years. Unemployment rose to nearly half the work force, four million peasants remained without land, and a tense controversy broke out with the United States over the treatment of illegal Mexican entrants into the American southwest, who, by 1980, had reached a million people. Always a leader in Latin America, conscious of its ties to Europe as well as of its long historical experience as a North American nation, Mexico appeared poised for significant change to either the political and social right or to the left. With a population of 72,000,000 in 1980, and 46 percent of that population under age fourteen, Mexico was growing twice as fast as the United States; in 1983 it had the highest rate of natural increase of any nation in the world.

III THE EASTERN BLOC

The Soviet Union and the countries of eastern Europe were not exempt from the cycle of prosperity, growth, economic stagnation, and social and political unrest, even though they could prevent the unrest from getting

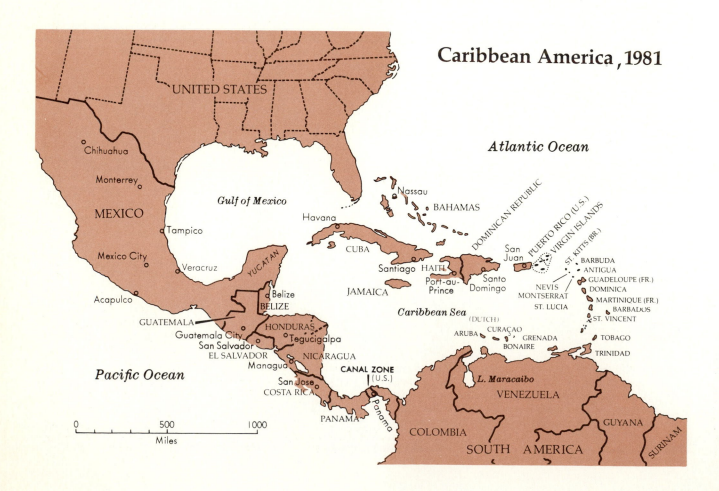

Caribbean America, 1981

KHRUSHCHEV SMASHES THE IDOL

Khrushchev's speech in 1956, which was intended to be secret, was meant to break Russia out of the Stalinist mold while preserving the purity of Leninism.

Stalin originated the concept "enemy of the people." This term automatically rendered it unnecessary that the ideological errors of a man or men engaged in a controversy be proved; this term made possible the usage of the most cruel repression violating all norms of revolutionary legality, against anyone who in any way disagreed with Stalin. . . .

Lenin used severe methods only in the most necessary cases, when the exploiting classes were still in existence and were vigorously opposing the revolution, when the struggle for survival was decidedly assuming the sharpest forms, even including civil war.

Stalin, on the other hand, used extreme methods and mass repressions at a time when the revolution was already victorious, when the Soviet State was strengthened, when the exploiting classes were already liquidated and Socialist relations were rooted solidly in all phases of national economy, when our party was politically consolidated and had strengthened itself both numerically and ideologically. It is clear that here Stalin showed in a whole series of cases his intolerance, his brutality and his abuse of power. . . .

The New York Times, June 5, 1956.

out of hand or from being made known outside their borders. Problems for the Soviet leadership proved to be fully as difficult as those faced by the Western democracies, but totalitarian states did not have to engage in divisive public debate over how to allocate resources. Thus the Soviet Union was free to concentrate on postwar industrial recovery and parity in the arms race.

As Stalin grew older, the secrecy and censorship at the top of the Soviet state had intensified. Anti-Semitic propaganda reached its peak with an alleged "doctors' plot," in which Jewish doctors were accused of plotting to poison Stalin. When Stalin died, the stage seemed set for a full-scale anti-Semitic drive. But fear of the West and hatred of Zionism did not alone explain Soviet anti-Semitism. Despite long years of preaching cultural autonomy for nationalities, many Soviet leaders were personally anti-Semitic and perhaps recognized the latent anti-Semitism of the population at large. Official Soviet anti-Semitism would continue even into the 1980s, and the door would be periodically opened, then closed, to emigration to the West or to Israel. The Soviet Union viewed Israel as a client state of the United States, and therefore Russian foreign policy was generally pro-Arab.

After World War II, the reparations extracted from Germany and the industrial loot from eastern Europe gave massive stimulus to Soviet reconstruction. A fourth five-year plan saw the first Soviet atom bomb completed; the fifth saw further advances in armaments and the building of the Volga-Don Canal. In agriculture, the regime embarked on a policy of reducing the number and increasing the size of collective farms. In 1951 Nikita Khrushchev proposed a plan to create great agricultural cities in order to concentrate farm labor and abolish rural backwardness.

In March 1953 Georgi Malenkov (1902-   ), personally close to Stalin, succeeded him as premier but surrendered the party secretaryship to Khrushchev. It was thus made clear that no one person would immediately inherit all of Stalin's power. Soon the regime began to denounce the "cult of personality" (Stalin's despotic one-man rule) and proclaimed a "collegial" system (government by committee). The dreaded chief of the secret police, Presidium member Lavrenty Beria (1899-1953), was executed for treason. At a party congress early in 1956 Khrushchev denounced Stalin, emotionally detailing the acts of personal cruelty to which the psychopathic nature of the late dictator had given rise. Khrushchev thus echoed what Western observers had been saying for years. As the details of the speech leaked out to the Soviet public, there was some distress at the smashing of the idol they had worshiped for so long, but the widespread disorder that some observers were predicting failed to materialize. Abroad, however, the speech produced turmoil in the Soviet satellites in Europe and so gave Khrushchev's opponents at home an opportunity to unite against his policies. Within the Presidium they had a majority, but Khrushchev was able to rally to his support the Central Committee of the Communist party. A veteran party worker, Khrushchev had installed his own loyal supporters in all key party posts, repeating Stalin's strategy after the death of Lenin, and he emerged from this greatest test in 1957 with his powers immeasurably enhanced.

Already in his sixties, Khrushchev could hardly hope for a quarter-century of dictatorship such as Stalin had had. Moreover, in making himself supreme he had deprived himself of some of the instruments available to Stalin. After 1953 he had released millions of captives from prisons and slave-labor camps. Almost everyone in Russia had a relative or friend now freed. Within a year or two Soviet society at every level except at the very top of the bureaucracy had absorbed these sufferers from tyranny. The secret police no longer enjoyed independent power in the state, a power that might challenge the party or the army; Khrushchev himself had emotionally denounced police terror. It was still possible to prosecute people by terroristic means, but Stalin's mass terror as a system of government had disappeared. Under Stalin centralization had reached an intolerable tightness. Between 1953 and 1957 responsibility for many heavy industries was transferred from the ministries of the central government to local authorities. In May 1957 a decree abolished many central ministries and transferred their duties to newly created regional economic councils. Regionalism replaced loyalty to one industry above all others. But by 1960 a process of recentralizing had begun, and by the end of 1962 the number of regional economic councils was reduced from 105 to about 40. New state committees, which were soon reorganized as ministries, appeared to oversee their work. The pendulum had swung back almost the entire distance.

In October 1964 Khrushchev was removed from power and succeeded by two members of the Presidium. Leonid Brezhnev (1906-1982) replaced him as first secre-

In 1969 the first man walked on the moon, ushering in an age of exploration as exciting as the long period of discovery in the fifteenth and sixteenth centuries. By 1972 there had been six moon landings by American astronauts.

tary of the Central Committee of the Communist party, and Alexis Kosygin (1904-1980) as premier. Both were "Khrushchev men." The two, but especially Brezhnev, would provide the Soviet government with stability until Brezhnev became increasingly ill and, in the early 1980s, virtually a figurehead. Khrushchev was denounced for his failures in agricultural policy, for departures from the conventional wisdom on foreign affairs, and for personal rudeness, and for "commandism"—rule by fiat. He was not, however, executed, and until his death in 1971 continued to live in retirement in Moscow and in his country house. No large-scale purge followed his removal.

Most spectacular during these years were the successes achieved in rocketry and space. The Soviets successfully launched the first earth satellite (Sputnik, 1957) and first reached the moon with a rocket (1959). Their heavy payloads soared aloft before American engineers could get their lighter ones off the ground. The first manned orbital flight by Yuri Gagarin (1934-1968), in April 1961, was followed in less than a month by the first American flight, by Alan B. Shepard Jr. (1923-   ), and in February 1962 by the first American orbit, by John H. Glenn Jr. (1921-   ). By the mid-sixties the United States had caught up in most aspects of space technology, and American landings of manned space vehicles on the moon beginning in 1969 overshadowed Soviet accomplishments in space.

The exciting race for outer space commanded the world's imagination, though for both the Soviet Union and the United States it diverted millions of dollars from domestic programs. However, the great technological achievements of the space race had practical applications, which the United States was in a better position to apply to industry. In the 1970s both nations cut back on their space programs, placing greater emphasis on space satellites for monitoring the activities of other nations. After six moon missions, the United States turned to new experiments, with space walks, the placing of a Skylab in outer space, and the development of a reusable winged spaceship. The Russians set a new space endurance record of one hundred and seventy-five days in 1979, while the two countries engaged in a joint flight, including a link-up between their respective crews in space, in 1975.

But it was agriculture that presented the Soviet planners with apparently insoluble problems. In 1953 Khrushchev had embarked on a "virgin lands" scheme— a crash program to plow under more than 100,000,000 acres of prairie in the Urals region, Kazakhstan, and Siberia. Drought and poor planning and performance led to a clear failure by 1963. By the following year, the number of collective farms was down to about 40,000 from an original 250,000 and the average size of the new units was far larger. After Khrushchev's fall from power in 1964, the Soviet authorities enaged in an open debate about the best way to improve agriculture in view of the immense changes since 1936. Some economists argued for a free market economy; others vigorously defended centralized planning. Still, the Soviet authorities were recognizing the importance of capitalist incentives in agriculture and other fields. Soviet economic performance continued to fail to meet its goals. The party program of 1961 announced that per capita production was to overtake the United States, which was used as the yardstick, in 1970; not only did it fail to do so, but by 1977 there had been an actual decline in production. The Soviet standard of living remained low by Western measurements, and by the mid-1970s general stagnation set in followed by crop failures and the need to purchase grain from the United States.

De-Stalinization extended to arts and letters the same partial relaxation that occurred in other fields. It took Soviet writers some time to accustom themselves to the idea that it might now be possible to voice dissent. Two outstanding Soviet composers with followings in the West, Aram Khachaturian (1903-1978) and Dmitri Shostakovich (1906-1975), spoke out for boldness, and in mid-1954 Ilia Ehrenburg (1890-1967), veteran propagandist for the regime, hailed the relaxation of coercive measures over artists in *The Thaw*, which gave a name to the entire period.

Then Boris Pasternak's *Dr. Zhivago* (1958) became a *cause célèbre* throughout the world. Pasternak (1890-1960) took advantage of the "thaw" to offer for publication his novel about a doctor who, through all the agonies of the First World War and the Russian Revolution, affirmed the freedom of the human soul. Accepted for publication in Russia, the novel was also sent to Italy to be published. Then the Soviet censors changed their minds and forced Pasternak to ask that the manuscript in Italy be returned to him. The Italian publisher refused, and versions in Russian, Italian, English, and other languages appeared abroad, arousing great admiration. In 1958 the Nobel Prize Committee offered Pasternak the prize for literature. He accepted. But then the Khrushchev regime reverted to Stalinism. Pasternak's fellow writers reviled him as a traitor, and the government threatened him with exile if he accepted the prize. As a patriotic Russian, he then declined it. Pasternak's Jewish origins, his intellectualism, his proclamation of individualism had offended Khrushchev, making it impossible to publish *Dr. Zhivago* in Russia.

But the spirit of individualism found more vigorous expression among the younger poets and novelists who had grown up since the Second World War and who regarded the heroic age of the Revolution and the early Bolshevik struggles as simply history, not experience. A young Ukrainian poet, Evgeny Yevtushenko (1933-   ) denounced Soviet anti-Semitism in his *Babi Yar* (the name of the ravine near Kiev in which the Nazis, with the help of the Russians, had massacred thousands of Jews). When Yevtushenko recited his verses, the halls were crowded with eager, excited, contentious young people.

The Pasternak affair had shown the limits of the new freedom; the case of Alexander Solzhenitsyn (1918-   ) would be even more instructive to the new readership. A former army officer, Solzhenitsyn had been interned for eight years in a forced labor camp. When he published his autobiographical novel *One Day in the Life of Ivan Denisovich* in 1963, he described for the first time in print the camps of which all Russians knew but did not speak. Solzhenitsyn was immediately attacked for being concerned with "marginal aspects" of Soviet life, and the censor refused to pass his next important novel, *The First Circle*. After his expulsion from the Soviet Union in 1974, his best known work, *The Gulag Archipelago*, revealed extensive knowledge of the Terror and the great camps of Siberia. In 1970, to the embarrassment of

A WARNING FROM SOLZHENITSYN

Upon coming to the United States, Alexander Solzhenitsyn repeatedly issued warnings to the West that it had become too soft, too concerned with material pleasures, to be able to resist the Soviet challenge over the long run. Even while in Russia he had remained convinced that the liberation of the mass of people within the Soviet Union, including the minorities, must come from within:

> I put no hopes in the West—indeed, no Russian ever should. If we ever become free it will only be by our own efforts. If the twentieth century has any lesson for mankind, it is we who will teach the West, not the West us. Excessive ease and prosperity have weakened their will and their reason.

Solzhenitsyn, *The Oak and the Calf: Sketches of Literary Life in the Soviet Union*, trans. Harry Willetts (New York: Harper & Row, 1980), p. 119.

The Soviet Union, 1980

SOVIET SOCIALIST REPUBLICS

1. Russian Soviet Federated
   Socialist Republic
2. White Russia
3. Ukraine

4. Georgia
5. Armenia
6. Azerbaidjan
7. Turkmenistan

8. Uzbekistan
9. Tadjikistan
10. Kirghiz Republic
11. Kazakh Republic

12. Estonia
13. Latvia
14. Lithuania
15. Moldavia

Areas annexed since 1940
Other communist countries
Industrial areas (in U.S.S.R.)

Arctic Ocean

Bering Sea

ALEUTIAN IS. (U.S.)

Pacific Ocean

Sea of Okhotsk

KAMCHATKA

KURILE IS.

SAKHALIN I.

Petropavlovsk

Vladivostok

JAPAN

NORTH KOREA

SOUTH KOREA

TAIWAN (FORMOSA)

PHILIPPINE IS.

SIBERIA

Anadyr

Kolyma R.

Magadan

Aldan R.

Lena R.

Yakutsk

Tiksi

Khatanga

Dudinka

Igarka

Tunguska R.

Yenisei R.

Ob R.

L. Baikal

Irkutsk

Chita

Krasnoyarsk

KUZNETSK

Novosibirsk

Novokuznetsk

Barnaul

Omsk

Irtysh R.

L. Balkhash

MANCHURIA

Khabarovsk

Blagoveshchensk

Amur R.

MONGOLIA

CHINA

SINKIANG

Alma Ata

Frunze

Tashkent

Dushanbe

KASHMIR

INDIA

Bombay

Bay of Bengal

NEPAL

BHUTAN

BURMA

BANGLADESH

LAOS

THAILAND

CAMB.

NORTH VIETNAM

SOUTH VIETNAM

AFGHANISTAN

PAKISTAN

IRAN

Karaganda

Aral Sea

Magnitogorsk

Kuibyshev

Molotov (Perm)

Sverdlovsk

U R A L M T S.

Gorki

Moscow

Leningrad (Petrograd)

Smolensk

DONBAS

Kharkov

Don R.

Volga R.

Rostov

Dnepr.

Kiev

Odessa

CRIMEA

Black Sea

Caspian Sea

Baku

Tiflis

TURKEY

SYRIA

LEBANON

ISRAEL

JORDAN

IRAQ

SAUDI ARABIA

Arabian Sea

AFRICA

Mediterranean Sea

GREECE

ITALY

BULGARIA

ROMANIA

AUSTRIA

POLAND

WEST GERMANY

EAST GERMANY

CZECH.

HUNGARY

YUGOSLAVIA

ALBANIA

FINLAND

SWEDEN

NORWAY

Murmansk

Archangel

Vorkuta

Pechora R.

NOVAYA ZEMLYA

Kara Sea

Barents Sea

Arctic Ocean

Soviet leaders, Solzhenitsyn, like Pasternak before him, was awarded the Nobel Prize for literature.

In 1968 the repression of young writers fed a dissident movement that continued to grow thereafter. Soviet citizens would accuse their own government of violating the human rights provisions of the Helsinki accords of 1975. A Nobel Prize physicist, Andrei Sakharov (1921-), would join the dissidents, and in the late 1970s and early 1980s the Soviet leadership would attack those who sought to criticize cultural policy, or to emigrate to Israel, or to speak favorably of the outcast Solzhenitsyn, who had settled in the United States after being thrown out of the Writer's Union.

Despite the reversion to repression in literature, film, and art, the communist bloc was no longer monolithic, for the Soviet leaders were unable to prevent a drift toward *polycentrism* (the existence of independent centers of power in the satellites). Yugoslavia had already demonstrated that a communist state could pursue a relatively independent policy; other eastern European nations had tried to do the same and failed, until after the death of Stalin. Warsaw Pact members remained more uniformly aligned than those in NATO, but nonetheless cracks began to appear in the Iron Curtain. So long as the satellite countries pursued a foreign policy in common with the Soviet Union, they gained some freedom to make their own economic decisions. Hungary and Romania struck out on paths of their own— Hungary toward a consumer economy, and both countries toward heavier industry, tourism, and trade with the West. Though the Soviet Union crushed liberalization in Czechoslovakia in 1968, it had to accept a declaration by communist parties in 1976 that there could be several separate paths to the socialist state. This loosening of the Soviet hold was only marginal, however, as events in Poland made clear. The Polish Solidarity Movement, a liberalizing, labor-led movement, seriously challenged both the Polish Communist party and the hegemony of the Soviet Union. Under pressure from Moscow, the Polish army suspended Solidarity and took control of Poland in 1981.

With the death of Brezhnev late in 1982 and the selection of Yuri Andropov (1914-) as his successor, the Soviet Union appeared poised for renewed confrontation and repression. Andropov had presided over the crushing of Hungary in 1956; he had been head of the Committee for State Security (KGB) from 1967 to 1982, and he had demonstrated a willingness to silence dissent in January 1983, when he moved against the independent-minded and widely admired historian, Roy Medvedev (1926-), who since 1971 had spoken out for objective history in the Soviet Union. Yet there was some reason for hope. Well-read and relatively knowledgeable about the West, Andropov had shown tolerance for eastern Europe's tendency toward polycentrism, and he had worked closely with the Hungarian leadership to encourage the economic departures from Soviet-bloc uniformity there. He would, observers thought, be tough, clear, and consistent; he was also ill.

IV THE NON-WESTERN WORLD AND INTERNATIONAL AFFAIRS

During World War II the Japanese had seized Western possessions in the Far East and had initially defeated Western armies, ending the myth of Western supremacy. Even though Japan was defeated in the end, Western prestige did not recover. Everyone knew that the French and Dutch had not really won, that British power had been seriously weakened. The only real victors in the war were the United States and the Soviet Union, each in its way anticolonial.

The deeper causes of anticolonialism lay in the record of Western expansion and in the Western tradition itself. Westerners brought with them the Bible, the American Declaration of Independence, the French Declaration of the Rights of Man, *The Communist Manifesto*. It was hardly possible to keep on insisting that "all men are created equal" meant "white men are created superior." Western imperialism carried within itself the seeds of self-determination for all peoples. One great instrument for the spread of Western ideas was the education provided by the West to a relatively small minority of the colonial peoples. Though some of these men and women turned against Western education and reaffirmed the values of their traditional cultures, most came to feel that independence could be won only by learning the industrial, technological, and military skills of the West.

Even if stimulated by the West, independence movements in Asia and Africa were nonetheless authentic movements from within. Nationalism—sometimes simply a disguise for the desire of a dominant tribal group to rule, though equally often cutting across social and kinship lines—had been implanted in some lands, unleashed in others. At first modernization tended to take the form of imitation of the West, but such imitation was quickly combined with a desire to preserve traditional culture, so that an industrialized Japan, while clearly modern, also remained clearly Asian.

Educated non-Westerners wanted independence. Many were revolutionaries; some admired the Bolshevik revolution, and a few were trained in Moscow. A great many Westerners made the mistake of assuming that these people did not represent the local populations, and that the great colonial masses were indifferent to who governed them. Instead, the urban masses and then, more gradually, the peasant masses began to demand that the foreigner go. Often this demand was sharpened by the rapid increases in population made possible by the dramatically lower death rates resulting from the sanitary engineering, medical facilities, and law and order imposed by the imperialist powers. Thus, within two decades of the end of the Second World War, the British, French, Dutch, Belgian, and American empires were virtually dismantled, and only the Portuguese empire continued into the mid-1970s.

Through the Commonwealth of Nations, Britain continued to exert considerable influence in parts of its former empire, though some former colonies either declined to join the Commonwealth or resigned from it: Burma, South Africa, and Pakistan, for example. The French retained substantial influence in French-speaking West Africa, and the Americans in the Philippines and the Panama Canal Zone. But many former colonial dependencies formed a determined neutralist bloc that stood apart from the superpowers, or took strongly left-wing positions. Some looked to the Soviet Union, others to Communist China for technical assistance. Increasingly those parts of the former empires which were primarily Islamic began to unite in a common policy of opposition to Israel, which, since that new nation was viewed as a Western incursion into the Middle East, led them to take positions that were basically anti-Western. Of the great non-Western nations, only one aligned itself unequivocally and consistently with the West: Japan.

Japan

During the Second World War the Japanese had created a huge empire, the Greater East Asia Co-Prosperity Sphere. To rule it they had relied chiefly on puppet native governments. Because the Japanese were an Asian people, they might well have acted as the emancipators of Asians that their propaganda proclaimed them to be. Instead, their armies looted and committed atrocities; they behaved like conquerors, not liberators. They alienated the people they might have won over. When the war ended they were stripped of their overseas possessions.

The occupation of Japan was wholly American. Despite some strong opposition from American opinion, the emperor was left on his throne, deprived of his divine status, and subjected to the close control of General MacArthur and the forces of occupation. Americans found that, on the surface, at least, the Japanese seemed eager to learn what democacy meant. When the peace was signed in 1952, they had made a promising start on a democracy of the Western type. Their economy—the only well-developed industrial economy in the non-Western world—grew so rapidly that it overtook France and West Germany, to rank third in the world after the United States and the Soviet Union. Industrious, efficient, loyal to their employers, and well educated, the Japanese work force had by the 1970s displaced both West Germany and the United States in many critical areas of the new high technology. German leadership in automobile production (and thus in the use of steel and rubber and independently manufactured components) also passed to the Japanese, the Datsun overtaking the Volkswagen even in the American market. By 1980 the Japanese per capita income, long the highest in Asia, had reached $8,460, only slightly behind that of the United States.

Signs of change and of affluence multiplied. Programs of birth-control education were successful, and the birth rate dropped, to become one of the lowest in the world. Peasants migrated to the cities, especially to Tokyo, which surpassed London and New York as the world's largest city until Mexico City moved past it by 1980. Appalling smog settled over Tokyo, which was linked to Osaka, Japan's second city, by a new high-speed rail line, the fastest in the world. Weekend traffic jams resulted from the rush of Tokyo residents to the beaches in the summer and to the ski slopes in winter. Western styles of dress became customary in urban centers. Japanese tourists became known as the most avid and wealthy in the world as the yen soared in value. Thus, inflation appeared to be the main threat to Japan's continued prosperity and to its social and economic Westernization.

Politically, democratic parliamentary institutions flourished under successive cabinets of the conservative Liberal Democratic party. The left-wing opposition, including both socialists and communists, objected to the mutual security pact binding Japan and the United States after the official restoration of full Japanese sovereignty in 1952.

Anti-Americanism derived in part from resentment over continued United States occupation of the island of Okinawa until 1972, from bitterness over the atomic blasts over Hiroshima and Nagasaki, and from left-wing mistrust of American policy in Vietnam. To these factors in the late 1960s was added a particularly virulent case of student extremism. The Japanese university system—always intensely competitive and therefore full of emotional strain—was now halted for months at a time by armed conflicts between rival groups of students and between radical students and police.

The greatest strain between Japan and the United States arose over Nixon's trip to China in 1972. In going to China, Nixon was shaking the foundations of the special American relationship with Japan. And by failing to let the Japanese know about his plan before the public announcement in 1971, Nixon offended them seriously, leading them to ask whether the Americans were preparing to abandon them. The enormous economic success of the Japanese had stimulated the Chinese fear that Japan would rearm, and Chinese propaganda constantly stressed "renewed Japanese imperialism." To allay this fear, Nixon concealed his plans from the Japanese, hoping that he could later repair the damage.

But the United States followed the same tactics in proclaiming a series of surprising new economic measures. The president freed the dollar from gold, allowing it to float, and imposed a new customs surcharge on foreign goods. Both these measures were damaging to the Japanese, who were forced to revalue their undervalued currency, and whose enormous sales of manufactured goods in the United States would no longer be so profitable. The Japanese continued to feel betrayed despite all efforts to reassure them, and they began a systematic reconsideration of the entire question of Japan's role in international politics. Premier Eisaku

Worldwide, life was becoming better for the masses. Increasingly it was becoming standardized, and increasingly modernization appeared to be Americanization. A major innovation in eating habits—which would influence nutrition, social life, and the economy—was the proliferation of "fast food" enterprises, which by the 1960s had become worldwide chains. Here the Japanese buy "Big Macs" at a McDonald's in Tokyo.

Sato (1901-1975), who had presided over Japan's growth as a world power, now resigned, beginning a period of relative political instability for the island nation. After meeting with Nixon, the new Japanese premier went to Peking in September 1972, and regular Chinese-Japanese diplomatic relations were established. This meant that Japan would no longer recognize the Taiwan government. Upon its formal diplomatic recognition of the People's Republic of China in 1978, the United States also severed relations with Taiwan, leaving this island of eighteen million people isolated and fearful. Thus a complex relationship among Japan, mainland China, and the United States brought a diplomatic revolution and relative stability to East Asia for the first time since World War II.

Alone among the potential great powers of the world, Japan had originally limited its close relations since the war exclusively to the United States. Japan's economic power, combined with a lack of a substantial military force, since the postwar settlement had limited it to self-defense, had proved unique. Protected by the United States, not having to put any substantial part of its national income into arms, prohibited from developing the nuclear capacity for war, Japan had been able to catch up rapidly with its protector. Now the tension between wishing to continue the economic advantages of such protection and the apprehension that such protection was suspect, compounded by the American withdrawal from Vietnam, led the Japanese to explore new initiatives. Yet these initiatives were largely limited to new diplomatic and commercial ventures, including the hope that the two Koreas, so close to Japan, might ease their mutual hostilities. The Japanese also vigorously developed closer trade relations with Australia, becoming that nation's major trading partner, and sent whaling and fishing fleets throughout the Pacific. In 1978 a Japanese-Chinese friendship treaty completed the regularization of relations with the old enemy on the mainland, leaving Japan free to redouble its concentration on improving its already strong world trade position.

South Korea

South Korea had also attempted constitutional government in the Western manner but ran into serious difficulties. After the disruptive Korean War of the early 1950s, the government of Syngman Rhee (1875-1965), South Korean president since 1948, came under mounting criticism for corruption and arbitrary actions. In 1960 massive protests by students forced Rhee out of office and inaugurated a tumultuous period marked, first, by the political intervention of the army and, then, by another attempt at constitutional rule. While the economy boomed during the 1960s, political instability continued, and in 1979 the chief of the Korean CIA assassinated the head of state. Amidst American troop withdrawals by the Carter administration, South Korea again became a police state under martial law. There were, however, signs of hope in the lessening of tensions with North Korea, which though also strongly authoritarian, agreed in 1972 to seek the common goal of reunification of the two states by peaceful means, a goal toward which there had been little movement by the 1980s.

Southeast Asia

Once the Japanese occupation ended in Southeast Asia, the major Western colonial powers found that they could not revert to the prewar status quo. The United States had granted the Philippines independence in 1946. In 1949 the Dutch had to recognize the independence of the Netherlands East Indies as the Republic of Indonesia, with a population of a hundred million people. Britain gave Burma independence outside the Commonwealth (1948) and the Federation of Malaya independence within the Commonwealth (1957). The island of Singapore at the tip of Malaya, with a largely Chinese population, became fully independent in 1965, after a period of union with the former Malaya, now called Malaysia after the addition of certain Borneo territories. Singapore, the fourth greatest port in the world, soon experienced its own economic miracle, attaining the second highest standard of living in Asia, remarkable productivity and stability, and high standards of health, education, and housing under its brilliant long-term prime minister, Lee Kwan Yew (1923-   ), who held office from 1959.

The Dutch in Indonesia had not prepared the people for independence by education. Nevertheless, the Indonesians at first attempted to run their government as a parliamentary democracy. Almost everything went wrong; the economy was crippled by inflation, and by shortages, by administrative corruption and the black market, and by the expulsion of experienced Dutch business leaders. The Muslims, who made up the bulk of the population, proved unable to form stable political parties. The outlying islands of the archipelago, resentful of domination by the island of Java—which contained the capital, Jakarta (the former Batavia), and two-thirds of the population—rebelled against the central government. As the high expectations raised by the achievement of independence were disappointed, President Sukarno (1901-1970), the hero of the Indonesian struggle for independence, urged a "guided democracy" based upon indigenous rather than borrowed political institutions.

Sukarno suspended the ineffectual parliamentary regime in 1956 and 1960 and vested authority in himself and in the army and an appointive council. But "guided democracy" created still more turmoil. Inflation ran wild, necessities vanished from the market, pretentious new government buildings were left unfinished for lack of funds, and all foreign enterprises were confiscated. In external policy, Sukarno initiated an alternating hot and cold war with the new Federation of Malaysia for control of the island of Borneo, where both states had territory. He annexed former Dutch New Guinea (called West Irian by the Indonesians). When the United Nations recognized Malaysia early in 1965, Sukarno withdrew Indonesia from membership; he also rejected United States offers of aid and moved closer to Red China.

A coup planned by Indonesian communists misfired at the last moment in the autumn of 1965; 300,000 local communists were then slaughtered or executed. Anticommunist forces came to power under military leaders, among whom General Suharto (1921-   ) took the lead, becoming president in 1968, reaching a settlement with Malaysia and rejoining the United Nations. Inflation was brought under control, a five-year plan was launched, and parliamentary elections were held in which Suharto was elected in 1973 and 1978. In 1976 Suharto took advantage of civil war in Portuguese Timor to annex that colonial remnant, and a continuing war marked by massacres festered on the island. In the 1980s the military, together with a growing navy, remained the principal source of power in Indonesia, which, in part on the basis of its oil reserves, was again experiencing growth. This vast nation, stretching along the Indian and Pacific oceans on 13,000 islands, with 153,000,000 people—exceeded only by China, India, the Soviet Union, and the United States—held the promise of stability or chaos for Southeast Asia.

India and Pakistan

The Labour victory in Britain in 1945 made the emancipation of India a certainty. But the deep-seated tensions between Muslims and Hindus had assumed critical importance. When the Hindu Congress party and the All-India Muslim League faced the need to draw up a working constitution for the new India, they found themselves in complete disagreement. The Muslims had long been working for separate Hindu and Muslim states, which were in the end reluctantly accepted by the Hindus. In 1947 Hindu India and Muslim Pakistan were set up as separate self-governing dominions within the British Commonwealth.

Pakistan was a state divided into two parts, widely separated by Indian territory—the larger, arid West Pakistan in the northwest, and the smaller, more fertile, and far more densely populated East Pakistan in former East Bengal. The rest of the British Indian Empire and four-fifths of its inhabitants became the Republic of India. Pakistan, with its smaller population and its relatively poorly developed industry, was weaker than India, and at first kept closer political ties with the British.

Violence accompanied partition. It was not possible to draw a boundary that would leave all Hindus in one state and all Muslims in another. Bitter Hindu-Muslim fighting cost hundreds of thousands of lives, as Hindus moved from Pakistani territory into India, and Muslims moved from Indian territory into Pakistan. A particular source of trouble was the mountainous province of Kashmir. Though mainly Muslim in population, it was at the time of partition ruled by a Hindu prince, who turned it over to India. India continued to occupy most of Kashmir, to the economic disadvantage of Pakistan. The United Nations vainly sought to arrange a plebiscite.

In domestic politics the two states went through sharply contrasting experiences. The chief architect of Pakistani independence, Mohammed Ali Jinnah (1876-1948), head of the Muslim League, died shortly after independence. Thereafter Pakistan floundered in its attempts to make parliamentary government work and to solve its pressing economic difficulties. In 1958 the army commander, the British-educated Ayub Khan (1907-), took full power, attacked administrative corruption and the black market, and instituted a program of "basic democracies" to train the population in self-government at the local level and then gradually upward through a pyramid of advisory councils. For a long period Ayub's "basic democracies" proved more workable than Sukarno's "guided democracy." A new constitution in 1962 provided for a national assembly and also for a strengthened presidency, an office that Ayub continued to fill. But as Ayub grew older, charges of corruption were made against his family and his officials, and the depressed peoples of East Bengal protested loudly against policies that discriminated in favor of West Pakistan. Disorder spread, and in 1969 a new military government ousted Ayub.

The tension between West Pakistan, whose Punjabis had a disproportionately large role in the central government, and the underrepresented and miserably poor Bengalis of East Pakistan erupted in civil war in 1971. The East, assisted by India, declared itself independent. As fighting continued, ten million East Pakistanis fled into India, straining to the limit that nation's resources. War between India and Pakistan followed, ending in a pact in 1972. East Pakistan became independent as Bangladesh; West Pakistan, shorn of its eastern portion, turned increasingly toward Islamic nationalism. In 1979 the leader of Pakistan's People's party was executed by military rulers who had taken over in a coup, and the American embassy in the capital of Islamabad was stormed and burned. Even though the nation became more reactionary, the United States—alarmed by the Soviet invasion of Afghanistan begun in 1979 and continuing against guerrilla fighters in the 1980s—concluded a new agreement to provide Pakistan with economic and military aid.

Newly independent India had suffered a grievous loss when Gandhi was assassinated by an anti-Muslim Hindu in 1948. But Jawaharlal Nehru (1889-1964), a seasoned politician, at once assumed leadership. India successfully inaugurated a parliamentary democracy of the Western type. Its hotly fought elections were based on universal suffrage among voters who were mostly illiterate and rural. Understandably, Indians were proud of their accomplishment, though here too India experienced a drift toward authoritarian government. Nehru's daughter, Indira Gandhi (1917-), who became prime minister in 1966, successfully carried India through the war with Pakistan. Feeling that the United States was anti-Indian in the conflict, Mrs. Gandhi signed a twenty-year friendship pact with the Soviet Union in 1971. As the old Congress Party split into two camps, Mrs. Gandhi's New Congress party became less democratic; in 1975 she used the emergency provisions of the Indian constitution to arrest thousands of her opponents and to impose press censorship. However, she did not turn to dictatorship, and in 1977 she was defeated in federal and state elections, in part because of charges of corruption, in part because of a rigorously

imposed and highly unpopular attempt to institute birth-control measures that were repugnant to most Hindus. She was returned to office in 1980.

India faced an acute form of the problem of overpopulation; by 1975 it had over six hundred million people, with a projection of one billion for the year 2000. The threat of famine was always present. In 1950 the government launched the first in a series of five-year plans for economic development, permitting the expansion of private industry but stressing government projects: irrigation and flood control, transport and communications, and especially agricultural education. Low yields could be improved by more fertilizers, by small local irrigation projects, and by modern tools, equipment, and varieties of grain. In the late 1960s a new strain of high-yielding wheat was planted experimentally; the initial results were promising. But the very success of the new foods (the "green revolution") threatened a new form of crisis, as farmers displaced from the countryside by new agricultural techniques flooded into the cities of India, where there was no employment for them. Starvation and political unrest always threatened.

Political controversy also arose over the question of language. There were thirteen major regions in India, each with its own distinctive tongue. Believing that a common language was essential to national identity, the government supported Hindi as the national language, to which it gave official status in 1965. In also recognized English as an associate language, though nationalists deplored this as a concession to colonialism. Yet English proved indispensable, both because of its modern scientific and technical vocabulary, which Hindi could not fully provide, and because it was the only common language of educated Indians, who could not understand one another's tongues. Languages virtually unknown to the West, such as Kannada, were (by example) spoken by twenty-two million people—the population equivalent of Canada. The elevation of Hindi to official status aroused especially strong opposition among the speakers of Tamil in the south, who viewed it as an instrument of the central government's hostility to regional or provincial pride in language and political home rule. The government met the problem by making some concessions but without abandoning its aim.

The debate over the relative weight to be given to industry and agriculture also continued. In 1970 India dedicated a nuclear power plant near Bombay, built with American assistance. Canada helped build two nuclear reactors, and in May 1974 India exploded an underground nuclear device, contrary to its understanding with Canada, which then halted shipments of nuclear equipment. With massive Soviet help, India launched a space satellite in 1975, and the United States and Canada resumed nuclear shipments the next year. India was determined to pursue a path between the West and the Soviet Union, ably playing one against the other, hoping to be dependent on neither. Both superpowers found their relations with other states—notably China,

Pakistan, and all nations that wanted to limit the number of countries that could join the "nuclear club"—severely strained.

The Middle East

In Saudi Arabia, in the small states along the Persian Gulf, and in Iraq and Iran, the Middle East possessed the greatest oil reserves in the world. Developed by European and American companies that paid royalties to the local governments, these oil resources influenced the policies of all the powers. Many of the oil-producing states had banded together in 1960 to form a cartel of Oil Producing and Exporting Countries (OPEC), and they quickly discovered a powerful new weapon in international diplomacy. They used the mechanism of oil pricing and threatened increases both to frighten Western industrial nations dependent on a continued flow of oil and to manipulate Western foreign policies toward Israel. Not all OPEC nations were intent upon ousting Israel from the eastern Mediterranean, and not all OPEC nations were located in the Middle East, since Indonesia, Nigeria, and Venezuela were members, but oil diplomacy and the long hostility between most Arab states and Israel were nonetheless intertwined.

When the British withdrew their forces from Palestine in 1948, the Jews proclaimed the state of Israel and secured its recognition by the United Nations. The Arab nations declared the proclamation illegal and invaded the new state from all directions. Outnumbered but faced by an inefficient enemy, the Israelis won the war. A truce that was not a formal peace was patched together under the auspices of the United Nations in 1949. Israel secured more of Palestine than the UN had proposed, taking over the western part of Jerusalem, the spiritual capital of Judaism—but also of compelling religious importance to Christians and Muslims—a city the UN had proposed to neutralize. However, the eastern part, or "old city" of Jerusalem, including the site of Solomon's Temple, widely known as the Wailing Wall, together with eastern Palestine, remained in the hands of the Arab state of Jordan.

During the 1948 war almost a million Palestinian Arabs fled from Israel to the surrounding Arab states. The United Nations organized a special agency that built camps and gave relief to the refugees, and tried to arrange for their permanent resettlement. The Arab states, however, did not wish to absorb them, and many refugees regarded resettlement as an abandonment of their belief that the Israelis would soon "be pushed into the sea," and that they themselves would then return to their old homes. This problem made the truce of 1949 very delicate, frequently broken in frontier incidents by both sides.

The new state of Israel could not trust its Arab minority, which numbered about 200,000. It continued to admit as many Jewish immigrants as possible, from Europe, North Africa, and Yemen. The welding of these human elements into a single nationality was a formidable task. Much of Israel was mountainous, and some of it was desert. The Israelis applied talents and training derived from the West to make the best use of their limited resources, and they depended on outside aid, especially from their many supporters in the United

By 1983 the OPEC nations were no longer able to hold a common front on oil prices. Sheiks of Kuwait, the United Arab Emirates, Saudi Arabia, and Qatar met to discuss how to maintain the unity of the Persian Gulf states as Western nations were finding alternative sources of oil in the North Sea, Canada, and Mexico.

ROMANIA

Dniester R.

Dnieper R.

CRIMEA

Sea of Azov

BULGARIA

Black Sea

Istanbul

Batum

U.S.S.R.

Caspian Sea

Baku

Dardanelles

GREECE

Ankara

TURKEY

Izmir (Smyrna)

Tabriz

Teheran

Adana

Aleppo

Mosul

CRETE

CYPRUS

Banias

Kirkuk

Kermanshah

Tripoli

SYRIA

Mediterranean Sea

Beirut

Damascus

Baghdad

Isfahan

LEBANON

Sidon

Haifa

IRAQ

ISRAEL

Euphrates R.

Tigris R.

Basra

Port Said

JORDAN

Abadan

Alexandria

Suez Canal

Elat

KUWAIT

Cairo

Persian Gulf

LIBYA

EGYPT

SAUDI

NEUTRAL ZONES

Dhahran

BAHREIN

OMAN

QATAR

Aswan

Red Sea

ARABIA

Abu Dhabi

UNITED ARAB EMIRATES

Medina

Riyadh

Nile R.

Jidda

Mecca

RUB' AL KHALI (EMPTY QUARTER)

OMAN

Port Sudan

SUDAN

Khartoum

Arabian Sea

Asmara

YEMEN

PEOPLE'S DEMOCRATIC REPUBLIC OF YEMEN

ERITREA

AFARS & ISSAS TERR. (Fr.)

Bab el Mandeb

Aden

SOMALI REPUBLIC

ETHIOPIA

Addis Ababa

Inset map:

CYPRUS

Baniyas

Mediterranean Sea

Tripoli

Beirut

LEBANON

Saida (Sidon)

Haifa

SYRIA

ISRAEL

Tel Aviv

Amman

Jerusalem

Port Said

Gaza

Suez Canal

JORDAN

NEGEV

SINAI

EGYPT

Cairo

Nile R.

Gulf of Suez

PEN.

Elath

Aqaba

Gulf of Aqaba

TIRAN

SAUDI ARABIA

Red Sea

N

Legend:

▲ Oilfields

— Pipelines

Arab League

Occupied by Israel, June 1967

The Middle East

461

States. Most Arabs viewed Israel as a new outpost of Western imperialism; therefore, it was difficult for the United States and other Western nations to retain cordial relations with the Arabs, who were in a highly nationalistic phase.

In 1952, less than four years after the Arab defeat in Palestine, revolution broke out in Egypt, where the corrupt monarchy was overthrown by a group of army officers led by Gamal Abdel Nasser (1918-1970). They established a republic, encouraged the emancipation of women, and pared down the role of the conservative religious courts. Only one party was tolerated, elections were closely supervised, and press campaigns were orchestrated by a Ministry of National Guidance. As an enemy of the West, which he associated not only with colonialism but with support for Israel, Nasser turned for aid to the Russians. Czechoslovak and Russian arms flowed into Egypt, and Russian technicians followed. Nasser was determined to take the lead in uniting the disunited Arab world to destroy Israel.

Nasser's chief showpiece of revolutionary planning was to be a new high dam on the Nile at Aswan. He had expected the United States to contribute largely to its construction, but in mid-1956 John Foster Dulles, Eisenhower's secretary of state, told Nasser that the United States had changed its mind. In retaliation, Nasser nationalized the Suez Canal, previously operated by a Franco-British company, and announced that he would use the revenues thus obtained to build the dam. For several months, contrary to expectations, the new Egyptian management kept canal traffic moving smoothly. The French and British governments, however, concealing their intentions from the United States, determined to teach Nasser a lesson, and secretly allied themselves with Israel.

In the fall of 1956 Israeli forces invaded Egyptian territory, and French and British troops landed at Suez. The Israeli operations were skillful and successful; the British and French blundered badly. The Soviet Union threatened to send "volunteers" to defend Egypt, even though Soviet troops were at the very moment of the Suez crisis engaged in putting down the Hungarian revolution. Nor did the United States, angry at its British and French allies for concealing their plans, give its support. With the United States and the Soviet Union on the same side of an issue for once, the United Nations condemned the British-French-Israeli attack, and eventually a United Nations force was moved into the Egyptian-Israeli frontier areas, while the canal, blocked by the Egyptians, was reopened and finally bought by Nasser.

Nasser experienced some disillusion with Russia during the summer of 1958, when revolution broke out in Iraq, where Soviet-sponsored communists were oppos-

In 1956 three neutralist leaders met in Brioni, Yugoslavia: Gamal Abdel Nasser, president of the United Arab Republic; Jawaharlal Nehru, prime minister of India; and Josip Broz Tito, president of Yugoslavia.

ing Nasser's own pan-Arab aims. Prompt American intervention in Lebanon and British intervention in Jordan temporarily countered the threat of the spread of Soviet influence. The Russians provided the aid that eventually made possible the high dam at Aswan and much armament for the Egyptian armies, but thereafter Nasser remained unaligned with either major bloc.

After the Suez crisis, Nasser's economic policy was governed by the grim struggle to support a fast-growing population (the birth rate in Egypt was double that in the United States). He undertook programs to reclaim land from the desert by exploiting underground water, and to limit the size of landholdings for redistribution to landless peasants. To provide more jobs and to bolster national pride, he also accelerated the pace of industrialization, often at very high cost. Most foreign enterprises in Egypt were nationalized.

In 1967 Nasser demanded that the United Nations troops that had kept the Egyptians and Israelis separated since 1956 be removed. UN Secretary General U Thant complied. The Egyptians began a propaganda barrage against Israel and closed the Strait of Tiran, the only water access to the newly developed Israeli port of Elath. The Israelis then struck the first blow in a new war, destroying the Egyptian air force on the ground and also hitting at the air forces of the other Arab states. In six days they overran the Sinai peninsula, all of Palestine west of the Jordan, including the Jordanian portion of Jerusalem, and the Golan heights on their northern frontier with Syria, from which the Syrians had been launching raids for several years. This third Arab-Israeli war in nineteen years ended in an all-out Israeli victory.

It was a humiliation not only for Nasser, but for the Soviet Union, which had supplied much of the equipment that had been abandoned as the Egyptian army retreated. The Russians moved vigorously to support the Arab position, arguing their case in the United Nations, transferring token naval forces to the Mediterranean, denouncing Israel, and rearming Egypt. Israeli armies remained in control of all the territory they had occupied. Had negotiations begun soon after the war, much of this territory could perhaps have been recovered, but as time passed the Israeli attitude hardened, and it became difficult for any Israeli government to give up any part of Jerusalem or the Golan heights, whose possession ensured Israeli territory against Syrian attack. Sinai, the Gaza strip, and perhaps the West Bank of the Jordan might be negotiable.

But the Arabs, led by Nasser, refused to negotiate directly with the Israelis or to take any step that would recognize the existence of the state of Israel. Rearmed and partly retrained by the Russians, the Egyptians repeatedly proclaimed their intention of renewing the war. Israel existed as an armed camp, its men and women serving equally in the military forces, ever prepared for an attack. The Suez Canal, blocked again, was now less crucial because of the development of huge oil tankers that went around the Cape of Good Hope, transporting oil more cheaply because of their great

capacity. Perhaps the most important result of the war of 1967, however, was not the Israeli victory but the naval bases that the Soviets had gained at Alexandria and in Algeria, giving them a firmer position in the Mediterranean than ever before.

In 1969 and 1970 tension again mounted dangerously in the Middle East. Arab Palestinians organized guerrilla attacks on Israel or on Israeli-occupied territory from Jordan, Syria, and Lebanon. The Lebanese government—precariously balanced between Christians and Muslims and hitherto a moderating influence among the Arab regimes in the area—was threatened by the Palestinian guerrillas and forced to concede Lebanese territory nearest the Israeli frontier. In various airports—Zurich, Athens, Tel Aviv—terrorists attacked planes carrying Israelis, and Israel tried to avenge such murderous acts and prevent their recurrence by such measures as a parachutists' raid on the Beirut airport. At times the Palestinian Arab terrorist movement took on the aspects of an independent power, negotiating with the Chinese, compelling Nasser to modify his pronouncements, and demanding that its leaders be heard in the United Nations. In the autumn of 1970 terrorists hijacked four large planes—Swiss, British, German, and American—in a single day, holding the passengers as hostages in Jordan for the release of certain captives of their own. During the tense negotiations that followed, full-scale hostilities broke out between the Arab guerrillas and the Jordanian government. The Syrians intervened on the side of the guerrillas, and the threat of American intervention on the side of Jordan's King Hussein (1935-   ) and of a Soviet response was suddenly very real. Jordanian successes, Syrian withdrawal, and American and Soviet restraint helped the critical moment pass. The Arab guerrillas could no longer use Jordanian territory.

Just as grave was the continual Arab-Israeli confrontation in Egypt. Here Egyptian raids across the Suez Canal into Israeli-occupied territory in the Sinai were followed by Israeli commando raids into Egyptian territory on the west side of the canal and by Israeli air raids deep into Egypt. During 1970 the installation of Soviet missile sites near the canal forced the suspension of the Israeli attacks. But the Soviet involvement in Egyptian defense also threatened open confrontation between the Soviet Union and the United States. To avoid this danger and to create a situation in which the Russian military could be withdrawn from Egypt without forcing the Russians to lose face, the United States, Britain, and France held four-power discussions with the Russians on the Arab-Israeli conflict. With the Russians totally committed to the Arab side and the French increasingly pro-Arab, with Britain balancing between the two sides, and with the United States trying to help Israel but determined to avoid another entanglement like Vietnam, the Israelis regarded with skepticism the possibility of any favorable solution emerging from the big powers' discussions, and firmly insisted that only direct talks between themselves and the Arabs could lead to a satisfactory settlement. Arab insistence that a return of all occupied territory must precede any discussions rendered such meetings impossible. In the summer of 1970, however, the Egyptians and Israelis agreed to a cease-fire. But as hopes were renewed that discussions might at least begin, President Nasser died suddenly, to be replaced by Mohammed Anwar el-Sadat (1918-1981), who pledged himself to regain all occupied territories.

But Sadat surprised the world. He became suspicious of Russian intentions, as their military and technical advisers grew increasingly arrogant, and in 1972 he expelled them from Egypt. Determined to regain Egypt's lost lands, he attacked Israeli-held territory, in concert with Syrian forces, on the Jewish holy day of Yom Kippur in October 1973. For the first time the Israelis, whose military intelligence was among the best in the world, were caught by surprise, and the Egyptians inflicted heavy losses. An Israeli counterattack turned the Egyptians back, however, and in November a truce was signed in the Sinai by the government of Israel's able prime minister, Golda Meir (1898-1978). Oil diplomacy now demonstrated its force. At the outbreak of the war, the Arab oil-producing states cut off the flow to Europe and the United States to force the West to bring pressure on Israel. While Americans had alternative, though expensive, sources of supply, many European nations had none, and the Arabs' policy had the desired response of pressure on Israel, though exerted more tentatively than they had hoped.

Sadat, however, was disturbed by the ultimate failure of the Egyptian attack and convinced that his people needed relief from constant conflict. In 1977 he committed himself personally and with great courage to achieving Egyptian-Israeli peace. Flying to Israel, he addressed the parliament and met with the new Israeli prime minister, Menachim Begin (1913-   ). Begin had taken a particularly hard line on all issues relating to the Arab states, including the question of a homeland for the Palestinians. Though immediately condemned by most Arab states, Sadat persevered, and both he and Begin later accepted an invitation to meet with the American president, Jimmy Carter, at Camp David outside Washington. There a series of accords were worked out in September 1978 as the basis for future negotiations on a wide range of Middle Eastern questions.

But the "spirit of Camp David" did not last. The Arab states refused to join Egypt in negotiations. The Palestine Liberation Organization (PLO), as the principal spokesman for the Palestinian refugees, mounted an increased terrorist campaign, combined with demonstrations of the growing desperation felt by the homeless Palestinians. PLO leader Yasir Arafat (1929-   ), helped by oil diplomacy and western disenchantment with Begin's tough bargaining positions, began to make inroads into Western support for Israel. Then three blows disrupted the delicate peace once again. In October 1981 Sadat was assassinated in Cairo by Muslim extremists. Two months later the Israeli parliament annexed the Golan heights, while Europe and the United States were distracted by the Solidarity crisis in Poland. Charges of bad

faith—since the United States believed that Begin had promised there would be no such annexation—drove a wedge between the new Reagan administration and Israel. Then in 1982 the long-explosive situation in Lebanon was ignited.

Determined to drive the Palestinians out of south Lebanon, which they used as a base for raids on Israel, the Israeli army had previously staged a massive invasion in 1978 and had withdrawn in favor of a United Nations peace-keeping force. However, Israel continued to aid Christian forces in Lebanon, as it had done in 1975-1976 during the Lebanese civil war. A second Israeli occupation of southern Lebanon occurred in 1980 in retaliation for a raid on a *kibbutz* (Israeli collectivist agricultural settlement). Israel next declared Jerusalem to be its capital, despite the embarrassment this would cause Western powers, who generally kept their embassies in Tel Aviv. In response to an Israeli attack on Syrian helicopters, Syria moved Soviet-built surface-to-air missiles into Lebanon. In June 1981 an Israeli air strike on an Iraqi atomic reactor near Baghdad, without previous consultation with Western nations, was widely condemned even by Israel's friends. Israel, long the underdog in the Middle East, was now deliberately, or through poor judgment, cast in the role of the aggressor at a time when oil diplomacy made it vulnerable to a loss of support in the Western democracies.

Even though the new Egyptian leader, Hosni Mubarak (1929-   ), stood by the spirit of Camp David, the Arab-Israeli conflict continued to make the Middle East the world's most unstable region. Begin, narrowly reelected in 1981, was determined not to appease the Palestinians. Having in his youth been a leader of a terrorist group against the British, Begin was unwilling to weaken his stance now. In the fall of 1982 he and his military advisers decided that they must at last clear the Palestinians out of all of Lebanon. After they mounted a massively destructive attack on the city of Beirut, support for Israel in the West declined even further. In September 1982, in the immediate aftermath of the destruction of Beirut, a Lebanese Christian Phalangist militia was allowed—probably with Israeli knowledge, and clearly without sufficient Israeli supervision—to move into two large Palestinian refugee camps and massacre men, women, and children. As the world learned of the slaughter, Israel found itself on the defensive even with its staunchest supporters.

The conflict in the Middle East had been marked by unremitting terrorism, by attack and counterattack, by escalation and miscalculation; because of television this violence was made known daily to the Western world. Massacre, always horrible, is nonetheless frequent in time of war, as Americans had learned at My Lai, in South Vietnam, where American soldiers had killed three hundred unresisting civilians. Britain had massacred Indians at Amritsar, and persistent massacres during the Congolese civil war, and by Ugandan dictator Idi Amin (1925-   ) between 1972 and 1979 had accustomed the public to the spectacle of widespread and indiscriminate killing. Even as Israel moved to institute a full inquiry into the killings at the Lebanese camp, tensions ran high in Israel and throughout the world. The investigating commission found several top Israeli military and government officials "indirectly responsible," which led to their demotion or dismissal. Weary and in poor health, Begin resigned in October 1983.

Iraq, at first closely aligned with the British after World War II, had ousted its monarchy and proclaimed a republic in 1958. Extremists of the left and right thereafter subjected the country to a series of coups and abortive coups. Rebellious Kurdish tribes in the northern mountains contributed to the disorder, which resulted in the abrupt slackening of economic development after 1958. In 1969 and 1970 Iraq developed the most terror-ridden regime of the Arab states, publicly executing from time to time amid general celebration its resident Jews or members of earlier Iraqi governments on charges of working for Israel or the American CIA. In 1979 Iraq carried its war against the Kurds into Iran, bombing Kurdish villages there. In 1980 Iraq and Iran went to war.

Africa

The rebellion against imperialism reached Africa in the 1950s, although there had long been ominous rumblings, such as an uprising in 1947 on the island of Madagascar, which the French had bloodily suppressed. Ethiopia was taken from its Italian conquerors after the war and restored to Emperor Haile Selassie, who had been ousted in 1935; in 1952 he annexed the former Italian colony of Eritrea. Selassie embarked on various programs of internal modernization though not liberalization, and he worked hard to assist in the development of the Organization of African Unity. However, like the shah of Iran, he misjudged both the speed and the nature of his reforms. As serious droughts took thousands of lives in the early 1970s, Selassie's suppression of all political parties that might have provided a response to the emergency led to widespread disillusionment with the aging emperor. An army mutiny, strikes in Ethiopia's cities, and massive student demonstrations in the capital, Addis Ababa, led to his imprisonment in 1974. The military junta then turned to local Marxists and the Soviet Union for support. In 1978 Soviet advisers and twenty thousand Cuban troops helped rout a Somalian independence force; in the same year a plague of locusts took an estimated million lives by famine. Now governed by a provisional military administrative council, Ethiopia was clearly far worse off in the 1980s than it had been under Selassie's autocratic rule before the revolution.

Among the Muslim and Arabic-speaking states bordering the Mediterranean, the former Italian colony of Libya achieved independence in 1951, and the French-dominated areas of Morocco and Tunisia in 1956. Morocco became an autocratic monarchy and Tunisia a republic under the moderate presidency of Habib Bourguiba (1903-   ), a veteran nationalist leader educated at the Sorbonne. Algeria followed, but only after a severe and debilitating war of independence against the French. Its first ruler after independence, Ahmed Ben Bella (1916-   ), was allied with the Chinese communists. Colonel Houari Boumédienne (1925-1981), who ousted Ben Bella in 1965, in large part because of the slumping economy, favored the Russians. Algeria and Libya strongly supported the Arab cause against Israel; Morocco and Tunisia did so hardly at all. Bourguiba occasionally called for a reasonable accommodation between Arabs and Israelis.

In Libya a colonels' coup d'état in 1969 brought to power a group of army officers who modeled their movement on Nasser's. In 1970 they confiscated Italian- and Jewish-owned property. American evacuation of a huge air base in Libya and Libyan purchases of French and Soviet arms added to the general apprehension in North Africa. A temporary "union" of Egypt, Libya, and the Sudan in 1970 had little political importance, but it marked the emergence of Colonel Muammar el-Qaddafi (1942-   ), the Libyan political boss and prime minister, as the most fanatic Muslim fundamentalist and most dictatorial ruler in the Arab world. He was also one of the richest, and he used his oil riches to instigate rebellion and political assassination throughout the Arab world, reaching out to the streets of Rome, Paris, and London with hired killers to eliminate Libyan exiles who might attempt to oppose him. After 1975 he purchased billions of dollars worth of modern Russian arms and became the supplier to terrorist groups in much of the world. Mercurial and unpredictable, Qaddafi waged border wars against Egypt in 1977 and Chad in 1977-1979. In 1980 he conscripted civil servants into his army, casting the economy into chaos and paralyzing administration.

South of the Muslim tier of nations lay the former colonies of the French, British, and Belgians. The West African climate had discouraged large-scale white settlement, except in portions of the Belgian Congo; but in East Africa—in Kenya and Uganda especially—many Europeans had settled in the fertile highlands, farmed the land, and regarded the country as their own, as did the large white population of the Union of South Africa. Here too were substantial Indian populations, usually small merchants, who carried on trade across the Indian Ocean.

In the areas with little white settlement, independence came quickly. The Gold Coast, with a relatively well-educated population and valuable economic resources, became the nation of Ghana in 1957. Its leader, the American-educated Kwame Nkrumah (1909-1972), the pioneer of African emancipation, made a hopeful start on economic planning within a political democracy. But he grew increasingly dictatorial, jailing his political enemies and sponsoring grandiose projects that personally enriched him and his followers. A promising democracy became a dictatorship in the 1960s, while the economy was in serious disarray, the Ghanaian foreign debt having mounted from $16.8 million in 1959 to $853.5 million in 1966. This trend, and Nkrumah's inability to persuade the rich and populous Asante people to submerge themselves in a greater Ghanaian nationalism, led to his overthrow by a military coup early in 1966. Nkrumah went into exile in nearby Guinea and continued to oppose the austerity program by which the new government tried to bring Ghana back to economic stability. One election and three coups later, however, Ghana remained economically stagnant and overpopulated.

The French colonies all achieved independence in 1960, except for Guinea, which broke away in 1958 under the leadership of a pro-Russian, Ahmed Sekou Touré (1922-   ). After independence, most of the colonies retained close economic ties with France as members of the French Community. Guinea did not; the French left in 1958, and the country virtually came to a stop. The neighboring states of Mali (formerly French Sudan) and Mauritania also pursued a general pro-Russian line. In the late 1960s Touré began to regret his economic dependence on the Russians, for he accepted United States and World Bank loans to finance a major bauxite mining complex.

Of the newly independent former French colonies, two proved especially important. Senegal was under the able leadership of Leopold Senghor (1906-   ), a noted poet who spoke of the beauties of negritude, helping give rise to the slogan "black is beautiful" around the world. The Ivory Coast, whose leader Félix Houphouët-Boigny (1905-   ) had long parliamentary experience as a deputy in Paris, also proved to be stable and prosperous. The Ivory Coast led a pro-Western bloc within the Organization of African Unity, while Senegal often played the role of intermediary between factions, developing a multi-party system and full democratic elections at home.

In 1960 Nigeria, most important of the British colonies, achieved independence. With sixty million people and varied economic resources, it represented a great hope for the future. The British had trained many thousands of Nigerians in England and in schools and universities in Nigeria itself. The country was divided into four regions, each semiautonomous, to ease tribal tensions, of which perhaps the most severe was that between the Muslim Hausa of the northern region and the Ibo of the eastern region. In the Hausa areas, the well-educated, aggressive, and efficient Ibos ran the railroads, power stations, and other modern facilities, and formed an important element in the cities. When army plotters led by an Ibo officer murdered the Muslim prime minister of Nigeria and seized power in 1966, the Hausas rose and massacred the Ibos living in the north, killing many thousands, while others escaped in disorder to their native east.

By 1967 the Ibo east had seceded and called itself the Republic of Biafra, and the Nigerian central government embarked on full-scale war to force the Ibos and other eastern groups to return to Nigerian rule. Misery and famine accompanied the operations, and the war dragged on until 1970, with both Britain and the Soviet Union helping the Nigerian government. The Biafrans got much sympathy but no real help, except from the

NKRUMAH ON AFRICAN UNITY

For a time Kwame Nkrumah's was the major voice calling for African unity. Well after he established a one-party socialist state in Ghana, he attacked neocolonialism, arguing that Europe had systematically underdeveloped Africa and was responsible for most of its economic woes:

Every state emerging from colonialism has to face, sooner or later, the threat to its independence of an alliance between local, reactionary elements and imperialist and neo-colonialist interests. The problem is serious, but not insurmountable, once its true nature is assessed and adequate steps are taken in time to prevent it from becoming deep-rooted.

We must be constantly vigilant. Imperialist intelligence organizations are hard at work in Africa, manipulating political pressures internally and externally within developing, independent states. Evidence of their activities may be seen in the conspiracies, subversions, coups and assassinations hitherto virtually outside our political experience. . . .

Government officials, police and army officers, party leaders, newspaper editors and others have been bribed and blackmailed. Local bourgeois reactionaries, dishonest intellectuals and retrogressive chiefs are being used to subvert progressive governments. The tragedy is that some African Heads of State are themselves actually aiding and abetting imperialists and neo-colonialists.

In Africa, the resistance of the masses to imperial aggression grows daily. African freedom and unity have become their watchwords. In that alone lies their fulfillment. The higher the level of a people's political awareness, the greater is their understanding of their historical mission. Africa is ripe for armed revolution.

Kwame Nkrumah, *Dark Days in Ghana* (New York: International Publishers, 1968), pp. 157-58.

DECOLONIZATION

In addressing the Houses of Parliament of South Africa on February 3, 1960, British Prime Minister Harold Macmillan (1894-   ) spoke of the "winds of change" he felt blowing across Africa, then the last bastion of empire. His address is usually taken to mark the Conservative party's acceptance of full decolonization, which began with great rapidity the following year. That Macmillan chose South Africa for his address was significant, since that nation was already independent, though its large black majority clearly was not:

Ever since the breakup of the Roman Empire one of the constant facts of political life in Europe has been the emergence of independent nations. They have come into existence over the centuries in different forms with different kinds of government. But all have been inspired by a deep, keen feeling of nationalism, which has grown as the nations have grown.

In the twentieth century, and especially since the end of the war, the processes which gave birth to the nation states of Europe have been repeated all over the world. We have seen the awakening of national consciousness in peoples who have for centuries lived in dependence on some other power. Fifteen years ago this movement spread through Asia. Many countries there, of different races and civilisations, pressed their claim to an independent national life. Today the same thing is happening in Africa.

The most striking of all the impressions I have formed since I left London a month ago is of the strength of this African national consciousness. In different places it may take different forms. But it is happening everywhere. The wind of change is blowing through this Continent.

Whether we like it or not, this growth of national consciousness is a political fact. We must all accept it as a fact. . . .

Harold Macmillan.

Nicholas Mansergh, ed., *Documents and Speeches on Commonwealth Affairs, 1952-1962* (London: Oxford University Press, 1963), p. 347.

French, who were interested in future oil concessions. When the war finally ended, the mass slaughter that had been feared did not materialize, and the nation devoted its energies to reconciliation and recovery. The most important nation in black Africa, Nigeria was able to use its growing oil revenues for economic development. In 1979 it nationalized the holdings of the primary private enterprise involved, British Petroleum. In the same year it returned to civilian government after thirteen years of military rule.

In east Africa, the British settlers in Kenya struggled for eight years (1952-1960) against a secret terrorist society formed within the Kikuyu tribe, the Mau Mau, whose aim was to drive all whites out of the country. Though the British imprisoned one of its founders, Jomo Kenyatta (1893-1978), who had studied at the University of Moscow, and eventually suppressed the Mau Mau with far more loss of life to black Kenyans than to British settlers, Kenya became independent in 1963. Kenyatta became its first chief of state and steered Kenya into prosperity and a generally pro-Western stance. In 1961 under the leadership of Julius Nyerere (1922-   ), educated at Edinburgh, Tanganyika became independent. A violent pro-Chinese communist coup d'état on the island of Zanzibar was followed in 1964 by its merger with Tanganyika as the new country of Tanzania. Nyerere, who had been pro-Western, thereafter became notably more neutralist. He solicited assistance from Communist China to build the Tanzam railroad from Dar es Salaam, the Tanzanian capital, to Zambia, to help that new nation achieve greater economic independence from South Africa. Nyerere also nationalized the banks, established vast new cooperative villages to stimulate more productive agriculture, and sought to play a major role in holding African nations to a neutralist course. Efforts to create an East African federation failed, as Kenyatta pursued a generally capitalist path, Nyerere a socialist one, and Uganda an intensely

Africa

- Independent
- French
- Portuguese
- Spanish
- Member countries of the British Commonwealth
- Member countries of the French Community

Dates indicate year of independence

Eritrea: united with Ethiopia in 1952

Atlantic Ocean

Mediterranean Sea

MOROCCO 1956

Ifni

WESTERN SAHARA

ALGERIA 1962

TUNISIA 1956

LIBYA 1951

EGYPT

0   500   1000
Miles

Red Sea

MAURITANIA 1960

MALI 1960

NIGER 1960

CHAD 1960

SUDAN 1956

ERITREA

AFARS & ISSAS TERRITORY (Fr.)

SENEGAL 1960

GAMBIA 1965

GUINEA BISSAU 1975

GUINEA 1958

SIERRA LEONE 1961

LIBERIA

UPPER VOLTA 1960

IVORY COAST 1960

GHANA 1957

TOGO 1960

BENIN 1960

NIGERIA 1960

CENTRAL AFRICAN REPUBLIC 1960

ETHIOPIA

SOMALI REPUBLIC 1960

EQUATORIAL GUINEA 1968

CAMEROON 1960

GABON 1960

1960

CONGO

Congo River

ZAIRE 1960

RWANDA 1962

BURUNDI 1962

UGANDA 1962

KENYA 1963

CABINDA (Angola)

ANGOLA 1975

ZAMBIA 1964

TANZANIA 1964

ZANZIBAR (Tanzania)

SEYCHELLES 1976

MALAWI 1964

NAMIBIA

ZIMBABWE 1980

MOZAMBIQUE 1975

MADAGASCAR 1960

MAURITIUS 1968

BOTSWANA 1966

Venda

SWAZILAND 1968

1966

REPUBLIC OF SOUTH AFRICA

Baphuthatswana

LESOTHO

TRANSKEI

nationalist and isolationist policy under Amin, before he was overthrown by Ugandan exiles and Tanzanian troops in 1979.

In contrast to the British, who had tried to prepare the way for African independence by providing education and administrative experience for Africans, the Belgians, who had since the late nineteenth century governed the huge central African area known as the Congo, had made no such effort. When the Belgian rulers suddenly pulled out in 1960, leaving a wholly artificial parliamentary structure, it was not long before regional rivalries among local leaders broke out. A popular leftist leader, Patrice Lumumba (1925-1961), was assassinated (the Russians named their university for Africans in Moscow after him); the province of Katanga, site of rich copper mines with many European residents, seceded under its local leader, who was strongly pro-Belgian; other areas revolted. The United Nations sent troops to restore order and force the end of the

Katangese secession, while the Chinese supported certain rebel factions and the South Africans and Belgians others. By 1968 the military regime of General Joseph Mobutu (1930-   ) was firmly in control. Soon after, Mobutu renamed the cities and people of his country to erase all traces of the colonial past: the Congo became Zaire, and he changed his own name to its African form, Mobutu Sese Seko.

The Congolese troubles overflowed the borders of the Congo into Portuguese Angola to the south, where a local rebellion, at first supplied from the Congo, forced Portuguese military intervention. Angola, which provided Portugal with much of its oil, together with Mozambique on the east coast and the tiny enclave of Portuguese Guinea on the west, remained under Lisbon's control despite guerrilla uprisings. The Portuguese regarded these countries as overseas extensions of metropolitan Portugal. But the guerrilla war proved expensive and unpopular at home, and in the mid-1970s

Portugal abandoned Africa. Thereafter Angola became a center for African liberation groups aimed at South Africa. The Angolan government invited in many thousands of Cuban troops, to the dismay of the United States.

Most stubborn of all African problems was the continuation and extension of the policy of apartheid in South Africa, where whites were a minority of about one in five of the population. The nonwhites included blacks, "coloureds" (as those of mixed European and African ancestry were called), and Asians, mostly Indians, who were usually shopkeepers.

The Afrikaners, who had tried unsuccessfully to keep South Africa from fighting on Britain's side in World War II, had emerged after the war as a political majority. Imbued with an extremely narrow form of Calvinist religion that taught that God had ordained the inferiority of blacks, the ruling group moved steadily to impose policies of rigid segregation: separate townships to live in, separate facilities, no political equality, little opportunity for higher education or advancement into the professions, and frequent banning of black leaders. Supported by some of the English residents who were fearful that the black upheaval to the north would spread to South Africa, the Afrikaners also introduced emergency laws making it possible to arrest people on suspicion, hold them incommunicado, and punish them without trial. Severe censorship prevailed, and dissent was curbed. In 1949, in defiance of the United Nations, South Africa annexed the former German colony and League mandate of South-West Africa, where the policy of apartheid also prevailed. The International Court of Justice in 1971 ruled that South Africa was holding the area illegally; by 1983 South Africa had relented under UN and American pressure and was preparing the former mandate for independence as Namibia.

One possible solution to the Afrikaner problem—how to maintain segregation, prevent rebellion by the black majority, assure South Africa of a continuing labor force, and satisfy world opinion—seemed to be a combination of modest liberalization of the apartheid laws and the establishment of partially self-governing territories, known as Homelands, to which black Africans would be sent. Begun in 1959 as *Bantustans*, or Bantu nations, the plan called for pressing most blacks onto 13 percent of the country's land area. Virtually no African nation would support such a plan, and much of the West was also opposed, though until the 1970s Portugal stood by South Africa, as did Rhodesia after its unilateral declaration of independence in 1965. The United States equivocated. It saw South Africa as a strategically important potential ally in case of war with the Soviet Union, and appreciated its staunch anticommunist position on world affairs, but it also realized that any unqualified support to the South African regime would cost the United States nearly the whole of black Africa and would also be opposed at home. Thus when South Africa finally created its first allegedly independent Homelands—the Transkei in 1976, Bophuthatswana in 1977, and Venda in 1979—not one nation, including the United States, gave them diplomatic recognition. However, the South African government appeared secure in the 1980s, with an efficient and well-equipped military force, an able Bureau for State Security (mockingly called BOSS), a viable if weakening economy, and the support of many white South Africans for the very gradual liberalization that was being extended to Asians and "coloureds," though denied to blacks throughout the republic.

Latin America

Although most of the Latin American republics had by 1945 enjoyed political independence for more than a century, they had much in common economically and socially with the emerging nations of Asia and Africa. Like the Asians and Africans, the Latin Americans had been suppliers of foods and raw materials to the rest of the world. Bananas, coffee, sugar, beef, oil, nitrates, and copper fluctuated widely in price on the world market; before the Latin Americans could raise their standards of living, they would have to build on a more stable and diversified economic base. Most of Latin America had a racially mixed population: some native-born whites or immigrants from Europe (like the Italians in Argentina), some descendents of the indigenous Indians, and some blacks (chiefly in Brazil and Haiti). Nominally governed under a democratic system of elected officials and parliaments, they had all too often lived under military dictatorships that shifted whenever a new army officer felt strong enough to challenge the one in power.

Latin Americans traditionally felt a mixture of envy, dislike, and suspicion toward the United States. Upper-class Latin Americans educated in Europe believed that North Americans lacked true culture; North Americans generally seemed to know little about Latin America. Whenever the United States ceased to be indifferent and devoted some attention to Latin America, it did so by intervening in their affairs. Upper-class Latin Americans were well aware of the miserable poverty in which most of their people lived, but they hoped that social revolution would not disturb the system. They were fearful of the periodic North American attempts at reform in Latin America, and on the whole they preferred that the United States leave them alone. Thus, when President Carter applied his test of "human rights" to the authoritarian regimes of South America, they were deeply resentful and confused as well, since they believed themselves to be committed anticommunists.

Some earlier attempts—President Franklin Roosevelt's "Good Neighbor" policy after 1932 and the Pan American Union in 1910—were primarily cultural in emphasis. After World War II the Pan-American Union became the Organization of American States (OAS). Somewhat looser than an alliance, the OAS provided a means for consultation among all the American nations on all important matters of mutual concern. The United States was accused by its enemies of having forged just another instrument of its imperialistic policies, yet OAS did in fact enable all the American states (except Canada, which did not join) a chance to reach joint decisions. The Alliance for Progress—launched under President Kennedy and designed to enable the United States to help the Latin Americans to help themselves—proved a disappointment, in part because it was difficult to allay Latin American suspicions of American intentions, in part because of the deeply entrenched ruling families that dominated most Latin American countries.

Not every Latin American country was invariably a dictatorship, however. Uruguay, for example, a small country with a population largely European in origin, had created a welfare state more advanced even than the Scandinavian countries or Britain—so advanced that the Uruguayan economy by 1970 collapsed, largely because of the payment of state funds to individual citizens for the many types of benefits available. The eroding economy gave the terrorist Tupamaros an opportunity to win some support, and in 1974 the military succeeded in defeating the Tupamaros at the cost of imposing a virtual military dictatorship on Uruguay. Venezuela, with rapidly developing oil resources, in 1959 ousted the

Much of Latin America was in upheaval in the 1960s. In Venezuela a week of revolt in June 1962 left twelve hundred casualties. Rebel marines had seized the naval base at Puerto Cabello, sixty miles from the national capital of Caracas. Under sniper fire, a navy chaplain is shown here giving final rites to a dying soldier.

last of a long line of military dictators and made the transition to moderate democratic rule. As a member of OPEC, Venezuela moved in the 1970s into an era of prosperity and stability.

Colombia underwent a lengthy terrorist campaign in the countryside—virtually a civil war—in which many thousands were killed, and even when this ended was still experiencing extremes of wealth and poverty. Brazil, the enormous Portuguese-speaking land larger than any other Latin American country, suffered from recurrent economic crises and military coups. Its poverty-stricken northeast, where many thousands lived in virtual serfdom on big plantations, contrasted sharply with the luxurious apartment-house and beach life of the big cities; but these too had their festering slums. Brazilian government was a tight military dictatorship that stood accused of torturing its political prisoners.

Chile too was plagued by military intervention. In 1970 Chileans elected a Marxist, Salvador Allende Gossens (1908-1973), as president. Though Allende was a minority president, having won less than 40 percent of the votes, he took office in relative calm and moved gradually to expropriate foreign properties. But some of his supporters felt he was not nationalizing rapidly enough, and the United States feared that he would not provide just compensation for the properties he expropriated. In a still controversial series of events in which the American CIA and possibly the International Telephone and Telegraph Corporation were involved, the Allende administration was toppled by a military coup in September 1973. By then the economy was in chaos, whether from Allende's poor planning or from deliberate sabotage by right-wing enemies of his regime. The military junta declared that it would exterminate Marxism, and it resorted to mass arrests and kidnappings. The economy did not improve, and charges of American complicity in the military's oppressive measures further damaged the United States' image in Latin America.

Argentina—peopled almost entirely by European immigrants and their descendants and dependent on the export of beef and grain to Europe—continued to have a social system that gave power to a small landlord class. The beginnings of industrialization, and especially the growth of the capital city, Buenos Aires, into a great metropolis of nearly five million, increased the numbers of working-class and middle-class people and deepened popular dissatisfaction with the regime. Brought to power in the national election of 1946, Colonel Juan Perón (1895-1974) became a dictator on the model of Mussolini, Hitler, and Franco. In 1955 he was removed by a military coup. He had begun to appeal to the poorer masses, the *descamisados* ("shirtless ones"), and thus lost much of his following among the conservative upper classes. Moveover, he had quarreled with the Roman Catholic church and put through anticlerical measures that cost him further support. Nor could he solve the grave economic and financial problems arising out of his country's essentially colonial position; indeed, his ex-

A NEW REVOLUTIONARY PHILOSOPHY

Fidel Castro and Ernesto Che Guevara were the activists of the Cuban revolution, and Guevara was an emissary to revolutionary groups throughout Latin America, where the Cuban leaders hoped to create similar rebellions. Less known was the theoretician of Marxist revolution for those Latin American states, a young French philosopher, Régis Debray (1942-1969). Debray sought to provide a handbook for guerrilla warfare and revolution that marked out a path to goals that, by being neither Russian nor Chinese, would be especially applicable to the situation in Central America in particular:

The armed revolutionary struggle encounters specific conditions on each continent, in each country, but these are neither "natural" nor obvious. So true is this that in each case years of sacrifice are necessary in order to discover and acquire an awareness of them. The Russian Social Democrats instinctively thought in terms of repeating the Paris Commune in Petrograd; the Chinese Communists in terms of repeating the Russian October [Revolution] in the Canton of the twenties; and the Vietnamese comrades, a year after the foundation of their party, in terms of organizing insurrections of peasant soviets in the northern part of their country. It is now clear to us today that soviet-type insurrections could not triumph in prewar colonial Asia, but it was precisely here [in Cuba] that the most genuine Communist activists had to begin their apprenticeship for victory. . . .

Fidel once blamed certain failures of the guerrillas on a purely intellectual attitude toward war. The reason is understandable: . . . the intellectual will try to grasp the present through preconceived ideological constructs and live it through books. He will be less able than others to invent, improvise, make do with available resources, decide instantly on bold moves when he is in a tight spot. Thinking that he already knows, he will learn more slowly, display less flexibility. . . .

The Latin American revolution and its vanguard, the Cuban revolution, have . . . made a decisive contribution to international revolutionary experience and to Marxism-Leninism.

Under certain conditions, the political and the military are not separate, but form one organic whole, consisting of the people's army, whose nucleus is the guerrilla army. The vanguard party can exist in the form of the guerrilla force itself. The guerrilla force is the party in embryo.

This is the staggering novelty introduced by the Cuban Revolution. . . .

That is why the guerrilla force must be developed if the political vanguard is to be developed.

That is why, at the present juncture, *the principal stress must be laid on the development of guerrilla warfare and not on the strengthening of existing parties or the creation of new parties.*

That is why *insurrectional activity is today the number one political activity.*

Régis Debray, *Revolution in the Revolution? Armed Struggle and Political Struggle in Latin America,* trans. Bobby Ortiz (New York: Grove Press, 1967), pp. 20, 106, 116. Italics from the original.

travagant spending on public works and welfare projects, and the extravagant lifestyle of his wife, Eva Duarte, virtually bankrupted Argentina.

During the years that followed, many Argentines continued to support Perón, who lived in exile in Spain. Twice (1962 and 1966), a weak elected government was overthrown by a military coup. The army regime installed in 1966 promised to purge Argentina of corruption but aroused much opposition by its repression of academic freedom. The old problems remained unsolved, indeed almost untackled. Perón returned to Argentina in 1973 and was again elected president, but he died before he could initiate new policies. He was succeeded by his second wife, Isabel (1931-   ). She too was removed by a military coup in 1976 and placed under house arrest. The military government turned to widespread repression, killing perhaps five thousand Argentines, suppressing civil liberties, using torture to

extract confessions, and becoming increasingly anti-Semitic. Inflation ran out of control, unemployment reached the highest levels since the depression, and the peso was devalued. To distract attention from the economy, the Argentine military attempted their ill-fated invasion of the Falkland (or Malvinas) Islands and suffered a humiliating defeat at the hands of the British in 1982.

Political unrest, however, was at its greatest in the Caribbean states and in Central America. The United States viewed these nations as in its backyard and made strenuous efforts to defeat communist movements there, often at the cost of bolstering right-wing military regimes. The United States was deeply stung by the failure to anticipate Castro's successful revolution in Cuba, and was determined not to recognize his regime and to force Cuban submission by prohibiting American trade. The Cuban situation proved divisive at home,

KALÂT
NUNA
(Den)

ALASKA
(U.S.)

CANADA

UNITED STATES

Pacific Ocean

Atlantic Oc

MEXICO

HAWAIIAN ISLANDS

CUBA
HAITI
DOM. REP.
JAMAICA
PUERTO RICO (U.S.)
BELIZE
DOMINICA
HONDURAS
ST. VINCENT
ST. LUCIA
GRENADA
BARBADOS
TOBAGO
TRINIDAD
GUATEMALA
EL SALVADOR
GUYANA
NICARAGUA
SURINAME
COSTA RICA
FR. GUIANA
PANAMA
VENEZUELA

COLOMBIA

KIRIBATI   Equator

NAURU   ECUADOR

SOLOMON IS.

B R A Z I L

TUVALU

PERU

VANUATU   WESTERN SAMOA

BOLIVIA

FIJI   TONGA

PARAGUAY

NEW CALEDONIA

The Modern World

CHILE   ARGENTINA   URUGUAY

NEW ZEALAND

■NATO   ■WARSAW PACT

472

ICELAND

UNITED
KINGDOM

EIRE

DENMARK
NETH.
BELG.
LUX.
FRANCE
SWITZ.

W.
GER.
E.
GER.
POLAND

CZECH.
AUST.
HUN.
ROM.
YUG.
BUL.
ALB.
ITALY
GREECE

NORWAY
SWEDEN
FINLAND

U. S. S. R.

MONGOLIA

N. KOREA
S. KOREA

PORTUGAL
SPAIN

MALTA
TUNISIA

CYPRUS
LEBANON
ISRAEL

SYRIA

TURKEY

IRAN

AFGHANISTAN

KASHMIR

TIBET

PEOPLE'S REPUBLIC OF CHINA

IRAQ

JORDAN

PAKISTAN

NEPAL

BHUTAN

TAIWAN

MOROCCO
IFNI

ALGERIA

LIBYA

EGYPT

SAUDI
ARABIA

UNITED
ARAB
EMIRATES

OMAN

INDIA

BURMA

BANGLA
DESH

N. VIETNAM

PHILIPPINE IS.

MAURITANIA

MALI

NIGER

CHAD

SUDAN

YEMEN

SOUTHERN YEMEN

THAILAND

KAMPUCHEA

VIETNAM

BRUNEI

UPPER
VOLTA

NIGERIA

CENTRAL
AFRICAN
REPUBLIC

DJIBOUTI

ETHIOPIA

SRI LANKA

MALDIVES
IS.

MALAYSIA

Singapore

(WEST IRIAN)

ONE
IBERIA
ORY COAST

GHANA
TOGO
BENIN

EQUAT.
GUINEA

CAM.

GABON

REP
OF
CONGO

UGANDA

RWANDA

KENYA

SOMALIA

BORNEO

PAPUA
NEW
GUINEA

SUMATRA

INDONESIA

CABINDA

ZAIRE

BURUNDI

TANZANIA

MALAWI

DIEGO GARCIA

Indian   Ocean

JAVA

(TIMOR)

ANGOLA

ZAMBIA

ZIMBABWE

MOZAMBIQUE

MADAGASCAR

MAURITIUS

NAMIBIA

BOTS
WANA

SWAZILAND

AUSTRALIA

REPUBLIC OF
SOUTH AFRICA

LESOTHO

■OAS

■SEATO ■ARAB LEAGUE

bringing as it did thousands of anti-Castro Cuban exiles and poverty-stricken refugees into Florida. While the United States boycotted Cuban goods, hoping to destroy the Cuban tobacco and sugar economy, other nations filled the trade gap. Castro, who had come to power in 1959, remained firmly in control, expanding Cuban influence by sending troops to many potential battle-fronts in Africa and fostering revolution in Central and South America.

In 1965 the United States concluded that a revolution in the Dominican Republic, a neighbor of Cuba, was inspired by Castro. Between 1930 and 1961 the Dominican Republic had been ruled by a ruthless and corrupt dictator. After his assassination, the first freely elected government in a generation took office under Juan Bosch (1907-   ), but increasing tension between the army and the new reformers led to military coups and finally to a civil war in 1965. Fearing that communists might take over, President Johnson sent in American troops, and then tried to internationalize the intervention by appealing to the Organization of American States. By a narrow margin, the OAS responded, and five of its member states, all with conservative military regimes, sent troops to join the Americans. The Dominican Republic was pacified sufficiently for constitutional elections to be held in 1966. A moderate, Joaquin Balaguer (1907-   ), became president and retained his office when the next elections were held in 1970 and 1974.

It would have been political suicide in 1965 for any president of the United States to allow another Caribbean country to fall into pro-Soviet hands. But the Dominican episode aroused much opposition among Americans; and in Latin America, where Mexico, for example, had opposed intervention, the reappearance of an American occupation force served to heighten the suspicion that the United States was still determined to intervene in Latin America when its interests appeared threatened. Although the United States did not intervene directly in Trinidad, Jamaica, or Guyana, despite strongly anti-American governments, it did provide "advisers" to any mainland Central American nation that considered itself threatened by Cuban communists. In 1975 a guerrilla war in Guatemala was launched against the military government there; by 1981 the dictatorial Somoza family in Nicaragua had been overthrown by the Marxist Sandinista guerrillas, who established a five-member junta to shape a socialist state. In 1979 a military coup in El Salvador was followed by a protracted guerrilla war, political assassinations, numerous atrocities, and the prospect of deepening American involvement. By the 1980s Central America was in ferment, war was widespread, and once again television presented Europeans and Americans with the vision of a perpetual battlefield.

If, as many argued, the cold war between the Soviet Union and the United States was over, then its legacy continued, for in the Middle East, in Central America, and potentially in southern Africa prolonged instability and the prospect of involvement by one or more of the major powers remained a daily threat to the world. Our times were, in standard of living, the best of times; our times were, in terms of stability, peace, and safety, not the worst of times but they nonetheless seemed so to millions. Western civilization had arrived at the present with little prospect that the immediate future would differ greatly from the immediate past. Indeed, few could wish that it would do so, for only the most dramatic and catastrophic of events—nuclear holocaust, the widespread collapse of liberal democracies—would be likely to bring quick changes, changes most of the world would consider undesirable. Current events and history had become indistinguishable.

SUMMARY

After World War II the nations of western Europe maintained their sovereignty and nationalist outlook but formed an economic union, the Common Market. In Britain a social revolution was accomplished with the nationalization of some industries and the extension of social programs. In the 1980s, however, Britain still faced economic difficulties and the unresolved problem of Northern Ireland.

In France, General de Gaulle reestablished republican government after liberation. Although he left office in 1946, he returned in 1968 to preside over the birth of the Fifth Republic.

In the postwar period the West German economy benefited from the building of new, modern, industrial facilities. Democratic government was established, but the question of eventual reunion with East Germany remained unanswered. Brandt's *Ostpolitik* resulted in better relations with eastern Europe and the entry of both Germanies into the United Nations.

Italy experienced turmoil in the postwar years although it enjoyed economic growth. The Italian Communist party increased in size but declared its willingness to enter into a coalition government. The Catholic church took bold initiatives in politics, especially during the reign of Pope John XXIII.

Dictatorships in Spain and Portugal were replaced by constitutional governments. The Scandinavian countries enjoyed prosperity and stability in the postwar period.

The United States experienced unprecedented

changes after World War II. Instead of isolation, it organized worldwide alliances and became involved throughout the globe. It was forced to deal with the existence of the poor within its own borders and recognize that the traditional notion of an economy of abundance had its limitations. It was challenged by the Soviet Union in foreign affairs. The assassinations of three political leaders, the radical youth movements of the 1960s and 1970s, antiwar protests, and demands for social change reflected serious tensions.

To the north, Canada experienced growth but faced the demands of French-speaking Canadians. In Mexico, serious economic troubles in the 1980s threatened the nation.

As elsewhere, the Soviet Union and the nations of eastern Europe experienced cycles of prosperity, growth, and economic stagnation, as well as social and political unrest. In 1956 Khrushchev denounced Stalin and ended the policy of mass terror. Soviet leaders emphasized production, but agricultural production remained below desired levels.

In the non-Western world, educated people as well as urban and rural populations wanted independence. Britain, France, the Netherlands, Belgium, the United States, and eventually Portugal were forced to dismantle their empires.

In Asia, Japan established a democratic government during the American occupation. Its economy was rebuilt, resulting in spectacular growth. Tensions between the United States and Japan developed in the 1970s as a result of the American decision to recognize China and of economic measures that hurt Japanese trade with the United States. South Korea suffered through political instability in a time of economic growth.

In Southeast Asia, new nations emerged, although some, such as Indonesia, were poorly prepared for independence and faced political turmoil. In 1947 South Asia was partitioned between India and Pakistan. The divided nation of Pakistan was torn by civil war in 1971 when East Pakistan became the independent nation of Bangladesh.

Oil and tensions between Arab nations and Israel caused frequent international crises in the Middle East during the postwar period. Oil was used as a weapon in international diplomacy. Despite Egypt's recognition of Israel, conflict between other Arab nations and Israel continued to make the region unstable.

African nations achieved independence but faced the problem of political instability. In South Africa, the white-controlled government imposed a rigid separation of races known as apartheid.

As in Africa and Asia, the nations of Latin America had traditionally been exporters of raw materials and food crops. Independence and industrialization caused economic strains and political unrest that threatened many nations of the region and resulted in military coups, even in countries such as Chile and Uruguay, which had democratic traditions.

chapter twenty-eight

TWENTIETH-CENTURY THOUGHT, LETTERS, AND ART

History is constantly changing. So too is the way that we view history. Obviously, history extends forward in time, each day bringing new events that make a mockery of any attempt to survey the entire historical past of any one culture, much less of all cultures, or of all Western civilization. Even this last term has now lost much of its meaning, for in many ways there is now a world culture from which it is not possible to isolate any singular culture. Japanese prints deeply influenced the French impressionist painters; postimpressionists such as Van Gogh and Gauguin sought inspiration in so-called primitive art, especially that of the South Pacific; Picasso was deeply influenced by African art and sculpture. Popular art forms in Africa, Latin America, and major portions of Asia were in turn, deeply influenced by the music, fashion, political thought, or economic policies that originated in the West. Thus, any history that attempts to recount the human past "from Plato to NATO"—as a properly mocking term describes the conventional survey—is in itself an artifact, a document that represents the modern age in its hunger for facts, for order, and for meaning. History changes by virtue of its existence.

History also changes by virtue of the dynamics of its own discipline. New facts are found about old events, new documents discovered, new artifacts unearthed by archaeologists. Old facts are reinterpreted, their meaning changed, both by the simple passage of time, which permits more distance from and more objectivity toward an event, and by the discovery of new facts. Today the historian writes quite differently of ancient Greece and Rome than historians did only twenty years ago, in part because society now permits open discussion of subjects, such as the use of slaves in classical civilization, that were once reserved to the specialist. Today the historian writes quite differently of sixteenth-century England or eighteenth-century France than twenty years ago, in part because new insights into social organization, population movements, the history of climate, disease, sexuality, or of the role of women and the family have forced a reassessment of what was truly significant about those centuries. Today the historian writes quite differently of the nineteenth-century United States or of the growth of the European empires because new techniques, derived in part from the social sciences, and new interdisciplinary methods have made a history based on comparisons more nearly possible. Today, four decades removed from the first years of the cold war, the historian writes differently of those years, for recent events have—usually in subtle ways but at times in major ones—changed judgments about the significance of intervening events; and also quite simply because a new generation of historians who were not eyewitnesses to those events or even contemporary with them has arisen. And history is written differently today because the pervasive influence of the media, and especially of television, has shaped a generation accustomed less to learning by reading than learning by looking, while the steady advance of the computer and the word processor into education and learning is producing a generation rather more numerate and somewhat less literate.

None of these developments is in itself harmful, nor can history yet judge their real significance; they all represent history as process. There are more scientists alive today than lived throughout the entire history of the world, and the impact those scientists will have on the future, and thus on the past, cannot be imagined.

I THE MODERNITY OF HISTORY

"Modern" history is an elastic term that depends upon the questions asked. All historical questions have at least four aspects: social, political, economic, and intellectual; this is no less true of popular cultures than of elite cultures. For all cultures and for all aspects, the "moment of modernity" will differ. North Americans, for example, are sometimes said to have become modern in the 1920s, when they first began to wonder if their lives would catch up with their dreams. The world, some argue, became modern with the first atomic explosion, when the capacity for humanity to destroy itself was

Family patterns of entertainment and education changed drastically and rapidly with the introduction of television into the average Western home. Potentially an enormous force for education, television was generally used as a tool for leisure and entertainment. Where once the kitchen had been the center of the household, the television room now became the family gathering place. Many commentators argue that television, by bringing graphic scenes of war and crime into the home, reduces the sense of community and increases the individual's tolerance for violence.

THE AGE OF THE COMPUTER

We live today in an information society. Such a society is the result of a long evolution from the development of writing, to movable type, to the high-speed printing press, to the typewriter and carbon paper and the office duplicating machine. More than any other development, however, it has been the exceptionally rapid growth of computer technology—and the application of that technology to education, information retrieval, and word processing—that has changed the way we look at learning. The sociology of knowledge has changed.

Today much of humanity, especially in the West, is visually oriented. People learn from images—whether on television or a computer console—rather than from linear type. This new mode of learning has changed speech, promoted new skills, and made it possible to assemble, sort, and retrieve incredible amounts of data. It has also led some people to confuse *data* (items of information) and *creative thinking*. Thus, many observers of the new high-technology societies of the West and Japan feel that the period since about 1975 (when historians of the computer say that society entered an "advanced third-generation computer age") has brought more rapid changes than any single generation has experienced before. These changes relate to technological unemployment and the threat of such unemployment, to vast transformations in the city as a communications center, to transportation, social relationships, finance, the arts, the use of leisure time, and to the nature of government and the challenge that pervasive government knowledge about its citizens poses to concepts of individuality and privacy.

Cooperation among individuals will become increasingly necessary and probably will be enforced by strong central—perhaps totalitarian—governments aided by computers acting as sources of information. Who shall this all-powerful and pervasive government be? Political scientists have suggested that some form of worldwide government is inevitable. Only time can prove the accuracy of these predictions. One thing, however, is certain—that government, whether a single global or a variety of national ones, will rely increasingly on the computer. The nature of any form of government requires that its citizens be kept track of. For, even in a feudal system, a knowledge of the subjects—their financial states and their major concerns—as well as a possession of some degree of their good will is mandatory. When the number of people being governed becomes as large as that with which future states shall have to contend, some extraordinary means of tabulation will be vitally necessary. The computer is that means.

Some people believe optimistically that not even a computerized spy ring would be able to control all

dramatically demonstrated. Yet some societies today are still referred to by those who study them as premodern, and others are said to have entered a postmodern phase.

History, as a body of written material or even as oral tradition, can of course be manipulated, so that a new generation may learn quite different "facts" about the past and can be led to quite different conclusions. For example, in 1983 Japan issued a new authorized textbook for use in its schools; the text gave rise to protest in China, since it referred to the invasion of the mainland in the 1930s as an "advance." There was concern not so much because it was an effort to whitewash the past, but because the whitewashing was taking place in the present. Societies reveal much about themselves in what they choose to take pride in—what they consciously preserve from their past and from their environment. Societies also reveal much about themselves in what they exclude, as when history until recently passed over the underclasses in near silence or neglected the role of women in national development.

Indeed, this lack of balance led to the fall of Western Civilization courses in many universities in the West, and reflected a crisis of conscience, a sense of doubt about Western values. The suspicion that such courses had been systematically neglecting much that was significant undermined the very notion that to know history was, in some measure, to know oneself. The renewed popularity of such courses, with their new balance between elite culture and popular culture—those who prefer Tarzan to King Lear, comic books to opera, rock to Mozart, and are not necessarily the worse for it—is itself a historical development in the 1980s.

Three Americans—Walt Disney (1901-1966), Frank Sinatra (1915-   ), and Elvis Presley (1935-1977)—may have done as much to shape modern society as, for example, Sigmund Freud or Adolf Hitler. Yet because possible movements of all people at all times. The past decade has witnessed the rise of an "underground" that is not really limited to newspapers and political movements. . . . Certainly, it is easy enough for an individual to lose himself among the masses of an urban area; this has been demonstrated more than once. All that need be done is to conform to certain surface expectations, such as dress and overt behavior. What you do in your own cubbyhole or in your own mind cannot be traced. Individuality, despite governmental control of so many facets of life, thus might be maintained to some extent.

A more pessimistic approach suggests that no degree of individual freedom would be possible. The cashless society [of the credit card] would mean that no one could "hide." The government might find it expedient to create the illusion of freedom and even permit the existence of some rebellious groups, but these would be carefully controlled and manipulated. . . .

Quite possibly, there will be choice enough, perhaps too much, at least in most areas of life, simply because it would require too much effort, even using the most advanced technology, for a government to control every aspect of the existence of every individual under its power. Consequently, the majority of activities might be observed, but restrained only loosely. When given a choice of flying to the Bahamas, London, Tokyo, or Greece, of attending lecture or discussion sessions on several hundred different topics, of painting a picture or reading a book, of going to the gym, the museum, or to a circus all in one day, the average person might stay in bed and sleep, simply to avoid making the decision. However, once again the computer could come to the rescue. Having been programmed according to the individual's tastes, the home computer could simply set up a schedule of activities for the person to follow. Thus, computers could limit man's freedom, but only under his orders. . . .

Possibly the only limitation on the computer's usefulness is man's imagination. Dependence on the computer, whether developed with moderation or whether indulged to the fullest extent, places the responsibility for the course of society on the persons who program, coordinate, and oversee the workings of those computers. Thus, we are brought back full circle to the question: who shall the government be? The answer is that the government will be the person or persons who control society's major tool, the computer. Never before in the history of man has one machine played such a crucial role in so many facets of life. . . .

The "Frankenstein complex" seems to be as integral to man's nature as the Oedipus complex, for humanity has certainly devoted enough verbiage to the horrors of his creations' getting the upper hand. However, just as the Oedipus complex is outgrown by the healthy individual, so the Frankenstein complex should be outgrown by the healthy society. The key to this maturity is the knowledge that the computer is just a tool. We can use it for good or ill; the choice is up to us.

This is not the first time that humankind has faced such a choice. When the gun was invented it could have been used to kill game to feed the starving or to kill people to feed the power hungry. The latter use was by far the more common. But centuries have passed. There is the hope that man has matured emotionally as well as technologically. And since mankind is composed of individuals, the hope for the world rests on the shoulders of people with conscience. . . . Knowledge is futile without wisdom, as is science without conscience.

Ralph J. Kochenburger and Carolyn J. Turcio, *Computers in Modern Society* (Santa Barbara, Cal.: Hamilton Publishing Co., 1974), pp. 236-39. Copyright © 1974 John Wiley & Sons, Inc. Reprinted by permission of John Wiley & Sons, Inc.

the significance of popular culture is less clear and the impact more diffuse and democratic, the historian cannot yet be sure. Leisure time spent watching a great worldwide professional sport such as soccer, or a more limited national sport such as baseball or cricket—both of which are increasingly internationalized though still associated with a single culture—may shape history far more than leisure time spent listening to Beethoven and Bach, or attending the plays of Shaw and Ibsen, or examining the art of Munch and Bacon. Such matters cannot be measured. In a sense, their significance relative to each other cannot be known. Yet all are part of history, and to be uninformed about either elite or popular culture is to be isolated from the broad flow of historical reality.

Of all the major "modern" or industrial nations, the United States and the Soviet Union have been the most insulated against a comparative awareness of historical trends elsewhere—the first largely by geography and nationalism, and the second largely by physical isolation and ideology. Yet the changes in both nations have been enormous in the last four decades, though they are more easily seen in the United States, the more open society. Syndication and wire services have turned once-parochial American newspapers into a national press; censorship and controlled news have made Russian papers fully national rather than local, an equally significant role for the press.

In the United States, the old party system appeared to be in an advanced stage of dissolution by the 1980s, and few could predict what new coalitions would emerge, though most likely under traditional labels. In the Soviet Union, historians lacked the information to judge even the immediate significance of most events. By the 1980s the United States was experiencing an industrial slump much like that of Great Britain in the 1950s, for its

World War II and the period of rapid industrial growth that followed it meant that populations shifted increasingly to the cities. They were seeking the amenities that could be provided by great concentrations of people and by the municipal governments they created. Many psychologists felt that the city also tended to increase anonymity and to bring the rich and the poor closer together physically, with the result that vast differences in income became more noticeable. Crime rates were higher in cities, and the advantages of city living were often offset by the risks of collective destruction. By the 1980s there were seventy cities with a population of over two million and with corporate headquarters of many great companies. Contrast this with Japanese survivors searching through the ruins of the city of Nagasaki, destroyed by an atom bomb in 1945.

productive equipment was not being replaced or remodeled rapidly enough, and America's share of the world's Gross National Product had fallen from 40 percent—a staggering figure for a single industrial power—to 20 percent. Religion in the United States—always stronger than virtually anywhere else in the modern West—was undergoing changes as yet unpredictable, in which evangelical religion was acting as a safety valve for groups whose prejudices had been stifled by shifts in population and opinion—a change not unlike the safety valve provided to Britain by the Methodists and other dissenters in the first several decades of the nineteenth century.

By the 1980s life was more uniform for much of human society, and the individual was subject to more laws than ever before. The twin contenders for the obedience of secular humanity—nationalism and ideological internationalism—appeared more and more mythical or visionary, neither nationalism nor socialism having produced the security of life it had appeared to promise. Determinisms, whether of Freud or Marx, the

fatalisms, whether of hydrogen bombs or of the collapse of democracy, seemed less certain. However, it also seemed less certain that the world could be improved simply by finding out what was wrong with it and then taking steps to put it right, for there were deep disagreements over the remedies.

The arms race and the prospect of nuclear annihilation offered a frightening security; deeply held beliefs, whether in a resurgent Islam or a reforming Christianity, to name only two, offered a no less frightening insecurity. The medieval concept of the treasury of merit had given way to the treasury of guilt: the son must be punished, even killed, for the mistakes of the grandfather, as when terrorists struck against innocent representatives of a given nationality because of the atrocities visited upon the terrorists' ancestors seventy-five years or more before. This was history with a vengeance.

As we move toward the twenty-first century, now less than a quarter century away, the myriad problems of all societies, the opportunities of some, the individualized fascination and mystery of most, continue to be ana-

Increasingly, English became the international language of speech and print, though French held its own as the language of diplomacy, and various forms of Chinese were spoken by huge numbers of people. An international language of signs and symbols developed, so that a traveler might recognize the command "No Parking," whether in Japanese or in English.

lyzed by philosophers, visually reshaped by artists, reconstructed by historians, questioned by theologians, attacked and defended by politicians and political thinkers. In the end, all history continues to be intellectual history, in the sense that humanity continues, no less in the 1980s than in the first century B.C., to be motivated by what it believes to be true, by what people think and hope for, fear and admire. The main currents of thought, perhaps best expressed by an elite culture, though just as deeply felt throughout popular culture, are ever more universal. One Western society and its language (and the thinkers who use the structure of that language to present their concept of reality) influences other Western societies and their languages, even as East influences West.

II MODERN THOUGHT ABOUT HUMAN NATURE

Psychology

Taking its cue from biology, especially the Darwinian theory of evolution, the nineteenth century emphasized *process*, the dynamics of change in time. Taking its cue from psychology, the twentieth century has put its emphasis on the role of the unconscious in human thought and action, on the nonrationality of much human behavior. Foremost among the thinkers responsible for this shift of emphasis was Sigmund Freud, a physician trained in Vienna in the rationalist medical tradition of the late nineteenth century. His interest was early drawn to mental illness, where he found cases in which patients exhibited symptoms of very real organic disturbances for which no obvious organic causes could be found. Under psychoanalysis, as Freud's therapeutic treatment came

---

FREUD ON MODERN CIVILIZATION

Though not his most famous book, *Civilization and Its Discontents*, written in 1929-1930, is probably the most frequently read work by Sigmund Freud (1856-1939), for it appears to speak directly to the human condition in the 1980s.

It seems certain that we do not feel comfortable in our present-day civilization, but it is very difficult to form an opinion whether and in what degree men of an earlier age felt happier, and what part their cultural conditions played in the matter. We shall always tend to consider people's distress objectively—that is, to place ourselves, with our own wants and sensibilities, in *their* conditions, and then to examine what occasions we should find in them for experiencing happiness or unhappiness. This method of looking at things, which seems objective because it ignores the variations in subjective sensibility, is, of course, the most subjective possible, since it puts one's own mental states in the place of any others, unknown though they may be. Happiness, however, is something essentially subjective. No matter how much we may shrink with horror from certain situations—of a galley-slave in antiquity, of a peasant during the Thirty Years' War, of a victim of the Holy Inquisition, of a Jew awaiting a pogrom—it is nevertheless impossible for us to feel our way into such people. . . .

For a wide variety of reasons, it is very far from my intention to express an opinion upon the value of human civilization. I have endeavoured to guard myself against the enthusiastic prejudice which holds that our civiliza-tion is the most precious thing that we possess or could acquire and that its path will necessarily lead to heights of unimagined perfection. . . . One thing only do I know for certain, and that is that man's judgments of value follow directly his wishes for happiness—that, accordingly, they are an attempt to support his illusions with arguments. . . .

The fateful question for the human species seems to me to be whether and to what extent their cultural development will succeed in mastering the disturbance of their communal life by the human instinct of aggression and self-destruction. It may be that in this respect precisely the present time deserves a special interest. Men have gained control over the forces of nature to such an extent that with their help they would have no difficulty in exterminating one another to the last man. They know this, and hence comes a large part of their current unrest, their unhappiness and their mood of anxiety.

Sigmund Freud, *Civilization and Its Discontents*, from *The Standard Edition of the Complete Psychological Works of Sigmund Freud*, trans. James Strachey (New York: Norton, 1961), pp. 11, 36, 92. Reprinted by permission from the Sigmund Freud Copyrights Ltd., The Institute of Psycho-Analysis, The Hogarth Press Ltd., and W.W. Norton & Co., Inc.

MOVING TOWARD AN UNCERTAIN FUTURE

The twentieth century, like the nineteenth, has been a time of enormous population upheaval, as millions of people have migrated from one part of the earth to another. These migrations have immensely enriched different societies, bringing them the most energetic and ambitious as well as the downtrodden of other nations. Mobility and uncertainty about the future have marked modern humanity.

Czeslaw Milosz (1911-   ), who won the Nobel Prize for literature in 1980, is representative of this sense of individually shifting perspective. Born in Poland, a leader of the avant-garde poetry movement there in the 1930s, a Resistance fighter in World War II, a member of the Polish diplomatic service in the early years of the cold war, he subsequently moved to the United States to become a professor. His poem "Flight" (1973) speaks to the sharp and cruel dislocations faced by humanity today:

When we were leaving the burning city,
On the first field path, turning back our eyes,
I said: "Let the grass cover our footprints.
Let the harsh prophets be silent in the fire
And let the dead tell the dead what happened.
We are intended to give birth to new, violent tribe

Free from the evil and happiness drowsing there.
Let us go—" and a sword of fire opened the earth for us.

Czeslaw Milosz, *Selected Poems* (New York: Ecco Press, 1980), p. 108.
Copyright © 1980 by Czeslaw Milosz. Reprinted by permission.

to be called, the patient was urged to pour out what could be remembered about earliest childhood; after many such treatments, the analyst could make the patient aware of what was so disturbing.

From his clinical experience Freud worked out a system of psychology that has greatly influenced basic conceptions of human relations. Freud started with the concept of a set of drives with which each person is born. These drives, which arise in the unconscious, are expressions of the *id* (the Latin word for "it," which Freud used to avoid the moralistic overtones in words like "desires"). These drives try to find satisfaction and pleasure, to express themselves in action. Infants are uninhibited; that is, their drives well up into action from the id without restraint from the conscious mind. But as infants grow, as their minds are formed, they become conscious that some of what they want to do is objectionable to those closest to them—to parent or friend or brother or sister—on whom they are dependent. Therefore they begin to repress these drives.

With dawning consciousness of the world outside, the child develops another part of the psyche, which Freud at first called the censor and later divided into two phases, which he called the *ego* and the *superego*. The ego is a person's private censor, the awareness that, in accordance with what Freudians call the reality principle, certain drives from the id simply cannot succeed. The superego is what common language calls conscience; it is a person's response as a member of a social system in which certain actions are considered proper and others are not. These drives of the id and most dictates of the superego are for Freud a great reservoir of which a person is not normally aware—that is, the unconscious.

In a mentally healthy person, enough of the drives of the id succeed to provide a sense of contentment and security. But even the healthiest individuals repress many drives from their ids by a process Freud called *sublimation*, or substituting for a repressed drive a new and socially approved outlet or expression. Thus a drive toward forbidden sexual relations might be sublimated into poetry, music, war, or athletics. In the neurotic person, however, the drives are driven down into the unconscious without a suitable outlet or sublimation and continue to fester in the id, trying to find some outlet. They display themselves in *neuroses* and *phobias*, which have in common a failure to conform to the reality principle. Neurotic individuals are maladjusted, and if the failure to meet the reality principle is complete, they are psychotic, living in an utterly unreal private world.

Freud's therapy rested on the long, slow process of psychoanalysis, in which the patient day after day reached back to memories of earliest childhood for concrete details, and the listening analyst picked from this "stream of consciousness" the significant details that pointed to the hidden repression that was expressing itself in neurotic behavior. Freud gave special importance to the patient's dreams, in which the unconscious wells up out of control or is only partly controlled by the ego. Once the patient became aware of what had gone wrong with a hitherto unconscious part of life, the patient might then adjust to society and lead a normal existence.

What was important in all this to political and cultural theory lay in the wider implications of Freud's work, particularly his concept of the role of unconscious drives. Ordinary reflective thinking was, for the Freudian, a very small part of existence. Much even of what is considered to be the exercise of reason was, according to the Freudian, what psychologists call *rationalization*—that is, thinking dictated not by an awareness of the reality principle but by the desires of the id. The difference between eighteenth-century rationalism and Freudian psychology can be seen by contrasting the earlier belief in the innocence of the child—the moral neutrality of the "blank slate" of Locke's newborn infant—with the Freudian view of the child as a bundle of unsocial or antisocial drives. For the Freudian, then, truth cannot be distilled into a few simple rules of conduct that all people, being reasonable and good, can use as guides to individual and collective happiness. The Freudian is at bottom a pessimist who does not believe in human perfectibility.

The modern age has often been called the age of anxiety. Humanity's constant search for a sense of security is constantly being challenged by psychology, by art and music, by foreign affairs and war, by social policy. One artist who brooded on the themes of madness, death, and human alienation was the Norwegian Edvard Munch (1863-1944). Though well regarded in his lifetime, Munch's coruscating use of line and color seemed to speak most directly to the late 1970s and early 1980s, when major retrospective exhibits of his work made him even more widely known. Perhaps most representative of Munch's vision were the several different versions he prepared of the same theme, *The Cry*, first developed as a lithograph as long ago as 1895. The panic-stricken scream, the sexlessness of the sufferer, spoke of a primal terror that, as Munch later wrote, revealed "modern psychic life."

Freud, to whom religion was an illusion, was himself a cult leader. His faithful disciples still form an orthodox nucleus of strict Freudian psychoanalysts. Other disciples parted with him. The Austrian Alfred Adler (1870-1937) rejected Freud's emphasis on sex and coined the familiar phrase "inferiority complex" to explain human compensations for perceived inadequacies. The Swiss Carl Gustav Jung (1875-1961) attempted to expand the horizons of psychology by studying the evidence of the past in literature, mythology, and religious faith. His studies convinced him that there was a "collective unconscious," a reservoir of the entire human experience that is reflected symbolically in the *archetypes* such as prophets, seers, and saviors that appear and reappear in art, literature, legend, and religion.

Such views of the nonrational origins of human action have deeply influenced daily life, from the relatively mundane, as in advertising, to the highly significant, as in organization of political systems, the gratification of economic wants, and the satisfaction of human desires. The Freudian influence on imaginative writing has been especially great, as shown by stream-of-consciousness fiction. It has also deeply affected philosophy and the arts generally. Freud reinforced the intellectual reaction against scientific materialism and against nineteenth-century bourgeois optimism, and he strengthened the revival of intuition and sensibility in a kind of neo-romantic and neo-Stoic protest against unbridled reason.

The Freudians hold no monopoly of psychology. Indeed, the eighteenth-century tendency to regard human nature, if not as wholly rational, at least as wholly adaptable by those who would manipulate the human and nonhuman environment, still had many representatives in the midtwentieth century. The long debate in Plato and Aristotle, in the evolutionists and eugenicists of the nineteenth century, in social theorists in both democratic and totalitarian societies, continued: did nature or nurture most influence the indivdual or groups of individuals? Intelligence testing, efforts to make prisons more comfortable, experiments with open classrooms, and a variety of theories in education all attested to the continued struggle between those who felt that humanity could be improved by reshaping the environment and those who felt that only through genetic engineering could humanity be made stronger or more intelligent—and thus perhaps more "moral."

Sociology and Political Science

In the social sciences, the twentieth century continued to question its inheritance of faith in the basic reasonableness and goodness of human nature. In fact, some social scientists found the term *human nature* to be so all-embracing as to make no sense. The specific programs and values of twentieth-century thinkers in this broad field were very varied. Yet most of them had a sense of the subtlety, the complexities, the delicacy—

MORAL ENLIGHTENMENT OR ESCAPE?

One of the remarkable developments of the twentieth century is the tendency to hide from the pressures of modern life through various forms of escape: in music, in romantic film, in travel, in drugs, in alcohol, in physical and mental activity. All these forms of escape have been present for centuries. Some commentators would regard religion as a form of escape; others would regard it as a higher reality. The same can be said for all forms of escape, since no two people necessarily agree on the direction to take in life, and an escape must imply a movement away from something, if not toward some goal.

The modern form of escape that seems to have most catastrophically changed modern society, rendering it even less predictable than it has ever been before, is the use of drugs, either for religious experience or for pleasure, rather than for medical purposes. The Russian writer Leo Tolstoy (1828-1910), author of *War and Peace*, wrote of this phenomenon in 1890:

All human life, we may say, consists solely of these two activities: (1) bringing one's activities into harmony with conscience, or (2) hiding from oneself the indications of conscience in order to be able to continue to live as before.

Some do the first, others the second. To attain the first there is but one means: moral enlightenment—the increase of light in oneself and attention to what it shows. To attain the second—to hide from oneself the indications of conscience—there are two means: one external and the other internal. The external means consists in occupations that divert one's attention from the indications given by conscience; the internal method consists in darkening conscience itself. . . .

What is the explanation of the fact that people use things that stupefy them: vodka, wine, beer, hashish, opium, tobacco? . . . Why did the practice begin? Why has it spread so rapidly, and why is it still spreading among all sorts of people, savage and civilized? . . . Why do people wish to stupefy themselves?

Meredith Murray, ed., *Why Do Men Stupefy Themselves? and Other Writings by Leo Tolstoy* (New York: Steinerbooks, 1975), pp. 44, 39.

and the toughness and durability—of the forces that bind human beings together in society but also hold them apart. In the work of many different thinkers—the German Max Weber (1864-1920), the Frenchman Emile Durkheim (1858-1917), the Italian Vilfredo Pareto (1848-1923), and others—sociologists found a common aim to study humanity in society "objectively" and still give full place to the role of the subjective and nonrational in human life, separating the rational from the nonrational in human actions.

What interested Pareto, for example, was the kind of action that is expressed in words, ritual, symbolism of some kind. For example, buying wool socks for cold weather is one such action. If they are bought deliberately to get the best socks at a price the buyer can afford, that is a rational action in accord with self-interest; it is the kind of action the economist can study statistically. If, however, they are bought because the buyer thinks wool is "natural" (as contrasted with synthetic fibers), or because the buyer finds snob value in imported English socks, or because the buyer wants to help bring sheep-raising back to Vermont, then the buyer has moved into a field less "rational" than that of price. The practical economist will still study marketing and consumer demand, but will have to cope with many complex psychological variables. In such situations, behavior becomes the subject of study. In time *behavioralism* would dominate much of the study of politics (now called political science), as well as aspects of psychology, economics, and medicine.

The psychology of motivation interested Mussolini and Hitler, both of whom had pretensions to philosophy, and also many democratic politicians and a host of experts employed by advertising agencies to persuade consumers. Something of the same emphasis on the need to go beyond abstraction to practical psychology in politics appeared in the writings of the American Walter Lippmann (1889-1975), whose *Preface to Politics* was published in 1913, and who thereafter continued to profoundly influence American political thought and foreign policy. Lippmann was a new type of intellectual, the syndicated newspaper commentator, who was read and respected throughout a nation.

Perceptive political leaders knew that planning was needed to deal with such essentials as education, health care, social security, and the conservation of natural resources and the environment. All were expensive, and the planners knew that in a democracy the government could not simply impose its plans. Ideas from the social sciences helped persuade the electorate to want, ask for, and pay for what the planners thought it should want. This was particularly so in economics, which while in no

In the second half of the twentieth century, owning your own automobile became a symbol of success, maturity, and mobility throughout the Western world. Before the fuel shortages of the 1970s and 1980s, it was the prime status symbol in most societies. The average American, as depicted here in front of his 1961 Pontiac, assumed virtually as an economic right that the typical family would consist of two children, and that the family would own, first, its personal automobile and, second, its own home. This theme was captured in this painting by the artist Robert Bechtle (1932-   ).

sense a science, came to be regarded as one by many in both democratic and communist societies (though only in the latter would explicit claims for the scientific validity of economics be openly asserted).

Philosophy

In formal philosophy, the movement was away from the presumptions of science. In particular, a philosophy known as *existentialism* developed from such nineteenth-century sources as Nietzsche and the Danish theologian Søren Kierkegaard (1813-1855), who assailed the depersonalizing and dehumanizing effects of the secularized and increasingly materialist society of his day. In such works as *Fear and Trembling* (1843) and *Either/Or* (also 1843), he argued that Christian truth was not to be found in churches but in experiencing extreme human conditions through the act of existence.

The central theme of existentialism was stated by the French writer Jean-Paul Sartre (1905-1980) in the phrase "existence precedes essence." This meant that human awareness of living, of being, precedes in time, and is therefore more important than, thinking or labeling reality with words. Clearly existentialism, which has been described as more a mood than a systematic world view, is part of the anti-intellectualism of the twentieth century. Yet the existentialists respected the instrument of thought and used it in making the hard choices and commitments they felt the act of being demanded.

Still, the most original and most typical philosophic movement of the twentieth century is variously called

logical analysis, logical positivism, linguistic philosophy, or, in some of its phases, symbolic logic. The movement accepted most of the new psychology and went ahead to insist that, although only a tiny bit of human experience could be defined as rational thought, that tiny bit should be protected and explored carefully. This somewhat varied school can be considered as beginning early in the twentieth century in Vienna with such distinguished pioneers as Ludwig Wittgenstein (1889-1951) and Rudolf Carnap (1891-1970), who both emigrated, Wittgenstein to England and Carnap to the United States. The school's basic position held that when, applying the methods of scientific practice, a problem can be answered by an "operation" and the answer validated by logical and empirical tests or observations, knowledge can be achieved. But when no such "operation" is possible, as in such problems as whether democracy is the best form of government, whether a lie is ever justifiable, or whether a given poem is good or bad—in short, almost all the great questions of philosophy, art, literature, history—then the problem is "meaningless" for the logician. To be without meaning does not signify that the problem should be dismissed, however, as most of humanity must still discover "operable truths" by which to make decisions, guide their lives, and act on their decisions with a sense of guidance.

Most logical positivists would admit that nonlogical or pseudological methods for resolving such problems, though they do not result in the kind of final answers scientists expect to get, are nonetheless useful and necessary for normal life. Approaching their problems in a very different way from Freud and Pareto, these logical analysts nevertheless came to a similar conclusion about the reasoning capacity of most human beings. Most human beings, they concluded, are at present incapable of thorough, persistent, successful logical thinking. Rather, they are open to manipulation.

Historicism

Probably the most widespread philosophical movement of the century developed on the margin of formal philosophy and the social sciences. This movement is called *historicism*—the attempt to find in history an answer to those ultimate questions of the structure of the universe and of human fate that the philosopher has always asked. Once Judeo-Christian concepts of a single creation in time and of a God above nature were widely abandoned along with the rest of the traditional world view, people looking for answers to questions about these ultimates had to fall back on the historical record. Humans are not made by God but by nature, the historicists said, which amounts to saying that humanity makes itself in the course of history. Humanity gets its only clues about its capacities here on earth—clues as to how to behave, clues to the future—from the record of the past.

But many of the thinkers who appealed to history found much more than indications of what might be, much more than the always tentative, never dogmatic or absolute "theories" the scientist produces. Many of these philosophers of history found in the course of history a substitute for the concepts of God or Providence. They found substantially the equivalent of what Christians had found in revelation—an explanation of humanity's nature and destiny. Of these historicisms, the most important and most obviously a substitute for Christianity was Marxism. For God, absolute and omnipotent, the Marxist substituted the absolutely determined course of dialectical materialism.

Another type of historicism was put forward by the German Oswald Spengler (1880-1936) in *The Decline of the West*, published at the end of World War I. Spengler argued from the historical record that societies or civilizations had an average life span, a thousand years or so for a civilization being the equivalent of seventy years or so for a human being. He traced three Western civilizations: a Hellenic from 1000 B.C. to about the birth of Christ; a Levantine or Middle Eastern from then to about A.D. 1000; and a modern Western, which began (according to him) about A.D. 1000 and was, therefore, due to end about A.D. 2000. This type of history, already being written at the turn of the century, became highly popular between the two world wars, when many commentators, though few trained historians, spoke widely of the decline of the West, by which they often meant, in a disguised form of racism, the collapse of all civilization.

Paralleling *The Decline of the West* but written by a trained historian was the enormously influential, multivolume *Study of History* (1934-1954) by the Englishman Arnold Toynbee (1889-1975). Toynbee was a classicist with a Christian background and a strong family tradition of humanitarian social service. World War I aroused in Toynbee a hatred for war and a conviction that nationalism was evil. His work was an attempt to trace the causes of the rise and fall of dozens of societies in the past. Concluding his history at the height of the cold war, he argued that Western society was facing a very serious challenge, that in terms of the cyclical rise and fall of societies, it looked as if the West was stagnating. Societies grew, he said, when challenged and able to respond; if not challenged or incapable of a sufficient response, they declined. This dialectic of challenge and response proved attractive to western Europe and the United States, which felt challenged by the Soviet Union and improved by their competitive response. Thus for a time Toynbee became the most discussed historian in the West.

More lasting, however, was the work of historians who asked questions not previously asked. Under the impact of the cold war, of the rising civil-rights movement, of the feminist movement, of all the events that shape the historiography of nations, French, British, and American historians in particular developed new fields of inquiry. Perhaps most representative was the enormous growth of interest in the history of slavery. In the United States the study of slavery had been seen as a branch of the history of the South, and thus truly of a "peculiar institution"—that is, an institution peculiar to a single region; and openly racist histories had dominated the field until World War II. American scholars as a whole had favored the "consensus" view of certain progressive historians, especially Frederick Jackson Turner (1861-1932) and Charles A. Beard (1874-1948), the latter regarded as radical for his time. They maintained that American development was marked far more by cooperation than by conflict, and that slavery was peripheral to an understanding of the rise of American civilization. From the 1950s, however, many scholars challenged the consensus argument, detecting much conflict in the American story, and pointing to the centrality of the problem of finding and retaining a predictable supply of labor in a rapidly growing agricultural and industrial nation, thus moving the issue of slavery into the center of American inquiry. In this and many other examples, historians in the West roundly condemned the conventional wisdom by which British or American history was viewed as a compilation of unalloyed success stories.

III TWENTIETH-CENTURY SCIENCE

In the twentieth century each science, each branch of each science, continued its ever more intense specialization. Cooperation among pure scientists, applied scientists, engineers, bankers, business people, and government officials produced exponential increases. The rate of travel is an example: in 1820 the fastest rate was still 12 to 15 miles an hour; railroads made it 100 miles or so by 1880; piston-engined airplanes made it 300 miles or so by 1940; jet planes broke the sound barrier in 1947, making speeds of close to 1,000 miles per hour possible; and starting in 1969 rockets propelled men to the moon at speeds exceeding 20,000 miles an hour. Even without mechanical assistance, humans moved faster, leapt higher and further, than ever before. To run a mile in four minutes was once thought to be virtually unattainable; when this essentially psychological barrier was broken in 1954, runners steadily lowered the mark by tenths of a second, to only 3:47.33 in 1981.

Scientific respect for nature and natural laws, and scientific skepticism toward the supernatural, have added powerfully to the modern drive toward rationalism, positivism, materialism. Science continued to promote the world view that arose in early modern times and culminated in the Enlightenment of the eighteenth century. Thus the hopeful views once attributed to Voltaire or other philosophers or social scientists became increasingly, though not unfailingly, the preserve of science.

The Revolution in Physics

The great scientific event of the twentieth century was the revolution in physics symbolized for the public by Albert Einstein (1879-1955) and also made possible by the contributions of many other experts. This revolution centered on radical revisions made in the Newtonian world machine, the mechanistic model of the universe that had been accepted for more than two centuries. Many nineteenth-century scientists were convinced that light moved in waves and was transmitted through the ether, which supposedly filled outer space. In the 1880s, however, experiments demonstrated that there was no ether. If the ether did exist, then it would itself be moved by the motion of the earth, and a beam of light directed *against* its current would travel with a velocity less than that of a beam directed *with* its current. But experiments showed that light traveled at 186,284 miles per second, whether it was moving with or against the hypothetical current.

In 1905 Einstein, who was then twenty-six years old, published a paper asserting that since the speed of light is a constant unaffected by the earth's motion, it must also be unaffected by all the other bodies in the universe. This unvarying velocity of light is a law of nature, Einstein continued, and other laws of nature are the same for all uniformly moving systems. This was Einstein's Special Theory of Relativity, which had many disconcerting corollaries. In particular, it undermined the idea of absolute space and absolute time, and made both space and time relative to the velocity of the system in which they were moving. If a rod moves at a speed approaching that of light, it will shrink; at 90 percent of the velocity of light, it will contract to half its "normal"

length. The motion of a clock carried aboard the rod will slow down commensurately; if astronauts should ever travel at such speeds through space for what seemed to them six months, they would discover on returning to earth that they had been absent for a year.

Einstein maintained that space and time, therefore, are inseparable linked; time is a "fourth dimension." An air-traffic controller needs to know the position of an airplane not only in longitude, latitude, and altitude, but also in time, and the total flight path of a plane must be plotted on what Einstein called a "four-dimensional space-time continuum"—a term he also applied to the universe.

Einstein equated not only space and time but also mass and energy. His famous formula $E = mc^2$ means that the energy in an object is equal to its mass, multiplied by the square of the velocity of light. It means also that a very small object may contain tremendous potential energy. Such an object, for example, can emit radiation for thousands of years or discharge it all in one explosion, as happened with the atom bomb in 1945, when a way was found to unlock the potential energy in uranium.

The problem of mass also involved Einstein in a review of the Newtonian concept of a universe held together by the force of gravity—the attraction of bodies to other bodies over vast distances. Einstein soon concluded that gravity—that is, the weight—of an object had nothing to do with its attraction to other objects. Galileo had demonstrated that both light and heavy bodies fell from the leaning tower in Pisa at the same speed. Einstein proposed that it would be more useful to extend the concept of the *magnetic field*, in which certain bodies behaved in a certain pattern, and speak of a *gravitational field*, in which bodies also behaved in a certain pattern. Einstein did not penetrate the mystery of what holds the universe together, but he did suggest a more convincing way of looking at it. This was the essence of his General Theory of Relativity (1916), which stated that the laws of nature are the same for all systems, regardless of their state of motion.

One of these laws of nature had been formulated in 1900 by Max Planck (1858-1947), a German physicist, who expressed mathematically the amount of energy emitted in the radiation of heat. He discovered that the amount of energy divided by the frequency of the radiation always yielded the same very tiny number, which scientists call Planck's Constant. The implication of this discovery was that objects emit energy not in an unbroken flow, but in a series of separate minute units, each of which Planck called a *quantum*. Quantum physics suggested a basic discontinuity in the universe by assuming that a quantum could appear at two different locations without having traversed the intervening space. It seemed almost absurd; as the philosopher and mathematician Bertrand Russell (1872-1970) noted, it was as if a person could be twenty years old, or twenty-two, but never twenty-one. Other physicists soon made discoveries reinforcing the idea of continuity, with all physical phenomena behaving like waves. The old dilemma of whether light consisted of particles or of waves was therefore greatly extended. Einstein and others suggested that the only useful procedure was to grasp both horns of the dilemma—and teach wave theory Mondays, Wednesdays, and Fridays, as one British physicist put it, and particle theory Tuesdays, Thursdays, and Saturdays.

During the 1920s it became evident that scientists might never be able to answer the ultimate questions about the universe. They could not fully understand the behavior of the electron, the basic components of the atom, because in the act of trying to observe the electron, they created effects that altered its behavior. Study of the electron led Werner Heisenberg (1901-1976), a German physicist, to propose the principle of indeterminacy or uncertainty, which concludes that the scientist will have to be content with probabilities rather than absolutes. Although the universe is no longer the world machine of Newton, its activity is by no means random, and it can still be expressed in the mathematical language of probabilities. Indeed, the new sciences of probability theory, molecular biology and biochemistry, and plasma physics, together with the discovery by Murray Gell-Mann (1929-   ) of the *quark*, which is any of three types of elementary particles believed to form the basis for all

matter in the universe, have nonetheless led scientists once again to feel that they may be on the verge of a unifying theory by which creation, matter, and even life may at last be explained.

The development of twentieth-century astronomy has been closely linked to that of physics. To the nonscientist, such astronomical concepts as the finite but expanding universe, curved space, and the almost inconceivable distances and quantitites of light years and galaxies have made astronomy the most romantic science. A light year is the distance traversed by light in one year, or roughly 5,880,000,000,000 miles. The Milky Way galaxy, of which our universe is a part, has some thirty thousand million stars and nebulae, in the form of a disk with a diameter of about a hundred thousand light years. To humanize these dimensions, and to make them comprehensible, Western writers produced works of science fiction and created television series and motion picture films that attempted to make sense at the level of popular culture of such abstract concepts as the light year. One such program, originally to be called "Wagon Train to the Stars," became one of the most popular television programs of all time as "Star Trek." It posed moral dilemmas in outer space to a generation of the young for whom the customary means of presenting moral issues, whether in church or through literature,

In the 1980s, the use of computers was creating a new technology, new employment opportunities, new forms of education, new means of storing and retrieving information, and new challenges to humanity. The microchip, smaller than an ordinary paper clip, could store as much information as an entire library. Advances in technology also made it possible to manufacture automobiles by remote means—that is, by robot, as in this scene from a factory in Japan.

seemed ineffective, and to whom the romance of outer space had replaced the romance of the old frontier. Politicians too were caught up in the popular fascination with space, referring to their policies as New Frontiers and using metaphors in their speeches derived from the new language of space travel and space conquest.

Science and the Quality of Life

Chemistry, which made possible plastics, synthetic fibers, and many other innovations, also greatly affected daily life by its impact on food, clothing, and most material objects. Chemistry assisted the very great gains made by the biological sciences and their application to medicine and public health. In the United States and elsewhere, infant mortality fell and many contagious diseases were conquered so successfully that the average expectancy of life at birth increased by over twenty years since 1900. More children were being born and living longer worldwide, so that the problem of feeding an expanding population remained acute. Some relief resulted from the new technologies of irrigated farming, chemical fertilizers, and highly productive new hybrid strains of wheat and corn.

The advance of science created problems as well as solved them. Some of the problems were of the first magnitude, notably the prospect that the modern military technology, with its hydrogen bombs, its missiles, and its biological warfare, could destroy humanity. Pesticides, detergents, and plastics, which were originally thought to be purely beneficial to the quality of life, also threatened life by their harmful effects on ecology. Scientists and technicians came under attack as cold, inhuman, and unable to control the awesome gadgets they created. Financing scientific education and research became a major and expensive problem. Yet twentieth-century science accomplished many wonders, not the least of which was to demonstrate the continued vitality and inventiveness of Western civilization, despite all the prophets of doom.

IV MODERN LITERATURE AND THE ARTS: ELITE AND POPULAR

Literature

Twentieth-century writers surprised the prophets of doom. Poetry remained, for the most part, what it had become in the late nineteenth century: difficult, cerebral, and addressed to a small audience. An occasional poet broke from the privacy of limited editions to wide popularity; but more symptomatic was the wide attention given to T.S. Eliot (1888-1965). His difficult yet moving symbolic poem, "The Waste Land," or his invocation to "The Hollow Men," which closed with the lines

This is the way the world ends
Not with a bang but a whimper

captured for a whole generation its sense of quiet despair, its anguish hidden in boredom, and its expectation of a cleansing flame to purge society.

However, the novel remained the most important form of contemporary imaginative writing. Although no one could predict which novelists of our century would be read in the twenty-first century, the American William Faulkner (1897-1962), the German Thomas Mann (1875-1955), and the Frenchman Albert Camus (1913-1960) were already enshrined as classics. Mann, who began with a traditionally realistic novel of life in his birthplace, the old Hanseatic town of Lübeck, never really belonged to the avant garde. He was typical of the sensitive, worried, class-conscious artist of the age of psychology. Camus too was sensitive and worried, but with an existentialist concern in his novels and plays over human isolation and the need to engage oneself in life. Camus nicely illustrated the problem of history as it related to literary trends; highly popular in his time, he remained a significant author in the eyes of the Americans and the English, even as, by the 1980s, he was virtually neglected by the French and no longer seen to be as important as once thought.

The most innovative novelist of the twentieth century surely was the Irishman James Joyce (1882-1941). Joyce began with a subtle, outspoken, but conventional series of sketches of life in the Dublin of his youth, *Dubliners* (1914), and an undisguised autobiography, *Portrait of the Artist as a Young Man* (1916). Then, in exile on the Continent, he wrote a classic experimental novel, *Ulysses* (1922), an account of twenty-four hours in the life of Leopold Bloom, a Dublin Jew. *Ulysses* is full of difficult allusion, parallels with Homer, puns, rapidly shifting scenes and episodes, and it is written without regard for the conventional notions of plot and orderly development. Above all, it makes full use of the recently developed psychology of the unconscious, as displayed in the stream of consciousness. The last chapter, printed entirely without punctuation marks, is the record of what went on in the mind of Bloom's wife, Molly, as she lay in bed waiting for him to come home. What went on in her mind was too shocking for most contemporaries, and *Ulysses*, published in Paris, had to be smuggled into English-speaking countries. The later widespread popularity of Joyce indicated the extent to which sexual mores and attitudes toward explicit language changed after World War II. Joyce's influence was pervasive; even Gell-Mann's quark was taken from Joyce's language.

Painting

Even more than literature, the fine arts confronted the cultivated Westerner with the problem of aesthetic modernism. Although a few popular painters still worked in the representational tradition, the mainstream of painting flowed into the many channels first explored by the French impressionsists and their contemporaries.

No painter could better serve as a representative of the endless variety and experimentation of twentieth-century painting than the versatile and immensely productive Pablo Picasso (1880-1973). A native Spaniard and adopted Frenchman, Picasso painted in many styles and periods. For example, the paintings of his "blue period" in the early 1900s, with their exhausted and defeated people, had a melancholy, lyrical quality that reflected the struggling young artist's own poverty. These pictures are said to have been influenced by the work of El Greco, the sixteenth-century Spanish master; certainly both artists conveyed a sense of concentrated emotion by exaggerating and distorting human proportions.

Around 1905-1906 Picasso turned to more daring innovations and distortions, much influenced by exhibitions of masks from black Africa and of large-eyed archaic sculptures newly discovered in the Mediterranean world. Picasso strove, as Cézanne had in the nineteenth centry to capture in the two dimensions of a picture the three dimensions of the real world. Sometimes he used the techniques of abstractionism—the reduction of figures to a kind of plane geometry, all angles and lines—and sometimes those of cubism—a kind of solid geometry, all cubes, spheres, and cones—and somtimes collage (pasteup), in which he glued onto a picture fragments of real objects—a bit of newspaper or caning from a chair.

In his later years Picasso often returned to more traditional representational painting, as in the almost classical portraits of his "white period" after World War I and in innumerable sketches of friends. Yet he also persisted in his more radical vein of showing the human or animal figure from two or more angles simultaneously, hence the misplaced eyes and other anatomical rearrangements that he employed with such telling effect in *Guernica* (1937), which depicted the havoc wrought by an aerial attack upon a defenseless town during the Spanish Civil War (p. 343). At his death Picasso was the most widely known artist in the world.

Art, like life, remained idiosyncratic, diverse, unwilling to be regimented. Some viewers denounced such art as decadent; this was Hitler's position. Others wished art to contribute in a direct way to the state; this was Stalin's position. Many found art simply irrelevant. The more it moved away from representing objective and visual reality, the less they could understand it. But many were fascinated by the new freedom, the new themes, and the new techniques. In varying ways this art sought to capture the courage and the anguish of modern humanity.

Perhaps the most arresting of Picasso's innovative paintings is *Les Demoiselles d'Avignon* (*demoiselles* were prostitutes, and Avignon was the name of a street in the red-light district in Barcelona). The women have huge, staring eyes, as though able to see through all human frailty, and their simplified features—similar to archaic sculpture from ancient times—suggest primitive masks that hide true feelings. As an artist, Picasso could comment through his work on the so-called "forbidden" side of history, for until the 1960s and 1970s, historians did not write about human sexuality, about death, or about madness—subjects that societies did not wish to see explored. Artists like Picasso prepared the way for the new, more candid, historiography of social movements so popular by the 1980s.

FAULKNER ON COURAGE

Courage in the face of adversity has marked the human condition. On any objective, material basis, the condition of life has steadily improved over the centuries: the infant mortality rate has fallen, the longevity rate has risen, the caloric intake has increased, a wide range of diseases that once devastated humanity have been conquered, and labor-saving devices have taken the sweat from the brow of millions. At the same time, human ability to inflict grievous wounds has also increased: wars that once took thousands of lives can now take millions, and new forms of warfare can destroy all life on this planet. The forms of courage the human condition demands have also changed, even as the demand continues. An American writer who won the Nobel Prize for literature in 1949, William Faulkner (1897-1962), in his brief address in Stockholm while accepting the award, discussed this long human search for security and courage:

Our tragedy today is a general and universal physical fear so long sustained by now that we can even bear it. There are no longer problems of the spirit. There is only the question: When will I be blown up? Because of this, the young man or woman writing today has forgotten the problems of the human heart in conflict with itself which alone can make good writing because only that is worth writing about, worth the agony and the sweat.

He must learn them again. He must teach himself that the basest of all things is to be afraid; and, teaching himself that, forget it forever, leaving no room in his workshop for anything but the old verities and truths of the heart, the old universal truths, lacking which any story is ephemeral and doomed—love and honor and pity and pride and compassion and sacrifice. Until he does so, he labors under a curse. He writes not of love but of lust, of defeats in which nobody loses anything of value, of victories without hope and, worst of all, without pity or compassion. His griefs grieve on no universal bones, leaving no scars. He writes not of the heart but of the glands.

Until he relearns these things, he will write as though he stood alone and watched the end of man. I decline to accept the end of man. It is easy enough to say that man is immortal simply because he will endure; that when the last ding-dong of doom has clanged and faded from the last worthless rock hanging tideless in the last red and dying evening, that even there there will still be one more sound: that of his puny inexhaustible voice, still talking. I refuse to accept this. I believe that man will not merely endure: he will prevail. He is immortal, not because he alone among creatures has an inexhaustible voice but because he has a soul, a spirit capable of compassion and sacrifice and endurance. The poet's, the writer's, duty is to write about these things. It is his privilege to help man endure by lifting his heart, by reminding him of the courage and honor and hope and pride and compassion and pity and sacrifice which have been the glory of his past. The poet's voice need not merely be the record of man, it can be one of the props, the pillars to help him endure and prevail.

From Frederick J. Hoffman and Olga W. Vickery, eds., *William Faulkner: Three Decades of Criticism* (East Lansing, Mich.: Michigan State University Press, 1969), pp. 347-48.

For a brief time a protest movement in art known as Dada scandalized the critics after World War I. This group protested the slaughter of millions in war not only in their work but in their chosen name, for Dada was a meaningless word, probably babytalk for the hobby-horse, that the artists and the makers of war all rode upon in the destruction of sanity and security. Although it has been argued that Dadaist protest was more political and social than aesthetic, most of the artists associated with it made distinguished contributions to the arts. Jean Arp (1887-1966), who fled his native Alsace for Switzerland to avoid service in the German army, was a pioneer in abstractionist painting and sculpture. Max Ernst (1891-1976) experimented with surrealism in an attempt to transfer to canvas the Freudian world of dreams and nightmares. George Grosz (1893-1959) made bitter sketches satirizing the foibles of German society between the two world wars. Marcel Duchamp

(1887-1968) created a sensation at the New York Armory show of 1913, which introduced avant-garde art to the American public, by exhibiting his *Nude Descending a Staircase*, a cubist attempt to depict the human figure in rapid motion.

Duchamp, Grosz, and Ernst eventually moved from Europe to the United States as part of the wave of artistic emigration that reached its peak in the late 1930s and early 1940s and ended the old dominance of Paris as the center of the avant garde. In the 1940s and 1950s New York became the capital of abstract expressionism, which communicated ideas or moods by entirely non-representational means through color, form, and a sense of movement or action. The American Jackson Pollock (1912-1956) dripped or hurled automobile enamel on huge canvases, which he laid out on his studio floor, creating an arresting effect of ordered chaos. In the 1960s the New York spotlight shifted to pop art, a neo-

Dadaist reaction to mass-produced and mass-marketed commodities. Pop artists depicted boxes of Brillo, cans of Campbell's soup, road signs, soap operas, comic strips, and blurred pictures of movie stars from magazines or the television screen. Pop artists, together with the American Robert Motherwell (1915-   ) and the British Francis Bacon (1909-   ) took up the dominating positions of their time.

The Other Arts

Pop sculpture featured plaster casts of real people surrounded by actual pieces of furniture in a three-dimensional comic strip of devitalized, defeated humanity. At the other extreme, sculpture in the grand manner experienced a rebirth, in good measure due to the work of two British artists. Barbara Hepworth (1903-1975) made classically fashioned standing abstract forms of great beauty, like the memorial to her friend Dag Hammarskjold outside the United Nations building in New York. Henry Moore (1898-   ) came to be

Alberto Giacometti (1901-1966), painter, sculptor, and poet, used simplified human forms to emphasize technology's growing control over human actions, and the themes and methods of his abstractions were taken up by other artists twenty years later. In *Chariot* (1950), his diminished symbol of mankind (shown below) is nonetheless monumental in the way in which it occupies space.

Henry Moore's *Family Group,* completed between 1945 and 1949, emphasized the strength and continuity of the family at a time when it was under attack.
The work of Constantin Brancusi (1876-1957) also contrasted sharply with that of the artists of despair. Soaring, calming, tactile—in the sense that the viewer longs to touch his work—and representative of the aerodynamic visions of modern flight, Brancusi's *Bird in Space* (1925) remained a peak of artistic expression. The very material itself—polished bronze—both expressed and depended upon the technology of the modern age. The version shown here, probably cast in 1928, is from the Museum of Modern Art in New York City.

In recent decades a growing fear of uniformity and homogeneity has been in conflict with a desire for comfort and security. As the standard of living in industrial societies rose around the world, the countervailing cost was the perception that everyone might be stamped from the same mold. Tract housing, which made it possible for lower income families to own their own homes, became the symbol of these competing values. Here an American suburb is shown in 1949: 17,447 homes, mass produced at a price well below the prevailing market level, closely packed onto five thousand acres of farmland on Long Island, New York.

widely considered the ranking sculptor of the century, possibly the greatest practitioner of the art since Michelangelo. His powerful renditions of monumental human figures, simplified and reduced to essentials, created an effect like that of a cubist or expressionist painting. In sculpture as in painting, the variety and vitality of innovations were remarkable—from the highly polished rhythmic abstractions of the Romanian Constantin Brancusi (1876-1957), to the disturbing, emaciated figures of the Swiss Alberto Giacometti (1901-1966), to the abstract or whimsical mobiles of the American Alexander Calder (1898-1976) and his larger, sometimes menacing, stabiles.

In architecture the twentieth century produced the first truly original style since the end of the eighteenth century. This functional style was no revival of the past, no living museum of eclecticism like many nineteenth-century buildings. It prided itself on honest use of modern materials and on adaptation to the site and to the demands of twentieth-century living, combined with avoidance of waste space and excess display. One of its pioneers was the American Frank Lloyd Wright (1869-1959), who spent his apprenticeship with the designers of early Chicago skyscrapers and then developed the "prairie" style of house, emphasizing the planes and the uncluttered simplicity that Wright admired in Japanese houses. Toward the end of his life Wright made a radical experiment in the designing of the Solomon Guggenheim Museum in New York, which consists mainly of one vast, open space through which visitors descend along a ramp that permits them to see the works dis-

played both close at hand and at several different removes of distance. If there was in the best modern architecture a touch of austerity, even puritanism, it was a reaction against nineteenth-century vulgarity, but there was in much of the less good a sterile uniformity. Travelers complained that all over the world they found the same unornamented steel and glass boxes, which, despite the credo of the functionalists, seemed to have been put up with no regard for the physical site or the traditions of the country.

Modern music, like modern art, moved away from what the general public could comprehend into atonal and experimental music, often based on electronics, or else it merged with a vast branch of the entertainment industry, represented by country and western, various forms of rock and roll, and modern jazz. All had their innovators who sought to develop fresh ideas and sounds, and jazz in particular was often both intellectually and emotionally creative in ways that broke with the essentially derivative modes of much popular romantic music. Music for the millions reached them through radio and television, and by traveling groups such as the Beatles. Sadly enough, the adored Beatles were not exempt from the irrational impulses of modern times, and a leading member of their group, John Lennon (1940-1980), was killed by an apparently insane admirer.

The words and sounds of popular music came to dominate the sensory world of young western Europeans, Americans, and Japanese, representing an internationalization of tastes as pervasive as the Sony Walkman on which the music was played. All art dis-

American popular music has become international in its appeal. Country and Western, once heard only regionally in the United States, is today heard everywhere, and rock music attracts large audiences throughout the Western world, in the Soviet Union, in parts of Africa, and in Japan. New cultural heroes who initially appealed to the young now attract all generations. Outstanding among the musical innovators over the years have been the Beatles and Frank Sinatra.

torts perspective in order to heighten concentration, and music, in distorting sound, commanded intense attention.

A Final Word

But then so too did all of the world and its complex realities. Many observers feared that there had been a slow breakdown in what was once understood to be the social contract. Much of humanity was struggling with dual goals: to achieve freedom and to create equality, to protect the rights of the individual and to meet obligations to others. But must individual liberty be given up to guarantee equality? Must a sense of service to others be abandoned to achieve self-realization? People more and more focused on devotion to self: a soaring divorce rate led to divided families; the desire for more and better material possessions led to greater materialism; a sense of entitlement to the good things of life led to anger at those who took without being entitled or those who had been rewarded with an excess of good things. In the 1980s the delicately balanced pendulum that moved back and forth across the face of Western history was beginning to emphasize duty in equal measure to rights, was beginning to place limits on the obligation of the state to the individual and of the individual to the state, in such a way as to create a sense of instability and uncertainty as to what values ought to be cherished.

One of the values under question was the study of history itself. History, it was agreed, attempted to demonstrate the relationship between cause and effect. Being itself about time, history attempted to show how people worked within the constraints of time to arrive at decisions. History sought to organize causes in some order of priorities, so that one could separate the important from the less important, the proximate from the remote, in a complex sequence of causation. But such efforts assumed that there were, in the end, *facts* that could be known, that there was a *rational* basis to decision making, that causes could be discovered and their effects could be charted, and that commonly held values could lead to agreement on priorities of action.

In some ways, Western civilization in the mid-1980s appeared to comprise a unity. To the extent that this unity was defined by high industrial capacity or serious attention to new art forms (such as the motion picture, which many regarded as the most significant development in art as well as in entertainment in the last fifty years) Japan was also a member of this Western world. Yet Western civilization also appeared more divided than it had been for many decades. The superpowers, the Soviet Union and the United States, were unable to agree on such fundamental matters as limiting the arms race. Some communist mass movements continued to stress the presumption of inevitability in history; they were "making history as we must," convinced that history would prove them right. The liberal democracies of Western Europe and Canada, as well as Japan, appeared less resilient than in the past, and despite

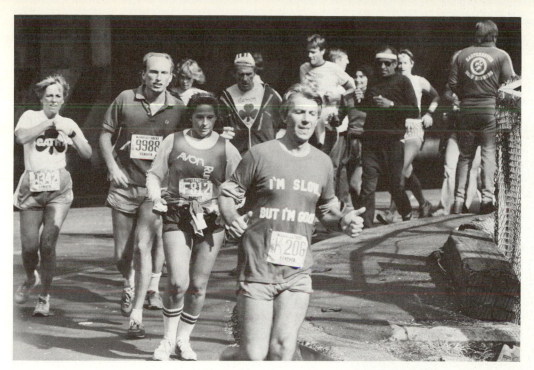

In the 1980s video games had become highly popular, especially in the United States, and a new entertainment industry was created. While some people feared that the games would confuse fantasy and reality in the minds of the young, and others argued that the arcade drew young people out into an environment where mind-affecting drugs were easily available, other commentators found that the games stimulated the imagination and fostered a healthy sense of competition. Another pervasive activity of the period was the health craze, as expressed in jogging, marathons, sports, and exercise programs.

significant international gatherings of their leaders—as in an economic summit in Williamsburg, Virginia, in May of 1983—they could not agree on how best to deal with inflation, high unemployment, and an angry electorate.

Germany and Japan had experienced remarkable recoveries from World War II, and other nations studied these "economic miracles," even as the miracles became tarnished, to see what might be learned from them. Both had been highly 'organized states under totalitarian regimes before their defeat, and in the postwar years they could draw upon a heritage of strong public commitment to the idea of the central state. Both were, to a high degree, ethnically homogeneous, so that neither experienced the far-ranging and debilitating effects of race conflict and racism. Both were aided after the war by those who had defeated them, so that they entered into economic competition with new industrial plants as the older industrial nations were falling behind by failing to replace their obsolete equipment. Neither Germany nor Japan was faced with large defense budgets, since as a condition of the peace settlements they were prohibited from maintaining forces capable of aggressive action against another nation. Nations with high industrial capacity looked to them as models of social and industrial reorganization.

Other contending models were authoritarian or repressive, and in the Third World the number of nations that followed such a pattern appeared on the increase. Totalitarian dictatorships usually involve single-party government, control over most forms of communications, a weapons monopoly within the state, a terrorist police force, a centrally directed economy, and usually a

single strong leader with an ideology attractive to a mass group. Some nations clearly met all these criteria—Kampuchea, North Korea, Libya, some of the smaller states of Africa—while others were simply repressive in relatively systematic ways, such as Poland, South Africa, or the Philippines. While most liberal democracies were firmly opposed to these contending models, even within

WHY STUDY HISTORY?

Historians continue to debate their own purposes and their own methods. Some detect clear patterns and may even attempt to predict general trends for the future from their study of the past; others find history to be simply one event after another. Between these positions there are other, more moderate, defenses for the value of history. One finds it poetic, even beautiful, for it gives humanity a sense of itself, of what it is that makes it human. Another finds that while history may seem to lack any grand design, there is a form of design in this random appearance.

The following extracts, from two British historians of the twentieth century, present these views. The first is from G.M. Trevelyan (1876-1962); the second is from H.A.L. Fisher (1865-1940).

The appeal of History to us all is in the last analysis poetic. But the poetry of History does not consist of imagination roaming at large, but of imagination pursuing the fact and fastening upon it. That which compels the historian to "scorn delights and live laborious days" is the ardour of his own curiosity to know what really happened long ago in that land of mystery which we call the past. To peer into that magic mirror and see fresh figures there every day is a burning desire that consumes and satisfies him all his life, that carries him each morning, eager as a lover, to the library and muniment room. It haunts him like a passion of almost terrible potency, because it is poetic. The dead were and are not. Their place knows them no more and is ours today. Yet they were once as real as we, and we shall tomorrow be shadows like them. In men's first astonishment over that unchanging mystery lay the origins of poetry, philosophy, and religion. From it, too, is derived in more modern times this peculiar call of the spirit, the type of intellectual curiosity that we name the historical sense. Unlike most forms of imaginative life it cannot be satisfied save by facts. . . . It is the fact about the past that is poetic; just because it really happened, it gathers round it all the inscrutable mystery of life and death and time. Let the science and research of the historian find the fact, and let his imagination and art make clear its significance.

* * * * * * * * * * * *

One intellectual excitement has . . . been denied me. Men wiser and more learned than I have discovered in history a plot, a rhythm, a predetermined pattern. These harmonies are concealed from me. I can see only one emergency following upon another as wave follows upon wave, only one great fact with respect to which, since it is unique, there can be no generalizations, only one safe rule for the historian: that he should recognize in the development of human destinies the play of the contingent and the unforeseen. This is not a doctrine of cynicism and despair. The fact of progress is written plain and large on the page of history; but progress is not a law of nature. The ground gained by one generation may be lost by the next. The thoughts of men may flow into the channels which lead to disaster and barbarism.

George Macaulay Trevelyn, *The Present Position of History: An Inaugural Lecture* (London: Longmans, Green & Co., 1927), pp. 28-29. These views of the discipline of history, together with many others, appear in Charles P. Curtis, Jr., and Ferris Greenslet, eds., *The Practical Cogitator: The Thinker's Anthology* (New York: Houghton Mifflin, 1983). Copyright Longmans Group Ltd.

the democracies groups appeared that wanted the greater stability that such methods could bring. The cost of democracy was high, and it was under heavy and persistent challenge. The liberal democracies had passed through periods of conflict over ideological commitment; the last such period had been in the late 1960s and early 1970s. In the mid-1980s public tolerance for ideological passion appeared relatively low.

To many observers, a fragmentation of knowledge seemed to put the basic assumptions of Western civilization at risk. Many commentators expressed fear that two distinct cultures were developing in Western societies: one based on the assumptions of humanists, the other on the assumptions of scientists. The explosion in knowledge—in what a person needed to know to be considered educated, in how society viewed and used knowledge, and in the technical means by which knowledge was transmitted, acquired, stored, and retrieved—led to increased specialization, which hindered communication among intellectuals, statesmen, and all who needed to communicate across the barriers of class, race, nation, or specialization. A worldwide resurgence in religious conviction was observed, whether in the nations that had long before embraced Islam, or in the nations that had evolved from the Judeo-Christian ethic. Other groups expressed their concern for the future of humanity in terms of environmentalism, or in seeking to establish new political coalitions. It was evident that fundamental convictions were under attack as seldom before.

New developments in Western thought challenged the older assumptions of rationality, and while most thinkers in the West probably held to a belief in ultimate order, trusting that explanations could be found for what happened, this trust had placed a new burden on history—itself rooted in the ancient Greek assumptions about what constituted the good life. To know thyself had been the Greek goal, and it still was the goal of historical study—though what one might truly know had been severely challenged in the 1980s. History continued to attempt to account to the self for the self, to explain why the world was as it was and is. Thus, paradoxically, as history provided some orientation on the relationship of the individual to the present, it also linked the individual to the largest and broadest community of all—the world of the past.

SUMMARY

Views of history change constantly. As historians view the last forty years, they face the difficulty of evaluating recent historical trends, such as economic cycles or the worldwide impact of the arms race. Today Western civilization can no longer be seen as separate from world culture.

Whereas nineteenth-century thought emphasized the dynamics of change in time, the twentieth century has focused on the role of the unconscious in human action and thought. The work of Sigmund Freud not only influenced the understanding of human relations but also had a vast impact on political and cultural theory. Sociologists such as Max Weber or Emile Durkheim sought to study society in the light of the subjective and nonrational elements in human life.

The three major philosophical movements of the twentieth century have been existentialism, influenced by such nineteenth century thinkers as Nietzsche and Kierkegaard; logical analysis; and historicism, an attempt to find in history an answer to the ultimate philosophical questions. In the twentieth century historians also have asked new questions and opened up new fields of inquiry.

Intense specialization occurred in the sciences in the twentieth century. Einstein and others revolutionized physics by radically revising the Newtonian view of the world. Major developments in astronomy were closely linked to those in physics and contributed to popular fascination with space travel. Great gains were also made in chemical and biological sciences and resulted in, among other things, greatly expanded life expectancy and increased food production.

In literature, the novel remained the most important form of imaginative writing. The new psychology influenced novelists as they examined the individual's unconscious drives. James Joyce's experimental novel, *Ulysses,* made use of the new "stream of consciousness" style.

In the past one hundred and fifty years artists have experimented with ways of expressing what lies beneath surface appearances. Led by Claude Monet, impressionist painters of the 1870s and 1880s experimented with the use of light and color, allowing the viewer to reassemble dabs of color into a recognizable scene. In the twentieth century a variety of artistic styles have held sway for a time, ranging from cubism, Dada, and surrealism to pop art. In the 1940s and 1950s New York became the capital of abstract expressionism, a nonrepresentational art that emphasized color, form, and a sense of movement.

Twentieth-century architects used modern materials adapted to the demands of space and function. Frank Lloyd Wright was a leader in this movement, designing buildings that embodied uncluttered simplicity.

Modern musicians experimented with atonality while popular music grew into a vast entertainment industry dominated by well-known stars with global followings.

Liberal democracies were challenged by totalitarian and repressive states, as well as by fragmentation and intense specialization within. The computer, perhaps the most significant change in technology in the last two decades, promised to change the very organization of knowledge, and thus of life. Confusion intermixed with dedication to the ideals of the past appeared to characterize most of the nations of the West as they approached the start of the twenty-first century.

SUGGESTED READINGS

Lists of supplementary or additional readings are usually intended to offer the student guidance into fuller, more specialized, or more advanced historical literature. These lists also include sources—that is, primary documentary materials—for students who want to enter into the spirit of the period under study by reading of that period in the words of contemporaries. Because footnotes have been used throughout the text to provide information on the origins of quotations, the following list is not intended to serve as a formal bibliography of books used in preparing the text. No titles are included that author Robin Winks has not read, but titles are not supplied to support all potentially controversial statements made in the text. Rather, the purpose of these lists, which are broken down by chapter and general subject matter, is to provide the student with a way to learn more about the major subjects.

Information listed refers to the latest edition available at the time this text went to press. Obviously there are dozens, even hundreds, of books on any of the subjects discussed in the text. The criteria for selection, therefore, have had to be clear: books, preferably short, written in a manner likely to be of interest to students of history, and when possible, books that are in print and in paperback editions. Clarity, accuracy, and availability were the primary tests. The most recent book on a subject is not always the best, though many titles published in the 1970s and 1980s have been included if they met the criteria. The authors believe that this list of suggested readings is therefore both up to date and useful, and books that have been included should be available in any good college library.

THE VALUE OF HISTORY AND OF HISTORICAL CONTROVERSY

Our first controversy was to define "civilization," and this was done in the introductory chapter. Readers wishing to pursue this thorny problem further might best begin with Robert Redfield, *The Primitive World and its Transformations* (Ithaca: Cornell University Press, 1953); move on to Lloyd Warner, *A Black Civilization,* rev. ed. (New York: Harper & Row, 1958); A. L. Kroeber, *The Nature of Culture* (Chicago: University of Chicago Press, 1952); and Arnold Toynbee, *Civilization on Trial* (Oxford: Oxford University Press, 1953), of which Kroeber was critical. Then explore Glyn Daniel, *The First Civilizations: The Archaeology of Their Origins* (New York: T. Y. Crowell, 1968) and *The Idea of Prehistory* (Cleveland: World Publishing Co., 1962).

CHAPTER 15: THE PROBLEM OF DIVINE-RIGHT MONARCHY

Europe in General

Maurice P. Ashley, *The Golden Century* (New York: Praeger, 1969). A valuable introduction to seventeenth-century Europe.

Richard S. Dunn, *The Age of Religious Wars, 1559-1717,* 2nd ed. (New York: Norton, 1979). Crisp, comprehensive survey.

Carl Joachim Friedrich, *The Age of the Baroque, 1610-1660* (New York: Harper & Row, 1952); Frederick L. Nussbaum, *The Triumph of Science and Reason, 1660-1685* (New York: Harper & Row, 1953); John B. Wolf, *The Emergence of the Great Powers, 1685-1715* (New York: Harper & Row, 1951). Detailed, scholarly volumes with very full bibliographies; in The Rise of Modern Europe Series (Harper & Row Torchbooks).

Eli Filip Heckscher, *Mercantilism,* 2nd ed. (New York: Macmillan, 1962). A famous and controversial work.

Frederick L. Nussbaum, *A History of Economic Institutions in Modern Europe* (New York: Kelley, 1967). An abridgement of Sombart's *Modern Capitalism,* which argues that war is economically creative. The arguments are attacked by John U. Neff, *War and Human Progress* (New York: Norton, 1968).

Nikolaus Pevsner, *An Outline of European Architecture* (London: Penguin, 1953). Clear, opinionated romp through the whole of western Europe.

France

Davis Bitten, *The French Nobility in Crisis, 1560-1640* (Palo Alto, Calif.: Stanford University Press, 1969). Sound study of their declining role.

Carl J. Burckhardt, *Richelieu: His Rise to Power and Assertion of Power and Cold War* (London: Allen & Unwin, 1940). Scholarly two-volume study of the great cardinal.

Charles W. Cole, *Colbert and a Century of French Mercantilism* (Hamden, Conn.: Archon, 1964). A solid, detailed study.

Albert Guerard, *France in the Classical Age: The Life and Death of an Ideal,* rev. ed. (New York: Brazillier, 1956). Stimulating interpretation of early modern France.

Ragnhild H. Hatton, *Europe in the Age of Louis XIV* (New York: Norton, 1979). Instructive study of the links among economic, social, and cultural developments.

James E. King, *Science and Rationalism in the Government of Louis XIV* (Baltimore: Johns Hopkins University Press, 1978). Monograph showing the relations between intellectual and political history.

W. H. Lewis, *The Splendid Century* (New York: Morrow, 1954). Stresses the nature of society in France under Louis XIV.

John D. Lough, *An Introduction to Seventeenth Century France* (New York: Longmans, Green, 1955). Designed for the student of literature.

Orest A. Ranum, *Richelieu and the Councillors of Louis XIII* (Westport, Conn.: Greenwood, 1976). An important monograph on administration.

Warren C. Scoville, *The Persecution of the Huguenots and French Economic Development, 1680-1720* (Berkeley: University of California Press, 1960). Enlightening evaluation.

W. J. Stankiewicz, *Politics and Religion in Seventeeth Century France* (Westport, Conn.: Greenwood, 1976). Illuminating study of their interrelations.

G. R. R. Treasure, *Seventeenth Century France* (London: John Murray, 1981). Full and lucid survey.

John B. Wolf, *Louis XIV* (New York: Norton, 1968). Detailed, scholarly biography; stresses politics.

England

Maurice Ashley, *England in the Seventeenth Century* (Totowa, N.J.: B & N Imports); and Christopher Hill, *The Century of Revolution, 1603-1714* (New York: Norton, 1982). Two sound surveys by experts.

Stephen B. Baxter, *William III and the Defense of European Liberty* (Westport, Conn.: Greenwood, 1976). Clear and sympathetic.

Carl W. Bridenbaugh, *Vexed and Troubled Englishmen, 1590-1642* (Oxford: Oxford University Press, 1968). A fuller study covering much of the same ground as Notestein's book listed below.

D. C. Coleman, *The Economy of England, 1450-1750* (Oxford: Oxford University Press, 1978). Short, clear look that combines the perspectives of historian and economist.

Godfrey Davies, *The Restoration of Charles II, 1658-1660* (San Marino, Calif.: Huntington Library, 1955). An authoritative monograph.

Godfrey Davies, *The Early Stuarts, 1603-1660,* 2nd ed. (Oxford: Oxford University Press, 1959); and George N. Clark, *The Later Stuarts, 1660-1714,* 2nd ed. (Oxford: Oxford University Press, 1971). More detailed scholarly treatments, in the Oxford History of England.

Christopher Hill, *The World Turned Upside Down* (London: Penguin, 1976). Sketch of the radical ideas advanced during the English Revolution.

Wallace Notestein, *The English People on the Eve of Colonization, 1603-1630* (New York: Harper & Row, 1954). Admirable social history.

Conrad Russell, *Parliaments and English Politics* (Oxford: Oxford University Press, 1982). The fullest, best look at the crucial Parliaments under James I.

Lawrence Stone, *The Crisis of the Aristocracy, 1558-1641* (Oxford: Oxford University Press, 1967), and *Social Change and Revolution in England, 1540-1640* (New York: Barnes & Noble, 1965). Important studies by a scholar who is an expert on the controversy over the role of the gentry. That controversy is neatly summarized in J. H. Hexter, *Reappraisals in History* (Chicago: University of Chicago Press, 1979).

Lawrence Stone, *The Causes of the English Revolution, 1529-1642* (New York: Harper & Row, 1972). Fine, very brief summary.

Joseph R. Tanner, *English Constitutional Conflicts of the Seventeenth Century* (Cambridge, Eng.: Cambridge University Press, 1962). Full and scholarly.

F. C. Turner, *James II* (London: Macmillan, 1948). Balanced treatment of a ruler generally subject to partisan interpretation.

Cicely V. Wedgewood, *The King's Peace, 1637-1641; The King's War, 1641-1647; and A Coffin for King Charles* (London: Macmillan, 1955-1964). Detailed study of the Great Rebellion.

Cicely V. Wedgewood, *Oliver Cromwell*, 2nd ed. (London: Duckworth, 1973); and Christopher Hill, *God's Englishman* (New York: Harper & Row, 1972). Perhaps the soundest of the general works on Cromwell.

David H. Willson, *King James VI and I* (New York: Holt, 1956). Sound appraisal of the first Stuart.

Perez Zagorin, *The Court and the Country* (New York: Atheneum, 1971). Appraisal of the origins of the English Revolution.

The Century of Genius

Samuel L. Bethell, *The Cultural Revolution of the Seventeenth Century* (London: Dobson, 1951). A literary study with fruitful suggestions for the historian of ideas.

Crane Brinton, *The Shaping of the Modern Mind* (New York: New American Library, 1953). A survey of intellectual history from the Renaissance on.

Ernest Mortimer, *Blaise Pascal* (Westport, Conn.: Greenwood, 1976). A sympathetic and well-written study.

Preserved Smith, *A History of Modern Culture*, Vol. 1 (New York: Holt, 1930). An older work that is a mine of information on aspects of culture often neglected in intellectual histories.

Basil Willey, *The Seventeenth Century Background* (New York: Columbia University Press, 1982). Essays on Descartes, Hobbes, Milton, and other figures in the intellectual life of the century.

The Baroque

Germain Bazin, *The Baroque* (New York: Norton, 1978). Less systematic but more suggestive assessment. Bazin is also the author of a brief introduction, *Baroque and Rococo Art* (New York: Praeger, n.d.).

Francis Haskell, *Patrons and Painters* (New Haven: Yale University Press, 1980). Enlightening examination of the relationship between Italian society and art in the baroque era.

Julius Held and Donald Posner, *17th and 18th Century Art* (Englewood Cliffs, N.J.: Prentice-Hall, 1972). A recent systematic survey of painting, sculpture, and architecture; handsomely illustrated.

Claude V. Palisca, *Baroque Music*, 2nd ed. (Englewood Cliffs, N.J.: Prentice-Hall, 1980). Fine, short survey.

A. Charles Sewter, *Baroque and Rococo* (London: Thames & Hudson, 1972). Compact introduction.

Victor L. Tapié, *The Age of Grandeur* (London: Weidenfeld and Nicholson, 1960). A review of baroque and classical art throughout Europe.

Rudolf Wittkower, *Art and Architecture in Italy, 1600-1700* (London: Pelican, 1980); and Anthony Blunt, *Art and Architecture in France, 1500-1700* (London: Penguin, 1977). Two scholarly volumes in The Pelican History of Art (Penguin).

Social Life

Richard L. Greaves, *Society and Religion in Elizabethan England* (Minneapolis: University of Minnesota Press, 1981). A full examination of the major differences in social outlook between Puritans and Anglicans before the English Revolution.

Christopher Hill, *Change and Continuity in Seventeenth-Century England* (Cambridge, Mass.: Harvard University Press, 1975). Stimulating essays on social attitudes.

Emmanuel Le Roy Ladurie, *The Peasants of Languedoc*, trans. John Day (Urbana: University of Illinois Press, 1977). A complex look at the life of the peasant in sixteenth-century France.

E. William Monter, *European Witchcraft* (New York: Wiley, 1969). Short collection of sources.

Roland Mousnier, *Peasant Uprisings in Seventeenth-Century France, Russia and China*, trans. Brian Pearce (London: Allen & Unwin, 1971). A close look at four peasant revolts in France between 1636 and 1675.

Lawrence Stone, *The Family, Sex and Marriage in England, 1500-1800* (New York: Harper & Row, 1977). Massive, much discussed work on an enormous range of topics in family history, from breast feeding to dealing with death.

Keith Thomas, *Religion and the Decline of Magic* (New York: Scribner's, 1971). Rich study of popular beliefs in sixteenth- and seventeenth-century England.

H. R. Trevor-Roper, *The European Witch-Craze of the Sixteenth and Seventeenth Centuries* (New York: Wiley, 1969). A short, clear-eyed view of the problem of witches.

Sources

William F. Church, ed., *The Impact of Absolutism in France* (New York: Wiley, 1969). Useful selections from source materials and commentaries on the era of Richelieu and Louis XIV.

Owen F. Morshead, ed., *Everybody's Pepys* (New York: Harcourt, 1926). A useful abridgment of a famous diary kept during the 1660s; a fascinating document of social history.

CHAPTER 16: THE OLD REGIMES

General Accounts

The following volumes in the series The Rise of Modern Europe (Harper & Row, Torchbooks), which comprise a detailed introduction to eighteenth-century war and politics, have elaborate bibliographies: Paul Roberts, *The Quest for Security, 1715-1740*; W. L. Dorn, *Competition for Empire, 1740-1763*; and Leo Gershoy, *From Despotism to Revolution, 1763-1789*.

M. S. Anderson, *Europe in the Eighteenth Century, 1713-1783* (London: Longmans, Green, 1976). A very good introductory volume.

The New Cambridge Modern History (Cambridge, Eng.: Cambridge University Press, 1957-1970). Two volumes of this ambitious but uneven publication contain materials useful for the present chapter. VI: *The Rise of Great Britain and Russia, 1688-1725* (1970); VII: *The Old Regime, 1713-1763* (1957).

Economics and Society

Thomas S. Ashton, *An Economic History of England: The Eighteenth Century* (New York: Methuen, 1972). Lucid introduction by an expert on the subject.

John Carswell, *The South Sea Bubble* (London: Cresset Press, 1960). An excellent monograph.

Carlo M. Cipolla, *Guns, Sails, and Empires* (New York: Minerva Press, 1965). Short, original inquiry into how specific technological innovations gave specific European nations dominance in the early phases of the great wars for empire.

Phyllis Deane, *The First Industrial Revolution* (Cambridge, Eng.: Cambridge University Press, 1980). Study of the British economy from 1750 to 1850.

Albert Goodwin, ed., *The European Nobility in the Eighteenth Century* (London: Black, 1953). Very helpful essays arranged country by country.

H. J. Habakkuk and Michael Postan, eds., *The Cambridge Economic History of Europe*, Vol. 6, Parts 1 and 2 (Cambridge, Eng.: Cambridge University Press, 1965). Scholarly essays by many writers on the economic revolutions.

Eli Filip Heckscher, *Mercantilism*, 2nd ed. (New York: Macmillan, 1962). A famous and controversial work; a mine of information on eighteenth-century economic developments.

Paul Mantoux, *The Industrial Revolution in the Eighteenth Century* (New York: Harper & Row, 1961). Classic study of the factory system in England.

David Ogg, *Europe of the Ancien Régime* (New York: Harper & Row, 1966). A social study, focused on Britain.

The Established Powers

Catherine B. A. Behrens, *The Ancien Régime* (London: Thames and Hudson, 1967). Readable and generously illustrated study which stresses French society.

Alfred Cobban, *A History of Modern France*, Vol. 1: *1715-1799* (London: Penguin, 1966). Good general survey.

Franklin L. Ford, *Robe and Sword* (Cambridge, Mass.: Harvard University Press, 1953). An instructive study of the French aristocracy during the generation following the death of Louis XIV.

George P. Gooch, *Louis XV* (London: Longmans, Green, 1956), and Nancy Mitford, *Madame de Pompadour* (London: Hamilton, 1954). Entertainingly old-fashioned biographies.

Hajo Holborn, *A History of Modern Germany,* Vol. 2 (Princeton: Princeton University Press, 1982). Succinct scholarly survey of the period from 1648 to 1840.

Olwen H. Hufton, *The Poor of Eighteenth-Century France, 1750-1789* (Oxford: Clarendon, 1974). Superb answer to the question, "Who were the poor?"

Henry Kamen, *The War of Succession in Spain, 1700-1715* (Bloomington: University of Indiana Press, 1969). Detailed study of the initial Bourbon impact upon Spain.

Louis Kronenberger, *Kings and Desperate Men* (New York: Knopf, 1942). Lively essays on eighteenth-century English society and personalities.

William E. Lecky, *A History of England in the Eighteenth Century,* rev. ed. (New York: AMS Press, 1968). A celebrated detailed study.

John Lough, *An Introduction to Eighteenth-Century France* (London: Longmans, Green, 1978). Clear and enlightening discussion of the Old Regime.

Lewis B. Namier, *The Structure of Politics at the Accession of George III,* 2nd ed. (New York: St. Martin's, 1957), and *England in the Age of the American Revolution* (New York: St. Martin's, n.d.). Detailed studies that revise the older concepts of eighteenth-century English political institutions.

Jack Plumb, *England in the Eighteenth Century* (Santa Fe, N.M.: Gannon, 1980). A good brief account by a scholar who has also written studies of Walpole, the elder Pitt, and the first four Georges.

William B. Willcox, *The Age of Aristocracy* (Lexington, Mass.: Heath, 1976). Fine, short history of England from 1688 to 1830.

Basil Williams, *The Whig Supremacy, 1714-1760,* 2nd ed., rev. (Oxford: Oxford University Press, 1962). A competent modern survey.

Arthur M. Wilson, *French Foreign Policy during the Administration of Cardinal Fleury* (Cambridge, Mass.: Harvard University Press, 1936). A sound monograph; one of the relatively few good books in English on the France of Louis XV.

The Newcomers

Francis L. Carsten, *The Origins of Prussia* (Westport, Conn.: Greenwood, 1982). Excellent monograph that carries the story through the reign of the Great Elector.

Gordon A. Craig, *The Politics of the Prussian Army, 1640-1945* (Oxford: Oxford University Press, 1964). Excellent scholarly study.

Christopher Duffy, *Russia's Military Way to the West* (London: Routledge & Kegan Paul, 1982). A careful examination of the emergence of Russia as a great European power in the eighteenth century.

Robert R. Ergang, *The Potsdam Fuhrer* (New York: Octagon, 1973). A splendid study of Frederick William I of Prussia.

Sidney B. Fay, *The Rise of Brandenburg-Prussia to 1786* (Melbourne, Fla.: Krieger, 1981). A lucid little volume packed with information.

V. Klyuchevsky, *Peter the Great* (New York: Vintage, n.d.). Stirring account by a Russian scholar.

Marc Raeff, ed., *Peter the Great Changes Russia* (Lexington, Mass.: Heath, 1972). Good cross section of judgments on the controversial czar.

Hans Rosenberg, *Bureaucracy, Aristocracy, Autocracy* (Boston: Beacon, 1966). A controversial analysis of Prussian history from 1660 to 1815.

Ferdinand Schevill, *The Great Elector* (Hamden, Conn.: Archon, 1965). A helpful study of the founder of the Hohenzollern despotism.

Benedict H. Sumner, *Peter the Great and the Emergence of Russia* (London: English Universities Press, 1950). A very good introductory account.

The International Balance

Christopher T. Atkinson, *A History of Germany, 1715-1815* (Westport, Conn.: Greenwood, 1970). An older account, particularly full on war and diplomacy.

Ludwig Dehio, *The Precarious Balance* (New York: Knopf, 1962). Reflections on the balance of power by a German scholar.

John F. C. Fuller, *A Military History of the Western World* (New York: Funk & Wagnalls, 1954-1956). The second volume of this stimulating survey covers the seventeenth and eighteenth centuries.

Lawrence H. Gipson, *The Great War for the Empire: The Culmination, 1760-1763* (New York: Knopf, 1954). Magisterial history of the war; Volume VIII of a detailed, sustained analysis.

K. M. Panikkar, *Asia and Western Dominance* (London: Allen & Unwin, 1965). Strong survey; emphasis on India.

Albert Sorel, *Europe Under the Old Regime* (New York: Harper & Row, 1964). A famous little essay by a French expert on the eighteenth-century balance.

Benedict H. Sumner, *Peter the Great and the Ottoman Empire* (Hamden, Conn.: Shoe String, 1965). A short and meaty monograph.

Leslie C. Tihany, *A History of Middle Europe* (New Brunswick, N.J.: Rutgers University Press, 1976). Straightforward survey.

Sources

Norbert Elias, *The History of Manners,* Vol. I: *The Civilizing Process,* trans. Edmund Jephcott (New York: Pantheon, 1982). Fascinating inquiry into changing forms of courtesy in daily life.

Robert and Elborg Forster, *European Society in the Eighteenth Century* (New York: Walker, 1969). Excellent anthology.

George P. Gooch, *Courts and Cabinets* (New York: Arno, 1972). A graceful introduction to the memoirs of some of the great personages of the era.

Carlile A. Macartney, ed., *The Hapsburg and Hohenzollern Dynasties in the Seventeenth and Eighteenth Centuries* (New York: Harper & Row, 1970). Helpful collection of documentary materials on Austrian and Prussian history.

Lady Mary W. Montagu, *Letters* (Oxford: Clarendon, 1965). By perhaps the best of the century's excellent letter writers; particularly valuable on the Hapsburg and Ottoman empires.

Arthur Young, *Tours in England and Wales* (London: Penguin, 1981). Reports of a prolific and perceptive agricultural expert.

CHAPTER 17: THE ENLIGHTENMENT

General

Walter L. Dorn, *Competition for Empire, 1740-1763;* and Leo Gershoy, *From Despotism to Revolution, 1763-1789* (New York: Harper & Row, 1944). These two informative volumes in the The Rise of Modern Europe series have very full bibliographies.

Leonard Krieger, *Kings and Philosophers, 1689-1789* (New York: Norton, 1970). Comprehensive survey; includes a succinct, up-to-date bibliography.

Robert R. Palmer, *The Age of Democratic Revolution* (Princeton: Princeton University Press, 1964). A thoughtful survey of political ideas and unrest in Europe and America at the close of the Old Regime.

The Ideas of the Enlightenment

Robert Anchor, *The Enlightenment Tradition* (Berkeley: University of California Press, 1979). A stimulating interpretation.

Carl Becker, *The Heavenly City of the Eighteenth-Century Philosophers* (New Haven: Yale University Press, 1932). A still-delightful essay, now much criticized. Its ideas are reassessed in Raymond O. Rockwood, ed., *Carl Becker's Heavenly City Revisited* (Hamden, Conn.: Shoe String, 1968).

Ernest Cassirer, *The Philosophy of the Enlightenment* (Princeton: Princeton University Press, 1951). An important and lucid study of the great principles of eighteenth-century thought.

Lester G. Crocker, *An Age of Crisis,* and *Nature and Culture* (both Baltimore: Johns Hopkins University Press, 1959, 1963). Penetrating criticisms of the implications of the Enlightenment.

Peter Gay, *The Enlightenment* (New York: Simon & Schuster, 1974). Comprehensive survey by a leading expert in the field; contains extensive bibliographies.

Norman Hampson, *The Enlightenment* (London: Penguin, 1977). Concerned chiefly with ideas and their background.

George R. Havens, *The Age of Ideas: From Reaction to Revolution in Eighteenth-Century France* (New York: Irvington, 1955). Most useful biographical sketches of the philosophes.

Kingsley Martin, *French Liberal Thought in the Eighteenth Century* (New York: Harper & Row, n.d.). A brilliant and opinionated survey of the philosophes.

Sidney Pollard, *The Idea of Progress* (London: Pelican, 1971). Stimulating look at why philosophers thought progress was inevitable.

Some Individual Thinkers

Alfred Cobban, *Rousseau and the Modern State,* 2nd ed. (Hamden, Conn.: Archon, 1964). A good introduction to the implications of Rousseau's thought. For a highly critical appraisal, see J. L. Talmon, *The Origins of Totalitarian Democracy* (New York: Norton, 1970).

Jean Guéhenno, *Jean Jacques Rousseau* (New York: Columbia University Press, 1966). A full-dress study. An excellent brief introduction is Ernest Cassirer, *The Question of Jean Jacques Rousseau* (Bloomington: Indiana University Press, 1963).

Frank E. Manuel, *The Prophets of Paris* (New York: Harper & Row, 1965). Turgot and Condorcet are among those considered.

Norman L. Torrey, *The Spirit of Voltaire* (New York: Russell, 1968); and Peter Gay, *Voltaire's Politics* (New York: Vintage, n.d.). Thoughtful studies.

Arthur M. Wilson, *Diderot* (Oxford: Oxford University Press, 1972). The best scholarly biography.

The Enlightened Despots

Paul P. Bernard, *Joseph II* (Boston: Twayne, 1968). Succinct appraisal by a scholar who has written more detailed works on Joseph's reign.

T. Blanning, *Joseph II and Enlightened Despotism* (London: Longmans, Green, 1970). Good brief introduction.

Walter H. Bruford, *Germany in the Eighteenth Century* (Cambridge, Eng.: Cambridge University Press, 1935). Stresses social and intellectual developments.

Edward Crankshaw, *Maria Theresa* (New York: Viking, 1969). A capable biographical study.

John G. Gagliardo, *Enlightened Despotism* (Arlington Heights, Ill.: Harlan Davidson, 1967). Informative and brief.

Richard Herr, *The Eighteenth-Century Revolution in Spain* (Princeton: Princeton University Press, 1969). Important reappraisal of the Enlightenment's effect upon Spain.

Carlile A. Macartney, *Maria Theresa and the House of Austria* (London: English Universities Press, 1969). Brief scholarly appraisal.

Gerhard Ritter, *Frederick the Great* (Berkeley: University of California Press, 1968). Well-balanced lectures by a German scholar.

Roger Wines, ed., *Enlightened Despotism: Reform or Reaction?* (Lexington, Mass.: Heath, 1967). All sides of the question examined by various authorities.

Catherine the Great

Jerome Blum, *The End of the Old Order in Rural Europe* (Princeton: Princeton University Press, 1978). Fine broad history of the relationship between seigniors and peasants.

P. Dukes, *Catherine the Great & the Russian Nobility* (Cambridge, Eng.: Cambridge University Press, 1968). Study of a most significant aspect of her policy.

Lewis B. Namier, *England in the Age of the American Revolution*, 2nd ed. (New York: St. Martin's, 1961). Study of British politics in the 1760s.

Lawrence J. Oliva, *Catherine the Great* (Englewood Cliffs, N.J.: Prentice-Hall, 1971); and Marc Raeff, ed., *Catherine the Great: A Profile* (New York: Hill & Wang, 1972). Instructive appraisals of the Russian empress.

Marc Raeff, *Imperial Russia, 1682-1825* (New York: Knopf, 1971). Survey from Peter the Great through Alexander I.

George Rudé, *Wilkes and Liberty* (Oxford: Oxford University Press, 1962). Analysis of the unrest in Britain during the early years of George III's reign.

Benedict H. Sumner, *Peter the Great and the Emergence of Russia* (London: English Universities Press, 1950). An able, quite short prelude to Catherine.

Gladys Scott Thomson, *Catherine the Great and the Expansion of Russia* (London: English Universities Press, 1961). A sound, short introduction.

Piotr S. Wandycz, *The Lands of Partitioned Poland, 1795-1918* (Seattle: University of Washington Press, 1974). Careful, full account of the aftermath of partition and the efforts to reconstruct a Polish state.

J. Steven Watson, *The Reign of George III, 1760-1815* (Oxford: Oxford University Press, 1960). Enlightening general account in The Oxford History of England.

R. J. White, *The Age of George III* (New York: Anchor, 1969). Short, clear study.

American Independence

Bernard Bailyn, *Ideological Origins of the American Revolution* (Cambridge, Mass.: Harvard University Press, 1967); and John C. Miller, *Origins of the American Revolution* (Palo Alto, Calif.: Stanford University Press, 1959). Illuminating studies of the background.

Carl Becker, *The Declaration of Independence* (New York: Random House, 1958). Stresses the influence of the Enlightenment upon Americans.

I. A. Christie, *Crisis of Empire* (London: Arnold, 1966). Very short analysis from the perspective of British concerns.

Robert Middlekauff, *The Glorious Cause* (New York: Oxford University Press, 1982). Fresh, full, well-written history of the Revolution.

Edmund S. Morgan, *The Birth of the Republic, 1763-1789* (Chicago: University of Chicago Press, 1977); Lawrence H. Gipson, *The Coming of the Revolution, 1763-1775* (New York: Harper & Row, 1954); and John R. Alden, *The American Revolution, 1775-1783* (New York: Harper & Row, 1954). Standard scholarly accounts.

The Arts

Frederick Antal, *Hogarth and His Place in European Art* (London: Routledge & Kegan Paul, 1962). Ingenious study which stresses parallels with earlier and later artists.

Germain Bazin, *Baroque and Rococo Art* (Oxford: Oxford University Press, 1964); and A. Charles Sewter, *Baroque and Rococo* (London: Thames and Hudson, 1972). Concise introductions.

Manfred F. Bukofzer, *Music in the Baroque Era* (New York: Norton, 1971). Survey through 1750.

Stephanie Faniel, ed., *French Art of the Eighteenth Century* (New York: Simon & Schuster, 1957). Valuable for its coverage of the minor arts.

E. M. and S. Grew, *Bach* (Totowa, N.J.: Littlefield, 1979); Alfred Einstein, *Gluck* (New York: McGraw-Hill, n.d.), and *Mozart* (Oxford: Oxford University Press, 1965); Edward J. Dent, *Mozart's Operas* (Oxford: Oxford University Press, n.d.). Enlightening works on individual composers.

Julius Held and Donald Posner, *17th and 18th Century Art* (Englewood Cliffs, N.J.: Prentice-Hall, 1972). A comprehensive survey which discusses rococo.

Tervio Pignatti, *The Age of Rococo* (London: Paul Hamlyn, 1969). Brief, but valuable for its stress on the Italian contribution and its unusual illustrations.

Charles Rosen, *The Classical Style* (New York: Norton, 1971). Perceptive study of Mozart, Haydn, and Beethoven.

Arno Schonberger and H. Soehner, *The Age of Rococo* (London: Thames & Hudson, 1960). Handsomely illustrated survey.

Jacques Thuillier and Albert Châtelet, *French Painting from Le Nain to Fragonard* (Geneva: Skira, 1964). Handsomely illustrated survey; covers from the midseventeenth to the late eighteenth century.

Ellis Waterhouse, *Reynolds* (New York: Phaidon, 1973). Sympathetic assessment of Sir Joshua.

Sources

Max Beloff, ed., *The Debate on the American Revolution, 1761-1783* (London: Kaye, 1949). Handy compilation of British speeches and writings for and against the rebels.

Crane Brinton, ed., *The Portable Age of Reason Reader* (New York: Viking, 1956); and Isaiah Berlin, ed., *The Age of Enlightenment: The Eighteenth-Century Philosophers* (Salem, N.H.: Arno Press, 1956). Two valuable anthologies.

Lester G. Crocker, ed., *The Age of Enlightenment* (New York: Walker, 1969); and Carlile A. Macartney, ed., *The Hapsburg and Hohenzollern Dynasties in the Seventeenth and Eighteenth Centuries* (New York: Walker, 1970). Volumes in the Documentary History of Western Civilization.

Robert and Elburg Forster, eds., *European Society in the Eighteenth Century* (New York: Walker, 1969). Well-selected anthology.

Ben R. Redman, ed., *The Portable Voltaire* (London: Penguin, 1977). A well-edited selection.

CHAPTER 18: THE FRENCH REVOLUTION AND NAPOLEON

General Survey Texts

Peter Amann, ed., *The Eighteenth-Century Revolution: French or Western?* (Lexington, Mass.: Heath, 1963). Selections both hostile and sympathetic to the Palmer thesis.

Crane Brinton, *A Decade of Revolution, 1789-1799* (New York: Harper & Row, 1934); and Geoffrey Bruun, *Europe & the French Imperium, 1799-1814* (New York: Harper & Row, 1938). Comprehensive volumes in The Rise of Modern Europe series; contain full bibliographies.

Jacques Godechot, *France and the Atlantic Revolution of the Eighteenth Century, 1770-1799*, trans. Herbert R. Rowen (New York: Free Press, 1965). A ranking French scholar comes to conclusions similar to Palmer's. Godechot's views on Napoleon may be sampled in Jacques Godechot, B. Hyslop, and David Dowd, *The Napoleonic Era in Europe* (New York: Holt, Rinehart, 1971).

Norman Hampson, *The First European Revolution, 1776-1815* (New York: Norton, 1979); and George Rudé, *Revolutionary Europe, 1783-1815* (New York: Harper & Row, n.d.). Two good general surveys.

Georges Lefebvre, *The Coming of the French Revolution,* trans. Robert Palmer (Princeton: Princeton University Press, 1976), and *Napoleon* (New York: Columbia University Press, 1969). Comprehensive accounts by an eminent French scholar with a modified Marxian point of view.

Robert R. Palmer, *The Age of the Democratic Revolution* (Princeton: Princeton University Press, 1959-1964). Defends the thesis that the French Revolution was part of a general democratic revolution in the West; particularly useful for detailed material on smaller European states.

Histories of the Revolution in France

William Doyle, *Origins of the French Revolution* (Oxford: Oxford University Press, 1980). Short, clear analysis of the range of causes, with an exceptionally fine survey of the historiography since 1939.

Ralph W. Greenlaw, ed., *The Social Origins of the French Revolution: The Debate on the Role of the Middle Classes* (Lexington, Mass.: Heath, 1975). Covers the range of views on whether the Revolution was essentially middle class in origin.

Norman Hampson, *A Social History of the French Revolution* (Toronto: University of Toronto Press, 1963). Excellent synthesis of recent scholarship.

Olwen H. Hufton, *The Poor of Eighteenth Century France, 1750-1789* (Oxford: Clarendon, 1979). Close inquiry into the meaning of poverty and crime.

Ernest John Knapton, *Revolutionary and Imperial France, 1750-1815* (New York: Scribner's, 1972). Short, balanced survey.

Gaetano Salvemini, *The French Revolution, 1788-1792* (New York: Norton, 1962). Colorful narrative.

William H. Sewell, *Work and Revolution in France: The Language of Labor from the Old Regime to 1848* (Cambridge, Eng.: Cambridge University Press, 1980). Superb, complex examination of the social history of labor.

J. M. Thompson, *The French Revolution,* 2nd ed. (Oxford: Blackwell, 1966). An informative one-volume history through the fall of Robespierre.

More Specialized Studies of the Revolution

Crane Brinton, *The Jacobins* (New York: Russell, 1961); and M. J. Sydenham, *The Girondins* (Westport, Conn.: Greenwood, 1973). Careful studies which greatly revise popular notions about the nature of revolutionary factions.

William F. Church, ed., *The Influence of the Enlightenment on the French Revolution,* 2nd ed. (Lexington, Mass.: Heath, 1972); and J. H. Shennan, *The Parlement of Paris* (Ithaca: Cornell Univerity Press, 1968). Appraisals of two significant factors in the background.

Richard C. Cobb, *The Police and the People* (Oxford: Oxford University Press, 1970). Important study of French popular protest from 1789 to 1820.

Alfred Cobban, *Aspects of the French Revolution* (New York: Brazillier, 1968), and *The Social Interpretation of the French Revolution* (Cambridge, Eng.: Cambridge University Press, 1964). Lively critiques of the Marxian interpretation.

Paul Farmer, *France Reviews Its Revolutionary Origins* (New York: Octagon, 1963). A history of writings about the Revolution by French scholars.

Jacques Godechot, *The Taking of the Bastille* (New York: Scribner's, 1970). Definitive monograph on July 14, 1789.

Jacques Godechot, *The Counter-Revolution: Doctrine and Action, 1789-1804,* trans. Salvator Attanasio (Princeton: Princeton University Press, 1981). An important study of the opposition to the Revolution.

John McManners, *The French Revolution and the Church* (London: S.P.C.K., 1969). Superb brief study.

Robert R. Palmer, *Twelve Who Ruled: The Year of the Terror in the French Revolution* (Princeton: Princeton University Press, 1978). Highly readable collective biography of the Committee of Public Safety.

George Rudé, *The Crowd in the French Revolution* (Oxford: Oxford University Press, 1959). Study of the participants in the great revolutionary "days" and of their motives.

Albert Soboul, *The Sans-Culottes and the French Revolution* (Princeton: Princeton University Press, 1980). Detailed French monograph. Based on police records, it examines the role of the Parisian sans-culottes in 1793 and 1794 from a Marxist perspective.

J. M. Thompson, *Leaders of the French Revolution* (Oxford: Blackwell, 1988), and *Robespierre and the French Revolution* (London: English Universities Press, 1960); Geoffrey Bruun, *Saint-Just: Apostle of the Terror* (Hamden, Conn.: Shoe String, 1966); and Louis Gottschalk, *Jean-Paul Marat* (New York: Gordon, n.d.). Biographies of major revolutionary figures.

Charles Tilly, *The Vendee* (Cambridge, Mass.: Harvard University Press, 1976). Revisionist study showing that much more was involved in the Vendean revolt than peasant devotion to throne and altar.

Alec R. Vidler, *The Church in an Age of Revolution* (London: Penguin, 1980). Survey from 1789 to the 1960s; especially good on the Gallican Church.

Napoleon

Herbert Butterfield, *Napoleon* (London: Duckworth, 1957). Very brief, impressionistic biography.

David G. Chandler, *The Campaigns of Napoleon* (New York: Macmillan, 1973). Thorough scholarly account.

Owen Connelly, *Napoleon's Satellite Kingdoms* (New York: Free Press, 1970). Informative studies of Spain, Holland, Westphalia, Italy, and Naples.

H. A. L. Fisher, *Napoleon* (New York: Holt, 1913); and Albert L. Guerard, *Napoleon* (New York: Knopf, 1956). Good shorter biographies.

Peter Geyl, *Napoleon, For and Against* (New Haven: Yale University Press, 1949). Survey of judgments passed on Bonaparte by historians.

Eli Filip Heckscher, *The Continental System* (Boston: Peter Smith, 1964). Old, still-important monograph by an economic historian.

Robert B. Holtman, *The Napoleonic Revolution* (Baton Rouge: Louisiana State University Press, 1979). Emphasizing institutional changes under Bonaparte.

Felix Markham, *Napoleon and the Awakening of Europe* (Mystic, Conn.: Verry, 1972). Brief survey; argues that European nationalisms were as yet underdeveloped.

D. H. Pinkney, ed., *Napoleon: Historical Enigma* (Princeton: Princeton University Press, 1972). A brief introduction to the contrasting interpretations of the man.

Edith Saunders, *The Hundred Days* (New York: Norton, 1964). On the next-to-last act of the Napoleonic drama.

J. M. Thompson, *Napoleon Bonaparte: His Rise and Fall* (Oxford: Oxford University Press, 1969); and Felix Markham, *Napoleon* (New York: New American Library, 1963). Readable biographies by careful scholars.

Sources

Edmund Burke, *Reflections on the Revolution in France* (several eds.). A celebrated indictment of the destructive character of the Revolution.

Armand de Caulaincourt, *With Napoleon in Russia* (Westport, Conn.: Greenwood, 1976), and its sequel, *No Peace with Napoleon* (Westport, Conn.: Greenwood, 1976). Vivid and revealing memoirs by one of Bonaparte's chief aides.

J. Christopher Herold, ed., *The Mind of Napoleon* (New York: Columbia University Press, 1955). Another fine collection; arranged topically.

M. Hutt, *Napoleon* (Englewood Cliffs, N.J.: Prentice-Hall, n.d.). A capsule biography; contains selections from his own words and a sampler of other views on his career.

Frank A. Kafker and James M. Laux, *The French Revolution: Conflicting Interpretations* (New York: Random House, 1968). Balanced selections of primary and secondary materials.

Jeffry Kaplow, *New Perspectives on the French Revolution: Readings in Historical Sociology* (New York: Wiley, 1965). A series of valuable case studies.

John H. Stewart, *A Documentary Survey of the French Revolution* (New York: Macmillan, 1951). Excellent collection of constitutional texts and other official documents.

J. M. Thompson, ed., *Napoleon's Letters* (New York: Dutton, 1954). A fascinating collection, arranged chronologically.

Arthur Young, *Travels in France,* C. Maxwell, ed. (Cambridge, Eng.: Cambridge University Press, 1929). Lively diary by an English farm expert who journeyed throughout France from 1787 to 1789.

CHAPTER 19: ROMANTICISM, REVOLUTION, AND REACTION

General Accounts

Frederick B. Artz, *Reaction and Revolution, 1814-1832* (New York: Harper & Row, 1969); and William L. Langer, *Political and Social Upheaval, 1832-1852* (New York: Harper & Row, 1969). Comprehensive volumes in The Rise of Modern Europe series; both have still-useful bibliographies.

Jacques Droz, *Europe between Revolutions, 1815-1848* (Ithaca: Cornell University Press, 1980). A survey which stresses the workings of economic and social forces and their political consequences.

Eric J. Hobsbawm, *The Age of Revolution, 1789-1848* (New York: New American Library, 1962). Provocative survey stressing economic and political developments.

The New Cambridge Modern History, Vols. IX and X (Cambridge, Eng.: Cambridge University Press, 1957-1970). Chapters by many scholars; uneven in quality, but provides information on topics and areas often neglected in general surveys.

George Rudé, *Debate on Europe* (New York: Torchbooks, 1972). Fine summary of conflicting and developing views on events from 1815 to 1850.

J. L. Talmon, *Romanticism and Revolt, 1815-1848* (New York: Norton, 1979). Stresses social and intellectual developments.

The Romantic Protest

The full texts of almost all the landmarks in romantic literature mentioned in this chapter are available in paperbound editions.

Jacques Barzun, *Berlioz and His Century* (Chicago: University of Chicago Press, 1982). Detailed examination of the career of a characteristic romantic composer.

Crane Brinton, *Political Ideas of the English Romanticists* (Oxford: Oxford University Press, 1926). A perceptive analysis.

Jacob Bronowski and Bruce Mazlish, *The Western Intellectual Tradition from Leonardo to Hegel* (New York: Harper & Row, 1970); Crane Brinton, *The Shaping of Modern Thought* (Englewood Cliffs, N.J.: Prentice-Hall, n.d.); W. H. Coates and H. V. White, *The Ordeal of Liberal Humanism* (New York: McGraw-Hill, 1969). Three lucid reviews of intellectual history.

Kenneth Clark, *The Gothic Revival* (New York: Harper & Row, 1974). Entertaining essay; focuses on architecture in Britain.

David L. Dowd, *Pageant-Master of the Republic* (Salem, N.H.: Arno Press, 1972). David's role as propagandist of the Revolution.

Walter Friedlaender, *David to Delacroix* (Cambridge, Mass.: Harvard University Press, 1952). Good study of neoclassical and romantic painting in France.

Lilian R. Furst, *Romanticism in Perspective,* 2nd ed. (Atlantic Highlands, N.J.: Humanities Press, 1979). Helpful interpretation; contains chapters on the historical perspective and on individualism, imagination, and feeling.

K. B. Klaus, *The Romantic Period in Music* (London: Allyn & Bacon, 1970). A useful introduction; goes well beyond the chronological limits of this chapter.

Thomas Prideaux, *The World of Delacroix* (New York: Time-Life Books, 1966). Relates the painter to the larger social scene.

M. Reynal, *The Nineteenth Century* (Geneva: Skira, 1951). Handsomely illustrated survey of painting.

Charles Rosen, *The Classical Style* (New York: Norton, 1972). Treats Beethoven in addition to Mozart and Haydn.

The Reconstruction of Europe

Guillaume de Sauvigny, *Metternich and His Times* (Atlantic Highlands, N.J.: Humanities Press, 1962). By a French expert on conservatism.

Russell Kirk, *The Conservative Mind* (Chicago: Regnery, 1957). A lucid, wide-ranging exposition.

Henry A. Kissinger, *A World Restored* (Boston: Peter Smith, 1973). Efforts of the conservative forces to restore the European balance from 1812 to 1822.

Arthur J. May, *The Age of Metternich,* rev. ed. (New York: Holt, Rinehart, 1967). Brief appraisal of Hapsburg history.

Harold Nicholson, *The Congress of Vienna* (New York: Harcourt Brace Jovanovich, 1970); Guglielmo Ferrero, *The Reconstruction of Europe* (New York: Norton, 1963). Detailed studies of the settlement of 1814 to 1815.

H. F. Schwarz, ed., *Metternich, the Coachman of Europe: Statesman or Evil Genius?* (Lexington, Mass.: Heath, n.d.). Instructive selection of contradictory interpretations.

Works on Individual States

Raymond Carr, *Spain, 1808-1939* (Oxford: Oxford University Press, 1982). Scholarly account.

Douglas Dakin, *The Greek Struggle for Independence, 1821-1833* (Berkeley: University of California Press, 1973). Definitive scholarly study.

Guillaume de Sauvigny, *The Restoration* (Philadelphia: University of Pennsylvania Press, 1966). Sympathetic, detailed interpretation of France under Louis XVIII and Charles X.

Theodore S. Hamerow, *Restoration, Revolution, Reaction* (Princeton: Princeton University Press, 1958). Scholarly reevaluation of German economics and politics from 1815 to 1871.

W. O. Henderson, *The Zollverein,* 2nd ed. (Totowa, N.J.: Biblio, 1968). A standard work on the subject.

Marshall G. S. Hodgson, *The Venture of Islam: The Gunpowder Empires and Modern Times* (Chicago: University of Chicago Press, 1974). Good coverage on the decline of the Ottoman empire.

T. E. B. Howarth, *Citizen-King* (London: Eyre & Spottiswoode, 1961). Biography of Louis Philippe.

Charles and Barbara Jelavich, *The Establishment of the Balkan National States, 1804-1920* (Seattle: University of Washington Press, 1977). Survey of Balkan nationalisms.

Douglas W. J. Johnson, *Guizot: Aspects of French History, 1787-1874* (London: Routledge & Kegan Paul, 1963). Illuminating biography of the French conservative liberal.

R. F. Leslie, *Polish Politics and the Revolution of 1830* (London: Athlone Press, 1956). Detailed analysis of the stresses and antagonisms that doomed the Polish movement.

Mary D. R. Leys, *Between Two Empires* (London: Longmans, Green, 1955). Brief survey of French social and political history from 1814 to 1848.

Carlile A. Macartney, *The Habsburg Empire, 1790-1818* (New York: Macmillan, 1969). By a ranking expert in the field.

Ted W. Margadant, *French Peasants in Revolt: The Insurrection of 1851* (Princeton: Princeton University Press, 1979). Trenchant analysis of the radicalization of the French peasant.

A. G. Mazour, *The First Russian Revolution* (Palo Alto, Calif.: Stanford University Press, 1937); and Marc Raeff, *The Decembrist Movement* (Englewood Cliffs, N.J.: Prentice-Hall, 1966). Valuable studies of the abortive coup of 1825 and its background.

David H. Pinkney, *The French Revolution of 1830* (Princeton: Princeton University Press, 1972). Important scholarly study which revises many older ideas about the nature of the July Revolution.

Gaetano Salvemini, *Mazzini* (Palo Alto, Calif.: Stanford University Press, 1957). Sympathetic analysis.

A. J. P. Taylor, *The Habsburg Monarchy, 1809-1918* (Chicago: University of Chicago Press, 1976). Spirited, brief treatment.

P. Taylor, *The Course of German History* (London: Hamilton, 1945). Clear and debatable.

R. Hinton Thomas, *Liberalism, Nationalism, and the German Intellectuals* (Westport, Conn.: Greenwood, 1975). Good study of the period from 1822 to 1847.

Arthur J. Whyte, *The Evolution of Modern Italy* (New York: Norton, 1965). Sound introduction.

The Revolutions of 1848

G. Fasel, *Europe in Upheaval: The Revolutions of 1848* (New York: Rand McNally, n.d.). Good, concise account.

Melvin Kranzberg, ed., *1848: A Turning Point?* (Lexington, Mass.: Heath, 1959). Diverse evaluations as to whether or not Europe failed to turn.

Arno J. Mayer, *The Persistence of the Old Regime* (New York: Pantheon, 1981). Brilliant explanation of why, despite revolutions, the Old Regime survived until the Great War.

Lewis B. Namier, *1848: The Revolution of the Intellectuals* (New York: Anchor, 1964). Trenchant essay castigating liberals, especially in Germany, for their illiberal attitudes.

P. H. Noyes, *Organization and Revolution* (Princeton: Princeton University Press, 1966). Enlightening study of working-class disunity in Germany.

Raymond Postgate, *Story of a Year: 1848* (Westport, Conn.: Greenwood, 1975). A lively and well-illustrated chronicle.

Reuben J. Rath, *The Viennese Revolution of 1848* (Westport, Conn.: Greenwood, 1977). Solid, clear monograph.

Priscilla Robertson, *Revolutions of 1848* (Princeton: Princeton University Press, 1952). Uneven social history; valuable for stressing the role taken by women and by students.

George Rudé, *The Crowd in History, 1730-1884* (Atlantic Highlands, N.J.: Humanities Press, 1981). Includes a chapter on the socioeconomic background of the Parisian demonstrators of 1848.

William H. Sewell, *Work and Revolution in France* (Cambridge, Eng.: Cambridge University Press, 1980). Especially good in describing the emergence of a class consciousness by 1848.

Jean Sigmann, *1848: The Romantic and Democratic Revolutions in Europe* (New York: Harper & Row, 1973). Revisionist study focused particularly on the economic, social, and political difficulties during 1846 and 1847.

Sources

Irene Collins, *Government and Society in France, 1814-1848* (New York: St. Martin's, 1971). Very useful collection of documents.

John B. Halsted, ed., *Romanticism: Problems of Definition, Explanation, Evaluation* (Lexington, Mass.: Heath, 1965). Informative samplings of many different points of view. Halsted has also edited a good anthology of romantic writing, *Romanticism* (New York: Harper & Row, 1969), a volume in The Documentary History of Western Civilization series.

Howard Hugo, ed., *The Romantic Reader* (New York: Viking, 1975). Imaginatively arranged anthology with an enlightening introduction.

James G. Legge, ed., *Rhyme and Revolution in Germany* (New York: AMS Press, 1972). Lively anthology of German history and literature from 1813 to 1850.

Ignazio Silone, ed., *The Living Thoughts of Mazzini* (Norwood, Penn.: Telegraph, 1982). Selections from his writings.

CHAPTER 20: THE INDUSTRIAL SOCIETY

The Industrial Revolution

Asa Briggs, *The Age of Improvement, 1783-1867* (New York: McKay, 1962). Fine summary of Victorian Britain.

Carlo M. Cipolla, *The Economic History of World Population,* 6th ed. (London: Penguin, 1975). Brief look at sources of energy.

Carlo M. Cipolla, ed., *The Industrial Revolution* (London: Penguin, 1973), and *The Emergence of Industrial Societies* (London: Penguin, 1973). Perhaps the best short summaries of the current scholarly position.

François Crouzet, ed., *Capital Formation in the Industrial Revolution* (London: Methuen, 1972). Excellent essays on how the Industrial Revolution was financed.

François Crouzet, W. H. Chaloner, and W. M. Stern, eds., *Essays in European Economic History, 1789-1914* (London: Arnold, 1969). Fascinating essays on the cotton trade, the railway age, and "how revolutions are born."

P. M. Deane, *The First Industrial Revolution* (Cambridge, Eng.: Cambridge University Press, 1980); Paul Mantoux, *The Industrial Revolution in the Eighteenth Century* (New York: Harper & Row, 1961); Thomas S. Ashton, *The Industrial Revolution, 1760-1830* (Oxford: Oxford University Press, 1948); R. M. Hartwell, ed., *The Causes of the Industrial Revolution in England* (New York: Methuen, 1967). Four useful, short works on the early history of modern industrialism.

P. M. Deane and W. A. Cole, *British Economic Growth, 1688-1959,* 2nd ed. (Cambridge, Eng.: Cambridge University Press, 1969). Good introduction.

Alexander Gerschenkron, *Economic Backwardness in Historical Perspective* (Cambridge, Mass.: Harvard University Press, 1962). Famous essay on why eastern Europe was slow to industrialize.

H. J. Habakkuk and Michael Postan, eds., *The Cambridge Economic History of Europe,* Vol. 6, parts 1 and 2 (Cambridge, Eng.: Cambridge University Press, 1965). Essays on the Industrial Revolution by ranking scholars. The contribution by David Landes has been amplified and issued separately: *The Unbound Prometheus: Technological Change and Industrial Development in Western Europe from 1750 to the Present* (Cambridge, Eng.: Cambridge University Press, 1969).

W. O. Henderson, *The Industrialization of Europe, 1780-1914* (London: Thames and Hudson, 1969); and Tom Kemp, *Industrialization in Nineteenth-Century Europe* (Atlantic Highlands, N.J.: Humanities Press, 1969). Valuable for developments on the Continent.

Eric J. Hobsbawm, *The Pelican Economic History of Britain,* Volume 3; *Industry and Empire* (London: Penguin, 1970). By the author of the provocative *Age of Revolution, 1789-1848* (New York: Praeger, 1969) and *The Age of Capital, 1848-1875* (London: Weidenfeld and Nicolson, 1975).

Paul Hohenberg, *A Primer on the Economic History of Europe* (New York: Random House, 1968). Short and clear.

Thomas McKeown, *The Modern Rise of Population* (New York: Academic Press, 1976). Striking synthesis of the present state of knowledge on demographic trends and disease.

Alan S. Milward and S. B. Saul, *The Development of the Economies of Continental Europe, 1850-1914* (Cambridge, Mass.: Harvard University Press, 1977). Excellent on France and Germany.

Sidney Pollard, *Peaceful Conquest: The Industrialization of Europe, 1760-1970* (Oxford: Oxford University Press, 1981). A careful examination of the phases through which the Industrial Revolution passed.

E. P. Thompson, *The Making of the English Working Class* (New York: Random House, 1966). Detailed, influential account of the impact of the French Revolution and the early Industrial Revolution on the shaping of class consciousness.

The Responses of Liberalism

Ester Boserup, *The Conditions of Agricultural Growth* (Chicago: Aldine, 1965). Significantly challenges Malthusian assumptions, arguing that historically, sustained population growth has been more likely to stimulate economic development than declining populations will.

Crane Brinton, *English Political Thought in the Nineteenth Century* (Cambridge, Mass.: Harvard University Press, 1949). Essays on Bentham, Mill, Owen, Kingsley, and other important figures.

Denis Mack Smith, ed., *The Making of Italy, 1796-1870* (New York: Walker, 1968). Excellent volume in The Documentary History of Western Civilization series.

Mack Walker, ed., *Metternich's Europe* (New York: Harper & Row, n.d.). Useful collection of sources; a volume in The Documentary History of Western Civilization series.

Louis Chevalier, *Laboring Classes and Dangerous Classes,* trans. Frank Jollinek (New York: Fertig, 1973). How society came to define crime in urban conditons in the first half of the nineteenth century.

Elie Halévy, *The Growth of Philosophic Radicalism* (New York: Faber, 1972). Celebrated older study of Bentham and his Utilitarian followers.

Robert Heilbroner, *The Worldly Philosophers,* 5th ed. (New York: Touchstone, 1980). A lively, clear introduction to the philosophy of laissez faire.

William L. Langer, *Political and Social Upheaval, 1832-1852* (New York: Harper & Row, 1969). Succinct look at "the social question."

M. Mack, *Jeremy Bentham* (London: Heinemann, 1962). A good biography.

Michael S. Packe, *The Life of John Stuart Mill* (New York: Macmillan, 1954). Sound biography. For a psychohistory of the father and son, consult Bruce Mazlish, *James and John Stuart Mill* (New York: Basic Books, 1975).

Donald Winch, *Classical Political Economy and Colonies* (London: Bell, 1965). Clear examination of the classical liberal economists.

The Socialist Responses

Shlomo Avineri, *The Social and Political Thought of Karl Marx* (Cambridge, Eng.: Cambridge University Press, 1971); and George Lichtheim, *Marxism: An Historical and Critical Study* (New York: Columbia University Press, 1982). Thoughtful recent evaluations.

Isaiah Berlin, *Karl Marx: His Life and Environment,* 4th ed. (Oxford: Oxford University Press, 1978). Brilliant study.

Julius Braunthal, *History of the International* (Boulder, Colo.: Westview, 1980). Sound, scholarly study.

John Foster, *Class Struggle and the Industrial Revolution* (New York: St. Martin's, 1974). An original look at early industrial capitalism in English towns.

John F. C. Harrison, *Quest for the New Moral World: Robert Owen and the Owenites in Britain and America* (London: Routledge & Kegan Paul, 1969). The standard study of the radical British businessman and of his impact.

Harry W. Laidler, *A History of Socialism* (New York: Thomas Y. Crowell, 1968). Updated version of an older standard account.

George Lichtheim, *Origins of Socialism* (New York: Praeger, 1969) and *A Short History of Socialism* (New York: Praeger, 1970). Highly useful introductions.

David McLellan, *Karl Marx* (London: Penguin, 1976). A very short study of the kernel of Marx's changing thought.

Nicholas V. Riasanovsky, *The Teaching of Charles Fourier* (Berkeley: University of California Press, 1969). The standard work on the French utopian.

Joseph A. Schumpeter, *Capitalism, Socialism, and Democracy* (New York: Harper & Row, 1967). Thoughtful survey; extends into the present century.

Joan Wallach Scott, *The Glassworkers of Carmaux* (Cambridge, Mass.: Harvard University Press, 1974). Study of an elite craft and its eventual radicalization.

Edmund Wilson, *To the Finland Station* (New York: Farrar Straus & Giroux, 1972). A sympathetic and balanced history of socialism.

Apostles of Violence—and Nonviolence

Michel Foucault, *Madness and Civilization,* trans. Richard Howard (New York: Vintage, 1973). Imaginative—perhaps too imaginative—analysis of how society coped with the idea of madness by instituting asylums.

James Joll, *The Anarchists* (Cambridge, Mass.: Harvard University Press, 1980). Helpful introduction.

A. B. Spitzer, *The Revolutionary Theories of Louis-Auguste Blanqui* (New York: AMS Press, 1957). Good study of the French agitator.

General Accounts of Intellectual Trends

W. H. Coates and H. V. White, *The Ordeal of Liberal Humanism* (New York: McGraw-Hill, 1969). A compact and useful survey of intellectual history since 1789.

William L. Langer, *Political and Social Upheaval, 1832-1852;* R. C. Binkley,

Realism and Nationalism, 1852-1871 (New York: Harper & Row, 1941); Carlton J. Hayes, *A Generation of Materialism, 1871-1900* (New York: Harper & Row, 1941); Oron J. Hale, *The Great Illusion, 1900-1914* (New York: Harper & Row, 1971). Four volumes in The Rise of Modern Europe series.

Roland N. Stromberg, *European Intellectual History since 1789* (Englewood Cliffs, N.J.: Prentice-Hall, 1975). A helpful textbook.

Science and Darwinism

Jacques Barzun, *Darwin, Marx and Wagner,* 2nd ed. (Chicago: University of Chicago Press, 1981). Suggestive study stressing the common denominators among three contemporaneous innovators once cataloged as very different from one another.

Loren Eisely, *Darwin's Century* (New York: Doubleday, 1958). Instructive study of the doctrine of evolution and of those who formulated it.

Charles C. Gillispie, *The Edge of Objectivity* (Princeton: Princeton University Press, 1960). Darwin and other nineteenth-century scientific innovators appraised. Gillispie has also written *Genesis and Geology* (Cambridge, Mass.: Harvard University Press, 1951). A study of the tension between science and religion prior to Darwin.

John C. Greene, *The Death of Adam* (Ames: Iowa State University Press, 1959). Assessment of the impact of evolution on Western thought.

Gertrude Himmelfarb, *Darwin and the Darwinian Revolution* (New York: Norton, 1968). Excellent critical introduction. For a rather different assessment consult Michael T. Ghiselin, *The Triumph of the Darwinian Method* (Berkeley: University of California Press, 1969).

Richard Hofstadter, *Social Darwinism in American Thought* (Boston: Beacon, 1955). An admirable study.

William Irvine, *Apes, Angels and Victorians* (New York: McGraw-Hill, 1955). A lively study of the social ramifications of Darwinism.

Nancy Stepan, *The Idea of Race in Science* (London: Macmillan, 1982). Fine examination of how science, and especially eugenics, fostered racism.

Frank Miller Turner, *Between Science and Religion* (New Haven: Yale University Press, 1974). Sensitive treatment of six figures who sought the middle ground.

W. P. D. Wightman, *The Growth of Scientific Ideas* (New Haven: Yale University Press, 1951). A most enlightening interpretation.

Literature and the Arts

Carlo M. Cipolla, *Literacy and Development in the West* (London: Penguin, 1969). On the expansion of the reading public.

Pierre Courthion, *Impressionism* (New York: Abrams, 1977). Well-illustrated introduction to the painters of light and color.

George H. Hamilton, *19th and 20th Century Art* (Englewood Cliffs, N.J.: Prentice-Hall, 1972). Encyclopedic, copiously illustrated survey.

Humphrey House, *The Dickens World,* 2nd ed. (Oxford: Oxford University Press, 1960). Excellent, brief introduction.

K. B. Klaus, *The Romantic Period in Music* (London: Allyn & Bacon, 1970). Organized by topic (melody, harmony, counterpoint, chamber music, vocal music); covers through the early 1900s.

Harry Levin, *The Gates of Horn: A Study of Five French Realists* (Oxford: Oxford University Press, 1965). Scholarly assessments of Stendhal, Balzac, Flaubert, Zola, and Proust.

Jean Leymarie, *French Painting: The Nineteenth Century* (Geneva: Skira, 1962). Well-illustrated survey through the mid-1880s.

J. Hillis Miller, *The Disappearance of God* (Cambridge, Mass.: Harvard University Press, 1976). A sensitive study of five nineteenth-century writers.

Fritz Novotny, *Painting and Sculpture in Europe, 1780-1880* (London: Penguin, 1973); and H. R. Hitchcock, *Architecture: The Nineteenth and Twentieth Centuries* (London: Penguin, 1958). Detailed and informative volumes in The Pelican History of Art.

Joseph C. Sloane, *French Painting between Past and Present* (Princeton: Princeton University Press, 1973). Stresses the years from 1818 to 1870, which marked "the birth of modern painting."

Francis Steegmuller, *Flaubert and Madame Bovary* (Chicago: University of Chicago Press, 1977). Illuminating portraits of the great French realist and his famous heroine.

G. M. Young, *Victorian England: Portrait of an Age* (New York: Oxford University Press, 1957); and Walter E. Houghton, *The Victorian Frame of Mind, 1830-1870* (New Haven: Yale University Press, 1963). Informative introductions to the English scene.

Philosophy and Political Thought

William L. Burn, *The Age of Equipoise* (New York: Norton, 1964). Stimulating study of the mid-Victorian intellectual climate.

Donald G. Charlton, *Secular Religions in France, 1815-1870* (Oxford: Oxford University Press, 1963). Scholarly survey of surrogate religions.

F. C. Green, *A Comparative View of French and British Civilization* (London: Dent, 1965). A look at morals and conventions through representative thinkers of the time from 1850 to 1870.

Walter Kaufmann, *Nietzsche: Philosopher, Psychologist, Antichrist,* 3rd ed. (Princeton: Princeton University Press, 1968). A fine book on the controversial German.

Karl Löwith, *From Hegel to Nietzsche* (Garden City, N.Y.: Doubleday, 1962). Analysis of the revolution in nineteenth-century thought, especially in Germany.

Frank E. Manuel, *The Prophets of Paris* (Cambridge, Mass.: Harvard University Press, 1962). Comte is the last of the five figures treated in this informative study.

Gerhard Masur, *Prophets of Yesterday: Studies in European Culture, 1890-1914* (New York: Macmillan, 1966); and H. Stuart Hughes, *Consciousness and Society: The Reorientation of European Social Thought, 1890-1930* (New York: Vintage, 1961). Two very suggestive studies of the twilight of the nineteenth century.

Walter M. Simon, *European Positivism in the Nineteenth Century* (Ithaca: Cornell University Press, 1963). Scholarly assessment of Comte and his disciples.

Sources

Henry D. Aiken, ed., *The Age of Ideology* (Salem, N.H.: Arno, 1977). Selections from nineteenth-century philosophers, with helpful introductory comments.

Edward Bellamy, *Looking Backward, 2000-1887* (several eds.); H. G. Wells, *A Modern Utopia* (Lincoln, Neb.: University of Nebraska Press, 1967); and William Morris, *News from Nowhere* (London: Routledge & Kegan Paul, 1970). Three contrasting visions of utopia in the light of science and industrialism.

Charles Darwin, *Autobiography* (New York: Norton, 1969); *Voyage of the Beagle* (New York: Dalton, 1979); *On the Origin of Species* (several eds.). Three key works for understanding the development of Darwin's ideas. His writings may be sampled in *The Darwin Reader,* ed. Marsten Bates and Philip S. Humphrey (New York: Scribner's, 1956).

Robert Forster and Orest Ranum, eds., *Food and Drink in History* (Baltimore: Johns Hopkins University Press, 1979). Fascinating collection of essays from the *Annales* school of historians in France; examines (among several subjects) the rise of cafe culture, the use of leftover food in Paris, and the role of the potato in the diet.

A. Fried and R. Sanders, *Socialist Thought: A Documentary History* (New York: Anchor, 1964). Informative collection of source materials.

V. A. C. Gatrell, *Robert Owen's A New View of Society and Report to the County of Lanark* (London: Penguin, 1969). Includes a fine introduction.

F. A. Hayek, *John Stuart Mill and Harriet Taylor* (Chicago: University of Chicago Press, 1951). Revealing correspondence on their friendship and marriage.

Vincent J. Knapp, *Europe in the Era of Social Transformation: 1700-Present* (Englewood Cliffs, N.J.: Prentice-Hall, 1976). Especially good on the idea of "mass society."

P. A. Kropotkin, *Selected Readings on Anarchism and Revolution* (Cambridge, Mass.: MIT Press, 1970). Useful introduction to his ideas.

Thomas R. Malthus, *Population: The First Essay* (Ann Arbor: University of Michigan, 1959). The original essay of 1798; states Malthusianism in its most undiluted form.

Frank E. Manuel, ed., *Utopias and Utopian Thought* (Cambridge, Mass.: Harvard University Press, 1979). A useful documentary collection. Manuel has written several studies of the utopians, the most detailed being *The New World of Henri de Saint-Simon* (Notre Dame, Ind.: University of Notre Dame Press, n.d.).

Karl Marx and Fredrich Engels, *Basic Writings on Politics and Philosophy,* ed. L. S. Feuer (Boston: Peter Smith, 1975). Good selection.

David McLellan, ed. and trans., *The Grundrisse* (New York: Harper & Row, Torchbooks, 1972). A selection from Marx's unpublished manuscript.

John Stuart Mill, *Autobiography* (several eds.); *Principles of Political Economy* (London: Penguin, 1962); *On Liberty* (New York: Norton, 1975); *On the Subjection of Women* (Cambridge, Mass.: MIT Press, 1970); *Utilitarianism* (Indianapolis: Hackett, 1978). Major writings of the great Victorian liberal.

Henri de Saint-Simon, *Social Organization, The Science of Man, and Other Writings,* ed. Felix Markham (New York: Harper & Row, 1964). Well-edited anthology.

Georges Sorel, *Reflections on Violence* (New York: AMS Press, 1970). The famous defense of direct revolutionary action and the general strike.

Herbert Spencer, *Man versus the State* (Indianapolis: Liberty Fund, 1982). Representative work by an English Social Darwinist.

Emile Zola, *Germinal* (London: Penguin, 1954). Famous French novel about a strike in a coal mine.

CHAPTER 21: THE MODERNIZATION OF NATIONS

General Accounts

R. C. Binkley, *Realism and Nationalism, 1852-1871* (New York: Harper & Row, 1935); and Carlton J. H. Hayes, *A Generation of Materialism, 1871-1900* (New York: Harper & Row, 1941). Volumes in The Rise of Modern Europe series.

Peter Gay and R. K. Webb, *Modern Europe since 1815* (New York: Harper & Row, 1973). A textook; contains very good bibliographies.

William L. Langer, *Political and Social Upheaval, 1832-1852* (New York: Harper & Row, 1969). Sensitive, synthetic treatment of a most difficult period.

George L. Mosse, *Toward the Final Solution: A History of European Racism* (New York: Fertig, 1978). Clear examination of racist thought, especially anti-Semitism.

W. E. Mosse, *The Rise and Fall of the Crimean System, 1855-1871* (London: Macmillan, 1963). Careful treatment of the diplomatic revolution associated with the war.

The New Cambridge Modern History, 14 vols. (Cambridge, Eng.: Cambridge University Press, 1957-1970). Volumes X, XI, and XII of this collaborative work are a handy source of information.

A. J. P. Taylor, *The Struggle for Mastery in Europe, 1848-1919* (Oxford: Clarendon, 1954). Crisp and provocative; a volume in The Oxford History of Modern Europe series. Informative sociological analysis.

Charles Tilly, Louise Tilly, and Richard Tilly, *The Rebellious Century, 1830-1930* (Cambridge, Mass.: Harvard University Press, 1980).

C. Vann Woodward, ed., *The Comparative Approach to American History* (New York: Basic Books, 1968). Enlightening essays comparing American with European developments.

France

Denis W. Brogan, *The French Nation from Napoleon to Petain* (New York: Harper & Row, 1957). Brilliant essay of interpretation. Brogan has also written a detailed and perceptive study of the Third Republic, *France under the Republic* (New York: Harper & Row, 1940).

Guy Chapman, *The Dreyfus Case: A Re-assessment* (Westport, Conn.: Greenwood, 1979); and D. Johnson, *France and the Dreyfus Affair* (New York: Walker, 1967). Scholarly appraisals.

Albert Guérard, *France: A Modern History,* rev. ed. (Ann Arbor: University of Michigan Press, 1969). By an American scholar of French background who also wrote sympathetic studies of Louis Napoleon: *Napoleon III* (Westport, Conn.: Greenwood, 1979), and a biography with the same title for the series Great Lives in Brief (New York: Knopf, 1955).

John H. Jackson, *Clemenceau and the Third Republic* (Westport, Conn.: Hyperion, 1979); and Geoffrey Bruun, *Clemenceau* (Hamden, Conn.: Shoe String, 1968). Succinct studies of a formidable politician.

John Rothney, *Bonapartism after Sedan* (Ithaca: Cornell University Press, 1969). Clear view of the complex political events of 1871 to 1879.

Frederick H. Seager, *The Boulanger Affair* (Ithaca: Cornell University Press, 1969). A revisionist refutation of myth.

Roger H. Soltau, *French Political Thought in the Nineteenth Century,* new ed. (New York: Russell, 1959). An older and still useful work.

J. M. Thompson, *Louis Napoleon and the Second Empire* (New York: Norton, n.d.). A standard scholarly synthesis. Other useful up-to-date works on the Second Empire are Theodore Zeldin, *The Political System of Napoleon III* (New York: Norton, 1971), and *Emile Ollivier and the Liberal Empire of Napoleon III* (Oxford: Clarendon, 1963); Roger L. Williams, *The World of Napoleon III,* rev. ed. (New York: Free Press, n.d.); and Benedict D. Gooch, *The Reign of Napoleon III* (Chicago: Rand McNally, 1969).

David Thomson, *Democracy in France since 1870,* 5th ed. (Oxford: Oxford University Press, 1969). Brilliant essay of interpretation; particularly good on the period from 1870 to 1914.

Eugene Weber, *Peasants into Frenchmen: The Modernization of Rural France, 1870-1914* (Palo Alto, Calif.: Stanford University Press, 1976). A complex, rich, and very significant achievement.

Roger L. Williams, *The French Revolution of 1870-1871* (New York: Norton, 1969). Study of the highly controversial period climaxed by the Commune.

Gordon Wright, *France in Modern Times,* 3rd ed. (New York: Norton, 1981); Alfred Cobban, *History of Modern France,* rev. ed., Vol. 2 (1799-1871), and Vol. 3 (1871-1962) (London: Penguin, 1962-1966). Enlightening surveys.

Theodore Zeldin, *France, 1848-1945* (Oxford: Clarendon, 1979). Richly detailed social and intellectual history.

Italy

D. Beales, *The Risorgimento and the Unification of Italy* (London: Longman, Green, 1982). Useful, clear appraisal.

Benedetto Croce, *A History of Italy, 1871-1915* (Oxford: Clarendon, 1929). A classic analysis by a famous philosopher-historian.

Clara M. Lovett, *The Democratic Movement in Italy, 1830-1876* (Cambridge, Mass.: Harvard University Press, 1982). A full, sophisticated examination.

A. W. Salomone, ed., *Italy from the Risorgimento to Fascism* (Garden City, N.Y.: Anchor, 1970). An informative survey of the background of totalitarianism.

Christopher Seton-Watson, *Italy from Liberalism to Fascism, 1870-1925* (New York: Methuen, 1967). Detailed scholarly study.

Denis Mack Smith, *Italy: A Modern History* (Ann Arbor: University of Michigan Press, 1959). Standard account by a ranking expert. He has also written other illuminating studies, including *Cavour and Garibaldi, 1860: A Study in Political Conflict* (Cambridge, Eng.: Cambridge University Press, 1954), and *Garibaldi* (New York: Knopf, 1956).

The United States

C. A. Beard and M. A. Beard, *The Rise of American Civilization* (Boston: Peter Smith, 1966). An early and influential economic interpretation.

Carl N. Degler, *Out of Our Past* (New York: Harper & Row, 1970). A sound consensus survey.

Richard Hofstadter, et al., *The United States,* 5th ed., 2 vols. (Englewood Cliffs, N.J.: Prentice-Hall, n.d.). A readable general text.

Walter LaFeber, *The New Empire* (Ithaca: Cornell University Press, 1965). Argues that expansionism and imperialism are the same, despite American efforts to use different terminology.

Robert F. Madgic, Robin W. Winks, et al., *The American Experience,* 3rd ed. (Menlo Park, Calif.: Addison-Wesley, 1979). Fresh look at themes and issues in American history.

Frederick Merk, *History of the Westward Movement* (New York: Knopf, 1978). Full, somewhat old-fashioned account.

S. E. Morison, *The Oxford History of the American People* (New York: New American Library, 1965). Reworking of a popular earlier book.

R. B. Morris, ed., *Encyclopedia of American History* (New York: Harper & Row, 1961); *Harvard Guide to American History,* rev. ed. (Cambridge, Mass.: Harvard University Press, 1974). Standard works of reference.

Douglass C. North, *The Economic Growth of the United States, 1790-1860* (New York: Norton, 1966). Controversial, much-debated, provocative interpretation of the significance of a market economy.

Russel Blaine Nye, *Society and Culture in America, 1830-1860* (New York: Harper & Row, 1974); David M. Potter, *The Impending Crisis, 1848-1861* (New York: Harper & Row, 1976); and Harold U. Faulkner, *Politics Reform, and Expansion, 1890-1900* (New York: Harper & Row, 1959). Well-written volumes in The New American Nation series.

J. G. Randall and David Donald, *The Civil War and Reconstruction,* 2nd ed. (Boston: Little, Brown, 1973). Balanced, general text.

William Appleman Williams, *The Contours of American History* (Chicago: Quadrangle, 1966). An important, controversial reexamination from the point of view of the New Left in American thought.

C. Vann Woodward, *Origins of the New South, 1877-1913* (Baton Rouge: Louisiana State University Press, 1972). Important reinterpretation of the role of the South in American history.

Germany

Gordon A. Craig, *Germany, 1866-1945* (New York: Oxford University Press, 1978). A fine, thorough, well-balanced survey.

Erich Eyck, *Bismarck and the German Empire* (New York: Norton, 1964). Translation and condensation of a large, standard work in German.

L. L. Farrar, Jr., *Arrogance and Anxiety: The Ambivalence of German Power, 1848-1914* (Iowa City: University of Iowa Press, 1981). Close look at the years immediately preceding World War I.

Eckart Kehr, *Economic Interest, Militarism, and Foreign Policy,* trans. Grete Heinz (Berkeley: University of California Press, 1977). Often complex, careful essays on the nature of bureaucracy in Germany.

Gerhard Masur, *Imperial Berlin* (London: Routledge & Kegan Paul, 1974). Lively social history.

W. N. Medlicott, *Bismarck and Modern Germany* (London: Hodder & Stroughton, 1974). A short biography.

Friedrich Meinecke, *The German Catastrophe* (Boston: Beacon, 1963). A useful antidote to Taylor by a German historian.

Otto Pflanze, *Bismarck and the Development of Germany* (Princeton: Princeton University Press, 1963). Only covers up to 1871; a brilliant study that sets the man in his time and digests the vast controversial literature about him.

James J. Sheehan, *German Liberalism in the Nineteenth Century* (Chicago: University of Chicago Press, 1978). Difficult, careful unraveling of the failure of German liberalism.

Walter M. Simon, *Germany: A Brief History* (New York: Random House, 1969). Clear, short, straightforward survey.

Fritz Stern, *Gold and Iron: Bismarck, Bleichroder, and the Building of the German Empire* (New York: Vintage, 1979). Superb, full examination of Bismarck and banking.

Michael Stürmer, *Regierung und Reichstag in Bismarck-staat, 1871-1880* (Düsseldorf: Droste, 1974). For those who read German, a fine interpretation of Bismarck's "Cäsarismus."

A. J. P. Taylor, *Bismarck: The Man and the Statesman* (New York: Random House, 1967). A provocative and often hostile reevaluation.

A. J. P. Taylor, *The Course of German History* (New York: Coward-McCann, 1946). A lively essay on the period since 1815, with strong anti-German overtones.

Hans-Ulrich Wehler, *Das Deutsche Kaiserreich, 1871-1918* (Göttingen: Vandenhoeck and Ruprecht, 1973). Complex, exciting reinterpretation.

The Hapsburg Monarchy

Robert A. Kann, *The Multinational Empire* (New York: Octagon, 1964). A monograph, arranged nationality by nationality; discusses national sentiments and the government's efforts to deal with them.

Claudio Magris, *Der habsburgische Mythos in der österreichischen Literatur* (Salzburg: Otto Müller, 1966). Imaginative look at Franz Grillparzer (1791-1872), an Austrian dramatist, and the implications of the Beidermeier style in decoration.

A. J. May, *The Hapsburg Monarchy, 1867-1914* (Cambridge, Mass.: Harvard University Press, 1951). Concise general account.

Robin Okey, *Eastern Europe, 1740-1980: Feudalism to Communism* (Minneapolis: University of Minnesota Press, 1982). Clear, short history for the beginner.

Steven T. Rosenthal, *The Politics of Dependency: Urban Reform in Istanbul* (Westport, Conn.: Greenwood, 1980). On the influence of the Tanzimat.

Carl E. Schorske, *Fin-de-Siècle Vienna: Politics and Culture* (New York: Vintage, 1981). Brilliant essays on the relationship between culture as politics and Vienna as power center.

A. J. P. Taylor, *The Hapsburg Monarchy, 1809-1918* (Chicago: University of Chicago Press, 1948). A spirited, brief treatment.

Russia

James H. Billington, *The Icon and the Axe* (New York: Vintage, 1970). Markedly rich, controversial interpretation of Russian culture.

Peter Brock, *The Slovak National Awakening* (Toronto: University of Toronto Press, 1976). Short essay on the intellectual history of cultural nationalism.

Ronald Hingley, *A Concise History of Russia* (New York: Viking, 1972). Very short illustrated survey.

Charles and Barbara Jelavich, *The Establishment of the Balkan National States, 1804-1920* (Seattle: University of Washington Press, 1977). Balanced, full account.

James Joll, *The Anarchists* (Cambridge, Mass.: Harvard University Press, 1980). Excellent chapters on Bakunin and Peter Kropotkin; a fine study of the movement.

Martin Malia, *Alexander Herzen and the Birth of Russian Socialism* (New York: Grosset & Dunlap, Universal Library, 1965). Excellent monograph on Herzen's life and thought.

Sidney Monas, *The Third Section: Police and Society in Russia under Nicholas I* (Cambridge, Mass.: Harvard University Press, 1961). Pioneering study of the repressive machinery.

Bernard Pares, *The Fall of the Russian Monarchy* (London: Jonathan Cape, 1939). An excellent study of the period from 1905 to 1917 by an authority who was frequently on the spot.

Nicholas V. Riasanovsky, *Russia and the West in the Teaching of the Slavophiles* (Boston: Peter Smith, 1980), and *Nicholas I and Official Nationality in Russia, 1825-1855* (Berkeley: University of California, n.d.). Useful studies.

Gerold T. Robinson, *Rural Russia under the Old Regime* (Berkeley: University of California Press, 1967). A splendid monograph on the peasant question.

Hugh Seton-Watson, *The Decline of Imperial Russia, 1855-1914* (New York: Praeger, 1956), sound and full, and *The Russian Empire, 1801-1917* (Oxford: Clarendon, 1967). Perhaps the fullest one-volume history of the period.

Benedict H. Sumner, *Russia and the Balkans, 1870-1880* (Oxford: Clarendon, 1937). A monograph including a helpful discussion of Panslavism.

Leslie C. Tihany, *A History of Middle Europe* (New Brunswick, N.J.: Rutgers University Press, 1976). Concise general survey.

Adam B. Ulam, *In the Name of the People: Prophets and Conspirators in Prerevolutionary Russia* (New York: Viking, 1977). Lively inquiry into the nature of nihilism and other contemporary movements.

Theodore H. Von Laue, *Why Lenin? Why Stalin? A Reappraisal of the Russian Revolution, 1900-1930* (Philadelphia: Lippincott, 1964). Fine, balanced examination of why the course of revolution ran as it did.

B. D. Wolfe, *Three Who Made a Revolution* (Boston: Beacon, 1956). A fine study of Lenin, Trotsky, and Stalin; emphasizes the period before 1914.

Sources

Helmut Böhme, ed., *The Foundation of the German Empire: Select Documents,* trans. Agatha Ramm (London: Oxford University Press, 1971). A wide variety of extracts.

Alexis de Tocqueville, *Democracy in America* (several eds.). The famous pioneering study by the great French observer.

Fyodor Dostoevsky, *The Brothers Karamazov* and *Crime and Punishment* (several eds.). Famous novels depicting the turbulent life of Russian intellectuals in the midnineteenth century; more romantic in tone than Turgenev's works.

Anatole France, *Penguin Island* (New York: New American Library, 1974). French history satirized at the turn of the century.

Nikolai Gogol, *The Inspector General* (several eds.) and *Dead Souls* (several eds.). Brilliant satirical play and novel.

Alexander Herzen, *My Past and Thoughts* (Berkeley: University of California Press, 1981). The classic picture of nineteenth-century Russia by its most distinguished rebel.

Frederic B. M. Hollyday, ed., *Bismarck* (Englewood Cliffs, N.J.: Prentice-Hall, 1970). Collection of diverse views on the Iron Chancellor.

Peter Kropotkin, *Memoirs of a Revolutionist,* ed. James A. Rogers (New York: Dover, 1970). An anarchist's story of his own life and times.

Thomas Mann, *Buddenbrooks* (several eds.). Novel of a family in imperial Germany.

Friedrich Meinecke, *The Age of German Liberation, 1795-1815,* trans. Peter Paret and Helmuth Fischer (Berkeley: University of California Press, 1977). A classic document of German cultural nationalism.

Robert Musil, *The Man without Qualities* (New York: Coward-McCann, 1953). A novel steeped in the atmosphere of pre-1914 Vienna.

Otto Pflanze, ed., *The Unification of Germany, 1848-1871* (Melbourne, Fla.: Krieger, 1979). Selections from conflicting views on German unification.

Marc Raeff, ed., *Russian Intellectual History: An Anthology* (New York: Harcourt Brace & World, 1966). Illuminating; contains full selections from the leading Russian thinkers of the time.

The Portable Chekhov (New York: Viking, 1947). A selection of the short stories and plays of Anton Chekhov, a skillful portraitist of the upper classes in czarist Russia.

Leo Tolstoy, *Anna Karenina* (several eds.). A celebrated novel set in late nineteenth-century St. Petersburg and the countryside.

Ivan Turgenev, *Fathers and Sons* (sometimes called *Fathers and Children*; several eds.), and *Smoke* (several eds.). Superb contemporary realistic fiction reflecting Russian intellectual and political life.

Sergei Witte, *Memoirs* (Garden City, N.Y.: Doubleday, 1921). The somewhat apologetic memoirs of the man who did the most to industrialize imperial Russia.

Emile Zola, *The Downfall* (New York: Appleton, 1902). Very good novel of the Franco-Prussian War. Arnold Bennett's *Old Wives' Tale* (New York: Grosset & Dunlap, 1911) has a superb account of life in Paris during the siege of 1870 to 1871.

CHAPTER 22: MODERN EMPIRES AND IMPERIALISM

Great Britain

C. J. Bartlett, ed., *Britain Pre-eminent: Studies in British World Influence in the Nineteenth Century* (London: Macmillan, 1969). A concise summary of the factors that made Britain the dominant power in the nineteenth century.

G. F. A. Best, *Mid-Victorian Britain, 1851-1875* (London: Weidenfeld and Nicolson, 1971). Solid account of a quarter-century of reform and resistance to it.

Robert Blake, *Disraeli* (London: Eyre and Spittiswoode, 1966); Phillip Magnus, *Gladstone* (New York: Dutton, n.d.); Donald Southgate, *"The Most English Minister . . .": The Policies and Politics of Palmerston* (New York: St. Martin's, 1966). Sound biographies.

Asa Briggs, *The Age of Improvement* (London: Longmans, Green, 1959). An excellent survey of the period from 1783 to 1867.

Maurice Bruce, *The Coming of the Welfare State* (North Pomfret, Vt.: David and Charles, 1974). Good study of the post-Victorian reforms. May be supplemented by Colin Cross, *The Liberals in Power, 1905-1914* (Westport, Conn.: Greenwood, 1976), and by studies of two Liberal leaders: Michael Gilbert, ed., *Lloyd George* (Englewood Cliffs, N.J.: Prentice-Hall, 1968); and Roy Jenkins, *Asquith* (New York: Dutton, n.d.).

John Cannon, *Parliamentary Reform, 1640-1832* (Cambridge, Eng.: Cambridge University Press, 1973). Balanced, clear, analytical treatment.

G. Kitson Clark, *The Making of Victorian England* (New York: Atheneum, 1967); and G. M. Young, *Victorian England: Portrait of an Age,* 2nd ed. ((New York: Galaxy, n.d.). Two very good introductions.

Norman Gash, *Aristocracy and People: Britain, 1815-1865* (Cambridge, Mass.: Harvard University Press, 1979). An excellent, up-to-date general survey.

Norman Gash, *Politics in the Age of Peel* (New York: Norton, 1971), and *Reaction and Reconstruction in English Politics, 1832-1852* (Westport, Conn.: Greenwood, 1981). Scholarly studies of an important epoch for reform and political change.

J. A. S. Grenville, *Lord Salisbury and Foreign Policy: The Close of the Nineteenth Century* (London: Athlone, 1970). Perhaps the best short history of the complex years between 1895 and 1902.

John Grigg, *The Young Lloyd George* (London: Eyre Methuen, 1973), and *Lloyd George: The People's Champion* (Berkeley: University of California Press, 1979). A fine, sympathetic biography.

Elie Halévy, *A History of the English People in the Nineteenth Century,* 2nd rev. ed. (Boston: Peter Smith, 1949-1951). Though incomplete—it covers only the years from 1815 to 1852 and 1895 to 1915—and often outdated, this study by a French scholar ranks as a classic. Halévy also wrote a standard work on the Utilitarians, *The Growth of Philosophic Radicalism,* 3rd ed. (New York: Faber, 1972).

Elizabeth Longford, *Queen Victoria* (New York: Pyramid, n.d.). Good standard biography.

Philip Mason, *The English Gentleman: The Rise and Fall of an Ideal* (New York: Morrow, 1982). A lively social history.

Lawrence J. McCaffrey, *The Irish Question, 1800-1922* (Lexington: University of Kentucky Press, 1968); Nicholas Mansergh, *The Irish Question, 1840-1921* (London: Allen & Unwin, 1965). Two balanced examinations of the Irish issue, the first in the context of British domestic politics, the second in the broader context of imperial issues.

Henry Pelling, *Popular Politics and Society in Late Victorian Britain* (London: Macmillan, 1968). Good essays on the origins of the welfare state.

Donald Read, ed., *Edwardian England* (New Brunswick, N.J.: Rutgers University Press, 1982). Enlightening collection of essays which revise several older views.

L. C. B. Seaman, *Victorian England: Aspects of English and Imperial History, 1837-1901* (London: Methuen, 1973). An original, even iconoclastic, interpretation which integrates domestic and imperial subjects.

Raymond James Sontag, *Germany and England: Background of Conflict, 1848-1894* (New York: Norton, 1969). Standard exposition of the sources of developing conflict.

E. P. Thompson, *The Making of the English Working Class* (New York: Random House, 1966). Complex, long, controversial, utterly fascinating analysis of the growth of class consciousness and class unity among British workers.

Martin J. Weiner, *English Culture and the Decline of the Industrial Spirit, 1850-1980* (Cambridge, Eng.: Cambridge University Press, 1982). Discusses Britain's industrial decline.

Cecil Woodham-Smith, *The Great Hunger* (London: Hamilton, 1982), and *The Reason Why* (New York: Atheneum, 1981). Dramatic accounts of the Irish famine and of British bungling in the Crimean War, respectively.

Ernest L. Woodward, *The Age of Reform, 1815-1870,* 2nd ed. (Oxford: Clarendon, 1964); and Robert C. K. Ensor, *England, 1870-1914* (Oxford: Clarendon, 1952). Two excellent volumes in the Oxford History of England series.

Imperialism in General

Winfried Baumgart, *Imperialism* (New York: Oxford University Press, 1982). Fine comparison of British and French expansion from 1880 to 1914.

Alfred W. Crosby, Jr., *The Columbian Exchange* (Westport, Conn.: Greenwood, 1973). Challenging look at the biological and cultural consequences of European contact with non-European peoples.

David K. Fieldhouse, *The Colonial Empires* (New York: Dell, 1971). An authoritative survey from the eighteenth century on.

Heinz Gollwitzer, *Europe in the Age of Imperialism, 1880-1914* (New York: Norton, 1979). Informative general survey.

Robert A. Huttenback, *Racism and Empire* (Ithaca: Cornell University Press, 1976). Examines laws intended to bar nonwhite immigrants in colonies of settlement.

Francis Jennings, *The Invasion of America* (New York: Norton, 1976). Fresh exploration of how colonialism affected the Indians of North America.

Richard Koebner and Helmut D. Schmidt, *Imperialism: The Story and*

Significance of a Political Word (Cambridge, Eng.: Cambridge University Press, 1964). An enlightening monograph.

William L. Langer, *The Diplomacy of Imperialism, 1890-1902,* 2nd ed. (New York: Knopf, 1951). Detailed case histories from a particularly complex period.

Kenneth S. Latourette, *A History of the Expansion of Christianity* (New York: Harper & Row, 1975). Volumes 5 and 6 treat its expansion into the non-European world.

O. Mannoni, *Prospero and Caliban* (New York: Methuen, 1964). Analysis of the psychology of colonization.

Philip Mason, *Patterns of Dominance* (Oxford: Oxford University Press, 1970). Examples of the varieties of colonial rule.

Wolfgang J. Mommsen, *Theories of Imperialism,* trans. P. S. Falla (Chicago: University of Chicago Press, 1982). Concise, short discussion of the range of theories—Marxist, anti-Marxist, and non-Marxist—on the causes of imperialism.

Ronald Robinson, John Gallagher, and Alice Denny, *Africa and the Victorians* (New York: St. Martin's, 1961). The classic formulation of the "collaborator thesis" which offers a non-Marxist, as opposed to pro- or anti-Marxist, analysis of the causes of expansion after 1870.

A. P. Thornton, *Doctrines of Imperialism* (New York: Wiley, 1965); and Tom Kemp, *Theories of Imperialism* (London: Dobson, 1968). Useful analyses of the ideological background.

Africa

Michael Crowder, *West Africa under Colonial Rule* (Evanston, Ill.: Northwestern University Press, 1968). Fine survey.

James Duffy, *Portugal in Africa* (London: Penguin, n.d.). The best study of an important and often-neglected colonial enterprise.

Peter Duignan and L. H. Gann, *Colonialism in Africa.* Vol. 1: *The History and Politics of Colonialism* (Cambridge, Eng.: Cambridge University Press, 1969). A comprehensive survey. The same authors have also published *Burden of Empire* (Stanford, Calif.: Hoover Institution, n.d.), a defense of the contribution of the colonial powers to the development of sub-Saharan Africa.

John Flint, *Cecil Rhodes* (Boston: Little, Brown, 1974). Fine, short biography.

Prosser Gifford and Wm. Roger Lewis, eds., *France and Britain in Africa* (New Haven: Yale University Press, 1971); *Britain and Germany in Africa* (New Haven: Yale University Press, 1967). Materials on their rivalry and their respective institutions of colonial rule.

John D. Hargreaves, *Prelude to the Partition of West Africa* (London: Macmillan, 1963). Best analysis of the idea of partition as it relates to the argument that the nature of imperialism changed after 1870.

C. Hollis, *Italy in Africa* (London: Hamish Hamilton, 1941). Good analysis.

A. G. Hopkins, *An Economic History of West Africa* (New York: Columbia University Press, 1973). Highly original reinterpretation of the economic impact of imperialism.

C. W. de Kiewiet, *A History of South Africa, Social and Economic* (Oxford: Oxford University Press, 1941). A good survey.

Lord Kinross (Patrick Balfour), *Between Two Seas* (London: Murray, 1969). Lively account of the creation of the Suez Canal.

David S. Landes, *Bankers and Pashas* (Cambridge, Mass.: Harvard University Press, 1980). Illuminating account of French economic imperialism in Egypt during the midnineteenth century.

Harry R. Rudin, *Germans in the Cameroons, 1884-1914* (Westport, Conn.: Greenwood, 1969). Valuable case study of an imperialist venture.

Ruth Slade, *King Leopold's Congo* (Westport, Conn.: Greenwood, 1974); and Roger Anstey, *King Leopold's Legacy* (London: Oxford University Press, 1966). These two critical volumes examine Belgian rule in the Congo from 1884 to 1960.

R. L. Tignor, *Modernization and British Colonial Rule in Egypt, 1882-1914* (Princeton: Princeton University Press, 1966). Full and balanced appraisal of the British record.

Monica Wilson and Leonard Thompson, eds., *The Oxford History of South Africa* (New York: Oxford University Press, 1969 and 1971). Authoritative history; Volume I ends at 1870, Volume II comes to 1966.

Asia

J. F. Cady, *The Roots of French Imperialism in Eastern Asia,* rev. ed. (Ithaca: Cornell University Press, 1967). Lucid scholarly study.

Michael Edwardes, *The West in Asia, 1815-1914* (New York: Putnam's, n.d.). Good introduction to the increasing involvement of the imperialist powers.

John K. Fairbank, *The United States and China,* 4th ed. (Cambridge, Mass.: Harvard University Press, 1979). With greater stress on Chinese history and culture than the title suggests.

John W. Hall, *Japan: From Pre-History to Modern Times* (New York: Delacorte, 1970). Fine survey.

Kenneth S. Latourette, *China* (Englewood Cliffs, N.J.: Prentice-Hall, n.d.). Concise introduction.

J. T. Pratt, *The Expansion of Europe into the Far East* (New York: Sylvan Press, 1947). Excellent introductory account.

E. O. Reischauer, *Japan Past and Present*, 4th ed. (New York: Knopf, n.d.). Admirable introduction.

B. H. Sumner, *Tsardom and Imperialism in the Far East and Middle East, 1880-1914* (Hamden, Conn.: Shoe String, 1968). Good short account.

The Middle East

R. H. Davison, *Turkey* (Englewood Cliffs, N.J.: Prentice-Hall, n.d.). Clear and concise introduction.

Albert Hourani, *Arabic Thought in the Liberal Age, 1798-1939* (Oxford: Oxford University Press, n.d.). Informative study; considerable stress on Western influences.

Marian Kent, *Oil & Empire* (London: Macmillan, 1976). Close look at oil imperialism to 1920.

Bernard Lewis, *The Emergence of Modern Turkey*, 2nd ed. (Oxford: Oxford University Press, 1968). A good study of the Ottoman empire in the nineteenth century.

The British Empire and Commonwealth

George D. Bearce, *British Attitudes toward India* (Westport, Conn.: Greenwood, 1982). Perceptive survey of the period from 1784 to 1858. Donald F. Lach, *India in the Eyes of Europe* (Chicago: Chicago University Press, 1968). Shows how sixteenth-century attitudes were shaped and carried over to subsequent times. Francis G. Hutchins, *The Illusion of Permanence* (Princeton: Princeton University Press, 1967). Describes how the British could imagine they would remain in India for all time. Christopher Hibbert, *The Great Mutiny: India 1857* (London: Penguin, 1980). Lively short history. R. J. Moore, *Liberalism and Indian Politics, 1872-1922* (London: Arnold, 1966). Discusses India in British politics.

Max Beloff, *Imperial Sunset*. Vol. I: *Britain's Liberal Empire, 1897-1921* (New York: Knopf, 1970). Useful, ironic account.

The Cambridge History of the British Empire (London: Macmillan, 1929-1940). With separate volumes on India, Canada, and Australia and New Zealand together.

Charles E. Carrington, *The British Overseas: Exploits of a Nation of Shopkeepers*, 2nd ed. (Cambridge, Eng.: Cambridge University Press, 1968). Detailed study.

J. B. Condliffe, *New Zealand in the Making* and *The Welfare State in New Zealand* (Westport, Conn.: Greenwood, 1959). These books constitute a good history from 1792 to 1957.

Gerald M. Craig, *The United States and Canada* (Cambridge, Mass.: Harvard University Press, 1968). Sound scholarly study with much stress on Canadian developments.

Donald G. Creighton, *History of Canada: Dominion of the North* (Boston: Houghton Mifflin, 1958); Charles Glazebrook, *Canada: A Short History* (Oxford: Oxford University Press, 1950). Two good general accounts.

Donald C. Gordon, *The Moment of Power* (Englewood Cliffs, N.J.: Prentice-Hall, 1970). Good survey of Britain at the height of imperial authority.

Gordon Greenwood, ed., *Australia: A Social and Political History* (New York: Praeger, 1955). Good collaborative work; includes bibliographies.

Paul Knaplund, *The British Empire, 1815-1939* (New York: Fertig, 1970). An authoritative text.

D. A. Low, *Lion Rampant* (London: Cass, 1973). Exceptionally fruitful essays on the impact of "social engineering" within the British Empire.

Keith Sinclair, *A History of New Zealand* (London: Pelican, 1959). Possibly the best short history of any Commonwealth country. W. H. Oliver, *The Story of New Zealand* (London: Faber, 1963). Emphasizes New Zealand as a social laboratory.

Russel Ward, *Australia* (Englewood Cliffs, N.J.: Prentice-Hall, 1965); and A.

G. L. Shaw, *The Story of Australia,* 4th ed. (New York: Faber, 1973). Two concise, short surveys.

Robin W. Winks, *The Relevance of Canadian History* (Toronto: Macmillan, 1979). A very short comparison between Canadian and American history.

Robin W. Winks, *Western Civilization: A Brief History* (Englewood Cliffs, N.J.: Prentice-Hall, 1979). Several paragraphs on the nature of imperialism were drawn from this short, general, and interpretive text.

Other Empires

Raymond F. Betts, *Assimilation and Association in French Colonial Theory* (New York: Columbia University Press, 1961). Best analysis in English of the policy of assimilation.

Henri Brunschwig, *French Colonialism: Myths and Realities, 1871-1914* (New York: Praeger, 1966). Perceptive study by a French scholar.

Ernest May, *Imperial Democracy* (New York: Harper & Row, 1973), and *American Imperialism: A Speculative Essay* (New York: Atheneum, 1968). By a scholarly expert; deals with America's emergence as a world power.

Dexter Perkins, *A History of the Monroe Doctrine*, rev. ed. (Boston: Little, Brown). Popular account by a leading specialist.

J. W. Pratt, *America's Colonial Experiment* (Englewood Cliffs, N.J.: Prentice-Hall, 1950). Good survey.

S. H. Roberts, *History of French Colonial Policy* (Hamden, Conn.: Archon, 1963). A valuable, detailed, older work.

Woodruff D. Smith, *The German Colonial Empire* (Chapel Hill: University of North Carolina Press, 1978). Clear, basic survey.

M. E. Townsend, *The Rise and Fall of Germany's Colonial Empire, 1884-1918* (New York: Macmillan, 1930). A standard account. May be supplemented by W. O. Henderson, *Studies in German Colonial History* (New York: Quadrangle, 1963).

Sources

R. F. Betts, ed., *The Scramble for Africa* (Lexington, Mass.: Heath, n.d.). Excerpts from varying opinions on the causes and dimensions of the competition.

Reginald Coupland, ed., *The Durham Report* (Oxford: Clarendon, 1946). The document that in a sense marks the beginning of the development of the British Commonwealth.

E. M. Forster, *A Passage to India* (several eds.). Classic novel on the gap between East and West.

H. Rider Haggard, *King Solomon's Mines* (several eds.). A splendid example of the rousing novel of imperialist adventure.

Louis Hémon, *Maria Chapdelaine* (New York: Macmillan, 1940). The best-known classic novel about rural French Canada.

John A. Hobson, *Imperialism: A Study* (Ann Arbor: University of Michigan Press, 1965). A celebrated hostile critique.

Benjamin Kidd, *The Control of the Tropics* (New York: Macmillan, 1898). A characteristic defense of imperialism.

Rudyard Kipling, *Kim* (several eds.), and *Soldiers Three* (several eds.). Famous works by the even more famous champion of imperialism.

V. I. Lenin, *Imperialism: The Highest Stage of Capitalism* (New York: International, n.d.). The classic Communist critique.

Wm. Roger Louis, ed., *Imperialism: The Robinson and Gallagher Controversy* (New York: Franklin Watts, 1976). Presents all sides to the Robinson and Gallagher thesis.

C. J. Lowe, *The Reluctant Imperialists* (London: Routledge, 1967). One volume analyzing British policy and a second containing documents.

Frederick J. Lugard, *The Dual Mandate in British Tropical Africa* (New York: Biblio, 1965). Significant detailed account of British policy in Nigeria.

Robin W. Winks, ed., *The Age of Imperialism* (Englewood Cliffs, N.J.: Prentice-Hall, 1969). A short volume in the Sources of Civilization in the West series, edited by Crane Brinton and Robert Lee Wolff.

CHAPTER 23: GREAT WAR, GREAT REVOLUTION

The Background

C. Andrew, *Théophile Delcassé and the Making of the Entente Cordiale* (New York: St. Martin's, 1938); and Samuel R. Williamson, *The Politics of Grand Strategy* (Cambridge, Mass.: Harvard University Press, 1969). Assessments of the Anglo-French rapprochement before 1914.

V. R. Berghahn, *Germany and the Approach of War in 1914* (New York: St. Martin's, 1973). Careful look at the war from the German perspective.

Oron J. Hale, *The Great Illusion, 1900-1914* (New York: Harper & Row, 1971). Stressing the economic and cultural background; includes full bibliographies.

Paul M. Kennedy, *The Rise and Fall of British Naval Mastery* (London: Allen Lane, 1976). Fine review of a subject central to the war.

Lawrence Lafore, *The Long Fuse* (New York: Harper & Row, 1971); and Joachim Remak, *Origins of World War I* (New York: Holt, Rinehart, 1967). Illuminating studies incorporating recent scholarship.

William L. Langer, *European Alliances and Alignments, 1871-1890* (Westport, Conn.: Greenwood, 1977), and *The Diplomacy of Imperialism, 1890-1902*, 2nd ed. (New York: Knopf, 1951). Detailed scholarly analyses; include valuable bibliographies.

Walter Laqueur, *Russia and Germany: A Century of Conflict* (Boston: Little, Brown, 1965). Yet another factor in the background scrutinized.

George Monger, *The End of Isolation* (Westport, Conn.: Greenwood, 1976). British foreign policy reviewed. For Anglo-American relations, it may be supplemented by Bradford Perkins, *The Great Rapprochement* (New York: Atheneum, 1968).

Gerhard Ritter, *The Sword and the Scepter: The Problem of Militarism in Germany,* 2 vols. (Miami: University of Miami Press, 1970). Volume II deals with the European powers and William II's Germany from 1890 to 1914.

Raymond J. Sontag, *Germany and England: Background of Conflict, 1848-1894* (New York: Norton, 1969). Excellent study of Anglo-German tension.

A. J. P. Taylor, *The Struggle for Mastery in Europe, 1848-1918* (Oxford: Oxford University Press, 1971). A crisp and suggestive survey.

Barbara Tuchman, *The Proud Tower* (New York: Macmillan, 1966). Instructive and readable account of the European societies that produced the great war.

The War

Frank P. Chambers, *The War behind the War* (New York: Arno, 1972). On the "home front."

Richard Collier, *The Plague of the Spanish Lady* (New York: Atheneum, 1974). The drama of the influenza pandemic that swept the world in 1918 to 1919.

C. R. M. Cruttwell, *History of the Great War,* 2nd ed. (Oxford: Oxford University Press, 1936); Cyril Falls, *The Great War* (New York: Putnam, 1959); Hanson Baldwin, *World War One* (New York: Harper & Row, 1962). Three sober and reliable accounts.

Fritz Fischer, *Germany's Aims in the First World War* (New York: Norton, 1968). A revisionist estimate of German policy that has caused considerable debate.

Paul Fussell, *The Great War and Modern Memory* (New York: Oxford University Press, 1977). Powerful study of how World War I was shaped in modern memory by major literary figures.

Ernest R. May, *World War and American Isolation, 1914-1917* (Cambridge, Mass.: Harvard University Press, 1959), and *The Coming of War, 1917* (Chicago: Rand McNally, 1963). The most reliable and balanced treatment of the events that made the United States a belligerent.

Elizabeth Monroe, *Britain's Moment in the Middle East, 1914-1956,* rev. ed. (Baltimore: Johns Hopkins University Press, 1981). Persuasive explanation of the contradictions in Britain's policy toward Arabs and Jews, particularly during World War I and the ensuing peace negotiations.

Alan Moorehead, *Gallipoli* (Annapolis: Nautical, 1982); and Alistair Horne, *The Price of Glory: Verdun, 1916* (London: Penguin, 1979). Excellent accounts of particular campaigns.

Gerhard Ritter, *The Schlieffen Plan: Critique of a Myth* (Westport, Conn.: Greenwood, 1979). Scholarly reassessment.

A. J. P. Taylor, *The First World War* (London: Penguin, 1978); B. H. Liddell Hart, *The Real War* (Boston: Little, Brown, 1964). Lively, opinionated surveys.

Barbara Tuchman, *The Guns of August* (New York: Macmillan, 1962). Well-written narrative of the first critical month of the War and the crisis preceding it.

Richard M. Watt, *Dare Call It Treason* (New York: Simon & Schuster, 1963). The story of the most concerted French attempt to break the deadlock of trench warfare and of the mutiny that resulted in 1917.

Zloynek Zeman, *The Gentlemen Negotiators* (New York: Macmillan, 1971). Study of diplomacy during the war.

The Peace

Thomas A. Bailey, *Woodrow Wilson and the Lost Peace* (Boston: Peter Smith, n.d.) and *Woodrow Wilson and the Great Betrayal* (Boston: Peter Smith, n.d.). Stress the setbacks Wilson's program suffered in Paris and in Washington, respectively.

Paul Birdsall, *Versailles Twenty Years After* (New York: Reynal and Hitchcock, 1941). Excellent appraisal by an American scholar.

John M. Keynes, *The Economic Consequences of the Peace* (several eds.), and Etienne Mantoux, *The Carthaginian Peace; or, the Economic Consequences of Mr. Keynes* (New York: Arno, 1979). Respectively, the most famous attack on the Versailles settlement and a thoughtful study of the results of that attack.

Arno J. Mayer, *The Political Origins of the New Diplomacy, 1917-1918* (New York: Random House, 1970), and *The Politics and Diplomacy of Peacemaking* (New York: Knopf, 1967). Two studies that stress the role played by the fear of Bolshevism. For another interpretation, see J. M. Thompson, *Russia, Bolshevism and the Versailles Peace* (Princeton: Princeton University Press, 1966).

Harold Nicolson, *Peacemaking 1919* (Boston: Peter Smith, n.d.). Informative study by a British expert on diplomacy.

The Russian Revolution: General

Robert V. Daniels, *The Nature of Communism* (New York: Random House, 1962). A valuable study of totalitarianism.

R. N. Carew Hunt, *The Theory and Practice of Communism* (New York: Macmillan, 1951). An excellent introduction to the subject.

Barrington Moore, Jr., *Soviet Politics: The Dilemma of Power* (Armonk, N.Y.: Sharpe, 1977). An illuminating analysis of the relationship between the Communist ideology and Soviet practice.

The Russian Revolution: Special Studies

Crane Brinton, *The Anatomy of Revolution* (New York: Random House, 1965). Comparison of the Russian Revolution with the French Revolution of 1789 and the English seventeenth-century Revolution.

Isaac Deutscher, *The Prophet Armed, The Prophet Unarmed, The Prophet Outcast* (Oxford: Oxford University Press, 1980). Biography of Trotsky in three volumes.

Merle Fainsod, *Smolensk Under Soviet Rule* (Cambridge, Mass.: Harvard University Press, 1958). A unique study, based on a collection of captured documents, of the actual workings of the Communist system in Smolensk in the 1930s.

Marc Ferro, *The Russian Revolution of February 1917,* trans. J. L. Richards (Englewood Cliffs, N.J.: Prentice-Hall, 1972). Close study of the fall of czarism and the defeat of the February revolution. Marc Ferro, *October 1917: A Social History of the Russian Revolution,* trans. Norman Stone (London: Routledge & Kegan Paul, 1980). Fine social history.

Alan Moorehead, *The Russian Revolution* (New York: Harper, 1958). A lively, generally sound survey.

M. C. Morgan, *Lenin* (London: Edward Arnold, 1971). Clear, short biography.

Richard Pipes, *The Formation of the Soviet Union* (New York: Atheneum, 1968). Excellent monograph on the question of national minorities in Russia from 1917 to 1923.

David Shub, *Lenin* (London: Penguin, 1977). A good biography of Lenin.

Nicholas Timasheff, *The Great Retreat* (Salem, N.H.: Arno, 1972). An account of the "Russian Thermidor."

Donald W. Treadgold, *Lenin and His Rivals: The Struggle for Russia's Future, 1898-1906* (Westport, Conn.: Greenwood, 1976). Examines the alternatives to Lenin.

Adam B. Ulam, *The Bolsheviks: The Intellectual and Political History of the Triumph of Communism in Russia* (New York: Macmillan, 1968) and *Stalin: The Man and His Era* (New York: Viking, 1973). Excellent detailed accounts.

Adam B. Ulam, *Expansion and Coexistence: The History of Soviet Foreign Policy, 1917-1967,* 2nd ed. (New York: Holt, Rinehart, 1974). The first six chapters of this excellent analytical work deal with the period to 1941.

Theodore H. Von Laue, *Why Lenin? Why Stalin? A Reappraisal of the Russian Revolution, 1900-1930* (Philadelphia: Lippincott, 1964). Thoughtful analysis of the causes of the Communist victory in Russia.

Bertram D. Wolfe, *Three Who Made a Revolution* (New York: Dell, 1978). Triple study of the careers of Lenin, Trotsky, and Stalin down to 1914.

Sources

Henri Barbusse, *Under Fire* (Totowa, N.J.: Biblio, 1975); and E. M. Remarque, *All Quiet on the Western Front* (New York: Fawcett, 1929). Two famous novels—by a Frenchman and a German, respectively—reflect the horror aroused in intellectuals by trench warfare.

John Buchan, *Greenmantle* (London: Nelson, n.d.); and W. Somerset Maugham, *Ashenden* (New York: Penguin, 1977). Tales of espionage and high adventure.

James Bunyan and H. H. Fisher, eds., *The Bolshevik Revolution, 1917-1918* (Palo Alto, Calif.: Stanford University Press, 1961). Substantial collection of documents and other materials.

e. e. cummings, *The Enormous Room* (New York: Liveright, 1978); and Arnold Zweig, *The Case of Sergeant Grischa* (New York: Viking, 1938). Respectively, discuss prisoners of war and the eastern front.

Robert V. Daniels, ed., *The Russian Revolution* (Englewood Cliffs, N.J.: Prentice-Hall, 1972). A well-chosen and well-discussed selection of sources.

John Dos Passos, *Three Soldiers* (Boston: Houghton Mifflin, 1964); and Ernest Hemingway, *A Farewell to Arms* (New York: Scribner's, 1982). Two American novels which reflect postwar disillusionment.

C. S. Forester, *The General* (Annapolis: Nautical, 1982). A careerist dissected.

SUGGESTED READINGS **511**

Dwight W. Lee, ed., *The Outbreak of the First World War,* 4th ed. (Lexington, Mass.: Heath, 1975); Ivo J. Lederer, ed., *The Versailles Settlement* (Lexington, Mass.: Heath, 1960); Theodore P. Greene, ed., *Wilson at Versailles* (Lexington, Mass.: Heath, 1958). Collections of primary sources and selections from secondary works; show the range of debated views prior to the opening of the most recent wartime archival collections, on which research is continuing.

Outbreak of the World War: German Documents Collected by Karl Kautsky (Oxford: Oxford University Press, 1924), and *German Diplomatic Documents, 1871-1914* (New York: Methuen, 1928-1931). English translations of some of the vast flood of documents released by the German republican government at the end of the War. May be compared with *British Documents on the Origins of The War, 1898-1914* (London: H. M. Stationery Office, 1926-1938).

Jules Romains, *Verdun* (New York: Knopf, 1946). Excellent and balanced novel about French troops on the Western front from 1914 to 1916.

Leon Trotsky, *The History of the Russian Revolution* (New York: Pluto, 1980). A brilliant but biased study by one of the leading participants.

CHAPTER 24: BETWEEN THE WARS: A TWENTY-YEAR CRISIS

Russia: General Accounts

Edward H. Carr, *A History of Soviet Russia* (New York: Macmillan, 1951-1964). The only attempt at a complete history of the Soviet Union from original sources.

Robert V. Daniels, *The Nature of Communism* (New York: Random House, 1962). A valuable study of totalitarianism.

Merle Fainsod, *How Russia Is Ruled* (Cambridge, Mass.: Harvard University Press, 1963). An analysis of the Soviet system, firmly rooted in the historical background.

Barrington Moore, Jr., *Soviet Politics: The Dilemma of Power* (New York: Sharpe, 1977). An illuminating analysis of the relationship between the Communist ideology and Soviet practice.

Donald W. Treadgold, *Twentieth Century Russia* (Boston: Houghton Mifflin, 1981). Good basic survey.

Russia: Special Studies

William L. Blackwell, *The Industrialization of Russia* (Arlington Heights, Ill.: Harlan Davidson, 1982). Full survey.

William H. Chamberlin, *The Russian Revolution, 1917-1921* (New York: Grosset & Dunlap, n.d.). Still the standard work on the later years.

Robert Conquest, *The Great Terror: Stalin's Purge of the Thirties* (New York: Collier, 1973). An examination of how the Terror came about and of the heritage it left.

Robert Conquest, ed., *The Politics of Ideas in the U.S.S.R.* (Westport, Conn.: Greenwood, 1976). Intriguing study of the mobilization of thought.

Naum Jasny, *Soviet Economists of the Twenties* (Cambridge, Eng.: Cambridge University Press, 1972), on the NEP and post-NEP economic thought, and *The Socialized Agriculture of the USSR* (Palo Alto, Calif.: Stanford University Press, 1949), especially good on the *kolkhoz.*

Moshe Lewin, *Russian Peasants and Soviet Power: A Study of Collectivization,* trans. Irene Nove (London: Allen & Unwin, 1968). Good study of the drive to collectivize.

Adam B. Ulam, *Stalin: The Man and His Era* (New York: Viking, 1973). Excellent detailed accounts.

The Roots of Fascism

Edward Hallett Carr, *The Twenty Years' Crisis, 1919-1939* (New York: Harper & Row, 1964). Clear exposition of the relationship between Fascism and foreign policy.

Alfred Cobban, *Dictatorship: Its History and Theory* (New York: Haskell, 1970). Highly suggestive survey, reaching well back into history.

George Mosse, *The Crisis of German Ideology: Intellectual Origins of the Third Reich* (New York: Fertig, 1981); and Fritz Stern, *The Politics of Cultural Despair* (Berkeley: University of California Press, 1974). Contrasting, solid studies of Hitler's forerunners.

Hans Rogger and Eugene Weber, eds., *The European Right: A Historical Profile* (Berkeley: University of California Press, 1965). A learned and stimulating collection of essays on right-wing movements in the various countries of Europe; includes good bibliographies.

Raymond Sontag, *A Broken World, 1919-1939* (New York: Harper & Row, 1971). A fine survey.

Henry A. Turner, Jr., ed., *Reappraisals of Fascism* (New York: Franklin Watts, 1975). Review of interpretations of Fascism, with emphasis on the arguments of the German scholar Ernst Nolte.

Italy

Herman Finer, *Mussolini's Italy* (Hamden, Conn.: Archon, 1964); and H. A. Steiner, *Government in Fascist Italy* (New York: McGraw-Hill, 1938). Two solid studies by political scientists.

G. Magero, *Mussolini in the Making* (Boston: Houghton Mifflin, 1938). A good study of Mussolini's early career.

Gaetano Salvemini, *Under the Axe of Fascism* (New York: Fertig, 1970). Lively work by an important anti-Fascist Italian.

Denis Mack Smith, *Mussolini* (New York: Viking, 1982), and *Mussolini's Roman Empire* (New York: Viking, 1976). Recent appraisals that, despite much new literature on Italian Fascism, remain essentially hostile to Mussolini.

Elizabeth Wiskemann, *Fascism in Italy: Its Development and Influence* (London: Macmillan, 1970). Very brief, clear analysis.

Germany

William Sheridan Allen, *The Nazi Seizure of Power* (New York: Franklin Watts, 1973). A close examination of how Nazism took over at the local level.

Karl D. Bracher, *The German Dictatorship* (New York: Holt, Rinehart, 1972). Excellent comprehensive study by a German scholar.

Alan C. Bullock, *Hitler: A Study in Tyranny* (New York: Harper & Row, 1964). A fine biography.

Erich Eyck, *A History of the Weimar Republic* (New York: Atheneum, 1970). A superb, full examination.

Joachim C. Fest, *Hitler,* trans. Richard and Clara Winston (New York: Harcourt Brace Jovanovich, 1974); and Norman Stone, *Hitler* (New York: Knopf, 1982). Two excellent, well-researched, and fresh appraisals.

Ruth Fischer, *Stalin and German Communism* (New Brunswick, N.J.: Transaction, 1982). A study of the role played by the Communist movement in the history of Germany between the Wars.

Samuel W. Halperin, *Germany Tried Democracy* (New York: Crowell, 1946). A reliable history of the Weimar Republic from 1918 to 1933.

Franz L. Neumann, *Behemoth: The Structure and Practice of National Socialism* (New York: Octagon, 1963). A good analytical description.

Henry A. Turner, Jr., *Gustav Stresemann and the Politics of Weimar* (Westport, Conn.: Greenwood, 1979). A fine inquiry into a failed leader.

Robert G. Waite, *Vanguard of Nazism* (Cambridge, Mass.: Harvard University Press, 1952). A study of the "Free Corps" movement.

J. W. Wheeler-Bennett, *Wooden Titan* (New York: Morrow, 1936), and *Nemesis of Power* (New York: St. Martin's, 1954). Two first-rate studies, the first dealing with Hindenburg, the second with the role of the German army in politics from 1918 to 1945.

Elizabeth Wiskemann, *The Rome-Berlin Axis* (New York: Oxford University Press, 1949). A study of the formation and history of the Hitler-Mussolini partnership.

Other Countries

Gerald Brenan, *The Spanish Labyrinth,* 2nd ed. (Cambridge, Eng.: Cambridge University Press, 1960). A useful study of the Spanish Civil War against its historical and economic background.

Raymond Carr, *Spain, 1808-1939* (New York: Oxford University Press, 1982). Includes a careful examination of Franco in the light of earlier history.

Carlo M. Cipolla, ed., *The Twentieth Century* (London: Fontana, 1977). Useful essays on demographic trends and the labor force.

Nicholas M. Nagy-Talavera, *The Green Shirts and the Others: A History of Fascism in Hungary and Rumania* (Stanford: Hoover Institution, 1970). Full examination.

Stanley G. Payne, *Falange* (Palo Alto, Calif.: Stanford University Press, 1961). Good study of the Falangist movement.

Frederick B. Pike, *Hispanismo* (Notre Dame: University of Notre Dame Press, 1971). A look at corporatism in Spain.

Hugh Seton-Watson, *Eastern Europe between the Wars, 1918-1941,* 3rd ed. (Hamden, Conn.: Archon, 1962). A useful account dealing with all the eastern European countries except Greece and Albania.

Hugh Thomas, *The Spanish Civil War,* rev. ed. (New York: Harper & Row, 1977). The best single work on the subject.

Sources

Adolf Hitler, *Mein Kampf* (several eds.). A complete English translation of the Nazi bible, the basic work to read for an understanding of the movement.

Adolf Hitler, *My New Order,* ed. R. de Sales (New York: Octagon, 1973). Speeches after the Fuhrer's coming to power.

Robert Payne, ed., *The Civil War in Spain* (Greenwich, Conn.: Fawcett, 1962). Original documents on the war.

Albert Speer, *Inside the Third Reich: Memoirs,* trans. Richard and Clara Winston (New York: Macmillan, 1970). Memoirs of Hitler's own city planner and architect; an invaluable picture of life among the Nazis.

Franz von Papen, *Memoirs* (New York: AMS Press, 1978). An apologetic autobiography by the right-wing politician.

Eugene Weber, ed., *Varieties of Fascism* (Melbourne, Fla.: Krieger, 1982). A short history with a selection of sources.

CHAPTER 25: THE DEMOCRACIES AND THE NON-WESTERN WORLD

The Political and Economic Climate

E. Fischer, *The Passing of the European Age* (Cambridge, Mass.: Harvard University Press, 1943); and Felix Gilbert, *The End of the European Era, 1890 to the Present* (New York: Norton, 1979). Reasoned defenses of the thesis that World War I cost Europe its old hegemony.

John Kenneth Galbraith, *The Great Crash* (New York: Avon, 1980). Wall Street, 1929, revisited by an articulate economist.

H. Stuart Hughes, *Contemporary Europe* (Englewood Cliffs, N.J.: Prentice-Hall, 1981); and A. J. P. Taylor, *From Sarajevo to Potsdam* (New York: Harcourt, n.d.). Surveys stressing intellectual and military-diplomatic history, respectively.

Great Britain

George Dangerfield, *The Damnable Question: A Study in Anglo-Irish Relations* (Boston: Little, Brown, 1976). A balanced account of the Irish Question in British politics.

Robert Graves and Alan Hodge, *The Long Weekend* (New York: Norton, 1963). Lively social history of interwar Britain.

Robert Rhodes James, *The British Revolution, 1880-1939* (New York: Knopf, 1977). A fine exploration of how Britain changed in fundamental ways.

Keith Middlemas and John Barnes, *Baldwin* (New York: Macmillan, 1970). A sound biography.

Charles L. Mowat, *Britain between the Wars, 1918-1940* (Chicago: University of Chicago Press, 1955); Arthur Marwick, *Britain in the Century of Total War, 1900-1967* (Boston: Little, Brown, 1968); W. N. Medicott, *Contemporary England, 1914-1964* (New York: McKay, 1967); David Thomson, *England in the Twentieth Century* (London: Penguin, 1965); A. J. P. Taylor, *English History, 1919-1945* (Oxford: Oxford University Press, 1965). Good general surveys.

Stephen Roskill, *Naval Policy between the Wars,* 2 vols. (New York: Walker, 1968). The first volume is especially good on the period of Anglo-American antagonism, from 1919 to 1929.

France

René Albrecht-Carrie, *France, Europe, and the Two World Wars* (Westport, Conn.: Greenwood, 1975). Illuminating study of French difficulties against their international background.

D. W. Brogan, *France under the Republic* (Westport, Conn.: Greenwood, 1974). Stimulating survey.

Nathaniel Greene, *From Versailles to Vichy* (Arlington Heights, Ill.: Harlan Davidson, 1970). Lucid survey of interwar France.

Stanley Hoffman, et al., *In Search of France* (Cambridge, Mass.: Harvard University Press, 1963); James Joll, ed., *The Decline of the Third Republic* (London: Chatto & Windus, 1959). Insightful essays.

Martin Wolfe, *The French Franc between the Wars* (New York: AMS Press, 1951). Enlightening study of France's chronic monetary difficulties.

The United States

Frederick Allen, *Only Yesterday* and *Since Yesterday* (New York: Harper & Row, 1972). Evocative social histories of the 1920s and 1930s, respectively. James M. Burns, *Roosevelt: The Lion and the Fox* (New York: Harcourt Brace Jovanovich, 1970). Analysis of FDR as a politician.

William E. Leuchtenburg, *Perils of Prosperity, 1914-1932* (Chicago: University of Chicago Press, n.d.), and *Franklin D. Roosevelt and the New Deal, 1932-1940* (New York: Harper & Row, 1963). Well-balanced studies.

Arthur M. Schlesinger, Jr., *The Age of Roosevelt* (Boston: Houghton Mifflin, 1957). Detailed study by a sympathetic though not uncritical historian.

The Non-Western World

George Antonius, *The Arab Awakening* (New York: Capricorn, 1965). The classic sympathetic account; stresses the rapid growth of Arab nationalism in the years during and immediately after World War I.

Yahya Armajani, *Iran* (Englewood Cliffs, N.J.: Prentice-Hall, 1972). A sound short history.

Erik Erikson, *Gandhi's Truth* (New York: Norton, 1969). Appraisal by a distinguished psychohistorian. May be supplemented by Robert Duncan, *Gandhi: Selected Writings* (New York: Colophon, n.d.).

J. K. Fairbank, *The United States and China,* 4th ed. (Cambridge, Mass.: Harvard University Press, 1979); Edwin O. Reishauer, *The United States and Japan,* 2nd ed. (Cambridge, Mass.: Harvard University Press, 1965); W. Norman Brown, *The United States and India, Pakistan, Bangladesh,* 3rd ed. (Cambridge, Mass.: Harvard University Press, 1972); W. R. Polk, *The United States and the Arab World,* rev. ed. (Cambridge, Mass.: Harvard University Press, 1969); J. F. Gallagher, *The United States and North Africa* (Cambridge, Mass.: Harvard University Press, 1963). These volumes in The American Foreign Policy Library furnish scholarly appraisals of the recent history of the countries indicated.

Francis Hutchins, *The Illusion of Permanence* (Princeton: Princeton University Press, 1967). Excellent critique of British imperialism in India.

Firuz Kazemzadeh, *Russia and Britain in Persia, 1864-1914* (New Haven: Yale University Press, 1968). Excellent background for understanding the persistence of Iranian fears of Russia and the West.

Jean and S. Lacouture, *Egypt in Transition* (New York: Methuen, 1958); Stephen H. Longrigg, *Syria and Lebanon under French Mandate* (New York: Octagon, 1972); and Joseph M. Upton, *The History of Modern Iran: An Interpretation* (Cambridge, Mass.: Harvard University Press, 1960). Perceptive studies of individual Middle Eastern states.

Gordon Lewis, *Turkey,* 3rd ed. (New York: Praeger, 1965); and Lord Kinross (Patrick Balfour), *Ataturk* (London: Weidenfeld and Nicolson, 1964). Respectively, a lively survey of the Turkish revolution and a clear biography of its chief architect.

Sources

F. Scott Fitzgerald, *The Great Gatsby* (New York: Scribner's, 1982). The famous novel about the jazz age.

E. M. Forster, *A Passage to India* (New York: Harcourt, n.d.). The classic novel detailing the obstacles impeding the meeting of East and West.

Frank Freidel, ed., *The New Deal and the American People* (Englewood Cliffs, N.J.: Prentice-Hall, 1964). Sampling of different views.

André Gide, *The Counterfeiters* (New York: Random House, 1973). French middle-class values put under the microscope by a talented novelist.

Ernest Hemingway, *The Sun Also Rises* (New York: Scribner's, 1982). Widely considered the classic novel about the "lost generation" of disillusioned American idealists after World War I.

Aldous Huxley, *Point Counterpoint* and *Brave New World* (several eds.). Mordant novels written in the 1920s appraising contemporary mores in England and forecasting their future, respectively.

André Malraux, *Man's Fate* (New York: Random House, 1969). Excellent novel about Chinese Communists in the 1920s.

Frances Perkins, *The Roosevelt I Knew* (New York: Viking, 1946). Perceptive appraisal by the Secretary of Labor in the Roosevelt years.

Howard Spring, *Fame Is the Spur* (New York: Viking, 1940). The career of the fictional hero, who is corrupted by political ambition, has many parallels with that of Ramsay MacDonald.

John Steinbeck, *The Grapes of Wrath* (several eds.). "Okies" journeying from Oklahoma to California in the wake of drought and depression.

Evelyn Waugh, *Decline and Fall* and *A Handful of Dust* (Boston: Little, Brown, 1977). Two corrosive short novels, published in one volume, on English society in the interwar years.

CHAPTER 26: THE SECOND WORLD WAR AND ITS AFTERMATH

General Accounts

Maurice Cowling, *The Impact of Hitler* (Chicago: University of Chicago Press, 1977). An original look at British policies from 1933 to 1940.

Jon Livingston, Joe Moore, and Felicia Oldfather, eds., *Imperial Japan, 1800-1945* (New York: Pantheon, 1973). Draws upon Japanese scholars to give their point of view.

Henri Michel, *The Second World War,* trans. Douglas Parmee (London: Andre Deutsch, 1975); and Peter Calvocoressi and Guy Wint, *Total War: Causes and Courses of the Second World War* (London: Allen Lane, 1972). Two superb, massive histories.

Samuel E. Morison, *History of United States Naval Operations in World War II,* 15 vols. (Boston: Little, Brown, 1947-1962). Official but detached and professional history; pays full attention to political and diplomatic problems.

Gordon W. Prange, *At Dawn We Slept* (New York: Penguin, 1983). The most nearly definitive account of the entry of the United States into the War.

Albert Seaton, *The Battle for Moscow, 1941-1942* (London: Hart-Davis, 1971). A model study of a crucial battle.

N. Sivachyor and E. Yazkov, *History of the USA since World War I,* trans. A. B. Eklof (Moscow: Progress, 1976). The War from the Soviet point of view.

F. L. Snyder, *The War: A Concise History, 1939-1945* (New York: Messner, 1960); and Kenneth S. Davis, *Experience of War: The U.S. in World War II* (New York: Doubleday, 1965). Relatively short histories with full notes and bibliographies.

Christopher Thorne, *The Approach of War, 1938-1939* (New York: Macmillan, 1969). Good short examination of the critical months that led up to war.

United States Army in World War II (Washington, D.C.: Department of the Army, 1947). The official history in many detailed volumes.

Gordon Wright, *The Ordeal of Total War* (New York: Harper & Row, 1968). A good survey.

Special Studies

Edward Bishop, *Their Finest Hour* (New York: Ballantine, 1968). A succinct illustrated history of the Battle of Britain in 1940.

Larry Collins and Dominique LaPierre, *Is Paris Burning?* (New York: Simon & Schuster, 1965). Deservedly popular account of the liberation of Paris.

Herbert Feis, *Churchill, Roosevelt, Stalin* (Princeton: Princeton University Press, 1967). A fascinating and fair-minded account of their wartime relationship.

Gerald Fleming, *Hitler und die Endlösung* (Munich: Limes, 1982). The best study of the systematic application, by Himmler, of Hitler's proposed Final Solution.

Otto Friedrich, *The End of the World: A History* (New York: Coward, McCann & Geoghegan, 1982). Through a close examination of Auschwitz, places the Holocaust into perspective.

Felix Gilbert and G. A. Craig, eds., *The Diplomats, 1919-1939* (Princeton: Princeton University Press, 1953). A helpful symposium.

David L. Gordon and Royden Dangerfield, *The Hidden Weapon: The Story of Economic Warfare* (New York: Harper, 1947). A good popular account.

William L. Langer and S. Everett Gleason, *The Challenge to Isolation, 1937-1940* (Boston: Peter Smith, 1978), and *The Undeclared War, 1940-1941* (Boston: Peter Smith, 1976). Solid studies of America's role.

Charles L. Mowat, ed., *The Shifting Balance of World Forces, 1898-1945* (Cambridge, Eng.: Cambridge University Press, 1968). A massive, synoptic history; Volume XII of *The New Cambridge Modern History.*

Alfred L. Rowse, *Appeasement: A Study in Political Decline, 1933-1939* (New York: Norton, 1963); and Neville Thompson, *The Anti-Appeasers* (Oxford: Clarendon, 1971). Controversial, lively arguments concerning the issue of appeasement.

S. R. Smith, *The Manchurian Crisis, 1931-1932* (New York: Columbia University Press, 1948). On the watershed between the postwar and prewar periods.

Charles C. Tansill, *Back Door to War: The Roosevelt Foreign Policy* (Westport, Conn.: Greenwood, 1975). Alleging that Roosevelt pushed America into war.

Barton Whaley, *Codeword Barbarossa* (Cambridge, Mass.: MIT Press, 1973). Discusses why Stalin did not believe Hitler would attack; a study in psychological warfare and military and political intelligence.

John W. Wheeler-Bennett, *Munich: Prologue to Tragedy* (London: Macmillan, 1948); and Lewis B. Namier, *Diplomatic Prelude, 1938-1939* (London: Macmillan, 1948). Good studies of the last international crises before World War II.

Roberta Wohlstetter, *Pearl Harbor: Warning and Decision* (Palo Alto, Calif.: Stanford University Press, 1962). First-rate monograph.

Sources

Hamilton F. Armstrong, *Chronology of Failure* (New York: Macmillan, 1940); "Pertinax" (André Géraud), *The Gravediggers of France* (Garden City, N.Y.: Doubleday, 1944); Marc Bloch, *Strange Defeat* (Darby, Penn.: Darby Books, 1981). Three perceptive studies of the French defeat in 1940.

Winston S. Churchill, *The Second World War,* 6 vols. (Boston: Houghton Mifflin, 1948-1953). Magisterial account by a chief architect of Allied victory.

Charles de Gaulle, *The Complete War Memoirs* (New York: Simon & Schuster, 1940-1961). Beautifully written first-hand account of de Gaulle's own experiences.

Desmond Flower and James Reeves, eds., *The Taste of Courage: The War, 1939-1945* (New York: Harper & Row, 1960). A good anthology of "war pieces."

A. J. Liebling, ed., *The Republic of Silence* (New York: Harcourt, Brace, 1947). Excellent collection of materials pertaining to the French resistance movement.

Esmonde M. Robertson, ed., *The Origins of the Second World War* (London: Macmillan, 1971). Documents and secondary extracts on the thesis of A. J. P. Taylor that Hitler was rational in his policy and that he was driven into war.

There are many memoirs of actors in this great war. The following make a good beginning: Dwight D. Eisenhower, *Crusade in Europe* (New York: Da Capo, 1977); Harry Truman, *Memoirs,* 2 vols. (Garden City, N.Y.: Doubleday, 1958); Bernard Montgomery, *Memoirs* (New York: Da Capo, 1982).

CHAPTER 27: OUR TIMES: ARRIVING AT THE PRESENT

General Accounts

C. E. Black, *Dynamics of Modernization* (Boston: Peter Smith, n.d.). Illuminating study.

Peter Calvocoressi, *World Politics since 1945,* 4th ed. (London: Longmans, 1982). Factual study.

Desmond Donnelly, *Struggle for the World* (New York: St. Martin's, 1965). A history of the Cold War, which traces it back to 1917.

Norman A. Graebner, ed., *The Cold War: Ideological Conflict or Power Struggle?* 2nd ed. (Lexington, Mass.: Heath, 1976). Divergent interpretations.

Samuel P. Huntington, *Political Order in Changing Societies* (New Haven: Yale University Press, 1969); Louis L. Snyder, *The New Nationalism* (Ithaca: Cornell University Press, 1968). Wide-ranging and provocative surveys.

The Free World

Francis Boyd, *British Politics in Transition, 1945-1963* (New York: Praeger, 1964). Solid account.

Crane Brinton, *The Americans and the French* (Cambridge, Mass.: Harvard University Press, 1968). Perceptive essay on the French in the postwar world.

Colin Cross, *The Fall of the British Empire, 1918-1968* (London: Hodder & Stoughton, 1968). Analysis of a central aspect of Britain's altered position.

Marton Dönhoff, *Foe into Friend: The Makers of the New Germany from Konrad Adenauer to Helmut Schmidt* (London: Weidenfeld and Nicolson, 1982). Useful journalistic study.

Alfred Grosser, *The Federal Republic of Germany* (New York: Praeger, 1964). Concise history.

Stanley Hoffmann, et al., *In Search of France* (Cambridge, Mass.: Harvard University Press, 1963). Essays on economics and politics in twentieth-century France.

H. Stuart Hughes, *The United States and Italy,* 3rd ed. (Cambridge, Mass.: Harvard University Press, 1979). Guide to postwar Italian politics and society.

Arthur Marwick, *Britain in the Century of Total War* (Boston: Little, Brown, 1968). Assessment of the impact of war on society.

Michael M. Postan, *An Economic History of Western Europe, 1945-1964* (New York: Barnes & Noble, n.d.). Comprehensive review.

Arthur M. Schlesinger, Jr., *A Thousand Days* (Boston: Houghton Mifflin, 1965). Memoirs by an aide of President Kennedy.

K. P. Tauber, *Beyond Eagle and Swastika* (Middletown, Conn.: Wesleyan University Press, 1967). Study of German nationalism since World War II.

Theodore H. White, *Fire in the Ashes* (New York: Sloane, 1953). Postwar economic recovery and the role of the Marshall Plan.

Philip Williams, *Crisis and Compromise,* 3rd ed. (Hamden, Conn.: Archon, 1964). Analyzing the failures of the Fourth Republic.

The Communist Bloc

C. E. Black, *The Eastern World since 1945* (New York: Ginn, n.d.). Instructive scholarly survey.

Zbigniew Brzezinski, *The Soviet Bloc,* rev. ed. (Cambridge, Mass.: Harvard University Press, 1967). Solid study of unity and conflict.

Leszek Kolakowski, *Main Currents of Marxism,* Vol. III, *The Breakdown* (New York: Oxford University Press, 1978). Rigorous analysis by a philosopher of past World War II problems in Marxist thought.

Leonard Schapiro, *The Government and Politics of the Soviet Union,* rev. ed. (New York: Random House, 1978). Short authoritative treatment.

Adam Ulam, *Expansion and Coexistence: The History of Soviet Foreign Policy, 1917-1967* (New York: Praeger, 1968). Lucid, brief account.

Robert L. Wolff, *The Balkans in Our Time* (New York: Norton, 1978). Informed survey.

The Emerging Nations

G. M. Carter, ed., *Politics in Africa: Seven Cases* (New York: Harcourt Brace Jovanovich, 1977). Informative.

Laing G. Cowan, *The Dilemmas of African Independence* (New York: Walker, 1964). A mine of information.

Charles C. Cumberland, *Mexico: The Struggle for Modernity* (Oxford: Oxford University Press, 1968); A. P. Whitaker, *Argentina* (Englewood Cliffs, N.J.: Prentice-Hall, 1964); A. Marshall, *Brazil* (New York: Walker, n.d.); Kai Silvert, *Chile Yesterday and Today* (New York: Holt, Rinehart, 1966); John E. Fagg, *Cuba, Haiti, and the Dominican Republic* (Englewood Cliffs, N.J.: Prentice-Hall, n.d.); Henry Bernstein, *Venezuela and Colombia* (Englewood Cliffs, N.J.: Prentice-Hall, 1964); Mario Rodriguez, *Central America* (Englewood Cliffs, N.J.: Prentice-Hall, 1965).

Roderick H. Davison, *Turkey* (Englewood Cliffs, N.J.: Prentice-Hall, n.d.); L. Fein, *Politics in Israel* (Boston: Little, Brown, n.d.); W. R. Polk, *The United States and the Arab World,* rev. ed. (Cambridge, Mass.: Harvard University Press, 1969); H. B. Sharabi, *Nationalism and Revolution in the Arab World* (New York: Van Nostrand, 1966). Introductions to the Middle East.

Vera M. Dean, *Nature of the Non-Western World* (New York: Mentor, n.d.). Brief overview.

Stewart C. Easton, *The Rise and Fall of Modern Colonialism* (New York: Praeger, 1962). Sweeping survey.

John K. Fairbank, *The United States and China,* rev. ed. (New York: Compass, n.d.); Edwin O. Reischauer, *The United States and Japan,* 2nd ed. (Cambridge, Mass.: Harvard University Press, 1965). Authoritative surveys.

Bernard B. Fall, *The Two Vietnams,* rev. ed. (New York: Praeger, 1965); and Robert Shaplen, *The Lost Revolution: The U.S. in Vietnam, 1946-1966* (New York: Colophon, n.d.). Outstanding.

J. F. Gallagher, *The United States and North Africa* (Cambridge, Mass.: Harvard University Press, 1963); W. Schwarz, *Nigeria* (New York: Praeger, 1968). Good studies.

Herman Giliomee and Richard Elphick, eds., *The Shaping of South African Society* (Capetown: Longmans, 1979). Excellent collection of original essays.

John Hatch, *A History of Postwar Africa* (New York: Praeger, n.d.). Clear and helpful guide.

Franklin W. Houn, *A Short History of Chinese Communism* (Englewood Cliffs, N.J.: Prentice-Hall, 1973). Useful recent introduction.

Walter Laqueur, *The Rebirth of Europe* (New York: Holt, Rinehart, 1970). Good, hard-headed history, reprinted with a new chapter as *Europe Since Hitler* (London: Penguin, 1982). Laqueur's *A Continent Astray: Europe 1970-1978* (New York: Oxford University Press, 1979), helps bring the account up to date.

John D. Legge, *Indonesia,* 2nd ed. (Sydney: Prentice-Hall, 1977); W. Norman Brown, *The United States and India, Pakistan, Bangladesh,* 3rd ed. (Cambridge, Mass.: Harvard University Press, 1972); Stanley Wolpert, *India* (Englewood Cliffs, N.J.: Prentice-Hall, 1965). Useful introductory studies.

The Cold War

Dean Acheson, *Present at the Creation* (New York: Norton, 1969). Beautifully written memoirs of the 1950s.

Olive Banks, *Faces of Feminism: A Study of Feminism as a Social Movement* (New York: St. Martin's, 1982). Good comparison of British and American feminist movements.

Lester R. Brown, *World without Borders* (New York: Random House, 1972). Interesting survey of major world issues without respect to specific nationalistic policies or views.

Curtis Cate, *The Ides of August: The Berlin Wall Crisis, 1961* (New York: Evans, 1979). A close look at the mechanics of a specific Soviet-American confrontation.

John Lewis Gaddis, *Strategies of Containment* (New York: Oxford University Press, 1983). Superb and restrained examination of postwar American national-security policy.

Louis J. Halle, *The Cold War as History* (New York: Harper & Row, 1971). An early attempt to take an historical perspective on the Cold War.

Richard W. Hull, *Modern Africa: Change and Continuity* (Englewood Cliffs, N.J.: Prentice-Hall, 1981). Balanced general survey.

Marion Kaplan, *Focus Africa* (New York: Doubleday, 1982). A journalist's account of issues in Africa in the 1980s which packs in good historical background.

Paul Kennedy, *The Realities behind Diplomacy* (London: Allen & Unwin, 1981). Thoughtful look at how a nation shapes its external policy; focuses on Britain.

Guenter Lewy, *America in Vietnam* (New York: Oxford University Press, 1978). While excessively defensive with respect to the American position, and illustrative of the perils of writing recent history, this provides a good chronological examination of the issues.

Evan Luard, *A History of the United Nations* (London: Macmillan, 1982). Covers "the years of Western domination," to 1955, with another volume yet to come.

John Lukacs, *A History of the Cold War* (New York: Anchor, 1962). Beautifully written survey; fully supportive of Western views on the origins of the Cold War.

Norman Luxenburg, *Europe since World War II: The Big Change,* rev. ed. (Carbondale: Southern Illinois University Press, 1973). Good general history.

Charles S. Maier, *The Origins of the Cold War and Contemporary Europe* (New York: Franklin Watts, 1978). Good collection of essays; some emphasis on views hostile to the American position.

Mary McAuley, *Politics and the Soviet Union* (London: Penguin, 1978). Excellent survey of economic as well as political events in the postwar Soviet Union.

Colin McEvedy and Richard Jones, *Atlas of World Population History* (London: Penguin, 1978). Quick examination of population changes across history.

Keith Middlemas, *Politics in Industrial Society* (London: Deutsch, 1979). Uses Britain as a case study for "postindustrial" political changes.

Theodore H. White, *The Making of the President, 1960; . . . , 1964; . . . , 1968; . . . , 1972* (New York: Signet). Highly informative analyses.

CHAPTER 28: TWENTIETH-CENTURY THOUGHT, LETTERS, AND ART

Unlike suggested reading lists for the other chapters, the list for Chapter 28 is intended only to provide titles that will illuminate generalizations made in the chapter itself, since no list of readings for contemporary intellectual trends can be more than superficial and indicative of themes worthy of further exploration.

Psychology

Ernest Jones, *The Life and Work of Freud* (New York: Basic Books, 1961). Detailed study; also available in an abridged version.

John Rickman, ed., *A General Selection from the Works of Sigmund Freud* (New York: Liveright, 1957). A well-chosen anthology.

R. L. Schoenwald, *Freud: The Man and His Culture* (New York: Knopf, 1956); and Philip Rieff, *Freud: The Mind of the Moralist* (Chicago: University of Chicago Press, 1979). Two good studies stressing Freud's place in contemporary culture.

Sociopolitical Thought

John Kenneth Galbraith, *The Affluent Society,* 3rd ed. (New York: Mentor, 1978). Lively assessment of consumerism by an economist.

H. Stuart Hughes, *Consciousness and Society* (New York: Octagon, 1976). Excellent study treating not only social thought but also other facets of intellectual history from 1870 to 1930.

Walter Lippmann, *A Preface to Politics* (New York: Macmillan, 1933). Another pioneering study.

Vilfredo Pareto, *The Mind and Society* (New York: Harcourt Brace Jovanovich, 1978). A major work in general sociology.

Talcott Parsons, *The Structure of Social Action,* 2nd ed. (New York: Free Press, 1949). A landmark in American sociological thinking.

Graham Wallas, *Human Nature in Politics* (New Brunswick, N.J.: Transaction, 1981), and *The Great Society* (Boston: Peter Smith, n.d.). Pioneering studies of the psychology of politics.

Philosophy

M. F. Ashley-Montagu, *Toynbee and History* (Boston: Porter Sargeant, 1956); and Isaiah Berlin, *Historical Inevitability* (Oxford: Oxford University Press, 1954). Criticisms of Toynbee in particular and historicism in general, respectively.

Albert Camus, *The Stranger* (New York: Vintage, 1946), and *The Plague* (New York: Random House, 1972). Modern existentialist novels by a gifted writer.

Ralph Harper, *Existentialism: A Theory of Man* (Cambridge, Mass.: Harvard University Press, 1949). A sympathetic introduction.

Walter Kaufmann, ed., *Existentialism from Dostoevsky to Sartre* (New York: New American Library, 1956). Instructive selections from existentialist writings; includes helpful editorial comments.

Arne Naess, *Modern Philosophers* (Chicago: University of Chicago Press, 1968). Carnap, Wittgenstein, and Sartre are among those discussed.

Morton G. White, ed., *The Age of Analysis: Twentieth-Century Philosophers* (New York: Mentor, n.d.). Excerpts and comments, very well chosen.

Science and Technology

Isaac Asimov, *The Intelligent Man's Guide to the Physical Sciences* (New York: Pocket Books, n.d.), and *The Intelligent Man's Guide to the Biological Sciences* (New York: Pocket Books, n.d.). Informative surveys by a prolific popularizer of difficult material.

C. T. Chase, *The Evolution of Modern Physics* (New York: Van Nostrand, 1947); and Lincoln Barnett, *The Universe and Dr. Einstein,* rev. ed. (New York: Bantam, n.d.). Helpful popular accounts of key developments in twentieth-century science.

R. Taton, ed., *Science in the Twentieth Century* (New York: Basic Books, 1966). Translation of a comprehensive French survey.

Literature and the Arts

H. H. Arnason, *History of Modern Art* (New York: Abrams, 1969). Encyclopedic introduction to twentieth-century painting, sculpture, and architecture.

John Cage, *Silence: Lectures and Writings* (Cambridge, Mass.: Harvard University Press, 1961). By an experimenter in extending musical frontiers.

Joseph Campbell and Henry M. Robinson, *A Skeleton Key to Finnegans Wake* (London: Penguin, 1977); and William P. Jones, *James Joyce and the Common Reader* (Norman: University of Oklahoma Press, 1970). Two guides to a baffling writer.

George H. Hamilton, *19th and 20th Century Art* (New York: Abrams, 1972). A lucid and less-detailed survey.

Henry-Russell Hitchcock, *Architecture: 19th and 20th Centuries* (London: Penguin, 1977). A meaty volume in The Pelican History of Art series.

Frederick J. Hoffman, *Freudianism and the Literary Mind* (Westport, Conn.: Greenwood, 1977). A suggestive exploration.

Claude Mauriac, *The New Literature* (New York: Brazillier, 1959). Essays translated from the French; treats mainly French writers.

Hans Richter, *Dada: Art and Anti-Art* (Oxford: Oxford University Press, 1978); Patrick Waldberg, *Surrealism* (Oxford: Oxford University Press, 1978); J. Russell and S. Gablik, *Pop Art Redefined* (New York: Praeger, 1969). Useful introductions to particular movements.

Harry Slochower, *Literature and Philosophy between Two World Wars* (New York: Octagon, 1973). (Originally titled *No Voice is Wholly Lost).* An informative study of the relations between intellectual and literary history.

Lael Wertenbaker, *The World of Picasso* (New York: Time-Life Books, 1967); and C. Tomkins, *The World of Marcel Duchamp* (New York: Time-Life Books, 1966). Informative attempts to relate two artistic pioneers to the cultural world of the twentieth century.

Edmund Wilson, *Axel's Castle* (New York: Scribner's, 1947). A study in imaginative literature from 1870 to 1930; extends to Joyce and Gertrude Stein.

ILLUSTRATIONS

INDEX